Sol Plaatje

Reconsiderations in Southern African History

Richard Elphick, Editor

Sol Plaatje

A life of Solomon Tshekisho Plaatje,
1876–1932

Brian Willan

University of Virginia Press
Charlottesville

University of Virginia Press
Originally published in 2018 by Jacana Media, South Africa. This edition of
Sol Plaatje is published by arrangement with Jacana Media.
© 2018 by Brian Willan
All rights reserved
Printed in the United States of America on acid-free paper

First University of Virginia Press edition published 2019

ISBN 978-0-8139-4209-4 (paper)
ISBN 978-0-8139-4367-1 (ebook)

9 8 7 6 5 4 3 2 1

Library of Congress Cataloging-in-Publication Data is available for this title.

Cover image: This portrait of Plaatje was taken in late 1916 by Lizzie
Caswall Smith (1870–1958), a fashionable society photographer, at her
studios in Oxford Street, London. It was commissioned by *The Christian
Commonwealth*, a weekly journal, and appears on the front page of its issue
of 3 January 1917.

Editing by Russell Martin
Proofreading by Lara Jacob
Design by Shawn Paikin and Maggie Davey
Set in Ehrhardt MT 10.3/14

This book is dedicated to the memory of Tim Couzens (1940-2016),
scholar and friend

Contents

List of abbreviations

AMEC	African Methodist Episcopal Church
ANC	African National Congress
AS/APS	Anti-Slavery and Aborigines' Protection Society
BMS	Berlin Mission Society, Berlin
BNA	Botswana National Archives, Gaborone
CAD	National Archives Repository, Pretoria
CMG	Companion, Order of St Michael and St George
DB	De Beers, Kimberley
DFA	*Diamond Fields Advertiser*
DSAB	*Dictionary of South African Biography*
HMV	His Master's Voice
ICU	Industrial and Commercial Workers' Union
ILP	International Labour Party
IOTT	International Order of True Templars
KAB	Western Cape Archives and Records Service, Cape Town
KC	King's Counsel
LMS	London Missionary Society
MFP	Molteno Murray Family Papers, University of Cape Town
NAACP	National Association for the Advancement of Colored People

NAD	Pietermaritzburg Archives Depot
OFS	Orange Free State
PSA	Pleasant Sunday Afternoon
SAIRR	South African Institute of Race Relations
SANNC	South African Native National Congress
SAP	South African Party
SGE	Superintendent General of Education, Cape Colony and Cape Province
SOAS	School of Oriental and African Studies, London
SSO	Southern Syncopated Orchestra
TAB	National Archives Repository, Pretoria (records of former Transvaal colony and province)
TLS	*Times Literary Supplement*
UCL	University College London
UCT	University of Cape Town
UM	University of Massachusetts, Amherst
UNIA	Universal Negro Improvement Association
Unisa	University of South Africa, Pretoria
USPG	United Society for the Propagation of the Gospel
UW	University of the Witwatersrand, Johannesburg
VAB	Free State Archives Repository, Bloemfontein
YMCA	Young Men's Christian Association

List of illustrations

Photographs in text

Plate sections

II Between pages 168 and 169

A note on terminology

Anybody writing on South African history has some tricky decisions to make regarding the use of terminology, particularly in relation to place names and the names given to African peoples.

On place names, I have generally adhered to contemporary usage, in line therefore with what was familiar to Sol Plaatje and reflected in his own writings: hence Bechuanaland for what is today Botswana, Basutoland for Lesotho, Rhodesia for Zimbabwe. Where place names have remained the same, but with slightly changed spellings, I have used modern variants: hence Mareetsane for Maritzani, Matobo for Matopo, Setlagole for Setlagoli, Mayakgoro for Majeakgoro. When quoting from historical documents, however, I have adhered to the original usage.

Mafeking, or Mafikeng (and, more recently, Mahikeng), which features prominently in this book, perhaps requires some further explanation. The name Mafeking, famous in the English-speaking world for its siege, was a corruption of the Setswana word 'Mafikeng', meaning 'place of stones'. I use 'Mafikeng' when referring to the original Barolong settlement, established well before the European township in 1885, or when I refer exclusively to the Barolong stadt, as it came to be known, after this date. I use 'Mafeking' for the European town specifically, and on occasion to encompass the two together, as was Plaatje's practice too.

The names used for African peoples have varied over time in response to changing orthographies and changing politics, and there have often been tensions between linguistic correctness and popular usage. As with place names, I have left terminology unchanged when quoting from original documents, reflecting therefore the wide variations that existed when signifying both the Tswana people as a whole and individual Tswana chiefdoms (for example, Tswana, Chuana, Cwana, Bechuana, Bechwana, Baralong, Barolong). Otherwise, in the body of the text, I have retained African prefixes in line with common usage: hence, collectively, Batswana, Barolong (rather than Tswana, Rolong,), and, individually, Motswana, Morolong. For their language I have used 'Setswana', although when this is subsumed within a broader conception of people and culture together, and used as an adjective, I have reverted to 'Tswana'. When referring to Nguni languages, I have preferred the more commonly used 'Zulu' and 'Xhosa' to 'isiXhosa' and 'isiZulu' just as I refer to 'German' rather than 'Deutsch'.

Today the term 'Kora' is sometimes used for people formerly known as Korana (or Koranna). I have adhered to the term 'Korana', in line with the terminology used by both Plaatje and German missionaries, quoted in this book.

Finally, my use of the terms 'Dutch' and 'Afrikaans'. During the period I write about, the 'Dutch' language in South Africa was in the process of becoming 'Afrikaans', but not in a unilinear manner, and usage and meaning varied according to context. Sometimes 'Dutch' really meant 'Dutch', sometimes it was taken to mean its South African variant. Where necessary, and where possible, I have clarified.

Preface

'One of the outstanding figures in the life of the people of South Africa: unveiling of tombstone on the grave of Solomon T. Plaatje: large and representative gathering at West End joins in impressive ceremonial.' So ran the headline over a report in the *Diamond Fields Advertiser* of 13 December 1935, on what had taken place in Kimberley's West End cemetery the previous day. Then as now the *Advertiser* was Kimberley's daily newspaper, and Kimberley the city where Solomon Plaatje had lived the greater part of his life. Compared to others close by, it was an imposing tombstone, the funds to pay for it raised by public subscription. A good-sized crowd, including Plaatje's widow, Elizabeth, and their four surviving children, were present to witness the unveiling, to honour the memory of a man who had died nearly three and a half years before.

Speaker after speaker praised his achievements. Z.K. Matthews, recently returned from study overseas and, like Plaatje, of Barolong descent, opened the proceedings and 'eulogised the work of the late Mr Plaatje, enumerating his qualities as a father, a friend of the people, an author, journalist, politician and leader'. Others echoed his sentiments: the mayor of Kimberley, speaking for the City Council and the people of Kimberley; Mr W. McLeod, representing the Non-European Association and the African People's Organisation, the voice of the Coloured community; and the Rev. Z.R. Mahabane, Methodist minister and a former president general of the African National Congress, today's governing party in South Africa.

The honour of unveiling the tombstone fell to George Simpson, editor of the

Diamond Fields Advertiser, invited to perform this task by Isaiah Bud-M'belle, Plaatje's brother-in-law. Plaatje, he said in his eulogy, 'was one of the best known and most highly respected leaders of native thought in the subcontinent', his premature death an irreparable loss. 'A man of lowly birth, he forced himself to the forefront by dint of his own exceptional abilities.' Nobody had 'contributed in greater measure to the cause of mutual understanding among the races without which there can be no true progress in South Africa'.

Before unveiling the tombstone, he concluded with an appeal to those around him, if they wished to show a true appreciation of Plaatje's work, 'to build upon the foundations he so well and truly laid'. 'He hath lit a torch, let us carry it high. In all reverence and humility, but with feelings of pride and thankfulness in having known him and shared his companionship and comradeship.' After all had had their say, the Bantu Musical Association Choir and the Lutheran Church choir led the singing of 'Nkosi sikelel' iAfrika', black South Africa's famous anthem, followed by what was then South Africa's official national anthem, 'God save the King'.

On the tombstone, standing there to this day, are inscribed the words 'We thank thee O Lord for lending us so rare a flower to bless our lives', followed by an injunction in Setswana: 'I khutse Morolong: modiredi wa Afrika'. Underneath is the English translation: 'Rest in peace Morolong: you servant of Africa.' Few but family would have noticed, when the tombstone was unveiled, that an unfortunate error had crept in: his date of birth, 9 October 1876 was given correctly, but he actually died on 19 June 1932, not 19 July, as the inscription mistakenly has it.

By any standards these were extraordinary tributes, from black and white alike. What would also have struck anybody present was how racially mixed the gathering was. On the face of it, given the segregated society South Africa had already become, this may seem surprising. But this is to project backwards the full force of what was still to come. Kimberley in any case was not Johannesburg or Pretoria, and racial lines were not so sharply drawn. Older traditions, more civil and more civilised, lingered on and, on occasions like this, would assert themselves.

Even so, the tributes were exceptional. They raise many questions. What was it about Plaatje that inspired such sentiments? Why had he made such an impact upon the memories of those who gathered that day? How had he risen from the 'lowly birth' George Simpson spoke of, overcoming the seemingly insurmountable barriers that lay in his way? What were his 'exceptional abilities'?

Was he just a genius, rising above his life and times – or is he best understood in the context of the tumultuous times in which he lived?

Today, eighty years on, the main contours of his life are well known. Born a Morolong, to Christian parents, and educated at a mission school near Kimberley, he worked first as a post office messenger in Kimberley, and then as a court interpreter in the smaller town of Mafeking. Caught up in the famous siege, during the South African War, his skills proved invaluable to the military authorities, and he wrote a diary, in English, of his experiences. After the war, as editor of a Setswana–English weekly newspaper, he emerged as one of South Africa's best-known political spokesmen. He was one of the founders of the South African Native National Congress (SANNC, precursor of today's African National Congress) in 1912, became its first general secretary, and twice travelled overseas. His *Native Life in South Africa*, published in London in 1916, set out the black South African case against the policies of their government, and had a huge impact. After travelling to the United States, he returned to South Africa in 1923 and resumed his career as a journalist. Then he devoted himself to literary concerns, writing in both English and Setswana and translating Shakespeare's plays into Setswana. His novel, *Mhudi*, was published in 1930, two years before his death.

It is small wonder people sometimes struggled to comprehend such a record of achievement and versatility, remarkable in a society which sought to exclude him, and others like him, from any meaningful role in its affairs. And all from a man who had a serious heart condition, contracted in the influenza epidemic of 1918, which often restricted his activities, and which in the end led to an early death.

In this book I have sought not only to describe these achievements, but to understand the man himself: to look into his origins and upbringing, his family and personal life, the source of his ideals and motivation, how he responded to the challenges he encountered along the way. Where the evidence allows, I have tried to interweave his private and public concerns, to explore his relationships with his wife, his family and his friends. Not out of mere curiosity but from a conviction that the one cannot be understood without the other.

Much of his adult life was driven by his response to change. He lived through a period that saw South Africa's transformation from colonial backwater into a modern unitary state. It developed an oppressive, racially exclusive form of governance which shaped the lives of all its inhabitants. In many of the events that ushered this in, Plaatje played a significant part: the South African War of 1899–1902; the creation of the Union of South Africa in 1910; the legislative programme that followed, implementing the legal and administrative framework for segregation; the vain attempts by the African people and their representatives to persuade the imperial government to intervene; the continued battle, in the 1920s, to preserve the non-racial Cape franchise, to resist the spread of segregation into every sphere of South African life. More than anybody else, in his journalism, in representations to authorities at home and abroad, in his books and pamphlets, he bore witness to what this meant for those who suffered the consequences.

Yet his interests and concerns went well beyond this. He devoted himself not just to resisting these changes, to opposing them as best he could, but to exploring the creative potential that lay in his country's multiplicity of cultural traditions. He set out an alternative vision to that propounded by the ideologues of segregation. He loved Setswana, his native language, and did all he could to preserve it from the threats he perceived to its survival. He loved Shakespeare too and thought it the most natural thing in the world to translate his plays into Setswana. In doing so he aimed to highlight its qualities and capabilities and became the first person to publish a translation of Shakespeare in any African language.

This is not my first attempt to write about Plaatje's life and work. When I did so, over thirty years ago, apartheid was at its zenith. Plaatje may have been in the public eye during his own lifetime, but by the 1970s and 1980s he had largely disappeared from view. Several biographies had been contemplated, and one – by Modiri Molema, a close friend – had been completed, but it had not been published. In the wider public sphere, apartheid had its own narratives and it cared little for the memory of those whose lives and ideals ran counter to its orthodoxies. South Africa had (and has) an extraordinary capacity to distort its past and Plaatje, I thought, was a notable casualty. His life and work needed to be retrieved, and I did my best.[1]

Thirty-five years on, that public sphere could hardly be more different. South Africa has once again been transformed, and so too have views of its history. Hitherto neglected dimensions of South Africa's past have begun to be rediscovered and memorialised. Statues to a new breed of pioneers have been erected, museums revamped, streets renamed, the historical experience of South Africa's black majority, so long neglected, has moved into the mainstream.

Plaatje has been caught up in this process. Today he is widely celebrated, his place in South Africa's history reclaimed. In 2004, for example, he was awarded the Order of Luthuli in Gold, South Africa's highest award, in recognition of his contribution 'to the cause of restoring the dignity of oppressed South Africans and exceptional contribution to the struggle for a free and democratic South

Africa'. In Kimberley, more recently, a new university has been named after him.

Such recognition is long overdue. The politics of memory and memorialisation are rarely straightforward, however. Opinions have varied over just what he is to be remembered for, how this should be done, and who should have a say. It has been a reminder of how the preoccupations of the present can shape both memories and representations of the past, and of the challenges for any biographer seeking to be sensitive to present-day concerns without being driven by them. Triumphalist new narratives, I have become increasingly aware, can be as damaging to historical understanding as the distortions, or neglect, that went before. It is one thing to pay tribute to the memory of past leaders and spokesmen, to see them as far-sighted pioneers of an ultimately successful struggle. It is another to know what they were really like, to understand their hopes and fears, to restore to them the agency they exercised. To see them, in other words, in the context of their own times, not ours.

Thus Plaatje has been celebrated for his association with the African National Congress. As its first general secretary and a key figure in its early campaigns, that is entirely right and proper – but not to the exclusion of all else. Little is heard today, for example, of his (longer-lasting) association with the interdenominational Brotherhood movement, or the International Order of True Templars (IOTT), promoters of the cause of temperance, or of his passionate concern for the future of Setswana and its literature. A rather more rounded view needs to be taken, in other words, if his life and legacy are to be properly understood, if we are to avoid being left with a rather one-dimensional view. Today both the Brotherhood and the IOTT may appear to have been dead ends, destined to failure, his concern for Setswana sometimes seen as a distraction from a wider struggle. This was not how it seemed to him.

This book started out as a modest attempt to update the biography I wrote in 1984. It has ended up, however, as a wholly new book and, I hope, the better for it. I have been able to uncover far more new evidence and information than I had imagined possible, shedding new light on almost every aspect of his life: for example, on his early years growing up on a German mission; his elopement with his wife Elizabeth in 1898; his intelligence work during the siege of Mafeking and his involvement in the little-known 'treason trials' that followed; the troubled history of the SANNC deputations of 1914 and 1919; his association with the Brotherhood movement in England and the many friendships he made there; his tribute to Shakespeare in 1916 and his work on Setswana with the eminent phonetician Daniel Jones; his travels in North America; the circumstances of the publication of his novel, *Mhudi*; his work in Setswana in the late 1920s; his relationship with his family.

Many new photographs have come to light, too, as well as a previously unknown recording of his spoken voice, which was discovered in London in 2010. Here, thanks to the serendipitous survival of a privately made 78 rpm record, dating from 1923, he can be heard reading out two tales from his *Sechuana Reader*. It lay undisturbed for nearly eighty years in a cupboard under the stairs in the Phonetics Department at University College London. Next door was the History Department where I spent three years as an undergraduate student.

This is not to say there have not been tragic instances of loss and destruction, too. Plaatje's daughter Violet preserved many of his papers, but after her death much simply disappeared, including the unpublished manuscripts of translations of a number of Shakespeare's plays. Z.K. Matthews, who intended to write about Plaatje in the 1960s, reported that some of his papers had been 'put in a bath and burnt'. Other valuable manuscripts, like his unpublished novel 'With other people's wives', and a notebook he kept in 1918 and 1919, were lost after that – fortunately not before copies were made.

New scholarship, as well as new evidence, has shed new light on many aspects of Plaatje's life and work, too. Two areas stand out. Firstly, Plaatje has been discovered by Shakespearean scholarship, both within South Africa and by the broader 'global Shakespeare' movement, concerned with what happens to Shakespeare's plays when they travel overseas. Plaatje, and others like him, it has been realised, could bring their own understandings and meanings to Shakespeare, to interpret him in their own ways. They did not have to take on board, willy-nilly, the cultural baggage that was assumed to come with Shakespeare, but could appropriate him for their own purposes. Secondly, several scholars, especially Tswana-speaking scholars, have looked closely at Plaatje's writings in Setswana, particularly his translations of Shakespeare. In doing so they have demonstrated the depth of his roots in Setswana culture, the pride he took in his origins and his language, as well as the characteristics and qualities of his writing in Setswana. They have helped to show, in important ways, how he viewed the world as a Motswana. I am indebted to the work of scholars in both these fields and I have drawn on their insights.[2]

Other new scholarship has shed light on the lives of people with whom Plaatje was associated – Daniel Jones, for example; John Dube, first president of the African National Congress; and African American figures like Marcus Garvey, J.E. Bruce, W.E.B. Du Bois and J.W. Cromwell, all of whom he encountered during his travels in North America. Studies of the black press, of *Native Life in South Africa*, of the 'Britishness' of the early Congress leaders, of the Barolong chiefdoms of Mafikeng and Thaba Nchu, of the 'ambiguities of dependence' that sometimes characterised the lives of Plaatje and his colleagues, have likewise enhanced my understanding of both the substance of Plaatje's life and work and the wider context in which this took place.[3]

All of this, and the encouragement of friends and colleagues, persuaded me to revisit Plaatje's life.

ONE

Beginnings to 1894

One hot summer evening, late in 1890, a horse-drawn wagon, carrying three people, made its way northwards from the mission station at Pniel, Griqualand West. Founded nearly half a century before by the Berlin Mission Society, for most of its existence this mission was not considered a success. Missionaries sent out from Germany had struggled to establish the kind of settled community they believed was essential if the Christian gospel was to take root. More recently, though, things had improved. New converts were made, a mission school finally succeeded in attracting some pupils, and the two resident missionaries were working well together. They attributed their success not only to their own efforts and the will of God, but to the arrival at Pniel of groups of Tswana-speaking Barolong. More receptive to their teachings than the nomadic Korana, the previous inhabitants of the region, these Barolong were willing to stay through the bad times as well as the good, and to make the mission their home. They were the hope for the future.

In charge of the small party was Gotthilf Ernst Westphal, the younger of the two missionaries. He was thirty-six years old, originally from Brandenburg in Prussia, and had been in South Africa for over a decade, nearly all of it spent at Pniel. Their destination was Mayakgoro, an outstation of Pniel, some sixty miles away, where adherents of the mission had established a new settlement; the purpose of the visit was to inspect progress, offer succour and support, and to preside over one of the regular church council meetings.

Accompanying Westphal on the journey was a 14-year-old Morolong by the name of Solomon Plaatje, a pupil at his mission school and a son of Johannes, one of his two black deacons. Solomon lived at Pniel with his elder brother Simon, both his parents having moved to Mayakgoro to join Gabriel, one of their other sons. Here they now worked to build up a new mission community.

As they set out from Pniel, so Westphal wrote in his mission diary, Solomon was cheerful and in high spirits, evidently excited at the prospect of seeing his family. When they ran out of things to say, they passed the time by singing hymns, but after a while both dozed off. Only Joshua, the coachman, and the third member of the party, remained awake, keen to make as much progress as possible in the cool of the late evening.

After that things did not go quite so smoothly. Two of the four horses fell ill, delaying their progress. Then they were caught in a heavy thunderstorm, and a violent thunderclap, directly overhead, frightened not only the horses and young Solomon but also – so Westphal admitted – himself. They eventually arrived safely, however, and Westphal was pleased with what he found at Mayakgoro. New church buildings had been erected, a school had been started, and there were more converts than before, thirty-two altogether. Such were the promising outward signs of the spread of the gospel.

Their return journey was less eventful but notable for the uplifting tale Westphal heard from '*klein Salomo Plaatje*', as he called him. Each morning, Westphal related, Solomon had to make an early start in order to get to school in time, since he lived on the edge of the mission, nearly three miles from the main mission buildings. His home was just off the main road between Kimberley and Barkly West, and the mail coach passed by at seven o'clock each morning. One day, setting off for school, he resolved to run along behind the coach and its six horses to see if he could keep up with it as far as the Bend Hotel, where he had to turn off to walk across the estate. Travelling in the coach were several Englishmen who, Westphal said, loved any kind of sport, and they watched his efforts with keen interest.

He managed to keep up with the coach all the way to the hotel and then sat down on the stoep for a rest. One of the Englishmen brought him a cup of coffee, and asked to look at the schoolbooks he had in his bag; these included not just his own work but that of two girls, most likely his cousins, who were coming on behind. Suitably impressed – Westphal was not sure whether this was by his schoolwork or his running – the unnamed Englishman rewarded Solomon with a shilling, and some sweets to give to the girls. Thereafter he made a regular habit of practising his '*Schnellläuferkünste*' ('fast-running skills') behind the mail coach, and with the money he collected was able to buy his own books as well as some other 'luxury items'.

Westphal saw a moral in the story. In fact he saw several. By getting himself to school in this way Solomon earned both praise and reward. Through arriving in good time, with his own books to read and study, and attending school regularly, he gained an advantage over the other pupils. Now he was top of his class, his efforts specially praised by the school inspector on his most recent visit. Hard work, natural ability and good character were thus all rewarded, young Solomon Plaatje's actions a demonstration of how it was possible to combine the useful (*nützliches*) with the pleasant (*angenehmes*).

At one level the story Westphal told can be seen as an unremarkable tale of missionary endeavour. Similar examples fill the records. It was the kind of individual success story that any mission needed to convey back to headquarters and to supporters beyond. Without them funds would dry up and they would fail in their efforts to spread the gospel. Nonetheless it is a revealing cameo, bringing to life a moment in a young man's engagement with a world of which he was not just a part but its very *raison d'être*. It is also specific enough in its details to suggest more than a hint of future promise. Since Westphal was relating what Solomon had told him, his voice is heard too. What comes through is a sense of an easygoing relationship between the two, founded upon participation in a common project – and far from a one-way process.[1]

Much was left unsaid, however. In reality Solomon Plaatje's fourteen years had been shaped not just by Westphal and the worldview he personified but by his own family history, by the lives they led as Barolong. Like them, he was born into this wider community, or nation, as Barolong often supposed themselves to be, and they took pride in a history that went back centuries before the arrival of any Christian missionary in South Africa. It was the interaction between these two worlds, and the manner in which they came together, that would shape his formative years. And it was the reason why, ultimately, the two found themselves together on that journey to the mission settlement at Mayakgoro.

Who, then, were the Barolong, and how did they encounter these Christian missionaries?

In the 1870s the Barolong lived across wide areas of what are today the Northern Cape, Free State and North West provinces of South Africa, and parts of Botswana. They depended on growing crops and raising cattle for their livelihood, in some places living within the colonial borders of the day, in some places beyond them. Most were attached to one of four chiefdoms. To the south lay the Seleka Barolong chiefdom of Thaba Nchu, numbering some 6,000 people, ruled by the elderly Chief Moroka, completely surrounded by the Orange Free State but still nominally in control of its own affairs.[2]

To the north lived the Tshidi branch of the Barolong, the most powerful section of the nation, and greater in number; they were ruled by the imposing figure of Chief Montshiwa, and throughout the 1870s fought against Boers from the Transvaal and Orange Free State for the right to occupy the area around the Molopo River, long regarded as their ancestral home. Here the greatest signs of 'civilisation' were to be found among the Christian section of the chiefdom, led by Montshiwa's younger brother Molema. To begin with they lived apart from the main body of the Tshidi Barolong, having been sent to found a defensive settlement in an otherwise uninhabited spot known as Mafikeng, or 'place of rocks'. Chief Montshiwa had other reasons too for dispatching them to Mafikeng, for he was finding that Christianity, while it had some very practical advantages, was also proving a disruptive influence in the affairs of the Tshidi as a whole.[3]

In the large region between these two main Barolong chiefdoms, lay scattered, less coherent groups of people of Barolong origin, belonging to the Rapulana and Ratlou as well as the Tshidi and Seleka branches of the nation, living on land now taken over by white farmers, land companies and missionary societies. It was here, on 9 October 1876, just inside the northern border of the Orange Free State, and on land occupied by one of these missionary societies – an outstation called Doornfontein – that Solomon Plaatje was born. Both his parents, Johannes and Martha Plaatje, were Barolong and, as their names proclaim, were Christians too, adherents of the Berlin Mission Society. This was their seventh child, all of them boys: Simon, the eldest, had been born in 1855, followed by Andrew, Samuel, Mmusi (Moses), Elias and then Joshua.[4]

Solomon was baptised four months later: not at the mission station at Pniel, of which Doornfontein was an outstation, but at the society's older mission at Bethanie, over a hundred miles away. Until recently Johannes and Martha had lived at Bethanie themselves and had left behind numerous friends and relatives, so their wish to return was understandable. At the same time their decision to make the long journey with a four-month-old baby to enable him to be baptised suggests a commitment to the Christian faith quite in keeping with what else is known of their circumstances.

The ceremony was performed on 14 January 1877 by the senior missionary, Carl Wuras, by now well advanced in years. Like most events that had some connection with the Berlin Mission Society, it was efficiently recorded. Entry number 795 in the Bethanie mission register set out the information required: the names of Plaatje's parents, and of the four godparents symbolically entrusted with care for the child's future Christian upbringing; his date of birth; and the Christian name his parents had decided to give him – Solomon, or Salomo in its German form, renowned in the Bible for his wisdom.

It was natural that they should want to give him a Tswana name too. They called him Tshekisho, meaning 'judgement', a reminder of one of Solomon's biblical attributes. The name also signified Martha Plaatje's acceptance of God's will and judgement in letting her have another boy rather than the girl she wished for. However, according to Martha Bokako, Simon Plaatje's daughter, and the source of much information on the Plaatje family history, there was a further layer of meaning in the name, derived rather from the term '*itshekisa*', meaning purity or purification. Overcome with remorse at having sought to anticipate God's will, the name Tshekisho emphasised Martha's repentance, her heart now purified for having presumed to express her own wish to have a baby girl.[5]

Important as their religion was to them, family and communal traditions, passed down from generation to generation, had far deeper roots. Fascinated by what he heard, later in life Plaatje took the trouble to write these down, being the first in his family, he believed, 'to put memory to paper'. At one time his ancestors, on the male side, had been kings of the Barolong nation until Modiboa, his 'last royal ancestor', was dispossessed 'during or about the years 1580–1600'; the kingship passed instead 'to the house of a younger brother and descended down to Tau (Lion), who ruled over the Barolong about 1770–1790'. On the other side, his mother was a direct descendant of a grandson of 'Tau's youngest and dearest wife, Mhudi', hence of the royal line of the Rapulana – one of the four sections or chiefdoms into which Barolong were now divided.[6]

Like every Morolong, Plaatje traced his ancestry back to Morolong himself, the eponymous founder of the nation, who was believed to have lived in the twelfth or thirteenth century. It served as their myth of origin. Although opinions differ on chronology, genealogies are largely in agreement on the line of succession, on the identities of Morolong's successors as paramount chief of the nation, and on the belief that they had once lived in the region of the Great Lakes of Central Africa before migrating south. Morolong was succeeded by Noto, then came Morara, Mabe, Mabua, Manoto and Mabeo, the reign of each chief being associated with a particular human quality, and a step in the direction of claiming the region around the Molopo River as their home.[7]

After Mabeo came Modiboa, the last Barolong chief to preside over a united nation. Accounts of his deposition vary in their detail but they have a common thread: he neglected his royal duties in favour of hunting and as a result was displaced by his younger brother Tsheshebe. Modiboa's descendants nevertheless continued to cherish the memory of their royal origins, becoming known as the Barolong *ba ga Modiboa* (the Barolong of Modiboa), those who did not desert the rightful heir of Modiboa, and they came to enjoy a reputation for loyalty. 'It is regarded as a special mark of distinction and reliability', wrote Modiri Molema, himself of the Tshidi Barolong royal line, 'to be recognised as being descended from this loyal stock, and the Barolong, with their punctiliousness in such matters, are ever ready to accord precedence to their brothers of Modiboa's stock.'[8]

Once the Barolong *ba ga Modiboa* became separated from the main body of the Barolong, they were able to retain an independent existence, remaining in the Molemane (Ottoshoop) and Mooka-osi (Slurry) districts, while the main body of

Barolong settled at Setlagole, forty-five miles to the south-west of present-day Mafikeng. Here the line of succession passed from Tsheshebe to Monyane to Setlhare to Mokgopha to Masepa to Thibedi, and then to Tau; with the *ba ga Modiboa*, in Plaatje's account, the line passed from Mooki to Mongale to Sehuba to Setlare to Mokoto to Dira and then to Selogilwe, who lived in the middle of the eighteenth century.

+~+

Tau's turbulent reign would be a turning point in the history of the Barolong. His ambitions brought him into conflict with the Batlaping, another Tswana-speaking chiefdom to the south, and the Korana, a mixed race of nomadic hunters. Together they proved to be more than a match for Tau's Barolong, many of whom were apparently opposed to his expansionist aims. It was a recipe for disaster. Tau was killed in about 1780, and in the ensuing confusion and dispute over the succession the Barolong broke into four sections – Tshidi, Ratlou, Seleka and Rapulana. They would retain a strong sense of a common ancestry and shared a common language, but they lived henceforth in independent chiefdoms, each of them taking their name from one of the sons of Tau. It was from the youngest of these, Rapulana, that Plaatje's mother was descended.[9]

The Barolong *ba ga Modiboa*, Plaatje's ancestors on the male side, were even more vulnerable and in no position to withstand the attacks of groups of Korana who flourished in the wake of Tau's defeat and death. Scattered among the newly forged divisions of the Barolong, they were forced to seek refuge and protection, ceasing to exist as an independent entity. From the time of Tau, the *ba ga Modiboa* largely ceased to have a recorded history of their own; we know only that it was with the Seleka branch of the Barolong that they were most closely associated.[10]

Then, early in the nineteenth century, the Barolong, along with many other peoples in the interior of southern Africa, found themselves caught up in one of the most far-reaching series of events in the history of the subcontinent, the *mfecane* ('scattering' or 'crushing'), which transformed the interior of southern Africa in the 1820s and 1830s. There were widespread migrations of peoples, bringing first the 'Mantatees' (the followers of the Tlokwa chieftainess, Ma Nthatisi) and then the Ndebele (Matabele) under Mzilikazi into the areas occupied by the Barolong. Weakened by internal divisions, and greatly outnumbered, the Barolong could offer little effective resistance and fled whenever they could.

Providentially, as it must have seemed to them, an unexpected source of protection materialised in the form of Wesleyan missionaries, first encountered in 1822. From that point onwards, the history of the Barolong was closely linked to that of missionary endeavour. Within a few years, the entire Barolong nation had gathered at Thaba Nchu under the leadership of the Seleka chief Moroka, living on land which the Wesleyans had succeeded in obtaining from Moshoeshoe, chief of the Basotho.

What drew the Barolong to Thaba Nchu was their need for refuge and protection. The aims of the missionaries were more far-reaching. Seeking to win adherents to their religion, they hoped to wean their potential converts from such traditional customs as polygamy and circumcision, to adopt Western styles of clothing and housing, and to foster a way of life built upon the virtues of monogamy, hard work and regular religious observance. They insisted on Sunday being set aside as a day of rest and worship; they encouraged regular church attendance and the reading of the Bible; and they expected the children of families living on mission stations to attend school so that they too could be taught the basic elements of the Christian religion.

The Barolong were not the only people in need of protection from their enemies. In 1836 Boer trekkers under Sarel Cilliers, making their way northwards from the Cape, encountered Mzilikazi's forces at Vechtkop, near present-day Heilbron. In the engagement that followed, they escaped with their lives but lost most of their cattle and provisions. When news of this reached Chief Moroka, he sent out his people to rescue them, bringing them back to safety in Thaba Nchu. It was the beginning, Plaatje would write later, of 'the tragic friendship' between Barolong and Boers.

After regaining their strength, the Boers joined with the Barolong and drove Mzilikazi and his Ndebele northwards into what would become Rhodesia and later Zimbabwe. But then the Barolong were betrayed by their allies. Joined by other trekkers, the Boers seized much of the land the Barolong had regarded as theirs, and in due course established the independent republic of the Orange Free State. It was an alliance, Plaatje would write, 'which cost the Barolong very dearly, and which involved sacrifices in men and materials for which history records absolutely no reciprocation on the part of the Boers'. The predicament of the Barolong nation as a whole thus mirrored that of Plaatje's own forebears, the Barolong *ba ga Modiboa*: exclusion from what was rightfully theirs. In Plaatje's memories of the past, there would always be this double sense of dispossession.[11]

+~+

Among those who gathered at Thaba Nchu during the early 1830s was Selogilwe Mogodi, Plaatje's paternal grandfather, remembered as 'the first Christian in the family'. From that time, family traditions agree, his direct descendants lived their lives in some form of association with Christian missionaries, albeit of different denominations and in different places, adopting a way of life whose values, beliefs and outward characteristics were increasingly influenced by this connection. As *ba ga Modiboa*, vulnerable dependants of one or other of the larger Barolong chiefdoms, it was an understandable choice to have made.

Selogilwe and his family did not remain long at Thaba Nchu. Before they departed, Selogilwe's son Mogodi was married to a woman called Magritta Morwagadi, who gave birth to their first son, Kushumane (Plaatje's father), in 1835, his date and place of birth – Maamuse, or Schweizer-Reneke – recorded in a prayerbook preserved by the family to this day. By the late 1830s, they had moved to the Philippolis district. Here Kushumane, who was given the Christian name Johannes, married Martha Lokgosi (a Motsieloa of the Rapulana clan), and on 28 February 1855 their first son, Simon (Solomon's eldest brother), was born. The family must have remained in the district for at least four or five years after that, for it was at Philippolis, as Martha Bokako recalled, that the next two sons, Andrew and Samuel, were born, there being two years between each child.[12]

Philippolis in the 1840s and 1850s was the centre of an independent state governed by the Griqua, a mixed race who had done much to maintain the balance of power, such as it was, between the different groups competing for land and power in the region between the Vaal and Orange rivers. Plaatje's parents and grandparents were part of the London Missionary Society settlement at Philippolis, comprising a mixture of Dutch-speaking Griquas and Basotho and Batswana pastoralists. For a while during the late 1830s and early 1840s, the missionary responsible for the Tswana-speaking congregation was Gottlob Schreiner, father of the novelist Olive Schreiner, whom Plaatje would encounter half a century later. In 1838, so the mission records reveal, Gottlob Schreiner baptised Plaatje's grandfather Selogilwe. In retrospect, it was, for Schreiner, a rare success in what was otherwise a troubled time for him.[13]

Family tradition has it that it was while living at Philippolis that Plaatje's forebears first acquired the name Plaatje. Meaning 'flat' in Dutch, the name was reputedly given to Selogilwe ('Au Plaatje'), by a Dutch-speaking Griqua farmer on whose land they lived. 'Au Plaatje' was supposed to have had a flat-looking head, and the Griqua to have been either unable or unwilling to pronounce the family name of Mogodi correctly. Whatever the exact circumstances of its acquisition, the name stuck and has been retained by one branch of the family ever since.[14]

The fact that 'Au Plaatje' was also known as 'Ryk Au Plaatje' ('Rich Old Plaatje') suggests that the family were beneficiaries of the period of relative peace and prosperity that Philippolis enjoyed in the 1840s and 1850s. Plaatje himself, writing many years later, had his own family history in mind when he wrote: 'Prior to the establishment of the Orange Free State our forefathers were trading grain for cattle and horses amongst the Griqua of Philippolis, and exchanging wheat for merino sheep among European pioneers around Colesberg and Victoria West.' Martha Bokako, too, recalled that this was when her grandfather and great-grandfather built up the size of their herds and stocks, on grazing lands owned by the Griquas. Tradition has it that Mogodi had a talent for healing sick animals, which would have further commended him to his Griqua neighbours.[15]

Philippolis's existence as an independent state came to an abrupt end in 1862 when the Griqua, threatened by the encroachments of the surrounding Boer state, departed for the district of Kokstad in what became known as Griqualand East, sandwiched between the border of the Cape and Natal colonies. At about the same time, most likely as a consequence, the Plaatje family moved northwards to the large mission estate at Bethanie, granted to the Berlin Mission Society some years earlier by the Griqua leader Adam Kok II. In some family accounts Mogodi and Kushumane settled for a while at a mission run by French missionaries on the border of Basutoland, and then accompanied Adam Kok on his epic trek, before deciding to return in the face of severe drought and the hostility of the Basotho chief Moshoeshoe.[16]

Bethanie proved to be a much safer haven. Established in 1834, it was the oldest mission station in the Orange Free State, although the missionaries had largely failed in their efforts to convert the nomadic Korana people to a Christian way of life. It was only in the 1850s and 1860s, when there was an influx of Tswana-speaking people (the Plaatje family among them) seeking access to land which was becoming increasingly difficult to find elsewhere, that the mission at Bethanie grew into the kind of settled, prosperous community that the missionaries hoped for.[17]

This period of consolidation took place under the autocratic guidance of Carl Wuras, who ran the mission according to the maxim 'Pray and labour', and it saw members of the Plaatje family rise to positions of authority and influence in its daily affairs. The ruins of 'Plaatje's Camp', solid stone buildings, can be seen there to this day. Names of members of the family appear regularly in the mission register for the late 1860s and 1870s, recording births, deaths, baptisms and marriages, collective tribute, in their way, to the way of life being forged by the residents of the mission. The Plaatje family was by now at the heart of this.[18]

On 17 July 1876, however, three months before Solomon Plaatje's birth, his grandfather Selogilwe Mogodi, 'Ryk Au Plaatje', the patriarch of the family, breathed his last. A resident of the mission for twenty years, and well on in his eighties, he lived long enough to be able to give thanks that his family could gather around him for his final hours. The entire mission community attended his funeral and heard Carl Wuras speak in glowing terms of his commitment to the Christian faith and his contribution to the life of the mission.[19]

Once he had been laid to rest, Plaatje's parents, Johannes and Martha, accompanied by others in their extended family, left Bethanie for Doornfontein, hoping to play their part in the creation of a new Christian community on this outstation. At the same time, so Martha Bokako recalled, Johannes Plaatje, unhappy about the dues he had to pay at Bethanie, was looking for suitable grazing land for his sheep and cattle. Such considerations, temporal and spiritual, were at the heart of life on any mission station.[20]

In the event the Plaatje family did not remain long at Doornfontein, and within a few years they had moved on yet again, this time to the mission lands at Pniel, some fifty miles further down the Vaal River. Plaatje did not return to the district for nearly forty years.[21]

So it was at Pniel that Plaatje would spend what he called the 'best and happiest days' of his childhood. Like many mission stations, it was ideally situated – set in attractive surroundings on a bend on the south side of the Vaal River, not far from the town of Barkly West. It occupied an area of some three square miles, its northern boundary formed by the banks of the river, which were lined by a row of tall willow and karee trees. The main mission buildings, the church, school building and missionaries' houses, lay close to the banks of the river, just high enough to avoid being washed away by occasional floods. A little further up the river, the ground was broken by clumps of rocky outcrops, but most of the estate, irrigated by dams and steam pumps constructed by the missionaries, possessed rich soils which made it suitable for either agriculture or grazing sheep or cattle. In fact the Pniel mission estate was recognised as one of the most fertile stretches of land for miles around, and visitors were often struck by its great natural beauty and abundance of flowers.[22]

Its apparent tranquillity belied an eventful past. Once the home of Korana and Griqua people, it was claimed by the government of the Orange Free State and was later annexed as part of the British colony of Griqualand West, itself incorporated into the Cape Colony in 1881. But as at Bethanie, so the Berlin mission at Pniel failed to build up a permanent, settled community, and it barely survived; in the 1860s, indeed, it appeared to be on the point of closure, and a severe drought forced almost all its inhabitants to leave.[23]

In 1867, however, life on the mission was transformed by the discovery of

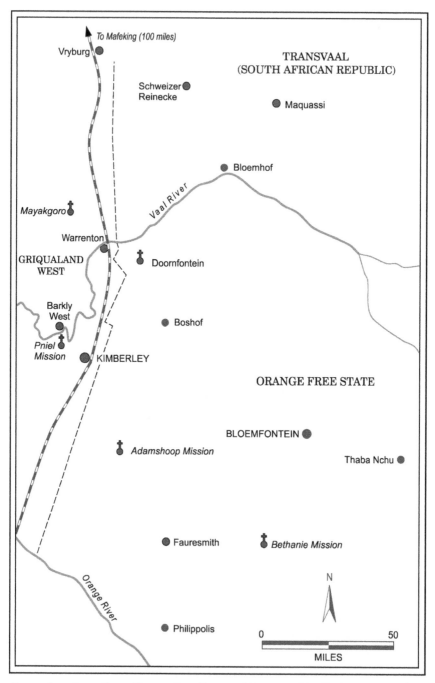

Parts of northern Cape, Orange Free State and Transvaal in the late nineteenth century, showing Berlin Society missions

diamonds along the banks of the Vaal River, on land occupied by the Berlin Mission Society. Thousands of people were drawn to this new scene of activity. For the missionaries it was a mixed blessing: on the one hand, it brought in a great deal of money, thanks to the dues they were able to extract from the diggers in exchange for the right to prospect on their property; on the other, it added to the already formidable task of establishing a godly life among the residents of the mission, and it led to a long dispute over the ownership of the Pniel estate, claimed by the society on the basis of a grant made to them in 1854 by the Korana chief Cornelius Kok.[24]

Although most of the diggers moved on, the affairs of the mission, in the early 1880s, gave little satisfaction in Berlin. Of the five hundred or so inhabitants of the mission, only a handful were regarded as 'serious Christians'; others would often resist the attempts of the missionaries to impose any kind of religious discipline.[25]

When the newly appointed missionary, Karl Meyer, took over at Pniel in June 1881, he faced a difficult task. Dues were not being paid, the mission school had virtually collapsed, and the spiritual life of the inhabitants – so he reported – had sunk very low. He did his best to re-establish some sort of order but a year later was forced to return to Germany through ill health. Responsibility for the task of reconstruction devolved instead to Martin Baumbach, who had been working at one of the society's stations in the Transvaal and who was now appointed senior missionary; and to a young probationer missionary, Ernst Westphal, who had arrived several months earlier.[26]

It was during this unsettled time that Johannes and Martha Plaatje and their family arrived at the mission, accompanied by several other Barolong families of the *ba ga Modiboa* clan. Johannes Plaatje's name first appears in the mission records in the second half of 1881. Further evidence of their presence comes in the form of an inscription in the Plaatje family Bible, dated 'Pniel, 2nd October 1881', one week, that is, before young Solomon's fifth birthday; and by a much sadder entry in the pages of the prayerbook set aside for the recording of family information, dated 30 October 1881, indicating that his elder brother Joshua, six years old, had drowned in the Vaal River.[27]

The Plaatjes and their fellow *ba ga Modiboa* prospered at Pniel. They owned substantial numbers of cattle and other livestock, and lived in a large, thatch-roofed stone building which they built on the edge of the estate, at the foot of a ridge which came to be known as 'Plaatje's Hoogte' (or 'Plaatje's Heights'), close to the main road from Kimberley to Barkly West. One year, according to the mission records, Simon Plaatje had 9 horses, 62 head of cattle and 245 sheep and goats – exceeded only by Philip Moyanaga, a relative and neighbour on the estate who had likewise moved to Pniel from Bethanie. They also grew vegetables in the grounds around their compound, and most years would make a good living from the sale of stock and produce, and wood for use as fuel, in the two nearby towns; part of the proceeds then had to go to the mission in return for their right to live there and to graze their livestock.[28]

At a time when many Africans in the northern part of the Cape Colony were being evicted from their lands, or forced to seek employment elsewhere, these *ba ga Modiboa* families enjoyed a relatively secure position, well placed to take advantage of the high prices paid for livestock and agricultural produce. For others it was very different. Several years before the Plaatjes arrived at Pniel, nearby groups of Batlaping, fellow Tswana-speakers, had resorted to desperate acts of armed resistance in a hopeless attempt to preserve a way of life now threatened by the demands of white colonists. Residence on a mission station undoubtedly provided some protection from the worst excesses of this new colonial order.[29]

Pniel's favoured position presented other opportunities. Plaatje would recall how the river used to overflow its banks and flood the surrounding valleys to such an extent that the pontoons could not carry the wagons across from one side to the other, their owners forced to wait for weeks on end until the floods subsided. This created a good market for fresh milk. The price rose to one shilling a pint, and 'there being next to no competition we boys had a monopoly over the milk trade', able to 'get six to eight shillings every morning for the pastime of washing that number of bottles, filling them with fresh milk and carrying them down to the wagons'. Not that he had much use for the money anyway, he added, 'as all we wanted to eat, drink and wear was at hand in plenty'. Unfortunately there would not be many more opportunities to profit from these floods, for in 1885 a road bridge was constructed across the Vaal River, putting an end to their lucrative milk-delivery business. Progress for some came at a price for others.[30]

More regular employment arose from the obligation to help tend the family's livestock, the customary task for small boys, whether they lived on a mission station or elsewhere. Solomon started with kid goats at the age of six or seven, and then graduated to the care of the family's highly prized cattle. He thus shared in the experience of what he later called 'the occupation most honoured among the Bechuana', pointing out that those who did so were likely to be 'the most intelligent and the best informed members of the community, rather than the reverse'. For cattle were universally revered, conferring both wealth and status upon their owners, and were central to everybody's lives. Soon he was exposed to the extraordinarily wide range of vocabulary and idiom associated with them. Tending cattle was not so much a job that had to be done as an integral part of growing up, of becoming a Motswana.[31]

Looking after animals would not always be so congenial. When he was a bit older, taking a year out from school, he found paid employment as a shepherd with a man called Bacchus who had land not far from the Pniel estate. From what he wrote of this later, it was a distinctly risky job to take on, for Bacchus was a brutal character who had once 'sjambokked a Hottentot herd to death', and it was also his practice to swindle his herdboys out of their wages by accusing them of losing sheep he had himself slaughtered, and then refusing to pay their wages.

Plaatje, however, was not deceived. 'I had been taught from childhood to calculate and could add up things just as quickly as a Dutchman can count his sheep', so every time a sheep was slaughtered or died from other causes he cut a nick in his walking stick. When 'Baas Bacchus' duly told him that sixty sheep were missing, he was able to point to the same number of nicks he had made in his stick and suggested instead that he look in his pantry and kitchen. The conclusion to Plaatje's account of his year's service with Baas Bacchus has not survived, but the implication is that he not only escaped retribution but secured the wages due to him. Here was experience of a type of white man very different from benevolent missionaries like Westphal and Baumbach.[32]

Plaatje left few memories of his parents. Almost the only time he mentioned his father was to say that he was 'a cattle farmer', and that 'he thought he knew a lot' – which did at least point to one of the main preoccupations of his life, and the reason he kept moving from place to place. He did not have much to say about his mother either, but he did remember her tale of an extraordinary incident she had witnessed in Fauresmith, a small town in the Orange Free State (not far from the mission at Bethanie), in the 1860s. It was apparently the custom for the ox-wagon drivers to give public displays of their skills when they visited the town, but Martha Plaatje saw one young driver come to grief in rather remarkable circumstances. While he was displaying his skills, one of the wheels of his wagon hit a boulder and knocked him off balance. As he fell to the ground, a wagon wheel passed over his neck, completely severing his head from his body. To everybody's amazement, the headless body then rose up, ran alongside the moving wagon and cracked a whip at the leading oxen before dropping down stone dead. It was not surprising the story remained in Plaatje's mind.[33]

Plaatje's mother was one of several women at Pniel who told him of family and tribal traditions, and from whom he learned Setswana, his first language.

'The best Sechuana speakers known to me', he observed later in life, 'owe their knowledge to the teachings of a grandmother, or a mother, just as I myself ... am indebted to the teachings of my mother and two aunts.' Among these 'teachings' was a fund of fables and proverbs, highly valued as repositories of the inherited wisdom of their people and passed on from generation to generation. Many involved animals with human characteristics. When he recalled, later in life, some of these fables 'overheard by us since early boyhood', it always struck him 'that the fox and the hare were the cleverest of animals' – a truth captured, so far as foxes are concerned, in the proverb 'Sebo ja phokoje oa matlhale-fetsa ga le fele' ('There is no limit to the sagacity of the super-wise fox').[34]

'Au Magritte', or 'Granny Masweamotho', Plaatje's grandmother (on his father's side), left a deep impression, and it was from her that he derived 'complete information' about the details of his own ancestry. When he wrote of having been 'taught almost from childhood to fear the Matabele', of being frightened with stories of the 'unreasoning ferocity' of their attacks upon the Barolong in the 1820s and 1830s, he was hearing them from a woman who must either have witnessed these scenes herself or learnt of them from her own parents. Among the casualties was Dira, one of his grandfather Mogodi's three brothers, and remembered as the last polygamist in the family, who was killed by the equally fearsome Batlokwa ('Mantatees').[35]

Another remarkable tale of female valour concerned the exploits of his great-grandmother, 'Au Magritte's' mother, from the same time. She was gathering wood one day with some other girls in the bush near the Kunana hills (so Plaatje himself related many years later) when they suddenly came upon a lion feasting on the carcass of a freshly killed eland. She rushed at the lion, waving her sheepskin in his face, causing him to turn tail and run off. When the girls returned home in triumph with the meat, the men would not believe their story. Only after returning to the scene were they convinced by the evidence of the spoors which revealed where the lion stood over the carcass, and how it ran away. Heroes, in Plaatje family tradition, did not have to be men.[36]

Young Solomon was not the only one to learn from these women about family and clan tradition, for it was to them, and especially to his mother Martha, that the missionaries at Pniel would turn when they needed information on such matters. This was a not infrequent occurrence. Far more than their English counterparts, German missionaries believed in immersing themselves in the language and culture of the people among whom they lived and worked, and they were prepared to spend long hours listening to stories of their lives and experiences, and learning about their customs.[37]

Underlying this was their concept of '*Volkschristianisierung*', or conversion of peoples as distinct from individuals. While they disapproved of such practices as initiation ceremonies and polygamy, and sought to eradicate them, they stressed the importance of preserving their converts' unique cultural identity ('*Eigentümlichkeit*') so long as this did not conflict with Christian doctrine. For the missionaries, influenced by a peculiarly German tradition of Romanticism, the '*Volk*' was akin to a living organism, manifest in the mother tongue as well as other aspects of culture and customs. It was vital, they thought, that this 'folk spirit', and the cultural bonds which held these societies together, should not be weakened. They worried about producing converts who had lost all connection with their indigenous cultures and they contrasted their approach with what they thought took place on English missions. It followed that the task of learning African languages was taken very seriously indeed. During their training in Berlin and then in the mission field, prospective missionaries were expected, before they were ordained, to master one indigenous language (as well as other European languages), and to be able to use it in delivering their first sermon.[38]

Such an approach to language was fine in theory but more difficult in practice. Inevitably it took a while for the missionaries to become fluent in the African languages concerned, especially in a situation as there was at Pniel where several quite different languages were spoken. They would always be dependent on the leading families – in the Tswana and Korana communities in particular – to enable them to communicate effectively with the inhabitants of the mission, and to deal with them as distinct communities.

Among the Korana they relied upon Teus Bloem. He was a grandson of Jan Bloem, founder of one of the Korana clans that once roamed the district, and he was one of the few who had decided to remain at Pniel. For the Batswana they looked above all to the Plaatjes. Along with the Sebotses, Mokaes and Moyanagas, they provided the deacons, elders, 'native helpers', the interpreters, the men and women whose job it was to help maintain discipline, to ensure the regular payment of dues, to support the missionaries with help and advice, visit the sick, admonish the weak in spirit – duties which, as the mission reports for Pniel suggest, did not always make them popular with other members of the mission community.[39]

Throughout the 1880s Johannes and Simon Plaatje were leading figures in the life of the mission. Johannes Plaatje was ordained as one of the two deacons responsible for the Tswana community at Pniel (about two hundred persons) in the latter part of 1881, having been a 'native helper' prior to this, and several months later Simon was made a church elder. It was Johannes's appointment that inspired the handwritten inscription, taken from Acts of the Apostles 20:28, written in Dutch and dated 2 October 1881, which appears at the beginning of the family Bible, and it reminded him of his new responsibilities: 'Take heed, therefore, with yourselves, and to all your flock, over which the Holy Ghost hath made you overseers, to feed the church of God, which he hath purchased with his own blood.'[40]

With a tradition of Christianity in the family that went back to the 1830s, it is not difficult to see why Johannes and Simon Plaatje should have assumed such responsible positions. Somebody who could address the church congregation on 'The advent of Christianity among the Barolong', as Plaatje's father did in 1883, or talk to Ernst Westphal's first 'Tea Meeting' (a popular means of raising money for church funds) about the history of the Pniel mission, was clearly a valuable asset to the two new missionaries. Over the next few years both their names appear regularly on the list of those who attended the monthly church council meetings. Often it was Johannes Plaatje who took the chair, and it became the custom, too, for him to say the prayer that closed the meeting. Once he was reported to have expressed his sadness at the sight of three boys, nephews of another member of the church congregation, who were brought before the council after they had been found drinking brandy. Outside these meetings, his single most important duty was the preparation of candidates for confirmation before presenting them to one of the missionaries for examination.[41]

To Simon Plaatje fell the task of assisting the missionaries in more temporal matters. He became, Erna Westphal wrote, 'my father's right-hand man in the management of the many and often very complicated situations not only among the Tswana and others on the Pniel estate, but especially between Europeans and Tswana on the diggings'. 'You see,' she added, 'the diggers were wont to imagine they could act just as they pleased, regardless of whether their acts were legally or morally permissible ... It was here that Simon showed both wisdom and tact, and father trusted him.' Her memories are borne out by the mission records. Throughout the 1880s there are frequent references to his work in collecting dues from both the diggers and the more permanent residents on the estate, and in acting as guide and interpreter for Westphal and Baumbach on their visits to the outstations that lay beyond the main mission at Pniel. Once, in 1884, Ernst Westphal expressed his concern that he might be tempted to leave for more money elsewhere. He remained at Pniel, however, as a result, Westphal thought, of his father's influence.[42]

Both Plaatje's father and eldest brother, in short, were closely associated with the two missionaries at Pniel: this relationship, and an awareness of the leading role of his family as intermediaries between the missionaries and the residents of the mission, must have impinged on his consciousness from an early age.

In 1883 or 1884, when he was seven years old, there was a far-reaching change in the family's circumstances. His parents decided to move away from Pniel to go and live at the outstation of Mayakgoro. Johannes Plaatje was keen for everybody to move, but he was unable to persuade his eldest son and his family to come with them. Simon was to spend the rest of a very long life at Pniel: he had found a secure niche in the life of the mission community, and he had no desire to leave. But he also insisted, as Martha Bokako recalled, on keeping his younger brother Solomon with him. Even at this age, it seems, he stood out as an able child, and was already attending the mission school at Pniel. When his parents and other brothers departed for Mayakgoro, therefore, Solomon remained at Pniel in the care of his eldest brother. From now on, it would be Simon and his wife Chrissie who would have the main responsibility for his upbringing. Instead of his brothers as companions, the closest to him now in age was his niece Lydia, just a year younger than himself.[43]

For a while the move opened up a rift within the family. According to the mission records, when Simon went to visit his mother after her move, he found her to be not only unwell, but to have lost all religious faith, blaming her husband for her misfortunes and wishing to prevent her younger children from going to school. Martin Baumbach was later happy to be able to report that she had recovered her faith, but she had evidently gone through a period of great distress. Doubts were raised, indeed, about her mental state. Johannes Plaatje, for his part, continued for a number of years to be deacon of the community at Mayakgoro, visiting Pniel from time to time in order to attend meetings of the church council.[44]

For the seven-year-old Solomon the immediate consequences of these family upheavals were clear: he was to remain at Pniel in the care of his elder brother Simon, and to attend the mission school. This, in turn, led to a close relationship with the man who was to be, outside his immediate family, the single most important person in this period of his life, missionary Gotthilf Ernst Westphal.

Ernst Westphal was in many ways a remarkable man, wholly committed to the life of the mission. Unlike most of the missionaries sent out to Africa by the Berlin Mission Society, who came from humble backgrounds, he was from a wealthy Brandenburg family. His father had owned a large textile business, which Ernst would, in the normal course of things, have inherited, had not both his parents died when he was very young. He was brought up instead by his uncle, also a businessman, and, when he was old enough, joined another firm, owned by a man called Metz. However, his career changed course sharply after he attended a conference of Christian students. He decided to become a missionary, joined the Berlin Mission Society, and then spent four years at the Berlin seminary, successfully completing its demanding course of instruction. Because of his business training and background, the society decided he would be the ideal person to take charge of the administration of the Pniel estate, and to restore some order to the chaotic state of affairs which existed there in the early 1880s. In order to familiarise himself with the diamond business, he was first sent to work in nearby Kimberley.[45]

In the event, the urgency of the situation at Pniel ensured that he joined the mission much sooner than had been expected. He set about transforming its finances, allowing the less worldly Martin Baumbach to attend to the religious life of the mission. It is clear that Baumbach, whose constitution was weakened by long exposure to malaria in the northern Transvaal, and who was more at home by all accounts in his book-lined study, welcomed such an arrangement. He hated having to collect hut tax and grazing fees and could never bring himself to apply the sanction of expelling defaulters from the mission. People consequently called him 'te Zachtmoedig', or the one who is too meek or too gentle.[46]

Ernst Westphal also assumed responsibility (as from 12 April 1882) for running the mission school and here too he quickly made his mark, his 'pleasant manners and quick intelligence' noted by one visitor. When he arrived, the school was in a sorry state. The school inspector from the Cape Education Department (responsible for the maintenance of standards at the school since Griqualand West became part of the Cape Colony in 1881) paid a visit early in 1882 and was not impressed. The general standard of attainment was 'low', attendance poor, and the school 'had not made the progress that might be expected, owing to several changes of teachers'; he added, though, that 'a new appointment had been made which is likely to be a permanent one', and looked forward to better things in the future.[47]

His optimism was borne out. When John Samuel, the school inspector, returned the following year he found 'a very remarkable improvement in the general condition of the school since I last visited', and particularly commended the work of the Korana school assistant, Thomas Kats. Under Westphal's guidance and the watchful eye of the Cape Education Department, the Pniel mission school went from strength to strength.[48]

Just how successful Westphal was is shown by an enthusiastic report written by no less a person than Dr Hermann Theodor Wangemann, the director of the

Berlin Mission Society, following his visit to Pniel a year later. When he examined the pupils, boys and girls, he was struck by their keenness, tidiness, punctuality and discipline (such were the qualities valued most highly), and compared them favourably with children of the same age in schools in Germany. Not only could they relate stories from the Bible, he found, but also explain their meaning. A few of the older children knew the catechism, could read in both English and Dutch, the two European languages spoken in the Cape Colony, and were able to take down dictation and write out on the blackboard what was read to them, making very few mistakes.

Dr Wangemann was pleasantly surprised, too, at the ability of the older children at mathematics, since he had often found this to be a weak point on other mission schools he had visited. He concluded his report with the observation that he had never seen a better-run school anywhere in either Africa or Germany. Both Ernst Westphal and Thomas Kats were commended in the highest possible terms, and the latter was awarded an immediate pay rise (from £18 to £24 per year) for his part in bringing this about.[49]

Such was the satisfactory state of affairs in the classroom at Pniel. Without doubt young Solomon Plaatje was fortunate to be reaching school age at a time when, thanks to these efforts, the school had improved out of all recognition; and then to be taken in hand by a teacher who was capable of recognising and encouraging a talented pupil. Of course the school had its limitations. The Berlin Mission Society may have regarded the provision of education for the children living on their missions as essential to the spread of the gospel, but this did not mean it set its sights very high. Heinrich Grützner, missionary at Bethanie and superintendent of the circuit to which Pniel belonged, summed up their approach a few years later: 'As missionaries, we do not think it advisable to make them big scholars. As long as they know how to read and write, know their Bible, know how to write a letter, we are contented as missionaries.' His society provided virtually no secondary education and pupils generally left school well before the age of fourteen.[50]

At Pniel things were never quite as bleak as Grützner's comments would suggest. Being situated in the older-established, more liberal Cape Colony, and subject to the influence and oversight of its Education Department, made a big difference. The regular visits of the school inspector brought not just extra funds and an expectation of higher standards but a more progressive, and more secular, approach to education. In the four 'government school-hours' of each day, a broader school curriculum, based on the English model, had to be followed and the practice of using religious texts for teaching purposes was forbidden. In contrast to the German missionaries' preference for the vernacular, and the

Missionsordnung's injunction that teachers should concentrate on turning pupils into Christians, they were urged to devote more time to the teaching of the two official languages of the Cape Colony and to use the standard textbooks that were now widely available. Two very different educational philosophies, in short, had to reach some accommodation in the classroom at Pniel.[51]

The profusion of different languages spoken on the mission – Setswana, Sesotho, Korana, Xhosa, 'Cape Dutch', Herero – only added to the difficulties. At any one time the vast majority of pupils would be below Standard I. Very few ever reached the pinnacle of Standard III, which was as far as the school could take them, most of them simply not there 'long enough to acquire either English or Dutch well enough to pass the various standards'. One school inspector was inclined to attribute the slow progress he found at Pniel to its isolation. 'The children are not nearly as bright as those in the town mission schools', he observed one year, the problem being that 'they seldom come in contact with people in a higher state of civilization than themselves'. Better results might be achieved, he thought, if the teachers concentrated their efforts on just one of the two official languages, preferably English. Acquiring even the most basic education was always going to be a struggle for the majority of those who attended the Pniel mission school.[52]

Young Solomon Plaatje, given the position of his family in the life of the mission, was much better placed than most. School for him was never an alien environment. He would have been expected to attend the Pniel mission school at an early age, starting in its kindergarten class. Nevertheless, his earliest recollections were of his time at a different school altogether – the Anglican Church's All Saints mission school in Beaconsfield, adjacent to the mining town of Kimberley, some seventeen miles away. Our knowledge of this comes from David Ramoshoana, a close friend later in life, who remembered Plaatje telling him that in 1886 'he attended the Church of England mission school, then housed in the little iron building which still stands near the large church building near the town hall of Beaconsfield'. Often, he added, 'when we went past that iron building, he fondly remarked that it was in that little house that he learned to spell English words and the rudiments of arithmetic. His teacher, whom he held in high esteem, was the late Reverend Herbert Crossthwaite.'[53]

Herbert Crossthwaite did indeed run the All Saints mission in Beaconsfield at this time. Like Westphal, he was another businessman-turned missionary, equally dedicated to an ethic of hard work, and remembered for bringing to his teaching duties 'the accurate and methodical habits acquired … in his life as a man of business'. To his pupils he was known simply as 'Crosbie'. Despite being dogged by ill health, and always short of funds, he managed to provide an elementary education for the 140 or 150 pupils who attended his classes each day – of every 'race, colour, language and creed', he said, and from an even wider variety of backgrounds than the mission community at Pniel. Apart from his exposure to such a polyglot collection of schoolchildren, its main significance for Plaatje, Ramoshoana's anecdote suggests, is that it was his first experience of learning English from a teacher who spoke it as a first language.[54]

Quite how it was that Plaatje came to attend this school – and how long he remained there – is a mystery. Such a step could only have been contemplated if there were good relations between the missionaries at Pniel and their Anglican counterparts in Kimberley. Westphal was known to have been on friendly terms with the Anglicans, and both missionaries at Pniel were regular visitors to Kimberley, being in close contact with Carl Meyer (son of the former missionary at Pniel) and Friedrich Ecker, who ran the Berlin Society's town mission (St Paul's) in Beaconsfield. They met regularly, sometimes for synod meetings, sometimes to take or to preach at one another's church services, or to cover for illness and temporary absences.[55]

In October 1887 there was an exchange of personnel: Carl Meyer departed for Germany on furlough and Ernst Westphal took charge of the St Paul's mission and its school until his return the following July, moving to Beaconsfield with his wife Marie (who had joined him at Pniel in 1884) and their two-year-old son. Friedrich Ecker, meanwhile, took Ernst Westphal's place at Pniel for the same period. It is entirely possible that this was when Plaatje was at school in Kimberley, and hence able to stay with the Westphals – and that Ramoshoana (or Plaatje himself) was simply a year out in his recollection of when this took place.

The links between these missionaries were part of a wider network connecting Pniel and Kimberley. Whatever doubts those at Pniel may have had about Kimberley's reputation and its capacity to ensnare the unwary, it was a major commercial and administrative centre and could not just be wished away. Residents of the mission went there to find work or to sell their stock and produce and to fetch the goods and provisions they needed. Simon Plaatje – the family home conveniently close to the main road – visited Kimberley regularly, and on occasions his younger brother accompanied him. An early memory was of the first time he went on a train ('to me it was a railway journey of intense interest') from Kimberley to Modder River and back, when he would have been nine or ten years old, soon after the opening of Kimberley's railway station.[56]

Later in life Plaatje liked to describe himself as 'a country boy', contrasting his early years with his experiences later in life. But in truth Pniel was no rural backwater. And while some of the children living on the mission may have seen little of the world beyond, that was hardly true in his case. Growing up in one of Pniel's leading families, closely involved in the work of the missionaries, as well as the pursuit of their own livelihoods, gave him a varied range of experiences. Attending an Anglican mission school in a novel and decidedly urban, industrial environment was just something to take in his stride.

His time at the All Saints mission aside, Plaatje's schooling took place at Pniel, and it was Ernst Westphal, not Herbert Crossthwaite, who would be the greater influence. Here he was among the eighty or so children – there were usually a few more boys than girls – who made their way each day to the mission school. School started at eight in the morning, and there was always a last-minute rush, so Westphal remembered, once the final bell was rung. They began with a hymn and a prayer, followed by some further religious instruction. Most of the day was then devoted to a curriculum approved by the Cape Education Department: it included reading, writing, mathematics, some geography (including South Africa and the Holy Land), music and singing, and sewing (for the girls). The older pupils learnt both English and Dutch, and there was an emphasis on reading and dictation. For Dutch they had the Elffers series of graded readers, for English the Nelson *Royal Reader* series, widely used throughout the British empire. Years later he was reminded of one of the stories in *Royal Reader* III, and remembered every detail.[57]

Ernst Westphal believed in good order in the classroom, his teaching style as much a product of his period of national service in the Prussian army, his daughter thought, as his training at the Berlin seminary. Ephraim Moyanaga, another of his pupils and a near contemporary of Plaatje's, remembered that the first thing Westphal taught them all was 'discipline and fairness'. 'Yes, he was very strict', he said, 'but he loved us', and always used to say that 'example was better than precept'. Moyanaga recalled, lest it be thought it was all discipline and nothing else, that 'he also taught us to laugh and sing'.[58]

One thing the pupils at Pniel did not get was competitive team games. Unlike many of their English counterparts, German missionaries considered them an entirely inappropriate form of acculturation. Turning out 'black Englishmen' was not on their agenda and they had no wish to make fools of themselves either. Ernst Westphal, so his son remembered, particularly disliked football and cricket. At Pniel, you would not encounter 'a flannelled fool at the wicket' or 'muddied oaf' in goal.[59]

Plaatje made rapid progress at school. He had a natural gift for languages, a keen appetite for reading, and an exceptional memory – inherited, it was said, from his mother Martha. At some point in 1891, when he was fourteen or fifteen, he was appointed as pupil teacher. This involved helping to instruct the youngest children while continuing to attend classes himself, and was normally for a period of three years. Pupil teachers provided a cheap means of resolving the acute shortage of properly qualified teachers. Nobody pretended the system was perfect, least of all the superintendent general of education: in his report for 1893 he commented that pupil teachers 'in one class of school are subsidized pupils, in another they are a cheap form of teaching drudge', and 'in very few indeed are they pupil-teachers so-called'. But for somebody in Plaatje's position, keen to continue with his education, and probably encouraged by the Westphals to think of a future career as a teacher, the pupil-teacher system had its advantages, and at Pniel at least it seems to have served its purpose.[60]

His appointment was especially timely in view of the death of Martin Baumbach, the senior missionary at Pniel, in October 1891, aged only forty-nine, days after his two youngest children succumbed to diphtheria. One thing Plaatje owed to his time at Pniel was an immense respect and admiration for what he always saw as the selfless, self-sacrificing work of the missionaries. Here, in Martin Baumbach, was an exemplary life dedicated, and sacrificed, to the service of God – and a sad end to a harmonious partnership between the two missionaries that had put the mission back on its feet.[61]

It was a setback for the school too. Westphal had to relinquish his teaching responsibilities when he became superintendent of the mission, and it would be some months before a new teacher arrived to take his place in the classroom. In-between the school inspector paid a visit and was unimpressed by what he found. The building (the old church) was 'in the same half-ruined state as on the occasion of my last visit', the education of the children 'not in a very satisfactory state' either as there had been 'no efficient assistant teacher' since Martin Baumbach's death, and there were far too many pupils below standard. A new schoolroom was being built, but it was not yet ready.[62]

Things improved with the arrival of August Schulz, the new missionary. A tailor in Regenthin in Prussia before finding his true vocation, Schulz came with some knowledge of Setswana, having been an assistant at the society's mission at Adamshoop in the Orange Free State. He also had the advantage of Plaatje's assistance in the classroom. Within days of his arrival he was writing about '*der bekannten klein Schulmeister*' ('the well-known little schoolteacher'), and particularly commended his excellent work with the children's choir. Several weeks later Plaatje was still helping him to find his feet. Unaware that the school usually had only a half-day's teaching on the last day of term, Schulz caused consternation by launching into a mathematics lesson after the break – until Plaatje intervened to put him right.[63]

Young Plaatje was popular with the children he helped to teach and they often surrounded him, so Modiri Molema relates, eager to hear the stories he told them. Westphal provided every encouragement, seeing with his own eyes how he could hold their attention. Most of these children were of Tswana or Korana origin but they did include, at various times, several of the Westphal and Baumbach children, the only white pupils at the school. One of them was Johannes Baumbach, who hoped to follow in his father's footsteps as a missionary, and continued to live on the mission with his mother, serving as a classroom assistant alongside Plaatje. Half a century later he would 'still remember those days when Plaatje and I as small boys went to school together on my father's Mission on the banks of the Vaal River'. There was less than a year between them.[64]

The Westphals' eldest son, Gotthardt, had happy memories too. Years later, a long career as a missionary behind him, he recalled that it was Plaatje who had first taught him the alphabet in the classroom at Pniel, a striking reversal of the usual roles. He also remembered singing German songs with his black fellow pupils, especially the traditional children's song 'Mit dem Pfeil, dem Bogen, durch Gebusch und Tal' ('With a bow and arrow through bushes and valley') – reminder, were any needed, that an education at Pniel would always have a distinctively Germanic flavour, whatever the colour of your skin.[65]

Not that other languages and traditions were neglected when it came to music and singing. One English visitor, after hearing the schoolchildren sing hymns in English, Dutch and Xhosa, was particularly struck by their rendering of a verse from 'God save the Queen', sung, he thought, 'with a vigour and heartiness promising well for the loyalty of their future lives'. They were, after all, subjects of the British empire.[66]

In June 1892 Ernst Westphal reported in some detail, and no little pride, upon the progress of his protégé. Young Solomon, he wrote in his *Tagebuch*, was the most talented child he had taught in his eleven years at the mission, and he read and spoke both Dutch and English with ease. One day, Westphal related, he also found him reading a German *Hosianna* booklet (a devotional periodical for children published by the Berlin Mission Society). '"Are you able to read German?" I asked him. 'Yes, I am trying to,"' was the answer. So Westphal gave him a German language primer to help him make sense of it, and then some further instruction of his own.

Solomon was just as gifted musically. As his classroom assistant, Westphal said, he displayed a particular talent for teaching singing to the younger children, using the Tonic Sol-fa system of musical notation which he had taught himself to use. He also used to practise playing the violin and the trumpet. Unfortunately, Westphal added, he couldn't let him keep his violin as he needed it himself. But even in the short time Plaatje had the use of it he progressed from practising the scales to playing some melodies – clearly, though scratchily, he thought. Given the status of the instrument in European musical culture, there was perhaps a hint here about his wider potential.[67]

Further commendation came from Richard Brune, the senior missionary at Adamshoop and an occasional visitor to Pniel. Describing him as 'a child of Pniel', he wrote later of Plaatje's many talents, especially his exceptional facility with languages, and remembered that even as a child the missionaries were able to call upon him for 'linguistic work'.[68]

Westphal's wife Marie took a close interest in him too. 'Minna' to her friends and family, she was the only daughter of a well-to-do Brandenburg family and used to call herself '*ein feines Stadtfräulein*' ('a proper city girl'). Leaving her cultured home for the wilds of colonial South Africa had been a shock to her system, but she threw herself into her new life, undeterred by the discovery – on arriving in 1884 – that her husband-to-be had no more than a suit and two shirts to his name; even his watch, it was said, had been sold to help make ends meet. She taught sewing to the girls in the school and concerned herself with the welfare of the women living on the mission, often visiting them in their homes. After a while she had the care and upbringing of four children of her own to see to as well. Like her husband, she was remembered as a stickler for discipline, insisted upon good behaviour, and was in no doubt that cleanliness was next to godliness.

Marie Westphal was also a trained teacher. Before coming to South Africa she had taught, for several years, at a prestigious girls' high school in Brandenburg which catered for the daughters of the city's leading families. Her subjects were English and French but she was also talented musically and artistically. She was thus unusually well qualified to help the able pupil she now encountered in the less promising circumstances of the Pniel mission, and evidently welcomed the challenge, seeing an opportunity to make use of her knowledge and teaching experience. When Plaatje approached her one day, as her daughter recalled, with the request 'I want to be able to talk English and Dutch and German as you do', she was not going to turn him down.[69]

Both Westphals gave him some extra tuition after school hours, realising he had outgrown what the school could offer. In August 1893 the school inspector commented upon 'the boy who passed in the third standard', a rare event at the school, but that was as far as it could take him, and a Standard III certificate would be his highest formal educational qualification. Before long Marie Westphal took over most of the extra tuition herself, her husband's time being fully occupied in running the mission.

There are some clues as to what this tuition involved. Gotthardt Westphal remembered that Solomon had learnt some French as well as German. Erna Westphal recalled her mother saying she had taught him to play the piano, and had also 'improved his English by lending him what books were at her disposal'. 'Together', she said, 'they read or studied Shakespeare and Scott's Waverley novels.' The school had a few copies of *Royal Reader* Book IV, which would have covered the requirements of Standard IV of the curriculum, but they must have gone well beyond this. French and German were not required in the primary standards, and Shakespeare didn't normally make an appearance until Standard VI. They may well have dipped into one of the volumes of the complete works of Shakespeare in German which the Westphals had on their shelves. Shakespeare after all worked rather well in translation, and for many educated Germans of the Westphals' generation Shakespeare was '*unser Shakespeare*' ('our Shakespeare'), as much a part of Germanic as English culture.

Sometimes Plaatje used to stay with the Westphals in their own home, treated as one of the family – as if he were their own son, Modiri Molema thought. Years later Plaatje would say that the Westphals 'loved him to a fault', and he once expressed to Marie Westphal his 'filial compliments', such was the nature of the bond between them. For the Westphals he was vindication of their untiring but often frustrated efforts in the mission field. They had only to think of Thomas Kats, their Korana assistant teacher, to be reminded of how easily things could go wrong. Within a couple of years of receiving those glowing reports on his work in the classroom, he had fallen victim to drink. This had been a desperate disappointment not only for the two missionaries at Pniel but also for Dr Wangemann in Berlin and the Education Department in Cape Town, for all hoped he would be the first Korana to qualify as a trained teacher. Young Plaatje's record, on the other hand, served only to vindicate the conclusion reached by missionaries at Pniel some while previously, that their efforts were much better expended on the Barolong.[70]

Like missionaries elsewhere, those at Pniel saw their school as a means to a higher end: imparting the Christian faith and equipping their pupils to live worthy and fulfilling Christian lives. For Plaatje, as for many of the other children, this Christian faith was not just something they learnt about at school, but practised in their daily lives. At home, prayers were said every morning and evening, and at mealtimes. There was Sunday school, Bible classes and, as he grew older, regular Sunday services as well as the great religious festivals like Christmas and Easter which marked out the Christian year. Both his elder brother and his father, while he remained at Pniel, took church services for the Tswana-speaking congregation. In their mother tongue this religion could be shaped by their own traditions and sensibilities, and there were quite distinctive liturgies and forms of worship. Their service of baptism, for example, gave a far more active role to godparents than in the European tradition, even when adults were being baptised, and it embodied a collective rather than an individual view of the ceremony, imbuing it with new meaning. The missionaries accepted this. They realised that the form of Christian worship at Pniel was a matter for negotiation, and that their congregation, especially the leading families upon whom they relied, wished to do things their way.[71]

For churchgoers at Pniel the singing of hymns was central to the experience of worship. Hymns were sung in five different languages, Lutheran musical practice combined melodiously with indigenous tradition, and Ernst Westphal, once a member of the Brandenburg Cathedral choir, insisted upon the highest standards. Such was the reputation of the choir, indeed, that visitors came from miles around to attend services. Often the singing could be heard long after the services had finished, for members of the congregation used to carry on singing their favourite hymns as they made their way home, the sounds echoing across the low hills surrounding the mission buildings. Once Ernst Westphal reported a conversation with a resident of Pniel, originally from Bethanie, who told him that they often considered moving elsewhere to earn more money, but they could not bear the thought of leaving behind the beautiful singing in church. Judging by Plaatje's love of hymns later in life, and the efforts he devoted to their translation, they were sentiments he might have shared.[72]

It was at this time, too, that he formed a deep attachment to the books used for worship, in particular the Tswana prayerbook and Bible, fruits of a tradition of scriptural translation in Setswana that went back to Robert Moffat in the 1830s. Both books had given shape and substance to the written form of the language, and they would provide an enduring source of imagery and inspiration. Later in life a friend recalled that he used to attribute much of his knowledge of Setswana to his constant reading of the Tswana translation of the Anglican Book of Common Prayer. He had in mind Canon William Crisp's highly regarded translation, originally published in 1887, which had the additional attraction of being rendered in his own Serolong dialect.[73]

The Bible made a huge impression too. Initially, this was through his mother Martha, remembered for being an avid reader, able to recite long passages, including complete psalms, from memory. He was soon struck by the parallels between what he read in the Bible and what he knew of the lives and history of his people. 'Passages in the history of the Jews read uncommonly like a description of the Bechuana during the nineteenth century,' he would write later, citing Psalm 144:11–14, with its references to prayers for sheep to multiply and for oxen to be strong, as an example: 'the similarity here', he thought, 'is so emphasized that it seems difficult at times to persuade oneself that the writer was not a Mochuana'. Nor was it difficult to make connections between his own family's recent history and the forty-year wanderings of the children of Israel in the book of Exodus. Stories from the Bible fitted in so well with Tswana traditions that it was often difficult to know where the one ended and the other began.[74]

Ernst Westphal was struck by these parallels too, and reported, at a time when he had Plaatje as his classroom assistant, that his pupils loved listening to Bible stories more than anything else. Tales of the shepherds Abraham and David and their flocks, he said, or the story from the book of Genesis of how Rachel and Leah looked after their sheep and goats, seemed entirely familiar to his pupils – though he did point out that 'our girls' had these responsibilities at a much earlier age. In similar vein, when he needed to explain the destruction of the wicked city of Sodom he had only to refer to the thunderstorms and flashes of lightning common in the summer months around Pniel – such as the two of them had experienced on that journey to Mayakgoro.[75]

At the heart of the life of any mission, physically and symbolically, was its church. At Pniel, during the late 1880s and early 1890s, it was a particular focus since much of the time of the missionaries, and the families who worked with them, was devoted to erecting a new structure, large enough to house a growing congregation. Hampered by shortage of funds, it proved an enormous challenge. Since they could not afford to buy the massive number of bricks required, the missionaries enlisted the help of the residents of the mission in making their own. Eventually, after nearly four years' work and numerous setbacks, the new church was completed, a pulpit carved in oak in High Gothic style was shipped out from Germany, and well over four hundred people attended the ceremony of consecration on 13 July 1890.

It was a memorable occasion. A procession made its way from the old church to the new to signify and to celebrate its opening, and several services were held during the course of the day. Plaatje's niece Martha was among the four infants baptised in a special service of baptism, and his father Johannes – back in Pniel for the occasion – had the task of carrying the baptism utensils. In the afternoon another service was held when 'the native deacons and helpers addressed the congregation' in their own languages. They included Teus Bloem, who brought tears to his eyes, and those of his congregation, when he recalled the sad history and current predicament of the Korana people; Johannes Plaatje, more positively, who gave thanks to God for their new church and for the work of their teachers; and Philip Moyanaga, who likened the entrance to the new church to the door into the sheepfold in John 10, and those who entered as shepherds of the sheep.[76]

Not long after the new church was consecrated, Plaatje began confirmation classes to prepare for his formal acceptance into the Lutheran faith, joined in these by his elder brother Elias, who travelled from Mayakgoro where he was living with his mother. They were confirmed together by Ernst Westphal on 6 June 1892, the first day after Pentecost. To their surprise, and delight, they found their mother at the service too. Despite having complained to Westphal that she had no money to enable her to travel to Pniel, she had nevertheless told him, 'I must be there. How can they be confirmed without me?' She managed to take the train to Kimberley, hoping then to get a lift on one of the timber wagons that travelled along the road towards Barkly West. Failing to do so, she set out instead on foot and reached the mission six hours later.

For Ernst Westphal, who related all this in his journal, it was a touching instance of religious faith and maternal devotion, and tribute to her perseverance and determination. For it seems Martha had renewed her faith with a new fervour. On two occasions she was reported to have thrown out the medicines of traditional healers (medicine men or witchdoctors in missionary parlance) from the huts of those who had resorted to them, believing rather in the Christian God and the power of prayer to heal body and mind.

Sadly, Elias died not long afterwards. He got a job with a white trader travelling northwards to Mashonaland. He returned home full of experience, according to the mission records, but without having been paid for his services, and with a fever which led to his death in September 1893. He was the third of Plaatje's brothers to have died since the family had moved from Bethanie.[77]

+~+

While Plaatje grew close to the Westphals and spent time in their home, he continued to live with his brother Simon and his family during the years he spent as a pupil teacher at Pniel. He recalled being paid 'the princely sum of £9 per annum', but considered himself quite comfortably off (in fact, he 'lived like a lord on it') 'because my elder brother not only gave me free board and lodging, but he also bought for me all my clothes, including luxuries, and I rode his horses, using his saddles and bridles'. Some additional earnings at the Bend Hotel, tending the horses of travellers, must have helped too.[78]

Plaatje's own parents were less settled. They had stayed on at Mayakgoro for some years, but in 1891, or soon after, his father Johannes decided to move on. Leaving behind sons at both Pniel and Mayakgoro, but taking his two youngest, Ramokoto (Johannes Daniel) and Monnapula (James), with him, he moved to a place called Ditlarapeng in the Mafeking district, just inside the border of the Bechuanaland Protectorate. Most likely this trek northwards was inspired, as before, by his desire to find the best place for his cattle. Perhaps too, like other black evangelists, he just preferred to be independent of any white missionaries, to pursue his faith – and his way of life – on his own terms, free of the obligation to pay for the privilege of residing on lands the mission societies claimed as their own.[79]

Ditlarapeng, prime grazing land, was an attractive alternative. One of the so-called Barolong farms, it had been the subject of a long dispute with the Bangwaketse, another Tswana-speaking chiefdom. When the Barolong claim was upheld by the Protectorate authorities in 1892, Montshiwa, the paramount chief, had the land divided into individual farms and distributed to his relatives and followers. Ditlarapeng went to Joshua Molema, his son-in-law and one of the leading Barolong headmen. Molema must then have reached an agreement with Johannes Plaatje, allowing him to reside there with his cattle and other livestock. Johannes accordingly found himself living under the jurisdiction not only of the British colonial authorities, but of the Tshidi Barolong paramount chief and his headmen. The connection thus established was to prove highly significant in years to come.[80]

Solomon probably visited his father at Ditlarapeng on several occasions. Once, in 1891, he travelled from Mafeking to Setlagole by ox-wagon, remembering the journey because, after heavy rains, it took five days to travel the distance of forty-five miles between the two places. Another memory which must date from this time is more revealing. Visiting the Tshidi Barolong settlement at Mafikeng 'when quite a youngster', he managed to steal into Chief Montshiwa's council and listened, fascinated, to the proceedings of a court case that was being heard. The case in question arose out of a man being accused of stealing the affections of another man's wife. What was of particular interest, and the reason he later wrote about it, was the way in which the married man had resorted to witchcraft to catch the adulterous couple in the act. As plaintiff, the married man won his case but was then publicly warned by Chief Montshiwa that if he ever employed such methods again he would be severely punished, since they constituted a threat to the well-being of the community as a whole.[81]

Quite apart from the interest of the case itself, the memory has a further significance. For it was evidence that Plaatje had direct experience, and at an impressionable age, of the functioning of an African chiefdom that still enjoyed a large measure of independence. Witnessing the great Barolong Chief Montshiwa giving judgment in council was far removed from anything he could have experienced at Pniel. Here it was the missionaries, with their deacons and elders, who laid down the code of behaviour by which people lived. Direct chiefly rule such as he found in operation at Mafikeng was something quite different.

To be a Morolong was to have a wider identity as a Motswana. This was defined by an attachment not to a particular chiefdom but to a wider set of shared traditions, above all by a common language, Setswana. Its recent emergence in written form meant that it had become an effective means of communication for literate Tswana-speakers throughout the region, connecting them in a way that had not been possible before. When Plaatje learned to read and write in Setswana, he thus joined an expanding literate community, giving new meaning to the very notion of being a Motswana. An important expression of this was the newspaper *Mahoko a Becwana*, a monthly review of current news and religious comment, published by the London Missionary Society at Kuruman. Each new issue was eagerly anticipated 'by the native peasants in Bechuanaland, and elsewhere', he would recall, and at Pniel he was 'frequently called upon as a boy to read the news to groups of men sewing karosses under the shady trees outside the cattle fold'.[82]

The memory speaks both to the spread of written Setswana and his relationship with those around him. But what he actually read in *Mahoko a Becwana* was interesting too, for here were aired views – particularly in the letters from readers that were published in its columns – on a range of concerns that would be his too. They addressed such issues as the transformation of Tswana customs in the face of increasing European influence, the differences between the Batswana chiefdoms, the standardisation of the written language of Setswana, the impact of the spread of Christianity on the power of the chiefs, or even – in 1893 – the machinations of Cecil Rhodes in relation to Bechuanaland. Here was a distinctive Tswana discourse developing, facilitated by missionary endeavour.[83]

Being part of a wider Tswana-speaking community co-existed, as it did for others, with being a British colonial subject. This had an important linguistic dimension too. English was an increasingly pervasive presence in the affairs of the Cape Colony, it was promoted enthusiastically by its Education Department, and it was sustained in the public sphere by an expanding English language press, the Kimberley *Diamond Fields Advertiser* being the most influential newspaper locally. Along with this came a host of beliefs and assumptions, common to the English-speaking world, including a strong sense of loyalty to the figure of Queen Victoria, an enduring symbol for black and white alike of the values and ideals of benevolent imperial rule. As a youngster Plaatje would have been aware of the celebrations surrounding her golden jubilee in 1887: if he was in Kimberley at the time, he could not have avoided them.

Importantly, as his own education testified, English was not just for those with a white skin. In other parts of the colony, especially in the eastern Cape, where English and Scottish missions were long established, Africans had taken advantage of what was on offer, mastering the English language and using it to communicate their views and concerns to their rulers and to their fellow citizens, black and white. Since 1884, indeed, they had their own bilingual weekly newspaper, *Imvo Zabantsundu (Native Opinion)*, published in King William's Town and edited by an African of Mfengu origin, John Tengo Jabavu. Unlike *Mahoko*, it was published in both English and an indigenous language (Xhosa), and was independent of missionary control, enjoying, as Plaatje later put it, 'a kind of monopoly in the field of native journalism'. *Imvo* circulated widely in Kimberley too and carried plenty of news of the doings of the town's mission-educated African community, as well as the social, religious and political affairs of the colony more generally. It would be surprising if Plaatje had not already encountered it.[84]

Imvo, however, was only one of a number of influences, secular and religious, that shaped the thoughts and aspirations of these emerging African communities as they were drawn into the life of the colony. Some were from much further afield. Most striking of all in its impact was a visiting African American musical company, the Virginia Jubilee Singers, which toured South Africa in the early 1890s. They proved extraordinarily popular among black and white alike. For black South Africans their music held a special fascination, not just for its intrinsic qualities but because it conveyed an inspiring message of educational uplift and advancement – and of racial solidarity too. Orpheus M. McAdoo, the charismatic leader of the troupe, added to its appeal by regaling his audiences with stories of black American achievements in education and the professions, of the progress they (and he, born a slave) had made since the era of slavery.[85]

Nowhere did they leave a greater legacy than in Kimberley. Plaatje would recall attending one of their performances, but for others, older than he, their visit – in August 1890 – proved to be life-changing. Charlotte Manye, for example, a teacher in a Wesleyan mission school, was inspired to join with friends to form a troupe of their own, and ended up performing before Queen Victoria. Titus Mbongwe, a clerk working in the town, so impressed Orpheus McAdoo with his desire for education that he was awarded a scholarship to study at the Hampton Institute in Virginia – only for his good fortune to end in tragedy when he died in a train crash en route to the United States. Others, like Josiah Semouse, a messenger at the Kimberley post office, were prompted to question their own circumstances. When would the African people 'stop being slaves and become nations with their own government?' he wondered, after hearing that African American schools and universities were run without the help of whites.[86]

Encountering the Virginia Jubilee Singers brought home to these young men and women the existence of a wider world of education, opportunity and advancement, and it confounded racial certainties and stereotypes. At the same time it created a powerful bond with Negro America, holding up a mirror to their own experiences. Orpheus McAdoo and his troupe were not easily forgotten.

Plaatje remained at Pniel until early in 1894 when he left the mission in order to take up a job as a messenger with the post office in Kimberley. According to a surviving fragment of an account he wrote about his departure from Pniel, there had been some discussion among both relatives and the Westphals about the possibility of his going on to one of the few colleges of secondary education open to Africans in the Cape Colony, most notable of which was the prestigious Lovedale Institution in the eastern Cape. Certainly this would have been feasible. Although Lovedale was run by Scottish Presbyterian missionaries, it did take in pupils from other denominations if they were considered able enough, so there was nothing in theory to prevent his admission, and he would not have been the first from a Berlin mission school to have studied there.[87]

Finding the required fees, however, proved to be a stumbling block. For some reason it seems Plaatje's father was unwilling to assist, despite being well able to do so. The Westphals nevertheless 'had something mapped out for me which they could not quite define', so Plaatje related, 'and it came as a terrible shock to them … when I left the old mission by way of the Cape Civil Service'. Tearful scenes accompanied his departure, and they appealed to him to change his mind, fearful 'he should fall an easy prey to the temptations of city life'. But he was intent on leaving. With his already proven abilities it was natural he should want to move on, and not altogether surprising he should have secured a job at the Kimberley post office, well known locally for its readiness to employ Africans possessed of a mission-school education. Colonial society, it should be said, did not otherwise offer a great deal in the way of career prospects for even the abler products of its mission schools.[88]

Sad as they were to see him go, the Westphals were soon reconciled to his decision. Ernst Westphal provided a testimonial for the post office in support of his application, as did Friedrich Ecker in Kimberley, and it was not long before he was writing proudly of Plaatje's progress in his new job. But it would be surprising, too, if his departure had not prompted some reflection about the failure of the Berlin Mission Society to provide anything in the way of secondary education for their more able students – and thus the opportunity to harness their talents to the service of the mission.[89]

Such was Plaatje's life, so far as it is possible to piece it together, up to the age of seventeen and a half. In many respects, it had been a comfortable, almost privileged, existence. Compared with the majority of other Africans of his generation who grew up in southern Africa during these years, he had enjoyed security and material comfort, and he was now equipped with the means of escaping from the unskilled, manual labour that was becoming for so many a necessary part of their livelihood.

Other Africans grew up in broadly similar circumstances on mission stations elsewhere in southern Africa. When they came together, as they did in places like Kimberley, they were conscious of a commonality in experience and outlook that cut across both ethnic identity and religious difference. Like them, Plaatje had been brought up to accept the values and beliefs of the Christian religion and, as happened on countless other mission stations, was greatly influenced by one particular missionary. It was almost in the nature of mission-station life, indeed, that close relationships of this kind should develop, although rather less common for missionaries' wives to be quite as influential as Marie Westphal.

It is clear that he left Pniel with a strongly developed moral sense, rooted in his upbringing with his family as much as the teachings of the missionaries, equipped with the self-discipline to cope with a challenging new environment. He feared letting down not only the Westphals but his own relatives, especially the two aunts who showed a greater concern for his future, he considered, than that of their own children. These 'four guardian angels', he called them, 'were always a circle around my bed'. They would die of sorrow were he to let them down, and he would be 'their killer'; while the thought of 'being seen at a place where fellas are drunk', or 'being implicated in a police case', 'struck terror into a fellow's heart'.[90]

Such an emphasis on inner strength and character was entirely in accord with the ethos of life on German missions, dedicated as they were to building the spiritual and personal resources to resist the temptations of the 'external world'. For the missionaries, and those who followed their teachings, this 'inner realm' was the key to salvation. Plaatje never forgot what Richard Brune, the missionary at Adamshoop, once told him. 'Salomo,' he said, 'all the knowledge of the world is only smoke and ashes. Jesus alone is the Wisdom.' In this inner realm, moreover, unlike the world outside, there was equality between black and white. Before God, if you believed in him, all were the same. That would remain with him too.[91]

What distinguished Plaatje's upbringing from that of many of his contemporaries was the depth of experience his family had accumulated in reconciling African and Christian tradition, in forging a distinctive way of life from a synthesis of the two. At Pniel, as later, there is nothing to suggest he was troubled by conflict between them: rather, it was a matter of the one enriching the other, of broadening the social and cultural resources that shaped his being. He was secure in his inherited identity and lived experience as a Morolong *ba ga Modiboa*, and fascinated by their traditions. At the same time he was well equipped by education and upbringing to explore the opportunities that beckoned in the late-Victorian colonial world around him. Being the third generation of his family since his forebears first came into contact with Christian missionaries undoubtedly helped.

To the Westphals, it is fair to say, he owed a special debt. They combined in an unusual way a genuine respect for the culture and traditions of the people who lived on the Pniel mission with a belief and confidence in what both Christianity and European culture had to offer. They had gone out of their way to foster his talents, and they treated him as one of their family. In their life and work, they exemplified selfless service to a higher cause. He would never forget what they did for him.

The Westphals, for their part, had simply to accept the inevitable, for it was obvious that their protégé had seen far too much of the outside world to wish to remain at Pniel any longer. If Ernst Westphal thought back to that trip they made to Mayakgoro in 1890, he might have guessed, with the advantage of hindsight, how things would work out.

TWO

'Full of pleasant anticipations'
Kimberley, 1894–1898

Kimberley in the 1890s was a world away from the chaotic mining shanty-town that had sprung up so rapidly in the early 1870s. Now it was very much a company town, dominated by one great corporation, De Beers Consolidated Mines Limited. Created by the logic of diamond mining as much as by the driving ambition of its founder, Cecil Rhodes, De Beers first of all bought up the small diggers, then the numerous other smaller companies, and finally, in the late 1880s, won control over its remaining rivals. With consolidation came control over the selling price of diamonds, tight control and regimentation of the labour force through the newly instituted compound system, and massive profits. By the 1890s the wealth this produced supplied more than half the revenues of the Cape Colony.

All this had transformed the character of the town of Kimberley. Fewer people were needed to work on the mines now they were run by a single corporation, and many of the whites who had come to the diamond fields had left to seek employment elsewhere. Most of the unskilled work was done by African migrant labourers, cheaper to employ than whites, and readier to endure the harsh discipline of the compounds. Kimberley now had the atmosphere and trappings of the company town it had turned into, its local institutions as much under the control of De Beers as the mining of diamonds. The 'old roughness', as one distinguished visitor put it in 1894, 'has been replaced by order and comfort' and Kimberley was no longer 'an adventure camp, but a town inhabited by intelligent people who read and study'; while its public library, in the opinion of another, was 'one of the largest and best stocked that I saw in the Colonies'.[1]

In addition to migrant labourers housed in closed, tightly guarded compounds – many of them from well beyond the borders of the Cape Colony – Kimberley was home to a larger and rather more permanent population of Indians, Coloureds and Africans, some twenty thousand strong in total. The Africans formed the majority, and mostly lived in the crowded residential areas (known as locations, numbered one to four) that had grown up around the four great mines, earning a living by small-scale trading, in working for De Beers, the larger trading stores or contractors, or the Kimberley municipality, or in servicing the domestic needs of the town's white residents.

Among this mixed community was a group of Africans, consisting of no more than a few hundred, at most a thousand people, who possessed a marketable commodity of a different kind: a missionary education. 'In the townships', noted the civil commissioner for Kimberley in 1892, 'a considerable number of educated natives are employed. They come principally from Lovedale, and belong to the Fingo or AmaXhosa tribes', and they occupied positions as clerks, messengers, teachers, police constables, interpreters and the like. These jobs were reasonably well paid, and since the 1870s their existence in Kimberley had been a powerful attraction for the graduates of mission schools, such as Lovedale, Healdtown, Morija and a handful of others, which provided Africans with the opportunity of acquiring a basic secondary education.[2]

The Mfengu ('Fingos') and Xhosa came from the eastern Cape, the earliest and most successful field of missionary endeavour in southern Africa, and consequently the region that produced the largest number of Africans with the best educational qualifications. Unable to find suitable employment nearer home, the more adventurous made their way to Kimberley in search of jobs commensurate with their ambitions and aspirations. The Mfengu in particular, close adherents of the missionary cause and relatively recent immigrants to the eastern Cape, proved most adept at exploiting the opportunities they found on the diamond fields; they more than anybody else were prepared to make a permanent home in this new urban environment.

A few of the incomers, if they could afford it, chose to live not in one of the locations but in the Malay Camp, a racially mixed residential area much closer to the centre of town. This took its name from the Malay artisans who arrived from Cape Town in the 1870s, but it was now home to people of European, Coloured, Indian, Chinese and African descent as well as the original Cape Malays and their descendants. Their homes ranged from solid brick and stone buildings to flimsy, ramshackle structures made from 'wood, canvas, iron, and even tin linings of packing cases neatly patched together'. There were gambling dens, saloons and dance halls, as well as mosques and Christian churches (of several denominations). Children played what one resident called 'paraffin cricket' in the streets (a paraffin tin served as the wicket, a strip of packing case as bat), disturbing the progress of passers-by. Overcrowded and disorderly it may have been, according to one unsympathetic observer, but the Malay Camp was a colourful, cosmopolitan place and people had the freedom to get on with their lives. Young Benjamin Tyamzashe particularly remembered 'the exuberant music and vibrant rhythms' he heard around him. Being the son of a Christian minister did not prevent him from joining in the singing and chanting at one of the mosques – or from helping himself to the curry and rice that was on offer. Sixty years later he had only to sing one of the tunes to be reminded of the taste.[3]

✦

Plaatje's new job in the post office began on 1 March 1894. He stayed initially with relatives, most likely his elder brother Samuel who worked for Cuthberts, a leading shoe retailer in town. After a short while, he got to know a young man called Isaiah Bud-M'belle, an Mfengu, who had just been appointed interpreter to the Griqualand West High Court, seeing him most days when he delivered telegrams to his office. Soon they were sharing lodgings in a boarding house in the Malay Camp, run by a man of Malay origin called Cumgalie and his wife. Here, in return for £2.10s a month (nearly half his salary) he got a room and an evening meal and had his washing done. The other main attraction of Cumgalie's establishment was undoubtedly its location, close to the town centre and no more than a few minutes' walk from the main post office building where he went each day. Since the High Court building and the post office were on opposite sides of the Market Square, it was just as convenient for Bud-M'belle too.[4]

The post office was popular with the town's mission-educated African community because it provided them with employment. This went back to 1880 when the general manager of telegraphs for the colony had approached Dr Stewart, the principal of Lovedale, with a request to send some 'native messengers' to Kimberley to deliver telegrams in the town. The need arose because it was found impossible to obtain white labour, delivering telegrams being considered too menial a job and the pay too low. A reasonable degree of literacy was nevertheless essential if the telegrams were to end up in the right place. So an 'experiment' was initiated in 1880, 'a staff of native messengers' came to Kimberley from Lovedale, and they proved a great success. Three years later the general manager of telegraphs wrote that it afforded him much pleasure to be able to state 'that from the day on which they took up their duties to the present, not so much as the shadow of a complaint has been urged against them, and not a single case of non-delivery or delay has been officially reported to me'.[5]

Similar circumstances encouraged the Cape civil service to take on mission-educated Africans elsewhere; government service, as a result, came to be a very highly regarded avenue of advancement – official recognition too of their place in colonial society. Most of the positions open to Africans were, it is true, at the lowest levels, but it was expected that in time, as they achieved additional qualifications and experience, further progress would be made. 'We are just emerging from barbarism', wrote John Knox Bokwe, one of the best-known

African spokesmen of the day, 'and have to find our way, and by degrees gain their [whites'] confidence. By and by we shall attain, if one here and there shows capacity for positions of trust and responsibility, and creditably discharge the responsibility.' Although not everybody would have gone along with quite such a cautious, gradualist approach, there nevertheless remained a widespread faith in the possibilities of government employment.[6]

By the time Plaatje took up his job in Kimberley white attitudes had hardened, however. In the late 1870s and early 1880s, if you had a white skin, jobs were easy to come by, but by the 1890s this was no longer the case. Unemployment had risen, and there was a campaign, led by a man called James S. Morgan, to replace African telegraph messengers and letter-carriers by whites. 'Surely with so many respectable white men and lads out of employment,' he argued, 'there should be no difficulty in procuring white labour to fill any vacancy that arises. It is the white population who contribute most largely to the revenue of the Post Office,' he said, 'and I maintain that they deserve a recognition of their just claims in the matter.'[7]

It was fortunate for Plaatje that the Kimberley postmaster, John Henry, was not persuaded to alter the policy of employing Africans as messengers and letter-carriers. They had given him good service and he knew they were better educated than the whites he could have got in their place. And in such men as Alfred Moletsane and Nelson Lindie, both of them working at the Kimberley post office when Plaatje started in March 1894, he had two most capable and long-serving members of staff. Both men were part of the original 'experiment' and had remained with the Kimberley post office ever since. Alfred Moletsane had, by dint of what Plaatje described as 'diligence and assiduous application to duty', achieved promotion to the rank of assistant postmaster, the only African among the usual complement of twenty Europeans in such positions, earning, like them, a salary of £110 a year. He had also managed to pay off the cost of his education at Lovedale through monthly instalments taken out of his wages.[8]

Nelson Lindie, too, had progressed up the local post office hierarchy, occupying the position, at the time Plaatje started work there, of 'sender-out', responsible for the direction and dispatch of the thirty or so messengers he had under his charge; he would have been, in all probability, Plaatje's immediate superior.

A little more is known about Nelson Lindie because an article about him appeared in the local newspaper, the *Diamond Fields Advertiser*, in March 1895. This is of interest not only for the details it gives about his background and ancestry (he claimed descent from a Xhosa royal family), but for what it reveals of the attitudes and behaviour considered desirable by his employers. Thus Lindie

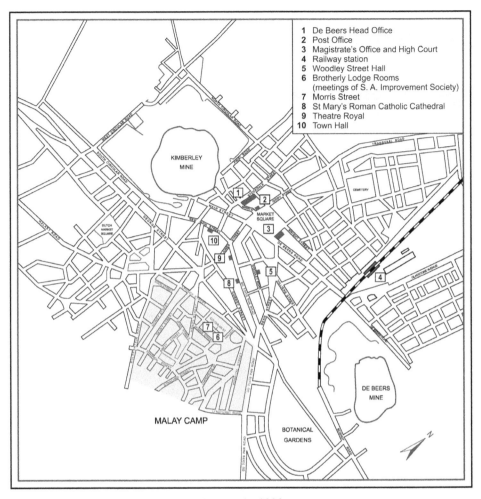

Kimberley during Plaatje's time there in the 1890s

was 'not overbearingly proud of his genealogical tree, but on the contrary is a well-spoken, well-educated native of respectable demeanour, and is as politely mannered as a large proportion of his fellow civil servants of European origin'; he was, moreover, 'to be commended for his extremely creditable record as a private citizen and as a servant of the Government', representing in his own person 'a satisfactory solution of the native problem', and who was in his 'usefulness and general conduct of life a complete answer to those who are strenuously opposed to native education'.[9]

In return for displaying such virtues, and for discharging their duties efficiently and responsibly, black employees at the post office were paid a decent salary and treated fairly. Such at any rate was how Plaatje remembered things some fifteen years later. Protesting in 1911 about the way Africans were being unfairly treated by the post office authorities, he drew a contrast with how things were in his day. Then, minor misdemeanours, when they occurred, were punished by a fine of a shilling, not used as a pretext for their dismissal and replacement by whites. And if all fairness had disappeared, so too had standards of efficiency. In his day, 'when a telegram came for "Robinson, Kimberley", Robinson had to get it or the Postmaster General would know the reason why'. You just had to use your initiative, in other words. Returning it to the sender marked 'insufficient address' was not an option.[10]

Plaatje and his colleagues may have been subject, as he recalled, to 'the strictest discipline', but it was applied to black and white alike. For somebody brought up on a German mission this was hardly a problem. Employers in Kimberley looked upon Pniel and other German missions with special favour precisely because of the reputation they had for strict discipline, something that undoubtedly helped him to get his job in the first place.

He started at the Kimberley post office on £72 a year, a figure that had risen to £96 a year by the time he left in 1898. Few other details of his time there have survived. We do know that, like his colleagues, he turned out each day in a smart grey uniform distinguished by three thin red stripes down each trouser leg; that as well as Nelson Lindie and Alfred Moletsane, his colleagues included, at various times, Moses Lassias, Boyce Skota, Abraham Smouse, Joseph Mikwalo, Aaron Nyusa, Simon Sondolo, Thomas Xipu, Hendrik Molschane, David Oliphant, Anthony Makubalo and Herbert Mizine, their very names a mark of their diverse ethnic origins; and that one of the white telegraphists who worked in the office at this time, a man called J.K. Bray, remembered that everybody was accustomed to 'working at high pressure'. But at least he did not have to face up to the occupational hazards of actually delivering letters or telegrams. Aaron Nyusa was once awarded £3 damages (plus costs) in the local magistrate's court after being bitten by a dog while delivering a letter to a house in Market Road. Things could be even worse in the neighbouring borough of Beaconsfield. Here Theo Binase, well known to Plaatje, requested permission (unsurprisingly refused) to carry a loaded revolver to protect himself while carrying out his duties.[11]

At some point Plaatje was promoted from the position of telegraph messenger to that of letter-carrier, which was better paid and carried a greater degree of responsibility. When he looked back on his time with the post office, however, other things seemed more important. Having commenced his career as no more than 'a semi-barbarian', he told an audience in Kimberley years later, the post office proved to be his 'educational institution'. 'An abnormal thirst for knowledge' had shown him that 'no-one was too humble or too young to teach him something', while 'a keen observation' of what he saw around him 'stood him in such good stead that he was soon able to gain a footing'.[12]

Such, indeed, was the impression formed by Ernst Westphal when he called in to see Plaatje one day in the middle of 1895. He considered he had surpassed all his other pupils 'in knowledge, skills and even in behaviour' and was relieved that so far he had not disgraced him – any missionary's worst fear. Most of Plaatje's colleagues at work, Westphal noted, had been to Lovedale or Morija, and he was delighted to find that his protégé was more than holding his own among them and had just been rewarded with a salary increase. All of which supports Modiri Molema's contention that Plaatje responded quickly to the demands of the job and the example of the people with whom he worked, and acquired a reputation as 'a speedy, industrious and energetic messenger, knowledgeable about his work, and impeccably well-mannered'. Here was a young man who wanted to get on.[13]

In the employment of the Kimberley post office Plaatje and his colleagues had to observe the myriad rules and regulations which governed their working lives. They were expected to know their place and to respect the conventions that prevailed in the workplace, particularly those that governed relations between black and white. If they failed to do so, they not only put their own jobs at risk but played into the hands of those – like James Morgan – who would rather see whites in their place: there was often quite a tricky path to negotiate between being considered part of 'the native problem' or the solution to it. Outside working hours, though, in the company of friends of their own colour and class, things were very different. Here they had far more control of their own lives and they could speak freely, their social interaction rooted in shared attitudes and experience. From the moment Plaatje arrived in Kimberley he was drawn into a natural association with the men and women who made up the town's mission-educated African community, and he was soon involved in the network of social and cultural activities which helped give them so distinct an identity.[14]

They were a well-established community, and some of them had been there for years. John Kosani, for example, a Wesleyan lay preacher of Mfengu descent, and one-time ox-wagon driver, now a cab-owner, took special pride in his claim to be the earliest African resident of the diamond fields, having arrived on the day the first diamond was discovered at Bultfontein in 1871. Gwayi Tyamzashe, a Congregational clergyman, remembered by Plaatje as 'the first ordained black minister I ever saw', arrived soon after, and for over two years, until his death in

1896, was a close neighbour in the Malay Camp. As a clergyman, he enjoyed an elevated status in the eyes of his community, and along with the other two African ministers on the diamond fields, Jonathan Jabavu and Davidson Msikinya, both of them Wesleyans, was often asked to become president, chairman or honorary member of the many societies and clubs which flourished in the life of this community. The three men assumed a natural role as spokesmen when representations needed to be made over some issue that affected their interests. One thing Plaatje particularly remembered about Davidson Msikinya was his frequent use in conversation, doubtless in his sermons too, of the phrase 'nooks and corners'.[15]

Then there were the court interpreters. Apart from Isaiah Bud-M'belle, these now included Joseph Singapy Moss, a man of Mfengu origin who had first come to the diamond fields in 1879, tried his hand at transport riding and teaching, became an interpreter in the Beaconsfield magistrate's court, achieved promotion to the Griqualand West High Court three years later, and was now a well-known public figure and a substantial property owner; George Polisa, a resident of No. 4 Location, who started work at the post office in Beaconsfield in 1885 before moving on to better things in the Kimberley magistrate's court; and Jonas Msikinya, one of the well-known Msikinya family (Davidson was a younger brother), educated at Lovedale, and interpreter and office messenger at the Beaconsfield magistrate's court since 1879.[16]

Like the smaller mission-educated communities in other parts of the colony, Kimberley's African community was bound together by a body of shared beliefs, values and assumptions as well as the close personal ties of friendship, marriage and a busy social life. Its members, almost by definition, were committed Christians and regular churchgoers, firm believers in the idea of progress, in the virtues of education, hard work and individual achievement, and they had a warm but far from uncritical admiration for the institutions of the Cape Colony and the British empire. Two things in particular they held on to: the notion of equality before the law, regardless of racial or any other distinctions; and the non-racial Cape franchise, the right to vote, enshrined in the laws of the colony, and open to any male citizen who possessed property worth £75, or an annual income of £50, and who could fill in a registration form in either English or Dutch.

It would be difficult to exaggerate the significance of these two constitutional facts in the perceptions of this community: they signified an entitlement to the privileges of 'civilised life' and the means of making a place for themselves in a society which otherwise put so many obstacles in their way. They gave substance to a vision of a common society in which merit and hard work, and not race, would prevail. Embracing these values, and expressing their loyalty to the British empire, was to assert their right to equal treatment and inclusion, to be considered as imperial citizens, not as voiceless subjects. In doing so they challenged the way most white colonists viewed the world. Queen Victoria remained for them, more than ever, the symbol around which these ideas cohered. Living on the diamond fields, they had special cause to join in the celebrations for the Queen's diamond jubilee in June 1897, and they took every opportunity to appropriate the image of 'the great white Queen' to their own ends – such as when raising money from the great and the good of Kimberley for a new 'Queen Victoria Jubilee Hall', which was opened, amid further celebration, several months later.[17]

To a greater or lesser degree the members of this community, like their compatriots elsewhere, believed they had a special role and duty in the leadership of their people as a whole. Certainly they were keen as individuals to succeed in their professional and personal lives and to prove themselves entitled to full citizenship and equal treatment in the life of the colony. But their personal ambitions and identities were tempered by an often deeply felt sense of responsibility towards the African societies from which they came, and whose interests they sought to both serve and represent. Sometimes the two things came into conflict. On the one hand, they were faced with constant pressures to reject and disown many of the features of their own societies in order to 'prove' their worthiness of entitlement to equal treatment with whites. On the other, they sometimes encountered widespread suspicion on the part of their less educated countrymen for appearing to do precisely this. It was not always easy to find the right course to steer, socially or psychologically.

But among Kimberley's African elite in the 1890s the overwhelming impression is one of optimism and self-confidence. Their communal life displayed an impressive vitality and sophistication. Both locally and nationally there still seemed reason to be hopeful about the future direction of the Cape's political affairs and the role they could expect to play in them. And Kimberley itself was so much of a self-contained society, situated far away from the rural societies from which most of its mission-educated community originally came, that the kind of social divisions that arose between town and country in the eastern Cape was barely an issue.

Plaatje's friendship with Isaiah Bud-M'belle was the ideal entrée into the social life of this community. Then aged twenty-five, seven years older than Plaatje, he was a man whose career was frequently held up as an example of what it was possible for Africans to achieve. Like the majority of mission-educated Africans living and working in Kimberley, Bud-M'belle came from the eastern Cape, and was of Mfengu origin, born in Burgersdorp in 1870. He attended the

Healdtown Institution, second only to Lovedale in its reputation as a college for secondary education for African pupils. After that he taught for a few years at a Wesleyan mission school in Colesberg, studying privately in order to take the Cape civil service examinations, open to black and white alike, and passing these successfully at the end of 1892. He was the first African to do so, and his achievement attracted a considerable amount of comment in the press at the time.

It made up for an earlier disappointment. When the Virginia Jubilee Singers visited in 1890, Bud-M'belle, like so many others, was struck by their message and approached Orpheus McAdoo about the possibility of studying in the United States. Unsuccessful in this – for McAdoo had already awarded his scholarship to Titus Mbongwe – he applied directly to the Hampton Institute in Virginia, explaining to the principal, 'Here in South Africa, a coloured man gets no sound education, but merely primary.' Nothing came of this, so he resorted instead to private study – with most impressive results.[18]

Bud-M'belle first came to Kimberley for a holiday over Christmas 1892, filling in for the interpreter in the local police station during his temporary absence. In March 1894, qualified by now in English, Dutch, 'Kaffir' (Xhosa) and Sesotho, he was appointed interpreter in native languages to the Griqualand West High Court, the Special and Circuit Courts, and clerk to the resident magistrate, and took up his duties three months later, earning a salary of £200 a year. It was not long before it was being said that he was one of the best interpreters, black or white, in the colony.[19]

Bud-M'belle was also a man of boundless energy and humour (he used to amuse his friends by telling them how he was once introduced at a meeting as the judge's 'interrupter'), a talented sportsman and musician, and was soon a leading light in the social life of Kimberley's African community, being at one time, according to a praise poem composed in his honour, secretary of no less than eight different clubs or societies. After the three African clergymen, nobody was held in higher esteem. He personified, indeed, the values which this community held dear, and he had demonstrated what could be achieved through natural ability, hard work and perseverance in the face of adversity.[20]

His profession was held in particularly high regard too. African court interpreters, it was believed, could make a special contribution to the institutional life of the colony by virtue of their familiarity with their own languages, unmatched by all but a handful of whites. Upon them, accordingly, depended both the proper functioning of the judicial system, and hence access to one of the institutions they valued so highly, and the means of making a practical reality of the Cape judiciary's claims to give equal treatment to every individual, black or white, in the courts of law. When this interpreting was done in the High Court rather than the magistrate's courts, as in Bud-M'belle's case, the burden of responsibility was all the greater. Nobody doubted he was up to the task.

No organisation, among the many clubs and societies that flourished in the life of this community, was more characteristic of their ideals and aspirations than the South Africans Improvement Society. Formed in June 1895, and meeting at 7.30 p.m. every second Tuesday in a room hired from a white organisation, it soon came to play an important part in Plaatje's life. The society's name is revealing in itself: 'improvement', like 'progress', was a key concept in these circles, while the decision on the part of the twenty members who attended the society's inaugural meeting to call themselves 'South African', rather than 'Native' or 'African', seemed to signify an aspiration towards an identity defined more by nationality than race. The society's objects, in the mind at least of its first secretary, Simon Mokuena, interpreter in the Beaconsfield magistrate's court, whom Plaatje remembered as 'perhaps the greatest linguist and orator I ever knew', were equally explicit: 'firstly, to cultivate the use of the English language, which is foreign to Africans; secondly, to help each other by fair and reasonable criticisms in readings, recitations, English compositions, etc. etc.'[21]

It would be difficult to exaggerate the importance that mission-educated Africans in the colony attached to a command of the English language, and there was nothing unique in the Improvement Society's view of the matter. Here is *Imvo Zabantsundu*, the English–Xhosa weekly, several months later: 'The key of knowledge is the English language. Without such a mastery of it as will give the scholar a taste for reading, the great English literature is a sealed book, and he remains one of the uneducated, living in the miserably small world of Boer ideals, or those of the untaught Natives. But besides, in this country where the English are the rulers, the merchants, and the influential men, he can never obtain a position in life of any importance without a command of English.'[22]

The point could not have been made more clearly: without good English, employment, 'improvement' and 'progress' were all impossible. The members of Kimberley's South Africans Improvement Society had every reason, therefore, to take their self-declared objectives very seriously indeed. This is not to say they followed slavishly every aspect of 'the great English literature', and every assumption that came with it, in their quest for knowledge. Rather, they brought their own linguistic and cultural traditions to an understanding of English and its peculiarities, playing around with the possibilities in a creative, often very humorous manner. In doing so they gave it a distinctive flavour of their own. They made it their language too.

Plaatje was a regular at the society's meetings and soon an active participant. He did not, however, contribute a paper or reading at the first meeting; this was taken up with a talk by Isaiah Bud-M'belle, entitled 'My ideas of a debating society', and was followed by the election of office-bearers. But at the society's second meeting, held on 16 July 1895, the secretary reported that Plaatje read out a chapter from *John Bull and Co.* by Max O'Rell, published the previous year, and written by a Frenchman (whose real name was Léon Paul Blouet), best described as a humorous celebration of the glories of the British empire. Plaatje had not been in Kimberley when Blouet visited the town in 1893, but many of the older members of the South Africans Improvement Society had, and it may well have been the chapter on Kimberley that he chose to read out. His rendering was by no means perfect: 'his style of reading and pronunciation', so Simon Mokuena thought, 'was fairly criticised', while 'the mistakes corrected did not only benefit the reader, but also the other members'.[23]

Such was Plaatje's literary debut. If, on the evidence presented above, it can be considered no more than a modest success, the other members present would have made some allowance for the fact that he had grown up on a German-run mission station and had received only a limited formal education. But at least his text proved a happier choice than that of the previous speaker that evening. Walter Kawa's admittedly able recitation from Milton's *Paradise Lost* was not, in Mokuena's opinion, 'highly appreciated by the majority of members, as it was too classical to be comprehended by the average native mind'. What Plaatje made of it was not recorded, but it was clear that Kawa had overstepped the limits of social and literary one-upmanship. For the secretary of the Improvement Society at least, Milton represented the point at which some doubts might be entertained as to the universality, not to say the comprehensibility, of high English culture.

Not everybody agreed with this. Joseph Moss, for example, had he been present that evening, would have seen things differently. As a founder member of the Lovedale Literary Society, that was perhaps to be expected. Of course, *Paradise Lost* posed some challenges but that just called for effort and application. The important thing, as Moss saw it, was to assert their claim to a literary tradition that was as much theirs as their white fellow citizens', and then to demonstrate their mastery of it. He was in no doubt, moreover, 'that a classical education is the right and necessary one for the Native people at the present stage', a view he had put forward in a series of 'Lectures on native education' some years before. Questions of literary taste raised quite big political and philosophical issues, so it was no surprise that opinions varied.[24]

Plaatje's contribution to the society's meeting a month later was rather better received. Certainly it gave an indication of an early interest that had developed at Pniel, and that was to continue to fascinate him later in life, the essay he read on this occasion being entitled 'The history of the Bechuanas'. 'Being a Bechuana by birth,' it was recorded, with perhaps just a hint of condescension, 'he showed great mastery over his subject.' However much he had in common with his audience that evening, to give a talk on this subject was a reminder that he was different. As a Motswana, and a Morolong, he was in a small minority among the society's predominantly Xhosa-speaking membership.[25]

Since the Batswana were very much in the news, the timing of his talk was probably not fortuitous. British Bechuanaland, which included Mafeking and the surrounding district, was in the process of being annexed to the Cape Colony. Chief Montshiwa had first of all consented, then changed his mind, and finally expressed himself in favour. While he prevaricated, the chiefs of the Bechuanaland Protectorate, to the north, facing another threat, prepared to travel to England to protest to the British imperial government about Cecil Rhodes's plans to annex their lands for his Chartered Company. Indeed, by the time Plaatje was enlightening his colleagues about the 'history of the Bechuanas' at their meeting on 13 August, the three Protectorate chiefs – Khama, Bathoen and Sebele – were already on their way south. Three days later they stopped briefly in Kimberley and 'a large crowd', so it was reported, gathered that evening to witness their welcome and departure; it would be surprising if Plaatje was not among them. Other members of the South Africans Improvement Society, if they were there too, would at least have a clearer idea of the historical background to their mission to England.[26]

At subsequent meetings of the Improvement Society, debating and musical performance featured too. The debates are especially revealing of the aspirations of the people with whom Plaatje now spent his time, helping to familiarise them – the younger members of the society in particular – not just with the finer points of the English language but the pros and cons of different aspects of 'civilised life': as when, for example, they debated the motion 'Is insurance a proper provision for life?' (Isaiah Bud-M'belle for, Joseph Moss against), as a result of which 'many who did not fully understand insurance made proposals to the various companies'.[27]

On occasions difficulties could arise when conventions of debating procedure ran counter to personal conviction. At a meeting of the society early in 1896 the subject debated was 'Is lobola as practised at the present time justifiable?' – Walter Kawa for, Henry Msikinya (a teacher at the local Wesleyan mission school) against. Not unexpectedly, Msikinya won the debate, but to Walter Kawa must go the credit for maintaining a stiff upper lip in what must have been a difficult situation for him: 'It is only fair to state that Mr W.B. Kawa, after having ably led his side, publicly stated that his own personal convictions were entirely against this relic of barbarism.'[28]

Perhaps the most striking feature of all about the meetings of the society was the blend of humour and self-confidence so often displayed. These were qualities which Plaatje would make his own, but it is evident that in this respect, as in others, he owed a great deal to the example of those around him. Much of their humour arose from the social situation in which they found themselves, and they were frequently willing to make fun not only of the 'ways of European civilisation' but of their own aspirations towards them.

It had no better exponent than one of Plaatje's friends, Patrick Lenkoane, a much-travelled resident of Kimberley, originally from Leribe in Basutoland, who had at one time been in personal service with Cecil Rhodes, then worked as a gardener, but now described himself as a boarding-house keeper. Plaatje remembered him as the 'humorous black Irishman', whose jokes and stories constituted a genre called a 'Lenkoanic'. Everybody found him funny. Nearly eighty years after Maud Zibi first met Lenkoane, the mere mention of his name brought on a big smile: he was, she remembered, 'very, very humorous, oh very humorous – we would all laugh when he came in the room'. His contributions invariably enlivened the proceedings of the Improvement Society. On one occasion it was in response to the paper, 'Civilisation and its advantages to African races', read by the society's vice president, W. Cowen, a West African now living in Kimberley: 'It was during the comment and criticism on this essay that the native Artemus Ward, Mr Patrick Lenkoane, said, in his inimitable and humorous manner, "That the natives of this country have caught hold of civilisation by the tail, and not by the head, and it is therefore dangerous to them."'[29]

When Patrick Lenkoane was around, it would seem, meetings of the Improvement Society were never too serious, and Plaatje would exchange 'Lenkoanics' with friends long after he had left Kimberley. That he was found funny by his colleagues is not only tribute to their willingness to make themselves and their situation the object of satire and humour, but a reflection of an underlying optimism and self-confidence. For Plaatje, Lenkoane, Bud-M'belle and the others, 'progress' and 'improvement' seemed assured, and the future held every promise: they could afford to laugh at themselves. Perhaps it was this shared taste for parody that lay behind Plaatje's choice of *John Bull and Co.* for his literary debut. He and his friends just had to remember to behave in the manner expected of them when they went to work the next day.

Alongside his participation in meetings of the Improvement Society, Plaatje studied hard in private, determined to bring his education up to the level of those around him. 'Constant reading after office hours', he recalled, helped to 'develop his knowledge' and to overcome 'the difficulties he experienced with the English language' when he first arrived in Kimberley. His aim was to become proficient not just in English but in the other languages used in court interpreting and thus to enhance his job prospects. It was a natural progression for somebody in his position and with his ability, and it cannot have taken him long to have formed such an ambition. Possibly it was in his mind even before he left Pniel, for he already had a keen interest in the law. 'As a boy', he wrote later, 'I was tremendously fascinated by the work of the Supreme Court', and he used to follow the progress of court cases in the law reports in the newspapers. Now he had only to turn to Isaiah Bud-M'belle for an insider's view of the challenges involved.[30]

Plaatje applied himself assiduously. By the time he left Kimberley in 1898, with a job as a court interpreter to go to, he could read and write, he said, in English, Dutch, Sesotho and Setswana, and speak 'Kaffir' (Xhosa) and German. By any standards it was an impressive array, and his list did not include several other languages, such as Zulu, Korana and Herero, with which he was familiar if not quite fluent in. It certainly helped to be surrounded by friends from a wide variety of ethnic backgrounds from whom he could learn, and on whom he could practise, his linguistic skills. In Ernst Westphal, too, he still had somebody to help improve his German. Once, in June 1896, he wrote him a letter in German: while it had a lot of mistakes, Westphal told him in reply, he nevertheless thought it a good effort overall, and complimented him on his zeal and application.[31]

Westphal was particularly impressed by his dedication to mastering the European languages. 'Drive and talent', in his view, had enabled Plaatje to build upon his education at Pniel, and he noticed, when he visited him in 1895, that he now had a good library of both English and Dutch books, and even a few in German. Judging from later references Plaatje made to them, they may well have included Arthur Conan Doyle's popular Sherlock Holmes stories, so his reading matter was unlikely to have been purely didactic and instrumental. Reading, after all, was for fun as well as enlightenment. It reminded Westphal of the time '*klein Salomo Plaatje*' used to run behind the mail coach, earning money to buy books.[32]

Plaatje had some way to go before he could match Isaiah Bud-M'belle in social and linguistic accomplishment, and in another sphere he didn't even try: sport. As well as everything else Bud-M'belle was a talented cricketer and rugby player, he organised competitions in both games (with Coloured, Malay and Indian as well as African teams), and managed to persuade De Beers to donate silver trophies for the winners of each. Cricket was particularly popular in Kimberley, as indeed it was among Africans elsewhere in the colony. The two African teams in Kimberley were called Eccentrics CC (Bud-M'belle's team) and Duke of Wellington CC ('Duke' as it was more familiarly known), and fixtures between the two were high up on the social as well as the sporting calendar.[33]

Plaatje was no cricketer, however. An upbringing on a German mission station may have got him his job but it was no preparation for cricket, and unlike Bud-M'belle he scarcely possessed the physique of a rugby player: he stood no more than 5'6" tall, lightly built, without the stockiness that would come later, but with thin, delicate-looking fingers, more suited to the concert hall than any kind of playing field. He did become, in September 1896, joint secretary of the Eccentrics Cricket Club, but that was as far as his sporting record went. His preference rather was for country pursuits like riding and later hunting – hardly suited to Kimberley.[34]

Plaatje made his mark in other ways, none more so than at the 'social gathering of Africans', fully reported in both *Imvo* and the *Diamond Fields Advertiser*, which took place on 21 August 1896. This was one of several events organised that week to provide a fitting send-off for Henry Msikinya and Chalmers Moss (a son of Mr 'Interpreter' Moss), both of whom had secured places at Wilberforce University, an African American college in Ohio, in order to continue with their education.

They owed their opportunity to the remarkable Charlotte Manye. Her exploits were already legendary. The star performer in the African Jubilee Singers, she was taken up with her friends by two white musical entrepreneurs, convinced they would appeal to audiences overseas. Their first European tour ended in some disarray but this failed to deter Charlotte from joining a second overseas tour two years later. This time she ended up in Ohio where she encountered a sympathetic bishop of the African Methodist Episcopal Church; his support enabled her to pursue her dream of an education in the United States, and she was accepted as a student at Wilberforce University in 1895. As news of this filtered back to Kimberley (via letters to her sister), along with glowing reports on her new surroundings, Wilberforce became the focus of the aspirations of other young men and women, responding to the almost mystical appeal of 'Negro America' and eager, like her, to further their education in the United States.[35]

Henry Msikinya and Chalmers Moss were fortunate to have parents who were willing to find the money that was needed. Not surprisingly, given the importance that was attached to education, securing admission to Wilberforce was an achievement of which they, their parents and the community as a whole could be very proud, and it was decided to give them an appropriate farewell – and also to raise some further funds to send them on their way. As was customary with important social events of this kind, an organising committee was formed. Plaatje was made its secretary, responsible therefore for the arrangements that needed to be made.

The evening surpassed all expectations. Isaiah Bud-M'belle considered their dinner 'an elegant affair in the fullest sense of the word', and found himself lost for words ('in this day of loose adjectives and thoughtless exaggerations') 'to convey that anything out of the ordinary has occurred'. He did feel, though, that since the function 'was carried on in a novel manner, judging it from an African standpoint', the after-dinner proceedings deserved to be reported in some detail, and from the account he wrote afterwards it is clear that Plaatje, still several months short of his twentieth birthday, was much involved. For after Bud-M'belle had taken the chair ('in obedience to the desire of the committee of arrangements'), and letters of apology were read from the Revs. Gwayi Tyamzashe and Jonathan Jabavu regretting their inability to be present 'owing to prior arrangements', it was Plaatje who commenced proceedings with a toast first to 'The Queen and Royal Family', and then another to 'The Acting Administrator'. It was quite a moment for him, and a remarkable demonstration of self-confidence and assurance from one so young. Not at all bad, those present must have thought, for a 'semi-barbarian' with no more than Standard III to his name, who had been in Kimberley less than eighteen months.

There followed a variety of further toasts – to 'Africa', 'Local black folk' and 'Our guests' – interspersed with musical interludes and songs, African and European, concluding, as was the custom on these occasions, with 'God save the Queen'. It had been, Bud-M'belle wrote, 'a function long to be remembered', and he ended on a note of thanks to those who had been involved in the arrangements. 'The entire success of this gathering', he said, 'is due to Messrs Sol T. Plaatje and E.J. Panyane who got up and prepared everything, to Mr T.J. Binase, who gave the use of his fine organ and accompanied most of the songs, and lastly, but not least, Mr Patrick Lenkoane, who superintended the waiting during the evening and seemed to be here, there and everywhere at the same time, arranging the details and looking after the introductions.'[36]

Three days later Msikinya and Moss departed for Cape Town on the first stage of their journey to the United States, taking with them the good wishes and hopes of Kimberley's African community. It would be surprising if Plaatje, denied the opportunity of a formal secondary school education, let alone the chance to go to a university, had not harboured some feelings of envy at their good fortune. Isaiah Bud-M'belle, too, must have thought of his own abortive attempt to get to the States six years previously. For all their loyal toasts and patriotic sentiment, the higher education these ambitious young men and women so desperately wanted in their own country was no closer.

Chalmers Moss, sad to say, never returned to Kimberley. Two years later news was received from Wilberforce that he had died, 'preparing for his life work', so the Rev. Davidson Msikinya wrote, 'the uplifting of his native land'. Great things were expected from Africans with an overseas education.[37]

Just a month later, in September 1896, Plaatje was involved in another characteristic initiative on the part of Kimberley's African community, this time involving an approach to De Beers. The company's own records tell the story. On 22 September, William Pickering, acting secretary at De Beers' head office, received a letter from a group of African residents of Kimberley, Plaatje among them, who had recently formed an African branch of the YMCA. They wanted money towards the construction of a meeting hall, and they had already constituted themselves into a building committee for this purpose. Their letter reminded the company of the number of Africans it had on its payroll ('Your worldwide known company has the honour of being the largest employers of native labour in this country'), and 'respectfully and humbly' put in a plea for 'financial aid towards defraying the necessary expenses connected with the building of and equipping the premises about to be erected in the Malay Camp'. 'We earnestly hope, nay believe, that our request will not be in vain', ended the appeal, 'as this is the first and only request from the native inhabitants of the Fields to you.'

At the end of the letter, carefully written out in Bud-M'belle's hand, were appended ten signatures, each with an indication in brackets after their name of their tribal, or racial, identity: T.J. Binase ('Fingoe'), John Cowan ('West African'), R.R.M.N. Gella ('Kaffir'), T.D.P. Lenkoane ('Basuto'), I. Bud-M'belle ('Fingoe'), J.J. Makwalo ('Mpondo'), S.M. Mokuena ('Basuto'), J.M. Ngcezula ('Fingoe'), E. Panyane ('Basuto') and, lastly, Sol T. Plaatje ('Bechuana'). Their ethnic diversity illustrates graphically the cosmopolitan nature of Kimberley's African community, and the signatories themselves clearly hoped the point would not be lost on De Beers; the more representative they were, the greater the chance – or so they hoped – of obtaining a contribution from the company. Perhaps because he had proved himself so successful as secretary of the committee of arrangements for the farewell dinner for Moss and Msikinya the previous month, it was agreed that Plaatje should become 'Secretary *pro tem*' of the YMCA committee, and it was he who wrote a short covering letter to accompany the petition, 'respectfully request[ing] you to submit the attached letter to the directors of your company', which he then delivered to the De Beers offices in Stockdale Street.

It is the earliest letter of Plaatje's to have survived. Although it has one crossing-out – he had got half-way through the word 'enclosed' before deciding that 'attached' would be more appropriate – it is written in a clear, bold hand and signed 'Your humble servant, Sol T. Plaatje', using the abbreviated form of his Christian name by which he was now known to his friends.

Later the same day he had some second thoughts. How, he wondered, were De Beers to reply to his committee's request? He decided to write again, apologising for having 'accidentally omitted to enclose the attached stamps for communication' and concluding: 'I therefore most humbly request that you must accept them for the said purpose.'

His concern for De Beers' postal budget was considerate, but somewhat misplaced. The company's net profit that year amounted to over two million pounds and it could well afford to forgo the six one-penny stamps enclosed in his letter. And if he thought a last-minute reminder might tip the balance in his committee's favour when it came to the directors' decision on their application, or simply to bring it to their attention in case it was overlooked, he was in for a disappointment. The directors' minutes note simply that the request was 'refused', and Plaatje and his friends got, as he would recall, not 'a brass farthing' towards their building fund. But De Beers did at least return the stamps to him, and therein perhaps lay a lesson not just in etiquette but in the realities of life in Kimberley in the 1890s: providing De Beers with stamps with which to reply to letters was simply not done.[38]

If there was one form of recreation which this African community really made their own, it was music, and unlike many of their other social activities it was one in which men and women participated on an equal basis – in the case of the talented Charlotte Manye, indeed, on a rather more than equal basis. One of the reasons the Jubilee Singers made such an impact on the diamond fields was that there was already a well-established local tradition of music making and appreciation. Partly this was nurtured, as elsewhere, in their churches and choirs, but in Kimberley there were opportunities to experience a much wider range of musical entertainment. It was a large enough town to attract a variety of visiting companies as well as supporting its own musical activities. In fact, they were often spoilt for choice, and Plaatje for one made the most of it. He would look back not only at the Jubilee Singers' 'quaint and classical oratorios' and the black-faced 'corner men of the Macadoo Vaudevilles', but also the 'mellifluous carols on Christmas eve at the Roman Catholic Church, and 'a member of the Payne family silencing a boisterous crowd with a selection she is going to give on the violin': testimony not only to the variety of musical entertainment on offer but to his manifest enjoyment and appreciation of it.[39]

Plaatje and his friends were fortunate that in Kimberley, more liberal than most places in the colony, their presence was generally tolerated by the predominantly white audiences who patronised the town's musical entertainments. Sometimes, it is true, the prejudices of their white fellow citizens would get the better of them. Once 'T. O'C' wrote to the *Diamond Fields Advertiser* disapproving of the presence of 'obviously full blooded Kafirs recognisable as such despite the glories of stand-up collars and evil-odoured manillas' at brigade band concerts and other public entertainments. Such racist sentiments may have surfaced from time to time, but they did not actually lead to Africans being excluded from public functions. Nor was there anything to prevent them from hiring the town's major venues, such as the Town Hall, for their own shows and concerts, or attending the splendid new Theatre Royal after it was opened in August 1897 – the venue several weeks later for McAdoo's Minstrels. 'Good behaviour and a ticket – not colour or race', Plaatje recalled of this time, were 'the only keys to the stalls'. It would not always be so.[40]

They also made their own music. As well as specially arranged concerts held in churches or on occasion at larger venues like the Town Hall, some form of musical performance was usual at almost every gathering of Kimberley's African community. Meetings of the South Africans Improvement Society, for example, frequently included some musical entertainment (often courtesy of Henry Msikinya until his departure to the United States), as did the annual prizegiving ceremonies of the African cricket and rugby clubs; and there had been a mixed and varied after-dinner musical programme at the farewell function for Moss and Msikinya.

Plaatje often participated in their concerts. Three months after the function for Moss and Msikinya, he took a part in the 'Grand Vocal Concert', held in the Kimberley Town Hall, given by the Wesleyan Native Church Choir, his talents clearly in sufficient demand for strictly interpreted denominational differences to be overlooked. His participation can be seen, moreover, as a gesture on the part of Kimberley's African community against their separation on denominational lines, which many saw as akin to the ethnic differences that sometimes divided them too. The far smaller Lutheran congregations were simply not in a position to organise anything as elaborate as this 'Grand Vocal Concert'. The majority of Plaatje's friends belonged to the Wesleyan or Congregational churches, and it was only natural that they should seek his participation.

The 'Grand Vocal Concert' proved to be a great success. Plaatje himself was one of the baritone soloists, and sang a piece called 'Chiming bells'. The *Diamond Fields Advertiser* described the evening's entertainment as 'excellent', a 'very good audience expressed its appreciation of the proceedings by frequent applause', and it commended Henry Msikinya upon the 'evident results of the careful training of this choir'.[41]

One of the most striking characteristics of events of this kind was the variety of influences – European, African and African American – reflected in their programmes: Negro spirituals ('Roll, Jordan, roll'; 'Pickin' on de harp') jostled for place with popular contemporary European songs ('The village blacksmith'; 'The gendarmes') and Xhosa compositions ('The Kaffir wedding song'; 'The Bushman chorus'; 'Intlaba Nkosi'). Plaatje and his friends considered themselves to be the inheritors of all these traditions, and explored with enthusiasm the rich cultural possibilities they saw in them. Thanks to the Jubilee Singers, the black American element was particularly strong, especially after Will P. Thompson, one of the leading members of the troupe, and highly regarded as a 'first-rate pianist', fell out with Orpheus McAdoo and decided to remain in Kimberley, along with several female members of the troupe, after they visited the town in July 1895. Over the next few years Thompson was much involved in the musical life of the town's African community, his 'invaluable services', so it was reported, in great demand.

One of Thompson's enterprises in which both Plaatje and Bud-M'belle participated was a new musical society, called the Philharmonic Society, whose debut took place in the Woodley Street Hall on 19 March 1897. Its programme, so the notice in the *Diamond Fields Advertiser* indicated, 'consists of modern part songs, selected solos, the famous Bushman Song, Kaffir ditties, with clicks, the Kaffir Wedding Song, and *Ulo Tixo 'Mkulu* ("Thou Great God") as sung by the first Christian converts among the AmaXhosa Kaffirs, whose name was Ntsikana Gaba'. There were some familiar names among the artistes. The musical director was Isaiah Bud-M'belle, also a baritone soloist, who rendered on this occasion the highly popular 'Close the shutters, Willie Boy's dead'. Plaatje himself sang a piece called 'Trusting'. Among the basses was the versatile Theo Binase, well known as a fine cricketer, and Henry Ngcayiya, a future head of the Ethiopian Church of South Africa.[42]

As well as having a fine baritone voice that was often in demand, Plaatje now earned enough money to buy his own musical instruments. When Ernst Westphal visited in 1895 he saw that he had bought a trumpet and a violin – a reminder of those first steps on his own violin several years earlier. Plaatje told him, however, that he had set both aside in order to concentrate on the harmonium. He must have put in a lot of practice, and by April 1896 was confident enough to give a public performance in the Malay Camp. The occasion was a fundraising concert for the Congregational Church, seeking to raise money for an extension to the church hall. Plaatje and Theo Binase were both reported to have played beautifully.[43]

Plaatje was passionate about music and an accomplished performer, and so were many of his friends. Few of them, though, came to share his fascination with drama and none – Isaiah Bud-M'belle perhaps came closest – developed quite such an enthusiasm for Shakespeare. For Plaatje, it would become a lifelong interest, and it was an important legacy of these years in Kimberley.

He wrote about his encounter with Shakespeare in a contribution to Israel Gollancz's *Book of Homage to Shakespeare*, published in 1916 to mark the three-hundredth anniversary of Shakespeare's death. 'I had but a vague idea of Shakespeare until about 1896', Plaatje began his piece, 'when, at the age of 18, I was attracted by the press remarks in the Kimberley paper, and went to see *Hamlet* in the Kimberley Theatre. The performance made me curious to know more about Shakespeare and his works. Intelligence in Africa is still carried from mouth to mouth by means of conversation after working hours, and, reading a number of Shakespeare's works, I always had a fresh story to tell.'[44]

The Merchant of Venice was the first of the plays he read, and he was struck – like others before and since – by Shakespeare's apparent universality, his capacity to transcend different contexts. To a perceptive observer like Plaatje, Victorian Kimberley did not seem a world away from Shakespearean Venice. 'The characters were so realistic', he related, 'that I was asked more than once to which of certain speculators, then operating around Kimberley, Shakespeare referred to as Shylock.' All of this, he went on, 'gave me an appetite for more Shakespeare, and I found that many of the current quotations used by educated natives to embellish their speeches, which I had always taken for English proverbs, were culled from Shakespeare's works.'

He did not elaborate upon the 'vague idea' he had of Shakespeare prior to this encounter, and it is understandable that he should have highlighted the dramatic impact of a single performance. What he already knew of Shakespeare must have come from the Westphals and from his own reading and private study in Kimberley. Quite likely he had also heard of the performances of scenes from Shakespeare's plays (in both English and Setswana) put on by Gabriel David, an Anglican clergyman and a Morolong like himself, with his school students in Bloemfontein.[45]

That said, there is no reason to doubt the impact of that performance of *Hamlet*. It was one of a number of plays put on in Kimberley by a travelling company from England responsible, so the *Diamond Fields Advertiser* reported, for the 'novel and somewhat daring experiment of importing Shakespeare into South Africa'. William Haviland, the leader of the company, came to Kimberley in 1896 (*Othello, Merchant of Venice*), and again in 1897 (*Merchant of Venice, Much Ado about Nothing, Taming of the Shrew, Hamlet*). On his first visit he declared himself most impressed by the appeal that Shakespeare had to his audiences in South Africa, many of whom, he was pleased to hear, had witnessed some of the great Shakespearean performances in the capitals of Europe. Most of his South African audiences would have been composed exclusively of people of European origin but in Kimberley, as with other forms of entertainment, there was nothing to prevent Africans from going along too.[46]

Plaatje, for one, saw no reason why Shakespeare should not be as accessible to him as to his white fellow citizens. If Shakespeare was England's greatest playwright, as readers of the *Advertiser* were reminded several times during Mr Haviland's two visits, then he was keen to know more. Acquiring a knowledge of English to the requisite standard not only gave an entrée to 'the great English literature', as *Imvo* had said, but made it possible to appreciate Shakespeare performed on stage. There was all the more reason to take advantage of the opportunity since William Haviland claimed a direct link with the great English tradition of Shakespearean acting: he and his leading lady, Amy Coleridge, he wanted it known, were 'Late leading members of Sir Henry Irving's Lyceum Company'.

The performance of *Hamlet* which Plaatje remembered attending, for it was the only one during either of the company's two visits, took place in Kimberley on the night of Friday, 17 December 1897, and the 'press remarks' that caught his eye must have been the long article entitled 'Hamlets I have seen', by 'an Old Stager', in the *Advertiser* on Wednesday, the 15th. By all accounts it was an impressive performance. The new Theatre Royal, opened by Sir Alfred Milner several months earlier, was widely regarded as the best in the country. Plaatje remembered it as 'the prettiest and most comfortable playhouse in South Africa', and that night it was reported to have been 'packed from floor to ceiling'. William Haviland's Hamlet was 'a scholarly, judicious, and temperate piece of acting', and Amy Coleridge 'a most sweet and gentle Ophelia'; 'the scenes and setting of the play', so the *Advertiser* thought, 'left nothing to be desired' and everything else 'was as satisfactory as it could well be'.[47]

Even more noteworthy were the prescient remarks of 'Old Stager' a few days earlier. The value of performances of this kind, he thought – he spoke with the authority of one who had seen the legendary Charles Kean play Hamlet on the London stage – was that 'it induced a study of the great dramatist's works, as when one has seen a play, there is no rest until a better acquaintance is acquired by reading', and it was 'so much easier to read a play after the several scenes are present to the mind's eye'. 'Many a young man in Kimberley', he confidently predicted, 'will date his most intimate knowledge of England's greatest dramatic bard to this and the former visit of the Haviland Company.' An uncannily accurate prediction, it would turn out, with respect to one 'young man' in the audience that evening – although scarcely of the race and colour he can have imagined.[48]

For all the opportunities and freedoms, the lives of Plaatje and his friends were subject to restrictions and constraints. Racial feeling was all-pervasive in the society in which they lived, and their situation was far from secure. Always there was a fear of losing their privileged status, of reduction to the ranks of the unskilled or unemployed if they put a foot wrong. However well they performed at work, there were always those who thought their jobs should be reserved for whites, that they had no business to aspire to anything beyond being 'hewers of wood and drawers of water'. Likewise in their personal and social lives, they carved out an imaginative niche for themselves in colonial society, and believed they had every right to do so. Others did not. Many whites, poor whites particularly, felt threatened by their very existence, and they had to learn to cope with an often hostile environment. Occasionally, the verbal abuse and offensive letters to newspapers spilled over into assaults and other acts of physical violence.

Their response was to avoid provoking their would-be detractors as best they could, and to stress their loyalty to the colonial authorities, for here at least there were potential allies. There were times, too, when it was necessary to distance themselves publicly from their 'less civilised' brethren. The most notable example of this, for those living in Kimberley, was in 1896 when the Batlaping chief Galeshewe and his followers were goaded into taking up arms against the colonial government. There was never much doubt about the outcome of this so-called Bechuana Rebellion: after a bitterly fought campaign in the remote Langeberg to the north-west of Kimberley, the 'rebels' were defeated, those of their leaders who were not killed in the fighting were brought to trial and either hanged or sentenced to periods of imprisonment, while several thousand of their followers were sent off to the western Cape as forcibly indentured labourers, their lands expropriated.

For Plaatje and his friends it was a lesson in the futility of any form of armed resistance, serving only to reaffirm their commitment to strictly legal and constitutional methods in defending their interests. Nevertheless, it was a challenging time, and it was natural that they should sympathise with the plight of their fellow countrymen, however ill-advised they considered their actions. Plaatje would have particularly felt it, since he had grown up among Batlaping, Tswana-speakers like himself; some of those who took up arms against the colonial government lived not far from the Pniel mission. The rebellion impinged on the lives of his friends as well. Patrick Lenkoane served with the colonial forces as a lieutenant in the Basuto Police contingent and did what he could to persuade the 'rebels' to surrender and to avoid further bloodshed, eventually receiving a medal for his efforts; Isaiah Bud-M'belle interpreted in court at the trials and hearings that followed; Jonathan Jabavu joined with his fellow clergymen, black and white, in condemning the government's treatment of prisoners and their compulsory indenturing.[49]

In seeking to protect their interests through such peaceful means as were available to them, Plaatje and his friends often looked – like others in the colony – to the leadership of John Tengo Jabavu and his newspaper, *Imvo Zabantsundu*. Both played an important part in their lives. *Imvo* carried a wide variety of news and comment in both English and Xhosa: of local political and religious developments; of the progress being made by blacks in the United States and West Africa, always a source of inspiration; detailed reports from local correspondents of the social and sporting life of mission-educated communities in the colony and beyond; and editorials advocating temperance, education, self-help and improvement along the lines pursued by Kimberley's South Africans Improvement Society.

Above all, *Imvo* urged Africans to become involved in the political life of the colony, arguing that they should be moderate and cautious in their attitudes and demands, exploit the differences that existed between white politicians in order to extract concessions, and place their trust in the various 'friends of the natives' who were sympathetic to their interests. 'Civilised' Africans, Jabavu also believed, had a special responsibility towards their less articulate brethren, and a duty to act as their spokesmen: *Imvo*'s guiding metaphor was the hope that it could serve as 'a rope to tow those stragglers to the desired shore'.[50]

Jabavu himself was an experienced politician and a skilful behind-the-scenes negotiator, and more than anybody else he helped formulate the political aspirations of a generation of mission-educated Africans. Plaatje was a great admirer of his weekly editorials in *Imvo*. One in particular we know left a lasting impression. In its issue of 23 April 1896, responding to a hostile editorial in the *Bloemfontein Express*, Jabavu warned of the dire consequences of the continued oppression by Boers of Africans living in the Transvaal, and predicted that in the event of war between the Transvaal and the British imperial government the African tribes of the Transvaal, 'on whose neck the foot of the oppressor has been pressing with inhuman severity, would rise for revenge and a scene might ensue which would make humanity shudder, but which must be expected when a host of conquered savages finds an opportunity to burst its bonds'. It was the phrase about making humanity shudder that particularly struck Plaatje, and it lodged in his memory. He would be reminded of it four years later when Boer and Briton were indeed at war – and when there seemed every prospect of Jabavu's prediction being realised.[51]

Jabavu's influence was at its greatest around election time when white politicians tended to pay rather more attention than usual to their African constituents. But in Kimberley, as in the other larger towns of the colony, there also developed a more continuous tradition of political activity, concerned with local as well as wider colonial issues and personalities. Here, too, great importance was attached to securing the support of 'friends of the natives'. In Kimberley, so Patrick Lenkoane was to recall, the local African community relied for assistance upon what he described as 'a saintly company', consisting of men like Advocate Richard Solomon, Advocate Henry Burton, Samuel Cronwright-Schreiner and Percy Ross Frames: 'a magnificent group', Lenkoane said, 'in whose hands the Natives of Kimberley entrusted their interests', and whose names were 'household words in native circles throughout the length and the breadth of the land'.[52]

Plaatje soon came to be involved in the discussions and deputations that drew Kimberley's African community and these 'friends of the natives' together, and the sympathetic response which he and his colleagues received – along with several notable successes in defence of their rights – would have a lasting effect upon his thinking. For two members of Patrick Lenkoane's 'saintly company' he developed a particularly warm admiration. The first was Samuel Cronwright-Schreiner, husband of the novelist Olive Schreiner, who established his credentials among Kimberley's African community with a famous address (later revealed to have been largely the work of his wife) on 'The political situation', which he delivered in the Kimberley Town Hall in August 1895. In essence it was a fierce attack upon Cecil Rhodes and the capitalist interest he represented, and it accused him of using the Afrikaner Bond, with whom he was in alliance, for his own purposes, and of maintaining it by 'retrogressive legislation on the Native question'.[53]

Although Cronwright-Schreiner did not actually come out with anything very concrete in the way of a more positive 'native policy', his sympathetic comments were nevertheless sufficient to earn the gratitude of, among other people, the Rev. Jonathan Jabavu. 'Those of us who knew Mr Cronwright-Schreiner and therefore attended his lecture on the 20th inst.', he wrote, 'knew a good word would be uttered against their oppression.' 'Few as they are, we believe that men of Mr Cronwright-Schreiner's stamp will some day succeed in emancipating us from slavery caused by such oppressive measures as the Glen Grey Act, the East London and Haarhoff's Curfew, Dear Bread and Cheap Brandy, and the Strop Bill. It only needs us to move and unite, and raise our voices against such unjust legislation, which aims at lowering the standard of the Queen's beneficent rule.'[54]

Jabavu's sentiments would have been shared by the other members of the Improvement Society (of which he was president) who came to hear what Cronwright-Schreiner had to say. Most of them, according to its secretary, were present that evening and they had to postpone their regular Tuesday meeting as a result. It would be very surprising if Plaatje, who came to know both Schreiners well, had not been among them.[55]

Cronwright-Schreiner's address had an interesting sequel. De Beers did not like what he had to say and wasted little time in arranging a public defence of the Rhodes–Bond alliance. They entrusted the task to the 25-year-old Jan Christiaan Smuts, recently returned from four years in Europe and struggling to establish himself in legal practice in Cape Town. In this, his first major speech, he set out what he called 'the general principles of a broader political platform as a reconciled basis for both the white peoples of the Cape Colony'. This rested upon the fundamental proposition, so he told his audience, that 'the theory of democracy as currently understood and practised in Europe and America is inapplicable to the coloured races of South Africa', and that 'you cannot apply to the barbarous and semi-barbarous natives the advanced political principles and practice of the foremost peoples of civilization': it was the case, in short, for the maintenance of white supremacy, albeit not delivered with much originality. The 'Native problem', he added, loomed ominously on 'the dark background of our future', and he thought 'native education' 'ought to be more physical and manual than intellectual'. Hardly a hopeful message, in other words, if you were a member of the South Africans Improvement Society. The *Diamond Fields Advertiser*, more concerned with party politics than prognostications about the future, gloomy or otherwise, welcomed the speech as 'the ablest and clearest exposition yet of the principles of the Bond–Rhodes alliance'.[56]

Subsequent events were to make a mockery of Smuts's hopes for so unlikely an alliance. In December 1895 Dr Leander Starr Jameson, a close associate of Cecil Rhodes, led an armed force into the Transvaal from his base in the Bechuanaland Protectorate, hoping to take control of Johannesburg, spark off a rebellion amongst the so-called Uitlanders ('foreigners'), and replace Kruger's regime with a government more sympathetic to the interests of certain of the mining companies. The raid was a fiasco: the planned rising of Uitlanders failed to materialise, and Dr Jameson and his men were forced to surrender to a Boer force at Doornkop, twenty miles from Johannesburg. Cecil Rhodes, involved in the conspiracy, had to resign as prime minister of the Cape Colony. Political life in the colony was transformed.

After Cronwright-Schreiner the figure to whom Plaatje was particularly drawn was Henry Burton, an ambitious young South African-born lawyer who had practised in Kimberley since 1892. Burton was a popular figure in the eyes of Kimberley's African community because he was ready to support their claims for fair and just treatment: 'he acted on our behalf directly on the platform, in the press and at the bar', so Plaatje would recall. They appreciated his willingness to accept briefs to fight test cases in the courts. This was a strategy in which they placed great faith, and they won several important victories. Most notable of them all was the decision in *Mankazana* v. *the Queen* which gave them legal protection against the rigours of pass law legislation, designed to control the movement of African labour, as embodied in Proclamation 14 of 1872.

At issue was the question of exactly who was supposed to carry a pass, and in what circumstances the police could demand to see it. According to *Imvo*, 'the more advanced natives' in Kimberley had been subjected to harassment by both police and magistrates, and prosecutions under the proclamation were 'fast becoming unbearable'. Their opportunity to mount a challenge came with the arrest of Saul Mankazana, a property owner, registered voter and chairman of the Eccentrics Cricket Club, hauled up for not having a pass when walking down Ross Street in the centre of Kimberley one day in May 1898. He was duly found guilty and fined 5s.[57]

It was the test case they were waiting for. In response to this 'lawless persecution of guiltless black men', as Plaatje related, 'the Natives retained Advocate Henry Burton and sought the "Higher Palace of Justice"' (the Griqualand West High Court) and appealed against the conviction. They won. The judge president, Perceval Laurence, ruled that 'it was not enough for a native to have no pass' for the police to make an arrest, and that there had to be other grounds for suspicion. Simply walking down the street did not amount to 'wandering or loitering'. A week later, again with the concurrence of his fellow High Court judges (Lange and Hopley), he applied his ruling in a second appeal case, *Ben* v. *the Queen*. As a result, respectable, law-abiding Africans like Mankazana, Ben, Plaatje and their colleagues were now spared this kind of harassment by the police; while the municipality, which had come to rely upon the flow of prison labour from these arrests to carry out the work of night-soil removal, had to employ contractors to compensate for its sudden disappearance.[58]

Plaatje saw it as a famous victory. More than any other case it showed how the courts could be used in defence of their rights, while engaging sympathetic lawyers like Henry Burton was a strategy he would advocate time and again. In contrast to the generally 'anti-native' drift of legislation emanating from the Cape parliament during the 1890s (such as the measures which Jonathan Jabavu had specified in his expression of thanks to Samuel Cronwright-Schreiner), in the law courts at least there was every prospect of securing justice and redress of grievance. The case illustrated the way in which an older, established tradition of Cape liberalism could be utilised to enable Africans of this class and background to resist being treated simply as units of labour, subjected to what the municipal authorities considered to be appropriate means of control. Such measures were already in effective operation in the gold-mining areas of the Transvaal, and in the Cape the pressures in this direction were growing all the time. But for the time being at least, Kimberley's African community had demonstrated that they could be successfully resisted. For Plaatje, *Mankazana* v. *the Queen* provided a lesson in political and legal strategy which he did not forget, and he would remain on friendly terms with Henry Burton for the rest of his life.

In June 1898, when *Mankazana* v. *the Queen* was heard in the Griqualand West High Court, Plaatje was nearly twenty-two years old and had been living in Kimberley for over four years. By now it must have become obvious to family and friends that their fears of him succumbing to the 'temptations of city life' were misplaced. Part of the reason, he was inclined to reminisce, was that he always remained very conscious of the hopes they had placed in him, knowing 'how it would grieve them if ever he went wrong'.[59]

His family at Pniel in any case had every opportunity to keep a watchful eye on his progress, since he used to spend many of his days off with them. Martha Bokako was only four years old when he left Pniel to go and work in Kimberley, but she had a clear recollection of his visits back home during the few years after that. Sometimes, she remembered, her father Simon travelled the seventeen miles into Kimberley on horseback to go and fetch him.[60]

For a while he used also to visit his father at Ditlarapeng in the Mafeking district. Old Johannes Plaatje died, however, in September 1896, far away, so the family prayerbook lamented, from his children. He had recently lost all but four of the 148 head of cattle he possessed, his herd devastated, like those around him, by the great rinderpest epidemic that swept across southern Africa in 1896 and 1897. The Mafeking district was very badly affected, and the Barolong lost virtually all their cattle. 'Many flourishing cattle posts were reduced to ruins', Plaatje wrote later: where once 'large herds of sleek fat oxen swarmed over the grasslands as a moving testimony to Barolong wealth', now 'only heaps of whitened skeletons remained'. The tragedy, and its devastating impact, very likely hastened Johannes's death, for his cattle were his life: the search for better grazing had driven his migration from one place to another, and ultimately to his final resting place.[61]

On the news of his death both Plaatje and his elder brother Simon travelled to Mafeking as quickly as they could. But they were too late to witness his burial. In accordance with custom, this had been arranged right away by two of Plaatje's uncles, Kokome and Kikana, the Molemas assisting too.

Plaatje returned to Mafeking the following year to wind up his father's affairs and to sell off his remaining cattle and other livestock, taking sixty-one days' leave of absence from the post office between June and August 1897 for this purpose. With the money raised from the proceeds of his father's estate, according to Modiri Molema, he sent his two younger brothers, Ramokoto and Monnapula, to school at Morija in Basutoland. He took this decision without consulting his other brothers – no doubt because he knew they would not agree to it – which then caused a rift, albeit one that was soon mended, with his elder brother Simon.[62]

Back in Kimberley, Plaatje was embroiled in a dispute of a different kind – with his former landlord, Cumgalie. He had left the boarding house shortly before travelling to Mafeking, but Cumgalie claimed he had not given sufficient notice and further payment was therefore due. Plaatje disagreed, claiming rather that his landlord had turned him out without himself giving proper notice. When they failed to resolve the matter, Cumgalie instructed his lawyer to recover what he said was owed, and a summons was issued. Well used to recovering debts by such means, Cumgalie would not have anticipated any difficulty in getting his money. In the previous year he had instituted proceedings in three similar cases. In two of them the magistrate ruled in his favour, and in the third the writ was withdrawn, almost certainly because payment was made before the defendant was brought to court. Cases of this kind were rarely contested, and in at least nine times out of ten, judging from the civil record book for this period, judgment was made in favour of the plaintiff.

But in young Plaatje, Cumgalie met his match. Confident in the strength of his case, Plaatje instructed an attorney, E.J. Sydney, to act on his behalf, denying Cumgalie's claim and putting in a counterclaim to recover the expenses he had incurred. He had a clear recollection of the sequence of events and, crucially, was able to produce a notebook in which he had written down the key dates and payments made. Thomas Xipu, who described himself as 'no. 1 delivery boy' at the post office, came forward to testify that Plaatje had left Kimberley at the beginning of June and could not therefore have been boarding with Cumgalie at the time he claimed. The magistrate, after considering all the evidence, found in Plaatje's favour, awarding him '9s/2d plus costs of writ' – the full amount he had claimed, and a rare instance of a civil judgment in favour of a defendant. The timing could scarcely have been better. The next day, Saturday, 9 October, was his twenty-first birthday.[63]

One person likely to have taken a keen interest in these proceedings was a young woman who had recently come into his life: Elizabeth M'belle, Isaiah Bud-M'belle's youngest sister. Elizabeth was several months younger than he. She had gone to the Lesseyton Girls' School in the eastern Cape, receiving what Plaatje later described as 'a much better schooling' than he. On leaving, she joined her brother Isaiah as an assistant teacher at the Wesleyan mission school in Colesberg, helping out temporarily at another school in De Aar when its teacher died suddenly. In August 1896, however, she moved to the Anglican mission school in Steynsburg, a small town some two hundred miles south-east of Kimberley, not far from her family home in Burgersdorp. She was the only teacher at her new school. It had been closed for nearly a year prior to her appointment, due to the lack of a teacher, so she had ground to make up with the forty or so pupils in her charge. But she was doing an excellent job: attendance was 'regular', discipline 'commendable' and the education inspector, who visited early in 1897, thought her 'energetic and ambitious'. She even caught the eye of the colony's superintendent general of education, who said she should be qualifying for a teacher's certificate. She spoke five different languages – English, Dutch, Xhosa, Sesotho and Setswana. She looked, in every sense, a very good prospect.[64]

Plaatje and Elizabeth first met when she came to Kimberley to visit her brother. Their relationship blossomed and they were soon exchanging letters, writing to one another in English. He explained their choice of language some years later. 'I was not then as well acquainted with her language – the Xhosa – as I am now', he said, 'and although she had a better grip of mine – the Sechuana – I was doubtful whether I could make her understand my innermost feelings in it.' Soon 'the daily epistles' became 'rather lengthy', he explained further, 'for I usually started with the bare intention of expressing the affections of my heart but generally finished by completely unburdening my soul'. English, in other words, was a key not only to knowledge, as *Imvo* had it, but to Elizabeth's affections too.[65]

From the start both would have been acutely aware of the difficulties they were likely to encounter with their respective families. He, after all, was a Morolong, she an Mfengu, and it was unlikely that any family members – Isaiah Bud-M'belle apart – would approve of their liaison. This was what Plaatje was alluding to, a couple of years later, when he wrote of the 'long and awful nights in 1897 when my path to the union … was so rocky'. For the problem, as he was to explain long after the matter had been satisfactorily resolved, was this: 'My people resented the idea of my marrying a girl who spoke a language which, like the Hottentot language, had clicks in it; while her people likewise abominated the idea of giving their daughter in marriage to a fellow who spoke a language so imperfect as to be without any clicks!'[66]

The linguistic problem was of course only part of it. Inter-tribal marriages may have been acceptable in the cosmopolitan African community in Kimberley, but they were not in either Pniel or Burgersdorp, where Elizabeth's mother and relatives lived. They were strongly opposed to any such liaison. Even worse, as they saw it, was the thought that with a Dutch-sounding name like 'Plaatje' he could be of Khoisan or 'Hottentot' origin. They therefore prohibited Elizabeth from visiting Kimberley and intercepted and destroyed her letters. Against this unremitting hostility she would have been able to count on her brother Isaiah's support: the previous year he had married Maria Smouse, a woman of Tswana origin, so was well placed to offer advice and encouragement on how to cope with what must have been a difficult situation all around.

Parental opposition was no deterrent. Once Elizabeth reached her twenty-first birthday on 13 January 1898, there was nothing to stop them marrying by civil licence, whatever their families thought. The 'civilized laws of the Cape Colony', Plaatje wrote later – he had in mind the Marriage Licence Act of 1882 – 'saved us from a double tragedy in a cemetery' such as befell Romeo and Juliet. They wasted little time. He travelled to Steynsburg and accompanied Elizabeth back to Kimberley. Then, on Tuesday, 25 January 1898, they obtained – at a cost of £5 – a special licence at the magistrate's office, authorising a minister of religion to solemnise their marriage without having to go through the normal procedure of banns being read – thereby preventing any objections being raised.[67]

The Rev. Davidson Msikinya performed the happy task in his church several days later. The young couple had to repeat their declaration that they knew of no 'just impediment or lawful objection' to their marriage, and called upon those present to bear witness. 'Not a soul', however, according to Modiri Molema, 'listened to the words of Rev. Msikinya's sermon' which followed. All eyes instead were on the young couple, the bride's face covered by a long white veil, the bridegroom resplendent in long coat and tails and dress shirt.[68]

In the eyes of Kimberley's African community the ceremony was conducted in a style and manner that was entirely in accord with the social standing of the young couple, for to them it was a manifestly suitable match. And like so many of their functions it was a formal and ostentatious affair. Not all the attention it attracted was favourable, however. 'Last evening', so the *Diamond Fields Advertiser* reported the next day,

a couple of 'swagger' looking natives resplendent in bell toppers, morning coats, white waistcoats, light pants, and patent leathers, with a number of females in holiday attire, were the centre of an admiring group in the Kimberley Railway Station. The rumour had gone forth that they were a couple of Lobengula's sons and certain of his wives, and the passengers and platform loungers were deeply interested in watching Master Lobengula making preparations for Mrs Loben's comfort for the journey, while when one of the princes of the blood royal deigned to take a long drink of water from an old lime juice bottle brought by one of the porters, excitement 'ran high'.

The report added that 'shortly before the train left, the police sergeant on duty at the station "spotted" one of the "princes" as an interpreter at a court down colony, while his companion was discovered to be a telegraph messenger', and it went on: 'It transpired that the former had come up to the Diamond Fields for the purpose of getting married, and that the buxom dusky lady who had been put down as one of the sharers of the late Matabili monarch's joys and sorrows was in reality a daughter of the people and the bride of the "got up regardless" interpreter.' Clearly the *Advertiser*'s correspondent was confused about which of the two 'princes' was getting married. And the reason why the interpreter, recognised by the police sergeant, was described as being from 'a court down colony' was that for the previous few weeks Isaiah Bud-M'belle had been seconded to the colony's Eastern Circuit, based in Grahamstown, but returned to the diamond fields for the wedding – ensuring that at least one other family member was present.[69]

The two newly-weds would probably have been much amused by the rumour that the bridegroom was one of the sons of Lobengula, the great Ndebele chief, and Elizabeth one of his wives. Less pleasing, though, was the tone of the report, a sharp reminder of white resentment at black social aspirations, and of the gulf that existed between the exuberant world of their own creation and the attitudes held by the majority of their white fellow countrymen. To them, the obviously well-educated, self-confident group of Africans who had been at Plaatje's wedding constituted not only an affront to their sensibilities but a threat to their livelihoods. In their encounter at the Kimberley railway station two very different worlds collided.

But for Kimberley's African community, the marriage of Sol Plaatje and Elizabeth M'belle gave romantic expression to many of their collective hopes and aspirations. They had always stressed the importance of achieving unity among themselves, of overcoming the tribal differences and jealousies that sometimes stood between them; Plaatje and Elizabeth M'belle, Morolong and Mfengu, were doing this in a particularly personal way. Family objections were in any case soon overcome. Presented with a fait accompli, both sets of 'erstwhile objecting relatives', as Plaatje called them, soon came to accept what had happened – a happy outcome to a romantic affair, and the beginning of what proved to be a happy and enduring partnership. Elizabeth's family were doubtless relieved that she had married a Morolong and not something worse.[70]

There remained, though, some loose ends to sort out so far as Elizabeth's teaching commitments were concerned. The chairman of the Steynsburg school committee, the Rev. D. Lomax, was expecting Elizabeth back in the classroom for the beginning of term, Tuesday, 1 February. Under normal circumstances she would have given him the agreed period of notice to enable him to recruit a new teacher. But these were not normal circumstances and it is clear that their decision to marry was taken in haste, and understandable that informing Mr Lomax of her intentions and her new situation had not been her first priority.

Four days after their wedding, however, Elizabeth wrote to Lomax with her notice, and to let him know that she had arranged for a substitute teacher, Thomas Ngcolomba, to take her place as she would not be returning. Ngcolomba accordingly set out from Kimberley to Steynsburg so he could be there for the first day of term. Unfortunately, Lomax was far from impressed with her chosen substitute. Elizabeth assured him that Ngcolomba had a teaching certificate from Healdtown, but he did not take it with him, and had no other testimonials or letter of introduction. Lomax therefore refused to accept him, preferring to go to Grahamstown to find an alternative. When Elizabeth heard this, she felt she had no choice but to resign with immediate effect, adding in her letter, 'I deeply apologise for whatever inconvenience I put you into.'[71]

Plaatje was of course on hand to help Elizabeth to deal with this awkward situation. So much so that of the three letters sent to Lomax in Elizabeth's name, two of them were in his hand, and in one of these he had even signed for her (as 'E.L. Sol Plaatje'). No doubt he took care of the telegram that had to be sent too. He was clearly doing his best to help – but perhaps this was also an early indication of who would be doing what in their future life together. They now settled into a new home, staying, for a while at least, at no. 9 Morris Street, in the Malay Camp. A few weeks later Elizabeth was pregnant.

Their romance unfolded against a troubled background in the wider affairs of the Cape Colony. Since the Jameson Raid, relations between the British imperial government and the South African Republic had deteriorated steadily and political opinion within the Cape Colony had become increasingly polarised on either side of the white racial divide. In these circumstances, the campaign for elections to the Cape House of Assembly in the middle of 1898 was always going to be a bitterly fought affair. Rhodes himself re-entered the political fray as the leader, in all but name, of the Progressive Party, and much of the electioneering revolved around the question of the future shape of southern Africa as a whole, rather than the more parochial concerns that had dominated political life in the Cape hitherto. It was the first general election in which Plaatje, over twenty-one years old, male, literate, and with a salary of over £50 a year, was qualified to vote.

The African vote was more important than ever before. For the first time, two opposing political parties, the Progressives and the Afrikaner Bond, competed openly for African support, and both Sir Gordon Sprigg, the outgoing prime minister, and W.P. Schreiner, his successor, campaigned personally among African voters. In Kimberley, as elsewhere, the candidates made the necessary gestures towards their African and Coloured constituents, but there was never much doubt here that all four Progressives would be returned with majorities that were anything less than overwhelming; the only opposition they encountered came from two independent candidates, and the Afrikaner Bond did not bother to put up any candidates of its own.[72]

Rather more intriguing from Plaatje's point of view was the contest for the Barkly West constituency: not just because it included the Pniel mission, where he may well have cast his vote, but because the main candidate standing against Cecil Rhodes, for the Afrikaner Bond, was Henry Burton, who only several weeks previously had fought and won the pass law case in the High Court in Kimberley. Had the Bond been represented by some other candidate, Plaatje might well have felt inclined, like his friend Patrick Lenkoane, to support Cecil Rhodes and the 'British' party, even against the advice of Tengo Jabavu, who had come out in favour of the Bond. But in the circumstances his personal admiration for Henry Burton, supported in his campaign by Olive and Samuel Cronwright-Schreiner, won out, and he was the candidate he thought it right to support. This was not a view shared by Ernst Westphal, a keen supporter of Cecil Rhodes. 'He sent me', Plaatje recalled a couple of years later, 'a hot letter going for me for having leanings towards the Transvaal and Krugerism, simply because I sympathised with Adv. Burton during the last election; and he could not be convinced by my reasons that the young QC earned my sympathies not because he was supported by the Afrikaner Bond, but simply because he was a negrophilist and did a lot for us while I was in Kimberley.'[73]

Whatever influence Westphal once had over his former pupil, Plaatje was plainly well able by now to make up his own mind on the political issues and personalities of the day, and not at all afraid to take a different line from his former mentor. Not surprisingly, Westphal found it hard to accept. Friendly with Cecil Rhodes for over fifteen years, and recently naturalised as a British citizen, Westphal believed that Plaatje's support for a Bond candidate, whatever the reasons for it, amounted to little short of treason.

The Barkly West constituency had one of the highest proportions of black voters in the colony, and the rival candidates went to considerable lengths to solicit their support. Cecil Rhodes personally addressed a number of African and Coloured meetings and deputations, and it was at one of these that he came out with his famous formula of 'equal rights for all civilised men'. The slogan was adopted at the last minute, on the advice of his election agent, in order to help secure African and Coloured votes ('equal rights for all white men', it was realised, did not have quite the same appeal). The amendment had the desired effect, especially when reinforced by the Rev. Davidson Msikinya, who campaigned energetically on Rhodes's behalf, moving a resolution at one meeting that was reported to have been 'carried unanimously and with great enthusiasm'.[74]

On the other side, Samuel Cronwright-Schreiner, seeking to secure the African vote for Henry Burton and his running mate, did his best to discredit Rhodes on the basis of his Chartered Company's treatment of Africans in

Rhodesia and declared himself in favour of raising 'the native to the very highest pitch of civilisation and culture'. Although in the end Rhodes and his Progressive running mate were returned with comfortable majorities, it was a fiercely contested election, and it received intense coverage in the press. Tengo Jabavu might now have found himself outflanked politically, and his influence diminished by the emergence of a rival newspaper, *Izwi la Bantu*, but his longstanding advocacy of African participation in the Cape parliamentary system was never more strongly vindicated.[75]

Plaatje drew similar lessons from what he saw. When questioned about his views on the Cape's franchise some years later, he referred back to his experiences of elections in Kimberley and Mafeking and expressed himself wholly in favour of the existing system. He had seen it work well, he did not think elections stirred up hostility between black and white, and he had no difficulty in casting his vote; 'everyone', he said, 'was only too anxious that every voter should record his vote'. Just as *Mankazana* v. *the Queen* vindicated his faith in its legal system, what he saw during the general election of 1898 served to reinforce his belief in the value of the non-racial Cape franchise, and the importance of participating in the political life of the colony. In Henry Burton, as it happened, these two things came together.[76]

There was an interesting postscript to the contest in Barkly West. Although defeated by a large majority, Henry Burton challenged the legality of the result on the grounds that Rhodes had offered illegal inducements to voters, in particular the numerous diggers with claims along the Vaal River; there were allegations, too, that money was offered to Burton's African election agent to change sides, and that Davidson Msikinya, who acted as intermediary, was also suitably rewarded. In the hearing that followed, Rhodes simply denied all knowledge of the details of his campaign, claiming he left all this in the hands of his election agents (though he did recall Msikinya's visit to the De Beers offices to 'collect a church subscription'), and in the end the result was allowed to stand.[77]

A rather more lasting legacy of the election was the slogan 'equal rights for all civilised men', which soon took on a life of its own. It may not have persuaded Plaatje to support Cecil Rhodes at the time but there was no denying its utility as a rhetorical device. Later he would uphold the famous slogan as evidence of Rhodes's support for African and Coloured rights, invoking his considerable authority and prestige when challenging the arguments of later generations of politicians for whom such sentiments constituted dangerous extremism. Whether or not Rhodes meant a word of what he said was beside the point.[78]

While the voters of the Cape Colony, black and white, decided the future complexion of their House of Assembly and government, Plaatje had a pressing concern of his own: his career. He had by now spent over four years delivering letters and telegrams for the Kimberley post office. Prospects for advancement were minimal and it is difficult to imagine that a job as 'no. 1 delivery boy' or 'sender-out', even if these positions were to become vacant, would have had much appeal. Financially, too, things cannot have been easy, now that he had his wife to support. As the postmaster general was prepared to admit in his report for the previous year, 1897, 'rinderpest, drought and other causes [had] enhanced the cost of living to such an extent that those who are married on small salaries find much difficulty in living in comfort'. Because of the high cost of living in the Kimberley district, all post office employees received a special cost-of-living allowance, which was increased, but for those at the bottom of the salary scale it was often a struggle to make ends meet.[79]

Plaatje's ambitions lay rather in becoming a court interpreter. He had worked hard to improve his knowledge of the languages he needed and had probably been on the look-out for a suitable position for some time. Possibly there had been opportunities to gain some experience in temporary interpreting work, deputising for Isaiah Bud-M'belle in the police station or the magistrate's office if this could be fitted in around his normal working hours at the post office. His recent experience of the potential of the law as a means of protecting African rights, not to mention his first-hand knowledge of the salary and status enjoyed by Isaiah Bud-M'belle, can only have strengthened his motivation.

So when he heard, sometime in July or early August 1898, that a clerk and interpreter was required at the Mafeking magistrate's court he hastened to apply. Such opportunities did not arise very often, and the position had only fallen vacant because of the departure of the previous incumbent, Jan Moloke, following the belated discovery that he once served a jail sentence for illicit diamond buying. 'My knowledge and ability to translate and retranslate into the English, Dutch, German, Kaffir, Sesuto and Sechuana languages qualifies me for the position I am applying for', Plaatje wrote in his letter of application, adding that, if accepted, he hoped it would be possible to be transferred to his new job (rather than having to resign from the post office) so as not to lose his pension. In the event of being successful, he said, 'I shall do my utmost best to discharge my duties satisfactorily'.[80]

The response was encouraging: Charles Bell, the magistrate and civil commissioner at Mafeking, first of all requested testimonials and then, on 12 September, asked Plaatje to come to Mafeking for an interview. Plaatje found, though, that he could not very easily take the time off work, and wrote to explain that 'pressure in our Department does not permit me to be absent for more than three days', two of which would be taken up with travel, and that he hoped 'the brevity of my visit will not inconvenience you'.[81]

Bell could hardly object to such an arrangement; indeed, Plaatje's evident commitment to his current duties must have created a favourable impression. After testing his competence in the languages in which he claimed to be qualified, Bell declared him to be 'fairly well educated', 'well suited for the appointment for which he applies', and recommended him for the position. Plaatje also had a good reference from the postmaster in Kimberley, who thought him 'suitable for the position of Interpreter', adding that 'he knows the native languages and is a good English scholar'. Just as valuable, in Bell's mind at least, was the verbal recommendation he had received from the influential local figure of Silas Molema, the Barolong headman, a younger brother of Joshua Molema. In a place like Mafeking such things counted for a great deal.[82]

Plaatje, in short, was ideally qualified for the position. A formal offer from the Law Department followed, and he accepted. The transfer problem was resolved satisfactorily, but in one respect there was disappointment: despite the more responsible duties he would be undertaking, the salary was to be no more than the £96 p.a. he had been getting from the post office in Kimberley. Since the cost of living in Mafeking was known to be higher even than in Kimberley this was not good news, and he must have known that Isaiah Bud-M'belle, now his brother-in-law, was earning more than twice as much. On the other hand, prospects for promotion were better, and there was no doubt he could look forward to a considerably enhanced status, the position of interpreter in magistrates' offices in rural areas being considered, in the opinion of one well-informed observer, 'second only in importance to the magistrate himself'.[83]

Plaatje intended to move to Mafeking at the beginning of October 1898. In the event he did not do so until later in the month because of illness, the first recorded instance of ill health which was to be, in one form or another, a fairly regular occurrence over the next few years, and which was to affect him throughout his adult life. Neither his own description of his ailment on this occasion ('a serious indisposition') nor that entered on his doctor's certificate ('fever') give much clue as to its nature. Possibly it was a bout of malaria from which he did suffer a couple of years later.[84]

A rather more worrying possibility was that he had some form of epilepsy, for about a year later a sharp-eyed clerk in the Cape Law Department noticed, as a batch of papers passed through from the Civil Service Commission, that he was certified by Dr Hayes, one of the doctors in Mafeking, 'to be suffering from epilepsy'. Most likely the diagnosis was just mistaken. There is no other evidence that he suffered from this disability either at this time or later in life, and he never subsequently applied for sick leave on these grounds. Indeed, had he done so he would have found himself in some difficulties, for in applying for his new job in Mafeking he had attached his signature to the statement that he did not suffer from 'fits or any other bodily infirmity'.[85]

Whatever the nature of this ailment, it was sufficiently serious to prevent him from beginning his new job when he had hoped. But it did at least enable him to spend his twenty-second birthday, 9 October 1898, at home with his wife Elizabeth. Their baby was due in a few weeks' time, and they had decided, in keeping with custom, that she should stay at Pniel with his family, and join him in Mafeking only after the baby was born. That they were both able and willing to contemplate such an arrangement suggests that the objections of Plaatje's family to his choice of bride were already a thing of the past. Personal contact and the passage of time had clearly broken down the barriers of prejudice that had once coloured their view of Plaatje's bride-to-be.

In retrospect, Plaatje came to see these years in Kimberley, defined by his period of employment in the post office, as something of a golden age. They had their sadnesses, particularly his father's death in 1896, and he would remember, twenty years later, the 'needlelike pangs' he felt when he heard the news. But then, he said, his 'physical organs were fresh and grief was easily thrown off in tears', and he lived 'in a happy South Africa that was full of pleasant anticipations'. Inevitably, when he looked back, his memories were coloured by what came after.[86]

Yet even at the time, it was clear that for a young man of his ability and ambition, Kimberley was a congenial place to be. Determined to make his own way, he had built upon his limited formal education, enhancing his job prospects, and engaged fully in the vibrant social and intellectual life going on around him. He had flourished in Kimberley's cosmopolitan atmosphere, relating easily to people from any number of different backgrounds. He had gained experience of public life and had built a network of friendships and contacts, not just with others of his own race but with a small group of whites, 'friends of the natives', who showed sympathy for their cause. He was well informed about the issues of the day, an avid reader of the newspapers, and he had a fascination with the law – what it was, what it meant and how it could be used. He knew his own mind and was ready to act decisively, above all in his love for Elizabeth.

For all the attractions of Kimberley and the vistas it opened up, he never for a moment forgot his roots. Spending time with Xhosa- and Sotho-speakers served to remind him not just of what they had in common but of how they differed – daily affirmation of his own quite distinctive identity as a Motswana. Family and kin remained as important as ever. Family ties had been sustained through visits to both Pniel and the Mafeking district, his marriage to Elizabeth seemingly no more than a temporary jolt to their equilibrium. In Mafeking he had encountered at first hand a largely self-governing African chiefdom, deeply conscious of its history and traditions, battling to preserve its independence and its cohesion in the modern world. To be able to reconnect to this Tshidi Barolong polity, building upon a relationship set in place by his father, must have been an appealing prospect. Here, after all, he would be with his own people.

THREE

'The essential interpreter'
Mafeking, 1898–1899

MAFEKING,
South Africa.

D. Taylor

There were not one but two Mafekings. The oldest, and the largest by far, was Mafikeng, the home of the Tshidi Barolong. Most of them resided in the area known as the stadt, or township. They were some five thousand strong and lived in 'an irregular aggregation' of traditional round huts with red walls and thatched, peaked roofs, interspersed with the giant boulders from which Mafikeng ('place of stones') got its name. There were, according to one who lived there, 'no regular streets' but plenty of 'sand and dirt, and all kinds of trees'. Mostly the residents made a living from cultivating small plots of land, or tending herds of livestock on communally held land around Mafikeng, their income supplemented as necessary by paid employment.[1]

On the other side of the railway line, a symbolic as well as a physical divide, lay the European township of Mafeking (its name simply a corruption of the Setswana) and the world of *makgoa*, the white people. Founded in 1885, and neatly laid out in a grid pattern adjacent to the Barolong settlement, it had become an important commercial and administrative centre, and it now had the amenities appropriate to a self-contained community in one of the remoter outposts of the British empire – a hospital, racecourse, Masonic Hall, four churches, tennis courts and the like. One of the oldest buildings served as the offices of the magistrate and civil commissioner, situated along one side of the expansive Government Square. This would be Plaatje's place of work for nearly four years, a daily walk of half a mile or so from his home in the stadt.

Distinctive as they were in appearance, Mafeking's two settlements were nonetheless closely connected, and each day growing numbers of men and women, Plaatje among them, left the stadt to go to work in the European township. Mafeking and Mafikeng were in reality part of a larger whole and increasingly interdependent economically. Everybody, black or white, had an obligation to observe the laws of the Cape Colony, and many shared a common religion, Christian churches and missionaries being quite thick on the ground. Coloureds, Indians, Mfengu, Basotho, even a few Chinese, had made Mafeking their home too, adding to the mix and giving a cosmopolitan feel to the place that was reminiscent of Kimberley, albeit on a much smaller scale. Where people lived was not entirely defined by colour. A handful of whites, for example, had settled in the stadt, among them Spencer Minchin, one of the town's attorneys, who had arrived in 1890. Plaatje would soon come to know him well.[2]

Visitors from Kimberley tended to be unimpressed by the place. One anonymous correspondent, writing for the *Diamond Fields Advertiser* in 1897, remarked that the small wooden market house in the centre of the market square might quite easily be mistaken for the 'municipal broom cupboard', and he was struck by the fact that the resident commissioner of the Bechuanaland Protectorate, which had its headquarters in Mafeking, administered the whole of his territory (an area of 220,000 square miles) from offices in a building which was originally built as the Anglican rectory. Just as pertinent were his observations about the main (Cape) government building where Plaatje would be working. This, thought the *Advertiser*'s correspondent, 'was not of much architectural pretension' and 'quite inadequate for the purpose required. In one gable end justice is dispensed, in the other – postage stamps.' At least Plaatje would be familiar with what went on in that end of the building.[3]

Just outside the European township of Mafeking, south of the Molopo River, were two other communities: the Cape Coloureds, whose men mostly made a living as craftsmen and artisans, or were employed by the railways and the police; and a slightly larger community of several hundred Mfengu, residents of the 'Fingo location'. Many of them had settled in Mafeking in 1890, arriving in the town as members of Cecil Rhodes's famous pioneer column, on its way northwards to occupy Mashonaland for the British South Africa Company. Once they reached Mafeking, however, the Mfengu contingent refused to go any further, decided to make their home there, and were subsequently joined by their families. Since then they had grown into a thriving community. Like their compatriots in Kimberley, they were regular churchgoers, sent their children to the local mission schools, and tended to regard themselves as considerably superior to the mass of the Barolong who lived nearby.

It was in this Mfengu community that Plaatje would find two of his closest friends, Patrick Sidzumo and David Phooko. Patrick was the son of a well-known Mfengu preacher, originally from the Tsolo district in the Transkei, who had taken his family to Bechuanaland in 1892, seeking a hot, dry climate as a cure for his tuberculosis. Close in age to Plaatje, and likewise married with a small child, Patrick had a job as a messenger with the CGR (Cape Government Railways) but would soon join Plaatje in the magistrate's office when a vacancy arose there. In fact, he replaced his elder brother Petrus, who had lasted no more than a few weeks, Charles Bell having found him to be 'useless for office purposes'. Patrick, by contrast, made a favourable impression and soon settled into his new job. Plaatje called him 'Sibale' (brother-in-law) since Elizabeth was related to his mother Sarah.[4]

David Phooko was in government employment too, as constable and interpreter for Mark Rushton, the inspector of native reserves, who had a general responsibility for the well-being of the areas of African settlement in the district, and a duty to collect hut tax. Like Patrick, he was a distant relation of Elizabeth, came originally from Aliwal North, and was some eighteen months older than Plaatje. He had lived for a while in Kimberley before coming to Mafeking, and they discovered they had plenty of friends in common – and a shared sense of humour too.[5]

Plaatje found his own people, the Barolong, in a parlous state. Two years earlier they had lost virtually all their cattle in the rinderpest epidemic, and since then had suffered further from the ravages of locusts and drought. Now, their remaining stocks of sheep and goats sold off to raise money, they suffered from a severe famine. Some people in outlying districts were reported to be dying of starvation, and Charles Bell had given up all hope of collecting any taxes that year. Others, younger men especially, had been forced to go and work on the gold mines of the Witwatersrand, something which hitherto they had managed to avoid. But early in 1898 labour recruiting agents were seen 'loofing about on foot collecting boys for the mines', the first time they had considered it worth coming to the district. Nothing demonstrated more vividly the manner in which the economic self-sufficiency of the Barolong had, within a short space of time, been undermined by rinderpest and the disasters that followed in its wake. Plaatje had known Mafikeng in more prosperous times and must have been struck by their desperate situation.[6]

Chief of the Tshidi Barolong at the end of 1898 was Wessels Montshiwa, successor to Chief Montshiwa, who had died, aged eighty-five, in 1896. The old chief, though dead for over two years, still cast a long shadow over the daily lives of the Barolong of Mafikeng. Chief of his people for nearly half a century, he had taken the Barolong to their present home in the 1870s and, through a mixture of stubborn courage, skilful bargaining and some good luck, had ensured for his people a measure of control over their land and independence from white rule. Boer forces from the Transvaal, who laid claim to the land around Mafikeng, had attacked and besieged the Barolong settlement on many occasions during the 1870s and early 1880s, but each time they managed to hold out. Montshiwa sought the aid of the British imperial government in his efforts to resist Boer expansion, and in the end his supplications bore fruit in the dispatch of the Warren expedition in 1885 and the subsequent declaration of a Crown colony over the area in which his people lived. It was this that led to the establishment of the adjacent European settlement of Mafeking.[7]

At the time, the Barolong regarded the securing of British protection in this way as a great achievement. Without it Montshiwa and his followers would have lost their lands, sharing the fate of other African communities who fell victim to the demands of white settlers, backed by force of arms. But British protection had itself led to a gradual diminution of their independence, and by the 1890s the municipal, district and protectorate authorities were all making inroads into the chief's sphere of jurisdiction. The British Bechuanaland proclamation of 1891 was an important stage in this process: it set up the legal machinery to handle civil and criminal matters, marriages, trade, taxation and various other administrative functions, and it effectively defined and limited the areas in which the Barolong chief was to be permitted to exercise jurisdiction over his people.

With the incorporation of British Bechuanaland into the Cape Colony in 1895, these powers were proscribed still further. The region around Mafeking became a magisterial and administrative district of the colony, and acquired its own magistrate and civil commissioner. The establishment of the local bureaucratic apparatus to carry out these functions was of course what brought Plaatje to Mafeking; his very presence in Mr Bell's office, a welcome opportunity for him, testified to the existence of the laws and regulations which now circumscribed the daily lives of the Barolong who lived in the district. Plaatje would have been aware, even before he took up his new job, that this was bound to be the source of some tension, and that he would be right in the middle of it. The disadvantage of enjoying a status second only to that of the magistrate was that sometimes you got the blame too.

For all the intrusions of the colonial authorities and local white settlers, Chief Montshiwa had remained an imposing, revered figure, and such was the degree of personal authority he exercised that the colonial government at first felt little need to intervene in the internal affairs of his chiefdom. But his son, Wessels Montshiwa, never looked like making a success of the chieftaincy he inherited on his father's death. He only became chief because all his older brothers had been killed fighting in wars against the Boers, and he was largely unprepared for the responsibility that came his way. He was unable to read or write, he suffered from continual ill health (being laid up for weeks on end with gout), was frequently drunk, and was never accorded anything like the respect that was enjoyed by his illustrious father. Indeed, it was not long before he was hauled before the magistrate for non-payment of debts and charged with 'committing a public nuisance'; such things had never happened in his father's time. All of which proved the wisdom of the Tswana proverb 'Kgosi e tsala diphera', or 'Chiefs often beget scapegraces'.[8]

Whatever Wessels's failings as an individual, and the encroachments of *makgoa*, the institution of chiefly rule remained the dominant factor in the daily lives of the

Barolong: neither could detract from the pervasive reality of tradition and custom, and the kgotla, the chief's court, remained the focal point both geographically and symbolically. It was here that the affairs of the chiefdom were discussed, and it was to the chief that people continued to bring their problems. As Plaatje himself summed it up several years later, 'Anything that crops up, or anything affecting the Natives here, we first advise the Chief about it and ask him to take steps in the matter.' In practice this meant referring any such matters to the chief's council as much as the chief himself, for this was the tradition too – and a truth captured in another proverb, 'Kgosi ke kgosi ka morafe', or 'A chief is a chief by the people'. No chief, to put it another way, could rule without popular consent. The ethos and character of life in this largely self-governing Barolong community were quite distinct from anything Plaatje had known in Pniel or Kimberley.[9]

When Plaatje took up his new job in Mafeking, he went to stay with Silas Molema. He was a headman, or sub-chief, a member of a family who occupied a special position in the life of his people, and would soon play a decisive part in his own future. Silas Molema was then forty-eight years old, the youngest son of Isaac Molema, the founder of Mafikeng. The old Chief Molema, a brother of Montshiwa and leader of the small Christian community among the Tshidi Barolong, had been sent to occupy Mafeking in 1847 as a stronghold against Boer invasion. Thirty years later Molema was joined by Montshiwa and the main body of the Barolong, and it was only then that it became their main home. Thereafter there was always a somewhat uneasy relationship between Montshiwa and the Molemas and their following, but they had been bound together in a mutual dependence in which the outward forms of unity, at least, were preserved. Each faction was only too conscious that it needed the other, and that disunity would endanger the survival of the Barolong as a whole.

Even more than their claim to be the original founders of Mafikeng and a leading chiefly family, the Molemas were known for their commitment to the Christian religion, their belief in the power of education, and their conviction that the Barolong must adapt and change in response to the new circumstances they faced in the world around them. It was therefore not surprising that it was to members of the Molema family – above all, to Israel, Joshua and Silas, sons of Chief Isaac Molema – that the task of negotiating with the outside world would devolve, for this required, among other things, the skills of literacy; nor was it any less surprising that these same skills would be applied with good effect to the advancement of the interests of the family too.

All these characteristics were evident in the career of Silas Molema. Educated at the Wesleyan Healdtown Institution in the eastern Cape, he became convinced of the importance of extending education among his people and returned to Mafikeng in 1878 to set up a school. He combined this task with performing the other chiefly duties expected of him, and regarded it as his duty to spread a knowledge of Western ideas among his people. Not that he ever neglected his more traditional functions: the school he ran, so Plaatje recounted later, 'was often interrupted by the several quarrels with the Boers, as the teacher, being a sub-chief, always went on active service at the head of the regiment'. He took particular pride, indeed, in having taken part in the defence of Mafikeng in every one of the six sieges it endured in the 1870s and 1880s.[10]

By the 1890s Silas Molema had also become a large landowner in his own right, harvesting his crops with a steam threshing-machine, and had built up an extensive range of business and property interests on both sides of the Bechuanaland Protectorate border. They included a stretch of land at Pitsane, on the railway line just north of this border, known to posterity for the fact that it was from here that Dr Jameson had launched his ill-fated expedition into the Transvaal in 1895. Rather less well known is that in return for the use of his land for training and assembling the raiders, Silas Molema had been promised, in the event of the raid achieving its objectives, a particularly fertile stretch of land at Lotlhakane (Rietfontein), occupied by Barolong *boo* Rapulana but long claimed by the Tshidi. As it was, he did not do badly: while the rest of Mafeking nervously awaited retribution after the raid ended in fiasco, Molema had quietly pocketed £300 for his services. It was a typical combination of the man's entrepreneurial instinct and loyalty to the British. Twenty years later he would look back upon these times with understandable regret: since the time his 'late lamented friends' Dr Jameson and Cecil Rhodes 'had left these parts', he recalled, 'as you know it has been very difficult to get on'. Nobody had been more adept at using the British to further the interests of his people – or his own family.[11]

Silas Molema had been careful to cultivate a good relationship with many of the other newcomers to the district, and he was highly regarded by Mafeking's leading white residents, private citizens and government officials alike. The manager of the local branch of the Standard Bank considered him 'a steady man', and with assets (according to the bank) worth nearly £10,000 was clearly one of their more valued customers. He got on well, too, with Charles Bell, magistrate and civil commissioner since 1897, who considered him 'one of the most trustworthy and respectable men in the district'. It was a relationship from which both men stood to benefit. If Bell was successful in gaining the confidence of the Molema family, then half the battle in securing the co-operation of the Barolong

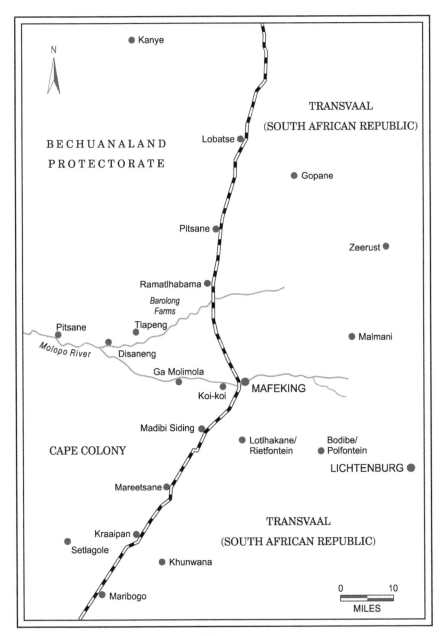

The region around Mafeking, late 1890s

in the administration of their affairs was won; without this, given the very limited resources at his disposal, it was a far harder task. And on the Molemas' side, being on friendly terms with the magistrate was bound to be helpful when it came to the finer points of interpreting government proclamations, assessing tax liabilities, granting trading or firearms licences, or benefiting from such patronage as lay within his gift.[12]

One expression of this mutually beneficial relationship was the understanding that Silas Molema could expect to be consulted whenever a vacancy arose in Bell's office for which an African employee was required – as was the case when Plaatje applied for his job as interpreter. The two men had probably been known to each other for some years before Plaatje came to live in Mafeking. Plaatje's father, it will be remembered, had lived on one of the Molema family farms until his death in 1896, and Plaatje himself must have encountered Silas Molema, and others in his family, on his earlier visits to Mafeking. Silas Molema was clearly quick to recognise the talents and potential of this able (and, by Mafeking standards, well-educated) young man to the Tshidi Barolong – and the advantages for his own family in having 'their man' so conveniently placed.

So it can have come as no surprise that Plaatje, when he arrived in Mafeking, should have moved in with Silas Molema and his family at 'Maratiwa' ('place of the lovers'), their expansive, European-style home in the stadt, well attended by the servants and hangers-on who formed a natural part of the entourage of so influential and progressive a member of the Barolong aristocracy. Socially this was now where he belonged. Soon, however, he found a place of his own to live close by, a 'hut' as it was officially described. It would be a while before he was able to build a proper home in which he and Elizabeth could bring up a family.

Among those who looked upon the new arrival with particular interest, albeit from the youthful perspective of an eight-year-old, was Silas Molema's son Modiri. Looking back on the occasion later in life, he recalled being at first slightly puzzled by the lightness of Plaatje's complexion (lighter than his other brothers, and lighter even than his own family, who were renowned for this characteristic themselves), and guessed that he might have been a Griqua or somebody else of mixed race. But young Modiri soon took a firm liking to the new house-guest, and he was struck by Plaatje's generosity and lively sense of humour. From these beginnings in 1898 there developed a relationship which would grow into one of close personal friendship.[13]

Plaatje commenced his duties at the office of the Mafeking magistrate and civil commissioner on 14 October 1898, evidently recovered from the illness that had delayed his arrival. In view of Elizabeth's condition his new job cannot have been the only thing on his mind. The good news from Pniel came five weeks later.

Elizabeth gave birth to a baby boy on 23 November, and Plaatje hastened back to the mission to see his young son. Several weeks later the personal columns of *Imvo Zabantsundu* conveyed the news to their many friends and acquaintances. Subsequently the new arrival was christened Frederick York St Leger ('Sainty' for short), after the well-known founder and editor of the *Cape Times*, a man whose liberal views on 'the native question' Plaatje held in high esteem. Elizabeth did not join her husband in Mafeking, though, until quite a while afterwards, leaving Plaatje to endure a rather lonely Christmas that year. He remembered spending 'three lengthy, solitary days in old Ma-Diamond's beautiful garden' where she consoled him for the absence of his wife and baby son and gave him newly ripened fruit from the trees. Next Christmas, he assured her, they would all be together in Mafeking.[14]

Their time apart did at least mean he could devote his energies to his new job. This promised to be considerably more demanding than anything he had been accustomed to in the post office in Kimberley. So it proved. From the records of the Mafeking magistrate's office it is clear that Charles Bell presided over a busy, overworked staff who struggled to keep abreast of the mountain of paperwork generated by his duties as both administrative and judicial representative of the Cape government. From time to time Bell would apply to the Law Department in Cape Town for more resources, but the response was rarely sympathetic. Earlier in the year he had put in a plea for a third clerk, since the two he had could not cope with the demands being made upon them. His first clerk (with whom he did not get on) had broken down with 'a severe attack of haemorrhage, the long hours in the office being too much for him', while Ernest Grayson, who had just arrived, was having to work long hours overtime, sometimes returning to the office in the evening. Any new employee, it was clear, could expect to be kept fully occupied.[15]

When Plaatje joined the office, the staff thus consisted of Charles Bell, the magistrate and civil commissioner; Herbert Cowie (when he was well enough), the first clerk and assistant magistrate, who deputised for Bell when he was away on tour in the district, but was soon replaced by a man called William Geyer; and Ernest Grayson, the second clerk, recently graduated from Balliol College, Oxford, whom Bell considered to be 'gentlemanly', 'inclined to be lazy', 'very slow', but 'has ability if he will make use of it'. Plaatje, the new junior clerk and court interpreter, had neither an Oxford degree nor a white skin, but he was better qualified in other respects, and he was keen to make his mark. There was also an office messenger, but a permanent appointment – his friend Patrick – was not made until some months later.[16]

Of Bell himself Plaatje had the fondest of recollections. He considered himself fortunate, he once said, to have 'served my apprenticeship under such a man', and he always remembered him with affection, holding him in the highest regard. Then in his mid-forties and married with a large family, Bell was one of the colony's most experienced magistrates, having joined the Cape civil service nearly thirty years previously as a clerk to the resident magistrate in Leribe, Basutoland (at that time part of the Cape Colony). Since then he had held several different magistracies and, before being appointed to Mafeking in 1897, had served on the commission set up to try to contain the rinderpest epidemic.[17]

In many ways Bell personified the finest traditions of the Cape civil service. 'Thoroughness and efficiency', so one of his friends wrote, 'were his mottoes throughout life. Under a genial disposition and kindly manner, he retained a firm resolve to see that those under him should do their duty to the public. He was a strict disciplinarian. He had no faith in civil servants who amplified red tape regulations or treated the public with indifference. Mr Bell insisted that persons coming to his office on business should receive prompt and courteous attention, no matter what their position in life might be. And he inoculated all those under him with this ideal.'[18]

Others who knew him pointed to his 'great tact and sound judgment' and considered that he 'imbued his subordinates with his spirit and zeal for work'. As one of those subordinates, Plaatje discovered that Bell was an unusually accomplished linguist too. As well as being fluent in Dutch, he had 'a clear grasp' (Plaatje's assessment) of four African languages (Xhosa, Setswana, Sesotho and Zulu), which made a big difference when it came to providing the guidance and support Plaatje needed during the first few weeks of his new job. It was a task Bell took very seriously.[19]

Not all magistrates were prepared to go to these lengths. Over the course of a long career, however, Charles Bell had formed a positive view of the potential of educated Africans like Plaatje, and he was used to working with them. In fact, if truth be told, he quite enjoyed their company. He was much less enamoured of traditional chiefs, and the powers they exercised, his views undoubtedly coloured by memories of the 'Gun War' in Basutoland in 1881 when his father was killed and he himself only narrowly escaped with his life. Subsequently, as his career took him into the Cape Colony proper, he often found the chiefs he encountered were reluctant to accept his authority, and he came to see them as a barrier to progress and efficient administration, two of his priorities in life.

His fractious dealings with Wessels Montshiwa only confirmed what he had long believed. The two frequently clashed, and once he simply walked out of a public meeting in the stadt after the chief had repeatedly interrupted him.

Another time Bell threatened to terminate his government allowance after finding him drunk. Chiefly power, as Charles Bell saw it, was best consigned to the past. He preferred to work with headmen he appointed himself, and if they had a decent education and were willing to embrace his efforts to assist the progress of their people, then so much the better. Without them, he once said, it was impossible to 'successfully manipulate' the district.[20]

Bell was popular with Mafeking's white community too. He took an active part in their social life, helped set up a public library, and was an automatic choice as president for Mafeking's numerous clubs and societies. 'His presence', it was said, 'enlivened whatever company he might be in, and was like a sunshine in a room.' People particularly remembered his sardonic humour. One of his colleagues thought him 'a very clever and amusing fellow', a view Plaatje soon came to share. 'Our Civil Commissioner', he thought, conferring upon him the highest accolade, 'is a white Lenkoane. His acumen in fixing sarcastic phrases and aptitude in putting comical jokes is beyond description. His mere silence gives him a very ferocious appearance.'[21]

Plaaje was impressed as well by the dutiful attitude that Bell took towards the welfare of the African population (some fifteen thousand people) for whom he was administratively responsible. Bell believed it was his duty as magistrate and civil commissioner not just to keep the peace in the district, but to actively promote the well-being and interests of its inhabitants. In contrast to those magistrates who never ventured outside their offices, he pointed out to his superiors on one occasion, 'a Magistrate who individualises himself, obtains a moral control over the people ... is consequently enabled to mould them into a condition of peace and prosperity and an observance of the laws and the regulations of civilised usage'.[22]

It was the kind of creed with which Plaatje could readily identify, and from the beginning the two men established a friendly, albeit necessarily unequal, relationship. Bell, for his part, was impressed with the qualities of his new court interpreter, and he found him a great improvement upon Jan Moloke, his predecessor. Whereas Moloke had not been considered sufficiently trustworthy and reliable to handle office records without supervision, Plaatje was, so Bell was to observe in April 1899, 'a steady, diligent person', and to be trusted in every respect. Unlike Moloke, Plaatje could speak and write in Dutch, and to a very high standard.[23]

Plaatje's duties at work were divided between interpreting in the magistrate's court when it was in session and attending to the more routine work of copying documents, issuing passes, witnessing statements, writing out charge sheets, typewriting (in which he was soon very skilled), and filing correspondence and other office records. Translating incoming letters written in Dutch and Setswana into English was another regular task, his skills at a premium given the limitations of others in the office. Geyer understood Dutch but not Setswana; Grayson understood neither, being by his own admission 'a blundering ass where languages are concerned'. Surviving examples of letters Plaatje translated for colleagues include one in Dutch from the landdrost (magistrate) of the Lichtenburg district in the Transvaal concerning the exact location of the customs gate on the road from Mafeking, and another in Setswana from Marumoloa Mothibi, headman at Tshidilamolomo, seeking to resolve a misunderstanding arising out of the recent visit to his stadt of a detachment of Cape Police.[24]

Routine tasks of this nature, even if they were beyond others in the office, posed few difficulties. Interpreting in court, however, provided a far greater challenge, and this was the part of his job Plaatje enjoyed doing most.

The magistrate's court in Mafeking sat for several days each week, according to need, and heard both civil and criminal cases. Working conditions were far from ideal. The courthouse was too small and, in the summer months, stiflingly hot. Julius Weil, the town's member of parliament, thought it was 'a miserable structure', Mr Justice Lange that it was 'cramped and badly ventilated and not fit to sit in'. In fact, he and his fellow Circuit Court judges simply refused to use it, removing instead to the more commodious Masonic Hall when they came to town. Mr Bell and his staff did not have this option, however, and must have welcomed the respite afforded by their monthly visits to Setlagole, a large Barolong settlement that lay on the railway line south. Here the periodical court, as it was known, sat in less cramped surroundings.[25]

Most of the cases that came before them, whether in Mafeking or Setlagole, could scarcely be described as serious: petty theft, drunkenness, trespass, committing a public nuisance and causing a breach of the peace were the most common criminal offences. Two cases (numbers 290 and 291) heard in Mafeking during Plaatje's first week at work in October 1898 give a flavour. First, there was that of *R* v. *Katje*, described as 'a Hottentot female', with no occupation, charged with being 'wrongfully and unlawfully on or about 19 October at Mafeking, drunk in a public place, to wit, Carrington St'; she was found guilty and fined 7s 6d, or a sentence of five days' imprisonment with hard labour. It was not the first time, nor would it be the last, that the unfortunate Katje was hauled up before Bell on the same charge. Next came the case of *R* v. *Moses Callan*, described as 'a Barolong labourer', charged with 'wrongfully and unlawfully on 18 October 1898 at Mafeking steal[ing] one fowl, the property of George Francis, Market Master'. He was found guilty and got fourteen days' imprisonment with hard labour.[26]

Such cases formed the staple of business in the Mafeking magistrate's court, the consequence not of an inherent criminality on the part of the inhabitants of the district but the product, more often than not, of sheer poverty. In 1898 and 1899, in the wake of the rinderpest, conditions were far worse than before, and it is scarcely surprising that most of those who appeared before the court in criminal session were both poor and black.

The magistrate's court was not the only place in Mafeking where justice was dispensed. In the stadt, Wessels Montshiwa and his council had jurisdiction in civil cases where customary law applied and where no whites were involved. This right to hear these cases was jealously guarded, being both an expression of chiefly power and independence, and an important source of revenue by virtue of the fines they had the power to impose. Typically, cases that came before them would concern the occupation of land under customary tenure or the ownership of livestock. One such case which Plaatje happened to witness, involving several claimants and considerable complexity, arose in connection with the distribution of stock that had belonged to a man called Mitsagosi, who had died at Kunana in June 1898. Because the case was referred initially to the magistrate's court, before being handed over to the chief to deal with, Plaatje was called upon to supply Bell with a handwritten summary of the decision of the kgotla, which resolved the matter successfully.

The approach to doing justice in the chief's kgotla was far less adversarial than in the magistrate's court. Plaatje's summary of the judgment in the Mitsagosi case reflected the primary concern of Wessels and his councillors to reach a consensus. Their ruling was sealed by agreement that 'according to native custom we select a fat animal, from among the small stock, to be slaughtered in the lekgotla'. These were Plaatje's words, and he includes himself in the 'we'. It was not quite how things were done in the magistrate's court. Admirer as he was of the Cape's judicial system, and now involved in its day-to-day operation, he was equally familiar with traditional ways of doing justice and held them in high regard.[27]

On occasions more serious cases – murder, rape, assault, robbery and the like – would come before Mr Bell. His task then was not to dispose of these himself but to carry out preparatory examinations on behalf of the Griqualand West High Court in Kimberley. If the Crown prosecutor considered the evidence strong enough to support a prosecution, the case would come to trial during the Circuit Court's next visit to Mafeking – always a welcome occasion for Plaatje since it was an opportunity to see Isaiah Bud-M'belle, who travelled with the court as its interpreter.

Among the cases that fell into this category, and that came before Charles Bell in 1898 and 1899, one stands out. It involved Louis Brink, a 19-year-old Boer farmer who lived with his family on the farm 'Faith', some twenty-five miles outside Mafeking. Here, early in the morning of 28 April 1899, he assaulted a 'Kalahari' herdboy employed by his father, striking him violently with a heavy stick. Two days later the victim of the assault, named only as Jacob, died from his injuries. In other circumstances Louis Brink might have expected to get away with this without further ado. The owner of the farm on which they lived, however, was a man called James Keeley, who happened to be the field cornet for the district. He took his duties seriously, called in the police as soon as he heard about the incident, and held an inquest, summoning the district surgeon to examine the injuries to Jacob's body. A preparatory examination was held in Setlagole the following month, during which Plaatje took down, and translated into English, statements from four Africans who had either witnessed the assault or seen the victim shortly afterwards.

Charles Bell, to his credit, believed there were sufficient grounds to bring a charge of murder, and the relevant affidavits and statements were sent off to Kimberley. After considering them, however, the Crown prosecutor decided to take no further action because Dr Hayes, the district surgeon who examined Jacob's body, could not be certain that the concussion which caused Jacob's death had resulted from a blow to his head. Young Louis Brink therefore faced a lesser charge of common assault in the magistrate's court, pleaded guilty and escaped with a £5 fine.[28]

Interpreting in such cases was a harrowing business. Gratuitous violence was part of everyday social relations in this part of the world, particularly when visited upon 'Kalaharis' like Jacob and his family, mistreated by black and white alike. When asked why he had not reported the assault to the police, Abraham (Jacob's brother-in-law, also employed by the Brinks) replied that he 'looked upon it as the ordinary beating we get from the white people', and he had not thought Jacob was going to die. Abraham clearly risked his livelihood, at the very least, if he gave damaging evidence against Louis Brink, and the same was true of the other witnesses. With remarkable unanimity they all stated that Brink had hit Jacob about the arms and body, and not the head – scarcely credible in the case of somebody certified to have died from the effects of concussion.[29]

Plaatje can have had few illusions that justice was always done. All he could do, in a case like this, was to turn what the witnesses said into the formal written testimony that due process required – a skilled and demanding task in itself – and await the outcome as the law took its course. Without him they would have had little chance of even making their voices heard. It was inevitable, notwithstanding the efforts of a conscientious and humane magistrate like Charles Bell, that the legal process was affected, and sometimes subverted, by the inequalities and prejudices of the society it served. J.W. de Kock, Brink's attorney, undoubtedly advised his client on just what the witnesses needed to say.

Plaatje could not know, in June 1899, that Brink's past would one day catch up with him and that justice, of a sort, would eventually be done.

One other case heard in Mafeking before being referred to the higher court is of particular interest, and it could have had serious consequences. The accused was an African by the name of Joseph Ephraim. He had worked for De Beers in Kimberley and was caught trying to sell diamonds in Mafeking, a serious offence in view of the strictly enforced legal monopoly which De Beers enjoyed over the selling of diamonds. The hearing took place early in March 1899, followed soon after by his trial by the Circuit Court, and both attracted a great deal of interest locally in view of the value of the diamonds involved. The unfortunate Ephraim, who arrived in court wearing a 'fashionable light suit and a soft felt hat', which would not have helped his cause, was duly found guilty and sentenced to five years' imprisonment with hard labour.

But for Plaatje the worrying aspect of the case was that Ephraim had actually been staying with him in the stadt, and it was here that the Cape Police, in the person of Private Henry Currie, discovered the diamonds, after receiving a tip-off. They were hidden inside a locked portmanteau which Ephraim admitted was his. There was nothing to suggest Plaatje knew anything about the diamonds and, luckily for him, Bell was quite satisfied that he was in no way 'acquainted with Ephraim's illicit intentions'. Clearly, though, he needed to be rather more careful about the kind of people to whom he extended his hospitality, and it was fortunate that Ephraim made no attempt to incriminate him. Needless to say, had Bell found any evidence that Plaatje knew what Ephraim was up to it would have been a swift end to a promising new career. Losing a second interpreter to IDB (illicit diamond buying) would scarcely have enhanced Bell's promotion prospects either.[30]

By the time the case was decided, though, Charles Bell had had every opportunity to form an opinion of the character and the qualities of his new court interpreter. He could see that Plaatje approached his duties in court with commendable seriousness of purpose, that he seemed genuinely concerned that justice should be done, and that he had already attained a high level of professional competence. All these things emerge very clearly from the account that Plaatje himself wrote about his experiences as a court interpreter in Mafeking. Entitled 'The essential interpreter', and some ten pages long, it was written in 1909, seven years after he had resigned from the position. It contains some vivid descriptions of what he had seen and experienced during his time in the magistrate's court in Mafeking, and gives a revealing picture not only of the attitudes he developed towards his work, but of the way he responded to the demands that Bell made upon him.[31]

In interpreting, as in other matters, Charles Bell insisted upon the highest standards. 'Mr Bell informed me', so Plaatje wrote, 'when I first came into his office, that interpreting in court and interpreting at the sale of a cow were two different things entirely, and that it was as necessary to cultivate the art as to acquire a knowledge of the respective languages.' And as he learnt to 'cultivate the art', so he found Bell's own proficiency in languages a source of security and comfort when he was called upon to perform his duties. 'I always made my translations with a perfect security, believing that he could rectify my errors, if any. I cannot express the satisfaction this gave me – always – not only because of the correctness of my renditions but on account of the knowledge that the chances of a miscarriage of justice were non-est.'

On one occasion, however, Plaatje had to interpret in a case involving German and Korana, two languages in which 'I was less familiar and in which Mr Bell was unversed'. Accordingly he felt a much heavier burden of responsibility. In court, he sensed a feeling on the part of those present that this situation 'gave me the greatest satisfaction since for the first time I was able to exercise a free hand having to perform a role in which I was not subject to criticism'. But this was not how he saw it. His mind was focused, rather, upon the difficult task before him, and in ensuring that no mistakes were made. 'I took much pains eliciting my facts and getting the deponent to revise his sentences if they contained a phrase of the meaning of which I was not quite certain' – however long this took. He continued: 'This retarded the proceedings in an unmistakable manner and my renditions, usually noted for their expeditiousness, were clearly boring. I felt that it was a tedious performance taking up the time of the court to ascertain minute details which could easily be left unresearched; however, I threw the approbation of the Court and its loafers to the winds and centred my attention in the correct administration of justice only, determined to tell the magistrate so should he remonstrate against me for delaying the court more than is my wont.'

It is a revealing account that says much about Plaatje's high-minded approach to his work, as well as the kind of pressures that existed in the courtroom, which could all too easily affect the judicial process. For the courtroom was undeniably theatre too. Each court of law, he said, had its audience, 'a motley crowd of white men, Natives and Hottentots, males and females, clean and unclean'. Some of them were 'very intelligent and appreciate a legal point – good, bad or indifferent – as quickly as any member of the court'. Often there would be 'a distinct, yet respectful bid for the plaudits of this "gallery" by "budding" lawyers and court attendants', scarcely an aid to concentration if you were the interpreter. Court proceedings, in other words, served up entertainment as well as justice. If you worked there, you just had to get used to it.

'Tedious performance' or not, on this occasion virtue had its reward. Plaatje happened to overhear Bell, in conversation with the mayor, express his satisfaction with his new interpreter, 'who preferred to be understood when he translates and who visibly feels grave and took extraordinary pains when interpreting into and from languages not known to any others, and when he knows that the course of justice depends on him entirely'. Other interpreters he had had, by contrast, 'considered it infra dig to invite correction, they seem to fear that patient eliciting of obscure facts will be mistaken for incompetence and are happier if they can easily gloss over mistakes in an inaudible tone'. Unsurprisingly, Plaatje was 'highly elated at the testimony'.

Several aspects of his work Plaatje found especially challenging, not least the problem of explaining legal terminology:

> My own difficulty when I was still a fresh attaché of the Court was the finding out of the real meaning of most of the least known of forensic phrases, including commitment for trial, and how to express them in the vernacular. I found out that this was too difficult a phrase to render into intelligible Dutch, or any of the native languages, in half a dozen words. A literal translation of it will be beyond the reach of the intellect of a person of mediocre intelligence so I found the following rendition rather roundabout but more satisfactory because better understood.

> Magistrate: 'You are committed for trial.'

> Interpreter: 'Kgetse ea gagu yaka e koaliloe e tla romeloa koa mosekising eo mogolo koa Teemaneng, fa a sena go a bala ke ene o tla holeling fa u tla sekisioa Magesetrata, kgona ke Liyoche eo o tla tlang, lefaele gore ga nke u Sekisoa gope' – 46 words to explain 5.

> I have often found English prisoners, after being told in this pithy official language, and despite the fact that the phrase is in their mother tongue, that they scarcely understood their fate as they did not know if 'Committed for trial' was something round or square. My translation just quoted would, if re-translated into English, read: 'Your case as recorded will be sent to the Crown prosecutor at Kimberley. After reading it he will see if you are to be tried by the Magistrate, by the next Circuit Court judge or if you are not to be prosecuted at all.'[32]

The tricky business of cross-examination in three languages caused Plaatje a few problems at first. This required not only a good command of the languages involved but also a detailed knowledge of procedure, the ability and patience to explain it to a witness or the accused, and of course absolute integrity: the slightest mistranslation, he was always aware, could result in the miscarriage of justice. Efficient court interpreting thus required a high level of skill and application, and it placed a heavy burden of responsibility upon the individual concerned. He clearly relished the challenge. From 'The essential interpreter' comes a picture of a confident, conscientious and able young man who responded with enthusiasm to the demands of his work in court, and believed implicitly in the importance of what he was doing. At the same time, there were aspects of the job of which he was not so enamoured, in particular the related questions of pay and status. On the former, he believed himself entitled, on the basis of an undertaking made to him by the postmaster in Kimberley, to an additional £1 per month as from the first day of March 1899, with further increases annually to take him to a maximum of £120 p.a. by March 1901 should he remain in the service. He wasted little time in drawing this to Bell's attention, writing to him on the day he believed the increase was due. 'As they seem not to have brought this matter to your notice, at the time of my transfer,' he wrote, 'I beg the honour to do so with the sincere but humble request that you will be pleased to use such influence as you may be empowered with to have the omission rectified.' He added that he hoped his application 'claims your first attention as I am the only married member of your staff'.

Unfortunately, the acting postmaster general in Cape Town, when consulted about the matter, denied that any such promise was made 'by any responsible officer of this Department'. And Bell himself, while perfectly satisfied with Plaatje's work, did not think he had been working for him long enough to justify an increase if no such promise had been made.[33]

Just as galling to his sensitivities was the question of status. He found it particularly irritating to be ordered about like the most junior office messenger, and not to be accorded the respect to which he thought his position entitled him. One such instance he remembered very clearly. It began with a request from the Bechuanaland Protectorate resident commissioner's office for the services of an interpreter. Plaatje went over 'as soon as my time allowed', officiated as requested, and then submitted his account. The resident commissioner queried this, however, 'His Honour expressing surprise', so Plaatje related, 'that I should claim any remuneration for my service, a claim that was never put forth by any of my predecessors'. Charles Bell agreed, informing Plaatje that 'as an employee of the Cape government I should render my services free as the Cape was bound to assist the Imperial government whenever necessary' – despite his protestations that he saw no reason why he should 'go and render free services to facilitate the work of well paid officers any more than I could afford to work in his office without a salary'. He had no choice but to accept the ruling.

Plaatje's case may not have been entirely watertight (he would have done the work during office hours rather than in his own time), but his sentiments were clear enough, and when a second request for an interpreter came from the resident commissioner's office he declined to make himself available. It gave him no satisfaction whatever to hear, shortly afterwards, that the resident commissioner had obtained 'a street boy to interpret "anyhow"', with predictably disastrous results. Plaatje could be very prickly when he felt that his skills and status did not get the recognition they deserved – and not afraid to say just what he thought.[34]

On two occasions during 1899 Plaatje found himself before the presiding magistrate in a different capacity from usual: as plaintiff in the first, defendant in the second. On the first occasion, 9 June 1899, he brought a civil action against one Alfred Ngidi, a local railwayman of Mfengu origin, for the recovery of the sum of 7s 6d which he had incurred on his behalf. What had happened was this: Plaatje had agreed to hire out his harmonium to Ngidi to enable him to use it one Saturday evening at a function in the location and, since Ngidi did not possess the means of transporting it, to hire a horse and cart (from Joshua Molema) for this purpose. It was arranged that Ngidi would go to Plaatje's house on the Saturday afternoon to pick up both horse and cart and harmonium. But he never showed up. Plaatje, obviously very annoyed and kept waiting all afternoon, was unable to recover from Ngidi the 7s 6d he had already paid Joshua Molema, so determined to take him to court. Judgment, with costs, was duly made in his favour. It also fell to Plaatje to personally write out the summons which brought Alfred Ngidi to court, since this now formed one of his official duties. The law, he was again reminded, was an accessible instrument that could be used for civil as well as political purposes.[35]

But on the second occasion, he was not quite so fortunate. This time he was the defendant, having been brought to court by one Joseph Whiffler, a Mafeking baker of doubtful integrity, for the alleged non-payment of 14s 6d owed for bread, cakes and ginger beer which he had ordered and had delivered to his home. Plaatje had declined to pay the whole of this amount since Whiffler owed him 9s on a separate account, which he had tried repeatedly to extract from him.

When Whiffler's collector, Mr Mahoney, went on his rounds, therefore, Plaatje's suggestion was that he should pay only the balance of 5s 6d. Mahoney, however, was unwilling to agree to such an arrangement, and applied for a writ. In the light of the circumstances of the case, Plaatje, frustrated at having had to wait so long for Whiffler to settle his debt with him, argued that he was 'entitled to the dismissal of the summons with costs', adding in court that he would have paid up 'had the plaintiff not been so precipitous'. Charles Bell did not see things in quite the same light, and judgment with costs was awarded to Joseph Whiffler.[36]

The two cases are of interest for what they suggest of Plaatje's sensibilities, for in both an impression is conveyed of a young man (he was still only twenty-two years old) determined not to allow any liberties to be taken with him. Whether the other party was black or white really did not matter. In the second case, he may have misjudged, in the heat of the moment, the consequences of refusing to pay the full amount of money demanded by Mahoney, but what had upset him was the manner in which it had been demanded. He would have paid up, he said, had not Mr Mahoney been so 'precipitous'. Clearly, he was not prepared to tolerate this kind of treatment without protest, just as, at work, he was quick to claim the recognition and remuneration he believed his due. There was a keen sensitivity in his make-up to anything he perceived as unfair treatment.

Throughout 1899 Plaatje applied himself assiduously to his work in Charles Bell's office and in court. But there were lighter moments too. In one incident, remembered years later, he walked into the courtroom one morning, ready to interpret, and to his surprise noticed that the magistrate was wearing a shirt of exactly the same line and pattern as his own. 'I quickly disappeared into one of the anterooms', he related, pondering the Tswana adage 'Never measure your straw with great places', 'and hid the offending garment before I returned to officiate'. Magistrate and court interpreter, after all, were not to be confused.[37]

It is unlikely to have been the only occasion when his appearance in court led to magisterial raised eyebrows – or worse. One evening, he recalled some months later, he decided to accompany his friend David Phooko on a journey to collect a horse from Pitsane, some forty-eight miles from Mafeking. It was a fair distance, but Plaatje had an exceptionally good pony, David would be picking up a fresh horse, and they were confident of being able to get back to Mafeking by eight the next morning, when he was due at the office.

Unfortunately, things did not quite work out on the return journey as they planned. David's horses made slow progress, holding them both up, so when they got to Libono, thirty miles from Mafeking, Plaatje went on ahead in a bid to get to work on time, arriving in Mafeking at eight minutes past eight, and after a long and dusty ride probably not quite ready to step straight into court. He was silent about the reception he received from Charles Bell ('sarcastic phrases' were the least he could expect), but the escapade can have done little to enhance his reputation for punctuality. David did not make it back until half-past eleven that morning.[38]

In addition to carrying out his normal duties at work, Plaatje was also busy, over the course of 1899, preparing to take some Cape civil service examinations, hoping to qualify himself for a higher salary and promotion. His intention was to take the papers in Setswana, Sesotho, Dutch, German and Typewriting, an impressive array given that candidates in these examinations rarely took more than two papers at any one session. These were not the entry examinations for the civil service in which Isaiah Bud-M'belle had distinguished himself, but the proficiency examinations for people already employed in government service, open to black and white alike. In July 1899 Bud-M'belle had gone a step further and taken two such papers, Setswana and Sesotho, and passed both of them. It can only have encouraged Plaatje to do the same.[39]

But as the year wore on, it looked more and more likely that wider political developments would disrupt the normal course of the lives of everybody in Mafeking. Tension between the British imperial government and the two Boer republics was increasing steadily. Sir Alfred Milner, the high commissioner for southern Africa, was convinced that their overthrow, by military means if necessary, was essential for the empire's long-term security, and he had the full support of Joseph Chamberlain, the British colonial secretary. The fragile social and political order of the Cape Colony, fatally undermined by the Jameson Raid, was under severe strain too. By the middle of 1899 there was open talk of war, and both sides, Britain and the Boer republics, prepared themselves for military conflict.

Although the government of the Cape Colony tried desperately to steer a neutral course, in Mafeking there were understandable signs of anxiety. The town's residents, black and white, while well disposed, for the most part, towards the cause of the British imperial government, were acutely aware that Mafeking, by virtue of its geographical location, was likely to be one of the first places to be attacked in the event of a declaration of war. The town's association with the Jameson Raid, moreover, had not been forgotten in the Transvaal, and in August and September 1899 it was daily becoming a more attractive target in view of the large quantities of stores and railway equipment being accumulated there.

For several months the Cape government, fearful of providing the Boers with a pretext to justify invading Cape territory, had refused to allow the nearest imperial military force, led by Colonel R.S.S. Baden-Powell and based in the Bechuanaland Protectorate, to station any of its men in Mafeking. In response, Mafeking's white citizens began to take some secret measures to defend the town themselves. In the middle of September, though, Baden-Powell, having finally secured the necessary permission from the Cape government, moved his entire Protectorate Regiment into Mafeking from their base at Ramatlabama, and preparations for the town's defence proceeded with a new urgency. A Town Guard was formed, earthworks were thrown up, trenches dug, forts constructed, and inner and outer defensive perimeters were established. Many white women and children began to leave the town to journey southwards to Kimberley, Cape Town and, so it was hoped, to safety. Mafeking prepared itself for a siege.[40]

Like Mafeking's white citizens, Barolong, too, grew increasingly concerned as they heard news of the mobilisation of Boer forces on the other side of the border, for they were bound to be drawn into any fighting that took place. As with the whites, there was a long-established pro-British tradition among the Tshidi Barolong, but they were by no means confident of the ability of the British forces in Mafeking to resist a Boer attack. Wessels Montshiwa and his headmen repeatedly asked Charles Bell for arms so they could defend themselves in the event of war breaking out, but each time they were refused. They put the same request to Mr Justice Laurence, judge president of the Griqualand West High Court, when the Circuit Court came to Mafeking late in September. 'Wessels remarked that there seemed a good deal of thunder in the air, and raised the question of guns', Laurence recalled. He responded by reminding Wessels that 'thunderstorms often cleared the sky and did no permanent damage', and that if he and his people 'remained loyal to the Queen and obedient to the local authorities, they might rely upon protection if need arose'.[41]

Unhappy at being fobbed off in this way, the Barolong demanded a further meeting with Bell in the stadt, at which Plaatje himself interpreted. It was a dramatic occasion, and he remembered it clearly: 'The chiefs told the Magistrate that they feared he knew very little about war if he thought that belligerents would respect one another's boundaries. He replied in true South African style, that it was a white man's war, and that if the enemy came, Her Majesty's white troops would do all the fighting and protect the territories of the chiefs. To which Chief Montshiwa and Joshua Molema responded by going round the magistrate's chair and, crouching behind him, said: 'Let us say, for the sake of argument, that your assurances are genuine, and that when the trouble begins we hide behind your back like this, and, rifle in hand, you do all the fighting because you are white; let us say, further, that some Dutchmen appear on the scene and they outnumber and shoot you: what would be our course of action then? Are we to run home, put on skirts and hoist up the white flag?' Chief Motshegare then reinforced their point by pulling off his coat, showing Bell an old bullet scar on his shoulder received in an action against the Boers over fifteen years earlier. 'Until you can satisfy me that Her Majesty's white troops are impervious to bullets,' he said, 'I am going to defend my own wife and children. I have got my rifle at home and all I want is ammunition.'

As before, Bell simply proffered confident assurances, and when he communicated the proceedings of the meeting to Cape Town, the response was the same. 'The reply from headquarters', Plaatje thought, 'was so mild and reassuring that one could almost think it referred to an impending Parliamentary election rather than to a bloody war.'[42]

Several days later, on 9 October 1899, Plaatje's twenty-third birthday, President Kruger issued an ultimatum to the imperial government, demanding the immediate removal of all imperial troops from southern Africa. With war now a certainty, Chief Wessels and his headmen made another desperate appeal to the Cape government for 'arms and ammunition sufficient for the defence of the town', since, they said, 'we are entirely defenceless'. This time their letter went no further than the magistrate's office, and within hours of the expiry of the ultimatum on 11 October the two towns of Mafeking, Barolong and white, found themselves surrounded by a force of several thousand men under the command of General Piet Cronjé.[43]

Plaatje laboured under fewer illusions than most as to what lay ahead. Immediately before the outbreak of hostilities he had predicted, in the presence of a disbelieving representative of the imperial government (he did not say who this was), that it would take a hundred and fifty thousand soldiers of the imperial government over twelve months to conquer the Boer republics. Such an assessment, in the view of the officer concerned, verged on 'disloyalty', his own estimate being that fifty thousand troops 'could within six months have made such a complete business of it as to have almost forgotten that there ever was war'. Time would show whose estimate was closer to the truth.[44]

Over one thing at least Plaatje could feel some sense of relief in the desperate circumstances in which Mafeking's inhabitants now found themselves: Elizabeth and Sainty, not yet a year old, were safely out of Mafeking and staying in the comparative security, or so it seemed at the time, of Elizabeth's parental home in Burgersdorp in the south-eastern part of the colony. They had left Mafeking on a visit there in August, staying for a few days in Kimberley on the way, and had not returned. From his position in the office of the local civil commissioner, Plaatje was in a better position than most to assess the likelihood of the town being attacked from across the border, whatever the reassuring public pronouncements Charles Bell felt obliged to make. If Mafeking was going to be attacked, there was no sense in risking the lives, if it could be avoided, of his wife and young son. He of course had no alternative but to remain at his post; this time there was not the luxury of choosing whether or not he cared to render his services to the imperial government.[45]

One communication Plaatje never did receive before Mafeking was cut off: his civil service examination registration papers. He had applied in August to take the papers in Dutch, German and Typewriting (he had wanted to take the papers in Setswana and Sesotho as well, but was told this would not be possible), intending to sit the examinations in Cape Town in December. Accordingly, the secretary of the Civil Service Commission dispatched the certificates of registration to him on 5 October. They never arrived. Nor, for reasons which were to become painfully clear, was he able to get to Cape Town that year. 'My intentions', he wrote later, 'were completely defeated' as 'unfortunately war broke out'. Mafeking was now completely surrounded by enemy forces. He found himself caught up in what was to become one of the most celebrated episodes in the history of the British empire.[46]

Upper: The new church at Pniel, early 1890s, before the old church *(far right)* was demolished. The Vaal River lies in the background.

Lower, left: Johannes Kushumane Plaatje (1835–1896), Plaatje's father, cattle farmer and deacon of the Berlin Mission Society.

Lower, right: Simon Plaatje (1855–1937), Plaatje's eldest brother.

Upper: The mission congregation at Pniel assembled in front of the new church, 1890s.

Lower, left: Marie and Ernst Westphal, missionary mentors.

Lower, right: Johan Martin Baumbach, senior missionary at Pniel, with his wife Julie and their children.

Upper, left: August and Elizabeth Schulz and children. Plaatje acted as Schulz's classroom assistant after his arrival in 1892.

Upper, right: Montshiwa (c.1815–1896), chief of the Tshidi Barolong. In the early 1890s Plaatje's father lived on a farm which fell within Montshiwa's chiefdom.

Middle: The Barolong stadt, Mafikeng, in 1890.

Lower: The Bend Hotel, Pniel, in the 1890s, which features in several of Plaatje's early memories.

ORPHEUS M. McADOO.
Sole Proprietor and Director of the Original Jubilee Singers,
Georgia Minstrels, and Alabama Cake Walkers.
Copyright
99 Swanston Street
Melbourne
and at Sydney

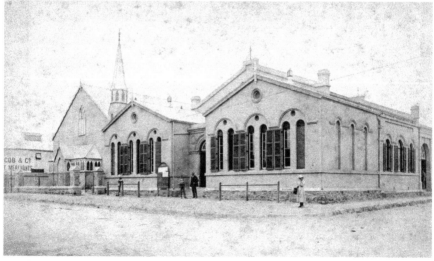

Opposite page: The Virginia Jubilee Singers come to Kimberley. *Upper, left:*
Advertisement for the Jubilee Singers' concert for 'Natives and Coloured People' in the
Kimberley Town Hall, 16 August 1890. *Upper, right:* Orpheus McAdoo (1858–1900),
born a slave in Greensboro, North Carolina, and leader of the troupe. *Lower:* The venue,
the old Kimberley Town Hall.

Upper: The post office in Market Square, Kimberley, where Plaatje worked from 1894 to
1898. 'Grewer's Fountain' is in the foreground.

Lower: African telegraph messengers in Kimberley in 1883, recruited from the Lovedale
Missionary Institute. Several of them remained when Plaatje joined the post office in
1894.

Upper: Charlotte Manye, seen here at Wilberforce University, Ohio, with other South African students. Henry Msikinya, standing behind to her left, and Joseph Moss, both from Kimberley, joined her late in 1896. Plaajie helped to send Moss and Msikinya on their way.

Lower, left: Rev. Gwayi Tyamzashe (1844–1896), Congregational clergyman and leading resident of the Malay Camp, Kimberley. Plaatje remembered him as 'the first ordained black minister I ever saw'.

Lower, right: John Tengo Jabavu (1859–1921), editor of *Imvo Zabantsundu*, the English–Xhosa weekly, and source of inspiration.

AMY COLERIDGE

Hamlet comes to Kimberley. *Upper:* the venue, the Theatre Royal. *Lower, left:* Notice in the *Diamond Fields Advertiser*, 17 December 1897. *Middle:* William Haviland, leader of the travelling company – his Hamlet 'a scholarly, judicious and temperate piece of acting'. *Lower, right:* Amy Coleridge, the female lead: 'a most sweet and gentle Ophelia'.

Upper: 'Equal rights for all civilised men'? Africans and Coloured people at a polling table in Barkly West during the general election in1898. Plaatje declared his support for Henry Burton, standing (unsuccessfully) against Cecil Rhodes, the sitting MP.

Lower: White sympathisers. *Left:* Samuel Cronwright-Schreiner and Olive Schreiner. Plaatje later credited Cronwright-Schreiner with encouraging him to become a journalist. *Right:* Henry Burton, attorney in Kimberley: he 'acted on our behalf directly on the platform, in the press and at the bar'.

FOUR

The siege of Mafeking,
1899–1900

It was supposed to be a white man's war. Both sides, Boer and British, said blacks should not be involved, at least in any combatant capacity. Otherwise, it was feared, they would learn to use guns against them and white supremacy would be threatened. In Mafeking there was never much chance that this unwritten agreement would be observed. Colonel Baden-Powell, Judge Laurence and Charles Bell himself may all have all rehearsed the official line when they met with the Barolong in September and early October 1899, but even as they spoke plans were being made to arm not only Barolong but units raised from Mfengu and Coloured communities too. As soon as war was declared and Mafeking was surrounded by Boer forces, these plans were implemented. 'The European inhabitants of the besieged town', Plaatje recalled, 'had a repugnance to the idea of armed Natives shooting at a white enemy' but soon changed their tune in the face of 'the business-like method of General Cronje in effecting the investment'.[1]

The Barolong stadt was far too close to the European town for it to be allowed to fall into Boer hands and it was always the intention to include it within the defensive perimeter. Baden-Powell was advised that the Barolong, like other Africans and Coloureds in Mafeking, could be relied upon to support the British and to defend their homes against the Boers. It turned out to be sound advice. Chief Wessels Montshiwa would occasionally vacillate, but the majority of his headmen remained steadfastly loyal to the British cause. Indeed they saw in the conflict the opportunity to defeat their local rivals, the Rapulana, who, as in the past, were allied with the Boers.

Plaatje moved back to 'Maratiwa', the Molema family home. It provided far more protection from stray shells and bullets than his flimsy hut, and more company. He was joined by his friend David Phooko and Ebie (or Ebenezer) Schiemann, his five-year-old cousin. Silas Molema, head of the household, was often away. As well as carrying out his normal chiefly duties, he now had command of a regiment defending the stadt, and was frequently summoned by headquarters staff to act as interpreter.[2]

In the European town, meanwhile, residents busied themselves in constructing shelters against the bombardment that was expected on the expiry of the ultimatum on 11 October. Those who could get out of Mafeking, especially women and children, escaped before it was too late. Several war correspondents came in the opposite direction, anticipating that Mafeking would soon be in the news. On 12 October a last train full of white women and children set off south. It got no further than Mareetsane, forced to turn back when it was discovered that the Boers had destroyed the line at Kraaipan, twelve miles beyond. The next day the armoured train, one of Baden-Powell's prize defensive assets, engaged in a skirmish with Boer forces just outside Mafeking. It was the first action of the war.

That night there was news of an imminent Boer attack. An unnamed African who had been with the Boer commando at Ramatlabama, north of Mafeking, and knew of their plans, made his way into the stadt and was directed to Plaatje, the recognised intermediary with the authorities. Realising the importance of the information he conveyed, Plaatje took him at once to Charles Bell, waking him from his sleep, and then to Baden-Powell. His men were accordingly well prepared for the Boer attack that came in the morning, successfully driving them off.[3]

Discouraged from making a further assault upon the town, the Boers prepared instead to shell it into submission. Surrender by six on the morning of Monday, 16 October, Cronjé demanded, or be subjected to intensive bombardment. Shells rained in all that morning before Cronjé offered the garrison a further chance to surrender. But little damage was done. Baden-Powell reported to the Boer emissary (and then to the rest of Mafeking) that only a chicken and a dog had been killed, and a donkey wounded. It was the kind of jaunty, insouciant response that did wonders for morale – and his own reputation.

Five days later there was another ultimatum. The Boers now had a much larger 94-pounder Creusot siege gun, just arrived from Pretoria, and it shelled the town on 24 October. Even this fearsome weapon inflicted only minor damage, and again nobody was killed or injured. Neither the ultimatum nor the size of the shells came as a surprise. A Barolong messenger had again slipped through the lines to alert the defending forces to the arrival of the new siege gun.

On the morning of the 25th, Boer forces launched an attack on the stadt. They advanced along the Molopo River valley, believing this to be the weakest point in the defences. Nearly five hundred Barolong, however, under the command of Captain Marsh, and supported by two squadrons of the Protectorate Regiment, barred their way. It was, Plaatje wrote later, their 'baptism of fire'. 'The Natives who were concealed behind the outer walls of Montsioa stadt waited with their rifles in the loopholes, according to Captain Marsh's instructions, till the Boers were quite near to them then returned the fire with satisfactory results', driving

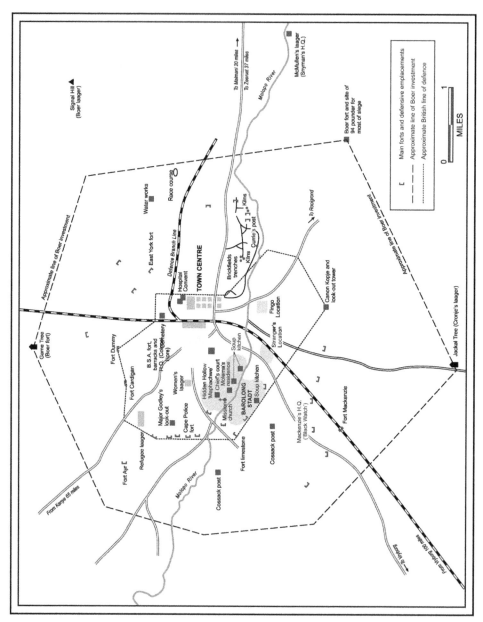

Mafeking during the siege, October 1899 to May 1900

them back. The only injury was when a splinter of rock grazed Chief Lekoko's temple after a Boer shell burst close by. The Barolong were not issued with much ammunition, Plaatje remembered, 'but it is doubtful if so little ammunition was

108

ever more economically used, and used with greater advantage'. It would be another six months before the Boers again tried this route into Mafeking.[4]

Besiegers and besieged settled into an uneasy routine. Cronjé's gunners shelled the town each day but there was no serious attempt to storm the town and the British made no attempt to break out: they just waited. To the relief of everybody in Mafeking the Boers observed Sundays as a day of rest, and both sides agreed not to undertake any offensive military operations during these twenty-four hours.

So it was that on 29 October, the third Sunday after the declaration of war, Plaatje was able to 'sit down and think', undisturbed by enemy action, before writing an account of his experiences of the previous week. Since these were not quite his first thoughts on the subject, he gave it the heading 'Continuation of my notes on the siege of Mafeking'. Unlike his earlier notes, written in pencil, he now used pen and ink, and foolscap paper, suggesting more serious intent. He began by writing in the day's date – he saw no need to add the month – and went on to review the week's events and what he had learnt from them. 'I have discovered nearly everything about war and find that artillery in war is of no use. The Boers seem to have started hostilities, the whole of their reliance leaning on the strength and number of their cannons – and they are now surely discovering their mistake. I do not think they will have more pluck to do anything better than what they did on Wednesday and we can therefore expect they will either go away or settle around us until the Troops arrive.'[5]

Such was the confident, optimistic tone with which he began. So far there had been few casualties and little damage, and all believed – if the Boers did not just 'go away' – that they would be relieved within weeks rather than months. Opinions varied over how long they would have to hold out. Plaatje initially thought until 20 November; others thought this unduly pessimistic. On 9 November Baden-Powell himself announced that 'we shall probably have to sit out another fortnight of siege before we can join the final defeat of the enemy'. Nobody imagined their siege would last until the following May.[6]

Quite why he began a diary he did not say. Plenty of others around him had the same idea. Charles Bell, better informed than most, had begun his on 1 October, and at some point asked Plaatje to type it out for him. William Geyer, the first clerk and assistant magistrate, had embarked upon his in a rather more desultory way (from 10 October), and so too had plenty of others in Mafeking, soldiers and civilians alike. With time on their hands, and a sense that momentous events were about to unfold, writing about their experiences and describing what they saw was just the natural thing to do.[7]

Even without their example Plaatje had little need of encouragement. He would have been very familiar, after all, with the genre. Published diaries, such as those of Samuel Pepys, John Evelyn and Queen Victoria, were read widely in the English-speaking world, and diary writing was a popular pastime. At Pniel, staying with the Westphals, he had first-hand experience of the missionaries' dedication to recording the events and progress of the mission in their *Tagebücher*, one of their most important tasks. Then he kept his own notebook, or pocketbook, whose entries had helped him to win the civil action brought against him in 1897. Quite likely this was a repository, not just for dates and details of expenditure, but of his thoughts on other matters too, or used to practise his written English. It would have been more surprising if on the outbreak of war, Plaatje had not resolved to put pen to paper.[8]

Unlike the war correspondents, all of whom kept diaries, he had no thought of writing for publication. What he embarked upon was a personal diary; something perhaps to share with Elizabeth when they were reunited, or to leave as a memento for her if he did not survive the siege. Mostly, though, he seems to have written it for his own enjoyment, recording his private thoughts and fears as well as describing the public spectacle unfolding around him.

He chose to write it in English but frequently used words and phrases from other languages – French, Dutch, Sesotho, Setswana, Xhosa and Zulu. Sometimes this was just to record what other people said in their original tongue. Sometimes he used a word which he found difficult to translate, or which he thought conveyed its meaning far better than in English – for example, the Xhosa term '*isiqu*' (which he used on several occasions), meaning 'body', but with a range of associations incorporating notions of self and personality. At other times he preferred to use indigenous terms because they sounded better than their English equivalents – like the Tswana term '*makasono*', derived from the sound of the Maxim gun.[9]

Essentially, though, it was in English. This seemed the natural medium for speaking in the first person, just as it was when writing to Elizabeth, and for engaging with the wider world around him. He had worked hard to improve his written English while he was in Kimberley, and it must have come on enormously in the year he had spent working for Charles Bell. Here, in a diary, was an ideal opportunity to practise what he had learnt and to take it to a higher level, free from the strict conventions of form and function that governed his work in the office.

He kept going with it for over five months. Apart from the period from 29 January to 5 February, he wrote something every day, even when – as over

Christmas 1899 – he was confined to bed with influenza. For a while he noted the number of shells from 'Au Sanna' (the Boers' 96-pounder siege gun) which landed in Mafeking each day. On some days he wrote only a few lines, on others half a page or more. Few were as long as the three pages of the first entry, a review of the events of the previous week written when he had time on his hands and was feeling in a particularly optimistic frame of mind. Some entries were in shorthand, a chance to practise a new skill.

Most of the diary is in his own hand, sometimes in ink, sometimes pencil. A number of entries, however – mainly in December 1899 and January 1900 – he dictated to David Phooko, who wrote them down in his own distinctive handwriting. It turned a solitary activity into a companionable one, and it helped to pass the time. For David it was a chance to practise his written English, and they enjoyed reminiscing about their time in Kimberley, sharing memories of mutual acquaintances like Patrick Lenkoane and of the 'Lenkoanics', or humorous stories, which his antics inspired. David's punctuation and grammar, especially his use of tenses, were less than perfect and Plaatje would sometimes go over the passages he had taken down, making a few corrections and additions. David had problems with spelling too. Words like 'miscellaneous', 'flabbergasted', 'innocent' were a challenge, but he had a good ear, and when he was unsure of the spelling of a word, his phonetic renderings were usually very accurate. It is easy to see why he thought Plaatje said 'lowest state' rather than 'low estate' ('I remember my low estate with an afflicted sense'), missing the biblical allusion (Luke 1:48, Romans 12:16) that was in Plaatje's mind – a trivial misunderstanding, perhaps, but a mark of rather different literary sensibilities.[10]

Plaatje was likewise keen to improve himself, but in a more expansive manner. His diary provided a means of articulating thoughts about his own behaviour and conduct, of reviewing a personal balance sheet. He could take pride in his achievements, admit failures, identify where he needed to do better. He was not afraid to acknowledge his shortcomings, such as a regrettable tendency to be late for work. 'This lateness appears to be a disease with which I am infected', he wrote, 'and I will see that it does not occur again as I feel very uncomfortable in consequence.'[11]

He was also keen to develop his literary skills, to experiment with vocabulary and narrative form. He would try out obscure new words (like 'funambulism', the art of tightrope walking), indulge in wordplay or elaborate, convoluted sentences – with varying success. He loved to construct self-conscious metaphors, often drawing upon the Bible for inspiration. Once he compared the attempt of a large group of black refugees to escape through Boer lines to the biblical exodus of the children of Israel: Charles Bell looked like 'their Moses', Sgt Abrams 'their

Aaron' and he doubted that there 'ever was an exodus so momentous as the one on the day on which Israel came out of Egypt'.[12]

Musical metaphors were another favourite. 'To give a short account of what I found war to be, I can say', he wrote, 'no music is as thrilling and as immensely captivating as to listen to the firing of the guns on your side. It is like enjoying supernatural melodies in a paradise to hear one or two shots fired off the armoured train; but no words can suitably depict the fascination of the music produced by the action of a Maxim, which, to Boer ears, I am sure, is an exasperation which not only disturbs the ear but also disorganises the free circulation of the listener's blood.' Warming to his theme, he compared the varied sounds of gunfire around Mafeking to musical performances he remembered in Kimberley: the 'boom' from the armoured train reminded him of the way one of the Payne family 'silenced a boisterous crowd with the prelude of a selection she is going to play on the violin'; the staccato sound of the Maxim brought to mind not only the organ of the Kimberley Roman Catholic choir but 'the Jubilee Singers performing one of their quaint and classical oratorios'.[13]

In truth the connection between the sound of a Maxim gun and the Jubilee Singers was somewhat tenuous, but by this point his convoluted metaphor had taken on a life of its own and he probably just wanted to find a way of including the Jubilee Singers in it. Here, as elsewhere, he liked to reflect upon his earlier life and experiences, making connections between past and present. So we hear about friends and family, memories of his time in Kimberley, of individuals like Ernst Westphal, Davidson Msikinya and Patrick Lenkoane, as well as those he was close to in Mafeking, such as Charles Bell, David Phooko, Wessels Montshiwa or the journalist Angus Hamilton. Implicit in all of this was the conviction that his own experiences and perceptions counted as much as anybody's: that they were a self-evidently valid frame of reference from which to view the events of the siege, and that he was at liberty to use the word 'I' as often as he pleased. Writing a diary was an assertion of both agency and identity.

It was also the opportunity to display a distinctive brand of humour. He was often struck by the incongruities of life under siege, the juxtaposition of the normal and the abnormal. The conduct of court cases, for example, departed radically from his notion of what constituted proper courtroom procedure and decorum. Thus his description of one court scene when a civil case was brought against Julius Weil & Co. for non-payment of wages to some of their workers: 'The parties concerned looked as usual, but not the court. The plaintiffs' attorney was in military attire; lawyer for the defence, never shaved since the siege, all hairy and dressed in a third-hand suit without a collar, looked more like a farmer than an attorney. Myself in knickerbockers and without a jacket, looked more like a member of the football team or a village cyclist than a court interpreter.'[14]

He was also amused by the way both sides claimed divine approval for their cause. 'The pulpit', he said, describing a church service held in the stadt, 'was occupied by Mr Lefenya, who warned his hearers to be very careful in their prayers, and remember that their God was the enemy's God; we, however, have the scale in our favour as we have never raised our little finger in molestation of the Transvaal Government, or committed an act that could justify their looting our cattle and shooting our children in the manner they are doing.'[15]

He was adept at conveying nuances of mood. Before long, as shelling and sniping took their toll on life and morale, there were signs of gloom and despondency. Several friends and acquaintances, black and white, were killed, among them Martha Sidzumo, the wife of his friend Patrick, and he had several narrow escapes of his own as shells landed close by. After one of these (on 3 January) he wondered how much more Mafeking would have to endure: 'I am inclined to believe that the Boers have fully justified their bragging, for we are citizens of a town of subjects of the richest and the strongest empire on earth, and the Burghers of a small state have successfully besieged us for three months and we are not even able to tell how far off our relief is.' By the middle of February things were a lot worse. The imperial government, Plaatje complained, 'may be as good as we are told it is, but one thing certain is that it does not care a hang over the lives of its distant subjects. It is distressing to hear that troops are still having a holiday at Modder River, even now after we had been besieged over four months.'[16]

At other times there were moments of loneliness, felt most keenly on traditional family occasions like Christmas. As well as being separated from Elizabeth and St Leger, he was also confined to bed with a severe bout of influenza. 'I am not even graced with as little as a congratulatory missive from both of them, but am nailed to a sick bed with very poor attendance – worst of all, surrounded by Boers.' The Christmas celebrations enjoyed by others served only to emphasise the pain of separation. Lady Sarah Wilson, he related, sent down a collection of toys and sweets for distribution among the children of the village. 'Contented little black faces musing over their gifts reminded me of a little fellow far away, who enjoys whatever he gets at the expense of the comfort of a bewildered young mother, deserving a Christmas box from his father but unable to obtain it.' It brought a tear to his eye, reminding him of the 'long and awful nights in 1897' when he had to overcome so many obstacles in his courtship of Elizabeth'. 'Surely,' he wrote, 'providence has seldom been so hard on me.'[17]

Feeling sorry for himself, however skilfully portrayed, was scarcely appropriate in the light of the events of the following day. Early on Boxing Day

Baden-Powell launched an attack against a well-defended Boer position at Game Tree. It was a disaster. Twenty-three men were killed and twenty-six wounded, heavy casualties which the defenders could ill afford. The Boers 'never hit so hard a blow on Mafeking since they besieged us', Plaatje wrote on the evening of the attack. Several days later he reflected on it further. 'The Game Tree fiasco appears to have been a heart-rending burlesque. Never was such a wilful suicide committed by a community in our condition. It was a lamentable affair and the least said about it the better. The consternation amongst the inhabitants was so deeply rooted that it is clearly visible amongst men and women and old and young of both white and black.' Baden-Powell learnt his lesson, and this would be the last offensive operation launched by the Protectorate Regiment. Charles Bell thought he had made 'the mistake of the siege, and one it is to be hoped he will not repeat'.[18]

For much of the siege Plaatje was kept very busy at work and he often struggled to keep his diary up to date. When the two other clerks, William Geyer and Ernest Grayson, joined the Town Guard and Protectorate Regiment respectively, Bell had only Plaatje to turn to, and his duties multiplied. He was in demand, too, with Baden-Powell's staff officers, some of whom he soon came to know well. Captain the Hon. Douglas Marsham, for example, he considered 'one of my dearest friends in the place', and he was very sad to have to report his death during the Boer attack on Cannon Kopje, one of Mafeking's key defensive positions, on 31 October. Sometimes he was summoned at short notice for translation and interpreting work, once being hauled out of a magistrate's court sitting when 'superior authorities (military) demanded my services'. Other tasks included translating written notices to convey information to the Barolong on arrangements for food rationing, and issuing passes and permits.[19]

Further interpreting work came with the establishment of a Court of Summary Jurisdiction. He wrote of officiating here for a second time on 22 November, understandably nervous about the threat posed by the Boers' 94-pounder siege gun. 'One is always wondering whether or not a shell from "Au Sanna" will not smash up the roof and crush our brains.' Nevertheless, he relished the challenge of acting as interpreter to this court, especially, he said, as they 'transact a lot of business in a very short time as evidence is taken by a shorthand writer, which causes one to extremely enjoy interpreting, as you have to fire away without stoppages'.[20]

A few days later he was summoned again but arrived in court late – not the first time, he was embarrassed to admit, although on previous occasions he didn't think the officers seemed too concerned. This time they lost patience and engaged another interpreter in his place. In the first case that came before them, however, most of the witnesses and prisoners were Boers, and the stand-in interpreter simply could not cope. 'The fellow being an amateur interpreter', Plaatje related with satisfaction, 'was completely flabbergasted when it came to cross-examinations, and I took his place to immense advantage.' 'He being incompetent in Dutch,' he explained, 'my services were procured', and he now became the 'unattached' – but frequently called upon – interpreter to the Courts of Summary Jurisdiction.[21]

Siege or no siege, Plaatje saw no reason why he should not be rewarded for the extra work. At the end of January, therefore, he wrote to Lord Edward Cecil, Baden-Powell's chief staff officer (and eldest son of the British prime minister, Lord Salisbury), to put his case. He had not previously troubled him about this, he said, 'for I had hoped that you would in the course of time remember me as in Colonial Courts Interpreters have the consideration of Heads of Department to a certain extent and are paid at the rate of 4/6 per hour if not permanently attached to the Court, and permanent interpreters are paid at that rate "extra", when they are engaged in other than criminal cases, besides their usual salary'. (Lord Edward could perhaps be forgiven for not knowing this.) He concluded with an appeal to his better nature: 'I hope your Lordship would remember that except during the week of my indisposition (last Christmas) I have never failed to act to the satisfaction of the Officers of the Court in that capacity; and also bear in mind that, although it would do me an amount of good, it will not hamper the Government in any way if you felt pleased to grant my request.'

This last flourish was entirely characteristic, but unfortunately he had breached protocol. 'I naturally thought you had told Mr Bell before you wrote to me,' Lord Edward replied. 'Never write to me again about Service matters except through Mr Bell.' His response was a contrite note to Mr Bell: 'I exceedingly regret the irregularity and humbly request that you will overlook it and kindly have the matter fixed up satisfactorily', adding that he was only making a claim for his work during sittings of the Courts of Summary Jurisdiction and not 'for such other assistance as I am able to render the staff, without prejudice to my Civil duties, the same as I have been since the commencement of the siege'.[22]

Charles Bell was far too aware of the value of Plaatje's assistance to make an issue of it, and he must have passed on a favourable recommendation since he was rewarded with an additional allowance of 5s per diem (6d more than he had been asking for), backdated to 17 November when the court first sat. It probably helped that Bell and Lord Edward Cecil were on good terms. They shared a distaste for Baden-Powell's autocratic manner, and Bell had recently prevailed upon Lord Edward to alter arrangements for the Court of Summary Jurisdiction so that the two of them could sit together (enabling Bell to avoid Colonel Vyvyan, the town commandant, whom he found frustratingly slow). Outside working hours both were accomplished raconteurs, entertaining themselves and their friends.[23]

～

When Plaatje spoke of 'such other assistance as I am able to render the staff', he was referring to military intelligence and to his part in it. One of his jobs was to issue passes, on behalf of Charles Bell, to dispatch runners, spies and armed raiders. When they returned he took down what they had to say, often in shorthand, translating their idiomatic Setswana into English, and then shaped their testimony into a coherent narrative suitable for intelligence purposes. Nearly a hundred such reports have survived, preserved in the papers of Charles Bell and Lt the Hon. Algernon Hanbury-Tracy, Baden-Powell's chief intelligence officer. Initially his reports were handwritten, and sometimes contained his own analysis and advice. When a man by the name of Thekisho arrived in Mafeking two weeks into the siege, claiming to be travelling from Windsorton (near Kimberley) to Mochudi (in the Bechuanaland Protectorate), Plaatje considered his statement 'most extraordinary' and doubted its veracity. 'Part of it may be true, or all of it may be; but besides instructing the officers to be on the alert so that such questionable people may under no circumstances be allowed through I think it would be more prudent than inhumane to give him a certificate to pass the outposts until we are relieved.'[24]

As time went on, a more fixed routine for this intelligence-gathering took shape. Plaatje would debrief spies and dispatch runners, typing up his report from his shorthand notes before presenting it to Charles Bell, who sometimes added his own comments and annotations before forwarding to Baden-Powell or Hanbury-Tracy. Occasionally Plaatje would add a few last-minute additions and corrections of his own. The result, for Baden-Powell and his staff, was a remarkably full and up-to-date picture of what was going on around Mafeking, often with information from inside the Boer laagers.

Chief Saane, a nephew of Wessels Montshiwa, was a particularly valuable intelligence source. Even when arrested by the Boers ('after they rightly suspected him of supplying the garrison with information'), and held in captivity by the Rapulana, he somehow managed to get messages through to Mafeking, including news of the surrender of Cronjé at Paardeberg and the capture of Bloemfontein by British troops. One of his reports, dated 30 January 1900, testified to the speed with which developments in the Boer laager were known inside Mafeking. 'On the day Snyman armed the Natives,' Plaatje noted, 'he received a letter from Mafeking, telling him what he was doing. He was quite perplexed by the suddenness with which the news reached Mafeking.'[25]

Being at the centre of this intelligence network gave Plaatje an unrivalled view of the work of these dispatch runners and the dangers they faced. He had a great admiration for Freddy Manomphe, whom he characterised as 'a black Sherlock Holmes'. Freddy arrived in Mafeking from Kunana on 12 November. He had encountered several parties of Boers on his journey, but each time he had hidden his dispatches, talked his way past them, retrieved his documents, and proceeded on his way. On his last encounter he was betrayed by another African he had met on his journey, but then 'lied so classically, and with such thoroughness and serenity that the Boers disbelieved the informer's testimony and let him go'.[26]

Dispatch runners to the south had to find other methods. At the end of January, Plaatje told Bell of the adventures of two dispatch runners who managed to reach Kimberley with the help of a 'Mr Honey', whom one of them had encountered by the Vaal River, and Plaatje's own brother Gabriel, who lived near Taungs. 'He and Mr Honey are old friends,' Plaatje explained, 'and the runners think that if in future dispatch riders are directed to my brother and the latter instructed to convey them to Honey, they would get through much safer. He is in excellent terms with the Boers, and they allow him to move about pretty freely.' It was not a task to be undertaken lightly. Plaatje reported that some runners sent by Ben Weil told him they had come across two other Africans who had been caught with dispatches from Mafeking and 'as a punishment for this offence the Boers had castrated both of them'.[27]

A number of Plaatje's reports ended up in the columns of the special siege edition of the *Mafeking Mail* (published daily, 'shells permitting'). If Baden-Powell thought them suitable for wider dissemination – taking into account considerations of security – he would mark the relevant passages and pass on to Hanbury-Tracy or Lord Edward Cecil to arrange publication with the editor of the *Mail*. 'By the courtesy of the Colonel we are enabled to print the following', the *Mail* said on 12 December, reproducing an extract about the successful exploits of 'three of our young men' who went out to raid cattle on the night of Friday, 8 December. A week later, reproducing another report, the editor commented that so much information from 'native sources' was subsequently corroborated by official intelligence that 'we feel disposed to give more credence to a Kaffir *ipse dixit* than we formerly have done'. Since the *Mail* 'regards the Native as a mere creature', Plaatje thought, this was quite an admission.

These reports provided much-needed copy for the *Mail*. News of the exploits of Mathakgong, cattle raider extraordinaire, boosted the morale of black and white alike, and the cattle he brought in were an invaluable contribution to food stocks, as the headline 'Our beef providers' recognised. 'We learned it was "Native Beef,"', so the editor of the *Mail* explained, and felt it best to give the account of this successful expedition 'in its own picturesque language'. There was never any indication of who had actually written these reports.[28]

✢

As well as carrying out his official duties, Plaatje was a valued source of assistance to several of the war correspondents. Charles Bell took a relaxed view of his desire to supplement his income in this way, and let him use the office typewriter. At the start of the siege he worked for E.G. Parslow, correspondent for the *Daily Chronicle*, whom he described as 'my dear friend'. The arrangement lasted until Parslow was famously shot by Lt Murchison in a drunken brawl at the beginning of November. 'This murder has not only deprived me of a good friend but it has wrecked me financially,' Plaatje lamented. 'He paid for my little assistance so liberally that I never felt the prices of foodstuffs that [have] reigned here since the commencement of the siege.'[29]

Fortunately, others were just as keen to have his 'little assistance'. One was the *Times* correspondent, Angus Hamilton, whose reports on goings-on in the stadt, and his account of the history of the Barolong, which interested him too, could not have been written without Plaatje's help. Early in December 1899 he took Hamilton around the stadt so he could take some photographs, which were eventually published in the London periodical *Black and White*. Several weeks later, Hamilton took another photograph, showing Plaatje interpreting, in the presence of Charles Bell and Major Hamilton Goold-Adams, as two dispatch runners conveyed the long-awaited news of the relief of Kimberley. Plaatje, gesturing with his right hand, is standing up in the middle of the photograph, while all the others are seated. It is a striking visual representation of his key role as intermediary, which Angus Hamilton, in setting up the photograph, seems to have fully appreciated.[30]

The other journalist with whom Plaatje struck up a profitable relationship was Vere Stent, the Reuters correspondent, who would become a lifelong friend and admirer. Over thirty years later Stent recalled how they had first met:

> One fine morning I became aware of a very smart, sprucely dressed young native standing to attention before me.

118

'Well?' said I.

'I hear you need a secretary-typist, sir,' he answered.

'Well, so I do. Is your master one?'

'I haven't a master,' said Plaatje, with a faint smile, 'but I write shorthand and can use the typewriter.' He spoke perfect English and I engaged him at a ridiculously low wage which he named himself and seemed glad enough to get.

Stent recognised in the young man before him ('an educated native, very rare in those days') 'an extraordinarily capable assistant'. 'To begin with, he could spell – which I can't and never could. He was quick on the machine ... quick-witted and understanding and quick to pick up and catch a new expression, ask the meaning and derivation of it and add it to his vocabulary.'

Stent found Plaatje invaluable as 'a liaison officer, between me and my little corps of native dispatch runners', and mentioned that he found in his diary 'entries of substantial sums of money paid to him for distribution amongst them'. His diary has not survived, but the claim is substantiated in a letter he wrote to H.D. Gwynne, the chief Reuters agent in Cape Town, seeking to justify his high level of expenditure. 'On January 31st 1900', he wrote, 'I issued a draft upon you in favour of Sol T. Plaatje for £30 for the payment of runners south and for services rendered to the Agency in connection therewith.'[31]

The high cost of runners reflected the risks involved. While some were shot or captured, the majority did get through, bringing the story of Mafeking's dogged resistance to the wider world. This had a huge impact on public opinion in the English-speaking world, the stirring tale of an isolated garrison holding out against superior enemy forces helpfully obscuring the bigger picture. The presence in Mafeking of army officers from some of England's aristocratic families – Lord Edward Cecil was just one of many – only added to its appeal.[32]

Plaatje was also able to call upon Vere Stent for help in arranging for some money to be paid to Elizabeth, and to send some messages of his own. Ben Weil did the same for him on another occasion. Later he wrote to Isaiah Bud-M'belle, via one of these runners, to ask for news of Elizabeth and Sainty and to reassure him that he was still alive ('I have never felt better in my life'), concluding with a request to 'remember me to Mr and Mrs Cronwright Schreiner' and to express the hope that 'the effects of this maze have not ramified their way'. Since neither was in Kimberley they probably never got the message, but it is nevertheless intriguing, five months into the siege, that he should think of passing on his compliments to the Schreiners in this way.[33]

Others were keen to take advantage of Plaatje's proficiency at the typewriter too. He never bothered to type out his own diary, but by early February he was busy with those of Charles Bell, William Hayes (Mafeking's senior medical practitioner) and Herbert Greener, the chief paymaster. Greener and Bell were friends, and Bell had probably recommended Plaatje to him, knowing that he was not only skilled at typing but could be relied upon to be discreet (some of Bell's comments about Baden-Powell, for example, were not for public consumption). For Plaatje it all provided extra income, typing practice which would be useful for future examinations, and some interesting insights into the minds of his white fellow citizens. He was pleased enough with what he got paid. Stent and Angus Hamilton may not have been quite as liberal as his 'late lamented friend' E.G. Parslow, but his earnings enabled him 'to keep pace with the hard times' – and good reason, he said, 'why I should sing the twenty-third psalm'.[34]

By January 1900 all the siege diarists were displaying signs of despondency. Relief had failed to materialise and the more historically minded among them were haunted by the memory of the siege of Khartoum fifteen years earlier: the relief column had been late in leaving, and General Gordon had been killed two days before it arrived. In Mafeking casualties were mounting, and food supplies were running low. Plaatje himself, in receipt of government rations, was relatively well provided for. On 22 February he reported that his week's rations consisted of '7 x 1 lb tins of preserved meat, 1 lb of sugar, half-a-pound of tea, ½ lb of coffee, some salt, pepper, rice, meal, etc', but in the stadt, and particularly among the black refugees who had sought shelter in Mafeking before the outbreak of war, starvation was rife. Plaatje had a close-up view of this and was directly involved in implementing the various measures announced by the military authorities to conserve food supplies, including restricting the sale and possession of various foodstuffs for the residents of the stadt.

It was not an altogether comfortable position to be in. He had loyalties both to his employer, the colonial government, and to his own people, the Barolong, and on issues like this they came into conflict. There was understandable resistance in the stadt to some of the measures proposed, and the officers who had the task of implementing them had scant regard for Barolong sensibilities. 'It came to their notice that some Barolongani were selling kaffir beer the other day', he noted on 5 January: 'They look upon it as wasting, and if the sale of this luxury was to continue, they were going to make a case against the party the other day, had the Civil Commissioner not been what he is – a white Morolong. They do not know that kaffir beer to a common Morolong is "meat and vegetables and tea" rolled into one, and they can subsist entirely on it for a long time.'

Plaatje was used to seeing all sides in such situations. 'From an official's viewpoint', he said of the restrictions being implemented, it was 'a wise policy, as it prevents the decrease of our supplies from passing faster than the days of the siege'; to 'a merchant it is a boon, in as much as it enables him to demand whatever he desires'; for the 'private individual a curse as the money is circulated at the expense of his pocket'. From 'a Serolong point of view', however, 'the whole jumble is more annoying than comforting. For this they may be excused, as the arrangement is in the hands of young officers who know as little about Natives and their mode of living as they know about the man in the moon and his mode of living.'[35]

On this occasion, thanks to the intervention of Charles Bell (who thought the commissariat 'were not to be congratulated' on the way they handled the matter), a serious confrontation was averted. It was by no means the only time Plaatje was caught up in tensions of this kind. Once there was a dispute with the official (a Mr Francis) who was allotted the task of running a grain store which had been set up in the stadt. He took over the church for this purpose, refusing to consider any alternatives when the residents of the stadt objected. Plaatje then drafted a strong letter of complaint on behalf of the 'chief and headmen of the Barolongs', criticising Francis's arbitrary behaviour and 'the most irregular manner' in which the store was being run. It can have left Bell in no doubt where his sympathies lay.[36]

Another tricky situation arose when the 'Black Watch', a unit composed largely of Shangaan refugees under the command of Lt McKenzie, took to intercepting Barolong cattle raiders as they returned to Mafeking, seizing their loot. Plaatje mentioned two such incidents in his diary. After the second, he wrote a strongly worded letter of protest to Lt McKenzie about the behaviour of his men and 'the ill treatment our people are subjected to under the Black Watch'. The 'Black Watch', he complained, 'seem to be particularly determined to leave no stone unturned in putting obstructions in their way in a manner tantamount to doing them more harm than good'. So pleased was Plaatje with this last turn of phrase – 'tantamount to doing them more harm than good' – that he repeated it in his diary when describing the incident. His representations were successful, 'superior members of the garrison' backed the Barolong, and the 'Black Watch' seem to have heeded the warnings.[37]

At other times Plaatje's sympathies lay elsewhere. In the middle of January he was called upon to interpret at a meeting between Charles Bell and Wessels Montshiwa in the stadt. Its purpose was to persuade the chief to allow his people to leave Mafeking in view of the shortage of food, but he was not inclined to co-operate. 'Things went on very smoothly', Plaatje wrote, 'until Wessels commenced to speak. He threw a different complexion on the otherwise excellent harmony which characterised the commencement of the proceedings. He misunderstood, misconstrued and misinterpreted everything said and an undesirable scene ensued.' Anybody who could interpret for Wessels when he was in this mood, Plaatje thought, 'ought to consider himself a professor', and it was 'an excellent thing that the CC is so patient' – otherwise 'things could happen that would cause great joy in the Boer laager'.[38]

But it was not just the chief who made his life difficult. Two months later, as large numbers of Barolong were finally leaving Mafeking, he was involved in taking a census to establish just how many people remained. The residents of the stadt did not welcome such official interference in their lives, however:

The people are vexing me exceedingly: one would ask me what I wished to do with the name of the owner of a place, another would object to a repetition of the census as they were counted (registered) twice already during the present siege. Another would say: 'No wonder the present, unlike all previous sieges of Mafeking, is so intolerable for the unfortunate beleaguered people are counted like sheep.' Another would stand at the door, empty herself of the whole of her stock of bad words, then threaten me to 'just touch my pen and jot down any numbers of her family'. The so–and–so![39]

Thus the voice of the harassed civil servant, exasperated at the unreasonable behaviour of the people he encountered as he went about his task – albeit not so serious as to prevent him from seeing the funny side of it.

This was not always the case. If things were too difficult to write about candidly, he would just skate over the details. Such was the case with the supposed 'deposition' of Chief Wessels Montshiwa at the end of December 1899. Baden-Powell had complained about the 'general unsatisfactoriness' of Chief Montshiwa and wanted him removed. Bell, no admirer of Montshiwa either, was present at the meeting to give effect to this, noting that its purpose 'was to tell Wessels, the Chief, that we would conduct business with his counsellors, in future, instead of himself'. Plaatje, who would normally have interpreted, is surprisingly reticent about the episode in his diary. He says only that 'The Colonel and Civil Commissioner were down to settle an issue amongst the Chiefs', and that 'the cause of the trouble was of course Thelesho' (Wessels Montshiwa). But he makes no mention of interpreting at the meeting, while his subsequent remark that 'we called in at 7 pm' after the proceedings had finished – by which time the chief was 'half-way at his cups and had a great many objections to make' – makes it clear he was not present earlier on. According to Angus Hamilton, an interpreter was present, but it must have been somebody else.[40]

Modiri Molema, however, remembered the episode well. Plaatje, he wrote, refused to interpret at the meeting when its purpose was made known. He was interpreter in the magistrate's court and not at the chief's kgotla, and he was not prepared to participate in the chief's deposition. Plaatje had his own mind, Molema said, and would not be forced into this. He was not a '*seraba*' (a bag of charms) that his employer could use to make him translate phrases from one language into another, nor could he be played at will like a '*serankure*' (a single-stringed bowed musical instrument). Only the Barolong themselves had the right to depose their chief, not an imperial military officer temporarily in authority over them. Here, it seems, was a line Plaatje was not prepared to cross.[41]

He did interpret at the meeting in the stadt three weeks later, but the situation was then different: the object this time was to encourage Wessels to let his people depart from Mafeking, not to depose him. And the very fact that a further meeting was arranged in order to secure his co-operation was tacit recognition that no mere fiat on the part of Colonel Baden-Powell could remove him from power if this was unacceptable to the people as a whole. All were as aware as Plaatje of Wessels Montshiwa's personal shortcomings, but this did not mean that Baden-Powell was entitled to act in so high-handed a manner, especially as the right to choose their own chief was enshrined in the terms of Bechuanaland's annexation to the Cape Colony in 1895. So they simply ignored his edict and continued to regard Wessels as their chief.[42]

Far more disturbing was the fate of those Africans who were executed after being found guilty of theft or of spying for the Boers. There were five such cases during the siege. Plaatje was expected not only to interpret at their trials in the Court of Summary Jurisdiction but at the place they were taken for execution. As they stood blindfolded, awaiting their fate, he had to translate their final words or requests and then convey back to them the response of the senior officer present. It was a harrowing ordeal, and Plaatje, so Molema recalled, was deeply affected by the experience. Not least because these hapless individuals who ended up before the firing squad had no conception whatever of the seriousness of the crime for which they had been convicted, or of the punishment they were liable to receive.[43]

Nothing about any of this appears in Plaatje's diary, and there is no mention of the execution of the supposed 'spy' at sunset on 25 January 1900. But others did describe what they saw. Charles Bell wrote that the man concerned 'was perfectly composed', 'saw no reason why he should be shot' and 'stood alongside the grave without the slightest sign of nervousness'. Angus Hamilton, who also witnessed the execution, reported that the condemned man, Piet, asked for one last opportunity to look around him, to have a final sight of the place he had lived all his life. His wish was granted, the bandages were removed from his eyes and then replaced before he was shot.[44]

Plaatje had tried to intervene earlier. According to Joseph Gape, a well-to-do Barolong farmer and Wesleyan lay preacher, Plaatje had appealed to the authorities to reprieve the condemned man but his appeal fell on deaf ears, earning the observation from Charles Bell that all Plaatje had 'inherited from those German missionaries was their absurd benignity and nothing more'. Just as likely, given his knowledge of legal procedure, his plea stemmed as much from a view that punishment for any crime should be proportionate to the seriousness of the offence as from a belief in the sanctity of all human life. He makes no mention of any of this, however, in his diary.[45]

Three Africans were also shot for theft. One of them, Hendrik Botetle, was sentenced to death for stealing 'and killing for food purposes' a horse belonging to Silas Molema, in whose house Plaatje was staying; 'an example was necessary', Baden-Powell considered, when confirming the sentence. Plaatje wrote simply in his diary for 10 March 'the horse thieves sentenced'. He did not mention what the sentence was, nor that it was carried out two days later.[46]

Later that month another case of theft of livestock came before the Court of Summary Jurisdiction. 'The prisoner pleaded something equivalent to "guilty under provocation,"' Plaatje wrote, the 'provocation' being extreme hunger. This time Lt-Colonel Hore, in command of the Protectorate Regiment, was one of the two officers presiding, and Plaatje commended his humane approach to the matter: 'The man could have been convicted had it not been for Colonel Hore. He always views things with the same light, and often makes as sarcastic remarks as the supreme court judges. When his brother justice was about to find the man guilty, he said: "The soup kitchen people are entirely to blame for these shameful deeds. Just look at him: his two legs are scarcely able to hold the fellow's body. They don't feed the people at all." He wouldn't agree to any verdict and it was decided his case would wait until the soup-kitchen affair has been investigated.'[47]

Hore, however, either changed his mind or was overruled. Before there was any time to investigate the shortcomings of the soup kitchen arrangements, the unfortunate prisoner, 'Jan, alias George Malhombe', was sentenced to death and executed on the evening of Monday, 2 April. Plaatje had no more to say about it: his diary had come to an end on Friday, 30 March.[48]

✦

Plaatje ended his last diary entry in mid-sentence, stopping some three-quarters of the way down the foolscap page. Most likely pressure of work had caused him to fall behind with his entries, and as the situation in Mafeking worsened there were simply more pressing things to attend to. On 20 March he mentioned being 'very busy officially', and there was no let-up in the stream of intelligence reports he had to prepare. It could well be that the unexpected execution of George Malhombe was just the final straw, prompting him to set aside what had become an increasingly burdensome and emotionally draining task.

For weeks past he had been busy with the problem of diminishing food supplies. 'We have very great difficulty in feeding the Natives', he wrote, identifying with Charles Bell in his efforts to address the problem. On 8 February Baden-Powell received a request from Lord Kitchener (chief staff officer to Lord Roberts) to try to make supplies last until 21 May, the earliest date a relief column was likely to arrive. More drastic rationing arrangements were accordingly put in place, and Baden-Powell decided to restrict the supply of food, so far as Africans were concerned, to 'the Barolong and defence natives', excluding several thousand black refugees who would now be encouraged, or if necessary forced, to leave Mafeking. This was the background to Plaatje's involvement in the attempted 'exodus' of nine hundred black refugees at the end of February. It failed because the promised armed escort never arrived, allowing the Boers to scatter 'the whole crowd in every direction', forcing them to return. Plaatje considered this outcome 'a serious blow to me particularly, taking into consideration that I have been on horseback from early to late during the last two days – and all for "niks"'. He recognised, as if this was perhaps not the right way to be looking at things, that their fate, and future, 'is of such a sweeping importance as put all other questions in the dark'.[49]

After that, he was involved in the efforts made by the authorities to keep these unfortunate black refugees from starvation. A soup kitchen was set up next to the residency but it proved to be too little, too late. It was a 'miserable scene', he wrote, 'to be surrounded by about 50 hungry beings, agitating the [engagement] of your pity and to see one of them succumb to his agonies and fall backwards with a dead thud'. These people, he explained, 'are made up of the blackish races of the continent – mostly Zulus and Zambesians. They venerate the Civil Commissioner and call me "ngwana's molimo"' (or young god). It was small wonder, given their situation and his, and the gulf that lay between, that this was how they saw him.[50]

Plaatje was also heavily involved in preparations for sending out armed Barolong parties into Boer-held territory. Mathakgong and his companions went on regular raids behind Boer lines, attacking Boer farmsteads as well as seizing cattle to run back into Mafeking. 'Mathakgong's name is a household word on every farm', he wrote on 18 March. 'They say he has killed many Boers at their farms during last month, including women and children.' In response General Snyman had already issued an order that all Africans coming from Mafeking were to be shot on sight. Some were, although not all his men were prepared to shoot unarmed refugees trying to make their way to safety. Plaatje's job was to issue Mathakgong and his men with passes and to check them in on their return. As it became easier to pass through the Boer lines, so the numbers increased. One day in the middle of March no fewer than eight dispatch runners arrived back in Mafeking. All had to be debriefed and reports written for the military authorities.

From the beginning of February he had also to prepare an 'official diary, all of the doings in connection with Native Affairs', as he described it. Probably Baden-Powell had requested this information, and Bell had simply delegated. Such a task would normally have fallen outside Plaatje's normal duties, but there was nobody better qualified. Whereas his intelligence reports were based on debriefings of individual spies and dispatch runners, taking down what they told him, he now had to summarise 'native affairs' more generally, both inside and (so far as he was able) outside Mafeking. In one he described the state of morale in the Boer laager, noting that while once the Boers 'appeared pretty jolly and thought that the food supply of the inhabitants was running out', now the sounds of 'dances and merry singing going on in the stadt' told a different story.[51]

There was no let-up in the daily shelling from the Boers' siege gun. On 13 March a shell struck the courthouse, making a 'terrible mess of everything inside', ruining what had once been Bell's private office. Nobody was in the building at the time, but the shell carried on through the building and burst against the outer wall, killing and wounding several Africans who had congregated outside, awaiting payment of their wages. Two days later he had a narrow escape himself. Riding his horse through the stadt, he heard the sound of a shell coming towards him. 'I have never felt so nasty as during that little period of my life, until it burst and the pieces flew overhead.' An old man named Letsie, in a nearby house, was not so lucky, and was killed instantly in the explosion.[52]

Their desperate situation continued into April. While large numbers of Barolong made their way out of the stadt, leaving it almost deserted, most of the black refugees remained. Some died of starvation, others were shot as they tried to pass through the Boer lines. At the beginning of April Colonel Plumer attempted to fight his way into Mafeking, but was repelled with the loss of a dozen men. Then an Mfengu cattle raiding party was betrayed by their Barolong 'guides' and led into a Boer trap. Heavily outnumbered and outgunned, they fell in a hail of bullets from two Maxim guns, although not before inflicting a number of casualties themselves. One of the two survivors was a man called Josiah Zulwana, whose sad tale Plaatje related in a report on the episode. He had managed to escape by hiding up a tree, and then 'crawled into Mafeking after dark'.[53]

Mathakgong, too, only narrowly survived an ambitious attempt to run over a hundred head of cattle into Mafeking supplied by Colonel Plumer at Sefikile, forty miles to the north. Unfortunately the Boers had advance warning of this plan, alerted by what Mathakgong described as 'the clumsy European method of always revealing their intention to the enemy', while Plaatje observed at the time that 'the Boers could not have been better prepared for them had they sent them a challenge'. Although they lost all their cattle, amazingly only two of Mathakgong's party were killed, the remainder owing their escape, so Mathakgong told Plaatje on his return, 'almost entirely to the good shelter afforded by dead carcasses of the cattle'. Aware of the trap Mathakgong's men were walking into, Plaatje sent out some men to try to warn him the night before, but they failed to get through.

Mathakgong reported that two of their party were wounded in the fight and taken prisoner but then killed in cold blood by the Boers. One of them, he said, was a man by the name of Moshen. In the margin of Plaatje's report Baden-Powell wrote in by hand: 'Bell, get evidence on this.' There would be a reckoning to come.[54]

Eventually, on 12 May, the Boers, aware of the progress of the long-expected relief column from the south, resolved to take Mafeking. Field Cornet Sarel Eloff (a grandson of President Paul Kruger) launched an attack through the stadt, passing very close to where Plaatje lived. It did not succeed. Reinforcements promised by General Snyman failed to materialise, Eloff was captured, and the combined forces of the Barolong, led by Silas Molema, and soldiers of the Protectorate Regiment killed or captured many of his followers after surrounding them in the stadt. Only a handful escaped back through the Boer lines. Two days later the besieging forces melted away as the relief column, led by a number of officers who had been involved in the Jameson Raid in 1895, made its way into Mafeking. After 217 days Mafeking was relieved.

The welcome the relief column received in Mafeking was dwarfed by the enthusiasm with which the news was greeted by the English-speaking world beyond. Extraordinary scenes of national rejoicing were enacted throughout

Britain and the empire. The popular press had a field day, celebrating its power to mould public opinion and to arouse patriotic fervour as never before. Henceforth Mafeking's seven-month siege made even the town's name a byword for the highest qualities of the British national character. Baden-Powell, instantly promoted to the rank of lieutenant general, was the hero of the day. A new word ('maffick': to exult riotously) was added to the English language.[55]

The Barolong had their own scores to settle. The day after the relief column entered Mafeking, Silas Molema led an expedition to Lotlhakane (Rietfontein) to capture Chief Abraham Matuba and his headmen, returning in triumph not only with the chief as their prisoner but with large quantities of livestock and loot – consisting, so Plaatje reported, of '200 head of cattle, 500 sheep and goats, a few horses, a buck wagon, a few old carts, and 49 rifles'. The last-mentioned included some British-owned Sniders which he thought had been taken from the Mfengu party massacred the previous month. 'Everybody in the stadt felt the Relief yesterday', Plaatje concluded his report, 'and the rebels are all in the Mafeking gaol', there to await their trial on charges of treason. Chief Saane 'very gladly joined the party and came home for the first time since October last year'.[56]

The relieving troops, and as many from Mafeking as could join them, likewise gathered up what they could find in the hastily abandoned Boer laager and trenches. Along with the more lootable items left behind – 'biscuits, butter, meat, jam and heaps of other things', so Bell reported – was a cache of documents that included 'all Snyman's official telegrams', brought back into Mafeking to be sifted through for intelligence purposes. Plaatje was on hand to translate. One telegram, dated 4 May, which he translated from Dutch into English, was from the state president in Pretoria to General Snyman, cancelling all leave and ordering that 'whoever is at home must leave immediately for the front'. Other telegrams, more recent, conveyed news of the occupation of Kroonstad by British troops on 12 May as well as 'demoralization of Boers all down the border and general unhappiness everywhere in the Transvaal'.[57]

Normal communication was soon restored with the outside world. Early in June trains were running once more and some of the white citizens who were evacuated in October made their way back into town. The inhabitants of the stadt who had departed over the previous weeks and months likewise returned home. Those who had persisted with their diaries drew them to a close. 'Although we have suffered many hardships and troubles,' Bell wrote in his last entry, 'we nevertheless all feel proud to think that each individual, both European and Native, has done his utmost to maintain the honour of the British Empire.' On the previous page he expressed his thanks to his 'faithful interpreter, Solomon T. Plaatje, who shifted about with his typewriter, in order to meet the requirements of the big gun and the Mauser bullets. And varied his accuracy according to the activity of the Boer fire.' He attached to his diary 'a few of the reports taken by Plaatje, from the Native Runners and Spies and those who went out to capture cattle'. 'His style, though naïve in its manner,' he said, 'conveys accurately what the Native meant and is a true record, of what happened, from a Native point of view.'

Plaatje may have wondered quite what was so 'naïve' about his style (Bell called his own diary 'crudely written' so there was no need to take it personally) and what he had to do to remedy this deficiency, but would have agreed wholeheartedly with the inclusive sentiments. He too had done his best to 'maintain the honour of the British empire' in its hour of need. Vere Stent wrote later that his 'weekly reports on the Native situation' 'were greatly valued by the military authorities', and that Plaatje had told him, 'with some sense of humour', that this arrangement 'was so satisfactory that Mr Bell was created a CMG [Companion of the Order of St Michael and St George] at the end of the siege'. Plaatje would not have begrudged Bell his CMG, but even then must have been well aware of the extent of his part in its award. Maintaining good relations between Barolong and British, after all, had been crucial.[58]

Plaatje had every reason to be proud of his contribution to the defence of Mafeking. He was fortunate to have escaped injury (though this could be when he picked up a scar on his chin), while his employment in government service ensured he was spared the worst privations of the siege. He had served both military and civil authorities to the best of his ability, and they had appreciated his work. A CMG was never a possibility, but he did have a certificate from Baden-Powell testifying to his 'services rendered to the Imperial Government … during the siege of Mafeking', and another from Major Hamilton Goold-Adams (resident commissioner for the Bechuanaland Protectorate, and commandant of the Town Guard). Along the way he had encountered a memorable cast of characters, often at very close quarters, thrown together in what was widely recognised as an imperial epic of heroic proportions. As ever, he made the most of the opportunities it threw up for him.[59]

As for his diary, it seems to have been just put away and forgotten. Apart from a brief mention in a court case, as evidence of the date a raiding party left Mafeking, he never referred to it again publicly. Unlike several of the war correspondents, he can have had no thoughts about getting it published. When he might have mentioned it later in life, in his account of the siege in *Native Life in South*

Africa, or a newspaper article he wrote celebrating the thirtieth anniversary of the relief of Mafeking, he didn't. Nor did others who must have known of its existence, such as his wife Elizabeth and brother-in-law Isaiah. It only came to light in the late 1960s when an anthropologist, John Comaroff, carrying out fieldwork in the Mafeking district, sent out an appeal for any old letters and documents that people may have preserved. In response one of Plaatje's grandsons, Victor Molema, brought him 'a tatty leather scrapbook' which, he said, had once belonged to his grandfather. Inside were the foolscap pages of the diary. Amazingly it had survived intact and was almost entirely legible, even the sections in pencil, protected by the sheath which the weight of the pages of the scrapbook had formed around it.

It is one of the most perceptive and most readable of the many siege diaries. Plaatje made no distinction between black and white when recording his observations, and was even-handed when it came to portraying acts of bravery, stupidity or cowardice. He nevertheless conveys a much fuller picture of the experiences of Mafeking's black residents than any of the other siege diarists, all of whom were white, and he was particularly interested in individuals and their stories: his friend David Phooko and his foibles; the unfortunate Miss Ngono, left destitute after the death of her lover, a member of the 'Black Watch'; 'that gallant Britisher – the Barolong herdboy', who displayed 'the tenacity of the African in all matters where cattle are concerned'; Emang Marumolwa, the fourteen-year-old daughter of Chief Lekoko who worked for a while as his housekeeper – 'I wonder what we can do without her'; or the seven-year-old Phalaetsile, who escaped from the Boers and made a model of the Big Gun fort, which Colonel Baden-Powell came round specially to look at – there was 'so much about this interesting little boy that I will never forget', Plaatje said.

We hear about the role of the Barolong contingents in defending their stadt; the 'Cape Boys' and their epic campaign in the trenches of the Brickfields; the situation of the black refugees and their desperate attempts to get out of Mafeking; the dispatch runners who risked their lives in keeping Mafeking in touch with the outside world; the exploits of Mathakgong and his band of cattle raiders; and, not least, his own role in liaising between the civil and military authorities and the African population, in supplying military intelligence, in interpreting at the Court of Summary Jurisdiction. It was emphatically not just a 'white man's war'.

At the same time his diary is revealing of his own sensibilities. What comes across is not just an engaging personality but a flavour of the social and intellectual worlds that shaped it. In his excursions into Barolong history, his dealings with Barolong notables, his evident sympathy with their concerns, we get an insight into one part of his being. In his references to the Bible and Psalms, the biblical parallels he drew with the exodus of the black refugees, the dutiful references to the Christian deity, there is another. And from his memories of living in Kimberley, a vivid sense of that optimistic world of improvement and advancement, of musical accomplishment, of dedication to mastering the English language. Nowhere were these worlds more powerfully or more eloquently validated.

If his diary gave expression to a distinctive personality, it was also an opportunity to fashion it, to enable Plaatje to play around with different ways of representing himself, of expressing his multiple identities: as the family man, missing his wife and young son over Christmas, marking their anniversaries; the vulnerable individual, aware of the danger of being blown to bits at any moment, dreading the prospect – if he survived – of having to eat horsemeat if relief did not materialise; or the privileged, conscientious servant of the colonial government, identifying with Charles Bell in his efforts to deal humanely with the unfortunate black refugees – but well aware that 'there is a very great difference between white and black even in a besieged town' when it came to food rationing.

At other times he speaks as a loyal British subject, upholding the cause of the imperial government, sharing the sufferings of his white fellow citizens, wondering like them whether they are to be relieved or abandoned to their fate. They are the 'civilised', the Boers the 'uncivilised': 'Surely these Transvaal Boers are abominable'. Implicit in this was the hope of a better future, that with the defeat of the two Boer republics the position of Her Majesty's loyal black subjects would be properly recognised – and a realisation that the events of the siege could be a powerful argument in their favour.

In the written form of his diary there is a sense in which these are all constructed identities. He revelled in creating this literary persona, representing himself in these different ways, often with an ironic, self-deprecating humour. And while it is clear that these constructions were rooted very firmly in his being, equally there were limits to what a diary could do. The very partial accounts and the omissions, such the deposition of Wessels Montshiwa and the executions, were revealing examples, but there must have been many more. Like any diary it was always selective in its self-portrayal.

Overall it is remarkable for its sophistication and virtuosity. With no concern for a wider audience or the conventions of published form, it is free from the inhibitions of style or intended audience, and from the kind of retrospective rationalisation or overt political purpose which would shape much that he wrote later in life. Which is not to say he had no concern with matters of style and presentation. He manifestly did. The difference, rather, is that in his diary he is addressing not a wider public but himself. And the great thing about a diary is that the writer does not know what is going to happen next. How can you shape the ending if you have no way of knowing what it would be?

FIVE

After the siege, 1900–1902

KORANTA EA BECOANA,

e Gatisioa mo Mafikeng Gangoe ka Tshipi.

MATLHACO, SEETEBOSIGO 15, 1901.

For their part in defending Mafeking against Boer forces, Plaatje hoped the Barolong would be suitably rewarded. In the immediate aftermath of the siege there were certainly encouraging signs. Compensation for injury and damage and loss of property was promised, and there was no shortage of words of praise. Charles Bell reported to his superiors that the Barolong had 'rendered invaluable services throughout the siege and defended their posts with energy and courage'. Lord Roberts, commander-in-chief of the British forces in South Africa, sent one of his senior officers, Sir Charles Parsons, to congratulate the Barolong leaders and people 'on the successful issue of their courageous defence of their homes and property against the invasion of the enemy'. It was followed by a moving ceremony, 'unprecedented in the annals of the history of the native tribes in this country,' Charles Bell thought, at which a framed address from Lord Roberts was presented to the Barolong chief, headmen and people.[1]

For Plaatje, who interpreted at this ceremony, it perhaps made up for the rather less than gracious (and less than honest) attitude which Baden-Powell had displayed hitherto. Determined to maintain the fiction that it was 'a white man's war', and that Barolong had not been involved in offensive operations, Baden-Powell had repeatedly prohibited the *Mafeking Mail* from giving a true account of the part they played in defeating the final Boer assault upon the town. Black and white alike were critical of his heavy-handed misrepresentations, and Plaatje later went so far as to accuse him of 'coolly and deliberately lying', in his evidence to the Royal Commission on the War, about the behaviour of the Barolong during the siege.[2]

Official expressions of gratitude were not accompanied by material or political reward. Baden-Powell did make a parting gift of a hundred heifers, but the promises of land he made during the siege remained unfulfilled. The Barolong were led to believe that land occupied by the Rapulana at Polfontein (Bodibe), in the Transvaal, would be handed over to them 'after the conclusion of hostilities', but no action was taken. Plaatje, Silas Molema and many others elsewhere were nonetheless hopeful of some wider recognition in the new political order that now looked imminent. As Chief Joshua Molema had put it in his speech of thanks at the presentation of Lord Roberts's address, 'They were British subjects, and they believed that although they were black the Queen regarded them as her subjects because she had honoured the work they had done for her.' For their 'loyalty' they now looked for tangible returns.[3]

Some patience would be necessary, however, for at the end of May 1900 British victory still lay two years in the future. For the moment, in the Mafeking district, martial law remained in operation and the Boers still controlled large swathes of the surrounding countryside. The Protectorate Regiment departed for service elsewhere, their place taken as the town's garrison by the rather less glamorous 4th Bedfordshires. Colonel Vyvyan remained as base commandant, though, and it was he who read out Lord Roberts's address to the assembled Barolong. He told Chief Wessels Montshiwa he should 'keep it and show it to your children and tell them why it was given to you and that they are to be proud of it'.[4]

In the office of the magistrate and civil commissioner, meanwhile, the staff set about tackling the administrative consequences of a seven-month siege, picking up the pieces as best they could. They were soon landed with two major new responsibilities: dealing with the numerous claims for compensation for losses and damage caused by enemy action, and collecting evidence and information about the activities of the 'suspected rebels', that is to say those citizens of the Cape Colony who fought alongside their compatriots from the Transvaal and Orange Free State against the imperial government, so they could be brought to court on charges of treason.

Early in June dozens of these rebels were rounded up and arrested, and the Mafeking gaol was full to bursting. Charles Bell applied once again for additional resources, an urgent need given the temporary absence of his two European clerks. William Geyer, his first clerk, had been seconded for 'special duty' in the Transvaal, while Ernest Grayson, the second clerk, was granted 'home leave' to see his elderly mother in England and to get over the 'insomnia' and 'nervous debility' brought on by the siege. Plaatje's friend David Phooko, working for the inspector of native locations, joined the exodus too. His move to Mafeking in August 1899 had been ill-timed, to say the least, as he often complained to Plaatje. He left at the earliest opportunity, delighted to have secured a job as constable and messenger to the magistrate's court in Aliwal North, his home town.[5]

Charles Bell, notwithstanding the new challenges his office now faced, had likewise had enough of Mafeking. He departed too, appointed to the position of magistrate and civil commissioner in Uitenhage in the eastern Cape, a step closer, he hoped, towards realising his ambition of becoming the colony's secretary for native affairs. Mafeking was not the place to be if one wanted to be noticed by head office in Cape Town.[6]

But Plaatje remained. His response was to apply himself with his customary diligence, and he wasted little time in putting in a request for an increase in salary. It was a carefully composed letter, and it must have afforded some amusement to Charles Bell, to whom it was addressed, and then to the attorney general's office in Cape Town, where it ended up. He began by explaining how his plans to qualify himself for promotion by taking the civil service examinations had been upset by the outbreak of war, and how his studies were 'adversely affected' by 'the class of shelling we were subjected to' during the siege. He then proceeded to demonstrate why £96 per annum was quite inadequate for the responsible position he held:

> I think it impossible from the very nature of things that a man, dressed in a cord suit of clothes, dwelling in a Native hut and living on mealies and Kafir corn could make a suitable person for the medium of speech, between a Magistrate and a community as we find locally; but I am sorry to say that this is the only mode of living that a man in receipt of my salary can manage to provide for himself and family, without the liability of falling into debts as is often the case.
>
> Nothing can improve an employee much more than recognition of his services, on the part of the Head of his Department, by way of stern encouraging remarks and by way of increase of emoluments. My present salary is £96 per annum. I have been in receipt of this since the beginning of 1897, when I was still a bachelor, and engaged at more inferior duties, in a Post Office. I have now got to perform higher duties, on a better situation, to keep a wife and child as well as an old mother of 60 years at the same salary. This is almost an impossibility in Mafeking, unless one adopts a mode of living, which may render him objectionable to the sight and presence of his senior officers.

And if Mr Bell needed some help in justifying his increase, here was a suggestion:

> In one office in the Colony we have an interpreter, very well known to me, who does not even know how to read (or much less translate) a Dutch letter, and who does nothing beyond barely interpreting in the Kafir and Sesutu languages, receiving £200 per annum: this ought to be an example that you would be quite within your rights to ask for a substantial increase for your Interpreter, who, besides being a faithful oral and documentary translator in the Dutch and Native languages, does the Office Typewriting

and as much of Shorthand writing as is within the requirements of your Office.

Summing up his case, he reminded Mr Bell once more of the experiences they had shared:

I have no doubt that up to the present, especially during the trying times we both had to endure for upwards of six months of the siege, you are aware that I have always endeavoured my utmost to perform my duties to your satisfaction; that you will feel pleased to give my application a favourable recommendation; and I am sure it will be the best incentive to better zeal, in improving myself for duty, in future.[7]

Charles Bell did as he was requested, commending Plaatje to the Law Department as 'a painstaking, hardworking man' and 'a thoroughly efficient interpreter' who 'rendered invaluable service during the late siege'. Doubtless, too, he was more than a little impressed by the comprehensive lecture on how court interpreters should be treated by their employers, for few requests for more money were as articulate or forthright as this. His reward was an increase of an extra £12 a year from the beginning of July: less perhaps than the 'substantial increase' he had in mind and hardly sufficient to compensate for the loss of his extra earnings from the (now disbanded) Court of Summary Jurisdiction or from the (now departed) war correspondents, but certainly better than nothing at all.[8]

He earned it. Over the next few months the treason investigations led to a huge increase in the volume of work for everybody in the office, and by early November over a hundred separate examinations had been carried out. This was not quite as impressive as it sounds since the new clerk, taken on to process the paperwork, was plagued by ill health and could not keep up with the demands made upon him. A stream of telegrams from the Law Department in Cape Town demanded to know why they were falling behind.[9]

In dealing with these investigations an important distinction was made between Class 1 cases, which dealt with ringleaders, and Class 2 cases for the rank and file. In the colony as a whole most of the individuals involved – in both categories – were allowed to return to their homes after being examined, although in some of the Class 1 cases bail conditions were imposed. In Mafeking, however, in view of the seriousness of the charges arising out of hostilities during the siege, a much higher proportion of Class 1 suspects were committed for trial and kept in custody.[10]

The politicians, meanwhile, had to decide exactly what to do with those charged with treason. It was a highly contentious issue, leading to the resignation of the prime minister, W.P. Schreiner, before the matter was resolved by the passage of legislation in August 1900. This set up a Special Treason Tribunal to try the more serious cases, including those where treason was accompanied by other charges such as murder, manslaughter or looting. There would be no juries and cases were to be decided by a panel of three judges. Those 'rebels' who had given themselves up, and who fell into the Class 2 category, were automatically disfranchised for a period of five years.

Plaatje's most important task at these hearings – some took place in Setlagole and Mareetsane as well as Mafeking – was to interpret what the Dutch-speaking 'rebels' wished to communicate to the authorities when making their statements. Many of these prisoners must have been surprised to find themselves dependent upon a black man, evidently in a position of some responsibility, to ensure they were understood by the court, their fate seemingly in his hands. A few may well have wondered what such a state of affairs signified for the future of their country. The fact that this young black interpreter spoke Dutch fluently, with no trace of an accent, and seemed equally at home in English, can only have added to their discomfort. From where they stood it was a world turned upside down.

Plaatje, for his part, clearly relished the challenge of such responsible work, pointing out – when putting in another request for a salary increase – that since 'the necessity for a better Dutch interpreter did not arise' when these hearings began, 'the fact speaks for itself as regards my competency'.[11]

The most serious cases were where Boer prisoners were suspected of having committed acts of murder. Among these, Plaatje would have noted with particular interest, was young Louis Brink, arrested, as he had been in 1899, by Field Cornet James Keeley and now charged with having unlawfully killed an unnamed African at the Boer laager in Rietfontein in March 1900. Unfortunately for him, this time there were several witnesses willing to testify to what they had seen, and without a sympathetic white jury or the means of intimidating witnesses, he was likely to be in some difficulty.[12]

There were also cases involving black as well as white 'rebels'. The most important was that of the Rapulana chief Abraham Matuba and his leading headmen, from Rietfontein, who had sided with the Boers and taken up arms against the Tshidi Barolong of Mafeking. They had languished in gaol in Mafeking since their arrest immediately after the siege, and would remain there until their trial in November 1901. The most damning evidence against them, taken down by Plaatje, came from Chief Saane, who told of his captivity at the hands of Matuba and his headmen, and provided details of how his captors had been issued with arms by General Snyman in January 1900.[13]

Whether a charge of high treason was really the most appropriate way of dealing with the chief and his followers was debatable. As Plaatje would comment a couple of years later, in reality it was only 'a longstanding family quarrel between them and ourselves which made up a case of treason', and in due course he would add his voice to the demands to have them released. To the English-speaking Victorian public, and in the chronicle of imperial feats of arms, there was only one siege of Mafeking: in the long history of conflict between Tshidi and Rapulana it was counted as the sixth. From such a perspective the events of 1899–1900 were just part of a much longer story – one, indeed, that could be traced as far back as the division of the Barolong kingdom in the 1780s.[14]

Determined as ever to improve himself and his prospects, Plaatje prepared once again to take the civil service examinations he had registered for the previous year. He wrote off to the Civil Service Commission early in August 1900 to enquire about this possibility, and heard in reply that they would be pleased to re-register him for the subjects he had applied to take before (Dutch, German and Typewriting) provided they received his completed application form by the end of the following month. Mark Garrett, the secretary of the commission, added that he could take 'Sesuto and Sechwana', in which he had also expressed an interest, 'if there should be other candidates for examination in those two subjects', but that 'the Commissioners cannot go to the expense of having papers prepared solely for one candidate'.[15]

Plaatje promptly sent off his completed application form, registering for Dutch, Typewriting, Sesotho and Setswana (he seems to have dropped the idea of taking the German paper). At the same time, mindful of what Garrett had just told him, he mentioned 'two friends' who were interested in taking the papers in Sesotho and Setswana: Patrick, the messenger in Charles Bell's office in Mafeking, and his brother Petrus, who now worked as interpreter to the magistrate at Vryburg. Patrick didn't in the end send in an application, but Petrus did. He applied to take the paper in Setswana, but the reply he got was even more discouraging: 'The Commissioners are not prepared to examine you in Sechuana', Garrett informed him, 'unless there is a Candidate for examination in that subject who takes the whole of the ordinary Examination', and since he thought that 'very unlikely' he was returning his registration fee.[16]

This was not quite what he had told Plaatje. The message then was simply that there had to be more than one candidate, not that that one other candidate had also to be taking the ordinary examination. Perhaps, if one is to be charitable, Garrett had failed to spell out clearly what the rules were. Since he already had Plaatje's application by the time he heard from Petrus, however, it is difficult to avoid the conclusion that he was making up the rules as he went along, and simply needed to find another reason to jettison a paper for which there would be only two candidates, with all the expense that entailed. Plaatje would have discovered the discrepancy if he compared notes with Petrus afterwards.

Plaatje was left, then, with the papers in Dutch and Typewriting to prepare for, although given his daily routine there can have been little need for extra practice or revision. As the time approached, he obtained two weeks' special leave of absence from the office to enable him to make the long trip down to Cape Town, his first visit to the city, and to sit the examinations. They were held, in the two weeks before Christmas, in the new Art School building in Queen Victoria Street, just opposite the Cape parliament buildings. He was given candidate number 27.[17]

He was not quite the only black candidate that year. Two other candidates, J.S. Olifant and J.Z. Zini, of Tswana and Xhosa origin respectively, had entered the ordinary examination, along with over two hundred whites, while David Nqwana, interpreter to the magistrate at Cradock, had registered, like Plaatje, for two special subjects, in his case Dutch and Xhosa ('Kafir' as it was still called). That year the examiner for this subject, as it happened, was Isaiah Bud-M'belle, recently appointed as interpreter to the Special Treason Court, and now based in Cape Town. Most likely this was where Plaatje stayed. The three other black candidates were, like Plaatje, employed as court interpreters.[18]

The Typewriting examination came first, on the morning of Saturday, 15 December, and candidates had to bring their own typewriters. They were required to type out a page of manuscript (this year it was on the subject of the physical properties of water), copy out a table showing the tonnage of merchant shipping built in different countries in 1895, construct a similar table of their own inserting new data, type out an official letter in the correct style, and, finally, type from dictation a passage on the subject of metaphysics (any candidate who could not spell this correctly would be in difficulty given the number of times the word was repeated).

Dutch was taken the following Thursday. It included an oral examination designed, according to the regulations, 'to test the ability to converse, sufficient for the ordinary business of a Magistrate's Court or a Civil Commissioner's Office', so nothing unfamiliar here. Candidates had also to translate a written passage from English into Dutch, another from Dutch into English, and then 'write a note (above 20 lines)' on the subject of the Transvaal War, the wild flowers of South Africa or the wild animals of South Africa (choose one). Finally, after the oral examination, consisting of 'interpretation of evidence given in a magistrate's court', they had to take down a short passage dictated to them in Dutch.[19]

What Plaatje made of the experience of taking these examinations, or what his impressions were of this first visit to Cape Town, is unknown, for he left no account of either. Like everybody else in the colonial capital that week, he could not have been unaware of the parades, speech-making and celebrations surrounding Lord Roberts's departure for England on 12 December. With the war apparently all but over, Roberts was now happy to hand over the command of British forces in South Africa to his successor, Lord Kitchener, leaving him with what, it was assumed, would be no more than a mopping-up operation.

What happened during Plaatje's trip back home suggested otherwise. He got as far as the town of De Aar, some three hundred miles south of Mafeking, only to be stranded for four days as a result of a major Boer incursion into the Cape from across the Orange Free State border. It threw both the Cape authorities and the military high command into a state of panic. British forces set off in hot pursuit, railway travel was severely disrupted, and the garrison at De Aar, an important railway junction, was hastily strengthened. Along with his fellow travellers or would-be travellers, Plaatje had simply to kick his heels until the way was clear, secure enough thanks to the presence of four companies of Imperial Yeomanry and two battalions of Coldstream Guards.[20]

Fortunately, he had not stumbled into another siege. The two Boer columns kept going westwards and railway services resumed a few days later. Their daring raid may have failed to achieve its main objectives but it did succeed in tying down thousands of British soldiers, and martial law was now extended to most of the Cape Colony. It was an inconvenient reminder that the Boers were far from beaten, and that the expectation of imminent victory was more than a little premature. Even around Mafeking, Boer commandos were still very much in evidence. For Plaatje, the immediate consequence was that for the third Christmas in succession, he found himself separated from Elizabeth and Sainty. By 27 December, though, he was back at work in Mafeking.[21]

His examination results came through a few weeks later. He had done spectacularly well. In Dutch he headed the list of eight successful 'Special Subject' candidates, obtaining maximum marks (50 out of 50) for the oral part of the examination, and

103 marks out of 150 in the written paper. His total of 153 put him comfortably ahead of the next candidate, Robert Kidman on 137. David Nqwana also passed, gaining a total of 100 marks, 25 above the pass mark, and he was successful in the 'Kafir' paper too.

Plaatje's performance in the Typewriting examination was just as impressive. Here he got 255 marks out of a possible 300, well above the pass mark of 200, heading the list of nine successful candidates. All that practice in typing out diaries and intelligence reports during the siege, and more recently the endless statements and affidavits from the treason investigations, had clearly paid off. Mr P.E. Potter, the examiner for the Typewriting paper, thought that, overall, candidates that year 'were of a much higher class than he had seen before in the Civil Service'.[22]

That was not quite the end of the matter, for when the results of these examinations were published in the *Government Gazette* some months later. Plaatje was disappointed to see that his name was not printed at the head of each list. In the list of successful candidates in the special subjects, for the Dutch paper he found himself in sixth place, sandwiched between David Nqwana and Robert Kidman; in Typewriting, a little higher up, in third place, between Albertina Centlivres and Alec Robb. Since he had already been sent details of his marks, and evidently those of the other candidates as well, indicating that he had come top in each, he wrote at once to the Civil Service Commission to express his 'considerable astonishment' at this apparent discrepancy, and to ask how this could be.

It is no wonder he was puzzled. In the ordinary examinations the practice of the commissioners, in publishing the results, was to list first-class passes in order of merit and second-class passes alphabetically, but in each instance this was made clear. For the special subjects, though, there was no indication one way or the other, but it was obvious that the names were not listed alphabetically. What, then, was the rationale?[23]

He can hardly have been satisfied with the reply that came from Mr Garrett: 'the only explanation I can offer', he said, 'is that in Special Subjects the names of successful candidates are not arranged in any order, nor does it appear necessary to so arrange them. The fact that a candidate has passed in any such subject seems to be sufficient to record, without reference to the position of any other candidate.' Why this distinction was made between special subjects and the ordinary examination was not explained. Nor did Garrett see any need to spell out in his letter what the basis for ordering the special subject results actually was. Plaatje had to work out for himself that it was simply determined by candidate number.[24]

So there was no public recognition of what was a considerable achievement, and there was none of the publicity that had accompanied Isaiah Bud-M'belle's success in the ordinary examination in 1892. Coming on top of the refusal to allow him to take the papers in Setswana and Sesotho, it was a disappointing conclusion to his dealings with the Cape Civil Service Commission. What he really needed in order to progress further, he must have been increasingly aware, was not just success in examinations, but a white skin.

Back in the office he remained as busy as before with the treason investigations. J.B. Moffat, a grandson of the famous missionary, took over from Bell as magistrate and civil commissioner in November 1900, sharing his predecessor's relatively enlightened views towards the African population he was responsible for. He was appreciative, too, of Plaatje's ability and hard work and supported his claims for remuneration from the military authorities, still stationed in Mafeking, when they sought his help. 'In addition to the very heavy extra interpreting work thrown upon him in connection with the treason investigation,' Moffat acknowledged, 'he was constantly being called upon to translate letters, etc, for the commandant as well as to interpret at interviews between the Commandant and native chiefs and headmen.' Happily, Colonel Vyvyan, the commandant, sanctioned payment of 5s per day for any such work, and the assistant provost marshal (whom Plaatje had assisted in issuing railway permits) rewarded him similarly.[25]

In other respects the continued presence of British forces in the district was much less welcome. They monopolised grazing land around Mafeking, they frequently clashed with the townspeople and the civil authorities, and there were complaints from the stadt and the Mfengu location about the behaviour of British soldiers, particularly towards women. Plaatje, too, had cause for complaint. Once he reported to the magistrate that he had been assaulted by a group of British soldiers. No further details of the incident have survived, but it seems to have had no lasting effects. Another time, not long after he returned from Cape Town, he submitted a claim for compensation after some cattle, belonging to the military transport department, had been allowed to stray onto the gardens around his house – not the first time this had happened. The 'transport herds had replied to my remonstrances with abuse', he added, suggesting that they had deliberately led the cattle onto his gardens.[26]

The officer in charge of the Ox Transport Department undertook 'to be more careful in future', but it seems it was not the end of the matter, for some weeks later he had to answer a charge of criminal assault, it being alleged that he had 'wrongfully and unlawfully assaulted one Indalo, a native herd in the employ of the Imperial Government by knocking him to the ground, by tying him with reins, by kicking him on the ground with his booted foot and by damaging his clothing'. What truth there was in Indalo's startling allegations it is impossible to know. Since no corroborating evidence was brought forward, it was a question of Indalo's word against Plaatje's, and the case was quickly dismissed by William Geyer, the assistant magistrate. In view of what had happened previously it seems likely that some altercation had taken place, occasioned by cattle being allowed yet again to trample over Plaatje's gardens. And that this time the altercation turned violent – whether or not it was in quite the manner Indalo alleged.[27]

Things were not easy in the office either. After Charles Bell's departure, office routine never really regained its equilibrium, the corrosive effects of the war heightened by the high level of staff turnover, always a problem in one of the colony's remotest and least desirable postings. Deteriorating relations between J.B. Moffat and William Geyer, the first clerk and assistant magistrate, only added to the difficulties. Moffat never really wanted to be in Mafeking. He regretted taking up the appointment from the moment he arrived and often found reasons to be elsewhere, desperate to return to Cape Town. It meant an unhappy William Geyer was left to deal with the bulk of the treason investigations, a particularly challenging task for somebody of Cape Dutch origin. A bitter dispute between the two men ensued. Moffat accused Geyer of neglecting his duties, insubordination and excessive drinking, the situation only resolved with his demotion and transfer to Kimberley late in 1901 (which ended in tragedy when he blew out his brains with a revolver eighteen months later). Nobody in the Mafeking magistrate's office, as they went about their business, can have been unaware of the tensions.[28]

Outside working hours Plaatje at least had his family to go home to, Elizabeth ('Ma-Sainty' as she was now known) having joined him permanently in Mafeking. It must have seemed to her a remote and somewhat uncivilised part of the colony to have to come to, but she soon settled in, her knowledge of Setswana a major asset in helping her to get on with her new neighbours. At first they lived at 'Maratiwa', Silas Molema's residence, but after a while they moved into a new home of their own close by – 'Seoding' ('riverside'), on the banks of the Molopo River, built on a plot of land provided by the Molemas.[29]

Elizabeth would have felt most at home in the company of the other Mfengu families living in Mafikeng, like the Sidzumos and Tyamzashes, many of them teachers at the local mission schools and regular visitors to their home. Music as ever was a common bond, and before long they got together to form a new musical company which they called the Mafeking Philharmonic Society, modelled upon the more illustrious Philharmonic Society in Kimberley in which her husband and brother had been leading lights.[30]

She was involved in the social life of the Tshidi Barolong too. By far the biggest function she attended was the wedding of Joseph Molema (eldest son of Israel Molema, Silas's brother) to Ntegogang, daughter of the Bangwaketse chief Bathoen, in February 1901. She was entrusted with the catering arrangements – quite a responsibility, and a clear indication of her acceptance into the life of this community. As befitted so significant a dynastic alliance, it was a huge affair, and nearly half the population of the stadt was reported to have travelled to Kanye for the celebrations. Unfortunately it was not the wedding feast that was remembered. On his way there the bridegroom was seriously injured in a riding accident, two horses falling down on top of him. He staggered through the service but had to be carried out before the end and died from his injuries a week later.[31]

Plaatje was even more involved in the communal life of the Barolong. For all the ways in which he was different – his education, his employment in government service, his easy familiarity with the ways of the white man – he was a Morolong through and through, and he lived among them. He may not have been of Tshidi descent like most of his neighbours, but his family was well known in the district and he was of the highly respected *ba ga Modiboa* line, renowned for their loyalty to their displaced royal ancestors. He shared their language, knew their customs, understood their concerns. Young as he was, people already looked to him for advice and guidance and he was a familiar figure at the kgotla, or chief's court. It must have been obvious to everybody that he enjoyed the confidence of the leading Tshidi families.

In immersing himself in the affairs of the Tshidi Barolong, and on occasion acting on their behalf, Plaatje was carrying on a well-established tradition. Chiefs and headmen had long been accustomed to utilising the skills of the handful among them who had acquired sufficient literacy and education, for they knew they could be trusted – unlike the various outsiders who sometimes offered their services. Prior to his arrival in Mafeking, the person upon whom the Barolong relied, more than anybody else, was Stephen Lefenya, a nephew of Chief Montshiwa. He had been educated at the Wesleyan mission at Thaba Nchu in the 1850s and held the position of tribal secretary for a period of some forty years. He was responsible for keeping records, for dealing with the paperwork generated by contact with the outside world, for briefing lawyers and others to represent Barolong interests when the need arose. Chief Montshiwa, in return, had rewarded him well for his services.[32]

But by the 1890s Lefenya was growing old and less able to comprehend the complexities of the world about him, the confused Barolong response to the threat of annexation to the Cape Colony in 1895 being symptomatic of the difficulties. This experience, and others that followed, suggested the need for somebody who was not only unquestionably loyal to the cause of the Barolong (as Lefenya certainly was), but who possessed, in addition, the expertise to guide them through the mass of laws and regulations that confronted them, and the ability to respond to new challenges and opportunities. Silas Molema would not have been alone in thinking that Plaatje, though still young in years, was the ideal person to be groomed for such a role. Now, as then, the talents of his young protégé seemed all the more necessary in view of the continued weakness and incompetence of the current paramount chief, Wessels Montshiwa.

Plaatje's privileged access to the local representative of the colonial government was a further asset. This had been evident, for example, in discussions about improving the supply of water before plans were interrupted by the outbreak of war, in conveying Barolong concerns to the military authorities during the siege, in helping to draw up compensation claims afterwards. Nobody was in a better position to brief chief and headmen on how to deal with the local authorities, be they magisterial, municipal or military. Given Plaatje's official position, though, and his obligation of loyalty to his employers, he was in a delicate situation, and had to be careful about the path he negotiated, publicly and privately, between these two potentially conflicting loyalties. He seems rarely to have put a foot wrong.

Not that there were always such concerns. Nobody could object to the presentation he organised, on behalf of the Barolong, to Benjamin Weil, the local storekeeper and contractor, on the eve of his departure for England in November 1901. He was presented with an elaborate silver shield 'as an appreciation', so its inscription reads, 'of never to be forgotten kindness shown to the Barolong Nation during the siege of Mafeking'. Accompanying the shield was a framed address, decorated by hand, inviting him to accept the gift 'as an appreciation both of your personal qualities, and of the valuable services which you rendered to us during the siege of Mafeking'. At the bottom stands the characteristically bold, confident signature of 'Sol T. Plaatje', responsible for organising the whole affair in his capacity as 'Hon. Sec.'. It stands in stark contrast to the simple cross made by Chief Wessels (and two of his headmen who also could not write) in the space Plaatje had provided. It all seemed to sum up in strikingly visual form the role he now had in the affairs of his people, as well as testifying to the cordial relations that existed between the Barolong and one of Mafeking's most prominent white citizens. Plaatje himself would not have forgotten Benjamin Weil's personal kindness to him during the siege in helping to get money sent to Elizabeth.[33]

✦

Quite when Plaatje decided that journalism might provide a more rewarding career is difficult to know. He certainly had a longstanding fascination with the world of newspapers. During his time in Kimberley he was, along with many of his friends, an avid reader of *Imvo*, Tengo Jabavu's newspaper, and had long been impressed with the role that the paper and its editor had played in the lives of Xhosa-speaking people. As we have seen, Jabavu's editorials left a deep impression upon him, as had those of Frederick York St Leger, the editor of the *Cape Times*. During the siege his contact with journalists like Vere Stent and Angus Hamilton was a further stimulus, and it must have been encouraging to see his intelligence reports appearing as news in the columns of the *Mafeking Mail* siege slip. At some point too, he later recalled, Samuel Cronwright-Schreiner, once a newspaper editor himself, had urged him to 'leave the Cape Civil Service and try journalism'.[34]

The first public indication that he may have resolved to act upon this advice came in the *Mafeking Mail* in its issues of 13 and 20 April 1901, when for the first time it included several columns in Setswana, summarising news on the progress of the war as well as carrying details of a case in the local magistrate's court. And then the following week, on 27 April, there appeared the first number of a separate single-page news-sheet, entitled *Koranta ea Becoana* (or 'Bechuana Gazette'), written entirely in Setswana, and selling for 3d a copy. According to information at the foot of the page, it was printed on the *Mafeking Mail*'s press and was both owned and edited by George Whales. He had only recently acquired proprietary rights to the *Mail*, and it may well have been this new financial responsibility that encouraged him to explore new possibilities. Since Whales could neither speak nor read Setswana, it was obvious somebody else had written it for him. Plaatje is the likeliest candidate. As an employee of the government, though, he was explicitly prohibited by the terms of his employment ('Acts, Rules and Regulations of the Cape Civil Service', section III, clause 32, to be precise) from 'becoming editor of a newspaper, or taking any part in the management thereof'; he needed to be careful, in other words, about just how far this involvement went – and how much people knew about it.[35]

This first issue of *Koranta* introduced itself as the first Tswana-language

147

paper to be produced by the Tswana themselves, but it did mention two earlier newspapers in Setswana produced by missionaries – *Mahoko a Becwana* ('News for the Bechuana') (printed by the London Missionary Society at Kuruman), which Plaatje used to read at the Pniel mission, and the more recent *Moshupa Tsela* ('The Guide'), produced by Lutheran missionaries of the Church of Sweden in the Transvaal. Both were published monthly. *Koranta*, however, was to be a weekly. In this way, so it said, it could be of even greater value to the Tswana people, whether they were Bamangwato of the Bechuanaland Protectorate or Seleka Barolong from the Orange River Colony, keeping them up to date with current affairs. Every Tswana chief, it urged, should do his best to popularise the paper among his people and inform them – a characteristic metaphor this – that the sun (enlightenment) had now risen among the Tswana people. *Koranta ea Becoana* aimed to speak to their concerns, and in their own language.[36]

After twelve somewhat undistinguished issues devoted largely to the progress of the war, there was a significant change in the direction of the affairs of the little news-sheet. By the terms of an agreement signed between Whales and Silas Molema on 5 September 1901, for a consideration of £25 Whales sold 'all his rights, title and interest' in *Koranta ea Becoana* to Silas Molema, who would thenceforth 'edit and be responsible for the same as from the next succeeding number to be published, to wit: No. 13'. At the same time, rates for printing were agreed (the initial circulation was to be five hundred copies), Whales was to take 20 per cent of advertising revenue, and Molema agreed to indemnify Whales for any action for damages brought against him as a result of anything printed in the paper. For Whales, such an arrangement promised an easier way of making money than retaining personal responsibility, and liability, for the affairs of a paper he was unable to read. For Silas Molema, on the other hand, it offered new possibilities, not so much any great hope of financial gain, but rather an opportunity, through control of a new medium, to foster the education and progress of his people: continuation of a tradition, in other words, that went back to the school he opened in the stadt in the 1870s.[37]

That Plaatje was by this time heavily involved behind the scenes is suggested by the surviving draft of a letter about the proposed agreement with Whales, purported to have been written by Silas Molema, but actually in Plaatje's handwriting. It outlined a programme of gradual expansion for the new paper, culminating in something about the same size as the *Mafeking Mail*, and with 'about 2 or 3 English columns like Imvo'. Meanwhile, said the letter, 'at the present there is only hard work to get Bechuanaland to know the paper'. The mention of *Imvo* is hugely significant: its combination of English and Xhosa signified exactly that intermediary role which Plaatje and Molema had in mind for their people. Nothing similar had yet been attempted among the Tswana. *Koranta* thus inherited a dual tradition: that of its Tswana-language missionary predecessors, mentioned in its first issue, and that exemplified by *Imvo*, the secular vehicle for the expression of African opinion, which was to provide the model for its future development.[38]

Once under Silas Molema's control, and with a newly arrived compositor in place, *Koranta ea Becoana* developed into a more ambitious publication. It first appeared on 7 September 1901, contained two pages, and for the first time carried advertisements, mostly inserted by local European dealers and traders in Mafeking, naturally keen to increase their business with a potentially lucrative African market. Over the next few months there was progress in other directions as well. Selling agents were appointed, and circulation started to increase in Tswana-speaking areas of the Cape, the Orange River Colony, the Bechuanaland Protectorate and the Transvaal; even in Johannesburg, so one of its readers would recall, 'it was almost marvellous to see how much the little sheet … was in demand out there'.[39]

One important step towards financial viability was achieved with the securing of regular notices and advertisements from the various governmental authorities in the area in which *Koranta* now circulated. The resident commissioner for the Bechuanaland Protectorate, for example, saw no objection to meeting Silas Molema's request. Scribbled in the margin of a letter he wrote about the matter was the comment 'I do not understand the paper but I presume it loyal and respectable'. This was evidently a view shared by the other governmental authorities, and before long *Koranta* was able to announce that it had become 'the only authorised medium for publishing Government Proclamations addressed to Natives by Colonial, Protectorate, and Imperial Military Authorities'. The regular income that such advertising provided was essential if *Koranta* was to survive and prosper.[40]

⁺↻⁺

Whatever the nature and extent of Plaatje's involvement in *Koranta ea Becoana*, his work on it had to be done in his spare time for he remained a paid servant of the colonial government, and he was not yet ready to give this up. A salary increase in August, bringing him up to £120 p.a., was a reminder of the benefits, and the need for caution. While the newspaper was the focus of his future ambitions, with a war dragging on for far longer than anybody had expected it was not an opportune time to relinquish his paid employment. In fact, the realities of war and the divisive legacy of the siege continued to dominate the lives of those who

149

lived in Mafeking, black and white. Nowhere was this more evident than when the Special Treason Court arrived in town in November 1901 to try the most serious cases that had been set aside for it to deal with. Several of these were of special interest to Plaatje, and the hearings – particularly the judgments – would have a lasting impact.[41]

The first case was that of *R* v. *Lottering and Maritz*. Both men were citizens of the Cape Colony and had joined General Snyman's forces around Mafeking. As well as being charged with high treason, they were accused of having murdered a Morolong by the name of Monthusetsi several miles outside Mafeking. They did not deny they had killed him. However, the case for the defence, ably conducted by Advocate Henry Burton, rested on the argument that in killing Monthusetsi, Maritz and Lottering were simply carrying out Snyman's order that all Africans leaving Mafeking were to be shot; that having joined Snyman's forces they were subject to his orders and commands; and that if Monthusetsi had come from Mafeking before meeting his death, he counted as an enemy. Maritz and Lottering were therefore justified in killing him.

As the trial progressed it became clear that proving Monthusetsi had come from Mafeking was going to be critical to the defence's case. For a while it looked as though the necessary evidence would not be forthcoming. Local feeling in Mafeking against the two accused 'was very high at the time', Plaatje recalled, due to 'memories of incidents connected with the recent bombardment of the place during the siege'. As a result, 'loyalists were not disposed to assist the defence in finding a loophole'. Local opinion in Mafeking, understandably enough, saw in the case the opportunity for judicial revenge for what had been inflicted upon the townspeople during seven long months of siege. By the second day of the trial it began to look as though they would get it.[42]

Then Plaatje stepped forward as witness for the defence to make the dramatic statement that he not only knew Monthusetsi as somebody who used to live in the stadt in Mafikeng, but had personally issued him with a pass to go out and raid cattle. The prosecution's case thus collapsed. 'At the last minute of the eleventh hour', Plaatje remembered, 'Mr H. Burton personally made the discovery that I held the key to the solution of the fateful riddle.' His evidence, he said, 'outraged loyalist sentiment' and turned the case. It was cited in the judge's summing-up (he referred to Plaatje as 'a respectable coloured witness about whose evidence there can be no shadow of doubt'), and the verdict (reached, said the judge, 'with the greatest reluctance') was that in killing Monthusetsi, Maritz and Lottering had the protection of the law, and had therefore to be acquitted. The two men were in no doubt as to whom they owed their lives. Although still held in gaol on another charge, they managed to send through to Plaatje 'a verbal message of thanks' for having come forward with his evidence.[43]

If Mafeking's white citizens were disappointed at this outcome, feeling among the black population was stronger still. Joseph Gape, a local farmer who lived in the Mafeking Reserve and a man of some standing, took issue with Plaatje's decision to give evidence as he did. He thought this amounted to a shameful betrayal of African interests, a gratuitous reward for 'a pair of the most rancorous Boers who cruelly murdered your countryman'. He went on: 'The three judges, the murderers' advocates and everybody else had given up hope and it only remained for the death sentence to be passed when, at nobody's invitation, you came forward and gave the most undesirable evidence which capsized the whole case, and the fiercest criminals were let loose.'[44]

Joseph Gape was inclined to attribute Plaatje's action to a sentimental distaste for the death penalty, and he recalled his unsuccessful appeal to Charles Bell during the siege to save the life of Piet, the alleged spy. In reality there was more to it than this. Plaatje was not opposed to the death penalty in all circumstances, only when he felt it was unjustified. He also knew he had a legal and moral responsibility to give evidence once Advocate Burton had discovered what he knew about Monthusetsi. Nevertheless, it took courage to do so and there were doubtless plenty of others who shared Joseph Gape's view of it. At the same time he would have realised, even then, that in the long run his people had far more to gain from the protection of a judicial system that operated without fear or favour than one that could be swayed by the passions of the moment – whether on the part of black or white.

In the next two cases, however, popular opinion in Mafeking was assuaged, for in both the accused were found guilty and sentenced to death. Young Louis Brink, first of all, was convicted of the murder of an unnamed (and unknown) African outside the Boer laager at Rietfontein in March 1900. This time the judge president, William Solomon, could find no extenuating circumstances. Brink had shot his victim in the head while some older men around him discussed what to do with him. He did not claim that his victim had come from Mafeking, nor did he state at the time – or so Judge Solomon believed – that he was acting on orders issued by General Snyman or anybody else. He just shot him in the head, Solomon said as he pronounced the death sentence, 'in utter callousness, regarding his life of no more value than the life of a dog'. 'You must know', he told Brink, 'that a man, although with a black skin, is still a man.'[45]

In the other case five Boers – Rinke, Burke, Bruwer, Van Rooyen and Moolman – were charged with murdering three 'Vaalpenses' (or 'Kalaharis') living on James Keeley's farm at Mosita on 16 February 1900, claiming that they suspected them of stealing cattle. The charge against Moolman was dropped, but the other four were found guilty and sentenced to death. In passing sentence Justice Solomon, so it was reported in the *Mafeking Mail*, had this to say: 'They, the Court, were satisfied that the prisoners hunted these natives, as if they were wild beasts, and shot them down. It was probable that the prisoners did not at the time, and do not now realise, that in killing these unfortunate natives, the offence was as serious as if those they were killing were white men; but it is necessary that they, and those who think with them, should know that the law does not recognise a difference between white and black. A black man has just as much right to live as a white man.'[46]

These words would remain with Plaatje for the rest of his life. It was a classic statement of the moral basis of the Cape's judicial system, and he would often quote the passage, from memory, when upholding the virtues, and principles, of a colour-blind judicial system. Such judgments vindicated his belief in the integrity of the high court judges involved, and they served to reinforce his commitment to the rule of law as an instrument for the protection of the rights and lives of his people.

Isaiah Bud-M'belle, who travelled to Mafeking with the Special Treason Court as its African languages interpreter, would have felt the same way. In such chilling circumstances was the ideal of equality before the law affirmed. Plaatje and Bud-M'belle, the two black court interpreters, had witnessed the Cape judiciary in one of its more impressive moments.

It was not the end of the matter, though. All death sentences had to be reviewed by Sir Walter Hely-Hutchinson, the governor of the colony. In practice this task was delegated to the attorney general and the secretary of the Law Department, and they in turn normally followed the recommendation of the court. In these two cases Mr Justice Solomon, the judge president, and his two fellow judges (Mr Justice Lange and Mr Maasdorp, KC) were unanimous in their view that the prerogative of mercy should be extended to all the condemned prisoners. Unusually, however, John Graham, the secretary of the Law Department, while he acknowledged that their views 'must necessarily carry great weight and should not be lightly overridden', nevertheless proceeded to do exactly that with regard to two of the condemned men, Louis Brink and Arnoldus Rinke, advising that 'a different course be followed to that recommended by the Court'. In the second case three of the four condemned men were reprieved, but Graham considered Rinke to be the ringleader and more guilty than the others, and so advised that his death sentence be confirmed.

He reached the same conclusion on Louis Brink. While mindful of his youth (still only twenty years old), and the court's recommendation for mercy on these grounds, Graham nevertheless thought he should hang. His was 'by far the most brutal crime' of those under review; he might have been 'of very youthful appearance' but he was 'old enough to go out and fight and old enough to act for himself in the most cruel manner', while 'his whole conduct shows that his character was hardened and not pliable'. What clinched it was Brink's earlier court appearance in 1899. This had come up during the course of his trial, prompting Graham to send for further details from the acting magistrate in Mafeking, which he had examined carefully. Since Brink had been convicted of assault and punished, Graham acknowledged that the case could only have 'a very indirect bearing upon the point now to be decided'; however, he believed it did 'to some extent show that Brink although young was by nature violent in his treatment of natives'. Taking account of all the circumstances, he therefore recommended 'that the death sentence in this case shall be carried out'. Had the earlier case not come to light he would most likely have reached a different conclusion.

John Graham's recommendations were accepted by the attorney general and the governor of the Colony, and the news communicated to the acting magistrate in Mafeking. The date set for their execution was 28 December 1901. Few in Mafeking would have considered this anything other than a fate richly deserved. If there were any regrets, it would only have been that the others were not included too.[47]

Plaatje, though, took a different view of the case involving Louis Brink. However much he was appalled by his actions, he nevertheless felt compelled to bring some further information to the attention of the attorney general. Three days after confirmation of Brink's death sentence arrived in Mafeking, he swore an affidavit to say that he had issued a cattle raiding pass to a man named Senyamotse, and that this was the man Brink had killed. He had consulted with two members of the cattle raiding party, Mathakgong, its leader, and another man by the name of Lecogi, and both testified that Senyamotse had gone out with them, then disappeared in circumstances that left them in no doubt he was Brink's victim. Lecogi also swore that Senyamotse carried 'an old muzzle loader gun', reported to have been seen with his body by one of the witnesses during the trial. Plaatje was sure of the date of the episode, he said, because he had consulted 'A Diary kept by me during the siege'.[48]

Plaatje must therefore have sworn his affidavit, and got Lecogi to do likewise, in the belief that what he knew of the circumstances had the same bearing on the case as his evidence in *R* v. *Lottering and Maritz*, that it proved that the man

Brink had killed had come from Mafeking. This time there was no defence lawyer on hand to remind him of his legal duty. The decision to act as he did must have been his alone. The two affidavits were telegraphed urgently to Cape Town, and a third followed several days later when he found another member of the raiding party to confirm his testimony. His action amounted to a sustained plea, in other words, to spare Brink's life – initiated when he heard that Brink, contrary to expectation, had not been granted a reprieve. He could see no difference between the two cases.

His efforts failed to save Brink from the gallows. Although the affidavits were laid before the attorney general and the governor of the Colony, they came with John Graham's advice that there was nothing in them that caused him to depart from the view he had already expressed: 'the facts alleged', he said, 'do not seem to me to alter either the legal or the moral nature of the prisoner's act'. The key difference between the two cases was that neither the judge president nor Graham was persuaded that Brink believed he was carrying out orders from a superior officer when he murdered his victim. The fact that Senyamotse was a member of an armed raiding party, and from Mafeking, did not alter this, nor did it detract from the exceptionally cold-blooded manner in which Brink had murdered his victim.[49]

Preparations were accordingly made for the execution of the two men. Gallows were sent from Kimberley, since Mafeking had none of its own, and then erected inside the gaol courtyard, the condemned prisoners, according to one account, being forced to carry them from the railway station to the gaol. The Rev. Mr Meyer, the Dutch Reformed Church minister, attended to the prisoners' spiritual needs during their last hours. As the two men mounted the scaffold, Arnoldus Rinke advised his younger colleague, 'Keep up your courage, we are going to appear before the Lord, and he is free.' Moments later both were dead. In a bizarre twist, Mr Blake, the colony's hangman, would claim a world record for the speed with which he performed his duties that day.[50]

Outside the gaol a large crowd had assembled and 'the natives especially', so it was reported, 'evinced great interest, this being the first palpable local punishment for the very frequent and cold-blooded shooting of natives during the siege'. For some at least it was a hugely symbolic moment, for it was one of the very few occasions on which whites found guilty of murdering blacks actually had their death sentence carried out. It was a first for the Special Treason Court, and it very rarely happened in any South African court of law. Was it a sign, Plaatje may have wondered, that a new kind of judicial dispensation could be expected when the war was won?[51]

The Mafeking trials were the last to be heard by the Special Treason Court as it was then constituted. By now the imperial military authorities preferred to deal with cases of treason by military tribunal – quicker, cheaper, not given to fits of excessive leniency, and free from the troublesome legal paraphernalia that gave at least a degree of legitimacy to the proceedings of the Special Treason Court.[52]

To some who witnessed the hangings in Mafeking the executions were not just deserved retribution for their sufferings at the hands of the Boers during the siege, but the legitimate exercise of the full force of the law in an ongoing struggle. In the surrounding countryside, violence between blacks and Boers was by now endemic and showed no signs of abating. Both sides took the opportunity to settle old scores. On the very day of the executions a party of sixteen Barolong had ventured into the Transvaal in search, so they said, of firewood. Despite being armed with Lee-Metfords, which must have been supplied by the British, they were surprised by a Boer commando and apprehended without a shot being fired. Three managed to escape but the remainder were taken to a hollow, lined up and shot. Left for dead, two of them nevertheless emerged unharmed and two others survived their wounds.

A week later Plaatje took down the harrowing testimony of Ephraim Marubani, one of the survivors. He identified the leader of the Boer commando as a man named David Louw, and recalled that he told him he would now 'prove to you that the English had no power and that they will no more get this country than they can help you today'. Marubani and his colleagues had agreed among themselves to fall down together as the shots were fired and to try to play dead if they were not killed outright. His affidavit, along with another from a man named Simon, who also survived the killings, was then sent to the attorney general and to the imperial military authorities, where it was added to the file they were compiling on 'Boer atrocities'.[53]

The violence didn't end there. On the night of 12 January 1902 Boer forces from the Transvaal crossed into the Mafeking district. Knowing that the British authorities had disarmed most of the Barolong after the siege, they were able to carry off vast numbers of cattle and other livestock, killing several people as they did so. British soldiers were nowhere to be seen. Well aware of the danger, the Barolong had repeatedly requested permission to carry arms to defend themselves and their property and were understandably bitter when their predictions of a raid were borne out – and 'extremely indignant', so the magistrate reported, 'at the way in which the Boers were able to almost completely devastate the District without the least resistance'. They lost more stock and suffered more damage, in fact, in that one night than during the entire seven months of siege. As Mr Green, the newly arrived acting magistrate, pointed out to his superiors, with regard to the compensation that would have to be paid, 'it would have been infinitely cheaper to have given out arms' as a deterrent. The year could scarcely have begun on a grimmer note. In this part of the country an end to hostilities seemed no closer now than it was when Mafeking was relieved – and that was over eighteen months before.[54]

✢✢✢

In circumstances of this kind the future of *Koranta ea Becoana* was an altogether more hopeful prospect to contemplate. The paper continued to appear on a fairly regular basis with Silas Molema as its proprietor, but they were finding their dependence on the presses of the *Mafeking Mail* increasingly costly and irksome. The rates they were charged, Plaatje recalled, were 'exorbitant', the printing was often very late (up to three weeks sometimes), and it was generally a 'horrid nuisance' being 'dependent upon somebody else for the issue of the paper'. So they decided to order a printing press of their own. It was a big step to take, and more than one person advised them, so Plaatje remembered, not 'to undertake anything so disastrous'.

The printing press and ancillary equipment cost Molema (for it was he who financed the enterprise) something in the region of £1,000, quite apart from the money that had to be found for renting or purchasing a suitable building from which to operate. There was then a frustrating delay before the press was actually delivered, and by February 1902 Silas Molema was writing to the local commandant in Mafeking asking that the existing weight restrictions on railway transport (the reason for the delay) could be waived so that the plant could be transported from Cape Town. It was, he pointed out, 'urgently required as the *Koranta ea Becoana* is the only channel through which the truth can be disseminated to the native population of Bechuanaland'.[55]

The words were Plaatje's: it was he who had typed out the letter, and the indent attached to the letter was in his hand. There could be no doubt now as to the full extent of his involvement in the venture, and it must have been agreed he would edit the paper once the new press arrived. Very likely he had been the driving force from the beginning. Such, at any rate, is the implication of a statement he made to a government commission in 1904: 'I just started it as an enterprise,' he explained, 'and one of the chiefs financed it'. Even if this statement was something of a simplification of what had actually happened, Plaatje must have been a strong influence, at the very least, in persuading Molema to commit his resources to starting the newspaper.[56]

At the beginning of April 1902, in anticipation of the arrival of the printing machinery from Cape Town, Plaatje and Molema signed a lease with Russell

Paddon, a Mafeking storekeeper, for the hire of part of a building in Shippard Street to house the press and offices of the newspaper. In the document recording the agreement, Molema and Plaatje are described as 'Proprietors and Publishers of the Koranta ea Becoana/Bechuana Gazette, Mafeking', but 'trading under the style or form of Silas Molema'; and the lease was for two years, commencing on 1 April 1902, the annual rent of £84 being payable in quarterly instalments. A week before signing the document, Plaatje handed in his notice of resignation from the Cape civil service, indicating his intention of leaving two months hence. He was committed to a new career.[57]

According to Vere Stent, writing some thirty years later, there was an intriguing denouement to Plaatje's civil service career. Once, when Plaatje 'was third or second clerk in Mafeking', Stent recalled, both the magistrate and his senior clerk went sick. Plaatje 'calmly mounted the bench', therefore, 'as the regulations then directed, and weighed off one or two Saturday night drunks'. Then 'the storm broke' as news spread of what had just occurred. 'The Bamangwato objected, for this was a man of no standing, and the Europeans shook their heads.' Plaatje was ordered to vacate the bench and a clerk, junior to him, but of European descent, replaced him. Plaatje resigned. 'Of what use', Stent asked, 'to remain in a service in which his colour barred him from promotion?'[58]

Stent's rhetorical question was no doubt one that Plaatje often asked himself. He had been in the Cape civil service long enough to know that he was unlikely to get any further. It was galling to say the least to see inexperienced young white men appointed to jobs he was far better qualified to do himself, and he also felt, rather strongly, that the status accorded the position of court interpreter was nowhere near commensurate with the responsibilities involved. Nor was the salary that came with it. He later described the £130 p.a. he was getting as 'a waste of time'.[59]

But what to make of the story itself? There are some reasons to be sceptical. Vere Stent was well known for his inventiveness as a journalist and he was not one to allow an undue concern for factual accuracy to get in the way of a good story. There were no regulations such as those he postulated, and, as Modiri Molema would point out, it was 'extremely improbable' that Plaatje would have 'mounted the bench' or that the Bamangwato, who lived hundreds of miles to the north, should have been in any kind of position to object.[60]

Yet Vere Stent's 'improbable' tale, it turns out on closer examination, was by no means pure invention. From 21 February to 12 March 1902 Plaatje is known to have acted as second clerk while the normal incumbent, Cyril Brooke, was on sick leave (dysentery aggravated by overwork, he said), and from 13 March to 19 May he acted as third clerk while a wholly inexperienced new appointee, C.W. Lloyd, BA, was 'endeavouring to learn something of his duties'. And while it is clear that the acting magistrate, Mr Graham Green, continued to fulfil his normal duties in court – it was he who 'mounted the bench' – the records do also reveal that for the first week of March, Plaatje acted not only as court interpreter and second clerk but as clerk to the court, entering the records of proceedings into the criminal record book, the first time he had done this. Normally this was the responsibility of one of the European clerks.[61]

Moreover, Stent was absolutely right about the first two cases, heard on 1 March, which Plaatje wrote up for the criminal record book. John Martin, 'European of no occupation', and Hendrik Johnson, 'Hottentot Labourer', were both guilty of 'appearing drunk in a public place, to wit the railway station' (except that they were most likely Friday night not Saturday night drunks).[62]

Plaatje knew Vere Stent well and met him on a number of occasions later in life. He must have told him about this incident, and it is not difficult to see how he could have retold the story, suitably embroidered, with Plaatje in the role of the magistrate rather than the clerk to the court. Nor indeed that Plaatje's appearance in court in this capacity – never mind that he was not acting as magistrate – could well have offended local sensibilities. Stent may not have got the details quite right, and he had evidently confused Bamangwato with Barolong, but it is fair to say he had captured a wider truth. Plaatje, he thought, was always destined for greater things than the lower rungs of the Cape civil service, and was not prepared to put up indefinitely with the racial barriers he routinely encountered.[63]

Three weeks after writing up the cases of the two drunks, Plaatje handed in his resignation. In reality, though, the timing of his decision was prompted less by any fracas that may have resulted from his appearance in court than by his plans, by now well advanced, to take up the reins of *Koranta ea Becoana*. And any frustrations there may have been were more likely generated by the inordinate amount of time it was taking for the new printing press to arrive in Mafeking than the self-evident restrictions on his progress up the civil service hierarchy. The truth of the matter was that he was already set on a new course.[64]

✦

Plaatje's letter of resignation, dated 27 March 1902, probably came as no surprise to Mr Green. Nevertheless, his request to leave two months hence (for permission had formally to be granted) was a matter of considerable inconvenience given the shortage of staff and his dependence upon Plaatje for the smooth running of his office, including – as Plaatje would remind him – the performance of 'duties of a delicate and responsible nature'. However, he recommended that Plaatje's resignation be accepted and started to think about finding a successor. A pity, he must have thought, it wasn't his first clerk, Ernest Grayson, unwisely promoted by his predecessor, who was moving on. Four years at Oxford was no preparation for the rigours of a colonial outpost like Mafeking and he was clearly not well suited to this kind of work. Green thought him just 'a muddler', 'unable to cope with much detailed work', and he was often off sick. After five years in South Africa he still knew no Dutch. Yet he was paid more than twice as much as Plaatje.[65]

That same day the rest of Mafeking woke up to altogether more momentous news: the death of Cecil Rhodes. The *Mafeking Mail* called him South Africa's 'greatest man, her greatest friend', to whom was due the credit for 'discovering the value of this continent', 'securing the greater part of it for Great Britain' and 'laying the foundation for the glorious future in store for her'. Nobody doubted that his passing symbolised the end of an era. For Plaatje, about to begin a new chapter in his own life, it must have brought back memories of the elections in 1898 when Rhodes was obliged to face up to his need for African and Coloured votes – and had set about buying them as he would any other.

Nine days later, in an extraordinary spectacle, the whole of Mafeking, black and white alike, turned out to pay their respects as the train carrying Rhodes's body stopped for a few hours at the station, en route to Bulawayo and his final resting place in the Matopo hills. Several thousand Barolong, led by Mr Green, Chief Wessels Montshiwa, Silas Molema and the other headmen, 'with seemly decorum' filed past the carriage in which his coffin lay, 'all baring their heads', so it was reported, 'fathers and mothers lifting up their children for a last sight of the white chief'. Since many Barolong saw Rhodes as their saviour, rescuing them from Boer territorial ambitions, it was only natural that they should wish to mourn his passing – and to remind his successors that they, as much as the white population, had a stake in the future that must soon emerge from the long years of war. Their very presence, in considerably greater numbers than the whites, was a statement that they too wished to be taken into account.[66]

Plaatje, meanwhile, had obligations to fulfil to his employer. During his last few months in the office he managed to overhaul its system of record-keeping, determined to end his eight years in the Cape civil service on a high note, and to leave a favourable impression upon Mr Green. This would have been a natural inclination but it was also a wise precaution from the point of view of *Koranta ea*

Becoana's future prospects. In the hazardous occupation of editing a newspaper he was likely to need all the friends and goodwill he could get, and in a small town like Mafeking the attitude of the local magistrate and civil commissioner was always going to count for a great deal. Like his predecessors, Green was pleased enough with the performance of his clerk and court interpreter: his confidential report that year recorded 'good' on every count except punctuality, which was only 'fair'. The difficulties Plaatje had recorded during the siege had evidently not been put fully behind him.[67]

His ability as a court interpreter and his industry in the office would be sorely missed. His replacement, Petrus Sidzumo, back from Vryburg, failed to measure up to his predecessor's high standards and, after persistent complaints about bad interpreting in court from the town's two attorneys, he was dismissed. Green had high hopes of the man he found to replace him, Ezekiel Bud-M'belle, an elder brother of Isaiah and Elizabeth; but he too was dismissed after only a few months' service, having arrived at the office one day in an intoxicated state and 'quite incapable', Green said, 'of performing his duties'. Court interpreters of Plaatje's ability and character were not easy to find.[68]

Nearly four years earlier Plaatje had arrived in Mafeking to hear Charles Bell explain to him the difference between interpreting at the sale of a cow and interpreting in court. Since then he had impressed a succession of different magistrates with his capabilities and had often carried out work that fell 'entirely outside the scope of his ordinary duties', as Green for one was ready to acknowledge. Rearranging his office's record-keeping systems during his final weeks there was just the latest instance of this. In these 'exceptional exertions', he pointed out to Mr Green, 'I have done my utmost to arrange them [the office records] in such a manner that you could expect to find something in its proper place, and if this rearrangement failed to gain your entire satisfaction it was owing to the manner in which they were originally placed away'. It was as though he was determined to leave his mark on the way the office functioned, to assert his mastery over the body of knowledge upon which it depended, to rearrange the records – and then to depart.[69]

He was ready for a new challenge. Editing a newspaper offered the opportunity to give freer expression to his talents, the means not only to realise a personal ambition but to fulfil a growing sense of responsibility for the leadership of a wider community that now looked to him to represent its interests, to be its voice. During the eight years' service to the government of the Cape Colony he had acquired a wide range of skills and an intimate knowledge of the way things worked. In its judicial system and the non-racial principles it espoused, he could see hope for the future, a potential arena for fair play and advancement. Now it was time to move on and to harness his experience to a wider cause.

SIX

Editor of *Koranta ea Becoana,*
1902–1904

F ive days after Plaatje left the Cape civil service, peace negotiations between the British imperial government and the Boer republics were finally concluded. To many, the war had appeared to be over nearly a year previously, but it had continued in the form of protracted guerrilla warfare as the Boer leaders held out for peace terms which would have fallen short of total surrender. In the end they were able to extract little in the way of concessions. Lord Milner, the British high commissioner, was intent on a programme of reconstruction designed to consolidate British control and he was determined not to have his hands tied in any way by concessions in the peace treaty. Despite the more conciliatory attitude of Lord Kitchener, the British military commander, he got his way. After three years of war, heavy casualties among combatants and civilians, and widespread devastation of large areas of the Transvaal and Orange Free State, peace finally returned to the subcontinent.

Many Africans, in the Cape as well as the Transvaal and the new Orange River Colony (as the old Orange Free State was now called), were optimistic about the future. Wartime propaganda had raised hopes of some form of recognition of the political rights of Africans living in the conquered Boer republics, in line with those already enjoyed in the Cape Colony, and reflecting the elevated claims made in the British press that the war was being fought in the interests of Christianity and an imperial order based on the idea of 'equal rights for all civilised men'. 'There must be no doubt', declared Lord Salisbury, the British prime minister, on the eve of war, 'that due precaution will be taken for the kindly and improving treatment of those countless indigenous races of whose destiny I fear we have been too forgetful.' Many other statements in a similar vein had followed, with varying degrees of sincerity.[1]

But clause 8 of the Treaty of Vereeniging disappointed those who had hoped for an immediate improvement in political status. It provided that no decision would be taken on extending the franchise to Africans until after the introduction of responsible government in the former Boer republics. Then, as later, Milner and the imperial government, despite their expressions of concern for the interests of the 'native races', were in no doubt that the question of extending political rights to Africans should not be allowed to stand in the way of reconciling Boer and

Briton. The contribution of black South Africans to the war effort, it seemed, was to go unrewarded.

In Mafeking, as elsewhere, the signing of the peace treaty was greeted with relief by black and white alike. The town's white business community looked forward to re-establishing normal trading relations with the Transvaal, and the Barolong too welcomed the opportunity to rebuild their stocks and herds after the succession of disasters, natural and man-made, of the previous few years.

Plaatje faced difficulties of a different kind. He had timed his resignation from the civil service to coincide with the expected arrival of the printing press he and Molema had ordered so he could assume the editorship of the enlarged *Koranta ea Becoana* in the new premises they had secured for the paper. Things did not work out quite as planned. They managed to obtain the licence they needed to transport the printing press by rail from Cape Town, and within a week it had reached Port Elizabeth. But then it took a further two months to get from Port Elizabeth to Mafeking. Having solicited money from subscribers and advertisers, *Koranta*'s proprietors were understandably frustrated at the time it was all taking: 'the plant could not have been delayed much longer had we inspanned our ox-waggon and personally went to fetch it'. The result would be a delay of four months between the last issue of the two-page Setswana-only version of *Koranta ea Becoana*, printed by the *Mafeking Mail*, and the appearance of the first bilingual edition from the new printing press.[2]

In-between there was one notable event: a concert, on the evening of 23 May, the public debut of the Mafeking Philharmonic Society. Both Plaatje and Elizabeth were involved. He was reported to have been 'indefatigable throughout the evening in "bossing up" the show', but in their duet he went 'shockingly flat'. Overall the evening was judged a success, though there were some complaints about the high admission prices, designed to raise as much money as possible for the Victoria Memorial Fund, recently set up by Elizabeth's brother Isaiah in order to raise funds for educational causes. Seats cost 4s and 6s, which might explain the disappointing attendance.[3]

The concert was probably a welcome distraction while plans for *Koranta* remained on hold. Several offers of employment, Plaatje recalled, came his way at this time, but he turned them all down, unimpressed by the low salaries on offer. For all his complaints about his salary in the Mafeking magistrate's office, it was obvious, he wrote afterwards, 'that the Cape Government was not the worst offender in this connection'. At last, the printing presses arrived and were speedily set up: the months of waiting and frustration were over.[4]

This, then, was the background to the dignified and well-attended ceremony that took place in Main Street, Mafeking, on the morning of 16 August 1902, formally opening the Bechuana Printing Works, as it was now called, and celebrating the publication of the first number of the enlarged *Koranta ea Becoana*. It differed from its predecessor in being published in English as well as Setswana, and accordingly carried the additional title of *Bechuanas' Gazette*, leaving no doubt as to who was envisaged as its main readership. The interest of Mafeking's white community, aware of the benefits that advertising in the new paper could bring to their business among the African population, was evident in the presence at the ceremony of the mayor, the town clerk, the manager of the local branch of the Standard Bank (somewhat concerned, one imagines, at the damage the enterprise had already done to Silas Molema's bank balance), and other local notables including, so *Koranta* was to report, 'a number of others we had not the pleasure of knowing'.

It was unfortunate that the Barolong paramount chief, Wessels Montshiwa, and most of his headmen were unable to be present because they had a meeting with Ralph Williams, the resident commissioner for the Bechuanaland Protectorate, concerning a land dispute, and the Barolong were represented instead by Chief Lekoko. Whether or not Wessels and his headmen would have come if they had not had this prior engagement is a moot point, but it was entirely fitting that it should have been left to Lekoko to represent the Tshidi royal family. A nephew of the late Chief Montshiwa, and educated at an Anglican training school in Grahamstown in the 1870s, he represented the Christian, 'progressive' section of the Tshidi Barolong: precisely those people who could be expected to support and identify with the new enterprise.

Mr E. Graham Green, the magistrate and civil commissioner, had agreed to formally open the new plant, and he offered some encouraging words. 'It is very gratifying', he said, 'to see how the Barolong are progressing in being able to publish and print their own paper', and he wanted to remind those 'connected with its publication to bear in mind that they have a powerful instrument in their hands, for in no way is the saying "the pen is mightier than the sword" more exemplified than in the publication of a newspaper (Applause).' He hoped that it would be published 'in the interests of truth, justice and charity (Applause). Of truth, that its news may be reliable and verified, before publication; of justice, that it will see that the weak are not oppressed, and that the law is upheld; and of charity, that its personal criticism will be for the public benefit, and not to satisfy the personal feelings of the writer (Applause)." If these principles are upheld,' he concluded, 'then the paper will certainly be a benefit to the general public and the Natives in particular', and he was very pleased to start the paper 'on its new course'. Having thus delivered what Plaatje remembered as a 'noteworthy speech on the duties of a journalist', he 'started the machine, pulled off one copy and said: "Gentlemen, this is the first copy of the first number of the 'Koranta ea Becoana and Bechuanas' Gazette",' before reading out aloud from the English section of the paper (occasionally punctuated, so it was reported, 'by a hearty Hear, Hear').[5]

Further words of congratulation and encouragement came from the Reverends George Weavind and Molema Moshoela. Both expressed themselves well satisfied with the degree of progress that the new venture demonstrated. Weavind hoped the paper would be 'a success from a literary point of view as well as financially', Moshoela that it 'would be of service to the Governments and people of this and of the Transvaal and Orange River Colonies, by explaining the laws to the Natives and maintaining a healthy feeling between them and the whites'. Nobody could argue with such sentiments, or indeed those expressed in more traditional idiom in the praise poem composed by the Rev. Jacob Monyatsi of Bloemfontein to mark the birth of the new paper. For the Batswana in general, and the Barolong in particular, it was a hugely important initiative, it bestowed honour on all those associated with it, and it was only fitting that it should be celebrated in such time-honoured fashion. There would be plenty of challenges ahead, Mr Monyatsi warned, but he urged Plaatje to persevere. Future generations, he predicted, would shower him with praise. Coming from a man Plaatje considered 'the first Chuana scholar', these words must have meant a lot to him.[6]

It was an impressive opening ceremony which *Koranta* itself described, in its second issue, as 'a success beyond our anticipation', and the blessing of the local civil commissioner as well as the town's white dignitaries augured well for the future. Others, it has to be said, were less optimistic. The editor of the *Bechuanaland News* in Vryburg, for example, while he thought *Koranta*'s first issue was 'creditable', could not see how it was going to pay. 'The editor and printer', he said, 'will work hard, and after a few months will find themselves with a long subscribers' list, no money to pay wages, and a lot of expensive type which nobody wants.' He spoke from experience.[7]

Whatever the future held, it was obvious that the launch of *Koranta ea Becoana* was a big moment in Plaatje's life. Still only 25 years old, he now found himself occupying a position of considerable influence and importance in the affairs of his people, and with every prospect of making his reputation as their spokesman on a far bigger stage than hitherto. Unlike several other African-run newspapers of the day, *Koranta* had no white shareholders, nor was it beholden to any political party for a financial subsidy. Plaatje really could not have asked for a better opportunity for the realisation of his ambitions or the exercise of his talents.

᨞

There was a wider context to this bold initiative. In assuming the editorship of *Koranta ea Becoana*, Plaatje joined the ranks of what was then a rather select band of black pressmen in South Africa. So select, in fact, that there were at that time only two other black newspapers being published on anything like a regular basis: A.K. Soga's *Izwi la Bantu*, printed in East London, written in English and Xhosa; and the *South African Spectator*, published in Cape Town, and edited by F.Z.S. Peregrino, a talented, if slightly eccentric, West African journalist from the Gold Coast, who had lived both in England and America before moving on to South Africa. One famous name was missing: that of *Imvo Zabantsundu*, still edited by Tengo Jabavu, but closed down by the military censors in August 1901 for expressing what were considered to be disloyal sentiments. Although *Imvo* would reappear in October 1902, it was a sad irony that the paper which more than any other had inspired Plaatje in his endeavours should have been suspended when *Koranta* made its debut in the bilingual form that *Imvo* had pioneered. At the same time its fate stood as a reminder of the need for caution, to be aware that there were limits to free expression – martial law or no martial law.

The editors of these newspapers had a strong sense of common purpose. They were the 'mouthpiece' of the communities they both served and represented, and they saw it as their duty not only to give expression to 'native opinion' but to formulate it too. They provided the means of conveying aspirations and grievances to the authorities, and in doing so they asserted their claim to leadership. Plaatje's perception of the role of his newspaper was no different, and it was not long before *Koranta ea Becoana* was proclaiming its dedication to 'the amelioration of the Native' and its commitment to the four principles of 'Labour, Sobriety, Thrift and Education'. All had been plainly evident in his life and career to date.[8]

From the beginning Plaatje was assisted in the *Koranta* office by a staff of four or five other people. All were Africans, an achievement in which Plaatje took much pride, given the scepticism expressed by many local whites that the paper could function without their help. By 1903 its staff included James (Ramokoto) Plaatje, his younger brother, who lived with the family in the stadt; Isaiah Makgothi, a recent graduate of Lovedale, and a member of a well-known Seleka Barolong family from Thaba Nchu, who was one of the compositors; James Mpinda, who

167

had worked on the *Mafeking Mail* as well as the earlier *Koranta* news-sheet, and had learnt his trade in the printing department at Lovedale; and another man by the name of Henry Mtotoba, described, like James Plaatje, as a 'labourer'. One other employee called Salatiele, working at the *Koranta* office when it opened for business, did not last long: two weeks later he was caught trying to cash a cheque upon which he had forged Silas Molema's signature, and was duly convicted and sentenced by the Circuit Court to ten months' imprisonment with hard labour.[9]

Silas Molema probably played little part in the day-to-day affairs of the newspaper. His financial backing of course remained vital, but given his many other commitments it seems he was happy to leave the running of the office, and decisions over the content of each issue of the paper, in Plaatje's hands. Plaatje wrote the editorials and a variety of other unsigned articles, in both English and Setswana, but he certainly kept Molema informed. One of Modiri Molema's early memories is of Plaatje coming around to their home in the evenings, carrying a pile of other newspapers with him, reading extracts to his father and then discussing their views on them.[10]

The format and character of the newspaper were soon established. It appeared at weekly intervals (on Saturday mornings), in English and Setswana, was often printed on brightly coloured newsprint, and it sold at 3d a time; a year's subscription cost 15s. From the beginning it claimed to be 'rapidly increasing in size and circulation'. Each issue consisted of an eclectic mixture of letters from readers, reports from local correspondents (often the same people as the agents), extracts from the local and international press selected for their interest to an African readership, as well as editorial comment and original articles upon the issues of the day. There was also an occasional column entitled 'Mma-Maitisho' ('fireside tales'), a light-hearted review in Setswana, whose author – despite heavy hints to readers that this was none other than Plaatje himself – was supposed to remain a secret.[11]

Advertisements, crucial to *Koranta*'s survival, took up about half of each issue, including the first page. Usually there were eight pages, but this varied and was eventually reduced to four when the page size was doubled. *Koranta* could be bought direct from the newspaper's office in Main Street, obtained on subscription, or purchased from one of the network of agents living in Tswana-speaking areas of the Cape Colony, the Bechuanaland Protectorate, the Transvaal and Orange River Colony.

Probably between one and two thousand copies of each issue were printed. The large towns of Johannesburg, Bloemfontein, Kimberley, the Seleka Barolong settlement at Thaba Nchu and Mafeking itself supplied most of its readers, the vast majority of them Tswana-speakers; but there were individual subscribers,

Upper, left: Wessels Montshiwa, chief of the Tshidi Barolong, 1896–1903. He failed to live up to the example of Chief Montshiwa, his illustrious predecessor.

Upper, middle: Charles Bell (1853–1908), magistrate and civil commissioner at Mafeking, 1897–1900. Plaatje considered himself 'fortunate to have served my apprenticeship under such a man'.

Upper, right: Spencer Minchin (1866–1935), Mafeking's leading attorney, who would end up as *Koranta ea Becoana*'s last owner.

Lower: Ernest Grayson, BA, second clerk in the Mafeking magistrate's office, seen here *(standing)* at Balliol College, Oxford, in 1896. Bell thought him 'inclined to be lazy', 'very slow', but 'has ability if he will make use of it'.

Family and friends, c.1900. The two figures standing are Isaiah Makgothi, from Thaba Nchu *(left)*, and Plaatje's brother James *(right)*. Sitting, left, is his nephew Ebie Schiemann, aged 6.

Three generations of the Molema family. Chief Isaac Molema (c.1809–1881), the founder of Mafikeng *(upper, left)*; Silas Molema (1850–1927), sub-chief, patron and friend of Plaatje *(upper, right)*; Modiri Molema (1891–1965) *(lower)*, shown here as a young man. He later became a well-known medical practitioner and public figure.

Sunday 29ᵗʰ. -- Divine Services. ~~a man~~
~~~~. No thunder. Haikonna terror;
And I have therefore got ample opportunity to sit
down and think before I jot down anything about
my experience of the past week. I have discovered
nearly everything about war and find that
Artillery in war is of no use. The Boers seem
to have started hostilities the whole of their
reliance leaning on the strength and number
of their cannon and they are no surely
discovering their mistake. I do not think
that they will have more pluck to do any
thing better than what they did on Vensday,
and we can therefore Expect that they will either
go away or settle round us until the troops
arrive. To give a short account of what I
found war to be I can say

No music is as thrilling and as immensely
captivating as to listen to the firing of the
Guns on your own side. It is like enjoying supernatural melodies in a paradise to hear one or two shots fired off the
armoured train but no words can suitably
depict the fascination of the music produced by the action of a Maxim, which
to Boer ears, I am sure, is an Exasperating
Artillery that not only disturbs the ear
but also disorganises the free circulation of
the listener's blood. At the Native City
of Kanya they have been entertained
(I learn from one just arrived) with
melodious tones of big guns, sounding
"Grand air" of war, like a gentle subterranean
instrument, some 30 fathoms beneath their feet and not so
remote

Upper: The Court of Summary Jurisdiction in session during the siege. Plaatje is standing alongside Lord Edward Cecil and Charles Bell, who are sitting at the desk. 'Myself in knickerbockers and without a jacket looked more like a member of the football team or a village cyclist than a court interpreter.'

Lower: Barolong chiefs and headmen. *Sitting, left to right:* Silas Molema, Wessels Montshiwa, Lekoko. The others are unidentified, though the man standing on the right, with the rifle, is believed to be Mathakgong Kepadisa, famous for leading Barolong raids behind Boer lines.

Upper: War correspondents in front of their dugout. *Left to right:* J.E. Neilly *(Pall Mall Gazette)*, Vere Stent (Reuters), Major F.D. Baillie *(Morning Post)*, J. Angus Hamilton *(The Times* and *Black and White)*. Plaatje was employed by both Stent and Hamilton.

Lower: An armed African raiding party preparing to 'fetch cattle', March 1900.

Left to right: 1, Runner   2, Mr. Bell, Resident Magistrate   3, Plaatje, native interpreter   4, Major Goold   Adams, the Administrator   5, Runner

NATIVE RUNNERS DESCRIBING THE RELIEF OF KIMBERLEY

Upper: 'Two Boer horses and rifles captured by natives', after what Plaatje described as 'a brief but very hot battle' near Madibi, fifteen miles from Mafeking.

Lower: Interpreting for Charles Bell and Major Hamilton Goold-Adams. Two unidentified African 'runners' *(sitting, front)* convey news of the relief of Kimberley, 15 February 1900.

Upper: Black refugees queuing for horse soup in the stadt.

Lower, left: Certificate for Chief Wessels Montshiwa, written out by Plaatje and signed by Bell, confirming that he was 'a fit and proper person to obtain and have one No. 1 Express rifle'.

Lower right: A white man's war? An unnamed armed guard, during the siege of Mafeking.

black and white, scattered all over southern Africa. Several of the latter, indeed, wrote encouraging letters to Plaatje when they heard about the new newspaper. Samuel Cronwright-Schreiner, who had encouraged Plaatje to embark upon the venture in the first place, offered his congratulations, and advised him 'to get a clear grip of your policy and support it through thick and thin, strenuously, but not racially'. Vere Stent, with whom he had remained in contact since the siege, also had some words of advice, along with a prediction: 'Steer clear of race hatred and beware of the Ethiopian Mission which is preaching mischief. Don't abuse white people, and I am sure you will some day be a power amongst your people.'[12]

Vere Stent's advice was well meant but in reality a little superfluous. Plaatje had not the slightest intention of indulging in 'race hatred' or abusing white people, and he had his own views of the so-called Ethiopian mission. Taking its name from the breakaway 'Ethiopian Church' which had seceded from a Methodist mission in the Transvaal, but was later associated with the African Methodist Episcopal Church from America, for many Africans 'Ethiopianism' embodied a more general aspiration towards independence from white control. For whites, by contrast, it was shorthand for their worst fears about the threats they perceived to 'white civilisation' in southern Africa and symptomatic of the heightened racial tensions that existed in the aftermath of the war. Any black newspaper had to handle the subject with caution.

It was in the nature of these weekly African newspapers that they should both reflect and project the personalities of their editors. *Koranta ea Becoana* was no exception. Appearing with impressive regularity after its launch in August 1902, it developed into a very professional publication, marked by exuberance, a sense of humour and an optimistic outlook which sprang directly from its editor. There was an assertiveness too, equally characteristic, which found expression in the biblical quotation from the Song of Solomon which soon appeared under the masthead of each issue:

I am black, but comely, O ye daughters of Jerusalem, as the tents of Kedar, and the curtains of Solomon.

Look not upon me because I am black for the sun hath looked down upon me; my mother's children were angry with me; they made me the keeper of the vineyards; but my own vineyard have I not kept.

169

Only Plaatje, Modiri Molema thought, really knew what this passage meant to him. He must have known of it since his time at Pniel, intrigued by the coincidence with his own name as well as its expression of race pride. When it appeared in *Koranta* for the first time in September 1902, it came with the added note 'With Apologies to the South African Spectator', a nod to its editor's well-publicised views. Thereafter Plaatje included the verse in every issue of *Koranta*, in both English and Setswana, and in other newspapers he would edit in the future. As well as asserting his own pride in his race, and urging others to the cause, it became a kind of motto, a reminder to his readers that he was really there.[13]

The greater part of each issue was in Setswana. In these columns, particularly Plaatje's editorials and his readers' responses to them, a distinctive conversation took place. More than anything it was about the existence of the Batswana as a people, what this meant in practice, and how they should order their lives. Editorials, embodying Plaatje's views, frequently appealed to Batswana to take pride in their language and culture, to respect and celebrate the history and traditions of their chiefdoms – but at the same time to pursue the education they needed to prosper in the modern world. Readers wrote letters to express agreement or to point to the difficulties of finding the right balance between old and new, of gaining new knowledge and skills without compromising their identities as Batswana. Inappropriate behaviour was often criticised, reflecting a deep ongoing concern with personal and communal morality. In June 1903, for example, one Peter Mothibeli wrote to express his disappointment at the rowdy behaviour of some people that he witnessed in a railway carriage, concluding that proper education was the solution. Without it, he thought, they would always be confronted with the question 'Where's your pass?' Plaatje, in response, pointed out that arrogance on the part of whites was often a factor too, and advised that it was just best to keep out of their way and avoid contact with them wherever possible.[14]

Batswana chiefs, it was widely accepted, had a special responsibility for the leadership of their people, and their doings were generally covered in positive terms in the Setswana columns of *Koranta*. Plaatje himself was deeply committed to the institution of chiefly authority, believing it essential to his people's future. Yet chiefs had to be progressive – like the Molemas – and they were duty bound to set an example to others. They had an obligation to ensure their own children were properly educated, not just for themselves but in the interests of the nation as a whole, for only in this way could they acquire the necessary knowledge and the clarity of vision to enable it to flourish and prosper. Besides, if they were not competent to lead their people, Plaatje asked, how could they expect their people to remain loyal?[15]

Plaatje believed *Koranta* had a similar educative role, contributing to this goal of progress and enlightenment but able, thanks to the use of written Setswana and modern printing technology, to reach a far wider audience, to exploit new means of building solidarity. To extend its reach further, those who could read were urged to read out its pages to those who could not. Subscribers were frequently reminded to pay their subscriptions. If they did not, *Koranta* would fail, a vital instrument of unity and modernity would be lost, and the Batswana would fall further behind. Preserving their cultural integrity was vital. 'Can we really be anything in the world if we do not know who we are?' he asked in one article, 'How can other nations respect us?' Look at the way the Xhosa and Basotho value their traditions and languages, he said, concluding with an exhortation: 'Batswana, rouse yourselves, wake up and be proud of Setswana. Teach your children to love and to learn Setswana, to obey and to pray in Setswana.'[16]

For Plaatje, building upon the Tswana language and the traditions associated with it was the key to developing the communal strength of the Batswana – and to his own platform as their spokesman. But it was fraught with difficulty. A common language did not of itself create a strong sense of common identity, and attachment to individual chiefdoms was often far stronger. Rivalries between them only complicated things further, especially when they intersected with competing white interests, as in the longstanding Tshidi–Rapulana dispute. Nor did it help that the Batswana were so widely dispersed, scattered across five different colonial administrations; that they lacked the centralising focus of a recognised paramountcy; or that the language itself was represented in several different forms orthographically, throwing up further obstacles to communication. Conjuring up a vision of Tswana nationhood in such circumstances was never going to be an easy task.

Bringing knowledge of the wider world to the Batswana was central to Plaatje's project. For the information he needed, and for much of the content of each issue, whether in English or Setswana, he relied upon exchange arrangements with other newspapers and periodicals. By 1904 he had sixty-one such exchanges in place, receiving, in return for a copy of *Koranta ea Becoana*, newspapers printed in eight different languages, sent in from West Africa, Asia, Britain, America and Europe, as well as all the main centres in southern Africa. From these he extracted news of the outside world, often reproducing verbatim reports and commentary he thought would interest and enlighten his readers. He built up a narrative that celebrated black progress and achievement in other lands, highlighting instances of racial injustice, challenging the use of offensive language, or applauding sympathetic whites when they stood up for black interests. Plaatje's exchange newspapers, for their part, would reciprocate by reproducing extracts from *Koranta* in their own columns. Sometimes this was in a spirit of solidarity, as with newspapers in India and West Africa. At other times, especially in several white-owned newspapers closer to home, the tone was more often than not one of mockery of 'native' pretensions.[17]

Articles and reports from African American newspapers from the United States held pride of place in *Koranta ea Becoana*. Plaatje's personal interest in the situation of black Americans, shared by many of his readers, went back over a decade, and he was soon giving prominence to reports about leading African American spokesmen and thinkers like Booker T. Washington, principal of the famous educational institution at Tuskegee, Alabama; later, indeed, he claimed credit for being the first black South African newspaper editor to have done so. Maud Sidzumo, a young teacher at one of the location schools in Mafeking, and sister of his late friend Patrick, shared this fascination. Years later she could recall the visits she used to make to the *Koranta* office to read these African American newspapers, being particularly interested, she admitted, in the fashion pages – these were 'our people', she said. It was striking testimony to the way in which these transatlantic networks could touch people's hopes and dreams even in as remote a place as Mafeking.[18]

His exchanges with John Edward Bruce, a well-known African American journalist, then living in Washington DC, were especially fruitful. Nearly twenty years later Bruce remembered receiving a copy of *Koranta ea Becoana*, only the second African newspaper he had ever seen, and was struck by the 'virile and well written editorials, its snappy editorial notes and contributed articles which, though brief, were instructive and to the point'. He 'then and there decided to get better acquainted with Africa and Africans' and wrote to Plaatje to thank him for putting him on his exchange list, 'and to tell him how well pleased I was with his newspaper'. Thus began what Bruce called 'a desultory correspondence' during which they came to know each other 'pretty tolerably well'. None of their letters, unfortunately, have survived.[19]

The 'virile and well written editorials' which so impressed Bruce tended to be of two kinds. Some commented upon the issues of the day as they affected African interests locally or nationally, and others took the form of general statements of editorial policy and principle. Of the latter, the most striking was the considered statement which appeared under the heading 'Equal rights' in the third number of *Koranta ea Becoana*, 13 September 1902, and repeated verbatim on several occasions thereafter:

We do not hanker after social equality with the white man. If anyone tells you that we do so, he is a lunatic, and should be put in chains. We do not care for your parlour, nor is it our wish to lounge on couches in your drawing rooms. The renegade Kafir who desires to court and marry your daughter is a perfect danger to his race, for if his yearnings were realised we would be hurrying on the path to the inauguration of a generation of half-castes, and the total obliteration of our race and colour, both of which are very dear to us.

For this reason we advise every black man to avoid social contact with whites, and the other races to keep strictly within their boundaries.

All we claim is our just dues; we ask for our political recognition as loyal British subjects. We have not demonstrated our fealty to the throne for £.s.d., but we did it to assist in the maintenance of the open door we now ask for, so it cannot be said we demand too much.

Under the Union Jack every person is his neighbour's equal. There are certain regulations for which one should qualify before his legal status is recognised as such: to this qualification race or colour is no bar, and we hope, in the near future, to be able to record that one's sex will no longer debar her from exercising a privilege hitherto enjoyed by the sterner sex only.

Presently under the British Constitution every MAN so qualified is his neighbour's political equal, therefore anyone who argues to the contrary, or imagines himself the political superior of his fellow subject, is a rebel at heart.

It was a political creed which was to sustain *Koranta* throughout its existence, and Plaatje too: 'political recognition as loyal British subjects', equality of opportunity, equality before the law, all were the product of a set of beliefs formed in Plaatje's mind well before he came to Mafeking. But there was an awareness now of the salience of political considerations, of the importance of distinguishing such claims from any aspiration to social equality, which most whites were apt to lump together as one and the same. Plaatje was anxious to ensure that the two things were not confused, well aware of the extent of concern in the white press, and among whites more generally, about the supposedly pernicious effect that the war had had upon African aspirations. Hence his concern to calm such fears, to adopt the path of caution without compromising his underlying principles, to stress that he was claiming no more than was due to his people as 'loyal British subjects'. Loyalist British rhetoric aside, it was a strategy that owed something to the ideas of Booker T. Washington and the cautious path he likewise advocated in advancing the interests of his people.[20]

Central to Plaatje's formulation, too, was a sense of pride in his own race: not just a denial of any aspiration to social equality as a means of disarming white criticisms and anxieties, but a positive statement of pride in a black, and a Tswana, identity. Creating 'a generation of half-castes' through social and sexual contact between black and white was as unwelcome a thought to Plaatje as it was to his detractors, a view shared by the vast majority of his contemporaries. Where he went further than most, however, was in his consistent support for gender equality, his belief that the time had come to recognise that gender should be no more a barrier to equal treatment than race. What possible justification could there be, he asked, describing the decision of the South African Native Convention in Queenstown in November 1902, not to accept women as delegates? Particularly, he said, as one of the women thus disqualified was Charlotte Maxeke (Charlotte Manye as she was in her Kimberley days), the only person at the meeting who had a university degree. 'Just as strongly as we object to the line of demarcation being drawn on the basis of a person's colour,' he said, 'so we abhor disqualification founded on a person's sex.'[21]

He saw himself fighting on other fronts too. If his people were to be justified in their claim to 'equal rights for all civilised men', then they needed to measure up to the second part of this formula. He was never afraid, therefore, to criticise his people when he considered they fell short – whether this was their failure to support progressive causes, to refrain from alcohol, to treat women as equals of men, or to abandon customs which were not compatible with Christian practice. A strongly worded article on the revival of '*bogwera*' (circumcision rites) was a case in point: 'In some pity we record that during this, the fourth month of the third year of the twentieth century,' he wrote, 'the Barolong have revived the ancient circumcision rites which had long since gone down beneath the silent power of Christian civilisation. Scores of young men have during the week been taken away from their profitable occupations into the veld to howl themselves hoarse and submit to severer flogging than is usually inflicted by the judges of the Supreme Court. The fact that in the year A.D. 1903 the sons of Montshiwa can safely solemnise a custom, the uselessness of which was discerned by their fathers, and which the rest of Bechuanaland has for years relegated to the despicable relics of past barbarism, shows that someone has not been doing their duty.'[22]

So, as editor of *Koranta* Plaatje saw himself with a dual task: to foster the education and advancement of his people along 'progressive', Christian lines while retaining and revitalising the best elements of their traditional cultures; and to fight, by strictly constitutional methods, with caution and moderation, for their just rights and fair treatment; to ensure that 'native opinion' was taken into account in the political future of the country in which he lived. This was a vision that stood in sharp contrast to one being articulated with increasing stridency in public discourse around him: the notion that South Africa was a 'white man's country', that blacks should be there only to minister to its needs, and that the necessary steps should to be taken to ensure that this was how things remained.

+∾+

Given the disparity in status and resources of the proponents of these opposing visions, it could scarcely be considered an equal struggle. Nevertheless, Plaatje found ways of making his influence felt, and as ever he was adept at taking advantage of the opportunities that arose. Nowhere was this more clearly demonstrated than in the part he played in the first major political campaign in which he was involved: the question of the proposed annexation of the Bechuanaland Protectorate and the Mafeking district of the Cape to the British colony of the Transvaal.

The demand for annexation originated late in 1902 with a group of traders and businessmen in Mafeking, the product of dissatisfaction with the high rates of tariffs on goods moving between the two colonies and an understandable desire for readier access to the markets of the Witwatersrand. Their idea was to present a petition to Joseph Chamberlain, the British colonial secretary, when he visited Mafeking at the beginning of 1903 during his tour of southern Africa. In order to strengthen their case and to make it appear more than just self-interest, they sought to enlist African support, and they persuaded some local African chiefs to sign their petition. Plaatje had been away from Mafeking when this took place, and he was extremely disturbed to hear the news when he returned. A great believer in the political and legal system of the Cape Colony, he was horrified at the implications ('by far the most appalling information we have heard since the war broke out'), and wrote a strong editorial in the next issue of *Koranta*, pointing out the dangers. 'In the face of the eighth clause of the final peace terms', he wrote, 'this action on their [the chiefs'] part is nothing but a terrible leap in the dark and never was there a more flagrant case of wilful political suicide than there is in this movement; and we earnestly trust that for the sake of themselves the Chiefs will see to its early withdrawal before it is too late.'[23]

Plaatje's editorial, combined with intense personal lobbying, proved most effective, and he was delighted to be able to announce in *Koranta* several weeks later that 'the Barolong Chiefs, who previously signed a petition in favour of Annexation, have discovered their mistake, as clearly explained to them in these columns, and they have withdrawn it in time for the arrival of Mr Chamberlain'. Attempts had also been made, he said, 'to obtain the signatures of the Ratlou Chiefs and headmen in the further ends of the District'. 'Acting on our advice,' however, 'these Chiefs have stoutly refused to associate themselves with the movement and it is right that this should be the case.'[24]

The proponents of the scheme were understandably aggrieved at this reversal, and Chief Badirile's letter of explanation to the *Mafeking Mail* on the subject can have come as scant consolation. 'The older headmen of the tribe', Badirile wrote, 'are a number of primitive men who know nothing about South African politics, which appear to be difficult to be understood by the white people themselves; and if anything affecting the welfare of the nation is under consideration we have enlightened men amongst ourselves whom we consult under such circumstances, and their counsel may be relied upon to be better than that of a solicitor, as their interests will also be at stake.' At least they were left in no doubt about the influence their adversary now commanded locally.[25]

Plaatje had good reason to be satisfied with this outcome, and Chief Badirile's comments about the 'enlightened men' among them described his role to a tee. When Joseph Chamberlain did arrive in Mafeking, he was presented with a petition requesting him to consider the question of annexation, but it carried no African support and found no favour with colonial or imperial authorities. The plan was soon dropped.

Not surprisingly, the Barolong themselves were keen to take advantage of the colonial secretary's visit, for they had matters of their own to lay before him. Plaatje, no less surprisingly, was heavily involved in the preparations. Chamberlain had agreed to receive a deputation and time had been allowed in his programme for a visit to the stadt. It fell to Plaatje ('as representing the Chief Wessels Montsioa and the Barolong tribe') to brief lawyers in Kimberley to draw up a petition which they intended to present to him, along with a decorated address of welcome. While he was in Kimberley arranging this, he also spoke to a representative of the *Diamond Fields Advertiser* and was able to secure some sympathetic coverage of the Barolong case in its columns ahead of the colonial secretary's arrival, explaining just why his people preferred to remain part of the Cape Colony and not become part of the Transvaal. 'Lighter taxation' and 'a less stringent pass law' were just two of the reasons he gave.[26]

Their petition contained effusive expressions of loyalty to the imperial government, reminders of their contribution to the defence of Mafeking and of their desire to remain in the Cape Colony, and a request that several of their more pressing grievances be attended to. In particular, that the stretch of land at Polfontein (Bodibe), just over the border in the Transvaal, which they had been promised during the siege and believed was theirs by right, should now be handed over; that the substantial war losses compensation due to them should be paid without further delay; and that there should be no variation whatsoever in the terms on which their autonomy – which ensured they remained outside the jurisdiction of the local municipal and divisional councils – was recognised when British Bechuanaland was annexed to the Cape in 1895.[27]

Chamberlain arrived in the stadt early in the afternoon of 28 January 1903, having spent the morning in the company of the chiefs of the Bechuanaland Protectorate. Prior to his arrival in Mafeking a banner with the words 'We want to be annexed' had appeared on one of the arches erected in his honour over the road into town, but was hastily removed ('by special request') just before he passed through it. In the Barolong stadt the message was the exact opposite. 'We do not want to be annexed', proclaimed their banner, alongside another one saying 'God save the King', as Chamberlain and his party passed by, cheered all the way to the chief's kgotla. Chief Wessels Montshiwa recited an address of welcome, Plaatje interpreted into English, and Chief Lekoko followed up with further expressions of loyalty.[28]

Then Chamberlain rose to address the mass gathering. 'You have been friends to the English', he said, 'and the English do not forget their friends.' He had received their address 'with very great pleasure'; he thanked them for their loyalty during the war, and had 'taken note' of the points they had put to him. While he could not undertake to hand over Polfontein, he nevertheless believed that the Cape authorities would be prepared to listen to representations about possible alternatives. On the question of compensation for war losses, he was willing to look into this further. But he then gave what was taken as a firm commitment on the future protection of the rights the Barolong currently enjoyed under the terms of their annexation to the colony. 'I have the assurance of the Prime Minister of the Cape Colony', he declared, 'that these rights shall not be altered in the slightest respect.' As Plaatje would point out later, the assurance seemed doubly secure since it was delivered in the presence not only of the prime minister, Sir Gordon Sprigg, but also the governor and attorney general, all three of them sitting on the platform as the colonial secretary spoke. Sir Walter Hely-Hutchinson, the governor, is unlikely to have made the connection between the capable young interpreter now before him and the affidavits that had passed over his desk a little over a year previously.[29]

Plaatje was delighted with the ways things had gone, for in truth the Barolong stole the show. Chamberlain spent as much time in the company of Africans as whites; he addressed the Barolong in their own surroundings in the stadt, one of the few occasions during his tour when he was prepared to make such a gesture;

above all, he had given an unambiguous public assurance on their future rights and status. The *Diamond Fields Advertiser* was in no doubt that the Barolong had scored a considerable political victory. On their future status, it said, they had obtained 'the fullest assurances' from the mouth of His Majesty's secretary of state for the colonies, while the 'noble stand of the Barolong against the disruption of the Cape Colony, should provide Sir Gordon [Sprigg] with material for an epic'. 'From the Ministerial point of view', concluded the *Advertiser*, 'they saved the situation.' The sight of half the Cape administration applauding the Barolong to cover up their embarrassment at the attitude of the whites of Mafeking, some of whom refused to meet with the colonial secretary, was most gratifying: Chamberlain's 'only friends', Plaatje wrote later, 'were the Barolong', while the prime minister, Sir Gordon Sprigg, found himself more at home with them 'than amongst his own people'. Apart from a predictable response on the question of Polfontein, things could hardly have gone better. Loyalty seemed at last to be paying dividends, even if the cost of the formal presentations expected of them stretched their resources to the limit.[30]

Ten days later Plaatje received a more personal memento of Chamberlain's visit to Mafeking: a signed testimonial stating that he had carried out the work of interpreting in the Barolong stadt that day 'in a very satisfactory manner'. Plaatje was of course no stranger to high-ranking British military officers – he had testimonials from them too – but it was not every day that one interpreted for a British secretary of state for the colonies. There would be one other bonus. Several weeks later Messrs Mallett and Bowen, the lawyers in Kimberley whom he commissioned to draw up the petitions to be presented to Chamberlain, wrote to take out a subscription to *Koranta ea Becoana*. Clearly they anticipated more business from the Barolong of Mafeking, and knew where it was likely to come from.[31]

✦✧✦

During the months following Joseph Chamberlain's visit to Mafeking, the war losses compensation question remained an urgent preoccupation. Nothing came of his vague undertaking to look into things, and Plaatje wrote several strongly worded editorials for *Koranta ea Becoana* complaining about how the Barolong had been treated. The very least the government could do to show its appreciation of the contribution and sacrifices of the Barolong during the siege, he argued, would be to pay full and proper compensation for the losses they sustained in defence of the empire in its hour of need. Plaatje had spent a lot of time when still employed in the magistrate's office in Mafeking in dealing with compensation claims and was familiar with the intricacies. He was determined not to let the matter drop without doing all within his power to help the Barolong obtain their due (although he did admit, in the Setswana columns of *Koranta*, that their case was not strengthened by some fraudulent claims).[32]

Eventually, in August 1903, the Barolong decided to send a deputation to Cape Town to press their case, as the whole subject was due to be discussed in the Cape House of Assembly. The deputation was composed of Chief Lekoko, Silas Molema, Badirile Montshiwa (shortly to succeed his father Wessels Montshiwa as paramount chief) and Plaatje himself. During the month they spent in Cape Town, they enjoyed the hospitality and support of F.Z.S. Peregrino, editor of the *South African Spectator*, and from his residence in Newlands they mounted an energetic lobbying campaign among sympathetic members of parliament. These included Henry Burton, now the member of parliament for Burgersdorp, who was highly critical of the treatment of the Barolong at the hands of the Compensation Commission; the three members of parliament who represented the Bechuanaland constituencies; and Dr Jameson, soon to become prime minister of the colony, well known to Silas Molema at least by virtue of their business arrangement of eight years previously.

The members of the deputation went about their task with skill and determination. They secured interviews with the prime minister and attorney general, enlisted the support and sympathy of the *Cape Argus*, refused to be satisfied with vague promises to look into their grievances, and managed to get the prime minister to sanction a formal reinvestigation of their claims. Even the *Mafeking Mail*, which rarely had a good word for the doings of the Barolong or the views of *Koranta*, was impressed: 'they exhibited an astuteness', declared the *Mail*, 'that must have called forth admiration from the Premier', and went on to express its own admiration for the way in which the deputation refused to be fobbed off with a promise by the prime minister that he would 'confer with his colleagues and see to it, etc. etc.'.[33]

Given Plaatje's recent record, the deputation's 'astuteness' probably owed much to his guidance. At the same time, their visit to Cape Town provided invaluable experience in refining his skills as a political lobbyist and negotiator at the highest levels of government. Few black South Africans, indeed, were to become so skilled in dealing with white politicians, so aware of the constraints upon them, so discerning of the possibilities that nevertheless existed. In a striking manner it marked, too, the distance he had come since he was last in Cape Town to sit those civil service examinations in December 1900, less than three years previously. As the *Cape Argus* commented at the time, 'the young Barolong editor' of *Koranta Becoana* had 'made good use of his opportunities'.[34]

✦

Over the next couple of years Plaatje came to be noticeably more concerned with issues which went well beyond the immediate interests of the people among whom he lived. From the beginning he had displayed a concern for the rights and well-being of the African population of South Africa as a whole, and he often emphasised, in the columns of *Koranta ea Becoana*, that their loyalty during the recent war deserved proper recognition. He was constantly criticising the actions of government departments or administrators, the utterances of illiberal white newspaper editors, the decisions of biased white juries; or commending, in contrast, sympathetic white missionaries prepared to make a stand for African rights, or high court judges prepared to uphold the ideal of equal rights before the law in the face of established custom and practice.

The high court judges in particular attracted his admiration, none more so than Johannes Lange and Perceval Laurence in two cases heard in the Griqualand West High Court late in 1902: *R* v. *Willem Gabriel Visser* and *R* v. *Jan Cloete and Johannes Koekemoer*. In both, Boer combatants were charged with murdering blacks in the latter stages of the war and found guilty, notwithstanding their plea that they had acted on the orders of superior officers. In the second case, where there was no recommendation for mercy, Judge Laurence stated, in the course of a lengthy judgment, that 'the fact that equal justice was meted out to all, irrespective of race and creed' was the most important thing in holding the empire together – scarcely a trivial matter.[35]

Plaatje reported the judgments at length in the columns of *Koranta*, and in both English and Setswana. Judge Laurence's peroration, he wrote, 'immensely captivated the minds of our readers', and he had received a number of letters 'teeming with words of highest praise'. Just as before, however, Plaatje now courted unpopularity by arguing that the two men in the second case were also entitled to a reprieve, pointing to the judgment of Justice Solomon in the Maritz case in which his own evidence had been so crucial. The two judges, Plaatje pointed out, had taken a rather different view over the circumstances in which it was reasonable to expect a combatant in wartime to know whether an order given to him was legal or illegal.[36]

Personal experience as much as legal precedent led him to his conclusion: 'From our observations of military rule during the last few years', he wrote, 'a soldier has no opportunity to reflect whether an officer's orders are obviously (or observedly) illegal, so we think that the two condemned prisoners are strongly entitled to a reprieve.' This was not a view that met with universal approval. Several people wrote in to express 'serious exception' to the line he took, including Joseph Gape, who thought Plaatje guilty of abandoning African interests, dismayed that he 'would suddenly give way and sacrifice our cause for the sake of a cruel and relentless race'. In due course the two men were reprieved, their sentences commuted to periods of imprisonment. Reconciliation between Boer and Briton was now the priority in government and there was no longer any reason to make an example of the two men.

Plaatje, however, had made his point and he was not swayed by the criticism. And of course it worked both ways. He followed up his plea for leniency for these Boer prisoners with a demand for the release of the Batswana chief Galeshewe, still imprisoned after his abortive 'rebellion' in 1897. If Boer rebels could be treated leniently, surely it was high time to release the chief from imprisonment? And if the Boer 'rebels' were allowed to retain possession of their farms, then surely Galeshewe had a case for restitution of the lands confiscated from him and his followers? Within months Galeshewe and his followers were set free.[37]

Liberal high court judges prepared to take seriously the notion of 'equal rights before the law' in the Cape Colony were one thing. The policies and behaviour of the new British administrations in the Transvaal and Orange River colonies, it was becoming clear, were quite another. For it was here that the contrast between the hopes engendered among Africans during the war and the realities of what happened in its aftermath was most marked. In the absence of any means of direct political representation for Africans living in these colonies, *Koranta* and its editor came to play an important role in drawing attention to their disabilities and grievances. Plaatje himself, indeed, spent an increasing amount of time travelling in these two colonies, observing conditions and campaigning personally on behalf of Africans who lived there over such issues as their treatment in the courts and on the railways, or the discriminatory practices condoned by the municipality of Bloemfontein and other bodies, often to very good effect. And, of course, the higher his profile the more *Koranta ea Becoana* was likely to prosper and attract new readers.[38]

Above all, it was the British administration of the Transvaal, devoted to the reconstruction of the colony in collaboration with the mine owners, that became the focus of his campaigning. One of the worst features of this administration, from the point of view of Africans living in the colony, was the way it implemented the pass laws. When British troops occupied Johannesburg during the war, many had celebrated by burning their passes, expecting to be freed from such burdensome controls on their movement. Instead they were now enforced far more vigorously than they ever were in the days of the South African Republic. 'The benefit of the Pass Law', Plaatje said in one editorial, 'is that thousands of useful unoffending black men, than whom His Majesty has no more law abiding subjects, are daily sent to prison, without having done harm to anybody, and they die as regular gaol-birds even though they had never, during their lifetime, dipped the tips of their fingers in the cup of criminality.' He contrasted the situation in Johannesburg with that of Mafeking ('where the jailor has no such snare and where revenue is raised by honest and lawful means'), concluding with the observation that if there was any 'Native unrest' in the Transvaal, 'it is the outcome of the callous and oppressive administration of the Pass Law'.[39]

Criticism of the arbitrary behaviour of native commissioners and sub-commissioners in the Transvaal also came to fill *Koranta*'s columns. Plaatje published a number of letters of complaint from those who had suffered at their hands, and he devoted several editorials to the subject. 'All the Natives who write to us from the Pietersburg district', *Koranta* said in April 1904, 'unanimously declare that they were far better off under the Field Cornets of the late Government than what they are under the sub-Native Commissioners, as we are sure that never was the name of her late Gracious Majesty, Victoria, dragged in the mire like now, when the cruelty of those officials drives it into the minds of the black people, who lost their life and property to establish British rule in their country, that her reign is worse than Krugerism.' Another time he witnessed this disillusionment himself, writing later of the misery and hardships which attended the Johannesburg municipality's removal of Africans to Nancefield, and of his memory of hearing 'Native viragoes loudly lamenting the fall of Kruger and cursing the new administration, which they termed "remorseless tyrants"' (*batana li-sitihogo*, literally, 'cruel beasts of prey').[40]

In one institution, though, Plaatje retained confidence, the courts of law, and he was heartened by the appointment of two well-known liberals to the key legal positions in the Transvaal: Sir Richard Solomon as senior law adviser and then attorney general, and Sir James Rose Innes, chief justice of the new Supreme Court. His response to nearly every instance of injustice he encountered or exposed was to advise those concerned to turn to the law to seek redress of their grievances. Nobody, indeed, had a keener eye for the contradictions between the theory and practice of British rule in the new colonies, and the possibilities that lay in exploiting the gap in-between; and the Supreme Court, it turned out, was by no means averse to overruling magisterial sentences on appeal. For many Africans, of course, the financial obstacles to legal recourse were too great a deterrent for them even to contemplate action of this kind, but on some occasions it did prove successful.[41]

One such episode in which Plaatje was involved concerned the rights of African residents of the Transvaal to purchase land in their own name. Until 1904 this had been prevented by native commissioners on the grounds that the laws of the Boer republics had prohibited it, and that the law in question had not been repealed and therefore remained in force. Plaatje, however, had not been convinced. He 'searched the Transvaal Law Book from cover to cover, but failed to find in it a single ordinance prohibiting the sale of land to Natives', and decided to take up the case. The opportunity arose in the refusal of the local native commissioner for the Johannesburg district to allow prospective standholders in the new Kensington Township to acquire proper legal title for the plots of land which they had already paid for. 'Acting on our advice', *Koranta* stated in its issue of 13 April 1904, the majority of them refused to be intimidated by the 'written word of a snow-white Government official that the laws of the country were against us', and Paulus Malaji, chairman of the Basuto Association in Johannesburg, made a test case of it. It was some months before the case was heard in court, but the decision, when it came, was in their favour. The letter Plaatje received from the solicitors who were involved, informing him of the decision, was, he said, 'the best letter that ever reached us by the Johannesburg mail since the declaration of peace'. Several weeks later one of *Koranta*'s readers composed a praise poem to celebrate the victory.[42]

᠊ᠬᡃᠵ

Within a couple of years of taking over the editorship of *Koranta ea Becoana*, Plaatje had built up a reputation as an influential journalist and the spokesman for a far wider body of people than had been the case before. If at one time he had been considered as a representative of the Barolong in Mafikeng – and he would always be regarded as their special spokesman – now he was coming to be accepted not only as one who spoke for the Batswana in the various colonies of South Africa where they lived, but as a man who could now claim a political constituency and readership for his paper, which extended well beyond this.

There were tensions, however, and the question of just who *Koranta* was for, and whose interests it should represent, was by no means uncontested. On one occasion John Tolk, one of the paper's agents in the Orange River Colony, wrote to complain that he was losing readers because the paper was too preoccupied with the affairs of the Barolong. He thought it would help to change the title of the paper to 'Koranta ea Bancho' ('The Black People's Gazette') and hence to appeal to blacks of all backgrounds.

Plaatje was not ready to do this. While it was difficult to deny that the Barolong had pride of place in his columns, he was clear his first task was to appeal to Tswana-speakers. This was his core readership. Addressing the concerns of Tswana-speakers in their own language meant he could speak directly to them, and it helped ensure the support of the chiefs, vital to the enterprise. Setswana was thus a crucial resource, the organic link between the educated leadership, chiefs and people, and the means of building up their communal strength and identity. To seek to go beyond Setswana in search of more readers, and to use other African languages in the columns of *Koranta*, was to risk satisfying nobody, Plaatje thought, and he responded to Tolk's complaint with the story of the man, the boy and the donkey (one of Aesop's fables) to illustrate his point. Try to please all and you will please none – you would no more want a newspaper without readers than to be left with a dead donkey.[43]

Koranta did of course use one other language – English. It was this that enabled him to reach beyond Tswana-speakers, and it was often the medium he used when taking up the grievances of Africans living in the Transvaal and Orange River Colony. Plaatje's own attitudes and outlook were also crucial in extending *Koranta*'s appeal. If one believed in the notions of equal opportunity for all subjects of the British empire and equality before the law, as he often stated in his editorials, then it followed that these had to apply to everybody, Tswana-speakers or not. Such a combination of factors also ensured that, politically speaking, Plaatje never became a prisoner either of the relatively privileged circumstances of the Cape Colony or of too exclusive an association with the interests of the Barolong or the Batswana more generally. His horizons extended well beyond the stadt in Mafeking and the intricacies of Cape electoral politics with which he had grown so familiar in the 1890s, and he never forgot his family's roots in the old Orange Free State.

For these same reasons he was also well placed to take the initiative in establishing a Native Press Association to seek to advance unity among the African press as a whole. Partly this was inspired by their recent growth in numbers. In April 1903 the Rev. John Dube, a Zulu, had founded *Ilanga lase Natal* ('The Natal Sun'), published in Ohlange, Natal; in Pietersburg, in the northern Transvaal, Levi Khomo, like Plaatje a former interpreter, now edited *Leihlo lo Babatsho* ('The Native Eye'), the only paper among all his exchanges, Plaatje remembered, which he could not fully understand; and in Pietermaritzburg, Natal, *Ipepa lo Hlanga* ('The Paper of the Nation'), closed down in 1901, was now being published once more.[44]

Despite their dispersal in the different colonies and regions of South Africa and their often considerable political differences, these newspaper editors shared an identifiable sense of common purpose. They all struggled financially, grappled with the same issues, quoted each other's opinions, rejoiced in their different triumphs, sympathised with their trials and tribulations. They were united in a desire to develop and give expression to 'native opinion', at a time in the affairs of the subcontinent when this seemed a particularly important and worthwhile thing to be doing. The more they could speak with a common voice, they believed, the more likely they were to be heard. Late in 1903, therefore, Plaatje, together with F.Z.S. Peregrino (his host on the Barolong war compensation mission to Cape Town that August), proposed that a Native Press Association be formed to develop and give institutional form to the sense of community that existed between them.[45]

Quite where the idea came from is uncertain. Possibly it was modelled on the National Afro-American Press Association, which Plaatje could have heard about from J.E. Bruce, or through the exchange newspapers he received from the United States. Plaatje, by far the youngest of these newspapermen, became secretary of the new organisation, Silas Molema its treasurer, while A.K. Soga (editor of *Izwi* and younger son of Tiyo Soga) and F.Z.S. Peregrino (*South African Spectator*) were president and vice president respectively. They called their new organisation the South African Native Press Association, its motto was 'Defence, not defiance', and their purpose, Plaatje declared, 'was to improve the press of the Natives generally'. Its constitution was more expansive: it aimed 'to encourage and to seek to aid all who are engaged in the laudable work of diffusing knowledge and in legitimate educational work among the Natives of South Africa, to seek to cooperate with the Government in the solution of the many difficult race problems by which they are confronted, and to help to bring about understanding, and to establish amiable relations between the various Governments of South Africa, and the Native population'.[46]

Several meetings of the South African Native Press Association were convened, but its subsequent history is obscure. It was in existence a year later, in October 1904, but probably ceased functioning effectively not long after. That it should have struggled is no surprise. Political unity remained an elusive goal, and it did not help that Tengo Jabavu, editor of *Imvo*, remained aloof from the organisation. They were all plagued by financial difficulties and the practical obstacles that stood in the way of an organisation representing newspapers from so wide an area posed a huge challenge. It is nevertheless revealing that Plaatje should have been so involved, and that his fellow editors were willing for him to take a leading role in its affairs. In several respects the Native Press Association, premature at the time, was a portent of things to come.

There was precious little fellow feeling between the black newspaper editors and their white counterparts, however. Often the European press portrayed them as jumped-up, semi-educated barbarians who ought to know better than to express views on current affairs or to criticise their superiors. The African newspapermen, for their part, coped well enough with the insults thrown at them, and Plaatje for one delighted in doing battle with his white contemporaries in the columns of *Koranta ea Becoana*. The Bloemfontein *Friend* – Plaatje christened it 'The Foe' – was a frequent adversary, and its editor and correspondents were not accustomed to restraint when commenting upon what they read in African newspapers. Missionaries, so one article proclaimed early in 1903, were to blame for giving Africans ideas beyond their station, the British army had contributed to the problem by 'chumming with niggers, and – I regret to say – negresses', and it was 'now time for us to bring the native back to the status he was placed in before the war'. 'The first step in that direction', it suggested, 'would be the suppression of all the nigger papers, for they are spreading a propaganda throughout the country which is the cause of all the trouble in the native question, i.e. the fact that the native is equal to the white man. I am not in favour of slavery, but I think the time has come to place a firm hand on the native and put him in his place, and keep him there.' Plaatje was singled out for special mention: 'I dare say if some of us could get at the editor of *Koranta ea Becoana*, what was left of him would be nil.'[47]

Such was the climate of opinion in at least some parts of post-war South Africa in which *Koranta* and the other African newspapers had to operate. Plaatje's response to 'The Foe' on this occasion was rather more dignified: 'Woe betide this country', he concluded in reply, 'if the farming colonist would be misled by the drift of mischievous penmanship, which is strictly guided by pernicious designs, the outcome of prejudice and misrepresentation.'[48]

The Bloemfontein *Friend* was the most intemperate of *Koranta*'s opponents (at least until there was a change of ownership late in 1903), but it was by no means alone in taking the paper's editor to task for exceeding his supposed station in life. The *Natal Witness*, for example, took exception to *Koranta*'s articles on 'the alleged harsh treatment of natives', accusing both Plaatje and Tengo Jabavu, editor of *Imvo*, of ingratitude towards the British, 'the race to which they and theirs owe everything, and which has fostered, to an almost continental extent, progress among the natives of the subcontinent'. The *Bechuanaland News* (Vryburg) went further. It thought *Koranta*'s attitude towards the government was 'to say the least, extremely discourteous, if not offensive', and that it 'encourages disaffection leading to disloyalty, and is evidently inspired by the Ethiopian ideas which are abroad, and becoming so prevalent in Native Society'.[49]

Closer to home there was the *Mafeking Mail* to contend with. Despite their former connection, the *Mail*'s occasional references to the pronouncements of its local contemporary would sometimes descend to outright abuse. Once it went further, describing an article Plaatje had carried in *Koranta* on the administration of the Transvaal and Orange Free State as 'seditious', and it quoted with approval some strong comments from one of the Johannesburg papers on the matter: 'Disloyalty, now-a-days, is the refuge of the ignorant. It has sunk down to the level of a Kaffir pastime. The editor of the Mafeking Kaffir newspaper, "Koranta ea Becoana", is a studious person who used to interpret at the Magistrate's Court. He got into the habit of thinking during the course of his duties, and a lot of stored up, compressed thought drove him into journalism as an outlet for it. Thinking, however, is a bad thing to get into late in life, if you haven't been used to it before. One is apt to get a wrong perspective, and when he complains of British rule it is an evidence of it.' The *Mail*'s solution to the problem? 'It would be merciful if a little of the cat o' nine tails were applied now.'[50]

The picture was not always one of outright hostility, however. Plaatje enjoyed a good personal relationship with G.A.L. Green, editor of the *Diamond Fields Advertiser*, which would sometimes include extracts from *Koranta* as bona fide expressions of 'native opinion' and worthy of a hearing. The *Cape Argus* supported the Barolong campaign for payment of war losses compensation, and reported in a friendly manner on their mission to Cape Town. Most striking of all were the favourable comments Plaatje received in the normally indifferent or hostile Dutch-language press when he argued in favour of a reprieve for Jan Cloete and Johannes Koekemoer, the two Boers sentenced to death in the Griqualand West High Court at the end of 1902.

From the official authorities in the colonies in which *Koranta* circulated, the response was generally quite measured and proper, even though Plaatje did not hesitate to criticise their actions when he felt this was necessary. In Mafeking he continued to enjoy a good relationship with the civil commissioner, E. Graham Green; it was on his recommendation that the government supplied notices and proclamations for publication in the columns of *Koranta*, and it was thanks to him that Plaatje got a useful government contract in 1904 to print ten thousand copies of a Tswana-language pamphlet explaining the purpose of the census that year. Plaatje valued this not simply for the revenue it brought in, but because it was implicit recognition of that intermediary role between government and people to which all the African newspapermen aspired.[51]

Plaatje provided the Cape authorities with a copy of each issue of his newspaper, and they seem to have been read carefully. From time to time he would also send them particular articles for their consideration. Once this was on the treatment of Africans on the railways. To this he received a comprehensive reply from E. Graham Green (instructed by the secretary for native affairs in Cape Town), advising him that 'exhaustive enquiries have been made into the matter represented by you', and that steps had already been taken to prevent a recurrence of the instances of ill-treatment, about which there had been other complaints. It indicated that the Cape authorities – and this was true of those of the Transvaal and Orange River Colony as well – were prepared to take seriously matters he brought to their attention, and to treat him with consideration and courtesy.[52]

On only one occasion during these years was this generally quite cordial relationship called into question. It happened when a letter from Segale Pilane, a Tswana chief living in the Transvaal, complaining about British rule in somewhat stronger terms than usual, was published in *Koranta* in August 1903. The authorities took strong exception to the 'disloyal' sentiments expressed, particularly as they came from a chief who had been a strong supporter of the British during the war. It turned out that the letter had been published when Plaatje himself was away in Cape Town; they were quite satisfied with a suitable expression of regret and a promise that such a thing would not happen again. Apart from generating an enormous amount of correspondence, the matter was not actually taken too seriously: 'if I gave currency to every utterance circulated in the "Koranta"', explained Ralph Williams, resident commissioner for the Bechuanaland Protectorate, in a letter to the high commissioner, 'Your Excellency would weary of my dispatches'. Whoever it was that deputised in the *Koranta* office when Plaatje was away in Cape Town had some lessons to learn about where the line was drawn between sedition and free speech and to be able to recognise when it was crossed.[53]

For the most part the colonial authorities were well aware of the value of the African newspapers in providing a channel for the expression of opinion that was far better expressed openly than suppressed, even at a time of intense official concern over the dangers of 'Ethiopianism' and more general fears of a 'native uprising'. Herbert Sloley, for example, Ralph Williams's opposite number in Basutoland, thought that since 'the native press in South Africa is always going to be with us', it was 'quite as well to know what they are thinking about'. In truth the colonial authorities had little need to worry. Plaatje and his fellow newspapermen were invariably moderate in their views and they chose their words carefully; Plaatje, moreover, was openly critical of ministers of the

African Methodist Episcopal Church, the organisation most closely associated with 'Ethiopianism', and he had not hesitated to express his concerns in person to Bishop Levi Coppin, head of the church in South Africa, when he visited Mafeking in May 1903.[54]

So the authorities saw the African press as a useful means of keeping potentially volatile African opinion on strictly constitutional lines in seeking redress of their grievances. Plaatje may have been critical of the British administrations of the Transvaal and Orange River colonies in the immediate post-war years, but it was criticism expressed in terms of common political assumptions and conventions. He would not for a moment have associated himself with the 'Ethiopian' fantasies of the white South African imagination, or advocated the kind of armed conflict that erupted in Natal at the time of the Bambatha Rebellion in 1906 – any more than he had supported Galeshewe's 'rebellion' in 1897. His preferred methods, rather, were reasoned discussion and argument and the presentation of irrefutable evidence, taking advantage of such constitutional channels as existed, resorting to the law courts when they did not.

There was good reason, therefore, for the various governmental authorities in southern Africa to tolerate Plaatje and his fellow newspapermen, however irritating they found the criticism directed towards them. Such, indeed, was the conclusion of the South African Native Affairs Commission, set up to try to find a basis for a common 'native policy' across the colonies of the subcontinent, when it reported in 1905. The 'native press' had 'on the whole proved itself to be fairly accurate in tracing the course of passing events and useful in extending the range of native information'; even if, it added, 'an infant press could not be expected to be wholly free from mistakes and indiscretions'. A minority of the members of the commission favoured the enactment of some form of legal control over the African press, but the resolutions to this effect were not carried: 'freedom of thought and speech within lawful limits', the report concluded, 'is not lightly to be assailed'. In this space Plaatje and his colleagues carried on their business of informing, educating, criticising. With the future shape of South Africa still to be decided there was every incentive for them to do so.[55]

⚬

The reasoned tone of government reports, and the civil behaviour of many politicians and senior administrators, rarely extended to the lower levels of officialdom, particularly in the Transvaal and Orange River Colony. Here well-educated Africans like Plaatje were liable to be regarded with suspicion or condescension, and sometimes subjected to personal abuse. Their very existence was an affront to poorly educated white employees whose main qualification for their job was often their white skin. A visit to a police station, pass office or the like was thus a hazard to be negotiated with some care, particularly if a successful outcome depended upon the discretion of the official concerned.

Plaatje was all too aware of the dynamics of such encounters, and willing where necessary to act in a suitably deferential manner. He knew 'exactly when and where', he said, 'to "take off his hat"' in accordance with prevailing custom and prejudice. But there were limits to what he was prepared to put up with and they were reached one day late in April 1904 when he had occasion to visit the police station in Lichtenburg, a small town just across the Transvaal border. He needed to establish whether his Cape passport required endorsement to enable him to travel in the Transvaal. On arrival, however, he was met with a stream of abuse from one of the officers on duty. Taken aback, his reaction was to step outside the building, take out his notebook, and write down ('in order that there should be no misunderstanding') exactly what was said to him, which included the following: 'Take off your hat you damned, bloody dirty black swine! And always wait till you are spoken to!!' He proceeded instead to Klerksdorp where his enquiry was satisfactorily dealt with, 'unaccompanied by thunder'.

Two weeks later, when in Johannesburg, Plaatje wrote to complain about his treatment to Sir Richard Solomon, the attorney general. Reporting the abuse he was subjected to and the circumstances in which it took place, he concluded: 'I may add for your information that I am not quite sure whether or not I am "damned", but of the following I am quite certain, viz., (1) I had no blood stains on me, at the time; (2) I was not dirty, while I need hardly add that (3) I was not a pig. I transacted business with half a dozen businessmen in Lichtenburg, directly before and after this episode, none of whom objected to my appearance.' 'I think, Sir, you will agree with me', he concluded, 'that it is lamentable that a stranger should be treated kindly by the villagers and that he should regret ever having set foot in a public office, and for this reason I trust that you will enquire into the matter.'

Since the attorney general did not have formal responsibility for police matters, his private secretary passed on the letter to the inspector general, South African Constabulary, informing Plaatje that Sir Richard was sure he would 'enquire into the matter and if the story told is true deal with the officer capable of using language such as is reported'. What happened thereafter, and whether the police officer concerned was ever reprimanded, is unknown, but he can have scarcely expected that details of his abusive language, doubtless an everyday occurrence, would have ended up on the attorney general's desk in Pretoria.

Plaatje's reaction to the incident, though, was quite in character. While he was outraged at the 'extraordinary treatment' he encountered, he kept calm, recorded the evidence in his notebook, and then wrote to the attorney general, the highest legal officer in the colony, fully expecting him to consider the incident as distasteful as he did. The tone of his letter was respectful but forceful and to the point. No doubt it helped that he had known the attorney general when both were in Kimberley in the 1890s. But now he was not so much asking Sir Richard a personal favour as drawing his attention to the incident and presenting him with what amounted to a detailed witness statement. His confident assumption that Sir Richard would wish to have the matter investigated was entirely justified.[56]

Of course things could get a lot worse. Plaatje had witnessed innumerable instances of assault that had ended up in the magistrate's court, and would have known of plenty that had not. He himself was once assaulted by British soldiers in Mafeking and was fortunate to have suffered no serious after-effects. Another time he was assaulted by 'the woman in charge of the Refreshment bar and her native servant' at Vryburg railway station. A year later, however, his brother-in-law Isaiah Bud-M'belle was seriously injured in an unprovoked assault in a Kimberley thoroughfare, and took many months to recover from the head injuries he suffered. The threat of physical violence, in short, was never very far beneath the surface in early twentieth-century South Africa, and the Cape Colony was clearly not immune. It was a constant reminder of the prejudices that festered in colonial society – and the scale of the challenge that faced Plaatje and his colleagues in attempting to bring about change. Taking off your hat was no answer to the bigger problem.[57]

Broader political developments gave little cause for optimism. The British imperial government, intent on reaching a rapprochement with the defeated Boer republics, was anxious to grant them self-government at the earliest opportunity. In contrast to the high hopes generated during the war years, there now seemed only the remotest prospect that Africans living in the Transvaal and Orange River colonies would be given any form of franchise in the new constitutions that would soon be devised. What Plaatje wanted was for the two colonies to adopt the non-racial Cape franchise, and it was only after this had been agreed, he felt, that the question of self-government should be considered. 'On this side of the border', he wrote in an editorial in *Koranta* in October 1904, referring to the situation in the Cape Colony, 'we have that expensive little asset, the franchise, which to us is worth a jew's eye. We ourselves are too few to do anything with it, but knowing that we possess it, the Colonists treat our people very well.'[58]

Just as disturbing were the signs of a new consensus in favour of segregation as the basis for a uniform 'native policy'. Segregation generally meant two things: separate occupation of land as between black and white, and the provision of separate means of political representation, designed to maintain white economic and political domination. Whatever the differences between Boer and Briton during the late war, the vast majority of whites were united on this last point. In such a scheme of things, Africans were to provide an adequate supply of labour for white farmers and mine owners, while their political aspirations were to be confined to the 'reserves' where most of them would live, and control of affairs of state would remain firmly in white hands. Both were part of the British scheme for a unified southern Africa, and to some at least it was clear that, in the long run, there could be no place for the non-racial Cape franchise or for those Africans who believed, like Plaatje, in the notion of 'equal rights for all civilised men' and who looked to play a role themselves in the affairs of their country.

The most important milestone on this path towards segregation was the South African Native Affairs Commission of 1903–5. Members of the commission travelled extensively throughout southern Africa, taking both written and oral evidence from a wide variety of organisations and individuals, black and white, before publishing their report in 1905. Plaatje, as it happened, was among those who gave evidence to the commission when it visited Mafeking in September 1904. Their encounter – the questions put to him, the answers he gave – was a revealing cameo of worldviews in collision, the segregationist assumptions of the commissioners at odds with the beliefs of an older Cape liberal tradition and the integrity of a self-governing African chiefdom, which Plaatje articulated.

He was not impressed by how they went about their task. He criticised the composition of the commission on the grounds that it was unrepresentative, and he was unhappy about the way they arrived in Mafeking unannounced. He was only able 'to attend at a sacrifice', he complained, while some of his 'friends who were prepared to give evidence only heard about them when they were leaving'. He regretted too that, unlike most visitors, they had not found time to visit the stadt or the offices of *Koranta ea Becoana* so as 'to see and encourage a small band of Bechuanas editing, printing and publishing their own newspaper under their own vine and tree'.[59]

But this was not a social visit. The commission's purpose was to elicit information that would help to frame their recommendations for a uniform 'native policy' for southern Africa, and the commissioners had done their homework. One of them, Captain Quayle Dickson, principal native commissioner in the Orange River Colony, was familiar with Plaatje's newspaper, knew he had 'written rather strongly ... about the treatment of Natives in the mines', and proceeded to question him about it. He was aware, too, that Plaatje had criticised the activities of some ministers of the Ethiopian Church and was pleased to discover that he had not altered his views on the matter.[60]

Questions from other commissioners on the subject of the franchise had an obvious enough agenda ('Do you not think that the time of election stirs up hostile feelings between black and white people?'), but they failed to deter Plaatje from offering a spirited defence of the existing non-racial Cape franchise, nor did they persuade him that a polygamist should be deprived of the franchise if otherwise qualified. 'While he has his obligations to the state as well as any other civilized man he is entitled to it,' Plaatje asserted, agreeing with a statement made by Chief Badirile Montshiwa. One of the other commissioners, F.R. ('Matabele') Thompson, complimented him on having answered his cross-examination 'very fearlessly and well' – before trying, without success, to get him to admit that not all Barolong were capable of exercising their right to the franchise 'intelligently and honestly'. Plaatje knew perfectly well that the existence of the Cape franchise was a central political issue, the major obstacle, as it was perceived in ruling circles, to the creation of a uniform 'native policy' for southern Africa. He was not going to allow himself to be seduced by flattery of this kind.[61]

Important as the Report of the South African Native Affairs Commission would be as a future blueprint, in 1904 and 1905 its practical implications were not fully apparent, and its transformation into government policy would come only after the unification of the four South African colonies in the Union of South Africa. That remained some years off. For now the political priority, as Plaatje saw it, was the incorporation of a franchise similar to that of the Cape into the new constitutions of the Transvaal and Orange River colonies while there was still a chance to do so – and meanwhile to build up the strength of the Batswana as best as he could.

By the beginning of 1905 Plaatje could look back on a very successful two and a half years as editor of *Koranta ea Becoana*. The paper had appeared regularly, it was read widely, and it carried an impressive range of articles and editorials in his characteristically vigorous prose, framing, as it were, his selections from other newspapers from home and abroad. It was a source of pride for all those associated with it, a beacon of hope for the future. In a relatively short space of time Plaatje had emerged as an influential public figure and a powerful, independent voice, experienced in dealing with politicians and administrators at the highest levels. He was accepted as a spokesman not only of the Barolong but of a much wider

African political constituency spread out across the northern Cape, the Transvaal and Orange River colonies, and the Bechuanaland Protectorate. He had done all he could to promote a sense of common feeling among those who spoke Setswana and to use English to reach out to those who did not. Few would now deny that Vere Stent's prediction that Plaatje would 'some day be a power amongst your people' had already been realised. And he was still not thirty years of age.

Only with hindsight would it be clear that the end of 1904 marked the high point of a very brave venture. From now on, simply keeping *Koranta ea Becoana* afloat would become an increasingly desperate and all-consuming struggle. A hint of what lay ahead came in *Koranta*'s issue of 21 December 1904: 'It is with great satisfaction', Plaatje announced, 'that we are able to tell our readers that we have survived the trial and financial struggle of a most trying year. Indeed, we confess that at one time we have almost felt inclined to throw up the sponge, but here we are at the beginning of the year, alive and kicking.' Only just, however.

SEVEN

Koranta ea Becoana and after, 1905–1910

K *oranta ea Becoana* always struggled to get enough paying readers. Its fundamental problem, as with its African contemporaries, was that its circulation, and accordingly its revenue from subscriptions and advertising, was limited by poverty and low levels of literacy. Given the relatively small size of the Tswana population, and the sparse missionary activity among them, the problem was more acute for *Koranta* than it was for the two eastern Cape newspapers. Moreover, *Koranta*, unlike *Imvo* and *Izwi*, did not receive a subsidy from one of the colony's main political parties, nor did it have wealthy white business backers such as sustained *Ilanga lase Natal*. Independence therefore came at a high cost. Several Batswana chiefs – Chief Bathoen of the Bangwaketse and Chief Israel Moiloa of the Bahurutse are known to be among them – were persuaded to purchase shares in the venture but this never raised sufficient sums, and *Koranta* always ran at a loss. It was kept afloat by the enthusiasm of those involved, and by Silas Molema's willingness and ability, so long as it lasted, to underwrite its costs of production.[1]

Plaatje was wholly committed to the paper. Before long he, like Molema, began to run up substantial personal debts to help meet *Koranta*'s running expenses, and he used to work extraordinarily long hours to ensure that it appeared regularly. At one time, so he recalled, he would work eighteen hours a day, including Sundays. Such a level of commitment arose from his conviction that 'our people need a mouthpiece' at what was a crucial time in their history, but also from the realisation that his own position of influence as a spokesman for his people was closely bound up with the survival of the newspaper. There were not many other means of earning a living open to him.[2]

In May 1903 Plaatje and Molema had felt sufficiently confident to purchase new freehold premises for *Koranta* (an office and workshop in Shippard Street, Mafeking). By the following year, however, they had run into difficulties and on at least one occasion Plaatje was forced to deny rumours that the paper was on the point of folding. It was only saved from going under by a huge £650 loan taken out jointly by Plaatje and Molema in July 1904 from Charles Wenham, a local trader, which involved mortgaging the entire printing works and paying interest at a rate of 12 per cent a year. Although no complete copies of *Koranta* have survived beyond the end of 1904, there are sufficient references to it in other newspapers to suggest that it appeared with reasonable regularity for most of 1905. In April the *Diamond Fields Advertiser* carried an extract from a recent issue of *Koranta* celebrating the defeat of 'Matabele' Thompson in the recent Barkly West election. Six months later it was complimenting *Koranta* on a 'new and amusing version of recent troubles in the Ethiopian church', reproducing a lengthy editorial criticising, not for the first time, the behaviour of some of the church's ministers ('For barefaced foolhardiness, some of the people commonly known as "Ethiopian Ministers" will take a lot to beat!').[3]

Two major issues are known to have preoccupied Plaatje at this time. Both must have have figured prominently in *Koranta ea Becoana*, and both in their different ways reveal much about the wider context and circumstances in which he carried on his work.

The first concerned the form and ownership of the Tswana language. There was no agreed orthography, no commonly accepted convention for representing the sounds of the Tswana language in written form, but plenty of conflicting views about what needed to be done. The only organisations producing books in Setswana were the missionary societies. Each had developed its own orthography, differing significantly from one another, and reflecting both the different Tswana dialects spoken in the areas in which they operated and the differing European languages (mainly English and German) used by the missionaries themselves. The orthography which Plaatje used in *Koranta ea Becoana* was different again, based upon that devised by Canon Crisp but adapted in accordance with his own views and the needs of his newspaper. It had been tried and tested in a corpus of written Setswana that by now far exceeded any other in extent and variety. His orthography, it is fair to say, had a bias towards the Tshidi Barolong dialect, justified in his view because he considered it one of the purest forms of the Tswana language.[4]

Although the need to achieve some measure of orthographic uniformity was widely recognised, there were a huge number of obstacles in the way. None of the interested parties was much disposed towards making concessions to other forms of usage. The issue became a pressing one, however, when it became known that the London Missionary Society (LMS), by far the largest missionary body operating among the Tswana, was revising the original Setswana translation of the Bible by J.S. Moffat. Along with missionaries from the Berlin and Hermannsburg societies, Plaatje was very concerned at the decision of the LMS to proceed with this without first seeking to ensure some wider agreement over its orthography, and at the end of 1906 he joined with a group of missionaries from the two German societies in broaching the matter with the LMS.

The move provoked a hostile response: A.J. Wookey, the missionary primarily responsible for the revision, expressed surprise that the Berlin and Hermannsburg missionaries should 'subjoin the signature of a man who calls himself "Sol Plaatje"'. Plaatje, he said, was 'the native editor of a not very respectable paper', who 'months ago [had] published a very scurrilous article on the revision and other things', and he thought he '*may* be engineering the present opposition'. His 'chief standing as expressed in his paper', he added, 'is not such as to recommend him for the work', and he regretted that he had been 'supported by those on the press who had attacked and tried to belittle the work of the B.S. [Bible Society] itself in Bechuanaland and Cape Colony'.[5]

Plaatje felt strongly over this linguistic issue, then as later, and criticised the LMS's policy of seeking to determine the form of the Tswana language without reference to native Tswana-speakers like himself. But there was already in existence, as Wookey's comments suggest, an undercurrent of bad feeling. Several of their missionaries, in particular W.C. Willoughby, principal of the LMS institution at Tigerkloof, near Vryburg, had come to resent the influence that *Koranta* and its editor had acquired, for the society had become accustomed to a near monopoly in the provision of education and literature for the Batswana, particularly in the Bechuanaland Protectorate itself. On one occasion, after *Koranta* reported (or misreported, claimed the LMS) hostile statements made by Willoughby about some former students of Lovedale, he had dismissed Plaatje's own very critical comments upon the affair as no more than 'the irresponsible utterances of the youth at the *Koranta ea Becoana* office'; and he took particular exception to the assertive motto that Plaatje carried at the head of every issue of *Koranta ea Becoana*. '"I am black but comely" was the proud boast', Willoughby would recall, 'that appeared in heavy type on the front page of every number of a Native newspaper that I often used to read.' Detecting evidence of 'Ethiopianism' in the whole business, Willoughby warned a fellow missionary that 'the influence of men like Sol Plaatje will prove harmful to you by introducing the spirit of Ba-Ethiopia even if it does not introduce the people themselves'.[6]

Missionaries like Willoughby and Wookey, it is clear, did not find it easy to accept forthright African spokesmen like Plaatje on anything approaching equal terms, whatever the issue involved. In their view, the expression of African aspirations was, for the time being at least, best left to their missionary mentors.

Plaatje, for his part, had on several other occasions carried articles in *Koranta* that were critical of the shortcomings of the LMS in the educational field, and at a meeting in Mafeking in October 1908 he was reported to have expressed the view that the LMS was a 'pioneer society which had outlived its usefulness' and now 'blocked the way to progress'. With such sentiments being freely expressed on either side, it is not surprising that the question of orthography should have been so contentious or that when, in 1910, a conference was eventually called at the behest of the British and Foreign Bible Society to try to resolve the issue, Plaatje should have found himself excluded from it.[7]

A second major preoccupation during these years was the treatment of Sekgoma Letsholathebe, a Batawana chief from Ngamiland in the extreme north of the Bechuanaland Protectorate. It was a sorry tale. Sekgoma was unfortunate to have been involved in a succession dispute in which his rival, Mathiba, had secured some powerful allies, not least Chief Khama of the Bamangwato. Sekgoma was arrested on the authority of Lord Selborne (Milner's successor as British high commissioner for southern Africa) and then imprisoned for over five years without ever being brought to trial. Plaatje first became aware of the issue in March 1906 when Sekgoma, stopping off at Mafeking on his way back from a trip to Kimberley to see a doctor, was detained by the Protectorate authorities and escorted to Serowe. The following month – 'in the interests of my journal', as Plaatje later wrote – he accompanied the high commissioner on an official visit to the Protectorate, one of only two journalists in the party. In Serowe, after witnessing an elaborate royal welcome laid on by Chief Khama, he heard at first hand how the high commissioner had conveyed to the unfortunate Batawana chief 'the comforting information that he was imprisoned for his own good and for the benefit of his tribe, as it is feared that if he was allowed to return to Ngamiland there may be fighting'. Mathiba was then installed in his place.[8]

Plaatje was appalled by the illegal actions of the British authorities. In an account of the affair written in 1909, when the unfortunate chief was still in prison, he characterised Sekgoma as 'the Black Dreyfus' (after the French cause célèbre) and condemned the judicial and administrative system of the Bechuanaland Protectorate in the strongest terms for permitting such arbitrary action to take place. In contrast to the mature legal system of the Cape Colony, he considered that of the Protectorate to be 'dictatorial', 'a country under the despotic rule of one man, a well-administered country but without any judges and where provincial courts sit in judgment over their own acts'. Lacking the judicial machinery to safeguard the liberty of the subject, 'the protection of the subject in the said Protectorate', Plaatje believed, 'exists in shadow only and not in substance'. The essential problem, he concluded, 'is the absence of a clear charter of justice for the protection from their rulers of the inhabitants of that portion of the British empire known as the Bechuanaland Protectorate.

This indeed is one branch of the Protectorate administration which calls for immediate consideration.'[9]

Plaatje's concern over the manner in which Sekgoma was treated was a characteristic example of the way in which his views were shaped by his deep attachment to a judicial system he knew so well from his experiences in the courts in the Cape Colony. As on many other occasions, his point of departure was the set of principles which underlay the Cape's legal system and the institutions through which they were expressed. Several years later the strong feelings he had about the affair would colour his views of the political developments that were to culminate in the creation of the Act of Union. He was more aware than many of his colleagues that the imperial government was just as capable of arbitrary, unjust behaviour towards Africans as any self-governing colony in the subcontinent.

⚬

By the time Plaatje returned from his visit to the Bechuanaland Protectorate in April 1906, he had some urgent concerns of his own: *Koranta ea Becoana* was in severe financial difficulty. Earlier that year he and Molema had been forced to contemplate transferring *Koranta* back to the *Mafeking Mail*. For a while this was averted, but in May or June 1906 *Koranta* ceased publication, overwhelmed by its burden of debt. Both Plaatje and Molema had exhausted all sources of credit available to them, unable to repay either the loans they had taken out or the interest payments due on them. An attempt was made in October 1906 to interest the Bechuanaland Press, the owners of the *Bechuanaland News* and several other small country newspapers, in taking over *Koranta*, but with no success. In the sparsely populated northern Cape they too were struggling. Then, on 26 November 1906, Molema and Plaatje received a letter from Spencer Minchin informing them that in view of the outstanding debts of their business, the most pressing of which was £200 now due to a Mrs Helen Moroney, 'he had no alternative but to take possession of the Printing Plant in terms of the Bond', adding that he would be 'obliged if you will kindly let me have the key to the building'.[10]

Somehow *Koranta* survived the confusing sequence of events that followed. Minchin tried first of all to negotiate the sale of the business to the Barolong paramount chief, Badirile Montshiwa. When this failed he began to make the necessary arrangements for the sale of *Koranta*'s offices on which there was already a bond in his favour. Shortly before this was due to take place, however, he managed to reach an agreement with George Whales to take over the paper

200

and all its assets. Although this was complicated by the fact that Whales was in the process of liquidating his own debts by transferring his business to the Bechuanaland Press, agreement was reached, and on 30 January 1907 the *Mafeking Mail* announced that *Koranta ea Becoana*, 'the only Sechuana paper published', which had been 'in temporary shade for some weeks', was to recommence 'under new editorship'.[11]

Plaatje and Molema had no choice but to accept these new arrangements, but they did not do so willingly. Minchin complained that Silas Molema had obstructed his attempts to sell the business to Chief Badirile, and at one point he instituted legal proceedings against him in order to secure possession of *Koranta*'s offices: that earlier request to hand over the keys had clearly not been complied with.

While this was going on, they explored other avenues to try to save the newspaper. One offer of help came from Francis Peregrino, still editor of the *South African Spectator*, who was in Mafeking in January 1907. According to a report in *Ilanga lase Natal*, John Dube's newspaper, Peregrino, 'the natives' old and trusted friend', 'came to the rescue, and devoted a special page or two to the Sechuana news' which would 'tide over their difficulties', adding that it particularly regretted that the 'stoppage of the Becoana newspaper ... appears to be the result of a disagreement between the persons particularly concerned'. In the *Spectator* itself, however, Peregrino seems to have gone further, announcing that *Koranta* and the *Spectator* 'were to be combined' – to the understandable consternation of George Whales. 'What does this mean?' he wrote to Silas Molema after he had seen this. 'I have purchased the copyright of the *Koranta* of you. How does this notice appear?'[12]

When *Koranta ea Becoana* reappeared under Whales's ownership in April 1907, *Izwi la Bantu* noted that its editor and policy remained as they were before. Whether Plaatje really continued as editor is not at all certain. In the immediate aftermath of Whales's takeover he would have nothing to do with its new owner and Whales was obliged to look instead to Chief Badirile to supply an alternative. Most likely Plaatje did then relent and offer his services, for an article in the issue of 10 May about a recent Circuit Court case in Mafeking – all that has survived of the issue – is certainly written by him. The truth was that there was nobody remotely as qualified to take on the task.[13]

Things would never be the same, however. *Koranta* was now owned by the Bechuanaland Press and it had lost the independence Plaatje prized so highly. Even in its new incarnation it faced a very uncertain future. The difficulties encountered by Plaatje and Molema had not gone away and the finances of the Bechuanaland Press were barely more robust than the newspaper it had just added to its stable. In pursuing his dream Plaatje now found himself heavily in debt – 'insolvent', indeed, according to E.C. Welsh, recently arrived in Mafeking as magistrate and civil commissioner.[14]

If Plaatje did have anything to do with *Koranta ea Becoana* after its transfer to its new owners, it cannot have been for long, for a few weeks later he left Mafeking altogether, having told Mr Welsh that he was crossing the Kalahari into German South West Africa 'on a trading trip', and was 'no longer connected' (so Welsh thought) with the newspaper. He was away for over three months, seeking to ameliorate his desperate financial situation by making some money from acquiring animal skins and then selling them at a profit. Perhaps it was also a chance to escape the attentions of his creditors, for a while at least, and to rethink his future.[15]

In his absence, editorial arrangements for the paper were left in the hands of Petrus Sidzumo and Mejana Tyamzashe, a local teacher, Sidzumo being responsible for the Setswana columns, Tyamzashe for the English. How many issues were actually published during these months is not at all clear. It is known to have come out in July and August, but by September Welsh thought 'that publication of this paper has now ceased'.[16]

In fact, several more issues did appear after that and there are indications that Plaatje, back from his 'trading trip', was again involved since issue no. 152, 15 November 1907, carried a poem (in English) which he had written, inspired by a trip into the country with Olive, his four-year-old daughter. By December *Koranta ea Becoana* was once again on the point of closure. Minchin tried to interest Chief Badirile but with no more success than before, and arrangements were accordingly made for its assets to be auctioned. But then, just before the auction was due to take place on 28 March 1908, Spencer Minchin himself stepped in with an offer to purchase the plant for the sum of £600, which was accepted. And there, for a year, the matter rested: Minchin was unable to sell off the assets of *Koranta* at a satisfactory price – or perhaps, close to the Barolong as he was, could not bring himself to do so.[17]

᠆᠊᠊᠊᠊

Koranta ea Becoana's struggle to stay afloat had its parallel in the experience of the Tshidi Barolong as a whole, for they too were engaged in a struggle to preserve their independence, or such of it as remained. For Plaatje, inevitably involved, often advising the chief and his headmen, and writing letters on their behalf, it was yet another challenge.[18]

Throughout the first decade of the twentieth century the Tshidi fought a long-running battle with the municipal and divisional councils over their autonomy and title to land. These were supposedly guaranteed in perpetuity by the provisions of the Annexation Act of 1895, and had been reaffirmed publicly by the secretary of state for the colonies, Joseph Chamberlain, during his visit to Mafeking in 1903. But this had done little to discourage the local authorities in Mafeking from seeking, at every opportunity, to extend their jurisdiction. In their view the autonomy enjoyed by the Barolong was a huge nuisance, an anomaly in the government of the colony, preventing them from administering the district as they thought fit.

Particularly contentious was the question of a tax on dogs, which the divisional council first sought to impose in 1903 in order to control what the *Mafeking Mail* called the 'numberless mongrels' who roamed the stadt. The Barolong challenged the council's legal right to impose the tax, took them to the Supreme Court in Cape Town, and won a famous victory in November 1904: Plaatje had celebrated with a special 'Dog Tax' number of *Koranta ea Becoana*. The following year, however, the local magistrate attempted to implement the Native Reserves Locations Act, legislation that was designed to give local authorities throughout the colony greater powers over African 'locations'. He, too, was challenged, first of all in his own court, then in the Supreme Court, and again the Barolong won their case. Relations with Mr Green, the magistrate, and then with his successor, E.C. Welsh, grew more and more strained.[19]

Despite their victories in the courts, the Barolong could not prevent the government from simply overturning court rulings by proclamation. There was a second deputation to Cape Town in 1906, and another interview with the prime minister, Dr Jameson, but they failed to achieve their objective, and each year the local authorities tried to make further inroads (though it was years before the district council actually managed to collect any dog tax). Along with the chief and his headmen Plaatje could sometimes delay the process through using the legal machinery open to them – although legal fees were astronomical – but they could not reverse it. It looked to be just a matter of time before the Tshidi Barolong were fully incorporated into the administrative structures of the Cape Colony. Success in the courts was one thing; the political power to resist government proclamations and the will of their rulers, quite another.[20]

Their situation was deteriorating in other ways. There was growing poverty and increased dependence upon the earnings of the young men sent out to work in the mines, and Badirile Montshiwa was proving to be even more of a disaster as paramount chief than his predecessor. 'Although this man did remarkably well during the first three years [1903–6] of his short reign,' Plaatje would recall, 'he soon after took to drinking and polygamy' and then 'shockingly mismanaged the affairs of the tribe', 'his actions giving rise to much anxiety'. The institution of chiefship may have remained central to the lives of this community, but Badirile Montshiwa did nothing whatever to enhance its reputation. What Plaatje was witnessing, like it or not, and in spite of his own best efforts, was the disintegration of a once independent and often prosperous community, unable to resist the encroaching colonial state. Witnessing the great symbol of Barolong independence, Chief Montshiwa, giving judgment in council was a very distant memory now. That vision of a proud Tswana people, with the Barolong at its core, leading the way into the modern world, inspiration for both Plaatje and Silas Molema during the heyday of *Koranta ea Becoana*, was disappearing before their eyes.[21]

In a way the decline of the Tshidi chiefdom simply underlined the need to find alternative ways of responding to the changes that were taking place. For Plaatje and others like him, in Mafikeng and elsewhere, education was the key, and they did their best to equip themselves, and particularly their children, with the means of making their way as individuals in the colonial state that was tightening its grip on their lives. It was a return in a way to the ethos of African life in Kimberley a decade earlier, albeit within a political and social context that looked much less promising than it did then.

'Seoding', the Plaatje family home, was at the heart of these shared aspirations, a focal point for the more 'progressive', mission-educated Africans who lived in and around Mafikeng. Here Elizabeth, having given up teaching to concentrate on the upbringing of the children, was remembered as a warm-hearted hostess. Friends often came round to socialise, or to make music, taking advantage of the opportunity – the younger ones particularly – to improve their proficiency in English. Regular visitors included Patrick Lenkoane and his wife, Johannes and Sarah Sidzumo, Philemon Moshoeshoe, Isaiah Makgothi, and various of the Molema, Ncwabeni, Tyamzashe, Xaba and Samson families. Many, like Elizabeth, were of Mfengu origin; they taught in the local mission schools, or worked for local government or businesses, replicating in microcosm that close-knit community Plaatje had once been part of in Kimberley. In a largely male-dominated society female teachers like Rose Samson, Elizabeth and Katherine Tyamzashe, Helen Make, Bessie Gontshi and Hayeni Twenty could expect to be treated, at the Plaatje residence at least, in a manner appropriate to their status. Maud Sidzumo, another young teacher, just out of Lovedale, always remembered the welcoming atmosphere of the Plaatje home, as well as

Elizabeth's excellent singing voice. Often she would help look after the children when both parents were away.[22]

Young Modiri Molema was a frequent visitor too. He came to know Plaatje very well during these years, and has left some vivid recollections of their encounters. He was always struck by Plaatje's loud, hearty laugh, and his habit of exclaiming in a loud voice '*mugalammakapa*' for emphasis, in the manner of Tswana elders. If you did well at something, like passing a school examination, Plaatje had a way, he said, of approaching you with his broad chest out, his shoulders held high, as if to sweep you up in the air. And if you had spoken or written something particularly well, he would show his approval by striding back and forth, repeating '*sseee*', the equivalent of 'fine' or 'excellent' in English.

But he noticed another side to his personality too. 'If he didn't like something, or was offended, he vented his feelings angrily at the time, then, like a flame doused with soil or water and immediately extinguished, he calmly carried on. When you saw him again he had forgotten the anger and the incident.' Perhaps it was this characteristic that had landed him in trouble in the dispute over his gardens being trampled on by cattle – and a second incident in 1907 when he again had a charge of assault laid against him in the magistrate's court. Both cases were dismissed, but the fact that charges were laid at all is consistent with Molema's observation that on occasion his anger could get the better of him.[23]

At the same time Modiri was struck by Plaatje's natural warmth and hospitality. When visitors came, he would slaughter a chicken in the traditional manner, and he noticed that when friends' children came round to see him they rarely went away empty-handed. And he could not bear to see anybody mistreated. If he saw children taunting one another, he would always step in to help the one being bullied.

Another thing he noticed was how persistent and determined Plaatje was, even about little things. He would never use a knife to cut a knot in a string, always finding a way to untie it, however long it took. And he would always persevere in his efforts to repair things like bicycles and typewriters when the need arose, determined not to be defeated. He displayed the same doggedness when it came to language, refusing to let a new word or phrase pass unless he was sure of its meaning and derivation – whatever the language. Vere Stent had noticed just the same thing when he was with Plaatje during the siege of Mafeking.[24]

◦~◦

In comparison with Kimberley, there was much less in the way of organised entertainment, though the Mafeking Philharmonic Society remained in existence and would put on concerts from time to time (at one of them Plaatje and Elizabeth were reported to have 'brought the house down' with their duets). Other forms of public entertainment were shared with the white people of Mafeking. In April 1906, however, this gave rise to an unfortunate incident. One Wednesday evening Plaatje and an unnamed friend decided to 'make the acquaintance of Mr Nelson Jackson, the entertainer', and went along to the Town Hall where he was performing. They paid their entrance fee and were let in without difficulty, but after a few minutes an usher requested them to leave since, he explained, the Town Council had passed a regulation forbidding the admission of people of colour to entertainment functions in the Town Hall.[25]

Plaatje, taken aback, nevertheless complied with the request, but then wrote a long letter to the *Mafeking Mail* to complain about the 'bigoted regulation' in question, concluding with a quotation from Shakespeare (slightly, but pointedly, adapted) to emphasise his point that Africans should be just as entitled to attend these shows as their white fellow citizens: 'in the words of Shakespeare's *Merchant of Venice*', he said, 'I will ask His Worship [the mayor], "Is not an African fed with the same food, hurt with the same weapons, subject to the same means, warmed and cooled by the same winter and summer as a European? If you prick us do we not bleed? If you tickle us, do we not laugh? If you poison us, do we not die? If you wrong us, shall we not revenge? If we are like you all in the rest, we will resemble you in that."'[26]

Plaatje's letter was discussed at the next meeting of the Town Council, when the mayor explained that there was no such regulation and that it was the lessees of the hall who had decided not to admit people of colour that evening; in the light of this, he therefore thought no further action was necessary. Unpleasant though the incident was, it was not a common occurrence, and relations between black and white in Mafeking, as Plaatje often pointed out, were generally quite cordial. He had not expected to be asked to leave the Town Hall on account of his colour, and was taken aback when this happened. He and his friends must have attended other forms of entertainment in the Town Hall without incident and they naturally found it hard to understand why the promoter, J.H. Winterbottom, should wish to do without their custom.[27]

Colour was by no means always the defining issue in broader political matters too. Black and white in Mafeking had common as well as separate interests, not least a wish to avoid being marginalised as the South African colonies drew closer together. Some saw Plaatje as a spokesman for both. In October 1907, when the Unionist Party (the 'Progressives') in Mafeking considered possible candidates to stand for the constituency in the forthcoming general election, the *Mafeking Mail* reported, in a matter-of-fact manner, that Plaatje was one of three possible candidates on its list. As editor of *Koranta ea Becoana*, it thought, Plaatje would be 'most useful', especially 'with his experience of law courts and compensation questions, and his knowledge of native matters'.[28]

Nothing came of the suggestion, however, and in the end J.W. de Kock, the existing member of parliament for Mafeking (whom Plaatje knew well), decided to stand again, and was re-elected with a slim majority. Nevertheless, the consideration given to Plaatje in the matter was perhaps as close as any black candidate came to standing in the Cape parliament, even if it made no headlines. Three years later, thanks to a new South African constitution and the colour bar it introduced, it would no longer be possible.

At home the children were a welcome distraction from the trials and tribulations of *Koranta ea Becoana* and the difficulties of earning a living. Elizabeth, remembered as being quite strict, had the main responsibility for their upbringing. Always proud of her Mfengu origins, she made a point of keeping in touch with her own family and relations and visited them regularly. Particularly, it seems, when she was pregnant, for after Richard (September 1901) the next two children were born outside Mafeking: Olive, born in Burgersdorp in December 1903, and named after Olive Schreiner; and then Violet, the second daughter, born in Kimberley in January 1907. Although the long hours in the *Koranta* office and frequent absences from Mafeking must have limited the amount of time Plaatje was able to spend with his young family, he loved being with them and watching them grow up, recalling some of his memories of them in an account he wrote some years later.[29]

Sainty, the eldest child, fulfilled all his father's hopes. He displayed signs of musical talent from an early age, attended the Wesleyan mission school when he was old enough, and was soon fluent in English, Setswana and Xhosa, the three languages spoken in the Plaatje household. He learned to read quickly and passed the first two standards, reading as well (so his father thought) as children at Standard VI. When he was 9, his parents still in Mafeking, he was sent off to Kimberley, in the care of Elizabeth's brother Isaiah, so he could take his higher grades at the Lyndhurst Road school, the only African-run secondary school in the colony supported by the Education Department.[30]

Richard, his younger brother, went to live with relatives in Bethanie when his health started to suffer from the hot, dry climate of the northern Cape, and he stayed on with them, only returning to Mafeking in 1909. Olive, though, became a special favourite, and Plaatje had a fund of amusing anecdotes about her. In one she showed she had, like many children of her age, a quite literal understanding of the religious beliefs which formed an important part of her (and her siblings') upbringing. Why, she wondered, when somebody died, could they not take a message to her cousin Winston, who had died recently, and would be in the same place? And with such a big house in heaven, she announced after evening prayers one day, surely it must be full of bread because 'wherever you go people are also asking for that bread'. Another time she caused great merriment by asking whether her uncle Isaiah, in town to interpret for the Circuit Court, was working at bags of mealies or bags of corn – not knowing that the word *tsheko* could also mean legal cases.[31]

Olive was also quite aware, from a young age, that she was named after Olive Schreiner. 'One afternoon', Plaatje recalled, 'she went to a Sunday School at Beaconsfield where we were visiting. She was asked for her name which she gave as, "Olive, Sir". The teacher wanted the full name and after a little consideration she gave it serene and seriously as "Olive Schreiner". Naturally, the class rocked with laughter at the serious yet funny answers of the newcomer.'

And it was Olive who inspired Plaatje to write a poem, 'Olive and I', which was published in *Koranta ea Becoana* in November 1907; not great poetry, perhaps, but a touching record of the day they spent together out in the country around Mafeking:

By the verdant bank of a country spring
Olive and I sat watching a pen of
Kalahari partridges on the wing.
In their Aerial trend they looked peculiarly well off:
They sipped the precious fluid with Elysian nod.
Thus Olive softly: LI THABILE.

O'er the grassy turf 'neath the desert sun
Olive and I walked picking wild flowers,
Up sprang a duiker and commenced to run,
Sprightly and hale he flew and darted across the bowers.
I speedily fired and shattered his back;
The nickel bullet also pierced his vivific pluck.
Said Olive dolefully: E SHULE.

In the western vale of Mahur'take,
Olive and I mused of break-(ing our)-fast,
'Neath the clear rural sky, our meat to take:

Comprising wild fruit, 'morama', a handy repast,
Porridge, winged–game, cocoa beans and cookies,
Displaying her neat set of youthful ivories,
Olive quoth SOTTO VOCE: MONATE.[32]

Overshadowing everything was an increasingly serious financial predicament. Between 1906 and 1910 Plaatje was issued with summonses on no less than sixteen occasions for the repayment of unpaid bonds (taken out to raise money for the newspaper) or bills. In some cases these were served on him in his capacity as a business partner of Silas Molema, who was forced to sell off both land and large numbers of cattle; in others it was as a private individual. Many of those suing for repayment of money owed were general dealers in Mafeking who had supplied goods on credit but had not been paid. The first summons had been for the relatively small sum of £3 13s 6d, which he owed to the firm of A.W. and A.E. Fincham for 'goods sold and delivered', but the sums grew in size until, by January 1908, he was being pressed for payment of £116 to S. Kemp & Co. *Koranta ea Becoana* may have been one of the finest, liveliest newspapers of its day; by the time it collapsed it had left its editor in a dire financial state.[33]

He also found himself in difficulties with the magistrate on two other matters. The first concerned the question of the 12s per annum hut tax which all African householders had to pay. According to the local inspector of native locations, the official responsible for its collection, Plaatje had been 'a habitual defaulter' since 1903, and gave him 'the same trouble every year before he pays his hut tax'. Early in 1907, however, Mr Welsh, the magistrate, felt it was time to issue a summons to try to extract payment for the previous year. For nearly five years Plaatje had dealt with the paperwork for such cases when he was employed in the magistrate's office; now he was on the receiving end.[34]

The second difficulty arose out of a disagreement over a borehole which Plaatje had arranged to have dug on his property in order to provide a regular supply of water. The work was carried out at his request by a government drill–operator in June 1905, but the operation was not a success. Plaatje's version of events was that the operator refused to drill in the place he wanted, persuaded him to agree ('much against my will') to start drilling on another spot, failed to find any water there, tried again in the original place, but then stopped drilling 'just when it promised to give satisfaction'. The outcome was that he failed to get his supply of water, but found himself liable for the very considerable expenditure (£90) involved, and refused to pay; so, too, for a while at least, did several other leading citizens in Mafeking, including J.W. de Kock, Mafeking's member of parliament, also dissatisfied with the results achieved by the government drill-operator.[35]

Unfortunately for Plaatje, though, his argument that he should not be held liable for the whole of the £90 did not persuade the magistrate, and by the end of the year (1905), still refusing to pay the balance of £38, he was threatened with legal action. Over the next three years a lengthy correspondence ensued between the magistrate, the secretary for public works and the Treasury, as they sought means of either recovering the outstanding debt or accounting for it satisfactorily. In the end they managed to retrieve a portion of it but wrote off the balance, reluctant to institute legal proceedings if there was little chance of success.[36]

Eventually Plaatje was obliged to resort to labour recruiting to try to earn a decent income and keep his creditors at bay. It cannot have been a very appealing prospect, but it was one of the few legal means now open to him to earn a living. At least one other African newspaper editor (A.K. Soga) had resorted to this occupation when his paper was in difficulties. He would have had a good idea of what was involved. Silas Molema had a longstanding relationship with a firm of labour agents, while his friend Patrick Lenkoane worked as an assistant to Charles Goodyear, the local representative of the Witwatersrand Native Labour Association.[37]

Plaatje secured an appointment as the local agent of another organisation, the Mines Labour Supply Company, which specialised in providing labour for the coal mines in the Transvaal. He ran into obstacles from the start. To carry out work of this kind he needed a licence from the government. It was on the point of being issued when it occurred to Mr Welsh, the magistrate, through whom his application went, that this provided the opportunity to get Plaatje to settle the debt he still owed to the government on the borehole. But Plaatje was in no position to do so. He had numerous other debts, and more summonses were on the way. Instead, an arrangement was reached whereby the Mines Labour Supply Company would guarantee that he paid off the money in monthly instalments, and on this condition, early in February 1909, Plaatje commenced work as the 'Bechuanaland Representative', according to the headed notepaper he had printed, of the Mines Labour Supply Company Limited, and advised that all communications be addressed to 'Box 11, Mafeking', so long the address familiar to readers of *Koranta ea Becoana*.[38]

In the event his new career could not have got off to a worse start. On 12 March, having contracted nine labourers in the Mafeking district for the South Rand Coal Mine and sent them on their way to Johannesburg, he was informed that when they got to Zeerust, in the Transvaal, they had been intercepted by the police, and turned back on the grounds that his recruiting licence did not extend to the Transvaal itself – a point subsequently upheld when Plaatje complained about the matter to the magistrate. It seems that labourers recruited from outside the Transvaal were only allowed to cross its borders at certain places, and that a 'conducting licence' was also required. Plaatje took up the matter with J.W. de Kock, his member of parliament, whose representations to Edward Dower, the secretary for native affairs, met with some success. While the Mines Supply Company had failed to obtain the proper authority it needed, the director of native labour in the Transvaal did acknowledge that 'the stoppage of the gang at Zeerust appears to have been unnecessary'. He promised that steps would be taken to 'prevent a recurrence of the irregularity', and expressed 'his regret at the occurrence'. From now on, it was agreed, Plaatje would send his recruits into the Transvaal via Fourteen Streams, a village on the Cape–Transvaal border some two hundred miles south.[39]

It turned out to be no more than a temporary solution, for several months later the ill-fated Mines Labour Supply Company went into liquidation. Plaatje seems then to have made arrangements to contract labourers for another recruiting organisation, and later that year his licence was endorsed for operation in the Transkei, although whether he actually visited the region for this purpose is not at all clear.[40]

In the midst of all of this came a surprising development: *Koranta ea Becoana* returned briefly to life. On 30 March 1909 Mr Welsh received a letter from Spencer Minchin informing him that he, Minchin, intended to restart *Koranta* in a few days' time. The printer and publisher, he explained, would be himself, and the paper was to be 'brought out in the interests of the Bechuana people', issued 'weekly or fortnightly according to demand', and printed and published at the 'old Koranta Building on Erf No. 74, Mafeking'. He gave no indication as to who was actually to edit the paper.[41]

Predictably, Spencer Minchin's venture into the hazardous business of newspaper publishing did not last very long. The first number appeared on 7 April, and there were several more before the end of May. Prospects of its ever becoming commercially viable were negligible, Minchin was obviously unwilling to run up the kind of debts that had all but ruined Plaatje and Molema, and he decided to call a halt a month later. He auctioned off the printing plant ('in working order') and all ancillary equipment, and on 14 June 1909 the following notice – an epitaph almost – appeared in the *Mafeking Mail:*

FOR SALE

Portion of Erf 74 in the Township of Mafeking, with
Buildings thereon, known as the KORANTA Offices.

Suitable for Shop or Dwelling
For particulars, apply to S. Minchin, Mafeking.[42]

This time there was no last-minute reprieve. It was a sad end for a venture that had begun with such high hopes at that formal inauguration in August 1902, nearly seven years earlier. Minchin had been among the guests present that day to witness the opening of the 'Bechuana Printing Works' and to hear those encouraging words from the then magistrate, Graham Green. He can scarcely have imagined that he would end up as *Koranta ea Becoana*'s last proprietor.

⁓

The year 1909 undeniably marked the lowest point in Plaatje's life to date. He was heavily in debt, *Koranta ea Becoana* had folded, its office and printing plant sold off, and he was encountering one difficulty after another in his attempt to earn his living as a labour agent. Plans for a new newspaper, his hope for the future, had yet to come to fruition. In view of the far-reaching political developments taking place around him it must have been an extremely frustrating time too, since he was in no position to make an effective contribution to the discussions and protests that accompanied them. For that year witnessed the realisation of the imperial government's plans for South Africa: reconciliation between Boer and Briton, and agreement upon the formation of a unitary, self-governing state, bringing together the four colonies in a new Union of South Africa which, it was hoped, would preserve long-term British interests in the subcontinent.

Plaatje had observed, commented upon and criticised the moves made in this direction over the previous six years. Now, between October 1908 and February 1909, a convention of representatives from all the colonies in South Africa – all of them white, all of them male – sat in a number of sessions in an attempt to reach agreement on a constitution. On this objective there was, not surprisingly, much debate, the nature of the franchise being the main difficulty. Was the Cape's non-racial franchise to be preserved, or should it defer to the practice of the other colonies and be made the preserve of whites only? Only a handful of whites who attended the Bloemfontein convention argued that the Cape franchise should become the model for the Union as a whole. Nor was this favoured by the imperial government. The priority rather was to effect reconciliation between Boer and Briton, and the divergent interests of the different colonies, and this was never likely to be achieved by imposing a franchise based on that of the Cape.[43]

The African people were not consulted over these arrangements. The moves being made by white politicians nevertheless provided a great stimulus to political discussion and activity. Protest meetings, in different parts of the country, passed resolutions against the colour-bar clauses in the draft South Africa Act and condemned the failure of the white policy-makers to extend the Cape franchise to the northern colonies. This movement of protest culminated in a South African Native Convention, held in Bloemfontein from 24 to 26 March 1909. Further resolutions were passed, the sixty delegates present called upon the British imperial government to intervene on behalf of the black population of South Africa, and they resolved to send a deputation to England to protest about the terms of the draft South Africa Act before it received the approval of the imperial government.

This Native Convention was the most representative meeting ever convened by black South Africans, and it was clear that the threat of Union, and the grave danger it posed to their future political status, had created an unprecedented sense of unity of purpose among them. But there were some notable absentees from the meeting, including John Tengo Jabavu, editor of *Imvo*. Although he would join the deputation to England several months later, and had initially supported plans for the Native Convention, by the time it actually took place he had reconsidered his position. He was fearful not only of the threat posed to his own influence by the emerging new movement, but that any attempt to secure an extension of the Cape franchise northwards could jeopardise its survival in the Cape. Upon this, as he well knew, his influence depended.

Plaatje, too, was absent. Exactly what prevented him from attending a gathering he would not have wanted to miss, and where his presence would have been invaluable, is uncertain. Most likely he simply had to stay in Mafeking in order to attend to the urgent problems confronting him with his labour recruiting work, for the dates of the convention coincided almost exactly with the detention of his labourers in Zeerust. The Barolong of Mafeking were represented instead by Silas Molema and Lekoko Montshiwa, and Molema in particular took a prominent part in the proceedings, concerned as ever to secure guarantees for the autonomy they still clung to through the terms of their annexation to the Cape in 1895. Interestingly, the day after the Native Convention finished its work, the *Mafeking Mail* published a letter from Plaatje appealing to voters in the Mafeking district to register as a matter of urgency in view of the impending redrawing of constituencies for the new Union parliament. It was addressed as much to white as black voters, a reminder of his continued commitment to parliamentary politics – and a belief that both shared an interest in ensuring that Bechuanaland was properly represented in the new Union.[44]

Little official notice was taken of the representations of the Native Convention, either in South Africa or in Britain. Nevertheless, the holding of the convention was a significant achievement, and its organisers resolved to set up a permanent organisation, keen to build upon the momentum they had created. Plaatje may have been absent from the first meeting of the Native Convention but he soon added his voice to the protests that followed, writing to W.P. Schreiner the following month to say that he had been 'ordered' by the Barolong paramount chief to thank him for his 'fearless championship of the cause of the Natives', and requesting him to 'peruse' their objections to the terms of the proposed Act of Union.[45]

By the time the convention held its second annual meeting, in March 1910, also in Bloemfontein, Plaatje was much involved, joining many friends and colleagues, from the Orange Free State particularly, in taking the new organisation forward. He attended the meeting (he was described in a newspaper report as 'formerly editor, *Koranta ea Becoana*', and to be 'representing Johannesburg and Pretoria') and became 'assistant secretary' of the new organisation. A week later he led a deputation to General Louis Botha, prime minister of the Transvaal, to compliment him on his decision to repatriate the last of the Chinese miners who had been imported into the country six years earlier. Like most African spokesmen, Plaatje had been opposed to this from the beginning. The following month Botha became the first prime minister of the newly created Union of South Africa.[46]

The South African Native Convention, it is clear, had ambitious plans, for on the same trip to Pretoria Plaatje addressed several other meetings, including two in the Marabastad Location, where he explained that it was the 'intention of the Convention to combine all Native organizations with a view to cooperation with the officials who will be entrusted with the administration of native affairs under the Union government'. He hoped to persuade the two main African political organisations in the Transvaal to bury their differences and combine, and at the end of one of the meetings it was accordingly resolved that the officers of the Vigilance Association and the National Political Association should meet so as 'to effect an amalgamation … with a view to early affiliation with the Native Convention'. With the inauguration of the Union of South Africa only weeks away, nobody was in any doubt about the urgency of the task. Black South Africans needed to make their voice heard – and to do so, if they could, through a single, united organisation.[47]

※

In the difficult personal circumstances Plaatje faced in Mafeking, with no newspaper, no money and no obvious outlet for his energies and ambitions, such a mission probably came more as a relief than a burden; a chance to escape from the increasingly limited role as adviser and general secretarial dogsbody for the hapless Barolong paramount chief. But as well as inspiring a new political organisation, the impending Union of South Africa also stimulated debate about the future governance of the country's African population, above all about segregation, which many in ruling circles took to provide the solution to 'the native problem'. Here too Plaatje made his mark, not least in the form of an essay he wrote in response to a competition, open to black South Africans, organised by C.F. Tainton, a prominent pro-segregationist from Johannesburg, late in 1909. 'Is it desirable', Tainton wanted to know, 'to encourage the racial development of the Natives of South Africa, socially, commercially, politically and territorially, apart from the white people?'

Tainton thought it was, and was inclined to favour those essays in which he could detect some support for his views. The first three prizes went to A.A. Moletsane, from Kolo in Basutoland, who shared first prize with Cleopas Kunene, from Natal, the second prize going to E.S. Mbele from the Transkei. Plaatje was awarded third prize, worth £1 10s (which can have done little to relieve his financial difficulties). His essay attracted the following comment: 'Greater care in the arrangement of his arguments', Tainton said, 'would have added much to their value. His paper is a clear but bitter protest against our present native policy and throws much light on the effect of a repressive policy on educated and able members of the Native races.'[48]

In fact, the arguments Plaatje put forward in his essay, subsequently published in the *Transvaal Chronicle* (a daily newspaper published in Johannesburg), which commented that Plaatje 'hits hard with lumps of truth', seem perfectly well arranged. His central point was clear: that however desirable or undesirable total segregation was in theory, any attempt to implement it would be quite impracticable. He conjured up an ironic vision of what complete geographical segregation would mean: 'What a glorious millennium! A city of black folks where Europeans, being excluded, the havoc wrought in the Native territories by attorney's fees will be a thing of the past. With black postmasters, black carpenters, black tax collectors and black shopkeepers, making money! In fact, black everything.'

But all of this, Plaatje said, was visionary. 'Has it ever occurred to the thousands of white officials that when the segregation idea becomes an accomplished fact they stand three chances to one of being retrenched? I think it has, and I am satisfied that when the natives begin to move the whites will stop them even if they have to use Martini rifles for the purpose.' For the economic interdependence of black and white, Plaatje went on to argue, would ensure that the complete segregation of black and white was an impossibility. 'Two things only you need give the native', he concluded, 'and two things only you must deny him. Keep away from him liquor and lawyers, give him the franchise, and your confidence, and the problem will solve itself to your mutual advantage.'[49]

The first recommendation was rooted very much in Plaatje's recent experiences in Mafeking; the second, that Africans should be given the franchise and the trust of their rulers, derived from a longstanding commitment to the ideals of the Cape constitutional system. To the extent that the non-racial Cape franchise was preserved in the Union constitution of 1910 he had reason to be optimistic about the future; that it had not been extended to the other former colonies – provinces as they now became – was cause for grave concern. Only the future would tell which system, which set of values, which theory of government, would gain the upper hand.

Plaatje left Mafeking with his family sometime in May or June 1910. There was little to keep him there. The Tshidi Barolong were in no position to support his ambitions for them, for himself or for the Batswana as a whole. He could no longer earn a living as a labour agent since Mr Welsh, the magistrate, had declined to renew his licence when it expired in December 1909 (he gave no reasons) and his financial position remained dire. In the early months of 1910 he faced yet more summonses, and at the end of April a warrant was issued for the seizure of property and furniture in his house: a dining-room table, letter press and stand, kitchen stove, bedstead, sofa, mirror, rocking chair and bookcase were all at risk. Plaatje was away from home when the bailiff called, so it was left to Elizabeth to deal with him. As she was unable to pay the sum required, the household possessions were 'attached' before she managed to find the money the following day. Nevertheless, it must have been a distressing business, and probably not the first time she had to attend to such a situation. This particular debt, for a relatively small amount, was settled, but it would be years before they were free of the much larger debts that hung over them.[50]

Plaatje's main reason for leaving Mafeking, however, was that he had found backers for a new newspaper, to be based in Kimberley, having been involved in discussions over a new venture from at least the middle of 1909. If he was to play any meaningful role in the affairs of the new Union of South Africa, or to find a way of reviving the fortunes of the Barolong, Kimberley was a better place to be. The beginning of a new era in the history of South Africa coincided almost exactly with a new phase of his own life. What, he must have wondered, would the future now hold?

EIGHT

Tsala ea Becoana, the South African Native National Congress and the Land Act of 1913

T he new newspaper was called *Tsala ea Becoana* (*The Friend of the Bechuana*) and it had the backing of a syndicate. Most of those involved were relatively wealthy landowners from the Seleka Barolong settlement in Thaba Nchu. They included Chief J.M. Nyokong, head of the Matlala section of the Seleka; Jeremiah Makgothi, an elder brother of Isaiah, who used to work in the *Koranta* office in Mafikeng; Chief W.Z. Fenyang, a man of considerable wealth and local influence, to whom Plaatje was related on his mother's side; Moses Masisi, who owned the farm 'Naauwpoort' in the Thaba Nchu district; and the now elderly but much respected Rev. Joel Goronyane, a Wesleyan minister and headman of the Thaba Nchu Native Reserve. All were very well known to Plaatje, had contributed in the past to *Koranta ea Becoana*, and had acted as its agents. Collectively they were – in social position – to the Seleka Barolong of Thaba Nchu what the Molemas were to the Tshidi of Mafikeng. None of them was in any doubt as to Plaatje's experience and ability as a newspaper editor or of the reputation he had established as a spokesman for the Barolong people.[1]

The idea for a new newspaper had gained momentum with the holding of the Native Convention in March 1909 and its subsequent establishment as a permanent political organisation, and it was this same group of people who took the initiative in each, Moses Masisi and Jeremiah Makgothi, for example, being treasurer and secretary respectively of the convention and Joel Goronyane its chairman. Underlying their involvement in both initiatives was a keen awareness of their precarious political position, particularly in relation to the security of their land. They were anxious to do all they could to ensure that their voice was heard, sensing that it was now time for them to assume leadership of the Barolong in the circumstances they now faced, to take up the baton, as it were, from the Tshidi of Mafikeng. As they were denied political representation in the Union, a newspaper remained one of the most effective means open to them, and they were evidently responsive to Plaatje's representations on the issue. And he, after all, was in urgent need of a new means of livelihood.[2]

Other members of the *Tsala* syndicate included Thomas Mapikela of Bloemfontein, a wealthy businessman of Mfengu origin, who had been a member of the W.P. Schreiner deputation to England in 1909, and who had had thoughts of establishing a newspaper himself; and, intriguingly, John Tengo Jabavu, editor of *Imvo*, whose credentials and experience as a newspaperman were greater than those of any other African alive.[3]

Jabavu's interest in the venture actually predated the formation of the syndicate and his company, Jabavu & Co, was *Tsala*'s first registered proprietor. Apart from a substantial printing contract, Jabavu was attracted by the prospect of establishing a stronger presence in the northern provinces for his business, well aware that the impending unification of the South African colonies was bound to bring about a change in the wider economic and political equilibrium. From a business point of view his company had every reason to look northwards, and if an able and experienced newspaperman like Plaatje was available, then so much the better. In fact Plaatje, describing himself as 'Editor, Tsala ea Becoana', with Jabavu & Co. as proprietor, printer and publisher, had completed the necessary registration formalities in Kimberley in July 1909 – well before leaving Mafeking and nearly a year before its first issue appeared.[4]

By the time this took place, however, Jabavu had become part of the larger *Tsala* syndicate, hoping to widen support for the new venture. For nearly a year his company would print the new newspaper on its press in King William's Town in the eastern Cape, nearly four hundred miles away. *Tsala*, meanwhile, set up its office at the corner of Brett and Shannon streets in Kimberley. It was hardly a convenient arrangement in terms of the day-to-day operation of the newspaper, and most frustrating to have to wait for copies to be shipped back from King William's Town and into its main markets.[5]

However awkward these arrangements, Plaatje was back to doing what he did best, and Kimberley once again was a good place to be. Although it was thirteen years since he last lived there, many friends remained, including Isaiah Bud-M'belle and his family. The move also brought him much closer to his elderly mother and his eldest brother Simon at Pniel. Kimberley itself was not much changed. If anything, the town's prospects were somewhat bleaker than they had been in his time. The low price of diamonds on the world market had led to a long-term local recession from which the town began to recover only in 1910 and 1911, its importance eclipsed still further by the growth of Johannesburg as an industrial and gold mining centre. Kimberley nevertheless promised to provide an altogether more satisfactory base than Mafeking from which to run a newspaper, and its political and social surroundings were, for somebody in Plaatje's position, as congenial as in any of the larger towns of the country. Its educational facilities, now that he had four children of school age, were an important consideration too.[6]

Plaatje did not share quite the degree of pessimism about the implications of Union as many of those who had attended the Bloemfontein Native Convention in 1909. His feelings were influenced partly by the change in his personal fortunes; after all, things could not have got very much worse for him in Mafeking in 1909 and 1910. In Kimberley he must have felt far more in the mainstream. There were other reasons too. Like Tengo Jabavu, he was inclined to the view that the liberal traditions of the Cape, in which both men were so strongly rooted, would gradually spread northwards, that they could yet prove to be the dominant force in the affairs of the Union. There could also be advantages, he thought, in having to deal with only one administration, unlike the situation before.

His attitude towards Union, moreover, was influenced by the Sekgoma case and the views he had formed of the administration of the three protectorates, Bechuanaland, Basutoland and Swaziland. The question of their inclusion within the Union was highly contentious. African opinion, broadly, was against the idea; the general preference was for continued direct rule from Whitehall rather than the uncertainties of incorporation into the Union of South Africa – the devil they knew. Plaatje saw things differently. He had had direct personal experience of arbitrary imperial rule in the Bechuanaland Protectorate and thought that the inhabitants of the protectorates would be better off if they were part of the new Union, for they would have the Supreme Court to protect them against arbitrary misrule. 'In my opinion', he wrote, 'the jurisdiction of the Supreme Court alone warrants the change as it will give to the common people the King's protection in practice as well as in theory.' The sooner the protectorates could be handed over to the Union, he thought, the better. [7]

It was a prime example of the way in which his experience in the law courts, the views he had formed about how they could be used to protect African rights, and his confidence in the legal system of the Cape Colony could colour his political judgement. Within a few years his view on the position of the protectorates would change dramatically: in 1910 and 1911, however, he felt there was reason to be optimistic about prospects in the new Union of South Africa.

The first number of *Tsala ea Becoana* appeared on 18 June 1910. With four pages, columns in both English and Setswana, an intended circulation (by the second issue this was claimed to be 'large and increasing') throughout Tswana-speaking parts of the Union and the Bechuanaland Protectorate, and a network of agents to distribute and sell copies, it is not surprising that *Tsala ea Becoana* was taken by many to be *Koranta*'s successor. *Ilanga lase Natal*, indeed, welcomed it as 'our old friend "Koranta" resuscitated'. There was a familiar balance of advertisements, local correspondents' reports, readers' letters, news items and editorial matter, and the popular 'Mma-Maitisho' column reappeared too. The main concern of *Tsala*'s early editions was with the new circumstances of Union, with the first general election (held in September 1910), and then with the composition and behaviour of the new government formed by General Botha's South African Party.[8]

Plaatje's early editorials were hopeful in tone. He argued that 'Native interests' would best be served if neither of the two major parties (the South African Party and the Progressive Party) achieved overwhelming majorities, thereby rendering criticism ineffective; and that is just how things turned out, although it was not, in practice, very easy to detect much difference in their policies. He also derived considerable satisfaction from seeing a number of vehemently 'anti-native' candidates (in both parties) defeated at the polls, and from the inclusion in the first Union cabinet of several well-known Cape liberals and 'friends of the natives': F.S. Malan (minister of education), J.W. Sauer (minister of railways and harbours) and, above all, Henry Burton, as minister of native affairs.[9]

Plaatje had known Burton since the 1890s when both lived and worked in Kimberley. He had been impressed by his willingness to defend African rights in the courts, and supported his candidacy in the elections of 1898. Later, in Mafeking, he encountered Burton during the post-siege treason trials, and thereafter Burton accepted several legal briefs for the Barolong – in connection with the 'dog tax' and war losses compensation issues particularly. Each was as steeped as the other in the traditions of the Cape legal system. They shared a common attachment to the non-racial Cape franchise and a belief that it had been seriously undermined by clause 44(c) of the Union constitution, which stipulated that parliamentary candidates had to be 'a British subject of European descent' (that is to say, white). For Burton this was 'a dreadful blot on a great national instrument, and an unnecessary blot', and privately he confessed to having 'forebodings about the future' whenever he thought about it.[10]

Plaatje was delighted to hear of Burton's appointment as minister of native affairs and quick to draw the attention of his readers to their good fortune. He looked forward not only to the development of favourable 'native policies' but to a sympathetic ear for the particular grievances of his own people, the Barolong. 'Well may the Natives ... congratulate themselves', said *Tsala* in October 1910, 'that the wonderful year of 1910 [has] brought what promises to be the inauguration of a sound system in the administration of their affairs, under the most sympathetic Minister who ever administered this Department'. This relationship with the minister of native affairs seemed, moreover, to place him in a pre-eminent position among his fellow newspaper editors and spokesmen who were coming to terms with the new political and administrative structures, and to justify his optimism that Union might provide the means of 'liberalising influences' from the Cape spreading northwards.[11]

Plaatje was likewise pleased by the appointment of Edward Dower, a senior Cape Native Affairs Department official and son of a missionary, as secretary of native affairs; and even more by that of W.P. Schreiner, a former prime minister of the colony, as one of the four 'Native Senators' whose duty, in terms of the new constitution, was to look after 'native interests'. Plaatje telegraphed his 'heartiest congratulations' as soon as he heard news of his nomination. Both were men Plaatje knew well and likely, he thought, to be sympathetic to his representations.[12]

He wasted little time in lobbying the new administration. One of the most pressing issues, of special concern to his backers in the *Tsala* syndicate, was the legal restrictions on landholding in the Seleka Barolong enclave of Thaba Nchu, their main grievance being that the laws of the Orange Free State, enforced by the post-war British administration, prohibited transfer of property to anyone other than an immediate blood relation. Plaatje first approached Henry Burton in November 1910, drawing his attention to the need for 'urgent redress', and requesting a meeting so he could provide 'particulars which will enable you to introduce a short measure abrogating the oppressive chapter' of the Orange Free State law book. Several weeks later he travelled to Cape Town to drum up further support, writing to W.P. Schreiner on 10 December. His letter provides a revealing glimpse into how he went about his task: 'My dear Sir', he said,

> As I will not see you before Tuesday and you will in the meanwhile be seeing the other three Native Senators on my behalf, I think that I should mention to you that I wrote the Rt Hon. J.X. Merriman at the same time as I wrote you and Colonel Stanford, and if you think that his influence will help us you might ask him also to reinforce us and help us to induce the Prime Minister to see the justice of introducing a short relieving bill.
>
> I was very much struck by the tactics of General Hertzog 20 years back when he addressed a Dutch jury at Fauresmith in favour of two Native prisoners. I was but a youngster then but I will never forget the episode and I have carried with me a warm admiration for the General all these years and I will be very much surprised if he also does not see the justice of our modest request for immediate relief.
>
> With such a combination I am sure we could favourably impress the Rt

Hon. the Prime Minister (who knows me) and the Minister of Lands; for it will be a pity, having regard to what has been done for the participators in Bambata's rising, if the law abiding Barolongs of Thaba Nchu cannot get the ear of the government in a matter which (judging from the *Gazette* I showed you) the Free State Government was also anxious to redress.

Yours respectfully,
Sol. T. Plaatje

P.S. For the present I am not seeing any of my friends about this for if it were voiced abroad the opposition press will make political capital out of it, and do our cause more harm than good.[13]

Letters like this, confidential in tone, written as one politician to another, were a speciality. He knew exactly the compliments to pay, the names to drop, the tone to adopt. And while there is no reason to doubt the favourable impression left upon him by General Hertzog in years gone by, he had few illusions about where the general's current priorities lay. The personal impression he conveyed was all-important: he had a knack of presenting himself in a friendly and astute manner, as an eminently reasonable, flexible spokesman for his people, understanding of the need to build support for a case, to recognise the need for give and take on either side.[14]

His meeting with the minister of lands, Abraham Fischer, referred to in the letter, could not have gone better. In response to his representations the minister replied that he 'appreciated the disability and promised to bring in an amending Bill during the present session of Parliament', and that in the meantime two young men prohibited from occupying farms they had inherited could do so pending the passage of the bill. He was as good as his word, and within weeks a draft bill to legalise the transfer of landed property in Thaba Nchu was published in the *Government Gazette*. His action created, so *Tsala ea Becoana* reported, 'the liveliest satisfaction'.[15]

But the gazetted bill got no further. White landowners, coveting the land themselves, were up in arms about the proposed legislation, and its further progress was put on hold in the light of rather more far-reaching proposals for land reform which the government was by now considering. It would take another decade, and much further lobbying, before the modest relieving bill eventually became law.[16]

Over the course of the next twelve months Plaatje took up a variety of other issues with the new administration. Some related to the interests of the

Barolong, always a priority for him. He was involved in several meetings with ministers, for example on the question of the 'dog tax' which the Tshidi Barolong of Mafikeng continued to resist, determined to maintain their challenge to the district council's claim to jurisdiction. Other issues were of broader, Union-wide concern. One that particularly exercised him, in the columns of his newspaper as well as in personal representations to ministers and senior civil servants, was the steps being taken by the government to replace African civil servants by whites – on the railways, in the post office, in the courts of law. This was the political dividend that white voters, Afrikaners especially, now expected.[17]

What upset him most was the assault on the employment of black court interpreters. Here the issue was not just unfair employment practice but the proper functioning of the judicial system. He made a point of gathering evidence about the miscarriages of justice that resulted from the use of unqualified or inexperienced interpreters, black and white, and was appalled by what he found. Travelling in the eastern Cape in the second half of 1911, in one Circuit Court case he witnessed an example of faulty interpretation which resulted in the accused being sentenced to twelve months with hard labour, set aside a month later, however, once Plaatje brought it to the attention of General Hertzog, now the minister of justice. If what he saw in court was called 'the administration of justice', 'why, it is an outrage on one's sensibilities', almost unbearable for somebody who had taken so high-minded an approach to his own courtroom responsibilities.[18]

In another case, this one in a magistrate's court, his representations again prompted an inquiry by the minister, and an eventual admission from the assistant magistrate concerned that he thought it 'quite possible for a Magistrate to be influenced by the eloquence of clever attorneys with the result that innocent Natives suffered, if they are not legally represented'. 'The Magistrate promised to be more careful in the future', Plaatje recalled, 'and so he was.'[19]

At least Plaatje's representations on these kinds of issues were listened to and action sometimes taken in response. This was also the case when he visited Pretoria, the new capital of the Union, in December 1911. Following up his earlier criticisms of the replacement of blacks by whites in government service, he secured a series of interviews with government ministers and heads of departments. During the week he spent there he was sympathetically received (twice) by Henry Burton, minister of native affairs, who in turn arranged for him to see Sir David de Villiers Graaff, the minister of posts and telegraphs (who, despite being 'very busy with great matters of State', so *Tsala* reported, nevertheless 'evinced the greatest interest in the representations made'). Thereafter, he saw J.W. Sauer, minister of lands, the postmaster general (with whom he reminisced about his own early days in the employ of that department), the government mining inspector, senior officials from the Department of Printing and Stationery, and Edward Dower, secretary for native affairs, whose department supplied Plaatje, when he went on to Johannesburg, 'with an Orderly to facilitate his day's work there'. He came away with promises to investigate all his complaints and to provide him with written replies when these had been completed.[20]

This was Plaatje in the watchdog role in which he was so effective. Careful to be in full command of the details of the matters he took up, he invariably left a strong impression upon the people he saw. Few people in South Africa, black or white, enjoyed this kind of access to senior members of the government and administration. Often, the personal instincts of these ministers and officials were sympathetic to the eminently reasonable representations, put to them in fluent English or Dutch, whichever they preferred, that Plaatje laid before them, either in correspondence or in person. So long as the Cape liberal tradition retained a foothold in the Union government, and so long as there were no major new initiatives in 'native policy', then Burton, Sauer, Malan, Schreiner and several others were prepared to accept him as a responsible spokesman for his people, to listen to his representations, and in some cases at least to take remedial action.

Of course it worked both ways: Plaatje's own influence, and the circulation of his paper, as he well recognised, could only benefit from the appearance of detailed reports in the columns of *Tsala ea Becoana* about his meetings with the highest government officials, especially when they appeared to be responding positively to the points he put to them. Such courteous consideration was not destined to last. It was nevertheless during these first two years of Union that Plaatje enjoyed his greatest personal influence and access to the machinery of government. 'He had a way particularly his own', Isaiah Bud-M'belle would write, 'of approaching, interviewing, and placing his case before cabinet ministers of all different shades, and other highly placed authorities of English or Dutch extraction – a rare and valuable quality not possessed by other Bantu leaders.'[21]

༺✦༻

As ever, there was a stark contrast between Plaatje's growing stature as a political leader and spokesman and his own financial circumstances, inseparable as these were from those of the newspaper he edited. Although *Tsala ea Becoana* managed to come out at weekly intervals for over two years, its finances, judging from the correspondence which has survived, were rarely less than precarious. In one letter Plaatje complained of not having been paid by the *Tsala* syndicate for three months. In another, in January 1911, Joel Goronyane, chairman of the syndicate, wrote to Silas Molema urging him, as an agent for the newspaper, to gather in all the money that was owed and to forward it to him without delay. Otherwise, he said, it would be impossible for them to pay the editor and compositors: 'any negligence on your part would mean the total ruins of *Tsala*'.[22]

Silas Molema was very familiar with the problems of running a newspaper, and had written similar letters himself during the previous decade. On this occasion, the prospect of 'total ruins' to which Goranyane alluded were averted, and *Tsala* continued to be published with no hint of these difficulties appearing in its columns. Other letters testify similarly to the seriousness of *Tsala*'s situation and the challenges this posed to those involved. In February 1911 Plaatje had to appeal to Joshua Molema for a loan to help keep the paper going and on several occasions wrote to his brother Silas for help too. Another time Isaiah Bud-M'belle stepped in to pay the rent due on *Tsala*'s offices.[23]

Against all the odds *Tsala ea Becoana* survived. In October 1911 the syndicate was reconstituted. Jabavu, who was in England for most of the second half of 1911, seems to have withdrawn from any further involvement and the printing contract with his company was terminated. Henceforth *Tsala* would be printed in Kimberley, resulting not only in more efficient and more timely distribution in its main area of readership but a much-improved printed page, thanks to the use of a new linotype typesetting system.[24]

But Plaatje continued to be pursued by his creditors from Mafeking. Isaiah Bud-M'belle again came to the rescue, on at least one occasion settling a debt resulting from another adverse judgment in the Mafeking magistrate's court. But it is clear that many other debts remained unpaid. It could make visits to Mafeking very awkward. Once, in May 1912, Chief Lekoko asked Plaatje to make 'a flying visit' so as to discuss a land case with him. Aware of the difficulties he faced, Lekoko suggested he got off the train at Madibe (fifteen miles from Mafikeng) where he could arrange for a cart 'to bring you privately to the Stadt, in order that you may avoid to be seen by some of your white creditors, and others whom you care not to see'.[25]

White creditors were not his only problem in Mafikeng. After he had moved to Kimberley, questions arose about his plot of land in the stadt and the validity of his continued claim to it, given that he no longer lived there. It had originally been granted to him through the Molema family but under traditional terms of tenure, which essentially meant at the pleasure of the chief: it did not give him freehold tenure. In his absence others now laid claim to it. Things seem to have come to a head in May 1913. That month Plaatje complained bitterly to Silas Molema that the plot had been taken from him, allocated instead to Ephraim

Molema, and that even the house he had built (in which his brother and family were living) was under threat of dispossession. He appealed to him therefore to take up the matter with his elder brother Joshua. Given his emotional and financial investment in the property over the past decade, this must have come as a huge blow; scant reward, he must have felt, for his services to the Barolong over the past decade. Quite how the matter was resolved is unclear, but the effect of the dispute was to complicate his relationship with the Tshidi chiefdom, compounding the other difficulties pressing upon him. Surely, he must have felt, he was entitled to this land and the house he had built on it if he was to continue to act as their spokesman?[26]

Plaatje did his best to find the money to meet his obligations. He took on as much extra work as he could manage, first as an insurance agent, earning commission on policies he sold, and then as a contributor to the *Pretoria News*, edited by Vere Stent, his old friend from the siege of Mafeking. This began in January 1911, an experiment, Stent said, 'if only we can persuade the more rabid negrophobes to adopt a moderate and sensible attitude', and commended Plaatje to his readers as 'a native correspondent of considerable education and ability'. Over the course of the year a dozen substantial articles appeared under the heading 'Through native eyes', covering such topics as the pros and cons of annexing the protectorates to the Union of South Africa, the Dutch Reformed Church Bill (which restricted African membership), the policies of the 'white Labour Party', the death of the Tswana chief Sebele, the notorious 'amalaita' bands in Johannesburg, and his own travels in Basutoland and the eastern Cape. It was a welcome opportunity to convey his views to a wider audience and to influence opinion, but the income the articles brought in was just as crucial. 'I work day and night just to have something at the end of every month to pay up these things', he told Silas Molema when informing him of this new commission.[27]

He also acted as a correspondent for the *African World*, a London weekly edited by Leo Weinthal, founder and first editor of the *Pretoria News*. Only one piece was published under his own name, however, a full-page article entitled 'The social pest: a native viewpoint', criticising the exaggerated and biased reporting of current 'black peril' scares. An accompanying editorial, presumably written by Weinthal, explained that Plaatje said 'some things with which many readers of the *African World* will not be able to agree', but on this 'grave issue' it was right that they should 'hear all sides'.

It was certainly a contentious issue. In the immediate aftermath of Union, as in earlier periods of political uncertainty, white anxieties had crystallised around the supposed danger posed to white women by African men, and led to sensational coverage in the press of cases of alleged rape and sexual assault. Plaatje condemned, without reservation, the perpetrators of any such crimes, whether they were black or white. But he was highly critical of the press for its selective reporting, and its almost total neglect of the far greater incidence of rape of black women by white men. He argued, in this article and elsewhere, that all such cases, when they came to court, should be heard by a judge alone, given the proven bias of all-white juries. Otherwise, he said, 'the administration of justice ... will become a farce if left in the hands of racialists under the influence of sensational newspaper reports'.[28]

Towards the end of 1911 the political outlook took a distinct turn for the worse. The Cape liberals in the Union cabinet found themselves in an increasingly tenuous position. It was no longer politically feasible, for example, for Sauer, Burton, Malan or Graaff to take action to halt, or even delay, the growing discrimination against Africans in the civil service, and their replacement by whites. It may have been distasteful for Burton to see this happening, but to have opposed it, he said, would have played directly into the hands of General Hertzog's Afrikaner nationalist supporters. They were already impatient at the Botha government's pro-British tendencies, critical of what they saw as his betrayal of the interests of Afrikaner workers and farmers. They called instead for harsher 'native policies' to reflect the reality of the new political balance of power.

J.X. Merriman, whom Plaatje would dearly have liked to see as the first prime minister after Union, could do little to help. 'What can I do?' he asked, when Plaatje complained about the dismissal of African waiters on the South African Railways, 'I can only talk and that does not seem to help your people at all.' Plaatje himself became increasingly alarmed at the passage of such discriminatory legislation as the Native Labour Regulation Act, which tightened controls upon African labour; the Mines and Works Act, which reserved certain categories of work for whites, the first time that such a principle was actually embodied in government legislation; and the Dutch Reformed Church Act, which prohibited full African membership. His protests could not stem the tide. Politically, the northern colonies now predominated in the Union. It was essentially their interests and their traditions which the first Union parliament gave expression to. Afrikaner nationalism had become a powerful force.[29]

It was against this background, and with a growing realisation among politically conscious Africans in all parts of the Union that there was probably worse to come, that the South African Native National Congress was formed in

January 1912. It was conceived as an attempt to provide a truly united forum for the representation of African opinion and interests, a response to the coming together of Boer and Briton in the Act of Union, and a reaction to their own exclusion from any effective representation in the new political entity that had come into being. An awareness of the importance of achieving unity among themselves was not of course new. Even before the Act of Union, considerable experience in seeking to reconcile the political and regional differences that existed had been gained in organisations like the South African Native Press Association of 1903 and 1904, and then in the Native Convention first held in Bloemfontein in 1909.

It was from the recent experience of this convention and the permanent organisation it spawned that the new Congress could be said to have emerged; and it is clear that a great deal of discussion and deliberation had taken place before Pixley ka Isaka Seme, a lawyer trained at Columbia University, in New York, and Jesus College, Oxford, who had recently returned to South Africa, was able to issue his now famous call for unity at the end of 1911. Indeed, it was a special meeting of the executive committee of the Native Convention, held in Johannesburg in August 1911, that provided Seme with his opportunity to expand upon his ideas about the need for a new organisation. Plaatje was not able to attend but wrote to express his support.[30]

Pixley Seme's contribution was that of a newcomer to the political scene. He was equipped with the training and prestige of an attorney, a noticeable American accent, a taste for expensive clothes, and a strong sense of mission to bring about the political unity of the African people. Some of his colleagues thought him over-ambitious and rather hot-headed. One well-publicised incident seemed to lend weight to their views. Shortly after returning to South Africa, Seme had drawn a loaded revolver on a group of whites who took violent exception to his decision to travel in the first-class compartment of a railway carriage ('Like all solicitors,' he subsequently explained, 'I of course travel first class'). He was taken to court for using a firearm in a threatening manner, found guilty and fined.[31]

Seme argued on grounds of self-defence that had he not drawn the revolver, thereby frightening off his assailants, he would most likely have been assaulted and ejected from the train. Nevertheless, his behaviour was not welcomed by many of the older-established African political spokesmen, more cautious in their approach and always worried about alienating their white sympathisers. This was certainly true of Plaatje, who was careful to avoid provoking incidents of this nature, concerned, as he had always been, to disarm accusations that Africans were seeking social equality with whites. When, nearly two years after Seme's conviction, he had reason to complain of his own mistreatment by the white conductor of a tram in Kimberley, his response was not to argue the case on the spot, let alone threaten to use a firearm, but to complain in writing to the manager of De Beers (the owners of the tram), pointing out the various ways in which he had always sought to avoid any provocation. Clearly, Plaatje and Seme were men of very different temperament and experience, an added complication to achieving unity in any new African political movement.[32]

Pixley Seme nevertheless had the advantage of being free of any earlier political involvement and associations, and he proved to be the right person to take the initiative in overcoming the obstacles and rivalries which had hitherto kept South Africa's leading black political personalities and organisations apart. At the August 1911 meeting and subsequently he was able to argue powerfully and eloquently for a new unity, and for a fresh, more vigorous political organisation that represented the interests of all Africans; indeed, he had already drafted a constitution for it. Like Plaatje, Seme was acutely aware of the importance of securing the support of the chiefs in any organisation that sought to represent the African people, and he knew their financial support would be crucial. Both envisaged a movement that would not only unite politically active Africans and their separate organisations in different parts of the country, but also achieve a social unity – of the chiefs, as representatives of traditional forms of authority and influence; of the new generation, or generations, of mission-educated Africans who were now ready to assume leadership in the political affairs of their people; and of the masses of the people who needed to be led.

Only by achieving this social unity, Seme argued, could Africans overcome the political disabilities recently confirmed in the Act of Union, and only with such an organisation would they be able to 'make their grievances known and considered', he said, 'both by the Government and by the people of South Africa at large'. With a momentum that combined high idealism with close attention to the thorny problem of reconciling existing political and personal differences, Plaatje, Seme and their colleagues moved haltingly, during the second half of 1911, towards the achievement of their goal.[33]

In November a further 'caucus' meeting was held in Johannesburg. Plaatje was reported to have made a closing speech 'exhorting the members to be united', and – along with Pixley Seme – was given a vote of thanks for his contribution. The meeting finally closed at 2.30 a.m., having agreed to hold an inaugural conference in Bloemfontein on 8 January 1912. Plaatje later claimed to have made this step possible by persuading the leaders of the two main Transvaal African organisations already in existence, the Transvaal Native Congress and the Transvaal Native Political Organisation, to set aside their differences and rivalries and co-operate in setting up a single, national political body: completion of a task, in other words, he had begun in Pretoria over a year before.[34]

Perhaps partly because the achievement of this unity seemed to many to have been so long delayed (at the November meeting Seme admitted that the idea of a united African political organisation was 'a very old idea'), most of the chiefs and delegates, representing organisations from all four provinces of South Africa (and the protectorates), were conscious that they were attending a conference of historic importance. Seme pointed out in his opening address that it was the first time that 'so many elements representing different tongues and tribes ever attempted to co-operate under one umbrella', and he went on to emphasise the difficulties they faced. The formation of Congress, though, was the 'first step towards solving the native problem, and therein lay the advancement of the dark races who had hitherto been separated by tribal jealousies'. His motion proposing the establishment of Congress was seconded by Chief Joshua Molema, and the two men were followed by a series of other speakers, chiefs and commoners, all urging support. When it was put to a vote, late in the afternoon of Monday, 8 January 1912, the motion was passed unanimously and met with loud cheers from all the delegates, who had risen from their seats. Even at the time they were in no doubt that they had taken a vital step forward in the history of their people, equivalent in significance, as many saw it, to the achievement of the 'whites only' Act of Union.[35]

The next business in hand, the appointment of office-holders, was a matter of some delicacy, for it was considered vital to the future of the organisation to achieve a satisfactory balance between the different regions and peoples represented. It was widely expected that Dr Walter Rubusana of East London, a Congregational minister, member of the Cape Provincial Council (the only African ever to be elected to this body), formerly president of the South African Native Convention, and already something of an elder statesman in African eyes, would be elected as president of Congress. However, Rubusana, for whatever reason – perhaps he just felt he had too many other commitments – decided against putting his name forward, and the presidency was offered instead to another clergyman, the Rev. John Dube, who was not actually present at the meeting, being represented instead by his brother Charles Dube.[36]

John Dube, a Zulu, undoubtedly had strong credentials. Ordained in 1899, as a young man he had travelled to the United States to further his education, and, perceiving the parallels between Natal and the American South, came to be strongly influenced by the ideas of the black American educator Booker T. Washington; so much so, that in his declaration accepting the presidency of Congress, he indicated that Washington was to be his 'patron saint' and 'guiding star'.[37]

Dube was renowned too as editor and founder of the English–Zulu newspaper *Ilanga lase Natal* and as principal of his own school at Ohlange, near Durban, a unique venture that was widely regarded as one of black South Africa's proudest achievements. He was acceptable as president of Congress because the majority of delegates at its inaugural conference wished to emphasise that African political activity would in future no longer be centred in the relatively privileged Cape. Dube, moreover, quite as much as Pixley Seme, seemed to be inspired by this new spirit of unity, writing on one occasion of 'the great work we have taken upon ourselves as Natives of South Africa to unite together and give up old differences and racial hatreds and tribal quarrels to stand as one man, to speak as a voice of one person, for the interest of all'.[38]

Of the other officers elected, Pixley Seme and Thomas Mapikela were to be the two treasurers, the attorney G.D. Montsioa of Pietersburg (northern Transvaal) became recording secretary, and twenty-two of the chiefs, including the Barolong paramount, Badirile Montshiwa, became honorary presidents; Dr Rubusana was the only 'commoner' to be honoured in the same way. Together with the provision in the constitution for an upper house of chiefs, these appointments emphasised the importance that the Congress leaders attached to their support and involvement. Plaatje, more than most, believed that Congress was likely to stand or fall on this question, and was reported to have remarked at the time that 'the Natives can never effect anything which is not supported by chiefs'. He undoubtedly had his own experiences very much in mind. Seme likewise, closely connected to the Swazi royal family, never failed to stress the importance of the chiefs, and believed that their involvement was what distinguished their new organisation from anything that had gone before.[39]

Plaatje himself was elected corresponding secretary, a position that was in many ways even more important than that of president. With his many years' experience as a newspaper editor and political spokesman, his clerical experience in the Cape civil service, a well-known capacity for hard work (likely to be essential to success in building up any new national movement), and his ability to speak all the major African languages of the country, there could have been little argument that he was the ideal choice for the position. An additional consideration was that he was known to be close to the politically sophisticated Africans of the eastern Cape (the fact that he had an Mfengu wife was a considerable advantage in this respect), without, however, being tainted with their degree of involvement in the party and ethnic rivalries of the region.

Plaatje was thus seen as the right person to bring to the new national movement the traditions and skills of African political life in the Cape, but to direct these to the wider political realities now imposed by Union. Of course he had his own following too, being widely accepted as a spokesman for Batswana living in the Transvaal and Orange Free State, as well as the Bechuanaland Protectorate, and he was in close contact with the new leadership in Johannesburg and Pretoria. More than any other African political leader, moreover, he had acquired the reputation of having ready access to the Union administration. If any of the delegates at Bloemfontein had any doubts on this point, they had only to look at the most recent issue of *Tsala ea Becoana*, which carried detailed reports of a series of interviews in Pretoria with government ministers and high-ranking administrators; or the editorial that appeared in *Ilanga lase Natal* several weeks later congratulating 'our good friend, Mr Sol Plaatje' on his recent efforts.[40]

So it was, as *Tsala ea Becoana* remarked in February 1912, that its editor, 'besides taking a leading part in the movement, has been saddled with nearly the whole of the secretarial work at the instance of the Native lawyers who convened the movement'. It is unsurprising, as this formulation suggests, that Plaatje should have been reluctant to take on the task. Knowing the amount of time and work that was going to be required to get Congress effectively off the ground, he must have given careful consideration to the adverse effects this was bound to have upon his newspaper business. At the same time, it was recognition of the part he had now come to play in the political affairs of his people, and of the talents that suited him so well to the position; it was not a responsibility he felt he could turn down.[41]

After the election of office-holders the delegates had two major concerns. First, they discussed a range of social and political issues with a view to framing resolutions to lay before the government. Committees were set up to address such questions as 'Native Schools and Churches', 'Hostels and Passes for Native Women', and 'Medical Examination of Women', with particular individuals being appointed to lead on specified topics. Plaatje dealt with 'native labour', Philip Modise (principal secretary to the Basotho chief, Letsie II) tackled segregation, Levi Mvabaza and E.T. Moeletsi the pass laws. The question of land was of special concern, particularly in the light of the so-called Squatters Bill, recently gazetted by the government, which proposed drastic new restrictions on African landownership and purchase. Congress considered the bill to be a serious threat to their common interest and denounced it in the strongest terms, claiming that if passed 'it would cause large numbers of them to become wanderers, people without homes, in the land of their birth'. They resolved to 'respectfully request the Government to withdraw the said Bill as its sole aim and object is to deprive the native of economic independence which is the inherent right of all His Majesty's subjects'.

Their second major concern was the constitution of the new organisation.

No agreement on this was reached, however, the main stumbling block being the question of its financial structure and the size of contributions from the local branches. The name of the new organisation also proved to be a point of some contention. Plaatje's proposal was that it should be 'known by a distinctive name, and a native name for preference', his argument being that so many similarly named councils and congresses were already in existence, another one would only confuse people further. He supported the suggestion of Cleopas Kunene, a well-known former newspaper editor from Natal, now living in the Transvaal, who had written a long letter to the conference setting out the case for the name Imbizo Yabantu (Bantu Congress).

Although Plaatje was strongly supported by Joshua Molema, the meeting decided by a small majority to adopt the recommendations of the Transvaal delegates that they should be known as the South African Native National Congress (SANNC). Plaatje clearly felt strongly about the issue, for when the executive committee was authorised (on his own motion) to remain behind and complete the unfinished work and review the constitution, he again urged that Congress's name be changed. Again his resolution was defeated, this time by a majority of two, and the name South African Native National Congress was incorporated into the draft constitution. The voting also reflected what everybody at the conference must have realised: that the Transvaal was likely to play the dominant role in the affairs of the new organisation.

Agreement was reached on the objects of the organisation, and these were defined as follows:

a. The promotion of unity and mutual co-operation between the Government and the Abantu Races of South Africa.
b. The maintenance of a central channel of communication between the Government and the aboriginal races in South Africa.
c. The promotion of the educational, social, economical and political elevation of the native people in South Africa.
d. The promotion of mutual understanding between the Native chiefs and the encouragement in them and their people of a spirit of loyalty to the British crown, and all lawfully constituted authorities, and to bring about better understanding between the white and black inhabitants of South Africa.
e. The safeguarding of the interests of the native inhabitants throughout South Africa by seeking and obtaining redress for any of their just grievances.[42]

By no stretch of the imagination could these aims be described as radical. There was no mention of the franchise. Industrial action was not contemplated as a means of obtaining redress for the growing number of grievances of which the Congress delegates now complained. Nor were they attracted by notions of 'passive resistance', though they were all aware of the recent use of such methods by South Africa's Indian community, under the leadership of Mohandas Gandhi. Congress hoped and believed that in bringing their complaints to the attention of the authorities through the tried methods of explanation, petition and deputation, they would be given a fair hearing and their grievances attended to. They resolved to strengthen their cause by demonstrating that the new organisation did genuinely represent the African people of South Africa; to make it impossible for South Africa's white rulers to dismiss their claims, as they so often did, on the grounds that they spoke only for the educated minority.[43]

At the same time they went out of their way to stress their loyalty to the government: they wished to work as partners with the government, not in opposition to it, and their language was moderate and respectful in tone. Even their condemnation of the Squatters Bill was measured in comparison with that of Dr Abdullah Abdurahman, president of the African Political Organisation (APO), a predominantly Coloured body. In a speech at the organisation's annual conference in Johannesburg two weeks earlier, he had criticised, in the strongest terms, the proposed legislation, together with the general direction of government policy in relation to both 'native' and 'coloured' races, and prophesied a clash 'whenever the whites think it advisable and practicable to begin a war of extermination'.

Dr Abdurahman was roundly condemned in the daily press for using such extreme language and 'severely taken to task', so he said later, 'for imputing such inhuman motives to Europeans'. Plaatje for one believed he had gone too far, and was being unnecessarily provocative, admitting that he was 'one of those who criticized Dr Abdurahman's speech when he prophesied a war of extermination in this country'. He was by no means the only African political leader to have felt the same way.[44]

White South Africa took rather less notice of the SANNC's inaugural conference two weeks later. While its proceedings were reported in both English and vernacular columns of the weekly African newspapers, there was little coverage in the mainstream daily press. Perhaps it was just not so newsworthy. Even the Bloemfontein *Friend*, which had taken an interest in the meetings of the earlier Native Convention when it met in the city, barely mentioned the conference, the presence of a well-known local Anglican priest (Edgar Rose) notwithstanding. One reason for the lack of coverage, it was suggested, was that the organisers had failed to send out the necessary information and invitations to newspaper editors prior to the conference. This at least was the view of F.Z.S. Peregrino, still living in Cape Town, who wrote afterwards that 'owing to a mistake the Press was not sufficiently represented at the gathering in Bloemfontein'.[45]

There was, however, a notable exception. Vere Stent's *Pretoria News* carried a series of reports over four issues, summarising the speeches made, the resolutions passed, the office-holders appointed. Plaatje, who had been charged during the first morning of the conference with the task of recording its proceedings and making 'full reports in the newspapers', was most likely their author. Stent himself, a fierce opponent of General Hertzog and the Afrikaner nationalists, was in no doubt about the significance of what had just taken place. In an editorial commenting upon the conference, he wrote that the time looked 'almost ripe for union amongst natives', and that when achieved it would be 'one of the most far reaching events in the history of South Africa'. He also predicted that more was likely to be heard from the new organisation on the land issue given the strong opposition that had been expressed on the Squatters Bill.[46]

In official circles there were certainly some concerns. A letter of Dr Rubusana's, relating to his visit to Chief Letsie of Basutoland a month after Congress's inaugural meeting, fell into the hands of the Basutoland authorities, raising fears about the reach of the new organisation into the High Commission territories as well as the Union of South Africa. Lord Gladstone, the governor general and high commissioner, was responsible for both, and he told Lord Harcourt, secretary of state for the colonies, in one of his regular confidential briefings, that this new body 'representative of all the natives in S. Africa wants watching'. Hard as the Congress leaders tried to allay official concerns with their protestations of loyalty, and to adopt a studiously moderate tone in all their public pronouncements, government officials, mindful of earlier 'Ethiopian' scares, often worried that there was more to them than met the eye.[47]

In practice the main responsibility for building up the new Congress, and establishing its legitimacy in the eyes of both government and people, fell to Plaatje and Dube. It was a challenging task. A new national organisation may have come into being, but actually it was no more than a loose federation of existing organisations. It had a cumbersome structure, no agreed constitution, and very little money. However much those involved professed a desire for unity, it was not so easy to wish away the personal, regional and ethnic differences and rivalries that the delegates brought to the movement. In fact they had no strong wish to do so, most of them regarding the new organisation more as a platform for mutual co-operation and the advancement of their separate interests than an expression of new national sentiment. Intellectually all could agree on the need for unity. Emotionally it was not so easy, for the most fundamental loyalties lay elsewhere. A delicate balancing act had also to be achieved between harnessing the support of the chiefs – vital financially – and a recognition that their views and priorities were not always going to coincide with those of a more self-consciously 'progressive' leadership.[48]

There remained, moreover, the problem of Tengo Jabavu and his following in the eastern Cape, among the Mfengu in particular. Although he had been away in England for much of the second half of 1911, he arrived back in South Africa a few days before the Bloemfontein conference and there were hopes that he would make an appearance. But he failed to do so, and it soon became clear that he had no desire to play any part in the new organisation, regarding its existence as a threat both to the survival of the Cape franchise and to his own influence. Soon afterwards, indeed, he set up a rival organisation of his own, a branch of the Universal Races Congress whose conference he had attended in London. It was a significant blow to the SANNC's claims to be fully representative of all the peoples of South Africa.

Nevertheless, Plaatje and Dube did their best to maintain the new momentum. Initially the government seemed quite responsive to their representations, providing some grounds for hope that it would be prepared to recognise the new organisation as a kind of consultative body on 'native affairs'. Intending to take up issues that had been discussed at Congress's inaugural meeting, Plaatje travelled to Cape Town in March 1912, in advance of John Dube and several other Congress office-holders, with a brief to arrange meetings with government ministers. In one of these, a deputation consisting of Plaatje, Mapikela and Sefako Makgatho met with J.W. Sauer, the minister responsible for railways, to lay before him their concerns about the appalling way Africans were treated when travelling on trains. Makgatho, the Pretoria correspondent for Plaatje's newspaper, had had direct experience of this himself, having been thrown off a train when making his way to the conference in Bloemfontein. Other Congress delegates suffered similar indignities when travelling home afterwards; several of them were 'hurled off the train at Brandfort', Makgatho told the minister, and court cases were now pending. Sauer, in response, expressed sympathy with their concerns and agreed to look further into the matter.[49]

The interview was preceded by an interesting exchange that served to illustrate the value of Plaatje's relationship with Henry Burton, the minister of native affairs, as well as his experience in handling junior government officials. 'The members of the deputation reached the office punctually at 10 a.m., the appointed time,' Plaatje related, 'and were ushered with great ceremony into the presence of a clerk who seemed all affability.' Unfortunately, the clerk informed them, the minister was too busy to see them, but promised to pass on their concerns to him. Plaatje was not so easily put off, however. 'No,' said our editor, 'we have come not to see you, we have come to see the Minister by arrangement with another Minister, and if he cannot see us we will go back and ask Mr Burton why he sent us at ten o'clock, sharp, to a Minister who is unable to see us.' That was the end of the clerk's obfuscations: 'It transpired that just at that moment Mr Sauer was expecting the deputation', and they duly made their way into the meeting.[50]

The most wide-ranging of the meetings Plaatje arranged was with Henry Burton and his secretary for native affairs, Edward Dower. He was accompanied by John Dube, who had just arrived in Cape Town, the Rev. Edward Tsewu and Thomas Mapikela, and they again raised the issues that Congress had discussed at its inaugural conference. Their strongest representations were on the Squatters Bill: 'We oppose the Bill and ask for its withdrawal until land has been provided for the natives', Dube told the minister after they had outlined their objections. Henry Burton replied that while the last thing the government desired to do was 'injustice to the natives', he 'could see no alternative but the adoption of the principle laid down' in the draft bill. He was 'prepared to adopt a most reasonable attitude when it is brought up for discussion in Parliament', but he nevertheless 'saw no other way of dealing with the state of affairs and something of this sort is absolutely necessary'.[51]

In fact the government decided not to proceed with the Squatters Bill and it was dropped during the course of the next parliamentary session. This is unlikely to have been the result of the group's representations. Of rather greater weight were the objections of the white landlords (particularly the influential large absentee landlords, who stood to lose most) and a speech in the House of Lords in England by Lord Selborne, the former high commissioner, opposing the proposals. It nevertheless suited Plaatje and the other Congress leaders, keen to establish the credibility of the new organisation, to claim that their own representations had been taken into account.[52]

The question of passes for women was another urgent concern. In most parts of the country pass laws applied only to African men, but in the Orange Free State several municipalities now sought to extend their use to women as well. It was regarded as particularly degrading and had aroused strong opposition. Thomas Mapikela told the minister that the women, despairing that the men were not properly representing their case, were now circulating a petition and intended sending a deputation of their own to Cape Town. Burton replied that he was 'personally against the idea of forcing women to carry passes', but said that it was difficult for him to intervene since the power to issue passes was vested in the municipalities. He thought the idea of a women's deputation was 'inadvisable', but had to see them when they arrived in Cape Town three weeks later. Not long after, Thomas Mapikela's wife Martha was one of a number of women arrested by the police as the campaign escalated and violence ensued.

On several other issues Henry Burton responded more favourably. On the subject of 'Natives employed on Railways' he told Plaatje that he 'ought to see Mr Sauer', and arranged the interview referred to above. To the request of Plaatje and Dube that the government set up a commission to look into the 'black peril', he indicated that he 'quite agreed with the sentiment', and a commission was indeed set up. To Thomas Mapikela's request that part of the imperial vote of funds that had been 'set apart for the natives in the Orange Free State' should be used for educational purposes, he agreed to 'try and help them' to arrange this.

These interviews represented the first direct, official contact between the newly formed SANNC and the government of the Union of South Africa. On the whole the Congress delegates went home well pleased with their reception and appreciated the time that ministers had taken to listen to their representations. The meeting with Henry Burton on 15 March had lasted nearly three hours. They had some reason to feel they were being taken seriously.

Plaatje was involved in one other significant initiative while in Cape Town, exploring with Dr Abdurahman the possibilities of co-operation between their respective organisations. This led to a meeting, reported to have been 'of considerable length', of the executives of the two bodies at the APO's offices in Loop Street, Cape Town. The meeting resolved that 'there should be closer co-operation between the Coloured and Native races of South Africa', declaring 'that the two bodies should keep in close touch with each other, and discuss matters directly affecting non-Europeans, and where necessary take united action'. They envisaged meeting at least once a year.[53]

Of all the Congress leaders Plaatje was the best equipped by temperament and experience to take this forward. Kimberley had a long history of co-operation between Africans and Coloureds, and Plaatje himself was an active member of the Kimberley branch of the APO. For Plaatje, the achievement of unity among Africans, however desirable and important in itself, was not something to be achieved at the expense of friendly co-operation with the Coloured people (or indeed of white sympathisers) in their common struggles. Plaatje and Abdurahman would enjoy a relationship of respect and friendship for years to come.

Plaatje returned home at the end of March, although not before delivering a farewell address to a well-attended meeting held under the auspices of the Cape

Peninsula Native Association. It was a characteristically eloquent survey of the political situation, and he was frequently interrupted by applause, or shouts of 'shame' or 'hear, hear', as he ranged widely over the disabilities and injustices his people faced, paying special attention to the Squatters Bill and the issue of passes for women. All in all, Plaatje and his fellow Congress leaders could feel well pleased at what they had achieved during the few weeks they spent in Cape Town. Similar sentiments were in evidence at the first meeting of the executive committee of the SANNC when it met to review their progress some weeks later.[54]

Plaatje's unpaid work on behalf of the SANNC of course ran alongside his role as editor of *Tsala ea Becoana*. Throughout the early months of 1912 *Tsala ea Becoana* appeared regularly (despite several changes that were made in its printing arrangements), but with its issue of 8 June 1912 publication ceased. Exactly what happened is unclear. There was the usual accumulation of financial problems, but the difficulties must have been exacerbated by Plaatje's heavy involvement in the affairs of the SANNC. For much of March, April and May 1912, he had been away in Cape Town, Johannesburg and elsewhere, and it is difficult to believe that these extended absences from the office, whatever the arrangements made to ensure the paper appeared regularly during his absence, were not a contributory factor in its demise.[55]

His travels also stretched him financially. When John Dube met Plaatje in Cape Town (for the first time it seems), he found that while he and the other Congress leaders had funds contributed by their 'respective districts', Plaatje had none and he therefore 'took it upon myself' to reimburse him for the £21 he had spent from his own pocket. Having done so, he then wrote to Chief Lekoko, the Barolong chief regent, with a request to repay this sum to him since 'we looked upon Mr Plaatje as a special representative of yourself', reminding him of the issues Plaatje had taken up on his behalf and of the 'good stand' he had made 'on behalf of the Bechuanaland chieftainship'. The letter is evidence not only of the constant financial difficulties Plaatje faced but of the new organisation's dependence upon the chiefs for support.[56]

But within three months Plaatje was back in business. He was able to relaunch his newspaper, gave it a new name, *Tsala ea Batho* (*The People's Friend*), and was now its sole owner and proprietor, having somehow – quite how remains a mystery – secured the necessary backing. He also acquired his own printing press. This opportunity arose from the bankruptcy of a short-lived

Johannesburg newspaper, *Motsualle ea Babatsho*, and he got it at a knock-down price. He had been heartened by the support he received for the project from some non-Tswana Africans, including Elka Cele, a well-known Zulu spokesman, then living in Johannesburg, who helped him raise the £200 that was needed.[57]

It was the kind of gesture that might have been taken to express a new spirit of inter-tribal co-operation had it not been for the opposition expressed by Pixley Seme to the loan being made. Seme had plans for a newspaper of his own, and he too was in need of a printing press. Whether Plaatje simply outbid him for it, or whether he had still to secure the funding he needed from his main backer, Queen Labotsibeni of Swaziland, is unclear. Plaatje, at any rate, prevailed and Seme's new newspaper, *Abantu-Batho*, did not make its appearance until November. Soon both would be claiming to be official organs of the SANNC: co-operation and competition coexisted rather uneasily in the precarious world of black South African newspapers.[58]

Pleased as he was to have acquired the printing press the circumstances in which he did so simply underlined, as he pointed out in a letter to Silas Molema, the inability of the Tswana to raise the funds themselves – or even to come up with the money to pay for the transport of the press from Johannesburg. It was hard to return home to Kimberley with no funds, he said, adding that 'it would not be so shameful if the train money had been paid for'. Always, in Plaatje's mind, was this powerful sense that the Batswana needed to at least hold their own among other African peoples in South Africa, and that he had a special obligation to help them do so. He worried that if they did not make a sufficient contribution to the new newspaper, they would have little say in how it was run.[59]

The sentiments he expressed pointed to a wider truth. Black South Africans might now have come together in a new political organisation, but ethnic and regional identities remained as strong as ever. Indeed, if anything, they had been strengthened as a result of the formal recognition of the role of the chiefs in an 'upper house', and their importance as a source of finance. Inevitably there were tensions as leaders sought simultaneously to speak with one voice and to advance the interests of the different constituencies they represented. Competing for the resources to support rival newspapers was just one expression of this reality.[60]

The first issue of the new combined newspaper, published in Sepedi as well as Setswana and English, appeared in the middle of September 1912. Its new title, *Tsala ea Batho* (*The People's Friend*), reflected the union of Tswana and Pedi peoples which the merger was taken to signify, as well as an aspiration towards a wider unity. New offices were acquired in Shannon Street (soon to become known as the Newton Printing Works) and formally opened on 7 September 1912, the very day Plaatje's wife Elizabeth gave birth to a son – promptly christened Johannes Gutenberg in celebration of the happy coincidence. Although it was not long before he was complaining that lack of capital was retarding the growth of *Tsala*, and preventing improvements being made to the machinery, the newspaper appeared regularly for the next four months and with a healthy amount of advertising. From the point of view of his newspaper business, Plaatje was able to start the new year, 1913, with some optimism about its future prospects.[61]

✦

Politically, however, things looked increasingly ominous, and there had been, since the middle of 1912, some significant developments. Foremost among them was the replacement of Henry Burton as minister of native affairs by General Hertzog, whose views on 'native policy' were sufficiently well known to cause considerable alarm to the Congress leadership when the news was announced. At the meeting the Congress leaders had with Henry Burton in March 1912, John Dube, though he can have had no knowledge of the ministerial changes soon to take place, told him quite bluntly, 'What we are afraid of is your successor in office.' His fears proved to be justified. After taking office as minister of native affairs in June 1912, Hertzog busied himself with preparing some comprehensive proposals to deal with the 'native problem' which went a great deal further than the abortive Squatters Bill.[62]

Henry Burton's replacement by General Hertzog in fact marked an important turning point in the composition and behaviour of General Botha's administration. It signalled the end of a period of relative inaction and lack of direction in 'native affairs', a sharp decline in the influence of the Cape liberals in the government, and the growing strength of Afrikaner nationalism both inside and outside parliament. What optimism Plaatje and his colleagues once had about African prospects in the Union evaporated in the face of the government's determination to implement a comprehensive 'native policy' that was acceptable to the country's two most powerful interests: the farmers and the mine owners, maize and gold.

One legislative proposal in particular sought to achieve this objective: the Natives' Land Bill, whose provisions were first made known in April 1913. Since the governor general had made no mention of it in his speech when opening the new parliamentary session in January, it came as a shock. 'It sneaked into Parliament as quietly as an evil deed of which its perpetrators were ashamed,' Plaatje wrote later. Unusually he was not sent the *Government Gazette* by the government printer, and it was only thanks to three sympathetic members of

242

parliament, who sent him copies of the bill, that he became aware of its detailed provisions. His initial reaction, when the government's plans were first mooted, was to urge his colleagues to be cautious in the language they used. He soon abandoned his own advice when he realised its full implications.[63]

The Natives' Land Act of 1913 (as it duly became) was one of the most important pieces of legislation in South African history, and one of the central events in Plaatje's life; over the next four years, indeed, its course was largely shaped by his response to it. When its provisions were first made known, the effect was to confirm the worst fears of the Congress leadership about the direction in which official 'native policy' was going. The Natives' Land Act was important above all for introducing into the legislation of the Union the principle of territorial separation, or segregation. Its central provision was to deprive Africans of the right to acquire land outside their existing areas of occupation, and to prohibit whites from acquiring land within these areas, now defined as 'Scheduled Native Areas'.

Few Africans at the time objected strongly to the principle of territorial segregation per se, provided it could be implemented in a reasonable and equitable manner and did not deprive them of any political or constitutional rights. At the same time, few had any illusions about the possibility of either condition being met, and many would have shared the views Plaatje had expressed in his prize essay on the subject in 1910. These views seemed to be fully vindicated with the publication of the Natives' Land Bill, for it was clear that in practice there was no possibility of territorial separation being implemented in anything like an equitable manner, while the debates in parliament suggested that the logical corollary to the bill, in the minds of many of its supporters, was the phasing out of the non-racial Cape franchise.[64]

Under the terms of the bill, only 7.3 per cent of the total land surface of the Union was to be set aside for African occupation, patently inadequate to support a population that was four times the size of the white population. To meet this objection, a commission was appointed under the provisions of the bill to find and purchase land for African occupation to add to what had already been set aside, consisting largely of the 'reserves' already in African occupation, most of them already very overcrowded. Under the chairmanship of Sir William Beaumont, a former administrator of Natal and a Supreme Court judge, the commission was charged with completing its investigations and presenting its report within two years. In the intervening period, though, before the commission reported, Africans were to be barred from purchasing land except from other Africans, or in existing reserves where, as Plaatje would point out, this could not be done anyway since most land there was held communally, not individually.

Neither the idea of territorial separation nor the wider philosophy of segregation which served to justify the Natives' Land Act was of course new. Some of its provisions gave expression to recommendations of the South African Native Affairs Commission of 1903–5; in this sense the Act implemented, albeit somewhat belatedly, one of the major objectives of British imperial policy as formulated during the post-war reconstruction period.

Implementing this grand design, though, was only part of the story. Other provisions of the Act, as well as the manner in which it was rushed through the House of Assembly, reflected the response of General Botha's administration to the acute political pressures it faced, particularly from white farmers in the Transvaal and Orange Free State whose demands for state intervention had become ever more insistent. The legislation they got went further than anything that had been proposed in the past and it threatened to have particularly drastic consequences in the Orange Free State. Here, the system of 'sowing on the halves' (widespread in the province since the South African War), whereby Africans living on white-owned farms gave half of their produce to the white landowner in exchange for the seed and the right to farm the land, was made illegal. What many white farmers in the Free State now wanted was not a share of the produce of 'squatters' living on their land, but their labour, and on the best terms possible. Commercial farming had, for a variety of reasons, become a much more attractive proposition than hitherto, but it depended upon an adequate supply of cheap labour. This the Natives' Land Act, by converting African producers in these areas from peasants into farm labourers, aimed to provide. The segregationist ideology in which the Natives' Land Act was framed, and with which it was justified, barely disguised the manner in which these provisions expressed the new-found political power of the white farmers, mobilised under the banner of Afrikaner nationalism, in the politics of Union. They now had the upper hand. In the words of J.G. Keyter, member of parliament for Ficksburg, his province was 'a white man's country' and the 'Native' needed to be 'kept in his place': he 'was not going to be allowed to buy land or hire land there, and … if he wanted to be there he must be in service'.[65]

Plaatje's reaction to the Natives' Land Bill, once its provisions became known, was one of shocked disbelief. If somebody had told him at the beginning of the year that the South African parliament was capable of passing such a law, he said, he would have 'considered him a fit subject for the lunatic asylum' and he quickly revised his opinion of Dr Abdurahman's Johannesburg speech the previous year. A 'war of extermination', he now agreed, was just what it was, and he condemned it as 'a legislative monstrosity', its objective no less than 'to steal a whole subcontinent'. He felt it particularly because it appeared to be aimed specifically at an area he knew so well: the Orange Free State, province of his birth. Like many of his colleagues, Plaatje had been lulled into something of a false sense of security, politically speaking, by the lack of direction in 'native affairs' during the first two years of Union. Perhaps, too, his own success in building relationships with government ministers and administrators, even if he did recognise the tenuous foundations upon which they were built, had created an illusion of influence in the administration that for a while disguised the highly vulnerable position in which the African people and their leaders now found themselves.[66]

Neither Plaatje nor his colleagues in the leadership of the SANNC were equipped to deal with so momentous and drastic a piece of legislation as the Natives' Land Act of 1913. They had been brought up to believe in notions of gradual progress and advancement. Setbacks they had certainly experienced in their adult lives – the Treaty of Vereeniging in 1902, the Act of Union more recently – but the ideal persisted. Being able to purchase land, with legally recognised freehold tenure, and to enjoy security as tenants in agreements freely entered into, was central to their idea of citizenship and to their vision of the future. Nothing prepared them for an Act such as this. It struck at the heart of their belief in a common society, at their conviction that, ultimately, a shared sense of decency and humanity, between black and white, rulers and ruled, would protect them from measures such as the one now before them. What could they do but respond in the manner to which they were accustomed?

But as Plaatje, for one, was quick to realise, the Natives' Land Act, by far the greatest threat yet faced by the SANNC, did at least provide the opportunity to mobilise support for the movement as never before. Unlike many of the earlier issues with which Congress had been concerned – travelling on railways, or employment in government service – the Land Act threatened the interests and well-being of virtually every section of the African population. It thus provided an opportunity to cement that social unity which Seme had talked of when calling Congress's inaugural meeting; now it was reinforced by a much stronger sense of common interest and the urgent need to resist the new legislation. For black South Africans, there was no more fundamental or emotional issue than land. A shared sense of grievance bound them together.[67]

Plaatje was in the forefront of organising African opposition to the Land Act. From the time the bill was first published in February, to its passage in June 1913, and his departure from South Africa as a member of a Congress deputation to

England a year later, it was to be his overwhelming personal preoccupation, that of his newspaper, and of the SANNC as a whole.

Congress's response from the beginning was to concern itself not with the principle of territorial segregation which the Land Act claimed to embody, but with the effects it was likely to have. At its first annual conference meeting in Johannesburg at the end of March, in a hall Plaatje described as 'packed to suffocation', delegates discussed the proposed legislation, scarcely believing the enormity of it. If it became law, they declared in one of their resolutions, 'it would constitute the cruellest act of injustice ever perpetrated upon their people'. They then appointed a deputation to go to Cape Town to bring their protests to the minister, J.W. Sauer, who had succeeded Hertzog as minister of native affairs. Plaatje himself was not able, for financial reasons, to travel with his deputation, which went in May, but was present at the special July meeting which was convened to hear its report. The delegates had, so Dr Rubusana related, four interviews with the minister, and further sessions with other members of parliament. Their protests made no impact whatever, and even their clear willingness to compromise had failed to elicit the slightest response.[68]

Lord Gladstone, the governor general and high commissioner, a keen supporter of General Botha's government, offered no hope either. Plaatje had written to him earlier, requesting that he withhold his assent to the bill until he had heard the 'native view'. To this, Plaatje recalled, 'His Excellency replied that such a course was not within his constitutional functions'. John Dube again approached him after the Act had become law, with a request for an interview in order to inform him of 'the nature of the damage that the Act was causing among the Native population'. He received the same reply.[69]

As the Congress leaders feared, the effects of the Land Act, once it came into operation on 20 June 1913, were immediate and devastating. In July a meeting of Congress heard from delegates from all four provinces of the way white farmers were taking advantage of the new law to rid themselves of unwanted tenants, or force away others who refused to accept arbitrary demands for their labour. Plaatje himself, on the journey from Kimberley to Johannesburg, came across some of its worst effects. He had set out from Kimberley in the first week of July in the direction of Bloemhof, on the Transvaal side of the Vaal River, and found there, barely three months after the Act had become law, a large number of African families with their stock, who had travelled from the Free State, thinking that the Land Act was only in operation in that province. Travelling by bicycle, he encountered many of these evicted families on the road, finding it 'heart-rending to listen to the tales of their cruel experiences derived from the rigour of the Natives' Land Act'.[70]

After hearing Plaatje and other delegates recount their experiences of the effects of the Act, Congress resolved to appeal directly to the King, to the British parliament and, if need be, to the British public, to secure the removal of so iniquitous a piece of legislation from the statute book. Since the passage of the Act of Union the constitutional position was that legislation passed by the South African parliament had still to be ratified by the imperial authorities, and then to receive the royal assent. In practice, these constitutional requirements were regarded in official circles as little more than formalities, and only in the most exceptional circumstances was the imperial right of veto thought likely to be invoked. When the legislation in question in any case owed so much to British policies evolved during the reconstruction period, there was never any doubt that the attitude of the imperial government – leaving aside the niceties of the constitutional position – would be one of warm support for General Botha's government. It was upon his shoulders, after all, that hopes of maintaining British influence in southern Africa now rested.

Most of the members of Congress, even if they did not see things quite in these terms, were well aware that the prospect of persuading the imperial government to veto South African legislation was remote in the extreme. An appeal to the imperial government was, though, the only constitutional option open to them and they decided that they had to take it.

They were well aware that other methods were available. The idea of some form of strike action was raised at this meeting by several delegates from the Transvaal, who pointed to the recent example of the white miners. Weeks earlier they had brought the mines to a halt following an attempt on the part of management to impose new working conditions; a general strike had ensued and only the intervention of imperial troops had ended the dispute. But those within Congress who wished to resort to such methods were in a small minority and easily outvoted. Plaatje was strongly against the idea. He had an instinctive distaste for any action of this kind, and personally drafted a resolution 'dissociating the natives from the strike movement'. Later in the year he would again take issue with several prominent Transvaal Africans who argued in favour of abandoning the deputation and resorting to strike action instead.[71]

Like most of his colleagues, Plaatje had few illusions about the chances of securing an imperial veto on the Land Act but believed it was essential to exhaust every constitutional option that existed. 'Let our delegates tell the Imperial Government that we have appealed to the highest authorities in South Africa,' he wrote, 'and both our appeals, and the church's representations on our behalf, have been ignored; and let the Imperial Government inform our delegates that His Majesty's kingship over us ceased with the signing of the Act of Union and that whites and blacks in South Africa can do what they please; then only will we have the alternative, and I too will agree that we had better have a general strike, and "damn the consequences". Till then I will maintain that the consequences of a strike are too serious, and the probable complications too dreadful, to contemplate.'[72]

+∿+

Once it was decided to send a deputation to England, an emergency committee was set up to raise the necessary funds. Then Plaatje, accompanied by Dube and Makgatho, travelled to Pretoria to convey these decisions in person to the new minister for native affairs, F.S. Malan. His response was to try to dissuade them from proceeding with their plan to send a deputation to England, but he had no concessions whatever to offer in return. Nor did the minister's words inspire any confidence in the prospect of any alleviation in the sufferings being caused by the Act. He advised the three of them to wait until the Beaumont Commission reported, 'as it was rather too early to judge an Act which has been in operation only one month', and wait until there were 'cases of real suffering'. Plaatje asked for a definition of the word 'suffering'. 'If the evictions of all the families he had already told the Minister about did not amount to "suffering",' he said, 'then what did the word mean?' It was difficult for Plaatje to believe that F.S. Malan, a man with a reputation as 'a friend of the natives', and like himself a product of the Cape and its traditions, could have displayed so callous an attitude.[73]

Bitterly disappointed at Malan's attitude, for he continued to hope against hope that a personal appeal to the human nature of those in power would cause them to think again, Plaatje travelled back home to Kimberley with his colleague from Thaba Nchu, J.M. Nyokong, by way of Vereeniging, Kroonstad and Bloemfontein. In all three places he addressed meetings about the Natives' Land Act, collected further evidence of its effects, and appealed for funds to enable the deputation to travel to England.[74]

At Kroonstad, where he spent a weekend, he also came face to face with the consequences of the women's protest against the pass laws. For weeks he had covered their campaign in the columns of *Tsala ea Batho*, reporting its progression from polite deputations through to passive resistance, confrontations with the police and mass arrests. He accused the authorities of waging a 'war of degradation' against the women. Now thirty-four of the women who had been arrested and sentenced in Bloemfontein had been moved to the gaol in Kroonstad. When he visited them that weekend he was appalled to find them in freezing conditions and subjected to forced labour, and he redoubled his efforts to publicise their plight. He would never forget their dogged resistance to injustice, the example they set in defence of their rights. He characterised them as 'black suffragettes', comparing their struggle to the militant campaign for votes for women then at its height in Britain.[75]

At the beginning of the next month, September 1913, he set out on a further tour to investigate the effects of the Act in other parts of the Free State, and found many more examples of what he had seen during those first few weeks in July: African families wandering from place to place, refusing to accept arbitrary conversion from peasant to labourer but unable to find anywhere else to live. Many of them had congregated around Ladybrand in the hope of being able to cross the border into Basutoland (where the Act did not apply), while many of those who actually lived in the area had been given notice to quit. The only advice Plaatje could give them was that they should travel to Thaba Nchu the following week and listen to an address from Edward Dower, the secretary for native affairs, who was travelling around the country advising on the implementation of the Land Act; and to seek the governor general's special permission to continue to live on their farms, as was provided for in Section 1 of the Act.[76]

But Dower had no relief whatever to offer. In his first speech, to the astonishment of the thousand or so people present, he failed even to mention the Natives' Land Act. When he finally did so, he gave no indication that the government was prepared to compromise in any way. He explained that the Natives' Land Act, through introducing the principle of territorial segregation, was in the best interests of the African population, and advised those present to do one of three things: become servants; move into the 'reserves' (he did not specify which he had in mind – there were none in the Orange Free State); or sell their stock for cash. He concluded by stating that in the Orange Free State, unlike the other provinces, there was in actual fact no provision for special cases being made through application to the governor general. This concluding statement, Plaatje reported, 'settled the minds of those who had expected from the Government any protection against the law, and the disappointment under which the meeting broke up was indescribable'.[77]

⊷⊷

In November 1913 Plaatje undertook yet another major tour of investigation into the working of the Act, this time to the eastern Cape. While other Congress leaders were collecting evidence and raising funds for the deputation to England in other parts of South Africa, nobody as yet had been doing this in the eastern Cape. Although there was some uncertainty in legal circles as to whether the

249

Natives' Land Act was applicable in the Cape, since its provisions impinged upon the land-holding qualifications for the franchise, itself entrenched in the Union constitution, he nevertheless found that in some places white farmers were taking advantage of the situation to rearrange their relationships with their African tenants in just the same way as was happening elsewhere.

Plaatje also wanted to meet with two prominent individuals who had expressed their support for the Natives' Land Act. The first was James Henderson, principal of Lovedale, his first port of call. Here he found that Henderson's views were 'based on second-hand information', and that he had little real knowledge of the Land Act and what it was about. He took advantage of the opportunity to set out his own views in Lovedale's influential journal, the *Christian Express*. The Act was, he said, 'a carefully prepared, deliberate and premeditated scheme to compass the partial enslavement of the Natives', and its effects devastating. 'I shall never forget', he wrote, 'the scenes I have witnessed in the Hoopstad district during the cold snap of July, of families living on the roads, the numbers of their attenuated flocks emaciated by lack of fodder on the trek, many of them dying while the wandering owners ran risks of prosecution for travelling with unhealthy stock. I saw the little children shivering, and contrasted their condition with the better circumstances of my own children in their Kimberley home; and when the mothers told me of the homes they had left behind and the privations they have endured since eviction I could scarcely suppress a tear.'[78]

What Plaatje saw of the effects of the Natives' Land Act remained with him for the rest of his life; it generated a deeper sense of anger and betrayal than anything hitherto, a feeling of disbelief, too, that fellow human beings could be so callous about the consequences of their actions. Perhaps he also felt a sense of culpability for having misjudged government ministers, many of whom he knew quite well, for having failed to realise that they were capable of supporting such inhuman legislation. His response to the Land Act was deeply emotional and deeply personal.

Next, after James Henderson at Lovedale, he hoped to meet John Tengo Jabavu, editor of *Imvo*, not far away in King William's Town. The Natives' Land Act was the point at which South Africa's two leading black newspaper editors finally parted company, and in bitter circumstances. Jabavu had been one of Plaatje's childhood heroes, a man whose career and position were both example and inspiration, always in his mind when he first became a newspaper editor himself. Thereafter, despite their differences in age, the two men had become good friends. Jabavu had become godfather to Plaatje's daughter Olive in 1904, and on several occasions had stayed with Plaatje and Elizabeth while visiting Mafeking and Kimberley. Jabavu was then involved in the establishment of *Tsala ea Becoana*, his company had printed the paper for over a year, and Plaatje edited *Imvo* for several months during Jabavu's absence in Europe in 1911. Taking place as it did at a time of intense discussion over forming a new political organisation, this last move had raised hopes that Jabavu, along with his influential newspaper, might be persuaded to lend his support to the new national movement.[79]

It did not, and in 1913 Jabavu came out in favour of the Natives' Land Act, the only African politician of any significance to do so. After so many years of involvement in the politics of the Cape Colony, after Union Jabavu found himself tied to the policies of General Botha's government, and three shareholders in his company were now cabinet ministers. His closest association was with J.W. Sauer, an old political ally and the man to whom fell the task of introducing the Natives' Land Bill in the House of Assembly. The measure broke both men. Sauer was reported to have been in tears after doing so. 'Why', Dr Rubusana had asked him, 'did you not resign in protest?' 'Because', replied Sauer, 'your position would have been infinitely worse.' Several weeks later Sauer died, his death hastened, so some believed, by the anguish of having to introduce a piece of legislation that went against all he had stood for in a long and distinguished political career.[80]

Jabavu, though, continued to support the measure. In doing so, he met with widespread condemnation from Africans inside as well as outside the Cape, and he rapidly lost what remained of a reputation built up over so many years. Given the position he had taken, this was all but inevitable; it was rendered all the more so, however, by Plaatje's determination to challenge him directly over the issue.

Plaatje reached King William's Town on 3 November, carrying with him an invitation to address a meeting there about the Natives' Land Act. Jabavu, whom he called on before the meeting was due to take place, refused to see him. Several days later *Imvo* carried a very disparaging report about the meeting, and Plaatje responded with an invitation to a public debate about the Land Act. Jabavu failed to accept the challenge. Details of the whole episode were then publicised in the press, black and white, and contributed further to the eclipse of Jabavu's political reputation.[81]

The episode perhaps illustrated more clearly than anything else the ambiguous legacy of the Cape tradition in the politics of Union. Plaatje's ideals and political philosophy were rooted in the Cape quite as much as those of Tengo Jabavu. As John Dube once remarked, 'if Mr Plaatje had had his own way, he would have torn up the Union constitution and re-enacted the old Cape constitution'. He was right. But Plaatje, unlike Jabavu, was able to emerge as a national political leader and spokesman after Union. He possessed a broader vision, he had a wider political constituency, and he was not tied in the same way to the interests and structures of the Cape. In the fraught process of forging a national African movement there were some sad casualties. Jabavu was the most notable among them. At such a critical moment in the history of his people, Plaatje was not prepared to allow sentimental attachments of the past to stand in the way of what he saw as his clear political duty. He had seen too many of the drastic effects of what he was by now describing as 'the Plague Act' to feel able to extend any degree of sympathy to a man he had once so admired. The very closeness of their past association only heightened the sense of betrayal. By the time Jabavu acknowledged his error of judgement several years later, his reputation was in tatters.[82]

Throughout late 1913 and early 1914 Congress's campaign to collect funds for the deputation to England continued apace. In February 1914 a further conference was called to discuss the government's response to their representations, to ratify their decision (if no satisfactory assurances were forthcoming from Pretoria) to send the deputation, and to elect its members. The conference was originally meant to take place in Johannesburg, but the venue was changed to Kimberley at the last minute because of the martial law regulations (imposed as a result of another white miners' strike) in operation in the Transvaal. After all the travelling of the previous months, it must have been some relief for Plaatje to have the conference in his home town, and the delegates enjoyed the kind of reception which would have been unthinkable in Johannesburg. De Beers assisted in various ways, the *Diamond Fields Advertiser* was generous in its coverage, and the proceedings of the conference were opened by the bishop of Kimberley and Kuruman, one of a substantial body of churchmen who had considerable sympathy for Congress's case on the Natives' Land Act.[83]

The conference's deliberations were then transformed as a result of a telephone call which Plaatje received from the local magistrate, informing him that he had a telegram from Edward Dower, the secretary for native affairs, which read as follows: 'Leaving tonight for Kimberley to attend the Native Congress. Inform Plaatje.' The effect of this surprising piece of news, which Plaatje conveyed to the assembled delegates, was to raise their hopes that the government was, at the eleventh hour, preparing to make some concession to them over the Land Act, for no government representative of his standing had ever accepted one of the invitations to attend its meetings that Congress routinely sent out. At last, it seemed, the government was showing some sign of taking Congress's representations seriously. The meeting therefore decided to postpone the election of the deputation until after Dower's arrival in the hope that he would make an announcement that would render it unnecessary.

Not for the first time Dower's message came as an intense disappointment. During the course of a long speech he argued the case for territorial segregation, emphasising that more land had been promised and that the Act of 1913 should therefore be seen simply as a first instalment. At several points his arguments brought forth disbelieving laughter from his audience. He accused the Congress of not being representative of African opinion; he criticised their leaders for 'beating the air' in their denunciations of the Act; and he told them, finally, that the idea of a deputation to England was 'a huge mistake'. Dower had been sent to Kimberley, it became clear to everybody in the crowded hall, to try to dissuade Congress from proceeding with its plan for the deputation, but with absolutely nothing to offer in return.[84]

So far from proffering the olive branch that was expected, Dower's speech, Plaatje said, 'was entirely barren of results' and it left the Congress as it found it, 'in bewilderment and gloom'. Among those present at the meeting was Modiri Molema, now 22, who had just completed a short spell as a teacher at the Lyndhurst Road Native School, and was about to leave for Scotland to take up a place to study medicine at Glasgow University. As the Congress leaders responded in a series of 'heartrending speeches' to Dower's message, and Plaatje, 'in a voice trembling with anger', spoke out against the iniquity and inflexibility of government policy, Molema recalled being struck by 'the silence that fell on the house'. He thought it was 'like the silence of death', the expression of a 'collective heavy sigh, the stifling of life in those gathered'. The seriousness of their situation was apparent to all.[85]

Although Dower succeeded in sowing some seeds of dissension by revealing that the Crown had already been advised by the British government to give its assent to the Act, a large majority of the delegates were in favour of proceeding with the deputation (for which the sum of £1,353 19s 3d had so far been raised), and five delegates were elected by the executive committee to accompany John Dube, the president, to England. Plaatje, with thirteen votes, topped the poll, followed by S.M. Makgatho (nine), Saul Msane (six), W.Z. Fenyang (three) and T.M. Mapikela (three). It was an emphatic expression of the esteem in which he was held by his colleagues on Congress's executive committee. More than anybody else, he had devoted himself over the past months to travelling the length and breadth of the land to investigate the effects of the Land Act, and to bring his observations to the attention of all those who would read and listen. The SANNC now prepared to take its case overseas.[86]

Since the Union of South Africa came into being, Plaatje's life had been driven by a political imperative, by the need to respond to the threat that the policies of South Africa's new rulers posed to the African people. In these few years he emerged as one of their leading spokesmen: arguably, indeed, by 1914, given his relentless campaigning against the Natives' Land Act, his travels up and down the country, he had a strong claim to be regarded as *the* leading spokesman. But he was not of course a professional politician in the sense that this provided him with a living. Throughout these years he remained editor of his newspaper and in charge of the business that published it. This was in itself a hugely demanding task, and would have been more than sufficient preoccupation for somebody less committed to the political affairs of his people than he.

Remarkably, *Tsala ea Batho* not only survived, but prospered. It had appeared without a break from September 1912, and at the end of the following year, 1913, Plaatje could look back with considerable satisfaction at this achievement, the grim political situation notwithstanding. 'Three native papers have ceased publication during 1913', he wrote, 'but we are still here to tell the story.' He attributed this not so much 'to any valour on our part' as to 'the liberality of advertising firms throughout South Africa, who stood by us when our natural customers, the native peasants of the "Free" State and Transvaal, were driven from pillar to post under the cruel provisions of an unprecedented law, and could not send us any money'.[87]

The disruptions caused by the Natives' Land Act may have had an adverse effect upon the number of paid-up subscribers, but *Tsala*'s coverage of the Act, which dominated its columns from mid-1913 onwards, brought it a new standing. By 1914 circulation had increased to four thousand. Unlike *Abantu-Batho*, which enjoyed 'the unique privilege of being financed by a black capitalist', Plaatje noted on one occasion, *Tsala ea Batho* ran on a shoestring, unable to afford some 'luxuries' such as 'a staff of some half-a-dozen sub-editors'. He did have some help, however. His staff included Arthur Matlala, a keen cricketer in his spare time, who was in charge of the typesetting; Eva Mahuma, a recent graduate of Lovedale who would go on to become the first black South African woman to be awarded a degree of Master of Arts (from Columbia University); and, in 1913 and 1914, James Dippa, son of a Thembu chief, also Lovedale-educated, who joined *Tsala* after a short teaching career in the eastern Cape.[88]

Despite its limited resources *Tsala ea Batho* nevertheless claimed, with some justification, to be 'the most accurately informed Native newspaper in South Africa', and by 1914 it carried regular reminders of a number of its notable 'scoops'. It had news of the death of J.W. Sauer, for example, 'a whole week before any other Native newspaper', and of the return of Dr Abdurahman as a member of the Cape Provincial Council 'simultaneously with the daily papers'; it then gave 'the first news to the natives of the result of the Tembuland election', Tengo Jabavu's defeat being 'known to the *Tsala* readers four days before it appeared in his paper'. Once one of Plaatje's editorials on the Natives' Land Act was read out by Theo Schreiner, the member for Tembuland and a brother of both W.P. and Olive Schreiner, in a debate in the House of Assembly. Despite the debts with which *Tsala* continued to be saddled, it had succeeded in establishing itself as an important and influential newspaper, providing Plaatje with exactly the independent platform that he wanted.[89]

Since April 1913 *Tsala* had also carried regular news and comment in Xhosa, thereby providing an alternative to Jabavu's *Imvo*. It appealed particularly to the large Xhosa-speaking diaspora outside the eastern Cape, not least in Kimberley. Few issues were without criticism of Jabavu and the line he was taking on the Natives' Land Act. At the same time Plaatje's views were becoming increasingly well known to white readers as well. The *Pretoria News* continued to publish his articles and on occasions these were reproduced in other newspapers, particularly the *Cape Argus* and the *Diamond Fields Advertiser*. In addition to these commissioned articles he often wrote letters to the editors of these and other newspapers in response to ill-informed reporting, or to draw attention to some instance of injustice or misrepresentation. Among both black and white in South Africa Plaatje had become probably the most widely read black journalist of his day.

In the light of this hard-earned reputation Plaatje must have given careful consideration to the possible consequences of his absence overseas as a member of the Congress delegation to England. Already there were signs of conflict between the demands of his newspaper and the no less pressing demands of Congress, and in February 1914, at the time of the Kimberley conference, he offered his resignation as secretary, owing, it was reported, 'to pressure of work'. However, he was persuaded to reconsider and stayed on as secretary until he departed for England, when he resigned for a second time.[90]

Family life had likewise suffered as a result of these heavy work commitments, probably a factor too in his offer to step down as secretary of Congress. For the last few years he had spent long periods away from home. Even when he was in Kimberley – the family were living now in a rented house in Shannon Street – most of his time was spent working in the newspaper office or in his library at home, or attending meetings in town (involving, among others, the local branches of the SANNC and APO, local liquor licensing meetings, the committee of the Lyndhurst Road Native School, the Lutheran Church). 'Working from 8 a.m. to midnight and often till later than 3 a.m. next day (with only short intervals for meals), and 5 or 6 hours sleep in 24 hours,' he wrote of this time, 'we cannot have the same time we formerly devoted to the children.' It was small wonder that Elizabeth was reported to have commented, early in 1914, that the only time she enjoyed the company of her husband was when he was unwell and laid up in bed.[91]

While Elizabeth's comments were not intended as criticism, there was no doubt she had the main responsibility for the care of the children and running the household. By all accounts she was happy to fulfil these domestic duties, allowing her husband to devote his energies to a cause to which she was, in her own way, every bit as committed. Occasionally she gave expression to her views on social and political affairs. In May 1912, at the height of the 'black peril' scare, and at a time when Plaatje was away from Kimberley, she wrote to the *Diamond Fields Advertiser* to condemn the recent 'outrages' in Johannesburg, pointing out that no such incidents had taken place in Kimberley. She attributed this to the fact that in Kimberley 'loyal natives are regarded as human beings', and that as the home of Cecil Rhodes it provided 'free institutions and fair opportunities for every civilized man' – to which she added, pointedly, 'I presume women too'. To make doubly sure that Kimberley preserved its 'clean slate' she recommended 'total and absolute prohibition of the white man's liquor to natives' – an issue she felt just as strongly about as her husband.[92]

Elizabeth did not attach her name to the letter. It was simply signed 'a Native Woman', although from what she says about her time in Mafeking it can be from no one else. Whatever her reasons for preferring to keep out of the public eye, her letter reflected a combination of eloquence and modesty that is quite consistent with what else is known about her. Nobody reading it could fail to recognise its easy command of the English language and a sensitivity to the audience, or audiences, she was addressing.

The children just had to get used to their father not being there. Sainty, the eldest, now doing well at the Lyndhurst Road Native School (and probably thinking of a place at Lovedale), was old enough to understand the reasons for his father's heavy involvement in political affairs, and was already helping out in the *Tsala* office after school hours and during school holidays. Sometimes articles appeared under his name in the newspaper itself, such as a report of the visit of the school inspector, the appropriately named Mr Oscar Satchel, in October 1911. Sainty was growing in confidence in other ways too. A talented pianist and vocalist, he helped entertain the delegates to the SANNC conference in Kimberley in February 1914, where his rendition of 'Put your trousers on', a ragtime chorus performed by the 'Troubadours', was reported to have 'brought down the house' at the evening concert.[93]

But for Halley, named after Halley's Comet which appeared at the time of his birth in 1910; for Violet, born in 1907, the 'accredited chatterbox of the family'; and for Olive, six years old when they moved to Kimberley, and still very much a favourite, their father's long absences from home must have been more difficult to understand. When he was around, Olive, at least, was determined to claim as much of his attention as she could. She used to walk into his study, he remembered, 'just when we could not afford to be interrupted', and offer him tea. When he told her that he was too busy for this, she persisted: 'But it is made by me, Pappa,' she announced. 'Well, let's have a cup,' he would reply.[94]

Along with these happy memories was a great sadness: the death of the youngest, Johannes Gutenberg, born on the day the new printing office opened in September 1912. Unlike the other children, he never recovered properly from an attack of whooping cough that Christmas, and died in January 1914, a family tragedy which affected Plaatje deeply and left, as he was to write later, 'an indelible gap … in our domestic circle'. W.P. Schreiner and Vere Stent were among those who sent letters of condolence when the news was announced. His death came just after that of Maria Baile, the eleven-month-old daughter of Isaiah and Maria M'belle, one of half-a-dozen cousins who succumbed to illness during these few weeks.[95]

Family life, for Plaatje, provided a secure haven, however incessant the demands of others upon his time. His own extended family, and Elizabeth's too, may once have disapproved of their respective choice of partner, but that was now past history. In a society that attached such a premium to raising children, of continuing the family line, the arrival of their children at regular intervals must have put paid to any lingering concerns, and certainly gave fulfilment for both parents. He would have had every sympathy with his fellow Congress leader, John Dube, and his wife Nokutela, who, as many who knew them would have been aware, were unable to have children of their own.[96]

Whatever his thoughts about leaving behind both family and newspaper business, Plaatje was committed to travelling to England with the Congress deputation. Much of his time between February and May 1914 was spent collecting funds to finance the trip and, together with the attorney Richard Msimang, gathering further information about the effects of the Land Act to lay before the British public. He took the precaution, too, of obtaining testimonials from the mayors of Kimberley and Mafeking and the secretary of De Beers. All three were happy to provide suitable references, Ernest Oppenheimer, the mayor of Kimberley, testifying that he was 'a much respected member of the native community'. Frank Ireland, editor of the *Diamond Fields Advertiser*, and a journalist in England before moving to South Africa – a man with whom Plaatje had always got on well – likewise provided a letter of introduction to the Institute of Journalists in London which would prove especially helpful.[97]

As the time for the deputation's departure approached, he wrote to Henry Burton, now minister of railways and harbours, 'declaring himself altogether ignorant of the necessary permits and passports required by one to leave the Province for foreign countries', and asking for his help in securing the 'requisite official documents'. In fact no passport was needed to travel to England, so Burton informed him, but it is nonetheless revealing of the nature of his relationship with Henry Burton that he felt able to approach him about the matter, his current ministerial portfolio notwithstanding. More than likely he had a good idea of what he would need, but could see that a friendly reply from Henry Burton might well be helpful in other respects.[98]

By the time he actually reached Cape Town there had been several quite interesting developments. John Dube, the president of Congress and the leader of the deputation, had been the first to arrive, his intention being to submit the final Congress petition to the South African parliament before the deputation took it with them to England to lay before the imperial government. He was told, however, that it would take at least a month for the petition to be heard and considered by parliament. This meant that it would be impossible for the deputation to be in England by 16 June, the date by which, in terms of the provisions of the Act of Union, the King could still disallow any South African legislation.

Dube also took the opportunity, once he had arrived in Cape Town, to get in touch with J.X. Merriman, to find out his views on the deputation, and if possible to secure some introductions to people in England, but also to reassure him that his primary personal interest still lay with his educational institute of Ohlange, and not in political agitation. He found himself, he said, in a rather 'delicate position', and did not want his true motives to be misunderstood.[99]

Merriman was not at all in favour of the idea of the deputation to England and did his best to dissuade him from going, having in the meantime communicated privately with the prime minister, General Botha, over the matter. Merriman's view was that Dube was by no means wholeheartedly behind the mission, but that he was 'associated with some hot heads' from whom it was difficult to dissociate himself. 'Bechuanas, I suppose,' Merriman had said to Dube. 'Yes,' apparently, was the reply. Since Plaatje was the only 'Bechuana' among the delegates, there was no doubt to whom they were referring. 'The impression was left on my mind', Merriman concluded from the meeting, 'that Dube sees he is in the wrong boat and would be glad if he could get some pretext for getting on dry land again.'[100]

Merriman was not alone in having formed such an impression. Edward Dower, the secretary for native affairs, had seen Dube a few months earlier and thought he had persuaded him not to proceed with the deputation, news he had passed on to the prime minister. 'I have reason to believe', so General Botha informed Merriman, mindful of what Dower had told him, 'that Dube is in the horns of a dilemma'; his 'better judgement' convinces him of the 'unwisdom' of appealing to the imperial government, 'yet he has pledged himself to the Native contributors [to the fund] to proceed to England', and found it difficult to escape from this commitment.[101]

Whatever doubts Dube had about his mission to England, he was not persuaded to abandon the idea. Several days after meeting Merriman, he saw General Botha, accompanied by Dr Rubusana, who had by this time arrived in Cape Town in order to join the deputation, taking the place of W.Z. Fenyang, who had agreed to stand down in his favour. The prime minister did his best to dissuade the two men from going to England, but had no concession to offer in return. Parliament, he said, simply could not suspend the operation of the Land Act as they requested. At the end of the meeting Dube agreed to 'consult with his colleagues', who were due to arrive in town that day, and a further meeting with the prime minister, for the whole deputation, was arranged for the next day. Plaatje's arrival seems to have stiffened Dube's resolve, but the government would not budge: 'If I went to Parliament now with a Bill to amend the law,' Botha told the delegates during the second meeting, 'they will think I'm mad.' 'The lengthy official arguments,' so Plaatje described them, 'so far from promising relief to the native sufferers under the Lands Act, may be summed up in five short words: "Give up going to England."' Later the same day they also met the governor general, Lord Gladstone; his attitude was precisely the same. There was now no alternative but for them to depart for England as planned.[102]

All these last-minute meetings and discussions, while they did not in the end alter the decision of Congress to send a deputation to England, are nevertheless of considerable significance. It is clear that John Dube, the leader of the deputation, had severe doubts about the wisdom of proceeding with it at all, and only did so because in the end he was left with no way out – in contrast to Plaatje who, of the five delegates, seemed the most determined, taking heart from the willingness of 'the two highest personages in the land' to meet with them. Such differences in attitude did not augur well for its future conduct.

Nor, it has to be said, did the acrimonious disputes that arose over the question of money. When the delegates met to review their finances just before they sailed, it was discovered that only £800 remained of the £1,353 that had been collected. Saul Msane had been paying himself, without proper authorisation in Plaatje's view, a salary of £25 a month from this fund, plus travelling expenses, and John Dube was doing the same. In Dube's case this was not so much a 'salary' for work done, Plaatje thought, as a 'bribe' to keep quiet about Msane's misdeeds, all of it authorised retrospectively by Pixley Seme, the treasurer, fearful of the consequences of public exposure. Plaatje, on the other hand, had not been reimbursed for the cost of his train fare from Kimberley to Cape Town or for other expenses incurred, while Saul Msane alleged that much of the money collected in the (Tswana-speaking) Rustenburg district had ended up in the coffers of local chiefs and was not passed on to Congress. No wonder, so Plaatje would observe later, the affairs of the deputation were in such disarray and relations between the delegates so strained – even before they set sail from Cape Town.[103]

Differences notwithstanding, it is clear that the government was a lot more concerned about the impact the deputation might make in England than it cared to admit (although even General Botha went on record as saying 'they might succeed in arousing a certain amount of public sympathy in England'). This was implicit in both Edward Dower's attendance at the February meeting of Congress in Kimberley, and the considerable time and effort the prime minister personally spent in trying to dissuade the delegates from going. It was not customary for a prime minister of South Africa to be seen requesting interviews with black South African politicians. The use of J.X. Merriman as an intermediary meant that no such impression was created publicly, but from the correspondence between the two men it is clear that General Botha was very glad of the opportunity to meet John Dube and the other delegates for this purpose – even if in the end he failed in his objective.[104]

One other precaution was taken by the government: A.P. Apthorp, a senior official in the Native Affairs Department who had been closely involved in monitoring the implementation of the Natives' Land Act (he had been present at the meeting at Thaba Nchu in September 1913), was now preparing to board the next ship to England with a brief to do everything possible to counter the arguments of the Congress delegates and to neutralise any impression that they might succeed in creating there. Here was further evidence of the government's concern about the impact the Congress might make.[105]

After addressing a public meeting in the City Hall, Cape Town, on 15 May, the members of the deputation duly departed, Dube and Rubusana on 16 May,

Plaatje, Mapikela and Msane on the *Norseman*, which sailed the following day. They had ample opportunity to ponder the hostile editorials which appeared in the two Cape dailies, but would have missed the spirited defence of their actions that appeared in the *Cape Times* on the 19th. This came in the form of a letter from James Wellwood Mushet, a successful Cape Town merchant, recently married into the Schreiner family, who sympathised with their cause and was appalled by the way the Natives' Land Act had been rushed through parliament. He was on particularly good terms with Plaatje, and would be a consistent supporter of his endeavours in years to come.[106]

Whatever the tensions, the delegates were at least agreed on the task that lay before them: 'to bring the facts of their grievances to the notice of the English public with a view to bringing influence to bear on the British government', as Dube had said to General Botha, and then to lodge their protest 'through His Majesty's Ministers with the King, and asking the King to exercise his powers by disallowing the Act'. They now had until 16 June to do so (which did not give them a great deal of time), but such constitutional niceties were really not the point. None of the delegates was under any illusion that the King, or his ministers, were likely to accede to their request. They nevertheless felt, with varying degrees of commitment, that they were discharging a responsibility that had been thrust upon their shoulders, and that it was important to exhaust the constitutional options still open to them. On the whole they preferred not to contemplate what happened next.

All had other objectives in mind as they packed their bags. While John Dube hoped the trip might enable him to raise funds for his school in Natal, Plaatje intended, once he had arrived in England, to press the claims of the Barolong in the matter of the legal status of the Imperial Reserve in Mafikeng, taking with him a letter of authority from the Tshidi Barolong paramount chief and headmen that clothed him 'with all the power to fully represent the Barolong Nation in England'. He also hoped to be able to raise some money for his newspaper, its debts by now accumulating alarmingly, and to support educational and community work in Kimberley. Beyond this he had a more ambitious plan still: to visit the United States once the work of the deputation in Britain was completed, an idea inspired, in part at least, by his knowledge of John Dube's success in securing a substantial flow of funds to support his educational work at Ohlange. He would have been well aware that such an opportunity was unlikely to present itself again in the foreseeable future.[107]

For now, all of this was subordinate to their immediate purpose in travelling to England: to present the case of the SANNC, representing the African people of South Africa, against the Natives' Land Act of 1913. Plaatje was the only one of the five not to have been overseas before. He expected to be away for no more than five months. It would be nearly three years before he saw his wife and family again.[108]

NINE

Appealing to empire

England, 1914–1916

The voyage to England did not begin auspiciously. Even before the *Norseman* set sail, a splitting headache forced Plaatje to retire to his cabin. When he woke up, feeling much better, he was just able to catch a last sight of the African coastline receding slowly into the distance. Not having travelled by sea before, he had some worries about seasickness, which were only exacerbated by the sight of Thomas Mapikela and many of the other passengers 'croaking and squirming' during the first night of the voyage. He shuddered, so he wrote afterwards in an amused tone, 'in anticipation of the impending onslaught on an inexperienced greenhorn like myself'. His anxieties were soon allayed: 'Just at this time a rugged-looking veteran of the seas came on deck and asked how I fared. It was with a sigh of relief that I listened to his, to me, interesting conversation, especially that part of it (which was afterwards over-corroborated), wherein he assured me that, having survived the first day and night, I need no more expect any trouble from seasickness. I felt like a discharged prisoner, and prepared for my work with an extra freshness and security.'

In the same account of the voyage, published in the *Diamond Fields Advertiser* as well as *Tsala ea Batho*, Plaatje enlarged upon the work he had in mind, and how it occupied him for the remainder of the voyage: 'I am compiling a little book on the Native Land Act and its operation which I hope to put through the press immediately after landing in England. It keeps me busy typewriting in the dining-room all forenoons and evenings; the afternoons I spend on deck, making notes, etc. With such a regular daily programme I can afford to sympathise with our fellow passengers who are always very busy doing nothing. Their inertia must be well-nigh maddening and, as I see the heavy loads of time hanging down their weary necks, it is to me strange that they can stand it so long.'

So accustomed had he become to working almost every hour of the day that it had become almost second nature, and he could see no reason to abandon the habit aboard ship. Rather, he considered the three-week voyage to be an ideal opportunity to complete his book. It was difficult even to contemplate a life without work.[1]

Most of Plaatje's white fellow passengers reacted favourably to the presence of three black men on board the ship. Many of them were Australians, with whom

Upper: Boer rebels captured after the siege, seen here outside the Mafeking gaol. Plaatje interpreted in Dutch and English during the preliminary examinations when they were charged with treason.

Lower: Crowds gather in the stadt to witness Colonel Vyvyan present a letter from Lord Roberts, commander-in-chief of British forces in South Africa, commending the Barolong on their part in the siege. Plaatje interpreted the speeches.

Upper: The Treason Court judges in Mafeking, November 1901: *Left to right:* Justice William Solomon, Justice Johannes Lange, Justice Andries Maasdorp, KC.

Lower: Loyal Mafikeng – photograph taken by Mary Chamberlain, wife of Joseph Chamberlain, British secretary of state for the colonies, on their visit to the Barolong stadt, January 1903.

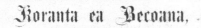

Upper, left: Front page of the first issue of the bilingual *Koranta ea Becoana (Bechuanas' Gazette)*, 16 August 1902.

Upper, right: Friend and supporter – the Rev. Jacob Monyatsi, of Bloemfontein, who welcomed *Koranta ea Becoana* by composing a praise poem in its honour.

Lower: Fellow newspapermen and colleagues of Plaatje's in the South African Native Press Association: A.K. Soga *(left)*, editor of *Izwi la Bantu* ('Voice of the People'), East London, and F.Z.S. Peregrino *(right)*, originally from the Gold Coast, editor of the *South African Spectator* (Cape Town).

Upper: Plaatje with a group of friends, male and female – probably a gathering of the Mafeking Philharmonic Society, c.1905.

Lower: Lord Selborne, high commissioner for southern Africa, addressing chiefs at Crocodile Pools, near Gaborone, April 1906. Plaatje accompanied him on his official tour of the Bechuanaland Protectorate and wrote about it in *Koranta ea Becoana*. He is seen here standing in front of the platform, right-hand side.

Dr. A. ABDURAHMAN,
Hanover Street.

THE SOUTH AFRICAN

NATIVE NATIONAL CONGRESS.

SPECIAL CONFERENCE

HELD IN THE

St. JOHN'S HALL, KIMBERLEY,

FEBRUARY 27th to MARCH 2nd, 1914,

IN CONNECTION WITH THE NATIVE LANDS ACT, 1913.

President: REV. J. L. DUBE.

Sr. Vice-President: MR. S. M. MAKGATHO.

Treasurer: MR. P. KA I. SEME, B.A.

Junior Treasurer: MR. T. M. MAPIKELA.

Hon. Secretary: MR. SOL T. PLAATJE.

Organising Committee of Protest against the Lands Act:

W. F. JEMSANA (*Chairman*).	B. G. PHOOKO.
ELKA M. CELE (*Treasurer*).	D. D. TYWAKADI.
D. S. LETANKA.	D. MOELETSI.
R. W. MSIMANG.	M. D. NDABEZITA.
H. D. MKIZE.	H. SELBY MSIMANG (*Hon. Sec.*)

S. MSANE, *Organiser.*

Upper: Friends and supporters – Chief Fenyang, seen here with his wife Lydia (*left*), and the Rev. Joel Goronyane (*middle*), both members of the *Tsala ea Becoana* syndicate.

Upper, right: Dr Abdullah Abdurahman, president of the APO, and proponent of black unity.

Lower: First page of the programme for the special conference of the SANNC, Kimberley, 1914, called to discuss the Natives' Land Act. Plaatje topped the poll in the election for the delegation to England.

Upper: Teaching staff and committee of the Lyndhurst Road Public School, Kimberley, 1913. Plaatje is in the back row, third from right; Isaiah Bud-M'belle, secretary of the committee, is in the back row, far right; Modiri Molema, recently arrived as a teacher, is sitting in the front row, far left.

Lower, left: Flyer advertising Plaatje's address to the Shern Hall Brotherhood, Leyton, 11 July 1915. He lived close by in Carnarvon Road.

Lower, right: Shown here with Charles Calvert *(left)* and James Kerridge *(right)*, two Coloured men from Kimberley who had travelled to England to enlist in the Middlesex Regiment. They appeared alongside Plaatje at a number of his meetings.

Upper, left: Lekoko Montshiwa, Barolong chief regent, who Plaatje hoped would help finance the publication of *Native Life in South Africa.* He died in 1915 before doing so.

Upper, right: Dr Alfred Salter, socialist, pacifist, medical practitioner – and generous supporter of Plaatje's cause.

Lower: Brotherhood friends and supporters – *Left:* Mr and Mrs E. Jefferies, from Pontypridd in south Wales; *Right:* William and Kate Dixon, from Leighton Buzzard, Bedfordshire.

With the Castle family in Heathfield, Sussex, 1915/16. *Upper:* with Henry and Louise Castle and their children, in their new Studebaker car. *Lower:* with Henry Castle's two sisters, Eleanor (second row) and Emmie, standing to his left.

he seems to have got on well. Among them was a woman called Ethel McDonald from Spicers Creek in rural New South Wales and, presumably, a Seventh Day Adventist since she presented him with one of their tracts 'as a souvenir', she said, of their voyage. With white South Africans, however, it was a different story. They found it difficult to accept with equanimity Saul Msane's pre-eminence at chess, or to repress their irritation at his good fortune in winning a sweepstake to which all had contributed. In normal circumstances these were people to be kept firmly in their place, so it was no surprise that the demands of civilised intercourse were often a distinct strain. For black passengers who had travelled overseas before, the racial attitudes encountered on board ship were a known hazard.[2]

After seventeen days at sea the *Norseman* called in at Tenerife, in the Canary Islands. It was, Plaatje said, the first time he had stepped on soil that was not British, and he was intrigued to hear a language spoken, Spanish, which he had not encountered before. Overall he was not greatly impressed by the place. He complained of the high postal charges he had to pay to send letters back home, and of being fleeced at every opportunity by souvenir sellers and tourist guides.[3]

Several days later, after a violent storm in the Bay of Biscay – an irritation because it prevented him from working for two days – the *Norseman* arrived in Plymouth, and most of its passengers boarded the special train to London. Plaatje thought its speed a revelation: while South African Railways could do the journey from Kimberley to Mafeking in twelve to fourteen hours, Plymouth to London, exactly the same distance, took just four. It was the reaction of any colonial citizen visiting 'home' for the first time, and his first impressions of London, sweltering in an exceptionally hot summer, were in similar vein. He was impressed by the crowds of people, the traffic, the London policemen and, when he had a chance to go there, the Houses of Parliament. It was 'a relief to get out of these moving crowds of an evening after a full day', and he soon moved from a hotel in central London to take up a friend's offer of accommodation in the suburbs.

The five delegates soon got down to work. Friends and sympathisers were already active on their behalf and Charles Garnett, secretary of the League of International Brotherhood, had met them on their arrival at Paddington station in London. John Dube, the leader of the deputation, had received a letter of welcome at Tenerife from John Harris, secretary of the Anti-Slavery and Aborigines' Protection Society, offering his assistance in organising their campaign and suggesting they get in touch immediately after arrival. Dube may have wondered about a request that he and his colleagues should 'say nothing to the press until we have had an opportunity of discussing matters', but it was nonetheless reassuring to hear of 'the deep sympathy of our Society in your efforts'. The Anti-Slavery and Aborigines' Protection Society was, after all, the leading humanitarian pressure group in England concerned with colonial matters and an experienced and seemingly influential organisation whose support was likely to be essential in making their case.[4]

When they duly met with the society to 'discuss matters', John Harris outlined to them his views on how they should proceed with their campaign. Again he stressed the importance of not talking to the press or seeking any publicity until after they had met Lewis Harcourt, the secretary of state for the colonies. Although this went against the instincts of Plaatje and Dube especially – both of them newspapermen and well aware of the power of the press in gaining publicity for their cause – they were nevertheless prepared to accept the advice of a man who exuded confidence and ambition, and gave every impression of being a highly professional lobbyist who had their best interests at heart.

Over two other issues they took more persuading. Harris's view was that since there was absolutely no chance whatever of the colonial secretary disallowing the Natives' Land Act, it would be better for them to express their support for the principle of territorial segregation, provided it could be 'fairly and practically' carried out, and to concentrate their efforts upon securing some minor improvements in several of the provisions of the Act. Against their better judgement the Congress delegates were therefore persuaded to sign a memorandum (drawn up by Harris) for presentation to Lewis Harcourt, with whom an interview had now been arranged. Far from requesting that the Land Act be disallowed, the document proposed instead that General Botha's policy of segregation should be given formal and public approval by the imperial government, 'or better still form the basis of an understanding as a native policy by the Imperial and South African Governments'.[5]

Like a number of whites in South Africa with an interest in the 'native question', Harris supported the principle of segregation because he believed it provided a guarantee against total dispossession, something he had seen in other parts of Africa, particularly the Congo where he had made his reputation. He regarded the Natives' Land Act, therefore, as an essentially progressive measure, defective not in principle but in some of its details. It is perhaps surprising that the delegates were prepared to append their signatures to such a document, and they quickly came to regret having done so, but they were put under strong pressure, and Harris made it clear that the prospect of an interview with the colonial secretary depended upon them signing. To have refused would have alienated the one organisation whose support seemed essential to their campaign. Plaatje was aware, too, that the help of the society's lawyers was essential if there were to be any hope of challenging government claims to jurisdiction over the Barolong reserve in Mafikeng. This matter remained very much on his agenda too. It was just a question of choosing the right moment to pursue it.[6]

The second issue discussed at their meeting related to land in Rhodesia, in which Harris appeared to be a good deal more interested. He outlined to the five members of Congress his plans for instituting legal proceedings against the British South Africa Company, challenging its claim to the title of 'unalienated' land in Southern Rhodesia. Since his society proposed to take up the case in the name of the colony's African population (who had not been consulted), he believed that the Congress delegates could provide him with at least a degree of legitimacy. They were therefore asked to sign a document giving power of attorney to a firm of lawyers, Messrs Morgan, Price & Co., to represent the interests of the African population of Rhodesia. Again, the delegates were persuaded to sign, fearful that a refusal would jeopardise their own campaign, even though Plaatje said at the time, so a friend recalled, that 'none of them were qualified to do this – neither being Natives of Rhodesia, nor possessing any mandate from the Natives of that country'.[7]

After a frustrating delay (during which time, Plaatje was told by several friends, 'the Right Honourable the State Secretary is still awaiting instructions from General Botha before deciding when, where and how to meet the deputation of the Native Congress'), the colonial secretary agreed to see them at the end of June. John Harris had wanted to accompany them to the meeting but the Colonial Office, who generally regarded his society as an irritating and interfering nuisance, saw no need for this, and told him his presence would not be required. This was to prove of some significance. Freed from Harris's influence and supervision, the delegates, speaking in turn, took the opportunity to express their own views on the Natives' Land Act, and in very forthright terms. Despite having signed the earlier document, they made it clear to the colonial secretary that they sought not the approval of the imperial government for a policy of segregation, but an investigation into the Act's operation, and the suspension of some of its clauses; or, as one of the Colonial Office officials put it, 'they clearly asked for certain impossibilities which they did not ask in their written demands'.[8]

It came as no surprise that the colonial secretary was unwilling to accede to any of their demands, written or spoken. South Africa was now a self-governing dominion; Harcourt held General Botha in high esteem and had no intention of causing him the slightest embarrassment. He felt that an undertaking to guarantee an alleged promise of General Botha's that Africans would be awarded more land under the provisions of the Land Act would be 'insulting' and that any attempt on the part of His Majesty's government to intercede informally on behalf of the delegates 'would be inconsistent with the responsible Government which has been granted to the Union of South Africa'. There was absolutely nothing, in short, he could offer them. 'At the interview', Plaatje wrote, after the delegates had set out their grievances, 'he took notes on nothing, and asked no questions. On every point he had "the assurance of General Botha" to the contrary'.[9]

Harcourt did at least agree to consider the delegates' request to 'pay their respects' to the King. 'Consider' in this case meant referring the request back to Pretoria where it was never likely to find favour. While General Botha indicated that his government did not wish to press their objections, both he and Lord Gladstone, the governor general, were in agreement that 'no useful purpose will be served if audience is accorded to these Natives by His Majesty and suggest for the consideration of the Right Honourable the Secretary of State for the Colonies that the result might be the establishment of an inconvenient precedent for the future'. Since the King's personal secretary had already intimated that His Majesty 'presumed there will be no necessity for him to receive this Deputation, which does not seem to be a representative one' (the Palace preferred visiting African royalty in traditional regalia), such an indication was more than sufficient. In view of the King's attitude, it was perhaps as well the meeting never took place.[10]

John Harris was greatly peeved at what transpired in the interview. As he pointed out to the Colonial Office afterwards, it was with a fear that the delegates might not confine themselves to the points in his document that he had suggested that he and several other representatives of the society might accompany them to the interview. He had done all he could to use his society's influence 'in the direction of securing a modification of their original programme and an abstention from public agitation pending the exhaustion of every constitutional means open to them' and he was disappointed to have secured no recognition for his efforts from the Colonial Office. He was left with no alternative but to accede to the increasingly impatient demands of the delegates to publicise their cause, and in particular to respond to attacks made upon them by the London weekly, *South Africa*. He now sought to ensure that the delegates created the right impression in the press and upon public platforms with a view to influencing the Colonial

Office vote in the House of Commons, due to take place in the middle of July, which would at least enable their grievances to be raised and placed on the official record. This, Harris told Dube, was 'your last chance of doing anything effective … when that is over you can do nothing more in the country at present'.[11]

In the three weeks that remained before this vote was to take place, therefore, the five delegates embarked upon a spirited attempt to convey their case to the British public. They had to compete for attention in the newspapers with political unrest in Ireland, the threat of industrial unrest closer to home, and the activities of militant suffragettes in their campaign to secure votes for women – and a seemingly distant crisis in Europe resulting from the assassination, on 28 June, of Archduke Franz Ferdinand, heir to the Austro-Hungarian throne. They prepared and distributed a printed statement of their grievances, wrote letters to the press, gave interviews and addressed meetings. Most of these were held under the auspices of various church bodies, but there was also a gathering at the House of Commons with some sympathetic members of parliament, and several evening receptions in the homes of their small band of supporters. Fresh invitations, Plaatje reported, were soon coming in 'at an inconvenient rate'.[12]

Mostly they elicited a favourable response. Plaatje in particular was gratified by the amount of sympathetic coverage in the press and by the unequivocal support of the National Brotherhood Council following their meeting with William Ward, its national secretary, early in July. Ward, impressed by their credentials, wondered whether in return they might be able to help introduce the Brotherhood movement 'among the South African tribes'. After attending the annual conference of the London Federation of the Brotherhood movement at Bishopsgate, other invitations flooded in.[13]

For Plaatje this was the beginning of what turned out to be a long association, and their warm support only confirmed his view that they should have embarked upon this kind of campaign from the beginning and ignored Harris's demands for restraint. Comments made by Will Crooks, a Labour member of parliament and a member of the Brotherhood movement, were especially encouraging, and he thought they had every chance of winning over the country, whatever the hostility of the Colonial Office. Plaatje wrote a piece for the *Brotherhood Journal*, the national organ of the movement, and it ran an editorial in support: 'Brotherhood is not only between man and man, but between nation and nation, and race and race', so there could only be one response to their appeal. 'If our Brotherhoods did not rise to a cause like this, it said, we might well question the reality of their fraternal pretensions.'[14]

The sympathy of press and public failed to influence the outcome of the

Colonial Office vote. But it did give Sir Albert Spicer and Percy Alden, two Liberal MPs whom the delegates had met earlier, the chance to bring the Natives' Land Act before parliament and to urge the Colonial Office to 'raise the question of the hardships being inflicted by it with the Prime Minister of South Africa'. Harcourt's reply was no different from before: he refused to contemplate taking any action, repeated his statement about the constitutional position, and drew the attention of the House to the recommendations of the South African Native Affairs Commission of 1905. Far from being a recent piece of Dutch-inspired legislation, he said the Natives' Land Act had a respectable English pedigree and was in the best tradition of British colonial policy. At least the Congress deputation had ensured, thanks to the two Liberal MPs, that a statement of their case now formed part of the official record of the British parliament.[15]

For a few weeks more the delegates continued with their campaign. John Dube had already returned to South Africa, promising the others that he would tour the country in order to raise money to support both the deputation's work and their families back home. He also took with him a request from John Harris to travel to Rhodesia to make contact with African leaders there and obtain the authorisation he needed to pursue the land case.[16]

Of all the delegates John Dube had been the least enthusiastic about going to England in the first place. When they met up in London, Plaatje found him strangely distracted in his manner, unable to look him in the eye. At first he thought this was due to his embarrassment about the way the 'expenses' matter had been handled. Only later would he realise that there was another reason for his puzzling behaviour: he had been having an affair with a female student at Ohlange, she had become pregnant, and a baby was due in November. Dube knew full well that when news of the scandal broke, it would not only destroy his personal reputation and threaten the future of his school, but was likely to cast a shadow over the reputation of Congress too – and undermine its mission to England. No wonder, Plaatje wrote later, he looked weighed down by 'such a terrible load on his mind'.[17]

Early in August the delegates in London were overtaken by a sequence of events they could not possibly have foreseen when they set out from South Africa in May. Following the assassination of Archduke Franz Ferdinand by Serbian nationalists, Austria-Hungary declared war on Serbia, the major European powers declared their support for one side or the other, and then, as Germany prepared to invade Belgium, Britain issued an ultimatum in fulfilment of its own treaty obligations to France and Belgium. When it expired, unanswered, at eleven o'clock on the evening of 4 August, Britain and Germany were at war. Plaatje, just six weeks in London, could never have imagined, he wrote later, that he would be witness to the sight of the capital of the empire 'under a war cloud filled with all the horrors of the approaching war storm and all the signs of patriotic enthusiasm'. 'We were about to see Mafeking over again', he said, 'but through the biggest magnifying glass.' It put an immediate end to his plans to visit Berlin. He had an invitation from the Berlin Mission Society and he had been looking forward to going there in September.[18]

The outbreak of war also ended the Congress's mission to England. It was already losing momentum. John Harris was quick to point out the difficulties of continuing when public opinion was bound to be focused upon the impending conflict, and when the empire needed above all to put on a display of unity in the face of a common enemy. Several days later a cable was in any case received from John Dube urging the delegates to come home, informing them of the decision of a meeting of the South African Native National Congress in Bloemfontein during the first week in August. This had learnt, half-way through its deliberations, that war had broken out between Britain and Germany, and so resolved 'to hang up native grievances against the South African Parliament till a better time and to tender the authorities assistance'. A demonstration of loyalty, the Congress thought, was the most effective gesture it could make. For the delegates in London the resolution provided a respectable pretext with which to draw their mission to a close.[19]

Rubusana, Msane and Mapikela accepted that they should call off their campaign. If this was the decision of the SANNC, meeting at its annual conference, they believed they had no alternative, and – with funds exhausted – they were keen to return home. Plaatje, however, was unhappy with the decision. He wanted to complete and publish his book about the Land Act, to fulfil his speaking engagements, and also to pursue the matter of the legal status of the Imperial Reserve in Mafikeng which he had discussed with lawyers. And he still hoped to be able to visit the United States, war or no war. A letter he received from Elizabeth may also have made him apprehensive about returning home. She wrote urging that he should not leave England until he was 'sure that the track was clear of German ships', and he had taken this to mean that 'they may know something that we do not quite know here'.[20]

The immediate problem was that none of the delegates had the money to pay for their passages back to South Africa. John Dube had promised to send money, but now he told them that because of the declaration of martial law in South Africa he was unable to hold any meetings to raise the necessary funds. Plaatje for one felt Dube had left them all in the lurch: 'It now amounted to this, that we must now look about and find the wherewithal to return home.' Dr Rubusana therefore volunteered 'to approach some friends, borrow money, and get us out of the tangle'.

What happened next would give rise to lasting controversy. Dr Rubusana, a Congregational minister, was successful in negotiating a loan from the London Missionary Society (LMS), but only under strict conditions. According to Plaatje, these were as follows: that the LMS would book and pay the delegates' passages, the loan being guaranteed by the Wesleyan Missionary Society and the Aborigines' Protection Society; that the LMS would also pay the delegates' board and lodging costs, up to the time they left the country, direct to their landlords; that the delegates had to depart by a particular ship – the *Borda* – due to sail in September; and that in the meantime they 'must not approach any other friends for assistance' or 'speak to any other African friends' ('goodness knows who they are', Plaatje said).

These conditions were imposed, so it transpired, at the instigation of John Harris, anxious to pack the delegates back home to South Africa and fearful that if they stayed any longer they would become both a financial burden and a political embarrassment for his society. His society then purchased four tickets in anticipation of their consent to the loan. Mapikela, Msane and Dr Rubusana accepted the terms, but Plaatje would not. 'When we got to the LMS offices,' he related, 'I told them on hearing this that I would never borrow money under such degrading conditions, with the added pleasure of having to repay it when I get back. Having come here to protest against bondage I could not very well go and sign away my liberty by undertaking not to speak to certain people and not to be at certain places at certain times.' He was beginning to understand, he said, 'why native deputations ... always start so well and then end in smoke immediately afterwards. It must be that they always get hard-up and borrow money under stop-gap conditions.'

Plaatje went to see John Harris to try to get these conditions altered, but to no avail. An argument ensued, Plaatje lost his temper, and finally stormed out of Harris's office, determined to have no more to do with a society which, he was now convinced, had sought to sabotage the efforts of the deputation from the moment they arrived in England. Harris's attitude made it all the more important, as Plaatje saw it, that his book should be published, that the iniquities of the Natives' Land Act should be brought to a wider audience, and that he must stay on in England long enough to see it through the press.[21]

Unpleasant though all this was, from Plaatje's point of view such a bad-tempered denouement was not entirely unwelcome, for it provided a convenient justification for ignoring the instructions of John Dube and the advice of the other delegates that he should return to South Africa. Staying on in England could thus be seen not as a quixotic or selfish desire to further his own ambitions, literary and otherwise, in defiance of a resolution of the SANNC, but as a principled attempt to retrieve a mission that had been curtailed prematurely, a casualty not of the outbreak of war but of a sustained campaign waged against it. He was able to pass on the ticket purchased on his behalf to Davidson Don Jabavu, the 29-year-old son of John Tengo Jabavu. He was in London but anxious to return home to South Africa after more than a decade away.[22]

Plaatje's determination to stay on to make his case was reinforced by his discovery, quite by chance, of the presence in London of Mr A.P. Apthorp, the Native Affairs Department official who had been sent over to counter their efforts. Late in July Plaatje had visited the popular Anglo-American Exhibition at White City in west London. Among the crowd of visitors he happened to see Apthorp, which surprised him since they had met in Bloemfontein shortly before he left South Africa in May, and discussed the deputation's intended visit to London. Apthorp had given no indication then that he was planning to travel to London too.

When Plaatje approached him at the exhibition, he claimed to be in England on 'a holiday trip'. It was hardly convincing. His suspicions as to his true purpose would be confirmed a year later when the expenses of his visit (£480) were set out in a published government Blue Book revealing, he said, that Apthorp was over not on a holiday 'but to counteract our propaganda at Downing St and to deny, in the name of the Union government, that the Land Act had hurt a single Native'. He would not have been surprised to learn that Apthorp had been along to the Anti-Slavery and Aborigines' Protection Society, as well as the Colonial Office, and had succeeded in making quite an impression upon John Harris.[23]

Before the other three delegates departed in the middle of September, there was another unseemly row over funds. Rubusana and Mapikela, it seems, objected strongly to Saul Msane's proposal that Plaatje, by now 'penniless', should be given £20 (which had just been received from South Africa) to keep him going. When Plaatje bade them farewell at St Pancras station on 17 September – 'as usual in England a dripping wet morning', Jabavu recalled – Mapikela did at least promise to try to get Congress to send him money for his eventual passage home, even though he made it clear that he ought to be returning now. Not that Plaatje can have held out too much hope on this score; he knew he was now on his own. Given the dire personal relations between the delegates, that can only have come as a huge relief – notwithstanding the equally dire financial predicament in which he now found himself.[24]

+∿+

Over the next few weeks and months Plaatje divided his time between work on his book on the Land Act and promoting his cause with a programme of public lectures and meetings. Mostly these were held under the auspices of the Brotherhood movement. To begin with these meetings were in and around London, relatively easy and cheap to get to, but before long he was venturing further afield. Early in October he travelled to Wales, and was delighted with his reception. He spent 'a very happy week', he related, 'among exceptionally kind Welsh people who took me for a pleasure trip in Cardiff and showed me around that interesting town and port', while at nearby Abertillery he 'addressed, in the Pavilion, the largest audience I ever spoke to'. All these meetings, he said, promised 'to pay earnest attention to the cause of the South African natives after the war'. In the circumstances this was as much as he could hope for.[25]

At these Brotherhood gatherings he found an instinctive sympathy for his cause. Firmly non-denominational, the movement drew its support from the nonconformist churches, and it claimed a national membership of over six hundred thousand people. Most were from 'respectable' working-class or lower-middle-class backgrounds, though its leaders were always keen to point to the landowners, solicitors, judges and the like who were part of it too. Along with a parallel Sisterhood movement, the Brotherhoods promoted teetotalism and self-improvement and they took the Bible as their text. There was also a genuine commitment to racial equality, in practice not just in theory, and in some branches, especially in London, black people were actively involved. At one meeting in Highbury, Plaatje remembered, there was 'a black man from South America in the chair', and his own presence as a speaker often prompted expressions of support for the idea of a universal, non-racial brotherhood. 'No one was debarred from addressing their meetings on account of either colour or race', it was reported, since 'they were of the opinion that God loved all men'.[26]

Their main activity was holding 'PSAs' ('Pleasant Sunday Afternoons'), regular Sunday meetings which were devoted to religious and educational instruction, usually accompanied by music and hymn singing, its members united by an evangelical zeal to promote the practical implementation of Christianity in everyday life. 'The Brotherhood', explained Arthur Henderson, president of the movement, 'must help not only the spiritual part of life, but also in social matters. They should always help the downtrodden, showing the brotherly feeling which was portrayed throughout the life of Christ.'[27]

It was a creed with which Plaatje could easily identify, and he often quoted Henderson's words. He had always tried to apply the basic tenets of Christianity in the political and social affairs of his own country. Now he found an organisation, a sort of domestic missionary society, committed to just such an ideal and achieving, it seemed, a good deal of success. Over the past decade, indeed, it had grown rapidly and spread to a number of other countries too. There was even a branch in Kimberley, although as elsewhere in South Africa it was for whites only. He shared the Brotherhoods' abhorrence of alcohol and their commitment to non-denominationalism, having long been a critic of the divisions within the churches and missionary societies.[28]

The Brotherhood movement wielded considerable political influence, especially within the Labour and Liberal parties, and in parliament too. Arthur Henderson was leader of the parliamentary Labour Party, and would soon become a member of the cabinet in Lloyd George's wartime coalition government, the first Labour politician ever to hold cabinet rank. Sir Richard Winfrey, Liberal MP for South West Norfolk and newspaper proprietor, was another committed Brotherhood man, and would become an enthusiastic supporter of Plaatje and his cause. Will Crooks, who had urged support for the deputation at the London Federation meeting, was an important labour leader as well as member of parliament for Woolwich in south London. The Brotherhood movement, in short, was an influential organisation whose support, Plaatje quickly realised, given his situation, was a godsend, and he was adept at cultivating contacts with its members.

None of this, however, could disguise an increasingly desperate financial situation. He had moved from Bloomsbury to cheaper lodgings in Leyton, some eight miles from the centre of London. His landlady was a woman called Alice Timberlake, and her home, 25 Carnarvon Road, would be his for over a year. Family tragedy, as well as a Brotherhood connection, had brought them together. Her husband Henry, a publisher's clerk, and the main breadwinner, had died in July, and she needed a lodger to help support her family. But Plaatje found it very difficult to keep up with his weekly board and lodging payments. He tried to get a loan from Ben Weil, once the saviour of Mafeking, who was now living in London, but he would part with no more than 30s – scant reward, Plaatje must have thought, for that solid silver shield he had secured for him in 1901. By the beginning of December he owed Mrs Timberlake £13 and appealed to Silas Molema for help, fearing eviction. Fortunately, despite the illness of her stepson, the only other breadwinner, Mrs Timberlake did not press him for the sums he owed and the crisis eventually passed.[29]

In fact Alice Timberlake showed him great kindness when he began to suffer from the extreme cold of the long, wet winter of 1914–15. It was, he wrote, 'the most strenuous winter' he had ever experienced, 'a dark, dreary winter of almost continuous snowflakes, cold, mud, and slush'. He was 'seriously troubled by colds and damp', he related after he had come through the worst of it, but added that 'its severity has been modified by the exceptional kindness of the people with whom I am living. I am afraid I will never be able to repay the painstaking manner in which they have carried me through this winter.' All the time he worked away at his book, depressed by the 'dismal gloom of the sunless days', compelled to work by gaslight even in the middle of the day. South Africa felt very far away.[30]

↜

Gradually things improved. His popularity as a speaker generated an increasing number of engagements and his circle of contacts widened. One of the most valuable proved to be Leo Weinthal, the genial editor of the *African World*, the journal Plaatje had written for several years previously. Plaatje spoke of Weinthal's generous spirit and found him 'as helpful to African callers as to Colonials of his own race'. After they met in person, Weinthal commissioned him to write some articles 'on Native topics', some of which appeared in the *African World Annual* as well as its regular weekly issues. They included an obituary of a white South African administrator, Allan King, native commissioner for the Pretoria district, whom he had got to know well during his visits to the capital. He was killed by Boer rebels when they took up arms against the South African government shortly after the outbreak of war. Plaatje described him as 'the best white friend in South Africa I ever had' and was greatly saddened by news of his death.[31]

This article, along with another entitled 'The South African coloured races and the war', evoked a lively response in South Africa itself. *De Volkstem*, a Dutch-language newspaper, took strong exception to what it considered its anti-Boer comments, and demanded that such material should be suppressed by the wartime censor. The *African World*, for its part, responded with an editorial in defence of the free expression of opinion, and continued to publish Plaatje's articles. In South Africa the effect of the controversy, noted in government as well as by the African press, was only to publicise the work Plaatje was doing in England.[32]

Leo Weinthal also helped Plaatje by providing a letter in support of his application for a reading ticket at the British Museum. 'I want some information with reference to a work on South Africa, which I am about to produce', Plaatje told the Museum's librarian early in December 1914, adding: 'When this is over I would like to compare some South African Native proverbs with analogous European equivalents which will form a separate little work.' Weinthal's letter of recommendation, in which he described Plaatje as 'our friend', and on a visit to England 'for special work', did the trick. He could now use the famous Reading Room and its unparalleled resources. Like other scholars of slender means, he also had a refuge from the bitter winter weather outside. And all free of charge.[33]

Plaatje's difficulties were greatly eased by the support of a wider circle of friends and sympathisers who began to form around him, providing a network that would sustain him during his time in England. Closest to him was a group of women who had a history of philanthropic and political engagement and some prior connection with or interest in South African affairs, drawn to him through their support for his cause and an admiration for his personal qualities. The most formidable of them was Mrs Georgiana Solomon, widow of the late Saul Solomon, one of the great figures of the Cape liberal tradition, a figure who ranked high in Plaatje's pantheon of distinguished 'friends of the natives'. The connection was strengthened by his memories of several other members of the Solomon family. One of her nephews was William Solomon, responsible for that treason court judgment in Mafeking in 1901 that had so impressed him; another was Richard Solomon, formerly attorney general of the Transvaal, who was South Africa's first high commissioner in London until his sudden death in 1913 – the man to whom Plaatje had once complained about his treatment by the police.

Since her husband's death in 1892, Georgiana Solomon had spent most of her time in England, devoting herself to a variety of liberal and radical causes before throwing herself with characteristic enthusiasm into the campaign for votes for women. She had participated, at the age of sixty-eight, in the famous march upon the House of Commons in 1909, chained herself to the railings, and had been arrested. Three years later she joined with others from the Women's Social and Political Union in smashing windows at the House of Lords, was again arrested, this time sentenced to a month in Holloway prison. For some years she had also been an active committee member of the Anti-Slavery and Aborigines' Protection Society, and shared with Plaatje not only a deep attachment to the ideals of Cape liberalism but a frustration with the position each shared in the societies in which they lived. In her mind, support for women's rights and African rights went hand in hand.[34]

Plaatje had met Mrs Solomon shortly after arriving in England (she held a reception for the Congress delegates in her home in Hampstead), and thereafter he became a regular visitor to her home, where she lived with her daughter Daisy, also a proud veteran of Holloway prison. Later he would visit Saul Solomon's grave in Eastbourne, Sussex, and arranged for a local photographer to take a picture of him standing before his memorial. The pose is unambiguously one of homage to a shared creed of Cape liberalism. To Georgiana Solomon, Plaatje was a living embodiment of her late husband's ideals.[35]

There developed a similar bond of friendship with the Colenso family, in particular Mrs Sophie Colenso, a daughter-in-law of the famous South African bishop, who had a long history of assisting visiting African delegations. All five Congress delegates had been invited to 'Elangeni', the family home in Amersham, some twenty-five miles outside London, soon after arriving in England, and after the others departed Plaatje became an eagerly anticipated visitor. He spent several weekends there in 1914 and 1915, relaxing from his campaign of public engagements, enjoying music and good conversation, finding friendship with people who had a deep interest in South Africa and shared his views on race and colour – a relationship inconceivable in South Africa itself where such familiarity would have been frowned upon by black and white alike. Irma and Sylvia, Mrs Colenso's two unmarried daughters, both talented musicians, enjoyed Plaatje's visits as much as their mother. For all of them it was a chance, as Plaatje said in one of his letters to Mrs Colenso, 'to divert one's mind from the stress and agony of these troublous times'.[36]

Another supporter was Jane Cobden Unwin, wife of the publisher T. Fisher Unwin, who likewise had a longstanding interest in African affairs. She, too, was a committee member of the Anti-Slavery and Aborigines' Protection Society, fought for votes for women, and upheld the liberal ideals of her late father, Richard Cobden. Over the years she had supported campaigns in favour of land reform, Irish home rule, the rights of Irish women, and freedom in Russia. At the time of the South African War of 1899–1902 she was a member of the South African Conciliation Committee, which opposed British policy. More recently she had become interested in land issues, having published a book on 'land hunger' in 1913, which would certainly have chimed with what she heard from Plaatje about the situation in South Africa.[37]

Plaatje used to meet Mrs Unwin at her residence in Adelphi Terrace, just off the Strand in London, next door to the offices of her husband's publishing company. Years later he spoke of his memory of 'her crown of beautiful white hair', and worried that he would be suspected of rudeness, 'for only with great difficulty' he said, could he keep his eyes off it. On at least one occasion, too, he spent a weekend at the Unwins' country residence, Dunford (Richard Cobden's birthplace), near Midhurst in Sussex, where he preached one evening at the local church.[38]

Finally, in this inner circle of female friends and supporters, was Alice Werner, lecturer in African languages at King's College London. An early graduate of Newnham College, Cambridge, her interest in South Africa was the result of her friendship, sustained in a regular correspondence, with Harriette Colenso, the best-known of the bishop's daughters. She had carved out a niche in the overwhelmingly male field in which she worked, could speak many different languages, African and European, and was also an accomplished journalist, a published poet and writer of short stories. Along with her sister Mary, with whom she lived, Alice Werner often befriended African visitors, including Pixley Seme when he was a law student in London. Though vexed by the differences between the Congress delegates in 1914 she supported their cause, wrote to the press on their behalf and, when not preoccupied with her own book about the language families of Africa, listened sympathetically to Plaatje when he told her about his book on the Land Act. Before long they were also discussing the intricacies of Setswana grammar and pronunciation, and she encouraged him in his plans for compiling a collection of Tswana proverbs.[39]

There were male friends too, and from a variety of backgrounds. The closest was William Cross, HM collector of taxes in the London borough of Ealing, and a leading light in the Southall branch of the Brotherhood movement. Plaatje often used to visit him at his home in Hanwell, in west London, where he lived with his parents and unmarried sisters (one of whom was much involved in the local Sisterhood). He was a popular and versatile speaker on the Brotherhood circuit, enjoyed both music and drama, and shared with Plaatje a concern about religious denominationalism and its attendant evils – and a belief that the Brotherhood movement had the potential to rise above them. He was also a committed internationalist and went out of his way, it was once reported, to invite speakers not only 'of all creeds and classes at home' but 'Indians, Canadians, West Indians, South Africans, and Americans'. The Southall branch of the movement, it was said, was 'a miniature International Brotherhood'.[40]

William Cross sometimes accompanied Plaatje on his engagements, and the two men formed what proved to be an enduring friendship. Once, when Plaatje was laid up with illness and unable to earn a living, William Cross took him to a farm in Buckinghamshire to recuperate, leaving the farmer with a cheque to cover the cost of looking after him till he was better. Plaatje would later cite this as an example of the warm hospitality he encountered in England, and 'a practical demonstration of the good Samaritan in action'.[41]

Another friendship was with Alfred Salter, a well-known socialist doctor and member of the Independent Labour Party who worked in Bermondsey in London's East End, and who was likewise committed to applying Christian principles in his personal and professional life. Plaatje did not share his militantly pacifist views, but this seems to have been no barrier to the warm relations that developed between them and with his wife Ada, a committed Quaker. After

Plaatje spoke at a meeting in Bermondsey, Dr Salter sent him a cheque for £25, informing him that everybody present was 'deeply impressed with the eloquence, humour and ability with which you presented your case'. He asked him to accept the money, 'a small gift' from his wife and himself, 'as an expression of our love and goodwill towards the people of your race who have so often been wronged by the people of my race'. It was probably the largest single donation Plaatje received.[42]

He also developed a range of contacts within London's African and African American community. They included Duse Mohamed Ali, an Egyptian who had lived in England since the age of ten and now edited the *African Times and Orient Review*, whose Fleet Street office became something of a social centre for London's African community. His main aim in the columns of his journal was to expose abuses of colonial rule, and he had recently written a book called *In the Land of the Pharaohs*, notable for a strongly anti-imperialist tone and some rather extensive borrowing from other published sources. He was always ready to lend a sympathetic ear to tales of colonial injustice, and was generous in his coverage of the SANNC deputation in May and June 1914. The two men kept in touch and for a while, until he found permanent lodgings in Leyton, Plaatje used 158 Fleet Street as his address for correspondence.[43]

He also had a group of friends from the colony of British Guiana. They included E.F. Fredericks ('a personal friend of mine'), educated in the United States, now at Gray's Inn training to be a barrister; and Samuel Cambridge, another lawyer, active in the Brotherhood movement, who lived in Acton, where he shared a house with John Barbour-James and his family. Barbour-James was also from British Guiana and had moved to west London with his family after being appointed postmaster in the Gold Coast. More than anybody else, he exemplified the opportunities the empire could provide for upwardly mobile black civil servants, and on his return to London, after taking early retirement, he would be for many years a leading spokesman for London's black community. Mostly he and his colleagues took a positive view of the British empire and what it stood for. They simply wanted to make sure it lived up to its promises of equal treatment for black and white alike.[44]

Another striking figure in Plaatje's circle was the Jamaican-born Dr Theophilus Scholes, a former Baptist medical missionary to the Congo, now well on in his fifties, and the author of several books about the British empire. Since he spent much of his life in the Reading Room of the British Museum, this may well have been where the two met. Scholes had ambitious plans for a six-volume vindication of the rights of 'the coloured races', two of which had been published. When he met Plaatje he had just completed volume 3, which was concerned with race relations in the United States. Like Plaatje, he now faced the challenge of finding the means to get it published.[45]

Other friends, including two from home, lived rather further afield. Several times he travelled to Scotland, combining his lecturing programme with spending time with two aspiring young doctors: Modiri Molema, Silas Molema's son, studying medicine at Glasgow University; and James Moroka, a descendant of the Seleka Barolong paramount chief Moroka, in Edinburgh. Plaatje first visit to Scotland was early in August 1914, immediately after Britain's declaration of war on Germany, and he was struck by the way towns along his route were 'swarming with Territorials in Khaki' – and distressed by 'the painful sight' of hundreds of horses being loaded onto railway trucks in preparation for war service. On a later visit, in 1915, so Modiri Molema recalled, Plaatje addressed a meeting of the African Races Association in Glasgow, and they managed to raise some funds for him.[46]

Plaatje's original intention, as he wrote aboard ship in May 1914, was to complete and publish 'the little book' he was writing 'immediately after landing in England'. Things had not of course worked out like that. He had been far too busy with the work of the deputation during the few months after his arrival to get it finished, and he decided in any case to expand it from being simply a book on the Land Act into something rather larger, including an account of the work of the deputation itself. With the outbreak of war in August he realised, if he was to have any chance of arousing British public opinion, that he would have to link his cause to the wider struggle in which the British empire was engaged. As he heard news of the Boer rebellion in South Africa following the outbreak of war, he perceived in this further ammunition for his argument, an opportunity to contrast 'African loyalty' with 'Boer disloyalty'. All this needed to be written up and incorporated into his manuscript. Inevitably it meant he had a much larger task on his hands.

But the other reason for the delay was more intractable: the question of funds to pay for the printing and publication of the book. It did not take long to discover that no printer or publisher would take it on without a substantial cash payment in advance. Of those he had approached by the beginning of November 1914, the prestigious firm of Longman, Green & Co. was the most expensive, quoting him a price of £120 to print a thousand copies of the book. Edward Hughes & Co., who had printed the deputation's pamphlet several months previously, were the cheapest at £87. Both required a down payment of £50 before they would embark upon the work of typesetting. Plaatje simply did not have this kind of money, and there was little immediate prospect of being able to raise it. His priority in any case had to be rent and subsistence. How could you write a book, let alone get it published, if you were hungry? An obvious source of funds would have been the Anti-Slavery and Aborigines' Protection Society but given his altercation with John Harris, and the views of his society, there was no hope here.[47]

Plaatje appealed, therefore, to the Barolong chief regent, Lekoko. Writing to him late in 1914, he explained his predicament, emphasised how much of a tragedy it would be if his book was not published in view of all the work of the deputation, and pointed out the ways in which the book could assist the cause of the Barolong. Should Lekoko provide the funds, Plaatje said, it would be a matter of pride to the chief and his descendants that he, chief regent of the Barolong, made possible the publication of the first book to state the case of the African people of South Africa, exposing the lies told about them by hostile white people. This might cause some jealousy among other African people, he added, but it would do much for the Barolong, and special attention could be given in the book to their land claims, and to the story of the part they played in the siege of Mafeking.

Nor was he above letting Lekoko know about the opposition he had encountered from Dr Rubusana and the other delegates, jealous, he said, that it should be a Morolong who succeeded in setting out the cause of the African people. Here was an opportunity, Plaatje put it to him, to vindicate the status of the Barolong vis-à-vis the other African peoples of South Africa, and to lay claim to their leadership. Finally, Plaatje asked, could the chief regent send him his photograph, along with a copy of the address presented to the Barolong by General Roberts in 1900, so that both could be reproduced in the book?

It was a carefully pitched appeal. Plaatje wrote as the chief regent's emissary, carrying out a mission on his behalf, approaching him in suitably respectful tone and register. Slipping into this kind of language came just as easily and naturally as if he had been in the chief's kgotla in Mafikeng: the fact that he was six thousand miles from home did not alter the underlying relationship. Since the chief had paid some of *Tsala*'s debts a few months before, there was some reason to be hopeful. This time, however, his appeal failed to elicit a response. No money came and there would be no photograph of Lekoko in the book.

Undeterred, he set about raising funds in England, and by February 1915 he was feeling a lot more optimistic. He told Mrs Colenso he was working hard on the book and expected to place it in the printer's hands 'this very quarter', his hopes raised by the favourable comments he had received from people to whom he had shown chapters. He wrote the final chapter over the 1915 Easter holiday and sent off the manuscript soon afterwards. He had agreed terms with the London firm of P.S. King & Son. They were well-established publishers, printers and booksellers with offices close to the Houses of Parliament, and he now had sufficient funds to persuade them to start typesetting. In May he had galley proofs to check, and sent copies to a number of people for comment and suggestion. Again the response was encouraging: Alice Werner ('I cannot tell you how much I like the manuscript of your book'), William Cross ('a good case against the South African policy') and Theophilus Scholes ('it will fill a great want') all wrote to congratulate him.[48]

Rather less encouraging, though, were the views of Sir Harry Johnston, the eminent (if somewhat eccentric) former explorer and colonial administrator, now living in Sussex, whom Plaatje had asked to write an introduction for his book. He knew Sir Harry was sympathetic to his cause, and the two men had met in the middle of August 1914 when Plaatje, accompanied by Saul Msane, travelled down to the south coast to visit him. Their meeting had gone well, and Sir Harry was impressed by his two visitors ('immensely helpful' in his work on Bantu languages, intellectually 'many grades above the average white man in South Africa', 'charming in their manners'). Plaatje must have discussed his own book with him, and Sir Harry expressed interest. In May 1915, therefore, Plaatje sent him a set of galley proofs to look at.[49]

His response was a disappointment. While Sir Harry was 'deeply in sympathy' with his views, and thought his command of the English language 'astonishing', he nevertheless had a number of objections, and would only write an introduction if changes were made. Otherwise, he said, 'if I was to write anything at the present moment it would of necessity criticize your presentation of the case so severely that it would nullify its purpose'. Some of Sir Harry's points were reasonable enough, such as his suggestion that it was a mistake to entitle the book *The European War and the Boer Rebellion*, which he thought was Plaatje's intention; others, including his notion that Plaatje should substitute the word 'Negro' for 'native' throughout the book, rather less so. He also recommended he should 'ruthlessly cut out every single poetical and scriptural quotation' and generally 'pull the whole work together'. Once all this was done, he said, he would be prepared to have another look at it.[50]

According to Alice Werner, Plaatje was 'greatly exercised' by the letter he received from Sir Harry, but he decided, with her encouragement, to do without the introduction. The idea that he should cut out 'every single poetical and scriptural quotation' was particularly unwelcome and it showed no understanding of his reasons for including them. Sir Harry thought they were simply to show how widely acquainted he was with English and European literature. This was not really the case. For Plaatje, quotations and epigraphs (at the beginning of each chapter) were an important means of establishing a relationship with his readers, of linking his case with the supposedly universal principles embodied in the literary and biblical canon. By juxtaposing his descriptions of the effects of the Land Act with some carefully chosen quotations, he could align the predicament of his people with the historical experience of the English and European world, drawing upon its literary heritage to make his point. Losing all this, he decided, was too high a price to pay for an introduction from Sir Harry, however helpful this might have been in getting the book noticed.[51]

It was in any case too late to be making extensive changes since this would only entail additional expense, the last thing he wanted given his circumstances. By the middle of June 1915, as he confessed to Philemon Moshoeshoe, his old friend in Mafeking, the situation was extremely worrying. 'I sometimes think that I am doomed,' he wrote. 'The Printer is threatening already and man if I and that Printer can fall out: the cause of the Natives will be irretrievably doomed.' He continued:

> I have written to the Chief just a week after I wrote you and I also telegraphed. If nothing is done by the time you get this please do your best. Things are serious … I address more meetings now and everywhere it's WHERE IS THE BOOK? And what a howling shame for the scheme to miscarry after they hear that I have been correcting proofs. Then the Natives can give up appealing to anybody with their grievances for a collapse of the scheme now would be a serious calamity. PLEASE do your best, man. Glad domestic affairs are somewhat easier with you.[52]

Moshoeshoe did his best to help, and he had already approached the chief. Unfortunately, Lekoko had fallen ill, and would not be able to do anything until he was better. All they could do was wait until he had recovered.

Plaatje met with no more success in London. Mrs Solomon tried to raise a loan to pay the £60 required, but to no avail. Then, a month later, came the worst possible news. Lekoko, far from making a quick recovery, had succumbed to his illness and died before taking any steps in the matter. With the printer now refusing to do any further work on the typesetting, their letters to Plaatje apparently unanswered, the prospect of publication receded further.[53]

At this point Alice Werner stepped in to help. An experienced author, she had become increasingly involved in the project, advising Plaatje and helping him to revise and correct proofs. Now she agreed to launch an appeal for funds, and sent out a circular letter to possible sympathisers. She explained the circumstances that made it necessary, stressed the loyalty of black South Africans to the imperial government in the current conflict, and ended with the assertion that it was 'of the greatest importance that Botha should be supported in the just and generous native policy to which I believe him personally to be inclined, though many of his supporters make his position difficult in this regard, so I understand'. Such a perception of the general was common enough in liberal circles, and was evidently hers too. It soon led, however, to serious complications, for her letter found its way into the hands of John Harris of the Anti-Slavery and Aborigines' Protection Society. Knowing Plaatje's views and the likely thrust of his book, Harris thought the appeal amounted to an attempt to raise money under false pretences, and that Plaatje must have deliberately misled Alice Werner as to its contents (quite unjustifiably as it turned out). He therefore advised potential contributors against donating money towards the book's publication, and took every opportunity to cast doubt upon Plaatje's character and integrity, suggesting that he had been living off funds collected specifically for the book's printing costs. Again, as Alice Werner was eventually able to demonstrate to him, this was quite without foundation.[54]

In John Harris, Plaatje had a determined and devious enemy. The two men had not met since Plaatje stormed out of that meeting in August 1914, but Harris was intent upon suppressing his book, fearful that his society would be associated with a cause it did not support, and that it would jeopardise his Rhodesian campaign. Plaatje's sympathisers believed Harris was perfectly capable of resorting to underhand methods: 'were Mr H. to get on the track of the printer', Alice Werner thought, he could 'do something to complicate matters' – a distinct possibility since P.S. King & Son, who printed pamphlets for the Anti-Slavery and Aborigines' Protection Society, appear to have kept Harris informed of the book's progress. Georgiana Solomon and Jane Cobden Unwin found Harris's behaviour quite reprehensible and were outraged by his personal attacks upon Plaatje's integrity. Alice Werner, more charitably, thought the society had done its best work for 'people who were absolutely helpless but they don't quite know how to take hold of people who are beginning to be articulate'. Soon she too concluded, as she wrote to Harriette Colenso, that 'Mr H. has his knife into P.'[55]

Plaatje's relationship with P.S. King & Son remained in a delicate state for the remaining months of 1915, but by the end of the year – Harris's efforts notwithstanding – he had managed to raise some more money. A week's employment in London just before Christmas had helped. He was engaged as a 'manager' to help with the 'Cape to Cairo Fair and Red Cross Fête', a charitable jamboree organised by the *African World*. Here he had a particular responsibility for the South West Africa stall, reported to have been 'a continuous centre of public attraction', and found himself working alongside Mrs R.C. Hawkin, a sister of Louis Botha, the South African prime minister. Clicko, the 'dancing bushman', one of the leading attractions at the fête, was at a stall close by. Charitable events in the imperial capital, it seems, brought together strange bedfellows.[56]

By the end of the following month, January 1916, Plaatje had made further progress with his fundraising. 'My troubles here have considerably abated since the New Year', he informed Mrs Solomon: 'I have already paid the printer £27, only £5 of which is borrowed and the binding of the book is now in progress.' At the same time, writing from Stockton-on-Tees, he was delighted to be able to report on how well his message was being received in the north of England. Addressing Brotherhood and Sisterhood meetings 'nearly every afternoon and evening', he found that 'the Yorkshire people are wildly enthusiastic with me and my question'; they sing 'much better than people in the south'; the 'weather is ideal, brilliant sunshine', and he had taken forty-two advance orders for the book. All he needed was printed copies to sell – these were not, however, quite as imminent as his comments about the binding suggested.[57]

Native Life in South Africa, as this book would be called, was Plaatje's major concern from the moment he arrived in England to its eventual publication in May 1916, nearly two years later. It was mostly written by Easter 1915, but for over a year after that he struggled to raise the funds to get it into print. All the time he was conscious of the consequences of failure, unwilling to contemplate returning home until he had achieved his aim. It would have been a challenge at the best of times, but in a time of war, and in the face of hostility from the one organisation that might have been expected to help, it must have seemed like a mountain to climb. Mounting war casualties on the Western Front, Zeppelin raids that were killing hundreds of civilians in London and other towns and cities, the controversy over the question of compulsory conscription, all were more urgent preoccupations for the British public than the affairs of a distant African dominion.

This posed problems for his public-speaking campaign too. He overcame them by stressing the patriotic support of his people for the Allied war effort, and making this his focus. On several occasions he was accompanied on the platform by two Coloured men in uniform, Privates Charles Calvert and James Kerridge, who had made their way from Kimberley to enlist in the Middlesex Regiment. Loyalty to the imperial cause could not have been more powerfully expressed, their presence 'in the familiar khaki' a fine tribute 'not only to the great diversity of the Empire's defenders, but also to the catholicity of the Brotherhood movement'. Calvert later joined the Machine Gun Regiment and survived the war; Kerridge, awarded both a Distinguished Service Medal and Military Medal for his bravery on the Western Front, did not.[58]

Although divided in its attitude towards the war, the Brotherhood movement remained steadfast in its support. In March 1915 there was a meeting in Southall to celebrate 'imperial Brotherhood Sunday', where Plaatje appeared alongside his friends William Cross and Samuel Cambridge. In July he delivered an address to the New England PSA in Peterborough, particularly impressing its president, Sir Richard Winfrey. In October he attended the annual conference of the National Brotherhood Council in London, speaking for South Africa at a much depleted international session, the only other delegates being from France, Russia and Japan.[59]

And all along, a host of smaller gatherings, often well reported in the local press, with such headlines as 'Loyal dark Africa: a native speaker at Hastings Brotherhood' (*Hastings and St Leonard's Observer*), 'Black man's pleas: coloured speaker at the Men's Own' (*Northampton Daily Echo*), or 'Visitor from the veldt: Kaffir speaker at Central Hall' (*East Ham Mail*). Plaatje was viewed with a mixture of exoticism and familiarity. Pronouncing his name correctly was sometimes a challenge for those who had to introduce him at meetings, but his patriotic message went down very well. He spoke with practised skill and humour and adapted easily to his English audiences. Invariably the meetings ended with an expression of sympathy for his cause, often in quite emotional terms, and he returned to several venues a second time, forming some close friendships along the way. These included William Dixon, president of the Leighton Buzzard Men's Meeting, where he spoke in July 1915 ('South Africa's patriotism in the war') and again in May 1916; and Henry Castle, an estate agent, keen amateur musician, committed Methodist and founding secretary of the Heathfield Brotherhood in Sussex. As with William Cross, these friendships would extend across two further visits to Britain, affirmation, as he often said, that the brotherhoods and their members 'know absolutely no distinction of colour, nor boundaries of race'. Three recently identified photographs, taken by a Heathfield photographer, also a Brotherhood member, provide a striking visual record of his encounter with Henry Castle and his family in 1915 and 1916.[60]

At some point in the late summer or autumn of 1915 Plaatje moved from Carnarvon Road, Leyton, to rented accommodation in Acton in west London: no. 33 Alfred Road, a quiet residential street just off Acton High Road. As well as being closer to central London, and with much better transport connections, it was easier to get to his friend William Cross in Hanwell, and it was no more than a few minutes' walk from where the Cambridge and Barbour-James families lived. They may well have encouraged him to make the move.

Meanwhile he heard regularly from Elizabeth. She supplied the newspapers he needed to write up developments in South Africa for his book (her assistance would be gratefully acknowledged in *Native Life*), and with her brother Isaiah managed to keep *Tsala ea Batho* going in his absence. She evidently coped well with the extra burdens placed upon her. 'I continue to hear from home every week', Plaatje told Mrs Colenso in February 1915. 'I thought when I left that my wife would manage very well, but she has surprised me in steering safely up till now, seeing that in our estimates before I left, we had provided for a five months' absence, and did not calculate that there would be a war, and a general retrenchment of income and an increase in cost of living.' In another letter Elizabeth had commented: 'it is strange that we should be separated each time there is a war'.[61]

News from home was not always so reassuring. One night in April 1915 fire destroyed the Lyndhurst Road Native School building, forcing the different classes to find temporary accommodation elsewhere. An even greater blow, perhaps half expected, was that *Tsala ea Batho* ceased publication, its last issue appearing in July 1915. It was impossible to absorb a 700 per cent increase in paper costs, a consequence of wartime shortages. One of its last issues reported that Pixley Seme had, without consulting him, put forward Plaatje's name for the presidency of the SANNC ('because of and on account of his own special merit and fitness for the position'). Plaatje could only hope to restart the paper when conditions were more favourable.[62]

More bad news followed. Shortly before Christmas, 1915, Elizabeth's mother passed away; then, on Christmas Eve, Isaiah Bud-M'belle was informed that his position as interpreter in native languages in the Griqualand West High Court was to be abolished with immediate effect, and that the Public Service Commission could find no other post for him. It was an abrupt end to a distinguished career with the judiciaries of both the Cape Colony and the Union of South Africa. He had numerous testimonials from a host of distinguished High Court judges. Now he simply had to find another way of making a living. For Plaatje, six thousand miles away, it can only have added to his worry about Elizabeth's financial situation, given her brother's support for her and the children.[63]

A few weeks later, though, there was much better news from home. 'God is so merciful that he has sent me a reward for the thankless sacrifice I am making for my fellow natives,' he wrote to Mrs Colenso. 'My boy has succeeded in capturing the ONE and ONLY little scholarship which is open to our people in South Africa and he left on March 5th for Lovedale FREE of charge. This is a considerable relief to me in the financial tangle awaiting my arrival in South Africa for which I thank the boy's boldness and Providence for inspiring him.'[64]

Sainty did indeed win his scholarship to Lovedale, but in one respect his father was misinformed. There were, as it happened, two such scholarships, and the other was won by Sainty's classmate, Z.K. Matthews, from the same Lyndhurst Road school in Kimberley. Since Plaatje and Bud-M'belle had between them done much to revive the school's fortunes, this could be counted a considerable triumph, and perhaps for Bud-M'belle it provided some consolation for the loss of his job. He then accompanied both children on the five-hundred-mile journey to Lovedale, seeing them to the separate dormitories that had been allocated to them. He also attended the formal opening of the nearby South African Native College, the future University of Fort Hare – the first post-secondary educational institution in South Africa to be open to black South Africans, and a cause with which he had long been associated. General Botha, back from the South West Africa campaign, performed the official opening ceremony, and Bud-M'belle interpreted for him with his usual skill and efficiency. This must have been encouraging news for Plaatje in his struggles in England, and of course it held out the welcome possibility for St Leger and 'Z.K.', should they fulfil their potential at Lovedale, of being able to pursue their education to a much higher level than had been possible hitherto.[65]

⌇

News of Sainty's success came at a promising time. Plaatje's debts may have been mounting but by now he had successfully established himself in London, gathered a large group of friends and supporters around him, and succeeded in raising the funds required by P.S. King & Son. The publication of *Native Life in South Africa* looked imminent. His appeal to the British imperial government had come to nothing, but his hopes of support for his cause now lay with the British public, and there seemed reason for optimism. Other literary opportunities, besides, were about to open up.

TEN

'A full-fledged scholar'
England, 1916–1917

N*ative Life in South Africa*, and the campaign that went with it, was unquestionably Plaatje's priority during his time in England, but it was not his only writing project. London was a conducive environment both intellectually and socially, and it threw up plenty of other opportunities. Paradoxically, given his distance from home, this proved to be particularly the case in relation to Setswana, his native language. Away from the personal and political obligations of his life in South Africa, he found the time and space to reflect upon his cultural identity. He was encouraged to do so by a small group of people who had an interest in African languages, who took it for granted that they were worthy of serious study, and who were ready to support him in his endeavours – particularly, it has to be said, when it benefited their own academic careers. London, moreover, offered possibilities for publication, once his work had progressed to that point, which simply did not exist in South Africa.

From this favourable combination of opportunity and circumstance, and his own persistence and hard work, three other publications emerged: *A Sechuana Reader*, written jointly with Daniel Jones, reader in phonetics at University College London; his own, solely authored *Sechuana Proverbs and Their European Equivalents*; and 'A South African's homage', a short tribute, in both English and Setswana, which he wrote for *A Book of Homage to Shakespeare*, published to commemorate the three-hundredth anniversary of Shakespeare's death. All were published within a few months of one another during the course of 1916.[1]

The first of these arose out of a lengthy period working with Daniel Jones on a comprehensive phonetic analysis of the Tswana language. Then in his early thirties, Jones already had a formidable reputation in his discipline. He had built up a successful department and had a long string of publications to his name, reflecting his interest in the characteristics not only of the main European languages but some of the more 'exotic' non-European languages as well, Cantonese, Gujarati and Ndau among them. He was promoted to the position of reader a few weeks before Plaatje started to work with him in April 1915.[2]

Alice Werner was the initial point of contact. She knew Daniel Jones well and they shared a professional concern with sub-Saharan African languages, albeit from different academic disciplines. She was intrigued by what she called 'the new science of phonetics' and alert to its possibilities; indeed, one of the aims of her new book, *The Language Families of Africa*, was to demonstrate how a knowledge of phonetics could help missionaries and others to master the languages they needed in their work. While she had some reservations about the particular system which Daniel Jones favoured – that of the International Phonetic Association (IPA) – she felt that on balance it was the best one to use, and included in her book an 'Introductory note on phonetics in relation to African languages' which he wrote for her, along with some examples of its operation in practice. One of these, in Setswana, was provided by Plaatje.[3]

She was not alone in being intrigued by this 'new science of phonetics', as the popularity of Bernard Shaw's new play *Pygmalion*, which had opened in London in April 1914, made very clear. Intended as a satire on the English class system, it tells the story of the relationship between a phonetician, Henry Higgins, and a cockney girl, Eliza Doolittle, whose accent he transforms into that of a duchess. Phonetics thus becomes the key to social mobility, and phoneticians, so Shaw claimed, were 'among the most important people in England'. Daniel Jones had provided Shaw with a good deal of the specialist knowledge he needed in writing the play but did not want this to be public knowledge. Shaw had gone along with the deception by letting it be known that another eminent phonetician, Henry Sweet (who had died in 1912), had been his main inspiration. None of this detracted from *Pygmalion*'s success in bringing an awareness of phonetics to a far wider audience than hitherto.[4]

Plaatje met Daniel Jones soon after he arrived in London, but it was only early in 1915, following a visit to the Phonetics Department at University College in the company of Alice Werner's sister Mary, that they began to work together. At that time, Plaatje said, he had no more than a 'vague acquaintance' with phonetics, and he was struck by the practical demonstration he was given. 'After some exercises I gave the students a few Sechuana sentences, which Mr Jones wrote phonetically on the blackboard. The result was to me astonishing. I saw some English ladies, who knew nothing of Sechuana, look at the blackboard and read these passages aloud without the least trace of European accent.' Just as Eliza Doolittle could sound like a duchess, so could these 'English ladies' pass as 'Bahurutse women on the banks of the Marico river', and he immediately saw the possibilities: 'I felt what a blessing it would be if missionaries were acquainted with phonetics. They would then be able to reproduce not only the sounds of the language, but the tones, with accuracy' – tones in Setswana being crucial to meaning as well as pronunciation. Just as important, he thought, was what phonetics could do to help the Batswana themselves 'to retain a correct pronunciation of their mother tongue', since many of them, especially in the south of Bechuanaland where European influence was strongest, were losing the original tones.[5]

Daniel Jones was equally enthusiastic. He considered Setswana 'an extraordinarily interesting language' and he realised that Plaatje, likely to be in London for some months yet, was ideally placed to help him carry out what would be the first comprehensive phonetic analysis of any African language. For Plaatje, likewise intrigued by the possibilities and desperately hard up, the promise of a regular income from such a collaboration could not have been more timely. Happily, from the point of view of his financial situation, it proved to be a lengthy task, and for well over a year, from May 1915 to September 1916, they had 'constant meetings' totalling, Jones estimated, between a hundred and a hundred and twenty hours, during which they worked together 'fairly continuously'.[6]

They launched straight into it. Daniel Jones began transcribing phonetically from Plaatje's dictation, believing that trying to get a general feel for the language was a waste of time. He made a point of not consulting any existing books on Setswana 'for fear of being misled', he said, 'by the inaccurate observations of other people'. It proved to be a more challenging business than he thought. Even with their frequent sessions, some of them in Jones's home in Ridgmount Gardens, a short distance from University College, it was a while before he got to grips with the complexities of the language. There were two vowels, for example – one between 'i' and 'e' and the other between 'o' and 'u' – which he could immediately identify, while a sound between 'd' and 'l' only became clear when Plaatje quickened the pace of a passage he was reading.[7]

Even then Jones struggled to pronounce it correctly. 'The analysis of the sound bothered us for a long time but by dint of looking at Mr Plaatje's tongue and trying [to] experiment myself, we found that in order to make it the tip of the tongue must be curled backwards and must touch the left hand side of the roof of the mouth.' It was, Jones, said, 'one of the most difficult sounds to make I have ever come across', and he 'practised it off and on when Mr Plaatje was here'. Another sound, a vowel which Jones described as being close to the French 'y', he only discovered after they had had over twenty sittings. In some sessions they used a wax cylinder phonograph which enabled Jones, so it was reported, 'to discover many curiosities in the pronunciation of the Sechuana language'. Plaatje particularly remembered the device because it enabled him to hear, for the first time, the sound of his own voice.[8]

Their greatest challenge was Setswana's tonal system, which 'gave more trouble than anything else'. Understanding it, however, was vital, since the use of different tones in speech could change the meaning of a word: 'Every syllable in a Sechuana sentence', Daniel Jones explained, 'has a certain definite musical pitch assigned to it; it has, in fact, to be sung on a certain note.' To ignore these tones in speech, he told Alice Werner, 'must be quite as bad, if not worse, than speaking English without making any differences between the vowels in *bed*, *bad*, *bird*'. They simply had to be represented accurately. He endeavoured to do so by means of musical notation but admitted he only began to 'get the hang of them' after he had got through 'something like ten sheets of music paper' and only after 'something like 10 sittings with Mr Plaatje'. Even then 'new features kept turning up unexpectedly ... so that it was a very long time before we really got the thing straight'. One feature of the language 'was not brought to light until we had well over 50 sittings'.[9]

Jones's observations on their work together come from a lecture he gave to his students in October 1916, shortly after his last session with Plaatje, and they provide some interesting insights into the nature of their relationship. Daniel Jones, it is clear, formed a high opinion of Plaatje's 'unusual linguistic ability' and regarded him quite differently from other 'native informants' with whom he had worked in the past, and about whom he was often very critical. By contrast, his work on Setswana, so he told his students, was carried out under 'rather favourable conditions', Plaatje was 'intelligent and observant' and 'most important of all soon understood what I was driving at and was able to help materially in the investigation'. Indeed, he soon mastered the business of writing phonetically himself.

Jones recognised, moreover, the part Plaatje played in the analysis as well as just the provision of linguistic data. As Collins and Mees, Jones's biographers, point out, it is very noticeable how he used the term 'we' in his lecture when referring to this aspect of their work together – as in the statement 'I hope and think that we have now got the analysis quite accurate'. The same point was made by Sylvia Colenso (Sophie Colenso's youngest daughter) when she recalled Daniel Jones telling her that the two of them had 'together threshed out all the difficulties of pronunciation which had hitherto baffled the missionaries and other teachers'.[10]

The main published outcome of these sessions was *A Sechuana Reader in International Phonetic Orthography* (*with English Translations*), jointly authored by Jones and Plaatje, and published by the University of London Press in 1916. It had a threefold objective, being intended '(1) as a collection of reading-matter suitable for native Bechuanas or for foreign learners, (2) as a guide to the pronunciation of the Sechuana language, and (3) to demonstrate the desirability and the feasibility of writing African languages on the "one sound one letter" basis'.

The book was in the University of London Phonetic Readers Series (edited by Daniel Jones), it followed the format established in earlier volumes on non-European languages, and it ran to seventy-five pages. The first thirty pages, written by Jones, provided an original, but highly technical, analysis of the phonetics and pronunciation of Setswana, followed by 'A few maxims for the transcriber of African languages' and suggestions for further reading. The remainder consisted of fifteen readings, each being made up of a phonetic transcription of a text in Setswana and two English translations, free and literal. Thirteen of these were fables or stories which Plaatje wrote specially for the book, four of them providing explanations of the context and meaning of proverbs that also appear in his *Sechuana Proverbs*. The other two were the Lord's Prayer and a fictional conversation between a teacher and pupil (which must have come from Daniel Jones).

Alice Werner was one of the few people in any sort of position to assess the merits of such a specialised work. Reviewing it in *Man*, the journal of the Royal Anthropological Society, she welcomed it as 'a new departure of a very interesting kind' and the most thorough study to date of 'Sechuana speech sounds, and more especially of the tones' (though she was less impressed by its neglect of the earlier work of German phoneticians). Not everybody, however, was persuaded that the use of the IPA script was the most appropriate means of representing the sounds and pronunciation of African languages. For nearly six months, between October 1916 and March 1917, the war with Germany notwithstanding, there was a long-running correspondence on the subject in the columns of the *Times Literary Supplement*. On one side were Sir Harry Johnston and several other former colonial administrators who thought it unnecessarily complicated, impossible to learn and unlikely to catch on; on the other, the purists like Daniel Jones for whom accuracy was everything and the IPA script a proven solution. He was supported, again with some reservations, by Alice Werner, both of them referring to the *Sechuana Reader* as an example of the successful application of the IPA script to an African language.[11]

The *Sechuana Reader* was recognised as a significant contribution to its discipline, especially for its pioneering analysis of tone. Daniel Jones considered it one of his most important pieces of work, and the most satisfying. He wrote later of having 'had the privilege' of working with Plaatje, regarded him as a 'personal friend' and was always appreciative of his part in their collaboration. He was also very much struck by the stories and proverbs he heard from Plaatje during the course of their work together, particularly the proverb that appears in the Reader as 'Alone I am not a man; I am only a man by the help of others', along with its accompanying text, contrasting the strength of a bundle of sticks with the weakness of its individual pieces. Friends and colleagues remembered him repeating it for years afterwards.[12]

Plaatje hoped that the book would be used both by missionaries and the Batswana themselves, but he would be disappointed. A friend later described it as 'a strange book in a strange spelling', and it was barely read outside specialist academic circles. Yet his collaboration with Daniel Jones did give him, quite apart from a vital source of income, an interest in phonetics he was to retain for the rest of his life – and the satisfaction of knowing that it was his own pronunciation of Serolong that would now constitute, as it were, the official record of the language. Judging from the inscription in the copy of *Sechuana Proverbs* he presented to Daniel Jones – with compliments and 'grateful recollections of helpful times at Ridgmount Gardens with English and Sechuana problems' – he greatly enjoyed their time working together. They had become good friends as well as colleagues.[13]

Just as important as the *Reader*'s contribution to the discipline of phonetics, in Plaatje's mind, were the stories he wrote specially for it. Most were drawn from his prodigious knowledge of Tswana oral tradition. He related the tale of the lizard and the chameleon, a parable of 'how death began'; of the traveller and the hartebeest, which gave rise to the proverb 'Take care that you don't mourn for the hartebeest and the hide', akin to the English proverb 'A bird in the hand is worth two in the bush'; and the proverb 'The ratel (honey badger) is suspicious of the honeycomb', accompanied likewise by an explanation of its context and meaning. Two other tales, unrelated to specific proverbs, illustrate human qualities of bravery and cowardice; one of them, entitled 'Hunters and beasts of prey', tells the story of the brave man who held onto the lion's tail, and the cowardly man who ran away, and the consequences of their actions. Several of the stories Plaatje relates were drawn from the more recent past: an incident 'that once took place in the region of the Molopo river after the introduction of firearms'; another was a tale of the experiences of Chief Gokatweng Gaealashwe and a party of his Bakwena people returning from a stint working on the mines in Rhodesia.

✦

Plaatje's collection of proverbs, published in July 1916 with the title *Sechuana Proverbs with Literal Translations and Their European Equivalents*, likewise had its origins in his longstanding interest in one of the most notable features of the Tswana language. The vast majority – 732 was his final total – came from memory, a considerable feat in itself, and reflecting his closeness to the oral culture of his people. He had often deployed proverbs in the Tswana columns of his newspapers and in both conversation and correspondence with other Tswana-speakers as it was natural to do, but there is no evidence that he had thought about a systematic compilation until he came to England.

Once in London, given the circles he moved in, there was plenty of encouragement. He thanked Alice Werner and William Cross for 'practical assistance received while compiling the proverbs', and he recalled the many 'helpful hours' spent at 69 Shakespeare Road, Cross's home in Hanwell. It was Alice Werner who provided the greater intellectual impetus, for she had a longstanding interest in proverbs and folklore, believing they provided a unique insight into the 'native mind' and that it was vital to preserve them in the face of the inevitable spread of European languages and culture. She was fascinated, too, by the equivalences she saw between proverbs and folktales across different cultures, validating their claim, she believed, to be taken seriously – and grist to the mill in the contemporary debate about whether such phenomena evolved independently or through a process of diffusion, one culture influencing another.[14]

When Alice Werner first met Plaatje she worried that he had become too 'Europeanized', too distant from his native culture. Once she got to know him, however, she revised her opinion, reassured, as she wrote later, that he, 'an educated native', should have appreciated the importance 'of this traditional lore', and she did what she could to encourage him. Judging from her later criticism of some of the European equivalents he came up with, she probably had little to do with the actual process of compilation, though like William Cross and Georgiana Solomon (to whom he would dedicate the book) she may have lent him reference books to help him in his task. With the resources of the Library of the British Museum at his disposal, however, it cannot have been too difficult to lay his hands on what he needed.[15]

One reference book he did have was Palmer's *National Proverbs* (*England*), published in 1912, one of the few books from his extensive library to have remained in the hands of his descendants. In it he inscribed the words 'Leyton, Essex, Whitsunday '15' (23 May 1915), suggesting serious engagement with the project, as he told the British Museum, once *Native Life in South Africa* was completed. When he went through it he wrote in Setswana equivalents against a number of the English proverbs. These duly made their way into his own manuscript. Thus the first proverb in Palmer ('There was a wife who kept her supper for her breakfast, and she was dead before day') becomes the equivalent to '*Bopelonomi bo bolaile Ma-Masiloanoke* / M was killed by her own hospitality (magnanimity)', proverb no. 53 in his own compilation. At other times he started the other way round, setting down Tswana proverbs from memory and then trying to find the closest European equivalent. He did not always succeed, and in the end was unable to come up with European equivalents for over sixty such proverbs.[16]

By January 1916 his compilation was well advanced and he had good news to report. 'You will be agreeably surprised', he wrote to Mrs Colenso on 28 January, 'that I have successfully fulfilled Mr Sonnenschein's conditions and that he has agreed to publish my proverbs and that I got him to improve the terms considerably in my favour so that my outlook is much brighter than in 1915.' William Swan Sonnenschein was the founder of the publishing company that bore his name, notable for having published, among other things, the works of Karl Marx and Friedrich Engels. By the time Plaatje met him, he had sold his company, and was commissioning books for the London publishing house of Kegan Paul, Trench, Trübner & Co., bringing to the task, according to one account, his 'ripe experience and shrewdness'. Plaatje did well to have extracted better terms for a book that was never going to be a money-spinner.[17]

As well as setting out the proverbs with their translations and equivalents, Plaatje wrote an informative introduction, setting them in the wider context of the Tswana language and its history. His main objective, he said, was 'to save from oblivion' the wealth of proverbial expression of the Tswana people, a task which had been undertaken for a number of other African languages but not, until now, for Setswana. And he elaborated upon their significance. Their wealth and variety, he believed, demonstrated fully the qualities and capacity of a language that was 'fully equipped for the expression of thought', while the many parallels to be found in European languages served only, in his view, to demonstrate the universality of cultural phenomena. The Tswana language, in other words, was as sophisticated as any other – a proposition which his friends in London could accept without difficulty, but which would have been anathema to many in South Africa. His collection of proverbs thus asserted the cultural worth and integrity of Setswana, complementing the political statement he was still struggling to get into print in *Native Life in South Africa*. Both were part of a larger whole, different aspects, as he saw it, of a way of life he sought to preserve from the worst effects of 'European civilisation'.

✦

A similar concern to validate the qualities of Setswana inspired his contribution to the tercentenary *Book of Homage to Shakespeare*. The driving force behind this project was Israel Gollancz, professor of English at King's College London and honorary secretary of the Shakespeare Tercentenary Committee. Plans to mark the anniversary of Shakespeare's death had long been in preparation, but the outbreak of war in 1914 put everything on hold. 'The dream of the world's brotherhood to be demonstrated by its common and united commemoration of Shakespeare, with many another fond illusion', Gollancz thought, 'was rudely shattered.' While there were some who felt that all commemoration should be held over until the end of the war, Gollancz and his committee did not, and came up with the idea for a Book of Homage as an appropriate and suitably modest means of marking the occasion. For Gollancz there was a pressing reason to at least do something. 'We dare not, under any conditions,' he wrote privately, 'allow the tercentenary to pass unobserved, lest the enemy mock at us, and have a commemoration at Weimar, while we are remiss.' Potential contributors, he thought, if they were English, had a patriotic duty to support the project and put pen to paper.[18]

Alice Werner was most likely instrumental in securing Plaatje's participation. She was a colleague of Gollancz's at King's College London, where both held academic posts. Her name is included in his list of acknowledgements to 'those who have helped me in various ways', and she would have been well aware by this time of Plaatje's interest in Shakespeare. Indeed, she was an enthusiast herself, far from unusual for somebody of her background and education. What really fascinated her were the connections between Shakespeare and folklore, one of her main academic interests. She was struck not only by the way Shakespeare drew upon oral traditions in his plays, but how the plays themselves fed into oral traditions elsewhere, including places 'beyond the bounds of the civilized and literate world', like Africa, where they 'filtered down into African tradition and became a part of current folk-lore'. Just as had happened, Plaatje told her, with the Batswana.

What she heard from Plaatje simply confirmed what she had discovered for herself. A few years earlier, during her travels in East Africa, she had been handed a manuscript of a Swahili version of *The Merchant of Venice* – something that 'took my breath away' when she realised what it was. From internal evidence she thought the tale originated in India, strengthening her belief in the Indian provenance of the printed sources upon which Shakespeare himself drew in *Merchant of Venice*. She thought it perfectly natural that this process of diffusion should work both ways: 'we now find his works dropping like seed into the virgin soil of the Bantu race', she wrote, thereby enriching 'the floating mass of tradition in those wonderful, melodious languages whose future possibilities some of us just dimly apprehend'. She saw no reason why at some point in the future 'Shakespeare and his mates' should not be to Africa 'what Homer and Sophocles were to the European Renaissance'. Who, better, then to contribute to a volume celebrating the universality of Shakespeare than a native speaker of one such 'melodious language'?[19]

Plaatje's tribute, entitled 'A South African's homage', which he submitted in the middle of March 1916, was one of a second batch Gollancz commissioned once he realised it was impossible to restrict their number to a hundred as originally envisaged. Mostly, the other contributors, 166 in all, were scholars, novelists, poets and literati from both sides of the Atlantic and around the globe, Germany and her wartime allies excepted; Thomas Hardy, Rudyard Kipling, John Galsworthy and Sir Henry Newbolt were among the well-known literary figures involved. Twenty-three different languages, living and dead, were represented, some of them appearing in their original form, others accompanied, as in Plaatje's case, by English translations. Apart from Setswana, other non-European languages were Bengali, Pali, Urdu, Burmese, Arabic and Sanskrit. Plaatje's was the only tribute from South Africa or in any African language, although interestingly Isaiah Bud-M'belle, doubtless at Plaatje's suggestion, was also invited to contribute; unfortunately his piece (in Xhosa) did not arrive in time to be included.[20]

Most of the tributes were distinctly reverential in tone. Plaatje, though, took a rather more personal approach. He described how he had first encountered Shakespeare in Kimberley, and how he was struck by the parallels between Shylock and 'certain speculators' in the city; he told the story of his romance with Elizabeth, and how English, 'the language of Shakespeare', enabled them to understand one another as they exchanged love letters; how he adopted the term 'William Tsikinya-Chaka' for William Shakespeare (literally, 'William Shake-the-Sword') after he had first heard it used 'by an educated native chief' in the kgotla in Mafikeng.[21]

But he did also have some more general observations to make about the nature of Shakespeare's appeal. The reason he so admired Shakespeare, he explained, was that his dramas 'show that nobility and valour, like depravity and cowardice, are not the monopoly of colour' – a point he illustrated by describing 'how feelings of an opposite kind were aroused in me' after seeing a highly biased film of the Crucifixion in which 'the only black man in the mob was Judas Iscariot'. More recently he had become even more 'suspicious of the veracity of the cinema and acquired a skepticism which is not diminished by a gorgeous one now exhibited in London which shows, side by side with the nobility of the white race, a highly coloured exaggeration of the depravity of the blacks'.

He was alluding, as many of his readers would have known, to the popular new film *The Birth of a Nation*, which glorified the activities of the Ku Klux Klan in the aftermath of the American Civil War, and made a huge impact upon audiences wherever it was shown. He had seen the film in London and was horrified by its racist representations of African Americans. He had then joined with Georgiana Solomon and Jane Cobden Unwin in appealing to the authorities to get it withdrawn, arguing that it was not only detrimental to good relations between the races but undermined the imperial war effort. They failed to get the film banned in Britain, but their protests did help persuade the South African high commissioner, W.P. Schreiner, to take steps to ensure that it was not shown in South Africa. Not surprisingly, Plaatje preferred Shakespeare, his 'keen grasp of human character', he wrote in his tribute, unequalled by more recent writers and playwrights.[22]

He ended his tribute by looking to the future. 'It is to be hoped that with the maturity of African literatures, now still in its infancy, writers and translators will consider the matter of giving to Africans the benefit of some at least of Shakespeare's plays. That this could be done is suggested by the probability that some of the dramas on which his dramas are based find equivalents in African folk lore.' Translating Shakespeare into Setswana was clearly in his mind. Nobody was better qualified to undertake such a task.

The published version of 'A South African's homage' differed significantly from the one he originally submitted to Professor Gollancz, and a rather intriguing passage was deleted. It followed a paragraph about his suspicions of 'the veracity of the cinema' (of which *Birth of a Nation* was a prime example), and ended with his observation about Shakespeare's dramas showing 'that nobility and valour, like depravity and cowardice' were not the monopoly of any colour. But Plaatje pursued this idea further, invoking the example of Othello to argue that blacks should be allowed to serve in the armed forces of the British empire, an important step, as he saw it, in justifying their claim to full citizenship. 'Being an Imperialist and subject of a great empire which is four-fifths black,' he wrote, 'I am convinced that if our Othellos were given an opportunity, in front as at the rear, they would serve this Empire as nobly as Toussaint L'Ouverture served his West Indian state, and as faithfully as Enver Bey and the other Beys served Germany in Gallipoli.' 'Knowing my people as I do,' he concluded, 'I am satisfied that given equal opportunities some of us could show in the cause of our Empire, a shining parallel to the wondrous deeds of Moriba, Mousa Sidi and the other "black tirailleurs" from West Africa', whose gallantry he then illustrated with a quotation (in French) from a book by Colonel Albert Baratier, extolling their deeds in past colonial conflicts.[23]

Quite why the passage was deleted is impossible to know. If there was ever any correspondence about the matter, it has not survived. The deletion could have been at Plaatje's instigation, or at Gollancz's, or the two of them together. It is not difficult, however, to see why Plaatje may have had second thoughts about it, or that Gollancz may have insisted on removing it, for he had touched on a number of sensitivities. The passage could be read as a clearly implied criticism of an important aspect of imperial – and South African – policy, namely the unwillingness to allow blacks to fight alongside whites on an equal basis. Enlisting Shakespeare to the cause of an empire of 'equal opportunities', as he wished to do, was hardly likely to go down well in official circles. South Africa was a valued partner in the war against Germany, and General Botha was widely regarded as an important symbol of imperial unity in the face of a common foe.

Other aspects of the deleted paragraph were just as controversial. What would the French, for example, Britain's principal wartime ally, make of Plaatje's reference to Toussaint L'Ouverture – bearing in mind that the 'West Indian state' he served (Haiti) fought and won its independence from the French empire of his day? Even more troubling were the complimentary remarks about 'Enver Bey and the other Beys' who had 'served Germany in Gallipoli' so faithfully, fighting for their Ottoman allies in what had been, for the British, a disastrous military campaign. This would have been about the last thing that Israel Gollancz, who saw the *Book of Homage* in distinctly patriotic terms, would wish to draw attention to in a celebratory volume of this kind. The sensitivities of his Australian and New Zealand contributors and readers, given Gallipoli's symbolic significance to them, would only have added to his concerns.

If Gollancz did intervene, it was no more than he had done with other contributors. Georg Brandes, for example, a Danish scholar and critic, had his draft returned with a request to revise his comments about the Baconians who denied Shakespeare's authorship. Douglas Hyde, an Irish nationalist, was persuaded to tone down the English translation of his poem in Gaelic. More drastically still, the poet Thomas Sturge Moore had his piece rejected in its entirety, being informed by Gollancz that 'our enemies are watching us very closely with regard to the Tercentenary'; that German propagandists would make capital out of his suggestion that the Germans venerated Shakespeare more than the British; and that the war effort needed to be prosecuted far more efficiently if victory was to be won. Gollancz went so far as to tell Moore that in time of war 'patriotism demands silence', that 'the Book of Homage is really a homage through Shakespeare to England', and that 'we dare not lose sight of this prime duty and indeed highest privilege'. Even Shakespeare, he concluded – appealing to the highest authority – knew when to remain silent for patriotic reasons too.[24]

Given such views, Gollancz is unlikely to have let Plaatje's tribute go through unchanged. The material excised from it, however this was done, undeniably robbed it of a sharper political edge. For here was Plaatje not just offering respectful homage, writing amusingly about his engagement with Shakespeare, of the nobility of Shakespeare's ideals and his grasp of human character, or of the possibility of translating his plays, but enlisting Shakespeare in support of a rather more subversive ideal: that of an empire of 'equal opportunities'. This was not what the rulers of empire thought they were fighting for.

One other textual matter remains a puzzle: the omission of any mention of Plaatje's name, 'A South African's homage' being the only unattributed contribution in the book. Plaatje's original intention was to have his name included, for he supplied it, along with his professional and literary credentials ('Editor of *Tsala ea Batho*, Kimberley, S Africa; author of *Native Life in South Africa*, *Sechuana Proverbs and their European Equivalents*'), on both English and Tswana versions of his text. In the English version his name and credentials have been crossed through by another hand. Israel Gollancz, for it must have been his, had no reason to take this action unless asked to, and he would not have welcomed the departure from the book's style which this entailed. It must be assumed this was in response to a last-minute request on Plaatje's part. Why, then, this desire for anonymity?

The most likely explanation is that he was worried that any hint of controversy could jeopardise the publication of *Native Life in South Africa*. This was still in the press, and there was good reason to believe that John Harris, intent on suppressing it if he could, would seize upon anything he could find to discredit the author.

Another fear was that the South African authorities, armed with the necessary wartime powers, might seek to prevent the book from being imported into the Union. Plaatje knew they were concerned about anything that threatened to undermine relations between Boer and Briton, at this time in a very fraught state. There had already been demands in the Dutch-language press in South Africa for his writings to be censored, and one of the things the *Volkstem* had particularly objected to was his argument that the military authorities should enlist blacks to fight in the South West Africa campaign; indeed, it had considered this 'a bitter provocation' (as it would the decision, later in 1916, to raise a Native Labour Contingent for service in France).

In particular, what Plaatje had written in his 'Othello' paragraph, if published, could only stoke controversy, and he may not have known at this point that it was to be edited out. Much wiser, at this delicate stage in *Native Life*'s protracted gestation, to keep a low profile and avoid anything that might jeopardise its prospects, even at the expense of rubbing shoulders publicly with the great and the good of the literary establishment.

Not that the removal of his name was carried through with any precision. On the contents page of the *Book of Homage*, the words 'William Tsikinya-Chaka'– seemingly the name of the author – and 'A South African's homage' appear together, but in a different order from every other entry. Perhaps this was just an error resulting from the last-minute changes, understandable given the haste with which the book was produced. At the same time it is quite possible that Israel Gollancz, under pressure, and with 165 other contributors to worry about, may never have been entirely sure whether he was dealing with Solomon Plaatje or William Tsikinya-Chaka: which could be the reason why, when he prepared his papers for sale some years later, he created a file cover with the title 'A South African's homage', indicating that this was 'by William Tsikinya-Chaka'. At least this uncertainty took the indigenisation of Shakespeare an interesting step further, even if by accident rather than design.[25]

The *Book of Homage* was published just in time for the tercentenary celebrations, one copy being formally presented to the King and Queen, patrons of the Shakespeare Tercentenary Committee. The lord mayor of London presided over a memorial meeting at the Mansion House, and the next day there was a special performance of *Julius Caesar* at the Drury Lane Theatre. Afterwards Frank Benson, the leading Shakespearean actor and producer, still in bloodied toga and smeared in greasepaint, was famously knighted by the King. The celebrations then moved to Stratford-upon-Avon, Shakespeare's birthplace, where (Sir Frank) Benson's company put on *A Midsummer Night's Dream* at the Memorial Theatre. At the end of the week, on the evening of Saturday, 6 May, festivities drew to a close with a pageant consisting of scenes enacted from nine of Shakespeare's plays.

Plaatje was in the audience that evening, witness therefore to 'the wave of emotion' that passed over 'the whole of that little theatre' as the tercentenary festivities reached their climax. Highlights of the performance included the conspirators' scene from *Julius Caesar*; the trial scene from *Merchant of Venice* in which Ellen Terry, the leading Shakespearean actress of her day, played Portia;

and this was followed by a grand finale, a 'Homage to Shakespeare', as all the players gathered together on the stage. Proceedings ended, just before midnight, with audience and players joining hands to sing 'Auld lang syne', 'ablaze with the flowers of Shakespeare's thoughts', foremost among which – in the view of the local paper at any rate – was 'patriotism'. The war, after all, was in everybody's thoughts.[26]

Such intensity of emotion was noticeably absent in the reviews of *Book of Homage*. Reviewers recognised its symbolic importance, but were not much impressed by the quality and coherence of what lay between its covers. Some dutifully noted the presence of leading lights like Thomas Hardy and Rudyard Kipling, but found it difficult to do justice to all the contributions: 'too big and too various for readable analysis', according to one. Nevertheless, several of the reviews did single out 'A South African's homage' for special mention. The *New Statesman* (its review was entitled 'A tombstone for Shakespeare') thought the tribute from 'a South African Sechuana' 'the most touching' of the foreign contributions, preferring its informality and humour to the platitudes to be found elsewhere. The *Times Literary Supplement* was even more fulsome in its praise. When, it suggested, 'you have read the papers of Lord Bryce, of Cardinal Gasquet, of M. Bergson, the minutiae of the scholars, the rapture of the poets, you may, not irreverently, wonder whether anything in the volume would have delighted Shakespeare so much as the paper in which a gentleman of the Chuana relates how he drew from Tsikinya-Chaka ("Shake-the-Sword") the language of his love-letters to his M'Bo bride'. The 'gentleman of the Chuana' had clearly struck just the right note – and was no doubt equally delighted at the thought of Shakespeare reaching out to him across time, space and cultures.[27]

A month later Plaatje's main objective in his mission to England was achieved with the publication of *Native Life in South Africa*. It was reward for his untiring struggles since arriving in England two years previously, and a notable victory, so he wrote later, after '11 months fighting Harris who was battling to suppress "Native Life" in the press'. The waiting, he said, was 'unbearable'. He had also to overcome the increasingly difficult conditions being faced by publishers and printers. Costs of book production, so P.S. King informed another of their authors, had risen 'enormously during the past year or so and are still rising', so it was as well there were no further delays. *Native Life* could easily have suffered the same fate as *Tsala ea Batho*, sunk by the massive wartime increases in the cost of paper.[28]

Native Life in South Africa before and since the European War and the Boer Rebellion was the final title Plaatje settled on, possibly taking his cue from a book of Alice Werner's called *Native Life in East Africa*, published a few years previously. She was also the intermediary in obtaining Harriette Colenso's assent to his request to be allowed to dedicate the book to her – 'in recognition of her unswerving loyalty to the policy of her late distinguished father and unselfish interest in the welfare of the South African Natives'. In fact Alice Werner worried that such a dedication might be interpreted as a hostile act in relation to John Dube, with whom Harriette Colenso had been closely associated, but it seems she had no objection to the plan.[29]

Native Life in South Africa was far from 'the little book' Plaatje once envisaged, and it now ran to over three hundred and fifty pages, good value for its modest price of 3s 6d. It described the events leading up to the passage of the Natives' Land Act, its effects when implemented, the campaign mounted by the South African Native National Congress, the story of the deputation to England and the reception it received, and several historical episodes illustrating the loyalty of African people in South Africa to the cause of the imperial government. At its heart are the chapters where Plaatje describes his own observations of the effects of the Land Act during the journeys he made in South Africa in 1913 and 1914.

Native Life in South Africa was formulated as a direct and often highly emotional appeal to the British public to right the wrongs being done to his people; to secure, above all, the repeal of the Natives' Land Act. Its opening words have become famous. 'Awaking on Friday morning, June 20, 1913 the South African Native found himself, not actually a slave, but a pariah in the land of his birth.' He justified his appeal not simply by reference to the constitutional responsibilities which Britain still retained for South Africa, but upon the grounds of shared humanity: natural justice and Christian belief alike demanded their intervention. Throughout the book he is concerned to demonstrate this common humanity, and to argue that as loyal subjects of the British empire his people were entitled to fair and decent treatment. He was conscious of the difficulties caused by the image they had in the eyes of the majority of the British public: 'This appeal', he wrote, 'is not on behalf of the naked hordes of cannibals who are represented in fantastic pictures displayed in the shop-windows in Europe, most of them imaginary; but it is on behalf of five million loyal British subjects who shoulder "the black man's burden" every day, doing so without looking forward to any decoration or thanks.'[30]

Plaatje counters these perceptions by presenting his case in terms that are meaningful to an English audience. In trying to convey what the Natives' Land Act meant, for example, he likened its operation to an imaginary decree of the

London County Council; he evoked memories of Daniel Defoe's *Journal of the Plague Year* by comparing the effects of the Land Act to those of the plague; he quoted Oliver Goldsmith's poem 'The deserted village' to emphasise the parallels between the evictions that followed the Natives' Land Act with those same consequences that followed the enclosures in England over a century previously. Possibly, too, he had in mind William Cobbett's *Rural Rides*, published nearly a hundred years earlier, more than any other book the record of the destruction of an independent English peasantry through the enclosures in the early nineteenth century. Plaatje believed that what he had witnessed in the wake of the Land Act was the destruction of a black South African peasantry, and he was aware of the similarity in historical process. His approach, throughout the book, was to emphasise this shared humanity.

The war and its relevance to his arguments were a central theme, too. In the circumstances this was hardly something he could have avoided. What he does, though, with both skill and style, is to turn a potential obstacle into a powerful argument in his favour. He emphasised the loyalty of his people to the cause of the imperial government in both past and present conflicts, arguing that this entitled them to 'fair play and justice' and relief from the 'tyrannical enactment' of 1913. Against this ideal stood the behaviour of the Boers, the instigators, as he argued, of the Land Act itself, who then rose in rebellion at the outbreak of the First World War. Africans, by contrast, were loyal to the imperial cause, their representatives, the South African Native National Congress, having resolved at their meeting in August 1914 to 'hang up their grievances' for the duration of the war.

Overall, *Native Life in South Africa* was a powerful and sustained polemic, shrewdly cast in the terms and language most likely to appeal to the conscience of a nation at war, and the first book-length statement of the grievances of the African people by one of their own leaders. Its significance was recognised by at least some of the reviews it received in the English press. The liberal *Daily News and Leader*, for example, thought the book ('though possibly open to criticism on points of detail') was nevertheless 'a very lucid and forcible – and, all things considered, not intemperate – statement of some very real and galling native grievances'. The *Birmingham Post* was likewise impressed by the strength of Plaatje's argument. 'It is a serious case, well and ably put and the evidence embodied in it is very disquieting. Here at any rate is a book which makes the native agitation intelligible and may conceivably have an influence on future events in South Africa – and at home, for by no legal fiction can the Imperial power dissociate itself from responsibility for Native affairs.'[31]

Other reviews took a similar line, several commenting on how remarkable it was that such a book could have been written by a black South African. Even the journal *South Africa*, so scathing of the Congress deputation in 1914, thought that 'there is the spice if not the charm of novelty about this book', that 'its author occasionally expresses himself well and forcibly', and that it was 'all to the good that South African publicists should have the advantage of reading the opinions of a native observer when dealing with legislation affecting his race'. Just as surprising was the approbation of *United Empire*, the journal of the Royal Colonial Institute. 'Mr Plaatje has marshalled his facts with considerable skill. He sets forth the case of his countrymen with energy and moderation. His conclusions seem to be warranted by the information at his disposal, and the facts he adduces seem to bear but one interpretation. And lastly, in the existing circumstances, he is fully justified in appealing to the court of public opinion.'[32]

Responses were not uniformly favourable, however. A reviewer in *New Age* thought *Native Life* was 'quite good journalism', but that its author 'does not make it easy for us to understand the real dimensions of his grievance'. 'Delta', in the *African World*, complained that the title of the book did not accurately reflect its content, that it was too long and in places 'melodramatic and childish', and full of 'unjust and illogical' generalisations. Overall 'Delta' sympathised with Plaatje's case but thought that 'all real sympathisers with Mr Plaatje and his friends' would wish he had presented it 'with more dignity'. 'Delta' was possibly one of John Harris's pseudonyms.[33]

Olive Schreiner, now living in London, had other objections. A friend of Georgiana Solomon, she sympathised with his cause but disapproved, on pacifist grounds, of what she had heard about the book: 'You know, I am a pacifist', she wrote to Georgiana Solomon, 'and from what I hear he advocates the natives coming over here to help kill.' She had evidently not, however (at least when she wrote this), read the book, but was now prompted to do so.[34]

Georgiana Solomon succeeded in eliciting a more substantial response from a man she still considered, their differences in political viewpoint notwithstanding, an old family friend: General Botha, prime minister of South Africa, whose Irish-born wife Annie had co-founded with her the Suid-Afrikaanse Vrouefederasie (South African Women's Federation) a decade earlier. Botha thanked her for the copy of *Native Life in South Africa*, and for 'her kindly opinion of myself', and told her that 'her appeal on behalf of the Natives has made a deep impression on me'. As to the book itself, he acknowledged that 'an opinion held by any man and constitutionally expressed is entitled to respect, however much one personally may differ from it', and that it 'will certainly not in any way adversely influence my Government in its dealing with the Natives of the Union'. Indeed, he went on, 'I welcome any criticism honestly given and the book may be of value in giving publicity to views, possibly held by a section of the Native community, which may perhaps be in conflict with those held by other sections of the Union's inhabitants; and where differences of opinion exist, full and free discussion is most desirable.'

Not surprisingly, however, he disagreed with the substance of the book. 'Mr Plaatje', he said, 'is a special pleader, and, consciously or unconsciously, in his book he has in my opinion been somewhat biased in his strictures on the Government in regard to the Natives' Land Act: he has exaggerated incidents which tell in his favour and suppressed facts that should be within his knowledge which would show the honest attempts made by the Government to avoid the infliction of hardship in carrying out a principle which, you must remember, was sanctioned by the Legislature.' He ended by saying that he believed there was 'a sincere desire to do justice to the Native Races in our intercourse with them', and that eventually relations between black and white would be worked out in an amicable manner – 'although to impatient souls progress towards this ideal may at times be slow and halting'. Mrs Solomon, he clearly felt, fell into just such a category.[35]

Plaatje did not of course accept Botha's arguments, but the generally moderate tone of his comments – one imagines Mrs Solomon showed him the letter – would have confirmed his view that the general's chief failing was his weakness in resisting the more extreme demands of Afrikaner nationalists, to whom he attributed the brutal excesses of the Natives' Land Act. Despite his criticism of Botha in *Native Life*, this was not meant personally, and he had got on well with him during their meetings in the past. They would always converse in Dutch, and at this level of personal contact, talking to politicians in their own language, Plaatje was often able to find some common ground with people who in public were far more hostile. Such an ability to get on with people of all shades of opinion was, indeed, one of his great attributes. It did much to sustain his faith in human nature and a continued hope for a change of heart on the part of South Africa's white rulers.[36]

Louis Botha's response to *Native Life* stands as an epitome of reasonableness and moderation when set against those of the man whom Plaatje by now considered to be 'the South African government's most sturdy defender': John Harris, 'the Organising Secretary of the so-called Aborigines' Protection Society'. Having failed to prevent the publication of *Native Life*, Harris proceeded to do all he could to discredit the book and its author, believing it his duty to give General

Botha 'a helping hand' in carrying out his 'great policy'. He sent out a stream of articles to the daily and periodical press in support of the policies of the South African government, comparing Botha variously to Moses and Abraham Lincoln and denouncing *Native Life* for its 'grotesque misrepresentations' and 'almost deliberate untruths'. In one of these articles, in the influential *Journal of the Royal African Society*, he argued that 'the attitude adopted at the moment by the natives' constituted 'by far the most formidable difficulty in relation to General Botha's native policies', and that such attitudes had 'just received most unfortunate emphasis by the publication of a book which shows that even now there is an intelligent, well-educated native who either cannot, or will not, grasp plain facts'. *Native Life in South Africa*, in Harris's view, was 'not merely full of the most unfortunate inaccuracies, but upon capital issues the distortions and misrepresentations are of such a nature that they can only do serious harm to the cause of the natives'.[37]

Despite his antipathy, Harris was nevertheless obliged to admit that it was not just Plaatje who constituted the problem. 'It cannot be overlooked', he acknowledged, 'that at the present time the natives as a whole are against General Botha's policy.' It was an extraordinary position for the organising secretary of the 'so-called Aborigines' Protection Society' to have arrived at.[38]

Plaatje's differences with John Harris were only intensified by the publication of the Report of the South African Land Commission (the Beaumont Commission) shortly after the first edition of *Native Life* came out. This was the commission which had been set up under the provisions of the Natives' Land Act in order to find further land for the African population. As both Plaatje and other African leaders had predicted, the commission had been unable to find any substantial areas of land for this purpose, and its recommendations were in any case soon rejected by the South African parliament. While Harris preferred to find reason for encouragement in the report, on the grounds that it offered further guarantees on the principle of segregation, Plaatje was fiercely critical, and took its findings as complete vindication of what he had been saying over the last three years and just what he predicted. 'Surely, Miss Werner,' he wrote, 'you never expected that a commission of five interested white men could pass a fair segregation measure between themselves and the blacks.'[39]

A generous donation from Mrs Solomon enabled Plaatje to have his thirty-page analysis of the Beaumont Report bound into the five hundred copies that remained from the initial print run of *Native Life in South Africa*. In it he subjected the report and its recommendations to detailed scrutiny, and left his readers in no doubt as to the depth of the deceit he believed to have been perpetrated: 'I must say', he wrote, 'that until this Report reached me, I never would have believed my white fellow countrymen capable of conceiving the all but diabolical schemes propounded between the covers of Volume I of the Report of the South African Land Commission, 1916, and clothing them in such plausible form as to mislead even sincere and well-informed friends of the Natives.' Fearful of the ultimate consequences for the future of South Africa if such policies were not altered, Plaatje again appealed to British public opinion to 'stay the hand of the South African Government, veto this iniquity and avert the Nemesis that would surely follow its perpetration'.[40]

They were not quite his final words. In the August 1916 issue of *The Crisis*, the monthly journal of the National Association for the Advancement of Colored People, there appeared a poem entitled 'Retribution' by Ida B. Luckie, warning of the inevitable outcome of oppression in the life of a nation. If injustices continued unchecked, she wrote, the result would be 'the blood-red tide of anarchy', to be followed by 'The wreck of Government, of home, and all / The Nation's pride, its splendour and its power'. Plaatje was clearly struck by the power of her words, commenting, as he reproduced two verses of her poem in his new chapter, that her mind 'must have been riveted on South Africa' when she composed them. He could find no better way to conclude his appeal 'for some outside intervention to assist South Africa in recovering her lost senses'.[41]

Harris, by contrast, sought to align his society ever more closely with the policies of the South African government, and a resolution to this effect, welcoming the Report of the Beaumont Commission, was passed in August 1916. It was opposed vociferously by Mrs Solomon and Mrs Unwin, Plaatje's two allies on the committee, but they were in a minority and unable to prevent it being adopted. Harris's reward was an approving letter from Edward Dower, the South African secretary for native affairs. He then stepped up his efforts to blacken Plaatje's reputation, discouraging newspaper and journal editors from giving him a hearing and complaining when they did. 'Months ago some of us were compelled to terminate relationships with him', Harris told Clifford Sharp, the editor of the *New Statesman*, and advised against allowing Plaatje to respond to his own article in the *Statesman*, assuring him of 'how unsafe a guide is this man whose activities are guided almost exclusively by sentiment'. He wrote similarly to Sir Harry Wilson, editor of the journal of the Royal Colonial Institute (and formerly colonial secretary in the Orange River Colony), expressing surprise that he should have carried so favourable a review of *Native Life in South Africa*.[42]

Such actions 'by means of confidential letters from behind closed doors', so Plaatje told Mrs Solomon, were typical of the way Harris operated. But he was not deterred. Denied the opportunity to reply personally to Harris in the columns of the *New Statesman*, he instead briefed John Hodgson, a friend of

Olive Schreiner's, who had read Harris's piece and proposed writing to the *Statesman* to point out its inaccuracies and bias. They had several meetings to discuss the matter in November and early December, Hodgson as a result forming 'a very high opinion of him [Plaatje] as a man, and of his honesty as a writer'. Suitably briefed, Hodgson wrote a long letter which the *Statesman* did eventually publish, criticising Harris's original article and pointing out why, apart from anything else, the comparison between Louis Botha and Abraham Lincoln was so singularly inappropriate.[43]

Harris, for his part, became more agitated by the day about the impact being made by *Native Life in South Africa*. Armed with information from Plaatje, Georgiana Solomon and Jane Cobden Unwin resisted every move he made. Matters came to a head at a conference the society convened in October 1916. Mrs Unwin tried at the last minute to secure an invitation for Plaatje to attend so he could present his case in person, only to be met with a point-blank refusal. Undaunted, the two ladies argued as powerfully and as emotionally as ever against the direction in which the society – *their* society as they saw it – was being taken, and personal relations with the two secretaries reached a new low. During afternoon tea at the conference Mrs Unwin went up to Harris and accused him of pretending to be 'a friend of the natives ... while all the time he was secretly working against them'. In response he demanded an apology and threatened to resign if he did not get it, confident that the society's committee would not countenance such a possibility. One committee member, the journalist and writer Henry Nevinson, thought the very future of the society was at stake, and sought unsuccessfully to broker a compromise. The crisis continued until the two ladies, unrepentant to the last, were finally removed from the society's committee, by a single vote, in April 1917. 'This Land Act is, as it has been all along,' said Mrs Unwin in her final appeal to the committee, 'a tyrannous law: and a Society like ours can only bring misfortune down upon our great cause by supporting in any way so un-British a return to oppression in South Africa.'[44]

With the publication of *Native Life in South Africa* in May 1916 and a revised edition several months later, Plaatje's main objective was achieved. Hopeful of interest and sales in the United States, he had some copies sent to W.E.B. Du Bois in New York for distribution through *The Crisis*, where it appeared in the new books list. He also took pleasure in sending copies to friends and family. Modiri Molema, for example, still studying in Glasgow, had his inscribed 'with the author's compliments and happy memories of the days spent together under the siege of Mafeking', and was inspired to write a book of his own (eventually published as *The Bantu Past and Present*). Mary Werner received a copy too, inscribed 'with the author's best wishes for her health and happiness, and pleasant recollections of Cartwright Gardens and Gower Street'.

Now Plaatje could travel to his meetings with copies of both *Native Life* and *Sechuana Proverbs*, selling as many as he could carry with him. Early in November he was in Stratford-upon-Avon to address a Brotherhood meeting (where he 'scarcely needed introducing to a Stratford audience', it was reported, 'as he was a well known Shakespearean scholar'), then it was to Birmingham under the auspices of the National Temperance Federation, and after that to Eastbourne on the south coast. In between he had an invitation from William Cross to join him in Oxford. 'You will thus see', he told Mrs Unwin, 'that in the Provinces (just like in London) I cannot get out of the University atmosphere, so that if I am not a full-fledged scholar by the time I get back to South Africa, it will not be the fault of the Natives of your beautiful island.'[45]

On his return to London he had a speaking engagement at the Robert Browning Institute in Walworth. He was accompanied to the meeting by Georgiana Solomon and an old friend of hers, Betty Molteno, recently arrived from South Africa. Now in her sixties, and a daughter of Sir John Molteno, first prime minister of the Cape Colony, she was a friend of Olive Schreiner too and an outspoken advocate in a variety of liberal and radical causes. She opposed British policy at the time of the South African War and supported Emily Hobhouse in her campaign on behalf of the Boer victims of the concentration camps. Since then she had taken up both African and Indian causes, particularly Gandhi's work in Natal. Once she was in England Plaatje, at Mrs Solomon's suggestion, hastened to introduce himself, meeting up with her a week before their trip to Walworth. It was the beginning of another long friendship.[46]

Meanwhile, he did all he could to support Georgiana Solomon and Jane Cobden Unwin in their battles with John Harris. One letter he wrote to Mrs Solomon on 8 December 1916 is especially revealing. In it he thanked her for 'writing so promptly of the latest bullyragging to which you seem to have been subjected at the last meeting of Denison House' (the London office of the Anti-Slavery and Aborigines' Protection Society), informing her that the 'disquieting information' it contained 'arrived just in time to upset me when (after a strenuous day) I wanted a peaceful evening for urgent correspondence, before leaving for Birmingham'.

The precise nature of this 'disquieting information' was not specified, but it was connected to Harris's allegation that Plaatje was deliberately working against the interests of his society, and that somebody was putting him up to this.

To which he responded: 'If to work with a University Professor, reducing an African language to phonetics is "to work against your Society" then I will plead guilty. Or if to address meetings in various parts of the country getting converts for the Native Cause, and selling copies of a book on the cause, is to fight your Society, well under those circumstances, I am culpable. But please bear in mind, Dear Mrs Solomon, that I have never hidden these occupations from, and I have uttered nothing at any of the minutes [*sic*] that I would not repeat inside the walls of Denison House.' He added that he was writing to 'the native paper at Johannesburg [*Abantu-Batho*]' to express his regret at the actions of Harris and his society – and doing so 'at my own initiative, using my own stationery and my own typewriter and my own stamps; and if anyone says I was employed by anyone to write it, he is a romancer of the superlative degree'.[47]

Recognition of his efforts came in the form of a farewell reception held at a Fleet Street hotel on 10 January 1917, ahead of his intended departure at the end of the month. Organised by Georgiana Solomon, it brought together many of the friends and sympathisers he had attracted to his cause over the last two and a half years, their presence a tribute to the personal impact he had made. Sir Richard Winfrey, MP, presided over the evening's proceedings, while Mrs Charlotte Despard, a leading figure in the campaign for votes for women and another old friend of Mrs Solomon's, whom Plaatje knew too, made the formal presentation.[48]

In response to the speeches and to the gift of a purse of money, Plaatje thanked all those who had befriended and supported him during his time in England, particularly 'the ladies'. 'There is one English custom that I have no difficulty in understanding and appreciating. That is the habit of a gentleman taking off his hat to a lady. For all that they have done for me both in my own country and in England I do most certainly and with the greatest pleasure take off my hat to the ladies!' Given his debts to them, back home as well as in England, it was an appropriate note on which to take his leave. *Native Life in South Africa* would not have seen the light of day without them.[49]

Just as welcome as the money was the decision of his band of sympathisers to form 'a committee to watch over native interests', 'to keep in touch with native affairs in South Africa', and 'especially to watch the workings of the Land Act'. As Alice Werner explained, the 'Anti-Slavery and Aborigines' Protection Society seem to have their attention occupied in other directions; moreover, they do not take quite the same view as to the gravity of the situation caused by the Land Act'.[50]

The composition of the new committee was a tribute to his work too. As well as Alice Werner, the secretary pro tem, it included Georgiana Solomon and Jane Cobden Unwin, soon to be thrown out of the Anti-Slavery and Aborigines' Protection Society; William Cross; E.F. Fredericks; John Hodgson; Dr G.B. Clark, the former MP, who had a longstanding interest in South African affairs; Dr Charles Garnett, founder of League of Universal Brotherhood, and a particular bête noire of John Harris; Josiah Wedgwood, a radical MP who had once spent two years as a magistrate in the Transvaal after the South African War; and Sir Richard Winfrey, recently appointed parliamentary secretary of agriculture in Lloyd George's government.

John Harris reacted with dismay when he heard about this – as well he might, for the committee posed a significant challenge to his society's position. He could not see, he complained, how Sir Richard Winfrey, 'a responsible Minister of the Crown', could allow himself to be associated with it, or how it was possible for him to 'take such an attitude in view of the obligations he had accepted'. For Plaatje, on the other hand, it was a highly promising legacy, a means of carrying on his work after he was gone. There was talk of starting up a newsletter and forming a deputation to put their case to General Smuts, recently appointed to the Imperial War Cabinet and due in London shortly.[51]

Two weeks later, on the eve of his departure, the Brotherhood Federation presented Plaatje with an illuminated address, a token of its appreciation for all his work in England. He had brought home to them an awareness of the 'grievous wrongs' inflicted upon his people, and they promised that 'at the close of the war we shall do all we can to help you regain that freedom and justice to which as loyal British subjects' they were entitled. The Brotherhood, it reminded him once again, had no colour bar. 'To us all men are brothers, and we hold out to them the right hand of fellowship.' Finally it wished him 'all success in the continuance of your noble work in the service of Christ, the cause of humanity, and on behalf of your people, to whom we send our fraternal greetings'. The address was signed by leading members of the Brotherhood Federation, along with William Cross (on behalf of the Southall Men's Own Brotherhood), William Dixon (Leighton Buzzard Men's Meeting), Henry Castle (Heathfield Brotherhood and Sussex Federation) and Sir Richard Winfrey (president of the New England PSA).[52]

The *Christian Commonwealth*, the leading weekly journal of progressive religious opinion, sang Plaatje's praises too. The first two pages of its issue of 3 January 1917 were devoted to an interview, and it included a fine studio portrait, specially taken by Lizzie Caswall Smith, a fashionable Oxford Street photographer. 'There is something touching in the picture of this gifted and earnest man toiling here in London without any resources save his own earnings and with none too many friends, in the interests of the race to which he belongs.' Here, in the case he had laid before them, were 'all the elements of a profoundly moving national tragedy', and 'even our preoccupation with the colossal crisis through which Europe is passing cannot altogether destroy the significance of Mr Plaatje's presence in this country'.[53]

This was all too much for the journal *South Africa*, critical of Plaatje and his colleagues from the moment the Congress delegation arrived in London in 1914. 'The less competent to discuss the native question', it announced, 'are curiously to be found in the ranks of educated natives, especially when they come to England and get their black heads swollen by negrophile adulation.' It was a reminder of the kind of racist sentiment he could expect back home, a world away from the warmth and Christian fellowship he so often encountered during his time in England.[54]

Plaatje sailed from Plymouth on 27 January 1917. During his time in England he had overcome adversity, poverty, bouts of ill health, official discouragement, lack of support from the SANNC, and the outright opposition of John Harris and his society. His great achievement was to have completed and published *Native Life in South Africa*, a pioneering statement of African claims. Nothing like it had been written before and it largely achieved the publicity he sought for it. Along with this he had addressed a total of 305 meetings, an average of nearly one every three days. Single-handed, he had done more than anybody before to convey to the British public a knowledge of the situation of his people and the injustices perpetrated against them, and he was convinced that he had strengthened support for his cause.

As if this were not achievement enough, he had made a vital contribution to the development of the Tswana language and its meagre written literature. Far fewer people were in any sort of position to appreciate this, but the opportunity to engage with the intricacies of Setswana had been highly significant too: not just because his collaboration with Daniel Jones provided the income which made *Native Life in South Africa* possible, but because of the academic and literary world it opened up for him, enabling him to consider himself, so he said, 'a full-fledged scholar'. This experience would pay dividends in years to come, and he would remain a disciple of Jones's approach to pronunciation, convinced of its value in preserving the true sounds of his native tongue.

For now, however, there were other priorities: a family to return to and to somehow provide for, debts to repay, and a political situation in South Africa which looked like going from bad to worse. And meanwhile, given the threat of German submarines, a potentially hazardous voyage back home.

ELEVEN

Back home

South Africa, 1917–1919

Wartime conditions ensured that the voyage home to South Africa, aboard the SS *Galway Castle*, took much longer than expected: twenty-nine days instead of the usual seventeen, the result of a lengthy detour that took the vessel almost across to South America. At least it arrived safely. The following year the *Galway Castle* was sunk in the Bay of Biscay by a German submarine with the loss of 143 lives (Henry Burton, returning to South Africa after attending a wartime imperial conference, was among the survivors).

Not that there was much likelihood of Plaatje wasting his time on this extended journey. Whereas in 1914 he had busied himself with writing the first drafts of *Native Life in South Africa* (which, he noted, received a 'cordial reception' among his fellow passengers), now he occupied himself in translating Shakespeare's *Julius Caesar* into Setswana, mindful of the challenge he had set himself. It was by no means a total preoccupation. Also aboard the *Galway Castle* was a group of twenty-three members of the South African Native Labour Contingent, who were being invalided back home to South Africa after service in France. Plaatje was naturally interested to find these men aboard the same ship, and keen to hear about their experiences, particularly as a number of his own friends and relatives in South Africa had joined the contingent. He found, however, that the attitude of the white (South African) non-commissioned officers towards him was far from friendly, and within a week he was served with notice not to visit the men. Their opposition was only overcome after an appeal to the ship's captain, and the support and assistance of two white missionaries who were also on the ship. Together, they succeeded in attending to the needs of the men, and were eventually able to hold religious services for them.[1]

Another of the passengers aboard the *Galway Castle* was a black American missionary, Herbert A. Payne, accompanied by his wife Bessie, travelling to South Africa to join an American Baptist mission in the eastern Cape. Both had enjoyed Plaatje's company during the voyage, but the Paynes expressed to him their fears that they would be prevented, on racial grounds, from disembarking when they arrived in Cape Town. These proved to be justified. Because of the secrecy surrounding the movements of all wartime shipping, there was nobody there to meet them, and it was left to Plaatje to take up their case when the Immigration Department informed them that they could not disembark. Within a couple of days of arriving in Cape Town he succeeded in getting the decision reversed, appealing personally to the minister concerned, Sir Thomas Watt, as well as J.X. Merriman, Advocate William Stuart and then General Botha himself, whom he managed to buttonhole during a break for tea during one of the parliamentary sessions. His success was a tribute to his ability to negotiate his way through to the highest levels of government, and an encouraging sign of his continued influence as a spokesman for his people, his reputation considerably enhanced by the publication of *Native Life in South Africa*. Botha was, besides, keen to enlist Plaatje's support in recruiting more Africans to join the Native Labour Contingent, to fulfil his commitment to the imperial war effort. To reverse the decision of the head of the Immigration Department was a small price to pay for Plaatje's active support in the recruiting campaign. It was an achievement Plaatje would remember.[2]

If his successful intervention in the Payne incident seemed to show that the government might prove more open to rational argument, the new legislation he found before the House of Assembly served only to confirm his worst fears concerning the direction of wider questions of policy. 'On landing at Cape Town', he wrote to Mrs Unwin, 'I found, besides other difficulties, that a horrible bill was before Parliament to confirm all the horrors of the Land Act. This meant hard work just from the moment of landing.'

The Native Administration Bill, to which he referred, represented the government's response to the Beaumont Commission's report. Accepting the report's recommendations about the division of land into areas of African and European occupation, it proposed to take the principle of segregation a stage further by separating the administration of the one from the other. In the 'Native areas' there was to be a uniform system of administration, and it was proposed that the governor general would legislate by proclamation, advised by a permanent commission headed by the minister of native affairs. Provision was also made for the establishment of councils to encourage African involvement in strictly local affairs, and several proposals were put forward to separate the administration of justice in 'European' and 'African' areas. Taken together, the provisions of the bill amounted to yet another nail in the coffin of the old Cape ideal, for so Plaatje saw it, of a society in which all citizens, black or white, were equal before the law. He was particularly concerned at the threat to prohibit access for Africans to the Supreme Court, a crucial bulwark, along with the Cape franchise, in the defence of African rights. Both were once again under threat.[3]

When he arrived in Cape Town, the bill was being given its first reading, but it soon ran into opposition in the House. J.X. Merriman, Sir Thomas Smartt and several others spoke out against the bill from the premises of the old liberalism of the Cape, and they were joined by members from Natal who believed that too much land from their province was being set aside for African occupation. It was a curious alliance and, as ever, the professions of concern for African interests masked a variety of interests and viewpoints. But one thing was clear: the bill was going to have a stormy passage in the various stages it needed to go through before it became the law of the land. One other development had an important bearing on the debate in parliament, the recent decision of the Supreme Court in the case of *Thompson and Stilwell* v. *Chief Kama*. This had the effect of rendering inapplicable in the Cape Province certain provisions of both the Natives' Land Act and the Native Administration Bill, on the grounds that these interfered with the qualifications required for the Cape franchise, entrenched constitutionally in the Act of Union.[4]

Encouraged by this, Plaatje remained in Cape Town for two weeks to try to rally support against the bill, both inside and outside parliament, staying with his old friend Dr Abdullah Abdurahman at his house in Loop Street, just a few minutes' walk from the House of Assembly. Even before he was reunited with his wife and family he had launched himself straight into the political affairs of his people.

When he did eventually complete the final leg of his journey home, by train to Kimberley, it was to a warm welcome from both friends and family. Elizabeth, Sainty, Halley, Olive and Violet were all there and, so Plaatje informed Mrs Unwin, in good health. But the 'financial tangle' he had anticipated a year earlier was every bit as serious as he had imagined. Both Isaiah Bud-M'belle and Simon Plaatje, the latter still living at the old Pniel mission, had helped support Elizabeth financially during his absence, but the South African Native National Congress (SANNC) had not made any contribution, and he had accumulated a personal debt of nearly £500 to finance his campaign in England. *Tsala ea Batho* had not appeared since the middle of 1915, but at least the printing machinery, he was relieved to find, had escaped the claims of his creditors. 'Mrs Plaatje', so he told Mrs Unwin, 'turned her house into a workshop, it has no appearance of a home. In fact, she shoved the machinery on one side and is doing ironing on my counter in the office also, until I can make a start with the paper.' Even Sainty had tried to do his bit for the family finances and the Allied cause by enlisting with the Native Labour Contingent, only to be rejected by the military doctors.[5]

Plaatje was not alone in recognising Elizabeth's vital contribution to the success of his campaign in England. Isaiah Bud-M'belle, living close by in Kimberley, wrote later of her 'loyal co-operation, assistance and encouragement', her willingness to cope with everything thrown at her. For Richard Selope Thema, too, she was an example for other African women to emulate, 'proof of the part which our young women are already playing in our national affairs'. While her husband, 'one of the greatest sons of our race, was in Great Britain fighting for our liberty and freedom', she proved herself 'an untiring supporter ... and in this way contributed largely to the success of Mr. Plaatje's book *Native Life in South Africa*'. Despite the 'difficulties and troubles which she encountered', she had managed to 'keep the home fires burning'. 'We need many more women of Mrs Plaatje's courage, faith and perseverance', he concluded.[6]

Despite his efforts over the ensuing months Plaatje was never able to raise the capital to resurrect his newspaper, though for well over a year he continued to call himself 'Editor, *Tsala ea Batho*'. This did not deter him from resuming an energetic role in political affairs, as the two weeks he spent in Cape Town before going home would suggest. Indeed, during the few months after his return to South Africa, his reputation and influence as a national political figure reached new heights, and he returned to something of a hero's welcome. 'Now let it be known', announced *Ilanga lase Natal*, 'that Mr Plaatje has performed the part of an intelligent and energetic champion for the cause of our peoples ... Let us show that we are not so dull as not to recognize his value as one of our leading men who can be trusted with the burden of a poor and suffering nation; he is one of whom Britishers of all kind are proud.' Abraham Twala, writing to the same newspaper, thought every teacher should pay Plaatje a 'hero's bonus' of five shillings in recognition of his efforts. Plaatje had 'risked himself' by producing *Native Life in South Africa*, and had succeeded in exposing injustice. The facts he had set out, he predicted, 'will make a New South Africa by and by!'[7]

Other laudatory letters appeared in the African press elsewhere, and praise was heaped upon him at the many meetings he addressed to tell people about his experiences in England, and to urge them to continue the fight against the Native Administration Bill. 'Mr Sol T. Plaatje, as a fearless defender and leader of his people,' so a leaflet advertising one of these meetings in Johannesburg said, 'has a wonderful and thrilling message, almost romantic, for the people of this country. The very interesting career of his 2½ years of campaign at an absolute sacrifice is worth the gratitude of his people.'[8]

His reputation was enhanced further by the publicity given to *Native Life in South Africa* in the press, especially after the book and several of his speeches were mentioned in the House of Assembly during the debates on the Native

Administration Bill. 'Last month', Plaatje informed Mrs Unwin on 18 May, 'a Boer member – Colonel Mentz, Minister of Lands – referred to it [*Native Life in South Africa*] as a "scurrilous attack on the Boers". A chorus of English members promptly defended it so vehemently that even in the subsequent days when the book was quoted by English members during the debates not one had the nerve to attack it again. I will not be surprised if the redoubtable Mr H[arris] makes capital out of the fact that a Boer member – a cabinet minister – attacked my book, and will say nothing about the unanimous defence of the phalanx of English members, including Mr James Henderson of Durban (who called it "a triumph for native education"), and Mr Van Riet, K.C., of Grahamstown, the only Dutch member who is a Unionist.' Another MP, Dewdney Drew, formerly editor of the Bloemfontein *Friend*, referred to 'the book written by Plaatjes [*sic*]' and his eyewitness reports of evictions in the Orange Free State in 1913, and 'urged that the natives be dealt with justly, so that they should be made to feel that it would not be necessary to look overseas for justice'.[9]

All this was very good for sales. The debates in parliament, Plaatje noted with satisfaction, 'brought forth orders from all over South Africa', and it was difficult to keep up with demand. With the help of William Cross, a third printing of *Native Life* was arranged in London, but copies didn't arrive in South Africa until late June. When a consignment of a hundred copies did eventually reach the Central News Agency in Johannesburg, they were all sold in two days, leaving Plaatje unable to obtain any copies for himself. Frustrating as this was, *Native Life in South Africa* had clearly struck a chord.[10]

Plaatje's activities particularly disappointed those who wanted to see agreement between Boer and Briton over a uniform 'native policy'. 'Sol Plaatje, and other natives', so one English-speaking supporter of the Native Administration Bill claimed, 'were already endeavouring to spread the belief that the Boer was the oppressor of the natives'; in his view, this was 'wholly unfounded in fact'. The inspector and protector of natives in Kimberley likewise thought him an unfortunate influence. *Native Life in South Africa*, he wrote, was 'in a sense an able exposition of the case against the proposals originally laid before Parliament'. While 'the language of the book is often exaggerated, and there are unsuitable innuendoes concerning Lord Gladstone, General Botha, and the Secretary of Native Affairs', he acknowledged that 'the undercurrent of the book is an endeavour which appears to have had a considerable measure of success, to create dissension between English and Dutch, rising from differences of tradition between the races with regard to the treatment of Native matters'.[11]

Other white commentators in South Africa appreciated the wider significance of *Native Life* and the impact it was making. One anonymous review which appeared in the Johannesburg *Star* early in June 1917, for example, thought the book was 'of unusual importance' and 'well worth reading' because it 'called attention to the scandalous way in which natives were treated under the Land Act'. 'Recently', it went on, 'several references have been made to the work in the Legislative Assembly, by speakers criticizing a proposed new Land Act. In reply General Botha and his supporters said that the book was "scurrilous", "miserable", etc., but it was noticeable that none of them ever denied the accuracy of its statements or questioned the authenticity of the details. The author has done his best to call attention to a great and crying scandal, and it is unfortunate that space is insufficient for us to recapitulate some of the happenings mentioned by him.'[12]

The Star's correspondent was also alive to the longer-term implications of the case Plaatje set out. 'It only needs this sort of thing to be persevered with', he continued, 'for the natives to become generally disaffected, and eventually to combine against us. Up to the present this has been prevented by tribal jealousy, but "adversity makes strange bedfellows" and this may soon be altered.' As if to underline the point, the government considered prohibiting Plaatje from addressing a series of meetings on the Rand in June. After the prime minister himself was consulted, however, it was agreed not to do so on the grounds that this would only increase the sense of grievance among the African population and provide Plaatje himself with further ammunition with which to criticise the government. He was thus able to address the meetings he had planned.[13]

✛✛

Plaatje's protests against the Native Administration Bill in the weeks after his return to South Africa complemented the efforts of the other leaders of the SANNC, John Dube and Richard Selope Thema in particular. During his absence overseas the organisation had, for the first two years after the outbreak of war, largely refrained from any criticism of the South African government as a demonstration of their loyalty to King and empire in their hour of need. It was in this spirit that the Rev. Walter Rubusana had offered, after his return from England in 1914, to raise five thousand black troops and accompany them to German South West Africa, which the Union had undertaken to invade. The offer was refused by General Smuts on the grounds that the war was one between white men only. Despite this rebuff, the Congress leaders were nevertheless prepared to assist the Native Affairs Department in recruiting twenty-four thousand Africans as non-combatant labourers for the campaign. When General Botha agreed to provide the imperial government with a Native Labour Contingent for the war in Europe, they supported that too, again in the hope that such a demonstration of loyalty would be rewarded. Although recruiting for the Native Labour Contingent had not so far been as successful as the government had hoped, it would have been very much worse had not the Congress leaders offered to co-operate.[14]

At the end of 1916, however, Congress had ended its period of restraint in attacking government policy by passing strong resolutions, in terms similar to those used by Plaatje in *Native Life in South Africa*, in denouncing the Report of the Beaumont Commission; and in February 1917, while he was en route back home, an extraordinary meeting was called in Pretoria to discuss the Native Administration Bill. In a crowded and very hot corrugated-iron hall the bill was discussed clause by clause, and the delegates heard the local native commissioner's exposition of its provisions and objectives. 'The opposition to the land provisions of the Bill', so Mr Barrett reported back to the secretary for native affairs, 'was very marked, and while sentiments of loyalty were freely expressed, words were not minced in denouncing the Government's proposals.' Even he professed sympathy for Congress's opposition to some parts of the bill, duly conveyed in the form of a resolution, proposed by John Dube, urging the South African government to repeal the Natives' Land Act of 1913. It failed to deter the government from launching the new bill on its passage through the House of Assembly.[15]

An unsympathetic government was not the only difficulty. While Congress did its best to maintain a show of unity, in reality it was racked by internal dissension. The financial irregularities surrounding the funds raised to pay for the deputation to England were a running sore, the delegates had failed to resolve their personal differences, and the broader issue of the relationship (and financial obligations) of the different branches of the Congress to its central body was likewise unresolved. Pixley Seme had sought to impose his own constitution in 1915 without proper discussion with the other members of the executive, and with the aim, as many saw it, of strengthening his hand against the president, John Dube, to whom he was bitterly opposed. Putting forward Plaatje's name in 1915 for the presidency of Congress had been part of his scheme to oust Dube. For an organisation whose professed aim was to unite the African peoples of southern Africa, it was not an edifying spectacle. That feeling of unity achieved at the time of the campaign against the Natives' Land Act was beginning to look a rather distant memory.[16]

Behind these unseemly personal differences lay several wider truths. The first was that the Congress leaders, having apparently exhausted the constitutional options open to them, were simply unsure of which way to turn, unable to conceive of any convincing alternative to the tried methods of appeal and rational argument, which had clearly failed to deflect the government from its course. At the same time there were signs that the Congress leadership was losing touch with the new, urban African population, concentrated heavily in the Transvaal, which had grown rapidly with the development of new industries during the war. To this emerging African working class, the immediate realities of wages and urban living conditions were a much higher priority than the Native Administration Bill and its various legal and constitutional ramifications. But with these material conditions the Congress leadership, drawn for the most part from an older generation rooted in rural, chiefly societies, had not seriously concerned itself. The scene was set for dramatic developments in African political life.

It was against this background that Plaatje, along with the other Congress leaders and delegates, made their way to Bloemfontein in May 1917 in order to attend Congress's fifth annual meeting. The Native Administration Bill dominated their agenda. Once again it was roundly condemned. Plaatje, his reputation largely untarnished by the public bickerings that had been taking place, made the opening speech, reiterating his opposition to the bill, and criticising the remarks that General Smuts had made in his much publicised 'Savoy Hotel' speech in London ten days earlier. The general had asserted that South Africa should be considered 'a white man's country', and that 'political ideas, which apply to our white civilization largely, do not apply to the administration of native affairs'. What he said was no different in its essentials, as Plaatje would have recalled, from the speech he made in Kimberley in 1895.[17]

A second speech Plaatje made at an evening reception aroused huge controversy. The *Rand Daily Mail*, not known for its sympathetic attitude towards African aspirations, was incensed: 'Sol Plaatje, the well known native orator, politician and journalist, made a vicious attack on the Government, and practically sounded the tocsin of a black v white propaganda.' 'He alleged', it went on, 'that the whole object of the bill was to erect huge reservoirs of servile labour for the Boers. The natives would have to come out of their little segregation plots or starve there. Economic conditions would force them to come out, and their labour would be sold at a cheap rate. They would be semi-slaves. The speaker said that his father and grandfather had helped to tame the Free State. "I am of this province", he continued, "and are we going to allow a Dutchman from Worcester to dictate to us where we shall live and how we shall exist?" Just at the moment when the Empire wanted the absolute, united support of all its peoples the Government of the Union had introduced the most contentious measure ever placed before a South African Parliament.'

All this was compounded, Plaatje said, by General Smuts's Savoy Hotel speech. 'Was this the way', he asked, 'to talk of a loyal section of the people who were giving their all in the war – making the supreme sacrifice in this struggle?' The general, he concluded, 'had done more harm to recruiting for the native labour battalion by that speech than it was possible to realize'.[18]

Plaatje's speech was cheered by the delegates in Bloemfontein and widely reported in the press. It also attracted the attention of the South African House of Assembly. It led to a 'savage attack' on General Botha, Plaatje recalled, by C.G. Fichardt, member of parliament for Ladybrand in the Orange Free State, 'who said that General Botha's policy was an insult to the whites since it permits a Kafir to criticize their policy'. Fichardt took Plaatje's comments as vindication of his opposition to the Native Labour Contingent, shared by all the other Nationalist MPs, and as evidence of 'the spirit created by the new policy'. Botha, in response, deprecated the fact that 'Sol Plaatje had said this or that', and looked distinctly uncomfortable in countering the arguments of one of his most persistent Nationalist opponents. In African eyes it all served to enhance Plaatje's stature as a leader and spokesman for their cause. Even the socialist *International* newspaper thought it 'gratifying to see a native leader standing up fearlessly without mincing words', although, it added, 'to us the hitting was a bit wild'. Plaatje needed to understand that 'the natives are exploited and oppressed not really as a race, but especially as workers'. Blame the capitalists, it advised, not the Boers.[19]

Congress duly passed formal resolutions condemning both the Native Administration Bill and Smuts's Savoy Hotel speech, which it called 'an insult to the natives'. The Native Administration Bill was still before a Select Committee (due to present its report in June), but the meeting discussed ways of raising funds to continue the campaign against it. Plaatje found himself on a committee charged with raising money for a special fund with which to launch a new campaign of agitation.[20]

The real drama at the Congress took place on the final day, sparked off by discussions about correspondence between the executive and the Anti-Slavery and Aborigines' Protection Society in England. This went back to the previous year when John Harris had written to Richard Selope Thema to thank him for sending a copy of the resolutions of the SANNC's Pietermaritzburg conference, praising the organisation for its adherence to the principle of segregation. The resolutions did no such thing, but this had not prevented Harris from misrepresenting them so as to better match his society's policy. When the letter was read out, so Plaatje told Mrs Unwin afterwards, there was 'an outburst of indignation' and 'delegates wanted to know when, where, and under what circumstances Congress "adhered" to the policy of separation'. 'I tried to point out that the whole thing could be rectified by writing a letter to the Society. I pointed out further that the Secretary of the Congress made the same mistake as I did, that is, mistaking Harris for a friend and thus became less guarded in his expressions he relied on the sympathy of a real sympathiser with the Boer policy – but Congress would not be appeased. They denounced Mr Dube for laxity in his management, which made possible the sending out of clumsy correspondence calculated to compromise the cause.'

It was the end of Dube's presidency. 'The result', Plaatje said, 'was that both Mr Dube and Secretary resigned on June 3rd and until June 23rd Congress had neither Head nor Scribe. They asked me to assume its leadership but I pointed out that the deterioration of my business during my enforced absence in England made the idea utterly impossible.'[21]

In fact there was rather more to this affair than Plaatje indicated. There had certainly been some confusion within the Congress in attempting to differentiate between the theory and practice of segregation, and John Harris had clearly exacerbated these difficulties in trying to get Dube and Selope Thema, the secretary, to commit themselves to the principle of segregation. It was equally apparent, though, that this correspondence was being used as a pretext to get rid of John Dube, the increasingly unpopular president, and that the moving spirits behind this were Pixley Seme, Saul Msane and Alfred Mangena. Richard Selope Thema, the secretary, who had written the supposedly compromising letter, was informed quietly that it was Dube's resignation that was required, not his, and that he could remain on as secretary if he wished. However, Selope Thema decided to step down too, thereby precipitating the break-up of the executive, and Dube, aware that a majority of Congress delegates were against him, followed suit. It seems unlikely that Plaatje was party to any of this (although he would have been well aware of the divisions within the Congress leadership), since Msane and Seme would surely have taken the trouble to approach him beforehand to make sure he was willing to assume the presidency. The meeting duly passed a resolution 'strongly and emphatically' denying that Congress 'at any time ever approved of the Natives' Land Act, its policy or principles, expressed or implied', and added: 'This Congress, having already recorded its thanks to Mr Plaatje and appreciation of his services since the commencement of the struggle, accepts the reference to him, contained in the Society's letter of March 29th, as a further tribute to his work.'[22]

After the mismanagement of the funds collected for the deputation to England, Plaatje remained one of the few individual figures within the Congress leadership who still commanded widespread popularity and respect, and many must have regretted that he was not willing to accept the offer of the presidency. S.M. Makgatho, president of the Transvaal branch of Congress, was the compromise candidate who became president three weeks later (his position confirmed at elections at the end of the year), but he had the confidence of neither the Dube nor Msane factions. Congress thus remained seriously weakened by its internal divisions at a time when it needed, more than ever, a strong and united leadership. Plaatje did agree to become senior vice president, but this was as much as he was prepared to take on.

At the heart of his decision to decline the presidency was the reason he gave Mrs Unwin: that 'the deterioration of my business during my enforced absence made the idea utterly impossible'. Anxious both to get his own financial affairs into some sort of order and to restart his newspaper, he simply did not believe he could take on such a demanding role without jeopardising these two aims. But his ambitions, it is clear, did not lie in political leadership for its own sake. In February 1914, it will be recalled, he had offered his resignation as secretary of Congress, citing similar reasons. He believed, rather, that he could render his greatest service as an individual spokesman, free from the burden, and frustrations, of leading a fractured and divided organisation.

Probably the sense of bitterness he felt at the failure of Congress to support either his family or himself during his absence in England was a factor too. Without a viable newspaper business or any other regular source of income, there were simply other priorities to attend to. It was an enormous honour to have been offered the presidency of Congress, but he was in no doubt he had to turn it down: 'there are only sixteen working hours in a day', he wrote later, 'and I could not possibly find the time to earn my living while trying to lead the unwieldy masses'.[23]

Shortly after Congress's annual meeting, during a trip to Johannesburg, he was arrested at the city's main railway station. He had boarded a train after twice being refused a ticket, and was detained after the railway authorities called the police. He was then charged, so he wrote to Mrs Unwin, 'with infringing half-a-dozen of the multifarious regulations by which natives are surrounded in this country, which constitute Mr Harris's "growing spirit of justice"'. He secured his release by payment of £5 bail and then 'prepared an elaborate defence that was likely to bring before the Courts these official outrages upon Natives'. At which point, he said, 'the authorities presumably discovered the publicity in store for their numerous pinpricky rules and regulations for when I appeared on July 5th to answer their peccadilloes, they failed to put in an appearance and the case was dismissed. I am now proceeding against them for wrongful arrest.' As ever, Plaatje saw salvation in the law courts, though quite what the outcome was in the case he brought against the railway authorities is not clear.[24]

+∾+

With no end to the war in sight, Plaatje travelled extensively in the countryside of the northern Cape, Orange Free State and the Transvaal during the following months. 'I have taken upon myself', he wrote in September 1917, 'as far as is humanly possible in this wide country, to enlighten the natives, who know absolutely nothing about the prohibitions and restrictions embodied in the new bill. They need no information on the Natives' Land Act which has, since 1913, made its provisions felt in an unmistakeable manner.' Nevertheless, he continued to collect evidence of its effects, having in mind to write 'a companion volume', as he described it, to follow on from *Native Life in South Africa*. In the Transvaal, he reported, '37 families in the Pretoria district will be evicted this month, 21 families in Potchefstroom district, and more round Heidelberg. I am only referring to those I have met. Of course some of them will become servants, others will give up country life and flock to the cities where this law [the Natives' Land Act] is not in force, while others will leave the Union altogether; but nobody cares for them.'[25]

In the Free State the Land Act continued to have even more drastic consequences. Here he found 'men who prior to 1913 rented land or ploughed on shares and gained from 500 to 1,600 bags of grain each year'. Now they had been 'reduced to servants and limited to the production of only a dozen (sometimes less) bags for themselves and the remainder for the landowner and, in addition, they have to render unpaid labour to the landowner for the right to stay on part of the land they formerly occupied by ploughing on shares'.[26]

Elsewhere, he told of the deserted churches and farms he encountered on his travels, of the reduction of once prosperous African farmers to little more than impoverished labourers. On one occasion, on his forty-first birthday, 9 October 1917, he returned, for the first time since he was a small child, to his place of birth, Doornfontein, in the north-eastern part of the Orange Free State. He discovered that the land was now owned by a man called Karl Woolf, a German subject whose movements had been restricted in accordance with wartime regulations. In the circumstances it struck him as grimly ironic that he, a loyal citizen of the British empire, should now be legally prohibited (under the terms of the Natives' Land Act) from purchasing the land upon which he was born, while its present owner and occupant was the subject of a nation with whom South Africa was at war.[27]

Until the end of 1917 Plaatje combined his self-imposed task of investigation and 'enlightening' with assisting in recruitment for the South African Native Labour Contingent. Like the other Congress leaders who had agreed to back the scheme, Plaatje hoped such a display of loyalty would bolster their demands for political and social rights. General Botha, it will be remembered, had done his best to persuade Plaatje to lend his support to recruiting for the contingent, having told him that 'this would help the native people better than any propaganda work in which he should engage'. Plaatje also perceived in the issue a means of keeping alive the differences between Boer and Briton (the very existence of the Native Labour Contingent being strongly opposed by the Afrikaner nationalists), and thus to help prevent agreement over a common 'native policy'. Such a strategy was implicit in both *Native Life in South Africa* and his campaign against the Native Administration Bill. 'The people who did not wish them to respond to the call', he said at one recruiting meeting, 'were the same people who were responsible for their grievances. By neglecting to answer the call they were therefore siding with their oppressors.'[28]

Unsurprisingly, such arguments did not always persuade potential recruits, who failed to come forward in anything like the numbers the South African government had hoped. Few Africans were prepared to draw such fine distinctions between English and Afrikaners, and many were instinctively suspicious of any scheme that had the backing of the South African government. News of the sinking of the troopship *Mendi* in February 1917 with the loss of over six hundred members of the Native Labour Contingent was a further disincentive – particularly, as Plaatje pointed out, when the government failed to communicate promptly with the relatives of those who had died or to compensate them adequately for their loss.[29]

Early in 1918 the South African government in any case suspended recruitment to the Labour Contingent. It was becoming increasingly difficult to attract further recruits without resorting to direct compulsion, and, as Nationalist opposition to Botha grew, the whole scheme was becoming more and more of a political liability. To this extent Plaatje's view that the Native Labour Contingent was an issue capable of being exploited in the interests of keeping alive differences between English and Afrikaner was wholly vindicated.

By this time, however, Plaatje had other preoccupations. As well as documenting the continued effects of the Land Act, he now investigated something even more sinister: a spate of shootings of blacks by whites in various parts of the Orange Free State in late 1917 and the early months of 1918. These arose out of growing tensions in the countryside and the violent, often fatal activities of white vigilante groups. When cases were brought to court, all-white juries ensured that perpetrators generally got off scot-free. Early in 1918 Plaatje visited the scenes of some of these murders, experiencing, so he recalled, 'some nasty encounters with discharged Boer murderers'. Nevertheless, he managed to persuade Johannes Brand Wessels, the member of parliament for Bethlehem, formerly a general during the South African War (and recently detained and tried for his opposition to the invasion of German South West Africa), to intervene on behalf of the widow of one of the Africans who had been shot; as a result of this, he said, 'the acquitted Boer was made to amply compensate the widow of the unfortunate native he shot'. Plaatje seems to have had a way with old Boer generals.[30]

Private lobbying went hand in hand with public campaigning. A special meeting of protest was held in Bloemfontein in April 1918, preceded 'by a solemn service in memory of John Kambule, Charli Mbelle, Tladi and other Natives, victims of recent shooting tragedies'. When Plaatje rose to address the meeting (in Dutch), 'as loudly cheered as usual', he spoke, outraged, of 'the suspicious frequency with which natives, armed with nothing but their ten fingers, are alleged to have attacked Europeans, holding loaded rifles and compelled them in self-defence to shoot and kill the unarmed black assailants', and he reminded his audience of the wholly different manner in which justice had been meted out to a white vigilante gang during the Mafeking treason trials in 1901. He called for the abolition of the jury system in cases of this kind and for civil proceedings to be instituted against the perpetrators. Resolutions of protest were sent to the prime minister, the minister of justice and the minister of native affairs. General Botha, when he read the report of the meeting, wanted it suppressed, but by then it was too late. It was already in the hands of the English-language press and Plaatje was soon addressing other audiences on the same subject.[31]

Plaatje's other main concern at this time was to establish the Brotherhood movement in his home town of Kimberley. He had returned home to South Africa in 1917 in a mood of keen appreciation for the support the Brotherhoods had extended to him during his stay in England, and he intended, as soon as the opportunity arose, to start up a branch in Kimberley. The idea attracted him for a number of reasons. As part of an international movement, he hoped that interest, and above all funds, could be generated overseas (especially in England), and channelled into schemes to foster the progress of Africans living in Kimberley and then in other parts of South Africa. He saw this as a form of missionary work, but carried out not on behalf of one or other of the missionary societies or churches but by a Christian organisation whose *raison d'être* was to challenge denominational divisions. This was one of the things that attracted him to the Brotherhood movement in the first place. Religious divisions among his people, he thought, were quite as serious as the ethnic divisions that often threatened unity too.

In a way Plaatje saw the Brotherhood movement as a counterpart to the SANNC. While the Congress existed to represent the political interests of the African people and to enable them to speak with one voice, the Brotherhood movement, in Plaatje's mind, had the potential to overcome religious divisions and to foster progress in religious, social and educational life. All were essential to the well-being of his people. Undoubtedly, too, he saw in the possibility of establishing the Brotherhood movement in South Africa an organisational basis for his own activities and campaigns, sorely needed given the dire personal and financial situation to which he had returned in 1917.

At first, preoccupied with other things, he made little progress with his Brotherhood plans. In January 1918, however, returning to Kimberley after a trip across the Transvaal and Orange Free State (there had been a meeting of the executive committee of the SANNC to attend in Bloemfontein just before Christmas), he noticed that demolition work had begun on an old tram shed, owned by De Beers and situated on the edge of the Malay Camp. If it could be saved from demolition and suitably modified, it could provide an ideal meeting hall for Africans in Kimberley, and the material foundation, as it were, for launching his Brotherhood. So he approached De Beers, first contacting E.C. Grimmer, the general manager, with whom he was on friendly terms. On his advice he then wrote a formal letter of application. 'At present', he said, 'the Natives have NO place of meeting. All the Native public meetings in Kimberley are churches of particular denominations who cannot be very well blamed for refusing to let them for secular purposes. If this prayer be successful, the Hall will be the property of all Natives, of any Church or no Church – and only the drunken and the rowdy will be barred.' Should he, Mr Grimmer, be pleased to support his application, 'it will only be typical of your numerous acts of generosity to the inhabitants of the Diamond Fields, irrespective of race or colour or creed'.[32]

It was the kind of letter Plaatje was well used to writing, appropriate in tone and style, and over the next few weeks he wrote more in similar vein. This time, unlike his request for a meeting hall in 1895, De Beers acceded to his request. On 9 May he heard that the directors of De Beers 'have now agreed to let you have the use of the building for the purpose mentioned, at an annual rental of 1/-, during the Company's pleasure and on the understanding that you will pay all rates and taxes of whatever description that may be levied on the said building and ground during your tenancy, which this year amount to £29 3s 4d, and that you keep the building in a good state of repair'. In addition, De Beers promised to replace the windows that had already been removed from the building, and later provided a cheque for £100 as a contribution towards the costs of improvements.[33]

Plaatje was understandably delighted, reward as it was for his skilful and persistent lobbying. But De Beers' generosity over the issue was not simply the result of his persuasive powers, considerable as these were, nor a wholly altruistic desire to meet the wishes of the local African population. As Sir David Harris, another of the directors whom Plaatje approached, said to the De Beers secretary: 'If possible I think it good policy to help the natives in the direction suggested by Plaatje'. It was 'good policy' because it provided De Beers with a convenient and relatively inexpensive means (the shed was valued at £573 6s), as Plaatje did not hesitate to point out, of 'enhancing their (the natives') loyalty to De Beers as a generous employer of labour'. Underlying the decision was a concern in the boardrooms of De Beers and other mining houses on the Rand about mounting industrial unrest in the early months of 1918. Although this was so far confined to the Rand, the spectre of a radicalised black working class, ready to resort to strike action, was very real. The gift of the old tram shed to Plaatje, acting on behalf of Kimberley's African population, was a product of their concern to discourage the spread of industrial unrest to Kimberley.[34]

Plaatje was well aware of what impelled companies like De Beers to acts of generosity of this kind. He was aware too that his success in persuading De Beers to donate a hall to the African population could be used to his considerable advantage locally to reaffirm a position of leadership and influence which was no longer unchallenged.

In part this had come about because he had spent so much time away from Kimberley, allowing other voices to be heard. There were signs of a growing dissatisfaction with the methods he advocated, with a style of leadership that some thought no longer appropriate to the needs of the majority of the people. In Kimberley, as in other urban centres, it was becoming clear that the interests of the unskilled and semi-skilled black workers were not necessarily those of the ministers, teachers, journalists, interpreters and the like who were accustomed to speaking for this wider African community. Plaatje himself was strikingly frank about this in one of his letters to De Beers: 'Let me add, Sir, at the risk of being too personal, that there is a belief among some of the native population here that I am in the pay of De Beers – employed to keep them quiet.' His appeal to the company was thus in a sense an appeal for assistance in shoring up his own position locally – as well as an opportunity for De Beers to respond in a way that 'enhanced their reputation as an employer'.[35]

There were further signs that Plaatje's influence was no longer unquestioned when opposition arose to his proposals to form a 'Native Brotherhood' committee to take over the management and running of the new hall. He had put his proposals to a series of meetings in the Kimberley 'locations' in June 1918, telling them of

De Beers' decision to donate the old tram shed for their use, and outlining in detail the purpose and nature of his proposed Brotherhood committee. Although he acknowledged, so the *Diamond Fields Advertiser* reported, that 'one or two friends think that the hall should be under the control of certain individuals among us, and kept distinct from any specific organisations', he was able to gain public approval of his scheme. He was elected chairman of the building committee to raise money to convert the hall into a venue for Brotherhood meetings, and for use as an additional classroom for the overcrowded Lyndhurst Road Native School. At last he had the physical structure to meet both needs.

His proposal to form the Native Brotherhood proper ('upon the lines of the P.S.A. Brotherhood Movements and Sisterhoods of England, and the Fraternité Societies of France and Belgium') was also carried. A month later it was formally established as 'The Diamond Fields Men's Own Brotherhood'. Plaatje was elected its president; Arthur Tsengiwe (of the Beaconsfield post office) was vice president; Dr J.E. Mackenzie, Plaatje's doctor since the 1890s, was treasurer; L. Mashoko, T.D. Mweli Skota, G.M. Motsieloa and T.G. Diniso were other committee members. The Brotherhood's headed notepaper carried the motto 'Bear ye one another's burden' and a logo of two clasped hands. It also gave a 'London address', that of William Cross of the Southall Brotherhood, an indication of the importance Plaatje attached to the link with the Brotherhood movement in England.[36]

The public meetings which launched the Brotherhood movement in June 1918 would be dwarfed by the celebrations that accompanied the formal opening of its new hall on 7 August. By this time, it had come to assume a rather more than local significance. The reasons for this are to be found in the rapid escalation of industrial and political unrest on the Rand in the intervening months, culminating in a successful boycott of mine stores by African workers and a series of strikes for higher wages to meet wartime increases in the cost of living. This was a matter of serious concern for the government and the mining houses, and it also led to renewed tension within the SANNC, complicating the divisions that had emerged in 1917. An influential section of the Transvaal branch of the organisation aligned itself with the demands of the strikers, and supported their methods. None of the other regional branches were prepared to go so far. They preferred to rely upon traditional methods of representing grievances to the authorities and were concerned that this new militancy threatened the legitimacy of their own leadership.[37]

There were signs of these tensions at Congress's sixth annual conference at Bethlehem, in the Orange Free State, at the end of March 1918. The 'old guard' nevertheless managed to retain control and S.M. Makgatho's presidential address was in much the same vein as its predecessors. It helped that the government had agreed to temporarily suspend the Native Administration Bill, but this had not prevented it from publishing another bill, the Natives (Urban Areas) Bill, which, Makgatho said, threatened to harass those victims of the Natives' Land Act who had sought refuge in the towns. Makgatho made a point of commending Plaatje, who was at the meeting, for the 'big sacrifices' he had made 'on behalf of his downtrodden countrymen and women', and for being 'a farsighted champion in the interests of the people he represented'. He also referred his audience to page 53 of *Native Life in South Africa* where Plaatje had predicted the contents and objectives of the new legislation. 'Even the very title of the Bill he has prophesied with accuracy.'[38]

On the Rand, industrial and political unrest intensified, exacerbated by a harsh sentence passed in court on 12 June by the Johannesburg magistrate, T.G. Macfie, upon 152 African strikers employed by the Johannesburg municipality's sanitary department. Congress launched a campaign for the prisoners' release, but the question of what form this was to take exposed the differences there now were. While Plaatje, Makgatho, Isaiah Bud-M'belle (now general secretary of Congress) and several others appealed to the government to quash the sentence, the more radical leaders of the Transvaal branch of Congress, urged on by a small group of white revolutionary socialists, turned the campaign to release the prisoners into a demand for an all-round wage increase of a shilling a day, and threatened a general strike from 1 July if their demand was not met. To the relief of the mining houses and the leadership of the SANNC, the government ordered the release of the prisoners, the Supreme Court reversed the magistrate's decision, and a commission of inquiry (the Moffat Commission) was appointed to look into the strikers' grievances. The immediate crisis was thus defused.

Plaatje drafted a petition to the governor general calling for the release of the prisoners and felt able to claim some of the credit. The general situation continued to be tense, however, and the position of several of the Congress leaders – Saul Msane and S.M. Makgatho in particular – remained precarious, propelled along a course that was not of their own choice or making, yet fearful of losing all political credibility among their people if they dissociated themselves completely from strike action. The Transvaal branch of Congress and the national executive were further apart than ever.[39]

Not surprisingly, therefore, the executive meeting of the SANNC that took place in Bloemfontein at the beginning of August 1918, which Plaatje attended, was a stormy affair. In the end, by virtue of their majority on the provincial congresses of the Cape, Orange Free State and Natal, the moderates prevailed over the ten delegates from the Transvaal. Instead of threatening strike action, resolutions were passed 'respectfully requesting' the Union government to 'make an urgent appeal to employers throughout South Africa to alleviate this distress by giving their native employees a rise of at least one shilling per day per worker of all various classes and grades'. They also commended the government for bringing about the reversal of the sentence passed upon the strikers by the chief magistrate of Johannesburg.

A further resolution, drafted by Plaatje, read as follows: 'The Executive of the South African Native Congress, in session at Bloemfontein, on August 2nd 1918, having been informed that H.E. the Governor-General, at the instance of the Rt Hon. the Prime Minister, is going to lay the foundation stone of the proposed Assembly Hall for Natives at Kimberley – a present from De Beers Company – desire to record its congratulations to our brethren of the Diamond Fields on their good fortune and appreciation of the generosity of the De Beers Company which we feel certain will go far towards removing the causes of friction between White and Black in South Africa.'[40]

Circumstances in the country at large had ensured that Plaatje's success in persuading De Beers to part with an old tram shed had assumed a significance far beyond what anybody could have imagined. Especially if it was to be formally opened, as Plaatje put it, by 'H.E. the Governor General, at the instance of the Rt Hon. the Prime Minister'.[41]

Plaatje claimed that this was the direct result of representations he made to the prime minister. Surviving records confirm that this was the case, tribute to the curiously close, albeit highly ambivalent, relationship he had with General Botha, as well as his keen eye for spotting an opportunity. He had written first to the governor general, Lord Buxton, knowing he was due to visit Kimberley, but was told that it would not be possible for him to open the hall. Several days later, disappointed by this response, he sent a telegram to the prime minister requesting him to intercede, alluding to the difficulties he knew he was facing in Johannesburg. It did the trick. The governor general would, after all, be able to open the new meeting hall, although two days later than originally proposed. Lord Buxton's aide-de-camp then asked for some suggestions for the formal speech that would need to be made. Plaatje was happy to oblige, recommending that Lord Buxton should pay special attention to the contribution of black South Africans to the war effort and their participation in the Cape Corps and Native Labour Contingent.[42]

Preparations for the ceremony, set for 7 August, then involved Plaatje in a huge amount of work and correspondence as he sought to extract maximum advantage from the governor general's visit. He wanted all the publicity he could get for his new Brotherhood organisation, and to remind everybody of his own role in securing the old tram shed from De Beers. He was determined to take full advantage of the presence in Kimberley of the many distinguished (and wealthy) visitors likely to be in attendance in order to raise money for the work that needed to be carried out on the building. To this end he devised a scheme whereby visitors to Kimberley on the day of the opening ceremony would pay for specific bricks to be used in the work.

Things did not go entirely smoothly. There was continued opposition to his plan to have the new assembly hall under the exclusive control of his new Brotherhood organisation. He attributed this to an unholy alliance of A.L. Barrett, the inspector and protector of natives in Kimberley, who thought Plaatje was 'on the high way to becoming a troublesome professional agitator', and a group of Africans living locally, including Boyce Skota, a long-established resident of the town, well known to Plaatje. It was a serious matter and it caused, so he told Silas Molema, three weeks' sleepless nights and a lot of unnecessary expense. At one point, after the dissidents had communicated their concerns directly to the governor general's office, the ceremony was at grave risk of being cancelled. Eventually the local magistrate, G.J. Boyes, after presiding over a meeting of the opposing parties, was able to report that differences had been 'amicably settled' and that all parties were now 'unanimous in their desire that His Excy should lay foundation stone of hall'. The governor general would therefore come as planned.[43]

All went well on the day. Suitably loyal speeches were made by Mr Boyes, by Plaatje himself and by Mesach Pelem, once a resident of Kimberley and now representing the SANNC. Then it was the turn of the governor general himself. He made good use of Plaatje's suggestions for his speech and went on to urge Africans in Kimberley not to take precipitate action in attempting to redress their grievances but rather to have confidence in the commission of enquiry being conducted into the unrest on the Rand by J.S. Moffat. The fact that Moffat was 'the grandson of the great missionary, Dr Moffat, who was loved by the natives so much … showed at all events that the Prime Minister and the Government and Parliament are anxious to meet the natives as far as they can in regard to matters affecting them'.[44]

This was a somewhat partial assessment of the nature and purpose of the Moffat Commission, but the stone-laying ceremony was hardly the occasion for this to be debated. Plaatje, as much as De Beers and the government, wanted it to be seen as an example of the harmonious relations between black and white that could be achieved through the kind of methods to which he was committed. As Edward Dower, the secretary for native affairs, put it in a letter to De Beers when conveying the prime minister's appreciation of their action, the gift was 'indicative of just that spirit of sympathy between Europeans and Natives in this country which it is so important to promote'. Plaatje, for his part, thanked both De Beers and the governor general for 'the rare honour' bestowed upon both himself and 'the Natives of these Fields', and asked Lord Buxton to accept a copy of his book of proverbs as a small token of his appreciation.[45]

Plaatje was in no doubt about the wider significance of the episode. He made this very clear in a letter to Mr Raynham, the De Beers company secretary, explaining that he had been away from Kimberley 'to attend the Native Congress at Bloemfontein to prevent the spread among our people of the Johannesburg Socialist propaganda'. He went on: 'I think you are aware of our difficulties in that connection since Mr Pickering, writing to me on an entirely different matter, ended his letter thus: "For God's sake keep them (natives) off the labour agitators."' The labour agitators certainly made their presence felt in Bloemfontein. 'The ten Transvaal delegates came to Congress with a concord and determination that was perfectly astounding and foreign to our customary native demeanour at conferences. They spoke almost in unison, in short sentences, nearly every one of which began and ended with the word "strike". It was not difficult to understand the source of their backing for they even preceded the Congress and endeavoured to poison the minds of delegates from other parts.'

But in the end, Plaatje told Mr Raynham, the proponents of strike action were outvoted and delegates persuaded that 'the Socialists' method of pitting up black and white will land our people in serious disaster, while the worst that could happen to the white men would be but a temporary inconvenience'. De Beers, however, could take some credit for this outcome. 'When they took the train for Johannesburg, at Bloemfontein station, I am told that one of them remarked that they would have "converted Congress had not De Beers given Plaatje a Hall". This seems intensely reassuring as indicating that Kimberley will be about the last place that these black Bolsheviks of Johannesburg will pay attention to, thus leaving us free to combat their activities in other parts of the Union. Only those who saw the tension at this Congress can realise that the building discussion of this hall of ours came at just the right time for South Africa.'[46]

Even allowing for some colouring to suit its recipient (Plaatje knew Raynham would be pleased to hear his company's money was well spent), this was nevertheless a frank and revealing letter which says much about the recent transformation of African political life, and the position in which Plaatje and other Congress leaders now found themselves. In a way Plaatje had successfully exploited the situation to his own ends, taking advantage of the concerns about the unrest on the Rand felt by both the prime minister and De Beers, and using this to launch his Brotherhood organisation in Kimberley. But it was a dangerous game to be playing and there were casualties. Saul Msane was perhaps the most notable of them. Throughout 1917 and 1918 he had sought to retain his influence with both the authorities and the radical Transvaal branch of Congress, of which he was president. In the end, as the two grew further and further apart, the task proved impossible. His conservative instincts got the better of him, he came out publicly against strike action in June 1918, and was rewarded with the epithet 'Isita sa Bantu', or 'Enemy of the people'. It was the end of his political career.[47]

Plaatje was fortunate to be based in Kimberley and to have had other sources of support, and it was always less likely that his reputation would suffer so total an eclipse. His position continued to be challenged, however, and after the stone-laying ceremony his opponents in Kimberley contacted the governor general's office once again with their complaints. Both locally and nationally things had changed. It was far more difficult for Plaatje and his colleagues on the national executive of the SANNC to claim to be wholly representative of the aspirations of the African people of South Africa. Tribal differences and divisions, regarded for years as the great stumbling block to the achievement of political unity, were now complicated by growing socio-economic cleavages. Six years on from its founding conference, Congress was deeply divided.[48]

The winter of 1918 brought some serious personal difficulties for Plaatje and his family. As though symptomatic of the troubled times in the country as a whole, in the midst of his preparations for the visit of Lord Buxton a telegram came from Lovedale informing him that St Leger had been involved in a student riot in which windows had been broken and furniture smashed; he was in serious trouble and in imminent danger of being expelled. The principal of Lovedale, the Rev. James Henderson, wanted Plaatje to go down there immediately, presumably to use his influence to calm the students down, but with Lord Buxton due in Kimberley in a couple of days' time this was impossible. Quite what happened at Lovedale is unclear, but the disturbances were most likely inspired by the industrial and political unrest on the Rand. Riots among the students at Lovedale were not infrequent, and at other times were sparked off by the poor food served to them, indicative, as they perceived it, of the second-class status in society for which they were being prepared.

Nothing could have been calculated to distress Plaatje more than the possibility of his eldest son being expelled from Lovedale. He wanted St Leger to have the first-class secondary education he had never had himself, and he thought this was achieved when he won that scholarship in 1916. Now, with his alleged participation in the riot, it all hung in the balance.[49]

It must have come as a very great relief to hear, several days later, that St Leger's punishment was not expulsion, but two weeks' extra work. When he returned home in December, having completed his time at Lovedale, he brought with him a certificate which testified to his 'very good' conduct, so it seems no lasting damage was done. But there were other domestic difficulties. While St Leger's fate hung in the balance, Olive, now thirteen years old, tripped over in the house when carrying a kettle of boiling water, and scalded her arm. It was a very painful accident, and she was unable to go to school for several weeks afterwards. Almost as soon as she had recovered from this, Kimberley was struck by the worldwide influenza epidemic. It was the first inland centre in South Africa to be affected, and over the next few weeks more than four thousand people, of all races, succumbed to its effects. The highest death rates were in the mining compounds and the crowded African locations, but over five hundred whites died as well. Men and women were reported to be simply dropping in the streets, and households in which entire families were stricken were asked to hoist a red flag so that help could be summoned. Inevitably, comparisons were drawn with the Great Plague of London.[50]

Plaatje lost several friends and relatives to the virus, and his own immediate family did not escape its effects. At one stage during October 1918 Elizabeth and all the children (except St Leger, away at Lovedale) were struck down, and Plaatje, recently returned from a visit to Basutoland, was kept fully occupied looking after them all and seeing to the needs of his neighbours. Eventually he too caught the virus, and it was for him and Olive, the elder of the two daughters, that the consequences were to be the most serious. In Plaatje's case, the influenza caused what he later described as an 'oppressive heart disease'. Its immediate effect was to lay him up in bed for several weeks, but after that one doctor after the other pronounced his condition to be incurable. It added to a long history of ill health, always aggravated by overwork, and it meant he would live the rest of his life in the knowledge that he had a weak heart, liable to worsen without warning. None of the doctors he consulted over the next few years were able to offer any reassurance, let alone provide a cure.[51]

In the aftermath of the epidemic, Olive's condition was even more worrying. She had attended selflessly to her family's needs when all were suffering, and appeared to have escaped the virus, but three months later she contracted rheumatic fever, becoming, in her father's words, 'literally shrivelled up by rheumatism', and no longer able to go to school. Their doctor put it down to the after-effects of nursing her family during the epidemic. Unable to recommend any other form of treatment, he advised Plaatje to take her to Aliwal North where there were some hot springs which he thought might alleviate her suffering. In the days before Union, Plaatje himself used to swim here for pleasure. When they arrived, he was informed that Olive would not be allowed to take to the water on account of her colour. It was now for whites only.

Few incidents brought home in so personal a manner the direction in which the country was going. Just as when he visited his birthplace the previous year to find it owned by a German subject, so now the memories of a more civilised past served only to highlight the oppressive realities of the present. The incident provided an unhappy postscript to a perception that struck him forcibly at the time of the epidemic: the capacity of whites and blacks to rediscover a common humanity in the face of an epidemic which, if it did not strike at everybody equally, nevertheless did not pay heed to the distinctions of colour and status that normally governed everyday life.[52]

✦

Armistice Day, 11 November 1918, was signalled in Kimberley by long-drawn-out blasts on the De Beers Company's hooters. Over the next few days the town celebrated both the ending of the war, which had claimed the lives of several hundred of the town's inhabitants of all races, and the passing of the influenza epidemic – which had claimed far more. For Plaatje, recovering from his illness, it was a time to think again about the wider political and constitutional position of his people. Like many of his colleagues in the SANNC, he had long looked forward to the end of the war, believing that a further appeal to the imperial government could prove more fruitful than the first. There remained a feeling that the Congress deputation of 1914 had been prevented by the outbreak of war from achieving its objectives, and that it would be a dereliction of duty not to try to capitalise upon the impact it had nonetheless made. It was Plaatje himself, of course, who had done most to convey its message to the British public, and he had returned home with many messages of support. The Brotherhood Federation, most notably, had promised to do all it could 'to regain that freedom and justice to which as loyal British subjects your people are entitled'. The fact that this undertaking was signed by, among others, Sir Richard Winfrey, a minister in Lloyd George's government, seemed to suggest that the British government itself might be more open to reason than before.[53]

Plaatje was ambivalent, however. His experiences in England had left him with no illusions about the magnitude of the task which any deputation would face, whether he was part of it or not. But what alternative was there? If he came out against a second deputation, it would inevitably encourage those who were urging direct industrial action instead. To this Plaatje remained firmly opposed. More positively, he shared the optimism generated by the wartime speeches of Lloyd George and the American president, Woodrow Wilson, which made much of the rights of 'small nations' and notions of 'self-determination', and of the need for a just settlement to ensure peace for the future. While neither statesman had the British colonies or dominions in mind, the arguments could easily be extended, and the African press, or such of it as had survived the war, was quick to point out the implications for the position of black South Africans.[54]

So for Plaatje, and others who thought like him, there now seemed an opportunity to claim the political rights to which, after four long years of war, they believed they were entitled. This had been one of the central arguments of *Native Life in South Africa*, but since this was published in 1916 other things could be added to the balance sheet. The most significant was the contribution of the Native Labour Contingent to the imperial war effort, and the apparent recognition of the justice of African claims in a speech made by King George V to members of the contingent in France in 1917. Like the rest of his troops, he said, they were 'fighting for the liberty and freedom of my subjects of all races and creeds throughout my Empire'.[55]

What also swayed his mind was his regular communication with friends in England, especially Mrs Solomon, Mrs Unwin, William Cross, the Colensos, Dr Salter and others involved in the committee formed after his departure. The committee had been thwarted in its attempt to lay its concerns before General Smuts (he had simply refused to see them), but Mrs Solomon was not easily deterred. When the general addressed a meeting in London on the subject of the Russian Revolution, she put a series of questions to him about his government's policies in South Africa, pointing out that what he had just said about freedom in Russia, and 'protecting the rights of the weak and of the struggling nationalities', must surely apply to South Africa too. His reply was as bland as she would have expected, and he assured her 'that there would be no revolution in South Africa'.[56]

The war over, Mrs Solomon and the others urged Plaatje to return to England to resume his campaign and to redeem the promises that had been made to him. If General Smuts offered no hope, as looked to be the case, they must appeal again to the imperial government and, if need be, to the British public.

A month after the armistice, the SANNC convened a special meeting in Johannesburg to discuss sending a second deputation to England. Plaatje, still feeling far from well, managed to attend. Loyal resolutions were passed expressing congratulations to the imperial government on the successful outcome of the war, but both *The Star* and *Cape Argus* were moved to devote lengthy editorials to the significance of the growing African national sentiment they detected. Their commentary reflected a conviction in church, business and government circles that something had to be done to defuse this potentially dangerous phenomenon, and both papers took the opportunity to draw the attention of the authorities, as well as their readers, to the need to devote rather more care to the development of 'native policy' than had been the case hitherto. They could see trouble brewing.[57]

The meeting itself was largely taken up with discussion of a draft memorial for presentation to the governor general, for transmission to the King, and then with arrangements for the deputation to England. Prefaced by a lengthy reminder of the loyalty of black South Africans during the recent war, and of the lofty statements of Allied war aims, the memorial reviewed the sad history of 'native policy' since the Act of Union and requested that the imperial government revise the South African constitution 'in such a way as to grant enfranchisement of natives throughout the Union'. Only in this way, it claimed, could Africans gain 'a voice in the affairs of the country, and have full protection so as to check reactionary legislation and unpopular one-sided laws'. Having decided in principle that a deputation should be sent to England, it was resolved to send a total of nine people, two representatives from each province, along with the president, S.M. Makgatho.[58]

Plaatje was one of those elected to the deputation, but he still had reservations about going. In a letter written to Silas Molema on 20 December, the last day of the meeting, he commented bitterly about the way Congress now expected him to participate in a second deputation after all the sacrifices that the first had entailed. The organisation had failed to defray his ruinous expenses, and he was reluctant to commit himself again. As he reminded Silas Molema, he had lost his newspaper business as a direct result of his enforced absence overseas, and he concluded: 'Unless they give ME only £1,000, I am going nowhere. Once bitten, twice shy.'[59]

But he was persuaded to go. 'Only common sense should guide us to send him back, now that the war is over', Sefako Makgatho thought, pointing to the many offers of support he had received. Plaatje agreed, and over the next weeks and months set about raising money for a new campaign overseas. Two new possibilities then emerged. The first was that the delegates should travel to Versailles in France where the post-war peace conference was to be held, and to present their case there. Support for this idea grew rapidly when it became known that the Afrikaner nationalists, led by General Hertzog, intended to do this too, and to argue that the right to national self-determination entitled them to secede from the British empire. Congress wanted the exact opposite, a reassertion of imperial control, and felt that if the Afrikaner nationalists were to be represented at the Peace Conference, then so should they.[60]

A second possibility was that the SANNC should attend the proposed Pan-African Congress. This was being convened by Dr W.E.B. Du Bois, the renowned African American scholar and politician who had, over the previous twenty years, led the struggle for black American civil and political rights. He believed that the struggles of black people worldwide were inseparable, and in bringing together representatives of African, West Indian and African American political organisations he hoped to develop this sense of unity and to strengthen their case for justice. Despite opposition from the American government, Du Bois succeeded in organising his congress in Paris in February 1919. He hoped to present it as a rival to the Peace Conference at Versailles, and to draw attention to the rights of black people as the leaders of the victorious Allied powers redrew European and colonial boundaries.[61]

The SANNC was not represented at the Pan-African Congress, however. News about it came too late and it was impossible to raise the money in time. Other plans had to be scaled down. Within weeks of the special meeting in December it was realised that sending nine delegates to England was too ambitious. Other problems arose too. In March 1919 Plaatje travelled to Cape Town to meet with Richard Msimang, a member of the executive of the SANNC, in order to present their memorial to the governor general. When he arrived, he got the distinct impression that Msimang resented his presence, and there followed an unseemly wrangle over the precise contents of the memorial. In a letter to Silas Molema, Plaatje told him he thought this deputation was in an even greater state of disarray than its predecessor in 1914.[62]

He planned to sail from Cape Town immediately after this, and passages for himself and three other delegates had been booked on the *Durham Castle*. But the money for the tickets could not be raised in time. Two delegates, Richard Selope Thema and Levi Mvabaza, did manage to get away on the *Voronej*, but Plaatje, by now appointed leader of the deputation, was unable to accompany them.

For the funds he still needed, he looked, as ever, to the Barolong. As in 1914, loyalties to traditional chiefdoms remained strong, and many thought their interests were best served not by subsuming their case within a wider African national movement, but in being represented separately, or at least as a distinct strand within a wider set of demands. The Tshidi never relinquished their claim to autonomy and they had continued, at ruinous cost, to fight the government through the courts to press their case. Now, in a second deputation to England, there was an opportunity, perhaps the last they would get, to bring their case to the British imperial government, to reassert their status as loyal allies of the British, and to remind the government and the British public of their continued mistreatment by the Union authorities. At the very least they wanted to ensure that Plaatje was there to represent their interests. Privately, Plaatje and Silas Molema could agree that later generations of Barolong would never forgive them if they failed to put their case as forcefully as the leaders of the Xhosa and Zulu peoples.[63]

In Mafikeng Silas Molema took the initiative in fundraising, convening several meetings. He also approached the local magistrate to ask if the government would agree to release £300 from the Barolong National Fund. This was a fund made up of contributions from the Barolong, collected and administered by the government and used to support educational and other causes; crucially, however, the government retained control over how it was spent. While the authorities considered their response to Molema's appeal, the Seleka Barolong in Thaba Nchu fulfilled an earlier undertaking. Writing on 14 March 1919, Plaatje was able to report that Goronyane, Fenyang, Nyokong and Makgothi, former members of the *Tsala* syndicate and long-time supporters of his endeavours, had somehow found the money to pay off his debts in England. More was needed for the new campaign, but it looked as if he would be able to join the other delegates after all.[64]

Meanwhile, he made some progress in building up his Brotherhood organisation in Kimberley. As in the rest of Kimberley, its work was severely disrupted by the influenza epidemic in the latter part of 1918. It caused, among other things, the death of Mr Lucas Mahoko, one of the committee members, and Mr Lindsay, the architect responsible for drawing up the plans for the conversion of the tram shed into a proper assembly hall. Despite its half-completed state, regular weekly meetings took place, all of them well attended. The Native Brotherhood Institute, as it was now called, was formally dedicated by the Rt Rev. Wilfrid Gore Browne, bishop of Kimberley and Kuruman, in April 1919. For Plaatje, the bishop's presence, along with that of a number of other local dignitaries, demonstrated how much better race relations were in Kimberley than on the Rand. Immediately before attending this ceremony Plaatje received news of a new wave of 'unrest'. Mounted police charged a crowd of anti-pass demonstrators, causing several deaths and a large number of injuries. The coincidence of these events served only to underline the importance of achieving 'brotherhood' between individuals and races, of helping to overcome the explosive tensions of the immediate post-war era through moral and religious, as well as political, change.[65]

At the beginning of May Plaatje was still in South Africa, having failed to get a passage, as he hoped, on the *Llanstephan Castle* the previous month. But he continued his preparations for his campaign, turning his attention to the 'companion volume' to *Native Life in South Africa* which he hoped to publish once he was in England. This led him to write to Sir Drummond Chaplin, the administrator of Southern Rhodesia, to congratulate him on the 'sound thrashing' he had recently administered to John Harris of the Aborigines' Protection Society, a reference to Chaplin's reply to Harris's new pamphlet on the case against the Chartered Company. Plaatje requested further information about laws relating to Africans in Rhodesia. He believed they were not subject to discriminatory legislation of the kind that existed in South Africa, and he intended to use this information in his new book in order to contrast John Harris's interest in Rhodesia with his 'role of defender of the Union Policy against a native publicist'. Sir Drummond's secretary, replying to Plaatje's letter, said that 'His Honour the Administrator' was 'greatly interested in the views expressed therein', and supplied the information he wanted.[66]

The delay in Plaatje's departure for England enabled him to attend the SANNC's seventh annual meeting, held in Queenstown between 6 and 9 May. Thanks to S.M. Makgatho's presidential address, he again attracted the attention of the House of Assembly. Makgatho described Plaatje's investigations into the Orange Free State shootings, and congratulated him for 'having managed to get at the Boers in his own way each time the courts had failed us'. As a result, he said, 'no shooting had been reported in the Free State since eight months ago, when he settled with the last Boer'. To one member of the House of Assembly, Brigadier General Myburgh, this kind of language, reported in the press, was as a red rag to a bull. Was the minister of native affairs aware of what had been said, he demanded in parliament, and what action did the government propose to take? F.S. Malan, the minister, replied cautiously that the matter was under consideration, and that he had brought it to the attention of the attorney general of the Orange Free State in view of 'insinuations' that had been made 'in regard to the administration of justice'. In the event no further action was taken. Malan said he thought the 'cryptic remark' about 'getting at the Boers' was a reference to the successful civil actions for compensation instituted against the perpetrators of the shootings – 'not to any blood for blood intimidation'.[67]

Back in Kimberley after the conference, Plaatje attended to his travel plans. From a letter he wrote to W.E.B. Du Bois on 19 May it is clear these were not confined to Great Britain alone. After expressing his regret at missing the

Paris conference ('all owing to the backwardness of our race – a backwardness intensified by our tribal and clannish differences'), he told Du Bois that 'to broaden my outlook I wish to visit the United States before returning', and asked him whether he thought 'a well arranged tour could pay expenses'. He would rely, he said, 'on your kind advice'.[68]

What Du Bois's advice was on this last point is unknown, but it is no surprise that visiting the United States was again in his mind. He intended to do this in 1914, and he remained as convinced as ever of the relevance of the experience of black Americans to the struggles of his own people. As the prospect of intervention by the imperial government receded, so the experience and the resources of black America became ever more attractive. He hoped in particular to raise funds to enable him to restart *Tsala ea Batho*, and to put his Brotherhood organisation onto a securer financial footing. As if he needed any reminder of the urgency of the situation here, he had several letters from De Beers drawing attention to the accumulation of unpaid rates and building bills on the new hall. It seemed impossible ever to escape from this constant shortage of funds. America, the land of wealth and black achievement, promised salvation.[69]

Plaatje finally left Kimberley on 6 June 1919, his passage booked on the *Kenilworth Castle*, due to sail from Cape Town five days later. As in 1914, he said, he embarked upon this mission 'against the personal persuasions of General Botha'. Prior to his departure he got the president and treasurer of Congress to agree to pay Elizabeth £6 a month for as long as he was away on Congress's mission. She was going to need it. He had just spent their remaining savings on his passage to England.

He was accompanied on the voyage by J.T. Gumede, a Congress delegate from Natal who had been to England twice before, the first time as a member of a Zulu choir in the 1890s. However, Gumede's travelling documents had not come through from Pretoria as expected, and it was only after some last-minute negotiations with the authorities in Cape Town that the difficulty was overcome, thanks this time to Plaatje's success in persuading F.S. Malan, the minister of native affairs (and acting prime minister), to intervene. Had it been somebody less sympathetic, Plaatje told Silas Molema, they could easily have delayed their response until the ship had sailed without them. Malan also promised Plaatje, when they had an hour's meeting on the morning of his departure, to look again at the issue of whether money might be released from the Barolong Fund for use by the deputation. On this note of official co-operation, the expressed views of General Botha notwithstanding, Plaatje departed for the United Kingdom to assume the leadership of the Congress deputation.[70]

꘠

It had been a difficult couple of years. Returning to South Africa in 1917, having achieved his ambition of publishing *Native Life in South Africa*, Plaatje struggled with his debts, turned down the offer of the presidency of the SANNC and, in inhospitable wartime conditions, tried but failed to restart his newspaper. Political unrest and class and racial tensions divided black and white alike, leaving African leaders of the old school in a precarious situation, their beliefs and methods no match for an uncompromising government – or the demands of an impatient new African constituency ready to try new methods to remedy grievances. In this fraught situation Plaatje saw his Brotherhood organisation in Kimberley as a means both of overcoming these tensions and providing himself with a platform, and he did what he could to place it on a secure footing. Given the poverty of his people and their reluctance to support an organisation that did not always seem to speak to their needs, it was not an easy task. In the end he could see no alternative but to return to Britain. While his mission was first and foremost on behalf of the SANNC, as in 1914 he travelled with several other objectives in mind. He still hoped to mount a legal challenge to the actions of the South African government in relation to the Imperial Reserve in Mafikeng, and he needed to raise funds for his Brotherhood organisation and his newspaper. The imperial metropolis was the inevitable first port of call as he prepared to navigate his way through these varied objectives.

TWELVE

Overseas again
England, 1919–1920

Richard Selope Thema and Levi Mvabaza, the two Congress delegates who had sailed from Cape Town in March, acquitted themselves creditably in London, securing an interview with Leo Amery, the under-secretary of state for the colonies. This was achieved not through the Anti-Slavery and Aborigines' Protection Society, which was not informed about the deputation, but with the help of W.P. Schreiner, the South African high commissioner in London. Schreiner was no stranger to deputations of this kind, having led the deputation which travelled to London in 1909 to protest about the colour-bar clauses in the draft Act of Union. Now he found himself on the other side of the fence. Although he accepted the official view that the imperial government had no right to intervene in the internal affairs of a self-governing dominion, and thought Congress misguided in sending a deputation to London, he was nonetheless prepared to intercede on their behalf with the Colonial Office.[1]

Leo Amery was never likely to do more than repeat the official line. He 'fully acknowledged the loyalty shown by the natives, but could not help regretting that the leader of the deputation had indicated that this loyalty might be diminished'. His government could not alter the South Africa Act and even if they could it 'would probably make the position of the natives worse, and not better'. Finally, 'he enlarged upon the nature of Responsible Government, and urged that the educated native should work patiently within the limits of the constitution of the Union, a constitution which being British necessarily contained within itself the power of development'.[2]

Privately, though, Amery was rather more concerned about the likely consequences of South African policy than he cared to admit publicly: 'it was very clear to me', he wrote in his diary, 'that trouble is coming this way, possibly much sooner than we have generally thought'. But the Colonial Office was careful to ensure that its dealings with the deputation were scrupulously fair. A good deal of correspondence was generated over the issue, and in the unsettled post-war period there was a distinct awareness in official circles of the need to avoid action that might provoke 'disloyal' sentiments, or worse, in any part of the empire. There was a concern, too, to avoid creating the impression that the African deputation was treated with any less courtesy than the Afrikaner

351

nationalist deputation, led by General Hertzog, which was also intending to present its case in Versailles.[3]

This last consideration seems to have persuaded the Colonial Office to allow passports to be issued to the delegates, when they applied, so they could travel to France to see the British prime minister, David Lloyd George, then attending the Versailles Peace Conference (along with, among others, Generals Botha and Smuts). While Selope Thema and Mvabaza failed to make the propaganda coup the Congress hoped for, their trip was not in vain. They managed, for one thing, to get noticed by General Smuts, something not easily achieved in South Africa. According to one observer, Smuts 'had been deeply impressed by the humiliating sight of a native deputation in Paris, praying for the intervention of the British government', calling their petition 'an appalling document', and symptomatic, as he saw it, of a new spirit of distrust between black and white.[4]

Secondly, while Selope Thema and Mvabaza did not get to see the British prime minister, who was too busy treaty-making, they did extract a promise from Philip Kerr, his private secretary, that he would meet them in the first week in July when he was back in London. With this the two men returned to England, and set about publicising their cause, preparing the ground for the more comprehensive programme that would be possible once Plaatje and Gumede joined them.[5]

Such was the situation when Plaatje and Gumede arrived in London at the end of June. Their first engagement was to attend the funeral of W.P. Schreiner, who had died on 28 June, the day the Treaty of Versailles was signed; theirs were the only black faces in a crowd of people who came to pay their respects, Lord Milner and Generals Botha and Smuts among them. Apart from the personal sadness Plaatje felt about Schreiner's demise, it was something of a blow to the hopes of the deputation in London, for he had hoped that his relationship with Schreiner ('our late lamented champion', he called him) might have opened more doors for them. The funeral was also, Plaatje would recall, the last time he saw General Botha: within weeks he too was gone to an early grave.[6]

The immediate priority was the question of accommodation. 'I am sorry', Plaatje told Sophie Colenso on 17 July, 'that the work kept me at such a high pitch, going at top speed, that I am only just able to communicate to you the greetings of myself and family. The position was intensified by the difficulty of obtaining lodgings, which are unobtainable in London.' He was glad to say, though, that 'after considerable trouble we have managed to secure lodgings and we are comfortably, though expensively, accommodated' at 13 Highbury

Terrace, a fine Georgian terrace building that looked out over Highbury Fields, and home to several prominent members of London's West African community. The apartments were not as good as those he had in Acton the last time he was in London, but at least they were more centrally situated: 'it is very convenient in that respect as one can get to the City at 2d and to Tottenham Court Road too at the same fare'.[7]

A week later Plaatje met up with the Colensos and other friends and supporters at a drawing-room reception held by Georgiana Solomon at her home in Hampstead. The meeting was chaired by Dr G.B. Clark, a sympathetic Liberal member of parliament, who agreed to convey to the prime minister a unanimous resolution urging him to fulfil the promise he made to Selope Thema and Mvabaza in Paris and grant the deputation an interview. The meeting itself went well. Olive Schreiner was among those present, and commented afterwards on 'How well Mr Plaatje and all the delegates spoke'; Sophie Colenso, too, was 'enormously impressed' by their 'splendid addresses'. Plaatje's only regret was that with so many people present and so little time he was unable to greet Mrs Colenso as she had to leave the meeting early. He wrote to her the following day: 'It pained me very much, especially after we came over, to have been separated not alone by war but by distance and the dislocated post – then to meet yesterday and part again like prisoners of war, without exchanging a single word.'[8]

A second drawing-room meeting a few weeks later, again hosted by Mrs Solomon, was notable for the impassioned debate that took place on the question of women. It was prompted by an explanation Mrs Solomon gave for not seconding the resolution passed at the previous meeting: 'the less advanced Natives', so Betty Molteno summed up her friend's lengthy argument, 'would not understand a woman taking such a role', hence she had deferred to a man to second a motion she of course fully supported. This was not something Betty Molteno could leave unchallenged. Her view was that 'we were in a new century which compelled women to spring forward, and that this should be explained to the Natives'. This was followed by 'quite an outburst from Plaatje', she reported, and a passionate account of the part that 'Native women' were now playing in South Africa. He told the meeting of the brave resistance of the African women of the Orange Free State in 1913, describing 'very dramatically' their 'spontaneous and marvellous outburst ... against the carrying of Passes', some being killed or injured. 'So we see', he concluded, 'that the Native Women are taking the law into their own hands.' He also expressed his regret that 'a Native Woman had not come over with the Deputation', especially since they had one 'who was a better, and abler, speaker than anyone'. He was referring to Charlotte Manye (Maxeke as she now was), star of the African Jubilee Singers who made such an impact in

353

the Kimberley of his youth. Now she was a leading figure in the newly formed Bantu Women's League.[9]

It was a revealing exchange: in the immediate post-war period, with votes for at least some women in the United Kingdom now achieved, along with their right to stand for parliament, it was an exciting time for Plaatje's circle of women supporters, and they were keenly interested in the campaigns of women elsewhere. For Plaatje, too, mindful as ever of the connection and parallels between issues of race and gender, the inspiring example of women's actions – in both England and South Africa – seemed to offer some hope at a time when it was desperately needed.

Support for the deputation's cause in London's liberal drawing-room circles was assured, thanks in part to Plaatje's efforts between 1914 and 1917. He nevertheless detected a stronger current of sympathetic opinion than before. He was encouraged, too, by the exchanges that took place in parliament at the end of July, when, as in 1914, the colonial vote came before the House of Commons. The most impressive speech this time came from Benjamin Spoor, a Labour frontbencher, who spoke of 'the existence of a definite tendency, since the Act of Union, 'to eliminate and destroy the rights of the natives', and urged the imperial government to 'exercise every power they have got in order to restore to the natives the conditions which existed before the Act of Union'. Supporting speeches came from Henry Cavendish-Bentinck, a Conservative backbencher who had served in the South African War, whom Plaatje had first met in 1914; from Captain Ormsby-Gore, member of parliament for Stafford; and from Josiah Wedgwood, a member of the committee set up to continue Plaatje's work in 1917, who claimed that what now existed in South Africa was 'only very thinly veiled slavery'. But even Josiah Wedgwood, sympathetic though he was, could only urge that the imperial government should dissociate itself completely from what was going on in South Africa – which was not going to change anything.

In reply to all these speakers, Colonel Amery simply told a thinly attended House what he had told Mvabaza and Thema in May, that the principle of responsible government bound the imperial government to a policy of non-interference. All he could offer was the slim hope that 'with a certain measure of faith in these matters' a solution to the 'very difficult problem of the relationship between the races' could be found. In reply to a final question from Cavendish-Bentinck, Amery did acknowledge, however, the effectiveness of Gandhi's intervention on behalf of the Indians in South Africa. This was a man, Amery said, who 'by his own personality, his persistence and his courage got much further in the solution of the problem of the Indians in the Transvaal than any official representations could have done'. What Plaatje, sitting in the visitors' gallery, made of these remarks is unrecorded: he was not, after all, short of the qualities to which Amery alluded, and he knew all about Gandhi. What he did not have, he often complained, was the advantage of a British Indian administration in the background, able to bring some influence to bear on the treatment of Indians in South Africa.[10]

A week later Plaatje wrote to Chief W.Z. Fenyang in Thaba Nchu to tell him about the debate in parliament. He was convinced that the coverage they achieved only underlined what he had said in a previous letter, 'namely that the English people are more amenable to reason than they were the last time'. Shortage of funds, though, threatened to cripple the whole campaign. 'When I arrived here I found that I could not get freedom of movement unless I paid part of the old accounts so I disgorged £54 and at least £200 is wanted immediately. It meant that I handed over everything – pocket-money included, and I am now standing between two fires – the old debts and my present expenses.' S.M. Makgatho had promised to send £100 to support their work, but nothing had come, and he worried about the consequences. 'As soon as English people find out that I have no money there will be a terrible set-back because they will consider me a d——fool if after what I endured in 1914–17 I came penniless again.'

The other delegates, he said, were losing all heart, 'disgusted' that he brought no money. 'The fact that I (their so-called leader) am penniless drives them more desperate and I hope that something could be done to get say £300 partly for old debts and partly for the present campaign. The position is really serious and I am beginning to tremble that the deputation will soon be disgraced – after which we will NEVER AGAIN manage the Boer. We have to strike out *now* or *never.*' He ended his letter with a request to Fenyang to check that Congress was paying Elizabeth the £6 a week it had promised. He had reason to be worried. As Isaiah Bud-M'belle would write later, Congress 'strangely and unaccountably failed to give Mrs Plaatje the support they had so solemnly undertaken to provide'.[11]

Despite these troubles Plaatje and his colleagues carried on with their campaign as best they could, and they began to widen the support for their cause. Unsurprisingly they got no further joy from the Colonial Office. Thanks to a private letter of introduction, Plaatje did manage to secure a meeting for Gumede and himself with Colonel Amery in the middle of August, but the outcome was no different from before. 'I told him [Plaatje] very much as I had told the previous deputation', Amery reported, 'that we were not prepared to go back beyond Union and that was our answer to Hertzog and if Hertzog had his way and the

Act of Union went, things would be much worse than they are today.'[12]

Outside the Colonial Office things looked more promising. From the time of their arrival the deputation had enjoyed the support of London's increasingly vocal black community. Their cause received wide coverage in the *African Telegraph*, which also distributed their publicity material, most notably a pamphlet entitled *A Summary of Statements Made to the 'African Telegraph' by the South African Delegation*. The black community also held several functions in their honour, including a well-attended musical reception organised by the 'Coterie of Friends' in west London in the middle of August. In these circles Plaatje and his colleagues were assured of the fullest encouragement and sympathy in their campaign, and for Plaatje particularly, hoping to travel on to the United States, these gatherings also provided a valuable source of contacts and information.[13]

Public interest in the deputation's cause extended well beyond natural sympathisers. To the support of London's black community and the Brotherhood movement was added, in August and September 1919, the backing of the Free Church Council, part of the women's suffrage movement, the Independent Labour Party (this after what Plaatje called 'a long and tedious round of negotiations and constant application'), the Union of Democratic Control, and the Church Socialist League. This was hardly the British establishment, but it was access to some sizeable networks, and the meetings which Plaatje and his colleagues addressed – and the interviews they gave – were widely reported in the daily and weekly press. Sometimes they attracted some international coverage too. Several American newspapers, for example, reproduced Plaatje's address on 'The condition of natives in South Africa', which he delivered to the British Dominions Women Citizens' Union late in September – 'the first purely women's meeting' he had addressed since landing in July. One of those present, the Australian feminist Vida Goldstein, thought 'this awakening of coloured and other subject races has been one of the wonders of the war period'.[14]

Often these gatherings were urged to send resolutions of protest to the Colonial Office and to the prime minister. The action of the Abney Brotherhood in Stoke Newington, north London, on 17 August 1919, was typical of many: 'having heard the statement of Mr Sol T. Plaatje, of Kimberley, on behalf of his fellow countrymen', it now wished to register its protest 'against the disabilities imposed upon the South African natives by the Union government, as contrary to the spirit and traditions of English government, and urges that prompt representations should be made by the Colonial Secretary, to secure their removal'.[15]

A similar resolution from the Church Socialist League, after Plaatje spoke at one of their meetings some weeks later, was noted in the 'Monthly review of revolutionary movements in foreign countries' laid before the British cabinet in

December. The very existence of such a report was a reflection of the widespread anxiety now felt by all Western governments about the impact of the Russian Revolution and its dangerous doctrines. Admittedly the British intelligence reports tended to be alarmist, and interpreted their remit in rather broad terms. In reality the SANNC was far from being a 'revolutionary' organisation and Plaatje, its principal spokesman, was certainly no 'revolutionary' himself. Nevertheless, in the unsettled post-war period there were very real fears about the spread of subversive doctrines in the empire, not just the UK, and definitions as to what was and what was not a revolutionary movement were not too carefully drawn.[16]

Racial issues, too, were becoming a significant concern, and there was already worrying evidence, from an imperial point of view, of the spread of Marcus Garvey's Universal Negro Improvement Association into the African colonies, indicating a growing dissatisfaction with colonial rule. Even in the UK there had been, for the first time, widespread racial rioting, particularly in port cities like Cardiff, Liverpool and Glasgow. Though there were local reasons for these disturbances, it was obvious, as news spread, that they posed a potential threat to peace in the African and Caribbean colonies. It all contributed to a much tenser atmosphere, as Plaatje and his colleagues sought to draw attention to South African grievances, than had been the case during his first visit to the UK.[17]

Throughout the autumn of 1919 Plaatje continued the campaign, addressing meeting after meeting. Sometimes, it was as many as three in one day. Such was the case on 9 October, his forty-third birthday. Describing his experiences in *The Clarion*, a journal published in Cape Town, he related how he addressed a 'drawing-room meeting at Kensington' in the morning, the National Liberal Club in the afternoon, and a Brotherhood meeting at St Michael's hall, Clapton, in the evening. The afternoon meeting was undoubtedly the highlight. Plaatje considered it the 'most exciting since we came here', largely because of the opportunity it gave him to demolish 'a South African Jew who styled himself "bosom friend of General Smuts" and warned the English people against offering any sympathies to Kaffirs'. Plaatje had little difficulty in ridiculing this man's ill-informed remarks. 'He fled when the meeting manifested its enjoyment of this rejoinder at the coward's expense, he did not stop to hear the end, but quickly took his hat and sneaked out of the place.'[18]

Despite his shortage of funds Plaatje did venture outside London and the home counties, sometimes accompanied by one or other of his fellow delegates. His visit to Tyneside, in the industrial north-east, albeit after a tedious seven-hour train journey, was a particular success. It came about because of a promise he made to councillor William Walker, a former mayor of Sunderland, whom he had met at a Brotherhood meeting in 1916, to visit his city if he ever returned to

England. So here he was, nearly three years later, addressing 'the biggest crowd I have ever faced', over four thousand people . He only just managed to get into the meeting. 'Reaching Sunderland just over an hour before the time we found the hall surrounded by policemen turning the crowds back as there was no room inside. A very good thing the advertisements mentioned that the speaker was black as our party would not have been admitted.' Sir Hamar Greenwood, the local MP, who was there too, 'simply could not believe that such barbarities were possible'. Plaatje was able to provide him, however, 'with documentary proof of the South African tyrannies exactly as published by the Government's own departmental printers'.[19]

Such an enthusiastic response served only to confirm his view of the benefits of concentrating his efforts outside London. But with so heavy a programme of engagements it is hardly surprising that he should have begun to complain, as he wrote to Mrs Colenso, of 'being frightfully overworked', or that several of his friends should have noticed how tired he was beginning to look. 'My doctor has been pressing me to take a few months rest to prevent a breakdown', he wrote, but it was advice he ignored: 'a month's break in the chain of appointments could upset the whole programme and perhaps adversely affect the whole mission'.[20]

Moments of rest and relaxation were few and far between, but there were several weekend visits to 'Elangeni', the Colenso's family home, and he did see quite a bit of Betty Molteno when he was in London. She had sought him out in the middle of October, so she told her friend Alice Greene, and met up with him twice in two days. 'He is a charming fellow to talk to', she said, 'and we have had much interesting conversation.' She supported his cause and attended his meetings when they were nearby, but it was his company she really enjoyed.[21]

His social contacts were by no means restricted to this white 'Anglo-African' community, supportive as it was. Another friendship was with George W. Lattimore, the African American manager of the Southern Syncopated Orchestra, a black jazz band which had arrived in London in July. A New York lawyer and businessman, and in his younger days a fine basketball player, Lattimore was no musician himself but he had a keen eye for the growing appeal of black American music in Europe; he took up residence in London and assumed control of the affairs of the orchestra when its original conductor, Will Marion Cook, returned to America. His path crossed with Plaatje's at several social functions organised by London's black community, and they got on well. Lattimore seems to have been attracted to the ideals of the Brotherhood movement, and he and his orchestra were, so Sophie Colenso reported after she met some of them, 'very sympathetic to their South African brothers'.[22]

Indeed it was in the company of the Southern Syncopated Orchestra, courtesy of George Lattimore, that Plaatje would spend the night of the first anniversary of Armistice Day, 11 November 1919, at the 'Great Peace Dance' at the Albert Hall in London. Their performance was spectacularly successful, and Plaatje, having earlier in the evening introduced them to a deputation of visiting Basotho chiefs, was struck by the enthusiastic applause they received in contrast to the more restrained reception given to the white orchestra which was also playing. The 'Negro Jazz Band' played on until 4.30 in the morning, 'putting such fire into their work', Plaatje thought, 'that the jovial revellers felt they were not only accompanied by a band but also driven by real artists': 'I too had a holiday', he added, 'and witnessed free, gratis a gorgeous palette that other people paid Five Guineas to see'. He had had 'a great time'.[23]

⌁

At the end of September 1919 there took place a thoroughly unpleasant incident which complicated the difficult financial situation Plaatje faced, threatened to upset relations between the Congress delegates, and occupied a great deal of his time and energy which could have been spent far more profitably on the campaign itself. The incident occurred aboard the Union-Castle liner the *Edinburgh Castle*, docked at Southampton, which Richard Selope Thema, Henry Ngcayiya and Levi Mvabaza, along with a South African student, Mdani Xaba, had boarded for their return journey to South Africa. The first three men were anxious to return home, having been in England since May, and it was agreed that it made more sense for their fast-diminishing funds to be used to support Plaatje and Gumede. Just before the ship was due to sail, however, an irate crowd of demobilised South African soldiers threatened to throw the four men ashore because they objected to them occupying third-class cabins, while they, because of the acute shortage of shipping accommodation at the time, were obliged to sleep in hammocks. Union-Castle officials just managed to prevent the four men being physically ejected, but felt they had to take them off the ship in the interests of their own safety. They then returned to London, without their baggage, to wait until another passage could be obtained for them.[24]

The whole affair generated a great deal of publicity and hundreds of pages of agitated correspondence between the Colonial Office, the South African High Commission in London, the Native Affairs Department in Pretoria, the Anti-Slavery and Aborigines' Protection Society, and, not least, Plaatje himself, as leader of the deputation. As the delegates contemplated legal action and questions were asked in the House of Commons, the most urgent question was who was to be responsible for the living expenses of the four men while they

359

awaited another passage back to South Africa. The High Commission intervened with the offer of a temporary loan on the understanding that it would in due course be repaid by the SANNC, who, it was assumed, would be able to claim compensation from either the Union-Castle shipping line or the South African authorities, whoever it was that ultimately accepted liability. From the start matters were complicated by the fact that, of the four men ejected from the ship, only Selope Thema and Mvabaza were actually Congress delegates; Xaba was a student at Edinburgh University and happened to be going back at the same time, while Ngcayiya, though president of the Ethiopian Church of South Africa, was in England to represent Africans from Rhodesia and was not an official member of the deputation. Worse would follow when the South African High Commission in London, instead of forwarding to Plaatje a remittance of £200 from S.M. Makgatho, president of Congress, to support the work of the deputation, used it to pay for the subsistence of the four men who had been ejected from the *Edinburgh Castle*.[25]

Plaatje, his hands full with the work of the campaign, had to become involved in trying to recover the money so it could be used for the purpose intended, and to spend a great deal of time in dealing with correspondence and visiting the offices of both the Anti-Slavery and Aborigines' Protection Society and the South African High Commission, to try to sort matters out. Since the High Commission was, as Plaatje saw it, withholding the means to enable him to pursue his campaign against the policies of the South African government, it is scarcely surprising that his frustration at the situation should have boiled over. 'On previous occasions', reported Mr Blankenburg, first secretary at the High Commission, 'Mr Plaatje exhibited much calmness and good reason; on this occasion he appeared to be very "warm" and most strongly protested that as Xaba and Ngcayiya were not delegates, they should not be aided out of the £200 provided by Congress.' Plaatje could get nowhere with them, however.[26]

Ngcayiya, Mvabaza and Xaba eventually found berths on the RMS *Briton*, which sailed from Southampton early in December, and there was no repetition of the *Edinburgh Castle* incident. Richard Selope Thema, the other Congress delegate, decided at the last minute to stay on in England to assist Plaatje and Gumede with the work of the deputation, hoping he might find the opportunity to embark upon some course of further education.[27]

Despite the difficulties and embarrassment caused to all the Congress delegates by the *Edinburgh Castle* incident, their extended stay in England did at least mean they were able to join Plaatje and Gumede in two notable meetings that followed. The first was with the archbishop of Canterbury, Randall Davidson, which took place at Lambeth Palace, in London, on 25 October. Quite what transpired it is impossible to know since the archbishop, concerned that he 'might be represented as having thrown myself into a cause in a manner which would give rise to misunderstanding both in the Colonial Office and in South Africa', insisted that it should be 'regarded as absolutely private, and that no account of it must appear in print'. Nor, it seems, did he or his advisers think it necessary to keep even a private record of the meeting.[28]

Plaatje had higher hopes of the second meeting – with the prime minister, David Lloyd George, who at last agreed to receive a Congress delegation. In many ways it was surprising that this took place at all, and it seems to have been Plaatje's connection with Arthur Henderson and Dr Clifford, two Brotherhood men who enjoyed some personal influence with the prime minister, which in the end brought it about. Until then, despite the promise made in France, the delegates' frequent reminders to the prime minister's office had been ignored, Dr G.B. Clark's request for a meeting was declined, and Plaatje for one would have known perfectly well that the idea would not have been viewed favourably, to say the least, by either the Colonial Office or the South African High Commission. When Lloyd George did finally agree to a meeting, Major Hugh Thornton, Lord Milner's private secretary, told Philip Kerr, Lloyd George's private secretary, that the feeling in the Colonial Office was that 'the less said to this Deputation by the Prime Minister the better'; he also suggested it would be 'a good thing' if Kerr could 'have a talk with Sir Henry Lambert', the assistant under-secretary in the Colonial Office, before the interview took place.[29]

Underlying all this was the fear that the delegates were quite capable of arousing the prime minister's sympathy. So it proved. The interview took place on the afternoon of Friday, 21 November 1919, in a committee room at the House of Commons. Led by Plaatje, the party included, apart from the South Africans, several leading figures in London's black community, including his friend John Barbour-James; Eldred Taylor, of the *African Telegraph*; and T.H. Jackson, editor of the *Lagos Weekly Record*, who happened to be in London at the time.

Levi Mvabaza began by summarising the historical background to their predicament; he enumerated in detail the discriminatory legislation that had been passed since the Act of Union, illustrating one of their complaints by showing Lloyd George a selection of passes which the delegates had brought along with them: 'Let me have a look at them,' Lloyd George said, 'I have never seen them.' He did at least seem interested.[30]

Then it was Plaatje's turn to explain how desperate they were. 'I am very sorry we have to weary you with our African difficulties but if we were to speak till tomorrow morning we would never succeed to enumerate them all.' He told of their visits to the Colonial Office and the advice they had received 'to go and settle affairs in their own country'. But how could they do that in a country where they had no footing, no rights, 'where we cannot even buy or hire a house'? He related how his own family had suffered from the restrictions now imposed upon them – his son St Leger no longer able to work in the post office where he had begun his own career, his daughter Olive prohibited from taking to the hot springs in Aliwal North, even to save her life. It is 'useless', he said, 'to go and tell our people that the home Government is absolutely powerless', and he pointed to instances where the imperial government had intervened in colonial affairs. All he requested was that 'you should consider us in the land of our fathers'. 'The native has no place to go. Our one crime is not that we want to be equals of the Dutch but that we are loyal to a foreign flag, the Union Jack. If it offers us no protection then our case is indeed hopeless.'[31]

In the view of one of the West Africans present, 'the tale of woe unfolded by Mr Sol Plaatje to the Prime Minister that evening was enough to melt the heart of the most callous negrophobe'. It certainly affected the prime minister. If the responsibilities of office had dimmed his earlier radicalism, Lloyd George remained one of the great orators of his day, and his sympathies were easily aroused. It was as though Plaatje, with his eloquent and very personal declaration about the injustices suffered by his people and by his own family, had touched a sensitive chord that brought back to the old Welsh radical his own more youthful tirades against the injustices of British society twenty years earlier. Dropping in the term 'land of our fathers', title of the Welsh national anthem, can only have helped stir his emotions.[32]

In reply, Lloyd George rehearsed the constitutional position but told them he had listened 'with some distress to the story you have told of restrictions which are imposed upon you in your native land', and he thought they had presented their case 'with very great power'. 'You have said enough', he said, 'to convince me that it is certainly a case which ought to be taken into the consideration of the South African government and I shall certainly take the earliest opportunity of presenting the whole of the facts to General Smuts', now prime minister of South Africa. They were the kind of words and sentiments which the Colonial Office officials, even in their unguarded moments, would never have uttered. Henry Lambert's concern about how the prime minister might react was entirely justified. Plaatje himself thought Lloyd George had been 'amazed' and 'greatly shocked' by what he had heard; Eldred Taylor, too, thought he looked 'visibly moved' and spoke afterwards of being struck forcibly by 'the sincere feeling' exhibited by the prime minister.[33]

Lloyd George was as good as his word about communicating with General Smuts. In two remarkable letters, filed away as 'secret' in the Colonial Office files, he wrote at some length to express his concern about the 'deep sense of injustice' which the Congress delegates had conveyed to him. They had been told they ought not to ventilate their grievances outside South Africa and that they should seek reforms by constitutional means. 'But, they asked, what was the use of calling upon them to obey the law and observe constitutional methods in their agitation for betterment and reform if they were given no adequate constitutional means for doing so?' 'If this is a correct statement of the facts', Lloyd George wrote, this 'seems to me a very powerful point', and he suggested that Smuts might meet with the delegates once they were back in South Africa. 'They presented their case with moderation, with evident sincerity, and with power. It is evident that you have in Africa men who can speak for native opinion and make themselves felt, not only within their country, but outside. I am sure you will be impressed by them, and I am equally sure that you will be able to remove the impression which seems to rest there at present, that they cannot get people in authority to listen to them with sympathy.'[34]

As though one letter was not enough, Lloyd George reiterated his concerns in a second, unofficial letter, marked 'Private and Confidential' and 'for your private eye', urging Smuts to do what he could to meet the legitimate grievances of the people he had seen. He mentioned again their 'very considerable oratorical gifts', and said that they made their case 'exceedingly well'. Recalling his ill-tempered meeting with the Afrikaner nationalists in Versailles, he drew an interesting comparison: 'The contrast between the case made by these black men and by the Deputation headed by General Hertzog was very striking', he wrote. 'They are evidently capable, not only of rousing their people, but of rousing public feeling in other countries. I am told that many of them have been going about the country lecturing at Labour Party meetings and Brotherhood meetings, and that they have produced some effect', showing themselves capable of securing 'the sympathy of people of power and influence in this country'.[35]

But there were bigger issues at stake and this is what really concerned Lloyd George. Having alluded to the stirrings of black nationalism in his first letter, he now emphasised the growing threat of 'Bolshevism' and 'Garveyism' to 'not only the British Commonwealth, but the whole existing structure of society', worried that unrest in South Africa could have much wider ramifications. He again urged General Smuts 'to see these people and consider if anything can be done to redress any real grievances from which they suffer, and to satisfy any legitimate aspirations'. 'If they do suffer under disabilities', he said, 'and if they have no effective mode of expression it is obvious that sooner or later serious results must ensue.' And not just for South Africa.

Smuts's reply, when it came, simply reiterated the points his government had made to the SANNC's original memorial (the 'appalling document') in December 1918: Congress was not a representative organisation; the claims of the delegates were 'more specious than true, and largely amount to *suggestio falsi*'; his government was working on what he described as 'improved machinery for voicing the needs and interests of the Natives'; and the delegates should in any case have availed themselves of the constitutional means available to them in South Africa before seeking to publicise their case outside by 'distortion and exaggeration'. Smuts, it is clear, was irritated by the seriousness with which the British prime minister had taken the complaints of the Congress deputation, and did not much care to be advised on what he should or should not do about it. What he made of the contrast Lloyd George drew between the Congress deputation, headed by Plaatje, and the Afrikaner nationalist deputation, led by General Hertzog, is unrecorded; the comparison would have caused consternation in South Africa had it been made public.[36]

It is a pity that Plaatje never knew of the letters that passed between the two prime ministers. He had always believed in his own ability to persuade even the most highly placed individuals to his way of thinking, and Lloyd George's reaction to their interview was striking, indeed spectacular, confirmation of this. At the same time the fact that the prime minister could do no more than write a worried letter or two to General Smuts demonstrated very clearly the limits to the effectiveness of personal appeals of this kind. Even the sympathy of the British prime minister could not alter the fact that Britain shared, by virtue of her colonial position, a common stance with South Africa, the inheritance of many years of careful policy development in 'native affairs' and imperial policy more generally. The people Plaatje really needed to convert were the hard-headed officials of the Colonial Office, and there was never much prospect of that. Henry Lambert, like Smuts, thought the prime minister took Plaatje and his colleagues much too seriously, especially when he realised that the letter to Smuts on 3 March was 'the first formal dispatch the PM has ever written to a Dominion', on any subject. Highly sensitive to accusations of interference in the affairs of the dominions, he did not consider this a welcome precedent.[37]

Plaatje's achievement was to have mobilised the support and connections required to secure the interview in the first place, in the face of opposition from the Colonial Office, and then to have so impressed the prime minister with the strength of their case that it prompted him to communicate his concerns to General Smuts. He had taken the technique of personal appeal to its furthest limits. It was a moment when one of his great strengths as an individual, and the weakness of the position in which he so often found himself, stood clearly revealed.

Unfortunately for Plaatje and his colleagues, the meeting with the prime minister had taken place on the strict understanding that its proceedings would remain confidential, and that nothing was to be said to the press – even though no such restrictions had been applied to Lloyd George's meeting with General Hertzog in France. The Congress delegates kept their word, denying themselves the opportunity to exploit what was by any standards a considerable coup – and the two West African newspapermen were likewise obliged to keep their silence on what would otherwise have been a scoop for them too.[38]

※

Levi Mvabaza and Henry Ngcayiya departed for South Africa shortly after this, but Plaatje, Gumede and Thema, encouraged by the prime minister's words, carried on with the campaign. Plaatje gave a long interview, published in the Independent Labour Party's *Labour Leader*, to a young left-wing journalist called Fenner Brockway, who was struck by the 'gentle refinement about his features' and the 'fire of passionate indignation against the wrongs committed upon his race'; he made a brief visit to France 'on deputation work', he said, most likely with the help of French Brotherhood contacts; and he compiled a pamphlet entitled *Some of the Legal Disabilities Suffered by the Native Population of the Union of South Africa and Imperial Responsibility*, notable for its attempt to draw attention to the so-called Byles Resolution of 1906, a noble (but hitherto forgotten) statement of imperial responsibility for the interests of the 'native races' who were without representation in the legislative assemblies of the colonies in which they lived.[39]

Interestingly enough, Plaatje seems to have written this pamphlet at the suggestion of John Harris, secretary of the Anti-Slavery and Aborigines' Protection Society – rather ironic in view of his energetic attempts to suppress and denigrate *Native Life in South Africa* in 1916. It is clear that Harris's views of the South African situation had altered considerably since Plaatje's first visit. He may have rid his committee of Mrs Solomon and Mrs Unwin, but it was a close-run thing, and he had been shaken by the whole episode. Now, with the emergence of several new organisations associated with the *African Telegraph*, he seems at last to have realised that his uncritical support for the policies of the South African government was distancing his organisation from progressive opinion.

Plaatje's antipathy towards Harris had mellowed too. Despite not being informed about the decision to send a deputation to London, Harris's attitude towards its members, once they arrived, was not unfriendly, and Plaatje appreciated his assistance in the *Edinburgh Castle* affair. The truth was they could not afford to ignore one other: Plaatje because of his deputation's desperate financial situation, Harris because he realised he had to change his stance if his society was to retain any credibility in a rapidly changing post-war world. Another sign of Harris's change of heart was that it was he who had arranged for Plaatje to address the National Liberal Club, using his influence as a member of its Foreign and Colonial sub-committee. After that he encouraged Plaatje to 'put in written form some of the principal grievances and disabilities from which the Natives are suffering in the Union territories' and was very pleased with the result: *Legal Disabilities* was 'excellent', he thought, and even suggested his society might be able to assist with printing costs. This was a world away from the unremitting hostility of 1916 and 1917.[40]

In the event Plaatje did not need Harris's help. *Legal Disabilities* was printed and published instead by the proprietors of the *African Telegraph*. 'Further information on this and cognate subjects', so the pamphlet advised, could be obtained not only from Plaatje at 43 Tavistock Square, but from Robert Broadhurst, secretary of the African Progress Union and a leading figure in London's African community, and from Audrey Jeffers, a young woman from Trinidad, training as a social worker, who was 'Hon. Sec of the West African and West Indians' Christian Union'. These were the people from whom Plaatje could now expect support in his campaign. The world was changing.

❧

On his return from France Plaatje went straight to Scotland, spending the second week of December 1919 lecturing and addressing meetings in and around Edinburgh and Glasgow, arranged for him by the Independent Labour Party and the Union of Democratic Control. 'I start there with a study circle of 500 members at 11.30,' he wrote, 'then I am to address a Brotherhood of 2,000 members at 3 p.m. and wind up the day with a Labour mass meeting in the large metropole at 8 p.m. Yet some people call this a holiday!'[41]

Scotland proved to be quite an eye-opener. On 'Red Clydeside' it was a time of unprecedented labour militancy and Plaatje's message went down well, confirming many in their belief in the iniquities of the capitalist system worldwide: that there should be 'Slavery under the British flag', the title of a lecture he gave on several occasions, came as no surprise at all to the kind of audiences who had come to hear him. Opposed as he was to the methods and doctrines of the socialists and communists among his own people in South Africa, in England and even more in Scotland, it was precisely in such circles that he now met with the most sympathetic response – even if, as he recalled, he 'never heard more arguments against Christianity than I did one week-end on Glasgow Green'. The paradox did not bother him unduly. 'I had great times in Scotland', he told Mrs

Colenso. 'There is much to do there if it could be revisited. Great times among the Socialists and U.D.C. members. Shared one Edinburgh meeting with Mrs Helen Crawfurd, the Socialist speaker. We stayed in the same hotel and sat till LATE exchanging views. I have learned MUCH from her while she thinks I have taught her a lot.'[42]

Plaatje knew he could ill afford to be too choosy about his friends and allies. Even so, he would have seen the irony in being acclaimed by *Forward*, the journal of the Scottish Independent Labour Party, as 'probably the first black lecturer to appear on the Socialist platform in this country'. And what, one wonders, would he have made of the following piece of advice which appeared in *The Workers' Dreadnought* ('For Revolutionary Socialism, the ending of Capitalism and Parliament, and the substitution of a World Federation of Workers' Industrial Republics')? 'The South African deputation has been well received by many sections of the labour movement. It will travel round the country, addressing enthusiastic meetings, and finally it will return to South Africa, if it is wise, to build up the International Socialists, a solid organization of black and white working together, without distinction of colour, race, or creed, to wrest power from the capitalists and to establish the African Soviets.' It was not quite what he had in mind.[43]

At the end of December 1919 Plaatje returned, tired out, to London and spent the New Year recuperating in the company of the Colenso family in Amersham. Physical exhaustion was taking its toll. Even before embarking upon his gruelling Scottish tour, Alice Werner had commented 'poor Plaatje is nearly worn out', and the few days he spent at 'Elangeni' provided some much-needed rest. Here he could relax in friendly company, a substitute of sorts for his own wife and family in yet another year spent away from them. There were long discussions over the affairs of the deputation and many other subjects, and conversations that alternated between English, German and Zulu as though this was the most natural thing in the world – all in an atmosphere in which the great Bishop Colenso, though dead for nearly forty years, was almost a living presence. 'Elangeni' provided for Plaatje an escape to a world in which he fitted easily, enjoying the company of people of comfortable means, sharing common values and attitudes to race, religion and politics. He appreciated the 'kindness and intelligent love' he encountered there; the 'exquisite music' Mrs Colenso's daughters played, 'the cozy coteries at meal times', 'the alfresco promenades to, from and through the beautiful grounds of Elangeni'.[44]

The Colensos, for their part, delighted in Plaatje's lively company, 'his unfailing humour and irresistible laugh' – and the amused pride he took in African custom and tradition when it differed from theirs. Modiri Molema remembered this too. Plaatje used to astound people in England, Molema said, by chewing or sucking the marrow out of meat bones when sitting down at a meal. Remonstrate with him and you would just get the response, 'Are you telling me to leave the best part of the meat? Not me!' Or if you offered him sugar to add to porridge and milk, he would exclaim in a loud voice, 'I am not going to spoil the pure natural taste of milk with sugar!'[45]

The few days Plaatje spent at 'Elangeni' to see in the new year, accompanied by Gumede and Selope Thema, provided only a brief respite from an arduous programme. They maintained their momentum over the next few weeks and continued to attract large audiences, especially outside London; in the third week of January, for example, Plaatje drew record numbers to a meeting of the Portsmouth Brotherhood (the largest in the country) and a generous donation to his cause. Indeed, it was to the Brotherhood movement that he now looked to sustain his campaign, particularly after attending the International Brotherhood Congress in London in September 1919. This was an impressive gathering, attended by delegates from many parts of the world, and his own address was warmly received. More than that, he was elected a member of the business committee of the International Federation, and was involved in drafting both a new constitution and the 'Brotherhood challenge', a stirring document calling upon nations and individuals to unite to construct a post-war world of peace and brotherhood.[46]

The International Brotherhood Congress also provided the opportunity to solicit support for his own Brotherhood organisation in Kimberley, now heavily in debt; and to seek contributions towards another scheme he had been working on, translating the *Fellowship Hymn-Book*, used by the Brotherhood movement, into Setswana and several other African languages. He had already prepared versions in Setswana and Xhosa by the time he arrived in England in 1919, and at the Brotherhood Congress he received a number of promises to finance their printing and publication, especially from the Canadian delegates who took a particular interest in his work.[47]

The support of these people was vital to his plans to travel to North America. S.M. Makgatho, president of the SANNC, was keen for him to take their case to the United States, but was in no position to provide any funds. He had been unable, in fact, to repay money advanced to the delegates by the Anti-Slavery and Aborigines' Protection Society, and the Congress had not paid Elizabeth the £6 a month as promised. The Brotherhood movement, by contrast, held out far more hope, particularly in view of his success in making contacts among the American and Canadian delegates who attended the International Congress. It was here that the idea of undertaking a lecturing and speaking tour in America under Brotherhood auspices took shape, and he hoped to get there in time to attend the next international Brotherhood Federation conference in Washington DC in May 1920.[48]

He began to make other preparations too, writing to several prominent African Americans to inform them of his plans and to seek their support. These included his long-time correspondent John E. Bruce, now working as a journalist in New York, who promised to do all he could to help. Bruce then wrote to John W. Cromwell, another well-known figure, who was at that time president of the American Negro Academy, asking him to get in touch with Plaatje immediately 'and take charge of him when he visits Washington as he hopes to do in May next'. Cromwell, to whom Plaatje also wrote separately, duly replied with a welcoming letter. These were just the people whose support he would need if his projected visit to the United States was to succeed, and the warmth of their initial reaction was most encouraging.[49]

In the middle of March 1920 Plaatje set about obtaining the travel documents he would need. It was the beginning of another long battle. He hoped the United States consul in London would issue him with the necessary passport. Inevitably it did not prove to be straightforward. When he visited the offices of the consulate he was pleasantly surprised to find several African American clerks working there, but bitterly disappointed at the response to his request. Clearance from the South African government would first be required, he was informed, and he would have to pay for the telegrams that had to be sent to South Africa to make the necessary enquiries.[50]

Unknown to Plaatje, his request was then dealt with at the highest level. George H. Murphy, the US consul general in Cape Town, acting for his counterpart in London, first of all telephoned Edward Barrett, the under-secretary for native affairs, to ask him what he knew of Plaatje. The answer, it seems, was a great deal. Barrett, since his appointment, had made it his business to keep abreast of Plaatje's activities, and was well aware of the impact he was capable of making both locally and internationally; indeed, a powerful reminder of Plaatje's capacity to cause trouble was about to land on his desk in the form of a request to draft a response to the letter Lloyd George had sent to General Smuts after his meeting with the SANNC delegates in London.[51]

Understandably, Barrett did not relish the prospect of Plaatje making his way to the US and responded immediately to Murphy's phone call, hurrying round to his office to make his views known. He then consulted with the minister to whom he was responsible, F.S. Malan. To his surprise and irritation, Malan, with whom he had a difficult relationship at the best of times, took a different view: 'he desires me to inform you', Barrett had to tell Murphy, 'that whilst not desirous of encouraging the enterprise in any way the Union Government does not wish to throw any difficulty in the way of Mr Plaatje'. The minister, who had seen Plaatje on the morning of his departure from South Africa in 1919, clearly took a more relaxed view of his travel plans.[52]

Murphy communicated this rather mixed message back to London, adding that he did not himself believe that it was advisable to allow Plaatje to visit the US. He suspected that 'his proposed lecturing tour has the double object of raising funds and of perhaps causing international bad feeling by appealing for sympathy for a movement which is not approved of by the government and people of South Africa'. And he suggested, in order to avoid controversy and to keep within the remit of their standing instructions, that in the event of the London consulate deciding to refuse Plaatje a visa, 'you base the refusal upon the object of his journey not being a sufficiently urgent one'.[53]

All of which left the US consul in London in a quandary. Unsure about whose advice to follow, he sought clarification from the British Foreign Office, who in turn referred the matter back to Pretoria with a request for a definite indication on 'whether the endorsement is to be granted or refused'. This time the response, left in the hands of Edward Barrett, was unambiguous: Plaatje's request was to be refused, and he set out the reasons why. 'Plaatje's lectures will no doubt consist of mendacious attacks upon the Union Government.' He had before him some press clippings of Plaatje's meetings in London, confirming, as Lloyd George put it in his letter to General Smuts, that they were men 'capable not only of rousing their people, but of rousing people in other countries'. Like Lloyd George, Barrett was concerned about the 'mischievous activities' of Marcus Garvey's Universal Negro Improvement Association: 'If Plaatje proceeds to the United States, he is pretty certain to link up Native activities here with this American organisation.'[54]

Barrett came up with two further reasons for denying Plaatje a passport: first, his presence was required in Kimberley to sort out the 'financial affairs of the "Brotherhood" founded by him which are seriously out of order'; secondly, Plaatje and the other Congress delegates in England were 'a constant source of embarrassment on account of their many difficulties'. 'I think', he concluded, 'that the passport might be refused and the reason might be alleged that apart from other considerations the financial difficulties already encountered show that the overseas peregrinations of political natives are likely to create trouble for themselves, embarrassment to the government and perplexity to responsible societies in the countries they visit.' A telegram was accordingly sent to the South African High Commission in London who in turn informed the Foreign Office and the American consulate of the South African government's decision.

370

Last to know was Plaatje himself, for whom this was a bitter disappointment. All he got for the $40 he was charged for the telegrams, he complained, was the bald message 'that it was not necessary for him to visit the United States'.[55]

Most likely the Americans would have reached this decision independently. They too had reason to be concerned at the rapid growth of Garvey's Universal Negro Improvement Association, and had they looked closely at the current files of the intelligence-gathering agency attached to the London consulate, busy at that time in monitoring the activities of American socialists in England, they would have found a report of a meeting held under the auspices of the Independent Labour Party in Falkirk which Plaatje had addressed during his Scottish tour. In the circumstances the American authorities can hardly have wished to encourage Plaatje's visit to the US either, if this was the company he kept: a socialist would have been unwelcome, a black socialist doubly so.[56]

With a visit to the United States ruled out, for the time being at any rate, Plaatje was forced to consider other options. On offer, if he wanted it, was a well-paid job in Johannesburg as editor of a new newspaper, *Umteteli wa Bantu* (*The Mouthpiece of the Native Peoples*), about to be launched by the Chamber of Mines. For a while he seems at least to have considered this possibility. The idea had originated the previous year when a group of conservative African political leaders in the Transvaal, Saul Msane and Isaiah Bud-M'belle among them, approached the Chamber of Mines for support for a new newspaper which would provide an alternative voice to *Abantu-Batho*, then controlled by the more radical Transvaal branch of the Native Congress. Their approach was not successful, however, and the Chamber turned down their request, preferring to take forward a plan of their own under the auspices of the Native Recruiting Corporation, part of their organisation, and thus to have direct control. By January 1920 they had purchased a second-hand printing press and prepared to launch a new paper with the objective, so they said, of dispelling 'certain erroneous ideas cherished by many natives and sedulously fostered by European and Native agitators, and by certain Native newspapers'. A massive strike by black miners the following month gave added urgency to the project.[57]

Who, then, was to be the editor? Since the Native Recruiting Corporation was doing its best to disguise its association with the new venture (having set up a 'Native Printing and Publishing Company' as notional proprietors) and to present the newspaper as a genuine organ of African opinion, an African editor was clearly a *sine qua non*. Saul Msane had wanted to edit the paper when the idea was first mooted, but he died at the end of 1919. In his place, when the first issue of *Umteteli* appeared in May 1920, was an altogether more impressive-looking line-up, for the names of John Dube and Sol Plaatje now appeared as joint editors under the editorial masthead. Here were two of the leading African political figures of the day, both of them experienced newspaper editors, both apparently involved. As a means of establishing *Umteteli*'s credibility, Henry Taberer, managing director of the Native Recruiting Corporation, could scarcely have done better.[58]

Quite what this meant is not at all clear. For a while John Dube was active on behalf of the new venture, notwithstanding the conflict of interest that arose from his being, at the same time, proprietor (and editor-in-chief) of his own weekly newspaper, *Ilanga lase Natal*. Plaatje's situation, six thousand miles away, was very different. It seems he had some discussions with representatives of the Chamber of Mines in London, but whether he ever seriously considered returning to South Africa to assume its editorship is doubtful: had he really wished to do so, they would surely have paid his passage back home.[59]

Possibly he allowed his name to be used on the understanding that there would be editorial independence, keeping his options open while he considered other possibilities. Once he became aware of the true nature of *Umteteli wa Bantu*, however, becoming its editor was out of the question. Although he was, in a general way, favourably disposed towards both the mining houses and business, regarding a hostile government as the main difficulty, he knew perfectly well that too close an association with them could destroy his own political credibility among his people, not all of whom shared his view of the potentially progressive nature of the mining houses. Whatever degree of editorial freedom Plaatje may have been promised, the fact remained that this new newspaper was owned by the mining industry, to be run in its interest and not that of the African people: they could not always be expected to be in harmony.

He had only to think of Tengo Jabavu to be reminded of the dangers. When Jabavu's long-established newspaper, *Imvo Zabantsundu*, ran into difficulties in the early years of the twentieth century, he had been forced to cede control to a group of shareholders who supported the policies of the first Union administration, including the Natives' Land Act of 1913. In coming out in favour of the Act, and following the views of his shareholders – three of them members of the first Union cabinet – Jabavu's reputation was all but destroyed. 'God forbid', Plaatje wrote, when recounting this in *Native Life in South Africa*, 'that we should ever find that our mind has become the property of someone other than ourselves'. Editing a newspaper funded by the Chamber of Mines, he knew full well, carried just that danger.

By August 1920 Plaatje had decided to have no more to do with *Umteteli wa Bantu*. Writing to Silas Molema, he told him of the offer he had received from Taberer, and that he was turning it down. He had no desire to live in Johannesburg ('that hell'), or to give up the vote that he enjoyed, as a resident of Kimberley and the Cape Province, in parliament, on the divisional and town councils, and on the local school board: 'if I go to Transvaal', he said, 'all that is finished'. Instead he appealed to Silas Molema for help in restarting *Tsala* once he returned to South Africa: to create a newspaper in which Setswana was the language used, where the cause of the Batswana would again be to the fore. If Molema could help in this way, so Plaatje wrote, 'everything will come right and we will resuscitate the *Tsala* again'. That was his dream.[60]

Declining the offer of the editorship of *Umteteli*, attractive as it must have been financially, was the right decision. Several months later he would learn of the underhand methods the management of *Umteteli* resorted to as they tried to put *Abantu-Batho* out of business. Plaatje could never have been a party to this and retained at the same time any degree of political credibility. He did well, in short, to end his association with the owners of *Umteteli*, and from August 1920 his name – as well as that of John Dube – disappeared from its masthead.[61]

So Plaatje remained in London, still living in lodgings at 43 Tavistock Square in Bloomsbury. Despite being refused a passport, he had not given up hope of getting to America, but he worried about the gloomy news he received from home about the difficulties of his Brotherhood organisation in Kimberley. His financial situation again became acute: 'I nearly died of hunger but Thaba Nchu came to my rescue on each occasion', he told Silas Molema. Daniel Jones, at University College, put some work his way, but it was much less frequent than before and cannot have brought in much. Alice Werner probably helped too. Once, when he visited the London School of Oriental Studies, where she now worked, he remembered meeting the famous West African educationist, J.E.K. Aggrey, on his way from America to Africa as a member of the Phelps Stokes Education Commission.[62]

In the middle of May 1920, there was welcome relief from an unexpected source: a £50 grant from the Royal Literary Fund to whom he had applied for help. The fund existed to support published authors who had fallen on hard times. His friend Dr T.E. Scholes had long been a beneficiary and this may well be how he heard about it. In making his case, Plaatje blamed his difficulties on the collapse of *Tsala ea Batho* during the war, and the impossibility of restarting it because of the continued high cost of paper. His savings, he told the fund, were exhausted and his current financial predicament 'precarious and uncertain'. His application had the support of Daniel Jones, who spoke highly of his 'personal character and of his ability', and William Cross, who said he was a particularly deserving case since his publications were 'valuable from an educational and literary point of view, and are remarkable considering that no other South African native has contributed to English literature'.[63]

With his finances at least temporarily repaired, Plaatje was able to make a second trip to Scotland, visiting Modiri Molema in Glasgow on the day the young doctor's first book, *The Bantu Past and Present*, was published. Subtitled 'an ethnographical and historical study of the native races of South Africa', it was an ambitious attempt to describe the life of his people, drawing largely on published sources, and Molema hoped that it might help mitigate the 'misunderstanding and contempt' to which he believed they were subjected. Plaatje was full of praise, and greatly enjoyed it: 'God only knows where you raked up these stories', he wrote to him after his visit: 'they are so humorously put that often when I took it up after working tired and late and lie down about midnight it has kept me roaring with laughter sometimes till the small hours; and I have felt lonely since Mr Cross took it away.'[64]

The long delays Modiri Molema had experienced before the book was published brought back memories of his own struggles. 'I had to wait 11 months fighting Harris who was battling to suppress *Native Life* in the press and the waiting was unbearable', he wrote, congratulating Molema on his patience in coping with the 'ordeal' of having to wait 'three whole years for the paper'. His only regret, he said, was that his book 'will excite the jealousies of the very Bantu for whose benefit you have laboured thus unselfishly for the book is BIG. Other tribes will maliciously belittle your efforts while the 200,000 Barolongs will offer you their lip loyalty instead of recommending the book to possible buyers.' Only to a fellow Morolong could he express such sentiments.

The six days they spent together gave plenty of opportunity to discuss his own literary plans, for over the last few months these had become a major preoccupation. After his visit to Scotland he wrote to Modiri's father Silas to put him in the picture too: 'I am still busy writing two books. One is a novel – a love story after the manner of romances; but based on historical facts.' These 'historical facts' related to the experiences of the Barolong in the 1830s and 1840s, beginning with their 'smash-up' by Mzilikazi's Ndebelele at the battle of Kunana in 1830, taking in the arrival of Boer Voortrekkers, their military alliance with the Barolong and ultimately the defeat of Mzilikazi's mighty army – all 'with plenty of love, superstition, and imaginations worked in between the wars'. It was, he added, 'just like the style of Rider Haggard when he writes about the

Zulus'. He had completed this book 'and it is looking for a publisher. Now I am finishing the political work something like *Native Life* which will bring the native troubles up to date.'[65]

The second of these books, 'the political work something like Native Life', was never published, and it seems unlikely it was ever completed. Plaatje probably conceived it as a narrative of political events in South Africa from 1915 or 1916, combined with an account of his own travels and observations in the rural parts of the country after his return in 1917. From his request for information to the administrator of Southern Rhodesia in April 1919, which he told him was for 'a companion volume' to *Native Life in South Africa*, and his remark that 'some mention will be made of Mr Harris's Society', it is clear he also intended to include an account of his differences with John Harris and his society during his time in England.[66]

Only a small part of this 'companion volume' has survived. In a notebook dating from this time there are ten pages of handwritten notes and a narrative for a section of the book. Although in a very rough draft, these pages provide a systematic account of the discriminatory laws then in operation in South Africa, broken down province by province. His starting point was his *Legal Disabilities* pamphlet, written at the end of 1919, and some of its pages, heavily annotated, have been pasted into the notebook and then added to by hand. He had most to say about the disabilities suffered by his people in the Orange Free State. Here, he wrote, 'a native is only tolerated when he works for a white man'; he was unable to 'own freehold property and he cannot trade'. 'Even if he works to the satisfaction of his white master he cannot even live in town.'

After describing the host of other restrictions that applied in the Free State, Plaatje then posed the question: 'Where do these natives come from? That they should be subject to a law unheard of in the annals of the Empire of a man being by law denied the right to purchase landed property in this interesting Province?' He answered as follows: 'Let's go to the beginning. In the year 1830 the Barolongs of Moroka had crossed over from Bechuanaland into a place called Platberg. It is just on the border of Griqualand West, Transvaal and Free State but it is in OFS property. The people had during the Matabele depredation met the Rev. Mr Broadbent, a Missionary sent by the Wesleyans among the Bechuana and after a few days at Platberg (at Motlana's pitse), as it was then called, decided that the place was unhealthy and many of the Barolongs were dying. So a movement was made to Basutoland and Chief Mosheshwe, the founder of the Basuto nation, gave the newcomers a refuge in his territory.'[67]

There follows a five-page account of the subsequent history of the Barolong: the attacks of the Matabele, the friendship between chiefs Moroka and

Moshoeshoe, the arrival in 1834 of the Boer Voortrekkers, their rescue by the Barolong and the military alliance that followed, the defeat of Mzilikazi, the subsequent proclamation of the Orange Free State. This was the same series of historical events that provides the setting for the other manuscript Plaatje mentioned in his letter to Silas Molema – the 'love story after the manner of romances; but based on historical facts', which would eventually be published, ten years later, as *Mhudi*.

There was thus an important connection between the proposed companion volume to *Native Life* and the romance novel. Both were written at around the same time, and pages of each appear in draft form in the same notebook, non-fiction and fiction set down side by side. The question he posed about the origins of the African people of the Orange Free State became a point of departure for *Mhudi* too. He seems to have arrived at the realisation, as he delved into the history of the Barolong, not only that he had far more material than he could reasonably include in a 'political work', but that he could only do it justice in a different literary form.

A knowledge of these shared beginnings may help to explain why the 'political work' has just disappeared. If it was ever completed, there is no evidence to suggest he tried to get it published, in contrast to his well-documented efforts over the next few years on behalf of both *Mhudi* and his translations of the *Fellowship Hymn-Book*. Perhaps he just recognised that the time for appealing to the British public, to plead for intervention in South African affairs, had now passed – and that without this immediate political purpose it was just not worth expending the huge effort that would be needed to get it into print. Better, rather, to concentrate his efforts on completing *Mhudi*, and to leave aside the 'political work', especially if he could achieve some of the same objectives.

What particular literary form, then, would work best for the kind of book he now envisaged? His letter to Silas Molema provides the essential clue. When he said his novel was 'just like the style of Rider Haggard when he writes about the Zulus', there is no reason to doubt his word. He must have been familiar with Rider Haggard's novels and had probably read many of them years ago. Haggard's South African romances, inspired by his stay in Natal and the Transvaal in the 1870s and 1880s, were popular in South Africa at the time he was busy improving his English in Kimberley in the 1890s, and were read by black and white alike. They would have been a natural choice of reading matter, along with other popular storytellers like Arthur Conan Doyle whose Sherlock Holmes novels he certainly knew. It is thus not hard to imagine that copies of *King Solomon's Mines* (1885), or *She* (1886), or *Nada the Lily* (1892), three of the best known of Haggard's novels, were among the 'English books' Ernst Westphal noticed on his shelves in 1895.

Since then Haggard had written over forty novels, a third of which could be said to be 'about the Zulus'. More than any other writer he had popularised their history, conjuring up powerful images of the Zulu past, and of their great king Shaka. Admiration for the Zulus' martial spirit and military prowess went hand in hand with a sense of the tragic inevitability, but ultimate justice, of their defeat by the British. His tales struck a rich seam in the British psyche, and he often returned to this subject. In 1919 he published *Finished*, the third in a new Zulu trilogy, following on from *Child of Storm* (1913) and *Marie* (1912). His books may no longer have sold in quite such vast numbers as before but they remained popular, and he had largely defined the genre. A number of his books were turned into films, keeping them in the public eye. *Child of Storm* was even dramatised for the stage, being performed when Plaatje was in London in 1914.[68]

Of all Haggard's Zulu novels, *Nada the Lily* was the one Plaatje was drawn to, and it served as both model and inspiration for *Mhudi*. Set in the time of Shaka and his successor Dingane, *Nada the Lily* tells the tale of Umslopogaas (an illegitimate son of Shaka) and his love for the beautiful Nada, drawing upon both real and fictional characters. Haggard's aim, so he said in his preface to the book, was 'to convey in narrative form some idea of the remarkable spirit which animated these kings and their subjects', to revisit long-lost 'incidents of history' and to make them 'accessible, in a popular shape' – all of it in a time 'when the Zulus were still a nation'. Unusually for a Victorian novel, it had an all-black cast, and the narrator, Mopo, the father of Nada, was black too. The result was a beguiling mixture of realism and fantasy, widely regarded as one of Haggard's best pieces of work. Haggard certainly thought so, as did his friend Rudyard Kipling, who told him that his own *Jungle Stories* were inspired by the fantasy of Galazi and the Wolves, one of his most imaginative creations in *Nada the Lily*.[69]

There are striking parallels between *Mhudi* and *Nada the Lily*. Both feature a peaceful pastoral idyll at the beginning, a town sacked, the wanderings of hero and heroine, lion stories to test courage, the entry of the Boers half-way through the narrative, an alliance of blacks and whites against a cruel oppressor, the device of a narrator to help convey a sense of realism, the use of prophecy. In both novels a love story provides the central motif, and it is the heroine who gives her name to each title. Both novels are set in a period in southern African history shaped by the expansion of the Zulu kingdom, and explore the lives of those affected by the violence and bloodshed that followed. There are distinct echoes too in some of the language used. 'Ah! Where is U'Faku now?' asks Mopo of the Amapondo chief, relating the exploits of Shaka's impis in *Nada the Lily*; 'Where is Chaka's dynasty now?' demands Mzilikazi in *Mhudi*, as he prepares to flee his foes. In *Nada*, a lion 'roared till the earth shook'; in *Mhudi*, the heroine confronts a lion that 'gave a startling roar that shook the earth beneath my feet'. In *Nada*, the heroine gathered 'many berries and a root that is good for food'; in *Mhudi*, she 'gathers some roots and wood berries about the slope'.[70]

Plaatje found in *Nada the Lily* both a style to follow and a narrative frame around which he could weave a tale of his own. Other aspects of *Nada*, it is true, were less appealing. For in *Nada*, as in Haggard's other African romances, were inscribed notions of African cruelty and savagery, crude justifications for white racial domination. All the more reason, then, as Plaatje would have seen it, to appropriate this genre, and where necessary to parody it, to counter such stereotypes and to convey a distinctive message of his own. To explore the historical experiences not of the Zulus but of the Barolong, to see the world from their point of view – and to suggest to his readers the lessons they might draw from this.

By drawing upon *Nada the Lily* in this way, selecting those elements he found useful, he could draw in potential readers with a sense of the familiar – but then undermine the conventions of the genre, twist them to his own purposes, and come up with something quite new and distinct. Just how he did this, and the response he elicited, we will return to in chapter 16. Meanwhile, given Rider Haggard's track record and the popularity of his books, he must have felt there was a good chance of finding a publisher for his own reworking of so familiar a fictional form.

For a good part of 1920 *Mhudi* was Plaatje's main priority. When Mrs Unwin wondered when he planned to return to South Africa, he told her he intended staying in England until he had finished the book and found a publisher. He must have hoped that her husband, the publisher T. Fisher Unwin, would express an interest, but there is no sign that he did. One person who did, however, was Alice Werner. As with *Native Life in South Africa* five years earlier, she now agreed to 'look over' the manuscript 'and revise for him'. In private she expressed some reservations. She told Agnes Colenso that it was a difficult task to revise the manuscript as she thought 'it really needs rewriting', and that parts of it were 'too unintentionally funny for anything'. Her main concern, though, which she conveyed to Plaatje too, was that he would have done better to write it in Setswana. 'I think it would have made quite a good piece of work if written in his own language, as Thomas Mofolo and others in Sesuto.'[71]

It was a predictable reaction. Alice Werner was a great enthusiast for African languages, convinced that only they were capable of conveying the inner-most thoughts of those who spoke them; English, by contrast, could 'never effectively express the African mind'. She was not the first, nor would she be the last, to put this kind of view to him. Indeed, by now he was quite used to people wanting him to be more 'authentic', to write and behave more like 'a native'. But English was always his choice of language for *Mhudi*. He was determined to reach an international audience, just as he had with *Native Life*, not least because he had a rather wider message to convey than Alice Werner perhaps realised. She characterised the book as 'a tale of the days of Mzilikazi – told of course from the Mochuana point of view and therefore not very favourable to M', which was true up to a point, but there was always more to it than that. Doubtless he would have agreed that a Setswana version would have been desirable too, but who would publish it? And which of the five existing Tswana orthographies, he might have asked her, was he to use?[72]

While he worked on *Mhudi* Plaatje continued to explore ways of supporting his Brotherhood work in South Africa. Aware of the need to put his fundraising efforts onto a more formal footing, early in July 1920 he met with a group of supporters and formed a South African Bantu Brotherhoods Committee. Its stated purpose was 'to establish and develop Brotherhood work among the South African natives by helping to erect, furnish and maintain meeting halls in some South African centres where regular Brotherhood and Sisterhood work could be conducted'; and also to 'promote Brotherhood amongst the tribes by the printing and circulation of suitable literature in English and the vernacular'. Plaatje and his wife Elizabeth were the 'missioners in South Africa'. Irma Colenso was the committee's secretary, William Cross its treasurer, and William Dixon, now president of the Bedfordshire Brotherhood Federation, an active vice chairman. Sir Richard Winfrey, whom Plaatje had sought unsuccessfully to include in his meeting with Lloyd George, agreed to be chairman.[73]

The committee made some headway in raising funds. On 6 September a successful benefit concert took place in London, courtesy of George Lattimore and his Southern Syncopated Orchestra, still performing in the capital. 'The programme, vocal and instrumental,' so it was reported, 'was delivered with a sprightly rendering and a good swing. The singers, who were in excellent voice, had a good reception.' In the interval William Dixon, on behalf of the committee, thanked both the venue (the Kingsway Hall) and the orchestra for their support; Plaatje, seconding, said that 'no place stood in greater need of brotherhood ideas than his homeland, the Union of South Africa'. Twenty members of the Leighton

Men's Meeting came along to lend their support too.[74]

Sitting in the front row of the audience that evening were the members of a delegation from the National Congress of British West Africa, visiting London in pursuit of a greater share in the administration of the several colonies they represented. Plaatje hoped they might be able to provide some financial assistance, and he enlisted the support of Robert Broadhurst, then lobbying on the congress's behalf. If they would grant Plaatje an interview, Broadhurst told them, he 'would willingly give an exposé of the case and what opposition he has experienced both in South Africa and recently in London in advancing the Cause of Africans'. They were unable, however, to help, 'save that it regrets to learn of the financial difficulties of Mr Plaatge [*sic*] and is entirely in sympathy with the native disabilities in South Africa'. Pan-African solidarity had well-defined limits when it came to matters of finance.[75]

Eventually, with the help of Betty Molteno and her niece Margaret Lennox Murray, Plaatje found the money to pay for his passage across the Atlantic; Mrs Murray, he acknowledged later, contributed 'the lion's share' of the cost of his ticket. At the end of September he again applied for a passport. This time he went straight to the South African High Commission in London, only to be told, as before, that it could not be granted to him. In response, and in 'a bitter mood', so he admitted later, 'I lost control of my temper and said things that I regretted afterwards'. He told Mr Sargeant, the official he was dealing with, that he resented being treated like a cow, 'the property of someone, and liable only to move at the behest of my owner', but that he intended to show him that 'you can no more keep me out of the United States than you could have prevented my birth'. In response Mr Sargeant simply 'laughed derisively and said, "I am just going to see how you will land in New York without a passport."'[76]

He had no intention of letting Sargeant know just how he intended to do this. While he needed a passport to enter the United States, this was not the case with Canada. If he could get over there, it would surely be possible to make his way south. He had remained in close contact with members of the Canadian Brotherhood Federation, and it was agreed that he would, for a period of six weeks, lecture and speak under their auspices. They were ideal friends to have, and they provided a cloak of respectability to deter over-zealous customs and immigration officials who might have wondered what else he intended to do in North America.[77]

Several of his English friends, especially Jane Cobden Unwin and Alice

Werner, were against his American venture. They thought he had spent far too long away from home and they worried about his wife and family. Alice Werner, moreover, was perturbed by his apparent enjoyment of life in England, which she thought made things worse. One of her language students, who had just seen him, told her 'Plaatje had said he didn't want to go home at all! but would prefer settling in England'. She admitted to Harriette Colenso that she 'didn't quite understand Plaatje', and was not sure how seriously to take this, recognising that it might just have been 'a polite way of saying how much he was enjoying himself'. She may have been right. Nevertheless, it was the case that he had, since 1914, spent considerably more time in England than South Africa, and in many respects he felt quite at home being there, his financial difficulties notwithstanding. The company of his English friends, freedom from the daily discrimination he faced in South Africa, the cosmopolitan atmosphere of the imperial capital, above all the opportunity to pursue his literary ambitions – living in London did have its attractions.[78]

Of course he had his family's welfare to consider too. Some of the news from home was reassuring. His Brotherhood in Kimberley may have been in difficulties, but his eldest son St Leger had won a bursary to enable him to go to Fort Hare, and Violet too would soon be at Lovedale, training to be a teacher. Overshadowing everything, however, was the continual worry over Olive. She never regained her health after contracting rheumatic fever in the wake of the influenza epidemic, and as time went on her condition deteriorated. Once, in July 1920, at the beginning of a new term, St Leger felt obliged to delay his return to Fort Hare on her account: 'the very serious illness of my younger sister', he told the principal, left him no alternative, and he could not 'leave my mother to face this as she is all alone at present'. Now twenty-one years old, he clearly felt a responsibility to support his mother in the difficult domestic situation she faced. Quite what his feelings were about his absent father at that point can only be guessed at.[79]

Had Plaatje been asked to justify his long absences from home he would have said that political circumstances demanded it, and that he had Elizabeth's support in what he was doing. South Africa was at a critical point in its history and the future of his people, as he saw it, hung in the balance. There was still a chance of outside intervention to help avert disaster, but this was not going to happen of its own accord. He was always adamant that Africans had to argue their own case and not rely on white sympathisers. He had the experience and the ability to do this. Until these bigger political and constitutional questions were resolved, his personal and family life, and that of others like him, would have to take second place. Besides, how was he to earn a living to support his family given the dire economic situation they faced in South Africa? Travelling to Europe, and now to America, would provide a rare opportunity, or so he hoped, to earn some money for his family as well as funds for his Brotherhood organisation.

Nevertheless, there were tensions: between the short term and the long term, between public duty and individual fulfilment, between a wider political cause and the well-being of his family. He would not be the first of his countrymen, nor the last, to have to wrestle with these kinds of conundrums, or to worry about the effects of his long absences on his children's upbringing.

He sailed from Liverpool aboard the Canadian Pacific liner SS *Melita*, bound for Quebec, on 22 October 1920. He took with him hundreds of copies of *Native Life in South Africa* (now in a fourth printing), his *Sechuana Proverbs* and his pamphlet on *Legal Disabilities*, all of which he hoped to be able to sell in order to support himself and his family. As he boarded the ship he picked up 'a nice telegram of well wishes' from Georgiana Solomon, perhaps his most loyal and wholehearted supporter.[80]

Despite the weather – 'dark, wet and foggy' the whole way – he enjoyed the voyage. His fellow passengers, he wrote to Betty Molteno, 'were a motley crowd … Poles from Germany and elsewhere, Irish men and women fleeing the pandemonium in their own country; Jews and other folks from all over the world and a large number of Canadians returning from their summer holidays in Europe'. The last, he thought, were a revelation: 'In the dining rooms, in the cabin and on deck, they came and went precisely as if there were no such thing as colour.' Besides himself there were two other Africans, two coloured women and one Indian – 'all mixed up with the other passengers and everyone was happy'. He shared a large cabin with four Canadians and two Englishmen. He was especially impressed by one of the Canadians, 'an old Ontario magistrate packed with information'; he called him 'a walking American Cyclopedia'. 'What he did not tell me about Canada and the USA was not worth knowing.' Later he admitted to Mrs Solomon that he owed this man a great deal for helping to prepare him for the ways of the new country in which he was about to disembark.[81]

The week-long voyage must also have been an opportunity to look back upon his time in England. There was no denying that the objectives of the original Congress deputation, his main purpose in coming to England, had not been achieved: there was never much prospect that the imperial government would intervene in the affairs of the new dominion, certainly not in the sweeping manner the Congress had demanded. But as no less a person than the British prime minister had acknowledged, Plaatje and his colleagues had made a considerable impact upon British public opinion; they had seen to it that the question of South Africa's policies towards the African population had been raised and discussed in the House of Commons; and they had deeply impressed the prime minister himself, causing him to communicate his concerns to General Smuts.

None of this brought about the changes they wanted, but there were signs that Smuts's tone had changed. He was worried by the growing black militancy of the immediate post-war period, appalled by the SANNC's petition and taken aback by the support the deputation aroused in England. He recognised the need to give responsible African leaders a greater voice, and went further than many thought in setting up both local and national consultative bodies in the Native Affairs Act, which became law in May 1920. Plaatje welcomed this as a step in the right direction. He was not alone in believing that Smuts was at last responding to pressure, and that the SANNC delegation, far from being considered a failure, could claim some of the credit. Smuts had also agreed to become an international vice president of the Brotherhood movement – enabling Plaatje, ever the optimist, to convey news of 'Smuts's conversion' to the cause. Whether a shared Brotherhood ideal carried any prospects of bringing about meaningful change in South Africa was another matter, however. Smuts was always more comfortable on the international than the domestic political stage.[82]

So now it was on to North America. A concern with the affairs of the SANNC had long since given way to a focus on to his own Brotherhood organisation, an inevitable outcome given the failure of the SANNC to support his wife and family or to fund his trip to America. His mission had an important personal dimension too: in his luggage he had his recently completed novel, his translations of the *Fellowship Hymn-Book*, and his translations, into Setswana, of three of Shakespeare's plays – *The Comedy of Errors*, *Julius Caesar* and *The Merchant of Venice*. All were in need not only of publishers but the funds to support their publication. Only the English-language novel was a remotely commercial proposition.[83]

On the eve of his departure he completed the form required by the Canadian immigration authorities. In response to the question about how much money he had with him, he replied '£100', and then gave the name of the Rev. Asher P. Latter, a Methodist clergyman in Winnipeg (and provincial secretary of the Brotherhood Federation of Canada), as the 'friend' he was 'destined to'. They must have met at the International Brotherhood Conference in London the previous year, though it is unlikely Plaatje had any real intention of going to Winnipeg. To question 6, asking him his 'object in coming to Canada', he replied: 'Educational Visit'. Quite why he then described his religion as 'Protestant (Moravian)' rather than 'Protestant (Lutheran)' is difficult to be sure. Most likely it was just to sound less German. His responses revealed his willingness to adjust his purpose and identity to the exigencies of the new challenge that lay ahead.[84]

THIRTEEN

'A wild goose chase'? Canada and the United States, 1920–1922

On arrival in Canada, Plaatje was surprised to encounter a language problem. 'Landing at Quebec', so he wrote to Betty Molteno, 'I was amazed to find that outside the Immigration Offices (where some of the officials speak very imperfect English) I could not get anyone to understand the plainest English question. The population, I am told, is 94% French. Young and old, I could almost always tell beforehand how everyone would answer me, viz: "Nose-peak Ingless"'. What little French he had once learnt at the hands of the Westphals was clearly no solution to the difficulty he faced.[1]

There was also an unfortunate misunderstanding over the arrangements made by the Canadian Brotherhood Federation. 'The Brotherhood', he explained, 'had telegraphed to a friend at Quebec from Montreal to meet me when the steamer arrives. When he reached the wharf I had already left, taken my baggage to the Rly station and was sightseeing in the city. Marvellous Roman Cathedrals and huge Presbyterian edifices in Canadian cities. Poor Mr and Mrs Henderson at Montreal were meeting the evening trains in which they had asked their Quebec friend to book me; but I did not leave Quebec till midnight and reached Montreal early next morning and put up at an hotel where some people speak English.'[2]

Nevertheless, he was delighted with the warmth of his reception by the Canadian Brotherhood Federation, first of all in Montreal where he spent two weeks and then, until the end of January 1921, in Toronto where the Federation had its headquarters. He was fortunate to have arrived at a time when the Canadian Brotherhood movement had achieved, albeit for a short period, a position of some influence in the religious and social life of the country. Founded in 1894, it drew its strength and support, as in England, from the nonconformist churches, and preached the same message of social concern and Christian involvement in the life of the country. The Canadians sent one of the largest delegations to the International Brotherhood Congress in London in September 1919, and were well represented, too, in the second world congress (which Plaatje had hoped at one time to attend) held in Washington DC a year later. Now he was to spend two months addressing church and Brotherhood meetings, aiming, so he said, to work himself 'into the hearts of the leaders of the Canadian Brotherhood Federation'.

Apprehensive about the rigours of a Canadian winter, he was relieved to find the country enjoying its mildest winter since 1863, the weather throughout being 'wonderfully congenial'. 'Beautiful sunny days and starry nights,' he thought, 'especially after the rain, made the chill very agreeable and bracing.'[3]

As ever he succeeded in making a deep impression upon his audiences. 'I once heard him preach to a congregation of about 1,500 white Canadians', recalled one observer. 'Except for occasional ripples of laughter (when he taps a vein of his irresistible humor even at the pulpit) he held them spellbound for 45 minutes, and at the close some said they could have stood another hour of his eloquence. His discourses are a revelation to people who had expected nothing but cannibals from Africa.'[4]

He was just as enthusiastic himself. 'I have been in the City of Toronto at the Brotherhood Headquarters for over a month now', he told Betty Molteno. 'Have spoken and preached at several halls and preached to a number of Methodist and Baptist Congregations. Last Sunday I had in my audience Mr Justice Coatsworth of the Supreme Court. He and his family came to shake hands and congratulate me on my sermon. I went to dinner with his son.' The Canadian Brotherhood Federation promised, moreover, that if he continued to speak for them 'they would make an allowance next February to the World's Brotherhood Conference in London and that when disbursements are made they would strongly recommend my South African work to the World Committee for liberal treatment'.[5]

Even more promising, bearing in mind his plans to take his campaign south to the large black populations of the cities of the United States, was his welcome by Toronto's own black community. One local leader, Arthur C. Holder, an office-holder in the Toronto branch of Marcus Garvey's Universal Negro Improvement Association (UNIA), has left a striking record of the impact Plaatje made during his stay in the city. Unlike many other distinguished African American visitors 'who came and went before many Torontonians had had a chance of meeting them intimately,' he said, 'Hon. Sol Plaatje has been with us now over eight weeks, and in that time he has revealed to us the true inwardness of African character and predilection. His humor, benevolence, good form and catchy conversation have earned for him a place in the hearts of many of us.' He had amazed them with his accounts of 'the sufferings of the lot of the persecuted South African negroes'. 'To hear Mr Plaatje on that subject – the subject of his great work – is to be convinced that the man is not out on his own but called by a higher power as well as by the votes of his people to be the Frederick Douglass of the oppressed South African slaves of today.'[6]

But it was Plaatje's personal qualities that counted most. 'Within a week after landing in the city he left the sumptuous hotel where he was placed by the

Canadian Brotherhood, and asked Dr Thomas, the UNIA President, to find him apartments in a colored household. And whenever the whites needed him they sent their automobiles to fetch him there. And since then, whenever he had an invitation to dinner he would take the first one that came and ask the others to take another occasion. He will not turn down a colored family for the sake of a grand time with a great white family at Hillcrest or Rosedale. If he is to give any preference it will rather be in favor of a poor black family in narrow apartments where he feels sure his presence is needed more; and he enjoys a conversation with the aged colored women and the kiddies, as thoroughly as the gay company of bright young ladies.'[7]

His experiences in Toronto augured well for his visit to the United States. 'I have very pressing invitations from Chicago, Pittsburgh, Detroit, and New York', he wrote after six weeks in Canada, and he believed 'the enthusiasm of the smaller Coloured Communities of Montreal and Toronto is an index of what one may expect below the line'. Meeting Marcus Garvey when he visited Toronto in January 1921 was a further bonus, bound to help in gaining access to UNIA platforms in the great cities of the United States and to the crowds of people who flocked to his meetings.[8]

'His further progress', as he called it, was nevertheless threatened on two fronts. The first problem was his health. He continued to suffer from the heart trouble he had contracted during the influenza epidemic, and none of the doctors he had seen in South Africa or England were able to do anything to improve matters or even to make a satisfactory diagnosis. When he consulted a heart specialist in Canada, the prognosis was even more pessimistic and he wondered whether he would make it through the winter: 'Your heart leaks so badly that we cannot help you. All we could do is prescribe something to ease the pain, while matters take their course.' There was no way, he was told, to 'mend or operate on a heart'. Five years later he would comment that this 'seemingly brutal frankness was altogether superfluous, for I had already been convinced that the end was not far off.' By the time he wrote these words he had recovered his health, but in Canada that winter he had good reason to wonder how much longer he would be able to carry on. How far he told Elizabeth of the seriousness of the situation will never be known: not one of the letters he wrote home to her has survived.[9]

Apart from his precarious health, his plans were also threatened by the fact that he still did not have the passport he needed to enter the United States. Obtaining this, one way or another, was a major preoccupation from the moment he arrived in Toronto. There were two possibilities. The first was that his friends in the Canadian Brotherhood Federation, some of them men of considerable standing locally, would be able to pull the necessary strings and prevail upon the

Department of External Affairs to issue him with a Canadian passport, endorsed as necessary. He courted them assiduously.

A second possibility was that Dr W.E.B. Du Bois, whom he had alerted to his difficulty, might be able to exercise some influence with the American authorities. Du Bois duly wrote confidentially to Louis F. Post, the assistant secretary of labor in the US administration and in charge of the Bureau of Immigration, reassuring him that Plaatje was 'in no sense dangerous or even radical'. Anxious to reinforce such an impression and keen to encourage Du Bois to further efforts on his behalf, Plaatje wrote to suggest that the translations of Shakespeare he had with him might be of some help. 'Let us say', he said, 'you want to print them in the States and also an American edition of "Sechuana Proverbs with English Translations" and nobody in the U.S.A. could see Native MSS through the press. Hearing that I am in Canada you wish me to come and see them through. Will that assist us somewhat through the mesh of regulations? After which I will return to Canada.'[10]

Even with this ammunition Du Bois made no headway, not surprisingly in view of the tough immigration controls recently put in place by the US authorities, alarmed as they were by the activities of undesirable extremists, black and white, in the unsettled post-war period. Louis Post's response was that the chances of making an exception in Plaatje's case were 'pretty close to the hopeless line', and equally negative messages came back from two US senators whom Du Bois had also approached. Just before Christmas 1920, however, the efforts of Plaatje's Brotherhood friends bore fruit. Passport no. 79,551 was issued in the name of 'Solomon Tshekisho Plaatje, Esquire, of Toronto, Canada', his profession recorded as 'missionary and author', and his 'national status' that of 'British subject'. 'With reference to your yeoman efforts to get me to the U.S.,' he wrote at once to Du Bois, 'I hasten to inform you that a second string to my bow has just responded. The Canadians have succeeded in obtaining a passport for me to go to the United States. It now remains for you to "cease fire" as they say in military signals, "the enemy has surrendered". If the efforts you are making at the White House are not relaxed they might fish out more information and just know enough to enable the enemy to stop me at the border for I won't be through with Canada until about the 25th January.'[11]

He had a busy last few weeks in Toronto. Apart from selling over four hundred copies (at $2 a time) of *Native Life in South Africa*, he had a promise of $7,000 from the Canadian Brotherhood Federation to cover the cost of publishing his African-language translations of the *Fellowship Hymn-Book*. Toronto's black community gave him a similarly generous send-off at a rally-cum-concert to bid him farewell on 24 January 1921. Held under the joint auspices of several local black churches and the Toronto branch of the UNIA, the 'vast assemblage gathered to do him honour' was 'tangible evidence of the new spirit of race consciousness among colored Torontonians', and considered an outstanding success. And while Toronto's black community, which numbered no more than several thousand people, could hardly have been expected to match the $7,000 promised by the Brotherhood Federation, his supporters nonetheless launched an appeal to raise $1,500 to purchase a pipe organ for his Brotherhood hall in Kimberley: 'all this to a man, said the *Negro World*, 'who landed two months ago at Quebec, knowing nobody in Canada, without a friend and without even a passport, as this was refused him by the South African Government – truly a remarkable achievement'.[12]

Plaatje never forgot the warmth of his reception in Toronto, and would often uphold it as an example for other communities to emulate. He bade farewell at further meetings of the UNIA and Brotherhoods on 31 January, and crossed the border at Niagara Falls the following day, armed with a US entry visa obtained from the American consulate in Toronto a week before. Given the fears he had expressed to Du Bois, he must have felt some nervousness at the prospect of the border crossing, but it went without a hitch. In fact, he told Mrs Solomon, the first thing that struck him about the US was 'the civility of the American Immigration Officers'.

Had he delayed his departure much longer it might have been a different story. Eleven days later the South African High Commission in London discovered, most likely from the columns of the *Negro World* or *The Crisis*, that Plaatje was in Canada and intended visiting the United States. It was a pity he could not see the agitated letter, marked 'urgent', that was dispatched from the South African High Commission to the chief passport officer, London, on 12 February 1921, requesting information on how he might have reached North America; and then the chief passport officer's reply, confirming he had not applied for a British passport, but noting in passing that 'the government of Canada does not insist upon persons proceeding to Canada being in possession of passports'. Of this the South African High Commission was evidently unaware. Often, later in life, he would regale audiences with the tale of how he outwitted the South African authorities.[13]

His first port of call in the United States was the city of Buffalo, in New York State, just over the border at Niagara. His host was Dr Theodore Kakaza, an African doctor originally from the eastern Cape who had qualified in Canada and was now practising in Buffalo, combining his professional duties with being president of the Buffalo division of the UNIA. He had first come to the United States in 1896, one of the group of students who had left South Africa to study at Wilberforce University in Ohio. Several of these Plaatje knew well: the indomitable Charlotte Maxeke, who had made the connection with Wilberforce in the first place; Chalmers Moss and Henry Msikinya, whose send-off in Kimberley he had organised so efficiently; Sebopia Molema, Modiri Molema's cousin, who had graduated in law but was ultimately frustrated in his ambition to practise in South Africa. In one respect Theo Kakaza was a living embodiment, twenty-five years on, of that Wilberforce dream: except that, far from returning home to serve his people, as was expected, he had married, raised a family and built a successful medical career in the United States. He never returned to his country of birth. For Plaatje, meeting up with him, and no doubt reminiscing about absent friends as he was shown the sights of Niagara Falls, was a reminder of the deep roots of his own fascination with Negro America.[14]

His reception at the hands of Buffalo's African American community was more than he could have wished for. He had intended to address one meeting in the city, to spend several days relaxing and sightseeing, and then to move on to New York. So successful was this first meeting, though, that he was obliged to repeat it every evening he was there. 'My first American meeting', he wrote afterwards, 'was crowded and it was painful to see for the first time in my life people turned away by the hundreds unable to hear me for lack of standing room. The Pastor told me he never saw his Church so crowded since 1906 when Booker T. Washington spoke there.'

Then it was on to New York. It was, he told Mrs Solomon, 'magnificent travelling': 'I had comfortable quarters on the train, no distinction of colour and at daybreak I looked out through the window from my bed and saw a beautiful panorama of the most fascinating view as the train sped along the edge of the frozen-up Hudson River for three hours before we reached New York City.' Later he described it as 'the most fascinating railway journey in my long experience'. Friends were there to welcome him as the train ended its journey at the Grand Central Terminal on 42nd Street.[15]

✛∿✛

He arrived in New York at a time of great ferment in the life of its African American community. Concentrated in the overcrowded district of Harlem, the city's black population had grown rapidly during the war years, partly in response to deteriorating economic conditions in the agricultural South, partly, as in South

391

Africa, to meet the new demand for labour that wartime economic and military activity had generated. Many new black immigrants came from Central America and the Caribbean islands too. One, from Jamaica, made a particular impact: Marcus Garvey, the charismatic president and driving force of the UNIA. Arriving in New York in 1916, Garvey proclaimed the 'redemption of Africa', he possessed a vision of achieving unity among black people everywhere in the world, and he promised to restore pride in being black for people who had little else. With his great gifts as an orator and organiser, Garvey succeeded in building up, in a remarkably short time, the largest mass movement among African and African American communities before or since. Linked to one another by its weekly newspaper, the *Negro World*, the UNIA established branches in every part of the world where black people lived, and a new spirit of pride and hope caused widespread anxiety to the authorities in Britain, the United States and elsewhere. Lloyd George's characterisation of Garveyism as a potential threat to 'the existing structure of society', in his letter to General Smuts after he met Plaatje's deputation, was just one manifestation of this.[16]

Garvey had his headquarters in Harlem. With a largely black population of about a hundred and fifty thousand, Plaatje thought it 'easily the biggest African city on earth' and it was natural that this was where he would want to find lodgings. Around him, as unemployment, recession and disillusionment replaced the cautious progress and optimism of the war years, Garvey's message of hope and solidarity was adopted enthusiastically by tens of thousands of blacks living in the city. Apart from the UNIA's offices on West 135th Street, often overflowing with queues of supporters and jobseekers, the most visible symbols of this new resurgence were Liberty Hall on West 138th Street, a cavernous meeting hall, seating six thousand people, which had once been the Metropolitan Baptist Tabernacle; and the *Yarmouth*, a steamship which Garvey had purchased for his Black Star Line to provide the means, physical as well as symbolic, of linking African Americans in different parts of the world. Throughout 1920 support for Garvey's movement had grown apace, its success marked by a massive convention held in Liberty Hall in August 1920, attended by delegates from all over the world, which drafted an ambitious 'Declaration of the Rights of the Negro Peoples of the World'. For many, the UNIA seemed the answer to the hopes and prayers of generations of oppressed and downtrodden blacks.

Whatever reservations Plaatje may have had about Garvey's populist style, or the extravagance of his oratory, the success of his movement and its influence in the life of New York's black community were undeniable. He would have had some reason, moreover, to believe it might be turned to his advantage. Central to Garvey's message was an emphasis upon the unity of black peoples and a fervent interest in Africa – the conditions in which African people lived and a fascination with their past achievements. Plaatje hoped to capitalise on both these things in order to arouse support and sympathy for his cause, and to raise money for his Brotherhood work in South Africa. His initial impressions of Harlem seemed only to underline the possibilities: 'the freedom is so intense you can almost feel it in the air'. He thought Harlem was infinitely more prosperous than any African township in South Africa, and he was struck by the 'crowds of clean and well-dressed black men and women, issuing from the underground stations in the blare of the electric lights at night, and pouring through the streets of Harlem like Londoners in Oxford Street'.[17]

Plaatje was fortunate to have the friendship of John E. Bruce, now an important figure in the UNIA, and a man who possessed an enormous network of contacts across the black diaspora. Unlike Du Bois, he had recognised in Garvey and his movement a positive force for the progress of America's black community, and along with a number of other black American intellectuals of the older generation – he himself was in his sixties – declared his support for this new 'race leader'. He became, indeed, one of the editors of the *Negro World*, as well as Garvey's private secretary, and contributed significantly to the intellectual respectability of the movement. His reward, in keeping with Garvey's penchant for giving impressive-sounding titles to his loyal inner circle, was to be knighted as 'Duke of Uganda' and awarded the 'Order of the Nile'.

Bruce and Plaatje had corresponded and exchanged newspapers over the years, and Plaatje had written to him from both England and Canada to keep him informed of his plans for visiting the US. He was, in short, an ideal contact for Plaatje to have in New York, in giving him access to UNIA platforms and providing the other introductions he needed, and the two men seem to have got on very well from the moment they met, sharing, among other things, a love of Shakespeare. Bruce, for his part, was pleased to hear from Plaatje that a review of *Native Life in South Africa* he had written several years earlier had generated a lot of orders, and that dozens of other people had referred to it when purchasing copies from him. A few months later Bruce would write that 'this Plaatje man from Kimberley ... has gotten closer to me than any African I have ever known personally', with the exception only of his 'late, lamented friend, Edward Wilmot Blyden', the famous West African intellectual. He soon discovered, as he told his friend John W. Cromwell, that Plaatje was 'a forceful and effective speaker' who could 'make a hit with any audience'.[18]

Bruce was able to help Plaatje in one other respect. Shortly after he arrived in New York, Bruce gave him a list of five doctors he recommended to treat his heart condition. If none of these could help, he said, then nobody could. 'More for his name than anything else', so Plaatje recalled, he selected a German-American by the name of George Sauer, who successfully treated his heart condition where all others had failed. After his consultations with Dr Sauer, who had a practice close to where he was staying in Harlem, he wrote afterwards, 'I never felt the pains in the heart that were such a handicap in my work and made life almost intolerable'; the effect of the doctor's treatment, he said, was 'permanent and really miraculous'.[19]

Plaatje arrived in New York with no fixed plans as to the length of his stay, intending that this should be determined by the nature of the reception he encountered. In the event he remained for three months, until the beginning of May 1921, hoping, as he wrote to Mrs Colenso soon after arrival, 'to turn my wild goose chase into a financial success'. This was never really achieved, at least on the scale he hoped, but he did manage to make quite an impact on black opinion. Throughout February and March the *Negro World* carried reports of the meetings he addressed in the city, many of them in private residences or churches (particularly those of the African Methodist Episcopal Church). Two such gatherings – he spoke on 'The black man's burden in South Africa' and 'The black women's burden in South Africa' – were at the Bethel AMEC church in West 132nd Street, the venue where, three years earlier, Garvey's own inspired address had launched the UNIA in America. 'Come and hear Mr Sol Plaatje, of Kimberley, South Africa', urged the bill posters: 'Gives a thrilling account of the conditions of the Colored Folk in British South Africa. A Touching Message well and luridly told. The story has gripped nearly a thousand audiences in England, Scotland, Canada and the USA. It will thrill you.' Three weeks earlier, at a meeting of the Brooklyn branch of the UNIA, he was reported to have held his audience 'spellbound'.[20]

By far the largest audiences Plaatje attracted, in New York or elsewhere, were at the packed meetings he addressed at Liberty Hall, six of them altogether; thousands more were able to read the verbatim reports of his speeches in the columns of the *Negro World*. The first took place the day after he arrived in New York, when he shared a platform with Garvey. The *Negro World*, interpreting his account of conditions in South Africa in its own idiom, could not have been more supportive. 'To hear this native of our motherland tell, in splendid English, with rounded periods, and in a coherent, logical, and delightful manner, of the needs of the South African people, and of the greatness of the African Continent, is worth anybody's while. It is instructive as well as entertaining, and no one can hear his message without becoming imbued with a desire as ardent and as enthusiastic and as great as even Garvey himself, in the cause of the redemption of this wonderful homeland of ours and as the only hope we, as a people, have for our salvation and that of posterity.'[21]

Plaatje presented his message in terms he knew would appeal to his audience – flattery for 'His Excellency' Marcus Garvey, enthusiasm for 'the new spirit of race consciousness which is gripping the Negro throughout the country' – and he urged his audience to emulate the example of the white man when it came to supporting causes in which they believed, and in maintaining unity among themselves. Otherwise, he said, 'the redemption of Africa will be delayed until we can be a little more trustful and a little more loyal to one another'. At the end of his speech, as on other occasions, he drew attention to the copies of *Native Life in South Africa* and the other publications he had for sale.

A week later he gave a second address at Liberty Hall, again sharing a platform with Marcus Garvey, and he returned for a third time over Easter, at the end of March, by which time the UNIA leader had departed for a tour of the Caribbean. He repeated his call for solidarity among black people everywhere. He told of his own work in South Africa on behalf of his Brotherhood organisation; and he appealed for financial aid to support it. He was at pains to present his Brotherhood as almost an extension of the UNIA in South Africa, preparing the ground, as it were, for the ultimate 'redemption of Africa':

A little while back I found it was impossible to organize the natives in South Africa, unless you can get them to forget the past, to remember that there should be no distinction between any of the tribes; that they should forget their tribal differences, forget that there is a Basuto or a Zulu, and combine and unite their resources, and they should unite and organize. But you cannot organize a people unless you have got places like this [Liberty Hall] where you can gather them together and tell them the facts. It is the organising of these places that I am after. It has pleased God to reward my efforts to such an extent, in this direction, that at Kimberley I had already got a sort of a Liberty Hall, where they gather together every Sunday afternoon. I get information from them while I am here, and they are fascinated by this gospel of the brotherhood of the natives, so that a Negro in one town is recognized as a brother in the other towns. But they have no facilities; they have no meeting places, and it is my endeavor to raise funds during my present trip, to raise money to enable me to get back and start another hall, the same as at Kimberley, at Bloemfontein, and erect building after building, first in one town and then in another.[22]

African Americans should support these schemes, Plaatje urged, since they could afford to do so. His own people, owing to low wages and lack of opportunities, simply could not. So that, as he concluded in a Garveyite flourish, 'when the time comes, and you … feel you have to make a rush for a jumping off place, you will know that there are people on either side calling you'.

As was evident on other occasions, one of the advantages of Plaatje's Brotherhood work was that it could be presented in a variety of forms, depending on whether his audience was black or white, South African or American, religious or secular. The directors of De Beers, for example, had been given a very different version of what his Brotherhood work was about, and they would no doubt have been somewhat perturbed to hear him describe the hall they had given to him in 1918 as 'a sort of a Liberty Hall'. His English friends, too, though some understood the constraints upon him and the guises he had sometimes to adopt, might also have wondered about the language he used, and it is significant that he made no mention of the UNIA in the account of his visit to the US which he afterwards wrote for them.

Whatever the concessions Plaatje made to Garveyite rhetoric, the financial support he received from UNIA audiences fell far short of his expectations. While the success of Garvey's movement had helped foster interest in Africa, which undoubtedly drew people to his meetings, the UNIA was always their first priority when it came to reaching for their pockets. There was precious little left over for any other cause.[23]

Possibly there were other reasons too. One of them he mentioned at the beginning of his Easter address at Liberty Hall when he referred to 'certain dubious remarks which were current in respect to his African nativity'. The reason for this, he explained, 'is because you have read from your childhood literature concerning South Africa and you are told about swarms of cannibals and gorillas that infest the African forests'. In New York he came up against those same barriers to comprehension that he had encountered in England. So conditioned were American blacks to an exotic image of Africa, which Garvey had in some respects only encouraged, that they doubted the identity of anybody who failed to correspond to the stereotype. It was a paradox Plaatje might have appreciated himself had it not been for the serious consequences such false ideas were likely to have in his efforts to raise money.[24]

When he arrived in New York, Plaatje set up a 'South African Bantu Brotherhood Mission' committee, enlisting the support of Ellen Wood, who had once worked as a nurse in Kimberley, and who was the sister of a Mrs Fawcus in whose house (in 135th Street, Harlem) he was staying. Its purpose was to regularise the collection of funds and to provide an American headquarters for his organisation. His idea was that all funds collected for his Brotherhood organisation should be sent here, while he sought to support himself and, so far as he was able, his family in South Africa, from the proceeds of the sale of his books and pamphlets.[25]

Initially he had some success, and he spoke positively of both the response to his message and the sales he was making. An added bonus was the favourable exchange rate: any remittance to his family 'in Canadian or American dollars increases by one fourth when it is paid to them in sterling', so he told Mrs Solomon after arriving in New York.

His most substantial offering was *Native Life in South Africa*, which sold at $2 a time. It may well have been the case, as Hubert H. Harrison, contributing editor to the *Negro World* believed, that 'no honest effort' had been made to sell the original batch of copies sent to *The Crisis* in 1916, and that since then they had been 'largely left to gather age and dust'. But now, with Plaatje in the country and busy promoting the book, sales picked up. It was favourably reviewed in the African American press, and it often left a big impression on those who took the trouble to read it. John E. Bruce, for example, wrote that 'if it doesn't make your blood boil, you are not of African descent'; Booker T. Washington's widow Margaret read it 'with a great deal of interest'; while John W. Cromwell, writing to Bruce shortly before Plaatje's arrival in the United States, confessed that the book had 'impressed him to no little degree'. 'It is a very sad story indeed which is told in this wonderful book by this very talented man, who comes here at a most auspicious moment to let the American people know of the conditions under which the Natives are now laboring in South Africa. I had not the slightest idea that such harrowing details could be told ... Plaatje will render a great service in his lectures throughout the U.S. as he has done in this wonderful book that displays such genius as well as literary brilliance. I thought I knew something of South Africa heretofore, but this book reveals the depth of my ignorance.'[26]

Later in the year, there would be a fifth edition of *Native Life in South Africa* (the price now increased to $2.50), an indication that the copies of the book Plaatje brought with him from England, or had sent previously, were all sold.[27]

Sechuana Proverbs (good value at $1 a copy) was on sale too, along with four pamphlets: an American edition of *Legal Disabilities*; two new pamphlets entitled *The Awful Price of Native Labour* and *Repressive Land Laws of British South Africa*, of which no copies appear to have survived; and a fourth, entitled *The Mote and the Beam: an epic on sex relationships 'twixt white and black in British South Africa*. All were advertised as being available from Plaatje's New York address, from J.E. Bruce (who lived further along West 131st Street), and from Young's Book Exchange at 135 W. 135th Street – 'The Mecca of Literature pertaining to Colored People', as it called itself, and the first African American bookshop in Harlem.[28]

The Mote and the Beam, at 25 cents a copy, was the biggest seller and by the time Plaatje left the United States in 1922 he had sold over eighteen thousand copies. A thirteen-page discourse on the hypocrisy of white South African attitudes towards the question of sex across the colour line, its purpose, as Plaatje explained to potential buyers at one of his meetings, was to expose the fallacy of the white man's claim 'that the Negro is such a low down scoundrel that he cannot trust him with his wife behind his back'. It was a subject with which, in its broader aspects, he had long been concerned. During the last 'black peril' scare in South Africa, in the aftermath of Union, he had been strongly critical of the sensational and misleading reporting in the white press of incidents of sexual assault, and had argued for the abolition of the jury system where such cases involved black and white, given the biased behaviour of white jurors.[29]

More recently, while in England in 1919 and 1920, white fears about black sexuality had again come to the fore, this time in a panic that developed around the presence of black troops in the French army of occupation of the Ruhr in Germany. It had generated a huge amount of publicity on both sides of the Atlantic. In England, E.D. Morel, with whom he had once shared a platform, exploited the issue in a quite shameful manner, publishing, in July 1920, a pamphlet called *The Horror on the Rhine*. Within a month it had sold ten thousand copies, eventually going into eight editions.[30]

It must have been around this time that Plaatje wrote what became *The Mote and the Beam*, most likely as a chapter in the 'political book' that was never published. An apparent trigger for it was a letter from a South African woman, then visiting the UK, to one of the London evening papers, criticising the behaviour of Africans in the Transvaal towards white women, and expressing outrage at the sight of black men courting white women in Europe. In the context of the ongoing campaign over the 'Horror on the Rhine' it was a highly topical issue, and Plaatje proceeded to counter her allegations in the course of a broader treatment of the subject, drawing attention to the hypocrisy of white South African attitudes and the injustices that often resulted.[31]

Once in America he would have realised that the issue of race and sexuality was every bit as toxic as in Europe and Africa: indeed, given the upsurge in the number of lynchings of African Americans, white fears about black sexuality took an exceptionally violent form, and black organisations campaigned vociferously on the issue. What he had written in London, therefore, even if its focus was on South Africa, proved to be of keen interest to African American audiences. The opinion of one of Plaatje's correspondents that it was 'of absorbing interest and should be widely circulated' was clearly shared by many others.[32]

A rather sourer note, though, was struck by Hubert H. Harrison, who reviewed *The Mote and the Beam* in the *Negro World* in April 1921. He thought that its 'chief value to Negro Americans is to demonstrate to them that their provincial notion of the unique character of race prejudice in this country is entirely wrong', and that on the whole it was 'a nifty little pamphlet' – but added that 25 cents for eleven pages was rather too expensive, 'and not a regular business proposition'. Leaving aside that he had miscounted the number of pages, Harrison's comments were of no great significance in themselves, and can have done little to damage sales. They did, however, provoke a revealing response from Plaatje in a letter to the *Negro World* three weeks later. What he particularly objected to was the description of *The Mote and the Beam* as 'a business proposition', and he complained that Harrison, and others like him, had 'failed to grasp the inwardness of my mission here'. He went on:

> Let me say again, Sir, that I am not here on business. I have travelled 9,000 miles purely in aid of the most oppressed Negroes of the world. I would gladly have stayed at home and earned $15 per week, like H.H.H., although I would have had to work all the week and a good deal harder for it; but the natives I represent are so oppressed they could not, even if they would, pay $15 or any other sum – worked they ever so hard. But, if anywhere, at one time, somebody had not left home and hearthstones and travelled to the Southern slave plantations in the face of the bitterest hostility on the part of the slave owners; or if, a hundred years ago, someone had not travelled to the South African wilds and made incredible sacrifices on our behalf, neither H.H.H. or I would be able to write. Somebody did it for us, so why not I for the black millions who lie so helplessly at the mercy of the South African Boers?[33]

Here was the clearest statement yet of that sense of mission that was so central to his make-up, that belief that it was his inescapable duty to speak out on behalf of his people. At the same time there was a palpable sense of frustration at the lack of understanding that he perceived around him, and disappointment that support for his cause, and the funds to finance his Brotherhood organisation, had not been as forthcoming as he had hoped. 'If we were any other race but Negroes', he said in the same breath, 'the heavens would long since have resounded with a diapason of war from our deliverance; but, because we are Negroes, clever penmen of our complexion stigmatize the efforts on our behalf as "a business proposition".' No doubt they were exaggerated hopes. Perhaps too his time in Canada had created unrealistic expectations about what he might achieve south of the border. Harrison's comments, even if intended 'as a neighborly act', clearly struck a nerve.

✛

By the time this letter appeared in the *Negro World* Plaatje had left New York for Boston to fulfil some speaking engagements, and stayed there for most of May. He attended, amongst other things, a public meeting to celebrate the banning by the city authorities of *The Birth of a Nation*, the notorious film of the Reconstruction period which he had first seen in London; it had been the focus of strong opposition from black communities since it was first released in 1915. From Boston he made his way to Atlantic City, New Jersey, and it was from here that he wrote to Dr Du Bois on 22 June, accepting an invitation to attend the annual meeting of the National Association for the Advancement of Colored People (NAACP).[34]

The two men, Plaatje and Du Bois, had met for the first time when Plaatje arrived in New York. Though some found him cold and aloof, the erudite, Harvard-educated academic was undoubtedly more to Plaatje's liking than the flamboyant, populist figure of Marcus Garvey, and they seem to have got on well. Besides inviting him to address the NAACP meeting, Du Bois promoted the new edition of *Native Life in South Africa* in *The Crisis*, the monthly magazine he edited. He also invited him to the next Pan-African Congress which he was planning to hold in Europe in July and August. Having missed the first congress in 1919, Plaatje was keen to attend, but lacked the means to get there. Du Bois wrote to S.M. Makgatho, president of the SANNC, to 'impress upon [him] the necessity of having South Africa represented at the Conference', and to try to persuade him to provide Plaatje with the £100 that he needed to get there. Plaatje had told him, Du Bois added, 'that as he was rather hard hit financially by the last two deputations to England he was unable to undertake any further expense on behalf of the native congress'; but that if Congress could finance his journey and attendance, it would be much cheaper than sending somebody else out especially from South Africa'. There is no evidence Du Bois received a reply to his letter.[35]

A couple of months later, resigned to being unable to travel to Europe himself, Plaatje asked Walter White, a colleague of Du Bois in the NAACP who was intending to go to the conference, to read out an address on his behalf. 'Wait till you get to Paris,' Plaatje advised, 'then stage an auspicious occasion when the best reporters are present to send it all over the world. The secret of the success of British policy in South Africa has been the suppression of the truth.' White agreed to undertake the task and to give it 'as wide publicity as possible'.[36]

In the meantime his speech to the NAACP conference in Detroit went down very well. He was brought on as a last-minute replacement for President King of Liberia, who failed to arrive, and impressed the assembled delegates with his account of conditions in South Africa. One of Bruce's friends who was there wrote afterwards that he 'covered himself with glory' with a speech 'which was marvelously phrased, powerful in argument, convincing in thought, eloquent in delivery and satisfying in effect'. Bruce was not surprised: Plaatje had this extraordinary ability to captivate any audience with the power of his oratory.[37]

A couple of months later, when he had moved on to Washington DC, there was tragic news from home: the death of his daughter Olive. She died on 14 July, but the news didn't reach him for six weeks. After contracting rheumatic fever in 1918 she had – the incident at Aliwal North notwithstanding – recovered her health sufficiently to attend the Indaleni Training Institution in Natal to train as a nurse. Once there, however, her health worsened, and she had to return home. According to her travelling companions, she was well enough to begin the journey, but when waiting in Bloemfontein for the train connection to Kimberley her condition deteriorated. During the three hours' wait for the train, she was prohibited from entering the 'whites only' waiting-room, and not allowed to lie down on one of the seats on the platform, also reserved for whites. She died not long afterwards, succumbing, so it was reported, to the effects of heart failure. For Plaatje, nine thousand miles away in the United States and without the means to return home, this added a bitter twist to what was a profoundly sad event. Olive occupied a treasured place in his thoughts, and what he learned about the circumstances of her death would remain a source of deep sadness. South Africa's discriminatory laws, which he had devoted his life to fighting, had never intruded upon his private, family life in so tragic a manner.

Olive was buried in Bloemfontein. A touching obituary, recalling the achievements of her short life, appeared in the *Brownie's Book*, a monthly magazine for African American children published by the NAACP in New York; Olive herself had been a reader and subscriber. The piece was written by Sarah Talbert Keenan, the daughter of Mary Burnett Talbert, one of the best-known African American women leaders of the day. Plaatje had met her in London in 1920 when she accompanied her mother on an international tour. He saw her again in New Jersey in 1921, just after Olive's death, when he gave her the information she needed for the obituary.[38]

Olive's more enduring memorial, however, was to be *Mhudi*, her father's as yet unpublished novel. It would be dedicated to 'the memory of our beloved

Olive, one of the many youthful victims of a settled system, and in pleasant recollection of her life work, accomplished at the age of 13, during the influenza epidemic'. Few people who read the book can have had any idea of the depth of meaning that Plaatje invested in the phrase 'a settled system', an allusion to the circumstances of her death as much as the kind of country she had grown up in.

<center>~~~</center>

Had Plaatje been in a position to return home after receiving news of his daughter's death he would have done so. His friends in Thaba Nchu made another effort to raise funds, and encouraged those in Mafikeng to do likewise, but it was too large a task. So he stayed on, continuing with his campaign. Thanks to Dr Du Bois he was able to convey his message to the Pan-African Congress in Europe. Du Bois himself read out Plaatje's typewritten address at the congress's London session, announcing only (thus it was reported in the press) that it came from a 'South African Native Propagandist now touring the States, but deciding to remain anonymous for the present'.[39]

It was one of the most impressive speeches he had written: a powerful account of the discrimination and oppression suffered by his people, fiercely critical of the pass laws and above all the Natives' Land Act, 'by far the most outrageous of the monstrous crimes that characterized the South African Parliament's crusade against law-abiding natives'. In the second half of his speech, anticipating what he imagined would be a major theme at the congress, he targeted those he believed were responsible for the oppression of his people: not the capitalists but a government that legislated 'at the behest of a relentless white league of lawyers, overseers, mechanics, and what not, who style themselves "The Labour Party of South Africa"'. It was a significant change of emphasis. At one time he regarded the Boers as the arch-villains; now they were joined by the white working class and their allies. But his solution to the problem remained as before: 'the extension of a reasonable franchise to all taxpayers irrespective of colour'. He concluded his address with an appeal to the delegates to do all in their power to ensure that South Africa was not given a League of Nations mandate to rule over German South West Africa.[40]

The address did not go unnoticed in South Africa. The *Cape Times* carried a long report on the conference, confused Du Bois's reading of Plaatje's address with his own 'Manifesto to the world', discussed on the same day, but nevertheless considered both to represent 'a rampant propagandism emanating from the least representative quarters and directed unmistakenly against European governments'. The *Christian Express*, picking up on this report, also

402

expressed its disapproval, condemning the manifesto of 'The South African Native propagandist' for resorting to 'agitator's stock phrases, catch words, and generalities, and sweeping denunciations, ignoring the progress being made in South African Native Affairs'.[41]

❦

At the time his paper was being read in Paris, Plaatje himself was on his way to Chicago. Here he enjoyed the hospitality of leading members of the city's black community, staying with Dr Mary Waring, an African American medical practitioner, whom he had met in England. An elaborate musical accompanied his talk at the Grace Lyceum, he was the guest of honour at a theatre party to see the popular black actor Charles Gilpin in Eugene O'Neill's *The Emperor Jones* (thought by many to have been inspired by the rise of Marcus Garvey), and he wrote a long article for the (anti-Garveyite) *Chicago Defender*, the largest-circulation black newspaper in the United States. Under the headline 'South Africa in grip of British Jim Crow rule: editor tells how British kill Natives', he told of the oppressive legislation his people suffered from, describing the violence that had occurred in a strike in Port Elizabeth late in 1920. 'Fortunately', he said, 'there are better and safer means of overcoming such legislative enactments and administrative tyranny. We are doing it by the native brotherhood, whose forte is the power of combined action. We do it through community service and social work and night school for adults. I started this work at Kimberley in 1918, and it has already proved such a blessing that other centers are calling me to help them to do likewise.' The purpose of his visit to the United States, he explained, was to raise funds to support this work, adding that 'anyone in sympathy with a downtrodden people striving for the fuller life cannot do better than communicate with Attorney J.A. Scott, 3710 Prairie Avenue, or R.L. Simmons, 3524 Michigan Avenue.'[42]

From Chicago he travelled to Washington DC to take up a long-standing invitation from John W. Cromwell. Then in his mid-seventies, Cromwell was a former newspaper editor, lawyer and teacher and a respected figure in the capital's well-established African American community, ideally placed to assist Plaatje with the contacts he needed. One major event he was able to attend was the 'Conference of Fundamentals' organised by the so-called Committee of Seven, representing seven of the major black American organisations. Its aim was to publicise the grievances of black people, in the United States and elsewhere, by presenting the International Armaments Conference, in session in Washington, with a comprehensive petition that set out the 'worldwide disabilities under which

403

we as a people suffer'. Its promoters claimed it was a 'Race meeting' that 'would go down in history as one of the most far-reaching toward inspiring race pride, race loyalty, and race confidence in the accomplishment of political, economical, educational, and civic justice ever held'. Exaggerated claims, no doubt – but for Plaatje another opportunity to convey his message.

He was delighted by his reception in Washington. He wrote afterwards, from Boston, to thank Cromwell for 'the nice introductions you gave my mission to Washington and the good people of the capital'; and also to ask if he might 'find a place in the corner of your basement somewhere' to store his 'bale of books', which always accompanied him on his travels, until he returned to the capital.[43]

While in Boston on this brief return visit, he participated in a successful African Pageant, held in the city's Symphony Theatre. It was called 'The Answer', and consisted of a sequence of tableaux dramatising the history of 'the Negro Race', the first half being devoted to 'Africa', the second to 'Negro Life in America'. Plaatje was one of six 'genuine native Africans' who had parts. Along with the inspired orchestration of H. Ballanta Taylor (from Sierra Leone), he particularly remembered the extremely severe weather outside. There had been a heavy fall of snow, followed by a blizzard, which had derailed some trains and brought down telephone lines, and when he reached the theatre on the evening of the performance, in a light drizzle, he found he could not close his umbrella because the rain had frozen. In view of the cold he was all the more surprised to find the theatre, which could hold three thousand people, was already completely full.[44]

Soon he was back in Washington, addressing yet more meetings. Their tenor differed sharply from the Garveyite gatherings in New York, the UNIA's stronghold. Washington had an older-established, more prosperous African American community and a reputation as the pre-eminent home of the black middle class, some of whom were educated at Howard University, which lay at their doorstep. At John W. Cromwell's invitation he attended the twenty-fifth annual meeting of the Negro Society for Historical Research, held at Howard during the holiday between Christmas 1921 and New Year 1922. Their journal, Plaatje thought, was 'one of the best quarterly magazines in existence'.[45]

One ambition he never did realise. Some months earlier, while in New York, he had told John Bruce that he wished, when he reached Washington, to meet Warren G. Harding, the recently elected president of the United States. Bruce wrote to Cromwell to see if this might be arranged, adding that he was sure such a meeting, were it to take place, 'will have its effect in South Africa'. If he could persuade the British prime minister of the strength of his case, then why not an American president – particularly as there were those who thought Harding was a man of relatively benign views so far as racial issues were concerned? Bruce, Cromwell and Plaatje would also have been intrigued, it is fair to say, by the widespread rumours that surfaced during the presidential election campaign that Harding's great-great-grandfather had been a black West Indian.[46]

Over the next couple of months there were further engagements in schools and churches, interspersed with visits to Baltimore and Philadelphia. Here his host was the Rt Rev. J.A. Johnson, formerly head of the AME Church in South Africa, who presented him with a piece of apparatus that was to play a large part in his life in the future: a portable movie projector, worth $420, suitable for showing 35 mm educational films. By March 1922 he was back in New York, at a new address (243 West 128th Street), but laid up for six weeks with neuritis and rheumatism. At the end of the month he was well enough to write an informative letter to Mrs Colenso, apologising for his 'long silence', explaining that this was 'all due to sickness and overwork'. He had 'not had much success financially' but had almost recovered his health 'at the hands of a very good German-American doctor'. 'It is such a pity', he continued, 'that I couldn't stop with him a long time. I had always to go away to earn money to pay board, lodging and travelling expenses, which are very high in this country. Had I the chance to remain in New York under his treatment for three months at a stretch, I could by now have been a new man physically; but circumstances are always beyond our control.'[47]

In the same letter he conveyed some impressions of his time in the United States. 'Besides my health the trip has been of very great educational value and I have stored up an immense amount of knowledge; which ought to be very beneficial to my work at home in South Africa.' He went on to describe the progress being made by African Americans, and how impressed he was 'to see the grasping manner in which Negroes reach out to take advantage of the several educational facilities' open to them. As for the women, 'They are progressive educationally, socially, politically, as well as in church work, they lead the men.' 'It is very inspiring to get into their midst', he said, 'but it is also distressing at times and I can hardly suppress a tear when I think of the wretched backwardness between them and our part of the empire, as compared with other parts.'

He commented only briefly on news from home and family. 'I continue to hear from Mrs Plaatje. She seems to have borne her bereavement since our daughter Olive's death much better than I do. They are only worried by my continued absence from home.' That was surely an understatement, and he failed to mention another devastating piece of news: after completing two years at Fort Hare, and shortly before he was due to sit his matriculation examination, St Leger was forced to give up and return home. It must have come as a huge disappointment and, especially for his father, cause for considerable soul searching. If only he had been around to help, perhaps things might have turned out differently.

According to the college records St Leger had to discontinue his studies 'owing to lack of financial support', and he himself said that he 'was forced by economic reasons to leave the Native College, Fort Hare and go to work to help my parents'. He had previously been awarded a bursary but this covered only part of the costs. His uncle Isaiah Bud-M'belle had paid the balance, and would probably have continued to do so. St Leger, however, must have felt he had no alternative given the dire state of the family finances and his father's prolonged absence. He had hoped to go on to study medicine. Instead he managed to get a clerical job in De Aar, helping to support his mother. Before long he was paying the school fees of his younger brother Richard, studying for a building apprenticeship at Lovedale.[48]

By the time his health broke down early in 1922, Plaatje's hopes of raising any significant sums of money for his Brotherhood organisation had all but evaporated, and he was finding it increasingly difficult to sell enough of his books and pamphlets to support himself, let alone his family in South Africa. Whereas he got '40 or 50 dollars in 1921', he complained, 'I could hardly get 8 or 10 this year [1922], and where I previously sold books like ice cream in August I could now scarcely sell a pamphlet'. Partly he put this down to deteriorating economic conditions and the fact that there was just less money around than before – but inevitably the novelty of his message was wearing off, too.[49]

Nor could he find a publisher for his novel, *Mhudi*. This was particularly disappointing as in many ways it seemed quite an auspicious time. 'Negro literature' was both fashionable and being published by mainstream publishers, and there was a growing interest in Africa in literary and cultural circles in Europe and America. This was exemplified by the publication in July 1921 of the novel *Batouala*, written in French by René Maran. He came originally from Martinique in the Caribbean, but the book is set in French colonial Africa where he spent much of his working life. *Batouala* was a literary sensation, controversially winning the Prix Goncourt, the leading French literary award of the day; an English edition, from the American publisher Thomas Seltzer, followed in 1922. African American intellectuals hailed it as a great achievement, as significant for its implied criticism of French colonial rule as its pioneering literary approach – it saw the world through the eyes of its central character, an African chief, and took a far more sympathetic view of African culture and customs than anything hitherto. Plaatje could have been forgiven for seeing his own unpublished manuscript as an anglophone equivalent – and just as publishable.[50]

Batouala struck a chord among African Americans because it came at a time of intellectual and artistic ferment. The term 'Harlem renaissance' had yet to be coined but New York was already the centre of a cultural awakening, expressed in literature, music, art and drama. In the early 1920s this was associated with the idea of the 'New Negro', conveying as it did a sense of assertion and racial pride; for some it also staked a claim to a wider pan-African identity. Many of the leading figures in this movement were associated with *The Crisis* and the NAACP. Several of them Plaatje had come to know quite well, and had corresponded with: Jessie Fauset, poet, novelist and literary editor of *The Crisis*; James Weldon Johnson, former diplomat, poet, lawyer and NAACP organiser; Walter White, novelist, journalist and NAACP staff member who had made his name by passing for white in order to expose, at great risk, the perpetrators of some of the brutal lynchings in the southern states in 1919 and 1920; and Du Bois himself, academic, polymath and political organiser.

Plaatje's experiences of the New Negro movement were by no means confined to those associated with the NAACP and *The Crisis*. He enjoyed both music and drama, and recalled meeting Florence Mills, star of the smash-hit musical *Shuffle Along*, which opened in New York in May 1921. He thought it 'the most spectacular and melodious musical comedy ever produced by Negro writers for Negro artists' and it ran for over a year, breaking all box office records. Florence Mills's talents, he added 'shattered the colour line'. He was also struck by the serious interest in 'Negro music' on the part of both black and white, evident in curricula and research in colleges and universities as well as in performance – in sharp contrast to the situation in his own country, where indigenous music had no place in the academy. If Americans had been like South Africans, Plaatje wrote later, 'the world would never have heard of the songs of the Jubilee Singers'.[51]

He was in contact with the Jamaican poet Claude McKay, who had returned to New York, at about the same time he arrived from Canada, after a year in London; it is possible their paths had crossed there too. McKay was best known for his haunting poem 'If we must die', written in the aftermath of the American race riots of 1919, a barely disguised appeal to his people to fight back against their oppressors. They had a mutual friend in New York in John E. Bruce, who evidently had some plans for them. 'We are going to give Plaatje and the poet McKay … a stag before Plaatje leaves New York', he wrote to his friend John W. Cromwell in March 1921. Whether such an event ever took place is unknown, but for a while at least Plaatje seems to have been close to a number of key figures in Harlem's vibrant cultural life, and fascinated by what he saw going on around him.[52]

But he had no luck in finding a publisher for his novel. Since arriving in the United States he had approached Macmillan, Harper Bros., Scribner's and Harcourt, all well-known American publishing houses, but all had declined it. Perhaps they just did not think it 'exotic' enough. At the beginning of February 1922, having despaired of placing the book with one of the established publishing houses, he approached Walter Neale, of the Neale Publishing Company in New York, who wrote back with a glowing report on his manuscript, a sales estimate of twenty thousand copies, and the proposal that Plaatje should pay him $1,500 to handle it. Encouraged at last by a positive response, but dubious about Neale's exaggerated sales forecast, he wrote to Du Bois for advice: 'Bearing in mind what you told me that there were publishers and publishers, do you think that Mr Neale's eulogy of this MS and his rosy forecast of the probable sales are worth the paper they are printed upon? "$5 for a novel" seems to me a clever dodge on his part to get $1,500 out of me. Supposing his extravagant expectations are realised, 25% royalty seems very small after I paid the initial printing cost plus the labour, anxieties and expense of authorship.' 'My reason for asking your advice in the matter', he added, 'is that if there is anything in his glowing forecast I could try and borrow the $1,500', and he asked him if he thought 'his appreciations are genuine'.[53]

Du Bois's reply, which can have come as no surprise, was that he thought Neale's claim was 'an out and out lie'; that there 'isn't one chance in a hundred thousand of a book like yours reaching a sale of 20,000'; and that if he was going to spend $1,500 he could use it to print and bind the book himself 'and not pay Neale a cent'. It was sensible advice, and Plaatje did well to avoid any further dealings with Mr Neale: another prominent African American figure who had signed a contract with his company several years earlier had come to the conclusion that the man was 'a wilful and deliberate fraud'. If part of Plaatje's purpose in writing to Du Bois was to interest him in the possibility of *The Crisis* publishing his novel, that didn't work either. Even less surprisingly, he was unable to find a publisher for his Tswana translations of Shakespeare.[54]

In his letter to Mrs Colenso in March 1922 Plaatje said he intended leaving the United States to return to England in May. It was not to be. After a further visit to Boston over Easter, he set off instead on a tour of the southern States. This was something he had wanted to do for a long time, but lacked the funds. In the event it was made possible by a grant of $100 from the Phelps Stokes Fund in New York. He was pleased to report that Dr T. Jesse Jones, the director of the fund, was 'intensely interested' in my mission, and the money was given to him, he said, 'on condition that I visited Tuskegee, which was just what I was anxious to do'; Jones also promised to pay part of the cost of his *Fellowship Hymn-Book* translations if he could secure some funding in England too. Founded in 1909 from the proceeds of the will of one Miss Caroline Phelps Stokes, the fund spent its money on promoting educational development for both Africans and African Americans. Recently it had been responsible for organising an education commission to survey colonial educational policies in Africa. One of its members was the West African J.E.K. Aggrey, whom Plaatje had first met in London in 1920 and saw again in New York where, he recalled, they 'shared some helpful evenings together while he was reading at Columbia University for his degree in philosophy'. It may well have been his support that helped secure the grant.[55]

Plaatje left New York early in May 1922, stopping to address several meetings (including the seventh annual session of the National Race Congress in Washington, his contribution described as 'an eye opener') on his way south, before visiting the Hampton Institute, Virginia. Six days later he was writing to Jessie Fauset to apologise for having left New York without seeing her, and informed her of the progress of his tour: 'I have spent a useful and strenuous time since I left you. Saw Hampton and other colleges and universities in Atlanta, Ga; all of them inspiring, and the young people went wild over my message.'[56]

More than any of the other colleges and universities, he was impressed by Tuskegee, his next port of call. Founded by Booker T. Washington, Tuskegee was the best known of the black educational institutes of the American South, and over the years small numbers of Africans, alongside the majority African American student body, came to acquire an education denied to them in their own countries. In accordance with Washington's philosophy, Tuskegee concentrated its efforts on building up the practical skills of its students. Only in this way, Washington believed, could the economic and social regeneration of African Americans (and Africans) be achieved; and only then, he thought, would it be practicable to lay claim to the political rights to which his people, as any other, were entitled. Founded in part upon what Washington had perceived to be a necessary compromise with dominant white interests in the American South (Plaatje would have appreciated the position here), his philosophy had come under attack from those – most notably Du Bois and the NAACP – who thought the struggle for equal rights was the first priority. Most African visitors, however, paid little heed to the increasingly acrimonious debates between the proponents of these opposing views: in their view both were necessary for their progress and advancement, and they simply took away what they could.

Despite these challenges, under Robert Russa Moton, Washington's successor as principal, Tuskegee nevertheless maintained its pre-eminent reputation, and Plaatje was one of a long trail of visitors who were deeply impressed by what they saw. He had devoted much of his life to fighting for the political rights of his people in South Africa, but always realised they needed the skills to progress economically too; as far back as 1903 and 1904, indeed, he had publicised Booker T. Washington's ideas in the columns of his first newspaper, *Koranta ea Becoana*. Things had changed greatly since then, but Plaatje was convinced that his people could benefit, as before, from the lessons he might learn during his short time in Tuskegee.

He formed an immediate rapport with Robert Moton. The two men would correspond intermittently over the next decade, and in time Moton's portrait came to adorn the living room of his home in Kimberley. He never forgot 'the happy and inspiring times' he spent during his brief visit to Tuskegee. What particularly struck him was the amount of money being channelled into Tuskegee by white philanthropists. When he saw the account books he was staggered to find that its budget for the previous year had been eleven million dollars. This was on a wholly different scale from the sums of money he had sought, let alone received, for his Brotherhood organisation in Kimberley. A couple of months later he heard that Tuskegee had been left another million dollars by a white benefactor from New Jersey.[57]

His admiration was reciprocated. 'I have been favourably impressed with Mr Plaatje', Moton wrote a year later, 'both as to his unselfish interest in his own people and his tactful dealing with the difficulties of the situation which he must face and endure.'[58]

Plaatje's letter of thanks after his visit, written from St Louis, Missouri, was further testimony to the impact of his brief visit: 'I have no words to adequately express my gratitude for the kind reception accorded me by the Principal and everybody at Tuskegee with whom I came in contact. I never felt so sorry to leave a place as I did when I had to turn my back on your great institution yesterday. Please convey my thanks to the Principal.' Albon Holsey, Moton's secretary, did as he was requested. 'It was very gratifying to us to have you with us for the visit', he wrote in reply, 'and many of us were inspired by the things you had to say. You certainly made a very fine impression here and made many personal friends, all of whom will look forward to hearing of your further achievements.'[59]

Plaatje left Tuskegee with the promised gift of several movie films, showing various scenes and activities at the institute, which he planned to show upon his return to South Africa. He wished to pass on the lessons he thought could be learnt from the experiences of African Americans in the United States, and to convey – to as many people as he could – that inspiration he himself took from

Tuskegee. Robert Moton's generous offer to supply several reels of Tuskegee, including one of the unveiling of the statue of Booker T. Washington in April 1922, a month before Plaatje's visit, was especially welcome. A similar, but rather vaguer, promise was also made by the Hampton Institute. He would have been particularly interested in the so-called *Hampton Epilogue*, a short film on the achievements of the institute which was sometimes shown as a counter to the notorious *The Birth of a Nation*.[60]

After a circuitous, zigzag trip northwards from Tuskegee, Plaatje spent his last few weeks in the United States in the city of Chicago, staying this time with Ida Wells Barnett, one of the best-known black women leaders of her day, only recently recovered from a serious illness. There was the usual round of meetings (he gave the 'Black man's burden' talk at the Unity Club on 25 June), and before he departed a permanent committee was formed by a group of local dignitaries, black and white, who wished to support his work. An attorney, James A. Scott, in whose house the meeting took place, became its chairman, and Dr Mary Waring the chairman of its executive board. They constituted themselves as the Chicago branch of the South African Bantu Brotherhood Committee, declared their intention to do all they could 'to assist Sol Plaatje in his great work in South Africa', and made preparations for a 'mass meeting' on 23 July to bid him farewell. Here he gave his final address in the United States – on 'Native conditions in South Africa'. In his audience, and also one of the musical performers in the 'Special Native African program' that formed part of the evening's proceedings, was a 29-year-old medical student from Thembuland, in the eastern Cape, studying at the School of Medicine at Marquette, Milwaukee, some fifty miles north of Chicago. His name was Alfred B. Xuma, later to become president general of the African National Congress of South Africa.[61]

Several days later Plaatje crossed the Canadian border, and spent a month in Canada before sailing from Montreal to Cherbourg, France, thence to Southampton, arriving early in September 1922. If he had hoped, on his return to Toronto, to redeem the promise made by the Canadian Brotherhood Federation to finance the printing of his *Fellowship Hymn-Book*, there was only disappointment. During his absence in the US the federation had gone into decline, and he probably never received a cent of the $7,000 that was promised on his first visit. The same was true of the $1,400 promised by Toronto's '3,000 Negro citizens', despite the assurances he had that they would 'double their efforts' in time for his return to the city.[62]

Awaiting his arrival in Montreal, instead, was a typewriter, a gift from the Corona company, some medicines from Dr Sauer in New York, and some further educational films from Henry Ford (founder and head of the Ford Motor Company), whom he had met personally. He was annoyed to find, though, that some spectacles he had ordered from an African American doctor he had seen in Chicago had not arrived. Since he had paid for them, he was understandably upset that Dr Scott, the doctor concerned, had not done as he had requested: 'Truly our folks in America are the limit!' he wrote to Alfred Xuma, almost a year later, still without the glasses – and exasperated that it seemed to be part of a pattern. Not one of the letters he had written to African Americans from Canada had produced a reply, in contrast to the prompt responses he had from his white correspondents. 'And yet we object', he added, 'when white folks call us inferior beings!'[63]

Plaatje told Xuma that his eyes had suffered while he 'wrote and appealed for glasses without getting an answer', and that he was 'even threatened with blindness if this lasts much longer'. Whatever his difficulties, they did not prevent him, after he had boarded the RMS *Antonia on* 29 August 1922, from embarking upon a Tswana translation of *Othello* to occupy himself during the voyage across the Atlantic.[64]

So ended Plaatje's mission to North America. In many respects, given the resources at his disposal, it was a remarkable achievement. Getting there in the first place required a great deal of persistence and ingenuity; the financial obstacles, and the opposition of the South African authorities, would have defeated anybody less determined. And once there, at meeting after meeting, at conference after conference, in conversation after conversation, he conveyed to anybody who would listen a knowledge of conditions in his country, impressing audiences with his ability as an orator, his natural warmth and humour, his transparently sincere commitment to his cause. But it had little lasting effect. Most of the people he convinced were without power or influence. African Americans had more than enough problems of their own, and there were many other calls on their limited resources.

It was a tribute to Plaatje's forceful personality that he was able to make this kind of impact, but once he was gone it quickly dissipated. Promises of financial support were always more forthcoming than hard cash, and easily forgotten once he had moved on. Even the special committee set up in Chicago on the eve of his departure soon collapsed. His campaign was far too heavily dependent on his physical presence, in short, to leave much of a permanent impression once he departed.

Nevertheless, he believed he learnt a great deal from his time in North America. What impressed him more than anything was the success of African Americans – the lynchings and grinding poverty notwithstanding – in building up their communities through self-help in education, business, and social and religious life, and through attracting donations from powerful and wealthy white benefactors. The comparison with South Africa was always his yardstick. 'He says we Negroes in America are living in Paradise compared with the lot of the natives of South Africa', so John Bruce reported to J.W. Cromwell after meeting Plaatje, 'and that our Jim Crow cars as they have been described to him are palace cars compared with those the natives have to ride in, in South Africa.' 'He is simply amazed at the condition of the blacks here', he added, 'and says if his people had our opportunities they'd own all South Africa, in the next 50 years.'[65]

What he saw subsequently, in nineteen different states, served only to confirm these first impressions, and he frequently reminded African American audiences of their good fortune. In private correspondence he was just as enthusiastic. 'You will be amazed at the freedom of Negroes in this country', he wrote to Mrs Unwin. 'No achievement is impossible under the liberal constitution of the United States. How I envy their opportunities when I think of the draconian restrictions by which my own people in South Africa are fettered.' 'They had a colour prejudice in America', he said on another occasion, 'but if it was so little in South Africa as it was in America, then his country would be a very happy one.' He often contrasted, too, the attention paid by the government and other organisations to black American leaders with the situation of their counterparts in South Africa. In the careers of men like W.E.B. Du Bois, John W. Cromwell and Robert Moton, he saw the kind of role which, were things different, he might himself have played.[66]

At times he painted an almost rose-tinted picture of African American life, but the truth was that he was far more interested in showing up the evils and iniquities of South Africa than providing an objective account of conditions in the United States. Even the southern states, 'famous throughout the world as a hot-bed of racial prejudice', he found to be a 'wonderful revelation', its system of segregation, in his view, altogether more benign than South Africa's. If he encountered instances of personal discrimination during his travels, in the southern States or elsewhere, he did not write about them. Even in the segregated South he was surprised at being able to stay, in defiance of local custom, in 'white' hotels.[67]

What remained to be seen was whether there would be any scope for applying the lessons he had learnt once he returned home. As he pointed out time and time again, black Americans did not suffer the political and legal disabilities that blighted the lives of his own people. However inspiring the example of African Americans, the fundamentals of South Africa needed to change if his people were to progress. Even if it was going to take more than fifty years.

FOURTEEN

Too long away, England, 1922–1923

Zonophone Records
BY
SOL T. PLAATJE.

The following Records have been made by Mr. Sol. T. Plaatje, who is well known to the South African Natives for his publications and lectures in connection with the Brotherhood movement, which he founded among them.

He has travelled widely in order to further the interests of this object, and lectured in many places during his visit to Europe and North America.

ZONOPHONE RECORDS
Double-sided 10-inch **3/6**.

4167	Hark 'tis the Watchman's Cry .. (Hymn in Sechuana) Lead Kindly Light .. (Hymn in Sechuana)	*Sol. T. Plaatje Piano acc. by Miss Sylvia Colenso* " "
4168	Pesheya Ko Tukela (Across the Tugela) Singa Mawela (We are Twins)	" "
4169	A band of hard pressed men are we .. (Hymn in Si-Xosa) The Kaffir Wedding Song (J. K. Bhokwe) (Sung in Xosa)	*Sol. T. Plaatje with Piano acc.* " "

Manufactured by
THE GRAMOPHONE COMPANY, LIMITED,
FOR
THE BRITISH ZONOPHONE COMPANY, LIMITED.

After 'a most delightful cruise across the ocean with a lot of Canadians whose behaviour made the voyage very pleasant', Plaatje arrived back in England on 21 September 1922, hoping to return home to South Africa in a few months' time. But as so often, things did not work out as planned, and in the event it was to be a frustrating and at times very depressing period of over a year before he was able to do so: 'circumstances', as he had written to Mrs Solomon a few months earlier, 'are always beyond our control'.[1]

One of his first tasks, while the experience was still fresh in his mind, was to write a thirty-page account of his American visit for Betty Molteno and her niece Margaret Lennox Murray. Since they had made it possible, he felt that providing 'some particulars of my trip' for the two of them was the least he could do in return. It was an informative but highly selective account, concentrating on his personal impressions of the United States and Canada, and the useful information he had obtained, but with nothing whatever to say about his contact with more radical organisations like Marcus Garvey's UNIA. Betty Molteno was delighted with it. 'To my surprise', Plaatje told Mrs Lennox Murray, 'she got a keen and extraordinary delight in reading it. Your aunt got so enthusiastic over it that she visited Mrs Saul Solomon and Miss Solomon at Hampstead and read it over to them. Next morning she hurried to my lodgings to thank me for it: in fact, rushed in here early before I even got up.' In such a mood Betty Molteno's enthusiasms knew no bounds.[2]

He promised to send his account to Mrs Lennox Murray too, though he told her she would have to wait until he had a chance to type out another copy, since he thought it unlikely her aunt would part with hers. She too was fascinated by what he had to say, so much so that she decided to pass on the typescript to General Smuts. His only response, in a belated letter of thanks, was to say he thought it was 'quite interesting'. Since he was prime minister at the time and still preoccupied with the fall-out from the so-called Rand Rebellion a few months earlier, a cursory reply was perhaps understandable.[3]

＋～＋

Plaatje's main purpose in staying on in England was to try to raise the money to print his African-language translations of the Brotherhood hymnbook. He had been at this, off and on, since 1919, but he was really no closer to achieving this objective than he had been then. For all the promises made, little or no money seems to have materialised. He thought the hymnbooks were crucial to the growth of his Brotherhood organisation in South Africa, a foundation to its religious life that was every bit as important as the halls and meeting places he wanted too, and he would often point to 'the immense influence exercised by the musical portion of a Brotherhood service'. In a way these hymnbooks seem to have assumed an almost symbolic importance in his mind. It was as if he felt he had to bring something back with him to South Africa, something to show for his long absence from home, something to justify all the time and energy he had devoted to the Brotherhood movement.[4]

However, other things now conspired to keep him from this task, including, as he explained in a letter to Betty Molteno, the general election that was due to take place on 15 November: 'I wish the Government had selected a better time to stage a general election', he complained, 'I can see nobody.' It was not the only problem. His educational films from Henry Ford had got no further than the customs house, while his film of Tuskegee was 'held up at Dover and they threaten to send it back if I don't at once pay some international nonsense'. 'It seems a pity', he said, 'that foreigners should give me moving pictures free gratis and for nothing – worth thousands of dollars – for the education of British subjects and then the British Government give me all this trouble.'[5]

These battles with the customs authorities continued for months to come, complicated by the fact that they first of all consented to his plans to show the films in England, then changed their minds. Convinced of the popular appeal of anything to do with Tuskegee and Booker T. Washington, he had hoped the films would be a means of raising some money and was bitterly disappointed at not being able to do so. 'It would have lightened my burdens considerably, and also hastened my departure for S Africa', he said.[6]

As to the elections, he was no mere observer, for he offered his services to one of the prospective Liberal candidates, none other than John Harris, still secretary of the Anti-Slavery and Aborigines' Protection Society, but now standing as Liberal candidate for the Camberwell North West constituency in south London. Writing to Mrs Colenso, he explained why he did so: 'You know, I am no personal friend of John H. Harris, but the position he occupied and the loyalty of his wife impelled me to go and offer them my assistance.'[7]

What Plaatje really had in mind is open to speculation. Partly, perhaps, it was a question of being able to forgive and forget their earlier battles in the interests of achieving parliamentary representation for a man who could be expected to raise colonial, and possibly South African, issues in the House of Commons. Perhaps, too, he hoped that his offer of assistance to Harris, especially if he were elected, might encourage him to take an interest in his Brotherhood work and open a few doors in return. As ever, he could ill afford to be choosy about his friends in the situation in which he now found himself, and their bitter personal battles were, after all, over five years old. Both were willing to forget their past differences.

Not that his assistance in electioneering proved sufficient to get Harris into the House of Commons. Harris had set himself 'the very difficult task of winning North West Camberwell for real Liberalism and progress'. He fought his campaign on 'the application of Christian principles to political life' (Plaatje would not have quibbled with that), but he finished at the bottom of the poll, blaming his defeat on Labour's decision to put up a candidate, thereby splitting the Liberal vote and allowing in Dr Thomas Macnamara, the National Liberal Party's candidate. Plaatje nevertheless considered his assistance had been of some help: 'It proved more valuable than I expected,' he wrote, 'and he [Harris] knows that I got him a number of votes; but he had very poor agents. I doubted if anyone could win with such amateurish canvassers. I was sorry but not surprised when he was defeated.'[8]

Plaatje did find some grounds for satisfaction in election results elsewhere. His letter to Mrs Colenso, written from the lodgings he now had in Tavistock Place, Bloomsbury, gave a typically humorous account of his observations:

> Wasn't it a foggy election, but I think that on the whole we came splendidly out of the fog. Everybody seems to be satisfied. The Tories because they are in power. The Labourites because they have doubled their strength; the Liberals have also doubled their number and Lloyd George thinks he had not been entirely obliterated. Was there ever an election that gave such widespread satisfaction?
>
> I was intensely interested in half a dozen candidates and all but two have come in with smashing majorities. Sir Richard Winfrey beat his opponent by 1,777. Dr Salter beat them by 2,325, as for [E.D.] MOREL his victory was as smashing as the effects of a 75 mile Krupp gun. Fancy kicking down to the bottom of the poll – Winston Churchill of all people in the world! I am glad to find that both Tories and Liberal papers are agreed that no election result was so sensational.[9]

Even when things were more settled after the election, and the people Plaatje wanted to see more accessible, he made precious little progress in raising money for the hymnbooks. He renewed contact with his Brotherhood networks, particularly in West London and Leighton Buzzard, but the organisation had lost some momentum during his time in America and he found it difficult to arouse interest in his cause. 'Unfortunately few people in this country are interested in South Africa', he complained. 'It is all the East Indies, the West Indies, and West Africans. Apparently, they have no time for the suffering toilers of the land where the gold and diamonds come from – if they only knew the truth!'[10]

Nor was it any easier to find ways of earning a living than it had been during his previous visit to London. As before, there were a few pounds to be made from writing for the *African World* and *South Africa*, and in assisting language students at the School of Oriental Studies. One of these was a very able 25-year-old South African called Gérard Lestrade, then studying for an MA in African languages and phonetics, of whom Alice Werner had a particularly high opinion; he would later refer to his 'notes of Plaatje's speech, taken down in London in 1922/3'. Plaatje also re-established contact with Daniel Jones at University College, and they had some further sessions on the phonetic study of Setswana.[11]

Employment of a different kind was provided by the visit to London of a deputation from Swaziland, which arrived in England in January 1923. It was led by the Swazi king, Sobhuza II (a one-time classmate of St Leger's at Lovedale). The delegation included Pixley ka Isaka Seme, moving spirit in the formation of the South African Native National Congress in 1912, and had come to London to lay its case in the complex land concessions issue before the Colonial Office. As befitted the long obsession of the British press and public with African royalty (they were much less interested in educated commoners), Sobhuza's presence in London was given a huge amount of publicity, and while Dr Manfred Nathan, his chief legal adviser, negotiated with the Colonial Office over the intricacies of the land question, the young king saw the sights of London, attended numerous functions – among them a fundraising concert in the Acton Town Hall organised by John Barbour-James – and was ultimately accorded a half-hour audience with the English king, George V.[12]

In much of this Plaatje was involved, acting as a guide and adviser on their various engagements. He appears in several of the photographs that were taken in London, and in a short Pathé news film of the members of the deputation ('here to confer with the Colonial Office', viewers were told) he is shown standing discreetly in the second row, partially obscured by the burly figure of Benjamin Nxumalo, Sobhuza's secretary. Plaatje, as well connected as anybody with potential sympathisers in London, black or white, was responsible for the introductions at the various functions the deputation attended. One was hosted by the recently formed (predominantly West African) Union of Students of African Descent; it was reported to have been 'largely attended' and to have extended a warm welcome 'to the guests from Swaziland'. Another, smaller but equally welcoming reception was held at Mrs Solomon's home in Hampstead. Here, according to Alice Werner, Mrs Solomon 'harangued poor dear Sobhuza [and] kept him standing for, I should think, 20 minutes while saying good-bye, to point out his and his people's duty to women in general', repeatedly drawing attention to what she called 'the law of the mother'. Plaatje knew Mrs Solomon well enough by now to have heard it all before.[13]

Plaatje approached the Swazi king with a request for financial assistance, and made no bones about his predicament. According to Chief Mandananda Mtsetfwa, one of the deputation, Sobhuza's response, when Seme told him of Plaatje's financial plight, was to say: 'Of course, we must help him. He is one of us.' A limited unofficial advisory role then followed, but any remuneration is unlikely to have extended much beyond his subsistence during the month they were in England.[14]

With the departure of the Swazi deputation at the beginning of February 1923, Plaatje returned to the task of fundraising for his Brotherhood hymnbooks. He could still attract good audiences, but donations were few and far between. William Cross, of the Southall Brotherhood, the treasurer of the appeal committee, did what he could to assist, but the prospect of raising the £862 required by the Aberdeen University Press (from whom a quotation had been obtained) looked more remote than ever. Plaatje's letter to Betty Molteno on 27 February was distinctly pessimistic: 'The flight of time and the slow response to our efforts on behalf of the hymn book are giving me much concern. I have long overstayed my time and the work is suffering on account of my absence.' He thought it essential, though, that he should stay on in England long enough to correct the hymn proofs and verify the metres since nobody could do this for him. To resolve the conundrum he asked: 'Is it not possible to find some benevolent sympathizer who could advance our Committee with £300 so that the printer may go to work while we prosecute our appeal? The Committee could guarantee the return of the loan and arrange the refund. Their efforts would be largely supplemented by the sales of the hymn book.'[15]

Betty Molteno did not have this kind of money herself but she was sympathetic to his appeal for help. She spoke with him at length about what he hoped to achieve with the hymnbooks, and her instincts warmed to anything she thought 'could help to move the soul of a people that it may better express itself in nobler life and deeds'. 'To take part in such a work', she told him, 'would indeed be a high honour. It would be a great call from God. And when God calls we must listen and try to understand and if we can obey the call.' She agreed to help: not just herself but on behalf of her late partner, Alice Greene, who had always asked for 'a profound sincerity' so far as religious belief was concerned, and whose last words, so she told Plaatje, were 'about the native peoples of South Africa'. Over the next few months, as she saw more of him, there were signs that her friendship with Plaatje was starting to fill something of the void left by Alice's death three years earlier.[16]

Nowhere was this more evident than in the free verse she used to write and circulate to her extended family. This included a poem, consisting of three typed pages, entitled 'Plaatje', dated 25 May, and inspired by a recent encounter with him. Much of it was almost mystical in tone, but in places she addresses him directly. 'O Plaatje, you rascal', she begins, 'What have I to you to say? / Do you think I have nothing else to do all day, / But busy myself with your affairs?' Nevertheless he fascinated her, she loved to listen to his stories, she enjoyed their walks around London, and he provided the emotional link with Africa she craved: 'I don't deny you are very interesting', she admitted, 'Bringing Africa to me, / In this little isle of the Northern Sea'.[17]

But she also found him an enigma, never sure what was really in his mind: 'O but you are a whole bag of tricks,/ A bit of quicksilver hard to fix. / What many ingredients are in you mixed? / Does anything in you fast stick?' At other times she envied him: for example, his skill at the typewriter, while she had to employ a secretary to rewrite her barely legible handwriting, and she thought he 'sometimes lives in a room very much better than mine', and dressed better too. Above all she thought him 'a child of nature', closer to his African roots than she could ever be, untainted – or so she hoped – by the corrupted Western civilisation she herself could not escape. 'I want him', she wrote in her private journal, to 'keep intact the purity of his own soul that the exquisitely pure spirit of Africa may be able to make use of him and guard him from the contaminations of European life'.[18]

She contrasted her view of Plaatje with that of Mrs Solomon. 'She really spoils him. She is like the Granny with the petted grandchild', and just thinking about it made her cross. Nothing pleased Georgiana Solomon more than 'when she is mothering her huge, black African family', she added, and when she did 'her blue eyes fierily sparkle and words flow out in abundance' (as they had done at her reception for the Swazi king). Betty Molteno saw her own relationship with Plaatje very differently: 'Plaatje and I are more on a level. I can't patronize him with too much sympathy', and she thought that in reality Plaatje was 'very well off compared with lots of people today' – including, she thought, herself.

His friendship with Betty Molteno was anything but straightforward, hugely complicated by her romantic sensibilities as well as the complex dynamics of gender, race and power – and to be negotiated with some care.[19]

Whatever went through Betty Molteno's mind, there was little she could do to boost his Brotherhood hymnbook fund. Writing to Albon Holsey at Tuskegee some weeks after raising the matter with her, he sounded no more hopeful. 'Perhaps you will be surprised that I am still in England', he wrote. 'So am I and so are my folks in South Africa. Of all the things I have ever undertaken nothing has worried me so much as the task of finding the money to print the Native Hymn Book and tonic solfa tunes for our Community Services in S. Africa. The task of translating the metres into African was child's play compared with the job of finding the money.'[20]

Seeking funds for these hymnbooks was not a total preoccupation. He found it difficult not to engage with other issues that affected black people. In the same letter he asked Holsey to send him a copy of 'the latest Negro Year Book' in order to help him support the novelist Charlotte Mansfield in her campaign against the continued stream of misrepresentations about black troops in occupied Germany, just as vitriolic as the last time he had been in England. Miss Mansfield, he said, was doing her best to counter this propaganda in the letters column of one of London's evening papers, but she was in need of more facts and information. 'Seeing her heroic stand,' Plaatje wrote, 'I sought her out and supplied munitions for her hammer blows.' He preferred to support her behind the scenes rather than join the fray himself as he thought that to do so 'would jeopardize the position of the S. African Natives'. The reason for this was that 'generally our best friends are the pacifists who are against France'. Yet some of them had cynically exploited the 'horror on the Rhine' controversy as a stick with which to beat the French. Among them was his old friend and supporter Dr Alfred Salter, recently elected as member of parliament for Bermondsey. He had intervened in the *Pall Mall Gazette* exchange, adding his own criticisms of the alleged behaviour of the black troops. Fault lines of race, were any reminder needed, ran every bit as deep in the UK and Europe as they did in the colonies and dominions. Even friends and supporters were susceptible to the insidious appeal of racial thinking.[21]

Plaatje's other major concern was his novel *Mhudi*, still without a publisher. Here at least there had been some encouragement. Having had no luck with publishers in North America he had, before he left for England, sent a copy of the MS to the firm of George Allen and Unwin, run by Stanley Unwin, who had left the firm of T. Fisher Unwin (his step-uncle) to strike out on his own in 1914. Stanley Unwin was sufficiently interested in *Mhudi* to send it out to his principal reader, Bernard Miall, a man remembered for his ability 'to turn his hand to almost any MSS for a competent first opinion'. Miall's report has not survived but it must have been positive, for Stanley Unwin then offered to publish the book. The only drawback, so Plaatje reported, was that 'he wants £75 if he is to handle it'. Worthy of publication, as Stanley Unwin saw it, but not sufficiently commercial to risk investing in without a subsidy.[22]

There the matter had rested. Plaatje did not have £75 and it was difficult to try to raise this while at the same time prosecuting his appeal for the Brotherhood hymnbooks. But he did, it seems, try other publishers in the hope that one might be prepared to publish without need of subsidy. Jonathan Cape, he was probably aware, had published an English edition of *Batouala* in 1922, so that was one possibility. Sophie Colenso and Georgiana Solomon did what they could to help push *Mhudi*, but to no avail. 'I have to thank you very much indeed for the trouble you took in reference to my novel', he wrote to Sophie Colenso in May 1923. 'And if the manuscript is not printed it will be in spite of your efforts. Nobody could have done more than you did; but these publishers are not of our way of thinking.' Some weeks later he wrote to Georgiana Solomon to ask her 'to do so kindly and let me have that copy of the novel back', as 'from next week I want to try some other publishers with it'. None, it seems, were interested.[23]

By the end of May 1923 Plaatje was intent on returning home, regardless of the fate of either hymnbooks or novel. Writing to Mrs Colenso he complained of being 'frightfully overworked', also that he had had 'two attacks of neuritis'. 'These illnesses do not advance my work at all; and, after each spell, the accumulation of work does not improve my health.' He continued to hear from 'Mrs Plaatje and the children'; they were – Sophie Colenso would not have been surprised to hear – 'much troubled about my long absence', but he added, 'I sincerely hope my efforts will succeed to effect my get-away'. 'If only the summer and better weather will bring health and enable us to move about and get something.' He promised his family he would be home by July.[24]

A month later his departure looked imminent. Writing this time to Betty Molteno, he told her he was 'so immersed in the sailing efforts that I have very little time to work', though he did manage to visit the Leighton Buzzard Men's Club to say his farewells. He gave a talk on 'the other man', a plea for people to give proper consideration to the wishes and needs of other people, concluding – as he often did on these occasions – by singing several verses in Setswana from his favourite hymn, 'Lead, kindly light'. He was reported to have received 'a great welcome and a very hearty send-off'. William Dixon, President of the organisation, had long been one of his keenest supporters.[25]

Then everything changed. An unexpected offer of employment came from George Lattimore, former manager of the Southern Syncopated Orchestra (SSO) whom Plaatje had first met in 1919. Since then Lattimore had been involved in a long-running legal dispute with Will Marion Cook, the original conductor of the SSO, over its ownership and control, and the orchestra had split into two factions, studiously avoiding one another as they toured the British Isles. Lattimore himself narrowly avoided being declared bankrupt. Then disaster struck: nine members of the SSO were drowned when the ship on which they were travelling to Ireland, the SS *Rowan*, sank after being struck by another vessel. The survivors resumed their tour, struggled on for a few weeks to fulfil their engagements, and finally disbanded early in 1922.[26]

Lattimore, however, stayed on in England, carving out a career for himself as an impresario who specialised in bringing black American bands and stage shows to Europe, his entrepreneurial instincts well attuned to the growing appeal of 'negro exotica'. In the middle of 1923, with a lease on the Philharmonic Hall in Great Portland Street (where the SSO had at one time performed), he had plans for something different. He had secured the rights to show a wildlife film, based on footage shot by a zoological expedition, led by Prince William of Sweden, which had travelled to Central Africa two years before. *Among Pygmies and Gorillas*, an account of the expedition, had just been published, and the film itself had already been shown in Sweden. Hoping to cash in on the recent popularity of other films of this kind, but recognising the need to come up with something to distinguish it from its competitors, Lattimore employed Plaatje to assist in preparing the film for commercial presentation in English, and to devise a live theatrical sketch to accompany it – a 'unique entertainment', he called it, to add to the audience's enjoyment and appreciation of the film. Lattimore also took every opportunity to stress his own African American origins to help market the film and persuade press and public that he was uniquely qualified to bring it to London audiences. If all went well, he hoped then to take it to North America.[27]

Plaatje, desperate for money, accepted Lattimore's offer of £10 a week, hoping, as he said, that it would 'solve my sailing difficulties by taking me out of the uncertainties of charity'. Initially he worked on the film itself ('cutting out the undesirable parts of which there are not a few') as well as preparing the musical accompaniment and theatrical sketch. He was 'frightfully overworked', he told Betty Molteno, but found the work 'intensely interesting'. Among his cast, it is interesting to note, were Kamba Simango and his wife Kathleen, who were in London with some time to spare and happy to help out. Both had taken part in similar productions in the US, and Kathleen devised one of the scenes that Plaatje incorporated into the sketch. Others reported to have had parts were 'Mr Kwa Minade, of Accra' and a 'Miss Gupta' from Abyssinia, taking a break from 'studying music in Paris where she has taken an arts degree'.[28]

A week later Plaatje wrote to Mrs Solomon, who was on holiday in Edinburgh, with a further progress report: 'It is a strenuous work preparing my inexperienced team. But when we settle down to the programme, I hope to have easier times for the actual work will be but half an hour afternoons and half an hour each evening. And if the play is a success, we are booked to the end of September so that I can now definitely say I will be sailing in October.' He went on: 'I had promised to be home by July and these postponements are very depressing. I hope however that this time we are on something definite. I get lugubrious letters from home, they wonder if I am ever coming home.' Finally, he told her, 'for the more expeditious performance of my work I have had to change quarters. I am now back again in Tavistock Square in a more spacious room, where rest is possible beside the green square. And every part of the city is so easily accessible to this place.'[29]

The letter perhaps provided some cheer for Georgiana Solomon: the day before she had written to a friend to tell her that 'Mr Plaatje's lonesome struggle and forsakenness painfully affects my spirit', and she couldn't understand why he did not get more support from the Brotherhood movement.[30]

The Cradle of the World opened at the Philharmonic Hall on 9 August, claiming to be the 'most marvellous and thrilling travel film ever screened'. Plaatje considered it a 'great show' and reported that they had received 'two tremendous standing ovations' on press night. He was optimistic about its prospects, considered it a striking contrast 'to the infamous Birth of a Nation', and was impressed by the technical quality of the film. So too, for the most part, were the critics, though one or two wondered whether the public might by now have had enough of this type of film. Nevertheless, the *Daily Express* thought it 'unquestionably the best wild animal and travel film ever seen in this country', the first of the 'many big game films in which the cinematographer came first and the hunter second', a view echoed by the *Pall Mall Gazette* ('without doubt far and away the most thrilling travel film yet shown'). The quality of the photography and the expertise of the expedition's chief photographer, Oscar Olsson, was widely praised. So too was his bravery. In one of the film's most dramatic moments a rhinoceros charges towards the camera. Olsson's colleagues fail to bring it down in time with their rifles, and he only just manages to jump clear. His tripod and camera are crushed by the dying rhinoceros, but the film in the camera was undamaged.

There was less unanimity, however, about the manner in which the film was presented. *The Times* thought it 'rather slavishly adapted to the convention that is now so familiar', and found the subtitles 'more than usually irritating' and 'written with a mixture of flippancy and condescension which is decidedly out of place' – by no means the only review to make this point.[31]

Opinions were mixed, too, about 'Somewhere in Africa', the theatrical sketch – or 'playlet' as one newspaper called it – which Plaatje devised and presented during the main interval. *Kinematograph Weekly* thought 'the African folk-songs and dances by native Africans contribute a novelty which affords no inconsiderable aid to the atmosphere of the presentation'; another reviewer was struck by the 'haunting boat song', its finale, and thought it 'deserves wider recognition'; while the *Morning Post* commended 'Intombi', the dancer ('exceedingly graceful in her movements'), and considered 'the songs in entire harmony with the spirit of the film'. *South Africa*, which provided the most detailed description, was impressed too, but had some reservations. Noting that the performers included 'Mr Sol Plaatje, the South African native author', who took the part of Chief Dumakude, it welcomed the opportunity, 'after seeing so many tribes on the screen, to see some Africans in the flesh'. 'To those of us who are acquainted with the wonderful part-singing of the South African natives, the four choruses at the Philharmonic Hall leave something to be desired, as they hardly give effective support to the soloists.'[32]

Overall, however, it was a lively production. 'Assegais describe circles in the air while the warriors recite their martial deeds. Miss Gupta dances to the pace of an expert tom-tom beater, and draws loud applause which earns for her a beaded necklace from the Chief. Two men subsequently fight over her in a wild scrimmage, during which spears fly and crash against the shields; and one wonders what would happen were the fight between 20 natives instead of only two.' Like other reviewers, *South Africa*'s correspondent was impressed by the boat song at the end of the sketch – 'more effective and reminiscent of the rhythm and harmony of the South African native vocalists'. Those interested in foreign lands, the review concluded, 'will enlarge their knowledge by spending an afternoon or evening at the Philharmonic Hall'.

Rather briefer, and more critical, remarks appeared in London's other major African journal, the *African World*: 'the theatrical scenes in which various grotesquely attired natives headed by our old friend, Mr Sol Plaatje, as a Chief, could, we think, be well dispensed with'. The *African World*'s critic surely had a point, and Plaatje himself must have been acutely aware of the paradox implicit in the *African World*'s comments. Here he was, an educated, 'civilised native', come to England to seek support for the cause of his people on the basis of their shared humanity and Christian faith, now employed to project exactly the kind of image he sought to demolish. Some months earlier he had told a meeting of the Union of Students of African Descent in London that he had been struck, when he was in the United States, by the 'extraordinary misconceptions' in currency about the African people. Many Americans, he said, supposed them to be 'a kind of baboon running about wild', so it was essential to spread a sound, informed knowledge of African people and institutions in order to counter such 'misconceptions'.[33]

But the harsh reality was that Plaatje was in no position to turn down the offer of work on *The Cradle of the World*, and he had to find some money from somewhere. Others involved in the sketch – all of them 'educated natives from East, West and South Africa' – no doubt felt the same way. They had to make the best of it and fit in with what was required of them. In the centre of the empire, more than anywhere, Africans were expected to conform to traditional stereotypes: witness, earlier that year, two photographs of King Sobhuza that were reproduced in *South Africa* when he visited London. In one he was in traditional dress, with the caption 'natural'; in the other, next to it, he was dressed in conventional Western attire, with the caption 'artificial'.[34]

Not that any of this bothered Betty Molteno, for in truth her image of Africa and Africans owed much to these stereotypes, albeit considerably modified by her idiosyncratic brand of spirituality. Seeing Plaatje in 'Somewhere in Africa' touched her deepest emotions and the next day she put pen to paper. 'O Plaatje! I saw you on the platform!' she wrote, 'O my friend I loved so, / Did I you in that strange scene know? / In a sense I was taken by storm.' She felt 'the vibrations of deep heart strings': 'O you lovely, native races, / Of Nature's teaching you show many traces'. The experience transported her to Africa: 'I wanted to go to Africa, / Well I have been taken there. / Answered has been my soul's prayer. / I have seen much of the land so divinely fair'. Her friendship with Plaatje went to the very depths of her psyche.[35]

The Cradle of the World did not prove to be a box-office success. Audiences were disappointing and a prolonged heat wave in the first half of August discouraged all theatre-going; its eight-week run was not extended, a blow to Plaatje's hopes of finding the money for his passage to South Africa. The cast of 'Somewhere in Africa' went their separate ways, and the film moved on to the provinces, more often than not showing a reel at a time in support of some more popular attraction; soon it disappeared from view and George Lattimore abandoned the idea of taking it to New York. As ever, though, Plaatje took full advantage of every new opportunity. 'I learnt a lot during the month', he told Mrs Solomon, 'and came in contact with people I otherwise would never have met – the greatest thing was to get acquainted with some film folks; and while I have educational films about Canada, West Indies and the United States, I was departing with nothing about England. Now I have found a man who gave me decent lengths about the Queen and King attending the races, the Prince of Wales visiting Indian schools, including his unveiling of his grandfather's monument at Calcutta, Lord Allenby entering Jerusalem during the war and a couple of incidents showing the London crowds.'[36]

The Cradle of the World threw up musical possibilities too. 'It gave me the facility of dictating our traditional music to the Director of the orchestra at the London Coliseum and he arranged some beautiful orchestration for it. When the Philharmonic Band played these melodies to illustrate some of the pictures on the screen, except for their weird repetition, they were scarcely distinguishable from the works of great European masters; and in my own songs I found the harmony of the English orchestral accompaniment very thrilling and opening up a new vision. Anglo-Africans, like Mlle Dumas and Dr Colenso, who heard my songs, informed me they could understand every word of the Sesuto and Zulu phrasing through the strains of the orchestra and the explosive clicks, which were to them a new thing on the concert platform.'[37]

Recalling this experience some years later, Plaatje compared the emergence of a distinctive and increasingly recognised African American style of music in the United States, with what he saw as the dire situation of black music in South Africa, neglected and unappreciated. The few weeks he spent working on *The Cradle of the World* convinced him, more than ever, that black South African music, if encouraged and nurtured, had enormous potential too. Plaatje's own musical talents deserved a better forum, it is fair to say, than in 'Somewhere in Africa'. It was a far cry from those performances of the Philharmonic Society in Kimberley twenty-five years before.[38]

While still engaged with *The Cradle of the World*, Plaatje and his friends made a last effort to raise funds for his hymnbooks with a concert one Sunday late in August. George Lattimore generously made the Philharmonic Hall available free of charge, while the promoter C.B. Cochran likewise agreed to release three African American members of the cast of *Dover Street to Dixie*, then coming to the end of a highly successful run at the Piccadilly Pavilion, to perform gratis. Since their normal fee would have been £77, Plaatje considered this an extremely generous gesture. Unfortunately, Florence Mills, the star of the show, was not among the three. Her presence alone would have guaranteed a large audience and perhaps made some inroads into the £800 that was still required to have the hymnbooks printed. In reality, according to Betty Molteno, whatever the press reports said, the concert was not very well attended. That, however, suited her quite well. The hall was 'wonderfully peaceful', she was inspired by the 'Negro spirituals', and she could meditate without interruption on being 'among the dark skinned people', believing that in such company she had found 'a sort of spiritual home'.[39]

No sooner had this concert taken place than arrangements were in hand for another: not in aid of Plaatje's Brotherhood work, but in honour of Plaatje himself. It was to take place on his forty-seventh birthday, Monday, 9 October 1923, and it was the opportunity for friends and supporters to bid him farewell, for he had now definitely decided to depart, regardless of the fate of his hymnbooks. Predictably these last few weeks were rather hectic and he had a lot to sort out. This was clear from his letter to Mrs Solomon a few days before the concert: 'You find me on your return from Scotland, in the hard work of preparing for Tuesday's concert. It was painful to come to the door on Saturday with tickets and then run off to Amersham without even waiting to pay my respects and tender to you my greetings. It is going to be a continuous run till this concert is over. It is so difficult to obtain good artistes and their accompanists. Then there are so many things to print and to pay and so many stringent Government regulations to comply with before permission can be obtained to run a Charity show – What between the hall, and Mr Cross at Hanwell, and the Customs authorities at Camden Town, whose requirements and payments are insatiable, to say nothing of my customary drudgery, I really wish these days had 36 hours instead of 24.'[40]

Among the artistes he had managed to engage were 'Miss Coleridge-Taylor (the great composer's daughter), a former member of the Jubilee Singers, one black American baritone, and, of course, the Colensos'. They would be joined by Evelyn Dove, a contralto, graduate of the Royal Academy of Music and daughter of a wealthy barrister from Sierra Leone and his English wife – and a lucky survivor of the *Rowan* disaster in 1921; Mary Lawrence, described as 'The West Indian soprano' (who more often went by the name of Marie); and 'Miss Winifred Procktor', probably the daughter of W.A. Procktor, a longstanding Brotherhood friend from Stoke Newington in north London. It was quite an impressive ensemble.[41]

Plaatje took a part in the concert himself, singing 'Lead, kindly light' in Sesotho and 'Singa mawele' ('We are twins') in Xhosa before the interval.

William Dixon, of the Leighton Buzzard Brotherhood, chaired the evening's proceedings, gave a short address during the interval, and congratulated Plaatje on his birthday. In response, Plaatje made a few humorous comments about other 'October babies' of note in South African history (Kruger, Rhodes, Milner), after which Mrs Sophie Colenso – in a touching ceremony – presented him with 'a large wreath' of laurels taken from the garden at 'Elangeni'. It carried the words 'With heartiest congratulations to the brave champion of the S. African natives, from the family of Gebuza ka Sobantu [Bishop Colenso]'. It was this moment, more than any other, that Mrs Solomon, unable to attend the function because of a severe chill, regretted missing. In the view of the journal *South Africa*, more friendly these days, the large audience present 'eloquently testified to Mr Plaatje's popularity'.[42]

Betty Molteno was almost overcome by the occasion. She had sought out 'a corner next to the wall where I was all alone' since she found it 'intolerable to be hemmed in among people when I am listening to moving music', and 'excruciatingly intense to me to listen to those African voices with their marvellous range and super-abundant volume'. She loved Coleridge-Taylor's 'Negro Melodies' played by the three Colenso sisters (on piano, violin and cello respectively), but was irritated by William Dixon, the chairman – 'tiresome', she thought, in the way 'he poured out his lavish abundant congratulations to Plaatje on the wonderful work he was doing for his people in England'. She felt she knew Plaatje better than anybody, and that there was rather more to him than this. In fact, she thought, that evening 'he looked sweeter and gentler than is usual with him. Very sensitive medium he is and is evidently suffering at the prospect at parting from his many English friends and admirers.' This was not so surprising. These friends had been an important part of his life for a long time now. It was unlikely he would ever see them again.[43]

In the midst of the preparations for his departure, there arose an unexpected but very welcome opportunity to make some sound recordings at the Gramophone Company's studios in Hayes in west London. The first of these involved Professor Daniel Jones, still interested in Setswana and keen to take advantage of Plaatje's expertise while he could. Sound recordings were important in the work of his department, he had already made a recording of his own for HMV (about 'The eight cardinal vowels'), so he was familiar with the possibilities. On the morning of 9 October, therefore, the two of them set off to Hayes to record Plaatje reciting, in Setswana, two of the tales which appear in their *Sechuana Reader* – 'The fable of the south wind and the sun' and 'Bulging cheeks are a characteristic of the cat family'. Introducing the two readings, Jones announces them as a 'Specimen of the Sechuana language, spoken by Mr S.T. Plaatje'. Curiously, for somebody for whom correct enunciation was everything, he pronounces Plaatje's name 'Plaat-ye', forgetting – or ignoring – the phonetic guidance provided in the *Sechuana Reader* itself.[44]

On the record label, above the famous HMV 'dog and trumpet' trademark, are the words 'private record', while the studio register describes it as an 'Educational test'. It was recorded on one side, and may have been the only copy made. What use, if any, Jones or his colleagues made of it in their work on Setswana is unknown, but it was an intriguing conclusion to the long collaboration between the two men, and a unique record of the pronunciation of Setswana from this time, capturing its musical qualities more vividly than any phonetic script. It is only through good fortune that the record survived. Having lain undisturbed for decades in a storage cupboard under the stairs in UCL's Phonetics Department in Gordon Square, it only came to light, along with a treasure trove of other unknown recordings, when the department moved to new premises in 2008.[45]

Plaatje was back at the studios in Hayes a week later. This time he was accompanied not by Professor Jones but by Sylvia Colenso, and their intention was to record some traditional African songs and hymns. He was to be the soloist and she was to accompany him on the piano. Unlike his first recording, this was a commercial venture, Zonophone being keen to add to their Zonophone Native Records series, for South Africa, which they had launched in 1912. Most likely this new recording came about through his work with the director of the orchestra at the London Coliseum, and then with the Philharmonic Band when they provided the accompaniment for *The Cradle of the World*. Zonophone records nos. 4167 and 4168, double-sided ten-inch discs, were the outcome. The first contained two hymns sung by Plaatje in Setswana, 'Lead, kindly light' (which he had sung at his farewell concert) and 'Hark, 'tis the watchman's cry'; while the second had two traditional songs in Xhosa – 'Pesheya ko Tugela' ('Across the Tukela'), a Hlubi folksong, and 'Singa mawele' ('We are twins'), described as a 'dance melody' (also sung at his farewell concert).[46]

There was something else too. After 'Pesheya ko Tukela', at the end of the first side of 4168, Plaatje can be heard singing 'Nkosi sikelel' iAfrika', the famous anthem composed in 1897 by the Xhosa composer Enoch Sontonga. It is just over a minute long, half the length of 'Pesheya ko Tukela'. Curiously, despite being listed in the studio's recording register, where it is described as a 'Native national hymn in Zulu and Suto' (though the version Plaatje sings is actually in Xhosa), it does not appear on the record label, nor is it mentioned in any subsequent publicity or advertising material.

Quite why is open to speculation. Although it would soon be adopted by the African National Congress as its official anthem, there is nothing to suggest the government was concerned about its use, or that by issuing it Zonophone had reason to worry about incurring their disapproval. More likely its omission from the label was just an oversight, or perhaps there was just insufficient space to include it. Whatever the reason, it was surely a missed marketing opportunity. It is difficult to imagine that drawing attention to 'Nkosi sikelel' iAfrika', the first time it had ever been recorded, and by so well known a public figure, would not have produced some extra sales had its presence on the record been made known and properly advertised.[47]

A week later, three days before his departure from the UK, Plaatje returned to Hayes for a last time to record what would become Zonophone no. 4169. This time Sylvia Colenso's place at the piano was taken by Madame Adami and a Mr P. Grant. On the first side of the record was a hymn in Xhosa, 'A band of hard-pressed men are we'; on the second an arrangement of John Knox Bokwe's celebrated 'Kaffir wedding song', which Plaatje had once sung with the Philharmonic Society in Kimberley in the 1890s. Most likely it was also among the Bokwe melodies reported to have been sung – with orchestration arranged by the director of the London Coliseum – as part of the programme of *The Cradle of the World*.[48]

↜↝

That same evening, 23 October, Plaatje made his way back to 'Clarensville', Mrs Solomon's house in Hampstead, for a farewell gathering in his honour. Betty Molteno had given him the money for a gramophone, a present for Elizabeth to celebrate their twenty-fifth wedding anniversary. During the evening they used it to play some 'negro music' records which he had bought to go with it, and he entertained them with some songs of his own. Betty Molteno was there too, and in reflective mood. She loved his company but, like the Solomons, she thought he had been away from home for far too long, and often worried about Elizabeth Plaatje, who, she thought, 'had to go through such hard times', while Plaatje himself 'had been enjoying himself here and in America'. 'Of course', she added, 'I know he has done a lot of work; but I am sure it is with difficulty that she has kept things going in Kimberley and I am glad he is to go by this week's mail.'[49]

Similar sentiments permeated her poem 'Good-bye, Plaatje', written a few days earlier. 'Mightily you have enjoyed / Your part on the London stage', she wrote, adding that in 'London's mighty whirlpool' it was 'Difficult for you to keep your head cool'. Again she admitted to being perplexed by him: 'I have studied you intimately / But there is much in you I cannot fathom', and she wondered whether there were not, in the relationship between them, echoes of a previous incarnation, 'old debts to be paid' from a 'long, long past'. She hoped his voyage home to South Africa might provide an opportunity for calmer reflection – but thought it unlikely: 'I fear the ship will not give you peace / Your ambitions they will not cease / You will want to make yourself felt / While in that circumscribed space.'[50]

Finding the money for his ticket (so as 'to take himself out of the hands of charity') proved beyond him. 'The two concerts and all the cinema work have not contributed in any way to the passage money', Betty Molteno discovered after speaking to him, but added that he had 'been before the footlights of the London stage – so he goes away with that satisfaction'. Fortunately Mrs Solomon came to the rescue. She was a relative of Lord Kylsant, chairman of the Union-Castle line, and through his influence was able to get Plaatje a second-class berth at a reduced rate (equivalent to the cost of going third class), and to get the company to agree that he could defer payment until after his arrival in Cape Town. She agreed to guarantee his promise of payment.[51]

With such an arrangement the Union-Castle Company were satisfied. In fact they owed Plaatje a favour. Six years earlier they had benefited from his intervention on behalf of the Rev. and Mrs H.A. Payne, the two black Americans who were refused permission to disembark from the SS *Galway Castle* in Cape Town. Had Plaatje not succeeded in persuading General Botha to reverse the decision of the Immigration Department, the Union-Castle Company would have been liable for the cost and inconvenience of taking them back to London. They had thanked Plaatje at the time for his efforts.

After a final round of farewells and an overnight stay at 'Elangeni', when he delighted Mrs Colenso by 'singing several native songs to trio accompaniment', and gave her some 'negro records', Plaatje sailed from Southampton on 26 October 1923. A day later the South African High Commission in London cabled Pretoria with news of his departure by the *Windsor Castle*, adding that he was 'full of agitation schemes, and should be kept under observation'. This time, it seems, wary of being caught out a second time, they were taking no chances. An alternative, had it occurred to them, might have been to enlist the help of one of Plaatje's fellow passengers in ascertaining his intentions. Also aboard the *Windsor Castle*, returning home after attending the recent Imperial Conference in London, was the Rt Hon. Nicolaas de Wet, South Africa's long-serving minister of justice, responsible for the department now being requested to keep Plaatje 'under observation'. He would not have forgotten Plaatje's intervention over the Orange Free State shootings in 1918 and 1919 – or the awkward parliamentary questions that resulted.[52]

On the morning of Plaatje's departure, the journal *South Africa* published the text of an interview with him, commenting upon it in an accompanying editorial. Little of it was very new or surprising. He contrasted conditions in South Africa with what he had seen in the United States and said this had made 'a profound impression' upon his mind. He criticised several new pieces of legislation in South Africa, in particular the Urban Areas Act of 1923, which in his view added still further to the disabilities imposed upon the African people. The editor of *South Africa* was not wholly impressed. While on the one hand he considered Plaatje to be a man of sincerity and 'a living (and eloquent) example of the potentialities of the South African Native, being himself a scholar, writer, and very pleasant company', on the other he was broadly in sympathy with the South African government's policies of segregation, and thought that the progress of 'native life' should always be 'within native capacity and in keeping with the pace of his evolution, skill and intelligence'. Not all Plaatje's brothers, he said, were as gifted as he, and he hoped that on the voyage home, as well as enjoying the sea air, he might 'think these things over'.[53]

In a way these remarks went to the heart of the dilemma that confronted him. In a society in which a philosophy of segregation was by now widely accepted in ruling circles, it was difficult to see what role there could be for somebody so fundamentally opposed to all it stood for. Plaatje hoped that what he had learnt in America would help his people to prosper in the increasingly industrialised, urbanised society South Africa had become. But was this a realistic hope? He had been away for over four years, and much had changed. There were many other unresolved questions. What place would there be for him among his own people? Who, indeed, could he now consider to be his own people? Was his Brotherhood movement, in which he invested so much, simply an anachronism, no longer relevant to the day-to-day realities of South Africa in the 1920s? And how, to return to harsh practicalities, was he to earn a living?

In the meantime, once the *Windsor Castle* set sail for Cape Town, there was always Shakespeare to fall back upon, and Plaatje was not one to waste an opportunity. By the time they arrived in South Africa on 12 November 1923, he had translated *Othello* into Setswana.

FIFTEEN

The 1920s

A leader without a people?

COMMUNITY HALL, Bloemfontein
Friday, Saturday and Monday,
September 26th, 27th and 29th.

ROLL UP AND SEE

The Coloured American Bioscope

DIRECT FROM CHICAGO LLL., U.S.A.

First-Class Animated Pictures of England, Japan, Coloured People in Brazil, America and the West India Islands.

PRINCIPAL FEATURE.

Booker Washington's School, TUSKEGEE and her thousands of young men and women students at Drill and Manœuvres.

The Immigration Department will not permit any Foreign Negroes not even the Jubilee Singers—beloved of our fathers—to land in the Union. You can only see Coloured Americans on the screen.

Don't Fail to see our FRESH FEATURES!

H.R.H. The Duke of York's Wedding at Westminster Abbey; King George's First Daughter-in-Law; The Late Chief Khama and his Bamangoato People at Serowe; Cricket and other Sports.

COME AND HEAR OUR RAG-TIME AND OTHER SONGS.

ADMISSION 1/-.   RESERVED SEATS 1/6.

Popular Children's Show, 5.30 p.m. Saturday and Monday,

Doors: Tickey per Child (3d.)

ORGANIZERS:	SOLOIST:
Waaihoek, Mr. P. PARLANE, (Sergeant at Arms)	Mr. F. Y. ST. L. PLAATJE,
	PIANIST:
CAPE STANDS:	Mr. CRAWFORD THOKA
Mr. J. J. PETERSON.	OPERATOR:
BANTU LOCATION:	Mr. GREYLING.
Mr. MAKGOTHI	LECTURER:
BANDMASTER:	SOL T. PLAATJE
J. G. NTLATSENG,	

He arrived in Cape Town at an interesting moment. It was the eve of polling day for the Cape Provincial Council elections and he found Dr Abdullah Abdurahman in the final stages of campaigning (on a South African Party ticket) for the local Hanover Street (District Six) constituency. When the results were declared it was clear he had scored an emphatic victory. 'Out of the 2000 votes cast', Plaatje wrote, 'he polled over 1300 and left his three opponents to divide the rest. Two of them forfeited £50 each for failing to poll 1/5 of the total votes cast; the third man escaped forfeiture just by 13 votes' – a result that gave Dr Abdurahman, remarkably, 'the largest majority in the whole Province'. Two days later Plaatje spoke at the victory celebrations, commending Abdurahman for his 'ability and commanding influence' and reminding him that for 'the Cape Province non-Europeans' he was not just 'the member for Hanover Street' but 'the spokesman for the whole Province'.[1]

His other thought, when he conveyed the news to Mrs Solomon a few weeks later, was on the injustice of the provision of the Union constitution that prohibited Dr Abdurahman, not being 'of European descent', from standing for the national parliament. He must also have been struck by the contrast between his own situation, returning to South Africa penniless and in debt, and that of the respected and well-to-do doctor, undisputed leader of the Coloured community as he was, supported by the South African Party, and now returned for a fourth time in a row.

The debt to the Union-Castle Company was his most urgent financial problem. He failed to raise the money from friends in Cape Town but was able to persuade the company to give him some extra time. It was clearly an emotional issue. Seeing the Union-Castle offices in Cape Town, so Isaiah Bud-M'belle recalled many years later, caused him to 'sob bitterly at the recollection that it was wholly through the graciousness of that Company that he found himself back again in his homeland'.[2]

His joy at returning home was tempered by the straitened circumstances in which he found his wife and children. At some point during his absence overseas, the family home – 14 Shannon Street – had been sold off to raise money for his family's subsistence, and they were living now at 32 Angel Street, owned by

Isaiah Bud-M'belle, who had moved to Pretoria. His letter to Mrs Solomon, written a month after landing at Cape Town, made light of what was a serious situation: 'Since landing I have been to Kimberley and had a family reunion of about three weeks. My children were living on next to nothing; but they looked as trim and healthy as others who eat three times every day – if not better. Truly "men shall not live by bread alone". Most of our furniture was sold and my credit pledged up to the hilt with grocers, butchers and cloth dealers and I must say creditors have been very patient with them. Now they will get restless since I have come back.'[3]

Elizabeth was not quite so well. Her eyesight had deteriorated to the extent that she was no longer able to read or write at night, and there had been no money to see an eye specialist. Plaatje realised how much he owed to her and the sacrifices she had made for him. 'Few men', he wrote, 'can boast of a spouse so faithful under such trying circumstances, she has been remarkably patient bringing up the children almost alone during the past eight years.'

Of the children, St Leger, the eldest, now had a job 'killing locusts' with a special magistrate in the De Aar district, employed there since leaving Fort Hare; Plaatje had stopped off to see him on the journey from Cape Town and reported that he 'looked very well'. Richard, his second son, was at Lovedale training to be a builder's apprentice but spending his summer holidays in Johannesburg trying to find a temporary job. Halley, who was thirteen, and Violet, nearly seventeen, were both aiming to qualify as teachers, and Violet had already spent a year at Lovedale where she had successfully completed the first part of her teacher's certificate. Now she was back in Kimberley continuing her training at the (Coloured) Perseverance Training School, one of a handful of African students allowed a place each year; she was also a talented musician but 'so sad', her father said, 'that the absence of an instrument prevents her from taking piano lessons'.

His own plans were uncertain. He told Mrs Solomon that he hoped soon to be writing to say he was 'showing bioscope films to native audiences', but he had first to retrieve both films and projector from the customs authorities in Cape Town where they had been impounded. Yet more money had to be found for the customs duties he owed. Restarting his newspaper business, his long-term aim, looked for the time being no more than a distant possibility. While he was away, the *Tsala ea Batho* printing press – like that of *Koranta ea Becoana* a decade before – had been sold off in order to pay the family's debts.

His Brotherhood organisation in Kimberley was in disarray. The committee he left behind in 1919 failed to keep up payments for municipal and provincial rates incurred by the Lyndhurst Road Native Institute, and Plaatje himself, for all his efforts overseas, had been unable to assist. By the end of 1922 it was nearly

£600 in arrears. Aware that such a sum was unlikely ever to be recovered, De Beers had agreed to a proposal from James Swan, treasurer of the committee, to alter the terms of the original agreement so as to vest control of its affairs in the hands of a new committee, which would give a firm undertaking to pay the rates and taxes that were required. In return De Beers wrote off the existing debt.[4]

Plaatje claimed never to have been consulted. While the new arrangement released him from a debt for which he was personally liable, it also meant he no longer had any control over the affairs of the institute, the Brotherhood's chief asset. What made this so galling was the fact that this action was initiated by a man whom he had himself installed as treasurer of the Brotherhood committee. All in all it was a difficult state of affairs to return to, and it simply underlined the consequences of the failure of his mission overseas to put the Brotherhood organisation onto a secure financial footing.[5]

It was by no means the only instance of the way whites were now assuming control in the field of 'native affairs'. He came up against the same difficulty when trying to promote the Brotherhood movement in Johannesburg several weeks after his return. He hoped to set up a national organisation and held several meetings, public and private, but got nowhere. Here, even more than in Kimberley, white liberals and churchmen were tightening their grip on urban African affairs, and they had no wish to encourage an initiative that was independent of their control. As one Methodist churchman on the Rand commented, Plaatje's Brotherhood 'is urging African people to a Christianity without the Church', his words exemplifying the narrow-minded denominationalism that Plaatje abhorred. At the other end of the political spectrum, the Communist Party opposed his plans on ideological grounds, criticising 'Mr Sol Plaatje and other Bible-punching natives' for failing to realise their true class interests.[6]

Displacement from the management of the Lyndhurst Road Native Institute in Kimberley, and the opposition he encountered in Johannesburg, were in reality part of a wider pattern, and his own experiences were far from unique. They are to be explained by the social and political changes that had taken place in South Africa during the years of his absence overseas, and they would have serious implications for the role that African leaders like himself could expect to play in the affairs of their people.

He had left South Africa at a time of intense political and industrial ferment among the African population. While he and his colleagues on the deputation to England sought external intervention, the South African government and leaders in mining, business and church circles were looking for other means to defuse a tense situation, the seriousness of which was dramatically underlined by the strike of black miners early in 1920. Several elements of the government's response were now in the statute book, most notably in the Native Affairs Act of 1920. While this piece of legislation was the product of a line of thought that went back to the South African Native Affairs Commission of 1903–5, and was conceived as a successor to the abortive Native Administration Bill of 1917, it was also seen as a means of addressing what was widely believed to be one of the main causes of discontent, the lack of any formal channel of communication between rulers and ruled.

The Act created a permanent (whites only) Native Affairs Commission which was supposed to represent African interests and to advise the government on matters of policy; it established local district councils on which Africans were to be represented; and it provided for a regular 'Native Conference', composed of chiefs and other African leaders selected by the government, to whom legislation on 'native affairs' was to be submitted for discussion and recommendation. The Act fell far short of the demands which the Congress deputation took to London, but it nevertheless established, for the first time outside the Cape, the principle of consultation between Africans and the government. While the Act was criticised for not going far enough, many in the South African Native National Congress (SANNC) welcomed it, believing it provided a platform and some degree of recognition and legitimacy from the government, something they had long sought. If the legislation was in part intended to separate African leaders from an increasingly coherent and volatile black working class, in part it succeeded precisely because many of them had become distinctly nervous about just such an association.

Richard Selope Thema was among those who took a positive view of it. He had left Plaatje in England in June 1920 and arrived in Cape Town just as the Native Affairs Bill was completing its passage through the South African House of Assembly. He thought it vindicated his mission to England and convinced him that the government was not, after all, oblivious to their demands. Plaatje agreed. Although he opposed the Act's wider purpose, he thought any form of representation was better than none, and he was willing to participate in the meetings between government ministers and African leaders that it proposed. At the very least, Plaatje thought, the Native Affairs Act of 1920 was the only 'native measure' passed since Union that had not posed 'additional humiliations' upon them.[7]

This concern to defuse African political and industrial discontent was echoed elsewhere. The Chamber of Mines, for example, was heavily involved in financing and promoting church- and missionary-inspired moves in the direction of inter-racial co-operation and consultation. These included the Joint Councils, established in 1921 and 1922, which sought to minimise racial friction through involving 'responsible' African leaders in consultation and discussion with sympathetic whites. As with the Native Affairs Act, the unspoken promise to African political leaders was a degree of recognition and legitimacy in exchange for dissociating themselves from African workers and the use of the strike weapon as a means of remedying grievances. The Joint Councils, established first on the Rand and then in many other towns throughout South Africa, were inspired by American ideas of racial co-operation and introduced into South Africa by American Board missionaries, and by the visit of the Phelps Stokes Commission in 1921: Plaatje would have heard all about this from J.E.K. Aggrey, one of its members, after his return to America later that year.

The Joint Councils were funded by the Chamber of Mines because they promised to furnish a means of damping down political and industrial discontent. The newspaper *Umteteli wa Bantu*, run by the Native Recruiting Corporation, could be seen in much the same light. Despite having failed to attract Plaatje from England to be its editor, *Umteteli* had, since its launch in 1920, built itself up into a well-produced and widely read newspaper, published weekly in English and several different African languages, an effective platform for the formulation and discussion of 'responsible' African opinion.

Plaatje's views on the situation he found on his return were expressed in a series of three articles which he wrote for the *Diamond Fields Advertiser* in January 1924. Economically, he thought Africans had been hardest hit by the prevailing economic depression, and by the continued effects that he perceived, as he travelled round the countryside during the few weeks after his return to South Africa, of the Natives' Land Act of 1913, which he held to be largely responsible for the growing influx of Africans into the towns – a point he was to make again and again over the next few years. Some things he saw happening in the towns, though, gave him cause for optimism. 'The better class of people on the whole seem to feel that these restrictions have gone far enough, and they are looking for a way out of the dilemma', and he commended the efforts that the mining companies, the municipalities and the churches – in particular American missionaries like Ray Phillips – were making to ameliorate conditions for the African population.[8]

With the state of African political and social life he was less impressed. The African press, he thought, no longer possessed its vitality of old. Reporting was often inaccurate or second-hand, based on clippings from the European press and often devoid of original comment. What he had seen led him to the conclusion that 'except to a limited extent in one or two instances', 'the native press' had almost ceased to fulfil its original function of giving expression to 'native opinion' and acting as 'interpreters of European thought and translators of Government policy'.[9]

He was no more impressed by the condition in which he found the African National Congress (as the SANNC had just been renamed). Certainly his views were coloured by its failure to support either his family or himself during his mission overseas, but to any observer it was clear that the Congress was nothing like the force it once was. The older generation of leaders, the original founding fathers like John Dube, Pixley ka Isaka Seme and Walter Rubusana, had moved on to other things and no longer played much part in its affairs; several others, like Saul Msane, had died, in his case discredited. No longer could it claim to express the aspirations of the African people of South Africa as a whole. The industrial and political discontent of 1918–20 had brought to a head the differences between the more conservative branches of Congress and the firebrands of the Transvaal, and since then many of those involved had found a niche with one or other of the organisations sponsored by the Chamber of Mines or the churches. Congress had only briefly represented the aspirations of the Witwatersrand's growing African workforce. Increasingly, its place was being taken by the Industrial and Commercial Workers' Union, led by an immigrant from Nyasaland, Clements Kadalie. Founded in 1920, the ICU, as it was widely known, was the first mass African trade union in South Africa, and it had already made a huge impact. Plaatje thought it was 'the best native association today', welcoming its efforts on behalf of 'that much despised fellow, the native labourer of South Africa'.[10]

Plaatje's impressions, as set out in the three *Diamond Fields Advertiser* articles, reflected these new complexities. What he saw around him was a country coming to terms with its transformation into an industrial society, with all the stresses and strains that came with this; black and white alike were in the process of making their adjustments. New structures had been created, new loyalties had emerged. Whether in these changed conditions Plaatje would be able to resume the position of leadership he had once had, or whether he could find a niche in the more complex society which South Africa had become, remained to be seen.

+∿+

By the middle of January 1924 Plaatje was back in Cape Town, hoping to collect the bioscope films he had been obliged to leave in storage, and to pay off the passage money he still owed. 'It was', he wrote to Betty Molteno, 'a difficult task trying to raise the wherewithal to pay the Union Castle for my ticket and release the films from the Customs'. But with the help of friends and sympathisers in the city, including Stephen Reagon, a well-known Coloured leader, he was very relieved to have achieved both objectives.

He was also able to enjoy a few days' relaxation with Elizabeth, who came with him for a short holiday. It was an opportunity to 'enjoy a few days of quiet in the changed air of the seaside' – and to get to know one another again after nearly five years apart. It was Elizabeth's first visit to the city, and the only time she had seen the sea in nearly thirty years. 'Naturally, Cape Peninsula and the City at the foot of Table Mountain – with Table Bay – Camp's Bay and Simon's Bay at Simonstown interest her immensely.' He took her to the docks to see the *Windsor Castle* when it arrived with the new governor general, the Earl of Athlone, showed her the cabin he had occupied on his passage, and introduced her to the '2nd class officers who befriended me on the voyage out'. Then they visited Henry Burton, now minister of finance in the Smuts administration. The 'warm reception' (as Plaatje described it) that they received from Henry Burton and his family was a tribute to the survival of a friendship which was feasible in the old Cape Colony, but which looked distinctly out of place in the harsher climate of South Africa in the 1920s. Henry Burton had only just returned from England himself, having attended the Imperial Conference. One evening the previous October Plaatje heard his live radio broadcast setting out his thoughts on the future of the empire.[11]

After a few days in Cape Town Elizabeth returned home to Kimberley, leaving Plaatje to attend to a variety of political matters. Apart from addressing meetings in and around the city, he spent much of his time at the House of Assembly, observing proceedings from the gallery, lobbying members on matters bearing on African interests, and writing to the press to try to influence opinion on the latest 'anti-native' legislative proposals. He spoke out against the injustices of 'Mr Nixon's Immorality Bill', and 'the irrelevant and extraordinary views' of Dr Visser, the National Party MP for Vrededorp, on the extent of the African contribution to government revenue; he criticised General Hertzog's comments about Africans (he said they were a 'menace' to whites and Coloured people) during discussion of the Women's Franchise Bill; and he lobbied vigorously in favour of one piece of legislation of special interest to his friends in Thaba Nchu, the Barolong Land Relief Bill, which had been originally gazetted over a decade earlier. Plaatje left those he met in little doubt that an articulate spokesman for African, and Barolong, interests was back on the scene.[12]

Among his many appointments during this extended visit to Cape Town was one which took place in Marks Buildings, Parliament Street, on the morning of 3 April: it was with the prime minister, General Smuts, then just two days away from a disastrous by-election defeat which precipitated his resignation and the holding of a general election.[13]

That Smuts should have been willing to see Plaatje is intriguing in itself, and understandable only in terms of the transformation of South African political life during his time overseas. For a great deal had changed since that troublesome correspondence with Lloyd George. Smuts had replaced General Botha as prime minister and was leader of the South African Party (SAP); he had found common cause with the old Unionist Party (which was dissolved, its members joining the SAP) to meet the growing strength of the Afrikaner nationalists, led by General Hertzog; and he now presided over a government which seemed every bit as responsive to the needs of the mining industry and the imperial connection as the Milner regime in the aftermath of the South African War. As if to prove these newfound credentials, he had not hesitated in putting down the white miners' strike in 1922 with all the force at his disposal.

Plaatje's view of the possibility of working with the general had changed too. In private he described Smuts as 'a subtle slippery eel' and 'as slim as ever with the native bills', and he had few illusions about Smuts's fundamentally illiberal instincts since being exposed to them in 1895. But circumstances had changed. Working with Smuts and the South African Party now seemed the only realistic means of resisting the political influence of the two groups of people he believed to be most hostile to the interests of the African people: the Afrikaner national-ists, to whom he attributed the most oppressive pieces of legislation since Union, and who were the most fervent advocates of policies of segregation; and the white working class, who sought the protection of the colour bar in employment and a guaranteed place for their labour, at the expense of African workers. Both groups had united in an electoral pact.[14]

So Plaatje believed there was a basis for co-operation with Smuts and his party; while Smuts, for his part, his government in an increasingly sticky position politically, would have seen the advantage of speaking with somebody who might be able to sway African voters towards the SAP in those Cape constituencies where they still possessed the balance of power. Plaatje may not have had the strongest of hands to play, but this was a familiar predicament.

Although no actual record of his meeting with the prime minister has survived, circumstantial evidence, together with a subsequent letter Plaatje wrote on the subject, would suggest that he raised the possibility of financial support from the SAP for the resuscitation of his newspaper, *Tsala ea Batho*; and in return offered to do what he could to deliver African votes for the SAP

– something which could not be taken for granted in view of General Hertzog's recent success in attracting African and Coloured support for the National Party with some well-judged policy statements. Whether Smuts let on to Plaatje that he had received, and read, a copy of his account of his American tour, one can only guess.[15]

Whatever consideration the prime minister gave to Plaatje's overtures, the general election was upon them before anything much could be done – although the fact the SAP reprinted and circulated one of Plaatje's articles attacking the Nationalists suggests some kind of understanding may have been reached. Soon he was busy electioneering. In the English-language newspapers in Cape Town and Johannesburg, as well as the *Diamond Fields Advertiser* in Kimberley, he urged their African readers, where they had the vote, to cast it for the SAP. While pointing to the relatively benign record of the Smuts government in the field of 'native affairs' (being election time, much was passed over), he castigated General Hertzog and the Nationalists in the strongest terms, holding them responsible for the Natives' Land Act of 1913, and condemning their proposals to abolish the Cape franchise. 'If the Nationalists are to attain power in the next election,' so Plaatje concluded one of these articles, 'let them get it by the votes of the Europeans, but let no coloured person be responsible for the orgy of tyranny that is to follow their ascendancy.'[16]

In the columns of *Umteteli wa Bantu*, too, Plaatje spoke out strongly against the Labour–Nationalist Pact, his particular concern being to discredit allegations that a meeting of the African National Congress at Bloemfontein had actually advised Africans to vote for the Pact. This had happened, but the meeting had been highly irregular, and took place in the absence of any senior Congress leaders. It had nevertheless sown discord and confusion, and underlined the state of disarray the organisation was now in.[17]

Closer to home, on the diamond fields, Plaatje did his best to mobilise African voters for the two SAP candidates, Sir David Harris and Sir Ernest Oppenheimer, chairman of De Beers. He knew both men well, and had every interest, personal as well as political, in seeing them elected. Whatever the current difficulties of the Lyndhurst Road Native Institute, he never forgot that it had been Sir David who recommended that the board of De Beers should give him the old tram shed in 1918. He had had dealings with Sir Ernest Oppenheimer too (he recalled 'courtesies during foggy nights in London') and would have hoped that his election as a member of the House of Assembly could strengthen the prospects of gaining SAP support for resuscitating *Tsala ea Batho*. Two weeks before polling day, at an election rally for African voters in No. 2 Location, Kimberley, he gave him his full backing. 'I feel certain we are going to win this election', Plaatje declared, 'and there is only one thing you want to do as a tribute to Sir Ernest and that is to return him with a big majority. There is no doubt about his return, but we want the biggest majority in the Union. We will give them such a result on the 17th that they will say, "This is what No. 2 Location did." (Loud cheers).'[18]

Sir Ernest, seeking election for the first time, and sitting next to Plaatje on the platform, was in fine form too, and he earned loud applause for his criticism of General Hertzog and his policies: 'I hear an attempt has been made to fool you, went on Sir Ernest. You have been told under this segregation policy you are going to have your own native Parliament (laughter). I suppose you will be drawing lots as to who is going to be your Prime Minister (more laughter). I am sorry to disappoint you, because General Hertzog said a few days ago at Potchefstroom he is going to give you proper Councils in these areas when you are segregated, but he has one condition, and that is that even these Councils must be under European supervision (A voice, "Oh"). So you see, even Mr Sol Plaatje cannot be Prime Minister (laughter). I am quite sure none of you will risk the loss of your votes by putting General Hertzog in power. ("No", and applause).'[19]

It was all good electioneering stuff, even if some doubts remained in the minds of those present about the intentions of a government headed by General Smuts should he be re-elected; in reality it was a question of choosing the lesser of two evils. The meeting concluded with the singing of 'God save the King' and 'thunderous salvoes of cheers for Sir Ernest'.

Two weeks later, as expected, both Sir Ernest Oppenheimer and Sir David Harris were elected with large majorities as members for Kimberley and Beaconsfield respectively. But overall the South African Party was now in a minority: it won only 53 seats against the Nationalists' 63 and Labour's 18, giving the Pact a parliamentary majority of 28. General Smuts lost his seat, and so too did a number of well-known politicians – 'real advocates of native well being', Plaatje called them – with whom he had worked closely in the past, including Henry Burton, F.S. Malan and Advocate Will Stuart, formerly the member for Tembuland. To his dismay, a government was now formed from the two parties, Afrikaner Nationalists and Labour, to which he was most strongly opposed. It looked to be only a matter of time before General Hertzog would proceed with his much publicised schemes to 'solve the native problem', implement the comprehensive ideas for segregation he had put to the electorate (admittedly in somewhat vague terms), and proceed to abolish the Cape franchise.[20]

In the months following the election Plaatje did his best to solicit support for his newspaper, but with no success. Then, in January 1925, he wrote to General Smuts for assistance. From the tone of his letter it is clear that he assumed Smuts was familiar with his plans: 'I am sorry to say that I have not been able to make any headway with the mining advertising requisite for the resuscitation of my paper. The Chamber of Mines seems willing; but such matters are controlled by their Native Affairs Department – the Great Native Recruiting Corporation – and they are not disposed to advertise; but I think they only require some one to determine and express the advertising value and possible party gains. Sir E. Oppenheimer is sympathetic but advised me to wait till the beginning of this year when he will occupy a higher position in the Chamber ... You should be doing a party stroke and incidentally benefiting the Natives if you took an early opportunity to remind Sir Ernest Oppenheimer to push the matter and strengthen his hands with any of the mining kings who have the authority to issue the word that would give us the annual financial vote.'[21]

Smuts agreed to talk to Sir Ernest about the matter as Plaatje requested, but since his plans for *Tsala ea Batho* depended upon support from the Chamber of Mines it is hardly surprising that this was not forthcoming. For the Chamber, more particularly its 'Great Native Recruiting Corporation', as Plaatje called it, ran its own newspaper, *Umteteli wa Bantu*, and can have had little desire to see a competitor. They had tried hard enough, after all, to kill off *Abantu-Batho*. Although they had not succeeded, support for another rival, even if it was unlikely to pursue so radical a line as *Abantu-Batho*, was never a possibility.

Plaatje's plans for resuscitating *Tsala ea Batho* nevertheless reveal the difficulties of the situation he was in. In the past, as editor of *Koranta ea Becoana* and later *Tsala ea Batho*, he had an independent platform, supported by a group of Africans who valued his services as a spokesman and somehow found the funds to keep him going. Now things were different. Their ability to support him had been undermined by the post-war recession and by ever more oppressive government policies. But it was also a question of what might be gained. With South Africa's major political and constitutional arrangements resolved, there was simply less scope for an individual spokesman like Plaatje to influence the actions of government, less reason for any backers to risk the ruinous expenditure that supporting a newspaper entailed.

So Plaatje was left with no alternative but to try to exploit such space as was left by the political realignments of the previous four years, and to make the accommodations that were necessary. At the same time he had to retain his independence as a spokesman for African interests or risk losing all credibility. It was a tricky balancing act. Accepting the editorship of *Umteteli wa Bantu* was an impossibility, especially given what he knew about the way the paper was run. But if he could secure financial support from the SAP and the Chamber of Mines for a newspaper of his own and retain editorial control – that would be different.

After the general election of June 1924 Plaatje undertook several extensive tours in the Orange Free State, the Transvaal and the eastern Cape, including the Transkei, to familiarise himself once again with conditions in the countryside, to tell audiences of his experiences overseas, and to show the films he had brought back with him, with such difficulty, on his bioscope apparatus.

Seeing him set off from home on these extended journeys was a sight to behold. Modiri Molema, now back in Mafeking and with a medical practice of his own, often witnessed it. He likened it to a person setting off on a long sea voyage, so loaded up was he with the equipment he needed – pen and ink, paper, typewriter, dictionaries, reference books, newspapers and the like. Plaatje himself used to call this his '*padkos*', or food for the road. It was as if he took an entire office along with him, so determined was he not to waste a minute of his time.[22]

On his bioscope tours he was usually accompanied by St Leger, who assisted with the operation of the projector and provided musical accompaniment as a vocalist or on the piano. In many ways this 'Plaatje bioscope', as it came to be known, was something of a curiosity and, as with so many of his activities, undertaken with a mixture of motives. He saw its main aim as educational but naturally hoped the film shows would also generate an income to help support himself and his family. Judging from his letters and the publicity material he circulated, the centrepiece was invariably the film he had acquired from Dr Moton, showing the work of the Tuskegee Institute. A leaflet advertising the show in Bloemfontein in September 1924, for example, urged people to 'roll up and see the Coloured American Bioscope, direct from Chicago, Ill., USA', and billed as 'its principal feature Booker T. Washington's School, Tuskegee, and her thousands of young men and women students at Drill and Manoeuvres'; in smaller print there followed the statement: 'The Immigration Department will not permit any Foreign Negroes – not even the Jubilee Singers, beloved of our forefathers – to land in the Union. You can only see Coloured Americans on the screen.'[23]

He met with his most enthusiastic response and his largest audiences in the smaller country towns where films of any kind were a novelty, and where Africans were generally refused admittance to European-run cinemas; or where he had a captive audience, such as in schools, hospitals or asylums. He received a particularly warm welcome when he visited the West Fort Leper Asylum in Pretoria late in August 1924, treating 'the inmates to a bioscope display of the scenes and people he visited in Canada and the United States'. 'None of the pictures', according to a press report, 'evoked so much enthusiasm as the work and drills of the students of the famous Tuskegee, Booker Washington's great institution in Alabama.' Isaiah Bud-M'belle, now living in Pretoria and working as senior interpreter in the Native Affairs Department, was on hand to help convey Plaatje's message to the audience.[24]

The programme was typical of many of his shows. But in the larger urban and industrial centres it was not nearly so popular. Several months earlier he had a show in the spacious Ebenezer Hall in Johannesburg, but fewer than a hundred people turned up, and his promised 'assistants' failed to put in an appearance. Elsewhere he found it difficult to hire suitable premises. In Pretoria, he complained about the attitude of the Indian proprietor of the only meeting hall available to Africans. He had first of all agreed to a contract with Plaatje for the use of the hall, then changed his mind and tried to cancel it. Only after the intervention of the location superintendent was he persuaded to honour the agreement. Even then nearly all the chairs he supplied, Plaatje complained, were broken. In the locations of other towns it was often difficult to attract enough people to cover his expenses, let alone make a profit.[25]

It was also clear that Plaatje's message of educational self-help and moral improvement was not to everybody's taste. Some people just preferred Charlie Chaplin, whose movies were on offer, free of charge, in the mine compounds of the Witwatersrand at least, thanks to the proselytising efforts of the Rev. Ray Phillips, the American Board missionary. To many, Plaatje's emphasis on individual uplift, in a situation where there were restrictions on so many aspects of people's lives, must have come across as strangely old-fashioned – in paradoxical contrast to the novelty of the equipment he used to convey his message. 'It is still difficult in some parts', he admitted a year later, 'to rouse the enthusiasm of our people.'[26]

Plaatje sought with his bioscope to pass on what he had learnt overseas, to implant the seeds of inspiration and motivation, to give hope where he often found despair. He called it 'a veritable moving school'. His shows for children were more popular than those for adults and he was always likely to leave a more lasting impression upon young minds, as several of those youngsters would later testify. Young Simon Lekhela, for example, a student at the Lyndhurst Road Native School in Kimberley, was captivated by the way 'the Negroes were pushing themselves up', how they 'rose up from slavery'. That's why, he said, 'every one of us who saw these films thought, one day I'll go to Tuskegee … be like Booker T. Washington, like Carver, his films were to inspire our people, to show that from poverty, from slavery, from nothing, we could become people.'[27]

It was the wide-eyed enthusiasm of Simon Lekhela and others like him that made it all worthwhile. 'I have been round a good deal with my films', Plaatje told Robert Moton in September 1924. 'With the poverty of the natives it is a profitless job: but when I see the joy, especially of the native kiddies, at sight of the thrilling drills of Tuskegee and my explanatory remarks enabling them to enjoy that which I have witnessed and they cannot, it turns the whole thing into a labour of love.'[28]

Plaatje's bioscope served other purposes too. It would provide the means of financing his travels, enabling him to carry on investigating social and economic conditions in the rural areas of the Cape, the Transvaal and the Orange Free State, and to report on what he found. For here, he instinctively recognised, was his real constituency. Things might have changed greatly in the towns and cities, but at least churchmen and missionaries were now attending to the conditions Africans faced there. Not so in the countryside. Here, 'away from the beaten track and far from the reach of enlightened sentiment', as Plaatje saw it, he was better placed to make a contribution to the life of his people; here too his authority and reputation, his tireless campaigning against the iniquities of the Natives' Land Act, gave him a measure of influence that was less easily achieved elsewhere.[29]

Plaatje's first year back in South Africa thus saw him involved in a variety of enterprises and activities. He had reminded the country once again of his stature and ability as a public figure and spokesman but was unable, as yet, to speak from the position he so wanted, as editor of his own newspaper. There were other disappointments. He had hoped to meet up with Dr Jesse Jones and Dr Aggrey, both of whom were travelling through South Africa on a second Phelps Stokes Education Commission, in order 'to enlist their material sympathy', as he wrote to Robert Moton, 'in the publication of our Native Fellowship hymnal still in the press through the lack of a few hundred pounds'. After nearly seven years and countless promises, he still hadn't found the money to publish his translations. The two men passed through without seeing him.

A note of pessimism runs through much of the rest of this letter. While conditions had improved somewhat for Africans living on the Rand, he said, in most other areas they were worse than ever. 'Johannesburg', he wrote, 'is only a speck in British South Africa.' In the countryside, by contrast, 'the lot of the South African native is not enviable. Since 1883, statisticians claim, South Africa never knew a drought like the one we have endured during the past ten years. Sometimes you have to call on a poor family in order to offer some Christian sympathy only to hear such a tale of woe as would force you to part with your last half a crown even if your family depended on it.' Yet whites were given generous relief – the jobs of blacks who'd been fired to make way for them.[30]

Few letters that Plaatje wrote, however, were without some expression of optimism to offset the gloom and despondency. In Kimberley, he was pleased to say, while 'every Department of our work is tottering, thanks to the acute economic depression', the Lyndhurst Road School was still flourishing because, 'Thank God, the Kimberley School Board pays the Teachers'. It was the only school board that supported an African-run school anywhere in the country; elsewhere, teachers in schools for Africans were paid for by churches, missionary societies or the parents of the schoolchildren.

Plaatje drew encouragement, too, from the belief that despite the change of government, he still retained some personal influence with members of the new administration. For this reason, he said in the same letter, he felt confident that should Dr Moton consider visiting South Africa (as he had planned to several years earlier), then he would be able, with the help of 'my Boer friends in the Ministry', to 'get General Hertzog to reconsider and rescind the ban' which the Nationalist government had imposed as soon as it came into office – just as he had persuaded General Botha to allow the Paynes into South Africa back in 1917. He then explained to Dr Moton, as one black man to another, just how, with the right kind of approach, this sort of thing might be done. 'There are places so hostile to the English and their Imperial rule', he said, 'that even General Smuts as Prime Minister never visited them for fear of being hissed off the platform for his loyalty to England; but I always manage to get by, taking good care however to hold my hat in my hand all the time, even when, to the bewilderment of local custom, I am invited in by the front door. Our Boer "crackers" are worse than Southerners. Only yesterday, a son of a Boer Senator and a cousin of a Crown Minister (member of General Hertzog's Ministry), brother of a judge of the Appellate Division of the Supreme Court of South Africa, said to me: "Man, your politics are putrid: too full of Smuts. But we like you as you are the only Kaffir who writes our language as beautifully as the other cheeky Kaffirs write English."'

Thus a black South African to a black American on how to act in accordance with 'local custom': in a white-dominated society this was just what you had to do. Dr Moton, like his predecessor Booker T. Washington, would have understood fully. It was an anecdote that sums up, in a way, the essence of Plaatje's style, exploiting to the full his personal qualities to carve out a niche for himself where by rights none existed. He was always careful, therefore, to keep open the channels of communication, even with people to whom he was strongly opposed politically.

This same concern lay behind the short letter he wrote to General Hertzog a month later. He enclosed a newspaper cutting describing one of his bioscope shows which he felt 'certain will interest the human side of your work in the Ministry of Native Affairs'; and he expressed his thanks, on behalf of the Barolong, for his refusal to allow 'pressure of other work and political differences' to stand in the way of passing the Barolong Relief Act during the previous parliamentary session. This, he said, would 'solve many a deadlock and smooth many difficulties among the Barolong at Thaba Nchu'. It was reward for a lobbying campaign that went back over a decade and only the second piece of 'native legislation' since Union, he pointed out on another occasion, that was actually of some benefit to his people.[31]

Strange as it might have seemed to those who read or heard Plaatje's denunciations of General Hertzog and his policies, he ended his letter with an expression of 'best wishes'. There is no reason to doubt they were well meant. Plaatje knew the general quite well and had met him on a number of occasions in the past. He always remembered an incident from the 1890s when, as a judge in the Orange Free State, Hertzog addressed a Dutch jury in Fauresmith in favour of two 'native' prisoners. It had encouraged him to believe that Hertzog was capable of recognising the justice of a case presented to him. Plaatje could never quite believe that even his greatest political opponents were inherently evil, whatever the nature and consequences of the policies they advocated. There was always a separation in his mind between the cause people stood for and an underlying human nature, and in this he never stopped believing. So he never lost his faith that men like General Hertzog might one day see the error of their ways, or that he was capable of persuading them to do so. Hence the importance of maintaining good personal relations – and his offer to intercede on Dr Moton's behalf should the need arise.[32]

He was careful to keep in with all shades of political opinion. Three months later he was writing to General Smuts to congratulate him on his 'signal success as leader of His Majesty's Opposition both in Parliament and in the country', and wished him 'greater success in the New Year'. Given the growing strength of Afrikaner nationalism, Smuts was going to need rather more than Plaatje's good wishes, or even the votes he could deliver, if he was to have any chance of returning to power.[33]

At the end of 1924 Plaatje broke his tour of the eastern Cape to attend two conferences: the third annual Native Conference, held in Pretoria and convened under the terms of the Native Affairs Act of 1920, which he attended as an observer rather than as an official delegate; and a Joint Councils Conference, in Johannesburg, in which he took a rather more active role.

The Joint Councils Conference was organised by Dr J.D. Rheinallt Jones, assistant registrar at the new University of the Witwatersrand and one of the moving spirits in the Joint Council movement. The conference was a characteristic manifestation of the burgeoning interest in 'race relations' on the part of white liberals and churchmen, and took place in a building which came to symbolise this new philosophy, the recently opened Bantu Men's Social Centre in Johannesburg.

In Plaatje's view any progress that could be achieved through inter-racial co-operation of the kind represented by this conference was welcome, and it had his support. But already in the paper he read to the gathering on 'The treatment of natives in the courts' he gave some indication of his reservations about the effects and scope of these kinds of initiatives. As he was to stress time and again over the next few years, far too little attention was devoted to what was going on in the rural areas, in relation to the administration of justice just as much as to the pernicious effects of the Land Act of 1913, and he urged the Joint Councils to extend their activities into the countryside.

Plaatje had another warning: that Africans should be prepared to fight their own battles, and not rely upon white sympathisers. He had lived much of his own life according to this principle, and he referred back to his own record to illustrate the point, enumerating several of his successes in securing ministerial intervention in cases of injustice and discrimination in the law courts. Fifteen years ago, he said, 'there was no welfare association ... we had here instead of a Joint Council what was known as "The University of Crime", and anyone interested in this kind of work had to finance it out of his own pocket like a hobby of his own'. But now well-meaning sympathisers threatened to displace African leaders like himself from any meaningful role in the affairs of their people. 'Most white men', he concluded, 'are interested in us because they are after our goods. Other white men are interested in us because they want to save us from exploitation but the best protection would be to stimulate the Natives' own interest in native life.'

He did not find it at all agreeable to see well-funded whites assuming the role of self-appointed advocates of the welfare of his people, and as time went on he would feel more and strongly about this process of displacement. Rheinallt Jones, for his part, did not much care to be lectured on what the Joint Councils

452

should or should not be doing: he thought Plaatje spoke 'with some, shall we say, excusable bitterness', the tone of his paper, in his view, not in accord with new inter-racial orthodoxies.[34]

There were also signs in Plaatje's remarks at the conference of what would become another insistent theme: criticism of his own people for their failure to take sufficient interest in their affairs, or to measure up to his own high standards of public service and leadership. To illustrate the point he gave several examples from his recent experiences. One arose from his visit to Cape Town at the beginning of the year, and concerned the implementation of the Natives (Urban Areas) Act of 1923. Attending a meeting of the Cape Peninsula Native Welfare Association, he recalled, he was the only person present to have been aware that magistrates in Cape Town had begun to enforce the Act despite the government having given an assurance that it would not do so. As a result some arrests had been made. 'Delicately and single-handedly', he said, 'I pulled some strings and brought the Chief Magistrate and the Town Clerk together on their behalf', adding: 'We shall never get better treatment in the Courts or outside if we show so little concern in the misery of our fellow men.'[35]

A further example he gave to illustrate what he called 'native indifference to native needs' was from the official Native Conference a few days earlier. A government spokesman at the conference had stated that Africans paid about two or three shillings per year in indirect tax, but not one person there spoke up to contradict what Plaatje, attending the conference only as an observer, readily saw was a quite unjustifiable claim, and based on a system of assessment whereby receipts for certain taxes were quite wrongly attributed solely to whites. 'If the Natives', Plaatje concluded, 'leave white people to fight our battle for equal treatment and equal recognition inside or outside the Courts I am afraid we shall continue to pay taxes and the Treasury will keep on mailing the receipts to white people.'[36]

While Plaatje grew frustrated at the shortcomings of other African leaders, the overwhelming threat was from General Hertzog's proposed legislative solution to the 'native question' which dominated the government's approach to 'native affairs' throughout the 1920s. Hertzog had made much of his plans for a comprehensive scheme of segregation at the time of the general election in 1924, and it had proved popular with the white electorate, particularly as it was linked with proposals to exclude Africans from certain occupations in the urban areas. It was not long before the new administration put its proposals before parliament.

In deference largely to the Labour half of the Pact, the first bill to be introduced, early in 1925, was the Mines and Works Amendment Bill, known more generally as the Colour Bar Bill, its objective being to legalise the industrial colour bar.

Over the next two years, until the Act finally became law in 1926, Plaatje frequently condemned the legislation and the principles underlying it, adding his voice to those of other African spokesmen, church leaders, white 'friends of the natives and, when it suited them, General Smuts and the South African Party. The campaign against the bill was co-ordinated by Dr Rheinallt Jones on behalf of the Joint Councils, and Plaatje was one of many to add his name to a distinguished list of protesters who signed a petition for presentation to the prime minister in May 1926. He then travelled to Cape Town during the first stages of the bill's passage through parliament (the degree of parliamentary opposition meant that it had to go before a joint sitting of the Senate and the House of Assembly) to offer Rheinallt Jones such assistance as he could, and to speak at a protest meeting organised by Dr Abdurahman's APO, but to no avail. In the past he had often been able to secure concessions on issues over which individual ministers had some discretionary powers, but on questions of national policy his voice counted for very little. Even the combined opposition of the South African Party and the Chamber of Mines (which financed the extra-parliamentary opposition) was powerless when the Pact government had a majority in the Houses of Parliament.[37]

General Hertzog encountered rather more difficulty with his plans to extend territorial and political segregation. Plaatje had denounced Hertzog's somewhat vague formulations at the time of the general election in 1924, but it would be well over a year before his proposals surfaced in any more concrete form. They did so in a famous speech at Smithfield in November 1925, and the prime minister took the opportunity to elaborate further at the annual meeting of the Native Conference in Pretoria the following month. Having received an official invitation to attend the conference, Plaatje was therefore among the fifty African delegates, or nominees as they really were, who listened to the prime minister set out his proposals. Addressing the delegates in Dutch, he laid before the conference four interdependent bills: the Coloured Persons Rights Bill, which proposed to remove Africans from the Cape common roll; the Representation of Natives in Parliament Bill, which provided for seven white MPs (with reduced status and voting powers) to be elected by chiefs, headmen and other prominent Africans nominated by the governor general; the Union Native Council Bill, designed to formalise the existing Native Conference by establishing a council of fifty members, fifteen of whom were to be elected in similar fashion to the above; and the Natives Land Act (Amendment) Bill, which proposed to make available additional land for African occupation as a quid pro quo for the loss of the franchise.

What the prime minister was offering, in effect, was more land, and a limited degree of indirect, separate representation in the House of Assembly, in exchange for the removal of the Cape franchise. Not one of the delegates present expressed themselves in favour, and speaker after speaker, Plaatje among them, opposed any attempt to remove Africans from the common roll in the Cape. 'The idea that the Cape Natives should surrender their present franchise to obtain seven European representatives in the Union Parliament', Plaatje emphasised, 'was absolutely unacceptable. Experience had shown the value of the Cape franchise in making friends for Natives in the House of Assembly. It was very observable how faithfully those members whom their votes had helped to place there had supported native interests – notably on the question of the colour bar.' Plaatje's entire political career had been founded on an appreciation of the value of the Cape franchise. On this there could be no question of compromise.[38]

There was considerable discussion, nevertheless, of the three other bills which the delegates had before them. Plaatje welcomed the proposal to make more land available for African occupation as a step in the right direction, provided this did not imply acceptance of the bill abolishing the Cape franchise. But this of course was the crux of the matter. The prime minister had made it clear that he regarded the bills as interdependent, and that they were to be considered and voted upon as such. The conference, while discussing each one in detail, resisted this idea, and ended by passing a resolution requesting the prime minister to enable them to vote on each one separately. It was as far as they could go. If Hertzog had expected African approval for the abolition of the Cape franchise in exchange for his meagre offerings, he had miscalculated badly. Plaatje and his colleagues certainly appreciated his willingness to address them personally and to lay his proposals before them, not least because it suggested that their attendance at the conference, denounced in more radical circles, might not be an entirely fruitless exercise. But even this relatively conservative group, unelected and only present by government invitation, would not compromise over the Cape franchise. It was the most effective means of political leverage they had, and they all knew it.

Also laid before the conference delegates was another part of the government's legislative programme, the Native Affairs Administration Bill. Plaatje condemned it without reservation, both here and on numerous other occasions before it finally became law (after passing through several Select Committees) two years later. Although not presented as one of Hertzog's four interdependent bills, it was nevertheless an integral part of his general programme of segregation. It took up the themes of the abortive Native Administration Bill of 1917, and it embodied a commitment to the notion of 'retribalisation': that is to say, the administrative refurbishing of African traditionalism, providing official government backing and authority for the institutions of tribal rule. The bill aimed to create a separate system of courts to administer African law in the rural areas and to extend to the other provinces of the Union Natal's system of incorporating the chiefs into the system of 'native administration', giving them far-reaching powers over their own people and recognising in law such elements of traditional practice as *lobola*, or bridewealth.[39]

For Plaatje this all amounted to a reversion to tribalism, it encouraged the survival of polygamy, and it proposed to remove many ordinary Africans from the ultimate protection of the law. Like the proposal to abolish the Cape franchise, the Native Affairs Administration Bill undermined one of his most cherished principles: equality before the law. He therefore found the bill quite unacceptable, and made his views very plain both at the conference itself and in the press in the weeks and months that followed. What saddened him, too, was the fact that at the conference, packed as it was with government-nominated chiefs, the bill predictably had some appeal to chiefs anxious to strengthen their powers. It threatened to drive a wedge between educated leaders like himself and the traditional leaders of the African people, and to undermine what was to him a crucial relationship. More than any other piece of legislation, the Native Affairs Administration Bill struck at the heart of the common society that Plaatje held so dear.[40]

Dr Modiri Molema, another of the delegates, shared these views. What he really remembered about the conference, though, was the chance to observe Plaatje in action, and in a forum that was ideally suited to the exercise of his talents. He was struck not just by what Plaatje said and the persuasive arguments he put forward, but by the way he spoke, especially when he did so in Dutch – as when he addressed General Hertzog in support of Professor Jabavu's motion of thanks to the prime minister for attending the conference. Plaatje's diction and intonation, Molema thought, were flawless, and carried no trace of an accent. He pronounced difficult words perfectly (like 'splinternuwe Duusman' – or 'brand-new white fellow'), and the Dutch-speaking officials and politicians present, amazed to hear this coming from the mouth of a black man, just sat up and listened, captivated. It was a surreal moment: the ideologues of segregation being spoken to in their own language by a black man as proficient in Dutch as they were themselves. Isaiah Bud-M'belle, interpreting at the conference, must have looked on with some amusement.[41]

Upper, left: Mrs Georgiana Solomon, suffragette and campaigner for African rights.

Upper, right: Alice Werner, writer and lecturer in African languages at King's College London.

Lower, left: Leo Weinthal, editor of the *African World*, who put work Plaatje's way.

Lower, right: Daniel Jones, reader in phonetics at University College London, collaborator in 1915 and 1916.

NATIVE LIFE IN
SOUTH AFRICA,

BEFORE AND SINCE THE
EUROPEAN WAR AND
THE BOER REBELLION

By

SOL. T. PLAATJE

Editor of *Tsala ea Batho*, Kimberley, S.A.
Author of *Sechuana Proverbs and their European Equivalents*

THIRD EDITION

LONDON
P. S. KING & SON, LTD.
ORCHARD HOUSE, WESTMINSTER
1917

Upper: Title page of *Native Life in South Africa*, published in London, May 1916. A third edition, seen here, followed early in 1917.

Lower, left: The Colenso family at 'Elangeni', Amersham, c.1916. *Left to right:* Lady Dickens, Sylvia Colenso, Sophie Colenso, Dusa, Irma Colenso.

Lower, middle: John Harris, of the Anti-Slavery and Aborigines' Protection Society, who did his best to prevent *Native Life* from being published.

Lower, right: Israel Gollancz, editor of the tercentenary *Book of Homage to Shakespeare*, which included Plaatje's contribution, 'A South African's homage'.

Upper: 'Fearless defender and leader of his people': flyer advertising Plaatje's reception in Johannesburg, 6 June 1917.

Lower, left: Betty Molteno and her partner Alice Greene, who died in 1920. Betty Molteno remained one of Plaatje's closest friends and supporters.

Lower, right: St Leger Plaatje *(sitting, left)* with fellow students at Lovedale, c.1917. Z.K. Matthews, from the same Lyndhurst Road school in Kimberley, is standing behind him.

Upper, left: Dr and Mrs Theo Kakaza, Plaatje's hosts in Buffalo, New York State, February 1921.

Upper, right: Marcus Garvey, president of the UNIA, speaking at Liberty Hall, Harlem, in 1920.

Lower, left: W.E.B. Du Bois, editor of *The Crisis* and founder of the NAACP, whom Plaatje met for the first time in New York in 1921.

Lower, right: Robert Russa Moton, principal of the Tuskegee Institute, Alabama. 'I never felt so sorry to leave a place as I did when I had to turn my back on your great institution yesterday', Plaatje wrote.

Upper: Swazi delegation to London, 1923, which Plaatje joined in an unofficial capacity. *Seated, left to right:* Benjamin Nxumalo, Mandananda Mtsetfwa, King Sobhuza II, Prince Msudvuka Dlamini, Pixley ka Isaka Seme. *Standing, left to right:* Amos Zwane, Loshina Hlope, Sol Plaatje.

Lower: 'Somewhere in Africa', the theatrical sketch which formed part of the *Cradle of the World* film production at the Philharmonic Hall, London, in August and September 1923. Plaatje is centre stage, holding a spear.

Upper: Addressing a meeting at the time of the visit of the Prince of Wales to South Africa in 1925.

Lower, left: David Ramoshoana, one-time teacher at the Lyndhurst Road school, Kimberley, Plaatje's collaborator in his work on Setswana.

Lower, right: Clement Doke, professor of African languages at the University of the Witwatersrand – and supporter of Plaatje's endeavours.

Upper, left: Tshekedi Khama, chief regent of the Bamangwato, 1930.

Upper, right: Halley Plaatje, Violet Plaatje and Westerfield Ncwabeni, Barkly West show, 4 August 1930.

Lower: 'On the way to the Barkly show'. *Left to right:* Miss Tutu Kosani, Mrs Elizabeth Plaatje, Mrs Z. Mahabane, Plaatje (at the wheel of his 14 hp Renault), Mrs Henry Mashuku.

Upper: Violet Plaatje *(seated, centre)* and her highly popular 'Rhythm Girls'.

Lower, left: Richard Plaatje, who worked as an interpreter in the magistrate's court, Kimberley, early 1930s.

Lower, right: At work outside with his typewriter and a young admirer.

Hertzog's four bills came before the Native Conference a year later in more or less the same form. Again meeting in Pretoria, but this time addressed by the jovial figure of Tielman Roos, who was both deputy prime minister and acting minister of native affairs, the conference nevertheless proved to be even more acrimonious than its predecessor. Tielman Roos began by rehearsing the provisions and objectives of the bills just as General Hertzog had done before, Professor D.D.T. Jabavu proposed a vote of thanks to him for his attendance, and Plaatje seconded in a long speech which Roos interpreted as one of complaint rather than welcome. Impasse on the issue of the interdependence of the Hertzog bills (as they were now known) was duly reached on the second day, and the conference very nearly broke up as the delegates sought to avoid any action that might be taken as indicating their acceptance of the disfranchisement bill. Eventually, after much toing and froing between the conference room and the prime minister's office, the delegates were persuaded to stay on and discuss the other bills, only for speaker after speaker to emphasise their opposition to the government's insistence upon their interdependence.[42]

The highlight of the discussion that followed, in the opinion of Professor Jabavu, was Plaatje's passionate speech on the subject of the Land Bill. Plaatje, said Jabavu, 'probably commands greater authority than any other single native individual in the country to speak on the subject', and his speech was 'admirable for its collation of arguments against the bill'. Again, Plaatje's point was not that Africans did not need more land – he knew better than anybody how desperately they did – but that the loss of the franchise was too high a price to pay. He illustrated the point with a widely quoted metaphor: 'When a Dutchman wants to trap a jackal,' he said, 'he gets a beautiful piece of mutton and puts poison in it, but the jackal usually walks round and round the meat and does not take it.' Were they to accept the bait of the land they were offered, and give up the franchise, said Plaatje, then they would show they had less sense than a jackal. They should accept neither the principle of the Land Act, which excluded Africans from acquiring land in 87 per cent of the Union, nor the sacrifice of the Cape franchise. The proposed land bill, Plaatje thought, simply added insult to injury, adding that the 'learned gentleman' who had drafted it 'must wonder they were human if they accepted the proposition'.[43]

Resolutions were framed to give expression to these sentiments and they were passed unanimously. It would be the last time the government sought African approval for the Hertzog bills; men like Professor Jabavu, Richard Selope Thema, above all Plaatje himself, were far too experienced politically to allow themselves to be used in this way. If the government had hoped to divide African opinion, then they failed here as well. It was for Plaatje a matter of considerable satisfaction that foremost in the defence of the Cape franchise, alongside himself, were Africans from the two northern provinces. Such a 'will to deny oneself for the sake of another', he wrote afterwards, 'is my idea of progress of civilisation', and the expression of 'a noble spirit on the part of the Northerners which does them credit'. None of them wanted to be remembered for being willing to exchange the Cape franchise for the paltry substitutes on offer. If it was forced upon them, then so be it; but never let it be said it was done with their approval and agreement. 'We shall this time let white politicians do their own fell work', Plaatje said, 'so that when the tears of the many victims of the Union's legislative efforts at length draw retributive justice from the heights, no Prime Minister may say that we, too, have had a hand in the transaction.' The government itself seems to have recognised the futility of trying to secure African approval for these measures, for the Native Conference was not summoned for another four years.[44]

Plaatje spoke with such authority on the question of land, as Professor Jabavu said, not only because of his long campaign against the Natives' Land Act, but because of what he had seen in the countryside during the three years since his return to South Africa. He continued to make this a priority, his ability to get to out-of-the way places considerably enhanced by the acquisition (with help from De Beers) of a Ford motor car early in 1926. This came complete with a portable generator which enabled him to operate his bioscope in places where there was no electricity, enabling him, he said, 'to work independently of other people's cars' and to bring both entertainment and his message of hope to remote rural communities.[45]

He also continued to watch the Circuit Courts in operation, reporting upon the frequent miscarriages of justice he encountered. Most often these occurred where white juries sat in judgement over fellow whites accused of crimes against blacks. He had witnessed, so he told the Joint Councils Conference in 1924, cases that 'seemed hopelessly incredible even in this land of discrimination'. What he saw subsequently served only to strengthen his belief in the need to keep a close watch over the horrors being perpetrated in the name of the law. As ever, he saw the law as the guardian of individual liberty, but he was convinced that trial by jury, in cases involving violence between black and white, should be replaced with trial by judge alone, or by judges and assessors. He raised the point at both Native Conferences. At the most recent one, in 1926, he presented Tielman Roos with details of a number of cases where there had been blatant miscarriages of justice as a result of biased white juries or incompetent interpreting, and demanded that he take action.[46]

At the same time he reported upon the evictions that were still taking place under the terms of the Natives' Land Act of 1913, often returning to this subject in the meetings he addressed and in articles he wrote for the press. He wished to draw attention to what he believed was the most iniquitous piece of legislation ever passed in South Africa. Now, as much as in 1913 or 1914, he saw it as his duty to speak out on behalf of the 'inarticulate natives of the rural districts of the Union'. As the years passed he became more and more critical, not only of the impact of government policy and legislation upon African life in the countryside, but at what he saw as the lack of concern of Africans living in towns for the condition of those who lived in the countryside. In one newspaper article he went so far as to accuse them of 'callous indifference to their own flesh and blood'. Plaatje, more than any other individual, earned a reputation as the spokesman for the interests of Africans struggling to make a living in South Africa's countryside.[47]

Plaatje's platform during these years, and his main source of income, was the press: not his own newspaper, for he failed to restart *Tsala ea Batho*, but the columns of almost all the major English-language newspapers of the day: the Johannesburg *Star*, the *Pretoria News*, the *Cape Times* and *Cape Argus*, the East London *Daily Dispatch*, the *Diamond Fields Advertiser*, and *Umteteli wa Bantu*, the newspaper published by the Chamber of Mines. Hundreds of his articles appeared in these newspapers, often under the headline 'Through native eyes'. Plaatje became known as the pre-eminent spokesman for moderate African opinion. His articles ranged widely over many different aspects of African life in South Africa. He had a characteristic style that combined strong moral indignation with meticulous documentary proof for the points he wished to make, and often his articles were enlivened by personal recollections of his own experiences. The strongest evidence, he always thought, was what he saw with his own eyes.

By now Plaatje's writings made quite acceptable reading for a significant portion of educated white opinion in South Africa. This was not just a matter of their intrinsic quality and his reliability over deadlines. As a result of the political realignments of the 1920s, his political views – seen in terms of the party politics of the day – were sufficiently close to those of the SAP-supporting English-language press for him to be given the freedom of the columns of their newspapers with little risk that he would upset their readers. Both the *Cape*

Times and the *Cape Argus*, for example, supported the maintenance of the Cape franchise, at least so long as the SAP was likely to need African votes to get back into power. Like the other English-language newspapers they were hostile to job reservation and the colour bar in industry, both of them subjects, along with the long-running constitutional progress of Hertzog's 'native bills', on which he frequently wrote. On occasions his pieces were accompanied by some additional editorial comment commending what he had to say to those readers who may not have been wholly convinced of the need to have the views of the 'well-known native publicist' aired in their daily newspaper.[48]

Some of these articles arose from his personal observations from the gallery of the House of Assembly in Cape Town, which, in the mid-1920s, he would visit at least once a year. He wrote in effect as an African parliamentary correspondent, 'Parliament and natives' being a frequent headline over his newspaper articles. When he could not be there in person, he relied upon the daily press for information on political developments, and always made a point of scrutinising relevant government publications. Sometimes he managed to refute arguments from government spokesmen (over such matters as the extent of the African contribution to the exchequer in taxation) by using information and evidence derived from their own published sources; this way it was difficult to accuse him of relying on unsound evidence. Many of his articles referred his readers to particular official publications, and in time he built up a large library of Blue Books, Select Committee reports, Hansards and the like at his home in Kimberley.

Not everything he wrote was political in its focus. Sometimes he tackled historical subjects, usually as a result of investigating the historical background to some topical issue. On more than one occasion he related the story of the first encounter of the Barolong with the Boers in the 1830s – and the tragic consequences, as he saw it, that ensued. He often pointed to the insidious dangers of misrepresenting and manipulating the past: 'Is Congress aware', he asked on one occasion, 'that school books are being changed and that white and black children are being taught that the extinct Bushmen and Hottentots alone were indigenous to South Africa; that the Bantu are interlopers from across the Zambesi and that they only landed here at the same time, if not later than, Van Riebeeck?' Another time he delved into aspects of missionary history in order to defend the contribution they had made to African 'civilisation', and to counter those who argued that the Christian missionaries had helped dispossess Africans of their land, offering them the 'dope' of religion instead. Plaatje, by contrast, always remained loyal to his missionary mentors, and had no time for arguments of this kind.[49]

Other articles took the form of travel writing, recording his observations as he travelled around the country. Hence, two articles entitled 'Native life at the alluvial diggings', published in several different white newspapers in mid-1927, following his visit to the Lichtenburg diamond diggings; 'In Bechuanaland today', another travel piece that drew attention to the economic disintegration of the Batswana and its consequences; and 'Native institutions revisited', a two-part account of his visit (in September 1928) to the Healdtown Institution and the St Matthew's Training Institution in the eastern Cape, which he had last visited in 1912. In the last one, he combined observation, analysis and personal reflection with a strong sense of how fortunate the eastern Cape was, in comparison with the northern Cape, when it came to education. 'Most notable after a dozen years absence', he added, 'is the striking absence of the red blanket population', though he was not sure whether this was attributable to 'the advance of civilization' or the effect of a new range of customs duties imposed on 'native blankets and all manner of Kaffir truck'.[50]

The obituaries he wrote were particularly striking. Many were of the great figures of Cape liberalism who were passing away, J.X. Merriman, J.W. Jagger, Sir William Solomon, Sir Perceval Laurence, men whom Plaatje had known in happier times, and who personified the values and ideals of a great tradition. In mourning their deaths, he was marking the passing of an era very different from the present: a time when the actions of individuals seemed to count for far more than they did now; a time when he enjoyed a fruitful association with men willing to recognise and accept him as a spokesman for 'native opinion'; a time when South Africa was not yet trapped in the segregationist orthodoxies of the 1920s. Above all, these obituaries, eulogies as they often were, reflected the importance he always attached to individual character and leadership. He recognised in the lives of these men an example for others to emulate. The same conviction had guided his own actions. He always believed that even the most severe disabilities and disadvantages could be overcome through sheer force of character and hard work, and that he was duty bound to set an example himself.[51]

He also wrote about the lives of his fellow Africans. Often they were people he had known well: J.E.K. Aggrey, the West African educationist whom he had encountered in both England and America; the Barolong chief J.M. Nyokong, once a member of the *Tsala* syndicate, who had given 'moral and material support' to 'every Progressive movement among Natives', and whose 'outstanding character' made it 'possible for a black man to command the high respect of the people of his race, and men and women of other races'; or the Basotho chief Makhaula Lerotholi, whom Plaatje recalled regaling his attendants, on one of his visits to Basutoland, with 'anecdotes of his and my own experiences in London, just ten years previously', memories of the Southern Syncopated Orchestra doubtless among them.[52]

Most heartfelt of all was his obituary of Chief Silas Molema, who died in Mafeking in September 1927, at the age of seventy-eight. Plaatje wrote of the many people like himself who had, over the years, regarded the chief as their 'guide, philosopher and friend', and 'often came to him for help and advice'. Silas Molema personified the independent, progressive, forward-looking Barolong chiefdom which once bore his own hopes and aspirations. It was Molema who had funded his first newspaper, *Koranta ea Becoana*, launching him on his journalistic career, and supported him ever since. Molema had been a father figure too. He always called him 'Rra', or 'Father': it was a conventional term of respect, but it expressed the fondness and closeness of their relationship; Molema, for his part, when he wrote to Plaatje in English, would begin his letters 'Dear Son'.[53]

Silas Molema's death thus brought back memories of a shared past, and he was deeply affected. 'You will not believe what a shock we got from your telegram conveying the news of Father's passing', he wrote to Modiri Molema. 'I was lying ill at the time and was simply beside myself. I saw him at home just four weeks back and there were no indications that the end was near.' 'It is indeed true', he added, by way of consolation, 'that in the midst of life we are in death – losho lo fa mojeng oa kabo'; literally, 'Death is at the end of the cloak'. It was entirely in keeping with the Christian faith the three men shared that he should have ended his letter with some words of comfort from the Bible: 'Blessed are the dead who die in the Lord, for they rest from their labours.'[54]

Much of what Plaatje wrote in the 1920s conveys the impression of a man whose ideas were being overtaken by new realities. In truth he was not well equipped to understand the dynamics of the complex industrialised society which South Africa had now become; few people were. His political ideas were formed out of a combination of Christian belief and Victorian liberalism (his views on individual character very much a product of this), grafted onto a powerfully felt sense of responsibility for the leadership of his people. But these ideas were powerless in the face of a government intent on implementing a social and political order which went against everything he stood for; while the notion that there was such a thing as a coherent, undifferentiated community of African interests was increasingly untenable in the fractured society South Africa had become.

On social and economic issues Plaatje found it difficult to come to terms with what was going on around him. He continued to regard the countryside as the 'natural environment' of the African people – a phrase he used on a number of occasions – and he always regarded African workers in towns and on the mines as essentially displaced rural cultivators. 'Failing anything better', he would tell a government commission in 1931, 'the principal industrial centres should have a reserve where an overworked Native or miners' phthisis victim could mind his own goat and spend the evening of his life under his own vine and fig tree.' In spirit, Plaatje was a man of the countryside, not the city, and it often showed in his writings; he sought not so much a new order as to preserve the best of what had gone before.[55]

A further consequence of his outlook was that he was inclined to attribute to political actions or legislation social and economic consequences which were in reality the product of wider processes of change. This was true above all in relation to the Natives' Land Act of 1913, about which he often wrote in the 1920s, invariably in the strongest terms. 'To me', he wrote on one occasion, 'it remains the most Draconian piece of legislation ever conceived, and it is responsible for the wholesale moral and economic degradation of our people in the country – including the high mortality of black babies.' There was of an element of truth in this, but it was not the whole story. Overcrowding in the towns certainly owed something to the effects of the Land Act in the countryside, but it was part and parcel of a wider process of industrialisation which Plaatje found difficult to comprehend.[56]

When Plaatje addressed an African audience it was generally in the columns of *Umteteli wa Bantu*, the weekly paper financed by the Chamber of Mines. While *Umteteli* was regarded by some Africans, and certainly by the Communist Party of South Africa, as simply a tool of the mining industry, it took a relatively liberal line. Its editorials advised against support for strike action as a means of redressing grievances, and precious little criticism of the mining industry ever appeared in its columns, but it did support the retention of the Cape franchise and its extension to the northern provinces, and opposed the Hertzog bills. It was also strongly opposed to the colour bar in industry and campaigned vociferously against the Mines and Works Amendment Bill. For *Umteteli* the villains of the South African political stage were not, as the Communist Party would have it, the mining capitalists, but overpaid white workers who possessed the political means to force the government to concede to their demands for a guaranteed place, protected by the colour bar, in industry; Afrikaner nationalists who demanded state handouts to subsidise inefficient farmers at the expense of the mining industry; and a Pact government that represented a cynical alliance of the two.

Such an outlook was shared by many African public figures, Plaatje included, and *Umteteli* found a receptive audience. Unlike its rival, the hopelessly under-capitalised *Abantu-Batho*, which somehow carried on, *Umteteli* was a well-turned-out newspaper, each edition packed full of news and features; it carried material in a variety of African languages as well as in English, and it appeared without a break. Ultimate editorial control, as most people were aware, remained with its white managers and it was this that had led Plaatje – probably on more than one occasion – to reject the offer of the editorship. He valued his independence far too highly to be willing to subject himself to restrictions of this kind.[57]

But he did write fairly regular letters and articles for *Umteteli* throughout the 1920s. These are among the most interesting of his extensive writings from this time, for they reveal, in a way that his articles in the white press often did not, a great deal about the personal as well as the political frustrations he now felt. Many of the topics he chose to write about were the same, but in addressing himself to an African audience there was a different emphasis. He was critical not only of the government for its wholly unsympathetic attitude to African aspirations and representations, but of his own people for their failure to unite, to support their political leaders, to demonstrate that collective strength of character and integrity that he thought vital to their well-being. He did not mince words in condemning the 'lethargy', 'fickleness' and 'wanton indifference' of people around him; the increasing incidence of alcoholism; the failure of delegates to conferences to prepare their arguments properly; a growing spirit of jealousy that he now detected among his people. With shortcomings of this kind, he often said, it was hardly surprising that African political and social life was in so sorry a state.[58]

Along with this there also developed a much more personal note of frustration: above all, on the subject of leadership, a much debated issue in *Umteteli*'s columns throughout the 1920s. His main charge was that leaders like himself were not supported by the people because they were swayed far more by tribal sentiment. 'Natives as a race only recognize one leader, namely, their hereditary prince.' Other leaders, however able, were simply ignored. 'A man may be a genius but the Native population will regard him very much like a clever actor on the stage – to be admired, not followed. This admiration – like the popularity of a new jazz tune – will last until its novelty has worn off, when the people look for fresh excitement in the shape of a different "leader". But, be he ever so faithful and self-sacrificing, they will desert him at the first sound of the call of the tribal chief, even if the latter implied nothing but a tribal chief and clannish tyranny.'

The failure of leadership, he concluded, 'is not on the part of the leaders of whom we have had several of outstanding ability; the fault lies with the Native masses who by nature object to follow one who is not their tribal chief'.[59]

With these frustrations came a new sensitivity to criticism. Several times he spoke out against the presumptuousness of 'the younger generation' to hold forth on such subjects as 'leadership', 'character' or 'sacrifice'. He pointed to his own record of service, to the sacrifices he had made, and to his independence from any political party. 'We of my generation', he wrote, replying to Archibald M'belle (a nephew of Isaiah), 'cannot go on working, lobbying among younger politicians and paying the cost.' He knew that others, both men and women, were able and willing take over the burden, but what encouragement was there 'to shoulder the thankless task, when busybodies who pay nothing and do less for the cause can stay at home and sow apples of discord among the Native masses by imputing unfounded motives and generally misrepresenting such voluntary sacrifices?' Not unnaturally he reacted when aspersions were cast on his integrity, when people failed to appreciate the value of what he had done in the past. More than ever, he thought he deserved better of his people. [60]

Many others joined this debate on the nature of 'leadership' in the columns of *Umteteli*. There was little agreement about the nature of the problem, let alone its solution. The variety of views expressed reflected the frustrations of several generations of African spokesmen, or would-be spokesmen, unsure on whose behalf they could really claim to be speaking. They saw themselves as leaders, but who were they leading? At one time Plaatje and his colleagues in the SANNC could claim with some justification to represent the African people as a whole. Now it was far harder to make this case, and his own public arguments with 'Enquirer' and 'Resurgam' made it clear that even his own, once authoritative views no longer went unchallenged.[61]

But it was not simply that the relationship between these African leaders and their political constituency was more ambiguous and tenuous than before. On one side, they were faced with an unsympathetic government, deaf to their representations, determined to implement its policies of segregation and retribalisation, with not a care for their careers or aspirations. On the other, they found that even that small space still left to them was being claimed by a new breed of white liberals and 'friends of the natives' – the 'self-styled native experts', as Plaatje called them on more than one occasion – who had moved into the 'race relations' arena, who controlled *Umteteli* and the Joint Councils, who possessed the resources denied to the Africans whose place they were taking. It was small wonder, in such circumstances, that 'leadership' should have been such a contentious and widely debated issue; that men like Richard Selope Thema,

Pixley ka Isaka Seme and others should have resorted to drink as a means of escape from the impossible position in which they found themselves; that African political organisation as a whole should have deteriorated to such an extent.[62]

+∿+

In Plaatje the effect of this collective sense of marginalisation led not to despair but to a renewed emphasis upon the need to set an example of individual service, to be more vigilant than ever as the Pact government pushed its legislative programme through parliament, to reiterate time and again that Africans must fight their own battles. Above all, he emphasised the need for moral regeneration. Nowhere was this more evident than in his involvement, from the middle of 1927, in temperance work on behalf of the Independent Order of True Templars, or the IOTT.

A committed teetotaller, he had long been concerned with the temperance issue. As a youngster he had witnessed in Kimberley the devastating effects that alcoholism could have on a people wrenched from the countryside to employment on the mines and in the towns; in Mafeking he had seen successive Barolong chiefs fall victim to its effects, and always supported calls for the total prohibition of sales of drink to his people. Later, in Kimberley, he used to attend the annual licensing sessions to argue against the extension and renewal of liquor licences. As time went on he became even more concerned about the issue. When he returned from England and America in 1923, he was shocked at the 'orgy of drunkenness' he encountered in Johannesburg and elsewhere, and he continued to regard it, whatever the reasons or mitigating circumstances put forward, as ultimately a question of moral failure on the part of those involved. Many of his articles in *Umteteli* singled out alcoholism as one of the primary reasons for the deterioration of the life of his people. Over practically no other issue, indeed, did he feel so strongly.

His work with the IOTT began in June 1927 when he was appointed special deputy ('A High Mogul of the Order', as he described it in a letter to Robert Moton) to the head of the movement, the Right Worthy Templar, J.W. Mushet, with a special brief to establish new branches of the organisation in the Transvaal, Orange Free State and eastern Cape. Mushet was an old friend who had long supported his endeavours. A wealthy Cape Town merchant and philanthropist, married to a niece of Theo Schreiner, he was one of a dwindling band of Cape liberals who remained active in South African public life in the 1920s, and he succeeded Schreiner as head of the order. He personified an older, more congenial Cape liberal tradition, willing to countenance collaboration with like-minded Africans on terms of greater equality than was true of most of the new breed of 'friends of the natives' on the Rand. The obvious point of comparison in Plaatje's life was the Brotherhood movement, and he was attracted to the IOTT for similar reasons. For like the Brotherhood movement, the IOTT was an inter-racial organisation which he upheld as an example in microcosm of what South Africa could be; and it held out the prospect of financial support, with few strings attached, to enable him to travel around the countryside, investigating and reporting, while furthering the aims of the movement itself. As with so many of Plaatje's projects, there was no single reason for his involvement. He was drawn to it by a mixture of both practical and moral considerations.[63]

Promoting the IOTT and setting up new branches was a major preoccupation in the second half of 1927 and for much of 1928. His work, in the opinion of J.W. Mushet, was of 'very outstanding merit' and he thought his visits to several African colleges had been especially valuable. After his visit to Fort Hare, for example, Mushet reported that he received 'a message from Professor Jabavu speaking in the highest terms of Bro. Plaatje's visit and of the impressive manner in which the claims of our work had been advocated'.[64]

The IOTT was far from his only concern. The government called no more Native Conferences, so that platform was denied to him, but he continued to write regularly for the press, and grew increasingly concerned at the implications of the Native Administration Bill. When the bill was before a Select Committee, tasked with refining its details, he wrote a long letter to the clerk of the House of Assembly to set out his views, in his capacity, he said, 'as member of the last Annual Statutory Conference at Pretoria, nominated thereto by unanimous decision of the rural natives of Griqualand West on the invitation of the Prime Minister, and on behalf of the other tribal and detribalised Natives unofficially represented in various capacities by me'. He thought the bill was a more serious threat to African interests than even the Natives' Land Act. Unlike any other measure of its kind it would 'effect some drastic changes in native life not only politically but even socially. Its aim is to put all natives under the same native law.' However, this was a hopelessly ambitious task, and bound to fail: 'One could no more draw up a single code for all the tribes than fix the same speed limit for Adderley Street, Cape Town, and the highways of the Karroo; and one cannot but foresee trouble in any attempt to apply the same social code to the Bapedi (under whose tribal laws it is permissible for a native to marry his first cousin) and the Tembus under whose tribal laws it is an abomination, purged only by death, for a native to marry a blood relation, however distant.'[65]

The Native Administration Bill was also one of the main subjects discussed at a conference which Plaatje attended in Kimberley in June 1927, a month later.

Organised by Dr Abdurahman and Professor Jabavu, and held in the Kimberley City Hall between 23 and 25 June, it was the first 'non-European conference' of its kind, and was attended by over a hundred delegates representing a wide range of African, Coloured and Indian organisations. Its aim was to secure 'closer co-operation among non-Europeans of all sections in British South Africa', one of the few concrete steps to have been taken in this direction since Plaatje had initiated talks between the executive of the SANNC and the APO back in 1912. Plaatje was prominent in procedural matters once the conference had opened, and it was fitting that it should have been he who moved the opening resolution: 'that the interests of South Africa can be best served by (a) closer co-operation among the non-European sections of South Africa, and (b) closer co-operation between Europeans and non-Europeans'.

A variety of matters of common interest to 'non-Europeans' was then discussed. From Plaatje himself there were contributions on familiar themes. Welcoming the delegates to the city of Kimberley, he spoke highly of the European, Indian and Coloured communities but had harsh words for 'the Kimberley Natives', about whom he regretted he could not do the same; they 'had better opportunities and educational facilities' than anywhere else, 'but they made little use of them', and he expressed the hope that the conference 'would wake them up'. On the Native Administration Bill, too, he reiterated his criticisms. Before moving a resolution condemning the bill (which was carried unanimously), he pointed out that if it were to become law 'the police could march into that Hall and arrest the whole conference, under the sedition clause, because it was called without the permission of the Governor-General'.[66]

The conference was considered a success, but it could do nothing to relieve the disabilities from which both Africans and Coloured people suffered. Both Dr Abdurahman and D.D.T. Jabavu, in their closing speeches, spoke of the historical importance they believed the conference would one day assume. For now, though, as Plaatje wrote to Robert Moton on the eve of the conference, it was no more than 'a vain hope' to believe that it could do anything to avert the 'drastic laws, most barbarous in character', designed to 'destroy the soul of the Native people', which parliament was intent on putting onto the statute book, since they lacked the political power to resist. It was small wonder he began his letter to Moton by saying 'the struggle for life in South Africa is so grim that I could scarcely remember whether I owe you a letter or the other way round'.[67]

He did have one positive piece of news to convey to Moton, however. During a recent visit to Cape Town, he said, 'I secured for my eldest son, St Leger, the head clerkship in the office of the location superintendent near Maitland, Cape Town. He starts on the new job on the first of July. It is the first time that a

South African municipality appoints a Native to such a position.' 'It is devoutly to be hoped', he added, 'that the splendid example set by the mother city may be followed by East London, Port Elizabeth, Johannesburg and other South African municipalities in the near future.'

It was an opportunity St Leger nearly missed. Plaatje only heard about the new position a week before the closing date for applications, and wrote to him right away, sure it would appeal to him. Worried his application would not arrive in time, he went ahead and applied on his behalf. He also had a quiet word with Dr Abdurahman, a member of the Cape Town City Council, and so ideally placed to help. St Leger, at this time, was in Pietermaritzburg, working for the firm of A.H. Todd, purveyors of patent medicines, where he had charge of 'correspondence in the native languages' – probably not quite the kind of 'career in medicine' he once aspired to. According to his father, St Leger 'never quite liked living in Natal' (he himself complained of 'rigorous pass laws and their attendant evils') so the position in Cape Town, which carried a salary of £240 a year, must have looked an attractive proposition. The main requirement for the new job was 'a knowledge of Bantu languages' which he had in abundance, being proficient, so Plaatje told the town clerk, in 'nearly all the native languages and dialects spoken south of the Limpopo'. He was appointed from a list of thirty-seven applicants.[68]

A year later there was another significant milestone in St Leger's life: he was married to a former school classmate, Mitta Ramhitshane, whose family lived in Beaconsfield. It was an elaborate affair, people came from far and wide and they received a huge number of wedding presents, among them the gift of a bullock from Sir David Harris and ten sheep from Sir Ernest Oppenheimer. After the ceremony at the Greenpoint Wesleyan Church, receptions were held in both Kimberley (at the Lyndhurst Road Native Institute) and, three days later, at Ndabeni in Cape Town. For Plaatje, his eldest son at last seemed settled both personally and professionally.[69]

Once the Native Administration Bill became law in September 1927, the defence of the Cape franchise was once again Plaatje's overriding concern – in the press, in lobbying politicians in Cape Town, in ensuring that as many Africans as were qualified for the franchise were actually registered. He had been cautiously optimistic about the consultative machinery established by the government in the 1920 Native Affairs Act, and was willing to participate in the new structures that were created. By the late 1920s his attitude had changed. The government had demonstrated its contempt for the whole notion of consulting representatives of the African people, even those it had nominated itself, by completely ignoring the views expressed at the 1926 Native Conference, and then by refusing to reconvene it. As a result, a number of measures affecting African interests were passed during the next few years without any official Native Conference ever having a chance to discuss them. Even the conduct of the Native Affairs Commission, supposedly composed of 'friends of the natives', proved a huge disappointment. During the last Native Conference Plaatje had said it simply 'interpreted to the natives the government point of view and pressed for its adoption'; thereafter it functioned as 'the political branch of the Native Affairs Department'. Early in 1931 he told a government commission that 'the Native belief is that in practice the Commission regards itself as the mouthpiece of the Government, appointed in the interest of the European population'.[70]

Plaatje's reaction to the attitude of the Pact government on the question of consultation was straightforward. It convinced him, more than ever, of the dangers of relying upon whites, even those who claimed to be 'friends of the natives', to represent African interests: 'only one person', he would often say, could truly represent their views, 'and that was the native himself'. And it only strengthened his belief in the need to defend, at all costs, the Cape franchise. He saw clearly that, despite the changed conditions of the 1920s, it was its existence that gave African spokesmen like himself some degree of leverage in the House of Assembly, some influence in the deliberations of the South African Party. So it was as a fervent defender of the Cape franchise that he spoke out most often in the late 1920s: against white 'sympathisers' who urged Africans to adopt a more flexible attitude towards the various alternative forms of representation that were being suggested, and to trust to General Hertzog's good faith; against people like Horatio M'belle, another of Isaiah Bud-M'belle's nephews, who thought he was in the pocket of the South African Party; against Coloured voters tempted by General Hertzog's promises of differential treatment from Africans.[71]

It was the reason, too, for his involvement in the Cape Native Voters' Association, whose vice president he became in 1927, and under whose auspices he played a characteristically energetic role, particularly during the provincial elections in 1928 and the general election of 1929, in mobilising Cape voters behind the South African Party, and in countering the efforts of National Party agents to prevent African voters from registering. In June 1929 he wrote of being busy 'electioneering and registering in 5 separate constituencies extending from Hopetown south of the Orange River to Mafeking on northern boundaries of the Union'. Protecting the Cape African franchise was never just a matter of composing eloquent articles for the English-language newspapers.[72]

For a short while, too, he became involved in the affairs of the African National

Congress, having hitherto kept his distance. He attended its seventeenth annual conference in Bloemfontein at the beginning of April 1929, drafting a reply to General Hertzog's notorious 'Black Manifesto' (which proposed, among other things, to abolish the Cape franchise). He condemned the general for describing 'the native people as something evil and subversive of European civilisation', and for making 'an authoritative appeal ... to the racial passions of all white people to unite in their suppression, and so create and perpetuate strife and friction between black and white in the Union of South Africa'. Such declarations could not obscure the fact that Congress was deeply divided, torn between conservatives and radicals. The conference threw out resolutions 'to adopt revolutionary methods', to take 'direct action' over pass laws, or to affiliate with the Communist Party, but feelings ran high. A Kimberley CID informant, reporting on proceedings, said Plaatje was 'suspected by the ANC of being in the pay of De Beers ... and is not trusted', not the first time such a view had been expressed. He and others of the old guard were denounced as the 'tools of the Capitalist oppressors and exploiters' in the columns of the Communist Party's newspaper, the *South African Worker*, and accused of dominating the conference and making decisions 'in the name of the African masses'. The 'only question', it said, was 'whether they serve capitalism from fear and servility or consciously'. But even the Communist Party, shortly to be muzzled by the 'sedition' clause of the Native Administration Act, decided to put up candidates for what it called 'the Parliament of the ruling classes'.[73]

To nobody's surprise the Pact government was returned to power at the general election in June with an increased majority for the National Party, giving it overall control in the new parliament. Plaatje called it 'a knockout blow for prejudice and repression'. Hertzog had appealed unashamedly to white fears of the so-called *swartgevaar* ('black danger'), condemning Smuts and his SAP for putting forward policies that would lead to the creation of 'a black kaffir state'. His alarmist rhetoric paid off handsomely with white voters. Plaatje and his colleagues were left to contemplate the grim prospect of a renewed assault upon the Cape African franchise. The political future looked bleaker than ever.[74]

A month later came even more devastating news. St Leger had lost his job in Cape Town, dismissed after it was found he had taken, on six different occasions, sums of money amounting to £7 10s 0d from the cash receipts at the office of the superintendent at Ndabeni where he worked. When confronted with the evidence, he at first made 'several attempts at evasion', so the mayor of Cape Town reported after the matter was investigated, but then admitted the offence, confessing that his wife had been ill and that he had been very pressed for money. He expressed regret and pleaded for leniency, but none was given. St Leger then returned to Kimberley, rejoining his parents at 32 Angel Street, and set about finding some other way of making a living. It would not be easy for any of them.[75]

The general election of 1929 can be seen as marking the end of another phase in Plaatje's life. He had returned home in 1923, forced to accept that there was no longer any prospect of outside intervention in the affairs of his country, and that he had no alternative but to work within the structures that existed. With his travelling bioscope he had done his best to convey something of the inspiration he had himself derived from his visit to the United States. He failed to resuscitate his old newspaper, *Tsala ea Batho*, but wrote extensively on the issues of the day in both black and white newspapers, and he sought to exploit white party politics to his own ends. He did all he could to foster that moral regeneration which he thought was the only way out of the deteriorating social, economic and political circumstances in which the African people now found themselves.

But for all his efforts, and through circumstances well beyond his control, he was far less of an influence in South African public affairs than before. It was no longer clear on whose behalf he spoke, and his involvement in such organisations as the IOTT seemed only to emphasise his isolation from any meaningful political constituency. The IOTT gave him a platform and a means of livelihood, but was no substitute for the existential chasm that now existed. The more he railed against the failings of his own people, and the more he stressed the need for individual uplift, the more lonely and isolated his own predicament appeared. And now, with St Leger disgraced, he must have wondered, more than ever, about the effect of the life he had chosen to lead upon the lives of his children. Moral rectitude was all very well, but it was difficult when your eldest son fell so far short of the standards you demanded from others.

In these circumstances his decision to turn his mind to other things, to devote himself to the preservation of the language and literature of the Tswana people, returning to earlier concerns, cannot have come a moment too soon. Over the coming months this would be his main preoccupation – and the overwhelmingly important theme of his life thereafter.

SIXTEEN

Setswana

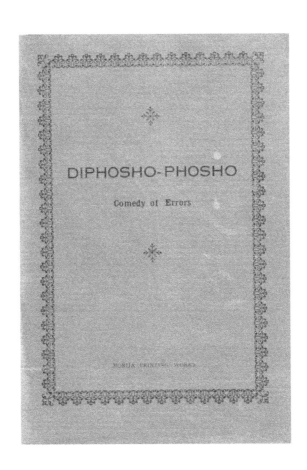

DIPHOSHO-PHOSHO

Comedy of Errors

MORIJA PRINTING WORKS

A love of Setswana was a constant throughout Plaatje's life. Growing up at Pniel, he had learnt, like many of those around him, to combine a deep attachment to Setswana, and the traditions that came with it, with the religion and values of the mission community of which he was a part. Together they shaped the person he was. Thereafter, he was always ready to uphold this Tswana inheritance, whether regaling the members of the South Africans Improvement Society in Kimberley with his talk on 'The history of the Bechuanas', entering the fray with the missionary societies about how Setswana should be represented in writing, or setting about translating Shakespeare's plays. Above all, in the newspapers he edited between 1902 and 1914, he demonstrated the capabilities and potential of his language as a medium of communication. In doing so he hoped to draw Tswana-speakers together, to strengthen bonds of community, to enhance their claims to nationhood. And in the tens of thousands of words in Setswana that appeared in these newspapers, written by himself and his contributors, he built up a treasure store of the riches of the language. The pages of *Koranta ea Becoana*, *Tsala ea Becoana* and *Tsala ea Batho* constituted between them the most extensive and most varied archive of written Setswana in existence.

Unsurprisingly, given his other commitments, it was only when he was in England during the First World War that he found the opportunity and the encouragement to engage systematically with a study of the language itself. *Sechuana Proverbs* and *A Sechuana Reader* were the two notable results. He was clear about his objectives in each case: the preservation of the proverbs by committing them to written form, and, with the help of Professor Daniel Jones and the new discipline of phonetics, recording the true pronunciation of the Tswana language. He thought Setswana was threatened by the spread of 'European civilisation' in southern Africa, and believed it his duty to do all he could to arrest this process. His translations of Shakespeare, paradoxical as it may seem, had this as a primary objective too.

By the 1920s, after his return to South Africa, he was more concerned than ever about the state of the Tswana language and its meagre literature. He no longer had a newspaper of his own with which to maintain a tradition of writing in Setswana, and there was simply no money to support the publication of literary and educational texts, even where they existed. He once complained to Robert Moton: 'I have seen many valuable MSS of useful works on natives – especially in the vernacular – which are needed in the schools but, like my own, they are kept out of print by lack of the printers' fees.' Lack of funds also stymied his efforts to collect the linguistic information in the first place. Once, he arranged to see an old man by the name of Maletisa who lived in the 'conquered territory' between Thaba Nchu and the Basutoland border, and who had an unrivalled knowledge not only of 'the praises of old Barolong chiefs and Bechuana hunters' but of the 'cryptic passages' and 'obscure Sechuana words' needed to understand them. Having neither time nor money, he was forced to keep postponing his visit until he eventually heard – in 1927 – that the old man had died, 'and all that treasure of Bantu folk-lore was buried with him'.[1]

At the heart of the unsatisfactory state of literature in Setswana was the unresolved orthographic problem. Each of the four missionary societies working in Tswana-speaking areas had developed their own orthographies, and over the years had failed to reach agreement on a single system. Plaatje regarded none of them as satisfactory, and as editor of *Koranta ea Becoana* and *Tsala ea Becoana* had used a further version of his own. For a while it seemed that the so-called 1910 orthography, the result of an initiative of the British and Foreign Bible Society, might gain wider acceptance, but these hopes proved short-lived. Vested interests were simply too strong and there was no proper consultation. His own efforts to promote the use of the International Phonetic Alphabet were no more successful. The *Sechuana Reader* may have been regarded as a pioneering scholarly effort, but the Tswana people, according to one of his friends, always regarded it 'as a strange book in a strange spelling', as well they might, and it never caught on.[2]

The dire state of written literature in Setswana contrasted with the progress being made by the other vernacular literatures of southern Africa. Although Setswana was one of the first Bantu languages committed to writing in the nineteenth century, and was fortunate in the quality of the linguistic and translating work carried out by the early missionaries and their collaborators, by the 1920s it had been overtaken by work done in other languages, particularly Xhosa and Sesotho. In both these languages orthographic obstacles had largely been overcome, and their writers had progressed a long way beyond the purely religious, didactic works that still, in the 1920s, constituted the bulk of published literature in Setswana. Aside from Plaatje himself, indeed, no native Tswana-speakers had written, or at least published, any books in their own language. Xhosa and Sotho, by contrast, could boast widely known authors like

S.E.K. Mqhayi and Thomas Mofolo, whose novel *Chaka*, published in 1925, had met with immediate acclaim, and was soon to be translated into English.[3]

For Plaatje, this only emphasised the extent to which Setswana had fallen behind. It possessed, in the 1920s, no literature beyond his own compilations and a limited number of religious and didactic books, an inadequate dictionary, no commonly accepted means of representing the language in writing, and no mission press that was either able or willing to publish anything other than its own denomination's religious output. The closest approximation to Lovedale or Morija among the Batswana was the London Missionary Society's institution at Tigerkloof, but this was severely handicapped by lack of funds; the orthography it used was not accepted by the other missionary societies; and what it did publish was based uncompromisingly upon the Batlaping dialect. In the past Plaatje had been very critical of the society's poor performance in the field of education; he saw no reason to change his opinion now.

Schools simply lacked suitable reading matter in Setswana, making it impossible to teach it properly. David Ramoshoana, a close friend and fellow Tswana scholar, shared his anxieties and the two men often discussed the state of Setswana during his regular visits to Plaatje's home at 32 Angel Street. A few others felt the same way. Peter Sebina, for example, a teacher living in Serowe in the Bechuanaland Protectorate, despaired at the way books written in Sesotho were being recommended for use in schools in Bechuanaland because there was nothing in Setswana. 'Bechuana children', he complained to the education authorities, 'are not Basuto children, nor are English children French children. Their colour may be the same, but not their languages. That means our children have to learn to read Sesuto (not by easy stages), and very often taught by a teacher who is himself ignorant of what he professes to teach.'[4]

Plaatje was concerned not just that Setswana was being distorted or neglected: he feared it could disappear completely. He was always conscious of the example of Korana, one of the languages spoken on the Pniel mission station where he had grown up, but by now well on the way to extinction, like the Korana themselves: it had been an extraordinarily rapid process. Against this there was an equally dramatic example of the reverse, of what could be done to rejuvenate, to create even, a language from seemingly inauspicious beginnings. That example was Afrikaans, recognised as an official language in 1925. 'The Dutch-speaking people of South Africa', David Ramoshoana wrote, comparing Afrikaans with Setswana, 'have pulled their Afrikaans – a baby among languages spoken in the Union – out of the fire and have launched it as one of the most important languages in the half-continent by writing it in newspapers, magazines, and books. Their ablest writers contributed articles, etc., and thus fixed its literary efficacy, and so it now faces the world as a cultural language.' Plaatje and Ramoshoana were convinced that the same needed to be done for Setswana.[5]

There was another dimension to Plaatje's concern to preserve Setswana. For it was also a response to his increasingly pessimistic observations of the effects of social and economic change upon the lives of his people – the lawlessness, alcoholism, the breakdown of parental control, a growing disrespect for authority. He attributed these things to a weakening of the constraints upon individual behaviour that were once imposed by the bonds of tribal society. 'Tribal organisation', he had said in 1924, commenting upon changes he perceived on returning home to South Africa from overseas, 'has undergone a marked deterioration during the last five years, and nothing appears to have replaced the disintegration.' What he witnessed over the next few years served only to underline his concerns, and much that he wrote during the 1920s emphasised this theme of disintegration in all spheres of the communal life of the African people. 'Rigidly excluded from all avenues of earning money,' he told Robert Moton in 1924, 'they are retrograding and degenerating while others go forward.'[6]

So Plaatje saw the preservation of the Tswana language as essential to cultural regeneration. Through preserving and valuing their language, the Tswana people could regain a sense of pride in their customs and traditions, and begin that process of moral regeneration of which he spoke so often. Instinctively, he looked to the past for the means to resist the changes taking place around him. Just as he regarded the countryside as the 'natural environment' of his people, so he saw their language and culture as a uniquely valuable resource that had, at all costs, to be nurtured and preserved.

There was a more personal element in this too: a sense not only that he was uniquely equipped to undertake this task, but that it could provide an escape from the worst of the frustrations and interference he experienced in his endeavours elsewhere. With the Pact's election victory in 1929 the political situation held out little hope for the future. He had done all he could to prevent this outcome but to no avail. Now was the time to apply himself to this project to preserve his native language and its culture.

He was not alone in finding this a congenial prospect. Elsewhere in southern Africa, as the dream of a common society faded and segregation gained the upper hand, others like him turned to the cultural resources of African societies to provide an outlet for their aspirations. Among the Zulu particularly, with their powerful tradition of a centralised monarchy, there was renewed interest in the Zulu language and in collecting and recording its traditions. The new sense of Zulu identity generated by this cultural renaissance had political implications too – which were not always predictable or easily controlled. While the government promoted policies of 'retribalisation', encouraging a return to traditional beliefs and values, they soon grew nervous at the prospect of a revitalised Zulu monarchy enjoying new levels of popular support, which presented them with a new set of problems.

Plaatje's situation was different. With the Batswana there was no tradition of a centralised monarchy, and mobilising ethnically for political purposes, given the varied circumstances in which they lived, was far harder. Any kind of cultural regeneration was a huge challenge too. The difficulty, as ever, was that the Batswana were fragmented, weakened by a multiplicity of small-scale, poverty-stricken chiefdoms, their separate traditions and loyalties generally stronger than a shared sense of being Batswana. Revitalising Setswana, their common language, remained, as Plaatje saw it, their only chance of salvation, their only hope of overcoming these divisions.

To this existential challenge were added the more immediate problems of lack of time and money. The two were of course related. Somehow he had to carve out time from his multifarious activities as well as to continue to make a living. Help was at hand, however, and from 1928 onwards he was able to obtain some modest financial support for his research and writing. The source was the Bantu Studies Research Committee at the University of the Witwatersrand in Johannesburg, and it reflected the growing interest in the universities – the University of the Witwatersrand and the University of Cape Town in particular – in finding out more about African languages and cultures.

Initially Plaatje sought funds for a new, enlarged edition of his *Sechuana Proverbs* and was awarded a grant worth up to £25. He owed this to a recommendation from Clement Doke, then a senior lecturer in the Department of Bantu Studies at the University of the Witwatersrand. He was a welcome ally. The leading African languages scholar of his day, Doke had an unusual background. He began his career as a Baptist missionary, and both he and his father had been supporters and admirers of Gandhi and his campaigns; Joseph Doke, indeed, became Gandhi's first biographer. Since then, after ill health prompted a change of career, Clement Doke had developed a passionate belief in the value and importance of African languages. Though not a Setswana specialist himself, he admired Plaatje's pioneering work, understood his predicament and did what he could to channel funds in his direction. Unlike some of his academic colleagues, he recognised the need to collaborate with Africans in his work on African languages and their literatures, and he was the first to employ African language assistants in his department.[7]

In July 1929 Plaatje reported back to the research committee. He had collected over 300 new proverbs and was actively seeking more, rescuing from oblivion 'as many as possible of these primitive native saws and preserving them for posterity', at the same time continuing his search for European equivalents. He also outlined the progress he had made on two other projects which he hoped the committee might support too. The first he described as 'Some Folk-Tales, Fables and Praises of Bechuana Chiefs'. He already had sixty pages of this in typewritten form – the remainder being 'still in rough notes' – but was holding off typing out more because of the unresolved orthographic situation. 'Meanwhile I am continuing to gather more stories etc.'[8]

The second project was to compile a new Setswana dictionary. He was inspired to embark upon this because his work on the proverbs and folktales had thrown up a host of new words that were not in the current English–Setswana dictionary by J. Brown, despite its recent revision. 'A serious study of this Dictionary', he said, 'shows that in many cases it teems with solecisms and mistranslations.' Consequently he had 'come to the conclusion that a useful purpose will be served if I added to my research work the recording of such omitted words and their translations besides a correction of the wrong rendering in the printed Dictionary'. He added that his friend David Ramoshoana – 'a keen student of Bantu lore with a wonderful command of English grammar' – was assisting in this task.[9]

Ramoshoana was an ideal collaborator. An experienced teacher, originally from Thaba Nchu, and now working at the Lyndhurst Road Native School, his knowledge of Setswana rivalled that of Plaatje, and he was fascinated by Tswana history and traditions. Like Plaatje, he had first learnt about these from his grandmother. In the late 1920s he wrote a series of articles for the *Diamond Fields Advertiser* on Tswana folklore, covering such subjects as spiritual belief, medicine, marriage, omens, beliefs about birds, and the months of the year. On other occasions he wrote about epic poetry, and about the derivation and characteristics of words themselves, sharing Plaatje's concern that Setswana's 'wealth of terms and idiomatic expressions' was no longer appreciated by educated Batswana, that schoolchildren were often taught 'a hotch-potch' in the name of Setswana. 'Provided the necessary help is forthcoming', Plaatje told the Bantu Studies Research Committee, they could together produce a more reliable and more accurate dictionary for Setswana.[10]

Three months later he had more progress to report. During October and November 1929, after spending some weeks in the eastern Free State, he had visited Morija, in Basutoland, obtaining 'valuable information and stories for his folklore collection'. The new edition of the proverbs, he was glad to say, was now complete, enriched by nearly 400 new items. There was good news on the dictionary too: with David Ramoshoana's help he had 'rescued and translated over 400 words'. 'With financial encouragement we can easily compile another 2,000 Sechuana words', he added, but it would 'require careful investigation in the interior of Bechuanaland where speech is less influenced by European ideas, so as to avoid the errors and omissions in Brown's Dictionary'.[11]

A new Setswana dictionary was just the kind of project likely to appeal to the Bantu Studies Research Committee and Plaatje was encouraged to apply for a grant for the following year too. In doing so, however, he crossed swords with the convenor of the committee, J.D. Rheinallt Jones, who queried his statement of disbursements. Rheinallt Jones did not think it was necessary to pay informants, either in cash or in kind, and told him that the committee would be unlikely to approve the £1 15s 0d paid to Ramoshoana for a fountain pen (this was 'beyond reason') or an annual subscription to the *South African Outlook* (which cost 6s 6d) for another informant. Plaatje, who knew what he had to do to obtain the information he was after, was outraged at Jones's attitude: apart from imputing dishonesty, it was clear he had no understanding of the social and personal complexities, and the reciprocal nature, of this kind of research. Other items of expenditure – not submitted in his claim – included a 55s portmanteau for Chief Lotlamoreng in Mafeking and '38/- plus free transportation for a length of underground garden piping for Mr Madingoana of Schmidtsdrift': thanks to such incentives he 'was still getting from them information which cheap informers can never supply', while the pen for David Ramoshoana 'definitely ensured his cooperation for the research work just completed', and for 'future work' too.[12]

In the event, thanks to Rheinallt Jones's timely departure for the United States on sabbatical leave at the end of 1929, the matter was satisfactorily resolved and his new grant 'in connection with researches in Chwana dictionary' was approved by the research committee. Unlike Rheinallt Jones, Clement Doke had carried out this kind of research himself, and when he took over as convenor he informed Plaatje that his explanation for the disbursements was acceptable after all. (He was also able to find another £5 to add to the £25 grant awarded to him.) It was a reminder not only of where power and resources lay, and the obstacles that had to be overcome, but also of the differences in attitude and experience that often existed among those charged with distributing funds.[13]

Helpful as these grants were, they did nothing to solve the bigger problem of finding the funds for printing and publishing his work. He had lobbied Dr Charles Loram, knowing he was well connected with wealthy philanthropic foundations in the United States, but to no avail. He also tried to raise funds locally in Kimberley through his Brotherhood organisation, but progress was painfully slow. Late in 1929, therefore, he appealed to De Beers, so often a source of funds for his projects in the past. Setting out his case, he stressed the need for suitable reading matter in schools, in Kimberley and elsewhere, and explained that he had a number of manuscripts that were now ready for publication. As well as the new edition of the proverbs and his 'Traditional Native Folk-Tales and Other Useful Knowledge', both of which had figured in his reports for the Bantu Studies Research Committee, he had three books which did not: his translations into Setswana of Shakespeare's *Comedy of Errors*, *Julius Caesar* and *Much Ado about Nothing*. He had obtained estimates from printers and publishers: Kegan Paul, Trench, Trübner & Co. in London, publishers of the original *Sechuana Proverbs*, had quoted £57 18s for the new edition, while the Morija Press in Basutoland wanted £125 for the three Shakespeare translations, and £205 for the 'Traditional Folk Tales'.[14]

How, then, to persuade De Beers to come up with the money? As ever it was not so much a matter of appealing to the altruism of the directors as reminding them of their shared interest in countering political extremists. 'It may perhaps be well to explain IN CONFIDENCE', he wrote, 'why our committee, which undertook the task last August, should thus far only have managed to raise £41 towards the printing of books that should be ready first thing after new year.' The reasons for this, he said, 'have been exceptional and varied'. 'To mention a few, the Pact vendetta against Sir E. Oppenheimer was launched by enemies of native welfare by sowing systematic dissensions among natives in the surrounding locations. It taxed our resources physically, mentally and financially to defeat their aims and keep the native vote intact. Again, besides our regular work we have had our hands full combatting and trying to keep the Communist movement outside Kimberley; this has been a stupendous task since Mr Bunting came here last September and left his agents here to spread his communistic propaganda.'

He drew attention to these 'confidential incidents', he said, 'only to show that while I was proceeding with the work of compiling these books, the committee was not idling; and if outside meddlers had only left us undisturbed the raising of funds would have kept pace with the edition of the books'. If the directors could see their way to meeting his request, they could rest assured that 'the books will be a continual benefit to future generations here and elsewhere and so merit the abiding gratitude of all respectable Natives': just as, so he recalled, the old tram shed they had donated ten years previously had proved of such value to the African community, and was now being used by the Kimberley school board for educating children.[15]

The De Beers directors were not persuaded. Plaatje had deployed similar arguments to good effect in 1918, but now things were different, the political and industrial situation – from the point of view of De Beers – much less worrying. Sidney Bunting, chairman of the Communist Party of South Africa, mentioned in his letter, may have been a nuisance, but he had not had much success in Kimberley, and the government was in any case now armed with the necessary powers to deal with 'agitators' of this kind. Neither altruism nor self-interest would persuade them to dip into their coffers. Yet again Plaatje was thrown back upon his own resources to try to find the substantial sums of money he needed.[16]

✦〜✦

Of the five books Plaatje mentioned in his letter to De Beers, only one – his translation of Shakespeare's *Comedy of Errors* – would be published in his lifetime. His *Julius Caesar* was published posthumously in 1937, but the other Shakespeare translations have all but disappeared. Only a single handwritten page survives of his translation of *The Merchant of Venice*, which he called *Mashoabi-shoabi*, and nothing at all of *Much Ado about Nothing* (*Matsapa-tsapa a Lefela*). Although not mentioned in his letter to De Beers, he had also translated *Othello* and *Romeo and Juliet*, of which a single handwritten page remains.

More encouragingly, most of the manuscript of the new edition of *Sechuana Proverbs* has survived intact but has yet to be published in the form he envisaged. On the other hand, *Traditional Native Folk-Tales and Other Useful Knowledge*, the most substantial of all these books, has disappeared, and so too has most of the work he and Ramoshoana carried out for a new Setswana dictionary. In this sad inventory of lost work lies one of the great tragedies in South African literature.

It could have been worse. Some of his manuscripts did survive, and, where they did not, there is at least some evidence to indicate what he had in mind, what his plans were. It is possible to retrieve, therefore, a sense of the nature of Plaatje's ambitious project to lay the foundations for a literature in Setswana – even if much of the work that was to form part of it has disappeared.

The new edition of *Sechuana Proverbs* was the first to be completed. It added a further 400 proverbs and sayings to the 732 that appeared in the original edition, ample vindication of Plaatje's assertion in 1916 that there were 'many unrecorded proverbs' of which he was unaware at the time. Once back in South Africa in 1923 he continued to note down new proverbs as he encountered them during his travels in the Tswana heartlands. In the late 1920s, encouraged by the grant from the Bantu Studies Research Committee and the assistance he received from David Ramoshoana, he redoubled his efforts. On occasions, his friend Michael van Reenen, who lived directly opposite his home in Angel Street, was able to assist by suggesting English equivalents to several of the new proverbs Plaatje found, even though he knew no Setswana. Over fifty years afterwards he remembered pondering hard over one proverb which Plaatje put to him – 'Ere u bona ngoana rra u tshabe, ere u bona ngoana mma u eme' / 'When you see father's son, run; when you see mother's son, stop' – before coming up with 'Like father, like son' as the nearest English equivalent he could think of.[17]

Taken together, Plaatje's two collections constitute a unique repository of Tswana proverbial sayings, the majority of them unrecorded in printed form elsewhere. He believed they encapsulated the unique traditions and accumulated folk wisdom of the Tswana people, and served important social functions too. They helped to educate young people about how to behave, they were central to public discourse and debate, and they permeated private conversation. He frequently used them in his own writings. Many, as he noted in the original edition of the *Sechuana Proverbs*, 'originated on the pastures or the hunting fields', reflecting the historical experience of a people traditionally dependent upon the tending of cattle and the hunting of wild game for their livelihood. Cattle, central to the way of life of Batswana, figure in many of them. Thus 'E mashi ga e itsale' / 'A good milch-cow does not always bear itself' (i.e. bear a calf that grows up to be a good milk-yielder) (no. 117); 'Go noa tse di choca, tse di dinaka dia faralala' / 'Only hornless cattle can reach the water, the horns will not permit the others to enter' (where 'hornless cattle' represent 'people without encumbrances') (no. 203). Or, from Plaatje's projected new edition, the wonderfully expressive 'Choana ea kgosing, u e thiba ke molato u e feta ke molato' / 'A heifer from the Chief's cattle-fold, drive it along and you are guilty, leave it alone and you are guilty'.[18]

Many of the proverbs involve wild animals too, often drawing comparisons between their behaviour and characteristics and those of human beings – for example, 'Nkoe go lacoana di mebala' / 'Spotted leopards lick each other' (similar in sense to the English proverb 'Birds of a feather flock together'). In some cases, the thrust of a proverb is to warn against allowing certain characteristics of animal behaviour to be adopted by humans, or to warn against over-confidence or recklessness when hunting – as in 'Moleleka kgama ea mariga o e leleka a chotse kobo' / 'He who chases an antelope in winter must do so carrying a cloak'. Other proverbs comment more directly upon human behaviour – on relations between men and women, and father and son, or the obligation of hospitality, or the nature of chiefs and chiefship, well represented in both of Plaatje's collections. Among the new ones he found were 'Bogosi bo botlhoko ke ntho e e sa phungoeng' / 'Chieftainship, like an unbroken abscess, is painful'; 'Bogosi mosima oa phiri'

/ 'Chieftainship is like a wolf's den'; 'Kgosi gae tsaloe' / 'A chief is not always born'.[19]

One thing that struck Plaatje about these proverbs was their contradictory nature – not only in the sense that one proverb would often contradict another, but also that there were contradictory meanings even within single proverbs. 'The whole truth about a fact cannot always be summed up in one pithy saying', he wrote. 'It may have several different aspects, which, taken separately, seem to be contradictory and have to be considered in connection with their surrounding circumstances. To explain this connection is the work of a sermon or essay, not of a proverb. All the latter can do is to express each aspect by itself and let them balance each other.' For context, as Plaatje saw it – 'surrounding circumstances' – was all-important, a knowledge of it essential to an understanding of the proverbs themselves. It is a point that comes out very clearly in the stories he included in his *Sechuana Reader* in 1916, for several of these serve to explain the origin and meaning of particular proverbs and sayings – 'Take care that you don't mourn the hartebeest and the hide', 'The ratel is suspicious about the honeycomb', 'Bulging cheeks are a characteristic of the cat family', 'Alone I am not a man; I am only a man by the help of others', and 'The mother of the child is she who grasps the knife by the blade'.[20]

Taken out of context, Tswana proverbs, like any other, could be almost meaningless, the literal translation or equivalent in another language no more than a pale reflection of the wealth of meaning and associations known to native Tswana-speakers. Hence the importance for Plaatje of preserving the integrity of that larger context, of overcoming the artificial divisions between different cultural forms. Indeed, this notion was at the heart of the wide-ranging work upon which he was engaged in all its different areas: the folktales and praise poems, the translations and the dictionary, as well as the proverbs themselves.

Only fragments remain of the manuscript of the book Plaatje described in his letter to De Beers as 'Traditional Native Folk-Tales and Other Useful Knowledge'. At other times he referred to it variously as 'Some folk-tales, fables and praises of Bechuana chiefs', 'Bantu folk-tales and poems – traditional and original', 'a volume of Native fables and traditional poems in the vernacular', and 'my book of folklore'. Originally he saw it as a development of the *Sechuana Reader*, speaking of his need 'to get information in order to sift and rearrange my collection of native stories, for my new Sechuana Reader'. As he did so and collected more material, so his ideas would sometimes change. He had to revise his earlier opinion, for example, that the fox and the hare were 'the cleverest of animals', concluding instead, in the light of his recent 'systematic investigations', that 'for right down shrewdness – not merely the cunning of the jackal, but the acme of sagacity – according to old Sechuana folk-tales, the majority vote and the first prize must be awarded to the TORTOISE'.[21]

But it is clear that this collection was not confined to animal tales. One of the few surviving pages contains a riddle of the kind that used to appear in the 'Mma-Maitisho' columns in *Koranta* and *Tsala* years before. Another lists some Tswana pronouns with advice on their use – which clearly fell into the 'other useful knowledge' category. Most significantly, too, Plaatje intended to include in this volume a substantial number of praise poems, or *maboko*, widely regarded as the highest literary form of the language and quite distinct from the fables and stories that had appeared in his earlier *Sechuana Reader*. In these *maboko* were encapsulated, in oral, poetic form, the heroic traditions of the Batswana. Many of them celebrated the military prowess of their chiefs or their fame as hunters, but they were concerned with the present as well as the past. Praise poetry was a highly flexible genre, rich in idiom and readily adaptable to changing circumstance. It could be applied to the attributes of trees and animals, for example, as well as to human beings. For Plaatje it was just as vital to collect and preserve as proverbs.[22]

Quite fortuitously, a list of the praise poems he collected survives in the papers of the late Z.K. Matthews, St Leger Plaatje's contemporary at Lovedale. In the mid-1930s, after studying at Yale University and the London School of Economics, Matthews undertook some anthropological fieldwork among the Barolong of Mafikeng, interesting himself, as he did so, in the collection of traditional Tswana praise poetry. Presumably he came across Plaatje's manuscript, for he made out a list of thirty praise poems and called it 'Plaatje's collection'. For each one he gave the name of the chief or other subject, the chiefdom from which the praises originated, the number of lines they contained (ranging from ten to a hundred), and the name of Plaatje's informant. Four were of Bangwaketse origin; four were Bahurutse; one Rapulana; three Bakgatla; eleven Bamangwato, and nine Barolong – three of the last-mentioned being in honour of Montshiwa, the greatest of the Barolong chiefs. His informant here was Gaeshele, one of Montshiwa's youngest wives, who lived into the 1930s and had a reputation for being particularly well versed in Tshidi law and custom. The majority of the praises were of particular chiefs, but other people and places were celebrated too: a successful raiding party (Hurutse); Thaba Nchu, the mountain in the Orange Free State where the Barolong had once gathered, and which was regarded as their spiritual home; and '*morulaganyi*', 'The Writer' or 'Editor' – Plaatje himself. One praise poem, the shortest, was to a woman, Mma-Matsetsenene, supplied to

Plaatje by the Rev. P. Motiyane, an old friend.[23]

Only traces of the poems themselves survive. Two extracts appear in a short biographical sketch of Chief Montshiwa which Plaatje wrote for inclusion in T.D. Mweli Skota's *African Yearly Register*, published in 1930. It seems reasonable to suppose these were drawn from the three praise poems to Montshiwa that Plaatje intended publishing in his own volume. The first extract bore tribute to Montshiwa's involvement in the execution of Bhoya, the Matabele tax collector whose killing in 1830 resulted in a fierce onslaught upon the Barolong, the point of departure for the historical novel he had written in London in 1920:

Re kile ra ineelela dichaba,
Ra ineela, ka lecogo, merafe;
Seja-Nkabo a sale mmotlana,
A sale mo tharing eaga Sebodio.
Jaana ke mmonye a tlhatlosa motho lekgabana
A mo pega ncoe ja Ga-Khunoana tlhogo
A nale mmaba, a ea go bolaoa,
Seje-Nkabo-a-Tauana.

Too long we've bent the knee to foreigners.
Too long we've yielded the arm to strangers;
Montshioa, at that time, was still a baby
Astride the back of his mother, Sebodio.
Now have I seen him lead a man up hill;
Leading him up to the crest of Mount Kunana;
Conducting a foeman up to his kill,
Seje-Nkabo, the son of Tauana.[24]

The second piece testified to Montshiwa's reputation as a fearless hunter and lion-killer – 'One of the few Bechuana', Plaatje wrote, 'who would follow a wounded lion straight into the thicket.'

Mogatsa Majang, tau ga di kalo!
Tau ga di kalo, moroa Mhenyana.
Ga di ke di bolaoa leroborobo,
Di ba di etsa dipholofolo tsa gopo,
Di ba di edioa pitse tsa gopo,
Lekau, ja Gontse-a-Tauana!

Tau di bolaoa dile thataro,
Lefa dile pedi dia bo di ntse.

That's not the way to kill lions,
O, husband of Majang!
That's not the way, O, offspring of M'Henyana!
Lions should not be butchered by the score
Nor like hunted animals at the chase;
Lions should not be slaughtered in such numbers,
To litter the field like carcasses of dead Zebra,
O descendant of Gontse, son of Tauana!
Six lions at a time are quite enough
For, even two at a time are not too few![25]

The two verses were part of a much larger whole, sixteen of the 125 lines Plaatje had on Montshiwa alone. Judging by the estimate he obtained from Morija (£205 as against £123 for each of his Shakespeare translations), it would have been a substantial volume. At one point he also intended to include a 'Chuana–English glossary' and 'minute explanatory notes', but later, so he informed Clement Doke in August 1931, he had to abandon both for reasons of cost. The challenge remained to find the funds to bring it to print. [26]

Compiling a dictionary was just as ambitious. This became Plaatje's priority once he had completed work on the new edition of the proverbs and the traditional folktales and, working together with David Ramoshoana, he devoted as much time to it as he could. By the end of 1930 they had collected 2,200 new words and Plaatje had embarked upon the correction of the substantial number of words in the dictionary which he thought were wrongly translated. Six months later they had over 3,000 new words. Even then, he wrote, 'fresh discoveries show we have only scratched the fringe'. Further demand for the dictionary had come with the publication of *Diphosho-phosho*, his translation of *The Comedy of Errors*, in the middle of 1930. He had included so many archaic and little-known words, few of them in the existing dictionary, that he reported being inundated with enquiries from people wanting to know their meaning. It would be the same, he told Clement Doke, 'when my book of folk lore appears'. A concern throughout was to redress what he considered to be the bias of Brown's Tswana dictionary in favour of the Batlhaping dialect.[27]

But it was not just a matter of correcting meanings and adding new words: just as vital was finding a means to ensure that their pronunciation was correctly represented. 'It should not be forgotten', he reminded Clement Doke in February 1931, 'that none of the diminutive and defective dictionaries now in circulation ever attempted any form of accentuation without which a Sechuana dictionary is all but worthless', something that was 'particularly true of the many words spelt alike and only distinguished by tone'. He gave several examples. Depending on the tone used in enunciation, the word '*sehudi*' could have three different meanings: an 'animal that feeds on grass as distinct from birds of prey', 'a crack shot', and a 'wild duck or water fowl'. Brown's dictionary listed only one meaning ('a wild duck'), exemplifying, so far as Plaatje was concerned, its inadequacies. Likewise the word '*mabele*', which could mean 'women's breasts', 'grain' or 'one who thinks much of himself'; Brown had the first two meanings (though he made no tonal distinction between them), but not the third.[28]

Plaatje's solution lay not in the use of phonetic characters, though he espoused these elsewhere, but in a form of accentuation based on that used by Daniel Jones in their jointly authored *Sechuana Reader*, and appropriate to a work of reference. In fact Jones had recently returned to the question of tones in Setswana himself, publishing a paper entitled 'The tones of Sechuana nouns' in 1928, drawing again upon his work with Plaatje. When Plaatje saw it, he was impressed by the fact that Daniel Jones, 'writing alone in London, has in his little brochure 126 Sechuana nouns not included in Brown's big Sechuana dictionary (the official dictionary of that language) and he has rendered correctly 30 other nouns which appear but are mistranslated by Brown'. He wondered how many more words he could have supplied had he dealt with verbs as well as nouns, and noticed only three words that were translated incorrectly – highly creditable, he thought, when compared to 'the "howlers" within the covers of the official dictionary', especially as Jones was writing from such a distance. All of which strengthened his determination to continue where the professor had left off and to apply his model of accentuation in his dictionary.[29]

It was a daunting challenge. Material had somehow to be collected at first hand, Plaatje pointed out, 'from the scattered tribes between the Orange River and Southern Rhodesia', a vast geographical area, if it was to be comprehensive and representative of the full range of Tswana-speakers. There were also more immediate practical difficulties. David Ramoshoana had left his teaching job at the Lyndhurst Road Native School in 1930 to take up a position in Hopetown, over seventy miles away, and was no longer able to call in at Angel Street on his way back from work to discuss their latest findings or agree on new words and their derivation. Another setback was the decision of the Bantu Studies Research Committee, in 1931, not to renew its grant. Plaatje and Ramoshoana applied for help with 'travelling expenses, gifts, index cards for future research in connection with the preparation of a Secwana Dictionary', but this time they were turned down. Owing to shortage of funds, grants were only being made to members of staff of the university. They were advised instead to apply for assistance from the Bechuanaland Protectorate administration.[30]

With such scant resources, compiling a dictionary was a near-impossible task, and it never came close to publication. All that remains is Plaatje's own annotated copy of the 1925 edition of Brown's Tswana dictionary, which reflects only his initial work on the project. This is of considerable interest, however. Altogether he added nearly 400 new words, written by hand on the pages of the dictionary, or on new leaves inserted into it, and made corrections to 200 or so of the existing entries. Now and again he added some marginal comments: 'Brown is confusing the two' (p. 18); 'Wrong', 'No' (p. 20); 'Nonsense' (p. 47); and – the only positive comment – 'Very good translation' (p. 25). His observations at the beginning of the book reveal the full extent of his dissatisfaction: 'Object of this Dictionary appears to be Quantity, not Quality'; and 'Hundreds of meaningless words, some of them wrongly translated, no end of duplications such as makgaha-mashaba, makgoa-makhoa, the right and the wrong'. A section of the preface, concerned with the differences between the Tswana dialects, he had crossed through with a bold line, adding the words 'very misleading' in the margin, while Brown's advice on how to pronounce the letter 'y' he dismissed as 'nonsense'. And on the blank page opposite the first entries he wrote: 'The Se-Ruti is not only affecting Sechuana speech but [influencing] Sechuana outlook in every respect. For instance, since Missionaries first translated the names of the Native "Moons", we find few old natives who know of the 13th month, and even they say the 13th name is interchangeable with one of the 12.'[31]

'Se-ruti' was not an original dialect of Setswana but a term used to describe Setswana as spoken by European missionaries, with all its imperfections, and as here embodied in Brown's dictionary. Plaatje had made a similar point in his introduction to the *Sechuana Reader* in 1916 when arguing the case for phonetic spelling as a means of preserving the true pronunciation of his language. Now, the method he proposed was different, but the sentiments and the motivation were the same: preserving his native language from neglect and from the attentions of those ill versed in its beauties and subtleties remained the constant throughout.

Compared with this ambitious scheme for a new dictionary, translating *The Comedy of Errors* was a more manageable proposition. Raising the funds needed to print it, however, once De Beers had declined to help, proved to be the familiar stumbling block. What particularly disappointed him was the lack of response to his appeal for support from Batswana, the people who would actually read and use the book. He was inspired to write *Diphosho-phosho*, he said, by their demands, by the cries of people exclaiming, 'Tau's Setswana will be of no use to us! It is becoming extinct because children are not taught Setswana! They are taught the missionary language! They will lose all trace of our language!' Yet these demands were not matched by a willingness on the part of well-do-to Batswana to dip into their pockets. He needed a loan of £30 to help pay printing bills, which could be paid back within three months from the proceeds of sales, but no money was forthcoming. If this was to be their attitude, he wrote in the preface to the book, it was hardly surprising that Tswana literature was in such a state.[32]

Approaching the Bantu Studies Research Committee for help would have been a waste of time. Apart from having very little money, the committee's priority was to support the recording of African linguistic forms and traditions before they were contaminated by the pervasive effects of 'European civilisation'. Translating Shakespeare could scarcely be said to meet this criterion; rather, it posed a direct challenge to the assumptions underlying the committee's work. The very idea of translating Shakespeare into any African language, it is clear, was out of step with current academic thinking, especially in anthropology and linguistics, the two disciplines that predominated in the committee.

In the end Plaatje managed to scrape together the money he needed from other sources: there were contributions from Herman Meysing, the Roman Catholic bishop of Kimberley; from Fr Francis Hill, of the Anglican Community of the Resurrection in Johannesburg, a long-time sympathiser; from Mr M. Sammy & Son, prominent Indian merchants in Kimberley; from Mrs W. Allan King of Pretoria (widow of the man killed in the Boer rebellion of 1914, whom he once counted his best white friend), and her sister-in-law, Mrs King-Botha. None of them, he noted ruefully, had any knowledge of Setswana. Unlikely midwives, perhaps, to the birth of Shakespeare in Setswana but undeniable tribute to Plaatje's persuasive powers when it came to fundraising for his projects.[33]

Diphosho-phosho (literally, 'mistake upon mistake') was printed by the Morija mission press in July 1930; it was a modest fifty-two pages long, came in a soft, brown cover, and sold for 2s 3d. Plaatje had left the manuscript at Morija when he visited late in October 1929, encouraged to do so by his discovery that they possessed the type for some phonetic characters. This, he said, had been 'a pleasant surprise', as this was his preferred solution to the problem of representing accurately the sounds and tones of many of the words he wished to use. In his introduction he thanked the supervisor and staff of the Morija Press for their dedication to the task of printing the book in a language that was not their own. The Reuters news agency, struck by the novelty of the venture when Plaatje told them about it, ensured considerable press coverage at both home and abroad.[34]

Plaatje envisaged *Diphosho-phosho* as the first of a series of translations under the general heading of *Mabolelo a ga Tsikinya-Chaka* ('The sayings of William Shakespeare'), the title page indicating that *Mashoabi-shoabi* (*The Merchant of Venice*), *Matsapa-tsepa a Lefela* (*Much Ado about Nothing*) and *Dincho-ncho tsa bo-Juliuse Kesara* (*Julius Caesar*) were to follow. In an interview for the Johannesburg *Star*, in July 1930, he offered some further reflections on the project. It was, he said, 'probably the first complete translation in any of the Bantu languages to be published in book form', and he had not found it easy. 'It is only natural that the translator must experience great difficulty in finding the equivalents for some of Shakespeare's phrases, in which case he has to rely on the general sense of the passage to render the author's meaning in the vernacular, and that has been my difficulty.' Without his experience as a court interpreter and as editor of a tri-lingual newspaper, he added, he simply could not have undertaken the task. He acknowledged the 'great help' provided by David Ramoshoana 'in the difficult Setswana which is needed in the translation of plays of a writer like Shakespeare', commending his 'pure Sehurutse' and 'the depth of his knowledge of English'.[35]

This fascination with Shakespeare had deep roots. Since his early encounters he had been struck by the universality of Shakespeare's characters and attended performances of the plays whenever he could. After that Shakespeare became a source of inspiration, as when (in 1910) the coincidence of Halley's Comet and the deaths of King Edward VII and two great Tswana chiefs, Sebele and Bathoen, brought to mind the prophecy from *Julius Caesar*, 'When beggars die there are no comets seen; / The heavens themselves blaze forth the death of princes'.

At other times he would invoke the authority of Shakespeare in order to counter the absurdities of racial discrimination – quoting Shylock's famous 'Hath not a Jew?' monologue from *The Merchant of Venice*, for example, in his protest against his exclusion from an evening's entertainment in the Mafeking Town Hall in 1906, and substituting 'African' for 'Jew'. He did the same thing in *Native Life in South Africa* a decade later, reproducing the same passage at the head of chapter 9, 'The fateful thirteen', appealing to his readers to recognise a common humanity and to support his cause.

Yet it was not just that Shakespeare carried this kind of cultural capital. As he became more familiar with the plays, so he was struck by the similarities between many of Shakespeare's themes and what he knew of the history and traditions of his own people. Kinship rivalries, divided kingdoms, exile and return, murderous ambition, superstition and sorcery, all had their counterparts. Even the dominant memory of his own family forebears – dispossession from their rightful claim to the Barolong kingship – had its echoes in several of Shakespeare's plays. By 1916 he had come to the view that 'some of the stories on which his dramas are based' were likely to 'find equivalents in African folk-lore', and that translating Shakespeare into Setswana 'could be done'. At the same time he saw that Shakespeare's plays could help him explore the riches of Setswana, providing a set of ready-made narratives that lent themselves well to adaptation. Shakespeare, after all, had an unparalleled track record in this respect: if his plays could be translated successfully into Urdu, Bengali, Mandarin and dozens of other languages, non-European as well as European, then why not Setswana?

He found the opportunity to embark upon this task on the voyage from England to South Africa in 1917, completing *Julius Caesar* by the time he arrived in Cape Town. *The Merchant of Venice* and *The Comedy of Errors* came next, both of them completed by the end of 1920. *Othello* kept him busy aboard the *Windsor Castle* between Southampton and Cape Town in 1923. *Much Ado about Nothing*, it seems, was translated some time after that.

How then, on the evidence of *Diphosho-phosho*, did he go about his task – and how successful was he?

The Comedy of Errors tells the tale of two sets of identical twins, separated at birth, who end up, unknown to one another, in the faraway land of Ephesus; here the father of one set of twins, Aegeon, a wealthy citizen of the rival city of Syracuse, had travelled in search of them, only to be arrested and sentenced to death for having strayed into hostile territory. He is unaware that his two sons, each accompanied by their servants, the other identical twins, are in Ephesus, and they are likewise unaware of his presence. Eventually, after much farce and confusion arising from their mistaken identities, including wrongful beatings, accusations of infidelity, witchcraft and possession, the twins realise who they are, families are reunited, Aegeon is released from imprisonment, and remaining loose ends are tied up.

The Comedy of Errors has never been among Shakespeare's most popular plays and is rarely ranked alongside his more accomplished comedies. But for Plaatje it clearly had its attractions. For one thing, as the shortest, by some margin, of all Shakespeare's plays, any translation would be the cheapest to typeset and print, an important consideration. But there were other things that may have drawn him to *The Comedy of Errors*. It is not difficult to imagine that its concern with the law chimed with his youthful experiences as a court interpreter, or that the death sentence hanging over Aegeon stirred memories of the treason trials in Mafeking in 1901. There is much in the play, moreover, that resonates with the customs and beliefs of the Batswana. Witchcraft and sorcery, for example, or relations between master and servant, both of them important preoccupations in *The Comedy of Errors*, had powerful echoes in the cultural universe of every Tswana-speaker.

There was also the question of twins. Traditionally Batswana regarded twins as an unsettling threat to normality, far more so than did Shakespeare's English audiences; they evoked feelings of fear and unease, they raised troubling questions of identity, and in the past it had been the practice to put one or both twins to death. So for Plaatje and other Tswana-speaking readers, the realisation that there were not one but two sets of identical twins in *The Comedy or Errors* must have aroused an immediate sense of foreboding. It brought to mind the well-known fable of Masilo and Masilonyana, twins whose wanderings end when Masilo slays Masilonyana after a dispute over a prized white cow. Masilo can never escape the consequences of his action, however. A bird settles upon the white cow and, like his conscience, sings constantly of his brother's murder, reminding the world of what had happened. Twins, in the cultural universe of the Batswana, did not have happy connotations.[36]

Most likely, though, Plaatje was drawn to *The Comedy of Errors* by its comic possibilities, confident that its central trope of mistaken identity, along with large doses of slapstick humour, would work just as well in Setswana as in English, and that it provided an ideal opportunity to explore Setswana's rich fund of comic idiom. Interestingly, *The Comedy of Errors* was a popular choice for contemporary translators of Shakespeare from the Indian subcontinent too – only *The Merchant of Venice* has been translated into more Indian languages. Perhaps there was just something about Shakespeare's brand of humour, and its setting in *The Comedy of Errors*, that had a particular resonance in a colonial context: that colonial subjects had an instinctive sense that misunderstanding was not only intrinsic to relations of domination and subordination, but a rich source of humour too.[37]

To call *Diphosho-phosho* a translation scarcely does justice to Plaatje's intentions – or his achievement. For Shakespeare is not just translated but transformed, freed from the dramatic and literary conventions of Elizabethan drama. The transformation lies not so much in what Plaatje did to the story – he remains faithful to plot and storyline – but in his ability to reimagine *The Comedy of Errors* in Tswana idiom, to draw upon the resources of Setswana to represent Shakespeare's tale in a manner, and in a context, that is meaningful to Tswana-speakers. It was a free, not a literal, translation, and he took plenty of liberties: dialogue is condensed, prose replaces blank verse, passages are omitted or paraphrased, word and sentence order are changed, speech is reassigned from one protagonist to another. Even his title, *Diphosho-phosho*, is suggestive of the creative thinking he brought to his task. He could have gone for a literal translation of 'Comedy of Errors', such as 'metlae/khomedi ya diphosho', but went instead for a distinctively Tswana term, far richer in onomatopoeia, conveying a sense of 'a series of blunders' or 'mistakes upon mistakes'.[38]

And if the text is to be transformed, then why not the persona of Shakespeare himself? The term 'Tsikinya-Chaka', literally 'Shake-the-Sword', derived not, as might be thought, from Plaatje's imagination but from an 'educated chieftain' who over twenty years before had suggested, in response to a question about the name of 'the white man who spoke so well', that this was, in the Tswana tradition, an appropriate Tswana praise-name for him. Plaatje agreed and adopted it on the spot. The 'educated chieftain' was most likely Cornelius Lekoko, chief regent of the Tshidi Barolong in Mafikeng from 1910 to 1915, who is known to have encountered Shakespeare when a student at the Anglican 'Kaffir Institution' in Grahamstown in the 1870s. Plaatje was by no means the first Morolong to have been exposed to Shakespeare – but, like Shakespeare himself, did not hesitate to appropriate somebody else's good idea when he saw one.[39]

This illusion that Shakespeare was really a Motswana is carried through in other ways. On the title page of the book, *Diphosho-phosho* is presented as the first in an intended series: 'Mabolelo a ga Tsikinya-Chaka', 'The sayings of William Shakespeare', suggesting an equivalence with the words of wisdom one might expect from a Tswana elder in a predominantly oral culture – not an alien cultural form dependent upon theatre and performance. Similarly, the summary of Shakespeare's life which Plaatje provides at the beginning of the book is not so much accurate biography as Shakespeare's life presented in a way that chimed with accepted Tswana values – and which bears more than a passing resemblance to the trajectory of Plaatje's own life.[40]

Plaatje also adapted the structure of *Diphosho-phosho*, introducing a number of new headings into the text. There were seventeen in all, set in a bold typeface, and superimposed upon the original divisions by acts and scenes, all of which are retained. Four of these headings are proverbs (e.g. 9 'Ditlhale-tlhale tse lobooa di bonana monoko-pele' / 'Familiarity breeds contempt', 17 'Mala a nku a tla ka bogamo' / 'The proof of the pudding is in the eating'), seven indicate where the action is taking place (e.g. 7 'Ko goora Antifoluse oa Efese' / 'At Antipholus of Ephesus's place'), six signify the action about to take place (e.g. 12 'Maoelana a santse a tshelepana a gakisa ben-gae mafoko' / 'Twins continue to miss one another and confuse citizens'). Another – 'Mafoko a Mosekisioa' / 'The statement of the accused', a familiar phrase to Plaatje from his court interpreting days – highlighted the seriousness of Antipholus's predicament. Plaatje's aim was to help clarify an often-confusing sequence of events and to divide the text up into more manageable portions, offering some help to the schoolchildren he expected to be among his readers. At the same time these new headings serve to highlight *Diphosho-phosho*'s relocation from one cultural context to another. Where they are also proverbs they suggest the passage concerned simply attests to what the Batswana already know. Shakespeare, it is clear, is being reshaped to fit a very different set of sensibilities.[41]

Above all, it is Plaatje's use of idiomatic Setswana and his imaginative engagement with the nuances of Shakespeare's text and its setting that give *Diphosho-phosho* its distinctive flavour. Deploying proverbs was central to this. In addition to the four proverbs in his new headings there are many more in the text itself, reflecting both their widespread currency in spoken Setswana and Plaatje's desire to use *Diphosho-phosho* as a repository, or showcase, for their display. Crucially, and unlike his collection of proverbs, they are now set in context. He is able to show how they are used, how they formed part of the texture of speech and conversation, how they could add weight and authority, and nuance, to the ebb and flow of debate and discussion. Sometimes he introduced proverbs in order to match an English proverb in Shakespeare's text. More often he simply introduced his own where there was none in the original, recasting speech in what was – to Tswana-speakers – a more natural and idiomatic form.[42]

On several occasions he has his protagonist relate a familiar proverb in order to illustrate, or to justify, what they have to say. In the scene where Ma-Noko (Shakespeare's 'courtezan') reflects upon the golden necklace she had been promised by Antipholus of Ephesus, she considers telling Adriana of their affair in order to secure the return of the ring she had previously given him. Otherwise she would end up with neither ring nor necklace, that is to say nothing, as in the proverb 'Eseŋ jalo, nka tla ka leleła kgama le morogoro' / 'Take care that you don't mourn for the hartebeest and the hide'. Few Tswana-speakers would have been unaware of its origin and meaning. Travelling through the countryside, the story goes, a hunter sees a lame hartebeest, an easy-looking prey. He drops the hide he is carrying, chases after the hartebeest but fails to kill it. He returns to pick up the hide but is unable to find it. Through his greed he ends up with nothing. Ma-Noko, the proverb implies in this context, is not to be sympathised with in her predicament.[43]

A similar example occurs when Adriana and her sister Luciana discuss the nature of men and marriage. In an impassioned speech Adriana urges Luciana to get married so she can at least understand what she, Adriana, has had to go through. In response Luciana says simply, 'Well, I will marry one day, but to try'. This is not good enough for Plaatje. He represents this as 'Baa pelo, gatoe kg ngo oa nna a lekoe. Ke tla tsamaea ke nyaloa le nna', or 'Just calm down, it is said that the kgengoe (a wild melon) must be tasted. I will get married at some point.' The proverb about the 'kgengoe' appears as no. 245 in Plaatje's published collection: 'It is best always to try the "kgengoe" by tasting it', where he explains further that the 'kgengoe' was a wild melon found in the Kalahari desert and used for quenching thirst, one variety of which was too bitter to use. In other words, one can only find out by being prepared to try – precisely Luciana's attitude to the question of marriage, though she was in no hurry to do so. The fact that this was also expressing traditional Tswana thinking on the subject is emphasised by the use of the construction '*gatoe*' ('it is said'), and by the knowledge on the part of readers of the book that Tswana elders would often deploy the proverb when encouraging young people to face up to their marital responsibilities. The exchange between Adriana and Luciana, when translated in this way, thus evokes a wide range of associations.[44]

Elsewhere Plaatje resorts to metaphor rather than proverb. Sometimes Shakespeare's metaphors work well enough in Setswana. When Antipholus of Syracuse, in search of his mother and brother, compares himself to a drop of water in the ocean, alone and lost, Plaatje is able to provide a direct but perfectly natural translation; likewise Dromio's jest, 'Marry, he must have a long spoon that must eat with the devil', which he translates literally ('Motho eo o jaŋ koo goora Satane o choanetse go ja ka dusho lo lo teleletelele'), confident, given the context, that even if his readers had not encountered the English proverb from which it derived, it still made perfectly good sense in translation.[45]

Sometimes he conjures up close equivalents, such as 'Fa kgomo di se na go mela diphuka, pitse di se na go mela dinaka' / 'When cattle have wings, and horses have horns', for Shakespeare's 'Ay, when fowls have no feathers and fish have no fin', or 'U logaga, monna oame, nna ke pota-dikgagane' / 'You are a cave my husband, I am the rock reptile' for 'Thou art an elm, my husband, I a vine'. At other times he adapts and imagines. When Antipholus of Syracuse, in one of the best-known lines in *The Comedy of Errors*, says to his servant Dromio, 'When the sun shines let foolish gnats make sport, / But creep in crannies when he hides his beams' – reminding him that there are times when he needs to know his place – Plaatje uses the same metaphor, but reverses it. In the northern hemisphere gnats may come out in the sunshine, but in southern Africa the opposite is true: so 'Kokobele li fofa gole longola; fa tlhaka di phaphalala, go nna sethukuthuku, di noaṇṃoaela di ee go iṃaralɛga', or 'Flying ants take wing when it is humid but when the grass on the riverbanks becomes dry and it becomes hot they go into hiding'.[46]

More often, though, Plaatje simply starts afresh when it comes to devising equivalents. When Adriana, in Plaatje's rendering, accuses Antipholus of sexual infidelity, she compares his behaviour to the image, familiar to Batswana, of a bull 'roaming about in winter', chasing after heifers. And on identical twins, where Aegeon refers to his two sons as 'the one so like the other, / As could not be distinguished but by names', Plaatje, in response, eschews any attempt to translate directly, resorting instead to an image of mice – 'ao a bo a choana fɛla jaka dipɛba' / 'They were as alike as mice', alluding to the proverb 'O itsetse fela jaka peba' / 'This child is as complete an image of its parent as a baby mouse is of its mother'. Similarly, when it came to conveying types of madness, rather than seeking direct equivalents to 'cuckold-mad' or 'horn-mad' (when Dromio of Ephesus and Adriana discuss Antipholus's state of mind), Plaatje comes up instead with 'gore o ja ditlhare ka mɛno' / 'biting trees by teeth', a far more meaningful and vivid metaphor in Setswana, and one to which he returns later on.[47]

Place names, laden with meaning and association in English, but none at all in Setswana, were another challenge. How, for example, to deal with a phrase like 'Poland winter', meaning 'a long period of extreme cold'? Plaatje's solution was the phrase 'maruru a kgoedi ea Seɛte bosigo' / 'the cold month of June', where, in Setswana-speaking regions, June was always the coldest month, and the word itself, in Setswana, was always associated with the injunction from which it is derived: 'Ser ete bosigo' / 'do not visit at night', itself a distillation of the aphorism 'Don't travel by wagon at night, at that time, if you do not wish your cattle to die, to be killed by the cold'. He faced a similar challenge with Antipholus's phrase 'And Lapland sorcerers inhabit here', alluding to their reputation as the most dangerous practitioners of the black arts. This time he did not have to look far for an equivalent: 'dikhurubɛrɛgɛ tsa Kgalagadi' / 'the spells of the Kalahari', i.e. inhabitants of the Kalahari desert, renowned, like Laplanders, for possessing the same kind of evil powers.[48]

He did not always need to jettison references to other countries if the context remained meaningful, preferring in such instances to indigenise their names. In the same passage that has the reference to 'Poland winter' – one of the funniest in the play – Dromio describes the enormously fat serving wench who has designs on him. Plaatje matches Shakespeare in conveying a sense of her awfulness, entering into the same journey around her fat, greasy body, finding France ('Fora') on her forehead, England ('Engelane') on her chin, Spain ('Sepania') in her breath, Scotland ('Skotlane') in her hand, Ireland ('Irelane') in her buttocks, America and the Indies ('Amerika' and 'India') on her nose, and 'Belgia' ('Belje') and the Netherlands ('Holane') ('Oh, sir, I did not look so low' – faithfully represented as 'Ga nka ka mo kɛlɛkɛla ko tlasetlase jalo'). Plaatje condensed some of this dialogue but, interestingly, changed the order in which the countries appear, starting with France and England rather than Ireland, perhaps because they were likely to be more familiar to his readers. Or perhaps he just thought it was better to save the best joke – about Ireland, buttocks and bogs – until later on.[49]

✦

He had a knack for finding just the right phrase, the ability to match Shakespeare's humorous tone in Setswana, to reinvent Shakespeare in a way that seemed both natural and enjoyable for his Tswana-speaking readers. 'It is as if he looked up from the text', one critic has observed, and then 'thinks and reformulates the context in Setswana. That is what makes it read like an original.' Reformulating the context did not mean distorting the narrative, however, for he remains faithful to the twists and turns of the original plot, and none of the cuts he made affect the storyline or its resolution. Plaatje shared Shakespeare's desire to entertain and amuse: he had no wish to twist Shakespeare's meaning, no desire to rewrite *The Comedy of Errors* in order to convey a radically different message of his own.[50]

Nevertheless, he was sensitive to those aspects of *The Comedy of Errors* that had particular resonances for Batswana and was alert to the possibilities. Sorcery is the prime example. *The Comedy of Errors* is shot through with it. Ephesus, the setting for its action, was well known historically for its association with witchcraft, mystery and magic, and they are soon invoked as an explanation for the otherwise inexplicable series of misunderstandings and misrecognitions which take place. Thus at the end of Act I, scene ii, Antipholus of Syracuse laments the evidence of witchcraft he finds around him: Ephesus, so it seems, is a town 'full of cozenage', 'dark-working sorcerers that change the mind', 'Soul-killing witches that deform the body', 'Disguised cheaters, prating mountebanks, / And many such-like liberties of sin'. For how else is he to make sense of the extraordinary situation in which he is treated familiarly by people he does not

498

know? His servant Dromio encounters just the same problem.

For Plaatje and his fellow Tswana-speakers, the answer is rather obvious: it is evidence of the presence of *boloi*, witchcraft of a malevolent kind which had a powerful hold over the actions and imaginations of many Batswana. Those who had been exposed to Christian teachings may have thought differently, but for most people *boloi* remained a pervasive reality, a necessary explanation for the misfortunes that befell them and their families. According to David Ramoshoana, *baloi* – the practitioners of *boloi* – were unremittingly evil. Traditionally they sought parts of the human body for their black arts; they were said 'to possess knowledge of a secret magic by which they strike dumb anyone who shouts, injures or speaks to them'; and members of the community were enjoined to do all they could to stamp them out and bring them to justice, which, in the past, invariably meant a swift execution. So when Plaatje translates Shakespeare's 'sorcerers' as *baloi*, his use of the term conjures up some powerful associations, and he contrasts *boloi*, rather more than does Shakespeare, with the countervailing force of Christianity. 'Now as I am a Christian, answer me', says Antipholus, demanding from Dromio an answer about what he had done with his money. Plaatje translates this as 'A ua nkutloa Dromio, ga ke mohaitane. Ke ikana ka Kresete, kare u nkarabɛ', or 'Do you hear me Dromio, I am not a heathen. I swear by Christ, answer me'. A few lines later, unable to get a satisfactory explanation for the disappearance of his money, he launches, exasperated, into his denunciation of the 'dark-working sorcerers', 'soul-killing witches' and the rest: the contrast is bound to resonate strongly with his readers.[51]

Often Plaatje goes well beyond Shakespeare in these allusions to witchcraft and sorcery. In the English tradition the devil may have had the best tunes, but in Setswana *baloi* could lay claim to the richer vocabulary, and Plaatje was keen to exploit this. In several passages he brings in references to witches and wizards where there are none in the original. Where Shakespeare has Antipholus of Syracuse remonstrate with Adriana about her claim that they had dined together at home, Plaatje has him exclaim, 'Ke jele tinare ko gagago, magalane kooena, a ua ntlholela?', or 'I had dinner at your place, you black snake, do you give me black omens?', referring to one of the most evil symbols in the world of *boloi*. A few lines earlier, where Antipholus calls Dromio a 'whoreson, senseless villain', Plaatje represents the insult as 'Ngoana' sethodi k'oena, moloi oa bosigo', or 'You child of the demon, sorcerer of the night'. For the Tswana, *baloi* can, and do, take hold of people. Plaatje makes the necessary adjustments, in translation, to reflect this widespread understanding.[52]

Strikingly, too, Plaatje turns statements about witchcraft and sorcery from the mouths of Shakespeare's protagonists into rhetorical questions, thereby confronting his readers directly with the reality of *baloi*, heightening its dramatic meaning. Thus in Act II scene ii, Dromio of Syracuse laments the sorcery in the 'fairy land' around him, exclaiming that if they did not obey the 'goblins, elves and sprites' they would 'suck our breath, or pinch us black and blue'. Plaatje instead makes this a question addressed directly to his readers: 'A jaana pholofolo tse re buanŋ naco tse e tsamile ke batho, a ga se bo tikoloshe, merubisi le badimo?' / 'Are the creatures we are talking to human beings – or are they demons, owls and ghosts?' He suggests, moreover, that rather more serious consequences will ensue: 'Fa re sa ee nabo ba tla re thubaka, ba re hupetse meoa, ba re je nanŋ, re thunye mebele' / 'If we do not go with them they will dash us to pieces and choke us and punch us so that our bodies turn grey'. In Plaatje's rendering, *baloi* are more evil, more menacing, than Shakespeare's 'goblins, elves and sprites' – and altogether more convincing as an explanation for the unlikely series of events and misrecognitions that occur.[53]

Another theme that resonated with the cultural universe of Batswana was that of relations between master and servant. *Diphosho-phosho* is suffused with a sense of hierarchy and the behaviour and modes of address that flow from this, reflecting Plaatje's intimate knowledge of Tswana custom and practice as well as his sensitivity to the tone of Shakespeare's text. Thus Aegeon, the duke of Syracuse – 'Agione, Morekisi oa Sirakuse' – is addressed as if he were a Tswana chief, his subjects displaying deference and respect in appropriate idiom. The 'most sacred duke' to whom Adriana appeals for justice in the final act becomes, in Setswana, 'Tau e tona, Senatla sa Matsha' / 'Big lion, the mighty one of the lakes', the allusion being not only to the traditional symbol of strength and power but to the mythical origins of the Batswana in the Great Lakes of Central Africa.[54]

Lower down the pecking order, the idiom is different. Poor Dromio is subjected to continued abuse from both master and mistress. Plaatje not only matches Shakespeare's colourful language but on occasions goes beyond it. When Luciana addresses Dromio contemptuously as 'thou snail, thou slug, thou sot', Plaatje enters into the spirit of the tirade and then goes further, using not three but five derogatory terms: *khukhu* (giant dung beetle), *seboko* (worm), *sefafalele* (careless person), *seapu* (fool), *seiaie* (idiot or moron).[55]

For both Plaatje and his readers the servile status of the two Dromios, and their frequent complaints about the way they are treated, were bound to recall the institution of *bolata*, meaning 'servitude', the term applied to the system of social relations that gave Batswana notables more or less complete control over the lives of their subordinates. The practice had been widespread in Bechuanaland during the nineteenth century but continued into the twentieth, particularly among the Bamangwato, the largest and most powerful of the Tswana chiefdoms. By the

1920s, however, it had become a very controversial issue, and the term 'slavery' was increasingly applied to describe the practice. In *The Comedy of Errors*, when Shakespeare uses the words 'slave' or 'slavery', Plaatje responds with several different terms in Setswana, reflecting degrees of servitude as well as regional variations in terminology: hence *molala/molata* and *motlhanka* for slave or serf, *bolata*, *botlhanka* or *bokgoba* for the system, whether it be deemed slavery or servitude. There was a crucially important ethnic dimension to *bolata*. It was always the Bakgalagadi or Masarwa ('Bushmen') who were the servants or slaves to wealthier Tswana tribesmen, never the other way round. In one scene Dromio of Ephesus reflects bitterly upon his servile status, agreeing that he must be 'an ass indeed' given the way he is treated; his life is one of constant cruelty and abuse, he complains, his suffering carried 'on my shoulders as a beggar wont her brat'. Plaatje renders this as 'Ke e roele ka marudi fela jaka mosada Mokgalagadi a belege molalana', or 'I bear it on my shoulder as a Bakgalagadi woman bears a little slave on her back' ('molalana' being the diminutive form of 'molala'). Reimagining *The Comedy of Errors* in Tswana idiom, even in jest, could raise some uncomfortable questions.[56]

In the opinion of the handful of people who were in a position to pass judgment, *Diphosho-phosho* was a huge success. One African living in the Bechuanaland Protectorate, who wrote to Plaatje to compliment him upon his achievement, thought *Diphosho-phosho* was 'the first Sechuana book that really speaks Sechuana'. Another, from the Cape, had this to say: 'Since the death of Robert Moffat and Canon Crisp, the Sechuana language never received such wonderful justice at the hands of a translator as you devoted to it in *Diphosho-phosho*.' The two university experts were likewise impressed. Clement Doke thought *Diphosho-phosho* was 'remarkably good', and was particularly struck by the many examples of Plaatje's 'magnificent wealth of Tswana vocabulary'. So too Gérard Lestrade, once taught Setswana by Plaatje in London, now a professor at the Transvaal University College in Pretoria. He compared *Diphosho-phosho* to Tiyo Soga's Xhosa translation of *Pilgrim's Progress*, and considered both works 'veritable treasure-houses of the linguistic riches of their respective languages, and show to a remarkable extent their authors' felicity for grasping not merely the language but the thought of the European originals and expressing that thought in idiomatic and vigorous prose'. Both men were struck by Plaatje's success in matching the puns, the epigrams, the colloquialisms, the distinctive tone of Shakespeare's language in *The Comedy of Errors*.[57]

Nobody, however, was in a better position to appreciate Plaatje's achievement than his friend and collaborator, David Ramoshoana. He expressed his views in a letter to *Umteteli wa Bantu* early in October 1930, concluding, once he had read *Diphosho-phosho* and discussed it with a group of friends, that it was 'a gratifying success'. He went on: 'The translator not only demonstrated his remarkable ability in English and complete mastery of the Sechuana language – a rare thing in these days – but he has also shown a clear understanding of the author's aims. Mr Plaatje has rendered the entire story in a language which to a Mochuana is as entertaining and amusing as the original is to an Englishman.' He had 'kept alive the sportive tenor of the play without distorting the author's ideas in any way, and without corrupting Sechuana idioms' – in contrast to that 'disagreeable and grating mess which is characteristic of certain books presented in Sechuana garb which yet remains foreign'. Rather, 'Shakespeare has inspired Mr Plaatje to bring into bold relief the etymological beauties of his mother tongue', and when reading *Diphosho-phosho* 'one feels as if one were reading the language of a Mochuana who happened to live in England. The pleading, or defence, of Aegeon before the Ephesian Court; the jokes, the treatment of servants and language in which they were ordered about, are very similar to the ways of the Bechuana of the last century. This is one of the features which make Mr Plaatje's translation so pleasant and entertaining.'

Lastly, in Ramoshoana's view, *Diphosho-phosho* was a milestone for what it signified about African capabilities and achievement. 'Many Englishmen hold the belief that Shakespeare's language and ideals are far above the intellectual scope of Africans and they defy translation into any African language because, they argue, European and African tongues, notions, and outlook, differ so irreconcilably that Shakespeare's elevated ideas must remain to the African an impenetrable mystery, even to those who have secondary training. It will be well for such sceptics to see how successfully a self-educated man has translated Shakespeare's "Comedy of Errors" into Sechuana. On seeing "Diphosho-phosho" they will revise their conclusions and change their opinions.'[58]

Such a concern to vindicate the claims and status of Setswana had been in Plaatje's mind from the moment he first thought of translating Shakespeare, conscious as he was of Shakespeare's symbolic importance in English culture. Now, more aware of the parallels and equivalences between the experience of the English and the Batswana, he was confident of the capacity of Setswana to comprehend and express Shakespeare's meaning. He was asserting not only Setswana's claims as a language but his own right, as an educated Motswana, fluent in both languages, to undertake the task.

By the time *Diphosho-phosho* was published in 1930 most whites in South Africa would have doubted such claims. By now the kind of cultural cross-fertilisation that came so naturally to Plaatje was at odds with the pro-segregationist sentiments that prevailed in political, literary and academic circles. Given such a climate of opinion, the very act of translating Shakespeare would have been regarded, at best, as misdirected effort; at worst, as a presumptuous statement of interest in the higher forms of a culture that no African had any business to be concerned with. Even those sympathetic to his endeavours expressed reservations. Clement Doke, for example, while full of admiration for the quality of Plaatje's translation and the importance of his work in preserving Setswana, nonetheless wondered whether 'other types of literature are not at present much more urgently needed in Chuana than this', and hoped that 'the Department of Native Education will give a clear lead to Chuana readers as to what type of literature is of immediate urgency'. Shakespeare, he implied, would not have been on their list.[59]

Stephen Black, editor of *The Sjambok*, a short-lived literary magazine published in Johannesburg, and by his own admission no devotee of Shakespeare, had other objections. 'I suggested to Plaatje the other day', he told a friend, 'that instead of wasting his time on translating Shakespeare, he should translate something which contains humanity, the one quality of which Shakespeare is entirely devoid … What in God's name the Bechuanas want to read Shakespeare for I don't know, unless it is that they want to feel more like worms than ever. Shakespeare, to my mind, is literature only, poetry only, and therefore untranslatable, because poetry is as much in the music of the poet's words as in any thought or ideas. This is very trite, but I can never understand why people want to translate Shakespeare.'[60]

Plaatje's reply to Stephen Black, if there was one, has not survived, but he would have disagreed with every point he made. Plaatje had his own very good reasons for being interested in Shakespeare; he admired Shakespeare precisely because he found in him a humanity that transcended boundaries of race and colour in a way that so many later English writers conspicuously failed to do; he thought many of the themes with which Shakespeare was concerned, far from making the Tswana people 'feel more like worms than ever', actually had a direct resonance with their own history and traditions; and in the act of translation he sought not to reproduce directly the poetic qualities of Shakespeare's language, but to match them, to find equivalents in Setswana, to demonstrate its own wealth of expression.

Stephen Black's views were not shared by everybody, however. Plaatje elicited a more positive reaction from the colonial authorities in the Bechuanaland Protectorate, thanks largely to the idiosyncratic figure of Charles Rey, the resident commissioner. Rey had seen a newspaper report announcing the publication of

Plaatje's Shakespeare translations and wondered who the author was and where he could be found. After he was reassured by one of his officials that Plaatje was 'so well known that probably the address "South Africa" would find him', a meeting was arranged. Rey described this, when it took place in November 1930, as 'a rather interesting interlude', noting that Plaatje 'had translated three of Shakespeare's plays into Sechuana!', that he was 'a useful fellow', and added, 'I want to get some of his books for our native schools'. In his job for little more than a year, Rey was a man in a hurry, keen to take Bechuanaland out of the dark ages, as he saw it, and to promote progress on all fronts. The consensus among experts was that primary schoolchildren should be taught in their first language. This was all very well if there was plenty of reading matter for them, but in the case of Setswana there was not. Plaatje, Rey thought, might help remedy this deficiency.[61]

Shakespeare, in whatever language, appealed to Rey for another reason: it was not religious. Personally agnostic, Rey had an intense dislike of missionaries, especially those of the London Missionary Society, whom he described variously, in his private diary, as 'pestilential dogs', 'children from hell' and 'vipers'. He wanted to reduce their influence in schools, and so welcomed any secular alternative to the religious texts and stories they used in the classroom. He urged his director of education, Henry Dumbrell, to pursue the matter further with Plaatje. Three months later, orthographic complications notwithstanding, *Diphosho-phosho* was on the reading list for Setswana for the upper primary classes of schools in the Bechuanaland Protectorate, Rey and Dumbrell being in agreement that it would be an interesting experiment. The new syllabus noted the 'great difficulty experienced in obtaining secular reading books' in Setswana, and expressed the hope that more would soon become available. It was a measure of the state of education in the Protectorate, after nearly fifty years of colonial rule, and sustained missionary effort, that there was not a single secondary school within its borders. It was small wonder Setswana was falling behind.[62]

Of Plaatje's other Shakespeare translations only *Julius Caesar* would see the light of day, albeit only after his death. It must have been a bitter disappointment not to have seen it in print as at one point its publication looked imminent. In May 1930, two months before *Diphosho-phosho* appeared, he wrote that the manuscripts of his translations of both *The Merchant of Venice* and *Julius Caesar* were 'in the hands of Longmans Green, Paternoster Row, who now make a speciality of School Readers in various languages'. There were hopes at this time that orthographic agreement on Setswana was in sight, and Longmans, Green was one of several publishing houses poised to enter the new market for school books that looked like opening up. Indeed J.W. Allen, one of the company's directors, visited South Africa in March and April 1930 with ambitious plans to expand in vernacular language publishing, and commissioned several new series of school textbooks, including one for Setswana (to be edited by Henry Dumbrell and G.H. Franz). Most likely this was when Plaatje interested Longmans in his two Shakespeare translations. Once it became clear that there was no agreement on Tswana orthography, however, Allen pulled out of both projects. There was never much chance that Longmans, or any other publisher, would take the financial risk of publishing in a language of which there was no commonly accepted printed form, particularly when the market was so small.[63]

Closely bound up in all Plaatje's work in Setswana and his struggle to get it into print was his involvement in an often vitriolic battle over the written form of the language itself. He was all too aware of the tragic effect of this lack of agreement on orthography upon the development of writing in Setswana, and that it was this more than anything else that made it impossible to find a publisher for his own work. He also had strong views on the particular form of orthography that was most appropriate for the true representation of the Tswana language. The fact that he was paying the printers did at least mean he could use the orthography he favoured, as he had done over the years when editing his own newspapers, and as he did now with *Diphosho-phosho*. In its introduction, indeed, he was at pains to explain and justify his preference, for it differed in two major respects from the various other missionary orthographies. Firstly, he used the letter 'j', so as to be able to distinguish between such words as *nyalela* (marry my daughter) and *njalela* (give me some), and to provide a more accurate form of representing the pronunciation of words like *bojang* (grass), *mojaki* (migrant labourer) and *dijana* (dishes).

Secondly, and more controversially, he believed that it was necessary to supplement the twenty-six letters of the Roman alphabet with additional characters from the International Phonetic Alphabet in order to represent accurately the sounds and tones of Setswana where this could not be done by a single Roman character, or any combination of them. In *Diphosho-phosho* he therefore introduced the phonetic characters ε, ŋ and ɔ in order to distinguish differences in pronunciation and tone in words in which the other orthographies made do with 'e', 'ng' and 'o' respectively. Often, he pointed out, the failure to make these distinctions could produce confusions in meaning: thus *mme* could mean either 'but' or 'mother', unless the latter meaning was signified by the phonetic symbol ε (*mmε*); and *botloco* could mean either 'illness' or 'want', unless the second meaning was signified by the use of the phonetic symbol ɔ (*botlɔcɔ*). Plaatje's interest in phonetics had originated in his work with Daniel Jones in London in 1915 and 1916; he felt every bit as strongly about the value of the phonetic script in preserving the true pronunciation of his language as he did then.[64]

His orthographic preferences and phonetic innovations did not please everybody. One M.M. Kendle, writing to *Umteteli wa Bantu* in December 1930 and again two months later, thought that *Diphosho-phosho* had 'deplorably digressed from the Sechuana orthography at present in vogue'; Clement Doke, too, thought it was 'a pity' that Plaatje had introduced 'his own modified orthography', thereby adding 'yet another to the many diverse methods in which Chwana is written'. Others were just puzzled. The district commissioner in Serowe, Bechuanaland, wrote to Plaatje to compliment him on *Diphosho-phosho* but thought his orthography 'a little strange'. In reply, Plaatje told him this was quite natural since 'educated Bechuana write to you mainly in English', and added that 'since the several se-Ruti orthographies are officially accepted as se-Cwana, you have in all probability never really have seen an indigenous Sechuana spelling'.[65]

There were similar reactions elsewhere in the Protectorate. Having agreed to include *Diphosho-phosho* in the new school syllabus, Henry Dumbrell soon complained of receiving criticism of the book on the grounds that it used a 'weird' orthography. In a report to the resident commissioner he did indicate that he would try to see Plaatje and find out if 'in the interests of the B.P. he would sacrifice his orthography to our wishes, in the interests of Native Education'. Dumbrell may well have pursued this with Plaatje but in view of the uncertainties of the situation it is unlikely that any action resulted. It was not, however, a matter on which Plaatje would have been keen to compromise.[66]

In fact, it seems he wanted to *extend* his use of the phonetic script, for late in 1930 he applied to the London-based International Institute of African Languages and Cultures (via Professor Daniel Jones, a member of its executive committee) for a grant to enable the Morija Press to purchase phonetic type for his 'book of folklore and poems written in Tswana'. Submitting Plaatje's request to the committee, Jones indicated that the total cost of providing the new phonetic type amounted to £36, a substantial sum which must have covered the cost of a number of additional phonetic characters, on top of the characters ɛ, ŋ and ɔ used by Morija in the printing of *Diphosho-phosho* several months previously. A grant of £10 was duly recommended by the committee, subject to the approval of its director, Professor Westermann; whether this sum, or a further £5 which Jones obtained from the Phonetic Association, ever reached Plaatje or the Morija Press is unknown.[67]

In retrospect it seems tragic that Plaatje's insistence upon the phonetic script as the only acceptable means of preserving the true pronunciation of his language should have helped delay the appearance of his collection of folktales and praise poems, with the ultimate result that they were lost entirely. It was clearly not an issue over which he was inclined to compromise if he could possibly avoid it, although he must have realised that a book heavily reliant on the phonetic script would be difficult to use in schools – that it risked being regarded, like the *Sechuana Reader*, as just another 'strange book in a strange spelling'. But his insistence upon using it suggests that in his own mind the act of preservation itself was his overriding priority. If his collection of folktales and poems was worth preserving, they had to be recorded and read in what he regarded as the proper manner. Whatever happened to the Tswana language in the future, then here at least, with the phonetic orthography, would be a permanent record of how he believed it should be.

✦✧✦

Alongside these desperate, often lonely efforts to create a written literature in Setswana there was a far more public campaign over the question of Tswana orthography, fought out at conferences and meetings, and in the columns of the press. Plaatje was a vociferous champion. His principal opponents were no longer the missionary societies with whom he had to contend in the past, but two different groups of people who had become involved: university academics and government officials, potentially more powerful adversaries. This new interest in the orthography of African languages was not confined to southern Africa. It owed much to a growing consensus in governing circles in the British empire in favour of policies of indirect rule, segregation being seen as a variant of this; and a concomitant realisation of the contribution that academics – anthropologists and linguists in particular – could make to the accumulation of specialised knowledge about the customs, languages and traditions of indigenous peoples. Only with this, it was thought, could indirect rule and the forms of administration it required be successfully implemented and managed.[68]

In South Africa, these ideas found institutional expression in the creation of several academic chairs in Bantu languages and the expansion of 'Bantu studies' (and a journal of the same name, founded in 1921), a process considerably accelerated by the reaction to the political and industrial unrest among Africans in the aftermath of the First World War. Confronted by the spectre of a militant African working class, government and industry responded by channelling money into academic disciplines that could yield information about how African societies worked and how, ultimately, they could be controlled. It was part, indeed, of that wider process of adjustment that led to the formation of the Joint Councils, the setting up of *Umteteli wa Bantu*, and the provision of officially constituted means of consultation for Africans in the Native Affairs Act of 1920.[69]

In Britain the concern was with Africa as a whole, but the response was comparable. Two institutions were of particular importance: the School of Oriental Studies, where Alice Werner, now a professor of African languages, continued to teach and write, imparting a knowledge of African languages to aspiring missionaries and colonial administrators; and the International Institute of African Languages and Cultures, founded in 1926 and presided over by the chief exponent of indirect rule, Lord Lugard. From its inception one of the new institute's primary concerns was with the possibility of standardising the orthography of African languages, initially on a regional basis, but ultimately with the objective of standardising linguistic forms for the entire continent – an ambition set out in its influential pamphlet, *A Practical Orthography of African Languages*, published in 1927.[70]

From Plaatje's point of view these developments were a mixed blessing. On the one hand, this new interest in African languages and cultures offered some hope that his own language, Setswana, would no longer be consigned to the general neglect it had experienced hitherto, and it helped him secure funds, however inadequate, for his research. On the other hand, when a scheme took shape to standardise the orthographies of the different African languages spoken in the Union and the protectorates, he was unrelenting in his opposition. Following the publication of *A Practical Orthography of African Languages*, a small group of government officials from the Education and Native Affairs departments initiated a series of meetings with university academics, Clement Doke included, with the aim of standardising the orthographies of the main African languages of South Africa. Their discussions took place under the aegis of the newly formed Union Advisory Committee on Bantu Studies and Research, and in July 1928 it appointed a subcommittee (known as the Central Orthography Committee) in order to 'take charge of the question of reform in the various orthographies'. Further subcommittees were then set up for the various language groups, including one for the so-called Sotho-Tswana-Pedi group.[71]

In principle Plaatje was in favour of orthographic reform. On numerous occasions he had pointed to the ways in which Setswana had suffered from the failure of the missionary societies to agree on a unified orthography. His own work, he believed, could have been published years ago if agreement had been reached. But he was totally out of sympathy with the moves being made in the direction of standardisation under the auspices of the Central Orthography Committee, because it was clear that its principal concern was with achieving a uniform orthography, not for Setswana but for a larger Sotho-Tswana-Pedi language group and, beyond that, all the other African languages in South Africa. For Plaatje the threat this posed to the integrity of Setswana was simply unacceptable. His great fear was that once linked with these larger language groups, Setswana, spoken by fewer than a million people and with virtually no literature of its own, would be forced to accept orthographic conventions that were foreign to it; that this would lead in practice to a distortion of its true pronunciation; that its unique qualities, and ultimately the language itself, would disappear. Having failed to unify its own orthography, Plaatje believed, Setswana would be in no position to resist the imposition of 'foreign' symbols and conventions. Pure Setswana, already distorted by missionaries and the influence of other languages and cultures, African and European, would cease to be a living language.[72]

Plaatje was nominated to the Sotho-Tswana-Pedi language group sub-committee, and attended its first meeting in Pretoria in February 1929, along with Professor Lestrade, the convenor; Dr Werner Eiselen; the Revs. Schwellnus, Baumbach and Ramseyer; Mr G.H. Franz, the secretary; and two other Africans, the Rev. P. Motiyane and Z.D. Mangoeala. Remarkably, four out of the six white members of this committee were sons of Berlin Society missionaries, and the Rev. Johannes Baumbach was once the young assistant teacher at Pniel with whom Plaatje shared classroom duties in the early 1890s. Common pasts and religious affiliations did not bring agreement on matters of orthography, however. During the course of the meeting it became clear that Plaatje's views differed sharply from those of the other people present, particularly on the question of how best to indicate pronunciation. On two occasions Plaatje proposed the use of phonetic characters for sounds which could not be expressed directly by the Roman alphabet, but on neither occasion could he find a seconder. Instead, the meeting voted by a majority of seven to one to adopt the use of diacritics – accents and stress marks, to be placed over letters of the Roman alphabet. These, Plaatje believed, both disfigured and misrepresented the language, and were in no way an adequate or accurate means of conveying the subtleties and variations in tones that were needed.[73]

Very little progress was achieved at the meeting, and its report was in any case rejected by the Central Orthography Committee, whose view was that the lack of unanimity indicated that 'the time is not yet ripe for unifying the orthography of the three languages'; it thought it 'most unlikely' that Sesotho would 'fall into line with the other two in the near future' and therefore recommended that separate district subcommittees should be set up for Sepedi and Setswana. When nominations were made for the Tswana subcommittee Plaatje's name was not among those put forward; he did not, therefore, attend its first meeting in October 1929. When the Rev. Motiyane, who was there, questioned why Plaatje had not been invited, pointing out that he had been 'a great help' at the previous meeting, the chairman, Professor Lestrade, replied that 'Mr Plaatje had not been reappointed by the Central Orthography Committee'. Motiyane felt Plaatje should have been reappointed, and attempted to raise the matter again at the end of the meeting, moving that 'the committee ask the Central Orthography Committee to reconsider whether he could not be reappointed to the Suto-Chuana-Pedi Committee'. He was unsuccessful: 'members of the committee felt', so it was recorded, 'that this would be a step beyond their powers and no vote was taken'. Plaatje was never again a delegate to any of the numerous orthography committees and subcommittees that sat over the next few years.[74]

Just who was responsible for the decision to exclude Plaatje, far and away the leading Tswana scholar of his day, is unclear. According to Alan Cuzen, resident magistrate at Kanye, who was present as a delegate at the second meeting, 'it was realized that an error had been made in the formation of the original committee of individuals called in their personal capacity', so this was changed to ensure that only those people 'representing governments, missionary societies and other bodies' were invited to attend – which provided a convenient pretext for excluding Plaatje. Having heard from Motiyane after the meeting, Plaatje reported that 'no one seemed to know who was responsible for my absence'. Gérard Lestrade, the chairman of the committee, must have known – and may well have engineered it – but decided to keep quiet, relieved to be rid of a disruptive influence. G.H. Franz, chief inspector of native education in the Transvaal and secretary of the committee, saw things in the same light. Once he accused Motiyane of allowing himself to be browbeaten by Plaatje, a charge Motiyane indignantly denied. 'I desire, first, sir, to say, it is no fear of Mr Plaatje that makes me write Secwana as I do.' Clement Doke, usually more sympathetic to Plaatje than most, was also a party to his exclusion from the committee, for it was he who had formally proposed its members.[75]

Unsurprisingly, Plaatje reacted angrily and was highly critical of the constitution of the various committees, especially as they were often composed of people who did not understand the languages whose futures they were deciding. Even the two Africans on the Tswana subcommittee, he thought, had been 'selected by virtue of their outstanding qualifications, viz. (a) neither of them ever wrote a Sechuana book or pamphlet; and (b) neither of them ever lived in Bechuanaland or in districts where the unadulterated Sechuana is spoken'. He was appalled by the orthography which was agreed upon and then ratified by the Central Orthography Committee. He believed that the proposal to replace the letter' 'c by 'ts' would cause endless confusions, and that the decision to use diacritics and circumflexes made writing Setswana 'irritating and cumbersome' and disfigured its appearance. 'Some one at Pretoria', he said, 'appears to have come across orthographic hieroglyphics and fallen head over heels in love with them. We admit that any man is entitled to his fads; but what right has he to embody his notions in our language? Anyone with a taste for diacritical hieroglyphs should incorporate them in his own language, not in ours.'

Beyond the differences of opinion over the details of orthography, Plaatje made the point time and time again that these self-appointed academics and government officials possessed neither the expertise nor the right to decide the future form of a language which was not their own, or to seek to impose it without adequate consultation with those who were going to be most affected by the changes – the Batswana themselves. 'Personally', he wrote, 'I have nothing but the highest respect for the sound learning of University professors. I yield to no one in my admiration for their academic distinction and high scholarship. The only trouble with the professors is that they don't know my language, and with all due deference, how could a string of letters behind a man's name enable him to deal correctly with something he does not understand? Only one man is capable of determining the spelling of this language. That man is the Native.'[76]

This ran directly counter to the predominant view shared by the professors and government officials involved in the orthography committee, as expressed on one occasion by Professor Lestrade: 'It is simply not done', he said, 'to consult people who are not expert in these matters, e.g. the natives.' This was simply confirmation of Plaatje's view that the whole orthography scheme carried 'the hallmark of true South African ideals, according to which anything of the kind must be evolved by white experts'.[77]

It is not difficult to see why he felt so strongly about this. Here, once again, the white man was taking over, assuming the right to take decisions that affected the lives of the African people, displacing men like himself from their natural role. Only now, since the issue at stake was the future of his own language, it was more personal. In the late 1920s he had made a conscious decision to devote himself to the preservation of the Tswana language and the creation of a written literature; nobody was better qualified for the task. But now these white academics and government officials, in an enthusiasm for orthographic unification that matched the commitment many felt to finding solutions to 'the native problem', claimed the right to decide even the future form of his native language. It denied Plaatje the right to interpret yet another area of the life of his people, one of the few, indeed, that were now left to him. At every opportunity he made his views clear in the strongest possible terms.

In fact, his outspoken campaign – in the press and at public meetings – contributed in no small measure to the groundswell of opposition to the new orthography for Setswana, especially when the authorities moved towards implementing the changes. In the Bechuanaland Protectorate he was also able to do a lot behind the scenes. When Colonel Rey's Education Advisory Board first met in November 1930, for example, Plaatje made sure he was on hand to provide advice: the orthography subcommittee it set up had the advantage, so it was recorded, 'of an informal and valuable talk with Dr Molema and Mr Sol Plaatje, the latter representing a group of Sechuana-speaking teachers in the Cape province'. As a result, it was noted, the members of the subcommittee were persuaded of the need 'to further explore native public opinion within the Territory', precisely his objective.[78]

He wasted little time following up this advantage. Within days of the meeting a detailed, four-page typed letter was delivered to the office of the government secretary in Mafeking, headquarters of the Bechuanaland Protectorate administration. It was from the Tshidi Barolong chief, Montshiwa, and his leading counsellors, and it complained in the strongest terms about the 'many unnecessary changes' being proposed for their language. The Bechuana 'cannot suppress their resentment', it said, 'that their mother tongue, alone among South African languages, is singled out as the plaything of University Professors'; with the help of the Transvaal provincial authorities these professors now sought to 'ram down the throats of the Bechuana an impossible and ungainly spelling', upsetting and confounding 'the simple Bechuana peasants in their efforts to study the Sechuana language'. Batswana living in South Africa therefore 'feel impelled to appeal to the Bechuanaland Protectorate Government – the only South African administration which deals solely with Bechuana tribes – to protect their mother tongue from the proposed mutilation by outsiders'. Plaatje was not a signatory to the letter but nobody else could have written it. It had the desired effect of ringing more alarm bells about the dangers of an over hasty acceptance of proposals that now looked like causing nothing but trouble.[79]

A second string to Plaatje's bow in this campaign was his friendship with Tshekedi Khama, the 25-year-old Bamangwato chief regent. Advising him privately, Plaatje's concern was not that Tshekedi failed to grasp the seriousness of the orthography issue but that outright opposition could be counterproductive, especially given the acrimonious relations that already existed between him and Colonel Rey, the resident commissioner. 'Among whites', he told the chief, 'a point blank refusal always creates the impression that one is obstinate.' 'Therefore Chief, say: "This is not merely a Mangwato language. I cannot decide alone. I must have plenty of time to confer with Bakgatla, Barolong, Ba-Hurutse, etc

etc."' And if delaying tactics of this kind needed reinforcement, he suggested the following form of words: 'Say further – "I found this language spoken when I was born; my fathers found it and left it when they died. I can't help you to reform it in two months."' Few people, Tshekedi would have well appreciated, had more experience than Plaatje in dealing with the whites who presumed to rule their lives – or had a better track record in subverting their designs.[80]

In the Cape, the education authorities were rather more responsive to African opinion than their counterparts in the Transvaal and Orange Free State, but opposition soon grew here too. African teachers' organisations and the different missionary societies, whatever their differences over the finer points of orthographic usage in the past, now found themselves united in condemnation of the proposals from Pretoria, the missionary societies increasingly concerned about the large stocks of books which would be made redundant. The unanimous resolution, drafted by Plaatje and passed by an African teachers' meeting in Kimberley in October 1930, reflected sentiment in Tswana-speaking areas: the proposals of the Central Orthography Committee were 'unduly cumbersome'; 'the complicated and unnecessarily numerous diacritical signs will occasion useless waste of time and space and, compared with the missionary orthography, at present in vogue (which is phonetically simple and easy to learn) ... will constitute a hindrance rather than an encouragement to the study of the vernacular'.[81]

Impasse was reached in November 1931. A conference was held in Bloemfontein in order to discuss implementation of all the new orthographies, but there was no agreement. Basutoland refused even to send a delegate, wishing to remain outside the scheme. The Cape authorities concluded that to go ahead in the face of the opposition that existed would be ill advised, and the Orange Free State followed suit. By then it was clear that there was simply not enough support for the scheme to have any chance of success, and amid much chaos and recrimination between local and central government the entire scheme for orthographic reform was shelved.[82]

The Bechuanaland Protectorate administration arrived at the same conclusion. Realising the extent of popular opposition, as well as that from the missionary societies, Rey had encouraged his officials to concentrate their efforts on finding an orthography acceptable for Bechuanaland alone, and not to wait until final agreement was reached by other administrations covering Tswana-speaking areas of South Africa. Even this more limited objective, though, proved to be beyond them; so too was a belated attempt at rapprochement – which had Plaatje's support – with the orthography of Basutoland Sesotho.[83]

Plaatje at least, as one of the most articulate voices of opposition, could take some satisfaction in the collapse of these ambitious schemes, but it nonetheless left the future of Setswana as a written language in as perilous a position as before. For the time being it had been preserved from the attentions of the 'would-be reformers of Bantu languages', but agreement on a more satisfactory and generally acceptable orthography seemed further away than ever. In so far as this related to Plaatje's own efforts to create a written language for Setswana, and to raise the money to publish what he had written, the net result was to throw him back once again on his own resources. The publishers who had been waiting in the wings quickly lost interest and transferred their attentions to more assured markets. For Plaatje and for Setswana, the challenge remained as daunting as ever.

⁓

Agreement on Tswana orthography would eventually be reached in 1937. A conference was convened in Johannesburg and, despite the misgivings of many present, a new orthography was officially adopted in the four territories concerned. Publishers prepared books in the new orthography and it achieved, for a few years at least, a degree of acceptance. Plaatje would have hated it: it incorporated diacritics, it dispensed with the letter 'c' in favour of 'ts', it insisted on capitalising the second person pronoun, and it contained a host of other features that would have been anathema to him.[84]

Agreement on this '1937 orthography' did have one especially significant outcome: it made possible the publication of *Dintshontsho tsa bo-Juliuse Kesara*, Plaatje's *Julius Caesar*, the first of Shakespeare's plays he had translated. Some time after his death the manuscript came into the hands of Clement Doke, who was keen to include it in the University of the Witwatersrand Press's new Bantu Treasury Series. This was dedicated to publishing texts in African languages and Doke was its founding editor. Doke then passed Plaatje's manuscript on to Gérard Lestrade, by this time a professor of African languages at the University of Cape Town, in order to prepare it for publication. Both recognised that its orthography would need to be brought into line with what had just been agreed. Both saw it indeed as a showcase for the new system, just as Plaatje had used *Diphosho-phosho* to demonstrate his own orthographic preferences seven years earlier.[85]

Dintshontsho tsa bo-Juliuse Kesara was published late in 1937, the third title in the Bantu Treasury Series, and the first in Setswana. It was perhaps just as well Plaatje never saw it. The new orthography was bad enough, but Lestrade's editorial intervention went well beyond that, as his introduction to the book makes clear. Here he provided a lengthy justification for the many other changes he felt it necessary to make. When he looked closely at the manuscript, he wrote, he found numerous problems. As well as inconsistencies in spelling, in the Tswana-isation of proper names, in the use of words of foreign origin – which could be put right without too much difficulty – there were also 'serious defects which could not be left unremedied'. The fundamental problem was that 'the rendering is but seldom of the nature of a translation, in the narrower sense of the word', and that 'throughout the sense rather than the language has been rendered in the Tswana version'. Words, lines and entire passages of text in the original were omitted, while there were additions 'for which no equivalent could be found' in the original: as well as being superfluous this was 'on other grounds also indefensible'.[86]

That was not the end of it: some passages, according to Lestrade, were translated inaccurately; others, 'while not positively erroneous, were so infelicitous or inappropriate that they seriously impaired the artistic effect of the passages in which they occurred'. In places, speeches had been rendered in 'highly condensed form – often done at the expense of meaning, or form, or both'; at other times 'speeches which in the English text are divided among several of the characters had been laid into the mouths of one character, and vice versa'. All things, of course, which Plaatje had done in *Diphosho-phosho*.

After such a litany of supposed defects it is a wonder Lestrade wished to proceed further. That he did so is attributable, to be fair to him, to his recognition of 'the remarkable qualities' of Plaatje's work. He commended 'its rich and expressive vocabulary, its idiomatic colour, its terse and vigorous expression, its highly individual style: truly an important contribution to the literature of the language of which he was so proud'. He hoped therefore that his work on the manuscript would be an appropriate tribute 'to the memory of a remarkable man', and 'in some small measure [help] to ensure that his courageous attempt at one of the most difficult things in the literary field should finally emerge in the form that would do it the most justice and gain for it the greatest measure of recognition and appreciation'.

In reality, Lestrade's views on Plaatje's rendering of *Julius Caesar* were the consequence not so much of its supposed defects and inadequacies but of a wholly different conception of the nature and purpose of translation. For Lestrade every word and line in Shakespeare had to be translated faithfully: authority resided in the original text and was to be followed as closely as possible, conceding only what was necessary to make it understood in Setswana, but no more. Shakespeare, as Lestrade saw it, needed to be rescued from the liberties Plaatje had taken with his text.

Plaatje had of course seen things differently. Shakespeare was not there to be followed religiously but to be reshaped in accordance with Tswana linguistic and cultural sensibilities. What he was after, to use David Ramoshoana's felicitous phrase, was 'a Sechuana book which speaks Sechuana'. Where Lestrade saw the rendering of the sense of the original as a deviation, for Plaatje that was the whole point – and absolutely essential if one was to avoid the grating mess that characterised so many other attempts to translate English into Setswana.

Out of such opposing views on the nature of translation emerged something of a hybrid, its integrity further compromised, Plaatje would have feared, by the involvement of Gideon Mangoaela, a Mosotho, who worked for Lestrade as 'Native Demonstrator in the Sotho Languages', and who helped edit and prepare the text for publication. Lestrade was at pains to stress that Mangoaela was qualified to undertake the task, aware that some might question why he had not chosen to work with a native Tswana-speaker. He was confident, however, that Mangoaela, 'through long residence among Tswana-speaking people', had 'a thorough knowledge of the Tswana language, and this knowledge he has placed unreservedly at my disposal'. The fact nevertheless remains that *Dintshontsho* was edited and prepared for publication by two people for whom Setswana was not a first language. Z.K. Matthews, by this time a lecturer at Fort Hare, and of mixed Bamangwato and Barolong descent, was asked to look at the manuscript, but this seems to have been something of an afterthought, and there is no way of knowing how thoroughly he did so.[87]

The ideal candidate for the task would undoubtedly have been David Ramoshoana. He had worked closely with Plaatje on his Setswana projects, including *Diphosho-phosho*, and Plaatje had once asked him to revise and correct *Dintshontsho* too. For whatever reason, however, Ramoshoana was not involved, though it had been thanks to his assistance that the manuscript had ended up in Clement Doke's hands. Perhaps he wasn't asked. Or perhaps he just couldn't bring himself to submit to the 'clumsy, tedious and ugly' new orthography that was now imposed upon his language, regarding this as betrayal. If written Setswana had done perfectly well for seventy-five years 'without the aid of those ugly marks', Ramoshoana wrote, why the need to introduce them now? On this issue he was at one with Plaatje.[88]

Dintshontsho's conflicted provenance is evident in its printed form. It was no longer part of Plaatje's projected 'Mabolelo a ga Tsikinya-Chaka' series, and the term 'Tsikinya-Chaka', for Shakespeare, is nowhere to be seen. Plaatje's name is on the title page as translator, along with that of Lestrade who 'corrected and arranged' the translation, the two names appearing in the same size type as if of equivalent importance (Mangoaela is mentioned only in the introduction).

Whereas in *Diphosho-phosho* Plaatje appears in the more informal style of 'Sol T. Plaatje', in *Dintshontsho* it is 'Solomon Tshekišô Plaatje', his middle name disfigured by both the new spelling and the diacritics above its final two letters. In the text itself there are no new subheadings of the kind he had introduced in *Diphosho-phosho*. Instead, it adheres to a conventional format, bringing consistency to characters' names, place names and stage directions. The overall visual impression, compared to *Diphosho-phosho*, is of Shakespeare in a straitjacket, at odds with Plaatje's conception of a resource to be shaped, played around with and utilised for the greater good of written Setswana.[89]

For all that, *Dintshontsho*'s qualities shine through. As in *Diphosho-phosho* there is the same imaginative use of Setswana proverbs and idiom, the same concern to explore the connections between the chiefly world of the Batswana and their counterparts in Shakespeare – the context this time being the power struggles of ancient Rome, the genre tragedy rather than comedy. Plaatje clearly rose to the challenge. In the view of two recent critics, his rendering of Mark Antony's famous speech in praise of Brutus ('the noblest Roman of them all') exploited to the full the musical qualities of Setswana, choosing words for their sound as well as their meaning, and then repeating them for dramatic and onomatopoeic effect. So seamlessly and sensitively is this done, say Matjila and Haire, and so expressive of a distinctive Batswana worldview, that 'Borutse' (Brutus), 'based on Plaatje's translation, might well have been a Motswana hero'.[90]

In fact, Lestrade's strictures about inconsistencies, loose translation and the like were not followed through in practice. There are numerous examples of wordy elaborations of short passages in the original, of which he especially disapproved, instances of speech being condensed and assigned to different characters, and of entirely new lines being introduced, often alluding to Setswana proverbs (none of course being present in the original). Even Plaatje's original title, *Dintshontsho tsa bo-Juliuse Kesara*, meaning, literally, 'the several deaths of Julius Caesar', was retained unaltered. Perhaps, when it came to it, Lestrade found it more difficult than he imagined to improve upon Plaatje's translation, however much it violated his rules. Or perhaps he was just more interested in making a statement about what he thought translation should aspire to, and to assert his own authority over all things Setswana, than to grapple with difficult and time-consuming practicalities.[91]

Dintshontsho met with a mixed reaction. As with *Diphosho-phosho* seven years earlier, there were those who believed Plaatje's efforts might have been better expended in other directions. Johannes Baumbach, for example, after reminiscing about their time together as schoolboys at the old Pniel mission, said he thought the new translation seemed 'quite successful', but that the great majority of

Batswana 'will not be able to comprehend and appreciate the happenings of two thousand years ago among people of a culture quite different from that of our days'. 'Would not a drama *Dintshontsho tsa bo-Tshaka* or *Moselekatse* or any other great Bantu chief', he asked, 'grip the African mind much more forcibly, provided a poet who is able to undertake the task?'[92]

Interestingly, given his subsequent reputation as one of the architects of Bantu Education, and indeed of apartheid itself, Professor Werner Eiselen, another son of a German missionary, expressed no such concerns. He thought the translation 'a fine piece of work, and one which has captured much of the dramatic force of the original', and commended Plaatje's 'marvellous command of the Tswana language, his easy flow of diction and his instinctive choice of the appropriate word'. Nobody, he said, had realised more than Plaatje the importance of developing African languages from the literary basis laid by missionaries, and so had 'set out single-handed to teach his countrymen that there was a literary future for Tswana'. 'Deeply impressed by the genius of Shakespeare', he had tried to do 'what no other African had yet attempted, to give a translation of Shakespeare's works'.

Eiselen, it seems, was unimpressed by Lestrade's lengthy catalogue of epistemological misdeeds. It would do no harm at all to *Dintshontsho*'s prospects of being prescribed for use in schools that he now occupied the position of chief inspector of native education in the Transvaal.[93]

⌁

In many ways Plaatje's two Shakespeare translations stand out as his finest literary achievement. Collecting proverbs and compiling a dictionary, vital as they were, were essentially projects of retrieval and preservation. His collection of Tswana folktales and praise poems may have gone beyond this, but it has not survived. *Diphosho-phosho* and *Dintshontsho* are of a different order. Here he drew upon the two languages and cultures in which he was so well versed to create something entirely new, the one informing and enriching the other. He drew upon Shakespeare to take written Setswana to new levels of subtlety and sophistication. He performed a service for Shakespeare too, freeing him, like pioneering translators elsewhere, from a dependence upon the original language and literary form of the plays, setting an example for others in Africa to follow.[94]

That so few people understood what he was doing was a source of frustration but it was not a deterrent. Committed to doing all he could to ensure the survival of Setswana as a written language, and to demonstrate its qualities and capabilities, he simply kept going. He was well used to the brand of racism that

518

would deny him the right even to attempt such a task as translating Shakespeare – and to the reservations of those who thought he should stick to something more useful, more practical. Hygiene manuals, for example, such as the missionary societies promoted.

Far harder to come to terms with was the seeming indifference of his own people. He told a poignant story to illustrate the point. One day, in the company of David Ramoshoana, working together on Setswana, they called out to an old man they saw walking past, hoping he could help with a problem they were puzzling over. The old man responded: 'What is it that you gain from your witchery, that after long and tedious journeys by train and lorry, you spend sleepless nights with the lights on, working tirelessly on your books, when the rest of the people are asleep?' Ramoshoana replied: 'There are presently about 300 African languages which have their own printed books. If I were to die having translated one of Shakespeare's plays into Setswana I shall rest in peace because I will have done something for you.'[95]

Should someone still want to know how we benefit from our toil, Plaatje added, that is our answer.

✢

Plaatje was not to know that both *Diphosho-phosho* and *Dintshontsho* would have significant afterlives. Sales of *Diphosho-phosho* during his lifetime were modest, and it did not long remain on the school syllabus in the Bechuanaland Protectorate. But in the 1950s, as primary and secondary education expanded, it acquired a new lease of life. A new edition was published by the Bechuanaland Book Centre (run by the London Missionary Society) in 1958, in a simplified new orthography, and in one twelve-month period in the early 1960s, for which a record has survived, over three thousand copies were sold. A 'quatercentenary' edition followed in 1964, expanded to include a glossary, biographical information on Plaatje, and a Tswana translation of the *Lambs' Tales from Shakespeare* summary of *The Comedy of Errors*. By 1990 this had gone into a fifth impression and it had become a fixture in both primary and secondary curricula of the newly prosperous independent state of Botswana. Only at the turn of the century, it seems, did it disappear from the curriculum, displaced by new writing in Setswana which Plaatje would have been delighted to see emerge.[96]

Dintshontsho tsa bo-Juliuse Kesara must have sold even more copies. Agreement on the new orthography in 1937 opened the way for sales to schools in South Africa and, with precious little else available in Setswana, it proved popular. In 1942 Clement Doke had *Dintshontsho* reprinted 'in order to supply its urgent requirement as a school-textbook for examination purposes', noting that it was the first title in the Bantu Treasury Series to have sold out its initial print run. With the coming of apartheid in 1948, and then Bantu Education, the teaching of African languages in schools gained new emphasis, schools were better funded than before and sales increased further; in 1953, according to Robert Shepherd (principal of Lovedale), it was widely read and 'used as a textbook in the upper classes of high schools and in Fort Hare University College'. Over the next two decades there would be regular prescriptions for the National Senior Certificate and for primary and secondary teachers' examinations, and for their equivalents in Botswana too. Professor D.T. Cole, a Setswana specialist, succeeded Clement Doke as editor of the Bantu Treasury Series and made some revisions as orthographies evolved, though he retained the original preface and introduction. Curiously, and inappropriately, they remain there to this day. *Dintshontsho* was the best-selling title in the series and was for years an important source of revenue for the Press as a whole.[97]

All told, Plaatje's two Shakespeare translations sold tens of thousands of copies, far more than all of his English writings. Generations of Tswana-speaking teachers and schoolchildren, as he had once hoped, would be exposed to his work. Perhaps that is who, in the end, benefited from his toil.

SEVENTEEN

Mhudi

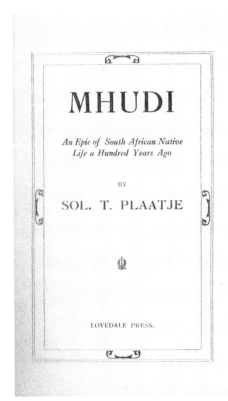

MHUDI

*An Epic of South African Native
Life a Hundred Years Ago*

BY

SOL. T. PLAATJE

LOVEDALE PRESS.

In May 1930 Plaatje wrote to his old friend Georgiana Solomon, now well into her eighties, the latest letter in what seems to have been a regular correspondence. His news was mixed. 'We are not too well physically, Elizabeth and I, but thank God we are still alive and about our usual efforts.' The children were all well. 'They frequently congratulate me on having an English mother abroad who is constantly praying for my safety and the welfare of my family – especially when they read some of your old letters to us!' The political outlook, he reported, 'is not too pleasant', but he had no wish to go into any detail, saying simply that 'we live in hopes', seeking solace in Samson's biblical aphorism, 'Out of the eater came forth meat and out of the strong came forth sweetness'.

Then came his real piece of news. 'You will both be glad to know', he said, addressing Mrs Solomon's daughter Daisy too, 'that after ten years of disappointment I have at length succeeded in printing my book. Lovedale is publishing it. I am expecting the proofs any day this week.' This was not one of his works in Setswana but *Mhudi*, the English-language novel he had written in London in 1920. With his next letter, he added, he hoped to be able to send her a printed copy. Mrs Solomon of course knew it well, having read the typescript and done her best to help him find a publisher for it in London. There was good news too on his Shakespeare translations: proofs of *Diphosho-phosho* were due from the Morija Press later in the week, while Longmans Green, the London publishers, had the manuscripts of *The Merchant of Venice* and *Julius Caesar*. 'This simultaneous opening of printing houses in 1930 is rather strange, after they have been blocked to me with ten years of hard writing on my hands. Completing arrangements with three different houses – one after the other – made me wonder whether my days are not drawing to a close.' In the middle of 1930, provided his health held up, Plaatje's literary ambitions at last looked like being realised.[1]

The Lovedale Press may not have been the international publishing house he once sought, but it was a good time to have approached them. Their decision to take on *Mhudi* stemmed from the arrival at Lovedale, a few years before, of a new chaplain by the name of R.H.W. Shepherd, who had a brief 'to assist in the publications work'. Until then, the Lovedale Press had concentrated on publishing books and pamphlets for religious and educational purposes, mostly in English and Xhosa. Shepherd, though, possessed a broader view of the literary responsibilities of a mission press, and believed that Lovedale should concern itself with providing more general reading matter for the African population. As convenor of the Publications Committee and later as director of publications, he largely decided what was to be published. Unlike his predecessors, he was quite prepared to take the risk of publishing fiction in English, one of the early beneficiaries of this new regime being the young Zulu writer R.R.R. Dhlomo, whose novella, *An African Tragedy*, came out in December 1928.[2]

Plaatje approached the Lovedale Press in November 1929. 'A letter was submitted from Mr Plaatje concerning a MS *Mhudi*, a story of the Bechuanas, in English', so it is recorded in the minutes of the Publications Committee meeting on 29 November, 'and also concerning a proposal to publish translations of some of Shakespeare's plays in Sechuana. Mr Chalmers [the vice principal] and the Convenor [Shepherd] were left to go into the matter with Mr Plaatje.' Nothing came of the Shakespeare plays – unsurprisingly in view of the confused orthographic situation – but they were keen on *Mhudi*. At the following meeting, on 4 December, 'Mr Chalmers and the Convenor reported that they were favourably impressed with Mr Plaatje's MS *Mhudi*, and it was agreed to accept it for publication at our convenience, should the missing chapter be furnished by the author and terms satisfactory to both parties be arranged.' By the next meeting, on 21 February 1930, agreement in principle was reached, and terms put to Plaatje. The committee accepted his suggestion that the book should be priced at 5s 6d, and a contract was drawn up, providing for a first edition of 2,000 copies, with a 10 per cent royalty payable when 700 copies of the book had been sold. Plaatje signed the contract on 19 March. Considering that overseas publishers had wanted him to contribute to the costs of publication, the terms must have appeared quite satisfactory, and the price of 5s 6d per copy – for a hard-cover book that was likely to run to over two hundred pages – not so high as to deter potential readers.[3]

Five months later *Mhudi* was printed and published, Plaatje having in the meantime supplied the 'missing chapter' (chapter 22, 'The exodus'). Evidence of Shepherd's personal interest and involvement is to be found in Plaatje's preface (dated August 1930), which concludes with an acknowledgement of Shepherd's assistance in 'helping to correct the proofs'. Shepherd, later in life, made it clear that he was very pleased to have been associated with the book's publication, and often referred to it. He remembered Plaatje 'as a man of strong and independent character, whose mind ranged widely in literature and African affairs', and as a 'man of much natural force', recalling the occasion Plaatje had first walked into his office to discuss the book.[4]

While Shepherd took a keen interest in *Mhudi* and its progress through production, there is nothing to suggest that he prevailed upon Plaatje to make any changes to his manuscript or that he made any himself, as some critics have argued. Since there was nothing in *Mhudi* that could be construed as being 'harmful to the missionary cause', there was no reason for him to do so. If he did have any concerns it is unlikely that the minutes of the Publications Committee would have recorded that both he and Chalmers were 'favourably impressed' with the MS, or that they would have agreed to publish it with no other provisos than that Plaatje should supply the missing chapter, and that terms acceptable to both parties were to be agreed.[5]

Nor is there any textual evidence to support any charge of interference. The typescript which Plaatje supplied to Lovedale, like earlier drafts that have survived, had numerous handwritten amendments, made at various times, but they are all in his own hand; this is simply how he worked, constantly revising what he had written. Beyond a very basic mark-up by the printer there is no sign of any editing or copyediting in any other hand. One consequence, in fact, of this lack of attention to the basics of manuscript preparation was a final printed product that was riddled with errors and inconsistencies in spelling and punctuation. Nobody, moreover, carried out a proper check of chapter headings in the text against their listing on the contents page, the most basic task of any copyeditor. Six of the chapter headings do not correspond, and different numbering systems – Roman for the text, Arabic for the contents page – are used.

Further changes and corrections were made at proof stage, after the book had been typeset, but most of these were minor in nature and did not affect sense or style. The two most substantial changes were the addition of two new pages, by Plaatje, at the beginning of chapter 11, 'A timid man'; and a new 'Exodus' chapter, chapter 22, only part of which had been supplied with the original typescript that Lovedale marked up for typesetting. None of this provides any reason to believe that the version of *Mhudi* which Lovedale published was not fully in accord with his wishes, or that there was some kind of 'psychological war' 'between Plaatje and his editors' over the text, as has also been suggested.

Michael van Reenen, Plaatje's friend and neighbour, also helped to correct proofs. His main memory, years later, was of Shepherd pleading with Plaatje to refrain from making any further changes, being concerned about the escalating costs. There is no doubt that it was Plaatje who was making these changes at proof stage, just as he had with his typescript.[6]

Mhudi

+~+

Even though *Mhudi*'s publication was delayed for ten years, it was nevertheless the first book of its kind, a full-length work of fiction, to have been written by a black South African. It was this that prompted Plaatje to offer a few words in justification and explanation: 'South African literature has hitherto been almost exclusively European, so that a foreword seems necessary to give reasons for a Native venture', he said. 'In all the tales of battle I have ever read, or heard of, the cause of the war is invariably ascribed to the other side. Similarly, we have been taught almost from childhood, to fear the Matabele – a fierce nation – so unreasoning in its ferocity that it will attack any individual or tribe, at sight, without the slightest provocation. Their destruction of our people, we are told, had no justification in fact or in reason; they were actuated by sheer lust for human blood.'

It turned out that this Matabele onslaught was not unreasoned or unprovoked, however. Plaatje only discovered the justification for it later in life, when he was told of 'the day Mzilikazi's tax collectors were killed', and that it was 'the slaying of Bhoya and his companions, about the year 1830' that 'constituted the casus belli which unleashed the war dogs and precipitated the Barolong nation headlong into the horrors described in these pages'.[7]

These events, action and reaction, were Plaatje's point of departure, and it is against this historical background of South Africa in the 1830s that he weaves his tale. There follows a dramatic account of the brutal destruction of Kunana, the Barolong capital, and an introduction to the two main characters, Mhudi and Ra-Thaga. Thereafter the scene shifts to the court of the victorious Matabele king, Mzilikazi. As his people celebrate their victory, Gubuza, commander of Mzilikazi's army, utters one of the prophetic warnings that build up an atmosphere of suspense and impending doom, predicting that the Barolong would not rest until they had their revenge.

Mhudi and Ra-Thaga, meanwhile, meet one another in the wilderness, fall in love, and after several encounters with lions, meet up with a band of Korana, and join them in the hope of discovering the fate of the rest of their people. Ra-Thaga then has a narrow escape at the hands of Ton-Qon, a Korana headman who is intent on taking Mhudi as his wife, but the couple hear that the survivors of the massacre at Kunana, together with the other branches of the Barolong nation, have now gathered and made a new home in Thaba Nchu. They set out to find them, and arrive to a joyous reception from Mhudi's cousin Baile, each amazed to find the other alive. Soon their arrival is eclipsed by that of another group of newcomers, 'a travel-stained party' of Boers travelling northwards from the Cape Colony, who are offered hospitality by Chief Moroka, the senior Barolong chief at Thaba Nchu. In due course, a friendship develops between Ra-Thaga and De Villiers, one of the Boer trekkers, and after much deliberation and the dispatch of a spying expedition, the Barolong and Boer leaders decide to form a military alliance and attack the Matabele.

The Matabele, for their part, prepare themselves for the onslaught. As they do so, a bright comet appears in the sky above them, an omen of defeat and destruction prophesied many times before by their witchdoctors and seers. In the battle that follows, the combined forces of Boers, Barolong and Griqua (also enlisted as allies) prove more than a match for the dispirited Matabele forces, and their triumph is joyously celebrated. In the opposite camp Gubuza brings news of the defeat of his army to the king, and advises him to 'evacuate the city and move the nation to the north'. Only in this way, he said, mindful of an earlier prophecy, could the complete annihilation of the Matabele nation be averted.

From the tragic scene of the court of the defeated Matabele king, the action returns to Thaba Nchu, where Mhudi has been left behind while her husband is away with the army sent out against the Matabele. It is not a situation she can long endure. Having a premonition of an injury to Ra-Thaga, she decides impulsively to make her way to the allies' camp, setting out alone on the hazardous journey. On the way there she encounters Umnandi, the former wife of Mzilikazi, forced to flee his court as a result of the machinations of her jealous rivals, and they arrive together in the allies' camp. Mzilikazi, meanwhile, prepares to move northwards, bitterly regretting his failure to heed the warnings and prophecies that had been made: 'I alone am to blame,' he acknowledges, 'notwithstanding that my magicians warned me of the looming terrors, I heeded them not. Had I only listened and moved the nation to the north, I could have transplanted my kingdom there with all my impis still intact – but mayebab'o – now I have lost all!' Then, in one of the most powerful passages of the book, Mzilikazi makes a prophecy of his own. The Barolong, he says, will live to regret the alliance they have made with the Boers.[8]

After so powerful and haunting a prophecy, the remaining two chapters of the book come almost as an anticlimax, and are devoted mostly to tying up loose ends in the personal relationships between the main characters. Umnandi rejoins Mzilikazi, welcomed back as his rightful queen; De Villiers, Ra-Thaga's Boer friend, marries the girl he loves, Annetjie; while Mhudi and Ra-Thaga, after declining an invitation to stay on with their new-found friends, De Villiers and Annetjie, set off in an old wagon in the direction of Thaba Nchu: 'from henceforth', says Ra-Thaga to Mhudi, in the final lines of the book, 'my ears shall be open to one call only besides the call of the Chief, namely the call of your voice – Mhudi'.[9]

In many ways the actual sequence of events, the development of the individual characters and the interaction between them are not of crucial importance. For Plaatje did not conceive of *Mhudi* as a realistic novel in the Western literary tradition. He gave his book the subtitle 'An epic of native life a hundred years ago', seeking to dignify his tale with the sense of grandeur and significance he felt it deserved. Just as in Shakespeare, he expected his readers to suspend a sense of realism to allow for the delivery of long set-piece speeches, dialogue, songs and poems; to allow him to bring historical events backwards and forwards in time as it suited him; and to exploit for dramatic purposes an assumed historical knowledge on the part of his readers. His characters are not realistic portrayals of human behaviour but rather vehicles for the expression of a variety of human qualities and ideas which he wished to explore.[10]

Mhudi was the outcome of a quite conscious and deliberate attempt on Plaatje's part to marry together two different cultural traditions: African oral forms and traditions, particularly those of the Barolong, on the one hand, and the written traditions and forms of the English language and literature, on the other. As noted in chapter 10, when he set about writing *Mhudi* in 1920 he looked to the imperial romance for inspiration and for a literary model, drawing in particular upon Rider Haggard's *Nada the Lily*. A further advantage of *Nada*, as Plaatje saw it, was that it showed how it was possible to explore and to incorporate oral traditions (Zulu), using them as the backdrop to the imagined tale of Umslopogaas and the beautiful Nada.

While Rider Haggard was able to go to published sources for his oral traditions, Plaatje got most of his at first hand. The slaying of Bhoya and his companions, for example, was unrecorded in any published histories, and Plaatje only heard about it 'from old people', 'by the merest accident', 'while collecting stray scraps of tribal history, later in life'. Other stories came from members of his own family. His use of proverbs and other idioms was likewise a quite deliberate attempt to convey something of the richness of the cultural resources upon which he was drawing. Often his technique of literal translation was strikingly successful. 'I would rather be a Bushman and eat scorpions than that Matabele could be hunted and killed as freely as rockrabbits', says Dambuza, one of Mzilikazi's warriors, at the Matabele court. Later he observes: 'Gubuza, my chief, your speech was the one fly in the milk. Your unworthy words stung like needles in my ears.'[11]

Plaatje was struck by the way Tswana oral tradition and the written traditions of English literature shared a common fund of literary and cultural symbols. In *Mhudi* he set out to explore this idea, not least in relation to omen and prophecy, and their association with planetary movements – preoccupations of both

Shakespeare and the traditions of his own people. This had always fascinated him. 'In common with other Bantu tribes', he had written in his newspaper at the time of the reappearance of Halley's Comet in 1910, 'the Bechuana attach many ominous traditions to stellar movements and cometary visitations in particular', and he had added: 'space will not permit of one going as far back as the 30s and 50s to record momentous events, in Sechuana history, which occurred synchronically with the movements of heavenly bodies'. Ten years later Plaatje found both the time and space to do exactly that in writing *Mhudi*, even if he had then to wait a further ten years before the results were published.[12]

This awareness of the literary possibilities that lay in the manipulation of symbols that had meaning in both Tswana and English cultures also found expression in the humorous lion stories that appear in the early part of the book. These serve as a means of testing the courage of Mhudi and Ra-Thaga, and are contrasted later on with the cowardly reaction of Lepane, a traveller faced with a similar challenge. That lion stories of this kind were a familiar motif in Tswana tradition emerges from the story that Plaatje himself reproduced in his *Sechuana Reader*. Like the lion story that appears in chapter 6 of *Mhudi*, its central point is the way in which the protagonist proves his bravery by holding onto the lion's tail. At the same time, lion stories of this kind, serving a similar function of demonstrating bravery and cowardice, appear in English literature too – in Bunyan's *Pilgrim's Progress* and Shakespeare's *Love's Labour Lost*, *Julius Caesar* and *A Midsummer Night's Dream*, all of which would have been very familiar to him.[13]

Another lion story came from Plaatje's own family history, albeit suitably reworked for his own dramatic purposes. 'I have had some exciting times in my young life', Mhudi tells Ra-Thaga in the middle of chapter 7, informing him that 'the day I met you was not the first occasion on which I had a narrow escape from a roaring lion'. She then tells him of the time she came face to face with a lion, stood her ground and emerged uninjured after her companions managed to frighten it off by shouting and waving their peltries (fur skins) at it. The story had come down to Plaatje from his great-grandmother: she had been the girl who, in the early 1820s, had faced down the lion in a bush near the Kunana Hills, just where the episode in *Mhudi* takes place.[14]

In 1916, as we have seen, Plaatje had expressed the view that he thought it likely that some of the stories on which Shakespeare's dramas were based 'find equivalents in African folk-lore'. When he looked into this question more closely he found this prediction to be correct. The lion stories, and his exploration of the symbolism and meaning of planetary omens and prophecies, were two of the outcomes. This was the kind of cultural borderland he loved to explore.

~~~

In writing *Mhudi* Plaatje had some broader objectives in mind, too. Foremost among them, as he stated in the preface, was his concern 'to interpret to the reading public one phase of "the back of the Native mind"': essentially, to write of a particular historical episode from an African and, more particularly, a Barolong viewpoint, rather than from the more familiar white, or European, perspective. It had long rankled in his mind that the Boers, to whom he largely attributed the misfortunes of his people, owed their survival to the succour and help which one branch of the so-called Great Trek had received at the hands of the Barolong chief Moroka at Thaba Nchu. It was a point he often drew attention to in his political writings. 'In the eyes of most Natives the Prime Minister's campaign of calumny,' he wrote in 1929, 'lumping us all as a barbarian menace to European civilisation was nothing but colossal ingratitude', and he went on to outline, as he had done in *Native Life in South Africa*, the way in which Moroka's Barolong came to their assistance and helped them defeat the Matabele. Even more disturbing to him was the way in which the historical record was distorted for political purposes. 'It is a standing complaint among educated natives', he wrote another time, 'that in South African history books (except where natives acted entirely under their own unaided initiative) tribal succour of Europeans is not even as much as mentioned, although tradition abounds with the stories of battle after battle carried by native legions in the cause of European colonisation in South Africa.'[15]

In *Mhudi* Plaatje set out to counter these kinds of misrepresentations by writing about a familiar historical episode from a novel perspective. One theme running through the book is an assertion that Barolong society prior to its contact with 'European civilisation' was not in the state of savagery invariably used to justify its subsequent conquest by white colonists – the familiar trope of the conventional imperial romance. At the very beginning of the book he implicitly contrasts the communal values of pre-colonial Barolong society with its later transformation under the impact of white settlement:

> Strange to relate, these simple folk were perfectly happy without money and without silver watches. Abject poverty was practically unknown; they had no orphanages because there were no nameless babies. When a man had a couple of karosses to make he invited the neighbours to spend the day with him, cutting, fitting in and sewing together the sixty grey jackal pelts into two rugs, and there would be intervals of feasting throughout the day ... But the anomaly of this community life was that, while the

many seams in a rich man's kaross carried all kinds of knittings – good, bad, and indifferent – the wife of a poor man, who could not afford such a feast, was often gowned in flawless furs. It being the skilled handiwork of her own husband, the nicety of its seams seldom failed to evoke the admiration of experts.[16]

The absence of extremes of wealth, and a tradition of communal hospitality, are portrayed as attractive features of Barolong society before its contact with white civilisation. Other aspects of Barolong life are presented in a favourable light too. At Thaba Nchu Chief Moroka is called upon to make a 'Solomonic' decision in a case involving two married couples who have exchanged partners; contrary to the precepts of Christian morality, his decision is that the new arrangement should continue since it was now obvious that this was the judgment that would give satisfaction to all parties concerned. Consensual justice, in other words, was preferable in certain circumstances to adherence to a rigid legal or moral code. In another decision made by Chief Moroka, the qualities emphasised were the seriousness with which physical assault was viewed in Barolong society, and a willingness to bestow mercy in dealing with those guilty of this offence.[17]

So Plaatje was concerned to offer a corrective to the stereotypes of white South Africans (and others), that his people were murderous savages, saved only by the coming of the white man. And he has a fresh perspective to offer upon the Boers too. In *Mhudi* they are viewed not as the embodiment of the advance of civilisation, but as a strange and far-from-heroic group of travellers who are forced to turn to Moroka for assistance. When they first make their appearance, over a third of the way through the book, they are seen from a Barolong perspective, their credentials somewhat open to question:

They were mounted and each carried a rifle. It was a travel-stained party, and the faces of the older men bore traces of anxiety. Apart from that they were well-fed on the whole, as the open air of a sunny country had impressed health, vigour, and energy on their well-clothed bodies, especially the younger men of the party. The spokesman of the riders was their leader, a Boer named Sarel Siljay, who headed a large band of Dutch emigrants from Cape Colony. They were travelling with their families in hooded waggons, and driving with their caravan their wealth of livestock into the hinterland in search of some unoccupied territory to colonise and to worship God in peace.

'But,' asked Chief Moroka, 'could you not worship God on the south of the Orange River?'

'We could', replied Siljay, 'but oppression is not conducive to piety. We are after freedom. The English laws of the Cape are not fair to us.'

'We Barolong have always heard that, since David and Solomon, no king has ruled so justly as King George of England.'

'It may be so,' replied the Boer leader, 'but there are always two points of view. The point of view of the ruler is not always the viewpoint of the ruled. We Boers are tired of foreign kings and rulers. We only want one ruler and that is God, our Creator. No man or woman can rule another.'

'Yours must be a very strange people,' said several chiefs simultaneously. 'The Bible says when the children of Israel had only one God as their ruler, they gave Him no rest until He anointed a king for them. We are just like them. There are two persons that we Barolong can never do without: a wife to mind the home and a king to call us to order, settle our disputes and lead us in battle.'[18]

This was a picture of the Boers far removed from the conventional image of the chroniclers of the Great Trek. It was no part of this story that the Boers were met at Thaba Nchu by Barolong chiefs quoting the Bible at them, and disputing their arguments on the nature of freedom and justice on biblical grounds. Thereafter, Plaatje presents the Boers in a distinctly unfavourable light, and with several individual exceptions they are portrayed as greedy, cruel and deceitful. They mistreat their Khoi servants, they fail to appreciate the hospitality accorded them at Thaba Nchu, and they try to strike a very unfair bargain over the spoils of war during the negotiations with the Barolong over mounting a joint expedition against the Matabele. On other occasions they are almost figures of fun: '"How long must it last, O God?" a group of Boer women demanded, 'as though expecting an answer by return post.' The Boers in Plaatje's *Mhudi*, in short, did not live up to the heroic image so carefully cultivated by their twentieth-century successors.[19]

Mhudi also has a more direct political message or warning. Although the action of the novel does not extend beyond the 1830s or the 1840s, it is clear that Plaatje expects his readers to draw a connection between the circumstances of the Barolong during the period covered in the book and the position in which they found themselves in the early part of the twentieth century when the book was written. In *Mhudi*, oppression and tyranny bring forth retribution with an inevitability emphasised throughout the book by the use of prophecy. When

Bhoya is killed, it is prophesied that Mzilikazi will seek his revenge, even if, when this duly took place, the devastation and destruction were on a scale that none had imagined. Then, among the Matabele, Gubuza is the first to warn that the Barolong would never rest until they had secured their revenge for punishment which he believed went far beyond reasonable retribution for the offence they had committed. Ultimately, that prophecy, too, is fulfilled: the Barolong ally themselves with the Boers, defeat the mighty Matabele in battle, and Mzilikazi is forced to flee northwards with his people. But before doing so – in that 'missing' chapter which Plaatje supplied after submitting his manuscript – Mzilikazi himself utters the greatest prophecy of them all, recovering his dignity and stature in a powerful exhortation to his people, warning the Barolong of the inevitable outcome of their fateful alliance with the Boers:

The Bechuana know not the story of Zungu of old. Remember him, my people; he caught a lion's whelp and thought that, if he fed it with the milk of his cows, he would in due course possess a useful mastiff to help him in hunting valuable specimens of wild beasts. The cub grew up, apparently tame and meek, just like an ordinary domestic puppy; but one day Zungu came home and found, what? It had eaten his children, chewed up two of his wives, and in destroying it, he himself narrowly escaped being mauled. So, if Tauana and his gang of brigands imagine that they shall have rain and plenty under the protection of these marauding wizards from the sea, they will gather some sense before long.

Chaka served us just as treacherously. Where is Chaka's dynasty now? Extinguished, by the very Boers who poisoned my wives and are pursuing us today. The Bechuana are fools to think that these unnatural Kiwas (white men) will return their so-called friendship with honest friendship. Together they are laughing at my misery. Let them rejoice; they need all the laughter they can have today for when their deliverers begin to dose them with the same bitter medicine they prepared for me; when the Kiwas rob them of their cattle, their children and their lands, they will weep their eyes out of their sockets and get left with only their empty throats to squeal in vain for mercy.

They will despoil them of the very lands they have rendered unsafe for us; they will entice the Bechuana youths to war and the chase, only to use them as pack oxen; yea, they will refuse to share with them the spoils of victory.

They will turn Bechuana women into beasts of burden to drag their loaded waggons to their granaries, while their own bullocks are fattening on the hillside and pining for exercise. They will use the whiplash on the bare skins of women to accelerate their paces and quicken their activities: they shall take Bechuana women to wife and, with them, breed a race of half man and half goblin, and they will deny them their legitimate lobolo. With their cries unheeded these Bechuana will waste away in helpless fury till the gnome offspring of such miscegenation rise up against their cruel sires; by that time their mucus will blend with their tears past their chins down to their heels, then shall come our turn to laugh.

Thereupon, Mzilikazi exhorts his people to move northwards to find a new home, 'far, far beyond the reach of killing spirits, where the stars have no tails and the woods are free of mischievous Barolong'. In *Mhudi* there is an inevitability about the overthrow of oppression and tyranny: prophecies, once made, are always realised. Mzilikazi's prophecy was the only one not to have been fulfilled within the pages of the book. But by the time Plaatje was writing his book it had been realised: in the South Africa of the early twentieth century the Barolong had become the oppressed; the Boers, as he saw it, the oppressors. In directing his readers to the lessons of history Plaatje's point was a straightforward one: unless tyranny and oppression were ended peaceably, it was inevitable that violence would remain the only alternative. It was not an outcome he welcomed or even wished to contemplate. His concern was simply to warn that this was what would happen. *Native Life in South Africa* had ended on exactly the same note.

Yet *Mhudi* also contains a message of hope as well as this fateful warning, and Plaatje put forward several ideas that might avert such an outcome. One is signified in the bond of friendship that develops between Ra-Thaga, a Morolong, and De Villiers, a Boer. In the relationship between the two, forged in confronting a common enemy, they discover a common humanity; as a result De Villiers is able to free himself from the otherwise characteristic Boer attitudes towards black people, whether they be Matabele or Barolong. 'But to tell you the truth', De Villiers eventually says to Ra-Thaga, 'I get on much better with you than with many of my own people.' For Plaatje, human brotherhood and individual, moral change provide a key to the resolution of South Africa's racial problems. The friendship between Ra-Thaga and De Villiers represents not only the 'literary wish fulfilment of what South African society could be if only the facts of the power struggle could conveniently be ignored', as one critic has it; in Plaatje's view, it is also the means of attaining such a society, of altering these facts of power by peaceful means, avoiding the violent but inevitable alternative. No stable, just South Africa, Plaatje said on another occasion, could ever be built 'on the rickety foundation of a race discrimination, which takes everything from a subject race without giving anything for it'.[20]

The ideal of brotherhood runs through *Mhudi* just as it sustained Plaatje himself. Indeed, the connection between the two is better understood when it is recalled that the book was written at a time when Plaatje was particularly hopeful of what might be achieved with his own Brotherhood movement: he enjoyed the support of members of the movement in England, he had promises of financial aid and support from the Canadian organisation, he enjoyed the hospitality of William Cross, president of the Southall Men's Own Brotherhood, one of his closest English friends. Having at that time just exhausted all constitutional options for bringing about change in South Africa through appealing for imperial intervention, Plaatje's commitment to the ideal of brotherhood and its material possibilities remained one source of hope. *Mhudi* can be regarded as the literary expression of this ideal, affirmation of a creed that was to be severely tested in the years to come.

Yet in *Mhudi* there is another, more fundamental source of hope and inspiration: the character of Mhudi herself. She is the central, life-giving figure of the book, a woman of great beauty, wisdom and determination. Her qualities stand in sharp contrast to the far weaker and less formed character of her husband, Ra-Thaga. Often Plaatje sets her qualities in a humorous way against the stereotypes of submissive female behaviour which he is intent on parodying and undermining. Thus his conclusion to the first lion-killing episode:

Leaving the dead lion, Ra-Thaga fetched his herbs and his buck, secured the openings to his enclosure with fresh wag-'n-bietjie bush, and followed Mhudi into the hut where he skinned his buck while sunning himself in the adoration of his devoted wife. Her trust in him, which had never waned, was this evening greater than ever. She forgot that she herself was the only female native of Kunana who had thrice faced the king of beasts, and had finally killed one with her own hand. Needless to say, Ra-Thaga was a proud husband that night.[21]

Thereafter Mhudi completely dominates the relationship with Ra-Thaga. Immediately after the lion-killing incident, Mhudi and Ra-Thaga discuss their attitudes towards Mzilikazi. Plaatje leaves no doubt whatever as to who emerges with the credit:

At times Mhudi and Ra-Thaga found fruitful subjects for animated discussion. On one topic there was a sharp difference of opinion between man and wife. Ra-Thaga at times felt inclined to believe that the land on which they lived belonged to Mzilikazi, and that Mzilikazi was justified in sending his marauding expedition against Kunana. This roused the feminine ire of Mhudi. She could not be persuaded that the crime of one chief who murdered two indunas was sufficient justification for the massacre of a whole nation.

'But', protested Ra-Thaga, 'all the tribes who quietly paid their dues in kind were left unmolested. Mzilikazi did not even insist that larger tribes should increase the value of their tax in proportion to their numbers. So long as each tribe sent something each spring in acknowledgement of its fealty, he was satisfied.'

Mhudi, growing very irritated, cried: 'I begin to think that you are sorry that you met and married me, holding such extraordinary views. You would surely have been happier with a Matabele wife. Fancy my husband justifying our exploitation by wild Khonkhobes, who fled from the poverty in their own land and came down to fatten on us!'[22]

Mhudi's judgement of people and character is far superior to that of her husband. Ra-Thaga, Plaatje says, 'benefited much from the sober judgement of his clever wife' during their stay in the wilderness; he nevertheless failed to heed her warnings about Ton-Qon, the Korana leader, who tries to kill him. As a result it is left to Mhudi to venture out and save his life, and then to nurse him back to recovery from his wounds. Later, when they encounter the Boers, Mhudi is sceptical of Ra-Thaga's uncritical enthusiasm for his new friends, and she is outraged by their cruelty; he, by contrast, turns a blind eye to the instances of cruelty he had witnessed.

Mhudi is also a woman of great courage. This is demonstrated at the beginning of the book through the lion stories and on numerous occasions thereafter, none more so than during the epic journey she undertakes from Thaba Nchu to the camp of the Barolong and their Boer allies. Her qualities, in short, dominate the book. But they are paralleled and given emphasis by the character of Umnandi, Mzilikazi's favourite wife, who is forced to flee his court as a result of the jealousies of her rivals. She, too, was a woman of great beauty, excellent at every royal duty except providing royal heirs. And like Mhudi, she is the source of strength of her husband, and it is her disappearance that coincided with the change in his fortunes. 'That daughter of Mzinyato', Mzilikazi exclaims to himself in his hour of defeat,

was the mainstay of my throne. My greatness grew with the renown of her beauty, her wisdom, and her stately reception of my guests. She vanished, and with her the magic talisman of my court. She must have possessed the wand round which the pomp of Inzwinyani was twined, for the rise of my misfortune synchronised with her disappearance.[23]

When Umnandi is reunited with her husband at the end of the book, the symbolism is clear: the future will see the rebirth of a nation beyond the reach of Boer and Barolong, and escape from what South Africa would become.

In the qualities displayed by these two women Plaatje seems to be offering a source of hope and inspiration for a South Africa of the future. The character of Mhudi was a composite, created in his imagination from a variety of people, ideas and associations. Part of this was undoubtedly the historical person. Although there is nothing in the book to indicate that Mhudi was a 'real' historical figure, in his account of his own ancestry Plaatje wrote: 'My mother is a direct descendant of a grandson of Tau from the house of his youngest and dearest wife, Mhudi.' Mhudi must have been, if he was right about this, his great-great-grandmother.

Family tradition thus provided Plaatje with a knowledge of Mhudi's existence; perhaps he also heard, from his mother and other relatives, more about her life and her character. At the same time he seems to invest her with qualities and characteristics which flow from his experiences and perceptions of the women in his own life. She can be seen as a tribute to his own wife Elizabeth, 'without whose loyal cooperation', so he acknowledged, his previous book, *Native Life in South Africa*, would not have been written; and to his daughter Olive, 'one of the many youthful victims of a settled system' to whom he dedicated *Mhudi*, who died, aged thirteen, having accomplished 'her life work' during the influenza epidemic of 1918.

But there can be little doubt that he also conceived of Mhudi as a kind of literary testimony to the women who gave him so much support and encouragement when the book was being written in London in 1920 – Georgiana Solomon, the Colensos, Betty Molteno, Jane Cobden Unwin, Alice Werner. From these women Plaatje had derived a keen insight into the parallels between racial and sexual discrimination. Through their actions and beliefs they strengthened his conviction that women, more than men, possessed the qualities from which a more just and humane society could emerge. He had once said as much, indeed, in a letter written to Mrs Lennox Murray, Betty Molteno's niece, when congratulating her upon the birth of her baby: 'The mothers of a past generation', he said, 'bequeathed to us a happy and beautiful subcontinent – the healthiest end of the Dark Continent: and it is the work of the mothers of tomorrow to save South Africa from degeneration if their dear ones are to live and enjoy the blessed privileges that once were ours.' *Mhudi*, in large measure, was the literary expression of this belief.[24]

Plaatje's humorous playing around with male–female stereotypes in *Mhudi* followed from this same awareness of male dominance in the society in which he lived. Much of this is very tongue-in-cheek, and on occasions he simply reverses the normal roles, subverting and parodying romantic convention. When the Boers first arrive in the Barolong camp it is the men who are the first to flee, the women who are the more curious to venture forth and meet them. Elsewhere, notions of submissive female behaviour are contrasted ironically with Mhudi's own actions, her statement 'Of course young women are timid and not as bold as men', for example, coming immediately after the account of her own bravery. Or later, when Mhudi first meets her long-lost cousin, Baile:

Baile (between sobs): 'And you escaped wholly unscathed?'
Mhudi (also sobbing): 'Yes, thanks to my husband.'[25]

– the point being, rather, that it had been thanks to *her* that Ra-Thaga was still alive, not vice versa. Plaatje took great delight, in other words, in exploiting the humour implicit in contrasting reality and stereotype, as well as making a more serious point about the potential role that women could play in South Africa's future. Just as he felt that individual, moral change was the key to the solution of South Africa's problems, so he believed women possessed particular qualities, transcending barriers of race, that gave them a special role and responsibility in bringing a more just society into existence. *Mhudi* stands as an eloquent, often very amusing testimony to this conviction.

So *Mhudi* – the book – was many things: the literary creation of a man of complex sensibilities, who found in writing it not just an escape from the day-to-day struggles that preoccupied him at the time he wrote it in 1920, but also the opportunity to give imaginative expression to many of his underlying values and beliefs. Just as a knowledge of Plaatje's life adds to an understanding of the book, so the book sheds light upon what it was that sustained him in a lifetime of endeavour. In this sense *Mhudi*'s value is that it brings all this together, and at a level of detachment from reality which provides a glimpse into a sensibility so often obscured by the many different guises Plaatje had to adopt in circumstances over which, as he often complained, he could exercise little control.

In *Mhudi* it is different. He is in control of both his characters and their circumstances, released from the constraints imposed upon his own activities and ambitions. Here there is scope for free expression of his imagination, his fascination with the traditions of his people, his exploration of the literary and cultural possibilities of mixing Tswana and English traditions, his admiration for the qualities he believed women to possess, his vision of the consequences of continued injustice in South Africa. Above all, there is an optimistic faith that things could yet come right. All this is conveyed in *Mhudi* in a manner not found elsewhere in his writings. The result is both a revealing personal testimony and a pioneering, eminently readable story which anticipates in many of its themes the preoccupations of later generations of writers from the African continent.

As to its more formal, literary qualities, several other things stand out. There is a breadth of vision which more than justifies Plaatje's description of *Mhudi* as 'an epic of native life', and a sense of grandeur which is conveyed in some of the great set-piece speeches – especially those of the tragic figure of Mzilikazi, who, from being the personification of cruelty and evil, ends up as a symbol of redemption and rebirth. Many of the descriptive passages, too, are finely drawn: the battle scenes, for example, and his descriptions of landscapes and natural phenomena, the product of a man who knew and loved the countryside, who felt a closeness to nature, who spiritually was far more at home here than in the towns and cities where he lived the greater part of his life.

❧

Mhudi's complexities may have largely eluded reviewers when it was published in September 1930, but it was certainly not ignored. The first review, a very favourable one, was in the new medium of radio, broadcast from the African Broadcasting Company's studios in Johannesburg just a few days after publication. Others soon followed in the daily press. The *Rand Daily Mail* thought *Mhudi* was 'a fascinating mixture' of fiction, history and anthropology, though some passages 'seem to betray Mr Plaatje's possibly too-great admiration for the stilted English of the early nineteenth century'. The East London *Daily Dispatch* did not care for Plaatje's handling of the relationship between De Villiers and Ra-Thaga ('no one who knows Boer character will take in the story of an intimate relationship between a young Boer and a native which is enlarged upon in the latter part of the tale') but thought that on the whole the book was 'a welcome contribution to South African literature, and is very pleasant reading'. Moreover, it added, 'the style is wonderfully good for a native'.[26]

Other people pointed to its significance as the first novel in English written by a black South African. Sir David Harris considered *Mhudi* to be 'as fascinating as it is enthralling' and 'a book of exceptional merit', and that anybody capable of such an achievement 'is capable of occupying high office in the Union'. Another old friend, Vere Stent, still writing for the *Pretoria News* (though no longer its editor), struck a similar note: 'If Mr Plaatje were a French subject', he wrote, 'he would be acclaimed in the *Academie*, and made a member of it. But he is merely a subject of South Africa, and so we refuse him the right to walk upon the pavements, to ride in a tram-car, or to own a single acre of ground in his own country.'[27]

When the reviews and notices concerned themselves with *Mhudi* itself, opinions were mostly favourable, if not very penetrating. 'M.S.S.' in the *South African Outlook* advised that 'all who are in search of a thrilling and well-written book should make a point of reading this work'. The *Diamond Fields Advertiser* approved too. Its reviewer, 'L.C.', thought Plaatje had accomplished his stated objective of 'interpreting one phase of the back of the Native mind' to Europeans 'with outstanding success', and had written 'a really readable narrative into the bargain which informs us of the conditions of life natives lived a century ago'. *Mhudi* was, moreover, 'a good honest tale told straightforwardly and without due artifice', and it contained 'some stirring episodes which would have appealed strongly to Rider Haggard'. If any criticism was to be made, it was of the dialogue, which 'occasionally reads a little stiltedly', a point made by several other reviewers. All in all, thought the *Advertiser*, *Mhudi* 'is a South African book for South Africans and it may cordially be commended to young readers whose parents, however, will probably refuse to hand *Mhudi* over till they have finished it themselves'.[28]

Few reviewers detected much of a political message. An editorial in *Imvo Zabantsundu*, now edited by Alexander Jabavu, one of Tengo Jabavu's sons, came closest. He complimented Plaatje on the 'virile style so familiar in his political polemics' but was particularly struck by the chapter entitled 'With the Boers at Moroka's Hoek': this, he thought, 'constitutes the political core of this novel because it demonstrates the root causes of the race problem in South Africa, showing just when the roads of racial amity part, and provoking hard thinking over the discovery of the necessary panacea for future race adjustments'.[29]

Mhudi was not a great deal noted in literary circles in South Africa, perhaps because it just fell outside any recognised literary tradition. A characteristic exception, though, was Stephen Black, editor of *The Sjambok*. He thought Plaatje was 'a highly interesting writer', had 'a marked sense of literary style' and 'knows English as perhaps no white man has ever known a Bantu language'. But he was also quite critical. Shortly after *Mhudi* was published, Plaatje was in Johannesburg and went along to see him – probably the same occasion they discussed his Shakespeare translations. In the office that day was a young Zulu writer by the name of H.I.E. Dhlomo, whose brother R.R.R. Dhlomo was now a regular and highly promising short-story writer for *The Sjambok*. 'I remember as if it were but yesterday,' H.I.E. was to recall, over fifteen years later, 'when that remarkable and talented man, Sol T. Plaatje (an admirer of Stephen Black), called at the *Sjambok* offices to get Black's opinion on his (Plaatje's) novel, *Mhudi*. Black told Plaatje quite frankly that one of his faults was to make all his characters speak in high-sounding language and advised the grand old man to read some of the sketches of Dhlomo already published. Here, although the characters spoke in English, their language was natural.'[30]

Black was another, in other words, who treated *Mhudi* as a realistic novel in the predominant Western literary tradition and judged its characters and their dialogue accordingly. In a letter to W.C. Scully, author of *Daniel Venanda* (the book which Black advised Plaatje to translate into Setswana), Black acknowledged that he was reading *Mhudi* 'with great interest and a good deal of pleasure' and that he thought there was 'a charming authority in this book'; but he added, as though such praise was too excessive, 'Of course it is crude.' Stephen Black, no lover of Shakespeare as we have seen, disliked Plaatje's Shakespeare-like monologues and dialogues and had no sympathy for the kind of cultural cross-fertilisation which is the essence of both *Mhudi* and the Shakespeare translations. His preference, rather, was for the realistic short stories of contemporary African life of the kind that R.R.R. Dhlomo was busy writing for him.[31]

Stephen Black voiced further criticism in the columns of 'The telephone conversations of Jeremiah', a regular feature that appeared in *The Sjambok*, which took *Mhudi* as its subject in its issue of 31 October 1930. The point he sought to make, in the convoluted style of the 'Conversations', was that Plaatje was inauthentic, too concerned with mimicking English literary styles. Plaatje had 'forgotten Bechuanaland sometimes', Jeremiah says, 'and remembered only the kingdoms of Shakespeare, and those two people, Mhudi and Ra-Thaga, speak like, like … literature'. *Mhudi*, Jeremiah explains, 'is composed of two parts … Sol Plaatje, the Bechuana writer, and all the white authors whom he has been reading'. In future, Jeremiah concluded, Plaatje should concentrate upon writing a novel that was about black life alone, and not involve whites. 'Stick to your own people' was his advice, 'and give up apeing the white man'.[32]

He was not alone in these views. When the *Times Literary Supplement* got around to reviewing *Mhudi* several years later, the view it expressed was that while the book was 'definitely memorable – a torch for some other to carry on', its author would have been better advised to steer away from 'Europeanism'. 'One wonders', said the anonymous *TLS* reviewer, 'what secret fountain of African art might not have been unsealed if, in interpreting his people, a writer of Plaatje's insight had thought and written "like a Native". That might well have been the first authentic utterance out of the aeons of African silence.' It was pretty much what Alice Werner told him after reading his manuscript in 1920.

Clement Doke was more concerned about the language issue. While he acknowledged (in a review in *Bantu Studies*) that 'Mr Plaatje has done a good service in writing this', he added that it was 'a great pity that for Bantu publications the demand is at present so small among the Bantu themselves that books such as this have to be written in English. *Mhudi* written in Chwana would have been a still greater contribution, and Chwana sadly needs such additions to its present meagre literature.' With this comment about the state of Tswana literature Plaatje would have been in accord. Indeed, Doke need have read no further for evidence of this than the preface to *Mhudi*, where Plaatje says he hoped 'with the readers' money to collect and print (for Bantu schools) Sechuana folk-tales which, with the spread of European ideas, are fast being forgotten, and thereby, to arrest this process by cultivating a love for art and literature in the vernacular'.[33]

But with the earlier part of Doke's remarks – that *Mhudi* would have been 'a still greater contribution' had it been written in Setswana – Plaatje would have been distinctly uneasy, for it carried with it the implication, explicit in what Stephen Black and the *Times Literary Supplement* said too, that Africans should concentrate exclusively on interpreting their own people and culture. This was a view Plaatje could never share. He contributed more to literature in Setswana than anybody, but he could not accept that he, and others like him, should be denied the right to explore to the full the cultural possibilities of English (or any other language) if they so pleased. Quite apart from the unacceptable political connotations bound up in this, the whole basis to his literary endeavours, in English or Setswana, was an insistence upon his right to interpret one culture to the other as he wished. It was the inevitable consequence of such a position that he was open to criticism on two fronts: and a sad paradox that it tended to be Africans who insisted upon the primacy of English, while whites sang the praises of Setswana and the other vernacular languages.

This would have its echoes, interestingly enough, in a tendency of later critics to overplay his reliance upon an unmediated (and therefore more 'pure') oral tradition in the telling of his tale – and to underplay his own agency in its creative reworking. Gray and Couzens, for example, thought that *Mhudi*, 'instead of being a novel written by an objective Victorian-Edwardian type of novelist is in fact a narrative told to the writer', and that 'we are dealing not with the abstract calculation of the Western historical novel, but with a document of living oral history'. Certainly, oral traditions were a vital source for Plaatje, but it was not a question of either/or. He shaped these traditions in a creative manner and to his own ends, taking account of the demands of his narrative and the constraints of the genre he had chosen to work in. Understanding these interactions is key to understanding what he was up to.[34]

Whatever the reactions *Mhudi* elicited, Plaatje was just pleased to see it published after so long a delay. He ordered 250 copies from Lovedale to sell or give away, a figure that would rise to 500, a quarter of the book's print run. A lot of copies went to old friends and colleagues, an appropriate way of repaying past debts of help or hospitality. Ernst Westphal, the missionary at Pniel, had died in 1922, but his widow Marie was still alive and well, and Plaatje sent her a copy for Christmas 1930, inscribed 'with the author's filial compliments and affectionate wishes for a blessed Christmas and a happy New Year'. Sir Ernest Oppenheimer received his copy 'with the author's compliments', as did Mr Harold Morris, Kimberley's chief electrical engineer, who had earned Plaatje's appreciation by persuading the City Council to instal street lighting in No. 2 Location. Likewise Selwyn Stokes, an attorney, whose copy of *Mhudi* came with an additional reminder of 'pleasant memories of old Barkly'. To other people he sent out copies of *Mhudi* in the hope that they might reciprocate. 'I should be glad to receive in exchange', he wrote to W.E.B. Du Bois, after sending him a copy of *Mhudi*, 'any Negro book – particularly *Darkwater* or *The Quest of the Silver Fleece*, as some sinners have relieved me of those two. I still treasure The Soul, The Gift of Black Folk etc.'[35]

This ploy didn't always work. He sent a copy of *Mhudi* to Professor Victor Murray, a well-known educationist at Selly Oak College in Birmingham, England, and author of a recent study on education in Africa, but he was reluctant to send his own book in return (since it was more expensive) and so mailed him a different one instead. 'Poor old Sol', he wrote afterwards, 'was very peeved, but what could he do? He wrote back very bad tempered but as he was 6d up on the transaction I doubt if he could convince anybody that he has a case against me!' It was not the most sympathetic of responses: Plaatje simply did not have the money to build up his library. Sending copies of *Mhudi* to people who had written books themselves, in the hope that they would reciprocate, seemed, in the circumstances, a good way of keeping up with subjects in which he had an interest.[36]

He was also keen that *Mhudi* should reach potential readers in England and the United States and not just South Africa, and so wrote to both Dr Du Bois and Dr Robert Moton to see what might be done. 'Can we not get a publisher over there to issue a SECOND edition?' he asked Moton. 'Any good publisher should successfully exploit the English and North American market with an overseas edition – 2nd print. Lovedale not being commercial have no agencies abroad and the field here is so limited that I am afraid by the end of the year when this edition is exhausted, every South African reader will have a copy of *Mhudi*.'[37]

The response was not encouraging: from Du Bois there is no record of a reply at all, and G. Lake Innes, Moton's assistant, who replied to the letter in Moton's absence, held out little hope. While Innes himself had enjoyed reading *Mhudi* (he found it 'delightful and informing', and was 'impressed with the fidelity of the narrative and particularly the sympathetic reflection of the heart and mind of the native people'), he was doubtful that *Mhudi* 'would find the circulation in America all that you would hope to achieve for it. It is true that Negro literature is in vogue at the present time, but not of the type which your book represents. I do not think any publisher would volunteer to issue it, but I am not sure that any of the Foundations would sponsor it. I think, however, that Dr Moton would be glad to feel them out and see what could be done.' Nothing further came of this, however, and it would be forty years before an American edition was eventually published.[38]

Mhudi was Plaatje's only English-language novel to have been published. According to Isaiah Bud-M'belle, in an obituary notice written immediately after Plaatje's death, he had also written another novel in English with the intriguing title of 'Monkey voodoo', which was 'as yet unpublished'. Bud-M'belle gave no further indication, here or elsewhere, as to what the book was about, and it seemed to have been lost. But in 1977 an incomplete seventy-page manuscript, partly written in Plaatje's hand, partly typed on his typewriter, came to light in the offices of the Bophuthatswana Education Department in Mmabatho; it had been lent to them by Morara Molema, husband of Plaatje's daughter Violet. It was located by researchers from the University of South Africa, who, fortunately, were able to make a photocopy of what they found before it once again disappeared from view.

Overall, the manuscript has the appearance of a rough, early draft, and does not have a definitive title. But it is clear that Plaatje played around with several alternatives. Some fifty pages into the manuscript he suggested 'With other people's wives: a romantic epic of the Baca, a South East African tribe', with 'A forty year's romance on the life of the Ama-Baca, a South East African tribe' as an alternative subtitle. A few pages further on he had 'The other fellows' wives' and 'Other people's wives' as possible titles, with 'an epic covering two generations in the history of the Baca, a South East African tribe' as his preferred subtitle. There is no mention here of the term 'Monkey voodoo', nor is it offered as a possible title anywhere else in the part of the manuscript that has survived. But it may well be that this was a thought Plaatje had later on, and there is some evidence to suggest, as we shall see, that 'With other people's wives' and 'Monkey voodoo' were most likely one and the same thing.[39]

But his source of inspiration is clear. His manuscript is concerned with the dramatic history and migrations of the Bhaca people of the eastern Cape. Historically, they originated in an area that was to become the colony of Natal. Most accounts and traditions agree that in the early nineteenth century, under the leadership of their great chief Madikane, the Bhaca fled from the Zulu king Shaka, and then travelled southwards, ultimately settling in the Mount Frere district of the eastern Cape. Madikane himself is believed to have been killed in battle with the Thembu some time between 1830 and 1834. He was succeeded by his elder son Ncapayi, another great warrior, who fought a further series of battles and acquired for his army a reputation which – in the view of the British naval captain and missionary, A.F. Gardiner, who visited Ncapayi's court in 1835 – would rival that of Shaka himself, were their population more numerous. Thereafter the Bhaca entered into a short-lived alliance with the Mpondo against the Thembu, and clashed with a Boer commando sent down from Natal, before Ncapayi himself was finally killed in battle in the mid-1840s during an attack upon the Mpondo chief Faku. Then, after a period of regency under Diko, Makhaula assumed the regency, and his people were incorporated into the Cape Colony, inhabiting the Mount Frere district where their descendants live to this day.[40]

Their history was a dramatic and eventful one, and Plaatje found it fascinating. He had some very interesting remarks to make about the reasons for this in a 'preface', although this does not actually appear at the beginning of the manuscript:

Why did I do it?

Outside the Baca tribe my limited reading has not disclosed another people whose history within living memory furnished miracles that approximate to Moses at the Red Sea and the destruction of Sennacherib's army. The more I investigated their history the prouder I felt that this South Africa of ours can show a tribe whose history includes epical topics paralleling those found in the annals of the ancient Israelites and I have often wondered why, apart from occasional sketches by Mr W.C. Scully, epical incidents like those of the Baca escaped the notice of all able writers.

So while many stories are written to provide readers with a thrill or a

shock and incidents are recorded to fill a gap in some narratives, this book
is the expression of pride – race pride – in the fact that South Africa ...[41]

Despite being tantalisingly incomplete, Plaatje's remarks are a revealing
indication of what was in his mind when he set out to explore the history of
the Bhaca. He recognised the quality of an epic in what he had found and, with
his knowledge of the Bible, could not fail to be struck by the parallels between
the historical experience of the Bhaca and the biblical story of the exodus of
Moses and the children of Israel from the land of Egypt. He had a fascination
in any case with the period of the *mfecane* in South African history, the forced
migrations of the 1820s and 1830s which did so much to create the identities of
the different African peoples of the subcontinent. For this was the heroic age of
African history: a time that saw great leaders arise and brave exploits performed,
when nations could be created or destroyed; a time of independence too, an era
before the white man began to assert his control over the lives of those who lived
in the interior of southern Africa. Plaatje was not alone in looking back upon
these years, for all their violence and turbulence, as a kind of golden age. In
literary terms he viewed them much as Shakespeare recalled and recreated the
histories of the medieval kings of England from the perspective of his day. Both
looked back to a heroic past for inspiration. For a man who knew Shakespeare so
well, it would be surprising if he was not struck by the comparison.

So Plaatje perceived in the history of the Bhaca material for the construction
of an epic. His stated intention was not 'to provide readers with a thrill or a
shock', or simply to fill in some gaps in an interesting historical episode, but to
demonstrate that in South Africa's neglected past there lay traditions that could
provide a source of 'race pride' for the African people; to suggest that they need
look no further than their own past for that sense of identity and pride which
South Africa's subsequent history had done so much to undermine.

Perhaps the single most important phrase that appears in this 'preface' was
the term 'within living memory'. When Plaatje spoke of investigating Bhaca
history, he must have been doing so at first hand, for at the time his manuscript
was written (during the course of 1931, judging from the evidence of a letter
and several newspaper clippings interleaved in the pages of his notebook) there
were no comprehensive written sources available upon which his account could
have been based. W.C. Scully's writings on the Bhaca – in *The State* in 1909, and
his *Further Reminiscences of a South African Pioneer*, published in 1913 – may
have provided Plaatje with some impetus to investigate the subject further, but
what Scully has to say bears little resemblance to Plaatje's own account; Bryant's
Olden Times in Natal and Zululand and J.H. Soga's *The South-Eastern Bantu*,

both of which Plaatje would have been familiar with, add little more. None of these accounts contain anything like the level of detail that Plaatje conjures up in his telling of the tale.[42]

Plaatje's manuscript was most likely the product, rather, of his own first-hand investigations into Bhaca tradition, reworked in dramatic form: similar in this sense to *Mhudi*, but closer in both form and content to oral tradition. From what survives of 'With other people's wives' it is clear that he was less concerned with individual characterisation than in *Mhudi*. Individual characters there certainly are, particularly Madikane and Ncapayi, but they are subordinate in importance to the epic story of the Bhaca as a whole; enough of 'With other people's wives' has survived to show that it is their history that is the real hero. But there are some similarities with *Mhudi*. There is the same technique of shifting perspective, alternating between the court of Shaka and that of the Bhaca. As in *Mhudi*, prophecies play a vital part in structuring the story and carrying it along. At the beginning of 'With other people's wives' an old Bhaca woman, on her deathbed, prophesies the departure of the Bhaca from the land of Shaka, and exhorts them to be prepared for the tribulations that lie ahead: 'Great are the battles that you will fight with your son, Ncapayi,' she says to Madikane, and she warns them to be ready to take in the women and children of other tribes whom they defeat in battle.

As in *Mhudi*, much of what follows sees the working out of these prophecies. Madikane and his people decide they can no longer endure the oppressive rule of Shaka; they plan secretly for their escape, and flee southwards. At the Tugela River they are saved from Shaka's pursuing army by a miracle. As the Zulu prepare to cross the river after them, a wall of water suddenly appears, blocking their route. They try to cross:

The Bacas watched and the Zulus surged. Swarms of Zulus lined the water's edge with shields poised and spears aloft. In obedience to the orders of the commanders to swim across they plunged side by side in a straight line into the angry waters. This was the signal for a second line and third to follow suit in like formation – the fourth line came to the water's edge and halted. These did not plunge in, for in five minutes the billows, having completely disorganised the ranks of the surviving pursuers, heaved and tossed with them. Already some Zulus were disappearing below the waves [and] myriad heads floated past, like balls with the bodies drowning some fathoms below the surface of the water, while the surface was tossing with myriad heads and bodies of dead or drowning Zulus, all rushing with the angry stream towards the Indian Ocean with a thundering sound.[43]

So the Bhaca are saved by the miracle of the Tugela River, 'an episode', Plaatje says, that 'in every respect resembled the flight of the Israelites at the Red Sea'. Then they press on southwards, celebrating their bloodless victory, composing praise songs to commemorate the event. In Shaka's court, in contrast, the loss of so many of his bravest warriors to the upstart Bhaca causes great consternation, for their escape is bound to have wider consequences given the number of other tribes under Shaka's dominion: 'the Baca became an abiding Zulu menace long after their exodus', Plaatje writes, 'for whoever mentioned them his tongue was forfeit because it mentioned a taboo, and whoever denied knowledge of their existence likewise forfeited his tongue because it told untruths'.[44]

Yet for the Bhaca their difficulties are only just beginning. Apart from the ever-present danger of Shaka dispatching a further expedition after them, as they travel southwards they encounter opposition from other people along their route. Among these are the Ama-Hola and Ama-Lala, but they avoid defeat at their hands because the Ama-Hola and Ama-Lala, intending to attack Madikane and his people, mistake each other for the intruders, and attack and destroy themselves. The Bhaca are left instead with their enemies' womenfolk and, in fulfilment of the prophecy, take the young women as wives for their warriors; hence it is 'with other people's wives' that the Bhaca build up their strength as a nation. They move on to find a new place of settlement near the Mzimvubu River, high in the mountains, but soon have to fight off further attacks from the people whose land they now occupy. Their survival is due to the ingenuity of their chief, Madikane:

> The consistent luck of Madikane's armies had acquired for their King the fame of being a great witchdoctor. Madikane, who knew that he was no doctor, but profiting by this reputation which made his neighbours fear him, had no intention of disillusioning them. His fertile brain was constantly devising methods of keeping the illusion alive. One day the [opposing] army, mouths watering for the possession of the numerous Baca herds, prepared to attack them and raid the cattle.
>
> Getting news of the impending attack, Madikane at once mobilised the Baca. They travelled across the mountains with outspread flanks and marching determinedly, and arriving in due time, forced the enemy's hand before his plans had matured. The consternation can be imagined when a people [who] had their whole training for a surprise attack on foreign [soil] suddenly finding themselves compelled to give a defensive battle on their own home and within view of their women and children amidst their own cattle posts.[45]

In the battle that follows Madikane once again displays his resourcefulness when he turns to his advantage the ominous appearance of a troop of monkeys, thereby defying the 'monkey voodoo':

> The evening before the delivery of the fatal blow a troop of monkeys made themselves very conspicuous on the mountain side below which position Madikane's army was encamped.
>
> Now among Bantu races these mischievous animals are regarded as walking voodoos and the proudest witchdoctor is he who can cleanse his path of any omen of evil and turn it to his enemy's detriment.
>
> The monkeys scampered and kept shouting at his men. So Madikane quickly thought of a plan. The Baca were really feeling disheartened as according to custom they knew that the die was cast against their enterprise and they were calmly awaiting the order to retreat and give up a hopeless battle. They had no faith that they could change the edicts of fate ... But Madikane, like a resourceful wizard, quickly thought of a plan without the aid of his [witchdoctors].[46]

The page containing the details of Madikane's scheme is missing, but as the narrative continues it is clear that it achieved the desired outcome:

> The running battle was swift and decisive, commencing with the race of the baboons by sunrise. The afternoon had [seen] Madikane ... collect a rich booty and next day began the march back to the banks of the Kinra with hundreds of women and their children too.[47]

Once again Madikane is able to build up the strength of his nation 'with other people's wives'. Ultimately he meets his death in battle with the Thembu. And just as Madikane had himself defied the 'monkey voodoo' in their earlier battle, so now his son Ncapayi, the new chief of the Bhaca, turned to his advantage the awesome effects of the total eclipse of the sun, which took place during the fighting between the two armies:

> 'They have killed Madikane!' yelled a leather-lunged Tembu, regardless of the orders of his army leader. 'They have killed Madikane and his spirit has stolen our sun. Madikane alive was always a dangerous being but Madikane dead – Hewu, he has blackened the sun.' This cry struck terror into the hearts of the bravest Tembu warriors. They could fight the Baca alive but an angry spirit that controlled the skies was surely too much.[48]

The tide of battle was turned. Ncapayi's warriors, though they were 'also wondering what was the matter with the sky', took full advantage of the fear struck into the Thembu army by the eclipse of the sun, and pressed home their advantage. But at this point, the moment that saw both the death of the great Chief Madikane and the decisive victory of his army over his foes, Plaatje's manuscript comes to an abrupt end, having covered only one generation of the two that he seems to have envisaged.

✦

It is impossible to reach any conclusive assessment of 'With other people's wives': the second half of it has disappeared, leaves are missing from the notebook in which it is written, sections of it are impossible to decipher, and virtually the whole of it is in an early draft. Nor is there any way of knowing whether Plaatje had completed the remaining part of the manuscript, or whether the death of Madikane was simply as far as he got. While his knowledge of the Bible and Shakespeare undoubtedly shaped his view of the epic nature of the story of the Bhaca people, there are no clues as to how or when he was able to collect the information upon which 'With other people's wives' is based. Perhaps he had been to the Mount Frere district on one or more of his visits to the eastern Cape in the 1920s and early 1930s and spoke to old people living there, just as Scully had done years before when he was magistrate for the district. Perhaps he heard about their story from the Basotho chief Makhaula Lerotholi, named after Makhaula, a descendant, so Plaatje wrote, 'of the great chief Madikane who, in the second decade of the last century, led the Baca out of Zululand, and inflicted on King Tshaka two of the most severe reverses ever suffered by that great military organizer'. Or perhaps his interest and curiosity had been aroused by Isaiah Bud-M'belle or Elizabeth, descendants of a Hlubi clan whose history was closely associated with that of the Bhaca.[49]

But whatever the sources of this fascination with the history of the Bhaca, even the incomplete, fragmentary manuscript that has survived provides an insight into the direction his future literary plans might have taken. It was significant, for one thing, that these were not confined to exploring the traditions of the Tswana people alone: there was a far wider body of historical tradition he was keen to investigate and to write about. It was a great pity that H.I.E. Dhlomo never elaborated upon the 'many literary plans' that Plaatje told him about during the several hours' conversation they had on the last occasion they met. Perhaps then he might have clarified, among other things, whether he had another manuscript entitled 'Chicago in the Bush' – which Modiri Molema

549

thought was the case – or whether this was just another title he considered for his epic tale of the Bhaca.[50]

EIGHTEEN

So much still to do

During the late 1920s and early 1930s Plaatje's most urgent preoccupation was with his literary concerns: working upon the Shakespeare translations, his collection of Tswana folktales, the new edition of the *Sechuana Proverbs*, collecting new words and meanings for his dictionary, writing – and, before that, researching – his epic on the history of the Bhaca; arguing his case over Tswana orthography; and, most time-consuming of all, seeking to raise the funds to print and publish all this work, and dealing with the various printers and publishers involved.

At times it was a lonely, dispiriting struggle. One letter he wrote to Robert Moton, in July 1931, reveals the depth of frustration he sometimes felt. 'There is much data that wants writing in the line of old Native research,' he told him, 'but valuable data lies unprinted, of immense historic and anthropological value; I have no financial aid to visit such localities and the old people are fast dying out and being buried with the information which is thus being lost to posterity.' All he needed was a couple of hundred pounds to bring his 'Sechuana Dictionary and a volume of Native fables and Traditional poems to the printing press', but he didn't have it. By contrast, he said, whites found no difficulty in securing the funds 'for half-cooked second-hand information (often distorted) about Natives', exemplified in his view by Bryant's *Olden Times in Zululand and Natal*, which had just been published with the help of grants from both the South African government and the Carnegie Trust.[1]

But there was increasing public recognition, too. In May 1931 *Imvo* commended him for being among those leaders who found 'the time and inclination for striving to attain achievement in literature notwithstanding their political activity and anxiety to rescue their people from the state of oppression that must obsess them', and thought that 'the Bantu race of the future, long after his political efforts have been forgotten, will place him in a position of high esteem as a pioneer of literature'. A few months earlier H.I.E. Dhlomo, an aspiring writer himself, reviewing the events of the previous year for *Umteteli wa Bantu*, pointed likewise to his achievements: 'Mr Plaatje', he said, 'is one of the new artists who deserve more support and sympathy for the priceless work they are doing for the nation'. In these circles, at least, Plaatje had acquired an honoured reputation as a writer. No nation with any claim to self-esteem, it was widely felt, could do without a literature of its own.[2]

Being a 'pioneer in literature' was never a total preoccupation. An important new theme was his involvement in the affairs of the Bechuanaland Protectorate, especially through his association with Tshekedi Khama, the Bamangwato chief regent. Partly this stemmed from a desire to seek new networks of support, given that so many of his activities now revolved around the Tswana language. In the Batswana of the Protectorate he saw his best prospect of derailing moves towards orthographic unification, and he enlisted Tshekedi's help, regarding the young chief regent as not only the Bamangwato's saviour but a potential source of support for his own projects, enabling him to tap into the strength and resources of a wider Tswana diaspora. In return he could offer favourable coverage of the Bamangwato in his journalism, advice on how to counter the efforts of Colonel Rey to undermine his authority, and support in the dynastic rivalries in which he was also embroiled. For Plaatje it must have brought back memories of his own experiences, twenty years earlier, when the Barolong battled with the colonial authorities of the day.

The possibilities were highlighted during a visit to Serowe in August 1931. This coincided with the official tour of Sir Herbert Stanley, the newly appointed high commissioner, which he wished to report upon. He also met up with Tshekedi Khama, travelled throughout the 'huge area' of the 'Mangwato Reserve', and immersed himself in local politics. 'I am indeed happy to have seen you at home and enjoyed your hospitality', he wrote afterwards, expressing his appreciation at being accommodated by the Sebina family: Peter Sebina was 'a man after my own heart', he said, and his company 'an education'. As a quid pro quo for Tshekedi's hospitality and help with his travelling expenses, Plaatje drafted a detailed defence of his position, drawing attention to the enlightened and democratic manner in which he ruled and denouncing 'the revolutionary inclinations against tribal authority' displayed by a small number of malcontents. Their idea then was to secure some publicity in the press. Rather than send a letter in his own name, Plaatje suggested that it would be much better coming from 'Peter Sebina or someone else', thereby pre-empting any charges of outside interference. A long letter from 'Peter M. Sebina' duly appeared in the Johannesburg *Star* on 8 October 1931, an important contribution to the public debate about the future of the Bechuanaland Protectorate. Just as in his campaign over orthography, he knew when it was better to operate behind the scenes – and how to do it.[3]

His visit to Serowe came with the customary social engagements. One Saturday evening he met up with a young LMS missionary, Alexander Sandilands, already an accomplished Setswana linguist. Over forty years later

Sandilands remembered Plaatje as a 'shortish stocky figure', and recalled their 'interesting talk' about orthographic matters. They were of a mind over the unrealistic proposals of the Central Orthography Committee, Sandilands's own view, expressed at the time, being that these white experts ('how one gets sick of that word') 'are rather inclined to think that all missionaries are obscurantist and stupid and prejudiced'. The next morning Plaatje took his sermon in the mission church in Serowe, the largest in the Protectorate.[4]

South Africa nevertheless remained his main focus. He had to earn a living, and so he continued to write, albeit not as frequently as before, for the *Diamond Fields Advertiser*, *Umteteli wa Bantu* and other newspapers on the issues of the day. He became increasing involved in the affairs of the Cape Native Voters' Association; he campaigned with growing impatience in the acrimonious orthographic debate; he travelled around with his bioscope apparatus, putting on shows in Kimberley and beyond; he continued to promote the cause of the International Order of True Templars, which now provided, thanks to his old friend J.W. Mushet, an important source of income.

In December 1930 there was an unexpected return to the national political stage. The government reconvened the Native Conference in Pretoria (for the first time since 1926), and Plaatje was one of those invited to attend. He didn't have as much to say as before. Perhaps it was that these days he saw his literary work as his priority; or that he just thought it was time for younger spokesmen to come to the fore. Z.K. Matthews, at this time headmaster of Adams College in Natal, recalled how impressed Plaatje had been by younger leaders like Richard Godlo, of East London, with whom he had worked closely in the Cape Native Voters' Association. Now Godlo was attending the Native Conference for the first time, he was happy to let him take the initiative. Unlike other leaders, Matthews thought, Plaatje positively welcomed the emergence of a new generation of leaders ready, when the time came, to take their place.[5]

Godlo certainly made an impressive debut during the debate over the proposed Native Service Contract Bill, a measure designed to give white farmers almost total control over their black labour force, and to prevent them and their families from departing for the towns. 'The service contracts, the contracting by parents for their minor children, the penalty of whipping all showed', he said, 'that the measure aimed at the introduction of slave conditions', and it was he who moved the conference's resolution on the subject, condemning the proposed legislation in the strongest terms. He recommended that the government look instead at the root causes of the problem, many of them in his view a consequence of the Natives' Land Act of 1913.[6]

Plaatje's sole contribution to this debate was to ask why the controversial 'whipping clause' (designed to help enforce the legislation) was to apply only to Africans living in the Transvaal and Natal, and not to those in the other two provinces. 'Are not the Natives of the Cape and Orange Free State cheeky?' he enquired, his words reproduced verbatim in the official record. Plaatje's wit now had a more biting, sarcastic tone, and people sensed, so Z.K. Matthews wrote, 'a note of despondency and a tone of harshness in his conversation about the trend of events in South Africa'. Vere Stent, too, remembered the time Plaatje was 'once rebuked by one of the Government nominees for ingratitude'. '"You should remember", said this maudlin person, "all the blessings the white man has bestowed upon you." "I do," said Plaatje, "always I do, especially brandy and syphilis."'. It was small wonder, Stent thought, that the government should have disliked so intensely 'his caustic tongue and unanswerable indictments of their native policy'.[7]

Richard Godlo's resolution on the Native Service Contract Bill was passed unanimously, defying a heavy-handed threat from Senator C.J. van Rooyen Smit, one of the 'Native Senators' appointed to look after African interests. He warned the delegates not to reject the various measures that were being laid before them, 'as in that case a Conference might not be called again'. He did not consider the 'whipping clause' – as one earlier speaker had characterised it – 'contrary to the principles of Christianity'. Since he was a missionary, Senator Smit perhaps thought he spoke with some authority on this matter.[8]

Plaatje did intervene in the discussion about the proposed extension of the 'tot' system (payment of workers in alcoholic drink) to the Transvaal, accusing the government of being in the pocket of liquor interests. He also made it very plain, during the debate on the codification of 'native laws', that he thought information about customary law and practice should be collected for historical purposes only and not used as a prop for policies of 'retribalisation'; delegates, he said, had allowed themselves to be 'influenced by publications by the Dept of Bantu Studies in the Witwatersrand University, all of which were written by European men'. Having made his point, he then walked out of the conference hall for the remainder of the session, accompanied by Richard Selope Thema, who shared his view. Edith Rheinallt Jones, seeing them depart, commented that they 'don't seem to be interested in codification'. Both saw that its function was to bolster the Native Administration Act of 1927, designed to exclude Africans from the protection of a common legal system and responsible, as they saw it, for holding back their progress.[9]

On the final day of the conference Plaatje raised the question of the delegates' attendance allowance, pointing out that the remuneration of 12s 6d per day was 'very small', especially when compared with the allowances paid for attending assemblies in the Transkei and Basutoland. The minister of native affairs, who at least took the trouble to attend most of the conference sessions, was not sympathetic. He 'did not think it was possible to increase the allowance of members at present', and he thought delegates should be prepared 'to make some sacrifice for their people'. Paying the expenses of attendants to accompany chiefs was another matter, since he quite realised that 'a Native Chief of high rank could not travel unattended'. It can have only confirmed Plaatje's view of the direction of government policy and the contempt with which he and his fellow (non-chiefly) spokesmen were regarded. He was, it is fair to say, the last person in need of a lecture from the minister of native affairs about making sacrifices for his people.[10]

Despite these acrimonious exchanges, both the minister and the chairman of the conference, J.F. Herbst, the secretary for native affairs, were thanked for their contributions. Few of the delegates present, however, can have returned home with any illusions as to the effect of their deliberations and resolutions. As they were reminded several times, the government was under no obligation to act upon any of their resolutions, or even to reconvene the conference – which it never did. Plaatje was angered, moreover, by the attitude of the members of the Native Affairs Commission, like Dr A.W. Roberts, who 'instead of supporting the natives, interpreted to the natives the Government's point of view and pressed for its adoption'. These commissioners did not share the disabilities of the people they were supposed to be representing, he pointed out, so how could they possibly tell the minister, or the government, or parliament, anything they didn't already know?[11]

⟊⟊

The following month, January 1931, Plaatje travelled to Johannesburg to attend another conference, rather more fruitful as it turned out, held under the auspices of the Independent Order of True Templars, for whom he had now been working, off and on, since 1927 in his capacity as 'Special Missioner'. Over the three days of the conference the successes and failures of the previous five years were debated and discussed, and Plaatje was given special credit for the progress of the movement among Africans in the Transvaal and Orange Free State.

By far the most significant outcome of this conference was the decision to launch a monthly or quarterly newspaper, the objective being 'to keep us all in touch with each other but even more than that to spread our message through such a medium'. The idea had been discussed on several previous occasions, but it had always been difficult to find the necessary financial backing, and it had not got off the ground. Now, however, the need had become more urgent, there were firm promises of support from the different branches and jurisdictions of the order, and the head of the order, the Right Worthy Templar, J.W. Mushet, was willing to put up the necessary capital. They accordingly resolved to 'start the paper as soon as arrangements could be made and to issue 3,000 copies to start with', the intention being, so Mushet explained, 'to publish the paper in English, but that Afrikaans items and any other items in Bantu languages would be published in these languages'. Mushet himself offered to act as its first editor.[12]

These arrangements took some months to put into place, and they were one of the reasons for Plaatje's visit to Cape Town the following May. Although his name had not been mentioned in connection with editing the paper in the minutes of the January conference, this soon changed. When the first number of *Our Heritage* (as the paper was called) appeared in June 1931, it gave two editorial addresses: Box 1432, Cape Town, for the IOTT's head office; and Box 143, Kimberley, Plaatje's personal box number. He seems to have started off as joint editor but it was not long before he was effectively in charge. From the contents of the first issue of *Our Heritage*, it was clear that the new paper was not going to restrict itself to the affairs of the temperance movement but would engage with issues of broader social and political interest too. Twenty-one years on from the Act of Union the launch of *Our Heritage*, it said, was 'a great and significant act'. More and more 'our Coloured and Native people' are 'being pushed back step by step', 'denied the inherent rights of mankind, and more and more they are being denied civic and political rights in their own birthland'. *Our Heritage* would therefore 'tell the world – and South Africa – just how they fare twenty-one years after Union and how they feel about it'.[13]

Over the next few months *Our Heritage* came to bear unmistakable signs of Plaatje's editorial imprint, including his 'I am black but comely, O ye daughters of Jerusalem' motto, which made its appearance in December. Certainly there was news of the affairs of the IOTT, but there was much else besides: a piece on 'Land hunger', for example, in the second issue, and several articles on the orthographic debate similar to those he wrote elsewhere. And plenty in Setswana: a familiar appeal to the Batswana to unite like other nations and support their new newspaper; a report on his travels in the Bechuanaland Protectorate; and an old friend from the days of *Koranta* and *Tsala*, 'Mma-Maitisho' ('Conversations') – all of it printed in the orthography that Plaatje was so anxious to protect from the university professors and the Central Orthography Committee, and not a diacritic in sight. *Our Heritage* was not quite *Koranta* or *Tsala* revived but there were distinct echoes. It was the first paper he had edited since departing on his first voyage overseas in 1914, and he hoped it would lead on to better things. In July he told Dr W.E.B. Du Bois in America that he hoped to turn it into a fortnightly 'very soon'.[14]

✦

This visit to Cape Town that May had one unexpected consequence. He happened to notice some advertisements for an international exhibition due to be held shortly in Elisabethville, capital of the Katanga province of the Belgian Congo. It provoked his curiosity. 'It struck me at the time', he wrote, 'that a visit up there and a study of race relationships on the spot might yield information of some value to Native Welfare Associations in the South. The General Manager of Railways obligingly concurred in the idea, and opened the way with a free press ticket to the Congo border, 2,165 miles away; so, without further ado, one wet and misty Wednesday, I bade goodbye to R.W.T. and Cape Town friends and boarded the mail train for the north.' He took with him a letter of introduction from the Belgian consul general in Cape Town, along with a request 'to refrain so far as possible from drawing comparisons between the Union and the Belgian administrations, as it was the latter's desire to keep on friendly terms with the Union'. Five days later, after stopping for only a few hours in Kimberley, and passing through Bechuanaland and Southern and Northern Rhodesia, and across the Victoria Falls, he was in Elisabethville.[15]

He reacted to what he saw in the Belgian Congo much as he did when in the United States ten years earlier, being struck above all by the differences with South Africa's 'native policies' and how it treated its African population. Contrasts in employment policies were evident even before he reached Elisabethville from the Northern Rhodesian border, for all the staff on the train he joined at Sakania, except for the ticket collector and chief steward, were black. Nor could he fail to be struck by the impression made by a passing shunting engine upon a group of white South Africans standing on the platform. 'At sight of the black crew', he wrote, 'one South African nearly fainted. Recovering from the shock, he protested vehemently against that method of keeping back the industries of the country. "In the Union we don't allow them to do it," he exclaimed.' It was the kind of story Plaatje delighted in recounting.[16]

Once in Elisabethville he visited the exhibition, witnessed some of the sports and athletics displays which accompanied it, and was then taken in hand by the Belgian authorities. They gave him VIP treatment. He met, among others, M.

Verbeken, the district commissioner, a 'wonderful administrator' who provided 'a useful mass of information', and then introduced him to His Excellency the governor (of Katanga province), the commissioner general and also the chief justice. Few of those he met, he discovered, spoke English, and he struggled with his rudimentary French. He felt a lot more comfortable in the company of Flemish-speakers, among them the chief of police and some nurses from the Roman Catholic Sisters of Mercy whom he met at a hospital. Their language, he thought, was 'a kind of Nederlandsch with which a South African could be more at home', and much easier to understand.[17]

Differences in labour and employment policies were also quite striking. While in South Africa the mining industry depended upon an institutionalised system of migrant labour, in Elisabethville the policy was one of labour stabilisation, designed to encourage the development of a skilled as well as unskilled labour force, for in the Belgian Congo there was to all intents and purposes no white working class to fulfil such a role.

The working of the Belgian Congo's judicial system, too, given his longstanding interest in such matters, provided more food for thought. Thanks to the chief justice, he spent some time in the law courts (listening, he wrote, 'to some very interesting forensic duels'), was impressed by the system of utilising assessors ('Juges Indigènes') from the different tribes involved in legal cases, and was assured that this system was 'giving the utmost satisfaction and inspiring a great respect for the laws of the country'. The contrast with what was being done within the South African judicial system, as he saw it, could not have been clearer. 'I hardly think', he wrote, 'that anyone in the Union could possibly object to a system of Native administration which inspires respect for law. Under such a system it would scarcely be possible to endure an unedifying spectacle like the Native Administration Act whereby the Union Parliament has legalised the sale of Native girls, like so many horses, and called the sale lobola! It is as if a Mohamedan power were to enact laws over Christians, and straightway dispensed with hymns and prayers, abolished sermons on Sundays, legalised only the collection, and called it divine service.'[18]

On policies and practices in education and taxation, both subjects in which he had a keen interest, his conclusions were broadly similar. On the latter topic, indeed, he pointed to 'the senseless taxation methods of my country in contrast with the thoughtful administration of the poll tax laws inspired by the Belgian authorities'. If Plaatje had any private reservations about what he saw in the Belgian Congo, he did not mention them publicly. He went there in search of new perspectives with which to view his own country, and this coloured all he wrote. Just as with his visit to North America ten years previously, his observations reveal as much about the perceptions he took with him as the objective realities of life in the Belgian Congo.[19]

After two weeks in the Belgian Congo he set off on the long journey home. Instead of travelling straight back to Kimberley, he broke his journey in Bulawayo, invited by the Native Welfare Society of Matabeleland to address one of their meetings. It proved to be a notable occasion. It was the first time any white Rhodesian audience had given a hearing to a black South African, the hall was full to capacity and the proceedings were given extended treatment in the local newspaper, the *Bulawayo Chronicle*. From its report it is quite evident that Plaatje had lost none of his customary eloquence on the public platform, or his talent for dealing with almost any audience imaginable.

The gist of his address, in which he confined himself to South Africa, was an attack on the policies of the government, and a warning of the dangers of abrogating the rule of law in favour of policies that discriminated against any section of the population. 'I can tell you from experience', he said, 'that if you allow the law to take sides with one group against another, it will not be many years before it takes sides with one section of the group.' At this point, so the *Chronicle*'s reporter considered, the speaker 'seemed to feel he was touching upon difficult ground, and complained that he was limited by the presence of a judge of the Supreme Court' (Mr Justice Russell, president of the Native Welfare Society, who was presiding at the meeting); whereupon he 'told a funny story to relieve the position', and suggested that proceedings should continue in the form of questions, to which he would then respond.

'What do you think of segregation?' was the first question. It depended on what you meant by the word, he replied. 'There was a time when the natives thought segregation would be a desirable thing – that was the segregation you read of in Johnson's dictionary. But poor Johnson did not know what segregation means. Segregation in practice does not mean that the white people should have their own area and sphere of control, and the natives theirs. No! It means that the native must live cheek by jowl with the white man, and the only segregation you have is between the native and his money. That is what we call segregation in action.'

The next question, no surprise given the composition of the audience, was on 'miscegenation'. In response he was 'vigorously outspoken', complaining that this was 'a point upon which the Native is very much misrepresented'. 'The task of the friends of the native', he said,' is rendered very difficult by some people who, whenever you suggest anything in the interests of the native, turn round and ask you whether you would like to see your daughter marry a kafir. That shows that some people in this world are absolutely good for nobody except their sons-in-law (laughter). I wish these people would understand that we natives have no intention of doing anything of the sort. We, too, have a proverb like your "birds of a feather". It is "the people know each other by their spots".' Not much had changed since he first began answering these kinds of questions decades before.[20]

✨

He returned home to the task of establishing *Our Heritage* as a viable concern. Early indications were not encouraging. Despite his professed hope that he might soon be able to turn *Our Heritage* into a fortnightly, the editorial in the second issue, July 1931, was already complaining that the response to it was 'a little disappointing', and that he had not yet heard from 'every Grand Secretary from Every Grand Temple'. The blank spaces on the pages set aside for advertising did not augur well, and *Our Heritage* failed to appear in August or September. 'We cannot fully go into the difficulties that arose accounting for this break', so it announced, 'but we can assure readers that we were up against, what were for the time being, insuperable obstacles. We trust we have now successfully overcome these and that the future publication of "Our Heritage" will be regular.' These 'obstacles', it was admitted, related to the question of which language, or languages, to use. English would remain the main medium; Afrikaans, spoken by many Coloured people, would in future be used too, but *Our Heritage* could 'not agree to have more than one Native language used'.[21]

Such disagreements were to be expected, given the different regions and languages represented in the International Order of True Templars (IOTT) itself. In particular, non-Tswana sections of the organisation and readers of the journal would have had reason to complain about the way in which Setswana had taken over as the 'one African language' to whose use the above-mentioned editorial could agree, and the very considerable amount of material in Setswana which then appeared in its columns. Even the English columns tended to be dominated by news of goings-on in Bechuanaland and other Tswana-speaking areas of the Union of South Africa. This may have suited Plaatje's interests and purpose, but was unlikely to commend itself to other sections of the IOTT whose support was essential to the journal's survival. From the beginning there was a tension between Plaatje's desire to reinvent *Koranta* and *Tsala* and the aims and objectives of the IOTT.

Even without this, *Our Heritage* would have struggled. Its goal of achieving an immediate circulation of three thousand was highly ambitious, particularly in a time of severe economic depression; as ever, the African population, its main prospective readership, was worst affected. Plaatje cast about for support elsewhere. He approached the Native Affairs Department in Pretoria with a request for a contract to carry government notices, explaining that *Our Heritage*, started by the IOTT, now 'catered for the social, political and industrial needs of Non-Europeans generally and more particularly for the Sechuana-speaking Natives of OFS, Northern District Cape and Western Transvaal up to Bechuanaland'. Since the demise of his 'older paper', he added, referring to *Tsala ea Batho*, 'the Bechuana section have had no news medium'. A 'favourable consideration of this application' would therefore be 'instructive to the most backward section of the Union's population'.[22]

He spoke in similar terms to Charles Rey, resident commissioner of the Bechuanaland Protectorate, when he called in to see him in August 1931. His problem, he explained, was that the owners of the paper had informed him that 'they could not continue to print the Secwana section as there is not enough circulation to justify it'. He wondered therefore whether the Protectorate authorities would subsidise the paper 'to the extent of £100 a year' so that the Setswana columns could be retained, enabling the paper to build up its circulation in Bechuanaland – and to serve the educational and social needs of the Tswana people as a whole. Just as, he would have reminded the resident commissioner, his Shakespeare translations were helping to meet the needs of his schools.[23]

Rey did at least consider the request. However, he had plans of his own for an African newspaper for the Protectorate, and it was unfortunate that he consulted J.D. Rheinallt Jones, now back from his sabbatical in the United States. Jones too was involved in discussions about launching a new newspaper in South Africa, and advised against supporting *Our Heritage*, which he considered in any case to be 'of indifferent quality'. *Our Heritage* appeared in November with an assurance that it had 'captured the imagination of our Native people', and again in December, promising more in the new year about the Belgian Congo, but this turned out to be its last issue. Readers wanting to know more would have to consult *Umteteli wa Bantu*, which carried Plaatje's piece about the Belgian Congo's system of taxation and justice late in January 1932.

Our Heritage was the last paper or journal over which Plaatje presided as editor. Ever since the demise of *Tsala ea Batho* he had cherished the hope of being able to edit his own newspaper, and over the years had sought various kinds of backing and support. For a while the IOTT provided this, but after just five issues *Our Heritage*, too, ceased publication. The resources he needed remained beyond his reach.

Towards the end of the year, he was offered the editorship of another newspaper, the weekly *Bantu World*, a new venture launched in Johannesburg – the outcome of the discussions in which Rheinallt Jones was involved. In many respects it represented an important new departure in the history of the African press in South Africa. The idea of a thirty-year-old failed farmer by the name of B.G. Paver, the *Bantu World* was conceived as the first in a range of publications which were to act as an advertising medium to enable white businessmen to reach the growing African market. Whereas *Umteteli wa Bantu* had been established ten years earlier for what were essentially political motives, the *Bantu World* heralded the arrival of European commercial interests in the African newspaper world. And unlike the under-capitalised African proprietors and syndicates who had struggled over the years to keep going, the Bantu Press (Pty) Ltd, the company set up to run the *Bantu World*, had the capital and the means of distribution denied to the dwindling band of independent African pressmen. It was the shape of things to come.[24]

Abantu-Batho was the latest casualty. It always found it difficult to compete with *Umteteli wa Bantu* and in the end was brought down by the debilitating effects of unpaid debts, antiquated printing machinery and disputes among those who ran it. Its demise marked the passing of an era of independent black journalism, no longer sustainable in the kind of country South Africa had become. A sympathetic white journalist, present at the auction of its assets, mourned its passing, alive to the poignancy of the moment, and paid tribute to the handful who struggled on. 'No panelled sanctums', he reflected, 'house the editors of South Africa's native newspapers; no special correspondents go scouring the country for news; no seats are provided for representatives in the press gallery in Parliament', their resources 'hopelessly inadequate to the size of the task they faced'. Yet they remained determined to 'educate themselves and improve their status in the eyes of the cultured world'. One day, he said, when African newspapers had achieved a secure place in the life of the country, people would look back upon 'the efforts of the pioneers of black African journalism, Jabavu, Dube, Plaatje and the others'.[25]

Plaatje was among those whose 'assistance and guidance' were acknowledged by the management and staff of the *Bantu World* when its first issue appeared in April 1932, but he declined the offer of the editorship, which went instead to Richard Selope Thema. His reasons for doing so were little different from when he turned down the opportunity to edit *Umteteli wa Bantu* in 1920. Now, as then, he valued his independence, and he preferred to live in Kimberley rather than Johannesburg. In his various literary ventures he had, besides, other priorities.[26]

+~+

So he remained in Kimberley. There were always those who thought him too close to De Beers, and not always to be trusted as a spokesman, but for the most part he was held in high esteem, and he had many friends of all races. To them he now owed a special debt of gratitude: the gift of his house, 32 Angel Street, purchased for him in 1929 by a committee, headed by William McLeod, a local Coloured leader – 'a tangible expression', so it was said, of Plaatje's '25 years of unsalaried service on behalf of non-Europeans'. Since Angel Street was a 'quiet and staid old residential thoroughfare' that had 'hardly any traffic', it would be particularly appropriate for the work he was now engaged in – producing literature in Setswana. De Beers, as so often in the past, made by far the largest donation to the fund. Plaatje, so his neighbour Michael van Reenen remembered clearly, was deeply moved by the gesture.[27]

What most people in Kimberley remembered was his unrivalled ability as a public speaker, somebody who could hold the attention of any audience. At election time he was particularly in demand. 'In those days', recalled one who used to attend these meetings, 'we had the SAP, the South African Party, Sol Plaatje was always the speaker. They always left Sol Plaatje to speak last. And whenever the meeting got a little boring, you know, they would say, "Sol Plaatje, Sol Plaatje", and in no time at all there would be roars of laughter … he was an eminent politician and speaker.' Plenty of others agreed. H.I.E. Dhlomo thought him 'the most forceful public speaker of his day, sharp-witted, quick of thought and a master of repartee'. His powers had clearly not diminished with age.[28]

One occasion stood out in people's memories: the 'non-European function' in the City Hall, held in honour of the Earl of Clarendon, the governor general of South Africa, and Lady Clarendon, during their visit to Kimberley in November 1931. The four non-European communities represented (Coloured, African, Indian, 'Mohammedan') gave a formal address of welcome, which Lord Clarendon acknowledged with a commitment to further, so far as he was able, 'the well being and happiness of all His Majesty's subjects, without distinction', an objective that was shared, he said, by Lady Clarendon. In response Plaatje moved a vote of thanks on behalf of the 'non-European' communities present. It was a typically witty speech. He expressed his sympathy for the governor general in the difficult task he faced in fulfilling his duties 'in a land of two official languages, two white races, two capitals hundreds of miles apart, and two flags', and concluded with the observation that he was 'particularly pleased to hear the King's English spoken by a representative of His Majesty'. It was just what the occasion required, and went down well.

What really struck those present, however, was what the Earl of Clarendon said in reply, for he singled out Plaatje for special mention. Glad as he was to hear his remarks about the King's English, he said, he 'was not altogether sure that he could not have learned a lesson from Mr Plaatje in the speaking of the English language'. Coming from the King's representative in South Africa, it was high praise indeed, and words which Simon Lekhela, a young teacher at Lyndhurst Road and relative of Plaatje, never forgot. 'You felt proud', he recalled, 'that you were related to a man of that stature.' His younger brother Ernest had reason to remember the occasion too. Sneaking into the crowded City Hall to listen to the speeches, he was spotted by a policeman but just managed to evade his grasp by ducking down and crawling through a forest of legs towards the exit, escaping into the throng outside.[29]

Others had more personal memories. Michael van Reenen, who lived just across the road, remembered the long discussions they used to have over Shakespeare, and about the proverbs Plaatje was collecting for the new edition of his book; and the late-night conversations, over a cup of coffee in his kitchen, about newspaper articles he had just completed. Simon Lekhela recalled the interest Plaatje took in his educational progress and the encouragement he was always ready to offer. Before he qualified as a teacher he was one of a small group of Africans who studied at the (predominantly Coloured) Perseverance Training School, there 'on sufferance', as they were often reminded whenever one of them stepped out of line. If they thought they were being treated unfairly, quite a regular occurrence, they used to complain to Plaatje: a quiet word with the principal of Perseverance, Mr Meadows (who also lived in Angel Street), and things would suddenly improve.[30]

Even closer to Plaatje was his daughter-in-law Mary (née Moikoatlhai), who had married his second son, Richard, in 1927, and lived for a while with the family in Angel Street. She had some vivid memories of the crowded household. Apart from herself and her husband, and Plaatje and Elizabeth, there was also Halley, the youngest son; Violet, a teacher at the Lyndhurst Road Native School; and, at various times, Jane Ntingana, Elizabeth's sister, who worked as a cook at the Kimberley Boys' High School; St Leger and his wife Mita; Gabriel Plaatje, one of Plaatje's nephews; and three girls from the Moyanaga family in Thaba Nchu, staying in Kimberley to attend the Lyndhurst Road school. There were often visitors, too, like Chief Fenyang from Thaba Nchu (whose daughter Morwa also stayed with the Plaatjes when she attended the Lyndhurst Road school), Dr Abdurahman from Cape Town, and the African American educator George E. Haynes, engaged (in 1930) in carrying out a survey of YMCA work in South Africa, who long remembered the 'pleasant day' he spent with Plaatje in Kimberley. It was no wonder one friend regarded the Plaatje family home as 'the asylum of visitors and strangers to Kimberley'.[31]

When he was there Plaatje would usually be at work in his study, often busy on his typewriter until the early hours of the morning. But it was not all work. Violet, like her father, was an accomplished pianist and, like her mother, had an extremely good singing voice. She and her father used to play together on the piano, and both were involved in the local Abantu Batho Musical Association. Fundamental to the daily routine of the household were family prayers, held each evening, after dinner. On Sundays there were sometimes family picnics, when Plaatje would drive the family in his car (for a while he owned a 14 hp Renault which took the place of the Ford he had earlier) to Modder River or to Pniel, where Simon Plaatje, by this time in his late seventies, was still living. Anybody wishing to come on these family outings had to be ready on time. If they were not, so Mary Plaatje recalled, Plaatje would simply depart without them. In his younger days punctuality had not always been his greatest strength; now, with a busy life to lead, it was a necessity. Paul Mahabane, son of the Rev. Z. Mahabane, a close family friend, was sometimes fortunate enough to join these outings as well.[32]

Mostly those who knew Plaatje in Kimberley during the late 1920s and early 1930s had fond recollections, inevitably coloured by the passage of time. There were warm memories of Elizabeth too, always a quietly supportive presence, sharing her husband's passions, engaged in social and temperance work locally when not busy just keeping things going in the home. Yet all were agreed that there was one thing which caused Plaatje much unhappiness: his sons' drinking – more particularly Sainty and Halley, the oldest and youngest. All three sons, St Leger, Richard and Halley, were able and talented young men, and had had a far better formal education than their father, all three having gone on to Lovedale after the Lyndhurst Road school. St Leger had a year at Fort Hare after that and then a well-paid job in Cape Town until his abrupt dismissal in 1929. Richard, who of the three most closely resembled Plaatje physically, had followed in his father's footsteps as an interpreter and secured a job in the magistrate's office in Kimberley. In his spare time he was a keen tennis player. His son, also named Richard, was Plaatje's first grandchild, born in 1928.

Halley was the playboy of the family. Popular with his friends, he dressed in the latest fashion, was a keen sportsman, and had, like his father, a marvellous aptitude for languages. Unlike his father, though, he saw no virtue in total abstinence, and he enjoyed a drink with his friends. Once this was in the company of several young teachers from Lyndhurst Road, celebrating the completion of their training. Among them was his friend Simon Lekhela. The memory of Plaatje's furious reaction when he encountered them after their night out remained with him for the rest of his life. 'From the old chap', he recalled, 'there was very strong talk about the evils of liquor. He likened alcohol to the blood of the lion, the blood of the fox, the blood of the pig: the lion in that it gives you a false sense of strength, the fox because it gives you a false sense of intelligence, but the only true representation is that of the pig. Because when you are drunk you grovel in the mire, like the ordinary pig. He couldn't understand how the young men could allow themselves to descend to that level. He was uncompromising on temperance, absolute temperance.'[33]

It was not an isolated occasion. Mary Plaatje and Michael van Reenen heard the furious rows when St Leger and Halley returned home after drinking sessions. Living as he did by the strict moral standards he set himself, Plaatje was bitterly disappointed that they did not share his attitude towards drink, particularly since he was at that time busy preaching the virtues of temperance in his work with the IOTT. If he could not persuade his own sons, he must have asked himself, why should anybody else heed his message? On such matters a tolerant understanding was out of the question. 'Sty and Halley can now be ruled out of the list of humanity and entered up as permanent liabilities', he wrote in his journal in January 1930, the only page to have survived. It was a desperately sad indictment to set alongside the good news of *Mhudi*'s acceptance by Lovedale and progress on his other literary projects, both noted in the lines immediately above. *Mhudi*, written during a long period of absence overseas and finally published after years of disappointment, perhaps came at a high price. In Plaatje's life public fulfilment and personal sadness were rarely far apart.[34]

He made no secret of his intense disappointment at his sons' lapses. Over forty years later Dr James Moroka, who knew Plaatje well, recalled him saying that he had done all he could for his sons, and just could not understand the way they had turned out. Perhaps he had tried to do too much for them, or had just expected too much of them. Or was it that he was just not around when he was really needed? Modiri Molema shared James Moroka's view, regretting for Plaatje's sake that he could not have had a son of whom he could be truly proud: this was, he thought, the gaping hole in his life.[35]

St Leger was his biggest disappointment. It was impossible not to compare his career with that of Z.K. Matthews, his classmate at the Lyndhurst Road school, both of them winners of that Andrew Smith bursary to Lovedale back in 1916. Since then young Z.K., despite his humble background, or maybe because of it, had outshone St Leger at every step, becoming, as Plaatje himself would point out, 'the first native BA, LLB of the University of South Africa', and a highly successful head of Adams College in Natal – somebody, he said, 'about whom local Bantu could feel justly proud'. If only he could have felt that about his eldest son.[36]

Yet St Leger's situation was hardly an enviable one. Quite apart from having to grow up in the shadow of so eminent a father, whose achievements were virtually impossible to emulate, his country had no place for him. Plaatje used to point out himself that his sons were now excluded by law from employment even as messengers in the post office in Kimberley where he began his career. Further education offered hope, but with Plaatje away in England and America, the family simply did not have the resources for him to continue at Fort Hare, and he felt an obligation to support his mother and younger siblings. Appreciative as his father was of this at the time, he could never condone his subsequent drinking, let alone dishonest behaviour. He himself had learnt to cope with what was happening to his country, with the frustration of so many of his hopes and ideals. It was far more difficult to cope with the pressures he saw getting the better of his children. Not everybody could have his own extraordinary strength of purpose and moral conviction.

Modiri Molema thought that of all Plaatje's children it was his daughter Violet who really took after him, and with whom he had the easiest relationship. She had excelled at Lovedale, completed her training at Perseverance and then, in the 1920s, taught at several different schools in Kimberley, much admired by her pupils. To her friends and family she was known as 'Teto' (from her middle name Nomteto), or – since she loved tennis – 'Doodles', after 'Doodles' Tapscott, a Kimberley sportsman who played tennis for South Africa. She brought in some extra income by giving piano lessons, she ran a group called the Rhythm Girls which performed at concerts and other local social events, and she was a leading member of both the Wayfarers (African Girl Guides) and the Band of Hope, a temperance organisation for young people, linked to the IOTT. When Plaatje wrote of the role that women might play in the redemption of his people, as he often did, it is difficult not to believe he had his own family circumstances in his mind.[37]

+∿+

Conscious as ever of the need to set an example to those around him, Plaatje never eased up in his work. Nor would he be deterred by the advice he was now receiving from his doctors to limit his activities so as to avoid putting unnecessary strain upon his weak heart. By the early 1930s, judging from several photographs which have survived, he was looking much older than a man in his mid-fifties, and he often complained of ill health. Yet he regarded his doctors' advice, according to Z.K. Matthews, 'as a counsel of perfection which he could not heed when there was so much to be done, and so little time in which to do it'. If anything, he pushed himself even harder.[38]

Late 1931 and early 1932 were a case in point. At the end of December he travelled to Aliwal North to give the presidential address (in the absence of Professor D.D.T. Jabavu, who was overseas) to the Cape Native Voters' Association, delivered, so *Imvo* thought, with 'his characteristic forceful eloquence', and widely noticed in the press. The threat of yet more repressive legislation, he said, would not so much undermine as completely demolish 'the liberty of the subject which, under the Constitution of the old Colony of the Cape of Good Hope, became the heritage of natives in this country'. During the previous year, severe economic recession and retrenchment had hit Africans harder than anybody else, leaving many quite unable to pay the £1 poll tax now demanded of them, regardless of income. They also faced a double standard of justice: the law turned them into 'a race of gaol birds', gaoled, on the one hand, for being poor, while on the other hand work – the only remedy to poverty – was denied them since it was now 'the prerogative of the white man'.[39]

He considered the proposed extension of the franchise to white (but not black) women, appealing to white women to behave in a more sensible manner than their sons and husbands. 'What we expect from them when the time comes is for women to clean up the man-made political mess from which the world is suffering today.' He had made much the same point in *Mhudi*, published six months previously. As an editorial in *The Star* pointed out, however, when commenting upon his speech, there was no evidence that white women were likely to behave any differently from their male counterparts when it came to defending white privilege.[40]

Plaatje concluded his address as he had so many others: with an appeal to his people not to despair, not to blame all their troubles upon the 'prejudice of the other race'. Many of their problems, he said, were 'due to our own inertia, or to false starts in the wrong direction'. He urged greater co-operation and understanding 'among the different groups of our community'. 'Let us subject ourselves to discipline, self control and sacrifice', he concluded, 'and strengthen the hands of our friends and sympathizers among another race. If standing shoulder to shoulder, with a pull together, we can manage to keep South Africa solvent we surely could combine in our own interest, for that power lies in our hands, as Shakespeare very truly put it:

Our remedies oft in themselves do lie
Which we ascribe to heaven the fated sky
Gives us free scope, only doth backward pull
Our slow designs when we ourselves are dull.'

There was no clearer exposition of both the strengths and weaknesses of Plaatje's philosophy, and it was entirely characteristic that he should have found in Shakespeare the words to conclude his address.[41]

✦

He began 1932 as he had 1931, attending the annual sessions of the Transvaal and Orange Free State jurisdictions of the IOTT. Then it was off to Cape Town to lobby the government on unemployment and education – 'their physical starvation by the policy of the Union Government and their mental starvation by the Provincial authorities'. It was, so he told Mr Grimmer, the De Beers general manager, on the eve of his departure, 'an involved problem with intricacies between the Union Government and the Cape Education Department and it may take weeks to clarify'.[42]

He hoped to see the minister of education over the provision of secondary education facilities at the Lyndhurst Road school. It was the latest phase of a lengthy saga. In 1925 Plaatje, David Ramoshoana and several others had managed to extract a promise from the Cape provincial authorities to provide Standards VII and VIII at the Lyndhurst Road school, but they had been unable to get the necessary funds from the Department of Native Education. African children completing their primary education thus had to go to a boarding institution like Tigerkloof (which very few parents could afford), or secure one of the handful of places that the (Coloured) Perseverance Training School in Kimberley reserved unofficially for Africans. After persistent lobbying over the issue, a deputation consisting of Plaatje, the Rev. Z. Mahabane and the Rev. C.B. Liphuko managed to see the minister of education in Cape Town in May 1931, just before Plaatje departed for the Belgian Congo, and extracted a promise of funds. Higher secondary education was begun, at long last, at the commencement of the new school year in January 1932, room for the classes being found in the Lyndhurst Road Native Institute. But at the last minute there was an unexpected setback. Although it had been understood that ninety-five places would be available, it turned out that there was provision only for forty: fifty-five unfortunate children had therefore to be turned away.[43]

With the help of Senator 'Matabele' Thompson, a large landowner in the Kimberley district, Plaatje managed to secure an interview with the minister of native affairs, E.G. Jansen, but he refused to take any action on the Lyndhurst Road school. On the question of unemployment the minister indicated that 'their distress was not escaping his notice', but made it clear that he felt this was a matter for the provincial authorities to deal with, not the central government. 'It will be seen', Plaatje concluded his subsequent account of the meeting, 'that natives unemployed would remain unemployed as long as the present Government remains in power.'[44]

He met with no more success in his lobbying over the Native Service Contract Bill, the measure which had been submitted for discussion in an earlier form at the last Native Conference. Even with the support of Sir James Rose Innes and Sir Clarkson Tredgold, ex-chief justice of Southern Rhodesia and now chairman of the Cape Town Joint Council, he was unable to get an appointment to see Oswald Pirow, the minister of justice, who had legislative responsibility for the bill. In parliament, Plaatje attended a number of sessions when it was debated. It passed through both Houses and became the law of the land, far fiercer in its provisions than the version condemned by the Native Conference. The white farmers could scarcely have asked for tougher legal controls over their labourers; its effect, in Plaatje's view, was 'to turn rural natives into so much property, to be, with their families, virtually owned by the European landowner'. Even the Native Affairs Department thought it so unjust as to be unenforceable.[45]

Plaatje was heartened, though, by one aspect of the debate, the strong speech made against the bill by J.H. Hofmeyr, the rising star of the liberal wing of the South African Party. Such, at any rate, was how Claire Goodlatte, secretary of the Cape Town Joint Council, described his reaction to it when she had him to lunch early in April. Besides this, she wrote afterwards in a letter to her brother, she got a number of other 'pleasant anecdotes' and 'scraps of interest' from him; she did not elaborate on what they were. Beyond securing one small amendment, however, Hofmeyr could do no more than Plaatje to prevent the passage of the Native Service Contract Bill.[46]

This visit to Cape Town was marred by one other incident, just as unsavoury in its way as the oppressive new legislation. It originated in an invitation from Miss Caroline Kemp, the principal of the (white) Rustenburg Girls' High School in Rondebosch, to address her pupils. Happy to accept, for he never tired of speaking to young people, he gave what Miss Kemp considered to be 'a balanced statement of conditions in South Africa', looking at, in turn, '(a) the benefits conferred on natives by Europeans' and '(b) the economic and educational disabilities of natives', concluding with an appeal to the pupils 'to give consideration to these disabilities, and if they thought well to use their influence in the future to remove them'.

News of this then reached Harm Oost, a Nationalist ideologue and member of parliament for Pretoria, once gaoled for his part in the Boer rebellion of 1914. He took a dim view of what he considered to be an inappropriate degree of familiarity between black and white, and tabled a question in the House of Assembly. Was it the case, he demanded, that 'a Native' had spoken to the pupils of Rustenburg Girls' High School, and that the gist of the address was that 'the natives are being badly treated by the white people'? Did the principal subsequently have 'tea with the said native in her sitting-room', and would the minister now 'take steps to prevent a recurrence of such incidents'? In reply, the minister of education confirmed that 'the said Native' (never named) had indeed addressed the pupils, but gave the principal's version of what he actually said, and indicated that he would be taking no further steps in the matter since it fell within the remit of the Cape provincial administration.[47]

Plaatje's reaction to this exchange, reported in Hansard, is unrecorded. He would have been pleased, though, by a couple of letters that appeared in the Cape Town press. One was from A.S. Williams, a well-known figure in Cape Town's Coloured community, who recalled Plaatje's success on the occasion of his first visit to Cape Town, and wondered how Mr Oost could possibly object to 'students listening to a native lecturer who outclassed their elders in the examination room 30 years ago'. A second was from an 'ex-Professor UCT' who, after making enquiries, found that the 'Native concerned' was 'my old friend, and your occasional contributor, Mr Sol Plaatje, known throughout the world to those interested in African development as the author of many valuable books of use to the anthropologist, the historian and the student of the native peoples and of social science'. As a parent of one of the pupils, he said, 'it seems to me that their distinguished principal is to be thanked for her idea of giving those pupils who, like our modern University students, wished to hear the native view at first hand (reasonably and moderately put), so good an opportunity of doing so'.[48]

Plaatje did have one very good piece of news to take back to Kimberley. He had persuaded Countess Labia, daughter of the mining magnate Sir J.B. Robinson (a one-time mayor of Kimberley), now married to the Italian minister plenipotentiary in South Africa, to write him a cheque for the £92 needed to pay for the printing of one of his unpublished Tswana manuscripts. It was a successful conclusion to a long struggle to raise the funds. Her donation supplemented those received from J.W. Jagger, Sir Abe Bailey and Mr J. Garlick (a wealthy Cape Town retailer and wholesaler), as well as the few pounds raised at a thinly attended meeting in Kimberley 'one cheerless evening' in August 1931. The *Bantu World*, in one of its first issues, contrasted the countess's generosity with the 'series of unpleasant questions in Parliament' that had recently been tabled.

'In one sense', it concluded, 'Countess Labia's generous gift is a striking answer to Mr Harm Oost, showing that the best people in the land recognize only merit in men, and not the pigmentation of the skin, nor the texture of their hair'.[49]

Plaatje returned home in May, and on Empire Day, 24 May 1932, he addressed a public meeting in Kimberley in the new Abantu-Batho Hall, in No. 2 Location, to communicate the results of his trip to Cape Town to those who were interested. He was received, so he noted in his own account of the meeting, 'with cheers', and was thanked for his efforts.[50]

Not long after, he set off for Johannesburg, intending to see to the printing of the books that were now ready, including the 'Bantu Folk Tales' for which he now had the funds. Among those who saw him off at the Kimberley railway station was Bahumi Motshumi, from Thaba Nchu, one of the girls who boarded with the family at Angel Street while she attended the Lyndhurst Road school. He had a limp, she noticed, as she bade him farewell.[51]

Mary Plaatje, Richard's wife, had a special reason to hope he would be back soon. He was planning, so she remembered, another trip to the United States, and had promised to take her with him so she could realise her ambition of training and qualifying as a beautician. His own objective was most likely to find an American publisher for *Mhudi*, and to raise funds for his other literary projects. As soon as he was back from Johannesburg, he told her, they would set off. It was an exciting prospect.[52]

Plaatje went to stay, as he usually did when visiting Johannesburg, with Mrs Maria Smouse, his sister-in-law, who had a house in Pimville, an African township some ten miles from the centre of Johannesburg. There were the usual social engagements. He had dinner one evening with A.W.G. Champion, a trade union leader from Natal now excluded from his home province by the provisions of the Riotous Assemblies Act of 1930. And he prepared obituaries of several 'friends of the natives' who died during the first week of June, among them Harriette Colenso, to whom he had dedicated *Native Life in South Africa*, and Henry Taberer, senior adviser to the Chamber of Mines, who had once tried to persuade him to become editor of *Umteteli wa Bantu*.[53]

On 8 June, along with hundreds of others, black and white, he attended Taberer's funeral service at St Mary's Cathedral in the centre of Johannesburg. Outside there was an icy wind, the temperature well below zero. Snow had fallen for the first time that year, the earliest anybody in Johannesburg could remember. Normally, if it came at all, it did not arrive until late July or August. 'Those people who have for years been advocating a white South Africa', *The Star* could not resist commenting, 'must have been rather astonished when they looked out of their windows this morning and realized their dreams had come true.'[54]

During this spell of bitterly cold weather, according to Modiri Molema, Plaatje caught influenza and had to retire to bed, though this did not stop him working on his manuscripts. Molema visited him on Thursday, 16 June, and considered him to be very ill. The next day, though, he felt rather better, and got up from his sickbed, anxious to keep appointments he had made with a bank and a printer. He walked to the nearby Nancefield station to catch the train into town, kept both appointments, but on the way back to the station in Johannesburg was taken more seriously ill and collapsed. Dr A.B. Xuma, the medical student he first met in Chicago in 1922, now a very well-known medical practitioner and public figure, was summoned, and he drove Plaatje back to Pimville in his car. Only a few weeks earlier they had met in much happier circumstances when Plaatje spoke at his wedding reception.[55]

It was obvious he was very ill, and that afternoon an urgent telegram was sent to Elizabeth in Kimberley to inform her of her husband's serious condition. It seems to have worsened quickly. What began as influenza had developed into double pneumonia. Elizabeth arrived on the morning of Sunday, 19 June, joining others who had gathered around his bedside, among them her brother Isaiah, who had come over from Pretoria. Plaatje died at five o'clock that afternoon. The cause of death, so it was officially recorded, was 'heart failure due to double lobar pneumonia'. His weakened heart, damaged in the 1918 influenza epidemic, had finally given up. Considering the way he drove himself, the wonder was that it had lasted so long.[56]

He was buried in Kimberley three days later. Isaiah Bud-M'belle had to resist demands that he be buried in Johannesburg, knowing, so he said later, that Kimberley would never forgive him if he allowed it. Instead, a large crowd of mourners and well-wishers had gathered at the Johannesburg railway station to pay their respects as his body was returned to the city with which he had been so long and so closely associated. For a last time De Beers were asked to make a donation, contributing substantially to the costs of transporting his body back to Kimberley. Plaatje had died, so his friends told the company, 'practically penniless'.[57]

Over a thousand people attended the funeral. It was an elaborate affair, and fitting tribute to his status as a public figure. The cortège, with the coffin on a wagon pulled by a team of oxen, set out from Angel Street early on the Wednesday afternoon. At the head of the long, winding procession were members and officials of the IOTT in their full red and blue regalia, proudly proclaiming Plaatje's adherence to their cause. They made their way first to the Lutheran Church in No. 3 Location, Plaatje's regular place of worship. Here the main part of the service was conducted not by a Lutheran minister, but by Rev. Z. Mahabane, the Methodist minister, an old friend, until recently president general of the African National Congress. Plaatje, a critic of denominational rivalries to the last, would have thoroughly approved such an arrangement.[58]

Plaatje's death, so Mahabane told his packed congregation, had robbed the African people of one of its ablest sons. He was a great writer, a great orator, but, above all, he said, a great leader of his people: 'A great patriot, he devoted his great talents to the service of his people and country. In this service he did not spare himself, but worked day and night. He lived not for himself, but for others, and ultimately laid down his life on the altar of national interests.'

Then it was on to the West End cemetery where Gerhard Kuhn, the Lutheran minister officiating at the graveside, 'delivered a stirring funeral oration', speaking in both English and Setswana. He took his text from the second book of Samuel, chapter 3, verse 38: 'And the King said to his servants, Know ye not that there is a prince and a great man fallen this day in Israel.' 'Our deceased friend, Solomon Plaatje,' he declared, 'may also be rightly called a prince and a great man, that is why we have gathered here in such numbers to pay him the last respect.' 'His one great desire and wish was to serve his people and better their conditions of life', his own 'person, interest and profit ... relegated to the background'. If we were to ask, he said, 'what was his never failing source of inspiration, then we must reply, his deeply rooted religious sentiment'; in his endeavours on behalf of his people he sought to serve 'the Highest Master', always ready to 'bear witness to his Christian faith'.[59]

Kuhn's words, and those of Mahabane before him, were echoed in the speeches and tributes that followed. W.B. Humphreys, MP, one of many prominent whites who were there, thought Plaatje's death 'had dealt a blow not only to the European and non-European people of Kimberley, but to the entire non-European people of South Africa', and had left a gap 'singularly difficult to fill'. G.A. Simpson, editor of the *Diamond Fields Advertiser*, considered he had 'done a great service not only to the race from whom he sprang, but to the whole community, both black and white, for he was a link between them, and enabled each to understand something of the nature, feelings and interests of the other'. He was 'proud to have counted him among his most cherished friends'. I.P. Joshua spoke on behalf of the Coloured community, Isaiah Bud-M'belle for the family. 'Sol Plaatje had fought against two things,' Bud-M'belle said, 'drink and racialism, and as an example of the latter he had broken the native custom of marrying inside his own tribe.'[60]

Over the next few weeks many more tributes appeared in the African press. For *Ilanga lase Natal*, 'the sad news of his demise' came 'as a thunderbolt from a clear sky', and 'the whole Native race' was poorer by his death'; for *Imvo Zabantsundu*, 'the ranks of recognised Bantu leaders' had 'suffered a severe depletion in the deplorable demise of a staunch patriot and indefatigable toiler in the service of his fellow men. His soul is departed but the memory of him and his works will live untarnished in the annals of Native history.' Both *Umteteli wa Bantu* and the *Bantu World* carried special commemorative supplements, recalling the many achievements of his career. His 'life motive', said *Umteteli*, 'had been the national weal', while his 'mature knowledge, quiet humour and innate kindliness had enriched his kind and built for himself a never-dying monument of public esteem. For Plaatje, Scholar and Patriot, the most fitting epitaph would be: "He loved his people."'[61]

Along with the public tributes came a flood of telegrams, letters and messages of condolence for Elizabeth and the family, from home and overseas. As the weeks passed, different aspects of his legacy were recalled. The IOTT, considering its participation in his funeral had not been enough, held a memorial service in Kimberley at the end of July – again at the Lutheran Church in No. 3 Location – in order to pay further tribute to Plaatje's 'distinguished service for the Temperance movement' and to celebrate 'the wonderful example of a humble, honest and radiant life'. Elizabeth, 'a worthy True Templar' herself, was commended for having been 'to a great extent responsible for the great achievements of her husband in the battles of life'.[62]

Others, like David Ramoshoana, drew attention to his contribution to the Tswana language and its literature, afraid that this would be neglected amid the eulogies for his better-known achievements as advocate and spokesman. Clement Doke spoke likewise of Plaatje's remarkable contribution to 'the advancement of Sechuana literature', but in private he was desperately worried about the fate of his unpublished manuscripts. 'Should Plaatje's widow and family desire it', he wrote to Ramoshoana two days after Plaatje's death, 'I believe the University would be prepared to negotiate for the purchase of certain of the materials which he has left.' He did not like to raise the subject so soon after his death, he added, 'but I am so anxious that his work should be preserved, as I fully appreciate the literary contribution he has made to Sechuana'. He had reason for concern.[63]

A characteristically controversial intervention came from Vere Stent. Writing in *The Star*, he said his death had 'passed almost unnoticed by the newspapers and people of South Africa' – which was hardly true – and went on to describe Plaatje's life, drawing upon his own memories of the time they first met during the siege of Mafeking over thirty years before. Like much that Stent wrote, his tribute was an entertaining mixture of fact and fiction, and nobody doubted he meant well. But it contained so many inaccuracies that it drew forth pained responses from Modiri Molema, David Ramoshoana and Michael van Reenen, all of them close to Plaatje and familiar with the details of his life. They were taken aback, especially, by the fanciful claim that he 'was of aboriginal not Bantu origin', that his parents were 'Vaalpense' ('Bushmen'), and that he was brought up by foster parents after he had been captured, as a small baby, during a raid by the Bamangwato (he probably meant Barolong).[64]

They also contested Stent's description of Plaatje as 'a lonely man', and his assertion that, for all his achievements, he 'should have been of so little use to his people'. 'Neither European nor Bantu, one of an intelligentsia, few in number, poor in circumstances, inhibited by lowly birth from commanding the confidence of their own people and again by their colour – another accident of birth – from appealing to those of European descent.' It was the kind of view that reflected the prejudices of many whites, even those, like Vere Stent, who had considerable sympathy for African aspirations but found it difficult to understand that educated Africans like Plaatje could both retain their African identity and find acceptance as their spokesman with the white authorities. Modiri Molema was quite sure Stent's view was mistaken: 'Plaatje's position and leadership had been established for over 25 years; his name and influence among the European and Bantu peoples were unquestioned.' Michael van Reenen, a pall-bearer at Plaatje's funeral, said that if Stent had been present, along with the hundreds of other people, of all races and creeds, and had heard the many tributes to him, he could not possibly have put forward such an opinion.[65]

In December 1935, three and a half years later, Plaatje's tombstone was unveiled at the ceremony I described at the beginning of this book. The sentiments expressed by the many speakers, and those inscribed on the tombstone itself, were fitting tribute. For decades this ceremony remained the high point of public commemoration, a striking tribute from friends, family and a wider community in Kimberley and beyond. In the era of segregation and then apartheid, his life and work stood as an indictment of the path South Africa had taken, his beliefs and achievements in direct conflict with official orthodoxies. In 1936 General Hertzog achieved his longstanding ambition of removing Africans from the common voters' roll in the Cape. It was perhaps as well that Plaatje did not live to experience what he would have considered the ultimate betrayal.

Of course he lived on in the memories of friends and family. For a few years, on each anniversary of his death, his daughter Violet would write a poem to help keep his memory alive and to preserve his legacy as best she could. But inevitably, as time passed, memories began to fade. His political career, in the context of the 1930s and 1940s, seemed increasingly irrelevant. His manuscripts were lost or destroyed, his published books little read. No biography appeared. His novel *Mhudi* formed part of no literary tradition, and was long regarded as little more than a curiosity, neither African nor European. Even to a later generation of black South African writers, like the talented *Drum* generation of the 1950s, it was a curiously old-fashioned, backward-looking book which could provide no inspiration for the elite of the new urban generation; they had no time for forging links with a past from which they sought, more than anything, to liberate themselves.[66]

Nor did Plaatje's work in Setswana receive much recognition. His two Shakespeare translations may have found a place in schools but the manuscripts of the others disappeared. David Ramoshoana wrote sporadically about Tswana words and idioms, but the dictionary the two of them had worked upon never materialised, and no more was heard of the Tswana folktales. Of the writers who might be considered his natural successors, a handful, in both South Africa and Bechuanaland, succeeded in getting their work published, but the quality was often indifferent. Compared with other African literatures in southern Africa, Setswana, as Plaatje had often lamented, made only slow progress. All were held back by the perceived association between the use of African languages and repressive government educational policies, particularly after 1948.

Only in the 1970s would he emerge from the shadows of the past – through a rediscovery of his works in English. For the first time literary scholars took a serious interest in *Mhudi*, rescuing it from the neglect that had been its fate hitherto. Tim Couzens, a lecturer at the University of the Witwatersrand, led the way. He showed how *Mhudi* presented a new view of African history, pre-figuring in many of its themes Chinua Achebe's famous novel, *Things Fall Apart*; how Plaatje used the past as an allegory for the present, warning of the inevitable consequences of continued injustices in the South Africa of his day. Stephen Gray, another writer and literary critic, looked more closely at Plaatje's use of language, identifying literary sources and influences, particularly Shakespeare, Bunyan and the Bible. Understand how Plaatje drew on these sources, Gray argued, and the shape and purpose of *Mhudi*, and 'the spirited linguistic game' he was playing, would become clear. Gray and Couzens then collaborated on the publication of a new edition of *Mhudi*, illustrated by Cecil Skotnes, one of the country's leading contemporary artists. Several years later it came out as a paperback in Heinemann's African Writers Series, bringing it to a far wider audience in South Africa and beyond.[67]

Not everybody was persuaded by the case for *Mhudi*'s rehabilitation. The most vociferous dissenter was Mazisi Kunene, poet and literary scholar. Echoing the views of earlier critics, he thought *Mhudi* was simply inauthentic, written in 'a cross-bred form that is neither African nor European', its uneasy mixture of genres 'sometimes producing total confusion'. He did not dispute Plaatje's right to use English, but he thought the 'romantic episode' of Mhudi and Ra–Thaga was 'totally infantile', out of step with what was, or should have been, the real purpose of the novel; overall it was a 'second-rate, badly organized hodge-podge of semi-history, semifiction, shoddy allegory – a pastiche combining fact and fiction in a most illogical manner'. Kunene missed *Mhudi*'s humour, its quite intentional adoption and parodying of the romance genre – and any sense of Plaatje's agency, of the stylistic choices he made.[68]

Kunene's view has not prevailed. Few other critics considered that Plaatje's choice of the medium of English meant that he was writing in 'a foreign language', or that he could be seen as little more than a pawn in the cultural politics of language and colonialism. Rather, they found in *Mhudi* a text for the new South Africa, highlighting instead its democratic credentials, its rewriting of history from a black perspective, its roots in oral history, the feminism of its heroine. Several new editions have been published since the 1970s and today *Mhudi* has a secure place in South Africa's literary canon, widely read and studied in schools and universities. Outside South Africa, too, it has come into its own with the rise of post-colonial literary studies, seen now as a pioneering novel in a much wider tradition of English-language writing from the African continent. Its literary reputation, in short, has been transformed.[69]

In the same decade that saw the start of *Mhudi*'s rehabilitation, Plaatje's Mafeking diary, miraculously, came to light and was published for the first time. South Africa was not quite ready for it. Here was an intensely personal testimony, in English, remarkable for its subtlety and sophistication, but distinctly at odds with dominant white conceptions of black Africans and their capabilities. It was at odds too with an African nationalist narrative that tended to see the past as a one-dimensional story of oppression and resistance, to disregard any form of expression that was not political in its focus. His diary was thus easily misunderstood. His patriotic, pro-British sentiments, his friendly relationships with Charles Bell and other white administrators, his pride in his work, his even-handed account of the efforts of the military authorities to deal with the black refugees – all could be seen, from the perspective of South Africa in the 1970s and a post-imperial mindset beyond, as at best puzzling, at worst a regrettable case of naivety or false consciousness.[70]

Then came *Native Life in South Africa*, republished in South Africa for the first time in 1982. It was recognised as an important political statement from the early days of the African National Congress, but its apparent moderation, and the politics of appeal it embodied, did not sit easily with the advancing political struggle and growing violence of the 1980s. Plaatje, and others of his generation, may have provided some inspiration for the campaigns of that decade, but his methods and his cultural universe were of another era. Upholding Cecil Rhodes's dictum of 'equal rights for all civilised men', for example, in his appeal to the British public, may have made sense in the early part of the twentieth century and with the audiences he was addressing, but it was scarcely an appropriate rallying call seventy years on.[71]

Only after the upheavals of the early 1990s, and the election of South Africa's first democratic government, would he come into his own as a political figure. Now the founding fathers of the ANC – Plaatje, Dube and the others – could be seen in a new light: not so much as cautious, sometimes misguided, spokesmen from a distant past but as far-seeing pioneers in an ultimately successful struggle, to be honoured for laying the foundations for today's democratic dispensation. 'Mr President, South Africa is now free,' President Mandela is reported to have said as he stood before a memorial to John Dube, after casting his vote in South Africa's first democratic elections in 1994. To a surprising degree, the founding fathers appeared to live on in the memories, the public pronouncements, even the gestures of President Mandela and others of his generation.[72]

For Plaatje, steeped in the legal traditions of the old Cape Colony, the adoption of South Africa's new Constitution in 1996, much admired through the world, was perhaps the real moment of vindication. Its Founding Provisions proclaim its commitment to the ideals of 'a common South African citizenship', 'non-racialism and non-sexism', and the 'Supremacy of the constitution and the rule of law'. These were Plaatje's ideals too. Of course he was far from alone in his attachment to them. Nobody, however, had defended them more eloquently and more passionately in the face of the dehumanising policies of segregation imposed by South Africa's rulers in the early decades of the twentieth century.

South Africa's new Constitution was vindication for Plaatje in one other respect. It recognised Setswana as one of the country's eleven official languages, stipulating that the 'state must take practical and positive measures' to elevate their status and use. This is just what Plaatje had tried to do, with a handful of others, for Setswana. His greatest fear was that Setswana would simply disappear or become so corrupted as to lose its identity. This did not happen. Today Setswana is spoken by far more people than in his day, and it has developed a substantial literature. Attempts to harmonise its orthographies continue, albeit with little sign of resolution, but its future as a language is no longer in doubt. New generations of writers have come forward to give it new life.

New times need new heroes and new forms of legitimacy. South Africa's public memory has been transformed, and so too has Plaatje's place within it. His tombstone and his house in Angel Street, which stands to this day, largely unchanged, have been declared national monuments. Awards and honours have been heaped upon him: an honorary doctorate from the University of North West; a posthumous national literary award; and the Order of Luthuli in Gold, South Africa's highest award, in recognition of having dedicated his life 'to the cause of restoring the dignity of oppressed South Africans and exceptional contribution to the struggle for a free and democratic South Africa'. Prizes for poetry and translation have been named after him, so have schools and streets in various towns and cities. Postage stamps have carried his image. In 2000 the Department of Education's headquarters in Pretoria was renamed 'Sol Plaatje House', in honour, according to the then minister of education, 'of a great South African with whom we can all identify, from whom we can all learn'.[73]

Of the places he was associated with, Kimberley has gone furthest in honouring his memory, renaming the greater Kimberley area as the Sol Plaatje Municipality and erecting a bronze statue on a spot that was once part of the Malay Camp (now the Ernest Oppenheimer Gardens); it was unveiled by President Jacob Zuma on 9 January 2010, the ninety-eighth anniversary of the founding of the African National Congress. Here Plaatje now sits at his writing desk, pen in hand, atop a plinth displaying images of him as newspaper editor, political spokesman and Shakespeare scholar. Close by stands the new Sol Plaatje University, which opened its doors to its first students in 2014, promising the kind of educational facilities the city has long needed.

The precise nature of his legacy is contested, however. It was over a decade before agreement was reached to place the statue in the Ernest Oppenheimer Gardens. A second statue, commissioned by the Northern Cape provincial government, showing Plaatje with one arm held aloft, fist clenched, was due to be unveiled in 2009. The plan was dropped at the last minute when the family and their representatives objected, pointing out that the 'amandla'-style pose was ahistorical and only became popular decades after Plaatje's death; it was quite wrong therefore to portray him in this way. They were not alone in believing that the (ANC-run) provincial government was seeking to appropriate the memory of a man whose achievements went well beyond his association with the African

National Congress; that a new national narrative failed to take account of local sensibilities; that representatives of the family should have been involved and consulted from the beginning.

Since then this statue has remained under cover and out of sight, lying on its side in a storeroom of the McGregor Museum in Kimberley, casualty of the unresolved tensions that have come with new notions of heritage, legitimacy and entitlement. Perhaps it serves as a metaphor, too, not only for the difficulties of coming to terms with the past, but of knowing just what to make of Plaatje, of reaching any kind of consensus about his place in a contested historical memory. Failure to erect statues sometimes says as much as pulling them down.[74]

Any understanding of Plaatje himself must start with his times, not ours. He rose to prominence in the early years of the twentieth century, but his ideas and beliefs were largely formed in the Victorian era. Born into a family of relatively prosperous Tswana pastoralists, he had deep roots in both family and clan traditions. As a Morolong *ba ga Modiboa*, direct descendants of the founder of the Barolong nation, he acquired a deep respect for the customs and institutions of chiefly rule, and he knew the Barolong chiefdom at Mafikeng at a time when it still enjoyed a measure of independence from white rule.

To his identity as a Motswana and a Morolong were added the values and beliefs that came with growing up on a mission station, participating in its project to forge a way of life that took the Christian gospel as its guide. From his own family, as well as the missionaries with whom they were associated, came not only a life-long attachment to the liturgy and rituals of the Lutheran faith, but an upbringing and education that laid stress on good character and behaviour, and on an inner strength that sustained him for the rest of his life.

His worldview was crucially shaped by the time he spent in Kimberley in the 1890s. Here, as a young man, he entered into a wider social world of improvement and progress, hopeful that the liberal institutions of the Cape Colony and the British empire could provide a future for educated Africans like himself. With its non-racial franchise, its colour-blind constitution, its commitment to equality before the law (in theory if not always in practice), the Cape Colony in the 1890s held out the promise of inclusion and advancement. Plaatje, and others like him, wished to claim their place, to exploit these opportunities – and then to extend them to their fellow countrymen. He developed a particular fascination with the law, perceiving in this a means of defending their rights against those who thought they should have none.

When war came at the turn of the century, many Africans believed that British victory would be their victory too, that it would extend the freedoms of the Cape Colony to a new South Africa. There appeared to be a window of opportunity after the Treaty of Vereeniging in 1902, just as Plaatje entered public life. As editor of *Koranta ea Becoana*, he became a tireless advocate of the interests of the Barolong, of the Batswana and of Africans more generally. His mission, as he saw it, was to intercede with the colonial authorities, to use the medium of print to promote solidarity, to help prepare his people for the modern world. He brought to this self-confidence, an exceptional facility with languages, and an independence of mind that sometimes left him at odds with those around him.

To the voices calling for South Africa to be 'a white man's country', Plaatje offered an alternative: a vision of a country that had a place for all its peoples, African and European, preserving their distinct cultural and racial identities, but incorporated into a new polity on the basis of common citizenship and a shared loyalty to King and empire. His watchwords were equality before the law and adherence to Cecil Rhodes's famous dictum of 'equal rights for all civilised men' – though he argued from the start that women should be included too. With goodwill, support from friends and allies, black and white, and by means of persuasion and reasoned debate, he hoped justice would prevail.

Everything changed with the Union of South Africa in 1910. For a while Plaatje was optimistic that disaster might be averted, that the Cape's liberal traditions might yet influence the direction of the new dominion's affairs. They did not. Afrikaner nationalism grew in strength, forcing through the Natives' Land Act of 1913, the greatest challenge by far for the newly formed South African Native National Congress. For Plaatje the Land Act was an existential threat to his fundamental beliefs, a triumph of racial chauvinism over the inclusive traditions of the Cape. Thereafter the political situation went from bad to worse. Neither Plaatje nor his colleagues could prevent South Africa's rulers from pursuing the course on which they were set, or of excluding them from any meaningful role in the affairs of their country.

Yet Plaatje continued to resist in every way he could. His historical achievement lay not in realising his objectives during his lifetime, though there were victories along the way, but in laying the foundations of what would follow, in keeping alive a tradition that would eventually prevail. Against those who would segregate and separate, he set out another way – in his speeches, in meetings with politicians and government officials, in missions and deputations at home and abroad. But, above all, he accomplished this in his writings – in his own newspapers, in his book *Native Life in South Africa*, in pamphlets and in his extensive journalism elsewhere. He left a remarkable written record. At different times he spoke for different people, for different constituencies, for different organisations, but at all times he spoke for himself, and in a voice that was always reasoned, eloquent and distinctive.

He devoted his final years to Setswana, intent on securing its future as a written language, determined to salvage something from the demolition of so many of his hopes and dreams. The political struggle, for his generation, may have been lost, but the cultural survival of his people was more fundamental, and it became his major preoccupation. His literary efforts came to fruition with the publication, in 1930, not only of his novel *Mhudi*, written ten years before, but *Diphosho-phosho*, his translation of Shakespeare's *Comedy of Errors*, the first in any African language.

Together they gave expression to what was perhaps Plaatje's greatest legacy: the idea that in South Africa's multiplicity of cultural and linguistic traditions, and the interaction between them, there lay not so much a problem as an asset, a source of creativity and human potential. In the life he led, in the peculiarly challenging conditions of early twentieth-century South Africa, he demonstrated just how that could be realised.

Acknowledgements

I began working on this book in 2010, building upon research that began in the 1970s which went into several earlier Plaatje-related projects. I am indebted to all those who helped me on this first time around, as it were, and I hope they will forgive me if my thanks to them individually are not repeated here. Even since 2010, I have accumulated a lengthy series of debts to many people, in several different continents, who have made this book possible.

First of all I owe a deep debt of gratitude to members and relatives of the Plaatje family who have continued to encourage and support me in my work, and who have provided invaluable information, particularly the late Mr Johannes Plaatje, Mr Daniel Plaatje, Mr Richard Plaatje, Elizabeth Molema and the late Mr Solomon Molema, Galefele Molema and Dr Leloba Molema. Both Mr Simon Lekhela and his brother, Professor Ernest Lekhela, very kindly shared their memories of the man himself.

Descendants and families of individuals who knew Sol Plaatje have been similarly generous in their responses to my enquiries. Mr Hermann Knothe, and Mrs Anna Knothe, a grand-daughter of Ernst and Marie Westphal, Plaatje's missionary mentors, very kindly allowed me access to Ernst Westphal's diaries and letterbooks, all of it written in Sütterlin script, and Mr Knothe translated material for me from his family archive as well as Berlin Society archives in Berlin and Pretoria. Harald and Marie Thiede, and the late Mrs Else Thiede, have been similarly generous with their hospitality, and in providing further information which they were able to pass on to me about the Westphal family.

In England, during the First World War, Plaatje was welcomed and supported by members of the Brotherhood movement, and formed some close friendships. A century on, their descendants, where I have been able to track them down, have responded generously to my requests for information and have shed new light on the relationships that developed. So I would like to thank Mr Graham Stapleton for information about his great-uncle, Mr William Cross, one of Plaatje's keenest English supporters; Tim and Richard Dixon, descendants of William Barber Dixon, from Leighton Buzzard; and Mr Grenville Williams, on his grandparents, Henry and Kate Castle from Heathfield, Sussex. I am grateful to them for their permission to reproduce photographs in this book. From an earlier episode in Plaatje's life – the siege of Mafeking – I thank Mr Richard H. Nicholson, grandson of the Hon. Algernon Hanbury-Tracey, Baden-Powell's chief intelligence officer, for his kindness in showing me the intelligence reports, prepared by Plaatje, which have been preserved in his family papers.

In the United States, I must thank Professor Adelaide Cromwell, for sharing with me several letters between Plaatje and her grandfather, John W. Cromwell, who Plaatje met in Washington DC in 1921 and 1922.

This book could not have been written without the help of librarians and archivists whose collections I have consulted. In Southern Africa, I am indebted to the staff of the National Archives of Botswana and the National Archives of Swaziland, and of the National Archives of South Africa at their repositories in Cape Town, Bloemfontein, Pretoria and Pietermaritzburg. I am particularly grateful to Erika Le Roux, Jaco van der Merwe, Thembile Ndabeni and other members of staff at the Western Cape Provincial Archive, where I have spent the most time, for the efficient and friendly service they have provided. My thanks also to the researchers who have helped me to track down material when I have been unable to do so myself – Loretha Du Plessis in Cape Town, André and Claudie Jooste in Bloemfontein, Zabeth Botha in Pretoria.

Other libraries and archives in South Africa have been just as vital to my research for this book. I am grateful to the staff of the Africana Library in Kimberley, where Bernice Nagel, a mine of information about Kimberley's nineteenth-and twentieth-century history, far exceeded her job description in the way she has responded unfailingly to my requests for information; to Gabriele Mohale, Zofia Sulej and Michele Pickover at Historical Papers, University of the Witwatersrand, which houses the invaluable Molema/Plaatje collection and much else besides; to Kathy Brookes, Special Collections, University of Johannesburg; Melanie Geustyn and Laddy McKechnie, Special Collections, National Library of South Africa (Cape Town); Charmaine McLean and the late Dr. M. H. Buys, De Beers Archives, Kimberley; Ammi Ryke and Marié Coetzee, Archives and Special Collections, Unisa, in Pretoria; Liz de Wet, Dr Cornelius Thomas,

Louise Vervey and Vathiswa Nhanha at the Cory Library, Rhodes University, Grahamstown; Colin Fortune, Sunet Swanepoel, Vida Allen and Robert Hart, McGregor Museum, Kimberley; Isaac Ntabankulu, Clive Kirkwood, Lesley Hart and Sandy Shell, Manuscripts and Special Collections, University of Cape Town; Jennifer Kimble, the Brenthurst Library, Johannesburg; Letitia Myburgh, Standard Bank Heritage Centre, Johannesburg; Mary van Blerk and Cedric van Dyk, Rustenburg School for Girls, Cape Town; Mosanku Maamoe at the Archives, University of Fort Hare.

Librarians and archivists in Europe have been similarly helpful and professional in all my dealings with them. Bettina Golz, archivist of the Berlin Mission Society, now located in the Kirklisches Archivzentrum in Berlin, enabled me to consult their wonderfully rich archive, while Berlind Lück and Ursula Unterumsberger, provided invaluable help with research and translation. Dr Andrea Schultze and Professor Ulrich van der Heyden kindly assisted too. In Sweden, the staff of the Swedish Film Institute and Sveriges Television (SVT) helped me to track down the wildlife film *The Cradle of the World*, with which Plaatje was involved in 1923.

In the UK, I am indebted to the archivists and librarians at the following institutions: the University of Cambridge; Balliol College, Oxford; the Bodleian Library, Oxford, and before that the Rhodes House Library, where Lucy McCann has been especially helpful; the British Library, including its former Newspaper Library at Colindale; the University of Reading; King's College, London; the London School of Economics and Political Science; the School of Oriental and African Studies; Senate House, University of London, including the archive of the Institute of Commonwealth Studies; University College London; the Cadbury Research Library, University of Birmingham; West Sussex Record Office; the Hull History Centre, including the Hull University archives; the National Archives, Kew; Ealing Central Library; British Museum (Central Archive); House of Lords Record Office; National Army Museum; University of Bristol; University of Leeds; Bristol Archives.

In the US, I am grateful to the staff of the following institutions: Folger Shakespeare Library, Washington DC; Library of Congress, Manuscripts Division; National Archives of the United States; Special Collections, University of Massachusetts Library, Amherst; Beinecke Library, Yale University; Buffalo and Erie County Historical Society; the Library, New York Academy of Medicine. Peter Limb, until recently Africana Bibliographer at Michigan State University, has gone out of his way to convey copies of relevant documents, newspaper articles and other material, and has been a source of encouragement throughout. Bob Edgar, Howard University, has done the same, over an even longer period.

They have been the most generous and supportive of colleagues.

Many other friends and colleagues, academic and otherwise, have helped in my research and writing. John Aldridge, John Comaroff, Catherine Corder, Andrew Dickson, Christopher Saunders, Harvey Feinstein, Heather Hughes, Martin Plaut, Janet Remmington, Kirsten Rüther, Keith Soothill and Charles van Onselen have all read one or more chapters, and provided invaluable feedback. Laurence Wright has read the entire manuscript, providing systemic and detailed comment and suggestion: this book is very much the better for it. Bill Nasson, Bob Edgar and an anonymous reader have performed the same task for the publishers of this book. All have contributed to a much improved final product.

Other people have helped in a variety of ways – with translation, passing on references, engaging in discussion and debate, providing friendship and hospitality. So thank you to Siemon Allen, Maitseo Bakwena, Fiona Bell, Grant Christison, Gwil Colenso, Beverley Collins, Tim and Diana Couzens, Johan Cronje, Stephen Curry, Peter Delius, Derek du Bruyn, Saul Dubow, Bob Edgar, Mark Freeman, Margrit Gander, Steven Gill, Stephen Gray, Jeff Green, Albert Grundlingh, Dawn Hamill, Brother Steven Haws, CR, Tim Jeal, Angela John, Barbara Josiah, Peter Kallaway, Alan Kelly, Moemedi Kepadisa, David Killingray, Veronica Klipp, Christopher Lowe, Hugh Macmillan, Margaret McCord, Peter Midgely, Henry Mitchell, Khumisho Moguerane, Colin Murray, Robert Molteno, David Morris, Paul Mulvey, Neil Parsons, Bheki Peterson, Mike Popham, Carina Ray, Andrew Reed, Janet Remmington, Kevin Ritchie, David Schalkwyk, Peter Seboni, Sandy Shell, Richard Smith, Liz Stanley, Jane Starfield, Jack Stokes, Les Switzer, Catherine Tackley, Nancy Taylor, Chris Thurman, Joe Tsonope, Lilian Serece Williams, Mary van Blerk, Cedric van Dyk, Stephen Volz.

A special word of thanks is due to Sabata-mpho Mokae, journalist, novelist, lecturer in creative writing, friend. We have shared an enthusiasm for Sol Plaatje and his work, and he has been a very generous host during my visits to Kimberley, and to the new Sol Plaatje University since it opened its doors to students in 2014. Like Plaatje himself, he has championed writing in Setswana: not just by talking about it, and teaching it, but by doing it. I look forward to our continued collaboration.

Jacana have done a splendid job in transforming my manuscript into a printed book, and they have not stinted on production values. Bridget Impey, publishing director at Jacana, believed in it from the moment she heard about it, as did Russell Martin from an earlier stage of its conception. Both have provided encouragement when needed and Russell has been a superb copyeditor. Others at

Jacana – Nadia Goetham, Lara Jacob, Tarryn Talbot, Sibongile Machika, Shawn Paikin, Stavi Kotsiovos – have all applied their professional skills to the project and have been great to work with. I believe we can all be proud of it.

As well as looking forward I must also look back. Firstly, in order to acknowledge my debt to Shula Marks who supervised my PhD thesis more years ago than either of us may care to remember, who supported my biographical researches at a time when this was not academically fashionable, and who has been a source of inspiration ever since.

Secondly, to salute the unique contribution that Tim Couzens has made to South African history and literature. We shared many interests, the life and work of Sol Plaatje among them. He taught me an enormous amount, and I will always treasure the memory of our research trips together. Tim was a fine, sensitive scholar, he wrote beautifully, and he was a very good friend. I am very sad that he did not live to see this book published. It is dedicated to his memory.

My thanks finally to my wife Jenny for reading every word of the manuscript of this book, and suggesting numerous improvements. And for everything else in our life together.

Notes

Preface

1 Brian Willan, *Sol Plaatje: South African nationalist* (London: Heinemann Educational Books, 1984) and *Sol Plaatje: a biography* (Johannesburg: Ravan Press, 1984). Modiri Molema's biography of Plaatje, written in Setswana, was completed and delivered to the Bechuanaland (later Botswana) Book Centre in 1965 but never published. An English translation was eventually published in 2012: Seetsele Modiri Molema, *Lover of His People: a biography of Sol Plaatje*, translated and edited by D.S. Matjila and Karen Haire (Johannesburg: Wits University Press, 2012).

2 See, for example, Andrew Dickson, *Worlds Elsewhere: journeys around Shakespeare's globe* (London: Bodley Head, 2015); Natasha Distiller, *South Africa, Shakespeare, and Post-Colonial Culture* (Lewiston: Edward Mellen Press, 2005); Laurence Wright (ed.), *The Shakespearean International Yearbook 9: special section, South African Shakespeare in the twentieth century* (Aldershot: Ashgate, 2009); D.S. Matjila and Karen Haire, *Bringing Plaatje Back Home: Ga e phetsolele nageng – Re-storying the African and Batswana sensibilities in his oeuvre* (Trenton, NJ: Africa World Press, 2015). (Fuller references to this literature are given in chapters 9 and 16.)

3 See particularly Beverley Collins and Inger Mees, *The Real Professor Higgins: the life and career of Daniel Jones* (Berlin: Mouton de Gruyter, 1998); Heather Hughes, *First President: a life of John L. Dube, founding president of the ANC* (Johannesburg: Jacana Media, 2011); Colin Grant, *Negro with a Hat: the rise and fall of Marcus Garvey* (London: Jonathan Cape, 2008); David Levering Lewis, *W.E.B. Du Bois: biography of a race*, 2 vols. (New York: Holt, 1993 and 2000); Adelaide M. Cromwell, *Unveiled Voices, Unvarnished Memories: the Cromwell family in slavery and segregation, 1692–1972* (Columbia: University of Missouri Press, 2007); Peter Limb (ed.), *The People's Paper: a centenary history and anthology of Abantu-Batho* (Johannesburg: Wits University Press, 2012); Janet Remmington, Brian Willan and Bhekizizwe Peterson (eds.), *Sol Plaatje's Native Life in South Africa: past and present* (Johannesburg: Wits University Press, 2016); Peter Limb, 'The subaltern's orb and sceptre: early ANC leaders and the British world', in Peter Limb (ed.), *Orb and Sceptre: studies on British imperialism and its legacies, in honour of Norman Etherington* (Clayton, Victoria: Monash University Press, 2006); Colin Murray, *Black Mountain: land, class and power in the eastern Free State,*

1880s to 1980s (Edinburgh: Edinburgh University Press, 1992); Khumisho Moguerane, 'A history of the Molemas, African notables in South Africa, 1880s to 1920s' (DPhil thesis, University of Oxford, 2014); Shula Marks, *The Ambiguities of Dependence in South Africa: class, nationalism and the state in twentieth-century Natal* (Baltimore and London: Johns Hopkins University Press, 1986).

Chapter 1

1   The story is told in Westphal's letterbook (Unisa Archives, Hesse Collection, Acc. 21, Ernst Gotthilf Westphal Collection, 7.1, June 1891) and the Pniel Tagebuch (Kirchliches Archivzentrum, Berlin, Berlin Mission Society Archive (BMS), Acta Pniel, 1885–1895, Bd. 5, III, 3, 10, June 1891). A further draft, upon which I have also drawn, is in Westphal Collection, 5.1, 'Morgengrüsse von allerlei kleinem Volk' (1890, no. 1). According to 'Berlin Mission Synod', *Diamond Fields Advertiser* (*DFA*), 23 January 1889, the journey from Pniel to Mayakgoro normally took fourteen hours.

2   Anthony Trollope, *South Africa* (London: Chapman and Hall, 1878), vol. 2, p. 275.

3   Trollope, *South Africa*, vol. 1, p. 7; S.M. Molema, *Montshiwa: Barolong chief and patriot* (Cape Town: Struik, 1966); J. Comaroff, 'Competition for office and political processes among the Barolong boo Ratshidi of the South Africa–Botswana borderland' (PhD thesis, University of London, 1973), esp. pp. 298–303.

4   Paragraph based on Bethanie Mission Register, entry 795, 9 October 1876 (microfiche copy in SOAS library); S.M. Molema, *Lover of His People: a biography of Sol Plaatje* (Johannesburg: Wits University Press, 2012), pp. 18–19; author's interview with Martha Bokako (daughter of Simon Plaatje, Sol Plaatje's eldest brother), Thaba Nchu, 26 March 1976; 'A brief history of the Plaatje (Mogodi) family' (unpublished) by Johannes L. Plaatje (grandson of Simon Plaatje and great-grandson of Johannes and Martha Plaatje), dated 10 May 1976.

5   Family traditions vary in their interpretation of the meaning of the name 'Tshekisho'. 'A brief history of the Plaatje (Mogodi) family' discounts on linguistic grounds any association with the notion of purity or purification, believing that the essential meaning of the term 'Tshekisho' relates only to the idea of 'judgement'. Martha Bokako, by contrast (interview, Thaba Nchu, 22 April 1976), emphasises the '*itshekisa*' (purity) derivation, and told me she knew this because Martha Plaatje had told her this. Her version is followed by Modiri Molema in *Lover of His People*, p. 19.

6   SOAS, Plaatje Papers, MS 375495, STP 1/2, 'Ancestry'.

7   University of the Witwatersrand (UW), Historical Papers, Molema–Plaatje Papers, Ccl, 'Historical account of the Barolong', pp. 1–2.

8   University of Cape Town (UCT), Lestrade Papers, BC 255, F7, 'Daniel Mokhatle and others *vs* Minister for Native Affairs', transcript of evidence of S.T. Plaatje, p. 221. For other accounts of the origins of the Barolong *ba ga Modiboa*, see Z.K. Matthews, 'A short history of the Tshidi Rolong', *Fort Hare Papers*, 1, 1945, p. 11; UW, Molema–Plaatje Papers, Ad6.1, S.M. Molema, 'History of the Barolong', pp. 31–2. Martha Bokako's version is from an interview, 22 April 1976.

9   SOAS, Plaatje Papers, STP 1/2, 'Ancestry'; Comaroff, 'Competition for office'; Matthews, 'A short history of the Tshidi Rolong', p. 12; Molema, 'History of the Barolong', pp. 39 et seq.

10 John Comaroff, Brian Willan, Solomon Molema and Andrew Reed (eds.), *The Mafeking Diary of Sol T. Plaatje* (Cape Town and Oxford: David Philip and James Currey, 1999), introduction, p. 9; Molema, 'History of the Barolong', p. 32.

11 S.T. Plaatje, 'Chief Moroko', in T.D. Mweli Skota (ed.), *The African Yearly Register: being an illustrated national biographical dictionary* (Johannesburg: R.L. Esson, 1930); see also, S.T. Plaatje, 'The case for the Barolongs: tribe's relations with the Voortrekkers: some wider issues', *Cape Argus*, 4 March 1924.

12 SOAS, Plaatje Papers, STP 1/2, 'Ancestry', Plaatje family prayerbook (courtesy the late Mr Johannes Plaatje), pp. ii and iii, for the places and dates of birth and marriage of Sol Plaatje's parents; gravestone in the cemetery at the former Pniel mission, and family register recording births and deaths in Plaatje family (photocopy courtesy of the late Mr Johannes Plaatje), for Simon Plaatje's date of birth; interviews with Martha Bokako, Thaba Nchu, 26 March and 4 April 1976, for the Plaatje family's time in Philippolis.

13 Evidence of Selogilwe's baptism by Gottlob Schreiner in 1838 is from a later report by one of the missionaries of the Berlin Mission Society at their Bethanie mission, 18 July 1876 (BMS, Bethanie: Acta 1872–1881, Abt. III, Fach 3, no. 9 (Blaue Bogenzahlung 114, S.5), bmw 1-5238, Tagebuch entries for 18 July 1876). This must have taken place in December 1838, the month Schreiner arrived at Philippolis. For Schreiner's time at Philippolis, see Karel Schoeman, *Olive Schreiner: a woman in South Africa 1855–1881* (Johannesburg: Jonathan Ball Publishers, 1991), pp. 29–35, and Robert Ross, *Adam Kok's Griquas* (Cambridge: Cambridge University Press, 1976). Martha Bokako believed that her grandmother Martha, when a child, attended the mission school at Philippolis, where Rebecca Schreiner (Olive Schreiner's mother) was for a while a teacher.

14 Interview with Mrs Bokako, 22 April 1976; SOAS, Plaatje Papers, STP 1/2, 'Ancestry'.

15 Ross, *Adam Kok's Griquas*, pp. 66–74; S.T. Plaatje, 'Descendants of the Koks', *DFA*, 7 December 1926. John Philip and James Read noted, in May 1842: 'The Bechuanas are all dependent on the Griquas, their cattle and flocks feed upon their pastures, and one half of them are as birds of passage': Karel Schoeman (ed.), *The Missionary Letters of Gottlob Schreiner 1837–1846* (Cape Town: Human and Rousseau, 1991), p. 89. Mogodi's talent for healing sick animals is from Molema, *Lover of His People*, p. 16.

16 Molema, *Lover of His People* (pp. 22–3) refers to the time the family spent at Patis (or Patisi), the site of the Paris Evangelical Society's Hermon mission, on the south side of the Caledon River, not far from the present-day town of Hobhouse.

17 SOAS, Bethanie mission register, misc. entries 1867–76.

18 J. Duplessis, *A History of Christian Missions in South Africa* (London: Longman, Green, 1911), ch. 22, 'The beginnings of the Berlin mission'; W.J. de Kock (ed.), *Dictionary of South African Biography* (Pretoria: National Council for Social Research), vol. 1, p. 891, entry for Carl Friedrich Wuras. The Bethanie mission register records the birth of Moses Plaatje, Johannes and Martha's fourth son, on 9 August 1870.

19 *Missionsberichte der Gesellschaft zur Beförderung der evangelischen Missionen unter den Heiden, Berlin* (*Missionsberichte*), 1878, p. 146, report for Bethanie; BMS, Bethanie: Acta 1872–81, Abt. III, Fach 3, no. 9 (Blaue Bogenzahlung 114, S.5), bmw 1-5283, Tagebuch entries for 18 and 19 July 1876.

20 According to Johannes Plaatje ('A brief history'), of Mogodi's children, Sarah and Leah accompanied Johannes and Martha to Pniel, while Elias, Elizabeth and William remained at Bethanie.

21 Plaatje described his return to the district in 1913 in his *Native Life in South Africa* (London: P.S. King & Son, 1916), p. 63: he had not been back here 'since infancy', he said, and while he remembered the name of the farm, he was unsure of its exact whereabouts.

22 E. Rosenthal, *Rivers of Diamonds* (Cape Town: Howard Timmins, n.d.), pp. 16–19, 26–7; Gardiner Williams, *The Diamond Mines of South Africa: some account of their rise and development* (New York: Buck, 1902), pp. 137–9; miscellaneous reports from Pniel in *Missionsberichte* in the 1880s; Plaatje, *Native Life*, pp. 61–2.

23 'The Pniel jubilee', *DFA*, 22 July 1895; *Missionsberichte*, 1891, pp. 134–8, report on Pniel for 1890; Dr G.J. Fock, 'An early history of Pniel', *DFA*, 1 March and 5 April 1963; *Report on the Land Question in Griqualand West* (London: Colonial Secretary's Office), June 1880, report no. 35, pp. 81–3.

24 For details of the dispute, see *Report on the Land Question in Griqualand West*, pp. 81–3.

25 Based on *Missionsberichte*, 1884, pp. 156–8, report on Pniel for 1883; 1882, pp. 107–9, report on Pniel for 1881; 1885, p. 154, report on Pniel for 1884.

26 Meyer's departure and the dire state of Pniel is from *Missionsberichte*, 1882, pp. 107–9, report on Pniel for 1881; see also L. Zöllner and J.A. Heese, *Die Berlynse sendelinge in Suid-Afrika* (Pretoria: Human Sciences Research Council, 1984), pp. 265–6. Meyer 'was shocked by the laxity of the tenants', but neither they nor Heinrich Kallenberg (who did 'not take kindly to being placed under the immediate authority of another man') co-operated with his attempts to reassert control.

27 The first reference to Johannes Plaatje is in BMS, Abt. 3, Fach 3, no.10, Stationsakten/ Tagebücher, Pniel, 1876–84 (vol. 4), Tagebücher, July–October 1881; Inventor, January 1882. Joshua Plaatje's drowning is recorded in Plaatje family prayerbook, p. ix, as well as Meyer's Tagebuch (November 1881–January 1882), BMS, D 49750, bmw 1-5277-4.

28 Interview with Mr Johannes Plaatje, Kimberley, 29 March 1976; Unisa, Westphal Collection, 2.0, Briefbuch 1890–1896, p. 13a, no. 52, 23 December 1893, details of stockholdings. Philip Moyanaga had married Sarah, a sister of Plaatje's father: see Colin Murray, *Black Mountain: land, class and power in the eastern Orange Free State 1880s–1980s* (Edinburgh: Edinburgh University Press, 1992), p. 192, and Notes of interview with Eric Moyanaga, Thaba Nchu, 2 June 1978 (courtesy Andrew Reed).

29 See especially K. Shillington, 'The impact of the diamond discoveries on the Kimberley hinterland', in S. Marks and R. Rathbone (eds.), *Industrialisation and Social Change in South Africa: African class formation, culture and consciousness 1870–1930* (Harlow: Longman, 1982).

30 Plaatje, *Native Life*, pp. 61–2. Flooding was reported in September 1884 (*Missionsberichte*, 1885, pp. 81–5, report on Pniel for 1884), when Plaatje would have been nearly eight years old, so this may well have been the time he remembered.

31 Molema, *Lover of His People*, p. 20; S.T. Plaatje, *Sechuana Proverbs with Literal Translations and their European Equivalents* (London: Kegan Paul, Trench, Trübner & Co., 1916), p. 7.

32 Plaatje's account of the 'Bacchus' episode appears on a typed page, part of what was intended as an article or chapter for a book (Unisa, Molema Papers, Acc. 142). According to Molema (*Lover of His People*, p. 7), Plaatje took a year out of school after Standard II to work as a herdboy, which is most likely when this incident took place.

33 Plaatje's evidence to the Native Economic Commission, 1931 (UW, South African Institute of Race Relations Archives (SAIRR), typescript evidence of S.T. Plaatje, p. 5326); S.T. Plaatje, 'Thirty years ago … Siege memories and others', *DFA*, 16 May 1930.

34 Plaatje, *Sechuana Proverbs*, p. 7, and proverb no. 611, p. 85. The two aunts concerned were probably Sarah and Leah who came with Plaatje's parents from Bethanie. Fox and hare: Plaatje to the Registrar, University of the Witwatersrand, 25 November 1929, reproduced in Brian Willan (ed.), *Sol Plaatje: selected writings* (Johannesburg: Witwatersrand University Press, 1996), p. 379.

35 SOAS, Plaatje Papers, STP 1/2, 'Ancestry'; Preface to *Mhudi* (Lovedale: Lovedale Press, 1930); Molema, *Lover of His People*, p. 16.

36 'Mixed-pars', *Tsala ea Becoana*, 21 February 1914. Although Plaatje described the heroine of the exploit as his 'paternal great-grandmother', if he is right in stating that the incident took place in the 1820s it may have been his grandmother 'Au Magritte', who could have been 'a girl' at this time (one of her sons, Plaatje's father, being born in 1835): in which case Plaatje could have heard the tale from the protagonist herself.

37 See Tagebuch entry for 8 November 1883 for evidence of Baumbach's interest in the customs and traditions of the different peoples living on the Pniel mission (BMS, D 49751, Tagebuch, p. 47, pdf p. 68). Martha Plaatje's importance as a source of information for the Westphals was recalled in 'Solomon T. Plaatje: as a very young man', unpublished account by Erna Westphal, August 1980, p. 2.

38 See particularly Gunther Pakendorf, 'A brief history of the Berlin Mission Society in South Africa', *History Compass*, 9, 2, 2011, pp. 106–18 and 'For there is no power but of God: the Berlin Mission and the challenges of colonial South Africa', *Missionalia*, 25, 3, November 1979, pp. 255–73, at http://www.oocities.org/athens/parthenon/8409/germiss1.htm, accessed 19 November 2011.

39 *Missionsberichte*, 1890–1, p. 164, report on Pniel for 1889 and Baumbach's Tagebuch for January 1884, report complaints about high dues (BMS, D 49753, p. 8, bmw 1-5277–7). Once Simon Plaatje was threatened with poison by one resident of the mission who disapproved of his close association with the missionaries (Baumbach Tagebuch, D 49762, 3 July 1889). On the Bloems and their adherents, see J.A. Engelbrecht, *The Korana: an account of their customs and their history* (Cape Town: Maskew Miller, 1936), esp. pp. 56–66.

40 BMS, Stationsakten/Tagebuch, Pniel, August–October 1881 and Inventor, January 1882 (D 49749, bmw 1-5277–3). The inscription in the Plaatje family Bible is in the hand of the Rev. Karl Meyer (senior).

41 BMS, Acta Pniel, Bd. 1, 1878–1891, II, 3, 12, Tagebuch (Baumbach), entries for 6 December 1882; 17 August, 14 October and 27 October 1883; 10 June 1885; 27 April 1888.

42 Erna Westphal, 'Solomon T. Plaatje: as a very young man', p. 3; BMS, Acta Pniel, Tagebuch (Baumbach), 1883; Tagebuch (Westphal), 25 May 1884.

43 Interview with Martha Bokako, 16 August 1980; Molema, *Lover of His People*, p. 21; Unisa, Molema Papers, handwritten fragment in Modiri Molema's hand entitled 'S.T. writes of early years'. Baumbach's Tagebuch for June 1883 (BMS, D 49752, p. 32, bmw 1-5277–6) makes it clear that his brother Moses attended the Pniel school too, but then joined his father and brother Elias in Mayakgoro.

44 BMS, Acta Pniel, Tagebuch (Baumbach), January–March 1886 and 19 September 1887; *Missionsberichte*, 1888, pp. 162–73. Martha Plaatje's mental state clearly concerned Martin Baumbach (BMS, Tagebuch, 8 September 1889, p. 181), and one of Modiri Molema's informants (probably Ephraim Moyanaga) told him many years later that she was 'half mad' (SOAS, Molema Papers, notebook, unpaginated).

45 Obituary of Rev. G.E. Westphal in *DFA*, 17 January 1922; interviews with Miss E.C.M. Westphal, October and November 1977; *Missionsberichte*, 1883, pp. 114–15, Pniel report, 1882. Westphal's letter of application to join the Berlin Mission Society, detailing his early life and his conversion experience, survives in the records of the Society (BMS, Ernst Westphal personal file, 4.1, bmw 1-4508, letter to Director Wangemann, 22 August 1873). Westphal explained that his father had, before he died, expressed the wish that he should be trained as a teacher but that his uncle had prepared him instead for a career in business.

46 BMS, Martin Baumbach personal file, bmw 1-2890, letter to Dr Wangemann, 26 June 1889, p. 77. *Missionsberichte* contains various reports of his ill health, and he was liable to fainting fits, sometimes in the middle of church services. For his well-stocked library, see 'A trip to the Bend: the Berlin Mission Station', *DFA*, 15 October 1886.

47 'A trip to the Bend'; Western Cape Archives and Records Service (KAB), SGE 1/130, Misc. letters received 1892, B–Cl, Westphal to SGE, Cape Town, 19 April 1892; *Missionsberichte*, 1885, pp. 151–3, Pniel report, January–June 1884; Cape Colony, *Annual Report of Supt.-General of Education for 1882* (G3-1883), Supplement, pp. xxxvi–xxxvii, report on Pniel mission school.

48 *Missionsberichte*, 1884 (Pniel report, 1883), p. 162; Unisa, G. Zittlau Collection, Acc. 15, 4.1.1.2, Tagebuch of Martin Baumbach, 1883, p. 21. In KAB, SGE 3/9 (Reports of Deputy Inspector, 1883) the education inspector, John Samuel, commended the 'hearty manner' of Thomas Kats and 'the readiness of the children', recommending that his grant be raised from £12 to £15.

49 H.T. Wangemann, *Ein zweites Reisejahr in Süd-Afrika* (Berlin, 1886), p. 63.

50 *South African Native Affairs Commission, Minutes of Evidence* (Orange River Colony), evidence of Rev. Heinrich Grützner, para 39,080. Grützner was superintendent of the Orange Free State synod in which Pniel (despite being in the Cape Colony) was included, so within the hierarchy of the Berlin Mission Society he was Westphal's and Baumbach's immediate superior. He was also responsible for carrying out inspections at the Pniel mission school (BMS, Westphal Tagebuch, D 49754, p. 4, bmw 1-5277–8).

51 Drawn up in 1881 by Director Wangemann, the *Missionsordnung* (Mission Regulations), which had to be followed by every Berlin Society mission, stipulated: 'In all school education it should be remembered that the instruction of young people to become Christians is the single main purpose and that everything else is subsidiary, and teachers have to guard with great diligence that subsidiary matters do not become primary ones nor that dispensable things are drawn into the area of teaching subjects.' (Quoted by Pakendorf, 'For there is no power but of God', p. 265)

52 KAB, SGE 2/6, Inspectors' Reports, 1894, vol. 1, A–B, report on Pniel mission school, 22 October 1894. The inspector, Henry Nixon, added that he felt 'certain that the teachers strive hard to obtain better results, but they have great difficulties to contend with from the fact that nearly all the children are Koranas or Bechuanas'.

53 Letter from D.M. Ramoshoana to *The Star*, 2 August 1932.

54 *Quarterly Papers of the Bloemfontein Mission*, 82, 15 October 1888, p. 147. Information about Crossthwaite is drawn from W.D. Crisp, *Some Account of the Diocese of Bloemfontein in the Province of South Africa* (Oxford: James Parker, 1895), pp. 73–4; also *Griqualand West Church Magazine*, 9, 104, December 1892, p. 7; C. Lewis and G. Edwards, *Historical Records of the Church of the Province of South Africa* (London: SPCK, 1934), pp. 483–4; obituary of Crossthwaite in *Quarterly Papers of the Bloemfontein Mission*, January 1901, pp. 29–33. Like Pniel, the All Saints mission school was inspected regularly by John Samuel: his conclusions can be found in issues of the *Griqualand West Church Magazine* for February 1886, October 1886 and June 1887 and in their original form in KAB, SGE 3/14. The report for 1886 was distinctly unfavourable, Samuel noting that 'the arithmetic is generally incorrect' and 'the children frequently do not understand the meaning of the written word when using their slates'.

55 Co-operation between missionaries and clergymen in Kimberley took institutional form in September 1885 with the formation of the Kimberley and Beaconsfield Ministers' Association. Its aim was to facilitate 'the discussion of various public matters, for mutual help, and the promotion of a more earnest spirit of unity' ('Kimberley and Beaconsfield Ministers' Association', *DFA*, 5 September 1885).

56 Plaatje's memory is from 'Native Congress mission to England', *DFA*, 17 July 1914. Modder River, twenty-two miles from Kimberley, was a popular picnic destination for school trips, which may have occasioned the train journey.

57 See Westphal's description of the school in his Tagebuch in June 1892 (Unisa, Zittlau Collection, 4.1.1.4). The use of the Elffers (I–III) and *Royal Readers* books (also I–III) is from SGE 3/23, Deputy Inspectors' reports, 1892, vol. L (A–M), report on Pniel: see Hubertus Elffers, *Leesboek voor Zuid-Afrika*, I–V (Cape Town: Juta & Co., 1890–) and *Royal Readers* I–III (London: Thomas Nelson, 1872–81). The Elffers graded readers were written for South Africa, the *Royal Readers* for use in the British empire as a whole. At Pniel, inspections generally rated the pupils' Dutch more highly than their English. The story from *Royal Reader* III was 'The wonderful pudding', recalled in Comaroff et al., *Mafeking Diary*, entry for 27 December 1899, pp. 77–8.

58 Quoted in 'A great missionary', by Anna Knothe, June 1997, unpublished account in author's possession. Mrs Knothe (a granddaughter of Ernst Westphal) added, 'Rev. Westphal used love – and understanding. He was strict – but very fair – and soon his scholars knew that his "no" was "no", and his "yes" really meant "yes".' Westphal's

period of service in the Prussian army (November 1877 to October 1878) preceded his joining the Berlin Mission Society. Ephraim Moyanaga and Solomon Plaatje were first cousins.

59 Gotthardt Westphal's recollection is from his letter to his daughter, Annemarie Knothe, 11 September 1960, p. 6, in Unisa, Westphal Papers, Gotthardt Westphal, 15.2.

60 *Missionsberichte*, 1893, p. 287; Molema, *Lover of His People*, pp. 21–2. On pupil teachers more generally, see Cape Colony, *Report of Supt.-General of Education for 1892* (G29-1893), p. 17.

61 Letter from Martin and Julie Baumbach to Kropf family, 19 October 1891, in BMS archive, bmw 1-2890; Personal file for Martin Baumbach, pp. 96–7, with details of the deaths of the two children; report in *Missionsberichte*, 1892, Pniel report 1891, pp. 199–202; death notice in *DFA*, 28 October 1891, p. 10; KAB, MOK 1/1/43 (4727), death notice for Johan Martin Baumbach, dated 4 November 1891. The Baumbachs had lost three other children before Julia and Wilhelm died in 1891.

62 Johannes Baumbach (1875–1961) was listed as an assistant teacher at Pniel, and in July 1893 applied to take the third class teacher's certificate. Westphal commended him as being of good character, an able teacher and 'kind to the children', and he himself expressed the wish to gain as good a certificate as possible as 'my mother is a poor widow' (KAB, SGE 1/144, Misc. letters received 1893 (B-C), Westphal to SGE, 26 July 1893 and Baumbach to SGE, 19 September 1893). The inspection report quoted is that of 12 August 1892 in KAB, SGE 3/23, Deputy Inspectors' Reports, 1892, vol. 1 (A-M). Late the following year, 1893, the school moved from the run-down old church building to new classrooms (*Missionsberichte*, 1894, report on Pniel for 1893, p. 11).

63 BMS, Acta Pniel, Bd. 5, III, 3, 10, Tagebuch, July–October 1892, entries for 4 September 1892, p. 58, and 27 September 1892, p. 60.

64 Review of *Dintshontsho tsa bo-Juliuse Kesara* in *South African Outlook*, 2 October 1939, pp. 229–30.

65 Letter from Gotthardt Westphal to his daughter, Annemarie Knothe, 11 September 1960 in Unisa, Westphal Papers, Gotthardt Westphal, 15.2. In August 1893, two of the 136 pupils at the school were classified as 'White', the remainder as 'Coloured' (KAB, SGE 2/1, Inspector's Report, vol. 1 (A-C), 1893–4).

66 'A trip to the Bend: the Berlin mission station', *DFA*, 15 October 1886.

67 Unisa, Zittlau Collection, 4.1.1.4, Pniel Tagebuch (Westphal), June 1892.

68 BMS, D 31952, bmw 1-1047-01, Acta: Eingeborene Helfer – Lebensläufe, 1.5.98 (Personal Records of Native Assistants, recorded by Richard Brune, c.1910).

69 Information about Marie Westphal (née Sack) is from her son Gotthardt's recollections in 'Erlebnisse in der Mission'; Gotthardt's letter to his daughter Annemarie Knothe (Unisa, Westphal Collection, 15.2, Gotthardt Westphal to Annemarie Knothe, 11 September 1960); 'A great missionary' by Annemarie Knothe, unpublished account; personal communication from Annemarie Knothe to the author, 10 June 1991; and interviews with Erna Westphal in October and November 1979. In a letter to the superintendent general of education in 1898, Westphal confirmed that Marie Westphal 'has German Certificates for Higher Girls School' (Westphal Collection, 7.1, Letter book of G.E. Westphal, Westphal to SGE, Cape Town, 21 March 1898).

70 Interview with Martha Bokako (22 April 1976); Molema, *Lover of His People*, p. 21; Erna Westphal, 'Solomon T. Plaatje: as a very young man'; interview with Erna Westphal, 11 November 1977, Plaatje's inscription in the copy of *Mhudi* presented to Marie Westphal in 1930 (formerly in the possession of the late Prof. E.O.J. Westphal). Confirmation that Plaatje received 'private lessons' from both Westphals comes in an article by Vere Stent in *Pretoria News*, 16 January 1911, quoted in Plaatje, *Native Life in South Africa*, p. 9. Martin Baumbach informed Dr Wangemann of Thomas Kats's failings in private letters dated 8 March and 30 August 1886 (BMS, bmw 1-2890, Martin Baumbach personal file,

pp. 55 and 56). The missionaries' preference for Batswana over Korana was expressed in *Missionsberichte*, 1884, report on Pniel for 1883, p. 166.

71 Gabriel M. Setiloane, *The Image of God among the Sotho-Tswana* (Rotterdam: Balkema, 1976), pp. 186–8, is especially illuminating about the coalescence of Sotho-Tswana and Christian rituals and traditions relating to baptism and '*patiki*'; see also Lamin Sanneh, *Translating the Message: the missionary impact on culture*, 2nd edn (Maryknoll, NY: Orbis, 2009) for a general account of the importance of vernacular translations of the Bible in defining the nature of African Christianity.

72 The distinctive service of baptism is described by Baumbach in *Missionsberichte*, 1883, report for Pniel for 1882, p. 118, and Ernst Westphal's conversation about the singing at Pniel in BMS, Tagebuch, June 1892. I am indebted to Erna Westphal's vivid recollections of the singing at Pniel (interview, 11 November 1977). Ernst Westphal's fine tenor voice and experience of the Cathedral choir is recalled by his son Gotthardt in his letter to his daughter in 1960 (Unisa, Westphal Collection, 15.2, G. Westphal to Annemarie Knothe, 11 September 1960).

73 Z.K. Matthews, 'Solomon T. Plaatje 1877–1932', *Imvo*, 24 June and 1 July 1961; Matthews himself considered this to be 'one of the best translations into a Bantu language of that English classic'.

74 Plaatje, *Sechuana Proverbs*, p. 11. Plaatje's familiarity with the book of Exodus is evident in his comparison, in his diary of the siege of Mafeking, of the flight of the Israelites from Egypt with the exodus of Africans from Mafeking (Comaroff et al., *Mafeking Diary*, p. 123, entry for 27 February 1900).

75 BMS, Bd. 5, III, 3, 10, Tagebuch, June 1892.

76 Details of the progress of the new church, and the setbacks it encountered, can be found in various issues of *Missionsberichte* from the mid-1880s onwards, and its consecration is described in *Missionsberichte*, 1891, report on Pniel for 1890, pp. 134–8 and in 'Opening of the new Lutheran mission chapel', *DFA*, 21 July 1890, p. 3. The words of Teus Bloem, Johannes Plaatje and Philip Moyanaga are reported in Unisa, Zittlau Collection, 4.1.1.3, Pniel Tagebuch (Baumbach), entry for 13 July 1890, p. 162. Unfortunately many of the bricks made by the residents of the mission proved to be useless and had to be discarded and remade. It then turned out that the new pulpit from Germany was too big to go through the door, necessitating some last-minute alterations. Within months of the opening ceremony, further defects came to light and extensive modifications had to be made. The church remained in use until 1924 when it was so badly damaged in a hailstorm that it could not be repaired.

77 Unisa, Zittlau Collection, 4.1.1.4, Pniel Tagebuch, June 1892; BMS, Acta Pniel, Bd. 5, III, 3, 10, Tagebuch, September 1893, pp. 79–81. Elias died at Mayakgoro but his body was brought back for burial at Pniel by his elder brother Simon.

78 Letter to the editor, *Christian Express*, May 1913.

79 The last mention of Johannes Plaatje in BMS records is in *Missionsberichte*, 1891, statistical tables for 1890, p. 237; also Molema, *Lover of His People*, p. 21 and interview with Martha Bokako, 16 August 1980. The role of black evangelists like Johannes Plaatje has been seriously neglected in comparison with the attention received by the missionaries. Stephen C. Volz's *African Teachers on the Colonial Frontier: Tswana evangelists and their communities during the nineteenth century* (New York: Peter Lang, 2011) provides an important corrective.

80 Details of the Barolong farms, and their history, is from I. Schapera, 'The system of land tenure on the Barolong farms' (unpublished report for Bechuanaland Protectorate Government), 1943, p. 1 (copy in Botswana National Archives, SMS).

81 'Along the road to Cairo land', *Our Heritage*, August–October 1931; SOAS, Plaatje Papers, STP2/2, unpublished notebook.

82 Plaatje, *Sechuana Proverbs*, p. 5. For the connection between African languages, print and

social identities, see particularly Derek R. Peterson, Emma Hunter and Stephanie Newell (eds.), *African Print Cultures: newspapers and their publics in the twentieth century* (Ann Arbor, MI: Michigan University Press, 2016), esp. pp. 1–48; John L. and Jean Comaroff, *Of Revelation and Revolution: the dialectics of modernity on a South African frontier*, vol. 2 (Chicago: University of Chicago Press, 1997), pp. 391–5; Stephen Volz, 'For sense of 40 or 50 missionaries: the development of written Setswana and colonization of the Batswana', in Ulrich van der Heyden and Andreas Feldtkeller (eds.), *Missionsgeschichte als Geschichte der Globalisierung von Wissen* (Stuttgart: Franz Steiner Verlag, 2012), pp. 417–28; and Adrian Hastings, *The Construction of Nationhood: ethnicity, religion and nationalism* (Cambridge: Cambridge University Press, 1997), esp. pp. 148–66.

83 Part T. Mgadla and Stephen C. Volz (eds.), *Words of Batswana: letters to 'Mahoko a Becwana', 1883–1896* (Cape Town: Van Riebeeck Society, 2006), esp. p. xv.

84 Plaatje, *Native Life*, p. 165. For Jabavu and *Imvo*, see particularly L.D. Ngongco, 'John Tengo Jabavu 1859–1921', in C. Saunders (ed.), *Black Leaders in South African History* (London: Heinemann Educational, 1979).

85 James T. Campbell, *Songs of Zion: the African Methodist Episcopal Church in the United States and South Africa* (Chapel Hill, NC: University of North Carolina Press, 1998), esp. pp. 127–31; Veit Erlmann, *African Stars: studies in black South African performance* (London and Chicago: University of Chicago Press, 1991), pp. 21–53; Veit Erlmann, *Music, Modernity and the Global Imagination: South Africa and the West* (New York and Oxford: Oxford University Press, 1999), esp. pp. 59–85; Chinua Akimaro Thelwell, 'Toward a "modernizing" hybridity: McAdoo's Jubilee Singers, McAdoo's Minstrels, and racial uplift politics in South Africa,1890–1898', *Safundi*, 15, 1, 2014, pp. 3–28, DOI: 10.1080/17533171.2013.864169.

86 Plaatje later recalled: 'I have met the Jubilee Singers when I was a boy and later on when I became a man' (*Negro World*, 12 February 1921). His initial encounter must date from the Jubilee Singers' visits to Kimberley in August 1890 and/or April 1891, for they did not then return until August 1895 and May–June 1896 (and again in November 1897 and April 1898 as 'McAdoo's Minstrels'). For Titus Mbongwe, see Erlmann, *African Stars*, p. 45: he died, along with eight other passengers, in a train crash just outside Taunton, Somerset, en route to London. Josiah Semouse's questions were in his article in *Leselinyana*, 1 October 1890, quoted (in translation) in Erlmann, *African Stars*, p. 44.

87 See J. Stewart, *Lovedale Past and Present* (Lovedale: Lovedale Press, 1887), pp. 224 (Paulus Makane) and 525 (August Tollie).

88 Unisa, Molema Papers, fragment in Modiri Molema's hand, and autobiographical fragment in Plaatje's hand; 'Mr Sol T. Plaatje honoured: tributes to his work for non-Europeans', *DFA*, 12 November 1928.

89 BMS, Acta Pniel, Bd. 5, III, 3, 10, Pniel Tagebuch (Westphal, July–September 1895), S.1–12.

90 Unisa, Molema Papers, autobiographical fragment.

91 BMS, bmw 1-5230-3 (D 49529), Beaconsfield Tagebücher, Report by G. Kuhn, Beaconsfield: II: Vierteljahr, 1932, pp. 13–14.

Chapter 2

1 James Bryce, *Impressions of South Africa* (London: Macmillan, 1897), p. 202; Max O'Rell (pseud. for M. Blouet), *John Bull and Co.* (London: Warne, 1894), p. 266. For Kimberley in this period, see also B. Roberts, *Kimberley: turbulent city* (Cape Town: David Philip, 1976).

2 Civil Commissioner's Report for Kimberley, 1892, *Blue Book on Native Affairs*, Cape Government, G7-1893.

3 Report by Sister Catherine (USPG), quoted in Edward Africa, *The Kimberley Malay Camp 1882–1957* (Kimberley: Sol Plaatje Educational Trust, n.d.), p. 50; 'The Malay

people and the Malay Camp', letter from R.W. Murray (Snr), *Diamond Fields Advertiser* (*DFA*), 23 September 1895; letter to the editor from James A. Domingo ('paraffin cricket'), *DFA*, 13 December 1889; 'The life and work of Benjamin Tyamzashe: a contemporary Xhosa composer' (Master of Music thesis, Rhodes University, 1968), p. 45; interview with Benjamin Tyamzashe, Zinyoka, King William's Town, 15 July 1976.

4 Interview with Martha Bokako, 22 April 1976; KAB, 1/KIM 2/1/44, Civil Records, case 899, *Cumgalie v. Solomon Plaatje*, 8 October 1897.

5 Based on *Report of General Manager of Telegraphs for the Year 1882*, Cape Government, G23-1883, reproduced in R. Young, *African Wastes Reclaimed* (London: Dent, 1902), p. 88.

6 Address by John Knox Bokwe to the Lovedale Training Society, *Imvo Zabantsundu*, 11 July 1894. Bokwe was in charge of the postal and telegraphic office at Lovedale.

7 *DFA*, 18 June 1892. Rev. James Hughes, an American Baptist minister, also lent his support to this campaign. See also *Imvo*, 9 and 16 June and 7 July 1892, also *DFA*, 15 July 1892.

8 'Mr Alfred S. Moletsane', *Koranta ea Becoana*, 13 April 1904; E.H. Kilpin (ed.), *Cape of Good Hope Civil Service List* (Cape Town, 1892), Post Office establishment; James Stewart (ed.), *Lovedale: Past and Present* (Lovedale: Lovedale Press, 1887), p. 226.

9 'A good example to his brothers', *DFA*, 4 March 1895. Lindie died later that year. See also Stewart, *Lovedale Past and Present*, p. 139.

10 *Official Post Office Guide (Cape Colony)*, no. 49, October 1895; 'The capital revisited: interview continued', *Tsala ea Becoana*, 16 December 1911.

11 'Interview with Henry Burton, Minister of Native Affairs, in November 1911' (editorial, *Tsala ea Becoana*, 2 December 1911); KAB, Attorney General's files, AG 739, 28/99, Annexure A, Plaatje to Resident Magistrate, Mafeking, 1 March 1899; 'Serious charge against a postman', *DFA*, 20 November 1901. Colleagues' names are from Cape Voters' Lists of 1895 and 1897, which list occupations (KAB, CCP 11/1/33 and CCP 11/1/3). Abraham Smouse began in the same year as Plaatje but his career ended in disgrace in 1903 when he was found guilty of stealing a letter and dismissed. Bray's recollections are in 'Worked day and night', *Pretoria News*, 1 April 1927; the experiences of the two post office messengers are from KAB, Kimberley Magistrate's Records, 1/KIM, 2/1/46 (Civil Records), record of case no. 1192, *Aaron Nyusa v. E. Street*, 29 November 1898, and 1/KIM, 4/1/2/11, RM to T. Binase, 18 March 1897.

12 KAB, AG 630, 120/98, Annexure A, Plaatje to RM, Mafeking, 5 August 1898 and Annexure B, Plaatje to RM, Mafeking, n.d. Plaatje's later memories, quoted here, are from S.T. Plaatje, 'Light and shade on native questions', *Umteteli*, 11 October 1924 and 'Mr Sol T. Plaatje honoured', *DFA*, 12 November 1928.

13 Westphal's visit took place at some point between June and September 1895. He reported that Plaatje's salary had been increased from 72 shillings a month to 96 shillings a month, equivalent to an increase from £72 a year to £96 a year. This conflicts, however, with a later statement of Plaatje's that he reached the figure of £96 p.a. only 'at the beginning 1897' (BMS, Pnieler Tagebuch, Westphal, July to September 1895, and KAB, AG 837, 3/1900, Annexure A, Plaatje to Resident Magistrate, Mafeking, 6 June 1900). Molema's description is from S.M. Molema, *Lover of His People* (Johannesburg: Wits University Press, 2012), p. 27.

14 The *Official Post Office Guide (Cape Colony)*, updated quarterly, and published during these years, sets out the most important duties, responsibilities and procedures.

15 Kosani: De Beers Consolidated Mines archive (DB), Kimberley, General Secretary's Correspondence (microfilm), S.T. Plaatje to De Beers, 25 September 1929. Tyamzashe: S.T. Plaatje, 'The Joint Council and the constitution', *Umteteli wa Bantu* (Johannesburg), 28 February 1925; interview with Mr Ben Tyamzashe, 15 August 1976; Msikinya: John Comaroff and Brian Willan (with Solomon Molema and Andrew Reed) (eds.), *The*

Mafeking Diary of Sol T. Plaatje (Cape Town and Oxford: David Philip and James Currey, 1999), p. 146.

16 KAB, AG 1984/1898, Record of Service of Messengers and Interpreters, entries for J.S. Moss and G.B. Polisa; AG 1970/1899, Record of Service, entry for J.S. Msikinya; Stewart, *Lovedale Past and Present*, pp. 230 and 239–40.

17 On the Queen Victoria Jubilee Hall, see 'Jubilee Commemoration Hall', *Imvo*, 18 November 1897; 'Native Wesleyan Church', *DFA*, 21 June 1897; 'Letters to the editor: the natives and the Queen', *DFA*, 23 May 1901.The hall was formally opened by John Tengo Jabavu, editor of *Imvo*, in November 1897. Fundraising efforts had been successful, and a number of local white individuals and organisations contributed (DB, 'List of contributions we have received from the European public', enclosure in letter from J.S. Msikinya et al. to the Directors, De Beers, 27 August 1897).

18 Hampton University Archives, Hampton, Virginia, I. Bud-M'belle to General Armstrong (principal of Hampton Institute), 16 September 1890. At least five other African students wrote to the principal of Hampton to apply for places and financial support but without success: see J. Mutero Chirenje, *Ethiopianism and Afro-Americans in Southern Africa, 1883–1916* (Baton Rouge: Louisiana State University Press, 1987), pp. 36–7.

19 For Bud-M'belle's career, see 'U Mr I.B. M'belle', *Imvo*, 5 January 1894; 'A government appointment', *Imvo*, 7 March 1894; T.D. Mweli Skota (ed.), *African Yearly Register* (Johannesburg: Esson, 1930), pp. 104–5; 'A scholarly native', *DFA*, 9 January 1893; 'Native interpreter retires' and 'Mr Bud-M'belle's retirement', *DFA*, 1 February 1916.

20 'Letter to the editor: a lofty tribute', *DFA*, 25 December 1901, p. 7, where it was said, on his departure from Kimberley in 1901, that his 'chief qualification' was 'perseverance under troubles, provocation, and misrepresentations'. The praise poem is in 'Umbolero e Kimbili', *Imvo*, 15 April 1897.

21 'The South Africans Improvement Society', *DFA*, 23 August 1895; S.T. Plaatje, 'An example to our youth', *Umteteli*, 17 October 1925. Part of the inspiration for the society came from two other local societies catering for the white population – the Kimberley Literary Society and the YMCA Literary and Debating Society, some of whose rules they adopted. Lovedale-educated members of the South Africans Improvement Society would also have had the Lovedale Literary Society in mind: see Isabel Hofmeyr, 'Reading debating/Debating reading: the case of the Lovedale Literary Society, or why Mandela quotes Shakespeare', in Karin Barber (ed.), *Africa's Hidden Histories: everyday literacy and making the self* (Bloomington, IN: Indiana University Press, 2006), pp. 258–77.

22 'Native teachers: the want of literature' (editorial), *Imvo*, 29 August 1895.

23 'The South Africans Improvement Society', *DFA*, 23 August 1895.

24 'Jubilee of the Lovedale Literary Society', *Christian Express*, 2 July 1917. Joseph Moss's 'Lectures on native education', published in the *DFA*, are noted in Stewart, *Lovedale: Past and Present*, p. 230 and also referred to in 'Sacrificing justice for respectability', letter from 'M.P.' to the editor, *Imvo*, 22 May 1890, p. 3. See also Michael Lambert, *The Classics and South African Identities* (London: Bristol Classical Press, 2011), pp. 101–5, and Leon de Kock, *Civilising Barbarians: missionary narrative and African textual response in nineteenth-century South Africa* (Johannesburg: Witwatersrand University Press, 1996), pp. 126–30, for the question of the place of the classics in African education.

25 'The South Africans Improvement Society', *DFA*, 23 August 1895.

26 See particularly Neil Parsons, *King Khama, Emperor Joe and the Great White Queen: Victorian Britain through African eyes* (London and Chicago: University of Chicago Press, 1998), pp. 64–8 and 148, and 'Khama and Kimberley: his mission to England', *DFA*, 17 August 1895.

27 'The South Africans Improvement Society', *DFA*, 23 August 1895. *Imvo Zabantsundu* also carried a report of the meeting in its piece on 'Beaconsfield' in its issue of 29 August

1895, referring to the 'South African Mutual Improvement Society'. It also announced that the Rev. Jonathan Jabavu was due to talk on the subject of 'Trade unions' at the meeting on 27 September.

28 'The Wesleyan Synod and ukulobola', letter from 'Biza' to *DFA*, 17 January 1896.

29 For Lenkoane, see *Leselinyana*, 1 March 1889; KAB, CCP 11/1/33, Cape Voters' List (Kimberley), 1896, entry no. 1571; Comaroff et al., *Mafeking Diary*, entry for 27 December 1899, p. 77; interview with Mrs Maud Zibi (née Sidzumo), Kayakulu, North West Province, 2 December 1981; 'The South Africans Improvement Society', *DFA*, 23 August 1895. Artemus Ward was the nom de plume of Charles Farrar Browne (1834–67), an American-born writer and humorist who was popular in both the UK and the US. Patrick Lenkoane was to assume command of the Basotho Native Contingent (with the rank of lieutenant) in the campaign against Galeshewe at the time of the 'Bechuana Rebellion' in 1897 and subsequently worked as an interpreter with the Cape Police before joining Plaatje in Mafeking after the South African War.

30 'Mr Sol T. Plaatje honoured', *DFA*, 12 November 1928; 'The treatment of natives in courts', address to 1924 Joint Councils Conference, Pretoria, reproduced in Brian Willan (ed.), *Sol Plaatje: selected writings* (Johannesburg: Witwatersrand University Press, 1996), p. 336.

31 KAB, AG 630, 120/98, Annexure A, Plaatje to RM, Mafeking, 5 August 1898; AG 630, 120/98, RM, Mafeking, to Law Department, Cape Town, 15 December 1898; Unisa Archives, Hesse Collection, Acc. 21, Ernst Gotthilf Westphal Collection, Letterbook, 7.1, Westphal to 'Mein liebe Salomo', 30 June 1896. Twenty years later Plaatje wrote that he was 'conversant with six native languages': S.T. Plaatje, 'The late Allan King', *African World Annual* (London: African World, 1915), p. 124, and another time specifically mentioned Herero as one of the languages in which he had 'a smattering' ('Suggested new Bantu orthography' in Willan, *Sol Plaatje: selected writings*, p. 397).

32 BMS, Pniel Diary (July–September 1895). Borrowing books from the Kimberley Public Library was not an option. Although it had been (since December 1894) 'open to the public' (rather than just the original subscribers), the definition of 'public' did not include Africans like Plaatje: see Rosemary Holloway, 'The history and development of the Kimberley Africana Library and its relationship with the Kimberley Public Library' (Master of Information Science thesis, Unisa, 2009), p. 122.

33 Bud-M'belle's achievements are set out in 'Umbolero e Kimbili', *Imvo*, 15 April 1897. For more on the sporting life of Kimberley's African community, see Brian Willan, 'An African in Kimberley', in S. Marks and R. Rathbone (eds.), *Industrialisation and Social Change in South Africa: African class formation, culture and consciousness, 1870–1930* (Harlow: Longman, 1982), pp. 250–2 and André Odendaal, *The Story of an African Game: black cricketers and the unmasking of one of cricket's greatest myths, South Africa, 1850–2003* (Cape Town: David Philip, 2003).

34 Plaatje's height is the figure he gave in applying for a Canadian passport in 1921 (SOAS, Plaatje Papers, STP 3/4); for his election as secretary of Eccentrics CC, see 'Beaconsfield-Eccentrics CC', *Imvo*, 22 September 1896.

35 James T. Campbell, *Songs of Zion: the African Methodist Episcopal Church in the United States and South Africa* (Chapel Hill, NC: University of North Carolina Press, 1998); Margaret McCord, *The Calling of Katie Makanya* (Cape Town: David Philip, 1995); Veit Erlmann, *African Stars: studies in black South African performance* (Chicago: University of Chicago Press, 1991); Alfred B. Xuma, *Charlotte Manye: what an educated African girl can do* (Johannesburg: AME Church, 1930); Zubeida Jaffer, *Beauty of the Heart: the life and times of Charlotte Mannya Maxeke* (Bloemfontein: Sun Press, 2016); Chirenje, *Ethiopianism and Afro-Americans in Southern Africa*.

36 'A little function', *DFA*, 25 August 1896. *Imvo* also carried a report of the function in its issue of 17 September 1896 ('Indaba kwele Mbokotwe').

37 'Death of a native student', *DFA*, 18 April 1898; personal communication from the Registrar, Wilberforce University, 11 October 1978. Henry Msikinya, however, returned to South Africa in 1901. For his subsequent career, see Campbell, *Songs of Zion*, pp. 266–7 and 271–2.

38 DB, General Secretary's Correspondence, YMCA appeal, 21 September 1896, and letter from Plaatje, 22 September 1896; *Koranta ea Becoana*, 11 October 1902.

39 Comaroff et al., *Mafeking Diary*, pp. 28 and 53. An advertisement for a performance of 'O.M. McAdoo's high class American Minstrel Vaudeville Compy' in Kimberley for the week beginning 17 November 1897 indicates that the programme includes '4 corner men with the latest songs, wheezes and dances, and high kickers and tricksters' (*DFA*, 12 November 1897, p. 4). For background, see David B. Coplan, *In Township Tonight! South Africa's black city music and theatre*, 2nd edn (Chicago and London: University of Chicago Press, 2008), esp. ch. 2.

40 T. O'C's letter was in *DFA*, 11 March 1896; Plaatje's memory is from 'Points of view: colour and the kinema', *DFA*, 30 June 1928.

41 'Concert', *DFA*, 23 July 1896.

42 'The debut of the Philharmonic Society', *DFA*, 13 March 1897; see also 'Umbolero e Kimbili: Philharmonic Society', *Imvo*, 15 April 1897.

43 BMS, Pniel Diary (July–September 1895); 'E Kimbili', *Imvo*, 20 April 1896.

44 S.T. Plaatje, 'A South African's homage', in I. Gollancz (ed.), *A Book of Homage to Shakespeare* (Oxford: Oxford University Press, 1916), pp. 336–9.

45 For Gabriel David and his Shakespeare performances, see Brian Willan, 'Whose Shakespeare? Early black South African engagement with Shakespeare', *Shakespeare in Southern Africa*, 24, 2012, pp. 3–24.

46 'Interview with Mr William Haviland', *DFA*, 16 October 1896. On their first visit in October 1896 Mr Haviland's company (the De Jong-Haviland Company) put on *David Garrick* and *The Lady of Lyons* as well as Shakespeare at the Queen's Theatre. They were back again in December 1897 as 'The Haviland and Lawrence Shakesperian and Dramatic Company', and performed at the new Theatre Royal, which had opened two months previously. William Haviland had previously been a member of the Holloway Theatre Company, which toured South Africa in 1895, its performance of *Othello* in Johannesburg in December 1896 coinciding famously with the Jameson Raid. See David Holloway, *Playing the Empire: the acts of the Holloway Touring Theatre Company* (London: Harrap, 1979), various issues of the *DFA* in June 1898, and Richard Foulkes, *Performing Shakespeare in the Age of Empire* (Cambridge: Cambridge University Press, 2002).

47 'Theatre Royal: Hamlet', *DFA*, 20 December 1897; 'Points of view: colour and the kinema', *DFA*, 30 June 1928.

48 'Hamlets I have seen', by 'an Old Stager', *DFA*, 15 December 1897. 'Old Stager' had seen Charles Kean on two occasions. 'So great was my desire to know more' after the first occasion, he added, 'that six months after I had seen Kean I knew the play of *Hamlet* by heart.' These performances probably dated from the 1850s, some forty years previously.

49 For the rebellion, see Kevin Shillington, *Luka Jantjie: resistance hero of the South African frontier* (Johannesburg: University of the Witwatersrand Press, 2011), and Brian Willan, '"Not calculated to increase their confidence in the government to whom they desired to be loyal": Kimberley's African intelligentsia and the Langeberg rebellion', in Sunet Swanepoel (ed.), *Resistance in the Northern Cape in the Nineteenth Century: proceedings of a mini-conference held at the McGregor Museum, Kimberley, 14–16 September 2011* (Kimberley: McGregor Museum, 2012), pp. 70–8. Reporting the arrival of Lenkoane's medal in 1902, Plaatje described it as 'an emblem of loyalty and an example to the rest of his countrymen' ('A black medallist: for valour in 1897', *Koranta ea Becoana*, 13 September 1902, p. 5).

50 Quoted in L.D. Ngcongco, 'John Tengo Jabavu 1859–1921', in C. Saunders (ed.), *Black Leaders in South African History* (London: Heinemann Educational, 1979), p. 146.

51 'War and the Matabele' (editorial), *Imvo*, 23 April 1896, p. 3, and Comaroff et al., *Mafeking Diary*, entry for 27 February 1900, p. 122.

52 'Mr P.R. Frames', letter from P. Lenkoane to *Koranta ea Becoana*, 29 November 1902.

53 Reproduced in *DFA*, 21 August 1895, later published as O. Schreiner and S.C. Cronwright-Schreiner, *The Political Situation* (London: T. Fisher Unwin, 1896); see also R. First and A. Scott, *Olive Schreiner* (London: Deutsch, 1980), pp. 218–21; S.C. Cronwright-Schreiner, *The Life of Olive Schreiner* (London, T. Fisher Unwin, 1924), pp. 274–5; S.T. Plaatje, 'Friends of the natives', *DFA*, 15 June 1925.

54 'Mr Cronwright-Schreiner and the natives', *DFA*, 27 August 1895. Plaatje knew both Cronwright-Schreiner and Olive Schreiner well enough to request a friend in Kimberley – while he was besieged in Mafeking in 1900 – 'to please also remember me to Mr and Mrs Cronwright Schreiner' (Willan, *Sol Plaatje: selected writings*, p. 45, draft of letter to Isaiah Bud-M'belle, n.d. [late February 1900]).

55 'The South Africans Improvement Society', *DFA*, 23 August 1895.

56 J.C. Smuts, *Jan Christian Smuts* (London: Cassell, 1952), p. 32; *DFA*, 30 October 1895, reproduced in K. Hancock and J. van der Poel (eds.), *Selections from the Smuts Papers*, vol. 1 (Cambridge: Cambridge University Press, 1966), pp. 80–100.

57 Comaroff et al., *Mafeking Diary*, entry for 18 March 1900, p. 141; *Imvo*, 15 June 1898; *Koranta ea Becoana*, 7 September 1904. The two appeal cases were reported in 'High Court: civil term', *DFA*, 10 June 1898 and 'Criminal appeal: Ben, appellant, *vs* the Queen, respondent', *DFA*, 15 June 1898. For Henry Burton, see W.J. de Kock (ed.), *Dictionary of South African Biography* (Pretoria: National Council for Social Research, 1968), vol. 1, pp. 138–9.

58 *Imvo*, 22 February and 15 June 1898; S.T. Plaatje, 'Natives and law and order', *DFA*, 10 November 1930; S.T. Plaatje, 'Transvaal and natives', *DFA*, 25 January 1928; 'Native rights under pass laws', *Cape Times*, 14 June 1928; S.T. Plaatje, 'The pass law in Kimberley', *DFA*, 26 March 1925. In 1899, after he had left Kimberley, arrests of 'respectable natives' under pass law legislation resumed, a further appeal case was heard and 'the Kimberley Natives' decided to petition parliament about the matter ('Natives and the pass law', *DFA*, 21 January 1899; 'High Court', *DFA*, 17 February 1899; 'In the courts: Kimberley', *DFA*, 28 June 1899; 'The natives and the Hofmeyr Act' and 'The Hofmeyr Voters' Act: its operation in Kimberley', *Imvo*, 3 July 1899).

59 'Mr Sol T. Plaatje honoured', *DFA*, 12 November 1928.

60 Interview with Mrs Martha Bokako, Thaba Nchu, 22 April 1976. In his evidence in Civil Record case no. 899, *Cumgalie v. Solomon Plaatje*, 8 October 1897 (KAB, 1/KIM 2/1/44) Plaatje confirmed that 'I used to go away sometimes on Saturdays'.

61 'Practical brotherhood', *DFA*, 17 January 1919; Plaatje family prayerbook, p. ix, entry recording Johannes Plaatje's death in Mafeking district, 26 September 1896; 'Chief Montsioa' in Willan, *Sol Plaatje: selected writings*, p. 418.

62 Molema, *Lover of His People*, pp. 27–8.

63 The three cases in which Cumgalie instituted proceedings in 1896 were *Cumgalie v. G. Nathan* (8 May 1896, entry 41); *Cumgalie v. G. Moses* (8 May 1896, entry 418); *Cumgalie v. J. Denoon* (4 December 1896, entry 1093) in KAB, 1/KIM 2/2/1/30 (Civil Record Book, 1895–6) and 1/KIM (Civil Record Book, 1896–8). The case of *Cumgalie v. Solomon Plaatje* is recorded as no. 899, 8 October 1897 (1/KIM, 2/2/1/31, Civil Record Book, 1896–7), and is one of only a small number for which the actual court proceedings have been preserved (in 1/KIM 2/1/44, Civil Records). It was reported in 'Civil court', *DFA*, 9 October 1897, p. 9.

64 This paragraph draws upon: S.T. Plaatje, *Native Life in South Africa* (London: P.S. King & Son, 1916), p. 92; 'Late Mrs E. Sol T. Plaatje', *Umteteli*, 30 January 1943; KAB, 1/

KIM, 8/1/18, Civil Marriage Affidavit, 25 January 1898; KAB, SGE 1/194, letters from Rev. A. Lomax to SGE, Cape Town, 1 and 22 July 1896. Details of the Inspection Report in March 1897 are in KAB, SGE 2/42 (Inspection Reports 1897, vol. VII – Richmond to Steynsburg). The overall assessment was 'satisfactory if it be taken into consideration that the school was closed for about a year'. A further inspection took place on 6 December 1897, the superintendent general of education himself adding the comment (in red ink) on the report, 'The teacher should qualify for a certificate'. For Elizabeth's time at the mission school in Colesberg, see KAB, SGE 2/1 and SGE 2/8, Inspection Reports, Colesberg, 1893 and 1894. Molema (*Lover of His People*, p. 68) attests to her knowledge of the five languages indicated.

65 Molema, *Lover of His People*, p. 29; interview with Mrs Martha Bokako, April 1976; Plaatje, 'A South African's homage', p. 336.

66 Comaroff et al., *Mafeking Diary*, entry for 25 December 1899, p. 76; Plaatje, 'A South African's homage', p. 336.

67 KAB, 1/KIM 8/1/18, Marriage Register (Kimberley), January 1898 – December 1899, affidavits of Solomon Tshekisho Plaatje and Elizabeth Lieby M'belle. The Marriage and Licence Act 1882 is reproduced, with commentary, in Daniel Ward, *A Handbook to the Marriage Laws of the Cape Colony, the Bechuanaland Protectorate and Rhodesia* (Johannesburg: Juta, 1902), pp. 10–11, 14 and 64–8. Elizabeth's date of birth is deduced from Plaatje's mention of her birthday in his *Mafeking Diary*, entry for 13 January 1900.

68 Molema, *Lover of His People*, pp. 29–30.

69 *DFA*, 26 January 1898. Several of Lobengula's offspring or relatives did in fact live on the diamond fields. His granddaughter Martha was the best friend of Katie Makanya (Manye), sister of the more famous Charlotte (McCord, *The Calling of Katie Makanya*, p. 27).

70 Plaatje, 'A South African's homage', p. 338.

71 The correspondence survives in KAB, SGE 1/222, thanks to Rev. Lomax having forwarded Elizabeth's letters (dated 29 January and 3 February 1898) and telegram (2 February 1898) to the superintendent general of education in order to explain why the school did not reopen at the normal time. The school remained closed for the first quarter of 1898 but reopened when a new teacher, Petrus Gabaka, arrived (SGE 2/54, Inspection Reports 1898, vol. VIII, Richmond to Steynsburg). Contrary to Molema's claim (*Lover of His People*, p. 32), it is clear that Elizabeth did not resume teaching at Steynsburg but resigned with immediate effect. Even if she had wanted to continue, this would not have been possible given the regulations that prohibited the employment of married women as teachers.

72 See, particularly, S. Trapido, 'White conflict and non-white participation in the politics of the Cape of Good Hope, 1853–1910' (PhD thesis, University of London, 1970), for the 1898 election and the significance of the African vote.

73 Comaroff et al, *Mafeking Diary*, entry for 18 March 1900, p. 141. Jabavu's support for Henry Burton, and for Bond candidates more generally, had caused concern to the *DFA*, which accused him of seeking to persuade the electors of Barkly West 'for the first time in their lives to cast in their lot with their political enemies' (editorial, 27 August 1898).

74 For the origins of the slogan 'Equal rights for all civilised men', see Robert I. Rotberg, *The Founder: Cecil Rhodes and the pursuit of power* (New York and Oxford: Oxford University Press, 1988), pp. 610–11; *DFA* (weekly edition), 6 August 1898, reports the meeting in Barkly West addressed by Cecil Rhodes, disproving Rotberg's claim (p. 608) that he did not 'appear before Africans'.

75 Cronwright-Schreiner's quote is from 'Mr Cronwright-Schreiner's volte-face', *DFA*, 25 July 1898, p. 3; see also First and Scott, *Olive Schreiner*, p. 232, for further detail on the election campaign.

76 Plaatje's views were expressed in response to questions put to him by the South African

Native Affairs Commission in September 1904, paras 37,621–37,757.

77 The proceedings of the inquiry are in KAB, CSC 2/1/1/355. Msikinya denied being paid £286 by Rhodes but admitted to having received £25 from him on an earlier occasion. When Rhodes was asked whether it did not strike him as odd that one of the two clergymen who came to his offices in Kimberley should also 'have addressed the natives and proposed a vote of confidence in you', he simply answered 'no'. He also denied all knowledge of the offer of payment to Pukwane, Burton's election agent, to change sides, despite a statement from Nathaniel Brown, Rhodes's election agent, that he (Rhodes) did indeed authorise this. The election accounts, conveniently, could not be found. Olive Schreiner was among those struck by the 'absolutely bare faced corruption' that was in evidence even before campaigning began, noting that Brown had lost 'a bag containing £400 in gold' from his cart when returning to Kimberley from a trip 'to water auriferously the electoral field of Barkly West' in November 1897. How much, she wondered, was in the bag when Brown travelled *to* Barkly West? (Liz Stanley and Andrea Salter (eds.), *The World's Great Question: Olive Schreiner's South African letters, 1889–1920* (Cape Town: Van Riebeeck Society, 2014), p. 90). In his ruling on the petition, the chief justice, Sir J.H. de Villiers, concluded that while 'the respondent's agents had not actually entered the forbidden ground of bribery, they have come perilously close to it'. For further reports on the proceedings, see *DFA*, 6, 7, 9 and 13 January 1899.

78 Plaatje, *Native Life in South Africa*, p. 162; see also Plaatje's letter to the *DFA*, 4 November 1910, on the subject of 'The native question', where he drew attention to Rhodes's responsibility for 'the formula which has made his name great, viz, "Equal rights for all civilised men irrespective of colour"'.

79 Cape Colony, *Report of Postmaster-General for Year 1897*, G39-1898, p. 92.

80 The discovery of Moloke's hidden past can be traced in KAB, 1/MFK, 5/1/9/2, misc. letters received (January 1898–October 1899), Detective Dept, Kimberley, to RM, Mafeking, 17 January 1898, and J.A. Moloke to RM, Mafeking, 28 February 1898; Plaatje's job application is in KAB, AG 630,120/98, Plaatje to RM, Mafeking, 5 August 1898.

81 KAB, AG 630, 120/98, Plaatje to RM, Mafeking, 13 September 1898.

82 KAB, AG 630, 120/98, RM, Mafeking, to Law Department, Cape Town, 15 September 1898; Annexure D, testimonial dated 9 September 1898; Annexure A, form of application for employment.

83 The words were those of future president Nelson Mandela, as true of Mafeking in Plaatje's time as when he was preparing for a career as an interpreter himself thirty years later, albeit by means of a course at the Healdtown Institution rather than by private study and practice. In the event Mandela left Healdtown before completing his course and never applied for a job as a court interpreter: Nelson Mandela, *Long Walk to Freedom: the autobiography of Nelson Mandela* (London: Little, Brown, 1994), p. 43.

84 KAB, AG 630, 138/98, Annexure C, application for leave dated 2 November 1898, and medical certificate dated 1 October 1898.

85 KAB, AG 630, 120/98, Annexure F, handwritten memo to chief clerk and Annexure A, form of application for employment.

86 Plaatje, *Native Life*, p. 63.

Chapter 3

1 S.M. Molema, *The Bantu Past and Present: an ethnographical and historical study of the native races of South Africa* (Edinburgh: W. Green & Son, 1920), p. 304.

2 For Minchin, see *Men of the Times: old colonists of the Cape Colony and Orange River Colony* (London: Transvaal Publishing Company, 1906), p. 288.

3 'The story of Mafeking', *Diamond Fields Advertiser* (*DFA*), 13 July 1897.

4 Information on Patrick Sidzumo and his family is drawn from: 'Dincho', *Tsala ea*

Batho, 17 July 1915, pp. 2–3; interview with Maud Zibi (née Sidzumo), Kayakulu, North West Province, 2 December 1981; KAB, AG 739/1899, Bell to Secretary, Law Dept, 17 July 1899, enclosing form of application for employment for Patrick Johannes Sidzumo. Patrick started at the magistrate's office in April 1899 on a salary of £60 p.a. (compared with Plaatje's £96 p.a.). Charles Bell's view of his brother Petrus is from KAB, AG 739/1899, Bell to Law Dept, Cape Town, 7 March 1898. For Patrick's family relationship with Elizabeth, see John Comaroff and Brian Willan with Solomon Molema and Andrew Reed (eds.), *The Mafeking Diary of Sol T. Plaatje* (Cape Town and Oxford: David Philip and James Currey, 1999), pp. 68 and 182 n.51.

5   KAB, 1/MFK, 5/1/2/1, W. Stanford to CC and RM, Mafeking, 9 September 1899, approving application of Phooko for job as constable to inspector of native reserves with effect from 1 August 1899; Andrew Reed's interviews with Herbert Phooko and Sheila Ramailane (son and daughter); see also Comaroff et al., *Mafeking Diary*, p. 171 n.8.

6   The local Methodist missionary estimated that the Barolong had lost £60,000 worth of stock (SOAS, Methodist Missionary Society Archives, Box 330/102, Rev. F. Briscoe to Rev. Marshall Hartley, 15 October 1898). Bell's assessment of the prospects of collecting taxes is from KAB, 1/MFK, 6/1/2/3, Letters Despatched, Departments (May 1898 – January 1899), C.G.H. Bell to Colonial Secretary, Cape Town, 9 November 1898. On the presence of labour recruiters, see K. Shillington, *The Colonisation of the Southern Tswana, 1870–1900* (Johannesburg: Ravan Press, 1985), p. 249, and KAB, 1/MFK, 6/1/2/3, Letters Despatched, Departments (May 1898 – January 1899), annual report from Inspector of Native Locations, 14 January 1899.

7   S.M. Molema, *Montshiwa: Barolong chief and patriot, 1815–96* (Cape Town: Struik, 1966); J. Comaroff, 'Competition for office and political processes among the Barolong boo Ratshidi of the South Africa–Botswana borderland' (PhD thesis, University of London, 1973); S.T. Plaatje, 'Montsioa', in T.D. Mweli Skota (ed.), *African Yearly Register* (Johannesburg: R.L. Esson, 1930), pp. 53–7; Jane Starfield, 'Dr S. Modiri Molema (1891–1965): the making of a historian' (PhD thesis, University of the Witwatersrand, 2001).

8   *Koranta ea Becoana*, 16 December 1903; reports in *Bechuanaland News* (Vryburg), 18 June and 6 July 1898; KAB, 1/MFK, 6/1/3/2, Letters Despatched (misc.) (August 1898–June 1899), Bell to Wessels Montshiwa, 6 October 1898. The proverb is no. 259 in Plaatje's *Sechuana Proverbs with Literal Translations and Their European Equivalents* (London: Kegan Paul, Trench, Trübner & Co., 1916), p. 47, the European equivalent being 'Sweet meat will have sour sauce'.

9   *South African Native Affairs Commission, Minutes of Evidence*, vol. 4, evidence of S.T. Plaatje, p. 264. The proverb is no. 260 in Plaatje, *Sechuana Proverbs*, p. 46.

10 S.T. Plaatje, 'The late Chief Silas Molema: passing of a progressive Barolong chief', *Cape Times*, 13 September 1927 and entry for Silas Thelesho Molema in Skota, *African Yearly Register*, p. 51. Molema's memory of past sieges is from 'When Eloff attacked Mafeking', letter from Silas T. Molema to *DFA*, 15 July 1902. See also Starfield, 'Dr S. Modiri Molema', chs. 1 and 2 for Silas Molema's life and role in Tshidi society, and Khumisho Moguerane, 'A history of the Molemas, African notables in South Africa, 1880s to 1920s' (DPhil thesis, Oxford University, 2014).

11 Plaatje, 'The late Chief Silas Molema'; De Beers Archives (DB), Lyndhurst Road Estate file, Silas Molema to S.T. Plaatje, 25 May 1918. See also Starfield, 'Dr S. Modiri Molema', ch. 2, p. 127 for Silas Molema's relationship with Dr Jameson prior to the Raid. For the history of Lotlhakane and the rivalry between Tshidi and Rapulana, Andrew Manson and Bernard K. Mbenga, *Land, Chiefs, Mining: South Africa's North West Province since 1840* (Johannesburg: Wits University Press, 2014), p. 95.

12 Standard Bank Heritage Centre, Johannesburg, INSP 1/1/243, Inspection report, Mafeking branch, as at 26 October 1903, Liabilities of Parties section, p. 4; KAB, 1/

MFK, 5/1/2/1 (Under Secretary for Native Affairs, Letters Received, January 1896 – December 1903), marginal comment by Bell re Molema's application for a firearms licence, Supt. of Native Affairs to RM, Mafeking, 20 October 1898.

13 S.M. Molema, *Lover of His People* (Johannesburg: Witwatersrand University Press, 2012), p. 10. Modiri Molema was intrigued to discover, much later, that Plaatje was known in his own family as 'whitey', or 'the little white one', being much lighter in complexion than his brothers.

14 Based on Molema, *Lover of His People*, p. 33; 'Iziqaneko zekaya', *Imvo*, 12 December 1898; Comaroff et al., *Makeking Diary*, p. 73, entry for 24 December 1899.

15 KAB, AG 630, 84/98, 'Application for a third clerk at Mafeking', Bell to Law Dept, Cape Town, 29 May 1898.

16 KAB, AG 630, 84/98, recommendation for Grayson to be placed on fixed establishment, 7 July 1898. Details of Grayson's less than distinguished record at Balliol – he obtained a third-class degree in Modern History in 1896 – are in Sir Ivo Elliott, *The Balliol College Register 1854–1950* (Oxford: Printed for Private Circulation by John Johnson at the University Press, 1924), p. 207. Grayson's Oxford degree, he was pleased to discover, exempted him from the need to take the civil service examinations in order to be taken onto the fixed establishment. In 1900, on a visit to the UK, he added an MA (Oxon) to his academic attainments (KAB, CLC 1/12, Mark Garrett, Secretary, Civil Service Commission, to Ernest Grayson, 10 and 23 June 1897, and CLC 1/13, Garrett to Grayson, 23 June 1901).

17 University of the Witwatersrand, Historical Papers, Molema–Plaatje Papers, Db2, 'The essential interpreter', IV, p. 7. Bell's career details are derived from E.F. Kilpin (ed.), *Cape of Good Hope Civil List* (Cape Town, 1902), p. 289; *Men of the Times*, p. 37; obituary in *Port Elizabeth Daily Telegraph*, 13 August 1908 (from which the passage quoted is taken).

18 Obituary in *Port Elizabeth Daily Telegraph*, 13 August 1908.

19 'The late Charles George Harland Bell, C.M.G.', *South African Law Journal*, 26, 1909, p. 209. Tobias Cekiso Mdula, who knew Bell in Port Elizabeth (quoted in the *Port Elizabeth Daily Telegraph* obituary), testified to his fluency in 'Sesuto and Kafir [Xhosa]'. Spencer Minchin, one of Mafeking's attorneys, spoke of the 'sterling common sense and fairness' of his magisterial decisions ('Departure of Mr Bell', *Mafeking Mail*, 31 October 1900).

20 'Mafeking notes: meeting of the Barolong', *DFA*, 27 September 1897, p. 8; KAB, NA 466, Bell to Chief Magistrate, 13 May 1890, quoted in William Beinart and Colin Bundy, *Hidden Struggles in Rural South Africa: politics and popular movements in the Transkei and Eastern Cape 1890–1930* (London: James Currey, 1987), p. 79.

21 'The late Charles George Harland Bell', p. 210; 'Departure of Mr Bell', *Mafeking Mail*, 31 October 1900; Comaroff et al., *Mafeking Diary*, p. 77, entry for 27 December 1899.

22 KAB, 1/MFK, 6/1/2/3, Letters Despatched (Departments), Bell to Secretary for Native Affairs, 15 September 1898.

23 KAB, AG 739, 28/99, Bell to Law Dept, Cape Town, 5 April 1899.

24 KAB, 1/MFK, 5/1/8/5, Letters Received, misc. (January 1898 – October 1899), F.H. Haarting, Landdrost, Lichtenburg, to RM, Mafeking, 31 October 1898 and Marumoloa Mothibi to CC and RM, Mafeking, 17 January 1899.

25 KAB, PWD 2/1/135, Bell to Secretary, Law Dept, 14 March 1898 and Julius Weil to Sir James Sivewright, 26 July 1898. Mr Justice Lange's complaint was reported in 'Mafeking Circuit Court', *DFA*, 22 October 1897, and he repeated it the following year (*Bechuanaland News*, 26 March 1898).

26 KAB, 1/MFK, 6/1/2/4, Letters Despatched, Departments (January 1899 – June 1900), schedule of types of cases heard in RM court, Mafeking, April 1898 and April 1899, and KAB, 1/MFK, 1/2/1/1/2, Criminal Record book, entries for cases 290 and 291, October 1898.

27 KAB, 1/MFK, A1/1/1/1, records of Setlagole periodical court, 'Decision of Wessels Lekotla in the matter of Mitsagosi's Estate, July 1899'. The majority of disputes heard by Wessels Montshiwa were resolved without reference to the magistrate, and no written records kept. Details of the Mitsagosi case have survived because two of the complainants initially came to Bell with signed affidavits in support of their case before Bell decided to refer the case to Wessels.

28 KAB, 1/MFK, A1/1/1/1, records of periodical court, Setlagole, 9 June 1899; KAB, CPK 251, Mafeking Preparatory Examinations, January–October 1899, case of *R* v. *Louis Mtys Brink*, May 1899 (no. 108 of 1899); KAB, 1/MFK, 4/4 (Inquests), inquiry into case carried out by J.J. Keeley at Farm Faith, 1 June 1899. Keeley's verdict at the original inquest was that 'the death of the deceased Jacob was caused by a wound on the forehead which caused congestion of the brain which may have resulted from blows alleged to have been inflicted by one Louis Martinus Brink'.

29 KAB, 1/MFK, A1/1/1/1, Evidence of Abraham, p. 8. Jacob's mother Martha testified that 'he told me he was dying from the wounds on the arms. He died on Sunday evening. He did not complain of pains in the head ... He only said he was dying because his arms was hurt' (pp. 17–18).

30 KAB, 1/MFK, 6/1/2/4, Letters Despatched, Departments (January 1899–June 1900), Bell to Law Dept, Cape Town, 29 March 1899; 'IDB at Mafeking', *Bechuanaland News*, 4 March 1899; KAB, CPK 251 (155/293), case of Joseph Ephraim. The reporter for the *Bechuanaland News* was struck by the largest ('absolutely perfect') diamond found in his possession, 'which would have been worth more than £200 at the very lowest estimate'. Plaatje himself acted in his normal capacity during the preparatory examination, witnessing and taking down statements. Private Currie went on to become one of the heroes of the defence of Mafeking, rewarded with a commission and the rank of lieutenant.

31 UW, Molema–Plaatje Papers, Db2, 'The essential interpreter' (original manuscript). It was first published in 1996 in Brian Willan (ed.), *Sol Plaatje: selected writings* (Johannesburg: Wits University Press, 1996).

32 Quoted passages are from Willan, *Sol Plaatje: selected writings*, pp. 54, 56 and 58.

33 KAB, AG 739, 28/99, Plaatje to Bell, 1 March 1899, enclosure (annexure A) in Bell to Law Dept, Cape Town, 5 April 1899, and marginal comment by Acting Postmaster General, Cape Town.

34 Willan, *Sol Plaatje: selected writings*, p. 52.

35 KAB, 1/MFK, 2/1/1/16, Civil records, case no. 91, *Solomon T. Plaatje* v. *Alfred Ngidi*, 9 June 1899; 2/2/1/2, Civil record book 1898–1903, case no. 91, p. 121.

36 KAB, 1/MFK, 2/1/1/16, Civil records, case no. 142, 29 August 1899, *Joseph Whiffler* v. *Solomon Plaatje*; 2/2/1/2, Civil record book, 1898–1903, case no. 142, p. 132. Joseph Whiffler was no stranger to criminal proceedings, appearing before both the magistrate's and circuit court on at least three other occasions. The most serious charge resulted in a conviction for receiving stolen property when he was involved, after the war, in a scam to relieve a government store of a quantity of oats, jam, milk, sausages and other foodstuffs (KAB, KSC 1/2/5, *R* v. *Daniel McGrath and Joseph Whiffler*, March 1903).

37 S.T. Plaatje, 'The Native Congress deputation', *DFA*, 17 July 1914.

38 David Phooko came to Mafeking in August 1899, so this episode must have taken place between August and early October 1899.

39 KAB, CLC 1/1, Records of Civil Service Commission, Letterbook (6 July 1899–31 December 1900), Secretary of Civil Service Commission to Plaatje, 10 August 1900; KAB, AG 837, 3/1900, Plaatje to Bell, 6 June 1900, enclosure in Bell to Law Dept, 8 June 1900; KAB, CLC 1/1, Records of Civil Service Commission, Letterbook (28 March 1893 – 5 July 1899), Secretary, Civil Service Commission, to I. Bud-M'belle, 23 May 1899.

40 For Mafeking on the eve of the siege, see T. Jeal, *Baden-Powell* (London: Hutchinson,

1989), pp. 223–8; I. Smith (ed.), *The Siege of Mafeking*, vol. 1 (Johannesburg: Brenthurst Press, 2001); Brian Gardner, *Mafeking: a Victorian legend* (London: Cassell, 1966); B. Willan (ed.), *Edward Ross, Diary of the Siege of Mafeking, October 1899 to May 1900* (Cape Town: Van Riebeeck Society, 1981), introduction; and issues of the *Mafeking Mail and Protectorate Guardian*, May–October 1899.

41 Comaroff et al., *Mafeking Diary*, prologue, p. 23; 'A quarter of a century on the diamond fields: some notes and recollections', *DFA*, Christmas number, December 1906; S.T. Plaatje, *Native Life in South Africa* (London: P.S. King & Son, 1916), p. 239.

42 Plaatje, *Native Life*; there was also a brief report of the meeting in *Mafeking Mail*, 7 October 1899.

43 KAB, 1/MFK, 5/1/9/2, 1028/99, Misc. Letters Received (January 1898–October 1899), Wessels Montshiwa to Secretary for Native Affairs, 9 October 1899. The letter was sent on behalf of 'Wessels Montsioa, Chief of the ra-Tshidi Barolong, by the consent of the headmen of the Barolong nation', and was in the hand of Stephen Lefenya.

44 S.T. Plaatje, 'Segregation: idea ridiculed', *Transvaal Chronicle* (n.d.), reproduced in *Tsala ea Becoana*, 28 January 1911. In fact, over 450,000 men served on the British side between the outbreak of war in October 1899 and the Treaty of Vereeniging in May 1902.

45 *Imvo*, 21 August 1899; Pietermaritzburg Archives Repository, Colenso Papers, Box 55, Plaatje to Mrs S. Colenso, 26 February 1915.

46 KAB, CLC 1/1, Records of Cape Civil Service Commission, Letterbook (6 July 1899 – 31 December 1900), Secretary of Civil Service Commission to Plaatje, 10 August 1899, and KAB, AG 838, 3/1900, Plaatje to Bell, 6 June 1900, enclosure in Bell to Law Dept, Cape Town, 1 June 1900.

Chapter 4

1 S.T. Plaatje, *Native Life in South Africa* (London: P.S. King & Son, 1916), p. 241.

2 British Library, Weil Papers, Add. MSS 46851, General Order dated 19 November 1899.

3 Charles Bell, 'Diary during the siege of Mafeking' (Rhodes University, Cory Library, MS 7347, p. 3).

4 Plaatje, *Native Life*, pp. 241–2.

5 John Comaroff and Brian Willan with Solomon Molema and Andrew Reed (eds.), *The Mafeking Diary of Sol T. Plaatje, Centenary Edition* (Cape Town: David Philip, 1999), p. 27. The fragment from Plaatje's initial notes is reproduced in *Mafeking Diary*, p. 169.

6 Weil Papers, General Orders, 9 November 1899.

7 William Geyer's unpublished diary is in KAB, A 1370, but is purely a record of events. He kept it up throughout the siege, his last entry being on 28 May.

8 For nineteenth-century diaries, see Rebecca Steinitz, *Time, Space and Gender in the Nineteenth Century British Diary* (New York: Palgrave Macmillan, 2011). Satirical fictional diaries like George and Weedon Grossmith's *Diary of a Nobody* (1892) were also popular.

9 The words '*siqu*' and '*isiqu*' are referred to respectively on 18 December (p. 70) and 6 February 1900 (p. 105); '*makasono*' appears in his first entry, 29 October 1899 (p. 28).

10 Passages dictated to David Phooko are listed in Comaroff et al., *Mafeking Diary*, p. 164, where a sample page of his handwriting is reproduced. That it is Phooko's is confirmed by a comparison with several of his later letters relating to his employment by the Cape civil service, while a letter from the Resident Magistrate, Aliwal North (where Phooko got a job as constable), to the Law Department, 15 September 1903, confirms that Phooko 'was in the siege of Mafeking during the Anglo-Boer War' (KAB, AG 1398, vol. 1: 1703). Plaatje's reference to his 'low estate' is from his entry on 24 December 1899 (p. 73) where he corrects David's rendering of his dictation.

11 Comaroff et al., *Mafeking Diary*, entry for 25 November 1899, p. 44.

12 Comaroff et al., *Mafeking Diary*, 27 February 1900 (pp. 122–4). His entry for 7 December 1899, where he reflects upon the impact of 'Au Sanna' on the inhabitants of Mafeking, has a similarly elaborate construction.

13 Comaroff et al., *Mafeking Diary*, entry for 29 October 1899, pp. 27–8.

14 Comaroff et al., *Mafeking Diary*, entry for 12 December 1899, pp. 65–8. Plaatje's description is captured in the photograph of the court scene taken by Edward Ross and published in his *Mafeking: siege views* (London: Eyre and Spottiswoode, 1900).

15 Comaroff et al., *Mafeking Diary*, entry for 12 November 1899, p. 38.

16 Comaroff et al., *Mafeking Diary*, entry for 18 February 1900, p. 117.

17 Comaroff et al., *Mafeking Diary*, entry for 25 December 1899, p. 76. Lady Sarah Wilson, a sister of Winston Churchill, and married to one of Baden-Powell's staff officers, had arrived in Mafeking earlier that month. After being captured by the Boers, she was exchanged for a Boer prisoner and arrived in town on 7 December. A letter of thanks to Lady Sarah for the toys and sweets has survived – written by Plaatje on behalf of Chief Lekoko and Matsetse, the queen mother (*Mafeking Diary*, p. 184 n.71).

18 Comaroff et al., *Mafeking Diary*, entries for 26 December (p. 76) and 29 December (p. 80); Bell, 'Diary', entry for 26 December 1899, p. 79.

19 Comaroff et al., *Mafeking Diary*, entry for 5 December 1899 (p. 52).

20 Comaroff et al., *Mafeking Diary*, entry for 23 November 1899 (p. 43). The Court of Summary Jurisdiction was formally constituted on 16 November, its purpose being to bring to trial 'persons not directly liable to trial by Court Martial and for offences not recognisable by such court' (Weil Papers, Add. MSS 46851, General Orders, 16 November 1899).

21 Comaroff et al., *Mafeking Diary*, entry for 25 November 1899 (p. 44); Plaatje to Edward Cecil, 26 January 1900, in Bell Papers (Rhodes University, Cory Library), reproduced in Brian Willan (ed.), *Sol Plaatje: selected writings* (Johannesburg: Witwatersrand University Press, 1996), p. 42.

22 Bell Papers, letters from Plaatje to Lord Edward Cecil, 26 January 1900, note from Cecil to Plaatje, 28 January 1900 and Plaatje to Bell, 30 January 1900.

23 Plaatje refers to his 'imperial allowance' in his letter to J.B. Moffat (Magistrate and Civil Commissioner, Mafeking), 18 July 1901 (KAB, AG 923, 10/1901); see also general orders, 17 March 1900 (Weil Papers, Add. MSS 46852, p. 159, General Order dated 17 March 1900). Bell's views on Baden-Powell are evident at several points in his diary, while his comment on Vyvyan's slowness, and his preference for sitting with Cecil in the Court of Summary Jurisdiction, is from his diary, 21 November 1899.

24 Statement of Thekisho (translated and signed by Plaatje), 24 October 1899, pp. 2–3 (Hanbury-Tracy Papers, privately held). I am most grateful to Mr Richard H. Nicholson for making these reports available to me.

25 Plaatje, *Native Life*, pp. 242–3; Hanbury-Tracy Papers, Report, 30 January 1900.

26 Comaroff et al., *Mafeking Diary*, entry for 12 November 1899, pp. 37–8.

27 Hanbury-Tracy Papers, Report (addressed to Charles Bell), 26 January 1900. Plaatje mentions this episode in his diary entry for 26 January, adding that Malno, one of the dispatch runners, had brought news of the death in Kimberley of Zakaria, Ebie Schiemann's elder brother.

28 'Latest news', *Mafeking Mail Special Siege Slip*, 12 December 1899; 'Our beef providers', *Mafeking Mail Special Siege Slip*, 16 February 1900; Comaroff et al., *Mafeking Diary*, entry of 15 December 1899, p. 69.

29 Comaroff et al., *Mafeking Diary*, entry for 1 November 1899, p. 32. Murchison was tried by the Court of Summary Jurisdiction, found guilty of murder and condemned to death. The sentence was commuted to life penal servitude, however, after it became clear that he had a long history of mental instability. In 1902 he was committed to Broadmoor Asylum in England and died there in 1917.

30 Plaatje mentions in his diary that news of the relief of Kimberley (15 February) was received in Mafeking on 26 February thanks to 'a spy returned from Lotlhakane this morning'.

31 Letter to the editor, *The Star* (Johannesburg), 5 July 1932; 'South Africa's first native novelist', *Pretoria News*, 8 November 1930.

32 TS carbon copy of letter from Stent to H.D. Gwynne, n.d. [February 1900], in Mafeking Siege records, A 1566, University of the Witwatersrand, Historical Papers. Some extracts from Stent's siege diary are reproduced in Sally and Betty Stent, *The Forthright Man* (Cape Town: Howard Timmins, 1972). In a letter to *The Star* shortly after Plaatje's death, Vere Stent mentioned that it contained 'frequent mentions of Mr Plaatje' ('Sol Plaatje: Mr Vere Stent's tribute', letter to *The Star*, 23 July 1932).

33 Plaatje preserved a draft of this letter to Bud-M'belle with the MS of his diary. It is undated, but from internal evidence must date from late February. Very likely it was never sent since this was when Plaatje heard news of the relief of Kimberley, which made redundant the suggestion he made about replying via letter to Gaborone. The letter is reproduced in Willan, *Sol Plaatje: selected writings*, p. 45.

34 Plaatje mentions typing out these diaries in his own diary entry for 8 February (p. 108). The original of Greener's diary has not survived, but his much later (1938) account based upon it is published in Robin Drooglever (ed.), *Inside Mafeking: Captain Herbert Greener's journal of the siege of Mafeking* (Honiton, Devon: Token Publishing, 2009). The typescript of William Hayes's diary is in KAB, MS A273. Parts of this diary, along with that of William Hayes's brother Tom, also a medical doctor, are reproduced in *New Contree*, 41, September 1997, pp. 25–161. Plaatje's references to his earnings from the war correspondents are from his diary entry for 18 November 1899.

35 Comaroff et al., *Mafeking Diary*, entry for 5 January 1900, pp. 89–91.

36 Draft of letter from the 'chief and headmen of the Barolongs' in Plaatje's hand (undated but January 1900), reproduced in Willan, *Sol Plaatje: selected writings*, pp. 40–1.

37 UW, Plaatje–Molema Papers, Cc2, draft of letter; Comaroff et al., *Mafeking Diary*, entry for 9 January 1900 (p. 94). Responding to Plaatje's representations, Baden-Powell wrote a note to his CSO, Lord Edward Cecil, saying (as had Plaatje) that 'This is not right and will stop the Barolongs going raiding', and that 'McKenzie's boys shd be told if they are afraid to go raiding themselves it is no reason why they shd try and stop others' (Weil Papers, Add. MSS 46849, p. 69, Baden-Powell to CSO, 10 January 1900).

38 Comaroff et al., *Mafeking Diary*, entry for 21 January 1900, pp. 99–100.

39 Comaroff et al., *Mafeking Diary*, entry for 21 March 1900, p. 144.

40 Baden-Powell's version of the 'deposition' of Wessels Montshiwa (he considered his 'general unsatisfactoriness' arose from 'having no authority over his people, being also generally drunk or ill') is from his Staff Diary (National Army Museum, London, 6411/1, entry for 31 December 1899); Comaroff et al., *Mafeking Diary*, entry for 31 December 1899, p. 81; J. Angus Hamilton, *The Siege of Mafeking* (London: Methuen, 1900), p. 197. Hamilton's account was first published in *The Times*, 20 March 1900, over six weeks after the event.

41 S.M. Molema, *Lover of His People* (Johannesburg: Wits University Press, 2012), pp. 35–6. In his original manuscript Molema gives the date for this as January 1901 but from his description there can be no doubt he is describing what took place at the meeting on 31 December 1899, for this was the only recorded occasion of its kind (Bell, central to Molema's account, had in any case left Mafeking by January 1901).

42 Wessels Montshiwa did not consider himself deposed. On 22 January a letter was written on his behalf to Baden-Powell requesting a pass for seven of his men to leave Mafeking for the purposes of cattle raiding (Weil Papers, Add. MSS 46849, no. 84). Later, on 26 March, Plaatje wrote out a certificate authorising Montshiwa to purchase a gun, describing him as 'Chief' of Mafeking.

43 Molema, *Lover of His People*, p. 37.

44 Bell, 'Diary', entry for 25 January 1900, p. 103. Bell added: 'Death was instantaneous. Six men fired, and 5 bullets went into him. He must have dropped before the sixth man fired.' Hamilton's description of the scene is from *The Siege of Mafeking*, pp. 216–19. He thought the accused had 'at no time seemed to understand the gravity of his offence' and 'had meant no harm'.

45 Editorial, quoting English translation of letter from Joseph Gape to the editor, *Koranta ea Becoana*, 6 December 1902. The English version of Gape's letter is a considerable elaboration upon the original in Setswana and so can be taken as Plaatje's own gloss on the affair.

46 Baden-Powell, Staff Diary, entry for 19 March; as in the previous case, Vyvyan wrote (10 March 1900) to Baden-Powell to ask him to confirm the sentence. Vyvyan's Diary (Brenthurst Library, Vyvyan Papers, MS 147, entry for 12 March 1900) confirms that the sentence was carried out that day.

47 Comaroff et al., *Mafeking Diary*, entry for 29 March 1900, p. 151.

48 George Malhombe's execution, like the others, was carried out by a firing squad from the Colonial ('Cape Boy') Contingent, under the command of Lt Henry Currie. Malhombe was found guilty of having stolen a goat, but the death sentence was justified, so Edward Ross reported, on the grounds that this was his second offence (Weil Papers, no. 179, note from Lord Edward Cecil to Baden-Powell, 30 March 1900, re 'death warrant of loafer of whom I spoke to you', and warrant for execution of George Malhombe, 31 March 1900); Brian Willan (ed.), *Edward Ross, Diary of the Siege of Mafeking, October 1899 to May 1900* (Cape Town: Van Riebeeck Society, 1980), entry for 2 April 1900, p. 206.

49 Comaroff et al., *Mafeking Diary*, entry for 27 February 1900, p. 123.

50 Comaroff et al., *Mafeking Diary*, entry for 21 March 1900, p. 144.

51 Plaatje refers to this 'official diary' for the first time in his own diary of 8 February 1900 (p. 108). The example quoted (undated) is from the Bell Papers.

52 Comaroff et al., *Mafeking Diary*, entries for 13 and 15 March 1900, pp. 136 and 138.

53 Plaatje's report dated 8 April 1900 (in Hanbury-Tracy Papers).

54 Based upon Plaatje's report dated 14 April 1900 (Hanbury-Tracy Papers). Plaatje described the same episode in *Native Life in South Africa* fifteen years later, recalling that Mathakgong's men 'said they owed their escape almost entirely to the carcasses of dead cattle, which they used as ramparts' (*Native Life*, pp. 246–7).

55 For how news of the relief of Mafeking was received, see Thomas Pakenham, 'Mafficking', in Iain Smith (ed.), *The Siege of Mafeking* (Johannesburg: Brenthurst Press, 2001), vol. 2, pp. 399–436.

56 Plaatje's report dated 20 May 1900 (Hanbury-Tracy Papers).

57 Bell, 'Diary', entry for 17 May 1900. Vyvyan subsequently added the note at the foot of Plaatje's translation, 'Copy of message found in Snyman's Camp 18-5-00'.

58 Plaatje, *Native Life*, p. 10, quoting from 'Through native eyes', an article in the *Pretoria News* in which Vere Stent introduces Plaatje to his readers. The 'letter written to a friend' was most likely to Stent himself, providing biographical details that Stent had requested for his article. A CMG (Companion of the Order of St Michael and St George) was awarded to individuals who rendered important service to the British empire.

59 The certificates from Baden-Powell and Goold-Adams have not survived, but Plaatje referred to them in his letter of 18 July 1901 when pressing his case for a salary increase (KAB, AG 923, 106/1901, Annexure A).

Chapter 5

1 KAB, 1/MFK, 6/1/2/4, Letters Despatched, Departments (January 1899 – October 1900), C.G.H. Bell, 'Report on the natives, state of"', p. 2; S.T. Plaatje, *Native Life in*

South Africa (London: P.S. King & Son), pp. 250–2.

2   B. Willan, 'The siege of Mafeking', in Peter Warwick (ed.), *The South African War* (Harlow: Longman, 1980), p. 160. Plaatje's accusation was in *Koranta ea Becoana*, 18 November 1903, and Baden-Powell's evidence in *Royal Commission on the War in South Africa, Evidence, vol. 2* (HMSO, 1903).

3   E. Graham Green, who became acting magistrate in Mafeking in 1901, accepted that Baden-Powell had made such a promise, but the Cape authorities refused to honour it on the grounds that he had no authority to do so (KAB, LND 884, L16461, Green to Native Affairs Department, Cape Town, 23 July 1903 and memo from Secretary for Agriculture, 2 September 1903). On the gift of the heifers, see Tim Jeal, *Baden-Powell* (London: Hutchinson, 1989), p. 285, quoting telegrams between Baden-Powell and Lord Roberts, 19 June 1900, and Plaatje's obituary of Silas Molema, *Cape Times*, 13 September 1927. Joshua Molema's comments were reported in *Mafeking Mail*, 13 September 1900.

4   Plaatje, *Native Life*, p. 251.

5   KAB, AG 837, 3/1900, 364, Bell to Law Dept, Cape Town, 29 June 1900. On Grayson, see KAB, AG 837, 3/1900, Bell to Law Dept, Cape Town, 19 May 1900, enclosing doctor's certificate and memo of services (leave taken) in Annual Report on Establishment, KAB, 7/7/06, JUS 39/6059/05. For Geyer's temporary absence (June to December 1900), see *Cape of Good Hope Civil Service List* (Cape Town, 1901), p. 298.

6   Bell's appointment to Uitenhage was from 2 August 1900 (*Civil Service List* for 1904, p. 328); for his ambition to become secretary for native affairs, see KAB, JUS 42, 6487/05, letter to Sir John Graham, 9 April 1907 – 'It is an appointment I have worked for for many years'.

7   KAB, AG 837, 3/1900, Plaatje to Bell, 6 June 1900. The other interpreter Plaatje referred to was Joseph Moss in Kimberley. On investigating Plaatje's claims, however, one of the officials in the Law Department wrote that 'Moss speaks Dutch well and has to my knowledge interpreted in that language in the High Court' (memo dated 23 June 1900).

8   KAB, AG 837, 3/1900, Bell to Law Dept, Cape Town, 15 June 1900.

9   KAB, AG 837, M728, K.R. Thomas to Magistrate and CC, Mafeking, 12 November 1900. Arriving in September as a supernumerary clerk, Thomas complained of being confronted 'with a heterogeneous mass of documents and contradictory instructions on the subject of treason'. Unable to cope, he requested a transfer to Cape Town to enable him to recover his health. It was not granted.

10 The *Bechuanaland News* (10 November 1900) reported that 106 examinations had been made up to that point. Many had been carried out by the assistant resident magistrate, W.F.G. Geyer. Although seconded to the Transvaal for a term of six months, he must have returned to Mafeking sooner than expected.

11 KAB, AG 923, 106/1901, Annexure A, Plaatje to CC and RM, 18 July 1901. Bill Nasson, *Abraham Esau's War: a black South African war in the Cape, 1899–1902* (Cape Town: David Philip, 1991), especially ch. 8, 'Treason offenders and their antagonists', illuminates the wider context in which these treason trials took place in the Cape.

12 Louis Brink was arrested by James Keeley on 1 June 1900. Keeley's statement, witnessed by Plaatje, along with those of the witnesses to the killing, are in KAB, AG 3418 (Mafeking: High Treason Preparatory Examinations, case 24/126) and 1/MFK, 1/4/1/2, High Treason Preparatory Examinations.

13 Saane's statement was made on 16 November 1900 in the case *R v. Abraham Matuba*, committed for trial on 16 November 1900 (KAB, 1/MFK, 1/4/1/2, High Treason Preparatory Examinations).

14 Editorial in *Koranta ea Becoana*, 20 December 1902, p. 7.

15 KAB, CLC 1/13, Records of Civil Service Commission, Letterbook (6 July 1899–

31 December 1900), M. Garrett (Secretary, Civil Service Commission) to Plaatje, 10 August 1900.

16 Garrett to Plaatje, 1 September 1900, and to Petrus Sidzumo, 21 September 1900 (CLC 1/13).

17 KAB, AG 837, 63/1900, Plaatje to CC and RM, Mafeking, 22 November 1900, enclosing application for leave; 'Bloemfontein: from our correspondent', *Koranta ea Becoana*, 21 March 1903. CLC 1/13, Letterbook (6 July 1899–31 December 1900), Garrett to all candidates taking special examinations, 15 November 1900, confirms the venue. A total of 243 candidates (ordinary and special) sat the examinations.

18 Information from KAB, CLC 1/1, results for December 1900. Nqwana had wanted to enter the ordinary examination too but, like a number of Africans who wished to do the same, was debarred on the grounds of age (candidates had to be under 25). Bud-M'belle's movements and status are deduced from Secretary of the Civil Service Commission to I. Bud-M'belle, 24 April 1899 and M. Garrett to I. Bud-M'belle, 30 November 1900, both in KAB, CLC 1/13, Letterbook (6 July 1899 – 31 December 1900); Cape Colony, *Report of the Civil Service Commission* (G20-1901). Bud-M'belle was appointed interpreter to the Special Treason Court on 12 October 1900 (KAB, AG 2036, no. 82, minute dated 21 November 1900), which is what brought him to Cape Town.

19 E.F. Kilpin (ed.), *The Cape of Good Hope Civil Service List 1901* (Cape Town: W.A. Richards & Sons, 1902), pp. 350–82. When defining the terms of eligibility for candidates, the Regulations, in clause 2(7), p. 350, state: 'But no person shall be deemed to be under any legal disability, merely by reason that he is a native, if he shall by virtue of the provisions of Act no 39 of 1887 [the Native Registered Voters Act] be exempted from the operation of the laws mentioned in Schedule A to the said Act'.

20 The delay to Plaatje's journey back home meant he had to be granted another four days' leave, detailed in KAB, AG 923, 65/1901, application for leave, dated 16 April 1901. Details of the Boer raids into the Cape Colony, and the garrison at De Aar, are taken from L.S. Amery (ed.) *The Times History of the War in South Africa, 1899–1902* (London: Sampson Low, Marston, 1907), vol. 5, pp. 127–8.

21 That Plaatje was back at work by 27 December is evident in his signature on a witness statement ('Jim') that day in the case of *R* v. *William* (Theft). Patrick Sidzumo deputised for Plaatje during his absence in Cape Town (KAB, CPK 250, Preparatory Examination no. 280 of 1900, also in 1/MFK, 1/1/1/1/28).

22 Civil service examination result sheets, KAB, CLC 1/1. The results were collated and signed off by Charles Murray on 17 January 1901, so Plaatje presumably heard his results soon after this. His claim to have come top in both papers is referred to in Garrett to Plaatje, 10 June 1901 (KAB, CLC 1/13) and his own letter to the CC and RM, Mafeking, 18 July 1901 (KAB, AG 923, 106/1901). In the unpublished results sheet, one candidate, Sydney Kingman, achieved a higher mark (257 to Plaatje's 255) in the Typewriting paper, but for unexplained reasons his name did not subsequently appear in the published results. Mr Potter's comment on the quality of Typewriting candidates is from the published *Report of the Cape Civil Service Commission for 1900* (G20-1901), p. 11. The special paper in Dutch which Plaatje sat was the same paper taken by the 243 candidates for the ordinary examination. Here Plaatje's total of 153 marks would have put him equal with two other candidates in 23rd place.

23 *Report of the Civil Service Commission*, 1900, pp. 4 and 5; Mark Garrett to Plaatje, 10 June 1901 (KAB, CLC 1/13).

24 Garrett to Plaatje, 10 June 1901 (KAB, CLC 1/13). Individual candidate numbers in turn seem to have been based on the order in which applications were originally received.

25 KAB, AG 837, 26/1901, J.B. Moffat to Law Dept, Cape Town, 19 December 1900; 1/MFK, 6/1/3/5, Letters Despatched, Misc. (October 1901–May 1902), Moffat to Commandant, 24 March 1901; 1/MFK, 5/1/9/4, Misc. Letters Received (January–

August 1901), Plaatje to CC and RM, 20 May 1901.

26 KAB, 1/MFK, 5/1/9/3, Letters Received, Misc. (May–December 1900), memo from Bell to Commandant, 5 September 1900, and reply from Commandant, 6 September 1900; KAB, 1/MFK, 5/1/9/4, Letters Received, Misc. (January–August 1901), Plaatje to CC and RM, Mafeking, 8 January 1901.

27 KAB, 1/MFK, 1/1/1/30, Criminal Records, 101-54 (February–April 1901), case no. 152, *R* v. *S.T. Plaatje*, 1 April 1901.

28 For the dispute between Moffat and Geyer, see KAB, 1/MFK, 6/1/2/5, Letters Despatched, Departments (October 1900–August 1901), Moffat to Geyer, 12 July 1901 where Moffat asked Geyer to respond formally to charges of being absent without leave and performing his duties 'in a negligent and careless manner'. Eighteen months later, while 'in a state of temporary insanity', according to the magistrate conducting the inquest, Geyer shot himself in the Public Gardens in Kimberley ('The late Mr W.F. Geyer: inquest and verdict', *DFA*, 15 May 1903).

29 Exactly when Elizabeth joined Plaatje in Mafeking after the siege is unclear, but she must have been there by February 1901 when Joseph Molema married Ntegogang: see n.31 below and S.M. Molema, *Lover of His People* (Johannesburg: Wits University Press, 2012), pp. 42–3.

30 The Mafeking Philharmonic Society was in existence by March 1902 and made its public debut on 23 May. The majority of those involved, male and female, were of Xhosa or Mfengu origin ('Opening of new Congregational Church', *Mafeking Mail*, 2 April 1902; 'Masonic Hall, Friday, May 23rd, 1902', *Mafeking Mail*, 21 May 1902; 'Philharmonic Society's concert', *Mafeking Mail*, 24 May 1902).

31 *Mafeking Mail*, 16 and 23 February 1901; Joseph Molema's accidental death was also reported in 'Joseph Molema of Mafeking', *Christian Express*, 1 April 1901, p. 62.

32 John Comaroff, 'Competition for office and political processes among the Barolong boo Ratshidi of the South Africa–Botswana borderland' (PhD thesis, University of London, 1973), pp. 237 and 304–5; S.M. Molema, *Montshiwa: Barolong chief and patriot, 1815–1896* (Cape Town: Struik, 1966), pp. 181–3.

33 The shield and framed address were described in *Mafeking Mail*, 5 November 1901. They can be seen today in the museum in Mafikeng, having been acquired from an antique dealer in London in 1977. The best reproductions are in Iain Smith (ed.), *The Siege of Mafeking* (Johannesburg: Brenthurst Press, 1999), vol. 2, pp. 284 and 448.

34 Plaatje mentioned Cronwright-Schreiner's encouragement to him to 'try journalism' on several occasions, including his article 'Friends of the natives', *Diamond Fields Advertiser* (*DFA*), 15 June 1925 and in an interview in *Christian Commonwealth*, 3 January 1917.

35 'Acts, rules and regulations of the Cape civil service', section III, clause 32, in E.F. Kilpin (ed.), *The Cape of Good Hope Civil Service List, 1892* (Cape Town: W.A. Richards & Sons, 1893), p. 167.

36 *Koranta ea Becoana*, 27 April 1901.

37 UW, Molema–Plaatje Papers, A3.6.1, Memorandum of Agreement between G.N.H. Whales and S.T. Molema, 5 September 1901.

38 UW, Molema–Plaatje Papers, A3.6.1, undated draft of letter from S.T. Molema to G.N.H. Whales, in Plaatje's hand.

39 'Our new departure', *Koranta ea Becoana*, 23 August 1902; see also KAB, CO 2535, Index (administrative) of letters received (individuals), 1901, entry re letter from S. Molema, 19 December 1901, re 'enlargement of paper and charges'. The compositor was James Mpinda, who arrived in response to an advertisement stating: 'Reliable and sober Native Compositor wanted to take charge of a small Sechuana Weekly Newspaper at Mafeking' (*Imvo*, 6 May 1901).

40 Botswana National Archives (BNA), RC 117, 3/10/01, Resident Commissioner, Mafeking, to Assistant Governor, Gaborone, 3 October 1901.

41 Plaatje's salary increase, awarded in response to his letter of 18 July 1901, supported by the magistrate, J.B. Moffat, was backdated to 1 August (KAB, AG 923, 106/1901, Plaatje to CC and RM, Mafeking, 18 July 1901).

42 S.T. Plaatje, 'A friend of the natives: the late Sir William Solomon', *Pretoria News*, 21 June 1930.

43 'A friend of the natives', *Pretoria News*, 21 June 1930; *Mafeking Mail*, 6–8 November 1901; KAB, AG 2038/9, Treason cases, *R v. B.C. Lottering and J.S. Maritz*, November 1901. For a discussion of the legal points raised by the judgment, and whether judgments in the Special Treason Court were to be considered part of the jurisprudence of South African courts more generally, see 'Rebels as belligerents', *South African Law Journal*, 21, 1904, pp. 119–23.

44 Editorial, quoting English translation of letter from Joseph Gape to editor, *Koranta ea Becoana*, 6 December 1902.

45 *Mafeking Mail*, 12 November 1901.

46 'Sentencing of four rebels', *Mafeking Mail*, 16 November 1901. Plaatje recalled the words on a number of occasions, including 'A friend of the natives', *Pretoria News*, 21 June 1930 and 'The treatment of natives in courts', in Brian Willan (ed.), *Sol Plaatje: selected writings* (Johannesburg: Witwatersrand University Press, 1996), pp. 385 and 334. The fact that there were some variations in the wording Plaatje quoted on each occasion suggests they came from memory rather than any printed source he had in front of him.

47 KAB, AG 2656, Letterbook, Graham to Attorney General, pp. 884–8. Graham added that this was 'the first instance within my knowledge where in capital cases the Governor has had before him the opinion of three judges on the question of whether the prerogative of mercy shall be exercised'.

48 KAB, AG 923, 189/1901 and 191/1901. Evidence that Senyamotse carried a muzzle-loader was also given by John Stephenson in his statement dated 22 November 1900 (KAB, AG 3418, case 24/126).

49 KAB, AG 2656, Letterbook, p. 947, John Graham to the Attorney General, 16 December 1901. Graham added, in seeking to distinguish this case from that of *R v. Lottering and Maritz*, that 'the condemned man is not shown to have had any special order from Corporal Herbst, nor does it appear that he believed he was carrying out any general order of Commandant Snyman'. From the evidence at the trial this last assertion was somewhat debatable.

50 According to Mr Blake, the double hanging took 4 minutes and 49 seconds. His claim to a world record is in *DFA* (weekly edition), 25 November 1905, citing a report taken from the *Bechuanaland News*, 18 November 1905.

51 The report of the execution of Brink and Rinke is taken from 'Mafeking murderers hanged', *DFA*, 30 December 1901. The hangings are described in Graham Jooste and Roger Webster, *Innocent Blood: executions during the Anglo-Boer War* (Cape Town: New Africa Books, 2002), pp. 140–1, although with some inaccuracies. The claim, which on the face of it seems unlikely, that the five condemned prisoners were forced to carry the gallows from the railway station to the gaol is in G. Jordaan, *Hoe zij stierven* (Burgersdorp: De Stem Drukkery, 1904), p. 165.

52 With the notable exception of Bill Nasson's exploration of the social and political context and consequences of the treason trials in the Cape (*Abraham Esau's War*, especially pp. 142–68), the work of the Special Treason Court has been largely neglected in the literature on the South African War, and the legal luminaries involved preferred to forget about their participation. Sir James Molteno, in two volumes of memoirs, ignores the treason trials completely, saying only that he 'did not propose to relate in this book my experiences in the course of the trials before the special Treason Court' because he considered there were others better qualified to do so. They never did. See Sir James Tennant Molteno, *The Dominion of Afrikanerdom: recollections pleasant and otherwise* (London: Methuen, 1922),

esp. pp. 215–17. I rely on H. Shearing, 'The Cape Rebels of the South African War 1899–1902' (PhD thesis, Stellenbosch University, 2004), p. 162, for the information that these were 'the only death sentences under the Indemnity and Special Tribunals Act'.

53 KAB, AG 2071, 1/26 Part 1 (Mafeking), affidavit of Marubani, enclosure in letter from E. Graham Green (Acting Resident Magistrate, Mafeking), to the Attorney General, Cape Town, 8 January 1902. I am most grateful to Carina Ray (Fordham University) for directing me to this file reference after drawing attention to its contents in 'Lest we forget', *New African*, 1 November 2007.

54 KAB, 1/MFK, 6/1/2/6, Letters Despatched, Departments (August 1901–March 1902), Green to the Secretary, Law Dept, Cape Town, 22 January 1902. Green reported the loss of 3,524 cattle, 3,380 sheep and goats, 45 horses and mules and 147 donkeys, with total losses estimated at £53,343 6s 9d. Green's report on the failure of local British forces to offer any effective resistance was so critical that he was obliged to rewrite it. Barolong views of the raid, and details of compensation claimed, are in KAB, 1/MFK, 6/1/2/7, Letters Despatched, Departments (March–December 1902), E. Graham Green (Acting RM, Mafeking) to Compensation Commission, Cape Town, 21 November 1902.

55 Standard Bank Heritage Centre, Johannesburg, Inspection Report (Mafeking branch), 26 October 1903, estimate of Molema's assets and value of printing machinery; SOAS, Plaatje Papers, STP 3/1, S.T. Molema to Commandant, Mafeking, 18 February 1902 (in Plaatje's hand).

56 *South African Native Affairs Commission, Minutes of Evidence, vol. 4*, evidence of S.T. Plaatje, p. 264.

57 UW, Molema–Plaatje Papers, Aa3.6.1, Memorandum of Agreement, March 1902 and 4 April 1902. Plaatje's letter of resignation, and Green's letter forwarding it to Cape Town, are in KAB, AG 1002, 37/1902, Green to Secretary, Law Dept, 27 March 1902.

58 Vere Stent, 'The strange life of Sol Plaatje: a leader without a people', *The Star* (Johannesburg), 5 July 1932.

59 'The essential interpreter', in Willan, *Sol Plaatje: selected writings*, p. 60.

60 Letter from Molema to *The Star*, 11 July 1932.

61 E. Graham Green to the Secretary, Law Dept, 11 June 1902, and Plaatje to CC and RM, Mafeking, 19 May 1902 (KAB, AG 1002, 53/1902). Plaatje wrote up entries nos. 93 to 105 (pp. 96–100) in the Criminal Record Book, between 1 and 8 March 1902, the record of each judgment and sentence signed and authorised by Mr Green. Cyril Brooke had entered his oath of office as clerk of the court in June 1901 prior to acting in this capacity but there is no record that Plaatje did the same.

62 *R v. John Martin* and *R v. Hendrik Johnson* were cases 93 and 94. The other cases were as follows: theft (two cases), failure to control a horse and vehicle (three), riding a bicycle on the sidewalk in Main Street (one), drunkenness in a public place (one), contravening martial law regulations (one), malicious injury to property' (one). Andrew Mitchell, a 'Cape Coloured Cook aged 27', as well as being convicted and fined in the last-named case, was also found guilty of 'Swearing and making use of obscene, insulting or threatening language to wit: "Damn you. Bugger you. Fade [*sic*] the bloody lot of you"' (Criminal Record Book, Mafeking, in KAB, 1/MFK, 1/2/1/1/3). Clearly Plaatje recognised when a euphemism was required.

63 Sally and Betty Stent, in their biography of Vere Stent, would perhaps have seen this as justification too: 'He was a superb story teller', they wrote, 'and on many occasions there were amongst his audience those doubting Thomases, who were confounded when the facts of his seemingly impossible tale were confirmed by his contemporaries': Sally and Betty Stent, *The Forthright Man* (Cape Town: Howard Timmins, 1972), p. 99.

64 SOAS, Plaatje Papers, STP 3/1, Silas Molema to the Commandant, Mafeking, 18 February 1902.

65 KAB, AG 1002, 37/1902, Plaatje to CC and RM, Mafeking, 27 March 1902, enclosure

in E. Graham Green to Secretary, Law Dept, 27 March 1902; KAB, AG 1002, 53/1902, Plaatje to CC and RM, Mafeking, 19 May 1902, enclosure in E. Graham Green to Secretary, Law Dept, 11 June 1902. Green's comment about Grayson is from his letter to the Secretary of the Law Department on 5 November 1905 in KAB, JUS 39/6059/05. As first clerk Grayson earned a salary of £260 p.a., supplemented by £75 a year local allowance, which Plaatje did not get (*Civil Service List*, 1903, p. 139).

66 *Mafeking Mail*, 27 March 1902; Francis Masey, *The Late Right Honourable Cecil John Rhodes: a chronicle of the funeral ceremonies from Muizenberg to the Matopos, March–April 1902* (Cape Town: privately printed, 1905), p. 41; *Mafeking Mail*, 7 April 1902.

67 KAB, AG 1986, Annual Confidential Reports on Messengers and Interpreters for 1902, 14 April 1902.

68 KAB, AG 1002, 106/1902, E. Graham Green to Secretary, Law Dept, Cape Town, 18 and 24 December 1902 and KAB, AG 1077, 79/03, E. Graham Green to Secretary, Law Dept, Cape Town, 6 October 1903. Eventually a satisfactory solution was found with the appointment of Jacob Moses as interpreter in November 1903.

69 KAB, AG 1002, 53/1902, Plaatje to CC and RM, Mafeking, 19 May 1902, annexure A, in E. Graham Green to the Secretary, Law Dept, 11 June 1902.

Chapter 6

1 Hansard Parliamentary Debates (House of Commons), 4th series, 77, 19 October 1899, quoted in Bill Nasson, *Abraham Esau's War: a black South African war in the Cape, 1899–1902* (Cambridge: Cambridge University Press, 1991), p. 33.

2 'Our apology', *Koranta ea Becoana*, 23 August 1902.

3 'Masonic Hall', *Mafeking Mail*, 21 May 1902; 'Philharmonic Society's concert', *Mafeking Mail*, 24 May 1902; 'The little peach dilates on the Philharmonic Concert', *Mafeking Mail*, 27 May 1902.

4 'The essential interpreter', in Brian Willan (ed.), *Sol Plaatje: selected writings* (Johannesburg: Witwatersrand University Press, 1996), p. 59.

5 'Our new departure', *Koranta*, 23 August 1902. Plaatje's later recollection of Mr Green's speech was from 'Mr. E. Graham Green', *Tsala ea Batho*, 18 April 1914.

6 'Our new departure', *Koranta*, 23 August 1902. Monyatsi's praise poem appeared in *Koranta*'s first issue, 16 August 1902, under the heading 'Lipako tsa Koranta'. I am indebted to Maitseo Bakwena for her translation. Plaatje's description of Monyatsi is from S.T. Plaatje, *Sechuana Proverbs with Literal Translations and Their European Equivalents* (London: Kegan Paul, Trench, Trübner & Co., 1916), frontispiece.

7 Editorial, *Bechuanaland News*, 23 August 1902, p. 4; see also 'Another native newspaper for Bechuanaland', *Diamond Fields Advertiser (DFA)*, 19 August 1902, p. 5.

8 *Koranta*, 25 October 1902 and subsequent issues.

9 Information about employees of the 'Bechuana Printing Works' is derived from the voters' roll, which lists occupations: KAB, CCP, 11/1/43, Cape Voters' Roll, electoral division of Mafeking (Native Reserves), 1903; KAB, Records of Supreme Court, Northern Circuit (September 1902 – September 1903), *R v. Salatiele*, 8 September 1902; *Mafeking Mail*, 8 and 27 September 1902.

10 *South African Native Affairs Commission, Minutes of Evidence, vol. 4* (Cape Town: Government Printer, Cmd 2399, 1905), evidence of S.T. Plaatje, p. 267; S.M. Molema, *Lover of His People* (Johannesburg: Wits University Press, 2012), p. 39.

11 *Koranta* claimed to be 'rapidly increasing in size and circulation' when advertising itself in the *South African Spectator*, starting some three months before the first issue actually appeared (*South African Spectator*, 31 May 1902, p. 6).

12 Union of South Africa, *Report of Natives' Land Commission, vol. II* (Evidence) (UG22-1916), p. 93; 'Englishmen and *Koranta*', *Koranta*, 13 September 1902.

13 Molema, *Lover of His People*, p. 81. The passage had a wide currency among African

American intellectuals, being quoted, for example, at the head of chapter 7 of W.E.B. Du Bois's *The Souls of Black Folk*, published in 1903.

14 'Tsa Bakoaleli', *Koranta*, 20 June 1903, p. 3. I am also indebted to the nuanced treatment of *Koranta ea Becoana* in K. Moguerane, 'A history of the Molemas, African notables in South Africa, 1880s to 1920s' (DPhil thesis, Oxford University, 2014).

15 *Koranta*, 28 February 1903, p. 3, English translation in Molema, *Lover of His People*, pp. 104–5.

16 *Koranta*, 27 June 1903, has a reminder of the need to pay subscriptions, pointing out that the paper was published weekly not annually and that it ran at a loss.

17 *South African Native Affairs Commission, Minutes of Evidence, vol. 4*, evidence of S.T. Plaatje, p. 264; 'Languages', *Koranta*, 30 March 1904.

18 'The negro question', *Koranta*, 7 September 1904; author's interview with Maud Zibi (née Sidzumo), Kayakulu, 2 December 1981.

19 'Bruce Grit's column', *Negro World* (New York), 16 July 1921.

20 Plaatje's concern to disarm white fears met with a positive response in some quarters: in May 1905 an article entitled 'The black problem in South Africa' (by Roderick Jones, chief Reuters correspondent in South Africa) appeared in the influential journal *The Nineteenth Century and After*. It commended *Koranta ea Becoana* for being 'an uncompromising foe' of 'Ethiopianism' and the African Methodist Episcopal Church, and 'singularly sensible' in other respects (pp. 774–5).

21 Reproduced in Molema, *Lover of His People*, pp. 92–3.

22 'Bogwera', *Koranta*, 11 April 1903.

23 The petition in favour of annexation to the Transvaal was headed by the mayor of Mafeking and was supported by 27 pages of signatures (KAB, CO 529/1, 17804); editorial, *Koranta*, 13 December 1902.

24 'Haikonna annexation' (editorial), *Koranta*, 17 January 1903.

25 'Translation', letter from Badirile Montshiwa to editor, *Koranta*, 7 February 1903; *Mafeking Mail*, 12 February 1903.

26 UW, Molema–Plaatje Papers, Bb3, invoice for Sol T. Plaatje from Mallett and Bowen (Solicitors), 29 January 1903; 'Address from the natives', *DFA* (weekly edition), 27 December 1902. 'The native editor explained, that the natives did not like the Transvaal regulations, which they thought too severe.'

27 UW, Molema–Plaatje Papers, Bb3, Petition to Joseph Chamberlain; *Koranta*, 31 January 1903; also National Archives (Kew), CO 529/1, 17754 and 17803, Petition and Supplementary Petition of Barolong to Joseph Chamberlain, January 1903.

28 'Mr Chamberlain's tour', *DFA*, 28 January 1903.

29 *An Account of the Rt Hon. Joseph Chamberlain's Visit to South Africa: a record of unique practical statesmanship* (London: St Martin's Press, 1903), p. 41; 'Mr Chamberlain's reply', *Koranta*, 31 January 1903. Chamberlain's speech was also reported in *Mafeking Mail*, 29 January 1903.

30 *Koranta*, 7 February and 9 September 1903. Mallett and Bowen's bill, dated 29 January 1903, amounted to 25 guineas, which Plaatje paid some weeks later (UW, Molema–Plaatje Papers, Bb3, invoice sent to Sol T. Plaatje, 29 January 1903).

31 Testimonial from Joseph Chamberlain dated 9 February 1903, in Plaatje to Emmett Scott, 27 August 1914 (Library of Congress, Washington DC, Booker T. Washington Papers, Con. 13); Molema–Plaatje Papers, Bb3, Mallett and Bowen to Plaatje, 23 April 1903.

32 'The compensation debate', *Koranta*, 1 August 1903.

33 This paragraph draws upon: 'Personalia', *Koranta*, 1 August 1903; 'Koranta "Special"', *Koranta*, 15 August 1903; KAB, NA 7/B1907 (Barolong claims), misc. correspondence between F.Z.S. Peregrino and W.C. Cummings, 20–29 August 1903; *Mafeking Mail*, 9 September 1903; *Cape Argus* (weekly edition), 12 August and 16 September 1903.

34 'The Argus plea', *Koranta*, 15 August 1903; the original piece ('Barolong chiefs: pressing claims') appeared in the *Cape Argus* (weekly edition), 12 August 1903, p. 25.

35 *DFA* (weekly edition), 22 November 1902, pp. 15, 26 and 27; *Koranta*, 22 and 29 November 1902.

36 *Koranta*, 6 December 1902, p. 5.

37 'Political prisoners released', *DFA*, 25 March 1903; *Koranta*, 18 April 1903, p. 4. Both the *Advertiser* itself and the (pro-British) South African League (Kimberley branch) supported the campaign for the release of Galeshewe, pointing to the disparities between his treatment and that of Boer rebels during the recent war: 'Native rebels', *DFA*, 7 April 1903.

38 For example, *Koranta*, 14 October 1903; editorial, *Koranta*, 6 June 1904, 'The Central S.A. Railways', *Koranta*, 30 March 1904.

39 'Whae's your pass?' *Koranta*, 13 July 1904.

40 'Occasional notes', *Koranta*, 13 April 1904; 'Segregation: idea ridiculed' (*Transvaal Chronicle*), reproduced in *Tsala ea Becoana*, 28 January 1911.

41 Plaatje's admiration for Sir Richard Solomon and Sir James Rose Innes was recalled in 'Lord Milner and the natives', *DFA*, 23 May 1925. Under their direction it was not long, Plaatje said, before the bench had succeeded in 'capturing the confidence of the Transvaal natives as completely as did the Cape Bench under Lord (then Sir Henry) de Villiers'.

42 Editorial, *Koranta*, 9 November 1904; 'Maitisho', *Koranta*, 9 November 1904. For the wider significance of this case and ensuing developments, see Jacob Dlamini, 'The land and its languages: Edward Tsewu and the pre-history of the 1913 Land Act', in Ben Cousins and Cherryl Walker (eds.), *Land Divided, Land Restored: land reform in South Africa for the 21st century* (Johannesburg: Jacana Media, 2015), pp. 40–55.

43 'Go Morulaganyi', *Koranta*, 19 October 1904.

44 L. and D. Switzer, *The Black Press in South Africa and Lesotho* (Boston: G.K. Hall, 1979), pp. 38, 44, 54.

45 *Koranta*, 16 September 1903; 'Notice', *Koranta*, 7 October 1903; 'SAN Press Association', *Ilanga lase Natal*, 25 December 1904, thanking *Koranta* for 'the proposal to establish a South Africa Native Press Association for better cooperation amongst the various native journals in the country', and offering its 'heartiest approval and support'; letter from F.Z.S. Peregrino, *Izwi la Bantu*, 24 March 1908 and editorial, *Izwi*, 14 April 1908; 'Native newspaper mania: letter to the editor of Imvo' (from Elijah Makiwane), *Imvo*, 7 January 1913.

46 *South African Native Affairs Commission, Minutes of Evidence, vol. 4*, evidence of S.T. Plaatje, pp. 267–9; KAB, NA 428 (Misc. letters received), Plaatje to Secretary for Native Affairs, 16 February 1904; Constitution of the Native Press Association (January 1904), in Willan, *Sol Plaatje: selected writings*, pp. 82–3.

47 'The educated nigger and his paper', *The Friend*, 9 March 1903. There was another tirade in its issue of 25 February 1903 ('The black man') where missionaries were again blamed, and *Koranta ea Becoana* was criticised for having complained about 'the way the Kafir is being treated by the British in the Transvaal and Orange River Colony'.

48 *Koranta*, 21 March 1903.

49 '*Imvo* and *Koranta*', *Imvo*, 8 September 1903; extract from *Times of Natal*, *Ipepa lo Hlanga*, 28 August 1903; editorial, *Bechuanaland News*, 17 December 1904.

50 Extract from 'A Johannesburg paper', *Mafeking Mail*, 9 May 1905.

51 KAB, 1/MFK, 6/1/2/9, Letters Despatched, Departments (September 1903 – May 1904), Green to Secretary for Native Affairs, 22 January 1904; Green to Director of Census, Cape Town, 4 March 1904.

52 KAB, 1/MFK, 6/1/3/8, Letters Despatched, Misc. (June 1903–March 1904), Green to editor, *Koranta ea Becoana*, 19 January 1904.

53 Botswana National Archives (BNA), RC 10/7, Resident Commissioner, Bechuanaland Protectorate, to High Commissioner, 19 November 1903. For more on the background to Segale Pilane's letter, see James Campbell, *Songs of Zion: the African Methodist Episcopal Church in the United States and South Africa* (Chapel Hill, NC: University of North Carolina Press, 1998), pp. 180–1.

54 Herbert Sloley (Resident Commissioner, Basutoland) to Howard Pim, 22 April 1908, quoted in Tim Couzens, 'A short history of *The World* (and other black South African newspapers)', African Studies Institute, University of the Witwatersrand, seminar paper, June 1976. 'I think I would be doing a very wrong thing indeed,' Plaatje told Bishop Coppin when he visited Mafeking, 'if I fail to draw attention to the existence in Bechuanaland of a very inferior class of black men who masquerade in the regulation cloth and the round collar and call themselves the pioneers of the African Methodist Episcopal Church' (*Koranta*, 23 May 1903).

55 *South African Native Affairs Commission, Report*, p. 65, para 322.

56 National Archives Repository, Pretoria, TAB, AG 2288/04, Plaatje to Attorney General (Transvaal), 13 May 1904, and copy of letter from Secretary, Law Department, to Inspector-General, South African Constabulary, 20 May 1904, reproduced in Willan, *Sol Plaatje: selected writings*, pp. 89–90.

57 KAB, 1/MFK, 6/1/3/6, Letters Despatched, Misc. (June 1902–January 1903), E. Graham Green to Resident Magistrate, Vryburg, 30 December 1902, re 'Complaint of Solomon Plaatje'; KAB 1/VBG, Records of Vryburg magistrate 2/17, Letterbook 14/10, 1902, RM (Vryburg) to CC and RM (Mafeking), 9 and 20 January 1903. 'As far as my knowledge of Plaatje goes', Green informed his counterpart in Vryburg, 'he has always appeared to me a quiet, inoffensive and reliable man.'

58 *South African Native Affairs Commission, Report*, p. 65, para 322. The two other Africans who gave evidence were Badirile Montshiwa, the Tshidi Barolong paramount chief, and Chief Khama of the Bamangwato, who had travelled south to meet the commissioners.

59 *Koranta*, 21 October 1903 and 21 September 1904.

60 Earlier in the year Plaatje had sent Dixon for his information a copy of the constitution of the South African Newspaper Press Association (Free State Archives Repository, Bloemfontein, VAB, CO 244: 711/04, J. Quayle Dixon to Acting Colonial Secretary, 1 February 1904).

61 *South African Native Affairs Commission, Minutes of Evidence*, pp. 264–70, reproduced in Willan, *Sol Plaatje: selected writings*, pp. 91–6.

Chapter 7

1 UW, Molema–Plaatje Papers, Aa3.6.2, De Kock & De Kock (attorney) to Silas Molema, 6 November 1914, and copy of letter from Chief Bathoen to Spencer Minchin, 26 May 1905.

2 *Koranta ea Becoana*, 27 June 1903.

3 'Journalistic amenities', *Central African Times*, 7 May 1904, p. 6, also *Cape Times*, 5 April 1904, p. 5; UW, Molema–Plaatje Papers, Ac3.6.1, general bond passed by Silas Tau Molema and the firm of 'Silas Molema' in favour of Charles Wenham; 'The native vote and Mr "Matabele" Thompson', *Diamond Fields Advertiser* (weekly edition), 8 April 1905, p. 22; 'The Ethiopian bishop and his flock', *DFA* (weekly edition), 23 September 1905, p. 23.

4 S.T. Plaatje, *Sechuana Proverbs with Literal Translations and Their European Equivalents* (London: Kegan Paul, Trench, Trübner, 1916), pp. 13–17; KAB, SGE 1/714, Misc. Letters, Mafeking, Plaatje to SGE, Examining Branch, Cape Town, 20 June 1908.

5 University of Cambridge, British and Foreign Bible Society Archives, Editorial subcommittee minutes, 1907–8, extracts from letters from Rev. A.J. Wookey, 3 December 1907 and 26 February 1908; Rev. A.H.W. Behrens, 26 October 1907; and Rev. G. Lowe, 8 May 1908.

6   W.C. Willoughby, *Race Problems in the New Africa* (Oxford: Clarendon Press, 1923), p. 238; Moeding College Archives (Botswana), W.C. Willoughby to W.O. Barratt, 21 September 1904.

7   'Bechuanas and education: meeting at Mafeking', *DFA* (weekly edition), 10 October 1908; Plaatje, *Sechuana Proverbs*, pp. 15–16.

8   'Sekgoma: the black Dreyfus', in Brian Willan (ed.), *Sol Plaatje: selected writings* (Johannesburg: Witwatersrand University Press, 1996), pp. 108 and 111. For a fuller account of the Sekgoma saga, see particularly A.J.G.M. Sanders, *Bechuanaland and the Law in Politicians' Hands* (Gaborone: Botswana Society, 1992), pp. 15–32, and Ralph Williams, *How I Became Governor* (London: John Murray, 1913), pp. 324–60.

9   Williams, *How I Became Governor*, pp. 116–17.

10 KAB, 1/MFK, 6/1/13/13, Letters Despatched, Misc. (July 1906–February 1907), RM (Mafeking) to Commissioner, Robben Island, 27 August 1906, states that *Koranta* had ceased publication. The approach to the Bechuanaland Press is the subject of UW, Molema–Plaatje Papers, Aa3.6.2, Minchin to Silas Molema, 25 October 1906. Subsequent difficulties are evident in Molema–Plaatje Papers, Aa3.6.2, Minchin to Molema, 25 October 1906 and 26 November 1906; KAB, 1/MFK, 2/2/1/3, Civil Record Book (12/6/03–5/1/09), case 134 (1906), *Helen Moroney* v. *S.T. Molema and S.T. Plaatje*.

11 UW, Molema–Plaatje Papers, Aa3.6.2, Minchin to Molema, 7 January 1907; the formation of the Bechuanaland Press (with a capital of £6,000 along with the 'printing plants, goodwill and copyrights' of the *Bechuanaland News*, *Mafeking Mail and Protectorate Guardian*, *De Boerenvriend* and *Koranta ea Becoana*) was reported in *Mafeking Mail*, 23 April 1907, and news of *Koranta*'s new start in *Mafeking Mail*, 30 January 1907.

12 'The Koranta trouble', *Ilanga lase Natal*, 1 March 1907; UW, Plaatje–Molema Papers, Aa3.6.2, Whales to Molema, 19 February 1907. For Peregrino's complex personality, see David Killingray and Martin Plaut, 'F.Z.S. Peregrino, a significant but duplicitous figure in the Black Atlantic world', *South African Historical Journal*, 2016, DOI: 10.1080/02582473.2016.1216158.

13 *Izwi la Bantu*, 30 April 1907; UW, Plaatje–Molema Papers, Whales to Molema, 19 February 1907; *Koranta*, 10 May 1907: cutting in Willoughby Papers, XDA 49 file 743, University of Birmingham, Cadbury Research Library. It is clear that the *Mafeking Mail* believed Plaatje to be 'editor of the Koranta ea Becoana' in its issue of 15 October 1907.

14 KAB, 1/MFK, 6/1/2/14, Letters Despatched, Departments (December 1906–September 1907), RM to Secretary for Public Works, Cape Town, 7 March 1907. Welsh replaced Green as magistrate and civil commissioner in November 1906.

15 KAB, 1/MFK, 6/1/2/14, Letters Despatched, Departments (December 1906–September 1907), CC and RM to Controller of Printing and Stationery, 4 September 1904. *Imvo* reported, in its issue of 22 October 1907, that Plaatje had left for the Kalahari three months previously and was expected back at any time.

16 *Imvo*, 9 July and 22 October 1907; *Koranta*, 16 August 1907 (Willoughby Papers, file 743).

17 UW, Molema–Plaatje Papers, Aa3.6.2, Minchin to Molema, 7 December 1907 and 13 February 1908; *Mafeking Mail*, 28 February 1908, announced the sale of the *Koranta* office and its printing plant, describing it as 'a good opportunity of acquiring one of the best properties in town and a First Class printing Plant'. The issue number attributed to *Koranta*'s issue of 15 November 1907 gives some idea of the rate and extent of its decline. Between 16 August 1902 and 21 December 1904, 108 issues were published, including 49 copies in 1903 and 37 copies in 1904. In the period of just under three years from the beginning of January 1905 to 15 November 1907, however, 44 copies were issued, fewer than during the whole of 1903.

18 Surviving letters in Plaatje's hand writing on behalf of the Barolong chief and people include those dated 15 January 1904, to the Mafeking CC and RM, and to an unknown

recipient (probably the governor or prime minister of the colony), n.d. [March 1904], both in UW, Molema–Plaatje Papers, A 979, Bc1-01.

19 *Koranta*, 23 November 1903; KAB, NA 752, F718, E. Graham Green to Secretary for Native Affairs, 29 November 1904; KAB, NA 752, F718, Commissioner of Taxes to Secretary for Native Affairs, 6 August 1906. Khumisho Moguerane, 'Black landlords, their tenants and the Natives Land Act of 1913', *Journal of Southern African Studies*, 42, 2, 2016, pp. 243–66, provides a detailed account of this saga into the second decade of the twentieth century.

20 Proclamations nos. 173 and 174, 21 May 1906, declared the Mafeking Reserve part of the Mafeking district (Moguerane, 'Black landlords', p. 252); *Mafeking Mail*, 15 May 1908; KAB, 1/MFK, 5/1/2/2, Letters Received, Secretary for Native Affairs (January 1905 –December 1910), Dower to CC and RM, Mafeking, 16 August 1906, re 'Complaints of Barolong'. In July 1909, in a confidential letter to the Secretary for Native Affairs, E.C. Welsh identified 'the extensive power of the Chiefs' and 'the uncertainty of the legal position in regard to the Native Reserve' as the two key problems he faced in administering the district: KAB, 1/MFK, 5/1/22/1, Letters Received, Confidential (July 1909 – December 1920), Welsh to Secretary for Native Affairs, 27 July 1909.

21 KAB, NA 752, K718, Plaatje to Secretary for Native Affairs, Cape Town, 2 April 1911; editorial, *Tsala ea Becoana*, 8 April 1911; J. Comaroff, 'Competition for office and political processes among the Barolong boo Ratshidi of the South Africa–Botswana borderland' (PhD thesis, University of London, 1973), pp. 362–7.

22 S.M. Molema, *Lover of His People: a biography of Sol Plaatje* (Johannesburg: Wits University Press, 2012), pp. 66–7; teachers' names are derived from Education Department inspection reports for 1908 and 1909 (KAB, SGE 2/227 and 2/252, reports for Mafeking, 1908 and 1909); interview with Mrs Maud Zibi (née Sidzumo), Kayakulu, North West Province, 2 December 1981.

23 KAB, 1/MFK, 1/2/1/1/5 (Criminal Record Book 1907–1909), case 74, 11 April 1907, 'R v. Solomon Plaatjes [*sic*], a Barolong Printer residing at Mafeking, adult'.

24 Molema, *Lover of His People*, pp. 8–9.

25 'Concert at the location in Wesleyan Church', *Mafeking Mail*, 3 July 1908, p. 3; 'Mafeking', *Imvo*, 28 July 1908.

26 'Correspondence: colour in the town hall', *Mafeking Mail*, 11 April 1906.

27 'Mafeking Town Council: proceedings', *Mafeking Mail*, 26 April 1906.

28 'Mems', *Mafeking Mail*, 15 October 1907.

29 Violet was born in Kimberley on 30 January 1907 ('Births', *Mafeking Mail*, 1 February 1907, p. 2). Elizabeth's investment in her Mfengu identity is evident in her subscription to the 'Fingo History Fund' several years later, recorded in John Ayliffe and Joseph Whiteside, *History of the Abambo (Fingos)* (Butterworth, 1912), p. 101.

30 Sainty's educational record is derived from his letter of application (2 May 1927) to the Town Clerk, Cape Town, in KAB, 3/CT, 4/1/5/1241, N7/5, and from his file (2/44) in the University of Fort Hare Archives (Administration), form of application dated 23 February 1920.

31 'With the kids', in Willan, *Sol Plaatje: selected writings*, p. 158. The reason for Richard's removal to Bethanie was confirmed for me by Mrs Mary Plaatje (Richard's wife) in an interview in Natalspruit, Johannesburg, November 1980.

32 'Olive and I', *Koranta*, 15 November 1907 (clipping in Willoughby Papers, file 743). Olive's three responses can be translated as: I'm happy; I'm sad; its nice.

33 KAB, 1/MAF, 2/2/1/3, Civil Record Book (12 June 1903–5 January 1909).

34 KAB, 1/MFK, 5/1/8/17, Letters Received, Misc. (January–December 1907), Inspector of Native Reserves, Setlagole, to Magistrate, Mafeking, 13 January 1907; KAB, 1/MFK, 2/2/1/3, Civil Record Book, case 1, 1907, *Colonial Government* v. *S.T. Plaatje*.

35 KAB, 1/MFK, 5/1/8/16, Letters Received, Misc. (January–December 1906),

Plaatje to RM and CC, Mafeking, 3 January 1906); KAB, 1/MFK, 6/1/2/14, Letters Despatched, Departments (December 1906–September 1907), CC and RM, Mafeking, to Controller and Auditor-General, 4 September 1907.

36 Conveniently collected in KAB, T 1942/67 (Treasury).

37 KAB, 1/MFK, 5/1/2/1, Letters Received, Under-Secretary for Native Affairs (1896–1903), Secretary, Native Affairs Dept to Civil Commissioner, Mafeking, 31 August 1903; CAD, NA 556/950, Captain G. Goodyear to RM, 15 August 1906.

38 KAB, 1/MFK, 6/1/2/16, Letters Despatched, Misc. (June 1908 – April 1909), RM to Plaatje, 21 January 1909 and subsequent correspondence; KAB, 1/MFK, 5/1/8/20, Letters Received, Misc. (January–December 1909), Plaatje to RM, 22 March 1909. Plaatje's recruiting licence, signed by Edward Dower, Secretary for Native Affairs, dated 11 February 1909, and valid until 31 December 1909, is in 1/MFK, 5/1/2/1.

39 KAB, 1/MFK, 5/1/8/20, Letters Received, Misc. (January–December 1909), RM, Mafeking to RM, Zeerust, 22 March 1909 (with reply of RM, Zeerust); KAB, 1/MFK, 5/1/8/18, Letters Received, Misc. (January–June 1908), telegram dated 8 April 1908; KAB, NA 7007, section D, F473 Dower to De Kock, 15 April, 7 June and 8 June 1909; KAB, NA 1008, F473, Dower to Pritchard, 13 May 1909.

40 KAB, T 1942/07, Secretary for Public Works to Assistant Treasurer, Cape Town, 8 September 1909; KAB, CMT 3/573, Circular no. 34, Assistant Chief Magistrate (Transkeian Territories), 15 October 1909.

41 KAB, 1/MFK, 5/1/8/20, Letters Received, Misc. (January–December 1909), Minchin to CC and RM, Mafeking, 30 March 1909.

42 KAB, 1/MFK, 6/1/2/17, Letters Despatched, Departments (April 1909–January 1910), RM to Controller of Printing and Stationery, Cape Town, 5 August 1909; RM to Under-Colonial Secretary, Cape Town, 9 August 1909; Notice, *Mafeking Mail*, issues between 14 and June 1909. The *Bulawayo Chronicle*, 19 June 1909, invited bids for the printing equipment by 30 June 1909, listing all the items available. According to Modiri Molema (*Lover of His People*, p. 48), the printing plant was purchased by the *Mafeking Mail*. Plaatje later recalled that he could have obtained it from Minchin for no more than £100 – if only he had the money.

43 L.M. Thompson, *The Unification of South Africa* (London: Oxford University Press, 1960), pp. 325–7; P. Walshe, *The Rise of African Nationalism in South Africa: the African National Congress, 1912–1952* (Berkeley: University of California Press, 1970), pp. 19–24; *The Friend*, 25–27 March 1909. André Odendaal's *The Founders: the origins of the ANC and the struggle for democracy in South Africa* (Johannesburg: Jacana Media, 2012) provides the most detailed and authoritative account of the African response to the threat of Union during this period.

44 *The Friend*, 25–27 March 1909 and Odendaal, *The Founders*, pp. 390–7; 'Correspondence', letter from Plaatje to the editor, *Mafeking Mail*, 27 March 1909, pp. 3–4.

45 National Library of South Africa, Cape Town, W.P. Schreiner Papers, MSC 27, Plaatje to W.P. Schreiner, 13 April 1909, no. 1430; the previous month the Barolong had communicated their concerns to the prime minister and colonial secretary: KAB, 1/MFK, 5/1/2/2, Letters Received, Under-Secretary for Native Affairs (January 1905–December 1910), Dower to CC, Mafeking, 24 March 1909 re 'Status of Natives under Draft Constitution'.

46 'Native Convention: meeting in Waaihoek', *The Friend*, 25 March 1910; 'Native Convention', *Pretoria News*, 6 April 1910, p. 7; 'Botha and natives', *Pretoria News*, 2 April 1910, p. 6; 'Natives and Chinese', *Mafeking Mail*, 6 April 1910; *Ilanga lase Natal*, 15 April 1910.

47 'Natives and Union', *Pretoria News*, 9 April 1910, p. 5.

48 'Prize essay competition on native segregation', *Christian Express*, December 1909 and July 1910; see also 'Prize essay competition', *Christian Express*, June 1910.

49 'Segregation: idea ridiculed' (*Transvaal Chronicle*), reproduced in *Tsala ea Becoana*, 28 January 1911; an extract from the essay also appeared in the *Rhodesia Herald*, 13 January 1911.

50 KAB, 1/MFK, 2/1/1/1/23, Civil Cases, case 57, 1910, *Kemp & Co.* v. *S.T. Plaatje*, 12 April 1910, warrant dated 28 April 1910.

Chapter 8

1 S.T. Plaatje, *Native Life in South Africa* (London: P.S. King & Son, 1916), p. 10; S.T. Plaatje, 'The late Chief J.M. Nyokong', *Umteteli wa Bantu*, 6 September 1930; S.T. Plaatje, 'Lesho ba morena mokitlane oa ga Motlala', *Umteteli*, 30 August 1930.

2 'The S.A. Native Convention', *Tsala ea Becoana*, 9 July 1910. For Jeremiah Makgothi, see Ellen Kuzwayo, *Call Me Woman* (London: Women's Press, 1985), pp. 55–62.

3 Free State Archives Depot (Bloemfontein), Colonial Secretary, ORC, 1192/1908, T.M. Mapikela to Colonial Secretary, Bloemfontein, 1 August 1908; Bloemfontein Municipality, MBL, Box 44, Mapikela to Town Clerk, Bloemfontein, 20 August 1908. The possibility of launching a newspaper was also discussed at the fourth annual meeting of the Orange River Native Association, held in Winburg on 17 and 18 February 1909 (*The Friend*, 27 February 1909).

4 KAB, Kimberley Magistrate's records, 1/KIM 9/4, Register of Newspapers (1884–1929), entry for *Tsala ea Becoana*, 13 June 1910.

5 In February 1910 Jabavu wrote to Silas Molema to solicit support for the new newspaper, conveying details of the shares he had on offer (UW, Molema–Plaatje Papers, Cc9, Jabavu to Molema, 5 February 1910).

6 B. Roberts, *Kimberley: Turbulent City* (Cape Town: David Philip, 1976), pp. 356, 360.

7 S.T. Plaatje, 'Through native eyes: annexation and the Protectorates', *Pretoria News*, 16 January 1911; see also 'The Protectorates and the Union', *Tsala ea Becoana*, 19 November 1910.

8 *Ilanga lase Natal*, 29 July 1910. 'Maitisho' in *Tsala*, 29 October 1910, reminded readers of its author's oath of secrecy, repeating a riddle that had first appeared in *Koranta ea Becoana* – along with a note that his birthday was 9 October 1876. An important step towards viability was a contract reached with the Government Printer to print government notices worth £50 for a six-month period: see CAD, CS 975, files 20012-20048/8, 'Publishing Notices Regarding Natives in Native Press', memo from Government Printer to Secretary for the Interior, 30 December 1910.

9 Editorial, *Tsala ea Becoana*, 8 October 1910.

10 'A native function: providing vernacular literature', *Diamond Fields Advertiser* (*DFA*), 11 August 1931; Burton to J.X. Merriman, 11 Feb 1909 (National Library of South Africa, Cape Town, Merriman Papers, MSC 15, 1910, no. 20).

11 *Tsala ea Becoana*, 8 October 1910.

12 Schreiner replied to Plaatje as follows: 'Thanks message of congratulations and good wishes' (National Library of South Africa, Cape Town, W.P. Schreiner Papers, J35, telegram from Schreiner to Plaatje, 16 October 1910).

13 W.P. Schreiner Papers, 1689, Plaatje to Schreiner, 17 December 1910. Colonel Walter Stanford, a former chief magistrate of the Transkeian Territories and under-secretary for native affairs in the Cape, was one of four senators in the Union parliament appointed to represent and protect African interests.

14 UW, Molema–Plaatje Papers, Da22, Plaatje to Silas Molema, 12 December 1912.

15 'ORC natives and land', *Tsala ea Becoana*, 7 January 1911; 'Native property in Thaba Nchu', *Tsala ea Becoana*, 28 January 1911.

16 'Thaba Nchu white men: up in arms against Rt Hon. A. Fisher', *Tsala ea Becoana*, 18 February 1911; see also 'Thaba Nchu native rights', letter from Plaatje to the Editor, *Cape Times*, 17 March 1911, p. 3.

17 See Khumisho Moguerane, 'Black landlords, their tenants and the Natives Land Act of 1913', *Journal of Southern African Studies*, 42, 2, 2016, pp. 243–66, for further details of the legal cases and appeals that ensued.

18 UW, Records of the Joint Council of Europeans and Africans file, Aa3.3.13, 'Natives in the courts', address by S.T. Plaatje to 1924 Joint Councils Conference, pp. 5–6; 'The administration of justice', *Imvo Zabantsundu*, 31 October 1911.

19 Plaatje, 'Natives in the courts', p. 6.

20 Editorial and 'The capital revisited', *Tsala ea Becoana*, 2 December, 1911; 'The capital revisited: interview continued', *Tsala ea Becoana*, 16 December 1911.

21 SOAS, Plaatje Papers, STP 1/1, typescript biography of Plaatje by I. Bud-M'belle, p. 14.

22 UW, Molema–Plaatje Papers, Aa2, Goronyane to Molema, 8 June 1911.

23 UW, Molema–Plaatje Papers, Da14, Plaatje to Silas Molema, n.d. [c. April 1911]; Da10, Plaatje to Silas Molema, 5 March 1911; Chief W.Z. Fenyang to S.T. Plaatje, 27 February 1911; Da16, Plaatje to Silas Molema, n.d. [c. 1911].

24 Editorial (Setswana), *Tsala ea Becoana*, 2 December 1911. Once the contract with Jabavu & Co. was terminated, *Tsala* was printed in Kimberley, first by J.C. Looney (from September 1911), then by the *Diamond Fields Advertiser* (from February 1912 to April 1913) and finally on *Tsala*'s own press (from April 1913).

25 KAB, 1/MFK, 6/1/3/19, Clerk to the Court, Mafeking, to Isaiah Bud-M'belle, Kimberley, 9 March 1910, re 'Dawson versus Plaatje', acknowledging receipt of payment from Bud-M'belle; Sebopia Molema Papers (in possession of Galefele Molema, Mahikeng), Chief Lekoko to S.T. Plaatje, 29 May 1912. I am most grateful to Dr Khumisho Moguerane for drawing this letter to my attention and to Mr Galefele Molema for giving me access to it.

26 UW, Molema–Plaatje Papers, Da30, Plaatje to Molema, 12 May 1913.

27 'Through native eyes', *Pretoria News*, 16 January 1911; UW, Molema-Plaatje Papers, Da14, Plaatje to Molema, n.d. [c. January 1914].

28 'The social pest: an African viewpoint', *African World*, 8 July 1911. An editorial in *Tsala ea Becoana*, 2 December 1911, explained that Plaatje 'worked on other newspapers for the whites in Pretoria and London at night' (English translation from Setswana). He had addressed the same subject, in response to a leading article in the *Diamond Fields Advertiser*, in 'The native outrages', *DFA*, 10 February 1911.

29 S.T. Plaatje, 'Natives and Mr Merriman: an appreciation', *DFA*, 10 August 1926.

30 'I konyenslani yabantsundu', *Imvo*, 29 August 1911; 'I konversheni yabantsundu', *Imvo*, 5 September 1911; 'Bloemfontein', *Tsala ea Becoana*, 26 August 1911; 'Izindaba ze komiti lokuhiela le South African Native Convention', *Ilanga lase Natal*, 1 September 1911. For Seme's life, and his role in the early SANNC, see Bongani Nqulunga, *Seme: the man who founded the ANC: a biography of Pixley ka Isaka Seme* (Century City: Penguin Books, 2017).

31 Letter from Pixley Seme to editor, *Ilanga lase Natal*, 15 December 1911; *Imvo*, 21 November 1911; 'Kafir attorney convicted', *Transvaal Leader*, 8 November 1911; 'The educated native', *Transvaal Leader*, 13 November 1911. See also R.V. Selope Thema, 'How Congress began', in Mothobi Mutloatse (ed.), *Reconstruction* (Johannesburg: Ravan Press, 1981), p. 108. Seme's 'slight American accent' is noted in a report which appeared in *The Star* (Johannesburg) when he first appeared in court as attorney (reproduced in *Tsala ea Becoana*, 18 February 1911). Seme was treated leniently by the magistrate, who took account of the provocation he was subjected to and fined only £12 – the maximum penalty for the offence being a fine of £75 or six months' hard labour.

32 De Beers Archives (DB), General Secretary's correspondence, Plaatje to De Beers, 17 July 1913.

33 'Native union', letter from Seme to editor, *Ilanga lase Natal*, 20 October 1911; 'Native

union', letter from Seme to editor, *Tsala ea Becoana*, 28 October 1911.

34 'Proposed Native Congress: caucus meeting', *Imvo*, 5 December 1911; 'Native union', *Ilanga lase Natal*, 1 December 1911; S.T. Plaatje, 'Umfiko e kaya', *Umteteli*, 15 December 1923; S.T. Plaatje, 'Kgakala ko Amerika', *Umteteli*, 22 December 1923.

35 'Native Congress: doings at Bloemfontein', *Pretoria News*, 11 January 1912: 'Native Congress to emulate the whites', *Pretoria News*, 13 January 1912; also, 'SA Native National Congress', *Tsala ea Becoana*, 10 and 17 February 1912; 'The South African Native National Congress', *Ilanga lase Natal*, 26 January 1912. 'S.A. Native National Congress', *Tsala ea Becoana*, 10 February 1912, lists the 62 delegates present.

36 See André Odendaal, *The Founders: the origins of the African National Congress and the struggle for democracy* (Johannesburg: Jacana Media, 2012), p. 471, for a discussion of the issues surrounding Rubusana's position.

37 On John Dube, see Heather Hughes, *First President: a life of John L. Dube, founding president of the ANC* (Johannesburg: Jacana Media, 2011). Earlier treatments include S. Marks, 'The ambiguities of dependence: John L. Dube of Natal', *Journal of Southern African Studies*, 1, 2, 1976; P. Walshe, *The Rise of African Nationalism in South Africa: the African National Congress, 1912–1952* (Berkeley: University of California Press, 1970), pp. 35–6.

38 UW, Molema–Plaatje Papers, Cc9, Dube to Chief Lekoko Montshiwa, 13 April 1912.

39 Editorial, *Tsala ea Becoana*, 10 February 1912; see also H.J. and R.E. Simons, *Class and Colour in South Africa* (Harmondsworth: Penguin Books, 1969), pp. 134–5.

40 'The capital revisited', *Tsala ea Becoana*, 2 and 16 December 1911; 'Mr Sol Plaatje', *Ilanga lase Natal*, 5 January 1912.

41 Editorial, *Tsala ea Becoana*, 10 February 1912.

42 'S.A. Native Congress', *Tsala ea Becoana*, 17 February 1912.

43 The question of the relationship between the SANNC leadership and the Indian community in South Africa has been the subject of considerable debate: see Hughes, *First President*, pp. 110–11 and 178–9; Odendaal, *The Founders*, pp. 298–9; and Howard Phillips, 'Mahatma Gandhi under the plague spotlight', in Poonam Bala (ed.), *Medicine and Colonialism: historical perspectives in India and South Africa* (London: Pickering and Chatto, 2014), pp. 75–84. Like Dube, Plaatje admired individual Indian leaders but saw few grounds for political co-operation, tending to regard the Indian community as outsiders who were not wholly committed to South Africa and reluctant to engage fully with its 'indigenous' inhabitants (see particularly, 'Through native eyes: Indians and natives', *Pretoria News*, 12 December 1912).

44 'Along the colour line', in Brian Willan (ed.), *Sol Plaatje: selected writings* (Johannesburg: Wits University Press, 1996) p. 167). Abdurahman's speech was reproduced in full in the *Cape Argus*, 2 January 1912, and widely reported elsewhere. His comment about reactions to it was in his presidential speech at the APO's annual conference in 1913, reproduced in Plaatje, *Native Life*, p. 138.

45 F.Z.S. Peregrino, 'The SA Native Congress: what it is', *Tsala ea Becoana*, 30 March 1912.

46 *Pretoria News*, 8, 11, 13 and 15 January. The reports are reproduced in Brian Willan, 'The founding conference of the South African Native National Congress: as reported in the *Pretoria News*', *Quarterly Bulletin of the National Library of South Africa*, 66, 4, October–December 2012, pp. 29–41.

47 Bodleian Library, Oxford, Lewis Harcourt Papers, Herbert Gladstone to Lord Harcourt, 13 May 1912, enclosing copy of letter from Chas E. Boyes to Cecil Rodwell, Imperial Secretary to the High Commission, 4 March 1912.

48 The description of Congress as a 'loose federation' appears in the preamble to its first constitution (UW, Molema–Plaatje Papers, Cc9), and in a letter from H. Selby Msimang to *The Star*, 16 January 1912. Khumisho Moguerane, 'A history of the Molemas: African

notables in South Africa, 1880s to 1920s' (DPhil thesis, Oxford University, 2014), p. 14, characterises the early SANNC as 'less a broad nationalist organisation and more a platform of mutual cooperation towards multiple and plural ethnic nationalisms'.

49 Makgatho's case was fully reported in the *Transvaal Leader*, 19 February 1912. Makgatho had taken action against one Field Cornet J.B. Wolmarans, who had ejected him from the train. Hundreds of white farmers surrounded the courtroom during the hearings, expressing their support for his action. Plaatje reported details of the deputation's meeting with Henry Burton in 'Natives on railways: an interview with Sauer', *Pretoria News*, 6 April 1912.

50 'Deputation to government', *Tsala ea Becoana*, 6 April 1912.

51 'Deputation to government', *Tsala ea Becoana*, 6 April 1912; CAD, NA 3250, 11/F1131, 'Notes of interview with the Minister of Native Affairs of representatives of the South African Native National Congress', Cape Town, 15 March 1912.

52 On interests threatened by the Squatters Bill, see P. Rich, 'The agrarian counter-revolution in the Transvaal and the origins of segregation, 1902–1913', in P.L. Bonner (ed.), *Working Papers in Southern African Studies* (Johannesburg: University of the Witwatersrand, 1977).

53 'A memorable meeting: the first step to union of non-Europeans', *Tsala ea Becoana*, 6 April 1912; see also 'The Native Congress and the APO', *Ilanga lase Natal*, 29 March 1912 and 'Native Squatters Bill', *Cape Argus*, 18 March 1912.

54 'Natives and government: the Squatters' Bill: mass meeting last night', *Cape Argus*, 27 March 1912; S.T. Plaatje, 'South African Native Congress: the business reviewed: sidelights on native opinion', *DFA*, 26 June 1912; 'Mr Plaatje', *Tsala ea Becoana*, 1 June 1912.

55 KAB, 1/KIM 9/4, Register of Newspapers, records the changes in printing arrangements.

56 UW, Molema–Plaatje Papers, Cc9, Dube to Chief Lekoko, 13 April 1912. Dube referred to Plaatje's 'intimate knowledge of Native affairs, particularly Bechuanaland', mentioning the issues of 'forest regulation, and proper care of sythilitic [*sic*] people in Mafeking, and the combatting of location laws'.

57 UW, Molema–Plaatje Papers, Da19, Plaatje to Molema, 8 August 1912

58 Peter Limb (ed.), *The People's Paper: a centenary history and anthology of 'Abantu-Batho'* (Johannesburg: Wits University Press, 2013), esp. pp. 10–11 and 188–94. Seme had put forward the idea of a new multilingual newspaper in 1911, prior to Congress's inaugural conference, but doubts were expressed about the viability of such a newspaper and Seme was unable to take it forward as quickly as he hoped. Plaatje mentions Seme's opposition to the loan from Elka Cele in his letter to Silas Molema, 14 August 1912 (UW, Molema–Plaatje Papers, Da20).

59 UW, Molema–Plaatje Papers, Da19, Plaatje to Molema, 8 August 1912.

60 See particularly the perceptive comments of Chris Lowe on 'historically rooted identities' within the early SANNC in 'The Swazi royalty and the founding of *Abantu-Batho* in regional context', in Limb, *The People's Paper*, p. 175.

61 Plaatje, *Native Life*, pp. 123–4; UW, Molema–Plaatje Papers, Da22, Plaatje to Molema, 12 December 1912. No copies of *Tsala ea Batho* have survived for the period October 1912 to March 1913 but its continued publication is clear from references in other newspapers, and from a numbering sequence that indicates that issues 94 to 119 appeared between these dates.

62 Dube's statement is from 'Notes of interview'.

63 In March 1913 Plaatje sent a telegram to Tom Zini, convening a protest meeting in Cape Town, saying 'Please urge our people not use language calculated to inflame.' ('Mr Sauer's native policy: condemnatory resolutions', *Cape Argus*, 17 March 1913, p. 7 and 'Meeting of natives', *Cape Times*, 17 March 1913, p. 11).

64 For the text of the Act, see Plaatje, *Native Life*, pp. 46–51; and more generally, C.M. Tatz, *Shadow and Substance in South Africa* (Pietermaritzburg: University of Natal Press, 1962), pp. 17–22 and Harvey M. Feinberg, *Our Land, Our Life, Our Future: black South African challenges to territorial segregation, 1913–1948* (Pretoria: Unisa Press, 2015), pp. 19–35. In an important recent article Khumisho Moguerane attributes the timing of the introduction of the legislation to the Barolong's legal challenge to the government over their chief's right to exercise jurisdiction over the Barolong Reserve: see Khumisho Moguerane, 'Black landlords, their tenants and the Natives' Land Act of 1913', *Journal of Southern African Studies*, 42, 3, 2016, pp. 243–66. Peter Delius and William Beinart, 'The historical context and legacy of the Natives' Land Act of 1913', *Journal of Southern African Studies*, 40, 4, 2014, pp. 667–88, provides an important overview, one hundred years on.

65 On the Land Act and its wider context and implications, especially in the Orange Free State, see Tim Keegan, 'The sharecropping economy, African class formation and the Natives' Land Act of 1913 in the highveld belt', in S. Marks and R. Rathbone (eds.), *Industrialisation and Social Change in South Africa: African class formation, culture and consciousness, 1870–1930* (Harlow: Longman, 1982), pp. 195–211; 'The restructuring of agrarian class relations in a colonial economy: the Orange River Colony, 1902–1910', *Journal of Southern African Studies*, 5, 2, April 1979; *Rural Transformations in Industrializing South Africa: the southern highveld to 1914* (London: Macmillan, 1987); and Harvey M. Feinberg, 'The 1913 Natives Land Act in South Africa: politics, race and segregation in early twentieth century', *International Journal of African Historical Studies*, 26, 1, 1993, pp. 65–109. J.G. Keyter's speech is reproduced in *Native Life*, p. 37.

66 Editorial, 'The war of extermination', *Tsala ea Batho*, 10 May 1913, reproduced in Willan, *Sol Plaatje: selected writings*, p. 151; 'Along the colour line', in Willan, *Sol Plaatje: selected writings*, p. 167.

67 S.T. Plaatje, 'Along the colour line', *Kimberley Evening Star*, 23 December 1913.

68 Congress's resolution was reported in the account of the meeting ('The S.A. Native National Congress: some of the resolutions') in *Pretoria News*, 1 April 1913 and in 'Mr Sauer's native policy: what the natives think', *Cape Argus*, 31 March 1913.

69 Plaatje, *Native Life*, pp. 172–3.

70 Plaatje, *Native Life*, p. 68.

71 'Natives and Federation of Trades: the Congress and the strike', letter from Plaatje to the editor, *DFA*, 18 February 1914, referring back to the events of the meeting on 25 July 1913; 'Along the colour line', *Kimberley Evening Star*, 23 December 1913, where Plaatje mentioned 'some prominent Natives favouring an abandonment of the deputation' in favour of a general strike, believing this would provide 'a more rapid way of obtaining redress'.

72 'Along the colour line', *Kimberley Evening Star*, 23 December 1913.

73 'Natives and the government: the new land Act', *Tsala ea Batho*, 9 August 1913.

74 'The war of extermination: now in full swing', *Tsala ea Batho*, 23 August 1913.

75 For the women's anti-pass campaign, see Julia C. Wells, *We Now Demand! The history of women's resistance to pass laws in South Africa* (Johannesburg: Witwatersrand University Press, 1993), pp. 32–49; for reports on the campaign in *Tsala ea Batho*, see issues of 14 June, 21 June and 23 August 1913; and Plaatje's later account of his speech to the APO annual conference in Kimberley in October 1913 ('Passive resistance: coloured women's movement in Free State', *DFA*, 2 October 1913, and Plaatje, *Native Life*, pp. 91–101).

76 Plaatje, *Native Life*, pp. 102–16.

77 Plaatje, *Native Life*, p. 116.

78 S.T. Plaatje, letter to the editor, *Christian Express*, December 1913, pp. 187–9.

79 *Umteteli*, 23 July 1921; Plaatje, *Native Life*, p. 168.

80 'Sub-rosa', *Tsala ea Batho*, 30 August 1913.

81 Plaatje, *Native Life*, ch. 13, reproducing correspondence published previously in *Cape Mercury* and *Tsala ea Batho*; 'Kingwilliamstown and the Land Act', letter from Plaatje to the editor, *APO*, 6 December 1913.

82 'Native Congress: delegates assemble in Kimberley', *DFA*, 28 February 1914.

83 Plaatje, *Native Life*, pp. 181–93; SAB, NA 3248, 13/F814, E. Barrett (Under-Secretary for Native Affairs) to Plaatje, 19 February 1914; S.T. Plaatje, 'S.A. Native National Congress: special conference in Kimberley', *DFA*, 26 February 1914. Plaatje was also in contact with W.P. Schreiner, seeking special permission for Congress to hold the conference in Johannesburg (W.P. Schreiner Papers, telegrams L.15, L.18 and L.22, January and February 1914).

84 Plaatje, *Native Life*, pp. 185–7; 'Native Congress', *DFA*, 28 February 1914; 'Native Land Act', *DFA*, 2 March 1914; 'S.A. Native Congress', *DFA*, 3 March 1914.

85 Molema, *Lover of His People*, p. 61.

86 Plaatje, *Native Life*, p. 188.

87 'A happy new year', *Tsala ea Batho*, 3 January 1914.

88 Union of South Africa, *Report of Natives' Land Commission, vol. 2* (Minutes of Evidence), evidence of S.T. Plaatje, pp. 93–4. Circulation had increased from 1,700 in 1910 (as *Tsala ea Becoana*). Plaatje's comments about *Abantu-Batho* are from 'Native papers and missionaries', *Tsala ea Batho*, 21 March 1914. Arthur Matlala and Eva Mahuma are mentioned in several issues of *Tsala ea Batho*, Matlala's proficiency at cricket being alluded to in Plaatje's dedication in *Diphosho-phosho* (Morija, 1930). Eva Mahuma's later achievements are celebrated in 'Ability of Bantu women proved', *Bantu World*, 28 January 1933. Details of James Dippa are from 'Mr James M. Dippa: brilliant Eastern Province scholar', *Umteteli*, 30 May 1936.

89 T.L. Schreiner's speech in the House of Assembly (on 4 June) is reproduced in *Native Life*, p. 40; see also *Cape Times*, 5 June 1913.

90 'Resignation', *Tsala ea Batho*, 23 May 1914; *Tsala*, 7 March 1914.

91 SOAS, Plaatje Papers, MS 375495, STP 2/2, unpublished notebook, passage headed 'With the kids'; 'Along the colour line', *Tsala ea Batho*, 10 January 1914. For important insights into the position of women in the African nationalist movement, and of Elizabeth Plaatje in particular, see Heather Hughes, 'Women and society in *Native Life in South Africa*: roles and ruptures', in Janet Remmington, Brian Willan and Bhekizizwe Peterson (eds.), *Sol Plaatje's* Native Life in South Africa: *past and present* (Johannesburg: Wits University Press, 2016), pp. 158–74.

92 Letter from 'Native woman, Kimberley, May 8', *DFA*, 10 May 1912. I am indebted to Neil Parsons for drawing this letter to my attention.

93 KAB, 3/CT, 4/1/5/1241, N7/5, Plaatje to Town Clerk, Cape Town, 4 May 1927; 'Lyndhurst Road Public School, Kimberley, by "Sainty"', *Tsala ea Becoana*, 28 October 1911; the concert for SANNC delegates was reported in 'The Native Congress', *Tsala ea Batho*, 7 March 1914.

94 SOAS, Plaatje Papers, unpublished notebook, 'With the kids'.

95 Plaatje, *Native Life*, p. 126. Other sources drawn upon here are 'In memoriam', *Tsala ea Batho*, 7 February 1914; 'Domestic notices: in memoriam', *Tsala ea Batho*, 17 January 1914 ; and UW, Molema–Plaatje Papers, Da27, Plaatje to Silas Molema, 5 February 1913.

96 For John Dube's marital situation, see Hughes, *First President*, esp. pp. 190–1.

97 See R.W. Msimang, *Natives' Land Act 1913: specific cases of evictions and hardships (collected and compiled by R.W. Msimang by the authority of the records committee of the South African Native National Congress)*, n.d. [1913]; 'Land Act, 1913', *Abantu-Batho*, 22 May 1913, reporting meeting of Preparation Committee (English translation in CAD, NA 3248, 13/F814). Sir Ernest Oppenheimer's testimonial, dated 25 April 1914, is in SOAS, Plaatje Papers, STP 1/3, typed sheet of references. Frank Ireland's help

is acknowledged by Plaatje in an obituary, 'In memoriam: a native journalist's tribute', *South Africa*, 28 September 1923.

98 CAD, NA 3248, 13/F817, Plaatje to Henry Burton, 7 May 1914.

99 J.X. Merriman Papers, 1914, 236, Dube to Merriman, 6 May 1914. For Dube's position at this time, see Hughes, *First President*, pp. 184–5.

100 Based on Merriman Papers, 1914, 241, Botha to Merriman, 8 May 1914 and 244, Memo of conversation with Dube, 9 May 1914.

101 Merriman Papers, 1914, 241, Botha to Merriman, 8 May 1914.

102 'Natives' Land Act: deputation to England', *Cape Times*, 16 May 1914; Plaatje, *Native Life*, p. 192; S.T. Plaatje, 'Native delegation to England', *DFA*, 29 June 1914.

103 Plaatje conveyed his version of events to Alice Werner, who recounted the details in a letter to Harriette Colenso on 21 January 1916 (NAD, Colenso Papers, Box 63). He also set out details in a letter to *Abantu-Batho* early in 1916: this has not survived but Richard Selope Thema, in a letter of his own to *Abantu-Batho* (reproduced in *Ilanga lase Natal*, 28 April 1916), says that 'according to Mr Plaatje's letter, the money was squandered even before the Congress meeting of Kimberley which took place in February 1914'. Plaatje's version of events is substantially confirmed in the recollections of Selby Msimang, who was secretary of the committee charged with raising funds for the deputation (Interview with Mary Benson in 1961, Benson Papers, SOAS). Plaatje's comment about the 'disarray' of the deputation was in an undated (c. Feb. 1919) letter to Silas Molema, comparing the situation of the 1919 deputation with that of 1914 (Unisa, Molema Papers). Saul Msane's complaint about the misappropriation of money (£200) collected in the Rustenburg district appears to be substantiated in Plaatje's letter to 'Morolong', 9 July 1914 (Unisa, Molema Papers).

104 'Natives' Land Act', *Cape Times*, 16 May 1914.

105 'The cult of leadership', *Umteteli*, 25 April 1925; National Archives (Kew), CO 551/64, H.Cr. 20147, Report of Apthorp's meeting with CO, 2 June 1914.

106 'The Natives' Land Act', *Cape Times*, 16 May 1914; 'The native deputation', *Cape Argus*, 16 May 1914'; 'Natives' Land Act', letter to the editor from James Wellwood Mushet, *Cape Times*, 19 May 1914. For further biographical details, see C.J. Beyers (ed.), *Dictionary of South African Biography* (Pretoria: Human Sciences Research Council, 1981), vol. 4, pp. 384–5. S.M. Makgatho, also elected a member of the delegation, at the last minute decided not to go.

107 UW, Molema–Plaatje Papers, Da38, Paramount Chief of the Barolong Nation to Plaatje, 13 May 1914; Plaatje to Emmett J. Scott, Booker T. Washington's secretary, 27 August 1914 (Library of Congress, Booker T. Washington Papers, Con 13).

108 NAD, Colenso Papers, Box 55, Plaatje to Mrs Colenso, 26 February 1915.

Chapter 9

1 S.T. Plaatje, 'Native Congress mission to England', *Diamond Fields Advertiser (DFA)*, 14 July 1914.

2 I am grateful to the late Solomon Molema for showing me a copy of this book – Ellen G. White's *The Great Controversy between Christ and Satan during the Christian Dispensation* (Melbourne: Signs Publishing Company, n.d. [original edition 1888].

3 S.T. Plaatje, 'The Native Congress deputation', *DFA*, 17 July 1914.

4 Bodleian Library, Oxford, Papers of Anti-Slavery and Aborigines' Protection Society (AS/APS), MSS Br. Emp. S19 D3/11, Harris to Dube, 18 May 1914.

5 AS/APS, S22 G203, deputation's memorandum to the Colonial Secretary, Lord Harcourt, 15 June 1914.

6 For a fuller treatment of the position of John Harris and the AS and APS in relation to the Land Act, see B.P. Willan, 'The Anti-Slavery and Aborigines' Protection Society and the South African Natives' Land Act of 1913', *Journal of African History*, 20, 1, 1979, pp.

83–102. See also University of Bristol, Papers of Jane Cobden Unwin, DM 851, Box 3, Jane Cobden Unwin to J.H. Harris, 25 October 1916, and Plaatje to Silas Molema, 9 July 1914 (Unisa, Molema Papers, Acc. 142).

7   AS/APS, S22 G180, Congress delegates to Messrs Morgan Price & Co. (Solicitors), 6 July 1914; S19 D3/8, Mrs S. Solomon to Travers Buxton, 29 March 1917; see also S19 D3/15, Harris to Mrs J. Cobden Unwin, 25 October 1916.

8   S.T. Plaatje, 'The Native Congress deputation', *DFA*, 17 July 1914; National Archives (Kew), CO 551/64, H.Cr. 20301, comments on dispatch cover, 4 June 1914; CO 551/67, H.Cr. 24531, comments on dispatch cover on letter from AS and APS to CO, 6 July 1914. The meeting took place on 24 June.

9   AS/APS, S22 D4/4, Harcourt to Harris, 11 July 1914; Central Archives Depot (Pretoria), Governor General (GG) 50/452, report on meeting with Congress deputation, 26 June 1914; S.T. Plaatje, *Native Life in South Africa* (London: P.S. King & Son, 1916), pp. 194–5; 'An appeal to the British Brotherhoods', *Brotherhood Journal*, August 1914, pp. 226–7; 'No room to live: South African natives and the land law', *Daily Chronicle* (London), 14 July 1914.

10 CAD, GG 50/448, telegram from Governor General, Cape Town, to Colonial Secretary, London, 4 July 1914, and minute from General Botha, 3 July 1914; National Archives (Kew), CO 551/67, 20301, Sir A. Ponsonby to CO, 13 June 1914.

11 National Archives (Kew), CO 551/64, 23292, Harris and Buxton to CO, 26 June 1914, and AS/APS, S19 D3/12, Harris to Cecil Beck, MP, 9 June 1914; AS/APS, S19 D3/12, Harris to Dube, 14 July 1914 (private). *South Africa* had expressed its disapproval in its issues of 13, 20 and 27 June 1914, characterising Congress's decision to send a deputation to England as 'utter folly'.

12 Plaatje, *Native Life*, pp. 194–5; S.T. Plaatje, 'The Native deputation', *APO*, 5 September 1914.

13 Plaatje, *Native Life*, p. 225.

14 'Our deputation in England', *Ilanga lase Natal*, 28 August 1914, quoting *Westminster Gazette*, 20 July 1914; Plaatje, *Native Life*, p. 225; 'An appeal to the British Brotherhoods: shall injustice be sanctioned under the British flag?' and '"Bear ye one another's burdens": an opportunity for British Brotherhood', *Brotherhood Journal*, August 1914, pp. 225–8.

15 Plaatje, *Native Life*, pp. 195–8; Hansard, House of Commons Debates, 28 July 1914, 1161–9.

16 NAD, Colenso Papers, Box 54, Plaatje to Mrs S.J. Colenso, 31 August 1914; CAD, GG 50/403, Louis Botha to H.J. Stanley, 4 March 1914; Heather Hughes, *First President: a life of John Dube, founding president of the ANC* (Johannesburg: Jacana Media, 2012), pp. 188–9.

17 Colenso Papers, Box 57, Alice Werner to Harriette Colenso, 10 May 1916; for further details of Dube's situation at this time, see Hughes, *First President*, pp. 188–91.

18 Plaatje, *Native Life*, p. 248; Colenso Papers, Box 54, Plaatje to Mrs S.J. Colenso, 31 August 1914.

19 AS/APS, G203, Harris to Sir H. Johnston, 6 August 1914; Colenso Papers, Box 54, Plaatje to Mrs S.J. Colenso, 31 August 1914; *Native Life*, p. 261.

20 Colenso Papers, Box 54, Plaatje to Mrs S.J. Colenso, 31 August 1914.

21 SOAS, Council for World Mission Archive, Home Correspondence, 1914, Box 15, folder 2, W. Lamplough (Secretary, Wesleyan Missionary Society) to Rev. F. Lenwood (London Missionary Society), 21 August 1914; AS/APS, G203, APS to Dr H. Haigh, Wesleyan Missionary Society, 12 January 1917; S.T. Plaatje, 'Why I remained in England and what I am doing', *Abantu-Batho*, 30 September 1915, and letter from J.H. Harris and T. Buxton to *Abantu-Batho*, 5 November 1915, both enclosures in AS/APS, S22 D4/8, Mrs G. Solomon to J. Harris, 27 January 1916.

22 D.D.T. Jabavu, 'England to the Cape: voyage notes, by a native passenger', *Imvo*, 17 November 1914.

23 S.T. Plaatje, 'The cult of leadership', *Umteteli wa Bantu*, 25 April 1925; 'Reception to Mr Sol T. Plaatje', *DFA*, 28 March 1917. See also National Archives (Kew), CO 551/64, H.Cr. 20147, report of meeting between A.P. Apthorp and Henry Lambert and letter from R. Blankenberg, Secretary, South African High Commission, to Under Secretary of State, Colonial Office, 2 June 1914; AS/APS, S22 G203, Harris to A. Wynne, 5 June 1914, re meeting with Apthorp at AS and APS offices.

24 S.T. Plaatje, 'Why I remained in England and what I am doing', *Abantu-Batho*, 30 September 1915, enclosure in AS/APS, S22 D4/8, Mrs G. Solomon to Harris, 27 January 1916; Colenso Papers, Box 54, Plaatje to Mrs S.J. Colenso, 31 August 1914; 'England to the Cape', *Imvo*, 17 November 1914.

25 Colenso Papers, Box 54, Plaatje to Mrs S.J. Colenso, 24 October 1914. Meetings which Plaatje addressed close to his home in Leyton were reported in 'Shern Hall Brotherhood', *Walthamstow, Leyton and Chingford Guardian*, 25 September 1915, p. 2; 'Brotherhood', *Walthamstow, Leyton and Chingford Guardian*, 5 March 1915, p. 2; 'Brotherhood Movement', *Walthamstow, Leyton and Chingford Guardian*, 9 April 1915, p. 2.

26 'Greetings from South Africa', *Brotherhood Journal*, October 1915, p. 311, and 'Brotherhood Movement: West Ealing welcomes a speaker from South Africa', *Hanwell Gazette*, 18 July 1915.

27 Arthur Henderson's words are quoted by Plaatje in *Native Life*, p. 223. For a movement of its size and influence the Brotherhoods have been seriously neglected in the literature: see, however, David Killingray, 'Hands joined in Brotherhood: the rise and decline of a movement for faith and social change, 1875–2000', in Anthony R. Cross (ed.), *Pathways and Patterns in History: essays on Baptists, Evangelicals, and the modern world in honour of David Bebbington* (London: Spurgeon's College, 2015) for a recent assessment.

28 The Diamond Fields PSA Brotherhood was formed in June 1908, inspired by the visit of the Rev. F.B. Meyer, the first national president of the Brotherhood Federation in England. Membership was 'open to all Europeans over 16 years of age': see 'PSA Brotherhoods', *DFA*, 13 June 1908.

29 Information on Alice Timberlake (1867–1957) and Henry Timberlake (1857–1914) are from the 1911 census and death certificate for Henry Timberlake; *Native Life in South Africa*, p. 226, mentions Brothers Timberlake (probably Alice Timberlake's 29-year-old step-son Albert) and (Frank) Martin, both of the Shern Hall Brotherhood; 'Mr and Mrs Sol T. Plaatje in the Transvaal', *Abantu-Batho*, 28 June 1917. Plaatje's financial difficulties are detailed in his letters to Morolong (Chief Lekoko), 6 November 1914 (UW, Molema–Plaatje papers, Da31) and 10 December, 1914 (Unisa, Molema Papers, Acc. 142).

30 Quotations from Plaatje, *Native Life*, p. 351 and Colenso Papers, Box 55, Plaatje to Mrs S.J. Colenso, 26 February 1915.

31 S.T. Plaatje, 'Friends of the natives: death levying a heavy toll', *Pretoria News*, 30 June 1930; 'The native press', *Tsala*, 17 April 1915; S.T. Plaatje, 'The late Allan King', *African World Annual* (London: African World, December 1915); 'The late Allan King', *African World*, 5 December 1914.

32 'The "Volkstem" and colour', *African World*, 20 March 1915; CAD, NA 3248/13/814, 'Translation of extract from *De Volkstem*, dated the 12 January 1915'. For coverage in *Tsala*, see 'A native journalist' and 'Volkstem vapour', *Tsala*, 27 February 1915, and 'Moooane oa "Volkstem"', *Tsala*, 6 March 1915.

33 British Museum Central Archive, record of application of Plaatje, Solomon Tsekisho: letter from Weinthal to the Librarian, British Museum, 1 December 1914, and Plaatje to the Librarian, British Museum, 3 December 1914. Plaatje became a regular visitor to

the Reading Room, renewing his ticket on 24 June 1915, 6 January 1916 and 17 August 1916.

34 For Georgiana Solomon, see W.E.G. Solomon, *Saul Solomon, the member for Cape Town* (Cape Town: Oxford University Press, 1948), pp. 348–50; Elizabeth van Heyningen, 'Solomon, Georgiana Margaret (1844–1933)', *Oxford Dictionary of National Biography*, online edn, Oxford University Press, May 2006. Her views on the iniquities of the Land Act were expressed in forthright manner in 'The South African Natives' Land Act', a letter written to *The Nation*, 18 July 1914, pp. 602–3. Heather Hughes, 'Women and society in *Native Life in South Africa*: roles and ruptures', in Janet Remmington, Brian Willan and Bhekizizwe Peterson (eds.), *Sol Plaatje's* Native Life in South Africa: *past and present* (Johannesburg: Wits University Press, 2016), pp. 159–74, provides a sensitive portrayal of this group of women.

35 UW, Molema–Plaatje Papers, Photograph Fca 7, 1916 and note on postcard to Mr Morgan, the Eastbourne photographer, 28 November 1916.

36 Colenso Papers, Box 54, Plaatje to Mrs S.J. Colenso, 31 August 1914; Plaatje to Mrs S.J. Colenso, 24 October 1914; Box 55, Mrs S.J. Colenso to Harriette Colenso, 23 April and 26 November 1915; Sophie Colenso was a widow of F.E. Colenso, Bishop Colenso's second son, who had died in 1910. Gwilym Colenso, 'The 1907 deputation of Basuto chiefs to London and the development of British–South African networks', *International History Review* (2013), DOI: 10.1080/07075332.2013.836123, describes the role played by the Colenso family in supporting other visiting African delegations. See also 'Mrs Colenso' (obituary), *Bucks Examiner*, 30 April 1937.

37 See A.C. Howe, 'Unwin, (Emma) Jane Catherine Cobden (1851–1947)', *Oxford Dictionary of National Biography*, online edn, Oxford University Press, May 2006; Sarah Richardson, '"You know your father's heart": the Cobden sisterhood and the legacy of Richard Cobden', in Anthony Howe and Simon Morgan (eds.), *Rethinking Nineteenth-Century Liberalism: Richard Cobden bicentenary essays* (Aldershot: Ashgate Publishing, 2006), pp. 230–46; and *The Land Hunger: life under monopoly* (London: T. Fisher Unwin, 1913), compiled and with an introduction by Mrs Cobden Unwin.

38 Philip Unwin, T. Fisher Unwin's nephew, remembered Jane Cobden Unwin (in the 1920s) as 'a handsome old lady, broad in the beam like Queen Victoria, with warm eyes and beautiful white hair – in middle life, with her great vitality, she must have been very attractive', adding that she 'could suddenly lash herself into embarrassing furies over the Bread Tax of the 1840s, birth control, or the Bolsheviks': Philip Unwin, *The Publishing Unwins* (London: William Heinemann, 1972), pp. 40–1. Mrs Unwin considered Plaatje to be a 'personal friend' to both her husband and herself. For the weekend at Dunford, see his letter to Sophie Colenso, 3 April 1916 (Colenso Papers, Box 55) and Georgiana Solomon to Alice Werner, 4 April 1916 (Colenso Papers, Box 63).

39 For Alice Werner's life and career, see her obituary in *The Times*, 11 June 1935; P.J.L. Frankl, 'Werner, Alice (1859–1935)', *Oxford Dictionary of National Biography*, online edn, Oxford University Press, May 2006. Her book *The Language Families of Africa* (London: Society for Promoting Christian Knowledge) was published in 1915. Her support for the cause of the Congress delegates was expressed in her letter to *The Nation*, 1 August 1914, p. 670.

40 'Fifty years' service: retirement of Mr W.C. Cross: many-sided interests', *Middlesex County Times and Gazette*, 4 January 1941; obituary, *Middlesex County Times and Gazette*, 27 March 1954; *Brotherhood Outlook*, 1, 2, March 1920, p. 36. I am indebted to Mr Graham Stapleton for further information about Mr Cross. Cross was a regular visitor to the east London Brotherhoods, speaking at meetings of the Marsh Street Brotherhoods and Sisterhoods in July 1914 and (with Plaatje) January 1915: *District Times (Leyton, Lea Bridge, Leytonstone)*, 3 and 10 July 1914; *Walthamstow, Leyton and Chingford Guardian*, 3 and 10 July 1914, 29 January 1915 and 16 January 1916.

41 'Reception to Mr Sol T. Plaatje', *DFA*, 28 March 1917.
42 Dr Salter's letter was quoted by Plaatje in a flyer for *Native Life in South Africa* (British Library, Royal Literary Fund Loan, 3094/3). For Alfred and Ada Salter, see Fenner Brockway, *Bermondsey Story: the life of Alfred Salter* (London: George Allen and Unwin, 1949) and Graham Taylor, *Ada Salter: pioneer of ethical socialism* (London: Lawrence and Wishart, 2016).
43 For Duse Mohamed Ali, see Immanuel Geiss, *The Pan-African Movement* (London: Methuen, 1974), pp. 221–8 and Mustafa Abdelwahid (ed.), *Duse Mohamed Ali 1866–1945: the autobiography of a pioneer Pan African and Afro-Asian activist* (Trenton, NJ: Red Sea Press, 2011); 'Native deputation from South Africa', *African Times and Orient Review*, 26 May 1914 and 'Natives Land Act, 1913', *African Times and Orient Review*, 16 June 1914. The letter carrying the Fleet Street address was to Chief Lekoko, 9 July 1914 (Unisa, Molema Papers).
44 For Fredericks, see Special Collections and University Archives, University of Massachusetts (UM), W.E.B. Du Bois Papers (MS 312), mums312-b015-i129, Plaatje to Du Bois, 19 May 1919; Cobden Unwin Papers, DM 851, Box 3, E.F. Fredericks to Jane Cobden Unwin, 27 April 1917. He later became a member of the British Guiana Legislative Council. I am indebted to Dr Barbara Josiah, City University of New York, for further information on Fredericks's life and career. For Samuel Cambridge and the Barbour-James family, see Plaatje, *Native Life*, pp. 227–8; 'War address at the Brotherhood', *Southall-Norwood Gazette*, 20 November 1914, p. 1; Jeffrey Green, 'James, John Alexander Barbour-James (1867–1954)', *Oxford Dictionary of National Biography* (Oxford: Oxford University Press, 2004).
45 For Scholes, see David Killingray, 'The Revd Dr Theophilus Scholes (1856–1940?): black Baptist critic at the heart of empire', in Anthony R. Cross and John H.Y. Briggs (eds.), *Freedom and the Powers: perspectives from Baptist history marking the 400th anniversary of Thomas Helwys'* The Mystery of Iniquity (Didcot: Baptist Historical Society, 2014).
46 UW, Molema–Plaatje Papers, Ad1.2.3, Modiri Molema to Silas Molema, 7 August and 9 October 1914; author's interview with Dr James Moroka, Thaba Nchu, 19 April 1976; S.M. Molema, *Lover of His People* (Johannesburg: Wits University Press, 2012), p. 69; Plaatje, *Native Life*, pp. 258–9.
47 Unisa, Molema Papers, Plaatje to Lekoko Montsioa, 6 November 1914.
48 Colenso Papers, Box 55, Plaatje to Mrs S.J. Colenso, 26 February 1916; UW, Molema–Plaatje Papers, Da42, Plaatje to Silas Molema, 15 July 1915. Founded in 1819, P.S. King & Son made much of the parliamentary connection, reproducing in full colour a map of Westminster on their letterhead so as to show their proximity to the Houses of Parliament. 'Messrs. P.S. King & Son, Ltd.', according to their 1919 catalogue, 'make a speciality of Publications dealing with Economics, Social questions, Politics, Local Government'.
49 AS/APS, S22 D4/6, Johnston to Harris, 16 August 1914, and S22 D4/4, Johnston to Harris, 14 March 1915. The magnum opus upon which Sir Harry was busy working was *A Comparative Study of the Bantu and Semi-Bantu Languages* (Oxford: Clarendon Press, 1919), a second volume following in 1922.
50 Colenso Papers, Box 63, Johnston to Plaatje, 4 June 1915, enclosure in Alice Werner to H. Colenso, 18 June 1915.
51 Jane Stafford, *Colonial Literature and the Native Author: indigeneity and empire* (London: Palgrave Macmillan, 2016), pp. 65–85.
52 Colenso Papers, Box 63, Alice Werner to H. Colenso, 18 June 1915; UW, Molema–Plaatje Papers, Da41, Plaatje to Philemon Moshoeshoe, 16 June 1915.
53 UW, Molema–Plaatje Papers, Da42, Plaatje to Silas Molema, 15 July 1915. Lekoko died on 20 June, but the news had not reached Plaatje when he wrote to Silas Molema on 15 July.
54 AS/APS, S19 D2/16, Circular letter signed by Alice Werner, 18 September 1915; S19 D3/13, D2/7, D2/16, D2/17, correspondence between Alice Werner, J.H. Harris and

T. Buxton, October–November 1915; S19 D2/7, A. Werner to T. Buxton, 28 October 1915; Colenso Papers, Box 63, A. Werner to H. Colenso, 18 February 1916; AS/APS, S19 D2/7, Mrs G. Solomon to T. Buxton, 5 February 1916.

55 Colenso Papers, Box 63, Alice Werner to Harriette Colenso, 18 February 1916 and 23 February 1917.

56 'The South African and Rhodesian stalls', *African World*, 1 January 1916, Supplement, p. vi; 'An exceptional concert', *African World*, 25 December 1915, Supplement, pp. xi and ix (photos); Cobden Unwin Papers, 'Notes of interview: Mrs Cobden Unwin and Mrs Saul Solomon and Mr R.C. Hawkin at 2 Harcourt Buildings, Temple, E.C., February 16th, 1917', p. 3. For Clicko, see Neil Parsons, *Clicko: the wild dancing Bushman* (Chicago: University of Chicago Press, 2009).

57 Colenso Papers, Box 56, Plaatje to Mrs Sophie Colenso, 28 January 1916.

58 'South Africans and the war', *APO*, 21 August 1915; 'Coloured men for Europe', *South Africa*, 4 September 1915, p. 355; 'Coloured men on the European front', letter from Plaatje to the editor, *Pretoria News*, 14 May 1917; *Walthamstow, Leyton and Chingford Guardian*, 16 July 1915. Calvert and Kerridge were at the East Ham Brotherhood in July 1915 ('Visitor from the veldt: Kaffir speaker at Central Hall', *East Ham Mail*, 30 July 1915, p. 1), and at the Tottenham PSA Brotherhood in January 1916 (*Brotherhood Journal*, February 1916, p. 62).

59 Plaatje, *Native Life*, pp. 226–9; 'A native African editor at New England: how native Africans love England', *Peterborough Citizen*, 20 July 1915, p. 4; 'International greetings', *Brotherhood Journal*, October 1915, pp. 311–13.

60 *Hastings and St Leonards Observer*, 11 December 1915; *Northampton Daily Echo*, 20 December 1915; *Hanwell Gazette*, 10 July 1915; *East Ham Mail*, 30 July 1915. For Plaatje's visits to the Leighton Men's Meeting, see 'South Africa's patriotism in the war', *Leighton Buzzard Observer*, 3 August 1915, p. 5; 'Leighton Buzzard: South Africa's patriotism', *Bucks Herald*, 7 August 1915, p. 5; 'LMM', *Leighton Buzzard Observer*, 16 May 1916. Plaatje addressed the Heathfield Brotherhood on 3 October 1915 and 30 January 1916 ('Black man's burden', *Sussex County Herald*, 9 October 1915 and 'Heathfield Brotherhood', *Sussex Express*, 4 February 1916). I am indebted to Mr Grenville Williams for information about his grandfather Henry Castle, and for identifying family members in photographs.

61 Colenso Papers, Box 55, Plaatje to Mrs Colenso, 26 February 1915.

62 KAB, SGE 2/432, Inspection Reports, 1916, vol. 9 (H–K), Report on Lyndhurst Road School, 9 September 1916; UM, W.E.B. Du Bois Papers, mums312-b015-i129, Plaatje to Du Bois, 19 May 1919; 'The Native National Congress', *Tsala ea Batho*, 17 July 1915; Colenso Papers, Box 63, Alice Werner to Harriette Colenso, 21 January 1916. Seme's machinations were not successful, and Dube remained, for the present, as president.

63 'Mr Bud-M'belle's retirement', *DFA*, 1 February 1916.

64 Colenso Papers, Box 55, Plaatje to Mrs Colenso, 3 April 1916.

65 Z.K. Matthews, *Freedom for My People: the autobiography of Z.K. Matthews* (Cape Town: David Philip, 1981), pp. 30–1.

Chapter 10

1 Daniel Jones and Solomon T. Plaatje, *A Sechuana Reader in International Phonetic Orthography (with English Translations)* (London: University of London Press, 1916); Solomon T. Plaatje, *Sechuana Proverbs with Literal Translations and Their European Equivalents* (London: Kegan Paul, Trench, Trübner & Co., 1916); 'A South African's homage', in Israel Gollancz (ed.), *A Book of Homage to Shakespeare* (Oxford: Oxford University Press, 1916).

2 Beverley Collins and Inger M. Mees, *The Real Professor Higgins: the life and career of Daniel Jones* (Berlin: Mouton de Gruyter, 1998), esp. pp. 136–63.

3 Alice Werner, *The Language Families of Africa* (London: Society for Promoting Christian Knowledge, 1915), pp. 28–30 and v–vii (Jones's 'Introductory note'). Alice Werner was immersed in German linguistic and phonetic traditions and an admirer of Professor Carl Meinhof, one of the leading figures. Shortly before completing *The Language Families of Africa* she had translated Meinhof's *Die moderne Sprachforschung in Afrika* (Berlin, 1910), published in English as *An Introduction to the Study of African Languages* (London: Dent, 1915). Daniel Jones's phonetic transcription of Plaatje's reading of the Lord's Prayer in Setswana appears on p. 80 of *Language Families*, preceded by his first published attempt to get to grips with the tones of Setswana – modified by the time his fuller analysis appeared in the *Sechuana Reader* in 1916.

4 Collins and Mees, *The Real Professor Higgins*, pp. 97–103.

5 Jones and Plaatje, *Sechuana Reader*, pp. vii–x. Jones and Plaatje both speak about meeting 'early in 1915', Plaatje's earlier visit to his department being described in an article ('Basetsanyana') in Setswana for his newspaper *Tsala ea Batho* on 29 August 1914.

6 University College London (UCL), Daniel Jones Papers, C1, 'How to use phonetics with little known languages', lecture delivered by D. Jones at University College London, 30 October 1916; MS annotation by Jones on typescript of 'Words distinguished by tone in Sechuana' (Daniel Jones Papers, D3.1).

7 Jones, 'How to use phonetics', pp. 25–6. Collins and Mees comment that Jones's unwillingness to read other people's work was a weakness, and that in his work with Plaatje 'he could have certainly speeded up his fieldwork had he done so' (Collins and Mees, *Real Professor Higgins*, p. 163).

8 Jones, 'How to use phonetics', pp. 26–7; 'Study of sounds: the use of the gramophone and kymograph', *Observer*, 5 November 1916 (in Jones Papers, G1.2, press cuttings); 'Basetsanyana', *Tsala ea Batho*, 29 August 1914.

9 Werner, *Language Families of Africa*, p. 56; Jones and Plaatje, *Sechuana Reader*, p. 40; Jones, 'How to use phonetics', p. 29.

10 Jones, 'How to use phonetics', p. 21; Collins and Mees, *Real Professor Higgins*, p. 161, quoting 'How to use phonetics', p. 29; NAD, Colenso Papers, Box 56, Sylvia Colenso to Harriette Colenso, 23 January 1917. Plaatje may also have had some sessions with Harold E. Palmer, who had joined the Phonetics Department in 1916 and had taken an interest in the role of tone in Setswana grammar. Jones reported that Palmer had collected several thousand sentences in Setswana, and that he had 'conducted important investigations into the grammar of the language' (report on work of department for 1916 and 1917, Jones Papers, B2). Unfortunately, this research was never written up and all trace of it has disappeared. For Harold Palmer, see especially Richard C. Smith, *The Writings of Harold E. Palmer: an overview*, http://homepages.warwick.ac.uk/~elsdr/WritingsofH.E.Palmer.pdf, accessed 6 February 2017.

11 Alice Werner, Review of *A Sechuana Reader*, *Man*, November 1917, pp. 180–2; shorter notice in *Journal of the Royal African Society*, 16, 63, April 1917, p. 267; letters from Sir Harry Johnston, *TLS*, 28 December 1916 (p. 637), Alice Werner, 4 January 1917 (p. 9), Daniel Jones, 11 January 1917 (p. 21).

12 Jones's work with Plaatje on tone in Setswana led directly to the phoneme, one of the most important concepts in twentieth-century linguistics: see Collins and Mees, *The Real Professor Higgins*, pp. 185–8, 433–4 and 428, and Beverley Collins and Inger Mees, 'Daniel Jones, the phoneme and the "Joneme"', *RASK: International Journal of Language and Communication*, 5, 6, 1997, pp. 161–76. Jones's recollections of working with Plaatje are from the MS of 'Words distinguished by tone in Sechuana' (Daniel Jones Papers, D3.1), published in *Festschrift Meinhof* (Hamburg: Friederichsen, 1927), pp. 88–98, but amended by hand by Jones in May 1942; and Collins and Mees, *The Real Professor Higgins*, p. 145.

13 D.M. Ramoshoana, 'Points of view: the late Mr Sol Plaatje', letter to the editor, *Diamond*

Fields Advertiser (DFA), 29 June 1932; inscription in *Sechuana Proverbs* in Brenthurst Library, Johannesburg.

14 Inscription from the copy of *Sechuana Proverbs* presented to William Cross (by kind permission of his nephew Mr Graham Stapleton).

15 Colenso Papers, Box 63, Alice Werner to Harriette Colenso, 21 January 1916; review of *Sechuana Proverbs* in *Man*, 18, 1917. Alice Werner's view of Plaatje was in response to Harriette Colenso's thoughts: 'I think myself that Plaatje and Seme are too advanced, Europeanized, to have the same grip on "the masses" that Dube has' (Killie Campbell Africana Library, Harriette Colenso Papers, KCM 50548, Harriette Colenso to Alice Werner, 15 December 1915).

16 I am indebted to the late Solomon Molema, Plaatje's grandson, for showing me his copy of *National Proverbs*. Other books Plaatje consulted are listed in the preface to *Sechuana Proverbs*, p. xi.

17 Colenso Collection, Box 56, Plaatje to Sophie Colenso, 28 January 1916; F.A. Mumby and Frances H. Stallybrass, *From Swan Sonnenschein to George Allen and Unwin Ltd* (London: Allen and Unwin, 1955), p. 81.

18 Gollancz, *Book of Homage*, preface, p. viii; letter from Gollancz to Austin Dobson, 17 November 1915, inviting him to contribute (in author's private collection). Weimar was the home of the German Shakespeare Society. Gollancz also set out his plans, more diplomatically, for 'a very simple and dignified observance of the Tercentenary in a manner consonant with the mood of the nation under present conditions' in a letter to *The Times* ('The Shakespeare Tercentenary', *The Times*, 23 December 1915). For Gollancz and his role in the *Book of Homage*, see Gordon McMullan, 'Goblin's market: commemoration, anti-semitism and the invention of the "global Shakespeare" in 1916', in Clara Calvo and Coppelia Kahn (eds.), *Celebrating Shakespeare: commemoration and cultural memory* (Cambridge: Cambridge University Press, 2015). Brian Willan, '"A South African's homage" at one hundred: revisiting Sol Plaatje's contribution to *Book of Homage to Shakespeare* (1916)', *Shakespeare in Southern Africa*, 28, 2016, pp. 25–34, explores the circumstances surrounding the publication of Plaatje's piece.

19 Alice Werner often returned to this discovery in her writings. An English translation of the story was first reproduced in her article 'Some notes on East African folklore', published in *Folklore*, 26, 1, 31 March, 1915, pp. 60–78, at a time when she was in contact with Plaatje, and again in 'Shakespeare in Africa' in *The Crisis*, 12, 3, July 1916, p. 144. Fifteen years later it would reappear in the concluding pages of her *Myths and Legends of the Bantu* (London: George W. Harrap, 1933), pp. 321–2. She believed that 'the story of the usurer and the pound of flesh seems to have come from the East to Europe through the Crusades; it is found in *Gesta Romanorum*, as well as in the *Pecorone* of Ser Giovanni, whence Shakespeare is supposed to have obtained it' ('Shakespeare in Africa', p. 144).

20 See Coppelia Kahn, 'Remembering Shakespeare imperially: the 1916 tercentenary', *Shakespeare Quarterly*, 52, 4, 2001, pp. 456–78 for an overview of the *Book of Homage*. The Gollancz collection in the Folger Library, Washington DC, has copies of several contributions which arrived too late to be included in the *Book of Homage*, but Bud-M'belle's is not among them.

21 Gollancz, *Book of Homage*, pp. 336–9.

22 For a fuller account of their protests against *Birth of a Nation*, see Brian Willan, '"Cinematographic calamity" or "soul-stirring appeal to every Briton": *Birth of a Nation* in England and South Africa, 1915–1931', *Journal of Southern African Studies*, 39, 3, 2013, 623–40, DOI: 10.1080/03057070.2013.826072.

23 For Gollancz and Hyde, see Kahn, 'Remembering Shakespeare imperially', pp. 465–7, and Werner Habicht, 'Shakespeare celebrations in time of war', *Shakespeare Quarterly*, 52, 4, 2001, pp. 441–55. Plaatje's original typescript is in the Folger Shakespeare Library, 'Tributes for Book of Homage to Shakespeare', edited by Israel Gollancz [manuscript],

y.d. 85 (58). Plaatje quoted from Colonel Albert Baratier's *Epopées africaines* (Paris: Arthème Fayard, 1912).

24 Willan, "'A South African's homage'", pp. 7–9, quoting Gollancz's letter to Sturge Moore, 3 March 1916.

25 There were no more than four weeks between the delivery of Plaatje's typescripts and a publication date that could not be missed. 'William Tsikinya-Chaka' lives on as author of 'A South African's homage' not only in the Folger Shakespeare Library's online catalogue but in Jonathan Bate's *The Genius of Shakespeare* (London: Picador, 2008) where William Tsikinya-Chaka is described as 'a black South African' (p. 224). Whatever the original intention, the result does seem to support the notion of 'a creative identification' between Plaatje and the playwright as Deborah Seddon has suggested: Deborah Seddon, 'The colonial encounter and *The Comedy of Errors*: Solomon Plaatje's *Diphosho-phosho*', in Laurence Wright (ed.), *The Shakespearean International Yearbook 9: special section, South African Shakespeare in the Twentieth Century* (Aldershot: Ashgate, 2009), p. 82.

26 For accounts of these celebrations, see Richard Foulkes, *Performing Shakespeare in the Age of Empire* (Cambridge: Cambridge University Press, 2002), esp. pp. 180–204. Plaatje's presence in Stratford, and at the pageant on 6 May, is deduced from his later memory of having seen *Julius Caesar* in Stratford 'together with several of his other pieces': see Sol T. Plaatje, *Diphosho-phosho (Comedy of Errors)* (Morija: Morija Printing Works, 1930), p. viii. Programme details for the pageant on 6 May are in the Stratford Memorial Theatre's 'Tercentenary Programme for 6 May 1916 (at 8 p.m.)' (copy in Shakespeare Centre Library and Archive, Stratford-upon-Avon); see also 'The closing scene of all: a unique spectacle', *Stratford-upon-Avon Herald*, 12 May 1916, p. 8.

27 'A tombstone for Shakespeare', *New Statesman*, 13 May 1916; 'Some tercentenary books', *Times Literary Supplement*, 11 May 1916, p. 223. *The Spectator* also reviewed the volume, noting the 'Bechuana dialect' as one of the 'less familiar' of the thirty different languages represented in it ('A Book of Homage to Shakespeare', *Spectator*, 27 May 1916, p. 7).

28 UW, Molema–Plaatje Papers, Da61, Plaatje to Modiri Molema, 11 July 1920; London School of Economics and Political Science, Library and Archives, Edwin Cannan Papers, correspondence with publishers (1019), W.H. Hulbert (a director of P.S. King & Son) to Edwin Cannan, 3 July 1917. In another letter, dated 11 July 1917, Hulbert spoke of the price of paper having 'quadrupled', and that his 'office staff has suffered through the war'.

29 Colenso Collection, Box 63, Alice Werner to Harriette Colenso, 21 January 1916; dedication in S.T. Plaatje, *Native Life in South Africa* (London: P.S.King & Son, 1916).

30 Plaatje, *Native Life*, p. 15.

31 Reviews of *Native Life* in *Daily News and Leader*, 12 July 1916, and *Birmingham Post*, 2 July 1916. The *Daily News and Leader* review was written by Alice Werner.

32 Reviews from *United Empire* and *South Africa* are quoted in a flyleaf in the second edition of *Native Life*. Although there is nothing to indicate the identity of the author of the review in *South Africa* (in its issue of 17 June 1916), Plaatje was able to attribute it to Sir Harry Johnston when quoting from it.

33 Review of *Native Life in South Africa*, *New Age*, 27 July 1916, p. 309; review of *Native Life* by 'Delta', *African World*, 3 June 1916. Alice Werner responded to the critical review in *New Age*, complaining that the reviewer 'must have given a very superficial perusal to this work', spelling out the central points Plaatje had made ('Native Life in South Africa', letter to the editor from A. Werner, *New Age*, 17 August 1916, p. 382).

34 Olive Schreiner to Mrs G. Solomon, 5 October 1916, in Liz Stanley and Andrea Salter (eds.), *The World's Great Question: Olive Schreiner's South African letters 1889–1920* (Cape Town: Van Riebeeck Society, 2014), p. 341.

35 National Library of South Africa, Cape Town, Solomon Family Papers, Box 4, General Botha to Mrs G. Solomon, 31 August 1916. Georgiana Solomon had also sent a copy of *Native Life in South Africa* to the British prime minister, David Lloyd George, and received a polite acknowledgement.

36 S.T. Plaatje, 'Through native eyes: the late General Louis Botha', *African World*, 6 September 1919.

37 National Archives (Kew), CO 417/629, 34975, Plaatje to Sir D. Chaplin, 6 April 1919; AS/APS, S19 D3/14, Harris to L. Moore, 21 July 1916; J.H. Harris, 'General Botha's native policy', *Journal of the Royal African Society*, 16, October 1916.

38 Harris, 'General Botha's native policy'; see also Harris's articles in *Manchester Guardian*, 27 December 1916, and *Fortnightly Review*, 101, January–June 1917.

39 Union of South Africa, *Report of the Natives' Land Commission*, UG25-1916; Colenso Papers, Box 63 (Notes and fragments), typed extract of letter from Plaatje to Alice Werner (n.d.).

40 Plaatje's analysis of the Beaumont Report was added in at the beginning of this batch of five hundred copies, which were then designated as a second edition: Colenso Papers, Box 63, Alice Werner to Harriette Colenso, 25 August and 15 September 1916. In subsequent editions and printings this analysis was moved to the end of the book.

41 *The Crisis*, 12, 4 August 1916, p. 173. Plaatje omitted one verse from the version which appeared in *The Crisis*. Ida B. Luckie was not an established poet or writer, and very little is known about her. The *Fort Gibson New Era* newspaper commented, however, in its issue of 12 October 1916, that the poem was 'a production of merit', and that its author was 'a sister of Dr Evans, of Fort Gibson', a small town in Oklahoma.

42 AS/APS, S22 G204, memorial to General Botha, 13 November 1916, quoting resolution passed at executive committee of APS, 3 August 1916; *Anti-Slavery Reporter and Aborigines' Friend*, series 5, 6, 4, January 1917; AS/APS, S22 G203, Edward Dower (Secretary for Native Affairs) to AS and APS, 15 December 1916. Harris's article in the *New Statesman* was published anonymously: 'General Botha's native policy', *New Statesman*, 16 September 1916, pp. 561–2. Harris's letter to Clifford Sharp, editor of the *New Statesman*, was in response to a letter from Sharp saying that it had been suggested to him (by John L. Hodgson) that 'I should offer the hospitality of our columns to S.T. Plaatje in order that he may reply to it'. Sharp knew nothing about Plaatje but was ready to accept Harris's views: 'I think I recognise the type from my experience in connection with the Indian Nationalist movement'. In South Africa, Harris's *New Statesman* article was picked up by both *Abantu-Batho* and *The International*: see 'The modern Voortrekkers', *Abantu-Batho*, 30 November 1916, reproduced in Peter Limb (ed.), *The People's Paper* (Johannesburg: Wits University Press, 2013), pp. 389–90. Harris's letter to Sir Harry Wilson, 14 August 1916, is in AS/APS, S19 D3/14.

43 West Sussex Record Office, Cobden Papers 974, 750g, Plaatje to Mrs Solomon, 8 December 1916; University of Leeds, Special Collections, New Statesman collection, BC MS20c (New Statesman: First World War Correspondence, 1915–1919), John L. Hodgson to Clifford Sharp (item 356), 7 December 1916. Hodgson explained privately to Sharp how Harris had gone about 'his subtle discrediting of Plaatje', aware of the extent to which Harris had influenced his views. Hodgson's letter was published in 'Correspondence: General Botha's native policy', *New Statesman*, 30 December 1916, pp. 800–2. Harris wrote to Sharp about the possibility of replying to it but in the end did not do so (BC MS20c, 345). Olive Schreiner's letters to Georgiana Solomon, 5 October 1916, and to John Hodgson, 6 December 1916, indicate their involvement too: see Stanley and Salter, *The World's Great Question*, pp. 341–2.

44 AS/APS, S19 D3/15, Harris to Mrs Unwin, 25 October 1916; West Sussex Record Office, Cobden Papers, 767G, Henry W. Nevinson to Mrs Unwin, 6 April 1921; University of Bristol Library, Cobden Unwin Papers, APS file, 'Statement' by Mrs

Unwin, April 1917. Henry Nevinson's involvement can be traced through the entries in his private diary (Bodleian Library, Oxford, MSS Eng. Misc. e.620/1, entries for 2 November and 7 December 1916, 3 January, 26 January, 1 February, 15 February, 27 February, 1 March, 20 March, 17 April, 24 April 1917).

45 'Mr Sol Plaatje at the PSA Brotherhood', *Stratford-upon-Avon Herald*, 10 November 1916. In this report (and in an advertisement for the meeting) Plaatje is described as 'joint editor' of the *Book of Homage to Shakespeare*. There is no evidence, however, that Plaatje's role was any different from the other contributors of tributes to the book. For his travels, see UCT, Molteno Family Papers, BC 330, Plaatje to Betty Molteno, 13 and 24 November 1916, and to Mrs Unwin, 31 October 1916, in West Sussex Record Office, Cobden Papers, 747-9g. For a later (4 December) meeting in Sudbury, Suffolk, where he addressed the Suffolk Sisterhood, see 'Sol T. Plaatje at the Sisterhood meeting', *Suffolk and Essex Free Press*, 6 December 1916.

46 Molteno Family Papers, Betty Molteno to Alice Greene, 17 November 1916 ('I had a v. interesting time yesterday afternoon at the Browning Institute at Walworth where Plaatje – a S. African native – addressed a meeting'; she also mentioned that Plaatje was due to depart for South Africa on 16 December, although he did not actually do so until six weeks later).

47 West Sussex Record Office, Cobden Papers, 750g, Plaatje to Mrs Solomon (copy), 8 December 1916.

48 'Farewell to Mr Sol T. Plaatje', *Brotherhood Journal*, 21, 1, January 1917, p. 9. According to Andro Linklater, the friendship between Charlotte Despard and Georgiana Solomon dated back to the time in the 1880s when they met on board ship en route to India: Andro Linklater, *An Unhusbanded Life: Charlotte Despard: suffragette, socialist and Sinn Feiner* (London: Hutchinson, 1980), p. 170.

49 'To the women of West Africa', by 'A.W.A.', *Sierra Leone Weekly News*, 24 February 1917, p. 13.

50 'Reception to Mr Sol Plaatje', *DFA*, 28 March 1917; AS/APS, S22 G203, circular letter from Alice Werner (secretary of the committee), 17 February 1917.

51 AS/APS, S22 G203, Harris to Dr Clifford, 20 February 1917; Colenso Papers, Box 63, Alice Werner to Harriette Colenso, 27 April 1917.

52 'Reception to Mr Sol Plaatje', *DFA*, 28 March 1917.

53 'The black man's burden: interview with Mr Solomon T. Plaatje', *Christian Commonwealth*, 3 January 1917, pp. 1–2.

54 'The white man's burden', *South Africa*, 27 January 1917.

Chapter 11

1 'Shakespeare in Setswana', *The Star* (Johannesburg), 26 July 1930; 'Coloured men on the European front', letter from S.T. Plaatje to the editor, *Pretoria News*, 14 May 1917. For the South African Native Labour Contingent, see Albert Grundlingh, *War and Society: participation and remembrance: South African black and coloured troops in the First World War, 1914–1918* (Stellenbosch: Sun Press, 2014).

2 National Library of South Africa (Cape Town), J.X. Merriman Papers, Plaatje to J.X. Merriman, 28 February 1917; Tuskegee University, Alabama, Archives Repository, R.R. Moton Papers, GC 109/810, Plaatje to Moton, 22 September 1924; National Archives of the USA, Washington DC, Dept of State, RG 59.848a, 55/20, 'Statement relative to Rev. H.A. Payne and his wife, missionaries, who are prohibited from remaining in the Union of South Africa'; RG 59.848a, 55/27, copy of letter from Rev. H.A. Payne to American Consul, Cape Town, 25 June 1917; S.T. Plaatje, letter to the editor, *Imvo Zabantsundu*, 24 April 1917; Robert Trent Vinson, *The Americans Are Coming! Dreams of African American liberation in segregationist South Africa* (Athens, OH: Ohio University Press, 2012), esp. pp. 27–33.

3 University of Bristol Library, Cobden Unwin Papers, APS file, Plaatje to Mrs Cobden Unwin, 18 May 1917. For the Native Administration Bill, see particularly C.M. Tatz, *Shadow and Substance in South Africa* (Pietermaritzburg: University of Natal Press, 1962).

4 Marian Lacey, *Working for Boroko* (Johannesburg: Ravan Press, 1981), pp. 86–8.

5 CAD, JUS, Dept of Justice, P3/527/17, 108, CID report of meeting at Boomplatz, near Lydenburg, Transvaal, 19 April 1917; Cobden Unwin Papers, APS file, Plaatje to Mrs Cobden Unwin, 18 May 1917; for St Leger's attempt to join up, see 'Lyndhurst Road Native School: closing concert', *Diamond Fields Advertiser (DFA)*, 17 December 1917.

6 SOAS, Plaatje Papers, STP 1/1, 'Solomon Tshekisho Plaatje', typescript biography of Plaatje by I. Bud-M'belle, p. 4, quoting Selope Thema's comments.

7 'A worthy defender', *Ilanga lase Natal*, 6 April 1917; 'Give honour to whom due: letter from Abraham Z. Twala', *Ilanga lase Natal*, 29 June 1917, quoted in Janet Remmington, 'Sol Plaatje's *Native Life in South Africa* (1916): the politics of belonging', in Dominic Davies, Erica Lombard and Benjamin Mountford (eds.), *Fighting Words: fifteen books that shaped the postcolonial world* (Oxford: Peter Lang, 2017), p. 115; see also 'U Mr Sol T. Plaatje uyabuya pesheya', *Ilanga lase Natal*, 16 February 1917.

8 UW, Molema–Plaatje Papers, Dd1, 'Mr and Mrs Sol T. Plaatje in the Transvaal'.

9 Cobden Unwin Papers, APS file, Plaatje to Mrs Cobden Unwin, 18 May; *Cape Times*, 17 April 1917. Drew further antagonised Free State members with the following statement: 'Nobody who knew the facts could say that justice was done to the natives of the Free State under the Bill. He referred to the assistance which the Barolongs had given to the people of the Free State in the past as allies, and said that they had been foully swindled out of their ground.'

10 Cobden Unwin Papers, APS file, Plaatje to Mrs Cobden Unwin, 10 July 1917. The Central News Agency had first advertised *Native Life* in January (see *Rand Daily Mail*, 5 January 1917).

11 Report of proceedings of parliament, *Cape Times*, 5 April 1917, *Eastern Province Herald*, 5 April 1917, *DFA*, 29 June 1917; CAD, NTS 619/17/1131, Inspector and Protector of Natives, Kimberley, to Director of Native Labour, Johannesburg, 12 May 1917.

12 'Native Life in South Africa', *The Star*, 4 June 1917.

13 CAD, NTS 619/17/1131, Acting Director of Native Labour to Secretary for Native Affairs, Pretoria, 15 May 1917, handwritten comments re opinion of General Botha.

14 S.T. Plaatje, *Native Life in South Africa* (London: P.S. King & Son, 1916), pp. 260–4; B.P. Willan, 'The South African Native Labour Contingent, 1916–18', *Journal of African History*, 14, 1, 1978, pp. 64–5.

15 CAD, NTS 2337/14/F1131, E. Barrett to the Secretary for Native Affairs, Cape Town, 20 February 1917; see also 'Native National Congress', *DFA*, 19 February 1917.

16 'No chance to lay proper foundations: inner history of A.N. Congress being revealed', *Bantu World*, 13 January 1934; R.V. Selope Thema, 'The African National Congress: its achievements and failures', *Umteteli wa Bantu*, 14 and 21 September 1929.

17 'South African Native Congress', *DFA*, 5 June 1917.

18 'Come out or starve', *Rand Daily Mail*, 2 June 1917; see also 'The native question: Sol Plaatje's speech', *The Star*, 2 June 1917.

19 S.T. Plaatje, 'The late General Louis Botha', *African World*, 6 September 1919; Report of proceedings of parliament, *Cape Times*, 29 June 1917; 'Sol Plaatje's outburst', *International*, 8 June 1917, p. 4.

20 'The Native Congress', *The Star*, 4 June 1917; 'Native Congress', *DFA*, 5 June 1917; S.M. Molema, *The Bantu Past and Present: an ethnographic and historical study of the native races of South Africa* (Edinburgh: W. Green & Son, 1920), p. 303.

21 Cobden Unwin Papers, APS file, Plaatje to Mrs Cobden Unwin, 10 July 1917.

22 R.V. Selope Thema, 'The African National Congress: its achievements and failures,

II', *Umteteli*, 21 September 1929; 'National Congress', *Ilanga lase Natal*, 15 June 1917. Dube told Harriette Colenso that he still held 'the confidence of the people and if I cared to stand again I have no doubt as to my success. However I have neglected my educational work so long that I feel I ought to devote more time to it now' (Colenso Papers, Box 56, Dube to Harriette Colenso, 3 October 1917).

23 S.T. Plaatje, 'The "good times" and the "New Native"', *Umteteli*, 9 November 1929; see also S.T. Plaatje, 'Leadership', *Umteteli*, 18 February 1928.

24 Cobden Unwin Papers, APS file, Plaatje to Mrs Cobden Unwin, 10 July 1917. An account of the incident also appeared in 'Ubotshiwe', *Ilanga*, 10 October 1917, reproducing an article from *Abantu-Batho*. I am indebted to Heather Hughes for her translation.

25 S.T. Plaatje, 'Through native eyes', *DFA*, 5 September 1917; National Archives (Kew), CO 417/629, 34975, Plaatje to the Administrator of South Rhodesia (Sir Drummond Chaplin), 6 April 1919.

26 S.T. Plaatje to the editor, *Imvo Zabantsundu*, 12 February 1918.

27 National Archives (Kew), CO 537/1197, 3473 (secret), 'Minutes of deputation of South African natives', statement by S.T. Plaatje, p. 11.

28 'The call for native recruits', *DFA*, 28 June 1917; see also 'Native grievances: a labour recruiting speech', *DFA*, 22 August 1917.

29 'Come out or starve', *Rand Daily Mail*, 2 June 1917; S.T. Plaatje, letter to the editor, 'The Mendi survivors', *Cape Argus*, 3 April 1917.

30 For a general account of these shootings, and the context in which they took place, see Martin J. Murray, '"The Natives are always stealing": white vigilantes and the "reign of terror" in the Orange Free State, 1918–1924', *Journal of African History*, 30, 1989, pp. 107–23. SOAS, Plaatje Papers, STP 2/2, Bound notebook. For Johannes Hendricus Brand Wessels, see D.W. Krüger and C.J. Beyers (eds.), *Dictionary of South African Biography* (Pretoria: Human Sciences Research Council, 1977), vol. 3, pp. 837–8.

31 CAD, JUS 7659, 10/332, 'Shooting of natives in Orange Free State, by R.F.S.' [R.F. Setlogelo], enclosure in letter to Prime Minister and Minister of Native Affairs, 30 April 1918. The *Pretoria News* ('The shooting of natives', 6 May 1918) and *Eastern Province Herald* ('Shooting of natives in Orange Free State'), 10 May 1918, were among a number of papers which carried the article on the Bloemfontein meeting. Plaatje addressed a meeting on the same subject at the Ebenezer Hall, Johannesburg, on 12 June 1918 (reported in 'Socialists in court', *The Star*, 17 July 1918).

32 Report of meeting of executive committee of the SANNC, *Ilanga lase Natal*, 28 December 1917; De Beers Archives (DB), Estate Records, Lyndhurst Road Native Institute file, Plaatje to W. Pickering, 15 March 1918.

33 DB, Native Institute file, De Beers General Secretary to Plaatje, 9 May 1918.

34 DB, Native Institute file, De Beers General Secretary to Plaatje, 9 May 1918 and Plaatje to A.S. Williams, 22 March 1918.

35 DB, Native Institute file, Plaatje to General Manager, 22 March 1918.

36 'De Beers Company and the natives', *DFA*, 25 June 1918; DB, Native Institute file, Plaatje to Estate Dept, 11 July 1918.

37 For the background to this unrest, see particularly, P.L. Bonner, 'The Transvaal Native Congress, 1917–1920: the radicalization of the black bourgeoisie on the Rand', in S. Marks and R. Rathbone (eds.), *Industrialisation and Social Change in South Africa: African class formation, culture and consciousness, 1870–1930* (Harlow: Longman, 1982), pp. 270–313; Peter Limb, *The ANC's Early Years: nation, class and place in South Africa before 1940* (Pretoria: Unisa Press, 2010), esp. pp. 155–99; Paul Landau, '"Johannesburg in Flames": the 1918 Shilling Campaign, *Abantu-Batho* and early African nationalism in South Africa', in Peter Limb (ed.), *The People's Paper* (Johannesburg: Wits University Press, 2013), pp. 255–81.

38 CAD, NTS 2337/14/F1131, J.M. McKenzie to District Commandant, South African

Police, Bethlehem, 6 April 1918, reporting proceedings of annual meeting of SANNC; typescript of presidential address by S.M. Makgatho, esp. pp. 7–8. Should the followers of General Hertzog be 'permitted to dragoon the Union Government into enforcing Free State ideals against the Natives of the Union,' Plaatje wrote, 'it will only be a matter of time before we have a Natives' Urban Act enforced throughout South Africa' (*Native Life in South Africa*, p. 53).

39 UW, Records of the Joint Councils of Europeans and Africans, Ac3.3.13, 'Treatment of natives in the courts', address by S.T. Plaatje to 1924 Joint Councils Conference, p. 7; Moffat Commission, evidence of Isaiah Bud-M'belle, pp. 267–9, indicating that Plaatje was among those he had summoned urgently to Johannesburg 'to calm the natives': quoted in Bonner, 'The Transvaal Native Congress, 1917–1920', p. 292.

40 CAD, NTS 2337/14/F1131, 'Resolutions passed by the executive committee of the National Congress at Bloemfontein on August 1st, 2nd and 3rd 1918', pp. 1–3; DB, Native Institute file, Plaatje to the Secretary, De Beers, 3 August 1918 and 2 August 1918; SANNC resolution reproduced in 'Natives' assembly hall', *DFA*, 9 August 1918.

41 An advertisement Plaatje inserted in the *DFA* similarly noted: 'His Excellency the Governor-General (by special request of General Botha) has graciously consented to perform the stone-laying ceremony at the above Hall' (*DFA*, 5 August 1918).

42 S.T. Plaatje, 'Through native eyes: the late General Louis Botha', *African World*, 6 September 1919. Plaatje's letter to Sir David de Villiers Graaff, 29 July 1918 (copied to Silas Molema), also alluded to General Botha's role: 'General Botha with his usual liberality and kindly interest has very generously urged His Excellency the Governor General to come and lay the foundation stone and His Excellency has graciously consented to come and perform the ceremony on August 7th next' (UW, Molema–Plaatje Papers, A 1893, Scrapbook). Plaatje's suggestions for Buxton's speech are in Molema–Plaatje Papers, A 1893, undated copy of letter to Buxton's ADC via John Orr, mayor of Kimberley. CAD, GG 1417, 45/75, has John Orr's letter to Buxton's ADC, 16 July 1918, passing these suggestions on.

43 CAD, NTS 619/17/1131, A.L. Barrett to Director of Native Labour, Johannesburg, 12 May 1917; UW, Molema–Plaatje Papers, Plaatje to Molema, 10 August 1918 (Da48) and 11 August 1918 (Da49); CAD, GG 1417, 45/75, Edward Dower, Secretary for Native Affairs, to Private Secretary to Viscount Buxton, 20 July 1918, and telegram from Mayor of Kimberley to aide-de-camp to Viscount Buxton, 23 July 1918.

44 'Assembly hall for natives', *DFA*, 8 August 1918; 'Natives' assembly hall', *DFA*, 9 August 1918.

45 DB, General Correspondence, Edward Dower to the Chairman, De Beers, 16 July 1918; CAD, GG 1417, 45/75, Plaatje to aide-de-camp to Viscount Buxton, 10 August 1918.

46 DB, Native Institute file, Plaatje to the Secretary, De Beers, 3 August 1918.

47 S.T. Plaatje, 'Mr Saul Msane: death of a Rand native leader', *African World*, 25 October 1919. For further details on Msane's position, see CAD, GNLB 90, 144/13/D205, 'Msane is undesirable', *Abantu-Batho*, 4 July 1918.

48 UW, Molema–Plaatje Papers, A1893, Scrapbook, annotated copy of letter from Magistrate, Kimberley, to Plaatje, 17 August 1918 regarding allegations made, and Plaatje's handwritten response.

49 UW, Molema–Plaatje Papers, Da47, Plaatje to Silas Molema, 3 August 1918; Da49, Plaatje to Silas Molema, 11 August 1918.

50 UW, Molema–Plaatje Papers, Da49, Plaatje to Silas Molema, 11 August 1918; Lovedale Archives, Leaving Certificate for F.Y. St Leger Plaatje, 18 December 1918. For the influenza epidemic in Kimberley, see B. Roberts, *Kimberley: turbulent city* (Cape Town: David Philip, 1976), pp. 365–7 and H. Phillips, *'Black October': the impact of the Spanish influenza epidemic of 1918 on South Africa* (Pretoria: Archives Year Book for South African History, 1990), esp. pp. 42–57.

51 UW, Molema–Plaatje Papers, Da51, Plaatje to 'Morolong', 6 November 1918; S.T. Plaatje, 'Native doctors at hospitals', *Cape Times*, 4 June 1927.

52 Sarah Talbert Keelan, 'Olive Plaatje', *The Brownies' Book*, December 1921, reproduced in Dianne Johnson-Feelings (ed.), *The Best of the Brownies' Book* (New York: Oxford University Press, 1996), pp. 107–9; National Archives (Kew), CO 537/1197, 3413 (secret), 'Minutes of deputation of South African natives', statement by S.T. Plaatje, p. 11; 'The natives and the epidemic', S.T. Plaatje to the editor, *DFA*, 12 November 1918.

53 S.M. Makgatho, 'Presidential address' to SANNC annual conference, 6 May 1919, in T. Karis and G.M. Carter (eds.), *From Protest to Challenge*, vol. 1 (Stanford: University of California Press, 1972), pp. 107–10.

54 See Plaatje's reported comments at 1918 annual SANNC conference in Bethlehem (CAD, NTS 2337/14/F1131, J.M. Mckenzie to District Commandant, South African Police, Bethlehem, 6 April 1918); P. Walshe, *The Rise of African Nationalism in South Africa: the African National Congress, 1912–1952* (Berkeley: University of California Press, 1970), pp. 61–2.

55 Speech by King George V to South African Native Labour Contingent at Abbeville, 10 July 1917, reproduced in SANNC petition to King George V, 16 December 1918, in Karis and Carter, *From Protest to Challenge*, pp. 139–40.

56 Makgatho, 'Presidential address', in Karis and Carter, *From Protest to Challenge*, p. 109; 'Mrs Solomon's questions', *Christian Commonwealth*, 20 June 1917.

57 'The Native Congress', *Cape Argus*, 23 December 1918; 'The Native National Congress', *The Star*, 23 December 1918.

58 'Native Congress', *Cape Argus*, 17 December 1918; 'Native Congress', *The Star*, 21 December 1918; 'Petition to King George V from the South African Native National Congress, December 16, 1918', reproduced in Karis and Carter, *From Protest to Challenge*, pp. 137–42.

59 UW, Molema–Plaatje Papers, Da52, Plaatje to Silas Molema, 20 December 1918.

60 Makgatho, 'Presidential address', in Karis and Carter, *From Protest to Challenge*, p. 139.

61 See especially I. Geiss, *The Pan African Movement* (London: Methuen, 1974), ch. 12, pp. 229–62.

62 UW, Molema–Plaatje Papers, Da55, Plaatje to Silas Molema, 14 March 1919; undated letter (no ref. number), Plaatje to Silas Molema [February 1919].

63 UW, Molema–Plaatje Papers, Da54, Plaatje to Molema, 14 March 1919.

64 CAD, NA 272, 466/1919/F639, Bechuana Deputation to England, especially letter from Silas Molema to Superintendent of Natives, Mafeking, 18 March 1919; 'Free State natives', *The Friend*, 19 February 1919 (reporting speech by S.T. Plaatje); CAD, Dept of Justice, F3/527/17, 108, CID report of meeting at Boomplatz, near Lydenburg, Transvaal, 19 April 1919; 'Natives in the Free State', *Cape Times*, 8 March 1919; CAD, Dept of Justice, 3/527/17/Part 6, police report of meeting of executive committee, SANNC, Kroonstad, 6 October 1919, referring to the £492 raised in the Orange Free State to pay off Plaatje's debts from his first trip to England; National Archives (Kew), CO 551/111, 15305, draft of minute from CO to SA High Commission, London, 14 April 1919; UW, Molema–Plaatje Papers, Da55, Plaatje to Silas Molema, 14 March 1919.

65 'Native Brotherhood Institute', *DFA*, 3 April 1919; 'Native Brotherhood', *DFA*, 18 March 1919; Basil Matthews (ed.), *World Brotherhood* (London: Hodder & Stoughton, 1920), p. 93.

66 National Archives (Kew), CO 417/629, Plaatje to the Secretary to the Administrator of Southern Rhodesia, 6 April 1919 and Secretary, Department of Administrator, to Plaatje, 24 April 1919.

67 UW, Molema–Plaatje Papers, Da56, Plaatje to Silas Molema, 10 May 1919; 'A native pamphlet, *Cape Times*, 21 May 1919; Makgatho, 'Presidential address', in Karis and

Carter, *From Protest to Challenge*, p. 110; quotations from *Christian Express*, 2 June 1919, pp. 2–3. See also CAD, 7659, 10/332, 'Volksraad', details of question asked in parliament, enclosure in Secretary for Native Affairs to Attorney-General, Bloemfontein, 20 May 1919; 'SA Native National Congress', *Queenstown Daily Representative and Free Press*, 8 and 9 May 1919; 'Ill-advised speech', *Imvo*, 27 May 1919.

68 Special Collections and University Archives, University of Massachusetts (UM), W.E.B. Du Bois Papers (MS 312), mums312-b015-i129, Plaatje to Du Bois, 19 May 1919.
69 DB, Native Institute file, Secretary, De Beers, to Secretary, Assembly Hall for Natives, 23 August 1920.
70 S.T. Plaatje, 'The native vote and other matters', *Umteteli*, 27 October 1928; UW, Molema–Plaatje Papers, Da58, Plaatje to Silas Molema, n.d. [June 1919]; CAD, NTS 1374, 3/213, Barolong Fund, Memorandum of meeting between Sol Plaatje, Rev. Mahabane, F.S. Malan and E.E. Dower, the Secretary for Native Affairs, 11 June 1919. On the recommendation of the secretary for native affairs, however, Plaatje was afterwards informed that the government was not prepared to sanction this; UW, Molema–Plaatje, Da 58, Plaatje to Molema, undated [June 1919].

Chapter 12
1 National Archives (Kew), CO 551/111, 2203, W.P. Schreiner to Colonel Amery, 6 May 1919.
2 CO 551/111, 22003, minute of interview, 8 May 1919.
3 J. Barnes and D. Nicholson (eds.), *The Leo Amery Diaries, vol. 1, 1896–1929* (London: Hutchinson, 1980), p. 260, entry for 8 May 1919.
4 CO 551/111, minutes dated 21 and 22 May 1919; Hugh Egerton, *British Colonial Policy in the Twentieth Century* (London: Methuen, 1922), p. 175; 'Native Affairs Bill: second reading debate in the assembly', *Cape Times*, 27 May 1920.
5 CO 551/114, 58532, minute from H. Thornton to Sir H. Lambert, 30 October 1919 and 21 November 1919; CO 537/1137, 3473 (secret), 'Minutes of deputation of South African natives to the Rt Hon. D. Lloyd George, MP (Prime Minister) on the colour bar and other questions', p. 12, statement by the Prime Minister.
6 Eric Walker, *W.P. Schreiner: a South African* (London: Oxford University Press, 1937), pp. 380–1; S.T. Plaatje, 'Through native eyes: the late General Louis Botha', *African World*, 6 September 1919 and 'Friends of the natives', *DFA*, 15 June 1925; 'Where is the Cape native delegation?', *Imvo*, 9 December 1919 (where Plaatje wrote that he attended the funeral in order to 'represent our people').
7 NAD, Colenso Papers, Box 56, Plaatje to Mrs Sophie Colenso, 17 July 1919.
8 Colenso Papers, Box 56, Mrs Sophie Colenso to Harriette and Agnes Colenso, 24 July 1919; UCT, Schreiner Papers, BC 27, Olive Schreiner to Mrs Solomon, 26 July 1919; CO 551/123, 60993, Mrs G. Solomon to Lloyd George, 15 October 1919; CO 551/123, 48382, Charles Garnett to the King, 12 August 1919; House of Lords Record Office (London), Lloyd George Papers, Series F, Box 227, folder 1, G.B. Clark to Lloyd George, 26 July 1919; Colenso Papers, Box 56, Plaatje to Mrs Sophie Colenso, 25 July 1919.
9 UCT, Molteno Family Papers, BC 330, Box 20, 'The woman question', notes made by Betty Molteno for Alice Greene, 22 August 1919.
10 Hansard, House of Commons Debates, 30 July 1919, p. 2198.
11 UW, Molema–Plaatje Papers, Da59, Plaatje to Fenyang, 2 August 1919; Isaiah Bud M'belle, 'Solomon Tshekisho Plaatje', p. 4.
12 CO 551/122, 3780, minute of meeting between Colonel Amery, S.T. Plaatje and J. Gumede, 20 August 1919.
13 'A London African gathering', *West Africa*, 16 August 1919; 'A "many-millioned cry for justice"', *African World*, 23 August 1919.

14 S.T. Plaatje, 'Our London letter', *The Clarion* (Cape Town), 17 January 1920; *Foreign Affairs* (journal of the Union of Democratic Control), October and November 1919, interview with Plaatje, where the interviewer, Herbert Bryan, described Plaatje as 'a most capable and cultured South African native gentleman' from whom, after two hours together, he 'would willingly have heard more'; 'Even in Africa: native Negroes are disfranchised, segregated and denied rights!', *Cleveland Gazette*, 3 January 1920, reproduced from *Christian Science Monitor* (n.d.). The comment about the 'awakening of coloured and other subject races' was by Vida Goldstein, quoted in Angela Woollacott, *To Try Her Fortune in London: Australian women, colonialism and modernity* (Oxford: Oxford University Press, 2001), p. 124.

15 CO 551/122, MI 49541, W. Procktor, President, Abney Brotherhood, to Walter Long, Secretary of State for the Colonies, 21 August 1919.

16 National Archives (Kew), Cabinet Office, CAB/24/95, 'Monthly review of revolutionary movements in foreign countries', Report no. 14, December 1919, pp. 23–4, which commented: 'South Africa has a long way to travel before effective political divisions on other than racial lines will become practicable'. A fuller report of the Church Socialist League meeting appeared in 'The peril of South Africa', *Church Times*, 28 November 1919.

17 The best treatment of this subject is Jacqueline Jenkinson, *Black 1919: riots, racism and resistance in imperial Britain* (Liverpool: Liverpool University Press, 2009).

18 S.T. Plaatje, 'Our London letter', *The Clarion*, November–December 1919; 'Rights of natives in South Africa', *Manchester Guardian*, 10 October 1919; also 'Britain's soul in danger', *West Africa*, 25 October 1919.

19 Plaatje, 'Our London letter'; Plaatje, 'Where is the Cape native delegation?'; 'Sunderland day by day: at the Sunshine Service', *Sunderland Daily Echo*, 17 October 1919. Plaatje had shared a platform with William Walker at a Brotherhood meeting in Southall in September 1916: 'Southall Brotherhood: address by ex-mayor of Sunderland, Councillor William Walker', *Southall-Norwood Gazette*, 21 September 1916, p. 1.

20 Colenso Papers, Box 56, Plaatje to Sophie Colenso, 12 September 1919; Plaatje, 'Our London letter', *The Clarion*, 22 November 1919, p. 12.

21 UCT, Molteno Murray Family Papers, BC 330 (MFP), Box 20, Betty Molteno to Alice Greene, 23 October 1919.

22 Colenso Papers, Box 56, Plaatje to Mrs Sophie Colenso, 12 September 1919. For the Southern Syncopated Orchestra, see particularly Catherine Parsonage, *The Evolution of Jazz in Britain, 1880–1935* (Aldershot: Ashgate, 2005), esp. pp. 121–62.

23 Plaatje, 'Our London letter', *The Clarion*, 22 November, 17 and 24 January 1920.

24 S.T. Plaatje, 'Mr Scully and native policy', letter to the editor, *Cape Argus*, 20 November 1919; CO 551/117, 5310, R. Blankenburg (Secretary, South African High Commission in London) to Minister of the Interior, Pretoria, 3 October 1919 (copy), and further correspondence in this series.

25 AS/APS, S19 D2/2, Plaatje to Travers Buxton, 5 and 7 November 1919, 22 January 1920. Questions were asked in the House of Commons by Aneurin Williams (Liberal MP for Consett) and Josiah Wedgwood (Liberal MP for Newcastle-under-Lyme) (CO 551/120, 61810, 27 October 1919 and 63629, 6 November 1919). The Union-Castle Company eventually paid a total of £237 in compensation to those ejected from the *Edinburgh Castle*.

26 See, e.g., CO 551/118, 69498, Plaatje to South African High Commission, 4 December 1919; CO 551/118, 3824, 'Memorandum: South African native delegation', 17 November 1919.

27 Colenso Papers, Box 63, Alice Werner to Harriette and Agnes Colenso, 4 December 1919 and 16 June 1920; Box 56, Plaatje to Mrs Sophie Colenso, 29 December 1919.

28 AS/APS, S19 H2/50, Gumede to Archbishop of Canterbury, 25 August 1919;

Archbishop of Canterbury to J.H. Harris, 13 October 1919; Harris to Plaatje, 21 October 1919. See also Raymond van Diemel, 'In Search of Freedom, Fair Play and Justice: Josiah Tshangana Gumede, 1867–1946, a political biography' (PhD thesis, University of the Western Cape, 1997), pp. 139–41.

29 CO 537/1197, 3473 (secret), 'Minutes of deputation of South African natives', statement by Prime Minister, p. 12; CO 551/114, 58532, minute from Major H.C. Thornton to Sir Henry Lambert, 30 October 1919, and from Lambert to Thornton, 31 October 1919, and copy of letter to Philip Kerr, 3 October 1919. At the end of October Arthur Henderson, referring to Plaatje, wrote of 'making arrangements to have a conversation with him myself': this may well have prompted the reminder the prime minister clearly needed (Bodleian Library, Colenso Papers, MSS Afr. s.1291/9b, vi, f25, Arthur Henderson to E.D. Morel, 29 October 1919). It had probably not helped that Dr Clark's letter had ended up in the prime minister's file on the Afrikaner nationalist delegation rather than that of the SANNC.

30 'The prime minister and South African native deputation', *African Sentinel* (London), 17 January 1920; Lloyd George Papers, Series F, Box 227, folder 2, L.T. Mvabaza to Philip Kerr, 24 November 1919.

31 CO 537/1197, 3473 (secret), 'Minutes of deputation of South African natives', statement by Plaatje, pp. 7–12. Drafts of the minutes, with handwritten corrections made by Plaatje and Mvabaza, are in Lloyd George Papers, Box 227, folder 2, 'South African native deputation'.

32 'Minutes of deputation', statement by Lloyd George to members of deputation, p. 13.

33 Plaatje, 'Our London letter', *The Clarion*, 17 January 1920, p. 11; 'The Brotherhood: a record attendance', *Evening News* (Portsmouth), 19 January 1920; 'The prime minister and South African native deputation', *African Sentinel*, 17 January 1920 and *Lagos Standard*, 14 January 1920, reproducing article from *African Telegraph*, December 1919; *African World* (Supplement), 30 September 1921, remarks of J. Eldred Taylor to Pan-African Congress, September 1921.

34 CO 537/1197, 1486 (secret), Lloyd George to Smuts, 3 March 1920 (also in CAD, NTS 8/326).

35 CO 537/1197, 1486 (secret), Lloyd George to Smuts, 3 March 1920, marked 'Private and personal' (also in CAD, NTS 8/326). Lloyd George wrote both letters early in January but it seems they were not actually sent off until 3 March.

36 CO 537/1198, 27397 (secret), Smuts to Lloyd George, 12 May 1920. Smuts's comment about the earlier SANNC petition was in a speech he made when moving the Native Affairs Bill in 1920, quoted by R.V. Selope Thema in 'The South African native policy', *Africa and Orient Review*, 1, 12, December 1920. Smuts said that he had 'never come across a more disappointing or graver document'.

37 See M. Chanock, *Unconsummated Union* (Manchester: Manchester University Press, 1977), pp. 132–4. Henry Lambert's comment was on the dispatch cover of CO 537/1197, 1486, dated 11 March 1920.

38 Philip Kerr reaffirmed the position in a letter after the interview to Levi Mvabaza: 'The Prime Minister has decided that the interview must be treated as a private interview, and that no public use must be made of it' (Lloyd George Papers, Box 227, folder 2, 'South African native deputation', Kerr to Mvabaza, 7 January 1920).

39 CO 551/118, 3824, Secretary, South African High Commission, to Secretary for Native Affairs, Pretoria, 10 December 1919, p. 3; 'Homeless! Landless! Outlawed! The plight of South African natives: interview with Solomon Plaatje', *Labour Leader*, 11 December 1919; author's interview with Lord Fenner Brockway, House of Lords, London, August 1978; 'Our London letter', *The Clarion*, 17 January 1920, p. 11; S.T. Plaatje, *Some of the Legal Disabilities Suffered by the Native Population of the Union of South Africa and Imperial Responsibility* (London: African Telegraph, 1919). My thanks to Peter Limb for

help in tracking down the UK version of this pamphlet.

40 AS/APS, S19 D2/12, Plaatje to AS and APS, 29 October 1919 and S19 H2/50, Harris to Plaatje, 20 November and 20 December 1919; University of Bristol, National Liberal Club Archive, DM 668, Minutes of Foreign and Colonial Subcommittee, 23 September 1919.

41 Plaatje, 'Our London letter', *The Clarion*, 17 January 1920.

42 Details of the meetings Plaatje addressed in Scotland can be found in 'Scottish Federation', *Foreign Affairs*, February 1920, p. 16 (in Hull History Centre, Records of the Union of Democratic Control, DDC/5/33/8); see also 'ILP lecture', *Paisley Daily Express*, 12 December 1919; 'In the Union of South Africa', *Falkirk Herald*, 13 December 1919; Colenso Papers, Box 56, Plaatje to Sophie Colenso, 29 December 1919; see also 'The colour bar: native leader describes his overseas tour', *The Star*, 13 December 1923, for similar comments, and CO 551/122, 71344, resolution passed at meeting of ILP in Falkirk, addressed by Plaatje, 12 December 1919.

43 'The colour bar', *Workers' Dreadnought*, January 1920; see also 'British government refuses to protect Negro subjects', *The Emancipator*, 20 March 1920.

44 Colenso Papers, Box 63, Alice Werner to Harriette and Agnes Colenso, 4 December 1919; Box 57, Mrs Sophie Colenso to Harriette and Agnes Colenso, 2 January 1920, and Plaatje to Mrs Colenso, 6 January 1920; Box 56, Mrs S. Colenso to Harriette and Agnes Colenso, 7 August 1919.

45 S.M. Molema, *Lover of His People: a biography of Sol Plaatje* (Johannesburg: Wits University Press, 2012), p. 10.

46 'The Brotherhood: a record attendance', *Evening News* (Portsmouth), 19 January 1920; Plaatje, 'Our London letter', *The Clarion*, November–December 1919; Basil Matthews (ed.), *World Brotherhood* (London: Hodder and Stoughton, 1920), pp. v–ix.

47 De Beers (DB), Estate Records, Lyndhurst Road Native Institute file, Griffiths Motsieloa to De Beers, 30 October 1920; National Adult School Union Minute Book (Drayton House, London), Minute 181, 27 October 1919; Minute 193, 19 November 1920; Plaatje, 'Our London letter', *The Clarion*, November–December 1919.

48 AS/APS, S23 H2/50, AS and APS to S.T. Plaatje, 1 March 1920.

49 Papers in private possession of Professor Adelaide Cromwell (Boston, US), J.E. Bruce to John W. Cromwell, 19 October 1919; Archives of the United States of America (Washington DC), Military Archives Division, File L0218-364/21, Report on Negro Subversion from Office of MID, New York, to Director of Military Intelligence, details of work of 'South African delegation' and summary of Plaatje's letter to J.E. Bruce, published in *Negro World*, n.d.; Moorland-Spingarn Research Center (Howard University, Washington DC), Cromwell Family Papers, John W. Cromwell Record Book, 1919–26, Box 24-3, folder 52, record of letter from Plaatje (January 1920) and to Plaatje (February 1920).

50 UM, W.E.B. Du Bois Papers, mums312-b016-i161, Du Bois to Louis F. Post, Assistant Secretary of Labor, 6 December 1920; Archives of the United States of America, General Services Division, Dept of State central decimal file (RG 59), request of Solomon T. Plaatje for US visa, 24 March 1920 (811.111); Diplomatic Section, Records of US Consulate, London, Register of Correspondence, p. 61, letter to Plaatje, 30 March 1920. Plaatje recalled the presence of the African American clerks in his 'Account of North American tour' in Brian Willan (ed.), *Sol Plaatje: selected writings* (Johannesburg: Witwatersrand University Press, 1996), p. 298.

51 Barrett was under-secretary for native affairs, but at this time was acting as secretary for native affairs. He was promoted to this position in August 1920. I am indebted to Saul Dubow for providing extracts from E. Barrett to Hon. PM 27/1/23 in CAD, PM 1/2/61, 18/1, which testifies to his difficult relationship with F.S. Malan (personal communication, 25 November 2013).

52 CAD, NTS 619/17/1131 (file on S.T. Plaatje), Secretary for Native Affairs to Consul General for the United States of America, Cape Town, 23 March 1920; Archives of the United States of America, RG 59, A1 Entry 705, 811.111, Plaatje, Solomon T., Box 193, 230/52/31/01, George H. Murphy to Robert P. Skinner (Consul General, London), 24 March 1920, and Barrett to Murphy (copy), 23 March 1920.

53 Archives of the United States of America, RG 59, George H. Murphy to Robert P. Skinner (Consul General, London), 24 March 1920. Deeming Plaatje's purpose as insufficiently urgent was designed to get around the instructions US consulates had to the effect that they were not to refuse 'to visa a passport of a friendly alien who desires to go to the United States for an urgent and legitimate purpose'.

54 CAD, NTS 619/17/1131, Barrett to Malan, 31 March 1920. For the activities of the UNIA in South Africa, see Robert A Hill and Gregory A. Pirio, '"Africa for the Africans": the Garvey movement in South Africa, 1920–1940', in Shula Marks and Stanley Trapido (eds.), *The Politics of Race, Class and Nationalism in Twentieth Century South Africa* (Harlow: Longman, 1987), pp. 209–53.

55 Barrett's claim about the financial affairs of Plaatje's Brotherhood organisation had some foundation: no rates or rent had been paid since August 1918, and at the time he wrote over £80 was owing (DB, Lyndhurst Road file, Secretary, De Beers, to Secretary, Assembly Hall for Natives, 23 August 1920).

56 Archives of the United States of America, Records of the Office of the Counselor, RG 59, 504.69-504.100, Box 30, report on address by Plaatje to Falkirk ILP meeting, 12 December 1919, enclosure in Wright to W.L. Hurley, 29 December 1919 (confidential).

57 Colenso Papers, Box 63, Alice Werner to Harriette and Agnes Colenso, 3 December 1920; SOAS, M. Benson Collection, MS 348942, transcript of interview with T.D. Mweli Skota (n.d.); Harold Mayer (Native Recruiting Corporation) to Secretary, Compound Manager's Association, 12 March 1920, quoted in *South African Review*, January 1923 and *International*, 2 February 1923. See also Chamber of Mines Archive, Minute Book of Board of Management of Native Recruiting Corporation, entries for 10 February 1919, 24 February 1919, 26 January 1920 and 12 April 1920; 'The objects of this paper', *Umteteli wa Bantu*, 1, 1, May 1920; 'Class hatred', *Umteteli*, 30 August 1924; and Peter Limb (ed.), *The People's Paper: a centenary history and anthology of 'Abantu-Batho'* (Johannesburg: Wits University Press, 2013), pp. 318–22 for the broader background, and in particular the impact of *Umteteli* on *Abantu-Batho*.

58 SOAS, M. Benson Collection, Skota interview transcript.

59 In a letter dated 17 May 1920, John Dube, using 'Native Printing and Publishing Company' headed paper, and describing himself as 'responsible editor' of *Umteteli wa Bantu*, wrote to Colonel Pritchard, director of native labour, to urge him to increase the amount his organisation was paying for advertising in *Ilanga lase Natal* (CAD, Pretoria, DNL/GNLB, letters from John Dube to Secretary for Native Affairs, 4 May 1920, and to Colonel S.M. Pritchard, 17 May 1920).

60 UW, Molema–Plaatje Papers, Da62, Plaatje to Molema, 25 August 1920.

61 SOAS, M. Benson Collection, Skota interview transcript.

62 UW, Molema–Plaatje Papers, Da62, Plaatje to Silas Molema, 25 August 1920; S.T. Plaatje, 'Departed friends of the natives', *Umteteli*, 17 September 1927.

63 British Library, Royal Literary Fund Archive, Loan 96 RLF, 1/3094.

64 S.M. Molema, *The Bantu Past and Present* (Edinburgh: W. Green & Son, 1920); UW, Molema–Plaatje Papers, Da61, Plaatje to Modiri Molema, 11 July 1920.

65 UW, Molema–Plaatje Papers, Ad1.1.3, Modiri Molema to Silas Molema, 2 June 1920; Da62, Plaatje to Silas Molema, 25 August 1920.

66 Drafts of parts of some chapters with the headings 'The tribes', 'Land tenure', and 'Superstition' suggest some broader context too (SOAS, Plaatje Papers, STP 2/2, Plaatje's notebook, unpaginated).

67 SOAS, Plaatje Papers, STP 2/2, Plaatje's notebook, unpaginated.
68 There is an enormous literature on Rider Haggard: see particularly Norman Etherington, *Rider Haggard* (Boston: Twayne Publishers, 1984); Lindy Stiebl, *Imagining Africa: landscape in H. Rider Haggard's romances* (Santa Barbara: Praeger, 2001); Kathryn C.S. Simpson, 'H. Rider Haggard, Theophilus Shepstone and the Zikali trilogy: a revisionist approach to Haggard's African fiction' (PhD thesis, Edinburgh Napier University, 2016).
69 H. Rider Haggard, *Nada the Lily* (London: Thames Publishing, 1956 [originally published 1892]), preface, pp. 1 and 2; for the link between Kipling's *Jungle Stories* and *Nada the Lily* see Lilias Rider Haggard, *The Cloak That I Left: a biography of the author Henry Rider Haggard* (London: Hodder and Stoughton, 1951), p. 147.
70 On *Nada the Lily* and *Mhudi* see particularly: Tim Couzens, 'Sol T. Plaatje and the first South African epic', *English in Africa*, 14, 1, May 1987, pp. 53–4; Peter J. Esterhuysen, 'Patterns of confluence: developments in selected novels in English by black South African writers' (MA thesis, University of the Witwatersrand, 1988); Laura Chrisman, *Rereading the Imperial Romance: British imperialism and South African resistance in Haggard, Schreiner, and Plaatje* (Oxford: Oxford University Press, 2000); Brian Walter, 'Plaatje's African romance: the translation of tragedy in *Mhudi* and other writings' (PhD thesis, Rhodes University, 2001). Quotations are from *Nada the Lily*, pp. 44, 69, 53 and S. Plaatje, *Mhudi* (Lovedale: Lovedale Press, 1930), pp. 208, 26, 61.
71 Colenso Papers, Box 63, Alice Werner to Harriette and Agnes Colenso, 3 December 1920 and to Agnes Colenso 1 September 1920. In referring to Thomas Mofolo, Alice Werner was thinking particularly of his first two novels, *Moeti oa Bochabela* ('The traveller to the East'), published in 1907, and *Pitseng*, published in 1920. His most famous work, *Chaka*, was written in 1910 but not published until 1925.
72 Alice Werner's comment about the use of English by Africans is from the review she wrote, shortly before her death, of Isaac Schapera's *Western Civilization and the Natives of South Africa* ('South African tribes', *Times Literary Supplement*, 10 January 1935, p. 5).
73 UW, A.B. Xuma Papers, AD 843, Box 5, file 38, 'South African Bantu Brotherhoods Committee'; see also 'Sevenoaks Brotherhood: facts about South Africa', *Chronicle and Courier*, 25 June 1920, p. 6; 'An African at the LMM', *Leighton Buzzard Observer*, 29 June 1920, p. 5; Colenso Papers, Box 11, Plaatje to 'Miss Colenso', n.d. [June 1920] and Box 56, Sophie Colenso to Harriette Colenso, 2 July 1920.
74 'A coaster's London log', *West Africa*, 4 and 11 September 1920; see also *Brotherhood Journal*, 1, 8, September 1920, p. 157 and 'The Bantu Brotherhoods', 9, October 1920, p. 175. The concert was also advertised in *Labour Leader*, 2 September 1920, and supported by editorial comment ('Help our black comrades') urging readers to attend since it was 'in aid of the South African Native Brotherhoods, organised by Comrade Sol Plaatje, who is well known as a Labour orator'.
75 J.A. Langley, *Pan-Africanism and West African Nationalism* (Oxford: Oxford University Press, 1973), p. 253; University of Ibadan Library (Ibadan, Nigeria), Herbert Macaulay Papers, Box 18, File 3, National Congress of British West Africa, 1920, minutes of meeting held on 8 October 1920.
76 Molteno Murray Family Papers, Box 50, A81.2.3, Plaatje to Mrs Lennox Murray, 17 November 1922; Colenso Papers, Box 80, Plaatje to Georgiana Solomon, 9 February 1921.
77 CAD, NTS 619/17/1131, Hubert S. Martin (Chief Passport Officer, UK) to Secretary, South African High Commission, 15 February 1921; UCT, Molteno Murray Family Papers, Box 50, A81.2.1, Plaatje to Miss Molteno, 16 December 1920.
78 Colenso Papers, Box 63, Alice Werner to Harriette and Agnes Colenso, 3 December 1920.
79 Fort Hare University, Student Records, St Leger Plaatje file, St Leger Plaatje to the

Principal, Lovedale, 10 July 1920.

80 Canada, Ocean Arrivals (Form 30A), 1919–1924, SS *Melita*, Plaatje's Passenger's Declaration form dated 28 September 1920, www.CanadaOceanArrivalsForm30A19191924_171011540, available via ancestry.co.uk, accessed 17 March 2013; Colenso Papers, Box 80, Plaatje to Georgiana Solomon, 9 February 1921.

81 Molteno Murray Family Papers, Box 50, A81.2.1, Plaatje to Miss Molteno, 16 December 1920.

82 'Our Brotherhood', *Portsmouth Evening News*, 30 August 1920 and '2,400 Brothers: progress of local society', *Portsmouth Times and Hampshire County Journal*, 3 September 1920, p. 6.

83 UM, W.E.B. Du Bois Papers, mums312-b016-i323, Plaatje to Du Bois, 19 December 1920.

84 Canada, Ocean Arrivals (Form 30A), 1919–1924, SS *Melita*, Plaatje's Passenger's Declaration form dated 28 September 1920; *World Brotherhood* (p. 276) lists 'Rev. A.P. Latter' as one of the Canadian delegates to the International Brotherhood Congress in London in September 1919; *The Christian Men's Brotherhood Federation of Canada (Incorporated): its aims and objectives* (Toronto, 1919), p. 1, indicates his position within the organisation.

Chapter 13

1 UCT, Molteno Murray Family Papers, Box 50, A81.2.1, Plaatje to Miss Molteno, 16 December 1920.

2 Plaatje to Miss Molteno, 16 December 1920. The 'Mr Henderson' referred to (with his wife) was Mr L. Henderson, secretary of the Calvary Men's Own Brotherhood, Montreal, 'the premier Brotherhood in Canada' ('Brotherhood in Canada', *Brotherhood Outlook*, January 1923, p. 182).

3 Colenso Papers, Box 80, Plaatje to Mrs Solomon, 9 February 1921; 'Account of North American tour', in Brian Willan (ed.), *Sol Plaatje: selected writings* (Johannesburg: Witwatersrand University Press, 1996), p. 289. On the Brotherhood in Canada, see R. Allen, *The Social Passion: religion and social reform in Canada, 1914–1928* (Toronto: University of Toronto Press, 1971) and William Ward, *The Brotherhood in Canada: the story of a Canadian Brotherhood campaign* (London: Brotherhood Publishing House, 1910).

4 'Welcome to Plaatje, a distinguished African; an appreciation by Arthur C. Holder, Toronto, Can', *Negro World* (New York), 5 February 1921.

5 Molteno Murray Family Papers, Box 50, A8.1.2.1, Plaatje to Miss Molteno, 16 December 1920.

6 'Welcome to Plaatje'.

7 'Welcome to Plaatje'.

8 Molteno Murray Family Papers, Box 50, A8.1.2.1, Plaatje to Miss Molteno, 16 December 1920; 'Hon. Marcus Garvey returns to Liberty Hall', *Negro World*, 12 February 1921; 'Hon. Sol Plaatje', *Buffalo American*, 3 February 1921, p. 1. I am most grateful to Cynthia van Ness, Buffalo History Museum, for supplying me with a copy of this issue of the *Buffalo American*. Marcus Garvey addressed UNIA meetings in Toronto on 5, 6 and 7 January 1921.

9 S.T. Plaatje, 'Native doctors at hospitals', *Cape Times*, 4 June 1927; 'Account of North American tour', in Willan, *Sol Plaatje: selected writings*, p. 292.

10 UM, W.E.B. Du Bois Papers, mums312-b016-i161, Du Bois to Louis F. Post, 6 December 1920 and mums312-b016-i323, Plaatje to Du Bois, 19 December 1920.

11 UM, W.E.B. Du Bois Papers, mums312-b016-i162, Louis F. Post to Du Bois, 9 December 1920 and mums312-b016-i139, Plaatje to Du Bois, 29 December 1920; Archives of the

United States of America, RG 59, A1 entry 705, 8111.111, Plaatje, Solomon T., Box 93, 230/52/31/01, Du Bois to Senator W.L. Jones and Senator William Calder, 16 December 1920; SOAS, Plaatje Papers, STP 3/4, Canadian passport no. 79551, issued to S.T. Plaatje, 21 December 1920.

12 'Welcome to Plaatje'; UM, W.E.B. Du Bois Papers, mums312-b018-i290, *The Daylight*, 15 January 1921.

13 Colenso Papers, Box 80, Plaatje to Mrs Solomon, 9 February 1921; UW, Molema–Plaatje Papers, Dbi, 'Account of visit to Canada and United States of America', p. 6; CAD, NTS 619/17/1131 (file on S.T. Plaatje), Secretary, South African High Commission, London, to Chief Passport Officer, 12 February 1921, and Chief Passport Officer to South African High Commission, 15 February 1921. For his border crossing, see Manifests of Passengers Arriving in the St Albans, VT, District through Canadian Pacific and Atlantic Ports, 1895–1954, Source 2: Roll 415, vol. 568–569, Feb. 1921, Record set: United States, Canadian Border Crossings (http://search.findmypast.co.uk/results/united-states-records?firstname=solomon&lastname=plaatje, accessed 17 March 2013).

14 For Kakaza's career and biography, see Robert A. Hill (ed.), *The Marcus Garvey and Universal Negro Improvement Association Papers: Africa for the Africans, 1923–1945* (Berkeley: University of California Press, 2006), vol. 10, pp. xcii–xciii and 139.

15 Plaatje, 'Account of visit', p. 7; *Negro World*, 26 February 1921, report from UNIA branch, Buffalo, NY; 'Hon. Sol Plaatje', *Buffalo American*, 3 February 1921. Lillian Serece Williams, *Strangers in the Land of Paradise: the creation of an African American community, Buffalo, New York, 1900–1914* (Bloomington, IN: Indiana University Press, 1999), esp. ch. 7, pp. 150–87, provides the broader context to black life in Buffalo at this time.

16 For the UNIA and Garveyism, see especially Colin Grant, *Negro with a Hat: the rise and fall of Marcus Garvey* (London: Jonathan Cape, 2008); Adam Ewing, *The Age of Garvey: how a Jamaican activist created a mass movement and changed global black politics* (Princeton: Princeton University Press, 2014).

17 Colenso Papers, Box 80, Plaatje to Mrs Colenso, 9 February 1921; 'Account of visit', p. 293.

18 'Bruce Grit's column', *Negro World*, 16 July 1921; letter from Bruce to J.W. Cromwell, 16 March 1921, in Adelaide M. Cromwell, *Unveiled Voices, Unvarnished Memories: the Cromwell family in slavery and segregation, 1692–1972* (Columbia: University of Missouri Press, 2007), p. 278. For Bruce, see Ralph L. Crowder, *John Edward Bruce: politician, journalist, and self-trained historian of the African diaspora* (New York: New York University Press, 2004); for his appointment as 'Duke of Uganda', see Grant, *Negro with a Hat*, p. 266.

19 Plaatje, 'Native doctors at hospitals', *Cape Times*, 4 June 1927; 'Account of visit', p. 292. An experienced general practitioner, John George Sauer (d. 1955) graduated from the University of Vermont Medical School in 1890 and was a fellow of the New York Academy of Medicine. The 1921 *Medical Directory for New York, New Jersey and Connecticut* (pp. 10 and 156) lists his practice at 106 East 136th Street, a short walk from where Plaatje was living at 67 West 131st Street. I am most grateful to Arlene Shaner, Acting Curator, Historical Collections, New York Academy of Medicine, and Prudence Doherty, Public Services Curator, University of Vermont, for information on Dr Sauer.

20 'Hon. Marcus Garvey returns', *Negro World*, 12 February 1921; Colenso Papers, Box 11, Plaatje to 'Mrs Gebuza' (Colenso), 15 February 1921; SOAS, Plaatje Papers, STP 3/5, poster advertising Plaatje's meetings; 'Mr Sol Plaatje addresses the Brooklyn UNIA', *Negro World*, 19 March 1921; see also 'Interesting Harlem notes', *Negro World*, 19 February 1921; 'A digest of Brooklyn happenings', *Chicago Defender*, 19 March 1921, p. 3; *New York Age*, 12, 19 and 26 March 1921.

21 'Hon. Marcus Garvey returns'.

22 'Special Easter services held in Liberty Hall', *Negro World*, 2 April 1921.

23 Colenso Papers, Box 57, Plaatje to Mrs Colenso, 31 March 1922, conveys his disappointment on the score of fundraising.

24 'Special Easter services', *Negro World*, 2 April 1921. Audiences at Liberty Hall had good reason to be cautious of the credentials of speakers: while Plaatje was in New York, a certain 'Prince Madarikan Deniyi', claiming to be 'a native prince of Lagos, Nigeria, West Africa', and seeking to raise funds under this pretext, was exposed as a complete fraud (*Marcus Garvey and Universal Negro Improvement Association Papers*, vol. 9, 1995, pp. 142–3).

25 Library of Congress, Manuscripts Division, NAACP collection, Box C8, General correspondence, Assistant Secretary NAACP, to Miss E.T. Wood, Treasurer, South African Bantu Brotherhood Mission, 5 and 15 July 1921; Ellen Wood to Secretary, NAACP, 12 August 1921; personal communication from Jeff Green, 30 March 1981, re interview with Miss Amy Barbour-James, London, 19 March 1981. Miss Barbour-James recalled that Ellen Wood had lived in London and worked as a nurse in the local hospital in Acton, close to where the Barbour-James family lived.

26 Schomburg Library, New York, J.E. Bruce Papers, John W. Cromwell to J.E. Bruce, 21 January 1921; Library of Congress, Manuscripts Division, Carter G. Woodson Papers, m/f reel 3, Mrs Booker T. Washington to Carter Woodson, 4 September 1922; Bruce to Mr J. Bronson, 7 January 1923.

27 Advertisements for *Native Life in South Africa*, in *The Crisis*, July and August 1921.

28 A fifth pamphlet, entitled *The Black Man's Burden in South Africa* – based on the text of Plaatje's address to the 1921 Pan-African Congress – was published by the Hunt Printing Company in 1922. For Young's Book Exchange, W. Burghardt Turner and Joyce Moore Turner (eds.), *Richard B. Moore, Caribbean Militant in Harlem: collected writings 1920–1972* (Bloomington, IN: Indiana University Press, 1988), pp. 161–4.

29 S.T. Plaatje, *Mhudi: an epic of native life a hundred years ago* (Lovedale: Lovedale Press, 1930), preface; 'Special Easter services', *Negro World*, 2 April 1921. See also Lucy Valerie Graham, *State of Peril: race and rape in South African literature* (New York: Oxford University Press, 2012), for the broader South African and American social and literary contexts.

30 E.D. Morel, *The Horror on the Rhine* (London: Union of Democratic Control, 1920); Iris Wigger, 'Black shame: the campaign against "racial degeneration" and female degradation in interwar Europe', *Race and Class*, 51, 3, 2010, pp. 33–46.

31 Textual evidence to support the view that the *Mote and the Beam* started life as part of a larger book comes in the following passage which Plaatje had left uncorrected: 'Here the reader may justly ask: "Your book claims to be a record of your own personal observations."'

32 'Mr Sol T. Plaatje explains his mission', *Negro World*, 18 June 1921.

33 'With the contributing editor', *Negro World*, 23 April 1921; 'Mr Sol T. Plaatje explains his mission'. For Harrison, see Jeffrey B. Perry, *Hubert Harrison: the voice of Harlem radicalism, 1883–1918* (New York: Columbia University Press, 2009).

34 For the campaign against *Birth of a Nation* in Boston, see 'Report on Equal Rights League meeting', *The Guardian* (Boston), 28 May 1921, quoted in Frederick G. Detweiler, *The Negro Press in the United States* (Chicago: University of Chicago Press, 1922), p. 95; S.T. Plaatje, 'Counteracting negrophilism in SA: race hatred and a film', *DFA*, 10 July 1931; Melvyn Stokes, *D.W. Griffith's 'The Birth of a Nation': a history of 'the most controversial motion picture of all time'* (Oxford: Oxford University Press, 2007), esp. pp. 237–8. For Plaatje's extended engagement with *Birth of a Nation*, see B.P. Willan, '"Cinematographic calamity" or "soul-stirring appeal to every Briton": *Birth of a Nation* in England and South Africa, 1915–1931', *Journal of Southern African Studies*, 39, 3, 2013, pp. 623–40. Plaatje's letter to Du Bois, 22 June 1921, is in NAACP

collection, Series B, Con. 4, 1921, Pan-African Conference file.

35 Advertisements for the new edition of *Native Life* appeared in *The Crisis* in July and August 1921; UM, W.E.B. Du Bois Papers, mums313-b017-i410, Du Bois to S.M. Makgatho, 6 April 1921.

36 NAACP collection, Plaatje to White, 6 July 1921 and White to Plaatje, 12 July 1921.

37 'Bruce Grit's column', *Negro World*, 16 July 1921; see also 'Negroes told to have unity', *Detroit News*, 1 July 1921; *The Crisis*, 22, 4, August 1921, p. 163; NAACP collection, Box C8, General correspondence, Plaatje to J.W. Johnson, 12 September 1921. Years later Plaatje's presence at this conference would be recalled by President Nelson Mandela in a speech to the NAACP in 1993, an early instance of pan-African solidarity, as he saw it, and 'an affirmation of the bonds of solidarity and common purpose that have united our people': *Speech of the President of the African National Congress Nelson Mandela at the Convention of the NAACP, 10 July 1993*, ANC Archives, Office of the ANC President, Nelson Mandela Papers, University of Fort Hare, NMS 1174 (accessed 30 September 2016 at http://db.nelsonmandela.org/speeches/pub_view. asp?pg=item&ItemID=NMS1174&txtstr=plaatje).

38 'Olive Plaatje', by Sarah Talbert Keelan, originally published in *Brownie's Book*, December 1921 (pp. 342–3), reproduced in Dianne Johnson-Feelings (ed.), *The Best of Brownie's Book* (New York: Oxford University Press, 1996), pp. 107–9. Plaatje also described the circumstances of her death in 'South Africa in grip of British Jim Crow rule: editor tells how British kill natives', *Chicago Defender*, 22 October 1921. *Umteteli wa Bantu*, 23 July 1921, and *Ilanga lase Natal*, 29 July 1921, reported her death and funeral.

39 UW, Molema–Plaatje Papers, Aa2.98, D. Goronyane to Chief William Letsapa, 18 July 1921; 'Pan-Africans in congress', *Cape Times*, 21 September 1921.

40 UM, W.E.B. Du Bois Papers, mums312-b018-i292mums312-b017-i410, Plaatje's address to the Pan-African Congress, 1921, esp. pp. 3, 8, 11.

41 'Pan-Africans in congress', *Christian Express*, 1 October 1921.

42 'South African entertained', 'Appomattox Club reception', and 'Grace Lyceum', *Chicago Defender*, 1 October 1921; also 'Savagery kisses civilization on cheek in S. Africa', 'Grace Lyceum audience hears African lecturer', *Chicago Defender*, 8 October 1921; 'Seen and heard in passing', *Plain Dealer* (Cleveland), 25 November 1921; 'Capacity audience hears W.H. Barrett at Lyceum', *Chicago Defender*, 22 October 1921. Like Sarah Talbert Burnett, Mary Waring had attended the conference of the International Council of Women in Norway in November 1920, meeting Plaatje in England en route. Attorney James A. Scott was the assistant state's attorney of Cook County, Illinois, and a popular local figure in Chicago (portrait in *Broad Ax*, 17 December 1921).

43 'Meeting of race leaders', *Washington Bee*, 19 November 1921; 'Conference on fundamentals in Washington', *Chicago Defender*, 3 December 1921; 'Conditions in South Africa described here', *Washington Tribune*, 3 December 1921; Cromwell Papers, Plaatje to J.W. Cromwell, 28 November 1921. Plaatje managed to have his pamphlet *The Black Man's Burden in South Africa* 'circulated among the delegates and international pressmen attending the Arms Conference, January, 1922'.

44 'The native's musical soul', *DFA*, 26 June 1926 and *Cape Argus*, 31 May 1926; *Chicago Defender*, 19 November 1921. Other African performers included Madikane Cele, Kamba Simango and Kathleen Easmon.

45 Plaatje, 'Account of visit', p. 20; 'Academy reads in Columbus' moldy diary', *Chicago Defender*, 7 January 1922.

46 Bruce to Cromwell, 16 March 1921, in Cromwell, *Unveiled Voices, Unvarnished Memories*, p. 278.

47 For Plaatje's movements at this time, see NAACP collection, Box C8, General correspondence (admin.), Plaatje to J.W. Johnson, 12 September 1921; UM, W.E.B. Du

Bois Papers, mums312-b017-i410, Plaatje to Du Bois, 1 February 1922. In Washington DC he addressed the pupils of Dunbar High School (probably arranged with the help of J.W. Cromwell's daughter Otelia, one of the teachers), the Nineteenth Street Baptist Church, Haven M.E. Church and the Armstrong Manual Training School, where he was announced as 'Dr Sol J. Plaatje' (see issues of *Evening Star*, 21 and 29 January, 12 February, 12 March 1921). On J.A. Johnson, see S.T. Plaatje, 'The "New Native" and the new year', *Umteteli*, 12 January 1929; Colenso Papers, Box 57, Plaatje to Mrs S. Colenso, 31 March 1922. Plaatje's letter to Mrs Colenso, 31 March 1922, is in Colenso Papers, Box 57; also, Plaatje, 'Account of visit', p. 292.

48 Fort Hare University, Student Records, St Leger Plaatje file, Principal (Fort Hare), 'To whom it may concern', 20 October 1926; St Leger signified his intention to do medicine in his application form (date-stamped 23 February 1920); KAB, 3/CT, 4/1/5/1241, N7/5, St Leger Plaatje to Town Clerk, Cape Town, 2 May 1927.

49 Plaatje, 'Account of North American tour', p. 299.

50 UM, W.E.B. Du Bois Papers, mums312-b017-i410, Plaatje to Du Bois, 1 February 1922.

51 S.T. Plaatje, 'The late Florence Mills', *DFA*, 14 November 1927; for Florence Mills and *Shuffle Along*, see particularly Bill Egan, *Florence Mills: Harlem jazz queen* (Lanham, MD: Scarecrow Press, 2004). Many years later Michael van Reenen, Plaatje's next-door neighbour in Kimberley, recalled that Plaatje told him he had also met Paul Robeson, another star of *Shuffle Along* (interviews with Michael van Reenen, Mitcham, 26 September 1976 and 29 March 1977). Plaatje's comments are from 'The native's musical soul: appreciation in America', *DFA*, 26 June 1926, and 'The law, the land and the native: South African questions and conditions', *South Africa*, 26 October 1923.

52 See especially A. Locke (ed.), *The New Negro* (New York: Albert and Charles Boni, 1925). Bruce's letter to Cromwell (16 March 1921) is from Cromwell, *Unveiled Voices, Unvarnished Memories*, pp. 278–80. McKay joined the staff of the radical *Liberator* magazine in March 1921, remaining in New York until his departure for the Soviet Union in September 1922: Wayne F. Cooper, *Claude McKay: rebel sojourner in the Harlem Renaissance* (Baton Rouge: Louisiana State University Press, 1987), pp. 134–70.

53 UM, W.E.B. Du Bois Papers, mums312-b017-i410, Plaatje to Du Bois, 1 February 1922.

54 UM, W.E.B. Du Bois Papers, mums312-b020-i103, Du Bois to Plaatje, 20 February 1922; Schomburg Center for Research in Black Culture, New York Public Library, William Pickens Papers, Box 1, File 8, James S. Stemons to William Pickens, 4 July 1916.

55 'Boston division celebrates Easter: Solomon Plaatje among speakers who praise UNIA', *Negro World*, 29 April 1922; Plaatje, 'Account of visit', p. 22; S.T. Plaatje, 'Departed friends of the natives', *Umteteli*, 17 September 1927.

56 'Sol Plaatje to lecture at YMCA', *Washington Tribune*, 22 April 1922; 'YMCA', *Washington Tribune*, 6 May 1922; 'Race Congress closes seventh convention here', *Washington Tribune*, 6 May 1922; 'Speakers discuss Negro's problems', *Evening Star*, 4 May 1922; 'African editor exposes Jim Crow laws', *Chicago Defender*, 3 June 1922; Hampton University, Virginia, Archives, Hampton Institute visitors' book, entry for 10 May 1922; 'Foreign visitors', *Southern Workman*, 51, 7, July 1922, p. 344; UM, W.E.B. Du Bois Papers, mums312-b020-i104, Plaatje to Jessie Fauset, 16 May 1922. Plaatje's address to the National Races Congress, *The Black Man's Burden in South Africa*, printed and published by the Hunt Printing Company in New York (1922), was a slightly revised version of his address to the Pan-African Congress in 1921.

57 Tuskegee University, Archives Repository, Papers of Robert R. Moton, GC 109/810, Plaatje to Moton, 18 June 1925; Plaatje, 'Account of visit', p. 19.

58 Hampton University, Archives, Gregg Papers, Moton to James E. Gregg, 29 December 1924 (I am most grateful to Professor Robert Edgar for providing me with a copy of this letter).

59 Moton Papers, GC 83, Plaatje to Holsey, 20 May 1922 and Holsey to Plaatje, 27 May

1922. The copy of *Native Life in South Africa* which Plaatje left with Moton carried the inscription: 'Dr R.R. Moton, with the author's compliments and pleasant recollections of my visit to Tuskegee, May 1922' (copy in Hollis Burke Frissell Library, Tuskegee University).

60 Moton Papers, GC 83, Plaatje to Holsey, 26 May 1922; Molteno Family Papers, A81.2.2, Plaatje to Miss Molteno, 8 November 1922; Moton Papers, GC 109/810, Plaatje to Moton, 22 September 1924 and Gregg Papers, Moton to Dr James E. Gregg (Hampton), 29 December 1924. For the *Hampton Epilogue*, see Stokes, *D.W. Griffith's 'The Birth of a Nation'*, p. 225 and Nickie Fleener, 'Answering film with film: the *Hampton Epilogue*, a positive alternative to negative black stereotypes presented in *The Birth of a Nation*', *Journal of Popular Film and Television*, 4, 1980, pp. 400–25.

61 'Mrs Ida B. Wells Barnett', *Washington Bee*, 28 May 1921; 'South African visitor', *Chicago Defender*, 17 June 1922; Moton Papers, GC 83, Plaatje to Holsey, 26 May 1922; 'African to speak', *Chicago Defender*, 24 June 1922; 'To help Africans', *Chicago Defender*, 15 July 1922; 'Africans on the program', *Chicago Defender*, 22 July 1922. On Xuma, see Richard D. Ralston, 'American episodes in the making of an African leader: a case study of Alfred B. Xuma (1893–1962)', *International Journal of African Historical Studies*, 6, 1, 1973, pp. 84–5, and Steven D. Gish, *Alfred B. Xuma: African, American, South African* (New York: New York University Press, 2000), esp. ch. 2, pp. 26–52.

62 For the decline of the Brotherhood Federation, see Allen, *The Social Passion*, pp. 237–8; Plaatje mentioned the assurances he had had from Toronto's black citizens in 'South Africa in grip of British Jim Crow rule', *Chicago Defender*, 22 October 1921.

63 UW, A.B. Xuma Papers, Plaatje to A.B. Xuma, 19 July 1923.

64 SOAS, Plaatje Papers, STP 3/4, passport; 'Shakespeare in Sechuana', *The Star* (Johannesburg), 26 July 1930; Allen, *The Social Passion*, ch. 14; UW, Xuma Papers, Plaatje to Xuma, 19 July 1923; Moton Papers, GC 83, Plaatje to Holsey, 20 Sept 1922.

65 Bruce to Cromwell, 16 March 1921, in Cromwell, *Unveiled Voices, Unvarnished Memories*, p. 279.

66 *Mhudi*, preface; UW, Rheinallt Jones Papers, AD 843/B, 53.1, copy (in Mrs Unwin's hand) of extract from letter from Plaatje to Mrs Unwin, undated [1921]; 'Native's view of Brotherhood', *Portsmouth Times and Hampshire Telegraph*, 16 March 1923.

67 'The law, the land, and the native', *South Africa*, 25 October 1923; see also, S.T. Plaatje, 'South Africans as others see them', *Umteteli*, 28 September 1929.

Chapter 14

1 Tuskegee University, Archives Repository, Moton Papers, GC 83, Plaatje to the Secretary, Tuskegee Institute, 20 September 1922.

2 UCT, Molteno Murray Family Papers, Box 50, A81.1.2, Plaatje to Miss Molteno, n.d. [November 1922].

3 Molteno Murray Family Papers, Box 53, Smuts to Mrs Murray, 31 August 1923. There is no trace of Margaret Murray's letter in the Smuts Papers.

4 'South African brother', *Norbury and Thornton Heath News*, 6 July 1923, p. 7.

5 Molteno Murray Family Papers, Box 50, A81.2.2, Plaatje to Miss Molteno, 8 November 1922.

6 Moton Papers, GC 93, Plaatje to the Secretary, Tuskegee Institute, 13 March 1923.

7 NAD, Colenso Papers, Box 11, Plaatje to Mrs Colenso, 20 November 1922. From Harris's letter to Plaatje on 9 November (AS/APS, S19 D3/13) it is clear that Plaatje had initiated the contact between them.

8 AS/APS, S19 D3/31, Harris to G. Gale, 25 October 1922; S19 D3/30, Harris to Mr and Miss Barlow, 16 November 1922; 'West Africa and the elections', *West Africa*, 18 November 1922; Colenso Papers, Box 11, Plaatje to Mrs Colenso, 20 November 1922.

9 Colenso Papers, Box 11, Plaatje to Mrs Colenso, 20 November 1922.

10 'Thinkers and thinking', *Leighton Buzzard Observer*, 17 October 1922 and 'LMM slate club', *Leighton Buzzard Observer*, 19 December 1922; Molteno Murray Family Papers, Box 50, SP1.2, Plaatje to Miss Molteno, 27 February 1922.

11 Colenso Papers, Box 63, Alice Werner to Harriette Colenso, 30 November 1922; S.T. Plaatje, *Dintshontsho tsa bo-Juliuse Kesara* (Johannesburg: University of the Witwatersrand Press, 1937), preface by G.K. Lestrade; 'Phonetic puzzles: harmless words that have two meanings', *Daily Mail*, 14 February 1922 (in UCL, Jones Papers, G1.2, press cuttings).

12 Hilda Kuper, *Sobhuza II: Ngwenyamu and King of Swaziland* (London: Duckworth, 1978), pp. 82–4; J.S.M. Matsebula, *A History of Swaziland* (Cape Town: Longman, 1976), pp. 140 and 168; 'Swazi chiefs in London', *South Africa*, 12 January 1923; 'Swazi chiefs and the king', *South Africa*, 2 February 1923; 'Swazi chiefs leave', *South Africa*, 9 February 1923; 'Swazi chiefs' visit', *African World*, 13 January 1923; 'Swazi ruler and chiefs say "au revoir"', *African World*, 3 February 1923.

13 'Pathé Gazette: Swazi chiefs arrive: Sobhuza II, Paramount Chief of Swaziland – here to confer with Colonial Office', issued 11 January 1923: http://www.britishpathe.com/video/swazi-chiefs-arrive/query/sobhuza, accessed 24 March 2013; 'The Swazi king and West African students', *West Africa*, 20 January 1923; Colenso Papers, Box 14, Alice Werner to Agnes Colenso, 21 February 1923; Colenso Papers, Box 57, Mrs Sophie Colenso to Harriette Colenso, 1 February 1923.

14 Kuper, *Sobhuza II*, p. 84; personal communication from Mr J.S.M. Matsebula, 1 June 1981, reporting conversation with King Sobhuza II.

15 *Brotherhood Outlook*, January 1923, advertising Plaatje's availability as a speaker; Molteno Murray Family Papers, Box 50, A81.2.5, Plaatje to Miss Molteno, 12 December 1922 and SP/1.2, Plaatje to Miss Molteno, 27 February 1923.

16 Molteno Murray Family Papers, Box 50, SP/3, E.M. Molteno to Plaatje, 26 February 1923.

17 Molteno Murray Family Papers, Box 9, 'Plaatje', 25 May 1923. An earlier poem, entitled 'My Bechuanaland friend', and dated 23 April 1923, was also inspired by a visit from Plaatje and their thoughts about the birth of Iona Murray, Margaret Murray's first child, in October 1922. Final quote is from Molteno Murray Family Papers, Box 10, 'What is coming this morning?', 23 August 1923. I am indebted to Catherine Corder for information on the readership of Betty Molteno's verse, and to Robert Molteno for ascertaining Iona's date of birth.

18 Betty Molteno, 'Plaatje', second verse. The remainder of the paragraph draws upon Molteno Murray Family Papers, Box 2, private journal, 28 September 1923, with the exception of her description of Plaatje as 'a child of nature', which is from her undated private musings in Box 9.

19 Molteno Murray Family Papers, Box 2, private journal, 28 September 1923, p. 1.

20 Moton Papers, GC 93, Plaatje to Holsey, 13 March 1923.

21 The evening paper concerned was the *Pall Mall Gazette*, which featured a lengthy exchange of correspondence between Charlotte Mansfield and A.J. Enstone, to which others also contributed, between 26 February and 23 March 1923. The day before Plaatje wrote to Holsey, Mr Enstone had seemingly answered Charlotte Mansfield's challenge to provide details of the employment by the French of black troops in the Ruhr ('Black troops challenge', *Pall Mall Gazette*, 12 March 1923, p. 7). Plaatje's hand, however, is evident in her response on 16 March, challenging Mr Enstone's claims that the black troops '"had authority" to suppress and humiliate' the civilian population in the Rhineland, and supplying other evidence from official British and American sources which discounted the exaggerated and distorted claims being made. For background, see particularly Robert C. Reinders, 'Racialism on the left: E.D. Morel and the "Black Horror on the Rhine"', *International Review of Social History*, 13, 1, April 1968, pp.

1–28.

22 University of Reading, Records of George Allen and Unwin Ltd, MS 3282, Register of Manuscripts, p. 115, entry for 2 August 1922. The title of the book was given simply as *Mhudi*, and Plaatje's address as 69 Shakespeare Road, Hanwell. Philip Unwin, *The Publishing Unwins* (London: Heinemann, 1972), p. 73, describes Miall as 'a scholarly recluse who lived on the edge of Exmoor', who was 'the translator of a vast number of books from German and French and was possessed of the most astonishing range of general knowledge'. Colenso Papers, Box 11, Plaatje to Mrs Colenso, 24 May 1923 and Molteno Murray Family Papers, Box 50, A81.2.9, Plaatje to Mrs Solomon, 2 August 1923.

23 Colenso Papers, Box 11, Plaatje to Mrs Colenso, 24 May 1923 and Molteno Murray Family Papers, Box 50, A81.2.9, Plaatje to Mrs Solomon, 2 August 1923.

24 Colenso Papers, Box 11, Plaatje to Sophie Colenso, 24 May 1923.

25 Molteno Murray Family Papers, Box 50, SP1.3, Plaatje to Miss Molteno, 26 June 1923; 'A Zulu speaker', *Leighton Buzzard Observer*, 24 July 1923, p. 5; see also 'South African brother', *Norbury and Thornton Heath News*, 6 July 1923, p. 7, where he appealed for funds for his *Fellowship Hymnbook* translation.

26 For the convoluted history of the Southern Syncopated Orchestra and its offshoots, see Catherine Parsonage, *The Evolution of Jazz in Britain, 1880–1935* (London: Ashgate, 2005), esp. pp. 143–62 and Howard Rye, 'Chronology of the Southern Syncopated Orchestra: 1919–1922', in *Black Music Research Journal*, 30, 1, 2010, pp. 5–17.

27 Prince William of Sweden, *Among Pygmies and Gorillas: with the Swedish zoological expedition to Central Africa 1921* (London: Gyldendal, 1923). The Swedish version of the film, 'Med Prins Wilhelm pa afrikanska jakstigar', was first shown in Stockholm in March 1922 (see the Swedish Film Database, http://www.sfi.se/en-GB/Swedish-film-database/, accessed 29 January 2017). The English-language version of the film has not survived but the original Swedish version has been preserved in the archives of Sveriges *Television* (SVT) in Stockholm. Lattimore outlined his plans for the film in a letter to W.E.B. Du Bois (UM, W.E.B. Du Bois Papers, mums312-b021-i417) on 13 August 1923, claiming it was now 'unanimously acclaimed the finest travel film ever exhibited in London'; he expressed his hope of taking the film to New York 'very shortly' in a second letter to Du Bois on 21 August (mums312-b021-i418).

28 Molteno Murray Family Papers, Box 50, SP/1.4, Plaatje to Miss Molteno, 21 July 1923; UM, W.E.B. Du Bois Papers, mums312-b021-i417, Lattimore to Du Bois, 13 August 1923. For Kamba and Kathleen Simango, see Leon P. Spencer, *Toward an African Church in Mozambique: Kamba Simango and the Protestant community in Manica and Sofala, 1992–1945* (Luwinga, Malawi: Mzuni Press, 2013) and 'Miss Easmon's wedding', *West Africa*, 29 July 1922. Names of others involved in Plaatje's sketch are taken from 'A new film of African life', *West Africa*, 18 August 1923 and 'Adventures of a hunter-prince', *Daily Express*, 9 August 1923, p. 7.

29 Molteno Murray Family Papers, Box 50, A81.2.9, Plaatje to Mrs Solomon, 2 August 1923.

30 Molteno Murray Family Papers, Box 50, A98.6, Mrs G.M. Solomon to Miss Colenso, 1 August 1923.

31 Molteno Murray Family Papers, Box 50, A81.1.10, Plaatje to Mrs Solomon, 8 August 1923 (copy for Miss Molteno); 'Marvellous wild animal film', *Daily Express*, 9 August 1923, p. 2; '"The Cradle of the World": an educative animal film', *Pall Mall Gazette*, 10 August 1923, p. 5; 'In wildest Africa', *Westminster Gazette*, 9 August 1923, p. 9; 'Film of the week', *The Times*, 13 August 1923. The story of the rhinoceros charge is related in 'The pygmy forest', *Morning Bulletin* (Rockhampton, Queensland), 21 February 1924.

32 *Reynolds's News*, 12 August 1923, p. 13, thought the 'playlet' 'unusual and interesting'; 'In darkest Africa: the newest big game picture', *Kinematograph Weekly*, 16 August 1923,

p. 62; 'Marvellous wild animal film', *Daily Express*, 9 August 1923; 'Central Africa: native tribes and wild animals', *Morning Post*, 9 August 1923, p. 9 (which referred to the boat song as 'the boat song of the Nile'); 'The Cradle of the World', *South Africa*, 24 August 1923.

33 'A great African film', *African World*, 25 August 1923, also 'A new film of African life', *West Africa*, 18 August 1923; 'Union of Students of African Descent', *West Africa*, 28 October 1922.

34 'Sobhuza II of Swaziland: the paramount chief in England', *South Africa*, 12 January 1923, p. 65.

35 Molteno Murray Family Papers, Box 10, 'What is coming this morning?', 23 August 1923, p. 3.

36 Molteno Murray Family Papers, Box 50, SP/1.5, Plaatje to Miss Molteno, 21 September 1923, enclosing copy of letter to Miss Molteno (n.d.).

37 'The law, the land and the native', *South Africa*, 26 October 1923.

38 'The natives' musical soul', *Diamond Fields Advertiser* (*DFA*), 26 June 1926 and *Cape Argus*, 31 May 1926.

39 'Brotherhood mission', *African World*, 25 August 1923; 'For a good cause', *West Africa*, 25 August 1923; 'Fellowship Hymnbook: need for translation into Bantu', *Brotherhood Outlook*, August 1923; 'The late Florence Mills', *DFA*, 14 November 1927. See also Bill Egan, *Florence Mills: jazz queen* (Lanham, MD: Scarecrow Press, 2004), pp. 94 and 97–8. Betty Molteno's observations are from Molteno Murray Family Papers, Box 10, 'Shoes off the feet', pp. 2–3.

40 Molteno Murray Family Papers, Box 50, A81.2.11, Plaatje to Miss Solomon (copy), c. 8 October 1923; see also Box 50, SP/1.5, Plaatje to Miss Molteno, 21 September 1923.

41 Molteno Murray Family Papers, Box 50, A81.1.11, Plaatje to Mrs Solomon, n.d. [c. 4 October 1923]; CAD, NTS 619/17/1131 (file on S.T. Plaatje), Programme of Farewell Concert, 9 October 1923. For further detail on participants at the concert, see Jeffrey P. Green, 'The Negro Renaissance and England', in Samuel A. Floyd, Jr (ed.), *Black Music in the Harlem Renaissance: a collection of essays* (New York: Greenwood Press, 1990), p. 159.

42 'Mr Sol Plaatje', *South Africa*, 12 October 1923; in fact two of these supposed 'October babies' (Rhodes and Milner) were born not in October but July (1853) and March (1854) respectively. Colenso Papers, Box 57, Mrs G.M. Solomon to Mrs Colenso, 11 October 1923; Programme of Farewell Concert.

43 Molteno Murray Family Papers, Box 7, Betty Molteno's journal, 9 October 1923.

44 For Jones's earlier recordings, see Beverley Collins and Inger Mees, *The Real Professor Higgins: the life and career of Daniel Jones* (Berlin: Mouton de Gruyter, 1999), p. 527. On the journey to Hayes, Jones reclaimed 7/9d 'Expenses for going to Hayes with Mr Plaatje to make gramophone record for Sechuana language' (UCL, Special Collections, Jones Papers, B3, petty cash book, 1923). I am indebted to Beverley Collins for his suggestion that Jones's pronunciation may have been influenced by his knowledge of Dutch rather than Afrikaans (personal communication, 9 October 2013).

45 For the background, see: http://www.ucl.ac.uk/news/news-articles/0805/08052102, assessed 20 March 2013. The only surviving copy of Plaatje's private recording of the two tales from the *Sechuana Reader* is now in the British Library National Sound Archive.

46 For the early history of Zonophone in South Africa, see John Cowley, 'UBungca (Oxford bags): recordings in London of African and West Indian music in the 1920s and 1930s', *Musical Traditions*, 12, summer 1994, available at http://www.mustrad.org.uk/articles/ubunca.htm, accessed 19 February 2012; for an account of the origins and subsequent history of the song, see David B. Coplan, *In Township Tonight! South Africa's black city music and theatre*, 2nd edn (Chicago: University of Chicago Press, 2008), pp. 56–61 and Siemon Allen, 'The South African national anthem: a history on record' at http://flatint.

blogspot.com/2013/10/the-south-african-national-anthem, accessed 23 October 2013. I am indebted to the late Dr Alan Kelly for making available to me his full transcription of information from the Hayes studio's recording register (personal communication, 11 October 2013), and to Siemon Allen for his suggestion about the lack of space on the label (personal communication, 8 October 2013).

47 See Janet Topp Fargeon, 'Sol T. Plaatje: the hidden recording', *Playback: The Bulletin of the National Sound Archive*, 12, autumn 1995, pp. 2–4.

48 S.T. Plaatje, 'The native's musical soul: appreciation in America', *The Star* (Johannesburg), 5 June 1926; 'The Cradle of the World', *South Africa*, 24 August 1923.

49 Molteno Murray Family Papers, Box 7, Betty Molteno's journal entries, 19 and 21 October 1923.

50 Molteno Murray Family Papers, Box 7, 'Good bye, Plaatje', 11 October 1923.

51 Molteno Murray Family Papers, Box 7, Betty Molteno's journal, 19 October 1923; Colenso Papers, Box 11, Mrs G.M. Solomon to Mrs S. Colenso, n.d. [c. December 1923].

52 Colenso Papers, Box 57, Sophie Colenso to Harriette and Agnes Colenso, 1 November 1923; CAD, J 269, 3/1064/18, telegram from South African High Commission, London, to Ministry of Justice, Pretoria; *Cape Times*, 13 November 1923, published a full list of passengers disembarking from the *Windsor Castle* at Cape Town.

53 'The law, the land, and the native', and 'Here and there', *South Africa*, 26 October 1923.

Chapter 15

1 UCT, Molteno Murray Family Papers, Box 50, SP/1.7, Plaatje to Mrs Solomon, 21 December 1923; 'Sol Plaatje returns', *APO*, 1 December 1923 (cutting in CAD, NTS 619/17/1131). The provincial elections were widely regarded as a rehearsal for the general election which had to take place by the end of 1925 (see 'Vote!', *Cape Times*, 14 November 1923).

2 SOAS, Plaatje Papers, MS 375495, Isaiah Bud-M'belle, 'Solomon Tshekisho Plaatje', p. 5.

3 Molteno Murray Family Papers, Box 50, SP/1.7, Plaatje to Mrs Solomon, 21 December 1923; for the loss of his Shannon Street home, see De Beers Archives (DB), General Secretary's correspondence, W.T. McLeod to De Beers, 31 August 1929.

4 DB, General Secretary's correspondence, General Secretary to Hon. Treasurer, Kimberley Native Institute, 8 June 1923; Hon. Treasurer, Kimberley Native Institute, to Secretary, De Beers, 15 June 1923; James A. Swan to Secretary, De Beers, 16 March 1932.

5 DB, General Secretary's correspondence, Plaatje to General Manager, De Beers, 15 March 1932.

6 For reports of these meetings, see 'The colour bar: native leader describes his overseas tour', *The Star*, 13 December 1923, and further reports in issues of 18 December and 1 January 1924; 'Native Brotherhood', *Umteteli*, 22 December 1923' 'Native Brotherhood: Sol Plaatje's address', *Daily Dispatch* (East London), 19 December 1923; *International*, 21 December 1923. The comment from the Methodist clergyman (G. Bottrill, Superintendent, Witwatersrand mission) is from SOAS, Methodist Missionary Society Archives (MMS), Transvaal correspondence 1921–4, Box 842, fiche 1201, 'Statement re Social Institute, Johannesburg', enclosure in J.W. Alcock to Amos Burnet, 8 January 1924. For the 'benevolent empire' of missionaries committed to the social gospel, see particularly Richard Elphick, *The Equality of Believers: Protestant missionaries and the racial politics of South Africa* (Charlottesville, VA: University of Virginia Press, 2012).

7 R.V. Selope Thema, 'The principle of consultation', *Umteteli wa Bantu*, 21 March 1925, p. 4; for Plaatje's view, see 'Nationalists and the natives: a scathing indictment', *Cape Argus*, 29 April 1924.

8   S.T. Plaatje, 'Native affairs after four years', *Diamond Fields Advertiser* (*DFA*), 19 January 1924.
9   Plaatje, 'Native affairs after four years', *DFA*, 22 January 1924.
10 Plaatje, 'Native affairs after four years', *DFA*, 22 January 1924. The SANNC resolved to change its name at its annual conference in May 1923.
11 Molteno Murray Family Papers, Box 50, SP/1.9, Plaatje to Miss Molteno, 1 February 1924; 'U S.T. Plaatje e Qonce', *Imvo Zabantsundu*, 28 October 1924. Plaatje's recollection of the live BBC radio broadcast in London (2 October 1923) is from S.T. Plaatje, 'Lord Milner and the natives', *DFA*, 23 May 1925.
12 S.T. Plaatje, 'The case for the Barolongs', *Cape Argus*, 4 March 1924; 'Native taxation: a reply to Dr Visser', letter from Plaatje to the editor, *The Star* (Johannesburg), 11 March 1924; 'Natives and taxation', *Imvo*, 1 April 1924; Plaatje, 'Nationalists and natives: a scathing indictment', *Cape Argus*, 29 April 1924.
13 CAD, NTS 619/17/1131 (Plaatje file), Secretary for Native Affairs to S.T. Plaatje, 2 April 1924.
14 Molteno Murray Family Papers, Box 50, SP/1.3, Plaatje to Betty Molteno, 29 June 1923.
15 University of Cambridge, Smuts Papers (microfilm), vol. 33, no. 43, Plaatje to Smuts, 19 January 1925.
16 Plaatje, 'Nationalists and the natives: a scathing indictment', *Cape Argus*, 19 April 1924, was printed and published separately as a leaflet by the South African Party (copy in National Library of South Africa, Cape Town); S.T. Plaatje, 'Natives and the election: why they should vote SAP', *DFA*, 16 June 1924.
17 S.T. Plaatje, 'Congress and the Pact', *Umteteli*, 14 June 1924.
18 Plaatje's recollections of 'courtesies during foggy nights in London' is from his inscription in the copy of *Mhudi* which he presented to Sir Ernest in 1930 (original in Brenthurst Library, Johannesburg).
19 'The native vote: strong support for Sir E. Oppenheimer', *DFA*, 7 June 1924.
20 S.T. Plaatje, 'Natives and elections: the piper and the tune', *DFA*, 27 June 1924.
21 Smuts Papers, vol. 33, no. 43, Plaatje to Smuts, 19 January 1925.
22 S.M. Molema, *Lover of His People* (Johannesburg: Wits University Press, 2012), p. 11; interview with Michael van Reenen, Mitcham, 6 September 1976.
23 KAB, Papers of the Town Clerk, East London, 3/ELN2: file 80, leaflet advertising Plaatje's bioscope in Bloemfontein (26, 27, 29 September 1924), enclosure in Plaatje to Town Clerk, East London, 9 October 1924.
24 'Natives at the films: leper asylum entertainment', *Pretoria News*, 1 September 1924, p. 3.
25 'Mr Sol T. Plaatje's bioscope', *Umteteli*, 31 May 1924; DB, General Secretary's correspondence, Plaatje to A.S. Williams (General Manager), 30 May 1925; Africana Library, Kimberley, Kimberley Municipal Records, Town Clerk's files, Plaatje to Kimberley Town Council, 7 March 1930; S.T. Plaatje, 'Natives in the capital: five years' progress', *Pretoria News*, 4 September 1924.
26 For Ray Phillips and his initiatives with the medium of film, see Ray E. Phillips, *The Bantu Are Coming: phases of South Africa's race problem* (London: Student Christian Movement Press, 1930) and Tim Couzens, '"Moralizing leisure time": the transatlantic connection and black Johannesburg, 1918–1936', in Shula Marks and Richard Rathbone (eds.), *Industrialisation and Social Change: African class formation, culture and consciousness 1870–1930* (Harlow: Longman, 1982), pp. 314–37. Plaatje's complaint about his difficulties is from his letter to Robert Moton, 18 June 1925 (Tuskegee University, Archival Repository, Moton Papers, GC 109/810).
27 Interviews with Mr Simon Lekhela (London, October 1978), Professor E.P. Lekhela (Mmabatho, July 1983, with Susan Newton-King), and Mr G. Hermans (New Brighton,

Port Elizabeth), 30 June 1976.

28 Moton Papers, GC 109/810, Plaatje to Moton, 22 September 1924.

29 For the activities and influence of missionaries in towns and on the mines, see particularly Elphick, *The Equality of Believers*, esp. pp. 132–48.

30 Moton Papers, GC 109/810, Plaatje to Moton, 22 September 1924.

31 CAD, Hertzog Papers, A 32, Box 35, Plaatje to Hertzog, 7 October 1924.

32 For Plaatje's memory of the incident in the 1890s, see p. 222.

33 Smuts Papers, vol. 33, no. 42, Plaatje to Smuts, 19 January 1925.

34 'Johannesburg conference on native affairs', *South African Outlook*, 1 December 1924, p. 273.

35 UW, Records of the Joint Councils of Europeans and Africans, AD 1433, Ac.3.3.13, address by S.T. Plaatje to the 1924 Joint Councils Conference on 'The treatment of natives in the courts'.

36 'The treatment of natives in court'; see also, for Plaatje's memories of this conference, 'Natives and the election', letter from Plaatje to the editor, *DFA*, 22 May 1930.

37 'Colour bill protest', *Cape Argus*, 7 May 1926; 'The colour bar: a final protest', *Cape Times*, 10 May 1926; UW, Records of the Joint Councils of Europeans and Africans, Cj2.1.6a, Plaatje to Rheinallt Jones, 23 April and 3 May 1926.

38 C.M. Tatz, *Shadow and Substance in South Africa* (Pietermaritzburg: University of Natal Press, 1962), pp. 49–52; 'Native policy of the Union', *DFA*, 4 December 1925; 'Native leaders' views', *Cape Times*, 4 December 1925; 'Division and removal of tribes', *Cape Times*, 5 December 1925.

39 For the Native Administration Act, see especially Marian Lacey, *Working for Boroko* (Johannesburg: Ravan Press, 1981), pp. 94–119 and Martin Chanock, *The Making of South African Legal Culture 1902–1936: fear, favour and prejudice* (Cambridge: Cambridge University Press, 2001), pp. 288–90.

40 For example, 'Recent Native Conference', *DFA*, 15 December 1925; 'Why segregation will not work', *Cape Times*, 21 April 1926.

41 Molema, *Lover of His People*, p. 75; UG17-1927, *Report of the Native Affairs Commission for the Years 1925 and 1926*, Annexure II, Minutes of Conference held in Pretoria, 3, 4 and 5 December 1925, pp. 13–42. Dr Molema attended the Native Conferences in 1925 and 1930, but not in 1926. The minutes recorded Plaatje's use of the term 'splinternuwe Duusman' on p. 36.

42 'Native Conference on premier's bills', *Cape Times*, 3 November 1926.

43 D.D.T. Jabavu, 'The government Native Conference', *Cape Times*, 19 November 1926; 'Native Conference on Hertzog's proposals', *Cape Times*, 4 November 1926; 'Scorpions for bread', *Pretoria News*, 4 November 1926.

44 S.T. Plaatje, 'The natives and the premier's bills', *DFA*, 19 November 1926; D.D.T. Jabavu, 'Native voting rights', *Imvo*, 6 May 1930, quoting Plaatje's words

45 'The Plaatje bioscope', *Umteteli*, 5 December 1925; DB, General Secretary's correspondence, Plaatje to Alpheus Williams, 30 May 1925; Moton Papers, GC 109/810, Plaatje to Moton, 18 June 1925.

46 S.T. Plaatje, 'Colour questions', *DFA*, 23 April 1925; 'Native Conference on premier's bills', *Cape Times*, 3 November 1926. Roos did respond to the detailed instances of injustice which Plaatje submitted to him but in a way, Plaatje thought, which 'ignores both the spirit of the complaint and the indifference of jurymen to native feeling outraged by their treatment of the social pest' (S.T. Plaatje, 'Natives and rural juries', *DFA*, 24 February 1927).

47 UW, Records of the Joint Councils of Europeans and Africans, Ac3.3.13, address by S.T. Plaatje to 1924 Joint Councils Conference; S.T. Plaatje, 'Light and shade on native questions', *Umteteli*, 11 October 1924.

48 'The colour bar bill', *DFA*, 11 April 1925; 'The native bills', *DFA*, 22 March 1927;

'Through native eyes', *Cape Argus*, 30 June 1926.

49 S.T. Plaatje, 'Should Nyandjas be deported?', *Umteteli*, 3 March 1928; S.T. Plaatje, 'Natives and the mission', *DFA*, 20 June 1925.

50 *Cape Times*, 7 and 9 May 1927; *Cape Argus*, 10 May 1927; *Daily Dispatch*, 7 and 10 May 1927; *DFA*, 11 May 1927; S.T. Plaatje, 'In Bechuanaland today: some recent travel notes', *DFA*, 17 April 1928 and S.T. Plaatje, 'In Bechuanaland today', *DFA*, 1 May 1928; S.T. Plaatje, 'Native institutions revisited', *DFA*, 11 and 29 September 1928.

51 S.T. Plaatje, 'Natives and Mr Merriman: an appreciation', *DFA*, 10 August 1926; S.T. Plaatje, 'Friends and helpers of natives: a tribute to Mr J.W. Jagger and Mr Weinthal', *Cape Times*, 3 July 1930; S.T. Plaatje, 'A friend of the natives: the late Sir William Solomon', *Pretoria News*, 21 June 1930. See also 'Lord Milner and the natives', *DFA*, 23 May 1925; 'Friends of the natives', *DFA*, 15 June 1925; 'Departed friends of the natives', *Cape Argus*, 30 August 1927.

52 S.T. Plaatje, 'Departed friends of the natives', *Umteteli*, 17 September 1927; S.T. Plaatje, 'The late chief J.M. Nyokong', *Umteteli*, 6 September 1930; S.T. Plaatje, 'Passing of great chiefs: Gaberone and Makhaola', *Umteteli*, 16 January 1932.

53 S.T Plaatje, 'The late Chief Silas Molema: passing of a progressive Barolong chief', *Cape Times*, 13 September 1927.

54 Plaatje to Modiri Molema, 10 September 1927 (original framed letter in Mafikeng Museum); the biblical passage is from Revelations 14:13.

55 University of the Witwatersrand, Historical Papers (UW), SAIRR Papers, AD 1438, B4.1, typescript of evidence to Native Economic Commission, p. 5292.

56 S.T. Plaatje, 'Self-help'; *Umteteli*, 28 February 1928.

57 Molema, *Lover of His People*, pp. 75–6.

58 For example, in S.T. Plaatje, '"The good times" and the "New Native"', *Umteteli*, 9 November 1929.

59 S.T. Plaatje, 'Leadership', *Umteteli*, 18 February 1928.

60 'The native vote and other matters', letter from Plaatje to the editor, *Umteteli*, 27 October 1928.

61 For example, S.T. Plaatje, 'The leadership cult from another angle', *Umteteli*, 14 March 1925; 'The race problem', letter to the editor from 'Enquirer', *Umteteli*, 4 May 1929; S.T. Plaatje, 'Statesmen and the natives', *Umteteli*, 11 May 1929; 'The vote', letter to the editor from 'Enquirer', *Umteteli*, 3 November 1928; 'The native franchise', letter to the editor from 'Enquirer', *Umteteli*, 20 October 1928; 'Resurgam', 'Bantu politics', *Umteteli*, 31 March 1928.

62 D.D.T. Jabavu, among others, was in no doubt about the harmful effects of alcoholism upon his people: 'It is no exaggeration to say that most of the best educated Bantu leaders, past and present, have been lost to Africa through drink' (quoted by William Hay in his letter to the editor, *Umteteli*, 19 May 1928). Professor W.M. Macmillan, a member of the Johannesburg Joint Council, likewise noted that Selope Thema was driven to 'hopeless drinking' and that African 'organisations and their leaders are in chaos': quoted in Alan Cobley (ed.), *From Cattle-Herding to Editor's Chair: the unfinished autobiography and writings of Richard Victor Selope Thema* (Cape Town: Van Riebeeck Society, 2016), p. xxx.

63 Moton Papers, GC 128/965, Plaatje to Moton, 29 June 1927; *Synopsis of Proceedings of the Thirteenth Session of the Right Worthy True Temple of the Independent Order of True Templars, held at Vrededorp, Johannesburg, 6–8 January 1931*, pp. 10–12 and xii; S.T. Plaatje, 'South Africans at the Ottowa conference', *Umteteli*, 23 April 1932; Editorial, *Our Heritage*, 1, 1, June 1931. Plaatje's salary was paid for with funds from a Schreiner Memorial Trust to which Mushet had access. Isaiah Bud-M'belle called Mushet a 'great friend' of Plaatje's.

64 *Synopsis of Proceedings*, p. 20.

65 Library of Parliament, Cape Town, Manuscript Annexures, Plaatje to Clerk of the House

of Assembly, 6 May 1927 and *Report of the Select Committee on the Native Administration Bill*, May 1927, SC11-1927, p. xxiv. For the best modern treatment of the Native Administration Act, see Saul Dubow, *Racial Segregation and the Origins of Apartheid in South Africa 1919–1936* (Basingstoke: Macmillan, 1989), pp. 87–93.

66 *Minutes of the First Non-European Conference Held in the City Hall, Kimberley, 23rd, 24th and 25th June 1927*, p. 32.

67 *Minutes of the First Non-European Conference*, p. 52; Moton Papers, GC 128/965, Plaatje to Moton, 29 June 1927.

68 KAB, 3/CT, 4/1/5/1241, N7/5, Plaatje to Town Clerk, Cape Town, 4 May 1927 and St Leger Plaatje to Town Clerk, Cape Town, 2 May 1927; Minutes of Council, 20 May 1927 and advertisement for post of clerk, N'dabeni Location, 12 March 1927; author's interview with Mrs Mary Plaatje, November 1981. St Leger's complaint about 'rigorous pass laws and their attendant evils' was from a letter he wrote to the principal of Fort Hare requesting references to enable him to apply for exemption (University of Fort Hare, Student records, file 2/44 (St Leger Plaatje), St Leger to A. Kerr, 15 October 1926). I am indebted to the registrar, University of Fort Hare, and to Ike Maamoe, Neo Ramoupi and Bob Edgar for their help in obtaining access to this file.

69 St Leger's wedding was reported in the *DFA*, 11 August 1928, p. 11 and in 'Umbulelo', *Imvo*, 16 October 1928, p. 6; see also 'Plaatje-Ramhitshane wedding', *Umteteli*, 6 October 1928.

70 Plaatje, 'Natives and taxation', *DFA*, 3 March 1931; UW, SAIRR Papers, B4.1, Native Economic Commission, Further Evidence of Sol T. Plaatje, 26 February 1931, p. 3; see also S.T. Plaatje, 'The native bills', *DFA*, 15 February 1929.

71 For example, S.T. Plaatje, 'Native conditions through European spectacles', *Daily Dispatch*, 9 July 1927.

72 For example, S.T. Plaatje, 'The Cape franchise', *Umteteli*, 29 September 1928 and *South African Outlook*, 1 October 1928; 'The native vote', *Umteteli*, 13 October 1928; 'The native franchise', *Umteteli*, 8 December 1928; 'Native voters', *Umteteli*, 19 January 1929; 'Native Voters' Association', *DFA*, 15 February 1929; UW, SAIRR, Kb32.2.1.5, Plaatje to Rheinallt Jones, 8 June 1929.

73 'African National Congress: bill of rights', *Umteteli*, 6 April 1929; 'Black man's place in the Union', *DFA*, 3 April 1929; UW, Saffery Papers, AD 1178, D3(iv), Report on the ANC conference held in Bloemfontein, 1929, p. 1; National Archives (Kew), FCO (Colonial Office) 141/499 (Basutoland series), Office of Divisional Criminal Investigation Officer, Kimberley, to Deputy Commissioner, South African Police, Kimberley, 12 April 1929; '17th annual convention of the ANC', *South African Worker*, 30 April 1929.' I am indebted to Professor Robert Edgar for the National Archives reference.

74 S.T. Plaatje, 'Another five years', *Umteteli*, 13 July 1929.

75 KAB, 3/CT, 4/1/5/1241, N7/5, report by mayor on interview with F.Y. St Leger Plaatje, 16 July 1929, and letter to St Leger Plaatje dated 6 August 1929.

Chapter 16

1 Tuskegee University, Archival Repository, Moton Papers, GC 109/810, Plaatje to Moton, 18 June 1925.

2 'Points of view: the late Mr Sol Plaatje', letter to editor from D.M. Ramoshoana, *Diamond Fields Advertiser (DFA)*, 29 June 1932.

3 For the state of literature in Setswana at this time, see C.M. Doke, 'A preliminary investigation into the state of the native languages of South Africa with suggestions as to research and the development of literature', *Bantu Studies*, 7, 1933, pp. 21–2, 31, 77–85; C.M. Doke, 'The linguistic situation in South Africa', *Africa*, 1, 1928; C.M. Doke, 'Vernacular textbooks in South African native schools', *Africa*, 8, 1935, pp. 197–99;

Tore Janson and Joseph Tsonope, *Birth of a National Language: the history of Setswana* (Gaborone: Heinemann Botswana, 1991).

4   Interviews with Mr Simon Lekhela, London, October 1978 and December 1981; Botswana National Archives (BNA), S.144/5, Peter M. Sebina to Resident Commissioner, Bechuanaland Protectorate, 26 February 1931. In Clement Doke's view, 'for more advanced reading, there is a calamitous dearth of books' in Setswana (Doke, 'Vernacular textbooks in South African native schools', p. 199).

5   'Experts and languages', letter from D.M. Ramoshoana to the editor, *Bantu World*, 16 June 1934.

6   S.T. Plaatje, 'Native affairs after four years', *DFA*, 22 January 1924; Moton Papers, GC 109/810, Plaatje to Moton, 18 June 1925.

7   University of the Witwatersrand, Historical Papers (UW), SAIRR, Kb32.2.1.3, 'Minutes of meeting of Bantu Research Committee held in the committee room on Friday the 23rd November, 1928, at 4 p.m.', p. 1. On Doke, see particularly G. Fortune, 'Clement Martyn Doke: a biographical and bibliographical sketch' in *Catalogue of the C.M. Doke Collection on African Languages in the Library of the University of Rhodesia* (Boston, MA: G.K. Hall, 1972).

8   UW, SAIRR, Kb32.2.1.5, Plaatje to the Registrar, University of the Witwatersrand, 3 July 1929.

9   J. Tom Brown's *Secwana Dictionary* (Tigerkloof: London Missionary Society, 1925) was a revised edition of J. Brown's original dictionary, first published in 1875.

10 Ramoshoana wrote thirteen articles for the *DFA* between 1 April 1927 and 20 March 1929. In 'Setswana witchcraft' (*DFA*, 7 September 1928) he recalled 'the indelible impression' left upon his mind by a frightening tale of '*boloi*' (witchcraft), dating from the mid-1830s, which he heard from his grandmother and his father, then a boy of seven or eight years. In 1942 it was reported that Ramoshoana had ready for publication 'a Tswana manuscript … dealing with Tales from Shakespeare' as well as 'a volume entitled "Dilekwana", a collection of valuable folk-lore material in Tswana about his folk' (*Sunday Times* (Johannesburg), 20 September 1942). According to D.D.T. Jabavu, writing a year later, Ramoshoana had in hand 'numerous manuscripts awaiting publication, comprising 1,700 proverbs, twenty-one heroic lyrics, nineteen essays, and six stories of various plays of Shakespeare': D.D.T. Jabavu, *The Influence of English on Bantu Literature* (Lovedale: Lovedale Press, 1943), p. 6. None of this was ever published.

11 UW, SAIRR, Kb32.2.1.5, Plaatje to the Registrar, University of the Witwatersrand, 25 November 1929.

12 UW, SAIRR, Kb32.2.1.5, J.D. Rheinallt Jones to Plaatje, 29 November 1929; 'List of presents and disbursements', attachment in Plaatje to the Registrar, University of the Witwatersrand, 25 November 1929; Plaatje to Dr Doke, 9 December 1929.

13 UW, SAIRR, Kb32.2.1.5, 'Minutes of meeting of the Bantu Research Committee held in the office of the Council of Education on Tuesday the 4th February, 1930', p. 2; Doke to Plaatje, 11 February and 7 April 1930.

14 In the 1920s, in line with international practice, the Cape Province Education Department laid increasing stress on the place of mother tongue instruction in the early years of primary education, culminating in a regulation in 1931 that provided that 'the home language of the pupils should be the medium of instruction during the first four years of a pupil's school life' (*Report of the Supt.-General of Education for the Year ended 31 December 1931* (CP3-1932), p. 46). The need for 'a good series' in Setswana had been identified three years earlier (*Report of the Supt.-General of Education for the Years 1927 and 1928* (CP2-1929), p. 87).

15 De Beers Archives (DB), General Secretary's correspondence, Plaatje to General Secretary, De Beers, 19 November 1929.

16 DB, General Secretary's correspondence, General Secretary to Plaatje, 25 November

1929.

17 'The late Mr Sol Plaatje', letter from D.M. Ramoshoana to the editor, *DFA*, 29 June 1932; interview with Mr Michael van Reenen, Mitcham, 6 September 1976. The original typescript of Plaatje's second collection is in SOAS, Plaatje Papers, STP 2/4 and has been published as *Other Proverbs of Sol Plaatje, the First Setswana Author* (Kimberley: Sol Plaatje Educational Trust, 2010), with a valuable introduction by D.S. Matjila. The proverb quoted is no. 43, p. 9. In January 1930 Plaatje wrote in his journal, 'Addtnl Diane [Proverbs] to London for its 2nd Edition', presumably to Kegan Paul Publishers, but no publication materialised, most likely because Plaatje was unable to provide the subsidy they required (UW, Scrapbook, A 1893, journal page for 1 January 1930).

18 S.T. Plaatje, *Sechuana Proverbs* (London: Kegan Paul, Trench, Trübner & Co., 1916), pp. 32 and 41; *Other Proverbs of Sol Plaatje*, no. 22, p. 5.

19 Plaatje, *Sechuana Proverbs*, pp. 76 and 64; *Other Proverbs of Sol Plaatje*, no. 13, p. 2; no. 16, p. 3; no. 105, p. 22.

20 Plaatje, *Sechuana Proverbs*, introduction, p. 13; D. Jones and S.T. Plaatje, *A Sechuana Reader in International Phonetic Orthography (with English Translations)* (London: University of London Press, 1916), pp. 4, 6, 10, 14.

21 Varying titles are from: UW, SAIRR, Kb32.2.1.5, Plaatje to Registrar, 3 July 1929; S.T. Plaatje, *Mhudi* (Lovedale: Lovedale Press, 1930), reverse of title page; Moton Papers, GC 60/130, Plaatje to Moton, 16 July 1931; University of Zimbabwe (UZ), C.M. Doke Collection, PL8752.P6, letter inserted in Doke's copy of *Sechuana Proverbs*, Plaatje to Doke, 6 August 1931. His 'November 1929' letter was to the Registrar, University of the Witwatersrand, 25 November 1929: Brian Willan (ed.), *Sol Plaatje: selected writings* (Johannesburg: Witwatersrand University Press, 1996), p. 378.

22 Fragments preserved in Unisa, Molema Papers, Acc. 142, file 1 (photocopies). For Tswana praise poetry, see particularly G.F. Lestrade, 'Bantu praise poems', *The Critic: A South African Quarterly Journal*, 4, 1, October 1935, pp. 1–10 and Isaac Schapera, *Praise Poems of Tswana Chiefs* (London: Oxford University Press, 1965).

23 Unisa, Z.K. Matthews Papers, Acc. 101, 'List of praise songs (Tswana)', available at http://hdl.handle.net/10500/8017 (accessed 3 January 2013). Recognising the importance of the praise songs he came across, but without the time to pursue them further himself, Matthews enlisted the help of a former student of his, Edison Bokako, to carry out the necessary fieldwork. Bokako compiled an invaluable collection of twenty-two praise poems, translated into English and extensively annotated, drawing upon information from both oral and written sources: see Z.K. Matthews Papers, 'Bo-Santagane: an anthology of Tswana heroic verse with notes and translations', accessible at http://hdl.handle.net/10500/10612 (accessed 3 January 2013). Information on Gaeshele (d. 1935) is from Z.K. Matthews, 'A short history of the Barolong', *Fort Hare Papers*, 1, 1, June 1945, p. 24.

24 S.T. Plaatje, 'Montsioa', in T.D. Mweli Skota (ed.), *African Yearly Register* (Johannesburg: R.L. Esson, 1930), p. 53.

25 Plaatje, 'Montsioa', pp. 53 and 57.

26 UZ, Doke Collection, Plaatje to Doke, 6 August 1931.

27 UZ, Doke Collection, Plaatje to Doke, 6 August 1931; UW, SAIRR, Kb2.1, 'Bantu Studies Research Grant 1930', 3(a), Annexure C to 'Minutes of the eighth general meeting of the Advisory Committee on African Studies and Research held at the Old University Buildings, Queen Victoria Street, Cape Town, on Monday, 16th March 1931, at 10 a.m.'

28 UW, SAIRR, Kb32.2.1.5, Plaatje to Doke, 13 February 1930.

29 Daniel Jones, *The Tones of Sechuana Nouns* (London: International Institute of African Languages and Cultures, 1928), reproduced in Daniel Jones and Solomon T. Plaatje, *A Sechuana Reader* (Farnborough: Gregg International Publishers, 1970); UW, SAIRR,

Kb32.2.1.5, Plaatje to the Registrar, University of the Witwatersrand, 25 November 1929.

30 UW, SAIRR, Kb32.2.1.5, Plaatje to Doke, 13 February 1930; SAIRR, Kb32.2.1.5, 'Minutes of a meeting of the Bantu Studies Research Committee held at the University on Tuesday, 9th June, 1931, at 3.00 p.m.', p. 2. Ramoshoana approached Doke again in October 1931 but with no more luck, and received the same advice. 'I am very sorry to have to write to you in this way', Doke said, 'but economy and retrenchment is the order of the day just now, and funds for research are not to be had' (University of the Witwatersrand (UW), University Archives, Clement Doke Papers, A1.2, Letterbooks, Doke to Ramoshoana, 13 October 1931).

31 Plaatje's annotated copy of J.T. Brown's *Secwana Dictionary*, pp. i–iv. I am very grateful to the late Professor D.C. Cole, formerly of the University of the Witwatersrand, for making a photocopy of this available to me. The present whereabouts of the original is unknown.

32 S.T. Plaatje (translator), *Diphosho-phosho / Comedy of Errors* (Morija: Morija Printing Works, 1930), introduction, p. iv.

33 Plaatje, *Diphosho-phosho*, introduction, p. 4. Francis Hill was director of native missions at the Community of the Resurrection in Johannesburg and also active in the Joint Councils movement.

34 Willan, *Sol Plaatje: selected writings*, Plaatje to the Registrar, University of the Witwatersrand, 25 November 1928, p. 378. For examples of overseas news reports, see 'Shakespeare in Negro dialect', *Belfast Newsletter*, 13 May 1930 and 'Shakespeare for Africans', *Charleston Gazette*, 15 June 1930.

35 'Shakespeare in Sechuana', *The Star* (Johannesburg), 26 July 1930.

36 Isaac Schapera, 'Customs relating to twins in South Africa', *Journal of the African Society*, 26, 102, January 1927, pp. 117–37, writes that 'almost everywhere the birth of twins is looked upon as something uncanny and out of the ordinary course of nature', and that 'Among the Bechuana, when twins were born one was invariably put to death'. William Crisp, *The Bechuana of South Africa* (London: SPCK, 1896), p. 45, likewise attests to the custom of killing 'one of all twin children and of children born deformed'. The tale of Masilo and Masilonyana, or at least a Tswana variant of it, is related by David Ramoshoana in 'Setswana folklore', *DFA*, 23 October 1928. See also Deborah Seddon, 'The colonial encounter and *The Comedy of Errors*: Solomon Plaatje's *Diphosho-phosho*', in Laurence Wright (ed.), *South African Shakespeare in the Twentieth Century* (Farnham: Ashgate, 2009), pp. 77–8.

37 For Indian-language translations of Shakespeare, see Poonam Trivedi and Dennis Bartholomeusz (eds.), *India's Shakespeare: translation, interpretation and performance* (Newark, DE: University of Delaware Press, 2004), esp. pp. 47–73 and 276–8. *Bhrantibilas*, the first Bengali translation of *The Comedy of Errors*, was published in 1869. *Angoor*, a Hindi-language film based on *The Comedy of Errors*, made in Mumbai in 1982, is widely regarded as one of Bollywood's finest comedies.

38 For examples of some of these changes, see particularly the seminal article by Shole J. Shole, 'Shakespeare in Setswana: an evaluation of Raditladi's *Macbeth* and Plaatje's *Diphoshophosho*', *Shakespeare in Southern Africa*, 4, 1990/91, p. 60, to whom I am indebted for the analysis of the meaning of the title. The most substantial excision is of nearly two pages of inconsequential banter between Antipholus and Dromio prior to the arrival of Adriana and Luciana in Act II, scene ii.

39 Deborah Seddon, 'Shakespeare's orality: Solomon Plaatje's Setswana translation', *English Studies in Africa*, 47, 2, 2004, pp. 82–5, provides an insightful discussion of Tswana praise-naming practice in relation to 'Tsikinya-Chaka'; for Cornelius Lekoko and the 'Kaffir Institution' see Brian Willan, 'Whose Shakespeare? Early black South African engagement with Shakespeare', *Shakespeare in Southern Africa*, 24, 2012, pp. 3–24.

40 I am indebted here to the insights of David Schalkwyk and Lerothodi Lapula, 'Solomon Plaatje, William Shakespeare, and the translations of culture', *Pretexts: Literary and Cultural Studies*, 9, 1, 2000, pp. 9–26 and Seddon, 'Shakespeare's orality', pp. 77–95.

41 N. Ndana, 'From Mafikeng to Stratford: Sol Plaatje's court interpretation, translation of Shakespeare and cross-cultural currents', in M.M. Bagwasi, M.M. Alimi and P.J. Ebewo (eds.), *English Language and Literature: cross cultural currents* (Newcastle: Cambridge Scholars Publishing, 2008), pp. 276–91.

42 Ndana Ndana, 'Sol Plaatje's Shakespeare: translation and transition to modernity' (PhD thesis, University of Cape Town, 2005), p. 160, identifies over fifty proverbs in *Diphosho-phosho*, more if a looser definition is applied. In addition to Ndana's PhD thesis, I also acknowledge the following key works of scholarship in assessing Plaatje's translation of *The Comedy of Errors*: Seddon, 'The colonial encounter and *The Comedy of Errors*'; P.D.K. Makhudu, 'Sol Plaatje and Setswana: contributions towards language development' (PhD thesis, University of Limpopo, 2010); Shole, 'Shakespeare in Setswana'. I have also drawn upon the unpublished English translation of *Diphosho-phosho* in the Lestrade Papers, UCT (BC 255, A6.31), using this unless otherwise indicated.

43 *Comedy of Errors*, Act IV, scene iii, lines 78–93; *Diphosho-phosho*, p. 35, lines 11–12; Plaatje, *Sechuana Reader*, p. 4. The proverb is represented slightly differently in *Sechuana Proverbs*, p. 87, where proverb no. 625 is 'Se lelele kgama lo mogogoro' / 'Do not lose the hide in the hand for the running hartebeest'. Ndana, 'Sol Plaatje's Shakespeare', pp. 167–9, provides an illuminating discussion of this proverb and its context. Quotations in Setswana from *Diphosho-phosho* follow Plaatje's orthography and use of phonetic characters: see pp. 505–6 for further discussion of this.

44 *Comedy of Errors*, Act II, scene i, line 42; *Diphosho-phosho*, p. 11, lines 1–3; Plaatje, *Sechuana Proverbs*, p. 46; Ndana, 'Sol Plaatje's Shakespeare', pp. 163–4. *Comedy of Errors*, Act I, scene ii, lines 35–40 (*Diphosho-phosho*, p. 7, lines 4–11).

45 *Comedy of Errors*, Act I, scene ii, lines 35–40 (*Diphosho-phosho*, p. 7, lines 4–11); *Comedy of Errors*, Act IV, scene iii, lines 61–2 (*Diphosho-phosho*, p. 34, lines 18–19).

46 *Comedy of Errors* Act III scene i, line 82 (*Diphosho-phosho*, p. 20, line 27); *Comedy of Errors*, Act II, scene ii, line 74 (*Diphosho-phosho*, p. 16, lines 26–7); *Comedy of Errors*, Act II, scene ii, lines 30–34 (*Diphosho-phosho*, p. 14, lines 10–12. I have drawn here upon Shole, 'Shakespeare in Setswana', p. 62, and Seddon, 'The colonial encounter and *The Comedy of Errors*', p. 70 (from which I have taken the English translation of Plaatje's 'gnats' metaphor).

47 *Comedy of Errors*, Act II, scene ii, lines 143–6 (*Diphosho-phosho*, p. 15, lines 24–9; *Comedy of Errors*, Act I, scene i, lines 51–2 (*Diphosho-phosho*, p. 3, lines 11–12); *Comedy of Errors*, Act II, scene i, lines 57–60 (*Diphoshosho-phosho*, p. 11, lines 13–15). Shole, 'Shakespeare in Setswana', p. 62; Ndana, 'Sol Plaatje's Shalespeare', p. 159; and Plaatje, *Sechuana Proverbs*, p. 78, for the mice metaphor; Ndana, 'Sol Plaatje's Shakespeare', p. 198, for the madness metaphor.

48 *Comedy of Errors*, Act III, scene ii, line 97 (*Diphosho-phosho*, p. 24, lines 25–6); I am indebted to Ndana, 'Sol Plaatje's Shakespeare', for his elucidation of the origins and associations of 'Seetebosigo'. The longer aphorism is from A. Sandilands, *Introduction to Tswana* (Tigerkloof: London Missionary Society, 1953), reproduced on p. 153 (Setswana) and p. 400 (English). 'Lapland sorcerers': *Comedy of Errors*, Act IV, scene iii, line 11 (*Diphosho-phosho*, p. 33, lines 10–12).

49 *Comedy of Errors*, Act III, scene ii, lines 114–45 (*Diphosho-phosho*, p. 25, lines 17–33).

50 Shole, 'Shakespeare in Setswana', p. 61.

51 D.M. Ramoshoana, 'Setswana witchcraft', *DFA*, 7 September 1928; *Comedy of Errors*, Act I, scene ii, lines 77–81 (*Diphosho-phosho*, p. 8, line 20–1).

52 The two passages are from *Comedy of Errors*, Act IV, scene iv, lines 63–6 (*Diphosho-phosho*, p. 37, lines 16–21) and *Comedy of Errors*, Act IV, scene iv, line 22 (*Diphosho-*

phosho, p. 36, line 11).

53 *Comedy of Errors*, Act II, scene ii, lines 188–92 (*Diphosho-phosho*, p. 17, lines 5–9). Shole (p. 61) points to other examples of the rhetorical form of Plaatje's translation.

54 *Comedy of Errors*, Act V, scene i, line 133 (*Diphosho-phosho*, p. 44, line 14).

55 *Comedy of Errors*, Act II, scene ii, line 194 (*Diphosho-phosho*, p. 17, lines 10–11); Ndana, 'Sol Plaatje's Shakespeare', p. 153.

56 *Comedy of Errors*, Act IV, scene iv, lines 27–37 (*Diphosho-phosho*, p. 36, lines 22–3); for *'bolata'* and the controversies that arose, see particularly Barry Morton, 'Servitude, slave trading and slavery in the Kalahari', in Elizabeth A. Eldredge and Fred Morton (eds.), *Slavery in South Africa: captive labour on the Dutch frontier* (New York: iUniverse, 2009), pp. 215–50; Suzanne Miers and Michael Crowder, 'The politics of slavery in Bechuanaland: power struggles and the plight of the Basarwa in the Bamangwato Reserve, 1926–1940', in Suzanne Miers and Richard Roberts (eds.), *The End of Slavery in Africa* (Madison, WI: University of Wisconsin Press, 1988), pp. 172–200; Ndana, 'Sol Plaatje's Shakespeare', p. 151. In June 1931 Plaatje reported on the case of Rajaba, a Mongwato, who 'had beaten to death an unfortunate Masarwa serf in his employ', his defence being that 'his action was the customary Bechuana way of dealing with Masarwa!' He was found guilty and sentenced to fifteen years' hard labour ('Native law and custom', *Our Heritage*, June 1931, p. 12).

57 BNA, DCS 14/6, Plaatje to Serowe District Commissioner, 25 September 1930; Doke, 'A preliminary investigation', p. 22; G.P. Lestrade, 'European influences upon the development of Bantu languages and literature', in I. Schapera (ed.), *Western Civilisation and the Natives of South Africa* (London: Routledge & Sons, 1934), p. 124. A further brief review in the *Pretoria News*, 11 October 1930, noted that the publication of *Diphosho-phosho* disproved those who 'said that the translation could never be done', and that Plaatje had 'put the sceptics to shame'.

58 D.M. Ramoshoana, 'Shakespeare in Sechuana', *Umteteli wa Bantu*, 4 October 1930; see also D.M. Ramoshoana, letter to the editor, *DFA*, 4 October 1930.

59 C.M. Doke, review of *Diphospho-phosho*, *Bantu Studies*, 5, 1931.

60 University of the Witwatersrand, Historical Papers (UW), W.C. Scully Papers, A 1312, Bf3, Stephen Black to W.C. Scully, 23 October 1930.

61 BNA, S.150/5, 1886. Rey had seen newspaper reports dated 7 May (title unidentified) and 26 July 1930 (Johannesburg *Star*); the comment about Plaatje being so well known came from the principal clerk, Mr E. Harris, in a note to Rey dated 21 July 1930. Rey was still demanding to know 'Who is this Plaatje?' when he saw an article by him in the *Diamond Fields Advertiser* on 'Spelling of African languages' on 15 October (BNA, S.68/13, 463/2). Rey's diary entry was from the period 3–9 November 1930, p. 48 in Neil Parsons and Michael Crowder (eds.), *Sir Charles Rey, Monarch of All I Survey: Bechuanaland diaries 1929–37* (Gaborone: Botswana Society, 1988).

62 Rey's dislike of missionaries runs through his diary, his particular bête noire being 'that poisonous person Jennings (known as Fat Albert)' whom he thought 'a fluent liar' (Rev. Albert Jennings, then chairman of the South Africa District Committee of the London Missionary Society). It extended, however, to all missionaries: 'I'd like to stick my missionary crowd down a mine on to a stick of dynamite and blow the whole damned lot to the heaven they're always bleating about' (Parsons and Crowder, *Sir Charles Rey*, diary entry for 28 November 1930, p. 51). The new primary school syllabus is in BNA, BNB 148.

63 NAD, Colenso Papers, Box 59, Plaatje to Mrs G. Solomon (copy), 13 May 1930. For evidence of publishers' interest in publishing Tswana school books, see correspondence in Lestrade Papers, UCT, BC 255, G2 (Longmans, Green & Co.) and BNA, S.68/14, H.J.E. Dumbrell (Inspector of Education, Bechuanaland Protectorate) to Stakesby Lewis, 8 December 1930 (Blackie's); for the broader history of Longmans publishing in

Africa, see Caroline Davis, 'Creating a book empire: Longmans in Africa', in Caroline Davis and David Johnson (eds.), *The Book in Africa: critical debates* (Basingstoke: Palgrave Macmillan, 2015), pp. 128–52. Plaatje had sent the manuscript of his translation of *Julius Caesar* to the Lovedale Press, but nothing came of this (see p. 522).

64 *Diphosho-phosho*, introduction, pp. i–ii; S.T. Plaatje, 'Letter to the editor: suggested new Bantu orthography', *South African Outlook*, 1 August 1931.

65 'Sechuana orthography', letter from M.M. Kendle to the editor, *Umteteli wa Bantu*, 20 December 1930; C.M. Doke, review of *Diphosho-phosho*, *Bantu Studies*, 5, 1931; BNA, DCS 14/6, Plaatje to Serowe District Commissioner (Capt. G.E. Nettleton), 25 September 1930.

66 BNA, S.150/5, 1886, minute from H.J.E. Dumbrell to High Commissioner, 19 February 1931; handwritten note from Dumbrell to the Government Secretary, 26 January 1931.

67 London School of Economics, Archives of International Africa Institute (London), Minutes of Business Committee, International Institute of African Languages and Cultures, 2 December 1930, pp. 155–6.

68 See, e.g., F.D. Lugard, 'The International Institute of African Languages and Cultures', *Africa*, 1, 1, 1928, pp. 1–2; also G.P. Lestrade, 'Some remarks on the practical orthography of the South African Bantu languages', *Bantu Studies*, 3, 1927–9, pp. 261–73.

69 W.D. Hammond Tooke, *Imperfect Interpreters: South Africa's anthropologists 1920–1990* (Johannesburg: Witwatersrand University Press, 1997), provides an invaluable account of the early development of anthropology and 'Bantu Studies' in South Africa.

70 International Institute of African Languages and Cultures, *A Practical Orthography of African Languages* (London, 1927); see also various articles in the first issue of *Africa* in 1928, esp. Lugard, 'The International Institute of African Languages and Cultures', pp. 1–2, and A. Lloyd James, 'The practical orthography of African languages', pp. 125–9.

71 International Institute of African Languages and Cultures, 'A practical orthography for Tswana', *Bantu Studies*, 11, 1937, pp. 137–8.

72 International Institute of African Languages and Cultures, 'A practical orthography for Tswana'; S.T. Plaatje, 'Suggested new Bantu orthography', *South African Outlook*, 1 May 1931, pp. 88–90.

73 UCT, Lestrade Papers, A1.7, Minutes of meeting of the Sotho-Pedi-Cwana subcommittee, 14 and 15 February 1929.

74 International Institute of African Languages and Cultures, 'A practical orthography', p. 138; BNA, S.68/12,463/1, Union Advisory Board on Bantu Studies and Research, Central Orthography Committee, Cwana District Committee, minutes of meeting held on 27 February 1930; Free State Archives (VAB), Dept of Education and Training (SOO), 1/1/16, N5/11 ('Sechuana orthography'), draft minutes of Tswana subcommittee, 1 and 2 October 1929. The final version of the minutes circulated omitted details of the reaction of the other members of the committee to Motiyane's motion: see UCT, Lestrade Papers, A1.1.1, minutes of meeting of Tswana subcommittee, 1 and 2 October 1929; also BNA, S.68/11, Cuzen (RM, Kanye) to Government Secretary, Mafeking, 26 November 1929, re October committee meeting.

75 BNA, S.68/12, 463/1, Cuzen to the Government Secretary, Mafeking, 7 April 1930, p. 2; Willan, *Sol Plaatje: selected writings*, Plaatje to the Registrar, University of the Witwatersrand, 25 November 1929, p. 379; VAB, SOO, 1/1/16, N5/11 ('Sechuana orthography'), Rev. P. Motiyane to G.H. Franz, 22 October 1928. At this point Franz was chief inspector of education in the Orange Free State, moving to the Transvaal in 1929.

76 Plaatje, 'Suggested new Bantu orthography', pp. 88–90.

77 Unisa, Molema Papers, 142/2, Minutes of conference on orthography, University of the Witwatersrand, Johannesburg, 28 April 1937, p. 3. Plaatje wrote elsewhere on the subject in: S.T. Plaatje, 'Uniform spelling', *Umteteli*, 15 November 1930; S.T. Plaatje, 'A

white man's native language', *Umteteli*, 5 December 1931 and 2 April 1932; 'Some native criticism of Bantu languages', letter from Plaatje to the editor, *The Star*, 2 December 1931; 'The Bantu orthography', *Our Heritage*, 1, 3, August–October 1931, pp. 10–11; 'Bantu orthography', *Our Heritage*, 1, 5, December 1931, p. 9.

78 BNA, S.98/9, 'Board of Advice on Native Education in the Bechuanaland Protectorate: minutes of the meeting held in Mafeking on Mon. and Tues., Nov. 10th/11th, 1930', p. 5: the orthography subcommittee consisted of Henry Dumbrell, Rev. A.J. Haile (LMS) and Chief Isang Pilane (Bangwaketse); BNA, S.69/1, 93, 'Minutes of orthography conference held in the office of the Acting Resident Commissioner, Captain R. Reilly, at Mafeking, on Thursday, the 10th September, 1931', p. 3.

79 BNA, S.68/13, Letter from Chief Montshiwa and counsellors to the Government Secretary, Bechuanaland Protectorate, re 'Orthographic innovation of Transvaal universities as applied to the Sechuana language', 15 November 1930. Plaatje had also drafted a resolution (probably for Dr Molema) for the Education Advisory Board in similar terms, expressing his 'resentment and disappointment at the action of the said European professors, of singling out our language and making it alone the plaything of their students while other native languages are apparently respected'. Rather than passing such a resolution itself, however, the meeting set up the subcommittee instead (Unisa, Molema Papers, typescript headed 'Resolution').

80 University of London, Senate House, Institute of Commonwealth Studies Archives, Michael Crowder Papers, 142/2, Plaatje to Tshekedi Khama, 11 August 1931.

81 S.T. Plaatje, 'Spelling of African languages: criticism of suggested reforms', *DFA*, 15 October 1930. Missionary concerns are well expressed in a letter from the Rev. R. Haydon Lewis (LMS) to Captain R. Reilly (Resident Magistrate, Lobatse), 23 July 1931, in BNA, DCL 7/2, drawing attention to the overbearing attitude of G.H. Franz as well as African opposition to the scheme, and 'endless expense and work for all the missionary societies', especially the LMS, which had 'alone invested enormous sums of money in getting the language from Kimberley to the Rhodesian border reduced to writing in accordance with an orthography which is now used by nearly all the natives in that area'.

82 'Spelling native languages', *The Star*, 19 November 1931; 'Bantu orthography', *South African Outlook*, 1 December 1931, p. 223; 'Spelling of native languages', *The Star*, 27 November 1931; 'Some native criticisms of Bantu languages', letter from Plaatje to *The Star*, 2 December 1931; BNA, S.68/15, G. Welsh (SGE, Cape Province) to Secretary, Provincial Education Dept, 30 July 1931; UCT, Lestrade Papers, A1.26, 'Second inter-provincial conference of introduction of new orthographies held at Bloemfontein on 18th November 1931'; 'Orthographies of native languages', comments in Report of the Chief Inspector for Native Education, Mr G.H. Welsh, BA, *Report of the Supt.-General of Education for the Year Ended 31 December 1931* (CP3-1932).

83 UCT, Lestrade Papers, F.125, 'Minutes of meeting of orthography committee appointed by his Honour the Resident Commissioner, held at Mafeking on Thursday, 4 December 1930'; S.68/13, 463/3/30, Government Secretary (Bechuanaland Protectorate) to Mr G. Welsh (SGE, Cape Province), 22 January 1931; S.68/13, 'Minutes of meeting held with certain representatives of the Barolong tribe on March 7th, 1931 with reference to Secwana orthography'; BNA, DCL 7/2, R. Haydon Lewis to Capt. R. Reilly, RM, Lobatse, 23 July 1931; S.68/5, H.W. Dyke (Principal Medical Officer) to G. Welsh (SGE, Cape), 25 July 1931, and H.W. Dyke and H.J.E. Dumbrell to the Government Secretary, Mafeking, 9 July 1931, mentioning that 'a letter was received by one of us from Mr Sol Plaatje stating that at a Meeting of LMS Native Ministers, held in June in Kanye, there seemed to be a very strong desire amongst them for Bechuanaland to tend towards the Basutoland orthography – a desire with which Mr Plaatje informed us he himself was in full accord'.

84 Derek Jones, 'A "resultant" Tswana orthography', paper prepared for a Bechuanaland Protectorate Education Department conference in May 1963 (in Unisa, Molema Papers, Acc. 142). A strong critique of its shortcomings is to be found in Sandilands, *Introduction to Tswana*, pp. 312–22.

85 For the background to the founding of the Bantu Treasury Series, see Elizabeth le Roux, 'Black writers, white publishers: a case study of the Bantu Treasury Series in South Africa', *E-rea* [online], http://erea.revues.org/3515, accessed 3 November 2015, DOI: 10.4000/erea.3515.

86 S.T. Plaatje, *Dintshontsho tsa bo-Juliuse Kesara* (Johannesburg: University of the Witwatersrand Press, Bantu Treasury Series, Johannesburg, 1937); UCT, Lestrade Papers, B2, 'Introduction'. Lestrade's introduction was translated into Setswana by G.L. Mangoaela and is published in this form. Quotations are from his original English draft.

87 Prior to his appointment at the University of Cape Town, Mangoaela taught Southern Sotho ('my mother tongue') and Setswana for a year at Adams College in Natal (UCT, University Archives, Gideon Mangoaela file, Mangoaela to D.P. Kunene, 13 May 1963). That Z.K. Matthews's involvement was only secured late in the day is deduced from the fact that this is not mentioned in the original English draft of Lestrade's introduction, dated July 1937 – only in the published version in Setswana. On the salience of Mangoaela's linguistic background, Makhudu ('Sol Plaatje and Setswana', p. 295) notes that his translation of Doke's preface and Lestrade's introduction 'is laced with Sesotho lexical items', for example employing the common Sesotho *lentswe/mantswe* (for 'word/words') instead of the standard Setswana equivalent, *lefoko/mafoko*.

88 Ramoshoana's role in securing the MS is acknowledged in Doke's preface (p. iv). Ramoshoana's comments on orthography are from 'The late Mr Sol Plaatje', *DFA*, 29 June 1932. He would never be reconciled to the use of diacritics.

89 I have benefited here from insights of Schalkwyk and Lapula in 'Solomon Plaatje, William Shakespeare and the translations of culture', and Ndana, 'Sol Plaatje's Shakespeare', esp. pp. 208–70.

90 D.S. Matjila and Karen Haire, *Bringing Plaatje Back Home: Ga e Phetsolele Nageng* (Trenton, NJ: Africa World Press, 2015), pp. 111–16.

91 Ndana, 'Sol Plaatje's Shakespeare', pp. 256–66, identifies 61 Setswana proverbs in the text – more than in *Diphosho-phosho*.

92 Review of *Dintshontsho tsa bo-Juliuse Kesara*, *South African Outlook*, 20 October 1939, pp. 229–30.

93 W. Eiselen, Review of *Dintshontsho tsa bo-Juliuse Kesara*, *Bantu Studies*, 12, 1938, pp. 153–6; for Eiselen, see C.J. Beyers and J.L. Basson (eds.), *Dictionary of South African Biography*, vol. 5 (Pretoria: Human Sciences Research Council, 1987), pp. 234–5. Eiselen took over the position of chief inspector of native education in the Transvaal from G.H. Franz in 1936.

94 See particularly Andrew Dickson, *Worlds Elsewhere: journeys around Shakespeare's globe* (London: Bodley Head, 2015), for an account of the global spread of Shakespeare and of the many forms this took.

95 *Diphosho-phosho*, introduction, p. iv.

96 Letter from Rev. A.E. Small (Manager, Bechuanaland Book Centre) to Morara Molema, Mafikeng, 9 August 1962, indicating that 3,268 copies were sold between August 1961 and July 1962 (courtesy of the late Mr Morara Molema). Janson and Tsonope (*Birth of a National Language*, p. 83) noted, in 1991, that Plaatje's two Shakespeare translations 'are still often read in school'. On the basis of interviews conducted in 2004, however, Ndana surmises that they disappeared from the secondary curriculum in Botswana in the 1990s ('Sol Plaatje's Shakespeare', pp. 277–81).

97 There were reprints in 1942, 1945, 1954, 1962, 1963 and 1967. 'Notes' in *African*

Studies, 1942, p. 152, announced the reprint, as did the *Sunday Times* (Johannesburg), 20 September 1942. Three years later there was a further reprint of 2,000 copies, leading to a request from Doke to the manager of the Lovedale Press, printers and distributors of the book, to 'consider holding up the type for a while' in view of 'the speed of sales' (Cory Library, Lovedale Collection, MS 16399, Doke to Manager, Lovedale Press, 12 May 1945). There was a substantial new edition in 1973, and further reprints in 1975 and 1985. Shepherd's comment on *Dintshontsho* is from his article, 'Bantu literature', in *Standpunte*, 7, 4, June 1953, p. 51 (I am most grateful to Stephen Gray for bringing this to my attention). The importance of the Bantu Treasury Series to the Press as a whole is reflected in the fact that, in 1980 and 1982, sales of books in the series as a proportion of total sales were 57% and 62% respectively, reprints of 10,000 or 20,000 being common (Le Roux, 'Black writers, white publishers', para 35). I am most grateful to Veronica Klipp, managing director of Wits University Press, for showing me their production file for *Dintshontsho* which records all reprints.

Chapter 17

1   Pietermaritzburg Archives Repository (NAB), Colenso Papers, Box 59, Plaatje to Mrs Georgiana Solomon (copy), 13 May 1930.
2   For Shepherd's role at Lovedale, see Jeffrey Peires, 'Lovedale Press: literature for the Bantu revisited', *English in Africa*, 7, 2, March 1980, pp. 71–85; R.H.W. Shepherd, *Lovedale, South Africa, 1824–55* (Alice: Lovedale Press, 1971), p. 122; Tim White, 'The Lovedale Press during the directorship of R.H.W. Shepherd, 1930–1955', *English in Africa*, 19, 2, October 1992, pp. 69–100.
3   Rhodes University, Cory Library, MS 16297, Minutes of Lovedale Publications Committee, 20 November 1929 to 18 September 1930; Contract between Plaatje and the Lovedale Institution Press, 19 March 1930 (photocopy in author's possession).
4   R.H.W. Shepherd, *Bantu Literature and Life* (Lovedale: Lovedale Press, 1955), p. 98; R.H.W. Shepherd and B.G. Paver, *African Contrasts: the story of a South African people* (Cape Town: Oxford University Press, 1947), pp. 279–80.
5   This argument that *Mhudi* was 'bowdlerised' was made by Tim Couzens and Stephen Gray, 'Printers and other devils: the texts of Sol T. Plaatje's *Mhudi*', *Research in African Literature*, 9, 2, 1978, pp. 198–215, and extended in Stephen Gray, *Southern African Literature: an introduction* (Cape Town: David Philip, 1979), pp. 171–82. In my 'What "other devils"? The texts of Sol T. Plaatje's *Mhudi* revisited', *Journal of Southern African Studies*, 41, 6, December 2015, I take issue with this, arguing that there is no evidence to suggest that Plaatje was forced to make changes against his will, and that the role of the Lovedale Press has therefore been misrepresented. References to *Mhudi* that follow are from the original Lovedale edition (1930). The typescript is in Cory Library, MS 16323. Shepherd explained in a letter in 1933 that he would not expect to 'publish matter which we consider harmful to the missionary cause' (letter to C.J. Uys, 1 December 1933, quoted in Peires, 'Literature for the Bantu revisited', p. 81).
6   Author's interview with Michael van Reenen, Mitcham, August 1976.
7   Sol T. Plaatje, *Mhudi: an epic of South African native life a hundred years ago* (Lovedale: Lovedale Press, 1930), preface (unpaginated).
8   *Mhudi*, pp. 208–9.
9   *Mhudi*, p. 225.
10 S. Gray, 'Sources of the first black South African novel in English', *Munger Africana Notes*, December 1976; T.J. Couzens, 'Sol Plaatje's *Mhudi*', *Journal of Commonwealth Literature*, 8, 1, June 1973; S. Gray, 'Plaatje's Shakespeare', *English in Africa*, 4, 1, March 1977.
11 *Mhudi*, pp. 42 and 45.
12 Editorial, *Tsala ea Becoana*, 10 July 1910. Plaatje did make the connections explicit

when he wrote, in 1931, of reactions to the appearance of Halley's Comet in 1910 and the memories it evoked: "'Seventy-five years!' They commented, "this must be Mochochonono – the star with a long tail – who heralded the fall of Mzilikazi, the Matabele king, once mighty ruler of Central South Africa, the star whose appearances synchronized with the disintegration of the Zulu dynasty'" ('Natives and eclipses', *Diamond Fields Advertiser* (*DFA*), 8 April 1931).

13 For the lion stories, see Gray, 'Sources', pp. 21–7 and William Crisp, *The Bechuana of South Africa* (London: SPCK, 1896), pp. 31–2.

14 *Mhudi*, pp. 59–61; *Tsala ea Batho*, 21 February 1914, p. 3. In Plaatje's retelling in *Mhudi*, the emphasis moves from the individual bravery of his great-grandmother/Mhudi to the collective courage of the girls who frightened off the lion. In each case they are not believed by the men until they returned to find the footprints and paw-prints next to one another.

15 S.T. Plaatje, 'Another five years', *Umteteli wa Bantu*, 24 August 1929; S.T. Plaatje, 'Should the Nyandjas be deported?', *Umteteli*, 5 March 1928; S.T. Plaatje, 'Descendants of the Koks', *DFA*, 7 December 1926.

16 *Mhudi*, pp. 3–4.

17 *Mhudi*, pp. 136–48, 115.

18 *Mhudi*, pp. 82–3.

19 *Mhudi*, p. 155.

20 *Mhudi*, pp. 208–9; for the connection between Plaatje's portrayal of events in the 1830s and twentieth-century South Africa, see T.J. Couzens, 'Sol Plaatje's *Mhudi*', *Journal of Commonwealth Literature*, 8, 1, June 1973, and his introduction to the Heinemann edition of *Mhudi*, pp. 17–19; Nadine Gordimer, 'English-language literature and politics in South Africa', in Christopher Heywood (ed.), *Aspects of South African Literature* (London: Heinemann, 1976), pp. 107–8; University of the Witwatersrand, Historical Papers (UW), SAIRR Archives, Evidence of S.T. Plaatje to Native Economic Commission (typescript), p. 5291.

21 *Mhudi*, p. 56. Feminist readings include Myrtle Hooper, 'Rewriting history: the "feminism" of *Mhudi*', *English Studies in Africa*, 35, 1, 1992, pp. 68–79; Laura Chrisman, 'Fathering the black nation of South Africa: gender and generation in Sol Plaatje's *Native Life in South Africa* and *Mhudi*', *Social Dynamics*, 23, 2, 1997, pp. 57–73; Laura Chrisman, *Rereading the Imperial Romance: British imperialism and South African resistance in Haggard, Schreiner and Plaatje* (Oxford: Oxford University Press, 2000).

22 *Mhudi*, p. 57.

23 *Mhudi*, p. 206.

24 UCT, Molteno Murray Family Papers, BC 330, A81.2.3, Plaatje to Mrs Lennox Murray, 17 November 1922.

25 *Mhudi*, p. 81.

26 'The Lovedale Press: a review of recent activities', *South African Outlook*, 2 March 1931, pp. 46–8: 'It is worth mentioning that a very favourable broadcast review [of *Mhudi*] was given out from the Johannesburg Studio a few days after it was published'; *Rand Daily Mail*, 7 February 1931; 'Overthrow of Mzilikazi', *Daily Dispatch* (East London), 17 December 1930.

27 'Tributes to Sir David Harris', *DFA*, 5 December 1930; Vere Stent, 'South Africa's first native novelist', *Pretoria News*, 8 November 1930.

28 Review of *Mhudi*, *South African Outlook*, 1 December 1930; 'The bookshelf' (review of *Mhudi*), *DFA*, 1 November 1930.

29 'Mhudi', *Imvo Zabantsundu*, 26 May 1931.

30 'Natives: don't ape white men!' (by Stephen Black), *The Sjambok*, 14 November 1930; H.I.E. Dhlomo, 'Three famous African authors I know: R.R.R. Dhlomo', *Inkundla ya Bantu*, August 1946 (reproduced in *English in Africa*, 2, 1, 1975, p. 9).

31 UW, W.C. Scully Papers, A 1312, Bf3, Stephen Black to W.C. Scully, 23 October 1930.

32 Stephen Black, 'The telephone conversations of Jeremiah: the first full-length black novel', *The Sjambok*, 31 October 1930, pp. 27–8.

33 Review of *Mhudi*, *Times Literary Supplement*, 31 August 1933; review of *Mhudi* by C.M. Doke, *Bantu Studies*, 5, 1931, p. 86. Doke hoped that 'Mr Plaatje's next effort in this direction will be in the vernacular'.

34 Couzens and Gray, 'Printers and other devils', quoted in Willan, 'What "other devils"?', p. 11. Eileen Julien, in *African Novels and the Question of Orality* (Bloomington, IN: Indiana University Press, 1992), argues that literary critics, in seeing oral tradition as a means of validating the genre of the African novel, lost sight of the ways in which authors shaped and appropriated oral traditions for their own purposes. Her arguments are very relevant here.

35 Cory Library, Lovedale Collection, S.T. Plaatje file, 'Statement of account: estate Solomon T. Plaatje', 14 July 1932; inscribed copies of *Mhudi* formerly in possession of the late Professor E.O.J. Westphal, University of Cape Town; Sir Ernest Oppenheimer (Brenthurst Library, Johannesburg); Mr David Morris, Kimberley; and Mr Jack Stokes, Port Alfred. UM, W.E.B. Du Bois Papers, mums312-b060-i315, Plaatje to Du Bois, 16 July 1931.

36 UW, Rheinallt Jones Papers, A 394, C1, Victor Murray to Rheinallt Jones, 20 May 1931. The book Plaatje wanted was Murray's *The School in the Bush: a critical study of the theory and practice of native education in Africa* (London: Longmans, Green, 1929).

37 Tuskegee University, Archival Repository, Moton Papers, GC 160/1304, Plaatje to Moton, 16 July 1931.

38 Moton Papers, GC 160/1304, G. Lake Innes (Special Assistant to the Principal) to Plaatje, 15 August 1931.

39 I. Bud-M'belle, 'Scholar and patriot', *Umteteli* (Supplement), 6 August 1932, also SOAS, Plaatje Papers, STP 1/1, 'Solomon Tshekisho Plaatje', by I. Bud-M'belle (unpublished biography), p. 14; Unisa, Molema Papers, Acc. 142, 'With other people's wives', unpublished manuscript of Plaatje's, p. 52 (page references are to the MS rather than the retyped copy). The late Professor Tim Couzens and I made several attempts to track down the original manuscript after these copies were made, but to no avail.

40 The most detailed modern account, drawing upon both oral tradition and archival research, is Anderson Makaula, 'A political history of the Bhaca from earliest times to 1910' (MA thesis, Rhodes University, 1988); also W.D. Hammond Tooke, *The Tribes of the Mount Frere District* (Pretoria: Ethnological Publications no. 33, Union of South Africa, Department of Native Affairs, 1955), pp. 32–43.

41 'With other people's wives', p. 8.

42 W.C. Scully, 'Fragments of native history: the AmaBaca', I–III, *The State*, June–August 1909; W.C. Scully, *By Veldt and Kopje* (London: T. Fisher Unwin, 1907), pp. 285–301; W.C. Scully, *Further Reminiscences of a South African Pioneer* (London: T. Fisher Unwin, 1913), pp. 259–70; J.H. Soga, *The South-Eastern Bantu* (Johannesburg: University of the Witwatersrand Press, 1930), chs. 21 and 22; A.T. Bryant, *Olden Times in Natal and Zululand* (London: Longmans, Green & Co., 1929), pp. 154, 352, 378–86. A further indication of the timing of Plaatje's work on 'Monkey voodoo' is suggested by his article 'Natives and eclipses', *DFA*, 8 April 1931, where he recalled that 'the total eclipse of the sun in the twenties of last century occurred on the day Madikane (the famous warrior-king of the Ama-Baca) was killed by the Tembus'.

43 'With other people's wives', p. 15.

44 'With other people's wives', p. 58.

45 'With other people's wives', p. 69.

46 'With other people's wives', p. 69.

47 'With other people's wives', p. 70.

48 'With other people's wives', p. 72.

49 S.T. Plaatje, 'Passing of great chiefs Gaberone and Makhaola', *Umteteli*, 30 January 1932. Plaatje had met Chief Makhaula on at least two occasions – in London in 1919 and again in 1929 when he visited Basutoland.

50 H.I.E. Dhlomo, 'An appreciation', *Umteteli*, 25 June 1932; S.M. Molema, *Lover of His People* (Johannesburg: Wits University Press, 2012), p. 76.

Chapter 18

1 Tuskegee University, Archival Repository, Moton Papers, GC 160/1305, Plaatje to Moton, 16 July 1931.

2 Editorial review of *Mhudi, Imvo Zabantsundu*, 26 May 1931; H.I.E. Dhlomo, 'Through *Umteteli*'s pages: a review of 1930', *Umteteli wa Bantu*, 3 January 1931.

3 Botswana National Archives (BNA), Bamangwato Tribal Administration, R-B1, Plaatje to Tshekedi Khama, 20 September 1931 (courtesy the late Michael Crowder); 'The Bechuanaland Protectorate: some further native comments', letter from Peter M. Sebina to *The Star*, 8 October 1931, p. 5. For details of Tshekedi's struggles, see Mary Benson, *Tshekedi Khama* (London: Faber, 1960) and Neil Parsons and Michael Crowder (eds.), *Sir Charles Rey, Monarch of All I Survey* (London: James Currey, 1988).

4 SOAS, Alexander Sandilands Papers, MS 38081, 3/2/4, Sandilands to his mother, 17 December 1930 and 3/2/5, Sandilands to his mother, 1 September 1931; letter from Sandilands to the author, 20 June 1976.

5 Z.K. Matthews, 'Continuing the Plaatje story', *Imvo*, 1 July 1961.

6 *Report of the Native Affairs Commission for the Years 1927–1931* (UG26-1932, Government Printer, Pretoria), Appendix D, Minutes of Native Conference held in Pretoria, 9–13 December 1930, pp. 22–3.

7 Minutes of Native Conference, p. 23; Matthews, 'Continuing the Plaatje story'; Vere Stent, 'The strange life of Sol Plaatje', *The Star*, 5 July 1932.

8 Minutes of Native Conference, pp. 22–3; for Senator Smit, see C.J. Beyers (ed.), *Dictionary of South African Biography* (Pretoria: Human Sciences Research Council, 1981), vol. 4, p. 577.

9 'Native chiefs in congress', *Pretoria News*, 11 December 1930, p. 6; University of the Witwatersrand (UW), SAIRR, AD 843, MS minutes of Native Conference (taken by Edith Rheinallt Jones), p. 17. Selope Thema was clear that the government wanted 'to preserve tribal organisation, not because it wants to prevent the disintegration of Bantu life, but because tribal organisation ensures control and enables the white race to impose its will upon our race': editorial in *Bantu World*, 27 April 1935, quoted in Tim Couzens, *The New African: a study of the life and work of H.I.E. Dhlomo* (Johannesburg: Ravan Press, 1985), p. 137.

10 Minutes of Native Conference, p. 28; S.T. Plaatje, 'Cheeseparing again: Native Conference', *Pretoria News*, 1 December 1930, p. 6; 'Native indaba: minister's address to chiefs', *Pretoria News*, 8 December 1930, p. 6.

11 'Natives and taxation', *Diamond Fields Advertiser* (*DFA*), 3 March 1931; UW, SAIRR, Plaatje, 'Further Evidence to the Native Affairs Commission', pp. 392–3.

12 *Synopsis of Proceedings of the Thirteenth Session of the Right Worthy True Temple of the Independent Order of True Templars, held at Vrededorp. Johannesburg, 6–8 January 1931*, pp. 10–12, and *Report of R. Worthy Secretary*, p. xii.

13 'Editorial notes', *Our Heritage*, 1, 1, June 1931.

14 UM, W.E.B. Du Bois Papers, mums312-b060-i315, Plaatje to Du Bois, 16 July 1931.

15 S.T. Plaatje, 'Along the road to Cairo land', *Our Heritage*, 1, 3, August–October 1931, p. 14; 'Taxation in the Belgian Congo', *Umteteli*, 23 January 1932.

16 S.T. Plaatje, 'Along the road to Cairo land', *Our Heritage*, 1, 4, November 1931, p. 11. *Leselinyana* also carried Plaatje's reports on his Belgian Congo visit in its issues of 23

January 1931, and 6, 13 and 20 January 1932.

17 'Through native eyes: a visit to the Belgian Congo', *Cape Argus*, 9 July 1931.

18 Plaatje, 'Taxation in the Belgian Congo', *Umteteli*, 23 January 1932.

19 Plaatje, 'Taxation in the Belgian Congo'.

20 'Native's definition of segregation', *Bulawayo Chronicle*, 20 June 1931; see also 'To succeed Sir Murray Bisset', *Our Heritage*, 1, 5, December 1931, p. 10.

21 'Editorial notes', *Our Heritage*, 1, 2, July 1931, p. 2; 'Editorial notes', *Our Heritage*, 1, 3, August–October 1931, p. 2.

22 CAD, GNLB, Plaatje to Secretary, Native Affairs Department, 19 November 1931, and ensuing correspondence. Plaatje asked for £100 a year to carry government notices but by the time a reduced amount of £30 was agreed to, *Our Heritage* had gone under.

23 UW, SAIRR Papers, Aa3.3.2.1, C.F. Rey to J.D. Rheinallt Jones, 22 September 1931 and Jones to Rey, 26 September 1931; BNA, Secretariat Register, 3890, 'Our Heritage: Sechuana newspaper', 1931, also alludes to Plaatje's request, but this file was destroyed.

24 See especially T.J. Couzens, 'A short history of *The World* (and other black South African newspapers)', African Studies Institute (University of the Witwatersrand) seminar paper, 1976, and Les Switzer, 'Bantu World and the origins of a captive African press', in Les Switzer (ed.), *South Africa's Alternative Press: voices of protest and resistance 1880–1960* (Cambridge: Cambridge University Press, 1997), pp. 189–212. Isaiah Bud-M'belle was on the original board of *Bantu World*, but stepped down when it was taken over by the Argus Printing and Publishing Company fourteen months later.

25 Charles L. Stewart, 'Black dabblers in the black art: natives who edit and print their own newspapers', *Cape Argus*, 9 April 1932. Charles Stewart was described as 'a young Cape Town journalist who signed on as an ordinary seaman, so that he might see something of the world' (*The Outspan*, 12 September 1930). On the demise of *Abantu-Batho*, see particularly Peter Limb, 'Conclusion: assessing the decline and legacy of *Abantu-Batho*', in Peter Limb (ed.), *The People's Paper: a centenary history and anthology of 'Abantu-Batho'* (Johannesburg: Wits University Press, 2013), pp. 318–30.

26 H.I.E. Dhlomo, 'Three famous African authors I knew', *Inkundla ya Bantu*, August 1946, reproduced in *English in Africa*, 2, 1, March 1975, p. 10.

27 'Mr Sol T. Plaatje honoured: tributes to his work for non-Europeans', *DFA*, 12 November 1928; De Beers Archives (DB), General Secretary's correspondence, W.T. McLeod to De Beers, 31 August 1929; interview with Michael van Reenen, Mitcham, Surrey, 6 September 1976.

28 Interview with Mr J. van Riet, Kimberley, April 1976 and interview (with Tim Couzens) with Mrs Madge Sesedi, 22 January 1975 (UW, AG 2738-64).

29 'Non-European function: address presented by the community', *DFA*, 3 November 1931; interview with Mr Simon Lekhela, London, 26 October 1978 and Professor Ernest Lekhela, Mmabatho, 30 June 1983 (with Susan Newton-King).

30 Interview with Michael van Reenen; interviews with Mr Simon Lekhela, 26 October 1978 and 18 December 1981.

31 Interview with Mrs Mary Plaatje, May 1976; Beinecke Library, Yale University, George E. Haynes Papers, Box 4, folder 37, Haynes to Plaatje, 7 August 1931. Morwa Fenyang (1912–86) left Kimberley for Healdtown in January 1930, trained as a nurse in England and in the 1970s worked as a matron at the women's hospital in Gaborone, Botswana: Colin Murray, *Black Mountain: land, class and power in the eastern Orange Free State, 1880s to 1980s* (Edinburgh: Edinburgh University Press, 1992), p. 191.

32 Interview with Mr J. van der Riet (formerly a mechanic at the garage that sold the vehicle to Plaatje), Kimberley, April 1976; interviews with Mrs Mary Plaatje, May 1976 and November 1981; interview with Mr Paul Mahabane, Thaba Nchu, 22 April 1976.

33 Interview with Mr Simon Lekhela, London, 26 October 1978. The drinking incident must date from 1930, the year Simon Lekhela completed his training. It did not prevent

him from joining the teaching staff at Lyndhurst Road, where he remained for a number of years. Halley joined him there in 1934 after a spell working as a court interpreter in Barkly West and a short-lived attempt to set up a taxi service based at 32 Angel Street (*Umteteli*, 24 July 1937 and 7 December 1934).

34 UW, Solomon Tshekisho Plaatje, A 1893, Scrapbook, journal entries for 1930.

35 Interview with Dr J.S. Moroka, Thaba Nchu, 19 April 1976; S.M. Molema, *Lover of His People: a biography of Sol Plaatje* (Johannesburg: Wits University Press, 2012), p. 82; interview (by Tim Couzens and Brian Willan) with Mrs Madge Sesedi, Kimberley, 22 January 1975 (UW, AG 2738-70).

36 'A native function: providing vernacular literature', *DFA*, 11 August 1931.

37 Information about Violet Plaatje is derived from a file kindly made available to me, courtesy of Tim Couzens, by Solomon Molema, and from 'The late Mr Sol Plaatje: a memorial service', *DFA*, 3 August 1932, which mentions that she was president of the Lig en Vrede [Light and Peace] Band of Hope, Lyndhurst Road. Her involvement in the Wayfarers, and the activities of the Rhythm Girls, were often reported in *Umteteli*, e.g. its issues of 9 June 1934, 24 November 1934, 4 May 1935, 9 November 1935.

38 Z.K. Matthews, 'Continuing the Plaatje story', *Imvo*, 1 July 1961.

39 'Cape native voters', *Imvo*, 5 January 1932; see also reports in *Ikwezi le Afrika*, 9 January 1932; *DFA*, 25 December 1931.

40 'The Native Voters' Convention', *The Star*, 24 December 1931.

41 'Cape Native Voters' Convention', *Ikwezi le Afrika*, 9 January 1932. The passage from Shakespeare is from *All's Well That Ends Well* (I, ii, 231–2).

42 'True Templars annual session', *DFA*, 8 January 1932; *Umteteli*, 6 February 1932; DB, Estate records, Lyndhurst Road Native Institute file, Plaatje to Mr Grimmer (General Manager), 15 March 1932.

43 'True Templars annual session', *DFA*, 8 January 1932; 'Secondary education for natives: limited openings in Kimberley schools', *DFA*, 21 March 1931; 'Kimberley secondary school: inadequate accommodation', *Umteteli*, 5 March 1932; *Our Heritage*, 1, 1, June 1931, p. 9.

44 'Native grievances: mass meeting in location', *DFA*, 26 May 1932; see also 'Unemployment: minister interviewed', *Umteteli*, 28 May 1932.

45 S.T. Plaatje, 'The crime factory', *Umteteli*, 13 February 1932; Saul Dubow, *Racial Segregation and the Origins of Apartheid in South Africa 1919–36* (Basingstoke: Macmillan, 1989), pp. 120–2.

46 National Library of South Africa (Cape Town), Special Collections, Claire Goodlatte Papers, MSB 618, letter to Jack Goodlatte, 13 April 1932; Alan Paton, *South African Tragedy* (New York: Charles Scribner, 1965), pp. 139–41.

47 Union of South Africa, *Debates of the South African House of Assembly*, 13 May 1932, 4602–3; for Harm Oost, see Beyers, *DSAB*, vol. 4, pp. 426–7. Plaatje's address, according to the school's history, was part of a 'catholic programme' of inviting distinguished outside speakers to address the pupils, and was not subject to the approval of the Department of Education: Josephine McIntyre, *White Stoep on the Highway: Rustenburg School for Girls, a history 1894–1994* (Rondebosch: Rustenburg School for Girls, 1994), p. 29. The school's logbook confirms that Plaatje's address took place at 3 p.m. on 20 April (my thanks to Cedric van Dyck and Mary van Blerk for help here).

48 'Mr Sol Plaatje', letter to editor from A.S. Williams, *Cape Times*, 16 May 1932; 'A native lecturer', letter to editor from 'Ex-Professor, UCT', *Cape Times*, 20 May 1932.

49 'A native function', *DFA*, 11 August 1931; 'Countess' gift to Bantu children', *Bantu World*, 4 June 1932; see also 'Countess Labia and the natives', *DFA*, 26 May 1932; S.T. Plaatje, 'Friends and helpers of natives: a tribute to Mr J.W. Jagger and Mr Weinthal', *Cape Times*, 3 July 1930; 'Mr J.W. Jagger and the natives', *DFA*, 20 June 1930.

50 'Native grievances: mass meeting in location', *DFA*, 26 May 1932.

51 Tim Couzens, *Battles of South Africa* (Cape Town: David Philip, 2004), p. 95.

52 Interview with Mary Plaatje, 19 May 1976.

53 Molema, *Lover of His People*, p. 86; *Umteteli*, 23 July 1932; Notes of interview with A.W.G. Champion, n.d. (courtesy of Sadie Foreman); 'Death of Mr Sol T. Plaatje', *DFA*, 21 June 1932; 'Occasional notes, by P. Choeu' (SOAS, Plaatje Papers, MS 375495, loose insert).

54 'Death of Mr Taberer', *The Star*, 6 June 1932, p. 14; 'Stoep talk', *The Star*, 8 June 1932. Plaatje's attendance at Taberer's funeral was confirmed by Isaiah Bud-M'belle in his 'Solomon Tshekisho Plaatje' (SOAS, Plaatje Papers, STP 1, p. 14). On 8 June Johannesburg was reported to be the coldest place in the Union, the temperature being between -4 and -5 degrees.

55 Molema, *Lover of His People*, pp. 86–7; *Umteteli*, 6 February 1932, p. 3, records Plaatje's attendance at Xuma's wedding reception in Johannesburg.

56 Mrs E.L. Plaatje to Mrs S.J. Colenso, 22 September 1932 (author's private collection); Plaatje family notebook recording deaths; Department of the Interior, full death certificate.

57 'Funeral of Mr Sol T. Plaatje', *DFA*, 23 June 1932; DB, Memorandum dated 20 August 1932, and letter from Secretary, De Beers, to Rev. Z.R. Mahabane, 18 November 1932. It had cost £60 to have Plaatje's body transported from Johannesburg to Kimberley. Plaatje's relatives thought that this could be covered by his insurance policy, but it turned out that he had allowed this to lapse. De Beers contributed £25 to the fund that was raised. I am most grateful to Charmaine McLean, of De Beers, for making these documents available to me.

58 'The late Mr Sol T. Plaatje', *DFA*, 22 June 1932; 'Funeral of Mr Sol T. Plaatje', *DFA*, 23 June 1932; Kirchliches Archivzentrum, Berlin (BMS), bmw 1/5230-3 (D 49529), Beaconsfield Tagebücher, Report by G. Kuhn, Beaconsfield: II: Vierteljahr, 1932, pp. 13–14; interviews with Rev. J. Dire, Edenburg, 29 April 1976 and Michael van Reenen, Mitcham, 6 September 1976.

59 SOAS, Plaatje Papers, STP 4/1, Funeral oration by Rev. G. Kuhn (typescript).

60 'Funeral of Mr Sol T. Plaatje', *DFA*, 23 June 1932.

61 'The late Mr Sol Plaatje', *Ilanga lase Natal*, 24 June 1932; 'Mr Sol Plaatje passes', *Imvo*, 28 June 1932.

62 'The late Mr Sol. Plaatje: memorial service', *DFA*, 3 August 1932, p. 7.

63 'The late Mr Sol Plaatje', letter to the editor from D.M. Ramoshoana, *DFA*, 29 June 1932; letter from C.M. Doke to the editor, *Umteteli*, 25 June 1932; UW, University Archives, Clement Doke Papers, Letterbooks, A1.2, Doke to Ramoshoana, 21 June 1932.

64 Vere Stent, 'The strange life of Sol Plaatje: a leader without a people', *The Star*, 5 July 1932. This myth was perpetuated by Clement Doke, who, fifteen years later, described Plaatje as 'that literary enthusiast of obscure and doubtful origin', and as being 'probably of Vaalpense Bushman parentage' (C.M. Doke, 'Bantu wisdom-lore', *African Studies*, 6, 3, September 1947, p. 115).

65 'Life of Sol Plaatje: Dr S.M. Molema corrects Mr Stent', *The Star*, 11 July 1932; 'The strange life of Sol Plaatje', letter from Michael R. van Reenen to *The Star*, 1 August 1932, p. 4; see also 'Sol Plaatje: Mr Vere Stent's tribute', letter from Vere Stent, *The Star*, 23 July 1932, and 'The late Sol Plaatje', letter from D.M. Ramoshoana, *The Star*, 2 August 1932, p. 9.

66 Among the poems Violet wrote were 'What is in a name?', *Bantu World*, 24 June 1933, p. 9, and 'In memory of the late Sol T. Plaatje', *Bantu World*, 27 June 1936, p. 16 (which ends, 'Yet fresh in speech and heart he lives – It seems but yesterday').

67 T.J. Couzens, 'The dark side of the world: Sol Plaatje's *Mhudi*', *English Studies in Africa*, 14, 2, September 1971, pp. 187–203; T.J. Couzens, 'Sol Plaatje's *Mhudi*', *Journal of Commonwealth Literature*, 8, 1, June 1973, pp. 1–19; Stephen Gray, 'Sources of the first black South African novel in English', *Munger Africana Notes*, December 1976; Stephen

Gray, 'Plaatje's Shakespeare', *English in Africa*, 4, 1, March 1977, pp. 1–6; Sol T. Plaatje, *Mhudi*, with introduction by Tim Couzens (Johannesburg: Quagga Press, 1975); Sol T. Plaatje, *Mhudi*, edited by Stephen Gray, with introduction by Tim Couzens (London: Heinemann Educational Publishers, 1978).

68   Mazisi Kunene, Review of Stephen Gray's 'Sources of the first black South African novel in English', *Research in African Literatures*, 11, 2, 1980, pp. 244–7; see also Kunene's review of the Heinemann edition of Mhudi in *Research in African Literatures*, 8, 3, 1977, pp. 410–15.

69   Key books and articles in this tradition include David Johnson, 'Literature for the rainbow nation: the case of Sol Plaatje's *Mhudi*', *Journal of Literary Studies*, 10, 3–4, 1994, pp. 345–58; Anthony Chennells, 'Plotting South African history: narrative in Sol Plaatje's *Mhudi*', *English in Africa*, 24, 1, 1997; Myrtle Hooper, 'Re-writing history: the "feminism" of Mhudi', *English Studies in Africa*, 35, 1, 1992; Laura Chrisman, *Rereading the Imperial Romance: British imperialism and South African resistance in Haggard, Schreiner and Plaatje* (Oxford: Oxford University Press, 2000); Phaswane Mpe, '"Naturally these stories lost nothing by their retelling": Plaatje's mediation of oral history in *Mhudi*', *Current Writing*, 8, 1, 1996. For *Mhudi* in the broader context of post-colonial literature, see Elleke Boehmer, *The Empire, the National and the Postcolonial 1890–1920: resistance in interaction* (Oxford: Oxford University Press, 2002) and *Colonial and Postcolonial Literature*, 2nd edn (Oxford: Oxford University Press, 2005).

70   John L. Comaroff (ed.), *The Boer War Diary of Sol T. Plaatje: an African at Mafeking* (London: Macmillan, 1973). There have been two later editions: Sol T. Plaatje, *Mafeking Diary: a black man's view of a white man's war*, edited by John Comaroff with Brian Willan and Andrew Reed (Cambridge: Meridor Books, 1990), and John Comaroff and Brian Willan with Solomon Molema and Andrew Reed (eds.), *The Mafeking Diary of Sol T. Plaatje: centenary edition* (Cape Town: David Philip, 1999).

71   Sol T. Plaatje, *Native Life in South Africa before and since the European War and the Boer Rebellion*, with a foreword by Bessie Head and an introduction by Brian Willan (Johannesburg: Ravan Press, 1982). Janet Remmington, Brian Willan and Bhekizizwe Peterson (eds.), *Sol Plaatje's* Native Life in South Africa*: past and present* (Johannesburg: Wits University Press, 2016) brings together a variety of perspectives and reflections in the year of the centenary of the book's publication.

72   Mandela's spoken words are those reported in Heather Hughes, *First President: a life of John L. Dube, founding president of the ANC* (Johannesburg: Jacana Media, 2011). In *Long Walk to Freedom: the autobiography of Nelson Mandela* (London: Little, Brown, 1994), p. 610, Mandela wrote that casting his vote near John Dube's graveside 'brought history full circle, for the mission he began eighty-two years before was about to be achieved'.

73   The most comprehensive account of Plaatje's memorialisation is Gabrielle Leflaive, 'Sol Plaatje: memory and history in South Africa (1932–2013): from oblivion to national recognition (MA thesis, University of Paris-Sorbonne, 2014), http://gabrielle-leflaive. gandi.ws/.

74   'Mounting confusion over statues', *New Age Online*, 22 February 2011.

Sources

This book is based upon research carried out over a long period. Listed below are details of archives and newspapers consulted, and interviews I carried out. I do not include here a consolidated bibliography of secondary sources, such as books, journals and official publications. These are referenced fully in the endnotes for each chapter, publication details being provided on first mention within each chapter and in abbreviated form thereafter. Full details of the sources of photographs reproduced in this book are set out separately.

Archives

United Kingdom and Europe

British Library
Weil Papers, Add. MS 46848–46855; Royal Literary Fund Archive, Loan 96 RLF

British Museum
Central Archive

House of Lords Records Office, London
Lloyd George Papers (LG)

Hull History Centre
Records of the Union of Democratic Control (U-DDC)

Kirchliches Archivzentrum, Berlin, Germany
Archive of Berlin Mission Society

London School of Economics and Political Science
Edwin Cannan Papers; Archives of International African Institute (IAI)

National Archives, Kew, London
Colonial Office (CO 417, CO 537, CO 551, CO 705 series); Cabinet Office (CAB); FCO (Colonial Office) 141/499 (Basutoland series)

National Army Museum, London
Baden-Powell staff diary, 6411/1

School of Oriental and African Studies (SOAS)
Bethanie mission register (microfiche); Solomon Tshekisho Plaatje Papers, MS 375495; Silas Modiri Molema Papers, MS 380269; Methodist Missionary Society Archive (MMS); Mary Benson Papers, MS 348942; Sandilands Papers MS 38081

University College London, Special Collections
Daniel Jones Papers

University of Birmingham, Cadbury Research Library
Chamberlain Family Collection; W.C. Willoughby Papers, DA 49

University of Bristol Library
Cobden Unwin Papers, DM 85; National Liberal Club Archive, DM 668

University of Cambridge
British and Foreign Bible Society (BFBS); J.C. Smuts Papers (microfilm)

University of Leeds, Special Collections
New Statesman Collection (BC MS20c)

University of London, Senate House,
Institute of Commonwealth Studies Archives, Michael Crowder Papers (ICS 123)

University of Oxford, Bodleian Library
Anti-Slavery and Aborigines' Protection Society Papers, MSS Br. Emp. s. 19; Colenso Papers, MSS Afr. s. 1291; Henry Nevinson Diaries, MSS Eng. Misc. e. 620/1; Papers of Lewis Harcourt, 1st Viscount Harcourt, MSS Harcourt 347-420; United Society for the Propagation of the Gospel Papers (USPG)

University of Reading,
Records of George Allen and Unwin Ltd, MS 3282

West Sussex Record Office
Cobden Papers 974

South Africa, Botswana, Zimbabwe and Nigeria

Africana Library, Kimberley
Kimberley Chamber of Commerce minutes

Botswana National Archives, Gaborone (BNA)
Bamangwato Tribal Administration files; Resident Commissioner (RC)

Brenthurst Library, Johannesburg
Vyvyan Papers (MS 147 and 598); inscribed copies of *Sechuana Proverbs* and *Mhudi*

Chamber of Mines Archive
Minute Book of Board of Management of Native Recruiting Corporation

Cory Library, Rhodes University
C.G.H. Bell Papers, MS 7347 and 7348; Lovedale Collection (LC)

De Beers Archives, Kimberley (DB)
General Manager's files; General Secretary's files; Estate files; Directors' minute books

Free State Archives Depot, Bloemfontein (VAB)
Colonial Secretary, ORC (CO); Town Clerk, Bloemfontein (MBL); Department of Education and Training (SOO)

Killie Campbell Africana Library, Durban
Harriette Colenso Papers

Library of Parliament, Cape Town
Manuscript Annexures

Moeding College, Otse, Botswana
Moeding College Archives

National Archives of South Africa, Pietermaritzburg (NAB)
Colenso Papers, A 204

National Archives of South Africa, Pretoria (CAD)
Director of Native Labour, Government Native Labour Bureau (DNL, GNLB); Governor General (GG); J.B.M. Hertzog Papers; Prime Minister (PM); Secretary of Justice (JUS); Secretary of Native Affairs (NTS); J.C. Smuts Papers

National Archives of South Africa, Pretoria (TAB)
Transvaal, Attorney General (AG) series

National Library of South Africa, Cape Town, Special Collections
W.P. Schreiner Papers, MSC 27; Merriman Papers, MSC 15; Solomon Family Papers, MSB 475; Claire Goodlatte Papers, MSB 618; Henry Burton Papers, MSC 38

Standard Bank Heritage Centre, Johannesburg
Inspection records

University of Fort Hare, Alice
Administration files

Western Cape Archives and Records Service, Cape Town (KAB)
Attorney General (AG); Cape Colony, Supreme Court (CSC); Chief Magistrate, Transkei (CMT); Civil Service Commission (CLC); Colonial Office (CO); Crown Prosecutor, Griqualand West (CPK); High Court, Griqualand West (KSC); Justice Dept (JUS); Lands Department (LND); Magistrate, Kimberley (1/KIM); Magistrate, Mafeking (1/MAF); Magistrate, Vryburg (1/VBG); Master of Supreme Court, Kimberley (MOK); Native

Affairs Department (NA); Public Works Department (PWD); Superintendent General of Education (SGE); Town Clerk, Cape Town (3/CT); Town Clerk, East London (3/ELN); Treasury (T); William Geyer diary, A 1370; William Hayes diary, A 273

University of Cape Town, Manuscript Collections
Lestrade Papers, BC 255; Molteno Murray Family Papers, BC 330; A.W.G. Champion Papers, BC 581

University of Cape Town, University Archives
Gideon Mangoaela file

University of Ibadan Library, Ibadan, Nigeria
Herbert Macaulay Papers

University of South Africa, Pretoria (Unisa)
Hesse Collection, Baumbach Collection, Acc. 27; Hesse Collection, Westphal Papers, Acc. 21; Hesse Collection, Zittlau Collection, Acc. 15; Documentation Centre for African Studies, Molema Papers, Acc. 142; Documentation Centre for African Studies, Z.K. Matthews Papers, Acc. 101

University of the Witwatersrand, Johannesburg, Historical Papers
Mafeking Siege records, A 1566; Silas Molema and Solomon Plaatje Papers, A 979; Plaatje Diary, 1899–1900, A 2550; Plaatje letter, 1930, A 1303; Plaatje scrapbook, 1918, A 1893; South African Institute of Race Relations records, AD 843B and AD 843RJ; Joint Councils of Europeans and Africans, AD 1433; J.D. Rheinallt Jones Papers, A 394; A.L. Saffery Papers, AD 1178; W.C. Scully Papers, A 1312; A B. Xuma Papers, AD 843

University of the Witwatersrand, Johannesburg, University Archives
Clement Doke Papers

University of Zimbabwe (UZ)
Clement Doke Papers

United States

Folger Shakespeare Library, Washington DC
Tributes for Book of Homage to Shakespeare, edited by Israel Gollancz [manuscript], y.d. 85

Howard University, Washington DC, Moorland-Spingarn Research Center
Cromwell Family Papers

Library of Congress, Manuscripts Division
Booker T. Washington Papers, MSS 44669; National Association for the Advancement of Colored People (NAACP), MSS 34140; Carter G. Woodson Papers, MSS 46342

Hampton University, Virginia, University Archive
Samuel C. Armstrong correspondence; James E. Gregg correspondence

National Archives of the USA, Washington DC
Department of State, RG 59 series; Office of the Counselor; Military Archives Division;

General Services Division, Diplomatic Section; Records of US Consulate, London, Register of Correspondence

Schomburg Library for Research in Black Culture, Manuscripts, Archives and Rare Books Division, New York Public Library
John Edward Bruce Papers

Tuskegee University Library, Archives Repository, Tuskegee, Alabama
R.R. Moton Papers

University of Massachusetts Library, Amherst, Special Collections and University Archives
W.E.B. Du Bois Papers, MS 312

Yale University, Beinecke Library
George E. Haynes Papers

Privately held papers

Hanbury-Tracy Papers (courtesy Mr Richard H. Nicholson, Whitchurch, Hants); Inscribed copies of *Sechuana Proverbs* (courtesy Graham Stapleton, the late Ellen Kuzwayo); Inscribed copies of *Mhudi* (courtesy David Morris, the late Professor E.O.J. Westphal, the late Mr Jack Stokes); J.W. Cromwell Papers (courtesy Professor Adelaide Cromwell, Boston, Mass.); 'Erlebnisse in der Mission', autobiographical account by Gotthardt Westphal (courtesy Mr Harald Thiede, Pretoria); National Adult School Union Minute Book 1919–23 (courtesy Dawn Hamill); Plaatje family prayerbook (courtesy late Mr Johannes Plaatje); Plaatje family register (courtesy late Mr Johannes Plaatje); Sebopia Molema papers (courtesy Galefele Molema, Mahikeng); Transcript of interview with A.W.G. Champion (n.d.) (courtesy late Sadie Foreman).

Newspapers and journals

Abantu-Batho, Acton Borough Post, Acton Gazette, Acton and Chiswick Express, Africa and Orient Review, African Sentinel, African Telegraph and Gold Coast Mirror, African Times and Orient Review, African World (London), *African World Annual, Anti-Slavery and Aborigines Friend, APO, Bantu World, Barking Chronicle, Barking, East Ham and Ilford Advertiser, Bechuanaland News, Berliner Missionsberichte, The Bioscope, Black and White* (London), *Black and White Budget* (London), *Bloemfontein Post, The Bookman, The Bookseller, Bucks Standard, Bulawayo Chronicle, Die Burger, Cape Argus, Cape Argus Weekly, Cape Mercury, Cape Times, Chicago Broad Ax, Chicago Defender, Christian Commonwealth, Christian Commonwealth and Brotherhood World, Christian Express, Chronicle and Courier* (Sevenoaks), *Church Times, Cleveland Gazette, The Crisis, Daily Chronicle* (London), *Daily Dispatch* (East London), *Daily Express, Daily Graphic, Daily Herald, Daily Mail, Daily Mirror, Daily News and Leader* (London), *Daily Telegraph, The Daylight, Detroit News, Diamond Fields Advertiser, Diamond Fields Advertiser Weekly Mail Summary, District Times* (Leyton, Lea Bridge, Leytonstone), *East Ham Mail, East Sussex News, Eastern Province Herald* (Port Elizabeth), *Evening News* (Portsmouth), *Evening Star* (Washington DC), *Falkirk Herald, Foreign Affairs* (UDC), *Forward* (Glasgow ILP), *The Friend* (Bloemfontein), *The Friend* (Society of Friends), *Griqualand West Church Magazine, Hackney and Stoke Newington Recorder, Hampshire Telegraph and Post* (Portsmouth), *Hanwell Gazette, Hastings and St*

Leonards Observer, Ikwezi le Afrika, Ilanga lase Natal, Imvo Zabantsundu, The Independent, Izwi la Bantu, Journal of the African Society, Journal of Negro History (New York), *Kimberley Star, Kinematograph Weekly, Koranta ea Becoana / Bechuana Gazette, Labour Leader* (ILP), *Lagos Standard, Lagos Weekly Record, Leighton Buzzard Observer, Leselinyana, Leytonstone Express and Independent, Mafeking Mail, Manchester Guardian, Middlesex County Times, Monmouthshire Evening Post, Morning Post, The Nation* (London), *Negro World, New Age, New Statesman, New York Age, News of the World, Northampton Daily Echo, Onward* (Portsmouth Brotherhood), *Opportunity: A Journal of Negro Life* (National Urban League), *Our Heritage, Outspan, Paisley Daily Express, Pall Mall Gazette, Peterborough Citizen, Port Elizabeth Telegraph, Portsmouth Times and Hampshire County Chronicle, Pose ea Becoana, Pretoria News, PSA Brotherhood Journal, Publisher's Circular and Bookseller's Record, Quarterly Paper of the Bloemfontein Mission, Queenstown Daily Representative, Rand Daily Mail, Reynolds's News, Rhodesia Herald, The Sjambok, South Africa* (London), *South African Outlook, South African Review, South African Spectator, South African Worker, South Wales Gazette and Newport News, South Wales Weekly Argus, Southall-Norwood Gazette, Southern Workman* (Hampton), *The Star* (Johannesburg), *The State, Stratford-upon-Avon Herald, Sunday Express* (London), *Sunday Pictorial* (London), *Sunderland Daily Echo, Sussex County Herald, The Times, Times Literary Supplement, Tonbridge Free Press, Tottenham and Edmonton Weekly Herald, Transvaal Leader, Tsala ea Becoana, Tsala ea Batho, UCT Quarterly, Umsebenzi, Umteteli wa Bantu, The Vote, Walthamstow, Leyton and Chingford Guardian, Walthamstow, Leyton and Leytonstone Weekly, Washington Bee, Washington Tribune, Weekly Free Press* (Kimberley), *West Middlesex Gazette, West Africa, Westminster Gazette, Workers Dreadnought.*

Interviews

Bokako, Martha (Thaba Nchu), 11 April, 22 April 1976, 10 May 1976 (with Tim Couzens), 26 May 1976, 14 November 1977, 16 and 28 August 1980 (with Tim Couzens)
Dire, Rev. J. (Edenburg), 29 April 1976
Lekhela, Ernest (Mmabatho), 30 June 1983 (by Susan Newton-King)
Lekhela, Simon (London), 26 October 1978, 23 February 1982
Mahabane, Paul (Thaba Nchu), 22 April 1976)
Matthews, John (Kimberley), 2 May 1976
Moroka, Dr J.S. (Thaba Nchu), 19 April 1976
Molefe, Rev. G. (Port Elizabeth), 30 June 1976
Moyanaga, Eric, Thaba Nchu, 2 June 1978 (by Andrew Reed)
Plaatje, Johannes and Simon Lekhela (Kimberley), 21 March 1997
Plaatje, Mrs Mary, Natalspruit, 19 May 1976 and November 1981 (with Tim Couzens), 7 December 1982 (with Tim Couzens)
Tyamzashe, Benjamin (Zinyoka), King William's Town, 15 July 1976
Van Reenen, Michael (London), 6 September 1976, 28 September 1976, 29 March 1977 (with Tim Couzens), 2 September 1977
Westphal, Erna (Johannesburg), 10 October 1977 (with Tim Couzens), 11 November 1977
Zibi, Maud (Kayakulu), 2 December 1981

Sources of illustrations

Cover photograph

University of the Witwatersrand, Historical Papers (UW), Plaatje-Molema Papers, A979-Fca 9.

Illustrations in text

Ch. 1: Unisa Archives, Hesse Collection, Acc. 27, Baumbach Collection; *Ch. 2:* S.T. Plaatje, *Native Life in South Africa* (London: P.S. King, 1916), frontispiece; *Ch. 3:* University of the Witwatersrand, Historical Papers (UW), Plaatje–Molema Papers, A979-Fcb3; *Ch. 4:* UW, A979-Fca2; *Ch. 5: Koranta ea Becoana*, issue 3, courtesy National Library of South Africa, Cape Town; *Ch. 6:* UW, A979-Fcb1; *Ch. 7:* private collection; *Ch. 8:* Africana Library, Kimberley, ref: V.A. 2080; *Ch. 9:* UW, A1384; *Ch. 10:* UW, A979-Fa2; *Ch. 11:* UW, A979-Fcc19; *Ch. 12:* UW, A979-Fa2; *Ch. 13:* private collection; *Ch. 14:* UW, A979-Dc-001; *Ch. 15:* W. Cape Archives, East London Municipal Archive, 3/ELN 2, no. 80, Town Clerk's correspondence, enclosure in Plaatje to Town Clerk, East London, 9 October 1924; *Ch. 16:* private collection; *Ch. 17:* private collection; *Ch. 18:* private collection.

Plate section 1 (between pages 104 and 105)

1: Missionsberichte, 1894 p. 144; *2:* private collection; *3:* private collection; *4:* private collection; *5:* Unisa Archives, Hesse Collection, Acc. 21, Ernst Gotthilf Westphal; *6:* L. Zöllner and J.A. Heese, *The Berlin Missionaries in South Africa* (Pretoria: HSRC, 1984), p. 524; *7:* M. Genischen, *Bilder von unserem Missionsfelde in Süd- und Deutsch-Ost-Afrika* (Berlin, 1902), p. 110; *8:* S.M. Molema, *Montshiwa: Barolong chief and patriot* (Cape Town: Struik, 1966), p. 22; *9:* Mafikeng Museum: Barolong stadt, Mafikeng l; *10:* McGregor Museum, Kimberley, mmkp2391: Bend Hotel, Pniel; *11: Daily Independent*, Kimberley, 15 August 1890, courtesy Africana Library, Kimberley; *12:* Africana Library, Kimberley; *13:* Wikimedia Commons; *14:* Africana Library, Kimberley, N13193.41; *15:* R. Bennett, *Reminiscences of the Cape Government Telegraphs* (Cape Town, n.d. [c.1908]), p. 34; *16:* Richard R. Wright, *Centennial Encyclopedia of the African Methodist Church* (Philadelphia: 1948), p. 288; *17:* T.D. Mweli Skota, *African Yearly Register* (Johannesburg: Esson, 1930), p. 104; *18:* D.D.T. Jabavu, *The Life of John Tengo Jabavu, Editor of* Imvo Zabantsundu, *1884–1921* (Lovedale: Lovedale Press, 1921), frontispiece; *19:* Africana Library, Kimberley, N13193.41; *20: Diamond Fields Advertiser*, 17 December 1897; *21:* V&A Museum, London. 2011FB3903_2500 William Haviland as Iago, late 19th century; *22:* New York Public Library, catalog ID (B-number): b15262620; *23:* W. Cape Archives CSC 2/1/1/355, no. 14, Illiquid Case. Henry Burton v Cecil John Rhodes and James Hill, 1899; *24:* Albany Museum, Grahamstown; *25: Men of the Times: old colonists of the Cape Colony and Orange River Colony* (Johannesburg: Transvaal Publishing Company, 1906), p. 480.

Plate section 2 (between pages 168 and 169)

26: UW, A979-Fa1; *27: South African Law Journal*, 26, 1909, p. 209; *28: Men of the Times*, p. 288; *29:* The Master and Fellows, Balliol College. Balliol College Archives, Oxford, PHOT. 21.23; *30:* UW, A979-Fcb5; *31:* UW, A979-Fb1; *32:* S.T. Plaatje, *Sechuana Proverbs* (London: Kegan Paul, Trench, Trübner, 1916), p. 8; *33:* UW, A979-Fb3; *34:* UW, A2550; *35:* Edward Ross, *Siege Views of Mafeking* (London: 1900), p. 6; *36:* Ross, *Siege Views of Mafeking*, p. 20; *37:* D. Taylor, *Souvenir of the Siege of Mafeking* (London: 1900); *38:* W. Cape Archives, image no. L1164; *39:* Lord Paden-Powell Papers, The Scout Association Heritage Collection, London, Frank Whiteley Album; *40: Black and White Budget*, 9 June

1900, p. 293; *41:* Ross, *Siege Views of Mafeking*, p. 20; *42:* Weil Papers, British Library, Add. 46848, f. 181 D40019-73; *43:* UW, A979-Fa2.

Plate section 3 (between pages 264 and 265)

44: Africana Library, Kimberley, P3247.3; *45:* 'Presenting Lord Roberts's letter to the chief of the Baralongs, 12 Sept. 1900' (photograph) MS.147/9/1/274, Brenthurst Library, Johannesburg; *46: Men of the Times*, p. 585; *47: Men of the Times*, p. 280; *48: Men of the Times*, p. 259; *49:* Cadbury Research Library: Special Collections, University of Birmingham, Chamberlain Papers, C/9/16 (original caption 'Native Stadt Mafeking'); 50 *Koranta ea Becoana*, 16 August 1902, courtesy National Library of South Africa; *51:* Plaatje, *Sechuana Proverbs*, frontispiece; *52:* Cadbury Research Library: Special Collections, University of Birmingham, Chamberlain Papers, C/9/13, Photograph album presented by SANNC; *53:* Cadbury Research Library: Special Collections, University of Birmingham, Chamberlain Papers, C/9/13, Photograph album presented by SANNC; *54:* UW, A979-Fc; *55: Diamond Fields Advertiser*, Christmas number, December 1906, courtesy Africana Library, Kimberley; *56: Mafeking Mail*, 26 March 1908; *57:* Plaatje, *Sechuana Proverbs*, p. xi; *58:* Plaatje, *Sechuana Proverbs*, p. 8; *59:* National Library of South Africa, Cape Town, JN49589; *60:* private collection; *61:* UW, A979-Fcb4; *62:* UW, A979-Dc; *63:* private collection; *64:* UW, A979-Fa2; *65:* UW, A979-Fcd25; *66:* UW, A979-Fcd14; *67:* Mr Richard Dixon; *68:* private collection; *69:* Mr Grenville Williams.

Plate section 4 (between pages 456 and 457)

70: London Museum, ID no. 53.14084; *71:* private collection; *72:* Leo Weinthal, 1922. W.E.B. Du Bois Papers (MS 312), Special Collections and University Archives, University of Massachusetts Amherst Libraries; *73:* UW, A979-Fcd21; *74:* private collection; *75:* private collection; *76:* AS and APS Papers, Bodleian Library, Oxford; *77:* National Portrait Gallery, London, NPG X 44047, by Walter Stoneman; *78:* UW, A979-Dd1; *79:* Robert Molteno; *80:* private collection; *81:* UW, A979-Fcd13; *82:* Wikimedia Commons; *83:* Wikimedia Commons; *84:* Wikimedia Commons; *85:* Swaziland National Archives; *86:* UW, A979-Fcb9; *87:* UW, A979-Fcb16; *88:* Mrs Ramoshoana, courtesy Andrew Reed; *89: Catalogue of C.M. Doke Collection on African Languages* (G.K. Hall, 1972), frontispiece; *90:* M. Benson, *Tshekedi Khama* (London: Faber, 1960), p. 97; *91:* UW, A979-Fcc18; *92:* UW, A979-Fcd4; *93:* UW, A979-Fcc14; *94:* UW, A979-Fcc2; *95:* UW, A979-Fcb11.

Index

members of 442
Native Administration Act (1927) 555, 559
Native Administration Bill (1917) 321, 439,
    455–6, 467–8
    debates regarding 322–3
    opposition to 322–4, 331
    suspension of 336
Native Affairs Act (1920) 439–40, 452
    provisions of 469
Native Affairs Administration Bill 455
Native Brotherhood Institute 346, 349,
    357–80, 437–8
    dedication of (1919) 346
Native Hymn Book 422
Native Labour Regulation Act 228
Native Press Association 184
Native Recruiting Corporation 371–2, 440,
    446
    personnel of 372
Native Reserves Locations Act 203
Native Welfare Association 558
Native Welfare Society 560
Native Service Contract Bill 554, 571
Natives' Land Act (1913) 253–4, 259, 261,
    264, 279, 281, 284, 306–7, 309, 314, 321,
    325, 328, 330, 402, 440, 444, 449, 459,
    463, 467, 555, 583
    impact of 330
    opposition to 243–7, 250–1, 261–2,
        265–6, 270, 272–3
    provisions of 242, 246, 250
Natives (Urban Areas) Act (1923)
    implementation of 453
Ndebele 8
Neale, Walter 408
Neale Publishing Company 408
Negro Society for Historical Research 404
Nevinson, Henry 312
New Age 308
New England PSA 287
New Statesman 305, 312
    editorial staff of 311
Newbolt, Sir Henry 300
Ngcayiya, Henry 59,
    travel to UK (1919) 359–60, 365
Ngcezula, J.M. 56
Ngcolomba, Thomas 72–3
Ngidi, Alfred
    civil action brought against 99–100
Non-European Association (Kimberley)
    members of xviii
Norseman 261, 264

Noto, Chief 6
Nqwana, David 142
Nxumalo, Benjamin 419
Nyokong, Chief J.M. 248
    support for *Tsala ea Becoana* 218, 346
Nyusa, Aaron 44

O
Olifant, J.S. 140
Oliphant, David 44
Olsson, Oscar 425–6
O'Neill, Eugene
    Emperor Jones, The 403
Oost, Harm 572
Oppenheimer, Sir Ernest 444–5, 469, 481
    Mayor of Kimberley 257–8
Orange Free State Shootings (1918/1919)
    347, 434
Orange, River 9
Orange River Colony 148–9, 181, 183,
    188–9, 193, 311
    formerly Orange Free State 163
    languages spoken in 168
O'Rell, Max
    John Bull and Co. 50, 52
Ormsby-Gore, Captain 354
Ottoman Empire 302
Ox Transport Department 143–4
Oxford University 159
    Balliol College 89
    Jesus College 229

P
P.S. King & Son 283, 285, 289, 305
Pact Government 445, 464, 466, 470, 477
    electoral victory of (1929) 471, 477
    opposition to 444
Paddon, Russell
    lease signed with Silas Molema and
        Solomon Plaatje (1902) 156–7
Pall Mall Gazette 422, 425
Palestine
    Jerusalem 428
Palmer, H.E.
    National Proverbs (England)(1912)
    297–8
Pan-African Congress (1919) 345
Panyane, E. 56
Parslow, E.G. 120
    shooting of 118
Parsons, Sir Charles 134
Pass Law 181–2

Reconsiderations in
Southern African History

Milton Shain, *The Roots of Antisemitism in South Africa*
Timothy Keegan, *Colonial South Africa and the Origins of the Racial Order*
Ineke van Kessel, *"Beyond Our Wildest Dreams": The United Democratic Front and the Transformation of South Africa*
Benedict Carton, *Blood from Your Children: The Colonial Origins of Generational Conflict in South Africa*
Diana Wylie, *Starving on a Full Stomach: Hunger and the Triumph of Cultural Racism in Modern South Africa*
Jeff Guy, *The View across the River: Harriette Colenso and the Zulu Struggle against Imperialism*
John Edwin Mason, *Social Death and Resurrection: Slavery and Emancipation in South Africa*
Hermann Giliomee, *The Afrikaners: Biography of a People*
Tim Couzens, *Murder at Morija: Faith, Mystery, and Tragedy on an African Mission*
Diana Wylie, *Art and Revolution: The Life and Death of Thami Mnyele, South African Artist*
David Welsh, *The Rise and Fall of Apartheid*
John Edwin Mason, *One Love, Ghoema Beat: Inside the Cape Town Carnival*
Eric Allina, *Slavery by Any Other Name: African Life under Company Rule in Colonial Mozambique*

Richard Elphick, *The Equality of Believers: Protestant Missionaries and the Racial Politics of South Africa*

Hermann Giliomee, *The Last Afrikaner Leaders: A Supreme Test of Power*

Meghan Healy-Clancy, *A World of Their Own: A History of South African Women's Education*

Ruramisai Charumbira, *Imagining a Nation: History and Memory in Making Zimbabwe*

Jeffrey Butler, edited by Richard Elphick and Jeannette Hopkins, *Cradock: How Segregation and Apartheid Came to a South African Town*

Hermann Giliomee, *Historian: An Autobiography*

Charles van Onselen, *The Cowboy Capitalist: John Hays Hammond, the American West, and the Jameson Raid in South Africa*

Robert R. Edgar, *The Finger of God: Enoch Mgijima, the Israelites, and the Bulhoek Massacre in South Africa*

Zachary Kagan Guthrie, *Bound for Work: Labor, Mobility, and Colonial Rule in Central Mozambique, 1940–1965*

Brian Willan, *Sol Plaatje: A Life of Solomon Tshekisho Plaatje, 1876–1932*

CPSIA information can be obtained
at www.ICGtesting.com
Printed in the USA
LVHW091621170419
614532LV00004B/265/P